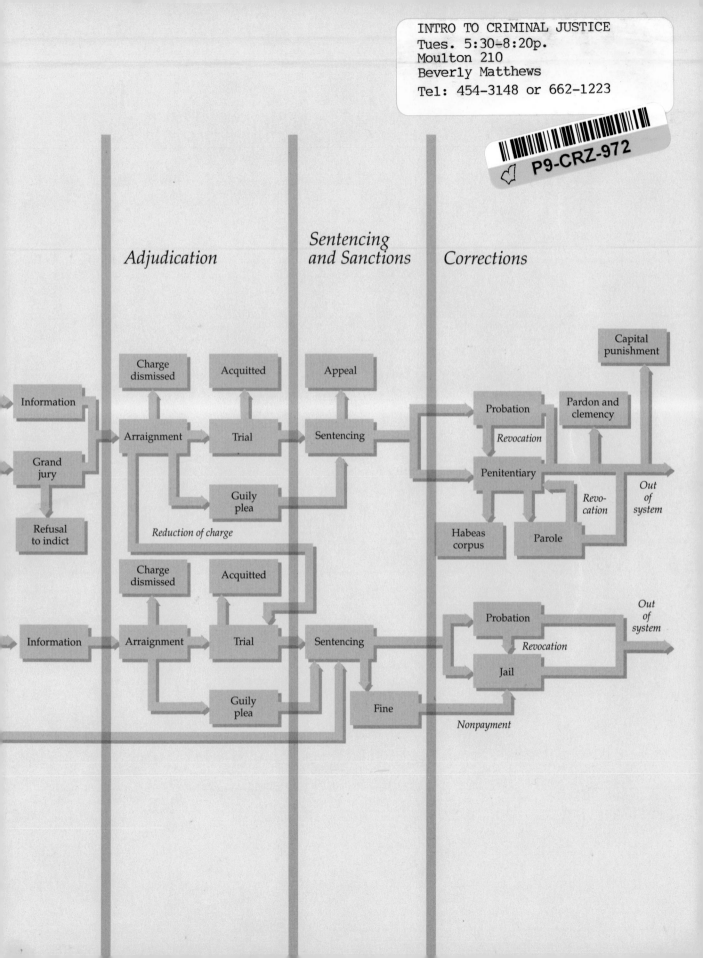

Adjudication

Sentencing and Sanctions

Corrections

Capital punishment

Charge dismissed

Acquitted

Appeal

Information

Probation

Pardon and clemency

Arraignment

Trial

Sentencing

Revocation

Grand jury

Penitentiary

Revocation

Out of system

Guily plea

Refusal to indict

Reduction of charge

Habeas corpus

Parole

Charge dismissed

Acquitted

Out of system

Information

Arraignment

Trial

Sentencing

Probation

Revocation

Guily plea

Jail

Fine

Nonpayment

6th Edition

The American System of Criminal Justice

George F. Cole
The University of Connecticut

Brooks/Cole Publishing Company
Pacific Grove, California

number do not have such aspirations, yet they still find the subject matter fascinating. Instructors thus must serve two constituencies. A successful text meets the needs of students who require the technical information that is the foundation for later courses in the criminal justice major; at the same time, the text must provide general knowledge for students whose contact with the system will be as citizens. Members of both groups need to be aware of the complexity of crime and the administration of justice and familiar with the policy issues that we as a society face.

REVISION HIGHLIGHTS

This sixth edition has been a major revision effort. The book has been completely updated and rewritten on a line-by-line basis. I researched the current literature and communicated with various specialists in the sub-fields of criminal justice to identify new approaches, research findings, and shifts of emphasis. More than thirty instructors were asked to review each chapter of the fifth edition. They pointed out portions of the text their students found difficult, made suggestions as to topics that should be covered, and noted those sections that should be dropped. Drafts of chapters were resubmitted for review, and further suggestions were incorporated into the final product.

Although the revisions in the sixth edition are too extensive to describe completely in this preface, the following ten examples illustrate some of the changes that have been made:

1. Chapter 1 starts the student thinking about the extent of crime in the United States. New international data raise the question of why violent crime is so much more extensive here than in other developed countries. Information on Iceland, a country with little crime, is used for comparative purposes. The section on the crime control and due process models of criminal justice, a feature of past editions, has been rewritten for clarity.

2. The war on drugs is having an enormous impact on the criminal justice system. The problem of drug enforcement and its impact on the police, courts, and corrections is addressed throughout the book. Questions concerning the relationship of drugs and crime, the new levels of violence being experienced in American cities, the use of the military to impede the foreign flow of illegal substances, and the reallocation of police and prison resources to fight this war are addressed.

3. Major changes are taking place in American policing. The law enforcement/crime-fighter emphasis is being supplemented by a greater focus on community policing and problem solving. Chapters 5 and 6 have been reoriented to illustrate this shift in police operations.

4. With prison crowding and overwhelming probation caseloads has come a search for intermediate punishments more restrictive than probation but less restrictive than incarceration. Chapter 13 on sentencing and Chapter 16 on community corrections: probation and parole introduce such new sanctions as intensive probation supervision, house arrest, boot camp, and restitution.

5. Students are now exhibiting a new interest in learning more about criminal justice systems in other parts of the world. Most chapters of this edition now include Comparative Perspective sections that describe a component of criminal justice in another country. By learning about others, we learn more about ourselves.

6. This is not a criminology text, yet criminal justice students need to know the logical policy implications of the major theories of criminal behavior—why some people commit crimes. If the evidence shows a bio-

logical predisposition to criminality, certain policies might follow. Chapter 2 has been rewritten to include this policy perspective.

7. Politics is an important influence on criminal justice, as the impact of the Willie Horton case on Dukakis's 1988 presidential campaign well illustrates. But there are other ways that politics play a role in the system. The definition of behaviors as criminal, the funding of criminal justice operations, and the election of judges and prosecutors all result from decisions that are politically influenced. Current examples of the influence of politics are given throughout the book.

8. Certain criminal justice policy issues are now being debated by professionals and by informed laypeople. Four of these issues have been chosen for special emphasis. The ongoing debates over drug legalization, handgun control, capital punishment, and incarceration are highlighted by special policy sections. These sections are supplemented with color graphics and photographs to assist students to fully understand the issues.

9. Criminal justice requires that decisions not only be made within the framework of law but also be consistent with the ethical norms of American society. Throughout the book scenarios place the student in the context of a decision maker faced with a problem involving a question of ethics. The aim is to make students aware of the many ethical dilemmas faced by criminal justice personnel and the types of questions that they may have to answer if they assume a role in the system.

10. The research on the governing of prisons that has emerged during recent years challenges many of the assumptions of the past. Chapter 15 on incarceration has been rewritten to show the importance of governance in maintaining secure, safe, and humane prisons.

THE GRAPHICS PROGRAM

Today's students have been greatly influenced by television. They are attuned to images that convey not only information but also values and emotions. We worked directly with a group of outstanding graphic artists and photographers to develop an extensive program of illustrations. Wherever possible, quantitative data have been converted into bar graphs, pie charts, and other graphic forms so that they will be clearly understood. Written summaries of the graphic presentations make them easier to grasp. Special care has been taken with regard to the placement of photographs and their captions so that the images are tied directly to the message of the text.

SUPPLEMENTS

An extensive package of supplemental aids accompanies the text. A full-fledged instructor's manual has been developed by Professor Charles Myers of Aims Community College. New to this edition are lists of resources, lecture outlines, and testing suggestions that will help time-pressed teachers communicate more effectively to their students. Each chapter has multiple-choice and true-false test items, as well as sample essay questions. The instructor's manual is backed up with a computerized test bank suitable for IBM or Macintosh personal computers.

To bring the graphic portions of the text to the classroom, forty-eight transparency masters for overhead projection are provided to help instructors fully discuss concepts and research findings with students.

Acknowledg

The valuable contributions
all of this book, are grateful

Michael B. Blankenship, M
State University

William Clements, Norwich
University

Gary Copus, University of
Alaska

Holly A. Dershem, Washing
State University

James Frank, Michigan State
University

Paul Friday, Western Michig
University

James J. Fyfe, The American
University

Gil Geis, University of Calif
Irvine

Marc Gertz, Florida State
University

Lynne Goodstein, Pennsylva
State University

John P. Harlan, Stephen F. A
State University

Paul H. Johnson, Weber State
University

Robert Johnson, The America
University

Nolan Jones, The American
University

Susan Katzenelson, U.S.
Sentencing Commission

To The Reader

Criminal justice emerged during the 1970s as a vital and unique academic discipline that simultaneously enhanced the professional development of students planning careers in the field and attracted those who wanted to know more about a difficult social problem and how this country responds to it. Criminal justice incorporates a broad range of knowledge from a variety of specialties, including law, history, and the social and behavioral sciences, each of which contributes to our fuller understanding of criminal behavior and of society's attitudes toward deviance.

Because of the vast amount of research that has been done during the past two decades, today's students of criminal justice must be familiar with a great deal of up-to-date literature. In preparing this text, I have drawn from monographs, government publications, scholarly journals, papers read at academic meetings, as well as the popular media. Although research reports are essential for developing an empirical foundation of criminal justice study, biographies and news accounts reflect the human dimension far more vividly. Before introducing my view of the American system of criminal justice, it is appropriate to discuss some of the assumptions on which this book is based and describe several of its special features.

Multidisciplinary Perspective

In this book I aim at comprehensiveness by describing the criminal justice system from the perspectives of several disciplines. Because criminal behavior is human behavior, key research findings and concepts are drawn from sociology, psychology, and political science, while history allows a comparison of past and contemporary issues and phenomena. Because the institutions of criminal justice make up an organizational system, concepts from the administrative sciences are employed. Criminal justice operates under law; accordingly, its boundaries are formed by jurisprudential responses to society's need for protection and the individual citizen's need for freedom. Because the criminal justice system is an arm of the government, it operates within the political context as well. Many criminal justice personnel obtain office by political means, and a form of bureaucratic politics influences how each portion of the system works. From this confluence of administration, law, and politics, decisions are made that define which behavior is criminal, determine the level of resources available to criminal justice agencies, and result in actions that affect the lives of citizens, crime victims, offenders, and officials.

Special Features

To make this introduction to American criminal justice informative, enjoyable, and rewarding (a tall order, but one worth attempting), I have included a number of special features.

1. Running glossary: One goal of an introductory course is to convey the terminology of a field. Because criminal justice is interdisciplinary, a number of terms used in law and the social sciences are fully defined in the margin, next to their first, boldfaced appearance in the text.

2. Graphics: Great care has been given to providing tables, figures, and photographs that focus and enliven information so that it can be accurately perceived and easily understood.

3. Policy Issues: Criminal justice issues are debated not only by policy analysts but also by citizens. There are four Policy Issue sections that present arguments concerning the vital topics of the legalization of drugs, the control of handguns, the abolition of the death penalty, and the use of incarceration. Full-color photographs and graphics make various kinds of information readily accessible and vividly bring alive competing perspectives on these issues.

4. A Question of Ethics: Criminal justice concerns raise a variety of ethical issues. Separate boxes on ethical questions related to the topic of each chapter are included to encourage the reader to consider these issues on a more personal level.

5. Close-Ups: At frequent intervals throughout the book, excerpts from magazines, newspapers, and other sources dramatize the topics under discussion with the vivid words of journalists, prisoners, judges, and attorneys.

6. Biographies: An introductory course usually highlights the many contributors to the development of the field. I have therefore included succinct descriptions of some of the most important figures in criminal justice. The student who knows something about the lives of these leaders will have a greater appreciation of their work.

7. Real-life experience: The story of a young man who was caught up in the criminal justice system is reprinted at the end of Chapter 4. "The People versus Donald Payne," first published in *Newsweek,* shows how the system operated in relation to one individual. While reading this selection, students can consider what they would have done in similar circumstances. New to this edition is a follow-up on Donald Payne, recapping some of what has happened in his life since the events described in the article.

8. Comparative Perspectives: Crime is a worldwide problem, and internationally there are various ways that justice is allocated. In each chapter there is a separate description of some aspect of criminal justice in a foreign country. A different view of American criminal justice is often possible when seen from an international perspective.

9. Other student aids: Each chapter opens with an outline and a list of the terms and cases to be discussed; each chapter concludes with a summary, discussion questions, and suggestions for further reading. The glossary items first encountered in the margins are presented alphabetically at the end of the text to facilitate quick reference. The appendix contains the criminal justice portions of the Constitution of the United States. The book concludes with a detailed index.

In the "Epilogue," I imagine the status of crime and justice in the year 2010, basing my projections on discernible trends that will affect policy. *The American System of Criminal Justice, Sixth Edition,* is neither a radical critique of its subject nor an endorsement of the status quo. I have tried to present contemporary, real-life aspects. Through this introductory text, I hope to challenge those who contemplate careers in the field to improve the system. For general readers, I have provided a foundation for participation in related policy decisions in their roles as voters, jurors, and informed citizens.

Criminal justice has been changing rapidly as new concepts and methods have come to the fore. The need for freedom and the need for order sometimes conflict in a democratic society, and this conflict creates both problems and opportunities. It is time for a new generation of criminal justice practitioners, scholars, and concerned citizens to provide the insight and leadership that will bring about long-overdue improvements.

Brief Contents

Contents

Policy Issue Number One: Should the Sale of Drugs Be Legalized?

**PART 2
POLICE**   **190**

Policy Issue Number Two: Should Handguns Be Regulated?

PART 3
COURTS   332

Chapter 12 Trial and Posttrial Processes   474

Chapter 13 Sentencing   506

PART 4
CORRECTIONS   504

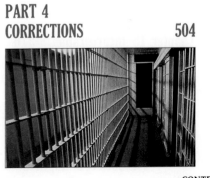

Policy Issue Number Three: Should the Death Penalty Be Abolished?

Chapter 14 Corrections   542

Chapter 15 Incarceration   576

Policy Issue Number Four: Should Less Use Be Made of Incarceration?

Chapter 16 Community Corrections: Probation, Intermediate Sanctions, Parole   632

Chapter 17 Juvenile Justice   676

PART 5
JUVENILE JUSTICE SYSTEM   674

EPILOGUE: Crime and Justice in the Year 2010   713

Appendix: Constitution of the United States Criminal Justice

6th Edition

The American System of Criminal Justice

THE CRIMINAL JUSTICE PROCESS

Crime is an enduring problem that has required attention since time immemorial. Today we want to understand the dimensions of this problem, how it has been defined, and how American society has attempted to deal with it. Is it possible that crime will never be controlled? What types of behaviors does the law define as "criminal"? What legal and administrative requirements must be met before a person can be labeled "guilty"? Part 1 explores such questions with a twofold aim: to give the reader (1) a sense of the nature of crime and what is currently being done about it and (2) a broad, general framework within which to analyze the more specific materials found in the rest of the book.

Crime and Justice in America

Key Terms

assembly-line justice
crime
Crime Control Model

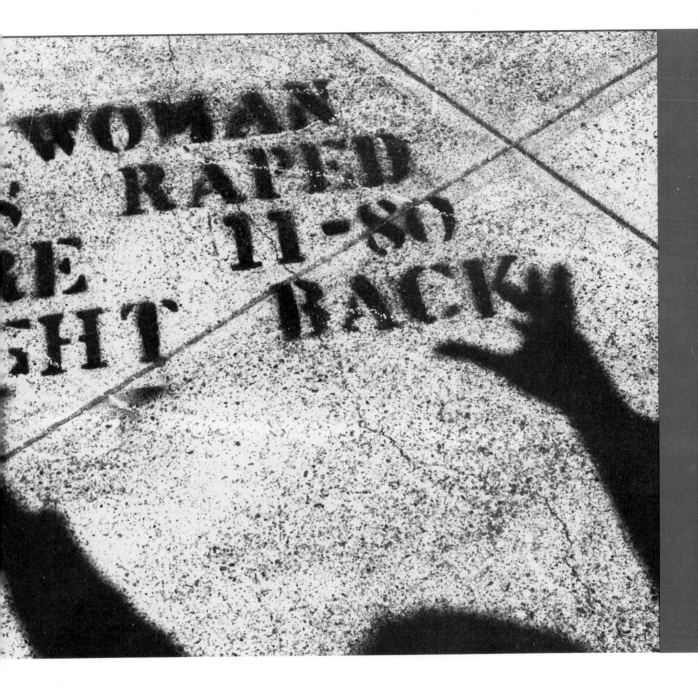

crime rate
dark figure of crime
Due Process Model

National Crime Surveys
political considerations
underclass

Uniform Crime Reports
victimization rate

There is much crime in America, more than ever is reported, far more than ever is solved, far too much for the health of the Nation. Every American knows that. Every American is, in a sense, a victim of crime.

*President's Commission on Law Enforcement and
Administration of Justice (1967)*

Newspaper headlines tell the story: "Killings Soar in Big Cities Across U.S.," "Shopowners Demand Foot Patrol," "Drug Turf War Yields Violence," "Neighbors Unite Against Crime," "Prison Population Reaches New High." Television news programs depict urban neighborhoods ravaged by drugs and crime, small towns where shoot-outs have occurred, and frightened citizens expressing fears about leaving their homes at night. But what is the reality of the American crime problem in the 1990s? Is it really increasing as the media portray, or has the amount of crime leveled out? The Bureau of Justice Statistics reports that violent crimes, personal thefts, and household crimes are down from their peaks in 1981, yet there are calls for increased use of the death penalty, for more police resources, for crash programs to build prisons. Is the United States in the 1990s really experiencing a criminal justice crisis? And if it is, what should be done?

Crime and justice are crucial policy issues in a country such as the United States in which a tension exists between the need to maintain public order and security and the need to protect such precious values as individual liberties, the rule of law, and democratic government. One might hope that citizens of the "land of the free" could live without having to devote great physical and psychological energies, let alone resources, to personal protection, but for many Americans the possibility of being victimized by criminals is ever present. When in 1973 the National Advisory Commission on Criminal Justice Standards and Goals set as a target the reduction of crime over the ensuing ten years, it stated that a time would come in the immediate future when

- A couple can walk in the evening in their neighborhood without fear of assault and robbery.
- A family can go away for the weekend without fear of returning to a house ransacked by burglars.
- A woman can take a night job without fear of being raped on her way to or from work.
- Every citizen can live without fear of being brutalized by unknown assailants.[1]

Almost two decades later, however, these goals are more elusive than ever.

CRIME AND JUSTICE AS PUBLIC POLICY ISSUES

Although there is widespread agreement in American society that crime is a serious problem, there is no consensus on the approaches to be taken to address this problem. Some people believe that the answer lies in stricter enforcement of the law through the expansion of police forces and the enactment of punitive measures that will result in the swift and certain punishment of criminals. The holders of this conservative view, politically dominant for the past decade, argue that we must strengthen crime control, which they assert has been hurt by decisions of the U.S. Supreme Court and liberal programs that have weakened traditional values of responsibility and family. In opposition are people who argue that the strengthening of crime control would endanger the cherished values of due process and justice. Liberals say that the conservative approach would also be ineffective in reducing crime because the answer lies in reshaping the lives of individual offenders and changing the social conditions from which criminal behavior springs.

Dealing with Crime

Changes in the direction of public policies do not occur suddenly, at specific points in time. With regard to crime, the conservative critique of the liberal policies of the 1960s gained in credence during the 1970s, in part because of findings by criminal justice researchers that cast doubt on many of the earlier ideas. Debate about "what works" forced a reconsideration of rehabilitation as the primary goal of the criminal sanction. Research was published that began to question many traditionally held assumptions about police work. Reformers recommended that greater weight be given to the goals of incarceration and deterrence. Questions were raised about the granting of bail to repeat offenders, the prosecution of career criminals, the lengths of jail and prison sentences, and the broader efforts to reduce crime through social reform.

More important than distinctions between these liberal and conservative approaches is the necessity that criminal justice policies be based on the fact that the United States is a democracy. The American democratic system requires that public policies be developed through the political process, that the rule of law prevail, and that the goals of criminal justice be pursued in an administrative context. It is in the political arena, at the local, state, and national levels, that democratic governments decide how to pursue such a problem. These requirements are a tall order, and we must recognize that differences of opinion exist over specific goals and the means by which they are pursued.

Debate over criminal justice policies is carried on daily in the press, in legislative assemblies, and in private conversations. In this book we will spotlight four policy issues that now concern Americans: Should drugs be legalized? Should handguns be controlled? Should the death penalty be abolished? Should less use be made of incarceration? These are questions about which there is much debate among researchers, policy makers, and citizens. They are questions

■

In a democracy criminal justice policies often result in extensive debate. In what ways might groups such as these death penalty abolitionists try to influence the process and policies?

that directly concern questions related to crime and justice. They are questions about which every citizen should be informed. What is your position on these matters?

Perhaps the most important question confronting American society is how to control crime while preserving due process and the elements of freedom and justice that quintessentially define a democracy. Citizens cannot enjoy their freedom, for example, if they are afraid to walk the streets and must spend a lot of energy and money protecting themselves against crime. However, freedom is too precious to be infringed on by unconstitutional actions of law enforcement agencies. Similarly, those wrongly accused of crime do not receive justice if they are convicted, nor do offenders who have paid their debt to society receive justice if they are treated as ex-convicts rather than as citizens. Though much of our crime problem would disappear if the police were to receive a massive allocation of resources and if limitations on their actions were to be removed, such a public policy would create a police state and a loss of freedom and justice.

Questions for Analysis

Although the press and the public decry the rise in crime and reformers argue that the administration of justice must be drastically changed, it is necessary to address a number of preliminary questions so that we can understand the problem before attempting to deal with it. First, we must know something about the causes of crime. Of equal importance is knowing something about how justice is dispensed by the legal system. Are rich and poor treated alike? Is the constitutional guarantee of a fair and speedy trial upheld? What are the purposes of correctional programs?

It is also necessary to learn how and why the criminal justice system operates. This means that we must take a hardheaded look at the history and operations of the police, courts, and corrections and the social forces that created them. The reality of criminal justice in the United States will shock many people, but only when the way the justice machinery functions is understood can proposals for change be considered.

Description of a social system is important, but criminal justice specialists must also be able to analyze why the process operates as it does. They must draw on the literature of a wide range of scholarly disciplines—among them law, history, and the social sciences—to bring together theories and concepts that will help them understand the reality of the system and predict the probable course of future actions. Social analysis is an ongoing search to determine why people act as they do. When the roles played by the multitude of actors in the vast criminal justice system are understood, new and different approaches can be explored to achieve the goal of maintaining both order and freedom.

The criminal justice system is one in which individuals make decisions about others. Although we emphasize the rule of law in our society, it must be recognized that criminal justice professionals—police officers, prosecutors, attorneys, judges, and correctional officials—ultimately must analyze situations in which the law is often only a guideline. Often the law does not help direct the right decision, with the result that officials must rely on their own sense of ethics, their own moral values, to determine what course of action to take. It is a system of *justice* that we are exploring, and thus the allocation of this precious value is greatly determined by questions of ethics that force officials to make decisions within the context of our moral heritage.

Chapter 1 introduces several of the underlying assumptions of the book, looking at such basic themes as the amount and type of crime in America, the war on drugs, the present condition of the system, and the role of politics in criminal justice. Conceptual tools for analysis are discussed in the final section. Succeeding chapters will consider the primary influences of law and administration on the practices of each portion of the system. Some people may view the challenge of crime in a free society as an unpleasantness to be avoided, but the rewards for those interested in understanding the system are many, because understanding provides the necessary basis for making appropriate changes.

CRIME IN AMERICA

Emile Durkheim, a nineteenth-century sociologist, made the classic observation that crime is a normal part of society:

> Crime is present not only in the majority of societies of one particular species but in all societies of all types. There is no society that is not confronted with the problem of criminality. Its form changes; the acts thus characterized are not the same everywhere, but, everywhere and always, there have been men who have behaved in such a way as to draw upon themselves penal repression.[2]

In view of the capacity of other eras to produce criminals, villains, deviants, and deeds of violence, ours is neither the best nor the worst

High levels of crime are not new to the United States. It seems that during every generation there are calls for a war on crime.

of times. There has always been too much crime, and virtually every generation since the founding of the Republic has felt threatened by it. References abound to serious outbreaks of violence following the Civil War, after World War I, during the Prohibition Era, and in the midst of the Great Depression. As the President's Commission on Law Enforcement and Administration of Justice pointed out in 1967:

> A hundred years ago contemporary accounts of San Francisco told of extensive areas where "no decent man was in safety to walk the streets after dark; while at all hours, both night and day, his property was jeopardized by incendiarism and burglary." Teenage gangs gave rise to the "hoodlum"; while in one central New York City area, near Broadway, the police entered "only in pairs, and never unarmed."[3]

That there has always been a great deal of crime does not mean that the amount and types of crime have been the same. During the labor unrest of the 1880s and 1930s, pitched battles took place be-tween strikers and company police. Race riots occurred in Atlanta in 1907 and in Chicago, Washington, and East St. Louis, Illinois, in 1919. Organized crime became a special focus during the 1930s. The mur-der and nonnegligent homicide rate, which reached a high in 1933 and a low during World War II, has actually decreased since 1982, as shown in Figure 1.1, even though the rate in some cities has risen dramatically during the last several years.

What is striking about crime in the United States is that the prob-lem is so much greater than it is in other industrialized countries. In per capita terms, about ten American men die by criminal violence for every Japanese, Austrian, German, or Swedish man; about fifteen American men die for every English or Swiss man; and over twenty for every Dane.[4] More than 150 countries, both developed and unde-veloped, have lower murder rates than the United States, as shown in Figure 1.2.[5] When we look at robbery rates, the data are even more dismaying. The robbery rate for New York City is five times greater than London's and, incredibly, 125 times higher than that of Tokyo.[6] In the 1980s crime in the United States stabilized at a very high level; however, by the 1990s arrests for drug sales and possession had sky-rocketed, causing dislocations in many parts of the criminal justice system. As the twentieth century draws to a close, our thoughts turn to the future. Will crime remain at today's levels? What will be the focus of criminal justice policies?

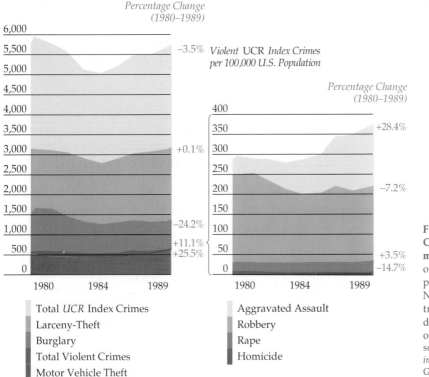

UCR *Index Crimes per 100,000 U.S. Population*

Percentage Change (1980–1989)

Total *UCR* Index Crimes
Larceny-Theft
Burglary
Total Violent Crimes
Motor Vehicle Theft

Aggravated Assault
Robbery
Rape
Homicide

FIGURE 1.1

Crime trends for index offenses as measured by the *UCR*. The number of crimes reported to the police is presented as a rate per 100,000 persons. Note that there is a general downward trend for most crimes but an increase during the last few years in crimes of violence.

SOURCE: U.S. Department of Justice, *Crime in the United States* (Washington, DC: Government Printing Office, 1986, 1990).

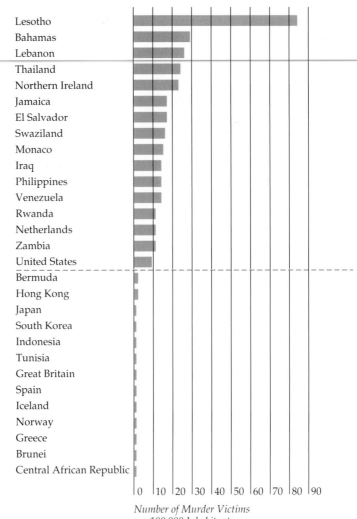

FIGURE 1.2
Comparing homicide rates in different countries. Why is the murder rate in the United States so much higher than in other developed, and some undeveloped, countries? What data collection problems might skew this figure? Is homogeneity of the population a likely factor?
NOTE: Only countries with the highest and lowest rates are included. The dotted line indicates where countries have been left out.
SOURCE: Interpol and United Nations Statistics, 1980–1986. Adapted from "Cross-national comparison of homicide: Age/sex-adjusted rates using the 1980 U.S. homicide experience as a standard," by G. Deane, *Journal of Quantitative Criminology*, 1987, 3(3): 215–227.

Number of Murder Victims per 100,000 Inhabitants

How Much Crime Is There?

One of the frustrations in studying criminal justice is the lack of accurate means of knowing the amount of crime in society. Surveys that ask members of the public whether they have ever committed a breach of the law indicate that much more crime occurs than is reported. Until very recently, the only criminal activities that were counted were those that were known to the police and that made their way into the Federal Bureau of Investigation's annual statistics. Since 1972, however, the Department of Justice has sponsored ongoing surveys of the public to determine the amount of criminal victimization experienced. A comparison of these studies with the FBI figures (published in the *Uniform Crime Reports*) reveals a significant discrepancy between the occurrence of crime and offenses known to the police. The large numbers of offenses never brought to the attention of the police, often referred to as the **dark figure of crime,** are of concern to the police and to criminal justice planners. Homicide and auto theft are the two offenses whose reported and estimated occurrences correspond. In the case of homicide, this correspondence can

dark figure of crime: A metaphor that emphasizes the dangerous dimension of crime that is never reported to the police.

be explained by the fact that a body must be accounted for; in the case of auto theft, by the fact that insurance payments require the police to be called in. But about 45 percent of U.S. rape victims do not report the attack to the police; almost half of robbery victims and 55 percent of those experiencing simple assault do not do so. Figure 1.3 shows the percentage of victimizations not reported to the police in the United States.

Many reasons have been advanced to account for nonreporting of crime. Some victims of rape and assault fear the embarrassment of public disclosure and interrogation by the police. Increasingly, evidence reveals that much violence occurs between persons who know each other—spouses, lovers, relatives—but the passions of the moment take on a different character when the victim is asked to testify against a family member. Another reason for nonreporting is that lower socioeconomic groups fear police involvement. In some neighborhoods, residents believe that the arrival of the law for one purpose may result in the discovery of other illicit activities, such as welfare fraud, housing code violations, or the presence of persons on probation or parole. In many of these same places the level of police protection has been minimal in the past, and residents feel that they will get little assistance. Finally, the value of property lost by larceny, robbery, or burglary may not be worth the effort of a police investigation. Many citizens are deterred from reporting a crime by unwillingness to become "involved," go to the station house to fill out papers, perhaps go to court, or to appear at a police lineup. All these aspects of the criminal process may result in lost workdays and in the expense of travel and child care. Even then, the stolen item may go unrecovered. As these examples suggest, multitudes of people feel that it is rational not to report criminal incidents because the costs outweigh the gains.

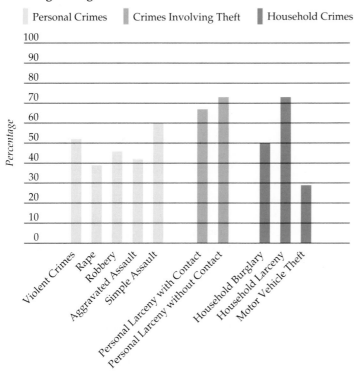

FIGURE 1.3
Percentage of victimizations not reported to the police. What are some of the reasons why people do not report their victimizations to the police? What can be done to encourage reporting? SOURCE: U.S. Department of Justice, Bureau of Justice Statistics, *Report to the Nation on Crime and Justice*, 2nd ed. (Washington, DC: Government Printing Office, 1988), p. 34.

Uniform Crime Reports

Uniform Crime Reports: An annually published statistical summary of crimes reported to the police based on voluntary reports to the FBI by local, state, and federal law enforcement agencies.

One of the main sources of crime statistics is the ***Uniform Crime Reports (UCR),*** which is maintained by the FBI and published annually. At the urging of the International Association of Chiefs of Police, Congress in 1930 authorized this national and uniform system of compiling crime data. The *UCR* is the product of a voluntary national network through which about 16,000 local, state, and federal law enforcement agencies transmit information to Washington concerning the twenty-nine types of offenses listed in Table 1.1. For eight major crimes—"index offenses"—the collected data show such factors as age, race, and number of reported crimes solved, whereas for the twenty-one other offense categories the data are not so complete.

Crime data is expressed three ways in the *UCR*: (l) as aggregates (there was a total of 578,000 robberies reported to the police in 1990); (2) as percentage changes over different time periods (this represented a 6.5 percent increase over 1989); and (3) as a rate for 100,000 people in the United States (the robbery rate was 233).

The value of the *UCR* has been questioned by a number of scholars. They point out that the data concern only crimes reported to the police, that submission of the data is voluntary, that the reports are not truly uniform because events are defined according to differing criteria in various regions of the country, and that many occupational crimes are not included. Finally, because of the shape of the graphs presented in the reports and the choice of baseline data, the untutored eye may not see the potential for distortion. In response to some

TABLE 1.1 ***Uniform Crime Reports* offenses**   The *UCR* presents extensive data on eight index offenses and twenty-one other offenses for which there is less information. When reading the *UCR*, it must be remembered that only crimes reported to the police are tabulated.

Part I (Index Offenses)	Part II (Other Offenses)
1. Criminal homicide	9. Simple assaults
2. Forcible rape	10. Forgery and counterfeiting
3. Robbery	11. Fraud
4. Aggravated assault	12. Embezzlement
5. Burglary	13. Buying, receiving, or possessing stolen property
6. Larceny-theft	14. Vandalism
7. Auto theft	15. Weapons (carrying, possession, etc.)
8. Arson	16. Prostitution and commercialized vice
	17. Sex offenses
	18. Violation of narcotic drug laws
	19. Gambling
	20. Offenses against the family and children
	21. Driving under the influence
	22. Violation of liquor laws
	23. Drunkenness
	24. Disorderly conduct
	25. Vagrancy
	26. All other offenses (excluding traffic)
	27. Suspicion
	28. Curfew and loitering (juvenile)
	29. Runaway (juvenile)

SOURCE: U.S. Department of Justice, Federal Bureau of Investigation, *Crime in the United States* (Washington, DC: Government Printing Office, 1991).

of the criticisms of researchers, the FBI has revised aspects of the program. These changes will be implemented nationwide during the early 1990s. Some offenses are being redefined, and police agencies are being asked to report more details about crime events. In addition, police agencies are to report all crimes committed during an incident, not just the most serious one as is currently the case.

As they now exist, the *Uniform Crime Reports* have limitations and must be used cautiously. But insofar as they contain information about what is known of crime, they are a valuable tool for the criminal justice scholar.

National Crime Surveys

In 1972 the U.S. Bureau of the Census began the largest series of interview programs ever conducted to determine the extent and nature of crime victimization. Sponsored by the Department of Justice, these surveys are designed to generate estimates of quarterly and yearly victimization rates for all index offenses except homicide and arson. The *National Crime Surveys (NCS)* are based on data collected through interviews with a national probability sample of 100,000 people representing 50,000 households. The same people are interviewed twice a year for three years about their experiences with crime in the previous six months. In addition, specialized surveys of twenty-six communities produce crime rates for many of the nation's largest cities. Separate studies of businesses are made. The results show that for the crimes measured (rape, robbery, assault, burglary, theft), 36 million victimizations affecting 22 million households (about 25 percent of all U.S. households) occur each year, a level much higher than that indicated by the number of crimes reported to the police.[7]

Each person interviewed in the national sample is asked a series of questions (for instance, Did anyone beat you up, attack you, or hit you with something such as a rock or a bottle?) to determine whether he or she has been victimized. For each affirmative response to these "incident screen" questions, detailed questions then elicit specific facts about the event, characteristics of the offender, and resulting financial losses or physical disabilities. The collection of such data permits the number of crimes that have occurred nationwide to be estimated and yields trend information on the offenders and indications of demographic patterns that may be emerging.

Data from victimization surveys have thus far helped to validate some hypotheses about the nature of crime. To illustrate, the Justice Department has created a series of estimates of the chance of a given person over the age of twelve becoming a victim of violent crime (rape, robbery, assault). For any particular year, the victimization rate is about 35.9 per 1,000 for males and 23.8 per 1,000 for females. Over a lifetime, of course, the chance is much higher, and the figures do not include such forms of victimization as murder, kidnapping, or harm from drunken drivers.

The surveys also shed light on the connections between sex, age, and race and the probability of victimization. With the exception of rape and personal robbery with contact (purse snatching), men are more likely than women to be victims of crime. An interesting finding is that a majority of the victimizations seem to occur within the lower age group of twelve to twenty-four years. Youths between

National Crime Surveys: Interviews of samples of the U.S. population conducted by the Bureau of Justice Statistics to determine the number and types of criminal victimizations and thus the extent of unreported crime.

Although they are vulnerable, the elderly are less likely than the young to be victimized. What might account for this fact?

twelve and fifteen are most likely to be the victims of such crimes as personal larceny without contact, robbery, and simple assault. Race is also an important factor, with blacks and other minorities being more likely than whites to be raped, robbed, and assaulted. In light of the current concern about crimes against the elderly, a notable finding is that they are less likely than the young to be victimized. Clearly, availability, vulnerability, and desirability determine whether someone or something is a likely target. Randomness also contributes to the process. Being near an armed person who is intent on robbing and who perceives an opportunity to do so greatly increases the probability of victimization.

Although the victimization studies have added to our scientific knowledge about crime, there are a number of difficulties with these data. For example, it is obvious that the surveys are unlikely to gather information about offenses in which the persons being interviewed participated. *NCS* representatives are undoubtedly seen as official representatives of government, and thus the data tell us little about such crimes as gambling, drug trafficking, prostitution, or the purchase of stolen property. It must also be remembered that the surveys are organized to document the victim's perception of an incident. Although the latter is perhaps important, it can be argued that laypersons do not have the legal background that would allow them to differentiate criminal from noncriminal behavior. The high number of incidents reported by the young, for example, is thought to be produced by defining schoolyard shakedowns or fights as criminal. Property thought to have been stolen may have been lost. Memories may grow hazy on dates and carry last year's crime into this year's data. Given the recent patterns of stability in **victimization rates,** however, this deficiency should not overshadow the analytical value of the studies. The Bureau of Justice Statistics has recently redesigned certain aspects of the *NCS* so as to improve accuracy and detail. Table 1.2 compares the *Uniform Crime Reports* and the *National Crime Surveys.*

victimization rate: The number of victimizations per 1,000 people or households as reported by the *National Crime Surveys.*

TABLE 1.2 How do the *UCR* and *NCS* compare? Compare the data sources. Remember that the *UCR* tabulates only crimes reported to the police, whereas the *NCS* is based on interviews with victims.

	Uniform Crime Reports	National Crime Surveys
Offenses Measured	Homicide Rape Robbery (personal and commercial) Assault (aggravated) Burglary (commercial and household) Larceny (commercial and household) Motor vehicle theft Arson	Rape Robbery (personal) Assault (aggravated and simple) Household burglary Larceny (personal and household) Motor vehicle theft
Scope	Crimes reported to the police in most jurisdictions; considerable flexibility in developing small-area data	Crimes both reported and not reported to police; all data are for the nation as a whole; some data are available for a few large geographic areas
Collection Method	Police department reports to FBI	Survey interviews: periodically measures the total number of crimes committed by asking a national sample of 60,000 households representing 135,000 people over the age of twelve about their experiences as victims of crime during a specific period
Kinds of Information	In addition to offense counts, provides information on crime clearances, persons arrested, persons charged, law enforcement officers killed and assaulted, and characteristics of homicide victims	Provides details about victims (such as age, race, sex, education, income, and whether the victim and offender were related to each other) and about crimes (such as time and place of occurrence, whether or not reported to police, use of weapons, occurrence of injury, and economic consequences)
Sponsor	Department of Justice Federal Bureau of Investigation	Department of Justice Bureau of Justice Statistics

SOURCE: U.S. Department of Justice, Bureau of Justice Statistics, *Report to the Nation on Crime and Justice,* 2nd ed. (Washington, DC: Government Printing Office, 1988), p. 11.

Crime Trends

Despite some skepticism about the accuracy during the past two decades of the data concerning crime, the impression that the U.S. **crime rate** has risen is generally accepted as accurate. What remain in dispute are crime trends. The *National Crime Surveys* showed a general stability of victimization rates until 1981, when significant declines began to occur. From 1981 to 1988 the number of victimizations fell 10 percent for violent crimes; personal thefts, 15 percent; and household crimes, 18 percent.[8] The *Uniform Crime Reports* tell a somewhat different story: a dramatic rise in crime rates beginning in 1964 and continuing increases for most categories until 1980, when the rates

crime rate: The number of reported crimes per 100,000 people as published in the *Uniform Crime Reports.*

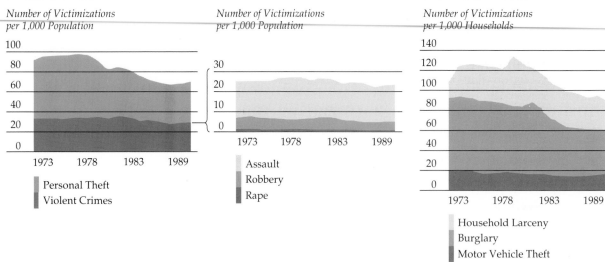

Trends in Victimization Rates of Personal Crimes

Number of Victimizations per 1,000 Population

Personal Theft
Violent Crimes

Number of Victimizations per 1,000 Population

Assault
Robbery
Rape

Trends in Victimization Rates of Household Crimes

Number of Victimizations per 1,000 Households

Household Larceny
Burglary
Motor Vehicle Theft

FIGURE 1.4
Crime victimization trends, 1973–1989.
Victimization trends, as recorded by the *NCS*, show a decline since the heights of the 1970s. Note how little variation there has been for certain offenses such as rape, robbery, and motor vehicle theft.
SOURCE: U.S. Department of Justice, Bureau of Justice Statistics, *Bulletin* (October 1989).

began to stabilize or decline. Crime trends, as revealed by the *UCR* in Figure 1.1, and the victimization rates from the *NCS* are illustrated by Figure 1.4.

The differences in the trends indicated by the *NCS* and the *UCR* are explained in part by the different data sources and different population bases on which their computations of crime rates are based. As discussed earlier, the "dark figure of crime" is an ongoing criminal justice problem, but this figure has declined for all of the index crimes since 1973. Over time the gap between the *UCR* data and those collected through the *NCS* has lessened. The Bureau of Justice Statistics found that in 1986, for the first time, more than half of all violent crimes were reported to the police, and significant gains in reporting were found in other categories.[9] This trend undoubtedly reflects an increase in citizen willingness to report criminal behavior. The introduction of "911" phone numbers, the augmented presence of police in many communities, and neighborhood watch programs have helped this effort.

The changing demographic characteristics of the American people constitute a major ingredient when analyzing crime trends. Age and urbanization are significant factors here. Criminologists have long shown that crime, especially the kinds the public fears most, is largely a function of youth and young adulthood. Persons in the fourteen-to-twenty-four age category have been the most crime-prone group in the country. In 1990, for example, the *UCR* disclosed that 30 percent of those arrested for serious crimes were under the age of eighteen, almost half of those arrested for robbery were under twenty-one, and 60 percent of those arrested for burglary were under twenty-one.[10]

The rise in crime during the 1970s has been attributed by some criminologists to the post–World War II baby boom. By the mid 1970s this high-risk crime group (fourteen to twenty-four years old) constituted a much larger portion of the U.S. population than "normal." It was thus predicted that between 40 and 50 percent of the total arrests during that period could have been expected as the result of population increase and the size of the "crime-prone" age group. Likewise the decline in crime rates during the 1980s has been ascribed to the maturing of the post–World War II generation. Demographers also cite those baby-boomers still committing crimes as contributing to the prison population explosion.

The impact of demographic factors on the extent of crime has been disputed by other researchers, who stress that arrest and sentencing practices play a more important role than age in crime reduction. These researchers say that the government's response to crime should be given greater credit for the decline. They argue, for example, that in the 1960s crime went up as the probability of being arrested for committing a serious crime and of being sent to prison after arrest went down. They assert that the lenient policies of that era contributed to the rise of crime. Because crime control policies were made more punitive in the late 1970s and 1980s, they contend, the probability of arrest and incarceration has been increasing. In this view, the tougher stance has paralleled the fall of crime rates.

Crime: An Urban Problem?

Urbanization has had an impact on the crime rate. Violent crime is primarily a phenomenon of large cities. Of the 14 million index offenses known to the police in 1989, more than 13 million occurred in cities. The greatest proportional increase in serious crimes has taken place in cities with populations above a half million. Although fewer than 18 percent of the American people live in such cities, they account for more than half the reported index offenses against persons and almost a third of all reported index property crimes.

Studies have shown that crime rates invariably rise in proportion to proximity to the center of an urban area. The highest incidence is in physically deteriorating, high-density urban cores, in which economic insecurity, poor housing, family disintegration, and transiency are most pronounced. These areas are where the poor live. Beginning in the 1960s, the populations of such districts tended to become predominantly African-American, as rural southerners moved to the cities to better their lives. Blacks are only a recent group to follow this pattern. In earlier periods, urban areas with the same characteristics were populated by various successive groups of immigrants: Irish, Jews, and Italians. Today some cities are experiencing a rise in crime among their newest immigrants, Asians and Central Americans. This has raised problems for the criminal justice system, where personnel are unprepared to deal with the language and culture of the new groups.

But it is important to recognize that it is not just because the residents of urban ghettos are poor that crime is so prevalent in their neighborhoods. When asking why some poor neighborhoods are crime ridden whereas other poor neighborhoods are not, it is necessary to consider a variety of ecological factors, including the physical conditions of the neighborhoods, the level of moral cynicism of the residents, the extent of the opportunities for crime, and the amount of social control by families and government agencies.[11]

The Urban Underclass

underclass: Disadvantaged members of the urban community, mainly blacks and Hispanics, who are at the bottom of the economic and social hierarchy. Membership is characterized by poverty, unemployment, criminal behavior, drug use, and welfare dependency.

Although U.S. history documents the upward mobility of the poor and immigrant groups, there is increasing concern that in today's cities there resides an **underclass,** the members of which seem unable to improve their condition. Sociologist William Julius Wilson describes the urban underclass as a "heterogeneous grouping of families and individuals in the inner city that are outside the mainstream of the American occupational system and that consequently represent the very bottom of the economic hierarchy."[12] It is estimated that about 5 million of the 33 million Americans with incomes below the official poverty line are members of this group. They are disproportionately African-American and Hispanic, a minority within these minorities. Being a member of the underclass is more a way of life than an economic condition. These people's behavior is typified by "chronic lawlessness, drug use, out-of-wedlock births, nonwork, welfare dependency, and school failure."[13] Without ties to families, churches, and other social institutions, members of the underclass seem to lack the values and direction attributed to the working poor. They do not have employable skills, and they tend to depend upon welfare subsidies and crimes, especially drug sales, to make ends meet.

In the inner cities with high drug use, murder rates have skyrocketed. Most of those slain, like their killers, tend to be young and black. Nearly one of every four black males between the ages of

COMPARATIVE PERSPECTIVE
Iceland: A Country with Little Crime

For the past several decades the increase in crime has been a major concern in the United States and Western Europe, yet there are countries where crime is not perceived as a problem. Iceland is one such country. Why is it that Iceland should differ so much from other countries in this respect? Is it the size of the population? The homogeneity of the people? The physical isolation from the major centers of Europe? What is it like to live in a country where there have been only twenty-one robberies over a twenty-year period, where there is an average of only two homicides per year, and where the first bank robbery with a firearm occurred in 1984?

Iceland, with a population of 253,000, is an island republic the size of Virginia. It has strong cultural ties to Denmark, which ruled it from 1380 until World War II, and to the other countries of Scandinavia. The Icelandic population is

ethnically homogeneous; there are relatively small differences along class lines, literacy is very high, and the Evangelical Lutheran Church is attended by about 95 percent of the population. The people enjoy a high standard of living, an extensive health and welfare system (reflected by the world's lowest infant mortality rate), and a 1 percent unemployment rate. To preserve the "purity" of the culture, governmental policies have been instituted to restrict immigration.

Even though 90 percent of the Icelandic people live in urban areas, the country is what the German social theorist Ferdinand Tönnies would call a *Geimeinschaft* (community) society, in which extended families, strong community ties, and a homogeneous culture seem to act as effective agents of social control. This *Geimeinschaft* society exists because of a cultural lag in Iceland in the shift to industriali-

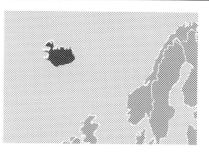

zation and urbanization that began at the turn of the century. As a result, Iceland has retained many of the aspects of a stagnant agrarian society.

When compared to the United States, Icelandic crime rates are extremely low. For example the assault rate per 100,000 people is 24; in the United States, 383. The rate for homicide is 0.8 for Iceland; for the United States, 4. For rape, Iceland's rate is 10, whereas the U.S. rate is 75. "Social density," homogeneous population, geographic isolation from other countries, and prohibition of handgun ownership are all factors contributing to the low level of violence in Iceland.

There has been an increase in

twenty and twenty-nine is under some type of correctional super-vision—probation, prison, or parole. In some inner-city neighbor-hoods, the rate is even higher. The homicide rate among this group is 100 per 100,000 population, about six times that for the same age bracket in the general popuation. These statistics describe what some have called a "lost generation of black men on a treadmill toward criminality and incarceration, cut off in the prime of their lives from society's mainstream like a diseased limb."[14] Young black urban women are also "lost" since they live in poverty without mates; their children grow up without fathers and without male role models. The cycle completes as these young people become both predators on their neighbors and dependents rather than productive citizens. A social time bomb exists in America's cities that unless changed can only lead to further crime and violence.

Impact of Crime on the Poor

One result of the presence of an underclass is that a jungle-like at-mosphere pervades such notorious urban areas as the South Bronx, Chicago's Robert Taylor Homes, and the Liberty City section of Miami. Within these ghettos and their counterparts in other large cities, criminals pursue their neighbors. This situation has prompted some scholars and policy makers to argue that crime causes poverty in the inner city.[15] They point out that low-income households are burglarized nearly twice as often as households with incomes of

---

drug use in Iceland during the past decade, but it is still minuscule compared with that in other West-ern countries. Cannabis use in-creased during the 1970s but has dwindled since then. In 1984 about 4 percent of Icelanders aged 16 to 36 said they had consumed ampheta-mines. It was not until 1983 that police found cocaine for the first time; they first seized a significant amount (one kilo) in 1987. Crack has not reached Iceland.

Undoubtedly, the size of Ice-land's population and its isolation from the major drug supply routes account for the low level of drug abuse. Also it is easy to "seal" the country, since import routes are few, and it is difficult for drug users to hide their habits in such a tightly knit community. There seem to be no organized drug rings in Iceland.

Whereas most Western countries are preoccupied with the war on drugs, this social problem is over-shadowed in Iceland by concern over alcohol abuse. Alcohol abuse, especially drunken driving, has been highly correlated with the

crime rate. Alcohol abuse is treated seriously in Iceland as it is in other Scandinavian countries. Total con-sumption of alcohol has increased during recent decades, and public drunkenness is the most com-mon violation of the criminal law. Having the highest number of au-tomobiles per capita in the world, Iceland strictly enforces drunk driving rules, with a resulting high arrest rate (1,400 per 100,000 versus 386 per 100,000 in the United States). Most arrests occur as a re-sult of intensive routine highway checks. Alcohol-related offenses are treated seriously. If blood tests re-veal 0.5 to 1.2 per milliliter alcohol, drivers lose their licenses for one month. Drivers with more than 1.2 per milliliter lose their licenses for a year. Incarceration is the sentence for a third offense. Given the low level of serious crimes and a policy of treating alcohol offenses se-verely, 20 percent of prisoners in Iceland are those committed for drunk driving.

The number of crimes reported to the Icelandic police has followed

the rapid transformation of the so-ciety over the past thirty years. As in other countries, the crime rate in-creased after World War II but lev-eled off during the past decade. The increases in crime can be accounted for by several factors. The growth of economic crimes seems to be a consequence of more complex busi-ness activities. Concern over the abuse of alcohol has resulted in proactive law enforcement policies that have contributed to the in-crease in criminality. It must be kept in mind that this increase ex-ists in the context of Iceland's very low rate of criminality as compared with those in other developed countries. As in Scandinavian countries and in low crime coun-tries such as Switzerland, there ap-pear to be cultural, geographic, economic, and public policy factors that explain the virtual absence of crime in Iceland.

SOURCE: Drawn from "Crime and the Crime Control System of Iceland," O. H. Krist-mundsson. University of Connecticut, unpub-lished paper, 1990. Reprinted by permission.

$25,000 to $30,000. The poor suffer the highest median economic losses from personal crimes such as robbery, assault, and theft. Since poor people often cannot afford insurance, and since personal property accounts for almost all of their capital, the theft of a TV, furniture, or a car can be devastating. A single robbery of cash, food stamps, or a welfare check may undo a family. Perhaps more important is the fact that with crime rampant, the poor are reluctant to avail themselves of opportunities—overtime, moonlighting, night school—that would improve their chances of escaping poverty.

Crime in the United States is not solely an urban problem. *NCS* data show that people living in rural areas are about half as likely as city dwellers to be victims of violent or property crimes. Although white Americans are fearful of being victimized by black strangers, most violent crime is intraracial; three of every four victims are of the same race as the attacker (see Figure 1.5). Similarly, in property crimes most victims and offenders are of the same race and economic group. Because social and economic factors largely determine where people live, work, and seek recreation, these same factors also influence the probability of people coming into close proximity with members of other groups. African-Americans and the poor thus bear a disproportionate risk of being victimized, for most are likely to live in the inner-city zones where street crime is greatest.

Research has suggested that it is extremely difficult to point to specific factors that have caused the rise in crime during the past two and a half decades. It is also vexing to try to determine why the crime rate in the United States should be so much higher than those in other industrialized democracies. It was once thought that the crime problem was amenable to analysis and solution, but social scientists

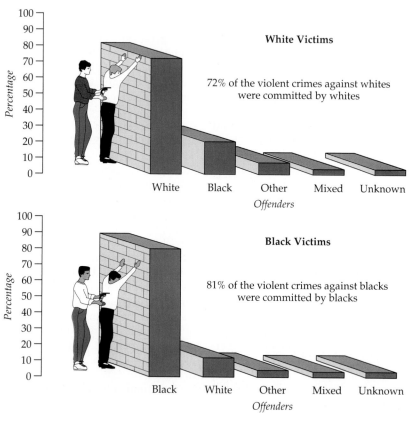

FIGURE 1.5
Victims and offenders are of the same race in three out of four violent crimes. Although whites seem most fearful of being victimized by blacks, the fact is that most violent crime is intraracial. Why do such misperceptions exist? SOURCE: U.S. Department of Justice, Bureau of Justice Statistics, *Report to the Nation on Crime and Justice*, 2nd ed. (Washington, DC: Government Printing Office, 1988), p. 21.

have discovered that it is an extremely complex phenomenon, requiring an understanding of some basic influences on human behavior. Does crime occur because of demography, unemployment, housing conditions, or family structure, or is it a result of the multiple interaction of these factors plus others that we are only now beginning to fathom?

Fear of Crime

Since 1965 public opinion organizations—Gallup, Harris, and others—have been asking Americans about their reactions to crime to determine whether they "feel more uneasy" or "fear to walk the streets at night." The results of these surveys show that the incidence of fearfulness closely matches the patterns of victimization and reported offenses. The trend rises sharply from the middle 1960s until about 1973 and then stabilizes. Although we may take heart that the proportion of people who fear crime has stabilized, the fact remains that fear of crime limits the freedom of more than 40 percent of the public. Many are forced to confine their activities to "safe" areas at "safe" times. Concern about crime leads people to spend money for protective devices. In addition, fear creates unmeasurable anxieties that have physiological and psychological ramifications. Perhaps most unsettling, some studies have shown that the very persons who have the least chance of being victimized by crime are the most fearful.

Fear of crime is primarily an urban phenomenon. In small towns and rural areas, fewer than 30 percent of the residents say that they are afraid to walk through their neighborhoods at night; in large cities, this figure is more than 60 percent. One impact of urban crime is that fear stimulates further movement of jobs, businesses, and middle-class people out of the central city, with the result that the core becomes hollow, deserted at night, and lacking in economic and social vitality. When city dwellers are timorous, neighborhood cohesiveness is eroded because residents curtail interactions with others, stop attending public gatherings, and view strangers with trepidation. Wesley Skogan and Michael Maxfield quote a black woman from South Philadelphia:

> People used to sit on their steps in the evenings, doors were open. Now the streets are deserted early in the morning and after dark. My mother used to go to church every morning—she stopped doing it— she is afraid of having her purse snatched. Many church and social activities have stopped—people won't go out at night.[16]

We know that when people talk about such fears, they are talking about street crime and particularly about being victimized by strangers. Robbery is perhaps the crime that citizens have uppermost in mind when they talk about their fears, for it is the violent crime most often committed by strangers (76 percent). But people are also apprehensive about being victimized by criminals when no face-to-face confrontation occurs. Burglary, a property crime without violence, also provokes fear because victims are conscious that there *could* have been a physical confrontation within the intimate setting of their households. The relationship between the victim and the offender is shown in Figure 1.6.

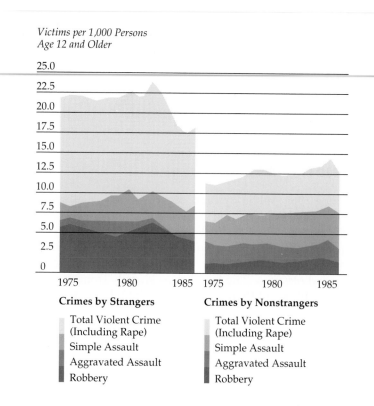

Victims per 1,000 Persons
Age 12 and Older

Crimes by Strangers

Total Violent Crime
(Including Rape)
Simple Assault
Aggravated Assault
Robbery

Crimes by Nonstrangers

Total Violent Crime
(Including Rape)
Simple Assault
Aggravated Assault
Robbery

FIGURE 1.6
**Strangers commit most violent crimes,
especially robbery.** Among violent
crimes, homicide and rape are most
frequently committed by acquaintances
or relatives. In such offenses as
robbery and assault, strangers are
more often the perpetrators.
SOURCE: U.S. Department of Justice, Bureau
of Justice Statistics, *Report to the Nation on
Crime and Justice*, 2nd ed. (Washington, DC:
Government Printing Office, 1988), p. 32.

Correlates of Fear

What are the individual and social characteristics of fear? One would
expect to find a strong relationship between victimization and fearfulness. Surprisingly, with the exception of crime victims who have
experienced personal offenses—rape, robbery, mugging—victims in
general are no more fearful than nonvictims. Victims of personal
offenses have a heightened level of fear, yet a crime of this sort is a
rare event in anyone's life (see Table 1.3). People evidently do not
assess criminal victimization in the same ways that they do other
risks, such as those caused by nature or by accident. Most research
also shows high levels of fear among nonwhites, people of low income, and those living in urban areas. This finding is not surprising,
given the concentration of street crime in sections of cities inhabited
by the poor and the nonwhite. However, women and the elderly—
groups that generally have low rates of victimization—are also more
frightened than the average citizen.

   How do we account for the fearfulness of social groups that have
not experienced victimization and do not observe crime in their
neighborhoods? Researchers point to vicarious or indirect victimization as an explanation. Some scholars believe that television viewing
shapes attitudes in regard to crime. Other researchers think that
personal communication networks report and materially magnify the
apparent volume of local violence. In all American cities there is
extensive newspaper and television coverage of crime and much publicizing of violence. Skogan and Maxfield found that people in
low- and high-income neighborhoods were equally attentive to crime
stories, but these researchers place greater weight on interpersonal
communication as a factor influencing levels of fear. In particular,
television reports and neighborhood conversations focus on and am-

TABLE 1.3 How do crime rates compare with the rates of other life events?
Crime seems to be on the minds of many Americans, but what are the risks of victimization compared to other life hazards?

Events	Rate per 1,000 Adults per Year
Accidental injury, all circumstances	290
Accidental injury at home	105
Personal theft	82
Accidental injury at work	68
Violent victimization	33
Assault (aggravated and simple)	25
Injury in motor vehicle accident	23
Divorce	23
Death, all cases	11
Serious (aggravated) assault	9
Death of spouse	9
Robbery	7
Heart disease death	4
Cancer death	2
Rape (women only)	2
Accidental death, all circumstances	0.5
Motor vehicle accident death	0.3
Pneumonia/influenza death	0.3
Suicide	0.2
Injury from fire	0.1
Homicide/legal intervention death	0.1
Death from fire	0.03

SOURCE: U.S. Department of Justice, Bureau of Justice Statistics, *Report to the Nation on Crime and Justice,* 2nd ed. (Washington, DC: Government Printing Office, 1988), p. 24.

plify crimes against women and the elderly, two groups perceived as vulnerable. Accounts about old, frail, or otherwise defenseless victims seem to heighten perceptions that criminals are rampant.[17]

Is it crime that makes people fearful or is it the perception of disorder in the neighborhood? Skogan's study of disorder and decay in selected neighborhoods of Chicago, Houston, Newark, and Minneapolis suggests that residents may be more fearful of disorder—rowdy youths, drunks, prostitutes, drug use, street harassment—than of crime itself. He found that there was a strong link between disorder and an index of perceived crime problems even when neighborhood stability, poverty, and racial composition were taken into account.[18]

Research has also shown that many say that they are fearful of crime in their own neighborhoods, but when they are asked to describe the local crime problem, their response is not specific. Dan Lewis and Michael Maxfield, for example, studied four Chicago neighborhoods. Although the perceptions by residents of dangerous areas matched official statistics, the people had difficulty pinpointing the types of crimes involved and their own risk of being victimized. Rather, their responses, similar to those found by Skogan, pointed to *incivility* in the community—signs of disorder such as abandoned buildings, vandalism, drug use, and loitering teenagers.[19] These views add weight to the thesis expressed by James Q. Wilson and George Kelling in their important article "Broken Windows: The Police and Neighborhood Safety."[20] They write that disorder in neighborhoods, if left unchecked, leads to physical and social deterioration. Such neighborhoods attract troublemakers and petty criminals, who then engage in theft, burglary, and street crime.[21] As we will see in

■ Fear of crime may lead to dramatic personal adjustments. Should this upper-class woman be fearful?

Chapters 5 and 6, this perspective supports the community policing approach, which claims that the problems of neighborhood deterioration, social disorder, and community disorganization must be addressed in order to stem the tide of crime and to make residents less fearful of their environment.

Responses to Fear of Crime

What do people do as a result of their fear of crime? As suggested earlier, many take what they believe are precautions by curtailing activities that they think may place them in a dangerous situation. Others attempt to reduce potential property loss by installing systems of one kind or another—more locks, window grilles, and alarms—that turn the home into a fortress. Those who can afford to do so may take refuge in apartment houses or residential enclaves that offer continuous surveillance, doormen or gatekeepers, and patrols. Still others flee to the suburbs or to the countryside, where it seems to them that crime is not a problem.

Most responses to the fear of crime are costly and require adjustments in lifestyle. The economically better off are able to take steps that will help alleviate their fear, whereas the poor must endure theirs. Paradoxically, those who are most vulnerable are also those least able to respond in ways that have a tempering effect.

THE WAR ON DRUGS

Crack cocaine arrived on the streets of New York, southern California, and Florida in 1985. Selling for ten to twenty dollars a vial, it became an immediate hit among users. Drug treatment centers were soon seeing addicts who had been using cocaine for several months only, not years. Beginning in mid-1986 the police of cities such as Washington, New York, Miami, and Los Angeles started to see sharp increases in murder, robbery, and other violent crimes in those neighborhoods where crack was in widespread use. New York's drug treatment centers were soon overwhelmed, and hospitals were registering an increase in the number of cocaine-addicted babies being born. In early 1987 Drug Enforcement Administration and Border Patrol officials reported increased drug trafficking on the Mexican border and the interception in Florida of large quantities of cocaine flown in from Colombia and Peru.

As magazines such as *Newsweek, Time,* and *U.S. News and World Report* featured the problem of drugs in lengthy cover articles and television networks told the crack story in hour-long specials, the U.S. public became aroused. The Gallup Poll registered a sharp increase in the percentage of Americans putting drugs as the number one national problem, way above the percentage ranking crime at the top. Political leaders, always ready to respond to the public pulse, soon were stressing the importance of doing something about drugs. In September 1987 President and Mrs. Reagan appeared together on nationwide television. The president asked Congress for $900 million for drug enforcement and treatment programs and stiffer penalties for drug sales, including life terms for major drug kingpins. The "War on Drugs" had begun.

Antidrug crusades have been a recurring theme in American politics since the 1880s.[22] Public concern about the use of marijuana, heroin, cocaine, and other drugs has come and gone as this issue has competed with others for attention. Antidrug campaigns are often described as "symbolic crusades" in that they seem to focus on groups and individuals perceived as a threat to traditional values. The rhetoric of the wars on drugs takes on an ideological aura that communicates the message that basic ideals concerning the nature of the community and individual responsibility are being challenged. In 1971 President Richard Nixon launched a campaign against drug abuse as part of an offensive for "law and order." By 1975 public concern about drugs seemed to have waned, but only seven years later President Ronald Reagan officially declared another war on drugs. In 1982 he requested that Congress appropriate more money for drug enforcement personnel, more prison space, stiffer sentences, and a more aggressive law enforcement stance against drug traffickers. The arrival of crack set the stage for another crusade.

The drug problem was high on the public's agenda throughout the presidential campaign of 1988. On reaching office, President Bush pressed Congress to appropriate $7.9 billion in the first year for drug enforcement, to build new prisons for drug offenders, to extend criminal penalties, to give military aid to drug source countries, and to create additional treatment and education programs. He appointed

President George Bush has used his office to emphasize the war on drugs. Critics have charged that the millions of dollars spent on drug enforcement should be diverted to deal with the problems that cause drug use.

America's first "Drug Czar," who was given the power to coordinate federal agencies in an all-out war on drugs.

One strategy in President Bush's war on drugs has been to focus on reducing the supply entering the country. This has traditionally been the job of the U.S. Coast Guard, the Customs Service, the Immigration and Naturalization Service, and the Drug Enforcement Administration. With the need to break up foreign and domestic drug smuggling, it was suggested that the Department of Defense be added to traditional federal law enforcement agencies. In the "peace lull" between the fall of the Berlin Wall and the Iraq conflict, officials debated the extent to which U.S. military forces should help interdict drugs arriving on American shores and the extent to which army and air force personnel should operate in Panama, Peru, Colombia, and Bolivia to reduce the supply (see Figure 1.7). All of this was taking place during a period when drug use, as measured by interviews with high school seniors, was on the decline.

Americans now spend about $40 billion a year buying illicit drugs. This is more than the combined expenditures for clothing, toys, sporting goods, and furniture. But consumers' expenditures on

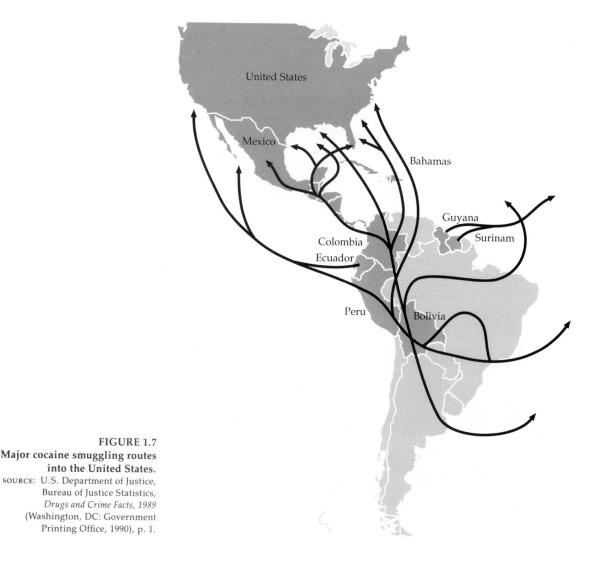

FIGURE 1.7
**Major cocaine smuggling routes
into the United States.**
SOURCE: U.S. Department of Justice,
Bureau of Justice Statistics,
Drugs and Crime Facts, 1989
(Washington, DC: Government
Printing Office, 1990), p. 1.

drugs is only a drop in the bucket compared to the total drug-related costs of the United States. In addition, more than $50 billion is spent on drug enforcement and corrections by federal, state, and local agencies; the impact on prosecution and courts; the billions of dollars spent on medical care for addicts; and the direct losses resulting from drug-related property and violent crimes. All of this is in addition to what Wilson cites as the loss of such important moral values as "temperance, fidelity, duty, and sympathy."[23]

Although some people argue that drug abuse should be treated as a health problem, most Americans consider it a crime problem. We may be concerned about the physical, economic, and social effects of drugs on individuals and their families, but the real concern seems to be about the link of drugs to crime. Because drugs are illegal, their cost is high. As a consequence, habitual users must acquire large amounts of money to obtain drugs. Since most abusers cannot amass through legitimate occupations the $200 per day they need to sustain their habits, they turn to crime. Researchers suggest that a majority of burglaries, robberies, and larcenies in many American cities are committed by addicts.[24] As shown in Figure 1.8, of males arrested for violent crimes in fourteen U.S. cities, between 54 percent (Kansas City) and 82 percent (Philadelphia) tested positive for drug use.[25] The increasing levels of violence in American cities are also attributed to drugs. Turf wars among rival gangs of dealers have been cited as the cause for the explosive increase of drug-related killings in Washington, Chicago, Atlanta, and Philadelphia.

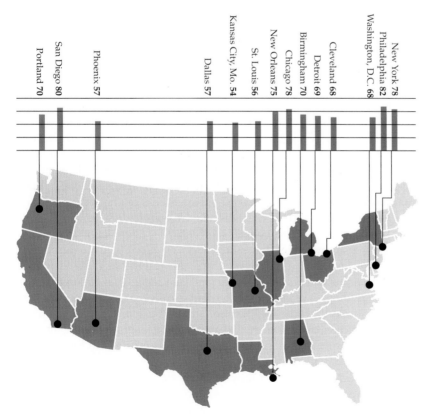

Portland 70 San Diego 80 Phoenix 57 Dallas 57 Kansas City, Mo. 54 St. Louis 56 New Orleans 75 Chicago 78 Birmingham 70 Detroit 69 Cleveland 68 Washington, D.C. 68 Philadelphia 82 New York 78

FIGURE 1.8
Percentage of male arrestees in fourteen cities who tested positive for any drug. Male arrestees for serious offenses in fourteen cities were tested for drug use. The majority of arrestees were charged with larceny-theft. The data not only support the belief that drug use is widespread among this group, but they also show that commission of crimes is necessary to support drug habits.
NOTE: All cities, except Washington, D.C., tested for ten drugs: opiates, cocaine, PCP, marijuana, amphetamines, Valium, Darvon, metaqualone, barbiturates, and methadone. (Washington does not test for marijuana.)
SOURCE: U.S. Department of Justice, National Institute of Justice, *NIJ Reports* (Washington, DC: Government Printing Office, (July/August, 1989), p. 8.

The importation, distribution, and sale of drugs is carried out by various organized crime groups such as the Colombia Medellin cartel, La Cosa Nostra, the United Bamboo Gang, Jamaican posses, and California street gangs. (Organized crime is fully discussed in Chapter 2.) Each of these organizations operates outside the legitimate financial and economic system, yet they must all follow the law of supply and demand, strive for efficiency in their operations, and follow rules. Being illegitimate, they cannot rely on the courts to enforce contracts, and thus violence is a business weapon. The "CEOs" of these drug organizations are usually insulated from public view by layers of protective subordinate operations. Typically, it is the young, poor street seller who is caught by the police while the "kingpins" remain untouched.

The largest of these groups have the ability, like legitimate corporations, to tap alternative sources of supply and to adapt readily to changing market conditions. Thus the Colombia cartel has been able to obtain coca leaf or paste in Peru, Bolivia, Ecuador, or Colombia itself. When Turkish authorities clamped down on the cultivation of opium-producing poppies, drug organizations shifted production to Southeast Asia. Because drug sellers deal only with cash, the organizations quickly invest their profits in the legitimate economy by "laundering" it through banks and other businesses.

Drugs and Crime

The current crack epidemic has had a devastating impact on inner-city communities. "Crack has greatly expanded the prosperity of the criminal underclass economy as well as incorporated and strengthened new elements into the criminal underclass subculture."[26] This has led to a great increase in violence and a decline of safety in American inner cities, which is related to the organization of the drug marketplace. Because heroin, cocaine, and crack are illegal, persons selling them have no recourse to law enforcement agencies when pressures are put on them by other sellers, their own "bosses," or organized crime operatives. Sellers are willing and able to use violence to maintain optimal selling conditions. Well-armed and well-organized drug organizations now exist in the inner cities of the largest American cities and in smaller urban areas as well. "They maintain effective paramilitary control much of the time in many inner-city streets and neighborhoods, although they generally cede control to police when they pass through."[27]

Drug use and sales have increased criminality in a number of ways. Heroin, cocaine, and crack use can rapidly lead some people into dependence. Because these drugs are illegal, they are expensive, and most users quickly exhaust their legally gained resources and must generate cash through crime (thefts, burglary, robbery, prostitution). Studies have shown that many drug users were engaged in criminality prior to their addiction, often committing up to 50 crimes per year. With drug dependence, they must commit up to 300 per year to maintain their habit.[28] Many become tied to drug organizations, become street sellers, and are paid off in drugs. Seller-users must protect themselves from predators and maintain their market turf, with resulting violence. Given the great economic returns to drug-selling organizations, the criminal underclass economy can rival or surpass the legitimate economic institutions in inner-city neighborhoods, which results in further devastation to the community.

The Criminal Justice Response

Throughout this book we will be examining the impact of the war on drugs on the American criminal justice system. The focusing of police resources on the sale and possession of illicit drugs has had an enormous ripple effect on the other parts of the system—prosecution, courts, and corrections. The one million drug arrests per year have clogged the courts so that in some cities, 75 percent of felony cases are now drug-related. In turn, the doubling of the prison population during the past ten years has been attributed largely to the drug war.

Critics have pointed out that governmental policies have not focused on reducing the demand for drugs and that treatment programs are sparse.[29] Others have said that the legalization of drug use would take the profit out of sales and that crime and violence would be reduced.[30] In turn, governmental expenditures could be shifted from law enforcement to treatment of addicts and education of the young about the perils of drug use. Such a shift in American policies and values is not likely to happen, but the debate has been useful in clarifying the goals of the war on drugs. The question is further discussed in Policy Issue 1: Should the Sale of Drugs Be Legalized?

The current war on drugs is not the first. During the early 1970s there was a similar war that focused on heroin use. Interestingly, that effort began as heroin use declined. David Musto points to other periods in American history when there has been much concern about the use of drugs. He argues that each generation experiencing drug abuse educates the next generation to its horrors. It is this collective memory that acts as a social control agent to suppress drug usage. Will the contemporary effort to "eradicate drugs" achieve its goal, or will it too fade as the public becomes concerned about some new aspect of crime and the threat to strongly held values?

CRIMINAL JUSTICE IN AMERICA

As crime has increased, the system of criminal justice has been unable to handle the demands made on it. In an oft-cited 1906 speech, "The Causes of Dissatisfaction with the Administration of Justice," Roscoe Pound, later dean of Harvard Law School (see Chapter 11), warned that a judicial system created within the framework of a rural America could not meet the needs of an urban society. In 1931 the Wickersham Commission reported that its national survey indicated a need for major reforms in the criminal justice system. It noted that the police were often ineffective in enforcing the law, that the courts were dispensing assembly-line justice, and that the resources allocated to the system were inadequate. More recently, the 1967 report of the President's Commission on Law Enforcement and Administration of Justice sounded the same theme: ineffectiveness, assembly-line justice, and inadequate resources. Although there has been much research and effort to improve the administration of justice during the past quarter century, the same problems persist.

Effectiveness

Of the 13 million serious crimes reported annually to the nation's law enforcement agencies, barely one in nine results in a conviction. The solution rate varies among crimes. Of the people arrested for murder, which is usually reported and 86 percent of the time leads to an arrest, only 64 percent are prosecuted and 43 percent convicted. Of people arrested for burglary, which leads to an arrest in only 19 percent of reported cases, four out of five are prosecuted and 56 percent of these are found guilty. These figures mean that for every twelve burglaries reported there is only one conviction. The data may be explained in large part by the nature of the crimes and the difficulty of a successful response by law enforcement agencies. An additional consideration is that unlike the police and courts in an authoritarian governmental system, those in a democracy must act within the law and uphold the civil rights of the accused.

Assembly-Line Justice

assembly-line justice: The operation of any segment of the criminal justice system with such speed and impersonality that defendants are treated as objects to be processed rather than as individuals.

Assembly-line justice is one highly visible result of problems in the criminal justice system. It can be seen in the heavy caseloads processed by metropolitan courts and in the attempt by harassed and overworked staffs to handle cases on a mass-production basis. For the most part, given the volume of cases, little attention is paid to the defendants as people. Rather, they are cases to be processed, items on court schedules to be moved.

The number of court officials and the size of facilities have been based on the premise that up to 90 percent of defendants will plead guilty. Lawyers have learned that court congestion can be turned to their clients' advantage: acceptance of guilty pleas to reduced charges and even outright dismissal of charges become attractive alternatives to jury trials when lawyers avail their clients of all the procedural delays the law permits. By invoking due process criteria—that is, the rights that ensure the accused will be prosecuted and tried according to law—lawyers may upset the fine balance that keeps the justice system in equilibrium. Demands for hearings and other formal procedures provided by the law slow down the process and often create turmoil in courts, which must dispose of cases as quickly as possible to prevent a backlog of untried defendants. Cases that are delayed usually weaken prosecution efforts, since evidence becomes "stale," witnesses are lost, and public interest lapses. The resulting advantage most often falls to the wealthy, who are able to employ aggressive counsel. Court congestion may seriously impede the due process rights of the poor and less fortunate.

The most recent federal census of city and county jails showed that 52 percent of the inmates had not been convicted but were awaiting the next step in the disposition of their cases.[31] In many cities where defense counsel has been provided for poor defendants, the percentage who plead guilty has been reduced, thereby necessitating a proportional increase in the number of trials, judges, and other court personnel.

To cope with these pressures, the legal system has placed greater emphasis on administrative decision making in the pretrial period, when the primary objective of law officials is to screen out cases that do not contain the elements necessary for speedy prosecution and conviction. In a democratic society, administrative practices often create a conflict between the needs for order and the preservation of civil liberties. Balancing this sensitive pairing is subject to political influences, because various groups hold different conceptions of the rights and duties of judicial actors. The defendant is often caught between demands for order and the inadequacies of the criminal justice machinery.

Inadequate Resources

Too often, law enforcement, court, and corrections personnel have not been given the resources to fulfill the constitutional obligation of carrying out justice and ensuring domestic tranquility. Until recently, the number and quality of criminal justice personnel were often inadequate for the job. Police officers were poorly paid, court employees were political appointees, and most courthouses and jails were products of the nineteenth century.

The problem of the criminal justice system has been described by former attorney general Ramsey Clark:

> If police are not effective in preventing crime, prosecution, courts, and prisons are flooded. If police fail to solve crimes, prosecutions cannot proceed and courts cannot do justice—the rest of the system never has its chance. . . . If courts have backlogs and are unable to reach criminal cases for many months, burdens are placed on police. . . . Prosecution offices face the difficult task of keeping up with witnesses. . . . Jails will be overcrowded with defendants who are not released pending trial. Additional burdens on manpower and facilities are costly, but more costly still is the loss of deterrent effect through delay.[32]

Why have the ills of American justice been diagnosed so frequently without apparent change in the "patient's" condition? Certainly we have the resources to minimize crime while maintaining the rule of law and the rights of citizens if we really wanted to do so. Is it because the public has focused its attention on other issues, such as the environment? Is it because we think that criminal behavior mainly affects the lower class and that the system is therefore not worthy of reform? Is it because the criminal justice bureaucracy has been able to withstand the pressures for change? These questions must be addressed by the makers of public policy. More important, they concern all citizens and should be of special concern to those who plan careers in criminal justice.

POLITICS AND CRIMINAL JUSTICE

The 1988 presidential campaign, a contest between George Bush and Michael Dukakis, also included the image of a previously obscure convicted murderer, Willie Horton. Much to the chagrin of the Dukakis camp, a campaign commercial pictured Horton, an African-American who had walked away from a Massachusetts prison furlough program and traveled to Maryland, where he raped a woman and assaulted her husband. The public response to that commercial contributed to Dukakis's defeat, since in the minds of many Americans, Willie Horton epitomized their fears about crime, especially crime committed by minorities. Many argued that Horton's criminality was possible because of the policies of liberal politicans who were "soft" on crime.

The impact of Willie Horton on presidential politics is one of the more dramatic aspects of the relationship between criminal justice and politics. But let us consider some of the more "routine" linkages: penal codes and criminal justice system budgets are passed by legislators who are responsive to the voters; many criminal justice officials are elected; and decisions by police, prosecution, judiciary, and corrections are influenced by community concerns. Candidates for public office use the issue of law and order to gain votes. A city council increases the budget of the police while cutting back on appropriations for social services. Congress appropriates millions to assist states and cities wage the war on drugs but prohibits any expenditures for indigent defense.

Although the relationship between law and politics has been recognized since ancient times, these illustrations reawaken us to the fact that like all legal institutions, the criminal justice system is political; that is, it is engaged in the formulation and administration of public policies in which choices must be made among such competing values as the rights of defendants, protection of persons and property, justice, and freedom. That various groups in society interpret these values differently is obvious. Decisions are influenced by the political power of decision makers and the relative strengths of competing elites (persons regarded as most powerful or influential). Criminal justice personnel are engaged in the determination of policy in the same sense as are other governmental decision makers whose positions are generally perceived as political. Broadly conceived, **political considerations** explain to a large extent who gets or does not get—in what amount and how—the "good" (justice) that is produced by the legal system in the setting of the local community.

political considerations: Matters taken into account in the formulation of public policies and the making of choices among competing values— who gets what portion of the good (justice) produced by the system, when, and how.

The administration of criminal justice is complicated by the fact that laws are often ambiguous, full enforcement of them is both impossible and undesirable, and many laws still on the books no longer have public support. The result is a somewhat selective process in which criminal justice officials are given a wide range of discretionary powers to determine who will be arrested, on what charges they will be prosecuted, and how their cases will be administered. Because these decisions are made on a daily basis within the context of the local community, the political aspects of the system are heightened.

Aside from the pervasiveness of politics in the administration of justice, political considerations exist in specific ways throughout the system. That political parties are a weighty ingredient in the recruitment of judges, prosecutors, and other legal personnel has long been recognized. In many American cities the road to a judgeship is paved with tasks performed for the party. Prosecuting attorneys are also recognized as important political actors. Because of their power of discretion and their political ties and obligations, prosecutors are pivotal figures with ties to both the internal politics of the justice system and the local political organizations.

Criminal Justice and the Community

In many ways the administration of criminal justice is a community affair. Although the FBI is much in the news, the national government plays a relatively minor role in the broad perspective of criminal justice. Most **crimes** are violations of state laws, but enforcement is left to a multitude of local-level agencies that have wide discretionary powers so that they may tailor their actions to be consistent with community norms.

crime: A specific act of commission or omission in violation of the law, for which a punishment is prescribed.

It is at the local level that people have contact with the legal process. Although most citizens will never appear in court or at the police station, their perception of the quality of justice will greatly affect their willingness to abide by the community's laws. Thus if people widely assume, for example, that the police can be bribed, that certain groups are singled out for harsh treatment, or that law-breaking will not result in punishment of offenders, the system will lose much of its influence over their behavior. As Roscoe Pound once said, criminal law "must safeguard the general security and the individual life against abuse of criminal procedure while at the same time making that procedure as effective as possible for the securing of the whole scheme of social interests."[33]

CRIME CONTROL VERSUS DUE PROCESS

Organizations do not exist in a limbo, untouched by the political and social environment. The behavior of criminal justice decision makers is influenced by the administrative structure and also by the values of the American culture. These norms provide legitimacy and justification for the ways in which criminal behavior is controlled and defendants' cases are judged. Given the organizational context of decision making, what are the goals or values that provide the foundation for the criminal justice system? How do these values influence the police officers, attorneys, and judges who must function within this administrative process? Does an understanding of the social norms underlying criminal justice help us analyze the activities that lead to the disposition of cases?

Ideally, one might hope to be able to describe a consistent and interrelated set of values that is the rationale for decision making, but such a description does not seem to be possible in the case of the justice system. In such cases, scholars often use models to organize their thinking about a subject and to guide their research, since models are ideal types that clearly characterize the values and goals that underlie a system. In one of the most important recent contributions to systematic thought on the administration of criminal justice, Herbert Packer describes two competing schemes: the Crime Control Model and the Due Process Model.[34] Packer's models are two ways of looking at the goals and procedures of the criminal justice system; they represent opposing views of how the criminal law *ought* to operate. He likens the Crime Control Model to an assembly line and the Due Process Model to an obstacle course and describes his models as polar extremes, the end points of a continuum.

Packer does recognize that the administration of criminal justice operates within the contemporary American society and is therefore influenced by cultural forces that, in turn, determine the models' usefulness. In addition, no one actor or law enforcement subsystem functions totally in accordance with either of the models; elements of both are found throughout the system. The values expressed within the two models describe the tensions within the process.

Crime Control: Order as a Value

Crime Control Model: A model of the criminal justice system that assumes that freedom is so important that every effort must be made to repress crime; it emphasizes efficiency and the capacity to apprehend, try, convict, and dispose of a high proportion of offenders, and it also stresses speed and finality.

Underlying the **Crime Control Model** is the proposition that the repression of criminal conduct is the most important function to be performed by the criminal justice system. Law enforcement's failure to control criminals is thought to bring about the breakdown of public order and thus the disappearance of human freedom. If there is a general disregard for laws, the law-abiding citizen is more likely to become a victim of the criminal. As Packer points out, to achieve liberty for all citizens to interact freely as members of society, the Crime Control Model requires that primary attention be paid to efficiency in screening suspects, determining guilt, and applying appropriate sanctions to the convicted.

In the context of this model, efficiency of operation requires that the system have the capacity to apprehend, try, convict, and dispose of a high proportion of criminal offenders whose offenses become known. Because of the magnitude of criminal behavior and the limited resources given to law enforcement agencies, emphasis must be placed on speed and finality. Accordingly, there must be a high rate of arrests, sifting out of the innocent, and conviction of offenders, all of which depends on informality, uniformity, and the minimizing of occasions for challenge. Hence probable guilt is administratively determined primarily on the basis of the police investigation, and those cases unlikely to end in conviction are filtered out. At each successive stage, from arrest to preliminary hearing, arraignment, and courtroom trial, a series of routinized procedures is used by a variety of judicial actors to determine whether the accused should be passed on to the next level. Rather than stressing the combative elements of the courtroom, this model notes that bargaining between the state and the accused occurs at several points. The ritual of the courtroom is enacted in only a small number of cases; the rest are disposed of through negotiations over the charges and usually end with defendants' pleas of guilty. Thus Packer likens decision making under the Crime Control Model to an assembly-line process. That is, an endless stream of cases moves past system actors standing at fixed stations and performing the small but essential operations that successively bring each case closer to being the finished product, a closed file.

Due Process: Law as a Value

If the Crime Control Model looks like an assembly line, the **Due Process Model** resembles an obstacle course. Although likewise valuing human freedom, the Due Process Model questions the reliability of fact finding. Because people are notoriously poor observers of disturbing events, the possibility of the police and prosecutors, the main Crime Control Model decision makers, committing a wrong is very high. Persons should be termed criminal and deprived of their freedom only on the basis of reliable information. To minimize error, hurdles must be erected so that the power of government can be used against the accused only when it has been proved beyond doubt that the defendant committed the crime in question. The best method to determine guilt or innocence is to test the evidence through an adversarial proceeding. Hence the model assumes that persons are innocent until proved guilty, that they have the opportunity to discredit the cases brought against them, and that an impartial judge and jury are provided to decide the outcome. The assumption that the defendant is innocent until proved guilty is emphasized by Packer as having a far-reaching impact on the criminal justice system.

Due Process Model: A model of the criminal justice system that assumes that freedom is so important that every effort must be made to ensure that criminal justice decisions are based on reliable information; it emphasizes the adversarial process, the rights of defendants, and formal decision-making procedures.

The models stress two very different kinds of guilt: legal and factual. Factual guilt is what people usually mean when they ask, "Did he do it?"—that is, is the person guilty of the crime as charged? Legal guilt, however, involves more than the factual situation: Can the state prove in a procedurally regular manner and by lawful authority that the person is guilty of the crime as charged? Judicial actors must therefore prove their cases under various procedural restraints dealing with the admissibility of evidence, the burden of proof, the requirement that guilt be proved beyond a reasonable doubt, and so forth. Forcing the state to prove its case in an adjudicative context functions to protect the citizens from undeserved criminal sanction. In the Due Process Model, the possibility that a few who may be factually guilty will remain free outweighs the possibilities in the Crime Control Model for governmental power to be abused, the innocent to be incarcerated, and society's freedom to be endangered. Table 1.4 compares the basic elements of the two models that lead to these views.

TABLE 1.4 Due process model and crime control model compared. What other comparisons can be made between the two models?

	Goal	Value	Process	Major Decision Point	Basis of Decision Making
Due Process Model	Preserve individual liberties	Reliability	Adversarial	Courtroom	Law
Crime Control Model	Repress crime	Efficiency	Administrative	Police, pretrial processes	Discretion

Reality: Crime Control or Due Process?

If someone from a foreign country should ask you to describe the way the criminal justice process functions, what would you say? Which of the value models would you use in your explanation?

The public's idea of democracy probably leads to an understanding of the criminal justice system in accordance with the ideals of the Due Process Model. According to this view, principles, not personal discretion, control the actions of police officers, judges, and prosecutors. Criminal justice is thus seen as an ongoing, mechanical process in which violations of laws are discovered, defendants are indicted, and punishments are imposed, with little reference either to the organizational needs of the system or to the personalization of justice. This perspective gives little opportunity for discretion in the criminal justice machine, and any attempt to induce flexibility must be carried out *sub rosa*.

Unlike the values expressed in the Due Process Model, in which decisions are made in the courtroom as a result of adversarial conflict, the reality of criminal justice in America is more comparable to the Crime Control Model, in which guilt is administratively determined early in the process and cases are disposed of through negotiation. Rather than emphasis on discovering the truth so that the innocent may be separated from the guilty, the assumption here is that those arrested by the police have committed *some* criminal act. Accordingly, efforts are made to select a charge to which the accused will plead guilty and that will result in an appropriate sentence.

SUMMARY

Law enforcement and the administration of justice are issues high on the agenda of national priorities. Events of the mid-1960s awakened Americans to the fact not only that crime was increasing but also that the forces of law and justice were encountering obstacles in achieving their goals. Even though crime victimization appeared to level off after 1973 and the number of reported crimes began to decline in 1981, the war on drugs begun in the late 1980s again aroused the public to demand that action be taken with regard to crime.

As a result of the extensive research carried on during the past two and a half decades, we have a greater understanding of crime and the administration of justice. Many of the earlier assumptions about criminals held by social scientists and government officials have been proved to be naive: The problem is much more complicated than was believed at the time.

It has been recognized in the United States that crime control is a pressing public policy issue, though measurement of the extent of crime and the reasons for the persistence of high crime rates are not as clear-cut. Although both the *Uniform Crime Reports* of the FBI and the *National Crime Surveys* have methodological problems, they are still the best sources of information. The criminal justice system has a number of problems, particularly involving effectiveness, assembly-line justice, and the lack of adequate resources. Criminal justice also operates in a political arena greatly influenced by public opinion, community elites, and competition among differing perspectives.

Two ways of conceptualizing the criminal justice system are described in the Due Process Model and Crime Control Model. These analytic tools help us understand how and why cases are disposed of. As one scholar has written:

> It is in the day-to-day practices and policies of the processing agencies that the law is put into effect and it is out of the struggle to perform their tasks in ways which maximize rewards and minimize strains for the organization and the individuals involved that the legal processing agencies shape the law.[35]

This book shows the links among law, politics, and administration in the criminal justice system. This first chapter has introduced the problem and set the direction for the discussions that follow.

FOR DISCUSSION

1. Increased criminal activity seems to come to the attention of the American people at different periods. Is this because more crime is being committed, or are other social forces creating this impression?
2. For many years criminal justice resources were neglected. What social and political influences have brought about greater attention to the system?
3. The public is troubled most by visible crimes (burglaries, thefts). Why?
4. If you had the power and resources to make improvements in America's criminal justice system, what would you do? Why? What values would be enhanced by your decision?
5. What is the major crime problem in your community? What could be done to reduce or eliminate it?

FOR FURTHER READING

Currie, Elliott. *Confronting Crime.* New York: Pantheon, 1985. A critique of conservative and liberal arguments about crime with particular emphasis on the work of James Q. Wilson. Urges development of social and economic programs to reduce crime.

MacDonald, Scott B. *Mountain High, White Avalanche.* New York: Praeger, 1989. Examines the impact of the cocaine trade on political power in Colombia, Peru, Bolivia, and Panama.

Musto, David F. *The American Disease: Origins of Narcotics Control,* 2nd rev. ed. New Haven, CT: Yale University Press, 1987. A historical analysis of drug policy in the United States. Argues that each generation that experiences drug abuse indoctrinates the next generation to its horrors.

Packer, Herbert L. *The Limits of the Criminal Sanction.* Palo Alto, CA: Stanford University Press, 1968. A classic examination of many of the assumptions underlying the American system of criminal justice.

Wilson, James Q. *Thinking about Crime.* 2nd ed. New York: Basic Books, 1983. Argues for policies to improve the criminal justice system and thus reduce crime. Examines various law enforcement, sentencing, and correctional strategies.

NOTES

1. U.S. National Advisory Commission on Criminal Justice Standards and Goals, *A National Strategy to Reduce Crime* (Washington, DC: Government Printing Office, 1973), p. 1.
2. Emile Durkheim, *The Division of Labor in Society,* trans. George Simpson (Glencoe, IL: Free Press, 1960), p. 102.
3. President's Commission on Law Enforcement and Administration of Justice, *Crime and Its Impact: An Assessment* (Washington, DC: Government Printing Office, 1967), p. 19.
4. Eliott Currie, *Confronting Crime* (New York: Pantheon, 1985), p. 25.
5. Dane Archer and Rosemary Gartner, *Violence and Crime in Cross-National Perspective* (New Haven, CT: Yale University Press, 1984).
6. Samuel Walker, *Sense and Nonsense about Crime*, 2nd ed. (Pacific Grove, CA: Brooks/Cole, 1989), p. 5.
7. U.S. Department of Justice, Bureau of Justice Statistics, *Bulletin* (October 1989).
8. Ibid.
9. U.S. Department of Justice, *Bulletin* (October 1989), p. 5.
10. U.S. Department of Justice, *Crime in the United States* (Washington, DC: Government Printing Office, 1990), p. 178.
11. Rodney Stark, "Decent Places: A Theory of the Ecology of Crime," *Criminology* 25 (1987): 893–909.
12. William Julius Wilson, "Inner City Dislocation," *Society* 21 (November–December 1983): 80; see also John J. DiIulio, Jr., "The Impact of Inner-City Crime," *The Public Interest* 96 (Summer 1989): 28–46.
13. Myron Magnet, "America's Underclass: What to Do?" *Fortune* 11 (May 1987): 130–150.
14. Chris Black, "America's Lost Generation," *The Boston Globe*, March 4, 1990, p. 69.
15. John J. DiIulio, Jr., "The Impact of Inner-City Crime," p. 28; James K. Stewart, "How Crime Causes Poverty in the Inner City," *Policy Review* 37 (Summer 1986): 2.
16. Wesley G. Skogan and Michael G. Maxfield, *Coping with Crime* (Newbury Park, CA: Sage, 1981), p. 48.
17. Ibid., p. 157.
18. Wesley G. Skogan, *Disorder and Decay: Crime and the Spiral of Decay in American Neighborhoods* (New York: Free Press, 1990), p. 74.
19. Dan A. Lewis and Michael G. Maxfield, "Fear in the Neighborhoods: An Investigation of the Impact of Crime," *Journal of Research in Crime and Delinquency* 17 (July 1980): 160–189.
20. James Q. Wilson and George L. Kelling, "Broken Windows: The Police and Neighborhood Safety," *Atlantic Monthly* (March 1982): 29–38.
21. Ibid., pp. 29–38.
22. David F. Musto, *The American Disease: Origins of Narcotics Control*, 2nd rev. ed. (New Haven, CT: Yale University Press, 1987).
23. James Q. Wilson, "Drugs and Crime," in *Drugs and Crime*, vol. 13, *Crime and Justice: A Review of Research*, ed. Michael Tonry and James Q. Wilson (Chicago: University of Chicago Press, 1990), p. 529.
24. Marsha Rosenbaum, "Just Say What? An Alternative View on Solving America's Drug Problem," National Council on Crime and Delinquency, San Francisco, n.d.
25. U.S. Department of Justice, National Institute of Justice, *NIJ Reports* (July-August 1989), p. 8.
26. Bruce D. Johnson, Terry Williams, Kojo A. Dei, and Harry Sanabria, "Drug Abuse in the Inner City: The Impact on Hard-Drug Users and the Community," in *Drugs and Crime*, vol. 13, *Crime and Justice*, ed. Tonry and Wilson, p. 27.
27. Ibid., p. 38.
28. Jan M. Chaiken and Marcia R. Chaiken, "Drugs and Predatory Crime," in *Drugs and Crime*, vol. 13, *Crime and Justice*, ed. Tonry and Wilson, pp. 203–241.
29. Peter Reuter, "Can the Borders Be Sealed?" *Public Interest* (Summer 1988): 51–65.
30. See Ethan A. Nadelmann, "The Case for Legalization"; John Kaplan, "Taking Drugs Seriously," *The Public Interest* (Summer 1988): 3–50.

31. U.S. Department of Justice, Bureau of Justice Statistics, *Bulletin* (June 1990), p. 1.
32. Ramsey Clark, *Crime in America* (New York: Simon & Schuster, 1970), p. 120.
33. Roscoe Pound, *Crime in America* (New York: Henry Holt, 1930), p. 11.
34. Herbert L. Packer, *The Limits of the Criminal Sanction* (Palo Alto, CA: Stanford University Press, 1968). For alternative models see John Griffiths, "Ideology in Criminal Procedures or a 'Third Model' of the Criminal Process," *Yale Law Journal* 79 (1970): 359; Thomas E. Reed and Larry K. Gaines, "Criminal Justice Models as a Function of Ideological Images: A Social Learning Alternative to Packer," *International Journal of Comparative and Applied Criminal Justice* (Winter 1982): 213.
35. William Chambliss, ed., *Crime and the Legal Process* (New York: McGraw-Hill, 1969), p. 86.

2 C H A P T E R

Defining and Understanding Criminal Behavior

Key Terms

Crime is . . . necessary; it is bound up with the fundamental conditions of all social life, and by that very fact it is useful, because these conditions of which it is a part are themselves indispensable to the normal evolution of morality and law.

Emile Durkheim

Rape. The very harshness of the word conveys the violence of the deed and the intensity of the fear and disgust with which society has traditionally viewed this crime. From ancient times, when developing cultures first became concerned about the purity of bloodlines and about the theft of property (the woman's virtue-value) and created regulations to govern sexual relationships, rape has been a taboo that has evolved into an offense formally labeled by criminal law.

Although forcible rape is generally understood to be sexual intercourse by a male with a female who is not his wife against her will and under conditions of threat or force, different countries have variously defined the offense and stipulated the penalties. For example, in England a decision of the House of Lords ruled that "if a man believes that a woman is consenting to sex, he cannot be convicted of rape, no matter how unreasonable his belief may be."[1] In some areas of the world rape is not charged if certain classes of women are involved. Forcible rape is an accepted form of sex relations for unmarried males among the Gusii, a large tribe in Kenya.[2] In Western countries a legal distinction is often made among rape, forcible rape, and statutory rape on the basis of such factors as the age of the

Publication of the name of the woman allegedly raped by the nephew of Senator Edward Kennedy brought forth a storm of protests. What does this say about American ambivalence concerning rape?

female, the level of force employed, and the nature of the sexual conduct. Until recently, death was the penalty prescribed for the offense of forcible rape in many American states; life imprisonment is now stipulated in thirty states, although most convicted rapists serve fewer than ten years in prison. However, many cases never result in conviction. For example, of 800 cases of forcible rape reported to the Indianapolis police, only 104 defendants were found guilty and only 83 were incarcerated.[3]

Before the rise of the women's movement, some states required that the victim's word be confirmed by evidence provided by some other person, and defense counsel could make reference to the victim's past sexual conduct. Under pressure from feminist groups, some legislatures have changed their penal codes to allow wives to accuse their husbands of rape.

Until recently in the United States, rape was thought to be the act of a stranger, not of an acquaintance or "date." Criminal justice officials and the general public viewed the act as an offense only when it was a "real" rape committed by a stranger.[4] Perpetrators and even victims did not believe that a rape occurred unless it fit that category, yet researchers have estimated that in up to 80 percent of sexual assaults the victim knows the offender. In a survey of 6,100 college undergraduates concerning "date" rape, 25 percent of the women described experiences that met the legal definition of rape, yet only 27 percent thought of themselves as rape victims. Among the men, 8 percent said that they had committed acts that met the legal definition, yet 84 percent of them said that they did not consider their actions as rape.[5] Such ambivalence by society as to what constitutes the crime of rape has important implications for the reporting of the offense and the willingness of the police and prosecutors to pursue such cases through the system.

Why does the law of rape take the form it does? Why does the criminal justice system treat rape differently from other assaults? Is something more involved here than the intensity of fear and disgust with which society has traditionally viewed this crime? Are the law's sanctions intended to uphold the sanctity of a husband's "property"? Is rape a special case because the crime violates the victim's personhood? Why is there differential treatment of those accused of rape and their victims?

The variety of definitions, evidential requirements, and penalties for rape helps to focus the text of this chapter. Societies in various places and at different times have attempted to deal with the problem of crime. An important point to remember is that laws are written by humans, they emerge from human experience, and they are administered by humans. Thus disagreements often occur concerning the exact nature of laws defining behavior as criminal. This is especially true in a heterogeneous society in which some groups do not believe that certain behaviors warrant criminal sanction and other groups wish to use the law to maintain the status quo.

In this chapter we examine three aspects of criminal behavior. We first look at the sources of criminal law—the ways societies have decided that certain types of behavior are criminal. Next we focus on the offender and explore theories that have been developed by criminologists to explain the causes of criminal behavior. Finally, we look at types of crimes and their legal definitions.

Behavior that is illegal during one era may be legal in another. The drinking of alcohol was made illegal through social and political processes, not because that behavior was inherently evil.

SOURCES OF CRIMINAL LAW

Many students ask, "Why is it illegal for me to smoke marijuana but legal for me to consume alcohol?" If the answer is that marijuana might be addictive, could lead to the use of more potent drugs, and is generally thought to be detrimental to health, the student may point out that alcoholism is a major social problem, that drinking beer may whet one's thirst for hard liquor, and that heart and liver disorders, not to mention highway fatalities, are caused by overindulgence in alcohol. If the argument persists, an exasperated "clincher" might be "Because pot smoking is against the law, and that's that!"

Why does the law declare some types of human behavior criminal and not others? What social forces are brought to bear on legislators as they write the criminal code? Why are activities that are labeled criminal during one era found to be acceptable in another? Why is the personal use of marijuana legal in some states but prohibited in others? Such issues need to be discussed because a theory explaining the sources of criminal law will have an important impact on assumptions concerning the nature of crime and the sources of criminal behavior.

For much of our history we have tended to think of crime as pertaining only to criminals rather than to other aspects of society. Most Americans do not separate the concept of crime from that of the criminal or believe that criminals are separate from the mainstream of society. In Puritan Massachusetts crime was viewed in theological terms, and the criminal was thus considered a creature of the devil. Most provisions of the Puritans' legal code bore notations showing their biblical source. In a later era the medically oriented professions saw crime as arising from some inherited abnormality. Some psychologists in the nineteenth and twentieth centuries, for example, have described crime as resulting from mental or personality defects. More recently, sociologists have looked to social situations—neighborhood, school, gang, family—as determining whether persons will be law-abiding citizens or criminals. Throughout these approaches runs the idea that criminality is a characteristic of the person and not a consequence of a label imposed by the community.

A most important point to recognize is that the definition of behavior as criminal stems from a social process and may have little to do with the individual criminal. Social groups create deviance by making rules the infraction of which constitutes deviance and by applying those rules to particular people and labeling them as outsiders. This means that in addition to the person who commits a crime, there must first be a community and a process by which the commission of that act has come to be called criminal. Second, someone must have observed the act or its consequences and applied the community's definition of it. Third, a crime implies a victim. Finally, punishment implies that someone is responsible for carrying out the community's will. Labeling behavior as criminal is thus a social phenomenon that arises from the complex interactions of a number of persons and social institutions. The criminal law is one manifestation of this social and political process.

A number of theories have been developed to explain the focus and functions of criminal laws and the social processes by which they evolve. These ideas can be divided into a consensus model and a conflict model. The **consensus model** argues that criminal law reflects the will or values of society. The **conflict model** emphasizes the role of political interests in the formulation of laws and points to the dominance of powerful groups in the structuring of law to meet their own needs.

Consensus: Law as an Expression of Values

The consensus position holds that criminal law reflects societal values that go beyond the immediate interests of particular groups and individuals and is thus an expression of the social consciousness of the whole society. Consensus theory has been greatly influenced by Emile Durkheim, who argued that groups in society—black and white, rich and poor—might have all sorts of different interests but be in underlying agreement on basic values. From this perspective, legal norms (the laws) emerge through the dynamics of cultural

consensus model: A legal model that asserts that criminal law, as an expression of the social consciousness of the whole society, reflects values that transcend the immediate interests of particular groups and individuals.

conflict model: A legal model that asserts that the political power of interest groups and elites influences the content of criminal law.

processes to meet certain needs and requirements that are essential for maintaining the social fabric. The laws are necessary to establish moral boundaries so as to differentiate the good members of the community from the bad. Legislators, as representatives of the people, formalize these values in the criminal law. As Jerome Hall, a leading exponent of this approach, said, "Criminal law represents a sustained effort to preserve important social values from serious harm and to do so not arbitrarily but in accordance with rational methods directed toward the discovery of just ends."[6] This position assumes that the society has achieved a well-integrated and relatively stable agreement on basic values. Criminal law reflects the kind of conduct that a community considers, at a particular time, to be "sufficiently condemnable" to impose legal punishments that restrict freedom and may even result in death. Thus, criminal law may be viewed as "a barometer of the moral and social thinking of a community."[7]

TABLE 2.1 **How do people rank the severity of crime?** Respondents to a survey were asked to rank 204 illegal events, from playing hooky from school to planting a bomb that killed twenty people in a public building. Severity scores were developed through mathematical techniques from the survey responses. For example, a severity score of 40 indicates that people believe that the crime is twice as bad as a crime with a severity score of 20.

Severity Score	Ten Most Serious Offenses	Severity Score	Ten Least Serious Offenses
72.1	Planting a bomb in a public building. The bomb explodes and twenty people are killed.	1.3	Two persons willingly engage in a homosexual act.
52.8	A man forcibly rapes a woman. As a result of physical injuries, she dies.	1.1	Disturbing the neighborhood with loud, noisy behavior.
		1.1	Taking bets on the numbers.
43.2	Robbing a victim at gunpoint. The victim struggles and is shot to death.	1.1	A group continues to hang around a corner after being told to break up by a police officer.
39.2	A man stabs his wife. As a result, she dies.	.9	A youngster under sixteen years old runs away from home.
35.7	Stabbing a victim to death.		
35.6	Intentionally injuring a victim. As a result, the victim dies.	.8	Being drunk in public.
		.7	A youngster under sixteen years old breaks a curfew law by being out on the street after the hour permitted by law.
33.8	Running a narcotics ring.		
27.9	A woman stabs her husband. As a result, he dies.		
		.6	Trespassing in the backyard of a private home.
26.3	An armed person skyjacks an airplane and demands to be flown to another country.	.3	A person is a vagrant. That is, he has no home and no visible means of support.
25.8	A man forcibly rapes a woman. No other physical injury occurs.	.2	A youngster under sixteen years old plays hooky from school.

SOURCE: U.S. Department of Justice, Bureau of Justice Statistics, *Report to the Nation on Crime and Justice,* 2nd ed. (Washington, DC: Government Printing Office, 1988), p. 16.

Given the multiplicity of racial, ethnic, and religious groups in American society, is there broad agreement on the moral values that are formalized in criminal law? A national survey of public opinion concerning the severity of various crimes sheds some light on this question.[8] The people interviewed were asked to rank the seriousness of 204 illegal events. The results showed that the planting of a bomb that exploded in a public building and killed twenty people was rated the most serious offense and that playing hooky from school was rated the least serious (see Table 2.1). Among the diverse groups of people who took part in the survey, there was generally broad agreement on the severity of specific crimes. Differences were noted, however, in that crime victims scored the acts higher than did nonvictims, and the severity ratings assigned by blacks and other minority group members were generally lower than those assigned by whites.

As an example of consensus theories in action, we can look back to Puritan Massachusetts. Kai Erikson argues in *Wayward Puritans* that three serious "crime waves" in seventeenth-century Massachusetts performed the important function of helping the colonists define the values of their society. During each of these periods—the Antinomian controversy of 1636, the Quaker persecutions of the late 1650s, and the witchcraft hysteria of 1692—the Massachusetts Bay colonists labeled certain types of behavior as criminal. As a result, they were better able to set the boundaries of their society, to clarify their doctrines, and to renew community norms.

■ The Salem witch trials are examples of Durkheim's view that deviance tightens community bonds. To what extent do such contemporary public concerns as drug use, missing children, and sexual abuse emerge because of weakened community ties?

The theoretical basis for Erikson's fascinating study is Emile Durkheim's idea that crime is a natural social activity and performs an important function in healthy societies. In Durkheim's view, violations of norms unite people in anger and indignation; that is, when a deviant breaks the rules of conduct that the rest of the community holds in high respect, citizens can come together to express their outrage:

> Crime brings together upright consciences and concentrates them. We have only to notice what happens, particularly in a small town, when some moral scandal has just been committed. They stop each other on the street, they visit each other, they seek to come together to talk of the event and to wax indignant in common. From all the similar impressions which are exchanged . . . there emerges a unique temper . . . which is everybody's without being anybody's in particular. That is the public temper.[9]

The deviant act, then, creates a sense of mutuality or community because it supplies a focus for group feeling. Much like a war or some other emergency, deviance makes people more alert to their shared interests and values. Erikson shows that at the time of each of the crime waves, the Puritans were being confronted with changes in their society and with challenges to existing values. Because of the theological basis of their value system, they interpreted deviant behavior in religious terms.

Also important is Erikson's argument that the amount of deviance a community encounters over time is likely to remain fairly constant. At any given time, a society focuses on people it considers to be criminals, regardless of how serious their behavior may appear according to some universal standard. The number of criminals the society actually deals with, however, is limited by its detection equipment as well as by the size and complexity of its apparatus for control. Thus Erikson found that among the Massachusetts Puritans, even during crime waves, the number of criminal offenders did not increase significantly; rather, the crimes that the society used its resources to manage shifted to those with a theological foundation.

BIOGRAPHY

Emile Durkheim

A French sociologist, Emile Durkheim (1858–1917) is one of the leading figures in the social sciences. The basic theme of his work is that society is a realm of unique social facts and that order and cohesion are of primary importance. As a criminologist, Durkheim maintained that crime is a normal, not a pathological, factor in society. He did not insist that criminals are always normal but believed that criminal acts reflect the community's dominant values. Crime will disappear, Durkheim asserted, only if the community's collective sentiments reach such a wide, nearly universal degree of acceptance that all persons concur with the same common values. Crime reflects a nonconcurrence with the dominant values and, as such, is necessary for the cohesion of the broader society. Although not condoning crime, Durkheim called attention to the function that it performs in cementing the ties that bind the members of a society.

Conflict: Law as an Expression of Power

In contrast to the view of the criminal code as a product of the society's value consensus, a relatively new approach emphasizes that the power of the dominant social groups influences the content of the code. Persons holding this conflict model argue that people generally pursue their own goals and that these interests reflect the diversity of their membership in subgroups based on race, social class, age, and economic level. They say that a community is better characterized by diversity and conflict rather than by consensus and stability. A second point they make is that the law is framed by the most powerful interests and is seldom the product of the values of the whole society.[10]

In this view, power, force, and constraint, rather than common values, are the basic organizing principles of society. Since there are unequal distributions of political influence, some groups will have greater access to decision makers and will use their influence to ensure that legislation is enacted to protect their interests. According to this approach, wrongful acts are characteristic of all classes in society, and the powerful not only shape the law to their own advantage but are able to dictate the use of enforcement resources so that certain groups are labeled and processed by the criminal justice system.

Since the power of groups ebbs and flows, the criminal law, its application, and its interpretation will reflect those tidal alternations.

> New and shifting demands require new laws. When the interests that underlie a law no longer are relevant to groups in power, the law will be reinterpreted or changed to incorporate the dominant interests. The social history of criminal law can be described according to alternations in the interest structure of society.[11]

In the United States we can point to various periods when the behaviors of certain groups were defined as criminal. Prohibition of alcohol earlier in this century is probably the best example. Joseph Gusfield has analyzed this movement as stemming from the political power of native-born Protestants concerned about the increasing number of immigrants from Catholic countries.[12] Likewise, in the 1940s young men in Los Angeles known as "zootsuiters" because of their distinctive dress, were labeled deviant and became the object of police action because they were perceived as flaunting traditional values. Conflict theorists would point to the fact that drug use by African-Americans (cocaine), Hispanics (marijuana), and Asians (opium) has been the focus of law enforcement efforts at various times. Today's war on drugs, to the extent that it focuses on the poor and powerless, is consistent with the conflict approach.

A look at fourteenth-century England provides a clear example of the conflict approach in action. Laws against vagrancy—that is, against wandering idly without means to earn a living—are a part of the penal code of most cities and states. William Chambliss argues that such laws originated in England and have changed over time to reflect shifts in social concerns and the power of influential groups. The first vagrancy law was enacted in England in 1349, when the Black Death (bubonic plague) killed a large part of the population and caused a severe labor shortage. This law regulated the giving of alms to able-bodied unemployed persons. With the need for cheap labor after the breakdown of the feudal system and after the labor force was again decimated by a recurrence of plague in the seventeenth century, the law was changed to read:

> Every man and woman, of what condition he be, free or bond, able in body, and within the age of threescore years, not living in merchandizing nor exercising any craft, nor having of his own whereon to live, nor proper land whereon to occupy himself, and not serving any other, if he in convenient service (his estate considered) be required to service, shall be bounded to serve him which shall him require. . . . And if any refuse he shall on conviction by two true men . . . be committed to gaol till he finds surety to serve.[13]

The rise of commerce and industry in the sixteenth century, Chambliss says, brought to life vagrancy laws that had lain dormant during much of the fifteenth century and directed them against any person who "being whole and mighty in body, and able to labor, be taken in begging, or be vagrant and can give no reckoning how he lawfully gets his living."[14] Where the earlier law had focused on the idle and was designed to provide labor, the new emphasis was on rogues and others suspected of criminal activities and was designed to protect travelers and goods on the highways. As Chambliss notes, only later did the vagrancy statutes stress the damage to persons or property that might be inflicted by the vagabond. This shift reflected the importance of a new group—the commercial class—and laws were altered to guard its interests.

The English vagrancy laws were adopted in the United States with only minor variations. In all the states, the statutes were written so that they more explicitly focused on the control of criminals and undesirables than was the case in England. Since the 1750s they have been used to clear the streets of people considered nuisances: prostitutes, derelicts, and others who "can be seen as a reflection of the society's perception of a continuing need to control some of its 'suspicious' and 'undesirable' members."[15] In contemporary times, vagrancy laws have been used for such purposes as controlling the movement of migrant laborers in California, civil rights workers in the South, and peace demonstrators in Washington, D.C. Under changing social conditions, dormant laws will often be revived to serve the newly powerful.

Chambliss's scholarship has been challenged by Jeffrey S. Adler, who says that although the work is "provocative and even suggestive, . . . it is far from conclusive."[16] Adler cites recent scholarship that challenges much of the historical foundation of Chambliss's research. He argues that it was widespread poverty, not crimes against property, that shaped the development of vagrancy laws in England. Adler believes that class anxieties did influence the law but that these concerns were embedded in the culture and cannot be understood solely in economic terms. The scholarly debate on this issue will undoubtedly continue; still, the analysis well illustrates the major themes of the conflict perspective.

Consensus versus Conflict: Emerging Theories

At this point in the study of the social processes involved in the development of criminal law, reaching a conclusion about the theoretical value of the consensus and conflict models is impossible. Certainly, with respect to some laws, especially those prohibiting acts that are *mala in se* (murder, rape, assault), consensus exists in most Western societies on the values expressed in the law. Yet conflict theorists will point to the fact that even for these crimes there is differential application of the law so that individuals with certain characteristics are processed more severely than others. In contrast, the laws prohibiting alcohol consumption, vagrancy, and the sale of pornography—*mala prohibita*—have their source in the political power of special interests. (These legal distinctions are discussed at greater length in Chapter 3.) Since most criminal violations are now of the latter type, attention logically focuses on the conflict model.

mala in se: Offenses that are wrong by their very nature, irrespective of statutory prohibition.

mala prohibita: Offenses prohibited by statute but not inherently wrong.

Jerome Skolnick has criticized Richard Quinney's assumption that the conflict model explains the source of all criminal law. He argues that in writing the criminal law, we evaluate various acts (heroin possession, robbery, rape) on the basis of some standard of crime. Since Quinney says that the standards of what ought to be criminal reflects various group and class definitions of conduct, an unanswered question remains relating to possible areas of consensus among portions of society. As Skolnick notes, "Surely, there is far greater negative consensus on the 'quality' of the behavior involved in forcible rape and armed robbery than in gambling or marijuana use. Shared definitions of crime exist, albeit variably, depending on the behavior in question, and the fact of sharing is also part of the social reality of crime."[17]

THEORIES ABOUT THE CAUSES OF CRIME

People have long pondered why some individuals conform to society's norms and values and others do not. References in ancient Greek writings indicate that speculation on this question was prevalent even then. Modern criminology is primarily concerned with understanding crime, the characteristics of criminals, and how the consequences of crime can be prevented or repaired. It is an interdisciplinary science, with scholars from sociology, political science, biology, economics, and psychology each viewing crime from a particular theoretical perspective. In this section we look at the two major schools of thought—classical and positivist—and then examine biological, psychological, and sociological theories of the causes of criminal behavior.

Two Schools: Classical and Positivist

It is important to place the development of the various approaches to criminality in a historical context. Speculation about the causes of crime does not take place in a vacuum. Each approach emerged through the ideas of particular scholars, but the pioneers of criminology were influenced by forces preeminent in their era, such as religion, philosophy, and science. To aid our understanding of theories about the causes of crime, the two leading schools of criminological thought, the classical and the positivist, will be outlined. Briefly, we will see that classical criminology was interested in explaining crime—why certain societies developed certain laws and legal structures. Positivist criminology, by contrast, has tried to explain criminal behavior—why certain people commit crimes. Each school was dominated by scholars who presented their views on the factors that caused criminal behavior and the means that society should use in dealing with criminals.

Classical Criminology

Until the eighteenth century most Europeans explained criminal behavior in religious terms. They saw crime as a product of the devil's work; persons who did wrong were in the devil's possession. One orthodox Christian view was that all humanity had fallen with Adam and had thereafter existed in a state of total depravity. Even up to the nineteenth century, indictments in both the United States and Europe often began "[John Doe], not having the fear of God before his eyes but being moved and seduced by the instigation of the devil, did commit [a certain crime]." Not only did religious ideas control thinking about crime, but also the concept of procedural rights had not yet been developed, the accused had little opportunity to put forth a defense, confessions were extracted through torture, and corporal punishment or death was inflicted for a multitude of offenses. Criminal law was administered in an arbitrary manner.

In 1764 Cesare Beccaria's *Essay on Crimes and Punishments* was published in Italy.[18] It was the first attempt to explain crime in secular, or worldly, terms as opposed to religious terms. The book also pointed to injustices in the ways in which criminal laws were being administered. Beccaria's ideas caught the attention of thinkers throughout Europe and North America because his philosophy meshed with other ideas then coming to the fore.

Beccaria argued that crime is rational behavior and that most people have the potential to engage in illegal activity. In other words, people may choose to commit a crime after weighing the benefits and consequences of their actions. It is the fear of punishment that keeps most people in check, and thus the severity, certainty, and speed of the criminal sanction is the controlling factor. He believed that the criminal justice system must be organized to ensure that punishment will deter crime, and hence he was most concerned that there be a rational link between the gravity of the crime and the severity of the punishment. To put these concepts into practice, Beccaria urged a new emphasis on utility, or usefulness, as a guiding principle in deciding on the laws to be enforced and the punishments to be exacted. The criminal justice system must be predictable, with laws and punishments known to the public. There should be no discretion in considering such factors as class, age, and aggravating or extenuating circumstances. A major theme of Beccaria's work is that the punishment should fit the crime. Others had made the same point earlier, but Beccaria's book was the first to integrate these aims into a consistent penological system. It was from this focus that the classical school of criminology emerged.

Essay on Crimes and Punishments made an immediate impact on public opinion, perhaps because the times were ripe for such a statement. Beccaria's notions were very influential, especially in France after the Revolution of 1789, when attempts were made to fashion the criminal code according to his principles. In England the notions struck a responsive chord with Jeremy Bentham, a leader of **utilitarianism.** He argued that the state must enact punishments that will deter criminals. Excessive force, however, might in fact encourage people to commit additional crimes, since if they were caught they would have nothing to lose.

utilitarianism: The doctrine that the aim of all action should be the greatest possible balance of pleasure over pain; hence, the belief that a punishment must achieve enough good to outweigh the pain inflicted on the offender.

Today there has been renewed interest in some aspects of classical theory. In particular, some scholars have argued that crimes may result from the rational choice of individuals who have weighted the benefits to be gained from the crime against the costs of being caught and punished.

Positivist Criminology

By the middle of the nineteenth century, the ideas of the classical school seemed old-fashioned. Many scholars declared that Beccaria and his followers had been too concerned with law and that the idea of free choice was mere speculation. Some pointed to the lack of proof that human beings are rational. Others said that the classical approach was too rigid, for it did not take into account individual characteristics of the criminal. Greatly influenced by such scientific works as Darwin's *Origin of Species* (1859) and *The Descent of Man* (1871), thinkers developed a new focus for criminological theory: Crime is a behavior determined by outside circumstances in which free will and responsibility play little part. The solution to crime is to use a positivist scientific approach to understand the causes of criminality and its treatment. Punishment should be tailored to the criminal. Positivist theories, with their emphasis on individualized, scientific study and treatment of the offender, have dominated criminology in the United States for much of the twentieth century. The central question of **positivist criminology** is 'Why do people commit criminal acts?'

positivist criminology: A school of criminology that views behavior as stemming from social, biological, and psychological factors. It argues that punishment should be tailored to the individual needs of the offender.

Three Italians stand out as the fathers of positivism and modern criminology: Cesare Lombroso (1835–1909), Enrico Ferri (1856–1929), and Raffaele Garofalo (1852–1934). Although Lombroso, a physician, Ferri, a legal sociologist, and Garofalo, a legal anthropologist, did not agree on the causes of criminal behavior, they greatly influenced the general development of the scientific study of crime. This Italian school, instead of emphasizing the legal and philosophical ramifications of the deviant act, as had been the classical tradition, focused on the people who committed crimes, on their behavior, and on the causes of that behavior. Positivists argue that behavior is determined by physical, mental, and social factors.

Today there are three main positivist approaches to criminality: the biological, the psychological, and the sociological. The latter two have dominated scholarly thinking in the United States during much of the twentieth century. It is only recently that the biological perspective has made something of a comeback. Theories that attempt to explain criminal behavior on the basis of characteristics inherent in the individual offender are based on biology and psychology. Theories that focus on crime-inducing conditions (poverty, social disorganization, subculture norms) in the community that influence the offender are based on sociological reasoning.

It is important to understand the leading explanations of crime causation, because their assumptions significantly affect the ways in which laws are enforced, guilt or innocence is determined, and misconduct is punished. When in Puritan New England the offender's behavior was believed to be the work of the devil, it became the practice for clergymen to use their powers to remove the curse, even if this meant hanging persons thought to be witches. Likewise, if it is believed that poor people are motivated to steal to provide food and clothing for their families, social welfare programs that meet these needs will appear to be the most effective government policy that can be adopted to prevent such crimes. As you read each of these explanations of criminal behavior, consider the types of crime control policies that might be adopted if credence is given to the approach.

Biological Explanations

Lombroso's training in medicine aroused his interest in the physical characteristics he believed differentiated the criminal from the law-abiding citizen. According to his explanation, criminals are born criminal and have traits that mark them as more primitive and savage people. Individuals so disabled have difficulty adjusting to modern

---

A QUESTION OF ETHICS

The auditorium at the university was crowded. The campus newspaper had publicized the fact that the nationally known scientist Herman Strong would lecture on his theory of a biological predisposition to criminality. Author of *Toward a New Crime Policy*, Strong linked crime rates among African-Americans to their low level of social development. Strong's controversial ideas made him a frequent guest on television talk shows and brought forth angry protests. Neo-Nazi groups and skinheads clashed with African-Americans and civil libertarians at demonstrations whenever Strong spoke in public. Most academic criminologists denounced Strong's ideas, noting that his training in physics had little to do with social theory, but they supported his right to speak.

As Professor Gregory Fishbein rose to introduce the speaker, a chant erupted from various parts of the auditorium: "No racists here! No racists here!" Fishbein attempted to speak above the din. "Ladies and gentlemen, a university has a responsibility to be a marketplace of ideas. . . ." He was drowned out by a mixture of shouts, as "Free speech here" competed with "No racists here." The campus police moved into the auditorium and quickly walked toward the stage; their presence seemed only to provoke the crowd. Fishbein and Strong left the podium.

Would you view this as a clash of rights or a clash of ethics? To what extent should ideas that deprecate a racial group be included in criminological debate?

society because they are frustrated by their social incompetence and by the rejection arising from it. Down this path the criminal is thrust into illegal activity.

Lombroso supported his theory with data he gathered by measuring the physical characteristics of Italian convicts. He believed that criminals have "stigmata": asymmetrical faces, ponderous jaws, eye defects, prominent cheekbones, and other such characteristics. These features do not actually cause the illegal behavior but are marks that allow the scientist to distinguish the criminal type.

With the development of psychology, however, interest shifted from physical characteristics to the importance of inherited traits that affect the intellectual level and mental health of criminals. Some criminologists believed that criminals were morally insane and committed crimes as a means of alleviating the pathological urges they inherited from mentally defective ancestors. Criminologists with this orientation studied family genealogies to determine the correspondence between these traits and the criminal records of family members.

Two studies of families given the fictitious names of Jukes and Kallikak presented evidence that genetic deficiencies reproduced in offspring could condemn succeeding generations to lives of crime.[19] Richard Dugdale located more than 1,000 descendants of the woman he called Ada Jukes, whom he dubbed the "mother of criminals." Among the family were 280 paupers, 60 thieves, 7 murderers, 140 criminals, 40 persons with venereal diseases, 50 prostitutes, and other types of undesirables. Similar data collected by Henry H. Goddard supported the belief that the Kallikak family, a group of relatives linked to the illegitimate son of Martin Kallikak, contained more criminals than the descendants of Martin's later marriage into a "good" family.

These early studies have been greatly criticized, but they were taken seriously in their time. In many states crime control policies were enacted requiring habitual offenders to be sterilized. This was done under the assumption that crime could be controlled if hereditary factors were not transmitted. This practice was declared unconstitutional in *Skinner v. Oklahoma* (1942).[20]

BIOGRAPHY

Cesare Lombroso

Born in Verona, Italy, in 1835, Cesare Lombroso became one of the most eulogized and attacked criminologists of all time. His work brought about a shift from a legalistic preoccupation with crime to a scientific study of the criminal. A professor of psychiatry and criminal anthropology at the University of Pavia from 1862 to 1876, Lombroso founded what became known as the biological school of criminology, often referred to as the Italian school.

Lombroso maintained that certain people are born criminals. These individuals are biological throwbacks to a more primitive stage of human evolution and can be identified by physical characteristics. He believed, too, that crime is a disease that can be inherited or brought on by anthropological and social factors. Much of Lombroso's work emphasized that the study of crime is a study of personality development. The work of Lombroso and his followers encouraged the development of more humane and constructive treatment programs for criminals. Lombroso's ideas are best expressed in his three most important books: *Criminal Man* (1876), *The Female Offender* (1895), and *Crime: Its Causes and Remedies* (1912).

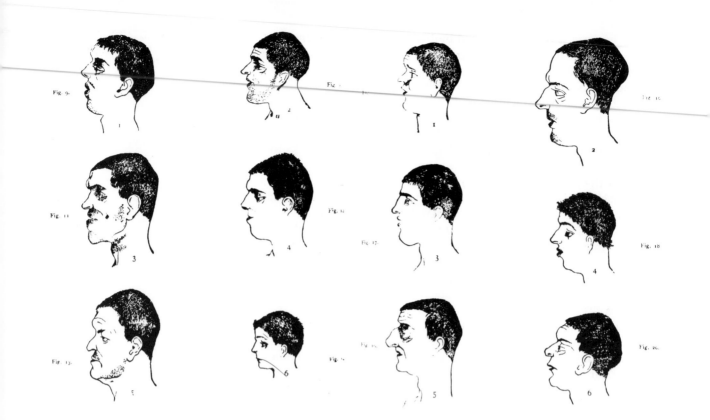

Cesare Lombrosco used these drawings to illustrate his theory that criminals could be distinguished by certain physical characteristics such as asymmetrical faces, ponderous jaws, and eye defects.

Although biological explanations of criminal behavior were ignored or condemned as racist during the period following World War II, they have attracted renewed interest in more recent years. Publication in 1975 of Edward O. Wilson's *Sociobiology: The New Synthesis* renewed interest in links between biological factors and behavior.[21] New research on nutrition, neurology, genetics, and endocrinology has indicated that these factors may be related to the violent behavior of some people. Studies in the 1960s pointed to the possibility that violence in men may be linked to the presence of an extra male sex chromosome. Richard Speck, who had been convicted of killing eight student nurses in Chicago, was found to have such a chromosomal structure. Additional research, however, has indicated that the smallness of the earlier studies' samples makes their findings unreliable. More recently, the defense in a Massachusetts case argued successfully that the accused had an endocrinological dysfunction that caused him to react violently when he consumed even small amounts of alcohol. Likewise, the modern technology of CAT scans, which allows scientists to study portions of the brain, has raised questions about the influence of neurological disorders on violent behavior.

These new perspectives have again brought biological explanations of criminal behavior to the fore. The 1985 book by James Q. Wilson and Richard J. Herrnstein, *Crime and Human Nature*, reviews the biocriminology literature.[22] Wilson and Herrnstein assert that certain "constitutional" factors, such as sex, age, body type, intelligence, and personality, differentiate the criminal from the noncriminal. But unlike the early positivists, these researchers do not point to single-factor explanations of criminality. They believe that biological tendencies interact in complicated ways with developmental and social

58

factors. The rejuvenated interest in biological influences on criminal behavior is a corrective to the psychological and sociological explanations that have dominated criminology for fifty years. Efforts to discover biological indicators of a propensity toward violence and criminality continue to be pursued by scientists.[23]

Psychological Explanations

Before the eighteenth century, madness was generally ascribed to possession by demons. Some scholars, however, eventually suggested that psychological deficiencies of the body caused a person to act "abnormally." One of the early advocates of this idea was Henry Maudsley (1835–1918), an English psychologist who believed that criminals were "morally insane." Maudsley argued that criminals as a group are defective in physical and mental organization and thus lack any sense of morality.[24] Moral insanity is an inherent quality, and crime is a way in which the deviant can express pathological urges. Without crime as an outlet for their unsound tendencies, criminals would become insane.

Sigmund Freud (1856–1939) is today looked on as one of the intellectual giants of the twentieth century. He developed a theory of the unconscious and stressed the role of early childhood experiences in later development. Freud also developed psychoanalysis, a technique for the treatment of personality disorders.

In the wake of Freud's revolution, psychiatrists have related criminal behavior to such concepts as innate impulses, mental conflict, and repression. According to such theories, crime is a form of substitute behavior that compensates for abnormal urges and desires. Although there are great divergences among the practitioners of this school, a main thesis is that personality is formed during early childhood and is a key determinant of later behavior.

Among the theories developed by psychiatrists is that of the person variously described as the "psychopath," "sociopath," or "antisocial personality"—a person who is unable to control impulses, cannot learn from experience, and does not experience normal human emotions such as love. This kind of person is viewed as psychologically abnormal and conforms to the popular image of the crazed killer or sex fiend. During the 1940s, with the rise of psychology and after a number of widely publicized sex crimes, state legislatures were pressured to pass "sexual psychopath laws" designed to remove these "homicidal sex fiends" who stalked the landscape and put them into institutions for treatment of their disorders. It was subsequently shown, however, that such legislation was based on false assumptions, revealing the political context within which the criminal law is fashioned.[25]

Psychological theories have been widely and variously criticized. Some critics talk about the difficulty of measuring emotional factors and of isolating persons thought to be **criminogenic.** Others point to the variety of theories, some conflicting, that have as a basis a psychological approach to crime.

Psychological explanations of criminality have, however, played a major role in criminal justice policy during the twentieth century. Correctional policies emphasizing rehabilitation have been largely

criminogenic factors: Factors thought to bring about criminal behavior in an individual.

based on the belief that personality is linked to behavior. Psychotherapy, group therapy, behavioral modification, and other "treatment modalities" were common in correctional programs from the end of World War II to the mid-1970s. These approaches sought to treat offenders so that they would not again commit crimes. Only during the past decade has there been a deemphasis of this approach.

Sociological Explanations

sociological explanations: Explanations of crime that emphasize the social conditions that bear on the individual as causes of criminal behavior.

Sociological explanations of crime assume that the offender's personality and actions are molded by contact with the social environment and such factors as race, age, gender, and income. People do not live as isolated individuals but as members of social groups, and it is these social influences that shape behavior. The sociological orientation developed along the ideas of such European social theorists as Adolphe Quetelet (1796–1874) and Durkheim. Quetelet's collection and analysis of data in France and Belgium showed that crime was related to a community's population density, income distribution, birthrate, and educational achievement. Like Quetelet, Durkheim believed that a certain level of crime is an intrinsic and natural part of social life. A group of researchers at the University of Chicago in the 1920s furthered development of sociological explanations of crime. Scholars looked closely at the ecological factors of urban life that gave

■
What theories of criminality are
illustrated by this scene?

rise to crime: poverty, inadequate housing, broken families, and the problems of new immigrants.

Sociological explanations of criminality emphasize that offenders are molded by societal forces; criminals are made, not born. Among the several theories that have arisen from this foundation, three deserve special mention: social structure theory, social process theory, and social conflict theory.

Social Structure Theory

Social structure theories ascribe criminal behavior to the stratified nature of Western societies, giving particular prominence to the fact that classes control very different amounts of wealth, status, and power. Those at the bottom of the heap tend to suffer from economic deprivation, lack of education, poor housing, and an inability to influence government agencies. Research has shown that during the 1980s the number of people living in poverty in the United States doubled, and today there is a wider spread between the rich and the poor.[26] Theorists argue that because of the structure of society, the lower-class lifestyle tends to create crime.

Durkheim emphasized that the structure of society often permits a situation of anomie to develop. By **anomie** he meant social conditions in which rules or norms to regulate behavior have weakened or disappeared. Persons may become anomic or frustrated when the rules are unclear or when they are unable to achieve what they expect. When the balance between cultural aspirations and social opportunities is lost or damaged, antisocial or deviant behavior may result. Thus it is said that American society places great emphasis on individual success but excludes some of its members from the possibility of achieving that goal; hence it follows that those caught in this trap choose crime as a way out. Theorists believe that the movement of some ethnic groups into organized crime has been one way of overcoming such anomic frustrations. Others argue that the social disorganization of urbanized and industrial society brings about conditions in which, among other things, family structure breaks down, alcohol or drug abuse becomes more common, and the incidence of criminal behavior rises. They assert that to reduce crime, poverty must be eradicated and the structures of society reformed. This was a major theme of the 1967 report of the President's Commission on Law Enforcement and the Administration of Justice.

Social Process Theory

Criminal justice statistics make clear that criminality is not a phenomenon exclusive to the poor. For many criminologists, the answers given by those accepting only a social structure approach are inadequate. **Social process theories,** although existing since the 1930s, came to be more widely known in the 1960s and 1970s, in part because more middle-class deviance was being recognized, as evidenced by self-report studies, participation in the drug culture, and political activism. Social process theories emphasize that criminality results from the interactions of people with the institutions, organizations, and processes of society. Unlike social structure theories, social process theories assume that everyone, regardless of education, class, or upbringing, has the potential to become a criminal.

social structure theories: Theories that blame crime on the creation of a lower-class culture based on poverty and deprivation, and the response of the poor to this situation.

anomie: Social conditions in which rules or norms to regulate behavior have weakened or disappeared.

social process theories: Theories that see criminality as normal behavior. Everyone has the potential to become a criminal, depending on the influences that impel one toward or away from crime and the ways in which one is regarded by groups and other persons.

These theories try to explain that the circumstances encountered in life influence some people to commit criminal acts and therefore become criminals.

A number of concepts and theories are grouped under the social process rubric. All share certain assumptions, yet there are important differences among them. The three major groups are learning theories, control theories, and labeling theories.

learning theories: Theories postulating that criminal behavior, like legal and normative behavior, is learned.

Learning theories hold that criminal activity is normal learned behavior. It is through social relations that some people have the chance or opportunity to learn how to be a criminal and to acquire the associated values. The assumption is that people imitate and learn from one another. Thus family and peers are viewed as primary influences on an individual's development.

differential association theory: A theory that people become criminals because they encounter a large number of influences that regard criminal behavior as normal and acceptable, with these influences outnumbering the influences hostile to criminal behavior.

In 1939 Edwin Sutherland clarified the learning process and proposed a **differential association theory,** which states that criminal behavior is learned through interactions with other persons, especially family members and others with whom close associations are maintained.[27] Criminal behavior occurs when an individual encounters strong prescriptions for behavior that are more favorable to than opposed to law violations. If a young person grows up in an environment of violence in which, say, an older brother is involved in crime, criminal behavior will be learned. If those in the family, neighborhood, and gang believe that illegal activity is nothing to be ashamed of, there is a greater probability that the young person will engage in crime. It is through these close associations that people learn what is expected and allowed. Someone who belongs to a social group that does not frown on criminal activity and has role models who conduct their lives outside the law will almost certainly become involved in crime as well.

control theories: Theories postulating that criminal behavior occurs when the bonds that tie an individual to others in society are broken or weakened.

Control theories recognize that all members of society have the potential to commit crime but that most are restrained by their ties to such conventional institutions and individuals as the family, church, school, and peer groups. Criminality results when these primary bonds are weakened or broken. Control theory, as developed by Travis Hirschi, holds that social links keep people in line with accepted norms.[28] Thus a person's sensitivity to the opinion of others,

BIOGRAPHY

Edwin H. Sutherland

An American criminologist, Edwin H. Sutherland had a profound impact on the development of the theory of crime causation. Born in Nebraska, Sutherland earned his doctorate at the University of Chicago (1913) and for a number of years was a member of sociology departments at leading universities (Illinois, Minnesota, Chicago) before becoming departmental chairman at Indiana University (1935–1949). His contribution to criminology was significant in shaping the substantive theory and methodological orientation of the field. His important works include *Criminology* (1924), *The Professional Thief* (1937), and *White Collar Crime* (1949).

A major theme of Sutherland's work is that personality and conduct develop as a result of the incorporation of the perspectives of the dominant culture surrounding the individual. From this view he developed the theory of differential association, which holds that criminal behavior is learned in essentially the same way as any other aspect of the culture. A person becomes a criminal through association with others, usually members of an intimate personal group, whose dominant culture is criminal. For Sutherland, the theory implied that on a societal level the cause of crime is *culture conflict*—that is, a conflict between the behavior patterns and values of different cultures within a society.

commitment to a conventional lifestyle, involvement of time and energy in that status, and belief in the standards or values shared by friends are all factors that bear on adherence to a law-abiding existence. Should a person's life be lacking in one or more of these behavior-controlling bonds, criminal behavior may result.

The third of the social process approaches to criminality are **labeling theories.** These approaches posit that to understand the causes of crime, we should look not at individuals but at the social process through which certain acts are labeled deviant. As Howard Becker notes, society creates deviance "by making the rules whose infraction constitutes deviance, and by applying those rules to particular people and labeling them outsiders."[29] Social control agencies, such as the police, courts, and corrections, are created to designate certain individuals as outside the normal law-abiding community. Having been labeled as deviant or criminal, the stigmatized individual comes to believe that the label is true, assumes the identity, and enters into a criminal career.

labeling theories: Theories emphasizing that the causes of criminal behavior are not to be found in the individual but in the social process through which certain acts are labeled deviant or criminal.

Labeling theory seems to have certain ideological and policy implications in that it suggests that criminals are not very different from other members of the community, except that the agencies of justice have labeled them as deviant. The approach also implies that we would be much better off if government did as little as possible with regard to crime. This theory suggests that during certain times, behavior previously viewed as normal is suddenly labeled deviant and therefore becomes the focus of attention for the police and the courts. It is thus argued that the criminal justice system creates criminals by labeling people as such because doing so serves their own bureaucratic or political ends. Policies to decriminalize certain offenses have been advocated by persons holding these views.

Social Conflict Theory

In the mid-1960s a new orientation challenged the biological, psychological, and sociological explanations of criminal behavior. **Social conflict theories** emphasize that criminal law and the criminal justice system are mainly the means of controlling society's poor and have-nots. The rich and well-educated commit as many crimes as the poor, it is argued, but the poor are more likely to be punished because they are powerless and unsophisticated. The rich use the law to impose their version of morality on the whole of society for the purpose of protecting their property and physical safety. By manipulating the law, the elite changes the definition of illegal behavior to encompass activities it views as threatening to the status quo.

social conflict theories: Theories that assume that criminal law and the criminal justice system are primarily means of controlling the poor and have-nots.

As with other approaches to criminal behavior, there are divisions among social conflict theorists. One group, referred to as critical, radical, or Marxist criminologists, argues that the class structure of society results in certain groups being labeled deviant. Thus, "deviance is a status imputed to groups who share certain structural characteristics (e.g., powerlessness)."[30] Thus the criminal law is designed to aim at the behavior of particular groups or classes. One result is a deep hostility among the poor toward the social order; this contributes to criminal behavior. It is argued further that when the status quo is threatened, legal definitions of criminal behavior are altered so as to ensnare those who challenge the system.

Although social conflict theories have affected U.S. criminal justice policies by making lawmakers aware of the problems of the poor and of the inequities in the system, the influence of this approach on the more conservative contemporary scene is uncertain. It will be interesting to see if this approach continues in the future to be an important theoretical perspective on crime and justice.

Like other explanations of the causes of criminal behavior, sociological theories have been thoroughly criticized. It has been argued that they are imprecise, are not supported by empirical evidence, and really do not constitute more than observations. Criticism notwithstanding, the fact is that sociological theories, together with portions of the psychoanalytic orientation, have served as the basis for many attempts to prevent crime and to rehabilitate offenders.

Assessing Theories of Criminality

Obviously, none of these approaches to the study of crime causation is powerful enough to predict criminality or clinically to link an offender's behavior with a specific cause, yet all contain a kernel of truth. Unfortunately, all focus on visible crimes, the illegal activities of the poor. There seems to be little relationship between any of the theories and upper-class or organized crime. What is missing and truly needed is an integrating theory that places all these disparate crime-causation ideas together. Only then will we be able to develop public policies that can deal with the crime problem. Table 2.2 sum-

TABLE 2.2   Major theories of crime causation and their policy implications

Theory	Major Premise	Policy Implications
Biological	Genetic, biochemical, or neurological defects cause some people to commit crime.	Identification and treatment or control of persons with crime-producing biological factors.
Psychological	Personality and learning factors cause some people to commit crime. Personality defects are developed early in childhood and are beyond the individual's control. Some people learn aggressive or deviant behavior by seeing the way others who have committed criminal acts are rewarded.	Persons with personality disorders should be treated so that their minds become healthy. Those who have learned illegal ways should have their behavior sanctioned so they will realize that crime is not rewarded.
Social Structure	Crime is the result of underlying social conditions such as poverty, inequality and unemployment.	Actions should be taken to reform social conditions that breed crime.
Social Process	Crime is normal learned behavior and is subject to either social control or labeling effects.	Individuals must be treated in groups, with emphasis on building conventional bonds and avoiding stigmatization.
Social Conflict	Criminal definitions and sanctions are used by some groups to control other groups.	Fundamental changes in the political economy should be made to reduce class conflict.

marizes the major theories of criminality that have been presented in this chapter and outlines the policy implications of the major thrust of each approach. We might not know much about the causes of crime, but many people think they have the answers!

You may have noticed that the theories discussed in this chapter are almost exclusively based on male offenders. The reason for this is that in the past, most criminologists studied the behavior of males. Female criminality, which has emerged within the past two decades as an area of study, poses new questions.

Female Criminality

The study of female criminality and of changes in female criminality emerged to a great extent as a result of the women's movement. Scholars investigating questions of female criminality base their research on several of the concepts and theories just discussed.[31]

Until recently, with the exception of such so-called female crimes as prostitution and shoplifting, little research was done on the half of the population that accounted for fewer than 10 percent of persons arrested. Two assumptions appear to have been operating. First was the assumption that most women were incapable of serious criminal activity; it was held that women by their nature were too gentle, nurturing, and dependent to commit crimes. Second was the assumption that those who did commit crimes were "bad" women; for some reason, women were viewed as moral offenders, as "fallen." The emergence of the women's movement has changed this orientation. Criminologists are focusing more intently on female offenders whose arrests for such offenses as fraud, robbery, and larceny, traditionally viewed as the province of males, have increased sharply, though arrest rates for women still lag far behind those for men.

FIGURE 2.1
How do the offense characteristics of men and women differ? Although most arrests are of males, the proportion of arrests of females is highest for larceny-theft.
SOURCE: U.S. Department of Justice, *Crime in the United States*, (Washington, DC: Government Printing Office, 1990), p. 189.

UCR **Index Crimes**

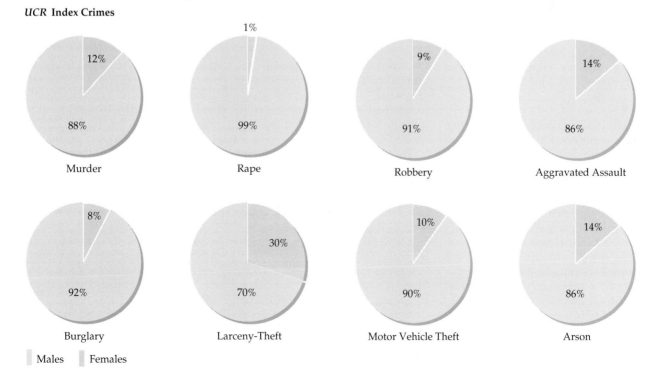

12% / 88%	1% / 99%	9% / 91%	14% / 86%
Murder	Rape	Robbery	Aggravated Assault
8% / 92%	30% / 70%	10% / 90%	14% / 86%
Burglary	Larceny-Theft	Motor Vehicle Theft	Arson

Males   Females

Why this increase? As Freda Adler noted: "When we did not permit women to swim at the beaches, the female drowning rate was quite low. When women were not permitted to work as bank tellers or presidents, the female embezzlement rate was low."[32] It is argued that as women take places of equality with men in American society, distinctions of criminality based on sex are diminished. Rita Simon nicely summarizes this trend by stating that because of the changes that have taken place since the 1950s, women are able to enjoy greater freedom, are less likely to be victimized and oppressed by men, and are less likely to be dependent on them.[33] She says that as a consequence, women will also be less likely to engage in crimes of violence but more likely to commit business-related and property crimes.

Has there been a change in criminality by women? Some scholars believe that the focus on female criminality is a product of the women's movement and that arrest data do not suggest major shifts.[34] Crime data show that there has been an increase to 30.4 percent for women arrestees for larceny-theft offenses (mainly shoplifting), and that female drug arrestees continue to mount. Yet for most other crimes, women remain minor players, constituting fewer than 14 percent of arrestees in all but the larceny-theft *UCR* crime categories, (see Figure 2.1). The link between drug addiction, prostitution, and AIDS is a new cause for concern. Public health as well as crime control are overriding issues with some leaders, who are calling for mandatory testing and even isolation.[35]

COMPARATIVE PERSPECTIVE
Theories of Criminality in the Soviet Union from Lenin to Gorbachev

Author's note: There has been a massive upheaval in the ideological perspective of the Soviet Union since Gorbachev came to power. What were the assumptions of Soviet criminologists until that point?

Early Soviet concern about crime was manifested by the initiation of criminological research very soon after the Revolution of 1917. The 1920s were innovative years that saw, for example, the opening of experimental penitentiaries. Studies were conducted on the personality of the criminal and the effect of social forces on crime. This work ended abruptly in 1936 with the political repression initiated under Stalin. It was only in the mid-1950s, after Stalin's death, that the study of crime resumed under the direction of the criminologists surviving from the 1920s. . . .

Most Western criminological theory builds upon the writings of Emile Durkheim, who saw crime as a "normal" and even necessary part of society. . . . Thus, few scholars in the West seriously entertain the possibility that crime (or at least "deviance") can be totally eliminated from society, since the environment of human action, society itself, demands it.

Starting from a totally different premise, Soviet criminology is in this respect far more optimistic. It is argued that crime can be eliminated, because it is possible to eradicate its primary sources—"vestiges from the past" and susceptibility to the influence of capitalist societies. Following the writings of Karl Marx, it is asserted that this will occur when the society moves from the current socialist stage of development to the ultimate achievement of Communism. This progressive change to Communism is seen as the way in which the social environment is corrected so as to eliminate the causes of crime. . . .

Some Western criminologists have investigated biological factors related to crime, but in the USSR, since the only acceptable causal explanations are those allowing for the complete eradication of crime, biological factors have no place. In the Soviet view, "If biology determines crime then criminal law and punishment are unnecessary, and it is only necessary to cure the individual." The few Soviet criminologists who consider biological factors are severely criticized by their colleagues.

While the Soviet criminologist may make the claim that there is "nothing in the nature of Soviet society which could give rise to crime," crime in capitalist society

Although one can discern some changes with regard to the criminality of women in the United States, what is the situation in other countries? As with other comparative strategies, research on this topic has a number of weaknesses that cannot be overlooked. Primarily there is a problem with the data. Although crime and gender data are extensively collected in the United States, Canada, and England, such is not the case in other developed countries. Research has generally depended on arrest data from the International Criminal Police Organization (INTERPOL). In a ground-breaking study published in 1975, Simon found that in only a few countries was there a trend toward higher female criminality. The highest female arrest rates were in a variety of countries, Western and Eastern, modern and traditional, industrial and agrarian. There were thus no predominant economic or social characteristics to distinguish these countries.[36] Adler sought to test her theories of changing female roles and criminality. If economic disparities were reduced, would male and female crime rates converge? Although fraught with methodological problems, Adler's study, like Simon's, focused attention on the need to recognize the importance of issues raised by the women's movement and arising from social change.[37] Single-country studies have also been conducted to examine the "new woman" and crime. Each tends to emphasize particular factors that are part of the country's culture and special circumstances. Summarizing international comparisons of women and crime, Ralph Weisheit and Sue Mahan noted that

is, of course, viewed in a very different light. The theory predicts that it will continue to grow and is rooted in exploitation, unemployment, and poverty—features inherent in the structure of capitalism. These economic and social shortcomings were supposedly overcome in the USSR in the 1930s. The program of the Communist Party of the Soviet Union states: "The rise in the material well-being, cultural level, and consciousness of the working people creates all the necessary conditions for uprooting crime."

If so many years have passed since the elimination of the economic and social shortcomings, how do the Soviet criminologists account for the fact that the Soviet Union has not yet achieved its goal of total liquidation of all crime?...

In private conversations many Soviet scholars reject the publicly espoused view that crime is withering away under socialism and will disappear with the achievement of communism. However, they still show fundamental agreement with the following dominant beliefs found in officially published

crime studies: Bourgeois influences from the past and from abroad are the only causes of crime in contemporary Soviet society . . . and the control of crime is most effectively achieved when offenders are subjected to a treatment that serves both to punish and rehabilitate.

Soviet criminologists include a great deal under the rubric of bourgeois vestiges of the past: the traditions and habits of certain groups in the population; individual characteristics such as cupidity, cynicism, coarseness, despotism, selfishness, philistine attitudes, egotism, lack of human dignity, and indifference to the fate of others; and conditions elsewhere commonly viewed as social problems, such as alcoholism, one-parent families, and low educational attainment. It is contended that vestiges remain significant even though presocialist conditions no longer exist, in part because of "lags of consciousness"—that is, because under certain conditions motivations may change more slowly than social conditions.

Along with vestiges of the past, the other primary Soviet explana-

tion for the existence of crime in Soviet society is the harmful influence of Western bourgeois society. But this explanation of criminality has become acceptable only since Stalin's death. . . .

The Soviet system is ideologically committed to fostering the development of the "new Soviet person," and the criminal justice system is viewed as a fundamental institution for achieving this end through its capacity to educate and coerce. But not all citizens yet (or probably ever will) conform to this model. . . . While the methods of control used in the Soviet Union have reduced crime in some regions, they have failed to confirm the Marxist prediction that "crime will wither away under socialism." Indeed, the evidence presented here supports Durkheim's view of the normalcy of crime, its inevitability within society.

SOURCE: Drawn from "Crime and Delinquency in the Soviet Union," by L. Shelley, pp. 208–224. In J. G. Pankhurst and M. P. Sacks (eds.), *Contemporary Soviet Society*. Copyright ©1980 by Praeger Publishers. Reprinted by permission of Greenwood Publishing Group, Inc., Westport, CT.

female criminality is less frequent than that of males and there is little evidence of dramatic changes in the nature and extent of crimes committed by women.[38]

Research on the backgrounds of female criminals shows that they tend to have been brought up in dysfunctional familes in which poverty and physical and substance abuse were present.[39] These characteristics, however, do not seem much different than those of male offenders. Earlier research posited biological explanations related to menstruation and menopause for some offenses committed by women. The defense of premenstrual syndrome (PMS) was successfully used in an English homicide case. This syndrome is based on some evidence that women are more violence-prone during certain points in their menstrual cycle.[40] With this exception thus far, the evidence does not appear to differentiate the cause of female criminality from that of men.

Victimology

victimology: A subfield of criminology that examines the role played by the victim in precipitating a criminal incident.

One of the newest areas of criminology is the subfield of **victimology.** There has long been a concern for the victims of crime, and proposals have been made to provide some form of compensation for the wrongs they have suffered. Revived interest in requiring the offender to make restitution to the victim is a contemporary manifestation of this orientation. The ways in which the criminal justice system treats victims will be more fully discussed in Chapter 4.

Another way of thinking about the victim has surfaced in recent years. Victimology has become concerned with the role the victim plays in the criminal incident. In this view, the crime is precipitated by something that the victim has or has not done. By analyzing the characteristics of a variety of victims, criminologists have advanced the idea that many of them voluntarily act in ways that incite their attackers to commit a violent act against them. The victim may bring about commission of a crime through consent, provocation, enticement, unnecessary risk taking, or carelessness with property.

Let us consider the type of city dweller who is more likely than another to become prey to a mugger. Morton Hunt has listed six elements that may predispose a person to attack.[41]

1. People who are on the sidewalks late at night are three times as likely to be victimized as those who stay indoors after dark.
2. Age and physical disabilities make the elderly more vulnerable to attack than the young and strong.
3. In addition, some people are more vulnerable because they are hampered by things they are carrying, by the attention they are giving to something, or by clothing that may block their view or make defense difficult.
4. Kinds of clothing worn can be a clue to likely amounts of cash being carried or jewelry being worn.
5. Although most street crime is intraracial, more than half the robberies on American city streets are interracial—white victims of nonwhite criminals, strangers to one another.
6. A person walking alone is more likely to be a target for a mugger than is someone with a companion.

Muggings occur between strangers, but there are other types of violence that occur between two persons who know each other, and these types add another dimension to the role that victims play in the administration of justice. A study of felony arrests in New York City focused on the many cases the prosecution drops because the complainant refuses to provide key testimony. It was found that in a high proportion of crimes of interpersonal violence, a prior relationship existed between offender and victim: manslaughter, 50 percent; rape, 83 percent; assault, 67 percent. When the victim knows the assailant, there is a high probability that an arrest will occur; yet the

CLOSE-UP *Marge: The New Female Criminal?*

Since her husband disappeared one day eighteen years ago, Marge has worked a total of fifteen years either as a waitress or a barmaid. During those years, she supported and raised two sons, one of whom eventually worked his way through a small state college and is currently a teacher. The other one, younger, died four years ago as a result of pumping a bad bag of heroin into his arm.

Deserted, with two small children, Marge was forced to get the first job she had ever had. It was as a barmaid in a small restaurant-lounge. Not long afterward, she gave her first serious thought to being a prostitute—like a fellow barmaid who was developing a very lucrative following among the bar's male clientele.

But soon Marge gave up the idea of prostitution—partly because of her figure, which she didn't feel was suited for the trade, and partly because of her "strong Catholic upbringing." She explained, "It didn't bother me that other girls I knew were turning tricks; I just couldn't bring myself to stay with it. I guess underneath it all, I was more straitlaced than I knew."

In place of prostitution, Marge found a more acceptable degree of reprehensibility in shoplifting. "Boosting" from department stores became a regular habit with her. At first she began by putting small items, like watches, into her pocket. Later, she progressed to more sophisticated methods. She wore large baggy coats that could conceal things like toasters and radios, then began to sew large bag-like pockets inside the coats to facilitate even larger load handling. She shoplifted for years and was caught only once. On that occasion she was allowed to go free on her own recognizance and, although threatened with further prosecution, never heard of the incident again.

Five years ago Marge robbed her first bank. The planning took her some months. "It was something that came to me all of a sudden. . . . I had a couple of big debts and I was getting tired of working. . . . I wanted a bit of easy time. I mean, the kids were getting older and I was still working and, after all those years, I needed a break. I guess maybe I got the idea from watching TV or something; I don't remember. But it surprised me; like, I first thought of it seriously and thought, 'No, I couldn't do that. . . . I'm a woman,' you know? But when I thought more about it, what the hell, it didn't seem so bad. The other girls I knew were boosting or [credit] carding. They said I must be crazy when we talked about it one day. We never really thought about a woman hitting a bank before. . . . But then soon after that, I heard on the radio of a lady who hit a bank and got away and I figured, what the hell, if she can do it, why can't I?"

After many months of careful planning and observation, Marge attempted to rob one particular bank. That first attempt was a failure. She walked in and approached the teller's window but was unable to go through with the robbery. "I just asked for change for a ten-dollar bill and felt like a real smacked-ass to myself." Two months later, though, she went through with it and went on to rob two more banks before she was finally caught. After the first one it seemed easy to her. "I just walked in, walked out, and went home to count the money. I always thought it would be a lot harder . . . a lot more dangerous. I did take a gun each time, but it was never loaded and I only really had to show it to one teller. The others just put the money in the bag when I asked them to. . . . I remember that first job. It was like a cheap high afterward. I went home and turned on the radio to see what they would say about me on the news."

To her disappointment, after that first heist, police described her to the news media as a "male dressed in women's clothing." That upset Marge a bit. "Well, I know I'm no beauty queen, but I didn't think I was that bad . . . and who the hell ever saw a man with plucked eyebrows?"

During her third try, Marge was stopped on her way out of the bank by policemen responding to a silent alarm. She gave up peacefully. ("What the hell else could I do, the gun wasn't loaded or anything.") She is currently serving an indefinite prison term for robbery.

SOURCE: From *Sisters in Crime*, by F. Adler, pp. 6–7 (copyright © 1975). Reissued 1985 by Waveland Press, Inc., Prospect Heights, Ill. Reprinted by permission.

complaint may well be dropped later. But these occurrences add new information on the causes of crime, because we can learn from them about the events leading up to the incident. The New York researchers concluded that much violent conduct is often the "explosive spillover from ruptured personal relations among neighbors, friends, and former spouses."[42] Interpersonal violence seems to result from such incidents as the family argument that escalates until one of the combatants picks up a kitchen knife or gun and commits an assault or homicide. In such circumstances, one can inquire about the responsibility of each of the parties for the final deed.

What do victimology studies tell us? First, there are instances in which citizens do not take proper precautions to protect themselves. Acting with common sense and regulating our behavior to prevent criminal attack may be one of the prices of living in contemporary society. Second, under some circumstances, the victim, by some action, may provoke or entice another to commit a criminal act. Third, the victims in certain types of nonstranger crimes are unwilling to assist official agencies in investigation and prosecution activities. All this does not excuse criminal behavior, but it forces us to think about other dimensions of the way in which the criminal act is perpetrated.

TYPES OF CRIMES

It is possible to divide crimes into various categories. Scholars interested in the development of societal reaction to crime often use the distinction between *mala in se* and *mala prohibita*. A legal division can also be made in which some crimes are labeled as **felonies** (those punishable by death or more than a year of incarceration) and others as **misdemeanors** (for which a lesser sanction is imposed). Criminologists have developed a third scheme that categorizes crimes according to the nature of the behavior and the type of person most likely to commit specific offenses. This scheme distinguishes five categories of crime: occupational, organized, visible, crimes without victims, and political. Each type has its own level of risk and profitability, each arouses varying degrees of public disapproval, and each has its own group of offenders with differing cultural characteristics. Though the community potentially can command the energy, resources, and technology to attack all crime, social and political processes somehow operate so that only certain offenders are thought suitable for processing by the criminal justice system.

felony: A serious crime carrying a penalty of death or incarceration for more than a year. Persons convicted of felonies lose the right to vote, to hold public elective office, and to practice certain professions and occupations.

misdemeanor: An offense less serious than a felony and usually punishable by incarceration for no more than a year, a fine, or probation.

Occupational Crime

occupational crime: Conduct in violation of the law that is committed through opportunities created in the course of a legal occupation.

Occupational crime is the violation of the law committed through opportunities created in the course of a legal business or profession. Often viewed as shrewd business practices rather than as illegal offenses, these are crimes that, if perpetrated "correctly," are never discovered.

The problem of crimes committed in the course of business was first brought to the attention of American criminologists by Edwin

■

Michael Milken, the "junk bond king," arrives for sentencing at U.S. District Court. He was given ten years in prison for securities fraud and for filing false information with the Securities and Exchange Commission.

Sutherland in 1939. Sutherland developed the concept of "white-collar crime," in which he emphasized the respectability of the offender and the occupational opportunity for the offense.[43] This orientation forced criminologists to recognize that crime was not primarily that of lower-class people but reached into the upper echelons of society.

As the white-collar/blue-collar distinction lost much of its clarity in our modern postindustrial society, scholars attempted to redefine Sutherland's idea. After reviewing this literature, Gary Green described four categories of occupational crimes:[44]

1. Occupational crimes for the benefit of employing organizations. These are crimes in which employers rather than offenders benefit directly. Price fixing, theft of trade secrets, and falsification of product tests are all examples in which an individual employee may commit the offense but, other than perhaps a bonus or promotion, does not individually benefit; the company reaps the profits. These are crimes that are "committed in the suites rather than in the streets." Well-known examples include charges that the Ford Motor Company knew that the Pinto's gas tank might explode and yet did nothing about it; a $2 billion overbilling of customers by the Exxon Corporation, the nation's largest oil company; and the seemingly continuous overbilling of the U.S. armed services by military contractors.

2. Occupational crimes through the exercise of state-based authority in which the offender has the legal authority to enforce laws or to command others. Included here would be the police officer who takes confiscated drugs from the evidence room, the politician who takes a bribe in exchange for a vote, or a notary public who falsifies a document. The 1978 ABSCAM case involving several congressmen and a senator who accepted bribes in exchange for introducing a private immigration bill and for obtaining government contracts for "Abdul Enterprises," an FBI sting operation, fits this category.

3. Occupational crimes committed by professionals in their capacity as professionals. Physicians, lawyers, and stockbrokers might violate their professional oaths or take advantage of patients by, for instance, sexually exploiting a patient, illegally dispensing drugs, or using confidential information for personal gain. The conviction of stockbroker Ivan Boesky for using confidential information to profit in securities trading is a good example of this category. Likewise, Michael Milken, the "junk bond king," was sentenced to ten years in prison for securities fraud and for filing false information with the Securities and Exchange Commission.

4. Occupational crimes committed by individuals as individuals in which opportunities are not based on governmental power or professional position. Examples of this type of crime include employee theft from the organization, filing false expense claims, and embezzlement. Jim Bakker of the "Praise the Lord" television evangelism ministry is a recent example of someone who was charged with committing fraud for personal benefit.

Take a moment to review Table 2.3. If you have heard of more than a few of these offenders, you are exceptional. Although highly profitable, most categories of occupational crimes do not come to public attention. Regulatory agencies, such as the Federal Trade Commission and the Securities and Exchange Commission, are often ineffective in their enforcement of the law. Many business and professional organizations "police" themselves, dropping employees or members who commit offenses. However, the low level of enforcement and prosecution of occupational crimes may result from the general public's view that these offenses are not of as immediate concern as, for example, purse snatching. As the President's Commission on Law Enforcement and Administration of Justice noted: "Most people pay little heed to crimes of this sort when they worry about 'crime in America,' because these crimes do not, as a rule, offer an immediate, recognizable threat to personal safety."[45]

Organized Crime

organized crime: A social framework for the perpetration of criminal acts, usually in such fields as gambling, drugs, and prostitution, in which illegal services that are in great demand are provided.

The term **organized crime** describes a social framework for the perpetration of criminal acts rather than specific types of offenses. Organized criminals provide goods and services to millions of people. They will engage in any illegal activity that provides a minimum of risk and a maximum of profit. Thus organized crime involves a network of enterprises, usually cutting across state and national boundaries, that range from legitimate businesses to shady involvement with labor unions to activities that cater to desires for drugs, sex, and pornography—things forbidden by the criminal code. It has recently become known that with increased regulation of the disposal of hazardous wastes, organized crime has entered into this business as

TABLE 2.3   Ten occupational offenders: what they did and what they got.
Most high-status occupational offenders receive mimimal punishments for the crimes they commit. Here are some examples. What might be appropriate punishments for such deeds?

Criminal	Crime	Sentence
Jack L. Clark	President and chairman of Four Seasons Nursing Centers, Clark finagled financial reports and earnings projections to inflate his stock artificially. Shareholders lost $200 million.	One year in prison
John Peter Galanis	As portfolio manager of two mutual funds, Galanis bilked investors out of nearly $10 million.	Six months in prison and five years' probation
Virgil A. McGowen	As manager of the Bank of America branch in San Francisco, McGowen siphoned off $591,921 in clandestine loans to friends. Almost none of the money was recovered.	Six months in prison, five years' probation, and $3,600 fine
Valdemar H. Madis	A wealthy drug manufacturer, Madis diluted an antidote for poisoned children with a worthless look-alike substance.	One year's probation and a $10,000 fine
John Morgan	President of Jet Craft, Ltd., Morgan illegally sold about $2 million in unregistered securities.	One year in prison and a $10,000 fine
Ivan Projansky	The former chairman of the First National Bank of Lincolnwood, Ill., Projansky raised stock prices artificially and then dumped the shares, costing the public an estimated $4 million.	One year in prison and two years' probation
David Ratliff	Ratliff spent his twenty-one years as a Texas state senator embezzling state funds.	Ten years' probation
Walter J. Rauscher	An executive vice-president of American Airlines, Rauscher accepted about $200,000 in kickbacks from businessmen bidding for contracts.	Six months in prison and two years' probation
Frank W. Sharp	The multimillion-dollar swindles of Sharp, a Houston banker, shook the Texas state government and forced the resignation of the head of the Criminal Division of the Justice Dept.	Three years' probation and a $5,000 fine
Seymour R. Thaler	Soon after his election to the New York State Supreme Court, Thaler was convicted of receiving and transporting $800,000 in stolen U.S. Treasury bills.	One year in prison and a $10,000 fine

SOURCE: From "America's Most Coddled Criminals," by B. Fleetwood and A. Lubow, *New Times*, September 15, 1975, p. 30. Reprinted by permission.

■

An example of the inequities of criminal justice in a capitalist system is the failure to vigorously prosecute for the illegal disposal of toxic wastes while focusing law enforcement resources on crimes committed by the poor.

well, finding sites for the illegal disposal of toxic substances for a high fee.

With minor exceptions, organized crime seldom provides inputs to the criminal justice process. Investigations by congressional committees and other governmental bodies of the crime "families" known as the Mafia and the Cosa Nostra have provided detailed accounts of the structure, membership, and activities of these groups, yet few arrests are made and even fewer convictions gained. The FBI has been especially vocal about the impact of organized crime on American society, but it, too, has failed to provide the evidence that would put this particular type of criminal behind bars.

Although the public currently associates organized crime with Americans of Italian ancestry, other ethnic groups have dominated this type of activity in the past. In fact, as a study from the seventies states:

> One group of immigrants after another has handed to each newly arriving immigrant group a "queer ladder of social mobility" which has organized crime as the first few rungs. The Irish were the first immigrant groups to become involved in organized criminal activity on a large scale in the United States. . . . As they eventually came to control the political machinery of the large cities, the Irish won wealth, power and respectability by expanding their legitimate business interests and gaining control of construction, trucking, public utilities and the waterfront. The Irish were succeeded in organized crime by the Jews, [whose names] dominated gambling and labor racketeering for a decade. The Jews quickly moved into the world of business as a more legitimate means of gaining economic and social mobility. The Italians came last and did not get a commanding leg up the ladder until the late thirties. They were just beginning to find politics and business as routes out of crime and the ghetto and into wealth and respectability in the fifties.[46]

■

Many of today's organized crime figures bear little resemblance to those of earlier periods. African-Americans, Hispanics, and Asians now engage in organized crime in ways that differ from the Mafia.

Today there is increasing evidence that African-Americans, Hispanics, and Asians have begun to manage these enterprises in some cities. Drug trafficking has brought Colombian and Mexican crime groups to U.S. shores, and reports from California document the emergence of Vietnamese-, Chinese-, and Japanese-led organizations.[47] These new groups do not fit the Mafia pattern. Law enforcement agencies have had to alter their tactics in dealing with the organized crimes of these non-Italian groups.[48]

The importation and sale of drugs, especially cocaine and crack, is a major source of income for a wide variety of organized crime groups.[49] Of these, the Colombia cartels, the Jamaican posses (major distributors of crack), and such street gangs as the Bloods and the Crips are the most heavily involved.[50] The Colombian drug traffickers, dominated by the Medellin and Cali cartels, control the production and wholesaling of cocaine, which is then sold on the street by organized crime groups. The Organized Crime Drug Enforcement Task Force, drawing on the resources of nine federal agencies, is primarily concerned with disrupting and dismantling drug trafficking organizations. It has been involved in the prosecution of organized crime figures involved in drug trafficking and the seizure of their assets.[51]

Visible Crimes

Visible crimes, often referred to as "street crimes" or "ordinary crimes" and committed primarily by the lower classes, run the gamut from shoplifting to homicide. For offenders, these crimes are the least profitable and, because they are visible, the least protected violations. These are the crimes that make up the FBI's *Uniform Crime Reports* and are the acts that most of the public regards as criminal. Included are crimes of violence, such as homicide, rape, and assault, as well as crimes against property, such as theft, larceny, and burglary. The extent to which society has allocated law enforcement, judicial, and correctional resources to deal with violators of these laws raises serious questions about the role played by political and social power in determining criminal justice policies. Theorists have argued that the decidedly lower-class characteristics of the inhabitants of American

visible crimes: Offenses against persons and property committed primarily by members of the lower class. Often referred to as "street crimes" or "ordinary crimes," these are the offenses most upsetting to the public.

■

Visible crimes are most often committed by the poor. The probability of arrest is high and the profits to be gained are low.

correctional institutions reflect the class bias of a society that has singled out only certain types of criminal activity for attention. They note that we do not prosecute occupational crimes with the same intensity as we do street crimes.

As noted in Chapter 1, the level of reported *UCR* offenses has remained fairly steady during the last decade. However, the current focus on drugs has raised concern about certain crimes, especially when drug users have been involved in robbery and burglary to sustain their habit. In one study New York City heroin users were found to have committed an average of 225 street crimes per year—robbery, burglary, shoplifting.[52] Drug-related homicides in cities such as New York and Washington, D.C., have provoked community outcries for greater police protection. Visible crimes of violence and against property are the focus of the criminal justice system.

Crimes without Victims

crimes without victims: Offenses involving a willing and private exchange of illegal goods or services for which there is a strong demand. Participants do not feel that they are being harmed. Prosecution is justified on the ground that society as a whole is being injured by the act.

Crimes without victims can be defined as offenses involving a willing and private exchange of goods or services that are in high demand but are illegal. These are offenses against morality, such as prostitution, gambling, obscenity, and drug use and sales. These crimes are victimless, since the participants do not feel that they are being harmed. Prosecutions for these offenses are justified on the grounds that society as a whole is being injured, since the moral fabric of the

---

CLOSE-UP *Portrait of a Mugger*

His world is small, a whirlpool of lower–New York street corners, tense friendships, family problems, small-change business deals, people without last names—and sudden violence. It is an insular world where "uptown" means a girlfriend's apartment north of Houston Street and "the Bronx" is your brother's apartment on 287th Street. When it suited him, Jones stayed at his parents' home, a tiny shelter in "the projects," and when it didn't he stayed with one of his women.

One day we decided to play a rather serious game: we would pretend to be muggers.

"I don't know all the rules and answers, but the ones I know I'm sure of," Jones is saying as we begin my guided tour of victimland. "Rule number one is that everything's okay as long as you don't get caught." He is pointing out areas of interest along the way—you and your wallet, for example.

I see a jowly, middle-aged man with wavy hair carrying a grocery bag toward a car. We are about fifty yards from him.

Jones sees the man but does not turn. His eyes seem to be aimed at the pavement.

"Yeah, he'd be good. He's got his hands full. You let him get in the car, and you get in with him before he can close the door. You are right on top of him, and

you show him the knife. He'll slide over and go along with it."

"After that?"

"If you think he's gonna chase you, you can put him in the trunk."

We turn toward a cluster of buildings. I see a man in a black suburban coat. He is taller and younger.

"Not him," Jones says, again without looking directly at him. "He looks hard. You could take him off in a hallway, but he would give you trouble in the street." . . .

We walk to Second Avenue, moving among crowds of shoppers—sad faces, tired arms filled with packages, coats, purses, flat hip-pocket wallets in the sunny afternoon . . . so much *money* in this speckled fool's gold afternoon. . . .

He looks across the street.

"There's a precinct house on that block. The check-cashing place near it is a good place to pull rips. Nobody thinks a dude would have the heart to do it so close to a cop station; so nobody watches it very closely."

We walk into a grimy side street between First and Second Avenues and stop across from a storefront. The red-and-blue sign—Checks Cashed/Money Orders Filled—is ringed with light bulbs, and the windows are

community is endangered. The use of the criminal law to enforce standards of morality is costly. Not only do these cases flood the courts, but also enforcement necessitates the use of police informers.

Some people feel that classifying goods as prohibited only encourages organized crime to develop an apparatus to supply the desired products. If the sale and possession of heroin, for example, were to be legalized, its price would probably drop immediately, underworld elements would move to more profitable business opportunities, and the crimes perpetrated by users to obtain money for their costly habit would be reduced. On the other hand, can crime truly be victimless? Perhaps we should allow individual adults to harm their bodies through drug use or to endanger their financial situation through gambling, but it can be argued that such activities do harm to family members. It can also be argued that purveyors of illicit goods and services depend on law enforcement activities to keep profits high. But are the costs of the prohibition worth their impact on the values emphasized?

Political Crime

Political crime includes activities, such as treason, sedition (rebellion), and espionage, that are viewed as threats to the government. Political freedom is always qualified, and American history has seen many laws enacted in response to apparent threats to the established

> **political crime:** Acts that constitute threats against the state (such as treason, sedition, espionage).

---

covered with wire and protective devices. Half a block away, the precinct house has patrol cars clustered in front. Brawny plainclothes detectives pass by every few minutes.

Jones looks at my watch and sees that it is 2:15.

"It's a little early now. Pretty soon, this place will be doin' business." We lean against a store window and wait.

Jones nudges me. "That dude's got cash. Watch him."

Across the street, I see a tall man with snow-white hair. He walks confidently, head erect, wearing a black cashmere coat; in profile he bears a striking resemblance to the late Chief Justice Earl Warren, the same bright eyes, broad nose, and prominent cheekbones. I mention this to Jones, who laughs, only vaguely familiar with the Warren Court.

Jones's street sense is astounding. The man hasn't moved directly toward the store, only stepped off the curb. He could be headed anywhere on the block.

Jones says he will cash a check.

He passes the storefront, then stops, steps backward, and disappears into the doorway.

"He is being careful. So he's got cash."

"A good victim?"

"Yeah."

Three minutes later, the man emerges and continues walking down the block.

"From the way he walks, I think he lives on this block."

"Why?"

"The way he moves. He looks like he knows where he's going. He's afraid to move too fast, but he looks like he knows where he wants to get to."

As Jones finishes the sentence, the tall old man turns on one foot and walks into a brownstone apartment building.

"When would you move?"

"I'd wait until he gets through the door. The building is old, so the second door won't lock fast. If you time it right, the lock won't stop you."

Jones drags on the cigarette he is holding.

"I'd be in there now. I'd let him start climbing the stairs. Then I'd take him."

And the old man, who looks like a statesman but lives on a bad block, would lose something. His Social Security check? A stock dividend? His life? . . .

SOURCE: From *JONES: A Portrait of a Mugger*, by James Willwerth. Copyright © 1974 by James Willwerth. Reprinted by permission of the publisher M. Evans and Co., Inc., New York, NY 10017.

order. The Sedition Act of 1789 provided for the punishment of those uttering or publishing statements against the government. The Smith Act of 1940 forbade the advocacy of the overthrow of the government by force or violence. During the turmoil surrounding the Vietnam War, the government used charges of criminal conspiracy as a weapon to deter the activities of those opposing the administration's policies. During the past quarter century the rise of international terrorism has had a political cast to it even though the acts (bombings, hostage taking, etc.) may be defined as visible crimes.

In authoritarian countries the mere making of statements critical of the government is a crime that may result in prosecution and imprisonment. In Western democratic countries, some criminologists would aver, there is virtually no political crime except for a rare offense like treason. As noted by Francis Allen: "Laws to proscribe political behavior are enacted in periods of strong public feeling, sometimes bordering on hysteria."[53] This is not to say that illegal acts are not perpetrated for political purposes but that such crimes are punished because of the nature of the act, not because of its intended impact. A terrorist who kills a government official will be prosecuted for homicide, just as will a woman who kills her spouse.

TOO MUCH LAW?

The United States has tended to use the criminal law for all sorts of social purposes. Each new technological advance, racial problem, or governmental program has resulted in another set of laws being placed on the books. In 1930 Roscoe Pound wrote that because of added laws, more than half of the 100,000 people arrested in Chicago in 1912 were accused of violating laws that had been written since 1887. It has been estimated that the number of crimes for which one may be prosecuted has more than doubled since the turn of the century. More striking than the number of offenses is the remarkable range of human activities now subject to the threat of criminal sanctions: "The killing of domesticated pigeons, the fencing of saltpeter caves against wandering cattle, the regulation of automobile traffic, the issue of daylight saving time versus standard time, to give only a few examples, have all, at one place or another, been made problems of the criminal law."[54]

overcriminalization: The use of criminal sanctions to deter behavior that is acceptable to substantial portions of society.

One of the current issues of criminal justice policy is **overcriminalization.** Some theorists have suggested that criminalizing actions that may not be regarded as deviant by substantial portions of the society contributes to disrespect for the law, to unequal enforcement, and to a drain on the resources necessary to control serious misconduct. Especially with regard to such victimless crimes as gambling, marijuana use, drunkenness, and prostitution, there have been calls for decriminalization.

Scholars have increasingly drawn attention to society's failure to distinguish between appropriate and inappropriate uses of criminal sanctions. Because we recognize that the activities mentioned above are crimes without victims, the question arises, Should the criminal law be used to enforce morality? Of equal weight is the question, Should behaviors be deemed criminal when there is no consensus about their harmfulness? In a classic statement, John Stuart Mill wrote in 1859: "The only purpose for which power can rightfully be exercised over any member of a civilized community, against his will, is to prevent harm to others. His own good, either physical or moral, is not a warrant."[55] Although Mill's view may sound logical, can it be said that vice does not harm others? A persuasive answer to Mill has been given by Patrick Devlin, who believes that harm does ensue when society fails to bring about adherence to a common morality.[56] From his standpoint, society has the right to use criminal law to bring about conformity to the majority's moral commitments and values. Further, criminal law serves to proclaim those values.

Although philosophers and legal scholars will continue to debate these problems, a more concrete and practical question asks, Is the enforcement of laws prohibiting these behaviors consistent with the goals of the criminal justice system? The National Advisory Commission on Criminal Justice Standards and Goals summarizes: "The criminal justice system is ill-equipped to deal with these [morality] offenses. These crimes place a heavy and unwelcome burden on law enforcement resources throughout the nation. And the laws regulating these offenses are open to abuse and, increasingly, to constitutional challenge."[57]

Reform

Numerous commissions and reform groups have suggested reviewing the criminal law with the intention of decriminalizing many aspects of behavior. Although some proposals reflect the humanistic belief that persons should be free to engage in any activity that does not harm others, most decriminalization proposals are based on the assumption that enforcement resources can be utilized more efficiently against "real crime" if they are not spent on crimes without victims.

Thus far, only such nuisance and illness statutes as those on vagrancy and drunkenness have been changed. Laws proscribing certain sexual activities will probably die a slow death through nonenforcement; sexual practices in private between consenting adults will undoubtedly be decriminalized in this manner. With the exception of laws prohibiting the possession of marijuana, most of the drug statutes will probably remain on the books and be objects of enforcement activity. As Thurman Arnold has said: "Most unenforced criminal laws survive in order to satisfy moral objections to established modes of conduct. They are unenforced because we want to continue our conduct, and unrepealed because we want to preserve our morals.[58]

What *are* the likely consequences of decriminalization? To be sure, certain classes of persons would not enter the criminal justice system for the offenses now charged against them, but would other charges be used to impose sanctions on those same individuals? Would decriminalization of particular types of behavior really bring about increased police effectiveness, or would it bring about increased frustration? Would the case loads of the courts become unclogged, or is a necessary level of inputs required to meet the organizational needs of the system? Such questions must be examined when reform is considered within the conceptual framework of an administrative system.

LEGISLATIVE PROCESS AND THE LAW

In a democracy, the people's elected representatives meeting as legislatures are charged with writing the statutes defining crime. Thus in the political arenas of the U.S. Congress and the legislatures of the fifty states, decisions are made as to the types of behavior that will come under the criminal code and the range of punishments that may be imposed on offenders. This is not to dismiss the contributions of constitutions and judicial decisions in the formation of the substantive and procedural aspects of the criminal law but to point to the fact that legislators write the statutes that define crime.

Ideally the legislative process is the instrument through which the public interest is expressed. Rather than being a rational process of decision making in which facts are clear, interests are identical, and unanimous agreement is easily reached on the nature of the common good, however, the political nature of the legislative process results in clashes, compromises, and bargaining. As a result, proposed statutes are often stated in vague and ambiguous terms to ensure that a majority of lawmakers will vote in their favor.

Statutory specifications of the punishments for criminal offenses demonstrate the ambiguity of the products of the legislative process. Although American legislatures have done a good job of defining proscribed behavior so that it is apparent which acts are forbidden, they have not done a good job of specifying punishments. Legislatures grant judges sweeping powers to fashion sentences. By giving this type of discretion to judges, legislators may appear to be mandating strong penalties, yet they may trust that more reasonable sentences will be handed down.

Interest Groups

The few studies of the way legislatures write the criminal law reveal that other than in connection with such highly publicized and emotional issues as drug traffic and obscenity, widespread citizen debate, with accompanying large, well-organized, and "well-oiled" pressure groups, does not exist. Most of the lawmaking activity leading to changes in the criminal code is monopolized by criminal justice professionals—lawyers, police officers, judges, corrections officers—and their occupational associates. However, social scientists have shown that lawmakers are influenced by **interest groups,** political leaders, community elites, and, on occasion, public opinion.[59] In addition, business interests that might be affected by legislative changes may become vocal.

interest groups: Private organizations formed to influence government policies so that they will coincide with the desires of its members. Such organized pressure groups operate at all levels of government.

Creating Criminal Law: The Case of Computer Crime

During the past three decades, computers have become an indispensable part of American society. The concept of computer crime developed during the 1970s, when it became evident that unscrupulous people could use this technology for theft, fraud, and to trespass or sabotage data archives. In 1978 Florida and Arizona became the first states to pass laws against computer abuse. Other legislative bodies followed, so that now forty-seven states and the federal government have laws on criminality related to the computer. As Richard Hollinger and Lonn Lanza-Kaduce note: "The rapid criminalization of computer abuse represents an exception to the gradual and reformist nature of typical law formation in common law jurisdictions."[60]

Hollinger and Lanza-Kaduce note that other than the American Society for Industrial Security, an organization of the private security industry, and the American Bar Association, few interest groups or concerned citizens played a dominant role in the legislative process. Rather, individual state and national legislators took the initiative. As they point out: "'Computer crime' presented activist legislators with an ideal issue to maximize personal media exposure without offending any major constituency."[61] Using technical experts who testified about computer abuse and drawing on media stories about this new threat, legislators urged their colleagues to pass the criminalizing statutes. In particular, the media played an important role, not by advocating the new laws but by reporting about them and the crimes they were expected to deter. Computer abuse was seen by editors and producers as a story that was newsworthy and would pique public interest. Stories about the invasion of computers to obtain or alter information, the abilities of "hackers," whether malicious or not, and the public's fascination with the new technology undoubtedly supported the politicians' efforts.

The impact of the new computer crime laws may be more symbolic than instrumental. Many aspects of computer criminality are already covered by laws concerned with theft and trespass, and prosecutions under the new laws have had less impact than one might have expected. What seems evident is that the new laws have been interpreted mainly to deal with the "browsing" activities of youthful hackers. As Hollinger and Lanza-Kaduce argue, it seems that the purpose has been to send a message to hackers about the importance of privacy interests without penalizing them.[62]

SUMMARY

Behavior that is defined as criminal varies from society to society and from one era to the next. Although it can be shown that throughout history certain crimes considered to be *mala in se* have consistently been part of the penal codes of Western civilization, their interpretation and enforcement have varied. Offenses classified as *mala prohibita* have increased greatly in number as legislatures have responded to pressures from an urbanized and industrial society. Although the criminal code may be thought to reflect the norms of society, we must remember that these laws are enacted by legislatures and are created in response to the political dynamics of the legislative system. The definition of behavior as offensive, this very basic element of the criminal justice system, is thus a product of the social and political environment.

Criminologists have developed a number of theories to explain the causes of criminal behavior. Members of the classical school, dominant until the middle of the nineteenth century, viewed crime in religious terms. The subsequent development of the scientific approach led to the positivist school, the adherents of which viewed behavior as stemming from social, biological, and psychological factors. Positivist criminology has characterized the study of criminal behavior in the twentieth century.

There are five broad categories of crime: occupational crime, visible crimes, crimes without victims, and political crime. Each type reflects characteristic behaviors and opportunities for illegal acts and has the potential for the perpetrator to benefit from the act instead of being caught and convicted. The objectives and opportunities of different segments of society lead to their being associated with particular kinds of crimes.

FOR DISCUSSION

1. Why does the law declare some types of human behavior criminal but not others?
2. Many states are now rethinking the legal status and penal sanctions for the possession and private use of marijuana. Why are these laws being reconsidered?
3. You are a state legislator. The public has called for very stiff penalties for drug sellers. You are aware of studies showing that the police will not make arrests and judges will not punish offenders when the penalties are too harsh. What aspects of the criminal justice system may allow you to remain popular with your constituents yet feel comfortable with new, stiff penalties?
4. States periodically revise their criminal code. What portions of the penal law in your state need revision? Why?

FOR FURTHER READING

Erikson, Kai T. *Wayward Puritans*. New York: Wiley, 1966. Analysis of three "crime waves" in Puritan New England.

Heidensohn, Frances M. *Women and Crime*. New York: New York University Press, 1985. An account and critique of criminological and sociological writings on women and criminality.

Katz, Jack. *Seductions of Crime: Moral and Sensual Attractions of Doing Evil*. New York: Basic Books, 1988. A challenge to positivist criminology that argues that there is an emotional appeal to "being bad" and "being hard."

LaFree, Gary D. *Rape and Criminal Justice.* Belmont, CA: Wadsworth, 1989. Research on rape based on interviews with police officers, prosecutors, and judges in Indianapolis.

Meier, Robert F., ed. *Major Forms of Crime.* Newbury Park, CA: Sage, 1984. An excellent collection of articles that discusses different types of crime.

Reinman, Jeffrey H. *The Rich Get Richer and the Poor Get Prison: Ideology, Class and Criminal Justice,* 2nd ed. New York: Wiley, 1984. A radical perspective on crime and criminality; well-written, provocative.

Sutherland, Edwin H. *White Collar Crime.* New York: Holt, Rinehart & Winston, 1949. The classic statement of the concept of white-collar crime.

NOTES

1. Susan Estrich, *Real Rape* (Cambridge, MA: Harvard University Press, 1987), p. 92.
2. Robert A. Levine, "Gussi Sex Offenses: A Study in Social Control," *American Anthropologist* 61 (December 1959): 896–990.
3. Gary D. LaFree, *Rape and Criminal Justice: The Social Construction of Sexual Assault* (Belmont, CA: Wadsworth, 1989), p. 60.
4. Estrich, *Real Rape,* p. 92.
5. *Washington Post,* September 4, 1990, Health Section, p. 14.
6. Jerome Hall, *General Principles of Criminal Law,* 2nd ed. (Indianapolis: Bobbs-Merrill, 1947), p. 1.
7. Wolfgang Friedman, *Law in a Changing Society* (Berkeley: University of California Press, 1959), p. 165.
8. U.S. Department of Justice, Bureau of Justice Statistics, *Report to the Nation on Crime and Justice,* 2nd ed. (Washington, DC: Government Printing Office, 1988), p. 16.
9. Emile Durkheim, *The Division of Labor in Society,* trans. George Simpson (New York: Free Press, 1960), p. 102.
10. Richard Quinney, *Crime and Justice in Society* (Boston: Little, Brown, 1969), p. 25.
11. Ibid.
12. Joseph R. Gusfield, *Symbolic Crusade: Status Politics and the American Temperance Movement* (Urbana: University of Illinois Press, 1967).
13. William J. Chambliss, "A Sociological Analysis of the Law of Vagrancy," *Social Problems* 12 (Summer 1964): 67–77.
14. Ibid., p. 68.
15. Ibid., p. 76.
16. Jeffrey S. Adler, "A Historical Analysis of the Law of Vagrancy," *Criminology* 27 (May 1989): 212.
17. Jerome Skolnick, "Perspectives on Law and Order," in *Politics and Crime,* ed. Sawyer F. Sylvester, Jr., and Edward Sagarin (New York: Praeger, 1974), p. 13.
18. Cesare Beccaria, *Essay on Crimes and Punishments* (Indianapolis: Bobbs-Merrill, 1963).
19. Richard Dugdale, *The Jukes: Crime, Pauperism, Disease, and Heredity,* 4th ed. (New York: Putnam, 1910 [1875]); Arthur Estabrook, *The Jukes in 1915* (Washington, DC: Carnegie Institute 1916); Henry H. Goddard, *The Kallika Family* (New York: Macmillan, 1902).
20. *Skinner* v. *Oklahoma* 316 U.S. 535 (1942).
21. Edward O. Wilson, *Sociobiology: The New Synthesis* (Cambridge, MA: Harvard University Press, 1975).
22. James Q. Wilson and Richard Herrnstein, *Crime and Human Nature* (New York: Simon & Schuster, 1985).
23. Diana H. Fishbein, "Biological Perspectives in Criminology," *Criminology* 28 (February 1990): 27.
24. Henry Maudsley, *Responsibility in Mental Disease* (London: Macmillan, 1974).
25. Edwin H. Sutherland, "The Sexual Psychopath Laws," *Journal of Criminal Law & Criminology* 40 (January-February 1950): 543.
26. *The Forgotten Half* (Cambridge, MA: William F. Grand Foundation, 1988).

27. Edwin H. Sutherland and Donald Cressey, *Criminology* (Philadelphia: Lippincott, 1970), pp. 71–91.

28. Travis Hirschi, *Causes of Delinquency* (Berkeley: University of California Press, 1969).

29. Howard S. Becker, *Outsiders: Studies in the Sociology of Deviance* (New York: Free Press, 1963).

30. Steven Spitzer, "Toward a Marxian Theory of Deviance," *Social Problems* 22 (1975): 639.

31. Sally S. Simpson, "Feminist Theory, Crime, and Justice," *Criminology* 27 (November 1989): 605. An excellent review of the literature.

32. Freda Adler, "Crime, an Equal Opportunity Employer," *Trial Magazine* (January 1977): 31.

33. Rita Simon, "Women and Crime Revisited," *Social Science Quarterly* 56 (March 1976): 658.

34. Joseph Weis, "Liberation and Crime: The Invention of the New Female Criminal," *Crime and Social Justice* 1 (1976): 17–26.

35. Richard Conviser and John H. Rutledge, "Can Public Policies Limit the Spread of HIV Among IV Drug Users?" *Journal of Drug Issues* 19 (Winter 1989): 113–128.

36. Rita Simon, *The Contemporary Woman and Crime* (Washington, DC: Government Printing Office, 1975), p. 94.

37. Freda Adler, "The Interaction Between Women's Emancipation and Female Criminality: A Cross Cultural Perspective," *International Journal of Criminology and Penology* 5 (1977): 101–112.

38. Ralph Weisheit and Sue Mahan, *Women, Crime, and Criminal Justice* (Cincinnati, OH: Anderson, 1988), p. 45.

39. Jill Leslie Rosenbaum, "Family Dysfunction and Female Delinquency," *Crime and Delinquency* 35 (1989): 31–44.

40. Joycelyn M. Pollock-Byrne, *Women, Prison and Crime* (Pacific Grove, CA: Brooks/Cole, 1990), p. 21.

41. Morton Hunt, *The Mugging* (New York: Atheneum, 1972). p. 135.

42. *Felony Arrests: Their Prosecution and Disposition in New York City's Courts* (New York: Vera Institute of Justice, 1977), p. 135.

43. Edwin H. Sutherland, *White Collar Crime* (New York: Holt, Rinehart & Winston, 1949).

44. Gary S. Green, *Occupational Crime* (Chicago: Nelson-Hall, 1990), pp. 10–15.

45. President's Commission on Law Enforcement and Administration of Justice, *The Challenge of Crime in a Free Society* (Washington, DC: Government Printing Office, 1967), p. 4.

46. Francis S. J. Ianni, *Ethnic Succession in Organized Crime* (Washington, DC: Government Printing Office 1973), pp. 1–2.

47. State of California, Attorney General, *Annual Reports to the Legislature: Organized Crime in California* (Sacramento: California Department of Justice, 1986).

48. Ko-lin Chin, *Chinese Subculture and Criminality: Non-traditional Crime Groups in America* (New York: Greenwood Press, 1990).

49. Howard Abadinsky, *Organized Crime,* 3rd ed. (Chicago: Nelson-Hall, 1990), ch. 7.

50. Edwin J. Delattre, "New Faces of Organized Crime," *The American Enterprise* (May-June, 1990): 38.

51. U.S. Department of Justice, *Drug Trafficking: A Report to the President of the United States* (Washington, DC: Government Printing Office, 1989).

52. Bernard Gropper, "Probing the Links between Drugs and Crime," *NIJ Reports* (Washington, DC: National Institute of Justice, 1984), pp. 4–6.

53. Francis A. Allen, *The Crimes of Politics* (Cambridge, MA: Harvard University Press, 1974), pp. 16–17.

54. Francis A. Allen, *The Borderland of Criminal Justice* (Chicago: University of Chicago Press, 1964), p. 3.

55. John Stuart Mill, *Utilitarianism, Liberty and Representative Government* (New York: Dutton, 1947), p. 72.

56. Patrick Devlin, *The Enforcement of Morals* (London: Oxford University Press, 1965), p. 13.

57. National Advisory Commission on Criminal Justice Standards and Goals, *A National Strategy to Reduce Crime* (Washington, DC: Government Printing Office, 1973), p. 131.

58. Thurman Arnold, *The Symbols of Government* (New York: Harcourt, Brace, 1935), p. 160.

59. See for example Pamela Roby, "Politics and the Criminal Law: Revision of the New York State Penal Law on Prostitution," *Social Problems* 17 (Summer 1969): 198.

60. Richard C. Hollinger and Lonn Lanza-Kaduce, "The Process of Criminalization: The Case of Computer Crime Law," *Criminology* 26 (1988): 101–125.

61. Ibid., p. 113.

62. Ibid., p. 118.

Criminal Justice and the Rule of Law

Key Terms and Cases

common law
double jeopardy
entrapment
exclusionary rule
inchoate offenses
incorporation

mens rea
procedural due process
self-incrimination
stare decisis
statutes
strict liability

substantive criminal law

Argersinger v. *Hamlin*
Barron v. *Baltimore*
Duncan v. *Louisiana*
Escobedo v. *Illinois*

Gideon v. *Wainwright*
Mapp v. *Ohio*
Miranda v. *Arizona*
Powell v. *Alabama*
Williams v. *Florida*

Danny Escobedo's conviction was overturned as a violation of his constitutional rights to an attorney during police interrogation.

Danny Escobedo, a trouble-prone Chicago laborer, was suspected of murdering his brother-in-law. No weapon was found, and there were no witnesses. He was held for questioning for fourteen hours, released, and then picked up again. Escobedo had been in enough trouble before to have a lawyer on call, and when he was brought in the second time, he asked to see his attorney but was refused. Meanwhile, his lawyer was in the station house and waited there for more than four hours to see his client. The police told Escobedo that his lawyer was not there and did not want to see him anyway. An alleged accomplice who was apprehended said that Escobedo had offered him $500 to shoot the brother-in-law. When confronted by the accomplice, Escobedo said to him in front of the police that the accomplice had pulled the trigger. By Illinois law, Escobedo was equally guilty. The judge said that the confession had been voluntary and sentenced Escobedo to twenty years in prison.

On appeal to the U.S. Supreme Court, Escobedo's conviction was overturned, not on the basis of a coerced confession but because he had been refused the right to see his counsel during his interrogation. As the opinion of the majority of justices noted, the police viewed Escobedo as the accused, and the purpose of their interrogation was to get him to confess his guilt despite his constitutional right not to do so. The Court said that once an investigation into an unsolved crime begins to focus on a particular suspect, our adversary system with its rights of due process begins to operate, and the suspect has a right to be represented by counsel.[1]

Danny Escobedo's troubles in Chicago serve to remind us that law is at the base of the criminal justice system. Law governs the conduct of officials, and law structures the behavior of citizens. Law thus performs two functions: (1) it defines those behaviors that are labeled criminal, and (2) it describes the procedures to be followed under our adversarial system by those with the responsibility for law enforcement, adjudication, and corrections. Persons may not be convicted of committing an illegal act unless the state is able to prove that the conditions specified in the law were met and that the procedures required by the law were followed. We have argued that criminal justice operates as an administrative system influenced by political and social forces; now the third necessary ingredient of our analysis—law—must be examined. This chapter explores the two aspects of criminal law: the substantive criminal law and the law of criminal procedure.

FOUNDATIONS OF CRIMINAL LAW

In our system of justice, violators of society's rules are prosecuted and tried according to law. As Chapter 2 emphasized, not all behavior that is offensive or considered deviant is criminal behavior. Only behaviors proscribed by the criminal code are illegal. We have seen that in different locations and times, different behaviors have been defined as criminal. What is basic to our system, however, is the assumption found in the ancient Latin saying *nullum crimen, nulla poena, sine lege*—"there can be no crime and no punishment except as the law prescribes." The criminal law, often referred to as the *penal code*, therefore embodies descriptions not only of the forbidden behavior and the punishment to be administered but also of the ways in which justice officials must deal with defendants.

Criminal law is thus divided into substantive law and procedural law. Substantive law embodies a view of the social order that the community desires to achieve. It is the specification, or stipulation, of the types of conduct that are criminal and the punishments to be imposed for such behavior. Substantive law answers the question *What* is illegal? Procedural law sets forth the rules that govern enforcement of the substantive law. It stipulates the procedures that officials must follow in the enforcement, adjudication, and corrections portions of the criminal justice system. Procedural law limits the activities of police officers, judges, probation officers, and guards. It answers the question *How* is the law enforced? In brief, the criminal law stipulates the nature of the offenses, thus defining the elements of a violation, and it also specifies the conditions of enforcement and punishment.

Development of Criminal Law

The earliest known codes of law are the Sumerian (3100 B.C.) and the Code of Hammurabi (1750 B.C.). These were written codes, divided into sections to cover different types of offenses. In classical Greece the Draconian Code was promulgated in the seventh century B.C., and the Law of the Twelve Tables existed among the Romans (450 B.C.). Although we can study these early sources of criminal law, the United States looks to England as the source of the greater part of its political and legal concepts. Of these concepts, the Anglo-American common law is probably the most important, for it is the major tie that binds the traditions of the two societies and differentiates them from the non–English-speaking world. **Common law** developed in England and was based on custom and tradition as interpreted by judges. In continental Europe, a system of civil law developed in which the rules were formulated in codes or specially written stipulations. By contrast, the common law was not written down as a code that one could easily consult to learn what was proper. Rather, it took its form from the collected opinions of the English judges, who looked to custom in making decisions. The judges thus created law when they ruled on specific cases.

These rulings then formed precedents to be followed in later rulings, in accordance with the policy of *stare decisis,* "to stand by things [that have been] decided." Even today *stare decisis* is the basic doctrine followed by American courts. Judges are thus expected to refer to prior opinions for guidance when they decide the cases before them. In other words, the prior decision is part of the law and is used to guide decisions on similar cases. Accordingly, for much of English history it was not possible to learn the law by consulting one source,

common law: The Anglo-American system of uncodified law, in which judges follow precedent set by earlier decisions when they decide new but similar cases. The substantive and procedural criminal law was originally developed in this manner but was later codified by legislatures.

stare decisis: "to stand by the decision." The principle that judges should be bound by precedents (decisions made in previous similar cases) when they decide the case before them.

such as a constitution or statute book. The law was found in many places, most of which were the leading opinions written by judges who had heard earlier cases. As new situations arose and more opinions were written to resolve conflicts, the common law grew. This stability combined with flexibility in the face of new circumstances is the uniquely valuable characteristic of Anglo-American law.

The emergence of criminal law in England paralleled the development of national sovereignty during the twelfth century. With the Norman invasion of 1066, the tribal law of the Saxons yielded to the authority of the central government, the crown. As the blood feud of the tribes had given way under the influence of feudalism and Christianity to a system of compensations for criminal wrongs, the reign of Henry II (1154–1189) marked the emergence of a common law for England. The system of compensations became a system of writs, procedures, and common law developed by a strong centralized court that made general rules for all the realm. This development marked the end of the concept that such offenses as murder were merely regrettable torts (wrongful actions) for which compensation should be paid. Under the common law, crime became an offense to be prosecuted by the community through its chief.

Among the contributions of England to the American colonies was the common law system. Originally the English precedents and procedures were maintained in the New World, but changes in the structure of the common law of crime began to occur with the American Revolution and subsequently with ratification of the U.S. Constitution. Starting in the nineteenth century, state legislatures began to incorporate the common law into written penal codes and rules of criminal procedure. We continue to speak of the United States as having a common law system because the concept of precedent is maintained; yet in most states judges now consult legislatively enacted criminal codes to ascertain how wrongdoing is defined and the punishments to be exacted. At the national level, there was never a common law of crime; rather, from 1789 on, Congress has passed statutes making various behaviors violations of federal law.

Mala in Se and Mala Prohibita

In the course of the development of the English common law, one of the primary distinctions made was between offenses considered *mala in se*—"ordinary" crimes, acts wrong in themselves (murder, rape, arson, theft)—and offenses considered *mala prohibita*—acts that are crimes because they are prohibited by law (riot, poaching, vagrancy, drunkenness). Ordinary crimes were considered felonies that could be tried in the central criminal courts; acts labeled *mala prohibita* were proclaimed by legislation, considered misdemeanors, and enforced by justices of the peace. C. Ray Jeffery quotes legal writers of the eighteenth and nineteenth centuries to show these differences:[2]

> Criminal law is related to acts which, if there were no criminal law at all, would be judged by the public at large much as they are judged at present. If murder, theft, and rape were not punishable by law, the words would still be in use and would be applied to the same or nearly the same actions.

Which has occasioned some to doubt how far a human legislature ought to inflict capital punishment for positive offences; offences against the municipal law only, and not against the law of nature. . . . With regard to offences *mala in se,* capital punishments are in some instances inflicted by the immediate *command* of God Himself to all mankind; as, in the case of murder.

The distinction between ordinary crimes and those that are prohibited serves the useful purpose of pointing to the sources of the criminal law.

Expansion of *Mala Prohibita*

By and large, the types of crimes classified as *mala in se* have remained static, whereas those known as *mala prohibita* have greatly expanded. Modern legislatures have added three major groups to the traditional offenses: crimes without victims, political crimes, and regulatory offenses. Today there are many more arrests and prosecutions for offenses belonging to these latter categories than for the traditional violations of the criminal law. William Chambliss and Robert Seidman make a valid point:

A common characteristic of these newer offenses [is] that, in one way or the other, the laws defining most of them have abandoned some or all of the devices by which the common law placed restrictions on policemen's discretion. These laws have in fact increased the policeman's opportunity to replace law with "order."[3]

In most of the situations involved in *mala prohibita,* law enforcement authorities are faced with the responsibility of determining not only *who* has committed the offense but, more important, *whether* an offense has been committed. Thus the number of arrests for these crimes is directly related to police efficiency.

The distinction between *mala in se* and *mala prohibita* helps clarify the principles of the criminal law, but not always. The problem lies in the perceptions or views of those who define criminal behavior. If an asbestos company fails to provide its workers with proper masks, is it violating governmental safety laws, or should it be charged with injury to persons? Is rolling back an odometer a commercial fraud or petty theft from a purchaser?

Felony and Misdemeanor

Another way of classifying crimes is according to their level of seriousness. The distinction between a felony and a misdemeanor is one of the oldest in the criminal law. Most laws define these terms with regard to the punishment that may be exacted. Conviction on a felony charge usually means that a prison sentence of more than a year is authorized; even death might be authorized. Misdemeanants are dealt with more leniently; the sentence might be incarceration for less than a year, probation, or a fine. Some states use place of punishment as the defining criterion: prison for felonies, jail for misdemeanors.

Whether a defendant is charged with a felony or a misdemeanor is important not only in terms of potential punishment but also in terms of how the criminal justice system will process the defendant.

Certain rights and penalties follow from this distinction. For example, the conditions under which the police may make an arrest, the right of indigents to have counsel provided by the state, and the trial level at which the charges will be heard are determined by whether a felony or misdemeanor is charged. Further, persons convicted of felonies may be barred from certain professions, such as law and medicine, and in many states are barred from other occupations (bartender, police officer, barber) as well. This sort of sanction can be carried to ludicrous extremes. In some states former felons are prohibited from working where alcoholic beverages are sold, refereeing professional wrestling matches, or even being a sanitarian.

Criminal Law versus Civil Law

It is also important that we clarify the distinctions between criminal law and civil law. A basic distinction is that a violation of criminal law is an offense against society as a whole; civil law regulates relationships between individuals. In the field of civil law known as torts, for example, the major concern is compensation to the individual wronged. If through your negligence your automobile collides with another, the owner of the other car may bring a civil suit against you to recover the amount of damages you have caused. In a separate action the state may charge you with a violation of the criminal law with regard to the operation of motor vehicles because your actions breached society's rules. There are thus occasions when actions can be both criminal and civil in nature.

Where Is Criminal Law Found?

One document that clearly stated the criminal law, both substantive and procedural, would be nice to have. It would allow citizens to know when they might be in danger of committing an illegal act and to be aware of their rights should official action be taken against them. If such a document could be written in simple language, society would probably need fewer attorneys. Compiling such a document would, of course, be impossible, and the criminal law must continue to be found in the four basic sources from which it is derived: constitutions, statutes, court decisions, and administrative regulations.

Constitutions provide the fundamental principles and procedural safeguards that serve as guides for the enactment of laws and the making of decisions. The Constitution of the United States was drawn up in Philadelphia in 1787 and went into effect in 1789 after it was ratified by the required number of states. The first ten amendments to the Constitution, the Bill of Rights, were added in 1791. Several of these amendments have a direct bearing on the criminal law since they include such basic protections from governmental action as the right against unreasonable searches and seizures, the right to due process, the right to counsel, and the prohibition against cruel and unusual punishments. Most state constitutions also list these protections, and since the early 1960s the U.S. Supreme Court has required that criminal procedures in the states recognize the protections set forth in the national constitution.

Statutes are laws passed by legislative bodies; the substantive and procedural rules of most states are found in their statutes. Although the law of crime is primarily an activity of state legislatures, Congress and city and town bodies also play a role. Federal criminal laws passed by Congress deal mainly with violations that occur on property of the U.S. government or with behavior that involves the national interest (treason) or the jurisdictions of more than one state (taking a kidnap victim across state lines). The states give cities and towns some authority to develop laws dealing with local problems. There is often an overlapping of jurisdictions among national, state, and local rules governing some criminal conduct. The possession or sale of narcotics, for example, may violate criminal laws at all three levels of government. In such situations, enforcement agencies may disagree as to which one will prosecute the offender.

If we want to know the definition of a crime covered by a statute, we consult a state's penal code. The behaviors that constitute each crime and the penalty to be imposed are clearly specified in each state's code. Although the laws of most of the states are similar, there are some differences. To encourage uniformity among the states in the substantive and procedural laws, the American Law Institute has developed a Model Penal Code that it urges legislatures to adopt.

Court decisions, often called *case law*, constitute a third source of criminal law. As noted, the major characteristic of the U.S. common law system is the principle that judges look to earlier opinions to guide their determinations. Although much of the common law of crime has been replaced by statutes, reference to precedent is still very much an aid to lawyers and judges in the interpretation of these codified rules.

Administrative regulations are laws and rulings made by federal, state, and local agencies. Such official bodies as departments of health have been given power by the legislative or executive branch to develop rules to govern specific policy areas. Most such rules have been promulgated during the twentieth century to deal with modern problems: wages and hours, pollution, automobile traffic, industrial safety, pure food and drugs, and the like. Many of the rules are part of the criminal law, and violations are processed through the criminal justice system.

When we talk of the criminal law, then, we refer to more than the penal code or some similar concise statement of rules. The criminal law, both substantive and procedural, is found in the four places described here.

statutes: Laws passed by legislatures. Statutory definitions of criminal offenses are embodied in penal codes.

SUBSTANTIVE CRIMINAL LAW

As we have seen, the **substantive criminal law** defines the misbehavior that is subject to punishment and specifies the punishments for such offenses. Underlying the substantive criminal law is the basic doctrine that no one may be convicted of or punished for an offense unless the conduct constituting that offense has been authoritatively defined by the law. In short, the substantive criminal law defines what is illegal. It is a basic principle that people must know in advance what is required of them, but this is more easily said than done

substantive criminal law: Law defining the behaviors that are subject to punishment, and the sanctions for such offenses.

because language is often confusing and ambiguous. In such instances, the judiciary is called on to interpret the law so that the meaning intended by the legislature can be understood.

Seven Principles

The criteria used to decide whether a specific behavior is a crime are more complicated than one might imagine from the language of the penal code. Jerome Hall has developed a seven-point formalization of the major principles of Western law.[4] This is a system of interlocking legal propositions that recognizes the existence of the same basic ingredients in every crime. Thus, for a behavior to be defined as criminal and subject to the penalties of the law, all seven principles must be present:

1. Legality: the existence of a law defining the crime. Antisocial behavior is not a crime unless it has been prohibited by law before the act is committed. For example, the United States Constitution prohibits *ex post facto* laws.

2. *Actus reus:* behavior of either commission or omission by the accused that constitutes the violation. This principle emphasizes that behavior itself is required, not just bad intentions. In a modern case involving the principle of *actus reus,* the United States Supreme Court declared unconstitutional a California law making it a criminal offense for a person "to be addicted to the use of narcotics."[5] As Justice Potter Stewart, speaking for the Court, said, the California law did not deal with antisocial behavior but rather with a status, that of being addicted, and thus involves no criminal act.

3. Causation: a causal relationship between the act and the harm suffered. If one person shoots another and the victim dies in the hospital from pneumonia, it is difficult to show that the act (shooting) resulted in the harm (death). In other words, did the act cause harm.

4. Harm: damage inflicted on certain legally protected values (such as person, property, reputation) as a result of the act. This principle is often relied on by persons who feel that they are not committing a crime because they may be harming only themselves. Laws requiring motorcyclists to wear helmets have been challenged on this ground. Such laws, however, have been written with the recognition that accidental injury or death may have a harmful effect on others—dependents, for example.

The principle of harm also includes those acts where there is the potential for harm. Thus, behaviors involving attempt, conspiracy, and solicitation to commit a criminal act, the **inchoate offenses,** are justified. For example, if you plan with someone to kill your spouse, you and your fellow plotter can be charged with conspiracy to commit that murder, even if the murder does not occur.

5. Concurrence: the simultaneous occurrence of the intention and the act. If two electricians enter a house to fix the wiring and while there commit a crime, they cannot be accused of trespass. The intent and the conduct are not fused.

6. *Mens rea* (a guilty state of mind): The commission of the act is not itself criminal unless it is accompanied by a guilty mind. This concept is related to *intent*—that is, the person's actions lead to the

inchoate offenses: Conduct made criminal even though it has not yet produced the harm that the law seeks to prevent.

assumption that the crime was committed intentionally and on the basis of free will. Persons who are insane when they perform a legally forbidden act have not committed a crime because *mens rea* is not present. Again, involuntary behavior is not criminal; there must be an intention to commit the act. (We will discusss the difficult concept of *mens rea* in more depth later.)

7. Punishment: the stipulation in the law of sanctions to be applied against persons found guilty of the forbidden behavior.

These principles can be combined in a single generalization: the harm forbidden by a penal law must be imputed to any normal adult who voluntarily commits it with criminal intent, and such a person must be subjected to the legally prescribed punishment.

Criminal law theory is concerned largely with the elucidation of these seven principles. They can be summarized as follows:

1. legally proscribed   (legality)
2. human conduct,   (*actus reus*)
3. causative   (causation)
4. of a given harm,   (harm)
5. which conduct coincides   (concurrence)
6. with a blameworthy frame of mind   (*mens rea*)
7. and which is subject to punishment. (punishment)

The seven principles of crime provide the basis for authorities to define individual behavior as being against the law and provide the accused with the basis for defense against the charges. From these principles flow the assumptions of the adversarial process.

Responsibility for Criminal Acts

Over the course of time, the seven principles that define a crime have been reinterpreted to meet changing conditions. Among the principles, that of *mens rea* is a crucial element of the substantive criminal law, because it is the key for establishing the perpetrator's responsibility for the act committed. To obtain a conviction, the prosecution must show that the individual not only committed the illegal act charged but also did so in a state of mind that makes the imputation of responsibility appropriate. This is a difficult task, because it requires that courts inquire into the mental state of the defendant at the time the act was committed.

In an earlier period, **mens rea** was closely linked through the influence of religion to the concept of sin. With the emergence of psychology as a prominent field of knowledge, the definition of *mens rea* as an actual consciousness of guilt has been abandoned "in favor of intentional, or even reckless or negligent conduct."[6] The new doctrine, called "objective *mens rea*," asks "not whether an individual defendant has consciousness of guilt but whether a reasonable man in his shoes and with his physical characteristics would have had consciousness of guilt."[7] Objective *mens rea* has thus replaced the traditional notion by requiring that the act be voluntary so that responsibility can be assumed, in this way tying the defendant to the act. It is the intentional quality of the illegal behavior that makes it blameworthy.

mens rea: "Guilty mind," or blameworthy state of mind, necessary for the imputation of responsibility for a criminal offense; criminal, as distinguished from innocent, intent.

Although many defendants in criminal cases openly admit that they committed the illegal behavior, they may still enter a plea of not guilty. They do so because they know the state must provide the evidence to prove them guilty and, more important, because they believe they are not responsible for the illegal act because the necessary *mens rea* element was not present. The clearest example of such a situation may occur when the defendant argues that it was an accident that the gun went off and the neighbor was killed or that the car skidded into the pedestrian. As Justice Oliver Wendell Holmes once said: "Even a dog distinguishes between being stumbled over and being kicked."[8]

We label events *accidents* when responsibility is not fixed; *mens rea* is not present, because the event was not intentional. But not everything that is claimed to be accidental is so judged by a court. In some situations the perpetrator is so negligent or reckless (the gun was kept loaded with the safety catch off) that the court may fix some degree of criminal responsibility.

Note that *mens rea*, or criminal responsibility, may be fixed without showing that the defendant was determined to do evil. In other words, it is not the quality of one's motives that establishes *mens rea* but the nature and level of one's intention. The Model Penal Code lists four mental conditions that can be used to satisfy the requirement of *mens rea*: The act must have been performed intentionally, knowingly, recklessly, or negligently.[9] There are offenses that require a high degree of intent. For example, the crime of larceny requires a finding that the defendant intentionally took property to which she knew she was not entitled, *intending* to deprive the rightful owner of possession *permanently*.

strict liability: An obligation or duty whose breach constitutes an offense that requires no showing of *mens rea* to be adjudged criminal; a principle usually applied to regulatory offenses involving health and safety.

But there are also so-called public welfare or **strict liability** offenses, acts that require no showing of intent to be adjudged criminal. The majority of such offenses are defined in legislation of a type first enacted in England and the United States during the latter part of the nineteenth century to deal with issues connected with urban industrialization, among them sanitation, pure food, housing, and safety. Often the statutory language did not include a reference to *mens rea*. Some courts ruled that employers were not responsible for the carelessness of their workers because they had no knowledge of the criminal offenses being committed in their establishments. An employer who had not known that the food products being canned by his employees were contaminated, for example, was not held liable for a violation of pure food laws even if people who ate the food died as a result. Other courts, however, ruled that such owners had a special responsibility to the public to ensure the quality of their products and therefore could be found criminally liable if they failed to do so.

The concept of strict liability was best described by Justice Robert Jackson in *Morissette* v. *United States* (1952), in which he upheld the right of legislatures to make certain acts criminal even if *mens rea* were lacking. Pointing to the need for health and welfare regulations, he stated that although the offenses did not threaten the security of the state, they were offenses against its authority because their occurrence impaired the efficiency of the controls necessary for social order. "In this respect, whatever the intent of the violator, the injury is the same. . . . Hence, legislation applicable to such offenses does not specify intent as a necessary element."[10]

The reasoning employed by Justice Jackson to uphold the principle of strict liability, however, has not been followed in all circumstances. Some people believe that the principle should be applied only to regulatory offenses that require no incarceration and that carry no social stigma. In practice the criminal penalty is usually imposed only after many attempts to induce compliance have failed. Some scholars believe that imprisonment would be unconstitutional for some strict liability crimes, but the incidence of such sentences has been so rare that the concept has not been tested.

In a technologically complex society, we may assume that the concept of strict liability will be expanded to a range of other acts in which a guilty mind is not present. It is also likely, however, that courts will restrict the application of the strict liability principle to situations in which recklessness or indifference is present.

Entrapment is a defense that may be used to point to the absence of intent. The law excuses the actions of defendants from criminal liability when it is shown that government agents have induced an individual to commit an offense. This does not mean that the police may not use undercover agents to set a trap for criminals, nor does it mean that the police may not provide ordinary opportunities for commission of a crime. But the defense of entrapment may be used when the police have crossed the fine line of encouragement and unacceptable inducement.

entrapment: The defense that the individual was induced by the police to commit the criminal act.

The defense of entrapment has evolved through a series of court decisions in the twentieth century. In earlier eras judges were less concerned with whether the police had held out bait to tempt a citizen into committing an illegal act than whether or not the citizen took the bait. Now when the police instigate a crime or implant the idea for a crime in the mind of a person who then commits the offense, entrapment may have occurred.

The critical question concerns the predisposition of the defendant. Was there criminal intent in the mind of the defendant at the time of the act? The courts have ruled that when the government induces a law-abiding citizen to commit a crime, the charges should be dismissed. The Supreme Court ruled in *Sherman* v. *United States* that the function of law enforcement should be to prevent crime, not to implant in the mind of an ordinary person the idea for an offense. The element of predisposition also means that a defendant with a criminal record would have a more difficult time using the entrapment defense successfully than a person who had never been in trouble.

In several recent cases the defense of entrapment has been raised. Automobile manufacturer John DeLorean was acquitted on drug charges after the jury was shown a videotape of his behavior and that of government agents. However, other sting operations such as "Operation ABSCAM," where undercover FBI agents paid bribes to several congressmen, resulted in convictions.

Entrapment is a defense that is difficult to prove in most cases. Such nebulous elements as the predisposition of the defendant and the circumstances under which encouragement or inducements were made by the police must be defined and proved.

The absence of *mens rea*, then, does not guarantee a verdict of not guilty in every circumstance. In most cases, however, *mens rea* may relieve defendants of responsibility for acts that, if intentional, would be labeled criminal. In addition to those defenses discussed above, seven defenses based on absence of criminal intent are recognized in appropriate circumstances: self-defense, necessity, duress, immaturity, mistake of fact, intoxication, and insanity.

Self-Defense

A person who feels that he or she is in immediate danger of being harmed by another person's unlawful use of force may ward off the attack in self-defense. The laws of most states also recognize an individual's right to defend others from attack, to protect property, and to prevent the commission of a crime. The law also specifies the manner in which one may protect oneself; generally one must use only the level of force necessary to defend oneself. Distinctions are made between deadly and nondeadly force (see Model Penal Code box on self-defense provisions).

One has the right to kill another person in self-defense if one believes that this amount of force is necessary to prevent one's own death, severe bodily harm, kidnapping, or rape. Courts would not uphold the shooting of an assailant armed with a broomstick unless, perhaps, it were shown that the accused thought that the weapon was a gun about to be fired. In most states self-defense is no justification for the use of force to resist arrest, even if it is later shown that the arrest was unlawful.

Bernhard Goetz, the "subway vigilante," argued the self-defense justification when he was tried on attempted murder and assault charges for firing on four young men who had approached him in a threatening manner on a New York City subway. This case, fully discussed in Chapter 4, resulted in the New York Court of Appeals

MODEL PENAL CODE:
Self-Defense Provisions

(Excerpts)

Section 3.04. Use of Force in Self-Protection.

1. *Use of Force Justifiable for Protection of the Person.* . . . the use of force upon or toward another person is justifiable when the actor believes that such force is immediately necessary for the purpose of protecting himself against the use of unlawful force by such other person on the present occasion.
2. *Limitations on Justifying Necessity for Use of Force.*
   a. The use of force is not justifiable under this Section:
      i. to resist an arrest which the actor knows is being made by a peace officer, although the arrest is unlawful; or
      ii. to resist force used by the occupier or possessor of property or by another person on his behalf, where the actor knows that the person using the force is doing so under a claim of right to protect the property. . . .

   b. The use of deadly force is not justifiable under this Section unless the actor believes that such force is necessary to protect himself against death, serious bodily harm, kidnapping, or sexual intercourse compelled by force or threat; nor is it justifiable if:
      i. the actor, with the purpose of causing death or serious bodily harm, provoked the use of force against himself in the same encounter; or
      ii. the actor knows that he can avoid the necessity of using such force with complete safety by retreating or by surrendering possession of a thing to a person asserting a claim of right thereto or by complying with a demand that he abstain from any action which he has no duty to take.

SOURCE: Model Penal Code, Official Draft. Copyright 1962 by The American Law Institute. This and all other excerpts from this source are reprinted with the permission of The American Law Institute.

■
Was the killing and eating of Parker,
the cabin boy, justified on the grounds
of necessity given that Dudley,
Stephens, and Brooks survived for
twenty-four days adrift in the Atlantic?

emphasizing that Goetz had to believe that deadly force was necessary and that the belief was reasonable.

Necessity

Outlawed acts are often committed because the perpetrators believe that they are necessary for their own preservation or to avoid a greater evil. Necessity is sometimes confused with self-defense. Jerome Hall explains the distinction: a person is acting in self-defense if he or she "injures the creator and embodiment of the evil situation"; the person is acting from necessity if he or she "harms a person who was in no way responsible for the imminent danger, one who indeed might himself have been imperiled by it."[11] In short, necessity may be claimed as a defense in situations in which the accused was confronted with a choice of evils. The person speeding through traffic lights to get an injured child to the hospital or someone breaking and entering a building to seek refuge from a snowstorm is violating the law out of necessity. But there are other more complex and serious situations in which it is difficult to exonerate the accused completely (see Model Penal Code box on necessity provisions).

MODEL PENAL CODE:
Necessity Provisions

Section 3.02. Justification Generally: Choice of Evils.

1. Conduct which the actor believes to be necessary to avoid a harm or evil to himself or to another is justifiable, provided that:
   a. the harm or evil sought to be avoided by such conduct is greater than that sought to be prevented by the law defining the offense charged; and
   b. neither the Code nor other law defining the offense provides exceptions or defenses dealing with the specific situation involved; and
   c. a legislative purpose to exclude the justification claimed does not otherwise plainly appear.
2. When the actor was reckless or negligent in bringing about the situation requiring a choice of harms or evils or in appraising the necessity for his conduct, the justification afforded by this Section is unavailable in a prosecution for any offense for which recklessness or negligence, as the case may be, suffices to establish culpability.

Since 1884, students have been considering the English legal case *The Queen v. Dudley and Stephens.*[12] Thomas Dudley and Edwin Stephens were accused of the murder of Richard Parker after the ship on which they were employed sank 1,600 miles from the Cape of Good Hope. The three, together with another seaman named Brooks, managed to get into a lifeboat containing no drinking water and little food. After twenty days, Dudley and Stephens proposed to Brooks that Parker, the cabin boy, be killed and that they eat his remains as a necessity for survival. Brooks would not agree. With Stephens's assent, Dudley then killed the boy, and all three ate from his body for four days, at which time a passing vessel picked them up. Dudley and Stephens were committed for trial, but the jury had to inquire of a higher court whether the behavior was murder. It was agreed that

> if the men had not fed upon the body of the boy they would . . . within the four days have died of famine. That the boy, being in a much weaker condition, was likely to have died before them. That at the time of the act there was no sail in sight, nor any reasonable prospect of relief. That under these circumstances there appeared to the prisoners that unless they then fed or very soon fed upon the boy or one of themselves they would die of starvation. That there was no appreciable chance of saving life except by killing some one for the others to eat.[13]

Given these arguments, one might think that the defense of necessity would have carried the day. But Lord Coleridge, the chief justice, argued that regardless of the temptation or the intensity of the suffering, standards had to be maintained and the law not weakened. Dudley and Stephens were given the death sentence, which the Crown later commuted to six months' imprisonment.

Duress (Coercion)

Closely related to the defense of necessity is that of duress. The distinction is made on the basis of coercion: a person who has been forced or coerced by another into committing an act has acted under duress. Defendants who present this defense are arguing that they are actually the victims, not the criminals. Bank tellers who give deposited money to an armed robber are excused because the tellers were acting under duress and thus should not be held responsible. By contrast, the defense of necessity is used when the environmental situation (natural rather than human forces) was such that a choice

MODEL PENAL CODE:
Duress Provisions

Section 2.09. Duress.

1. It is an affirmative defense that the actor engaged in the conduct charged to constitute an offense because he was coerced to do so by the use of, or a threat to use, unlawful force against his person or the person of another, which a person of reasonable firmness in his situation would have been unable to resist.
2. The defense provided by this Section is unavailable if the actor recklessly placed himself in a situation in

which it was probable that he would be subjected to duress. The defense is also unavailable if he was negligent in placing himself in such a situation, whenever negligence suffices to establish culpability for the offense charged.
3. It is not a defense that a woman acted on the command of her husband, unless she acted under such coercion as would establish a defense under this Section.

was made to commit an illegal act (cannibalism on the high seas). Courts normally uphold the defense of duress when it is shown that the defendant could not have done otherwise without the expectation of imminent bodily harm or death. Thus duress has not usually been allowed when it has been shown that defendants had opportunities to escape their plight or that there was a span of time between the threat and the act in which help could have been found (see Model Penal Code box on duress provisions).

John Charles Green escaped from the Missouri Training Center, where he had been imprisoned for a three-year term. He was apprehended the next day by a state highway patrol officer some distance from the center. Green contended that his escape had been justified, because

> prior homosexual assaults and threats near noon on the day of the escape of a homosexual assault upon him that night by other inmates caused the conditions of his confinement to be intolerable; and, that these conditions, together with the state's denial to him of access to the courts, made it necessary that he escape in order to protect himself from submission to the threatened assault or the alternative of death or bodily harm.[14]

Green offered evidence to show that he had been attacked previously and had feigned suicide in order to be taken to the prison hospital.

At a meeting of the center's disciplinary board, he was told by a member to "fight it out, submit to the assaults, or go over the fence." The Supreme Court of Missouri did not accept the defense; it said that the defendant was not being closely pursued by his assailants when he escaped and that he could have avoided the threatened consequences if he had reported to the authorities the names of those making the threats. Yet Judge Seiler in dissent noted that

> if the defendant here had been prosecuted for sodomy as a result of the first assault, it would seem clear that a defense of coercion would be available. In this case defendant sought to avoid committing the coerced act by resorting to escape. Because he was a prisoner, this action was a crime. The act of escape was just as much coerced as the prior act of sodomy. It is consistent with the principle underlying the defense to allow it to be asserted here.[15]

Immaturity

Traditionally, Anglo-American law has excused criminal behavior by children under the age of seven on the ground that they are immature

MODEL PENAL CODE:
Immaturity Provisions

Section 4.10. Immaturity Excluding Criminal Conviction; Transfer of Proceedings to Juvenile Court.

1. A person shall not be tried for or convicted of an offense if:
   a. at the time of the conduct charged to constitute the offense he was less than sixteen years of age (in which case the Juvenile Court shall have exclusive jurisdiction); or
   b. at the time of the conduct charged to constitute the offense he was sixteen or seventeen years of age, unless:
      i. the Juvenile Court has no jurisdiction over him, or,
      ii. the Juvenile Court has entered an order waiving jurisdiction and consenting to the institution of criminal proceedings against him.

and not responsible for their actions. At common law, it was possible to argue against the assumption that children seven to fourteen were not liable for their criminal acts. For example, prosecutors could introduce evidence of a child's criminal capacity by showing that the child had hidden evidence or had attempted to bribe a witness. As a child approached fourteen, the efficacy of the immaturity defense was weakened. Since the development of juvenile courts in the 1890s, children over the age of seven are not tried by the rules and procedures governing adults. There are, however, various situations in which children may be tried as adults—if, for example, they are repeat offenders or are charged with having committed a particularly heinous offense (see Model Penal Code box on immaturity provisions).

Mistake

The courts have consistently upheld the view that ignorance of the law is no excuse, but what if there is a mistake of fact? Can mistake be used as a defense if a person knows the law but believes that it does not apply in the context of a given situation? Certainly defendants could not plead ignorance of the fact that stealing is against the law, but they could use the defense that they mistakenly thought the property was their own. Intent to steal would not be present in the latter situation. In many jurisdictions the crime of statutory rape may result in conviction if the man had intercourse with a female under the age of consent even if he believed—because she looked older or had told him so—that she was over that age. The Model Penal Code rejects this position. What if you thought the white substance in your pocket was flour and police analysis showed it to be cocaine? (see Model Penal Code box on mistake provisions).

MODEL PENAL CODE:
Mistake Provisions

Section 2.04. Ignorance or Mistake.

1. Ignorance or mistake as to a matter of fact or law is a defense if:
   a. the ignorance or mistake negatives the purpose, knowledge, belief, recklessness or negligence required to establish a material element of the offense; or
   b. the law provides that the state of mind established by such ignorance or mistake constitutes a defense.
2. Although ignorance or mistake would otherwise afford a defense to the offense charged, the defense is not available if the defendant would be guilty of another offense had the situation been as he supposed. In such case, however, the ignorance or mistake of the defendant shall reduce the grade and degree of the offense of which he may be convicted to those of the offense of which he would be guilty had the situation been as he supposed.

3. A belief that conduct does not legally constitute an offense is a defense to a prosecution for that offense based upon such conduct when:
   a. the statute or other enactment defining the offense is not known to the actor and has not been published or otherwise reasonably made available prior to the conduct alleged; or
   b. he acts in reasonable reliance upon an official statement of the law, afterward determined to be invalid or erroneous, contained in (i) a statute or other enactment; (ii) a judicial decision, opinion or judgment; (iii) an administrative order or grant of permission; or (iv) an official interpretation of the public officer or body charged by law with responsibility for the interpretation, administration or enforcement of the law defining the offense.
4. The defendant must prove a defense arising under Subsection (3) of this Section by a preponderance of evidence.

Intoxication

The law does not relieve an individual of responsibility for crimes committed while voluntarily intoxicated. There are, however, situations in which intoxication can be used as a defense, as when a person has been tricked into consuming a substance without knowing that it may result in intoxication. More complicated are situations in which the law requires it to be shown that a defendant had a specific rather than a general intent to commit a crime. Drunkenness can also be used as a mitigating factor to reduce the seriousness of a charge. The fact of intoxication may be a complete defense against the charge of shoplifting on the ground that the defendant's condition was such that she simply forgot to pay and had not intended to steal (see Model Penal Code box on intoxication provisions).

Insanity

The defense of insanity has been controversial. The general public seems to have the view that great numbers of criminals "escape" punishment through the skillful use of psychiatric testimony. Yet only about 1 percent of incarcerated individuals are held in mental hospitals because they have been adjudged "not guilty by reason of insanity."[16] Thus the insanity defense is relatively rare and is generally advanced only in serious cases or where there is no other valid defense.

Over time, American courts have followed five tests of criminal responsibility involving insanity: (1) the M'Naghten Rule, (2) the Irresistible Impulse Test, (3) the Durham Rule, (4) the Model Penal Code's Substantial Capacity Test (see Model Penal Code box on insanity provisions), and (5) the test as defined in the Comprehensive Control Act of 1984. For a comparison of these tests, and the states in which they are used, see Table 3.1 and Figure 3.1, respectively.

Before 1843 the defense of insanity could be used only by persons who were so deprived of understanding as to be incapable of knowing what they were doing. In that year Daniel M'Naghten was acquitted of killing Edward Drummond, whom he had thought to be Sir Robert Peel, the prime minister of Great Britain. M'Naghten claimed that he had been suffering from delusion at the time of the killing, but the public outcry against his acquittal caused the House of Lords to ask the court to define the law with regard to delusional persons. The judges of the Queen's Bench answered by saying that a finding of

MODEL PENAL CODE:
Intoxication Provisions

Section 2.08. Intoxication.

1. Except as provided in Subsection (4) of this Section, intoxication of the actor is not a defense unless it negatives an element of the offense.
2. When recklessness establishes an element of the offense, if the actor, due to self-induced intoxication, is unaware of a risk of which he would have been aware had he been sober, such unawareness is immaterial.
3. Intoxication does not, in itself, constitute mental disease within the meaning of Section 4.01.
4. Intoxication which (a) is not self-induced or (b) is pathological is an affirmative defense if by reason of such intoxication the actor at the time of his conduct lacks substantial capacity either to appreciate its criminality (wrongfulness) or to conform his conduct to the requirements of law.

TABLE 3.1 Insanity defense standards. The evolution of the standards for the insanity defense can be discerned in this table. Compare the test, the date, and your understanding of developments in law and psychiatry as you note the differing standards.

Test	Legal Standard Because of Mental Illness	Final Burden of Proof	Who Bears Burden of Proof
M'Naghten (1843)	"didn't know what he was doing or didn't know it was wrong"	Varies from proof by a balance of probabilities on the defense to proof beyond a reasonable doubt on the prosecutor	
Irresistible Impulse (1897)	"could not control his conduct"		
Durham (1954)	"the criminal act was caused by his mental illness"	Beyond reasonable doubt	Prosecutor
Model Penal Code (1972)	"lacks substantial capacity to appreciate the wrongfulness of his conduct or to control it"	Beyond reasonable doubt	Prosecutor
Present federal law	"lacks capacity to appreciate the wrongfulness of his conduct"	Clear and convincing evidence	Defense

SOURCE: U.S. Department of Justice, National Institute of Justice, *Crime File,* Norval Morris, "Insanity Defense" (Washington, DC: Government Printing Office, n.d.).

guilty cannot be made if, "at the time of the committing of the act, the party accused was laboring under such a defect of reason, from disease of the mind, as not to know the nature and quality of the act he was doing, or if he did know it that he did not know he was doing what was wrong."[17] The *M'Naghten Rule,* often referred to as the "right-from-wrong test," is today accepted by many states.

Over the years the M'Naghten Rule has often been criticized as not conforming with modern psychiatric concepts of mental disorder. It has been argued that individuals may be insane but still able to distinguish right from wrong and that "disease of the mind," "know," and "nature and quality of the act" have not been adequately defined. Some states have supplemented the M'Naghten Rule by allowing defendants to plead that although they knew that what they were doing was wrong, they were unable to control an irresistible impulse to commit the crime. The *Irresistible Impulse Test* excuses defendants from responsibility when a mental disease was controlling their behavior even though they knew that what they were doing was wrong. Four states use this test in combination with the M'Naghten Rule.

MODEL PENAL CODE:
Insanity Provisions

Section 4.01. Mental Disease or Defect Excluding Responsibility.

1. A person is not responsible for criminal conduct if at the time of such conduct as a result of mental disease or defect he lacks substantial capacity either to appreciate the criminality (wrongfulness) of his conduct or to conform his conduct to the requirements of law.

2. As used in this Article, the terms "mental disease or defect" do not include an abnormality manifested only by repeated criminal or otherwise anti-social conduct.

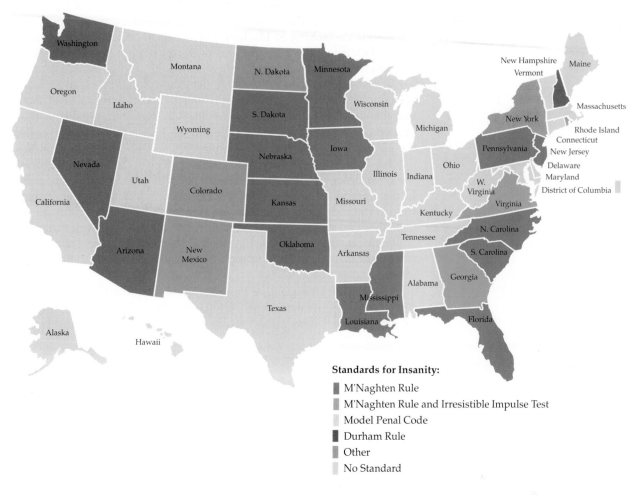

Standards for Insanity:

- M'Naghten Rule
- M'Naghten Rule and Irresistible Impulse Test
- Model Penal Code
- Durham Rule
- Other
- No Standard

The *Durham Rule,* originally developed in New Hampshire in 1871, was adopted by the Circuit Court of Appeals for the District of Columbia in 1954 in the case of *Durham* v. *United States.*[18] Monte Durham had a long history of criminal activity as well as of mental illness. At age twenty-six, he broke into a house with two companions. On appeal of his conviction, Judge David Bazelon rejected the M'Naghten Rule, stating that an accused is not criminally responsible "if an unlawful act is the product of mental disease or mental defect." The Durham Rule is based on the supposition that insanity is a product of many personality factors, not all of which may be present in every case.

The Durham Rule immediately aroused much controversy. In particular, it was argued that it offered no useful definition of "mental disease or defect." By 1972 (*United States* v. *Brawner*) the federal courts had overturned the Durham Rule in favor of a modified version of a test proposed in the Model Penal Code. By 1982 all of the federal courts and those of about half of the states had adopted the Model Penal Code's Substantial Capacity Test. This rule states that a person is not responsible for criminal conduct "if at the time of such conduct as a result of mental disease or defect he lacks substantial capacity either to appreciate the criminality [wrongfulness] of his conduct or to conform his conduct to the requirements of law."[19] The Substantial Capacity Test is essentially a broadening and modifying of the M'Naghten and Irresistible Impulse rules. Key terms have been

FIGURE 3.1
Standards for insanity used by the states
SOURCE: Adapted from Ingo Keilitz and Junikus Fulton, *The Insanity Defense and Its Alternatives: A Guide for Policy Makers* (Williamsburg, VA: National Center for State Courts, 1984), pp. 15, 88–89; U.S. Department of Justice, Bureau of Justice Statistics, *Report to the Nation on Crime and Justice,* 2nd ed., (Washington, DC: Government Printing Office, 1988), p. 87.

changed to conform better with modern psychological concepts, and the standards lacking in Durham have been supplied. By emphasizing "substantial capacity," the test does not require that a defendant be completely unable to distinguish right from wrong.

The attempted assassination of President Ronald Reagan by John W. Hinckley reopened debate over the insanity defense. The facts that television pictures showed Hinckley shooting the president, that he came from a wealthy background and was thus able to enlist the aid of psychiatric experts to substantiate the claim, and that the federal rules of procedure in the District of Columbia required the government to prove him sane all fed widespread public outcries. In the immediate aftermath of his acquittal, several states abolished the insanity defense, members of Congress introduced bills to do likewise, and three major national organizations—the American Bar Association, the American Psychiatric Association, and the American Medical Association—proposed changes in the legal definition of insanity.

Among the changes that have occurred since the Hinckley case is introduction of the defense of "Guilty but Mentally Ill," now adopted by eight states.[20] This allows a jury to find the accused guilty but to

CLOSE-UP Pitfalls Abundant in Insanity Plea

It was 3:30 A.M. on Jan. 29, 1976. Richard Hilliard Jackson had just taken three hours to explain his theory on the four states of "person" and his concept of death to a detective from the Metropolitan Police Department's homicide squad.

. . . Jackson claimed that the physical person is guided by a magnet-like uncontrollable power called The Force. The intellect remains after death, and the soul is the part of the intellect that lives forever. The After Death is a blessing, a state of freedom from pain, heartbreak, and defeat.

The Force could do anything, Jackson said, even kill.

The 37-year-old handyman . . . was charged with the murder and robbery of an elderly Northeast Washington woman who had been found dead two weeks earlier. Jackson denied any involvement in her death.

. . . Defense attorneys argued that Jackson was insane on Jan. 14, 1976, when the woman was killed.

The jury . . . did not accept [Jackson's] insanity defense and, after more than 24 hours of deliberation determined that Jackson was sane at the time of the woman's death.

The case typified the problems that prosecutors, defense attorneys and jurors face when law and psychiatry are mixed with the question of criminal responsibility.

In the Jackson case there was a major difficulty in distilling the testimony from six psychiatrists down into terms the jury could understand. And there is a risk, experts say, that when psychiatric testimony is reduced to layman's terms the significance can be lost.

The psychiatrists "said [Jackson] had a mental problem; OK, we all do," said one juror after the verdict was returned.

The psychiatrists testified that Jackson had symptoms consistent with paranoia and schizophrenia, but, said another juror, "there are other people walking around with these kinds of tendencies who don't commit any violent crime."

. . .

The jurors were instructed in the Jackson case that if they found him not guilty by reason of insanity, he would be committed to St. Elizabeth's hospital. After 50 days a hearing would be held to determine whether he was a danger to himself or to the community. If he was found no longer to be a danger, he would be released at the discretion of the judge.

Jurors are inclined "to lock somebody up who was crazy for the rest of his life," according to former public defender Jeffrey Freund. He said jurors may be reluctant to vote for an insanity defense knowing a defendant could be swiftly released.

The jurors actually heard two separate trials, which took over a month to complete. The first proceeding was on the merits of the case—whether Jackson in fact murdered and robbed the woman, with the burden of proof being on the government. After the jury found Jackson guilty of second-degree murder and robbery, the same jury then heard a second trial on the issue of whether at the time the offense was committed Jackson was sane and thus responsible for his act. Otherwise the jury could not decide that Jackson was not guilty on the two charges by reason of insanity.

Should the Sale of Drugs Be Legalized?

Imagine an America where adults legally purchase drugs; where government regulates the purity of heroin, marijuana, and cocaine in the consumer's interest; where government

Advocates argue that legalization would result in lower drug prices at better quality. Because drugs would be sold openly, organized crime, criminality, and related violence would drop.

taxes these products and ensures that they are not sold to minors. Growing numbers of people—including such notables as conservative commentator William F. Buckley, Jr., Nobel Prize-winning economist Milton Friedman, and the mayors of

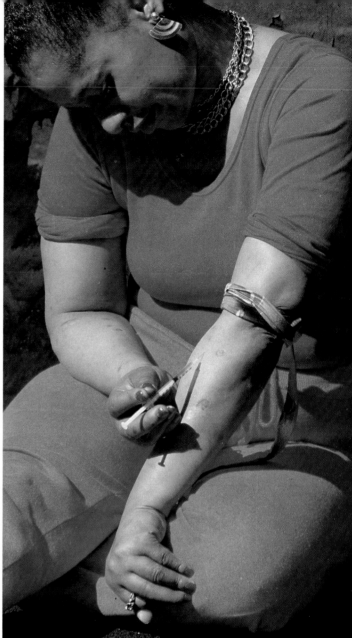

Baltimore and Hartford—are calling for the nation to consider the controlled legalization of drugs. These people are not advocates of the use of drugs. Instead, they believe that the costs of the War on Drugs—governmental expenditures, corruption, violence, and the power of organized crime—are simply too great (see Figure A.1).

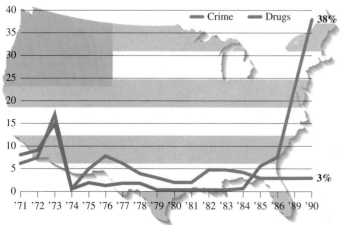

Percentage of Population

Data from Marsha Rosenbaum, *Just Say What?* (National Council on Crime and Delinquency, n.d.). U.S. Department of Justice, Bureau of Justice Statistics, *Sourcebook* (Washington, DC: Government Printing Office, 1991).

Figure A.1

Public Perceptions of Crime and Drug Problems (1971–1990)
The public's concern about the drug problem is reflected in opinion surveys. A 1990 Gallup Poll has found that 38 percent of Americans believe that drug abuse is the nation's most important problem. Compare this response to that of crime as the most important problem.

For Legalization

Supporters of legalization argue that the problems associated with drugs, particularly property crimes and violence, occur because drugs are illegal. Their argument is that if users would not have to obtain drugs on the black market, the price would drop precipitously and users would not have to commit crimes to secure the money to satisfy their drug needs. With drugs taxed and sold on the open market, governmental revenues could be used to further education and treatment programs. Addiction, it is argued, is a health problem; advocates contend that it should be dealt with through education and treatment, not criminalization.

The arguments in favor of legalization may be summarized as follows:

▶ Legalization would result in lower drug prices. As a consequence, users would no longer be forced to engage in street crime and prostitution to support their habits.

▶ Legalization would result in a significant lowering of crime with a resulting decline in crowded courts, jails, and prisons. Criminal justice resources could be reallocated to deal with the "real" criminals.

NORML, the National Organization for the Reform of Marijuana Laws, is an activist group that has demonstrated for drug reform.

▶ Legalization would mean that drug production and distribution would be handled by legitimate businesses and not by organized crime, which uses violence to control its operations.

▶ Legalization would mean that drug-related corruption of government officials in the United States and in other drug-producing countries would be eliminated.

▶ Legalization would mean that drug abuse would be treated as a public health problem. Addicts would therefore be more willing to accept treatment for their medical problem of addiction.

Growing numbers of people, including Hartford Mayor Carrie Saxon Perry, are calling for the nation to consider the controlled legalization of drugs.

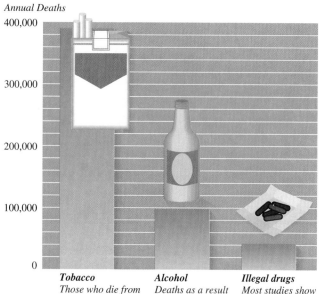

Annual Deaths

400,000

300,000

200,000

100,000

0

Tobacco	**Alcohol**	**Illegal drugs**
Those who die from a disease primarily caused by smoking	*Deaths as a result of drunken injury or disease linked to drinking*	*Most studies show that only a few thousand people a year are killed solely by ingestion of the drugs*

Marsha Rosenbaum, *Just Say What?*
(National Council on Crime and Delinquency, n.d.).

Figure A.2

Annual Death Toll Related to Drugs

Deaths from ingestion of illegal drugs account for less than one-tenth of the deaths related to the legal drugs of alcohol and tobacco. But, partially because drugs are illegal, there are no methods to tally additional deaths from drug-related homicides, drive-by shootings, and other violence (all of which has been on the increase), or from drug-related accidents.

Against Legalization

Although opponents of legalization recognize the costs of the current problem, they paint a very different picture of reality if drugs become legally available. They begin their critique by pointing to the vagueness of legalization proposals. They further emphasize the devastating impact of drug addiction on individuals, families, and society. They argue that if drugs are readily and legally available the number of users would increase, as would problems of vehicle and other accidents, antisocial behavior by persons under the influence of drugs, and addiction. Although criminal acts associated with the black market for drugs would decrease, violence to others would not abate, since some users under the influence of drugs (notably heroin and cocaine) engage in this behavior. Children raised by drug-using parents would live insecure lives that would greatly decrease their potential for a productive future. In particular, the inner-city poor would bear the brunt of the social costs resulting from the new freedom to freely buy drugs.

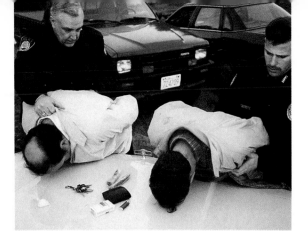

▶ Legalization would have a disastrous impact on the inner-city poor. The social fabric of the ghetto would be tattered still further. From this perspective, legalization can be viewed as a racist, neocolonialist strategy to manage the underclass.

▶ Legalization would create health and behavioral problems to a degree that would far outweigh the impact of drug prohibition. Drugs are damaging to the brain and to the immunity and nervous systems of users. Babies born to addict mothers present a wide range of medical and behavioral problems that we are only beginning to understand.

▶ Legalization would mean a total surrender of the standards of American morality and would greatly reduce such important values as temperance, fidelity, and community.

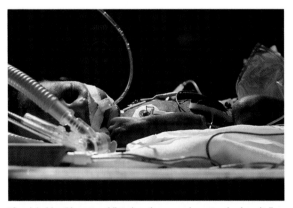

"Crack babies," born to addicted mothers, require extensive hospitalization and have a questionable future. Studies have shown that these children develop very slowly and will require special education.

The arguments against legalization may be summarized as follows:

▶ Legalization would mean a five- to sixfold increase in the amount of drug use, since firms would market their products to maximize sales by seeking out new consumers.

▶ Legalization would not eliminate the black market. Some groups (such as the young) would be prohibited from legal sales; others would seek out the black market to avoid paying taxes (as some do now with alcohol).

▶ Legalization would not mean a reduction in crime, since studies show that drug users were criminals first and users later.

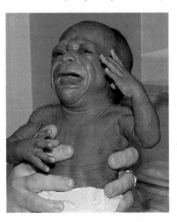

This six-month-old baby addicted to cocaine was born to a teenage mother.

Can we be guided by the experience of other countries? Two Western European countries, Britain and the Netherlands, have approached drugs mainly as a public health problem and have not imposed the rigorous prohibition found in the United States.

Until the 1960s there were few addicts in Britain, and doctors were allowed to prescribe heroin and opiates for maintenance purposes. With passage of the Dangerous Drugs Act of 1967, addicts had to register with the government, doctors were required to provide government with the names of their patients, and treatment clinics were set up. According to British policy the key individual is the physician, who can prescribe drugs, administer methadone maintenance, and provide counseling.

The focus of drug policies in Britain is to contain the use of heroin and other drugs but to stay within the public health modality of treating addiction, not focusing on law enforcement. Yet these policies have not eliminated the black market for drugs. Illegal dealers are subject to criminal penalties and an increasing number are being arrested.

Recognizing that drug use cannot be annihilated, the policy of the Netherlands seems to be to "reduce the harm" of drugs rather than to "conquer the evil." There is a concern that users not be harmed more by criminal proceedings and sanctions than by the use of the drug itself. Thus the Dutch prefer a policy of normalization by admitting that extensive drug use exists in society, as with the use of alcohol and tobacco. The 1976 Opium Act makes a distinction between "hard" (heroin and cocaine) drugs with "unacceptable risks" and "soft" (marijuana) drugs with "acceptable risks." Criminal penalties reflect this distinction. A sliding scale is used for those charged with dealing and importing/exporting both hard and soft drugs. There is no prosecution for possessing drugs for one's own use.

With regard to all drugs, including heroin and cocaine, the Dutch view the problem as a matter of public health. They have a policy of treatment and assistance for the users, but punishment for the commercial dealer. By focusing on reducing the risks to addicts and the community, the government has instituted methadone programs, needle exchanges, and street corner programs to assist users. With this range of services and easy access to them, an estimated 70 to 80 percent of Dutch addicts receive some form of assistance.

What Should U.S. Policies Be?

Are the costs of the present policy of criminalization of drug use and sale so great that the United States might shift to the public health models found in Britain and the Netherlands? Are there differences in our cultures that would preclude acceptance of legalization? What might happen if adults could obtain drugs from government-regulated stores? These are questions that until very recently have not been aired. Proponents of legalization have raised the issue. What is likely to be our response?

The internationalization of the drug trade is epitomized by General Manuel Noriega of Panama, arrested during the U.S. invasion of that country. General Noriega faces criminal charges in the United States for his role in drug trafficking.

require that correctional authorities provide psychiatric treatment during imprisonment. In fact, prison authorities already have the authority to decide if an inmate's psychiatric treatment will be within the prison walls or at a mental hospital.

Norval Morris suggested that the defendant's condition after the crime should be taken into account in the determination of the appropriate place of confinement, a hospital or a prison. Illness at the time of the crime should enter into the determination of the crime of which a defendant is found guilty; for example, a defendant found to be of diminished capacity would be convicted of manslaughter rather than murder.[21]

The Comprehensive Crime Control Act of 1984 changed the federal rules on the insanity defense by limiting it to persons who are unable to appreciate the nature and quality or the wrongfulness of their acts as a result of severe mental disease or defect. This legislation seems to eliminate the Irresistible Impulse Test. It also shifts the burden of proof from the prosecutor, who in some federal courts had to prove beyond a reasonable doubt that the defendant was not insane, to the defendant, who has to prove his or her insanity. The act also creates a new commitment procedure whereby a person found

Jackson, a chronic alcoholic who lived out of his 1965 Dodge, went to 1044 Grant St. NE on Jan. 14, in 1976, to repair a fuse box for Dorothea J. King, a 69-year-old cleaning woman. Jackson and a 15-year-old Maryland youth were seen drinking with Mrs. King in her house by a neighbor that evening. The following day Mrs. King was found dead on her living room floor. She had been beaten and strangled.

Jackson claimed that at some point when he was with Mrs. King he blacked out and had no recollection of what happened. The Maryland youth passed out during the evening and remembered nothing.

The medical examiner said Mrs. King died between 3:30 P.M. and 11:00 P.M. on Jan. 14, 1976. A neighbor testified that he saw Jackson's car outside Mrs. King's house at 11:00 P.M. that day. When he was arrested, Jackson had in his possession goods owned by Mrs. King. The Maryland youth testified that Jackson had also shown him other goods which police said were taken from Mrs. King's home.

"If he was insane at the time he committed the crime, why did he steal the property from this lady?" asked one juror. "This is what I think the majority [of the jurors] came around on."

"If he wasn't guilty, why didn't he get up [on the witness stand] and say something?" the juror asked.

Two days after Mrs. King's death, Jackson was arrested for disorderly conduct in a Maryland restaurant. According to police, he stood at the salad bar, waved his arms around, and screamed that someone was trying to steal his food. When his money was refunded in an attempt to calm him down, he began to rapidly shove lettuce into his mouth.

"He knew how to become insane at the right times," said one juror, who added that several members of the jury panel thought Jackson was feigning his illness. "I can't say he was faking," said another juror, "but I also thought [Jackson] knew what would be the best defense for him."

Beyond that skepticism, two other factors appeared to militate against the jury's acceptance of the insanity defense.

Jackson had pleaded guilty to manslaughter in connection with the death of his 9-year-old stepson in 1969. The child was slain after Jackson, who had been drinking, had an argument with his wife. He spent about two years in prison for the offense.

The jury was told about the earlier killing because defense psychiatrists thought the 1969 incident had some link to why Jackson killed the elderly Washington woman.

But perhaps the most damaging piece of evidence, and the key to the government's argument that Jackson had fabricated his mental illness, was a letter that Jackson wrote to a friend seven months after his arrest.

". . . be sharp and go along with the insanity moves my attorney and I will make and say nothing about anything else," Jackson wrote.

"That did it," said one juror.

SOURCE: From "Pitfalls Abundant in Insanity Plea," by L. A. Kiernan, *The Washington Post*, July 19, 1977, p. Al. © 1987, The Washington Post. Reprinted with permission.

The public was outraged by the decision that John B. Hinckley was not guilty by reason of insanity of the attempted assassination of President Reagan. Under federal rules, once the insanity defense is offered the prosecution must prove beyond a reasonable doubt that the accused was sane at the time of the action.

not guilty only by reason of insanity is required to be committed to a mental hospital until it is determined that he or she no longer poses a danger to society. These provisions apply only to prosecutions in federal courts and are now spreading to a number of states.

The problem with these alternatives is that the concept of *mens rea* is deeply rooted in our legal system. In addition, although there is much public discussion of notorious defendants who are found not guilty by reason of insanity, there are, in fact, few such cases. Persons who are ruled incompetent to stand trial because they are unable to assist in their own defense are committed to mental institutions until they are determined to be healthy enough to answer the charges. Civil commitment is also the usual route for defendants who successfully plead insanity. Some observers believe that this defense should be abolished, arguing that it is used to incarcerate legally innocent but dangerous people. Others emphasize that most criminals are somewhat unbalanced and that science cannot adequately measure the level of mental "disease" that allows borderline cases to use this defense. It is charged that the wealthy are able to pay for the testimony of psychiatrists in support of their defense, whereas the poor cannot. It is also erroneously believed that persons who use the insanity defense and are sent to mental hospitals somehow "beat the rap."

Elements of a Crime

Legislatures define certain acts as crimes when they are committed in accordance with the principles just outlined and in the presence of certain "attendant circumstances" while the offender is in a certain state of mind. Together, these three factors—the act (*actus reus*), the attendant circumstances, and the state of mind (*mens rea*)—are called the *elements of a crime*. Thus the section of one state's penal code dealing with burglary reads as follows:

Section 3502. Burglary.

1. *Offense defined*: A person is guilty of burglary if he enters a building or occupied structure, or separately secured or occupied portion thereof, with intent to commit a crime therein, unless the premises are at the time open to the public or the actor is licensed or privileged to enter.
2. *Defense*: It is a defense to prosecution for burglary that the building or structure was abandoned.
3. *Grading*: Burglary is a felony of the first degree.
4. *Multiple convictions*: A person may not be convicted both for burglary and for the offense which it was his intent to commit after the burglarious entry or for an attempt to commit that offense, unless the additional offense constitutes a felony of the first or second degree.

The elements of burglary are, therefore, entering a building or occupied structure (*actus reus*) with intent to commit a crime therein (*mens rea*) at a time when the premises are not open to the public and the actor is not licensed or privileged to enter (attendant circumstances). For an act to constitute burglary, all three elements must be present.

Even if it appears, according to the formal words of the applicable statute, that the accused has committed a crime, prosecution will be successful only if the elements correspond to the interpretations of the law made by the courts. The Pennsylvania judiciary has, for example, construed the *actus reus* of burglary to include entering a building, such as a store or tavern, open to the public, so long as the entry was "willful and malicious—that is, made with the intent to commit a felony therein." Thus one can be convicted of burglary for entering a store with the intent to steal even though entry was made during business hours and without force.

Statutory Definitions of Crimes

The laws of the United States and of each of the states often define criminal acts in somewhat different ways. To find out how a state defines an offense, it is necessary to read its particular penal code; this document will give a general idea of which acts are illegal. But a full understanding of the special interpretations of the code can be gained only by analyzing judicial opinions that have sought to clarify the language of the law, such as the opinion of the Pennsylvania court that interpreted the *actus reus* of the burglary statute.

To clarify the substantive criminal law, the following discussion focuses on two of the eight index crimes of the *Uniform Crime Reports*, homicide and rape. The Model Penal Code's definition of each offense is provided in the accompanying boxes. The elements of a crime may be interpreted somewhat differently in individual states.

Murder and Nonnegligent Manslaughter

A major problem in categorizing criminal behavior that has brought about death is that legislatures have subdivided the early common law definition of criminal homicide into degrees of murder and of voluntary and involuntary manslaughter. In addition, some states have created new categories, such as reckless homicide, negligent homicide, and vehicular homicide. Each of these definitions involves slight variations in the *actus reus* and the *mens rea*. The *UCR* counts murder and nonnegligent manslaughter as index offenses. These classifications correspond to murder and manslaughter in the Model Penal Code.

In legal terminology, the phrase *malice aforethought* is used to distinguish murder from manslaughter. The crime of murder is a deliberate, premeditated, and willful killing of another human being. In most states the definition of murder is also extended to circumstances either in which defendants knew that their behavior had a strong likelihood of causing death, showed indifference to life, and thus recklessly engaged in conduct that resulted in death, or in which their behavior resulted in death while they were engaged in committing a felony. Mitigating circumstances, such as "the heat of passion" or extreme provocation, would reduce the offense to manslaughter because the requirement of malice aforethought would be absent or diminished. Similarly, manslaughter would include a killing resulting from an attempt to defend oneself that was not fully excused as self-defense, as well as death resulting from a lesser degree of recklessness or negligence.

Rape

There has been a long and almost universal revulsion against the crime of rape. The victim suffers not only assault on the body but psychological damage as well. In recent years pressure has been

MODEL PENAL CODE:
Homicide Provisions

Section 210.1 Criminal Homicide.

1. A person is guilty of criminal homicide if he purposely, knowingly, recklessly or negligently causes the death of another human being.
2. Criminal homicide is murder, manslaughter or negligent homicide.

Section 210.2. Murder.

1. Except as provided in Section 210.3(1)(b), criminal homicide constitutes murder when:
   a. it is committed purposely or knowingly; or
   b. it is committed recklessly under circumstances manifesting extreme indifference to the value of human life. Such recklessness and indifference are presumed if the actor is engaged or is an accomplice in the commission of, or an attempt to commit, or flight after committing or attempting to commit robbery, rape or deviate sexual inter-

course by force or threat of force, arson, burglary, kidnapping or felonious escape.
2. Murder is a felony of the first degree (but a person convicted of murder may be sentenced to death, as provided in Section 210.6).

Section 210.3. Manslaughter.

1. Criminal homicide constitutes manslaughter when:
   a. it is committed recklessly; or
   b. a homicide which would otherwise be murder is committed under the influence of extreme mental or emotional disturbance for which there is reasonable explanation or excuse. The reasonableness of such explanation or excuse shall be determined from the viewpoint of a person in the actor's situation under the circumstances as he believes them to be.
2. Manslaughter is a felony of the second degree.

brought to bear, especially by the women's movement, to ensure strict enforcement of the laws against rape. Successful prosecution for rape is difficult, however, because corroborating evidence is often lacking, and the public humiliation to which victims are often subjected sometimes results in the withdrawal of charges. Some states have reformed their laws by removing the offending word *rape* and classifying the behavior as a sexual offense or an aggravated assault in an effort to encourage prosecution.

Traditionally, the statutory law has stipulated that the offense is committed if a male compels by force or threat a female who is not his wife to have sexual intercourse with him against her will. The charge may also be brought if the act is performed on a woman who is unconscious and therefore unable to resist. If the female is under ten years of age, common law regards her as unable to give consent. Note that this definition of the law does not cover homosexual rape or forced sexual intercourse with one's own wife, though statutory reforms and judicial opinions in some states have dealt with these two situations in recent years.

The charge of rape raises difficult questions of both *actus reus* and *mens rea*. Because the act usually takes place in private, prosecutors may have difficulty showing that sexual intercourse took place without consent; some states require corroborating evidence from someone other than the victim. Force is a necessary element in the crime of rape. In some courts, the absence of injury to the victim's body has been taken to show that there was no resistance, which in some jurisdictions implies that consent was given.

Unlike murder, rape is not usually divided by statutes into degrees; but other offenses are often charged when elements of proof or mitigating circumstances warrant. In some states "deviate sexual intercourse," "sexual assault," "statutory rape," or "aggravated assault" are charges that may be used to designate sexual offenses that do not contain all the criminal elements necessary to prove rape.

In our discussion of the crimes of murder and rape, we've seen that the substantive criminal law contains the basic doctrines stipulating the conditions that must be met before a person can be convicted of an offense. The so-called seven principles of Western law categorize these doctrines. Of primary importance are the various conditions that, if present, may relieve an individual of responsibility for committing a crime. Finally, the penal code of each of the states and the laws of the United States define offenses. Table 3.2 defines offenses according to the *UCR*.

MODEL PENAL CODE:
Rape Provisions

Section 213.1. Rape.

1. *Rape.* A male who has sexual intercourse with a female not his wife is guilty of rape if:
   a. he compels her to submit by force or by threat of imminent death, serious bodily injury, extreme pain or kidnapping, to be inflicted on anyone; or
   b. he has substantially impaired her power to appraise or control her conduct by administering or employing without her knowledge drugs, intoxicants or other means for the purpose of preventing resistance; or
   c. the female is unconscious; or
   d. the female is less than 10 years old.

PROCEDURAL CRIMINAL LAW

The opening of this chapter described the U.S. Supreme Court's decision that Danny Escobedo, in the Chicago police station, had been denied the right to counsel guaranteed him by the Constitution. This decision was based on the procedural criminal law. Escobedo did not contend that the substantive elements of the case against him had not been met. His legal brief presented to the Supreme Court did not mention the absence of an *actus reus*, attendant circumstances, or *mens rea*, such that he should not have been charged with the murder of his brother-in-law. Rather, improper police procedures were the basis of his appeal. Escobedo argued that he had been denied due process because of a procedural violation.

Although the Supreme Court's opinion in *Escobedo v. Illinois* was issued in 1964, its foundation lies in the history of Anglo-American law, with precedent going back to the Magna Carta. In that document, considered to be the first written guarantee of due process, the king promised that "no free man shall be arrested, or imprisoned, or disseized, or outlawed, or exiled, or in any way molested; nor will we proceed against him unless by the lawful judgment of his peers or by the law of the land." Persons must be tried not through the use of arbitrary procedures but according to the process outlined in the law.

procedural due process: The constitutional requirement that all persons be treated fairly and justly by government officials. This means that an accused person can be arrested, prosecuted, tried, and punished only in accordance with procedures prescribed by law.

In the United States, **procedural due process** of law means that accused persons in criminal cases must be accorded certain rights as protections in keeping with the adversarial nature of the proceedings and that they will be tried according to legally established procedures. As Chapter 1 explained, the Due Process Model is based on the premise that freedom is so valuable that efforts must be made to prevent erroneous decisions that would result in an innocent person's being deprived of it. As Packer put it, the rules of due process can be likened to an obstacle course in which decisions concerning the accused's guilt or innocence may be made only within the framework of the rules and rights stated in law as applying to all persons. Ac-

---

CLOSE-UP *Acquaintance Rape: Is It Really Rape?*

He was her friend. So the twenty-six-year-old real estate agent agreed when he asked to come over after work one night. Around midnight, she unlocked the door to her one-room apartment overlooking Connecticut Avenue. She listened indulgently to her friend, a former lover, complain about his job managing a local restaurant. Finally, she asked him to leave. He seemed to ignore her, so she decided to lie on her bed, fully clothed. She dozed off as her friend droned on. At one point, she slipped under the comforter of her bed and wriggled out of her jeans. Sometime in the next hour, she was aware that he was sitting on the bed. Suddenly she awoke with a start, as she realized he had climbed on top of her.

She screamed and tried to push him off the bed. He shoved her back, wrenching her neck and pinning her down. She began to cry. He placed his hand tightly over her mouth and penetrated her. Sobbing and unable to breathe, she began to choke. Blood vessels around her eyes popped from lack of oxygen.

Then she stopped fighting and went limp, psychologically retreating to a place where he could not hurt her. His hand slipped off her mouth; she gasped: "Just get it over with."

With that, he stopped. He rolled off her. He apologized. He swore at himself. He said he had made a mistake and threatened to kill himself. Then he ran out of her apartment carrying his clothes.

SOURCE: From "Rape," by C. Spolar and A. Walker, *The Washington Post*, September 4, 1990, p. 4. © 1990, The Washington Post. Reprinted with permission.

cordingly, the state may act against accused persons only when it follows due process procedures, thus ensuring that the rights of all are maintained.

CHAPTER 3
CRIMINAL JUSTICE AND
THE RULE OF LAW

113

From childhood we have been taught that defendants are entitled to fair and speedy trials, to have counsel, to confront witnesses, and to know the charges brought against them. They are protected against having to serve as witnesses against themselves, being subjected to double jeopardy, and enduring cruel and unusual punishment. Underlying procedural criminal law is the assumption that there are limits to the government's powers to investigate and apprehend persons suspected of committing crimes.

Like substantive law, procedural criminal law is found in many places: in the U.S. and state constitutions, in statutes, and in judicial opinions. Among these, the Bill of Rights—the first ten amendments to the U.S. Constitution—holds a primary position. In most respects, the due process assumptions found there provide the basis for the implementing procedures that have evolved and that constitute the rules ordering the daily practices of the criminal justice system. In particular, the Fourth, Fifth, Sixth, Eighth, and Fourteenth Amendments to the Constitution are especially important and are outlined in the following sections. More detailed discussion of each right is presented later; thus questions concerning the detailed prohibition of unreasonable searches and seizures and the limitation of self-incrimination are found in Chapter 6, the right to counsel is discussed in Chapter 9, fair trial in Chapters 11 and 12, and cruel and unusual punishment in Chapters 13 and 15.

TABLE 3.2 Definition of offenses in the *Uniform Crime Reports* (Part I)

1. *Criminal homicide*:
   a. Murder and nonnegligent manslaughter: the willful (nonnegligent) killing of one human being by another. Deaths caused by negligence, attempts to kill, assaults to kill, suicides, accidental deaths, and justifiable homicides are excluded. Justifiable homicides are limited to:
      (1) the killing of a felon by a law enforcement officer in the line of duty; and
      (2) the killing of a felon by a private citizen.
   b. Manslaughter by negligence: the killing of another person through gross negligence. Excludes traffic fatalities. While manslaughter by negligence is a Part I crime, it is not included in the Crime Index.

2. *Forcible rape*:
   The carnal knowledge of a female forcibly and against her will. Included are rapes by force and attempts or assaults to rape. Statutory offenses (no force used—victim under age of consent) are excluded.

3. *Robbery*:
   The taking or attempting to take anything of value from the care, custody, or control of a person or persons by force or threat of force or violence and/or by putting the victim in fear.

4. *Aggravated assault*:
   An unlawful attack by one person upon another for the purpose of inflicting severe or aggravated bodily injury.

   This type of assault usually is accompanied by the use of a weapon or by means likely to produce death or great bodily harm. Simple assaults are excluded.

5. *Burglary—breaking or entering*:
   The unlawful entry of a structure to commit a felony or a theft. Attempted forcible entry is included.

6. *Larceny-theft (except motor vehicle theft)*:
   The unlawful taking, carrying, leading, or riding away of property from the possession or constructive possession of another. Examples are thefts of bicycles or automobile accessories, shoplifting, pocket-picking, or the stealing of any property or article which is not taken by force and violence or by fraud. Attempted larcenies are included. Embezzlement, "con" games, forgery, worthless checks, etc., are excluded.

7. *Motor vehicle theft*:
   The theft or attempted theft of a motor vehicle. A motor vehicle is self-propelled and runs on the surface and not on rails. Specifically excluded from this category are motorboats, construction equipment, airplanes, and farming equipment.

8. *Arson*:
   Any willful or malicious burning or attempt to burn, with or without intent to defraud, a dwelling house, public building, motor vehicle or aircraft, personal property of another, etc.

SOURCE: U.S. Department of Justice, Federal Bureau of Investigation, *Uniform Crime Reports, 1990* (Washington, DC: Government Printing Office, 1991).

Bill of Rights

Although the Bill of Rights was added to the U.S. Constitution soon after its ratification in 1789, the amendments had little impact on criminal justice until the mid-twentieth century. Under our system of federalism, most criminal acts are violations of state laws, but for most of our history the Bill of Rights has been interpreted as protecting citizens only from acts of the national government. Hence important amendments—such as the Fourth, which guards against unreasonable searches and seizures; the Fifth, which outlines the basic due process rights in criminal cases; and the Sixth and Eighth, which cover procedures for fair trial and punishment—have been viewed as having no bearing on cases that arise out of state law. When it was drafted, the Constitution delegated certain powers to the new federal government, but the power to safeguard the rights of individuals from unjust enforcement of state laws was not among them.

COMPARATIVE PERSPECTIVE
Islamic Criminal Law

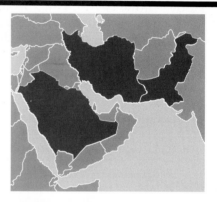

The 1979 revolution in Iran, the rise of fundamentalist Islam thought throughout the Arab world, and the conflict with Iraq has made Americans aware of great cultural differences between Westerners and people from the Middle East. Among Islamic institutions, the criminal law seems most at odds with justice as it is administered in Europe and the Americas. To the West, justice in such Islamic states as Iran, Pakistan, and Saudi Arabia, seems harsh and unforgiving. The practices of stoning for adultery and of amputation for theft are often presented as examples of the ferocity of Islam. What is unrecognized by most Americans is that there are judicial and evidentiary safeguards within the *Shari'a*, the law of Islam.

Islamic criminal law is concerned with (1) the safety of the public from physical attack, insult, and humiliation; (2) the stability of the family; (3) the protection of property against theft, destruction, or unauthorized interference; and (4) the protection of the government and the Islamic faith against subversion.

Criminal acts are divided into three categories. *Hudud* offenses are crimes against God whose punishment is specified in the Koran and the Sunna, a compilation of Muhammad's statements. *Quesas* are crimes of physical assault and murder, which are punishable by retaliation—"the return of life for a life in case of murder." The victim or the surviving heirs may waive the punishment and ask for compensation (blood money) or may pardon the offender. *Ta'azir* offenses are those for which penalties are not fixed by the Koran or the Sunna but are within the discretion of the *qadi* [judge]. As shown below, for the seven *Hudud* offenses the Koran defines the crime, specifies the elements of proof required, and sets the punishment.

Theft. Theft is the taking of property belonging to another, the value of which is equal to or exceeds a prescribed amount, usually set at 10 dirhams or about 75 cents. The property must be taken from the custody of another person in a secret manner, and the thief must obtain full possession of the property. "Custody" requires that the property should have been under guard or in a place of safekeeping.

Extramarital sexual activity. Sexual relations outside of marriage includes both adultery and fornication. They are believed to undermine marriage, lead to family conflict, jealousy, divorce, litigation, and the spread of disease.

Defamation. In addition to false accusations of fornication, this offense includes impunging the legitimacy of a woman's child. Defamation of a husband of his wife leads to divorce and is not subject to punishment.

Highway robbery. This crime interferes with commerce and creates fear among travelers and is therefore subject to punishment.

Use of alcohol. Drinking wine and other intoxicating beverages is prohibited since it brings about indolence and inattention to religious duties.

Historians have shown that at the time of the addition of the Bill of Rights, it was the power of the new national government that citizens feared; the constitutions of many of the states already contained protections against illegal procedures at the local level. This position was made clear in 1833 when the U.S. Supreme Court ruled in the case of **Barron v. Baltimore** that the first ten amendments to the Constitution were limitations only on the federal government and were not binding on the states. As Chief Justice John Marshall said:

Barron v. Baltimore (1833): Bill of Rights applies only to actions of the national government.

> Had the framers of these amendments intended them to be limitations on the powers of state governments, they would have imitated the framers of the original Constitution, and have expressed that intention. . . . These amendments demanded security against the apprehended encroachments of the general government—not against those of the local governments.[22]

This ruling meant that when individual rights had been trampled upon, only the states, and not the Supreme Court, could interfere.

Apostasy. This is the voluntary renunciation of Islam. The offense is committed by any Muslim who converts to another faith, worships idols, or rejects any of the tenets of Islam.

Rebellion. The intentional, forceful overthrow or attempted overthrow of the legitimate leader of the Islamic state.

Islamic *Had* offenses, required proofs, and punishments

Crime	Proof	Punishment
Adultery	Four witnesses or confession	Married person: stoning to death. Convict is taken to a barren site. Stones are thrown first by witnesses, then by the *qadi* and finally by the rest of the community. For a woman, a grave is dug to receive the body. Unmarried person: 100 lashes. *Maliki* school also punishes unmarried males with one year in prison or exile.
Defamation	Unsupported accusation of adultery	Free: 80 lashes. Slave: 40 lashes. Convict is lightly attired when whipped.
Apostasy	Two witnesses or confessions	Male: death by beheading. Female: imprisonment until repentance.
Highway robbery	Two witnesses or confessions	With homicide: death by beheading. The body is then displayed in a crucifixion-like form. Without homicide: amputation of right hand and left foot. If arrested before commission: imprisonment until repentance.
Use of alcohol	Two witnesses or confessions	Free: 80 lashes (*Shafi'i*, 40). Slave: 40 lashes. Public whipping is applied with a stick, using moderate force without raising the hand above the head so as not to lacerate the skin. Blows are spread over the body and are not to be applied to the face and head. A male stands, and a female is seated. A doctor is present. Flogging is inflicted by scholars well versed in Islamic law, so that it is justly meted out.
Theft	Two witnesses or confessions	First offense: amputation of hand at wrist, by an authorized doctor. Second offense: amputation of second hand at wrist, by an authorized doctor. Third offense: amputation of foot at ankle, by an authorized doctor, or imprisonment until repentance.
Rebellion	Two witnesses or confessions	If captured: death. If surrendered or arrested: *Ta'azir* punishment.

SOURCE: From *Islamic Criminal Law and Procedure: An Introduction*, by M. Lippman, S. McConville, and M. Yerushalmi, pp. 42–43. Copyright © 1988 by Praeger Publishers. Reprinted by permission of Greenwood Publishing Group, Inc., Westport, CT; From "Hudud Crimes," by A. A. Mansour. In M. C. Bassiouni (ed.), *The Islamic Criminal Justice System*, p. 195. Copyright © 1982 by Oceana Publications. Reprinted by permission.

Fourteenth Amendment

The ratification of the Fourteenth Amendment following the Civil War began a new period in the protection of citizens' rights. This amendment declares that "no state shall make or enforce any law which shall abridge the privileges or immunities of citizens of the United States, nor shall any State deprive any person of life, liberty, or property, without due process of law; nor deny to any person within its jurisdiction the equal protection of the laws."

The idea that the Fourteenth Amendment "incorporated" the first ten amendments and made them applicable to the states was not immediately accepted by the Supreme Court, which realized that it would have to supervise national standards for state justice. Although the Court used the Fourteenth Amendment to uphold property rights against state regulation, not until the 1920s did it begin to require adherence to the protections of the Bill of Rights in state criminal cases. For twenty-odd years a major dispute split the Court: a group led by Justice Hugo Black argued that the due process clause of the Fourteenth Amendment incorporated all the provisions of the Bill of Rights, making them applicable to state proceedings; a majority group led by Justice Felix Frankfurter said that the clause selectively incorporated only those protections necessary to "fundamental fairness." By 1970, however, the two sides had arrived at the same conclusion, and through a piecemeal process, all the major protections of the Bill of Rights have been incorporated.

Initially the justices used the Fourteenth Amendment to require that such fundamental democratic rights as freedom of speech, reli-

The 1932 Scottsboro case resulted in the Supreme Court ruling that the due process clause of the Fourteenth Amendment required that counsel be provided in a capital trial.

gion, and assembly, as specified in the First Amendment, be binding on the states. It was not until 1923, in the case of *Moore* v. *Dempsey*, that abuses of due process rights in Arkansas shocked them into reversing a decision of a state criminal court.[23] Five black men had been convicted of murder and sentenced to death in a forty-five-minute trial dominated by a howling lynch mob outside the courtroom. Nine years later the court again invoked the due process clause in the famous Scottsboro case (*Powell* v. *Alabama*), in which nine illiterate young blacks were convicted of raping two white women in an open railroad freight car. Because the defendants had not been given effective counsel, the Court overturned their convictions.[24] In 1936 the justices threw out a confession for the first time (*Brown* v. *Mississippi*), because the statements had been beaten out of two defendants by sheriff's deputies wielding metal-studded belts.[25] In all these early cases, the barbaric nature of the offenses perpetrated by state authorities provided reason for moral outrage and demonstrated that due process had been denied. In the opinions of the Court one finds little legal analysis but rather a feeling that the fundamental requirements of fairness had not been met.

Powell v. *Alabama* (1932):   Counsel must be provided defendants in a capital case.

The Case of Frank Palko

In 1937 Justice Benjamin Cardozo posed a test for determining whether a citizen had been denied due process of law by state action. Frank Palko had been charged by Connecticut with first-degree murder for the shooting of two policemen. The jury, however, found him guilty of second-degree murder, which carried life imprisonment rather than death. Under Connecticut law at the time, it was possible for a retrial, and this time Palko was found guilty of first-degree murder and received the death penalty. He appealed to the U.S. Supreme Court on the grounds that his second trial was a violation of the Fifth Amendment's prohibition against double jeopardy.

In *Palko* v. *Connecticut*, the Supreme Court upheld the state's rules. Justice Cardozo said that the test turned on the question "Does it violate those 'fundamental principles' of liberty and justice which lie at the base of our civil and political institutions?"[26] Frank Palko died in Connecticut's electric chair, and until the mid-1960s the dominant attitude of the Supreme Court was that the Fourteenth Amendment did not incorporate all the provisions of the Bill of Rights, only those that were fundamental. As Justice Frankfurter had noted, the doctrine of fundamental fairness meant that any state action that included "tactics which offend the community's sense of fair play and decency—conduct that shocks the conscience"—would be a violation of the Fourteenth Amendment's requirement of due process.[27] During those three decades, the Court slowly incorporated some of the provisions of the Bill of Rights, but only according to the fairness rule (see Figure 3.2).

The Due Process Revolution

Throughout the years when the fairness doctrine was supported by a majority on the Supreme Court, Justice Hugo Black had argued that all the provisions of the Bill of Rights should be applied to the states

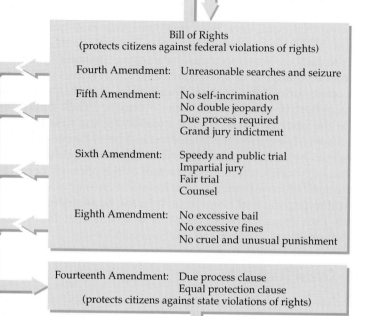

U.S. Constitution

Bill of Rights
(protects citizens against federal violations of rights)

Fourth Amendment: Unreasonable searches and seizure

Fifth Amendment: No self-incrimination
                      No double jeopardy
                      Due process required
                      Grand jury indictment

Sixth Amendment: Speedy and public trial
                      Impartial jury
                      Fair trial
                      Counsel

Eighth Amendment: No excessive bail
                      No excessive fines
                      No cruel and unusual punishment

Fourteenth Amendment: Due process clause
                       Equal protection clause
(protects citizens against state violations of rights)

Major Incorporation (Nationalization) Decisions

Fourth Amendment:	*Mapp* v. *Ohio* (1961)
Fifth Amendment:	*Malloy* v. *Hogan* (1964)
	Miranda v. *Arizona* (1966)
	Benton v. *Maryland* (1969)
Sixth Amendment:	*Powell* v. *Alabama* (1932)
	Gideon v. *Wainwright* (1963)
	Escobedo v. *Illinois* (1964)
	In re Gault (1968)
	Pointer v. *Texas* (1965)
	Duncan v. *Louisiana* (1968)
Eighth Amendment:	*Robinson* v. *California* (1962)
	Furman v. *Georgia* (1972)

FIGURE 3.2
Relationship of the Bill of Rights and the Fourteenth Amendment to the constitutional rights of the accused. For most of U.S. history, citizens were protected by the Bill of Rights only against violations by the federal government. The Warren Court began the process of interpreting portions of the Fourteenth Amendment (incorporation) so as to protect citizens from unlawful actions by state officials.

incorporation: The extension of the due process clause of the Fourteenth Amendment to make binding on state governments the rights guaranteed in the first ten amendments to the U.S. Constitution (Bill of Rights).

through the **incorporation** of the due process clause of the Fourteenth Amendment. It was not until 1953, when Earl Warren became chief justice of the United States and a new liberal majority began to form on the Court, that the due process revolution reached its full stride: "The essence of the due process revolution was an attempt by the Supreme Court to reform American justice—and particularly, to police the police of the nation—by imposing rigid constitutional rules from the top and requiring that they be followed in all cases."[28]

The Warren Court's revolution refined the meaning of the due process requirements of the Constitution, moving from the dictum that the state must observe "fundamental fairness" to a demand for absolute compliance by state and local officials with most of the specific provisions of the Bill of Rights. Where the fairness test had permitted states to fashion their own procedures, voiding only those that failed the fairness test, the new approach imposed in advance on state police and courts detailed and objective procedural standards. The justices were firm in their determination to void convictions obtained in violation of these rules.

The Case of Dolree Mapp

The change in the Supreme Court's attitude was probably first recognized in *Mapp v. Ohio* (1961).[29] On May 23, 1957, Cleveland police officers entered the home of Dolree Mapp without a search warrant, saying they were looking for a suspect in a recent bombing who was thought to be hiding there. Miss Mapp demanded to see the search warrant. One of the officers held up a piece of paper, whereupon Miss Mapp grabbed it and tucked it into her bosom. In an ensuing struggle, the officer recovered it. Miss Mapp was then handcuffed—because she had been "belligerent" in resisting the rescue of the "warrant" from her person—and led to her bedroom, where the officers searched a dresser, to other rooms in her apartment, and finally to the basement, where obscene materials were found in a trunk. At her trial no search warrant was produced, yet the Supreme Court of Ohio upheld the conviction because the evidence had not been taken from the defendant's person by the use of brutal or offensive physical force. By a narrow majority the Warren Court overturned Miss Mapp's conviction on the ground that the Fourth Amendment's injunction against unreasonable search and seizure, as applied to the states by the due process clause of the Fourteenth Amendment, had been violated. In the future, evidence gathered without a proper warrant was to be excluded from state trials.

As in most of the areas where the Warren Court broke fresh constitutional ground, federal procedures already guaranteed the specific right, and most of the states had placed on their books laws that met the Court's contemporary standards. The change was the new stricture that detailed procedural standards be followed by the

Mapp v. *Ohio* (1961): Fourth Amendment protects citizens from unreasonable searches and seizures by the states.

BIOGRAPHY

Earl Warren

The fourteenth chief justice of the United States (1953–1969), Earl Warren began his public career in 1919 as district attorney of Alameda County, California, a post he held for thirteen years. Having developed a reputation as a crusading, racket-busting prosecutor, Warren was elected California's attorney general in 1938. He was elected governor of California in 1942 and was twice reelected. In 1948 he ran for the office of vice-president of the United States as the Republican nominee.

When Warren was named chief justice, many observers of the Supreme Court expected him to be a moderate jurist with a cautious approach to the use of judicial power. But his appointment marked the beginning of an era of rapid development of the nation's constitutional law. The Warren Court had an enormous impact on American law and provided support and impetus to significant social changes. Several very important cases affecting American society were decided during this period: *Brown* v. *Board of Education* (1954) (desegregation); *Baker* v. *Carr* (1962) (reapportionment); *Mapp* v. *Ohio* (1961) (exclusionary rule); *Gideon* v. *Wainwright* (1963) (counsel); and *Miranda* v. *Arizona* (1966) (confessions).

Warren and his associate justices on the Court were often severely criticized. Critics focused on Warren's abandonment of precedent in favor of what he regarded as fairness and on what some observers saw as the Court's subordination of law to political preference. Others supported Warren's work, arguing that the Constitution must be used to uphold justice.

states to ensure that rights were not violated. This new insistence on the Bill of Rights approach to criminal justice differed from the doctrine of fundamental fairness, which had allowed the states to develop their own procedures, voiding only those actions that violated the ideals of fairness.

The significance of the *Mapp* decision is not only that the Fourth Amendment was incorporated but also that for the first time the Supreme Court imposed detailed constitutional restrictions on the actions of state law enforcement officials. It was a milestone opinion in that it breached the precedent against the Court's supervision of the nuts and bolts of state justice. Beyond the Fourth Amendment lay the Fifth, with its protection against self-incrimination, and the Sixth, which guarantees the right to counsel. If these three amendments should be applied by the Court to the states, almost the complete range of activities in the criminal justice system would come under the detailed control of the federal judiciary. With the retirement of Justice Felix Frankfurter in 1962 and the appointment of Arthur Goldberg, a firm liberal majority began to complete the task of incorporation. From 1962 to 1972 the Supreme Court, under the chief justiceships of both Earl Warren and Warren Burger, applied most of the remaining criminal justice safeguards to the states; incorporation was virtually completed.

Fourth Amendment

> The right of the people to be secure in their persons, houses, papers, and effects, against unreasonable searches and seizures, shall not be violated, and no Warrants shall issue, but upon probable cause, supported by Oath or affirmation, and particularly describing the place to be searched, and the persons or things to be seized.

The Fourth Amendment recognizes the right to privacy, but the application of this protection to the daily operations of the criminal justice system has caused a number of problems. First, not all searches are prohibited, only those that are *unreasonable.* Second is the problem of what to do with evidence that is illegally obtained.

Is it reasonable for the police to stop and search a vehicle without a warrant? Should a vehicle be treated differently than a house?

Should murderers be set free because a vital piece of evidence was seized without a search warrant? The ambiguity of these portions of the amendment and the complexity of some arrest and investigation incidents have created difficulties.

What Is Unreasonable?

With the rise in crime during the 1960s and the Supreme Court's increased interest in protecting the rights of defendants, many states passed laws permitting officers to stop and frisk persons who were thought to be about to commit a criminal act or who were believed to have just engaged in a criminal act. In *Terry* v. *Ohio* (1968), the Warren Court tried to deal with this situation.[30] Three men had been observed prowling in front of some store windows. An officer who had reasonable suspicion to believe they were planning a robbery stopped them and found guns on two of them. The state argued that stopping and frisking were not covered by the prohibitions of the Fourth Amendment, because such actions were tentative and preliminary procedures that might give rise to evidence that could then be the basis for a lawful arrest. Although the Supreme Court did not accept this argument, it upheld the police officer's action as a reasonable precaution for his own safety.

Since 1968 the Court has tried on numerous occasions to define what is meant by "reasonable" in the context of the search-and-seizure provisions of the Fourth Amendment (see Chapter 6). Its conclusion seems to be that a personal search incident to a lawful

---

A QUESTION OF ETHICS

The short, muscular black man strode through the Los Angeles International Airport carrying an attaché case and a small piece of luggage. He abruptly set down the bag and walked to a row of pay phones. His telephone conversation was interrupted by two Drug Enforcement Administration (DEA) agents, who grabbed the phone and started asking the man a series of questions. When the suspected "drug smuggler" did not respond, he fell or was thrown to the floor and was then handcuffed and led off for questioning. Only after his protestation that they had stopped the wrong person was Joe Morgan—a broadcaster for ESPN, former Cincinnati Reds second baseman, and National Baseball Hall of Fame member—released.

Los Angeles narcotics detective Clayton Searle and DEA agent Bill Woessner have claimed that they did nothing wrong; they merely responded to a DEA-developed profile of the characteristics of persons likely to be drug couriers. The fact that race is a major element of this profile has been justified as conforming to reality. Blacks and Hispanics, it is argued, are more likely to be involved in this aspect of the drug trade. Others have said that this is merely an expression of institutional racism—the darker your skin, the more likely that you will be stopped for questioning.

Is it ethical to base law enforcement actions on physical characteristics? Must the government stop and question only those whose behavior indicates they are committing or are about to commit a crime?

arrest is legal. But even if it is not incident to an arrest, a search is sometimes legally justified if an officer believes a suspect is armed. The extension of a search to the space surrounding an arrest has been ruled to be restricted to situations in which the suspect may reasonably be expected to obtain a weapon or destroy evidence. After an arrest has been made but before the suspect has been removed from the premises, the police have more discretionary power to make a search, because the defendant is now in custody.

Problems of the Exclusionary Rule

Paralleling the development of law in the search-and-seizure area are issues related to illegally obtained evidence. What remedy is available to a defendant who has been the subject of an unreasonable search and seizure? Since 1914 the Supreme Court has held to an **exclusionary rule**: illegally seized evidence must be excluded from trials in federal courts. The argument has been that the government must not soil its hands by profiting from illegally seized evidence and that without this rule the police would not be deterred from conducting raids in violation of the Fourth Amendment. In *Mapp* v. *Ohio* the exclusionary rule was extended to state courts, yet not all justices have agreed with this solution. Burger, for example, argued that the rule had not been effective in deterring police misconduct and that it exacted a high price from society—that is, the release of countless guilty offenders. On the other hand, Justice William Brennan has maintained that the justices who developed the exclusionary rule were well aware that it embodied a judgment that it is better for some guilty persons to go free than for the police to engage in forbidden conduct. In recent years, with a more conservative Court, there has been increased support for the idea that illegally obtained evidence should not be excluded if police officers made the search in the "good-faith" belief that they were acting legally (see Chapter 6).

In sum, of the amendments dealing with criminal justice, the Fourth appears to be the one most likely to undergo continuing inter-

exclusionary rule: The principle that the illegally obtained evidence must be excluded from a trial.

The state must prove its case beyond a reasonable doubt using lawfully obtained evidence.

pretation. Not only are several of its provisions ambiguous, but such technological developments as electronic surveillance lead to the need for new interpretations.

CHAPTER 3   **123**
CRIMINAL JUSTICE AND
THE RULE OF LAW

Fifth Amendment

No person shall be held to answer for a capital, or otherwise infamous crime, unless on a presentment or indictment of a Grand Jury, except in cases arising in the land or naval forces, or in the Militia, when in actual service in time of war or public danger; nor shall any person be subject for the same offense to be twice put in jeopardy of life or limb; nor shall be compelled in any criminal case to be a witness against himself, nor be deprived of life, liberty, or property, without due process of law; nor shall private property be taken for public use, without just compensation.

Clearly, the Fifth Amendment provides a number of rights that speak to various portions of the criminal justice process.

Self-Incrimination

One of the most important of these rights is the protection against **self-incrimination;** that is, persons shall not be compelled to be witnesses against themselves. This right is consistent with the assumption of the adversarial process that the state must prove the defendant's guilt. The right does not really stand alone but is integrated with other protections, especially the Fourth Amendment's prohibition of unreasonable search and seizure. The Sixth Amendment's right to counsel has also had an impact on the Fifth Amendment. The Fifth Amendment has its greatest force, however, with regard to interrogations and confessions.

self-incrimination: The act of exposing oneself to prosecution by being forced to answer questions that may tend to incriminate one; it is protected against by the Fifth Amendment. In any criminal proceeding the prosecution must prove the charges by means of evidence other than the testimony of the accused.

Historically, the validity of confessions has hinged on their being voluntary, because self-incrimination is involved. Under the doctrine of fundamental fairness, which held sway until the 1960s, the Supreme Court was unwilling to allow confessions that were beaten out of suspects, that emerged after extended periods of questioning, or that resulted from other physical tactics for inducing admission of guilt. In the cases of *Escobedo* v. *Illinois* (1964) and *Miranda* v. *Arizona* (1966), the Court added that confessions made by suspects who had not been notified of their due process rights could not be admitted as evidence. To protect the rights of the accused, the Court emphasized the importance of allowing counsel to be present during the interrogation process.

Escobedo v. *Illinois* **(1964)**: Counsel must be provided suspects when taken into police custody.

Miranda v. *Arizona* **(1966)**: Confessions made by suspects who had not been notified of the due process rights cannot be admitted as evidence.

In sum, the *Miranda* and *Escobedo* decisions fueled criticism of the Warren Court. These decisions shifted attention from due process rights in the courtroom to due process rights during the accused's initial contact with the police. Law enforcement groups claimed that the presence of counsel during interrogation would burden the system and also reduce the number of convictions. Research on this point has shown, however, that the fears of the police have not been realized. Confessions do not seem to be as important as the police stated, and informing suspects of their rights does not seem to have greatly impeded the police's ability to secure admissions of guilt.

Double Jeopardy

double jeopardy: The subjecting of a person to prosecution more than once for the same offense; prohibited by the Fifth Amendment.

Because of the limitations of the Fifth Amendment, a person charged with a criminal act may be subjected to only one prosecution or punishment for that offense in the same jurisdiction. As previously noted, illegal acts often violate both state and federal laws, so the prohibition against **double jeopardy** does not necessarily rule out prosecution in successive jurisdictions. The Supreme Court upheld this position in the case of *Bartkus* v. *Illinois* (1973).[31]

At what point in the criminal process does double jeopardy come into force? There have been a number of cases on this point, but the provision has generally been held to mean that if a case is dismissed before trial, a subsequent prosecution for the offense is permissible.

Sixth Amendment

In all criminal prosecutions, the accused shall enjoy the right to a speedy and public trial, by an impartial jury of the State and district wherein the crime shall have been committed, which district shall have been previously ascertained by law, and to be informed of the nature and cause of the accusation; to be confronted with witnesses against him; to have compulsory process for obtaining witnesses in his favor, and to have the assistance of counsel for his defense.

Right to Counsel

Gideon v. *Wainwright* (1963): Defendants have a right to counsel in felony cases.

Although the accused's right to counsel in a criminal case had long prevailed in the federal courts, not until the landmark decision in *Gideon* v. *Wainwright* (1963) was this requirement made binding on the states (see Chapter 9). In prior cases, relying on the doctrine of fundamental fairness, the Supreme Court had ruled that states must provide indigents (poor people) with counsel only when the special circumstances of the case demanded such assistance. Thus, when conviction could result in death, when the issues were complex, or when the indigent defendant was either very young or mentally handicapped, counsel had to be provided.

Argersinger v. *Hamlin* (1972): Defendants have a right to counsel when imprisonment might result.

At the time of the *Gideon* decision, only five states did not already provide attorneys for indigent defendants in felony cases, but the decision led to issues concerning the extension of this right. The next question concerned the point in the criminal justice process at which a lawyer had to be present. Beginning in 1963, the Supreme Court extended the right to counsel to preliminary hearings, to appeals, to a defendant out on bail after an indictment, to identification lineups, and to children in juvenile court proceedings. Although the *Gideon* case demanded counsel for indigents charged with felonies, this right was extended in 1972 to persons charged with misdemeanors when imprisonment might result (*Argersinger* v. *Hamlin*). The effect of these cases was to ensure that poor defendants would have at least some of the protections that had always been available to defendants with money. In sum, the rulings of the Court with regard to the right to counsel have been generally accepted throughout the nation with little criticism. Under most circumstances, counsel is made available, but the effectiveness of that counsel may still be open to question.

Speedy and Public Trial

The founders of this country were aware that in other countries the accused often languished in jail awaiting trial and was often convicted in the seclusion of the judge's chambers (see Chapter 11). At the time of the American Revolution, the right to a speedy and public trial was recognized in the common law and had been incorporated into the constitutions of six of the original states. But the word *speedy* is vague, and the Supreme Court has recognized that the interest of quick processes may be in conflict with other interests of society as well as with interests of the defendant.

The right to a public trial is intended to protect the accused against arbitrary conviction. The assumption is that if justice must be done in the open, judges and juries will act in accordance with the law. As with the matter of speed, the Supreme Court has recognized that there may be circumstances in which the need for a public trial has to be balanced against other interests. For example, the right to a public trial does not mean that all members of the public have the right to attend the trial. The seating capacity and the interests of a fair trial, free of outbursts from the audience, may weigh heavily. Likewise in trials concerning sex crimes in which the victim or witness is a minor, courts have temporarily barred the public to spare the child embarrassment.

Impartial Jury

The right to a jury trial was as well established in the American colonies at the time of the Revolution as it had been in England for centuries (see Chapter 12). In their charters, most of the colonies specifically guaranteed trial by jury, and thus references to this essential process are found in the debates of the First Continental Congress in 1774, the Declaration of Independence, the constitutions of the thirteen original states, and the Sixth Amendment to the U.S. Constitution.

From a historical and philosophical perspective, the jury constitutes a barrier between an accused individual and the power of the state. Because the crucial decisions in criminal—and civil—trials are made by an impartial jury of one's peers, a safeguard is erected against corrupt or overzealous officialdom.

The question of how to create juries that are representative of the community and inclusive of its various elements has not been answered with the unanimity expressed in regard to the principle itself. The Magna Carta stipulated that juries should be drawn from "peers" of the accused, and later, during the time of Henry II, members were selected from the immediate vicinity of the crime. Because *peer* and *community* in medieval England may have had meanings different from today's, scholars and the Supreme Court have advanced a number of definitions to clarify the nature and impartial composition of juries. Most scholars believe that impartiality can best be achieved when jurors are drawn at random from the broadest possible base, thereby balancing the different biases in the community against one another. The jury is expected to perform a representative function, and representativeness thus becomes the crucial concept permeating all aspects of jury administration. Because courts have prohibited the

Trial by an impartial jury is a basic element of our criminal justice system. To ensure that they are not biased, jurors are randomly drawn from the community. The judge instructs them to put aside their assumptions about a case and consider only the evidence.

systematic exclusion of any identifiable group of prospective jurors, random selection is the basis on which most trial juries in the United States are chosen.

State laws specify the offenses that can be tried by a jury, the size of the jury, and the types of decisions that can be made. The Supreme Court ruled in *Duncan v. Louisiana* (1968) that states must make jury trials available to defendants who are charged with serious offenses. This rule was further refined in *Baldwin v. New York* (1970) to mean that the option may be used when a crime carries a sentence of more than six months.[32] In other rulings, the Supreme Court has said that the size of the jury is left up to the state (*Williams v. Florida*, 1970)—six-person juries are thus allowed—and that a unanimous verdict is not necessarily required in a criminal trial.[33] In a number of states, primarily in the South, the jury not only decides matters of fact but is also charged with determining the type and length of punishment. The practice has been greatly criticized, principally because the brevity of jury service does not give citizens a perspective that would allow them to recommend sentences that are realistic and consistent with the goals of the criminal sanction.

Duncan v. *Louisiana* (1968): States must provide a jury trial for defendants charged with serious offenses.

Williams v. *Florida* (1970): Six-person juries are allowed in some cases.

Eighth Amendment

Excessive bail shall not be required, nor excessive fines imposed, nor cruel and unusual punishment inflicted.

Release on Bail

The purpose of bail is to allow for the release of the accused while he or she is awaiting trial (see Chapter 10). The Eighth Amendment does not require that release on bail be granted to all defendants, only that the amount of bail shall not be excessive. Many states do not allow bail to persons charged with some offenses, such as murder, and there appear to be few restrictions on the amount that can be demanded. In 1987 the Supreme Court in the case *United States* v. *Salerno and Cafaro* upheld provisions of the Bail Reform Act of 1984 allowing federal judges to detain without bail suspects considered dangerous to the public (see Chapter 10).[34]

The Issue of Capital Punishment

During recent decades the spotlight of public attention has focused on the Eighth Amendment's prohibition against cruel and unusual punishment—in particular, on the issue of capital punishment (see Chapters 13 and 15). In the case of *Furman* v. *Georgia* (1972), the Supreme Court ruled that the death penalty, as administered, constituted cruel and unusual punishment. Only Justices Thurgood Marshall and Brennan argued that the death penalty was per se cruel and unusual punishment, but a five-member majority could agree with Justice Potter Stewart that the death sentences being considered were cruel and unusual, "in the same way that being struck by lightning is cruel and unusual. For, of all the people convicted of rapes and murders in 1967 and 1968, many just as reprehensible as these, the petitioners are among a capriciously selected random handful upon whom the sentence of death has in fact been imposed."[35]

Following this decision, many states passed laws designed to maintain the death penalty by removal of the arbitrary aspects of the proceedings. These new laws were tested in the 1976 case of *Gregg* v. *Georgia*; the Court upheld those statutes that permitted a sentencing judge or jury to take into account specific aggravating or mitigating circumstances in deciding whether a convicted murderer should be put to death.[36]

Questions about racial bias in the administration of Georgia's law were addressed in the 1987 decision *McCleskey* v. *Kemp*.[37] In the face of statistical evidence showing that capital punishment was more likely in cases involving black killers and white victims, the Court ruled that exceptionally clear proof would be necessary to show that decision makers had been racially biased. It thus upheld McCleskey's sentence.

Since the reinstitution of capital punishment following *Gregg* v. *Georgia*, the death row population in the United States has soared to over 2,500, yet proportionally few people have been executed. Each year approximately 250 people are given the death sentence, but no more than 25 have been executed annually. The question remains one that the courts and society will be confronting for years to come. The policy issue "Should the Death Penalty Be Abolished" discusses this problem. (See Figure 3.3 for a summary of defendants' rights.)

From Warren to Burger to Rehnquist

With the retirement of Chief Justice Earl Warren and the appointment by President Richard Nixon of Warren Burger in June 1969 to be the fourteenth chief justice of the United States, liberals feared that the emphasis supporting the rights of defendants in criminal cases would end. Their disquiet was intensified with four additional appointments to the Court by Presidents Nixon and Gerald Ford, both Republicans. The Court did assume a much more conservative stance on social policy issues, especially those having to do with criminal justice. But

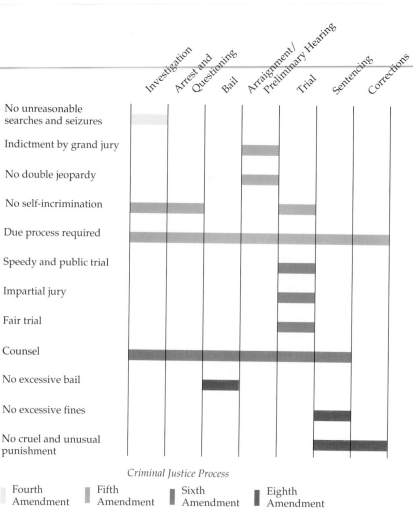

FIGURE 3.3
Protections of the Bill of Rights.
The Bill of Rights protects defendants
during various phases of the criminal
justice process.

most fears of civil libertarians were not realized during the seventeen-year period of the Court under Burger. It was not until Ronald Reagan's appointment of Sandra Day O'Connor and Antonin Scalia as associate justices and the 1986 elevation of William Rehnquist to the chief justiceship that significant shifts could be detected as the new six-to-three conservative majority began to consider such issues as preventive detention, the "good-faith exception" to the exclusionary rule, and administration of the death penalty. The appointment in 1988 of Anthony Kennedy strengthened the new direction of the Court. President Bush's nomination of Judge David Souter seemingly consolidated conservative power. With the remaining liberal justices now in their eighties, conservatives seem destined to retain power for the foreseeable future.

What can be said about the decisions of the Supreme Court since the due process revolution began under Warren? Will there be a retrenchment from the rights gained during the past three decades? In seeking answers to these questions, we must remember that even the newly reconstituted Court has upheld the basic thrust of rights dealing with counsel, fair trials, and juveniles. It is with regard to unreasonable searches and seizures, the exclusionary rule, and issues surrounding the death penalty that the Rehnquist Court can be expected to retreat from some of the positions of the Warren and Burger years.

Civil libertarians, however, have taken heart by the actions of some state courts. Law professor Ronald Collins has pointed to about 600 cases where state courts have interpreted their state constitutions to protect civil liberties more broadly than has the U.S. Supreme Court.[38] States cannot provide fewer protections on rights than those granted by the U.S. Constitution but they can provide more. For example, the Supreme Courts of New York, Connecticut, North Carolina, and New Jersey have refused to follow the Rehnquist Court with regard to the "good faith exception" interpretation of the Fourth Amendment's prohibition against unreasonable searches and seizures. It may be that during the new era of conservativism on the Supreme Court, state courts will continue the civil liberties revolution begun by Chief Justice Warren.

SUMMARY

Substantive law concerns the question What is illegal? For every criminal charge, it must be shown that the behavior of the accused was such as to be consistent with the seven principles that define crime. Such defenses as self-defense, necessity, and insanity may be used to show that the accused was not legally responsible for the offense.

Procedural law focuses on how the law is enforced. The manner in which evidence is collected, the admission of witnesses' statements at trial, the judge's charge to the jury, and the rights of prisoners are only a few of the matters in which the procedural law stipulates what can and cannot be done. In most states, attorneys can consult a practice book that describes the operational rules that must be followed in regard to the rights of defendants.

Many people believe that the substantive law and the rules of procedure have become so intricate that criminals escape punishment, court proceedings are unnecessarily drawn out, and the police are unable to do their job. Others contend that law and due process are essential for a just society. These positions remind us of the values summarized in Packer's Due Process and Crime Control Models and of the tensions existing between the rule of law and the administration of justice.

FOR DISCUSSION

1. We often talk about the rights of the accused, but what are the rights of the victim?
2. If very few persons have taken advantage of the rights enunciated by the Supreme Court, what is the importance of the Court's opinions?
3. You are a police officer. You have every reason to believe that if you search a certain automobile, you will find evidence that will result in an arrest, thereby solving a recent burglary. What actions can you take without violating the rights of the automobile owner, the suspect in the case?

4. You are a suspect. You have just been read the *Miranda* warnings by the arresting officer. What will be your response to the questions asked by officers at the station house? Why? How will your response affect your treatment by the police and your case when it comes to court?

5. How far can the rights of due process be extended? Are there any limits?

FOR FURTHER READING

Fletcher, George P. *A Crime of Self Defense: Bernhard Goetz and the Law on Trial.* New York: Free Press, 1988. An insightful examination of the legal issues involved in the Goetz case.

Graham, Fred P. *The Self-Inflicted Wound.* New York: Macmillan, 1970. Analysis of the Warren Court's "due process revolution" and its political impact.

Katz, Leo. *Bad Acts and Guilty Minds.* Chicago: University of Chicago Press, 1987. Exploration of questions raised by the insanity defense.

Lewis, Anthony. *Gideon's Trumpet.* New York: Vintage Books, 1964. A classic examination of the case of *Gideon* v. *Wainwright,* showing the process by which the issues came to the U.S. Supreme Court.

Morris, Norval. *Madness and the Criminal Law.* Chicago: University of Chicago Press, 1982. A stimulating and controversial examination of the insanity defense by a leading criminal justice scholar.

Simpson, Alfred W. Bain. *Cannibalism and the Common Law.* Chicago: University of Chicago Press, 1984. Exciting study of the case of *The Queen* v. *Dudley and Stephens* showing that there were many such incidents during the age of sail for which punishment did not follow.

NOTES

1. *Escobedo* v. *Illinois,* 364 U.S. 478 (1964).
2. C. Ray Jeffery, "The Development of Crime in Early English Society," *Journal of Criminal Law, Criminology and Police Science* 47 (March-April 1957):660.
3. William J. Chambliss and Robert B. Seidman, *Law, Order, and Power* (Reading, MA: Addison-Wesley, 1971), p. 230.
4. Jerome Hall, *General Principles of Criminal Law,* 2nd ed. (Indianapolis: Bobbs-Merrill, 1947), p. 18.
5. *Robinson* v. *California,* 370 U.S. 660 (1962).
6. Chambliss and Seidman, *Law, Order and Power,* p. 202.
7. Ibid.
8. Oliver Wendell Holmes, Jr., *Common Law* (Boston: Little, Brown, 1881), p. 3.
9. American Law Institute, *Model Penal Code* (Philadelphia, 1962), p. 32.
10. *Morissette* v. *United States,* 142 U.S. 246 (1952).
11. Hall, *General Principles,* p. 348.
12. *The Queen* v. *Dudley and Stephens,* 14 Q.B.D. 273 (1884).
13. Ibid.
14. *Missouri* v. *Green,* 470 S.W. 2d 565 (1971).
15. Ibid.
16. U.S. Department of Justice, National Institute of Justice, *Crime File,* Norval Morris, "Insanity Defense" (Washington, DC: Government Printing Office, n.d.).
17. *M'Naghten's Case,* 8 Eng. Rep. 718 (H.I. 1843).
18. *Durham* v. *United States,* 94 U.S. App. D.C. 228, 214 F. 2d 862 (1954).
19. *United States* v. *Brawner,* 471 F. 2d 969 (1972).
20. John Klofas and Janette Yandrasits, "'Guilty but Mentally Ill' and the Jury Trial: A Case Study" 24 *Criminal Law Bulletin* 424 (1989).

21. Norval Morris, *Madness and the Criminal Law* (Chicago: University of Chicago Press, 1982), esp. Ch. 2.
22. *Barron* v. *Baltimore*, 32 U.S. 243 (1833).
23. *Moore* v. *Dempsey*, 261 U.S. 86 (1923).
24. *Powell* v. *Alabama*, 287 U.S. 45 (1932).
25. *Brown* v. *Mississippi*, 297 U.S. 278 (1936).
26. *Palko* v. *Connecticut*, 302 U.S. 319 (1937).
27. *Rochin* v. *California*, 342 U.S. 172 (1953).
28. Fred Graham, *The Self-Inflicted Wound* (New York: Macmillan, 1970), p. 16.
29. *Mapp* v. *Ohio*, 367 U.S. 643 (1961).
30. *Terry* v. *Ohio*, 394 U.S. 1 (1968).
31. *Bartkus* v. *Illinois*, 411 U.S. 423 (1973).
32. *Baldwin* v. *New York*, 399 U.S. 66 (1970).
33. *Williams* v. *Florida*, 399 U.S. 78 (1970).
34. *United States* v. *Salerno and Cafaro*, 55 L.W. 463 (1987).
35. *Furman* v. *Georgia*, 408 U.S. 238 (1972).
36. *Gregg* v. *Georgia*, 96 S. Ct. 2909 (1976).
37. *McCleskey* v. *Kemp*, 55 L.W. 4537 (1987).
38. *Newsweek* (October 8, 1990):76.

The Administration of Criminal Justice

Key Terms

bureaucracy
criminal justice wedding cake
deterrence

discretion
dual court system

exchange
filtering process

plea bargaining
system

The case of Bernhard Goetz, the "subway vigilante," required the cooperation of the police, courts, and corrections at several levels of government.

Any criminal justice system is an apparatus society uses to enforce the standards of conduct necessary to protect individuals and the community. It operates by apprehending, prosecuting, convicting, and sentencing those members of the community who violate the basic rules of group existence.

President's Commission on Law Enforcement
and Administration of Justice

Three days before Christmas 1984, Bernhard Goetz, a thirty-seven-year-old, white, bespectacled electrical engineer boarded a New York City subway train headed for the Wall Street district. As the train rattled through the underground darkness, four black youths, two of whom carried long screwdrivers, suddenly surrounded him and asked for $5. Goetz is quoted as having said, "Yes, I have five dollars for each of you," whereupon he pulled a .38-caliber pistol from his coat and shot all four teenagers. A conductor rushed to the scene and demanded, "Are you a cop?" Goetz replied, "No. They tried to rip me off." "Give me the gun," said the conductor. Goetz refused, leapt from the train, and disappeared into the dark subway tunnel.[1] All four of the youths were rushed to the hospital; two of them were in serious condition, one paralyzed from the waist down. Nine days later Goetz surrendered to the police in Concord, New Hampshire, where he admitted the shooting, later saying that he had done it in self-defense.

The incident touched off one of America's most controversial criminal cases. Support for Goetz as someone who had stood up to lawlessness came from many quarters. The New York police were deluged with phone calls praising his actions. The "subway vigilante" received something like a hero's welcome when he returned to New York. The attack encapsulated many of the tensions in modern-day America: criminal versus victim, black versus white, and rule of law versus vigilantism. Some columnists called Goetz's reaction to the youths, whom he accused of being muggers, an understandable consequence of the failure of the criminal justice system to deal with violence, intimidation, and disorder in society.

From the shooting on December 22, 1984, until his sentencing in September 1987, Goetz's journey through the criminal justice system was long and complicated. Following his extradition from New Hampshire, Goetz was indicted by a grand jury on a charge of possessing an illegal weapon. Later, on the motion of the Manhattan district attorney, charges of attempted murder and assault were added. In January 1986 a judge dismissed nine of the thirteen counts, including the attempted murder and assault charges, on the ground that errors had been made in the presentation of the charges to the grand jury. Seven months later New York State's highest court unanimously reinstated all the charges and clarified the state's standards of self-defense (as discussed in Chapter 3). Jury selection began on December 12, 1986, and trial testimony on April 27, 1987. On June 16 Goetz was acquitted of all counts except illegal possession of a weapon, a decision criticized by African-American leaders as all but exonerating a white man for shooting four black youths. He was sentenced on this charge to six months in jail and five years on probation and was ordered to undergo psychiatric counseling. This sentence was overturned by a New York State appellate court and the case was sent back to the trial judge for resentencing. This time Goetz received a year in jail. With time off for good behavior, he was released in September 1989 after serving eight months.

In the course of the prosecution and trial of the "subway vigilante," Americans were given an elementary education in the functions and processes of the criminal justice system. With the help of the news media, persons who had never before paid attention to the activities of their local police and courts were soon debating issues of vigilantism, rule of law, self-defense, and the justice of punishment. Some may have been confused by the fact that so many different agencies of government, both state and local—New Hampshire, New York, and New York City—participated in the three major components of the justice system: police, courts, and corrections. Goetz committed the crime in New York City yet had to be formally extradited from New Hampshire by New York State to face investigation and prosecution. When Goetz was sentenced many felt the punishment was too severe and had resulted from political pressures brought by African-American leaders. Others said that the sentence was justified because it made Goetz an object lesson to all that the rule of law must prevail.

Before we examine the major components of criminal justice, let us take an overview of the system's administration and confront several crucial questions.

- What are the purposes of the criminal justice system?
- What organizations make up this system?
- What are the procedures by which a citizen may be arrested, found guilty, and imprisoned?
- What analytic tools can we use to understand the system better?

This chapter focuses on the operation of the criminal justice system, its agencies, and its processes. It is hoped that the description of formal relationships in this broad and complex system will add meaning to the theoretical and analytic chapters that follow. At the end of the chapter, several social science concepts are examined to determine whether they are useful in furthering our understanding of the way the system really works.

CRIMINAL JUSTICE AND SOCIETY

The concept of society implies that interpersonal relations are governed by measures of social control. Communities develop various ways that they keep the behavior of individual members within agreed-upon norms. Violations of these norms are followed by reactions that take a variety of forms, ranging from expressions of mild disapproval to the severest penalties, or sanctions, of the law. Although many of the actions of our fellow citizens may appear unpleasant, antisocial, or immoral, only certain types of behaviors have been labeled illegal. The criminal law specifies formal methods to enforce rules and a range of distinctive sanctions for violations. Of special importance is the fact that the criminal law and its agencies are authoritative; that is, the citizenry has given them certain legitimate rights and duties, including the ultimate sanctions that restrict freedom or even bring about death.

Crime is found in all societies, and each culture has developed some mechanism to control it. But the ways in which different peoples of the world attack crime vary considerably. Not only do dissimilarities exist in what is considered illegal, but a great variety of instruments is used to judge and penalize criminals. In many respects, a society's way of confronting its crime problem reflects its political and cultural values.

Because the United States is a democracy, the way we control crime represents a basic test of our ideals. The administration of justice in a democracy can be distinguished from that in an authoritarian state by the extent and form of protections provided for the accused as guilt is determined and punishment is imposed. Although the United States has one of the highest crime rates in the world, the efficiency of crime control may have to be sacrificed to preserve the rights of individual citizens.

Every year more than 14 million arrests are made in the United States. Although most of these arrests are for relatively minor violations, the fact remains that a sizable portion of the American population has direct contact with the official processes of criminal justice. When we add the victims and witnesses of crime, the number of people directly affected by the criminal justice process grows still further. Yet the system that the United States has developed to deal

A QUESTION OF ETHICS

After his jewelry store had been burglarized for the third time in less than six months, Tom Henderson was frustrated. The police were of little help, merely telling him that they would have a patrol officer keep watch during nightly rounds. Tom had added new locks and an electronic security system. When he unlocked his shop one morning he saw that he had been cleaned out again. He looked around the store to see how the thief had entered, since the door was locked and evidently the security alarm had not sounded. Suddenly he noticed that the glass in a skylight was broken.

"Damn, I'll fix him this time," cursed Henderson.

That evening after replacing the glass, he stripped the insulation from an electric cord and strung it around and across the frame of the skylight. He pulled the cord into a socket, locked the store and went home.

Two weeks later when he entered the store and flipped the light switch nothing happened. He walked toward the fuse box. It was then that he noticed the burned body lying on the floor below the skylight.

What are the limits that a person can go to "protect his castle"? If the police are unable to solve a crime problem, is it ethical for individuals to take matters into their own hands?

with crime is not uniform, and some critics say it is not consistent. The system is used to enforce the standards reflected in the laws we have developed to protect the individual citizen and the community.

GOALS OF CRIMINAL JUSTICE

For most Americans, the goals of the criminal justice system appear obvious: the prevention and control of crime; but such a broadly phrased statement does not tell us much about how these goals can be achieved. The criminal justice system operates to apprehend, prosecute, convict, and punish those members of the community who do not live according to the law. These functions are enhanced by the effect the sanctions imposed on one person have on the general population; that is, by observing the consequences of criminal behavior, others may be encouraged to live according to the law. Finally, we must recognize that our society can prevent and control crime only within the framework of law. The criminal law defines what is illegal and prescribes the procedures that officials must use as they attempt to achieve these goals. The rights of citizens are carefully outlined in the law.

In any city or town one can see the goals of the criminal justice system being actively pursued: a police officer speaking to elementary schoolchildren, a patrol car quietly moving through a darkened street, an arrest being made outside a neighborhood bar, lawyers walking into the courthouse, neon signs flashing the word "bail," the forbidding gloom of the county jail. While these images exemplify the broadly stated goals of the criminal justice system, they also point to nuances of meaning in the definition of these goals that require examination. It can be argued, for example, that prevention and control so overlap that they cannot be described as truly separate functions. The arrest outside the bar not only controlled the behavior but

Education about crime and justice begins at an early age. To what extent are the messages of teachers, parents, and police officers likely to overcome the competing messages of peers?

also may have prevented future violations by the offender and may have had a similar influence on bystanders.

In addition, questions can be raised about the boundaries of the criminal justice system. To what extent are criminal justice agencies responsible for pursuing the system's goals? If we believe that poverty causes crime, are the police and courts charged with curing poverty as a means of preventing crime? How do the stated goals of prevention and control shape the daily operations of the criminal justice system?

Control of Crime

One of the best ways to gain an understanding of crime control is to look at the processes by which offenders are apprehended, convicted, and punished. But a knowledge of how criminal justice agencies function tells us little about their contribution to the goal. Measures of effectiveness are needed so that observers can determine which activities are related to the achievement of this goal. This is where value conflicts occur among competing measures of effectiveness and among competing operational styles.

For example, is a police department that makes many arrests more effective than one that tolerates certain types of behavior in order to maintain an ordered community? Is the crime control goal of criminal justice better served by judges who sentence according to the letter of the law or by those who reduce the allowable sentences because of the characteristics of the individual offender? Are long periods of imprisonment under maximum security conditions more effective than the rehabilitative setting of a halfway house? The variety of ways in which criminal justice agencies can operate in the pursuit of crime control presents value dilemmas that must be faced by the individual patrol officer, judge, or correctional officer and by citizens and legislators who influence the making of public policy.

Prevention of Crime

The goals of criminal justice also include crime prevention—that is, preventing or deterring criminal behavior. As will be discussed more extensively in Chapter 13, **deterrence** means two things: (1) deterring offenders with whom the system has direct contact from committing further crime (special deterrence), and (2) deterring the public from committing crimes in the first place (general deterrence). As with the value choices that influence crime control operations, options are chosen in the pursuit of deterrence.

Considerable evidence indicates that criminal sanctions have not been particularly effective when it comes to special deterrence. Too many offenders continue in their former ways after they are released from prison. In addition, first offenders often become embittered and better skilled in criminal pursuits while imprisoned. Instead of being an effective institution for special deterrence, prisons have often been referred to as schools for thieves.

But even if the evidence should show that the criminal justice system had failed as a special deterrent, it might still perform the

deterrence: Discouragement of criminal behavior on the part of known offenders (special deterrence) and of the public (general deterrence) by the threat of punishment.

very important function of general deterrence. As long as the number of crimes committed by the public at large is smaller proportionally than the number of crimes committed by former convicts, general deterrence may be judged to have succeeded. But this is difficult to scientifically prove, since it is not possible to show the number of people who did not commit crimes who would not have offended even without the impact of deterrence.

The use of criminal sanctions for punishment or for rehabilitation provides the sort of value choice that will influence the deterrent effect of the criminal justice system. If the emphasis of a correctional institution is on the treatment and rehabilitation of offenders, the criminal justice system's capacity to act as a general deterrent may be diminished. The most obvious reason is that successful treatment programs must be conducted in an atmosphere in which the unpleasant aspects of prison life have been lessened or done away with altogether. To the extent that treatment is conducted in such an environment, rehabilitation efforts may succeed in deterring individual offenders from pursuing criminal careers. However, the general population may not be deterred from committing illegal acts, because the way the rehabilitation process is conducted does not seem especially unpleasant.

In the Pursuit of Criminal Justice Goals

The ways in which American institutions have been developed to achieve the goals of crime prevention and control lead to a series of choices. In the pursuit of criminal justice goals, decisions must be made that reflect legal, political, social, and moral values. As we try to understand the system, we must be aware of possible conflicts among these values as well as of the implications of choosing one value over another. The task of preventing and controlling crime would be eased considerably if the means of doing so could be clearly determined, so that citizens and officials are able to act with a forthright understanding of their responsibilities and obligations. Making such easy translations of wishes into reality is not characteristic of human institutions.

CRIMINAL JUSTICE IN A FEDERAL SYSTEM

How does the political system of the United States influence the enforcement of the law, the trying of defendants, and the correction of offenders? Of primary importance in the American system of criminal justice is the federal governmental structure created in 1789 with the ratification of the U.S. Constitution. This instrument created a delicate political agreement: The national government was given certain powers—to raise an army, to coin money, to make treaties with foreign countries, and so forth—but all other powers were retained by the states. Nowhere in the Constitution does one find specific reference to criminal justice agencies of the national government, yet we all are familiar with the Federal Bureau of Investigation (FBI), recognize that criminal cases are often tried in United States district courts, and know that the Federal Bureau of Prisons operates institutions from coast to coast.

Two Justice Systems

For conceptual purposes, thinking of two distinct criminal justice systems—national and state—is useful. Both perform enforcement, adjudication, and correctional functions, but they do so on different authority, and their activities vary greatly in scope. Criminal laws are written and enforced primarily by agencies of the states (including counties and municipalities), yet the rights of defendants are protected by the constitutions of both state and national governments. Although approximately 85 percent of criminal cases are heard in state courts, certain offenses—drug violations and transportation of a kidnap victim across state lines, for example—are violations of *both* state and federal laws.

As a consequence of the bargain worked out at the Constitutional Convention, general police power was not delegated to the federal government. Rather, it was kept as a power of the states. No national police force with broad enforcement powers may be established in the United States. The national government does have police agencies, such as the FBI, the Drug Enforcement Administration, and the Secret Service, but they are authorized to enforce only those laws prescribed under the powers granted to Congress. Since Congress has the power to coin money, it also has the authority to detect and apprehend counterfeiters, a function performed by the Secret Service of the Department of the Treasury. The FBI, a part of the Department of Justice, is responsible for investigating all violations of federal laws with the exception of those assigned by Congress to other departments. The FBI has jurisdiction over fewer than 200 criminal matters, including such offenses as kidnapping, extortion, interstate transportation of stolen motor vehicles, and treason.

When he shot President John F. Kennedy in 1963, Lee Harvey Oswald had violated only the laws of Texas. The U.S. Secret Service has the job of protecting the president, but Oswald was arrested by the Dallas police and would have been tried in Texas courts.

Jurisdictional Division

The role of criminal justice agencies following the assassination of President John F. Kennedy in November 1963 illustrates the federal–state division of jurisdiction. Because Congress had not made killing the president of the United States a federal offense, Lee Harvey Oswald, had he lived, would have been brought to trial under the laws of Texas. The U.S. Secret Service had the job of protecting the president, but apprehension of the killer was the formal responsibility of the Dallas police and other Texas law enforcement agencies.

As the constant movement of people and goods across state lines has become an integral part of American life, federal involvement in the criminal justice system has increased. The assumption that acts committed in one state will have no effect on the citizens of another state is no longer useful. Especially in the area of organized crime, for example, crime families and gangs deal with drugs, pornography, and gambling on a national basis.

Congress has passed laws designed to allow the FBI to investigate situations in which local police forces are likely to be less effective. Thus, under the National Stolen Property Act, the FBI is authorized to investigate thefts exceeding $5,000 in value when the stolen property is likely to have been taken across state lines. In such circumstances, disputes over jurisdiction may occur because the offense is a violation of *both* state and national laws. The court to which a case is brought may be determined by the law enforcement agency that makes the arrest. In some cases, a defendant could be tried under state law and then retried in the federal courts for a violation of the laws of the national government. In most instances, however, the two systems respect each other's jurisdictions.

It is important to emphasize that the American system of criminal justice is decentralized. As Figure 4.1 notes, two-thirds of all criminal justice employees work for local units of government. With the exception of corrections employees, the majority of workers in all of the

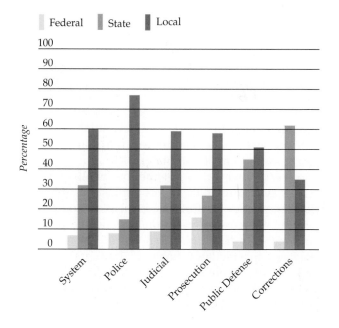

FIGURE 4.1
Percentage (rounded) of criminal justice employees at each level of government. The administration of criminal justice in the United States is very much a local affair, as these employment figures reflect. Corrections is the only category in which the state, rather than municipalities, shows a greater percentage of employment.
SOURCE: U.S. Department of Justice, Bureau of Justice Statistics, *Bulletin* (July 1990).

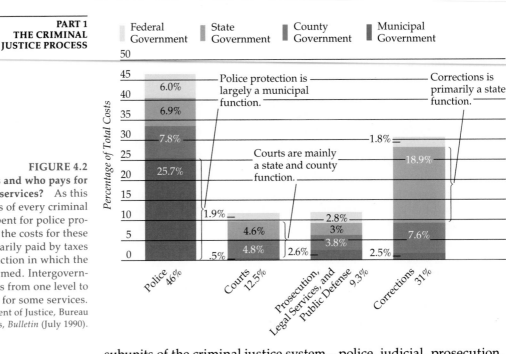

FIGURE 4.2
What are the costs and who pays for criminal justice services? As this figure shows, 46 cents of every criminal justice dollar is spent for police protection. Note that the costs for these services are primarily paid by taxes raised in the jurisidiction in which the services are performed. Intergovernmental payments from one level to another may also pay for some services.
SOURCE: U.S. Department of Justice, Bureau of Justice Statistics, *Bulletin* (July 1990).

subunits of the criminal justice system—police, judicial, prosecution, public defense—are tied to local government. Likewise, the costs of criminal justice are distributed in varying proportions among the federal, state, county, and municipal governments (as shown in Figure 4.2). It is in the states and local communities that laws are enforced and violators brought to justice. Consequently, the formal structure and actual processes are greatly affected by local norms and pressures—that is, by the needs and demands of influential local people and by the community's interpretation of the extent to which the laws should be enforced.

AGENCIES OF CRIMINAL JUSTICE

Society has commissioned the police to patrol the streets, prevent crime, arrest suspected criminals, and enforce the law. It has established courts to determine the guilt or innocence of accused offenders, to sentence those who are guilty, and to "do justice." It has created a system of corrections to punish convicted persons and programs to try to rehabilitate them so that they can eventually become useful citizens. These three components—police, courts, and corrections—combine to form the system of criminal justice.

We would be incorrect, however, to assume the criminal justice system to be uniform or even consistent. It was not fashioned in one piece at one time. Rather, various institutions, principles, and procedures were built around the core assumption that people may be punished by government only if it can be proved by an impartial process that they violated specific laws. Some of the parts, such as trial by jury and bail, are of ancient origin; others, such as juvenile courts and community-based corrections, are relatively new. The system represents an adaptation of the institutions of the English common law to the American social and political environment.

Police

The complexity and fragmentation of the criminal justice system are perhaps best seen with regard to the number and jurisdiction of the approximately 15,000 public organizations in the United States engaged in law enforcement activities. The police function is dominated by local governments, as can be seen in the fact that the federal government has only fifty law enforcement agencies, whereas each state except Hawaii has one; the remainder are dispersed throughout the counties, cities, and towns. At the state and local level these agencies have 757,000 employees and a total annual budget in excess of $28 billion.[2]

The responsibilities of police organizations fall into four categories:

1. Keeping the peace. This broad and most important mandate, or command by the people, involves the protection of rights and persons in a wide variety of situations, ranging from street-corner brawls to domestic quarrels.
2. Apprehending law violators and combating crime. This is the responsibility the public most often associates with police work, though it accounts for only a small proportion of law enforcement agencies' time and resources.
3. Engaging in crime prevention. By educating the public about the threat of crime and by reducing the number of situations in which crimes are most likely to be committed, the police can lower the incidence of crime.
4. Providing a variety of social services. In fulfilling these obligations, a police officer recovers stolen property, directs traffic, provides emergency medical aid, gets cats out of trees, and helps people who have locked themselves out of their apartments.

Federal Agencies

Entrusted with the enforcement of a list of specific federal laws, police organizations of the national government are part of the executive branch. The FBI has the broadest range of control, which encompasses investigation of all federal crimes not the responsibility of other agencies. Within the FBI is the semi-autonomous Drug Enforcement Agency (DEA). Units of the Treasury Department are concerned with violations of laws related to the collection of income taxes (Internal Revenue Service), alcohol and tobacco taxes and gun control (Bureau of Alcohol, Tobacco, and Firearms), and customs (Customs Service). Other federal agencies concerned with specific areas of law enforcement include the Secret Service Division of the Treasury (concerned with counterfeiting, forgery, and protection of the president), the Bureau of Postal Inspection of the Postal Service (concerned with mail offenses), and the Border Patrol of the Department of Justice's Immigration and Naturalization Service. Other departments of the executive branch, such as the U.S. Coast Guard, the National Parks Service, and the Environmental Protection Agency, have police powers related to their specific duties.

Agencies of the federal government also cooperate with Interpol, the International Criminal Police Organization headquartered in St.

■

Wearing civilian clothes or identifying jackets, agents of the Federal Bureau of Investigation have extensive power to deal with violations of federal crimes.

Cloud, France. Interpol has 146 member countries.[3] Its function is to foster cooperation among the police forces of the world with regard to crimes that are international in scope: drugs, terrorism, espionage, and fleeing from apprehension. Interpol maintains a data bank for intelligence on criminals and serves as a clearinghouse for information gathered by member agencies. The FBI, DEA, Treasury Department, Central Intelligence Agency, and the Internal Revenue Service all have strong ties to this international organization.

State Agencies

Each state except Hawaii has its own police force, yet here again we can see the traditional emphasis on the local nature of policing. State police forces were not established until the turn of the century and then primarily as a wing of the executive branch of state government that would enforce the law when local officials did not. The Pennsylvania State Constabulary, established in 1905, was the first such organization; by 1925 almost all of the states had an agency with some level of enforcement power.

In all the states these forces are charged with regulation of traffic on the main highways and in two-thirds of the states have been given general police powers. In only about a dozen populous states, however, are they adequate to the task of general law enforcement outside the cities. Where the state police are well developed—as in Pennsylvania, New York, New Jersey, Massachusetts, and Michigan—they tend to fill a void in rural law enforcement. The American reluctance to centralize police power has kept state forces generally from replacing local officials. For the most part they operate only in areas where no other form of police protection exists or where local officers request their expertise or the use of their facilities. In many states, for example, the crime laboratory is operated by the state police as a means of assisting all local law enforcement agencies.

BIOGRAPHY

J. Edgar Hoover

Born in Washington, D.C., J. Edgar Hoover received his LL.B. and LL.M. degrees from George Washington University in 1917. After admission to the bar, he began a career with the Justice Department and served as special assistant to the attorney general from 1919 to 1921.

President Calvin Coolidge appointed Hoover director of the Federal Bureau of Investigation in 1924, when that agency was racked by dissension and rife with politics. Hoover set out to eliminate politics from the FBI appointment process and to establish better training programs for new agents. Very early he recognized the importance of improved technical methods of police work and instituted such aids as a national fingerprint filing system and coordinated development of the Uniform Crime Reporting System. In his early career, Hoover became well known to the public as a G-man, pursuing such notorious criminals as Ma Barker, Machine Gun Kelley, Bonnie and Clyde, and John Dillinger, using these exploits to create an image of the FBI agent as the ultimate crime fighter. During the 1940s and 1950s, when Hoover became noted for his anticommunist views, the FBI's functions of control of subversives became prominent.

Hoover's long career sustained many criticisms of his management of the FBI, including accusations that the Bureau exceeded its jurisdiction, manipulated crime data, exaggerated reports of subversive activities, and tried to block activities in support of the civil rights movement. Nevertheless, Hoover's contributions to improved management of police work and to the effectiveness of the FBI are widely recognized.

County Agencies

Sheriffs are found in almost every one of the 3,080 counties in the United States.[4] They have the responsibility for policing rural areas, but over time many of their functions have been assumed by the state or local police. This is particularly true in portions of the Northeast. In parts of the South and West, however, the sheriff's office remains a well-organized force. In thirty-three of the states, sheriffs have broad authority, are elected, and occupy the position of chief law enforcement officer in the county. Even when the sheriff's office is well organized, it may lack jurisdiction over cities and towns. In addition to having law enforcement responsibilities, the sheriff is often an officer of the court and is charged with holding prisoners, serving court orders, and providing the bailiffs responsibile for maintaining order in court. In many counties, local politics determines appointments to the sheriff's office, whereas in other places, such as Los Angeles County (California) and Multnomah County (Oregon), the department is staffed by trained professional personnel.

Local Agencies

Though departments exist in more than 1,000 cities and 20,000 towns, only in the cities can they be said to perform all four of the police functions: keep the peace, apprehend law violators, prevent crime, and provide social services. Established by local government, the police of the cities and towns are vested by state law with general authority. The size of city police forces ranges from the more than 35,000 employees of the New York Police Department to the 987 localities with only one sworn officer. On a national basis this means that nearly 90 percent of the local police agencies serve populations of 25,000 or less; half of all sworn officers are employed in cities of at least 100,000.[5] The resulting ratio of officers to residents is 2.7 per 1,000, which is almost twice the average ratio for cities of fewer than 100,000.

In a metropolitan area composed of a central city and a number of independent suburbs, the policing function is usually divided among agencies at all governmental levels, and jurisdictional conflict may inhibit the efficient use of resources. In many large population areas agreements have been made so as to allow for cross-jurisdiction cooperation. America is essentially a nation of small police forces, each of which operates independently within the limits of its jurisdiction.

Courts

Although we may talk about *the* judiciary, the United States has a **dual court system,** consisting of a separate judicial structure for each state in addition to a national structure. Each system has its own series of courts, and the U.S. Supreme Court is the body in which the two systems are "brought together." Yet the Supreme Court does not have the right to review all decisions of state courts in criminal cases. It will hear only cases involving a federal law or those in which a right of the defendant under the Constitution is alleged to have

dual court system: A system consisting of a separate judicial structure for each state in addition to a national structure. Each case is tried in a court of the same jurisdiction as that of the law or laws broken.

been infringed—that is, a case in which the accused claims that one or more rights were denied during the state criminal proceeding.

With a dual court system, interpretation of the law can vary from state to state. Although states may have laws that are similarly worded, none of them interprets the laws in exactly the same way. To some extent these variations reflect varying social and political conditions. They may also represent attempts by state courts to solve similar problems by different means. But primarily, the diversity of legal doctrine results simply from fragmentation of the court system. Within the framework of each jurisdiction, judges have discretion to apply the law as they feel it should be applied until they are overruled by a higher court. The criminal law of auto theft, for example, thus depends not only on the laws written by the fifty state legislatures or by Congress but also on the development of interpretation in the judicial system of each state in addition to that of the federal government.

Each state's adjudicatory procedures have evolved through a blend of legislative enactments and judicial interpretation of both state and federal laws. Decisions made by criminal justice actors may be challenged as violating defendants' rights under the laws or constitution of the particular state or under the U.S. Constitution.

Federal Courts

Figure 4.3 shows the national court system arranged in a hierarchical manner, with the district courts at the base, the courts of appeals at the intermediate level, and the Supreme Court at the top. Ninety-four *U.S. District Courts* are the courts of original jurisdiction, or of first instance, in which federal cases are first heard and decisions of

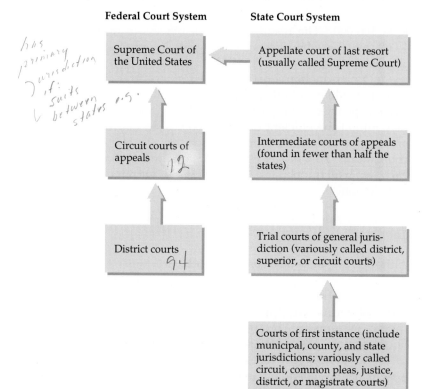

FIGURE 4.3
Dual court system of the United States and routes of appeal. Whether a case is processed through the U.S. or a state court system depends upon which law has been violated. There is the right of appeal to a higher court.

fact are made. Distributed throughout the country, with at least one in each state, one in the District of Columbia, and four in the U.S. territories, they hear the great majority of civil and criminal cases arising under federal law.

Above the federal district courts are twelve *U.S. Circuit Courts of Appeals,* each with jurisdiction for a geographic portion of the country and one for the District of Columbia. Created in 1891 as a means of reducing the case burden of the Supreme Court, this intermediate level of the judiciary hears appeals from the district courts and from such administrative bodies as the U.S. Tax Court and the National Labor Relations Board. From three to nine judges are assigned to each court of appeals, and normally three jurists sit as a panel.

The Constitution gives original (trial court) jurisdiction to the *U.S. Supreme Court* in only a few types of cases—suits between states, for example. The primary task of the high court is to hear appeals from the highest state courts and the lower federal courts. But as the highest court in the United States, it still retains discretion over the cases it will hear. Each year it rejects as unworthy of review 90 percent of the 2,000 cases that reach it. With nine justices appointed for life, the Supreme Court is probably the most influential judicial tribunal in the world. It reviews and attempts to maintain consistency in the law within the federal structure of the United States.

State Courts

One of the difficulties in describing the structure of state courts is that although they are all somewhat alike, they are all somewhat different. The laws of each state determine the organization of these courts; thus their names, their relationships to one another, and the rules governing their operation vary considerably. Still, one usually finds three levels of courts and a close resemblance between the pattern in the states and the organizational framework of the national judiciary. Note that state courts operate under the authority of state constitutions and should not be considered "inferior" to comparable courts in the national structure.

The powers of the approximately 13,000 *courts of limited jurisdiction,* often referred to as the "inferior" or "lower" trial courts, are limited to hearing the formal charges against accused persons in all cases, holding preliminary hearings involving crimes that must be adjudicated at a higher level, and conducting summary trials (where a jury is not allowed) and, in some states, trials of persons accused of some minor offenses. Generally, the law defines the court's jurisdiction according to the maximum jail sentence that may be imposed. Commonly, a fine of $1,000 and up to twelve months in jail is the greatest penalty that these courts may impose. About 90 percent of all criminal cases pass through these lower courts. In most places they are organized and funded by county government.

Especially in urban areas, the observer at these courts will find very little that resembles the dignity and formal procedures of higher courts. These are not courts of record (no detailed account of the proceedings is kept), and the activities are carried out in an informal atmosphere. In most urban areas, endless numbers of people are serviced by these courts, and each defendant gets only a small portion of what should be his or her day in court.

The *courts of general jurisdiction* have the authority to try all cases, both civil and criminal. With regard to criminal cases, they are often referred to as felony courts. They are courts of record in that the proceedings are recorded and they follow formal procedures specified by law. In large metropolitan areas, they commonly have divi-

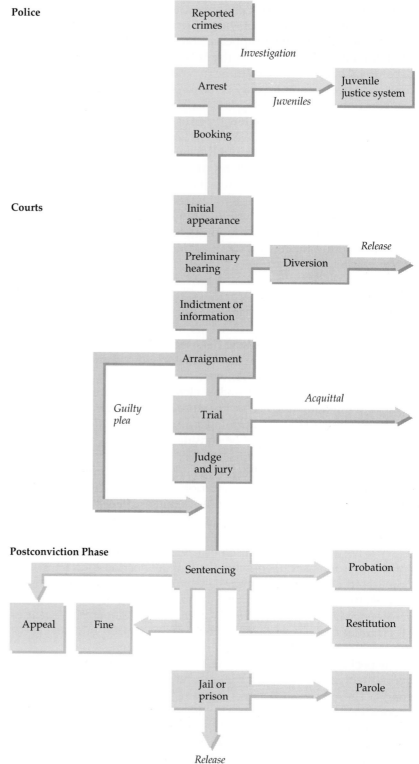

FIGURE 4.4
An overview of the criminal justice system. Note the various decisional points at which a case may be passed on to the next part of the process or may be dropped from the system.

sions that specialize in different kinds of cases. In addition to the original jurisdiction such courts exercise, which is their principal function, they also act on appeals by hearing defendants who contest decisions made at the inferior level. Most felony courts are funded by the state.

The *appellate courts* have no trial jurisdiction but hear only appeals from the lower courts. In some states only the state's supreme court—an appellate court of last resort—is found at this level; in others, an intermediate appellate court exists in addition to the state's highest judicial body.

One of the reforms undertaken during the past quarter century has been the development of intermediate appellate courts (IACs). In 1957 only thirteen states had such courts; today they are found in thirty-eight states, with plans being formulated in additional jurisdictions. These courts are designed to receive appeals from the trial courts so that the state supreme court (the court of last resort) has the discretion to hear only those appeals having widespread implications. Although the decisions of IACs may be reviewed by the supreme court, they are, in fact, final for most cases.[6]

State supreme courts normally sit *en banc* (as a whole), with all of the justices participating in the case, whereas intermediate appellate courts are usually divided up into groups of three judges, who sit as panels to hear cases.

Corrections

On any given day approximately 4 million Americans are under the care of the corrections system. Unlike agencies of the police and the courts, a "typical" correctional agency or activity is difficult to describe. The great variety of correctional institutions and programs are provided by public and private organizations, involving federal, state, and local governments and carried out in many different community and closed settings.

The average citizen probably equates corrections with prisons, but only about a third of convicted offenders are actually incarcerated; the remainder are under supervision in the community. Probation and parole have long been parts of the enterprise, as have community-based halfway houses, work release programs, and supervised activities.

The federal government, all the states, most counties, and all but the smallest cities are engaged in the corrections enterprise. Increasingly, nonprofit private organizations such as the YMCA have contracted with governments to perform correctional services. Of late, for-profit businesses have undertaken the construction and administration of institutions through contracts with governments.

THE FLOW OF DECISION MAKING

Although the flowchart of criminal justice decision making shown in Figure 4.4 may appear streamlined, with cases entering at the top and moving swiftly toward their disposition at the bottom, the route is long and has many detours. At every point along the way, decision makers have the option of moving a case on to the next point or dropping it from the system. The chart shows only the various processes involved at various points in the system. It is a blueprint of the criminal justice system, but it does not include the influences of the social relations of the actors or the political environment within which the system operates.

The popular "L. A. Law" image of an adversary system—in which the facts are determined in a public "battle" between defense and prosecution, with the judge acting as arbitrator of the contest— and even lawbook conceptions of due process goals are consistent with the ideal flow through the system presented in Figure 4.4. The police arrest a person suspected of violating the law and promptly bring the suspect to a judge. If the offense is minor, the judge disposes of the case immediately; if it is serious, the accused is held for further action and perhaps later released on bail. The case is next given to the prosecutor, who charges the offender with the specific crime after a preliminary hearing of the evidence. The defendant who pleads not guilty to the charge is held for trial. In the courtroom, the "fight" supervised by the judge is staged between the defense counsel and prosecutor. If the jury finds the defendant guilty, the judge announces the sentence, which is then carried out by corrections officials.

Although many cases do proceed in this way, this conception of the criminal justice flow is based on assumptions that do not correspond to the reality of most cases. It fails to take note of the many informal arrangements that are made through negotiation among the principal actors. Only a small number of cases ever reach the trial stage. Rather, decisions are made early in the process on the basis of discretion so that cases that may not result in conviction are filtered out by the police and prosecutor. In addition, in some jurisdictions up to 90 percent of defendants plead guilty, thus eliminating the need for a trial. Through **plea bargaining** between the prosecutor and defendant, a guilty plea is exchanged for reduction of the charges or for a recommendation of a reduced sentence. The enormous size of the prison population can be cited as justification of such practices.

plea bargaining: A defendant's pleading of guilty to a criminal charge with the reasonable expectation of receiving some consideration from the state for doing so, usually a reduction of the charge. The defendant's ultimate goal is a penalty lighter than the one formally warranted by the offense originally charged.

Many observers claim that these deviations from the formal blueprint have been brought about by the need to adapt a system created for a rural society to the realities of urban America, in which cases overload the system. More important, the use of shortcuts and other informal procedures reflects the adaptation of the criminal justice system to the personal and organizational needs of the administrators.

The Criminal Justice Wedding Cake

A linear depiction of the criminal justice process (such as shown in the flowchart of Figure 4.4) gives the impression that all cases are treated equally. What is not revealed is the third dimension of the system: the degrees of importance accorded to cases by the agencies and actors in the process and the ways in which this factor influences the allocation of justice.

FIGURE 4.5
The criminal justice wedding cake. This figure emphasizes the fact that different cases are treated in different ways. Only a very few cases are played out in the full dramatic "L. A. Law" style; the greatest number are handled administratively through plea bargaining and dismissals.
SOURCE: Drawn from Samuel Walker, *Sense and Nonsense about Crime Policy,* 2nd ed. (Pacific Grove, CA: Brooks/Cole, 1989), pp. 22–27.

Samuel Walker has suggested that although the flowchart is a notable aid to our understanding of the criminal justice system, an alternative model, the **criminal justice wedding cake,** is also enlightening.[7] According to this model, shown in Figure 4.5, criminal justice can be thought of as a set of layers, with different kinds of cases being handled in different fashions. The nature of a case has much to do with the way in which criminal justice officials and the public react to it. Four layers of the criminal justice wedding cake are described.

Layer 1 consists of those very few "celebrated" cases that are exceptional, get great public attention, result in a jury trial, and often run on in extended appeals. The cases of Leopold and Loeb, the Rosenbergs, Patty Hearst, John Hinckley, and Claus von Bülow are in this category. Not all cases in Layer 1 achieve national notoriety; from time to time local crimes, especially cases of murder and rape, are treated in this manner. The celebrated cases are like morality plays. Yet their importance lies in the fact that too often the public assumes that all criminal cases are handled in this manner.

Layer 2 consists of felonies that are deemed by officials to be serious: crimes of violence committed by persons with long criminal records against victims unknown to them. These are the cases that the police and the prosecutors consider important from the perspective of crime control and that result in "tough" sentences.

Layer 3 also consists of felonies, but the crimes and the offenders are seen as of lesser concern than those in Layer 2. They may involve the same offenses as in Layer 2, but the offender may have no record,

criminal justice wedding cake: A model of the criminal justice process in which criminal cases form a four-tiered hierarchy with a few celebrated cases at the top, and each succeeding layer increasing in size as its importance in the eyes of officials and the public diminishes.

There are very few "celebrated cases" such as that of Danish-born socialite Claus von Bülow, tried for the murder with insulin injections of his heiress wife.

and the victim may have had a prior relationship with the accused. When such cases occur, the primary goal of criminal justice officials is to dispose of them quickly. For this reason many are filtered out of the system, and plea bargaining is encouraged. It is at this level that we really begin to see the administrative rather than the adversarial system in operation.

Layer 4 is made up of misdemeanors. About 90 percent of all cases handled in the criminal justice system are found in this layer. They concern such offenses as public drunkenness, shoplifting, prostitution, disturbing the peace, and motor vehicle violations. Looked upon by officials as the "garbage" of the system, these cases are adjudicated in the lower courts, where speed is essential. Trials are rare, processes are informal, and fines, probation, or short jail sentences result. Assembly-line justice reigns.

The concept of the criminal justice wedding cake is a useful corrective to the flowchart perception of the system. Cases are not treated equally; some are viewed as very important by criminal justice officials; others as merely part of a mass that must be processed. When one knows the nature of a case, one can predict with some degree of confidence the way it will be handled and its outcome. Later we will emphasize the differential treatment of cases: for now, Figure 4.5 underscores for us the fact that officials' conceptions of what is "important" determine how cases are dealt with.

Movement of Cases

As we have seen, there are formal procedures for the handling of criminal cases, yet some offenders are given higher priority by justice officials because of the nature of their cases. At each step of the justice system, officials exercise discretion in ways that influence the defendant's fate. Many cases are filtered out of the system, others are forwarded with various charges, and still others go through informal processes.

We have seen that criminal justice is basically a function of local governments. Criminal justice policies and programs reflect local attitudes and values and change as attitudes and values change. Variations exist among cities and towns in the percentage of arrests for crimes that result in prosecution, conviction, and incarceration. Some of the differences can be explained by state laws and formal procedures; other differences may relate to the resources allocated to justice agencies; and still others arise because of special programs that have been developed in particular systems.

The process by which criminal justice agencies handle reported crime can be thought of as consisting of major steps of law enforcement, adjudication, and corrections. Although the terms used and the sequence of the steps vary in some parts of the United States, the flow of decision making shown in Table 4.1 is illustrative.

Law Enforcement

We may hold to the ideal of full enforcement, with resources allocated so that all criminal acts are discovered and all offenders caught, but the reality falls short of the ideal. Only a small portion of the crimes reported result in an investigation followed by arrest. This means that communities decide their enforcement policy and the allocation of police resources. Since the public is unable or unwilling to allow a policy of full enforcement (because it would be intolerable and expensive), decisions must be made as to the level of police resources desired and their distribution to various parts of the city.

Although the size of a city and the number of police it employs are closely correlated, measuring the level of needed law enforcement resources is difficult, and predicting the increase in protection that would result from the addition of police to the force is virtually impossible. A policy of concentrating patrol officers in sections of the city perceived as high-crime areas may become a self-fulfilling prophecy: more crimes may be discovered, thereby indicating a need for more officers. An independent study might reveal that any area with a large number of police officers will show a correspondingly high crime rate. Thus the policies of law enforcement decision makers have an important influence on the number of criminals caught and the types of cases solved.

Investigation

The flow of decision making begins when the police believe that a crime has been committed and an investigation is initiated. In this sense the police are the front-line agency charged with determining whether the criminal justice process should be invoked. This exercise of discretion is significant because a decision to do nothing may be as important as a decision to launch a full-scale investigation.

Only under special circumstances are the police able to observe illegal behavior. Thus law officers usually must react after receipt of information from a victim or other citizen who reports an incident. The fact that most crimes have already been committed and their perpetrators have left the scene before the police arrive places the police at an initial disadvantage. Since they have not witnessed the event, they must examine physical clues, question witnesses, determine whether a crime has been committed, and begin a search for the offender. Only in the case of certain categories of crimes, particularly those involving vice, can the police initiate the use of

TABLE 4.1 **Flow of decision making and responsible agency.** Each criminal justice agency is responsible for a portion of the decision-making system. Thus police, prosecution, courts, and corrections are bound together by a series of exchange relationships.

Criminal Justice Agencies	Process
1. Police	1. Investigation
	2. Arrest
	3. Booking
2. Prosecution and defense	4. Initial appearance
	5. Preliminary hearing
	6. Information or indictment (grand jury)
3. Court	7. Arraignment
	8. Trial or guilty plea
	9. Sentencing
4. Corrections	10. Probation or prison
	11. Parole or release

investigative techniques—for example, the use of informers, electronic surveillance, and undercover agents—to catch the criminal in the process of committing the illegal act.

Arrest

If a police officer finds enough evidence indicating that a particular person has committed a crime, an arrest may be made. From an administrative standpoint, arrest involves taking a person into custody, which not only restricts the suspect's freedom but also constitutes the initial steps toward prosecution.

What are the legal grounds for seizing citizens and putting them through the frightening experience of being taken into custody? Under some conditions, arrests may be made on the basis of a warrant—that is, an order issued by a judge who has received information pointing toward a particular person as the offender. In practice, most arrests are made without warrants. In some states, police officers may issue a summons or citation that orders a person to appear in court on a particular date, thus eliminating the need to hold the suspect physically until case disposition.

Booking

The immediate effect of arrest is that the suspect is usually transported to a police station for booking, the procedure by which an administrative record is made of the arrest. When booked, the suspect may be fingerprinted, interrogated, and placed in a lineup for identification by the victim or witnesses. All suspects must also be warned that they have the right to counsel, that they may remain silent, and that any statement they make may later be used against them. Bail may be set.

After arrest suspects are usually taken to the stationhouse for booking, a process during which key information and fingerprints are taken.

Adjudication

"Innocent until proved guilty" is a key concept of our criminal justice system. Although we tend to focus attention on the courts as the determiners of guilt or innocence, the process really begins when the police decide that a law has been violated and identify a suspect. These decisions provide the inputs to the adjudicatory process in which the evidence is closely examined by the prosecutor, judge, and jury. Throughout this process, the defendant, through counsel, may challenge the evidence, thereby creating adversarial tensions so that the case must be proved within the requirements of the law. Like the police, prosecutors and members of the bench may drop or dismiss the charges at any point in the process, thus filtering unsupported or doubtful cases out of the system.

Prosecuting attorneys provide the key link between the police and the courts. Their responsibility is to take the facts of the situation provided by the police and determine whether there is reasonable cause to believe that an offense was committed and whether the suspect committed it. The decision to prosecute is crucial because it sets in motion adjudication of the case.

Initial Appearance

Within a reasonable time after arrest, suspects must be brought for an initial appearance before a judge to be given formal notice of the charge for which they are being held, to be advised of their rights, and to be given the opportunity to post bail. Here the judge may determine that there is not sufficient evidence to warrant holding the suspect for further criminal processing, and the case may be dismissed.

Bail

The purpose of bail is to permit the accused to be released while awaiting trial. To ensure that the person will be in court at the appointed time, surety (or pledge), usually in the form of money or a bond, is required. In almost all jurisdictions, the amount of bail is based primarily on the judge's perception of the seriousness of the crime and the defendant's record. For accused persons who lack the necessary money for bail, a bondsman (a person who lends such cash) will provide the financing. Suspects may also be released on their own recognizance—a promise to appear in court at a later date—when the crime is minor and when it can be shown that they have ties in the community. In a limited number of cases bail may be denied and the accused detained because he or she is viewed as a threat to the community. Bail is extensively discussed in Chapter 10.

Preliminary Hearing

Even after suspects have been arrested, booked, and brought before a magistrate to be notified of the charge and advised of their rights, the evidence and probability of conviction must be evaluated before a decision is made that they should be held for prosecution. The preliminary hearing, used in about half the states, allows a judge to determine whether probable cause exists to believe that the accused committed a known crime within the jurisdiction of the court. If the judge does not find probable cause, the case is dismissed. If there is sufficient evidence, the accused is bound over for possible indictment, in grand jury states, or for arraignment on an information, in states without grand juries.

Jurisdictions vary in the nomenclature they use and in the order of each step during this stage of the process. What is uniform is that decisions are made at this point about whether the accused should be held to answer to the charges. The preliminary hearing is designed to prevent hasty and malicious prosecutions, to protect persons from mistakenly being humiliated in public, and to discover if there are substantial grounds upon which a prosecution may be based.

The preliminary hearing affords prosecutor and defense counsel an opportunity to get a glimpse of the cards held by the opponent. Here the prosecutor may decide that the probability of conviction is slight and that efforts directed against the accused would be more effectively expended elsewhere. Likewise, defense counsel may see that the accused does not have much of a case and thus may be more willing to seek a negotiated plea.

Information or Indictment

In the United States, people must be formally accused by means of either an indictment or an information before they can be required to stand trial on a felony criminal charge; the stated legal purpose of both is to make a preliminary finding that there is sufficient evidence to warrant further action by the state. The major difference between these procedures is that an information may be filed by the prosecutor on the basis of the findings of the preliminary hearing, whereas an indictment needs the concurrence of a grand jury. In states where the information is used, the grand jury proceeding is usually absent. In many states grand juries are used only for felony cases. The use of one form rather than the other is related in part to historical development.

The *grand jury* is composed of citizens (normally about twenty) who meet in closed hearings with the prosecutor. In the hearings they evaluate the materials gathered by the prosecutor on each case and issue an indictment if the evidence is sufficient. The grand jury originated in England as a device to gain knowledge from local people concerning matters of interest to the crown. It gradually became an instrument for the protection of the people against arbitrary accusations. This evolution brought about a reduction in the number of baseless allegations (statements without proof) presented to judges and allowed a degree of local control of prosecution.

Indictment through grand jury action has been criticized as costly and wasteful, yet the institution survives (see Figure 4.6). The grand jury's independence from the prosecutor has been questioned. As the only lawyer in the room, the prosecutor defines legal terms for the citizens on the grand jury and instructs them concerning their function. Not surprisingly, the relationship between them tends to be strongly influenced by the prestige and influence of the prosecutor and the inexperience of the jurors. The assembly-line aspects of the judicial process usually result in the waiving (giving up) of the right to a grand jury hearing in approximately 80 percent of cases; in the remainder, the prosecutor is usually able to secure the desired indictment. To the extent that the prosecutor is able to lead the members of the jury to feel that they are participating in the war against crime, he or she will be successful in securing the desired indictments.

From the defendants' standpoint, the information, with its requirement of a preliminary hearing, may have advantages over the indictment. They have the right to appear before the examining magistrate with counsel, to cross-examine witnesses, and to produce their own witnesses—rights they do not have before a grand jury. At the preliminary hearing, counsel is allowed to see the prosecutor's evidence against the defendant. With this knowledge, counsel is in a better position to structure plea negotiations.

Arraignment

During the arraignment phase, accused persons are taken before a judge to hear the formal information or indictment read and are asked to enter a plea. In addition, they are notified of their rights, a determination is made of their competence to stand trial, and counsel is appointed if they can establish their inability to pay for a lawyer. Defendants may enter a plea of guilty or not guilty, or in some states may stand mute. In some states they also have the option of pleading

FIGURE 4.6

Grand jury requirements. States use the grand jury for different offenses and in different ways. This once important part of the system has grown less important during the twentieth century. SOURCE: U.S. Department of Justice, *Report to the Nation on Crime and Justice*, 2nd ed. (Washington, DC: Government Printing Office, 1988), p. 72.

■ Grand Jury Indictment Required: All Crimes
■ Grand Jury Indictment Required: All Felonies
▢ Grand Jury Indictment Optional
■ Capital Crimes Only
▢ Grand Jury Lacks Authority to Indict

nolo contendere ("no contest"), which is the same as guilty except that the plea may not be used against them in later civil suits.

If a defendant enters a guilty plea, the judge must determine whether it is made voluntarily and whether the person has full knowledge of the possible consequences of the action. A judge who is not satisfied in these respects may refuse to accept the plea and enter "not guilty" in the record. The importance of the guilty plea is discussed in Chapter 10. Here we should recognize that when the plea is made, the accused is immediately scheduled for sentencing. At any time during the trial phase, the prosecutor may reduce the charge to a lesser offense that carries a correspondingly lighter sentence or may recommend that the judge deal leniently with the defendant in return for a plea of guilty, which eliminates the need for the time-consuming processes of a trial.

Courtroom

A visit to a criminal court in a metropolitan area is an educational experience. The noise and confusion that actually exist are in dramatic contrast to the dignified and precise procedure most visitors expect. The courtroom is often a cavernous space crowded with lawyers, defendants, and relatives. It is presided over by a judge sitting at one end, going through a procedure that can be heard only by those directly in front of the bench. Especially in misdemeanor cases, the informality and speed are startling to the observer and must be confusing to the defendant.

Trial

For the relatively small percentage of defendants who plead not guilty, the right to a trial by an impartial jury is guaranteed by the Sixth Amendment, but this right has been interpreted as an absolute requirement only when imprisonment for more than six months may result. In many jurisdictions, lesser charges do not command a jury. The use of juries is required in only a small number of cases; most trials are summary or bench trials—that is, they are conducted solely before a judge. National court statistics are unavailable, but it is estimated that only about 10 to 15 percent of cases go to trial and only about 5 percent of these are heard by juries. In felony cases the choice of a jury or bench trial is generally left to the defendant, with the nature of the crime, community norms, and the past record of the judge influencing the choice. Juries are waived in approximately 30 percent of murder prosecutions but in 90 percent of forgeries. It is widely assumed that because of court congestion, judges normally penalize defendants who do not waive their right to a jury trial by imposing longer sentences on the convicted.

Whether a criminal trial is held before a judge alone or before a judge and jury, the procedures are similar and are prescribed by law. A defendant may be found guilty only if the evidence proves beyond a reasonable doubt that he or she committed the offense. Rules prescribe the type of evidence that may be introduced, the way it may be obtained, and the way it is interpreted. The prosecutor's role is to present proof to substantiate the charge. The defense has an opportunity to challenge this proof by presenting alternative evidence or by questioning the validity of the prosecutor's case according to the rules of procedure. In a jury trial, the judge instructs the jurors concerning the laws applicable to the case before they depart to decide the defendant's fate. The elements of a trial are discussed in Chapter 12.

Sentencing

Judges have the responsibility of imposing sentences but, in the case of felonies, are usually assisted by an investigation and a presentence report prepared by the probation department. The report covers the offender's personal and social background, criminal history, and emotional characteristics, and studies show that judges usually follow the report's recommendation. In the sentencing phase, attention is focused on the offender; the intent is to make the sentence suitable to the particular offender within the requirements of the law and in accordance with the retribution (punishment) and rehabilitation goals of the criminal justice system. Although criminal codes place limitations on sentences, the judge still has leeway to consider alternatives: suspension, probation, prison, or fine. The level of the sentence also gives the trial judge tremendous choice, because legislatures typically set minimum and maximum limits but still allow for discretion.

Appeals

Defendants found guilty may appeal their conviction to a higher court. An appeal is based on claims that the rules of procedure were not properly followed by criminal justice officials or that the law forbidding the behavior that resulted in the charge is unconstitutional. Only recently have appeals of the terms of sentences been successful under some circumstances. In some states an appeal is automatically granted by the higher court; however, most law codes specify that the granting of an appeal is discretionary. The number of criminal trial verdicts appealed is small in comparison with the total number of convictions, and most such appeals (about 80 percent) result in an affirmation of the lower court decision.

Corrections

Execution of the court's sentence is the responsibility of the correctional subsystem. Apart from fines, which are usually collected by officers of the court, probation and incarceration are the sanctions most generally imposed.

Probation

Probation (fully discussed in Chapter 16) is a device to allow convicted offenders to serve their sentences in the community under supervision. Probation is used instead of incarceration, especially for the young first offenders and offenders convicted of minor violations. The conditions of probation require that offenders observe certain rules—be employed, maintain an orderly life, go to school—and report to their supervising officer as required. Probation officers are assigned to help offenders make their way in society and to see that the rules are followed. Violations of the conditions of probation may result in its cancellation by the judge and the imposition of a prison sentence.

Incarceration

Regardless of the reasons offered for incarceration (discussed in Chapter 15), prisons exist to segregate the criminal from the rest of society. Offenders convicted of misdemeanors usually serve their time in city or county jails, whereas felons serve their time in state prisons. Isolation from the community is probably the most overbearing characteristic of incarceration. Not only are visits from family members and correspondence restricted, but also supervision and censorship are ever present. In the name of internal security, prison officials justify unannounced searches and rigid discipline among the inmates.

Community Corrections

The idea of community corrections emphasizes that the goal of reintegrating the offender into society cannot be achieved behind prison walls. As a more realistic means toward this end, programs have been devised to give inmates opportunities to remake their ties to the community. Educational release, work release, and halfway houses are among the numerous alternatives to incarceration that are being explored.

Parole

Instituted in the United States near the turn of the century, parole is a feature of the criminal justice system of more than half the states, and a period of supervision after incarceration is required in most. After a portion of the prison sentence has been served, parole allows the offender to live in society under conditions similar to those of probation. Depending on the state's sentencing system, prisoners are given either a mandatory release after serving their time or discretionary release on the decision of the parole board. Parolees remain under supervision until the length of time represented by their maximum sentence has expired or for a period as specified by law. Parole may be revoked and the person returned to prison if the conditions of parole are not fulfilled or if the parolee commits another crime.

JUVENILE JUSTICE

Thus far attention has been focused on the processes by which adult offenders are arrested, judged, and punished. Until the turn of this century little effort was made to separate juvenile from adult offenders. With the rise of the Progressive movement in the early years of the century, states instituted separate criminal justice systems for juveniles. The focus of the reforms was on the courts, but special police units, detention facilities, and reformatories were also created to deal with juvenile delinquency. (See the back endpaper for a graphic description of the juvenile justice system.)

Until very recently a central emphasis of the juvenile courts was the appropriateness of a humanistic rather than legal perspective on the individual child accused of crime. Stress was placed on dealing with the juvenile much as a parent would deal with a child, searching for the reasons for the criminal behavior, and working out treatment programs that would be in the best interests of the individual. It was argued that the formal and adversarial aspects of the adult system, with its emphasis on rules, impeded efforts to reach the goals of juvenile justice. Thus juvenile courts were run in an informal manner, without attorneys, rules of evidence, juries, or observers. These elements of adult courts were to be replaced by a caring judge, a social worker, and the parents, who would work together to understand the child's problem and devise ways to prevent future waywardness.

Chapter 17 describes and analyzes the juvenile justice system in detail. As you examine the intervening chapters, bear in mind that adult—rather than juvenile—crime and the systems that deal with it are being discussed.

IMPACT ON THE VICTIM

In the concern about crime and the administration of justice, the victims are often forgotten. After crimes have been committed, victims often suffer loss, injury, and emotional trauma and are poorly treated by the agencies of criminal justice. Some say that they have been doubly victimized: by the criminal and by the system. Once the crime has been reported to the police, victims frequently say they are interrogated as if they themselves were responsible for the offense. Officials are rude to them, and they are called to appear in court repeatedly, only to be told that the case has been postponed, or, alternatively, they never hear another word about the incident and do not know if the criminal is still at large and ready to strike again. In addition, victims usually incur economic costs. Earnings may be lost because of court appearances, transportation must be paid for, and access to recovered property is denied pending trial. Unlike some European countries in which the victim may take part in the prosecution of the accused, the United States makes no provision for the victim's participation in the adjudicatory process other than as a provider of information to the police and prosecution or as a witness at the trial. It is society's interests that are being taken care of by the system, not the needs or desires of the victim.

During the past decade justice agencies have become increasingly sensitive to the interests of victims of crime. This sensitivity has resulted in part from the recognition that victims are often the only witnesses to the event in question, and their help is necessary if a conviction is to result. If economic and emotional costs are involved in assisting law enforcement and judicial officials, many citizens will not cooperate.

Abuse in the family presents the criminal justice system with a host of difficulties including detection of violations and the ability of children to provide evidence in court.

This awakened concern about the victims of crime is evident in the report of the President's Task Force on Victims of Crime.[8] The task force stressed the importance of achieving a balance between the needs and rights of the victim and those of the defendant. It urged that both be protected against intimidation, that restitution be required by the courts, and that the Sixth Amendment to the Constitution be changed so that the victim would have a right to participate in all of the critical judicial proceedings. In 1982 California voters passed Proposition 8, known as the "Victim's Bill of Rights" (see Table 4.2). As a result, California law now places greater emphasis on restitution, involves the victim more closely in the criminal justice process, and gives correspondingly less weight to the rights of the accused. Other states have followed this lead. In 1984 Congress

CLOSE-UP   *For Some Victims of Crimes, the Fear Never Leaves*

Blossom Jackson will never forget that November night when—at 10 minutes to 9—her sister-in-law pounded on the door of her small Brooklyn house screaming, "They've killed Jackson."

"I remember thinking, 'No. No. It's not Jackson, it's not my husband, it's not my Jackson,'" she said. "But it was. He was lying in the street, right across from our house. The police said a man shot him over a parking space."

Thousands . . . have had their lives shaken by violent crime, according to police statistics. And whether they have suffered through the murder of a husband or they themselves have survived an attack by a knife-wielding robber or a purse snatcher, the victims . . . have found their lives changed.

Some say fear and caution are now a part of their daily routine. For others, there is anger at a criminal justice system they believe has failed them. Still others say there is disappointment in their own cherished beliefs about people and a city they once loved.

Then there are . . . [those] who have been victimized so often that they have lost their fear and anger. Instead, they say, they have learned to live with threats and blows and thievery, as if these things were as natural as air and sun and rain.

For most, the crime itself is just the beginning.

It has been more than a year since Alfred Jackson, a thirty-eight-year-old Brooklyn plumber, was shot and killed by a neighbor because Mr. Jackson wanted to park in the spot where the man was walking his dog.

In the weeks that followed her husband's killing, Mrs. Jackson said she was numbed by shock. But gradually, the shock wore away, replaced by fear.

"I know now that anything can happen in this city," she said. "My husband was a good, hard-working man. He never carried a gun, he was never in trouble. But that didn't matter."

Mrs. Jackson said fear is now a part of her most ordinary days and her quietest nights. "I'm scared," Mrs. Jackson, the mother of five children, said. "I'm scared when I go to work, or go out shopping, or take the kids to school. I can't wait to get back home and lock the door."

"It's very hard," she said, sitting in the living room of her home. "Sometimes I feel like I'm falling apart."

The man who shot Alfred Jackson pleaded guilty to first-degree manslaughter, and last month he was sentenced to five to fifteen years in prison. With good behavior, he will serve ten years at the most.

Mrs. Jackson now works six days a week at two jobs to make ends meet. She lives in fear, and she worries about her children, who she said "spend too much time just staring at the walls and asking questions about Jackson's death."

Three months ago, Jan Chytillo, who works for the city, was mugged on a quiet street in a residential section of Queens. She said she and a friend had gone out to dinner that night and were walking home together at about 10 o'clock when a "very big, very tall man" accosted them and demanded their purses. When her friend resisted, he shoved her in the bushes, grabbed both purses, and then ran to a waiting car. He was never captured.

Today, just walking on a city sidewalk in broad daylight is a small ordeal that makes Mrs. Chytillo jumpy, nervous. "I feel very, very vulnerable," she said, "and I'm anxious, afraid, suspicious of almost everybody I see."

The twenty-eight-year-old woman said that for two months her husband had to meet her at the subway because "I was too frightened to walk home alone." Now, she said, "I'm always very aware of everything that's going on around me on the street, even in my own neighborhood, where I used to feel safe."

"When I leave the house, I watch out," she said. "I won't walk past a car that is double parked, and I won't walk on the side of the street where it happened."

"I'm convinced," she added, "that this is a very

passed the Federal Victims of Crime Act, which establishes a fund supported by fines; the states are to receive half for victim compensation programs and half for victim assistance programs.

Programs of information, assistance in time of crisis, and compensation have been inaugurated in many states to help meet the needs of crime victims. Information programs are designed to accomplish two goals: first, to sensitize justice officials to the need to treat crime victims courteously in order to secure their effective cooperation; second, to develop ways to let victims know what is happening at each stage of the case. In some states the investigating officer at the scene hands the crime victim a booklet containing information about the steps that will be taken and telephone numbers that can be called should questions arise. Assistance in time of crisis is most

scary city, and you have to have a lot more energy to live here—you have to be a lot tougher."

Edward Tede, a retired postman who lives in the Bronx, was attacked a month ago at a subway entrance in his neighborhood. It was late afternoon, he said, and he was returning home after visiting his wife in the hospital.

Suddenly, three young men jumped him. They grabbed his watch and his wallet, then hit him in the face. The blow sent him crashing to the ground and, when he got up, his glasses were smashed and a tooth was knocked out. Doctors later found that several of his cheekbones had been fractured.

Mr. Tede, a tall, strapping man even at age seventy-six, said that before the mugging, he went where he wanted, when he wanted, without fear.

Even though he said he is "determined not to dwell on this," he admitted, "I'm leery now when I go out." He said, "I try to stick with crowds of people. I don't want to be alone on the street or in the subway."

"I guess I'm more nervous," Mr. Tede said. "There is a tension—you can't get it out of your mind."

His wife, Jeanette, said the whole episode has left her "frightened and angry." She added: "You work hard all your life and try to be honest, then you get this."

She and her husband have lived in the same neighborhood for most of their lives. "And in one afternoon, those boys destroyed the sense of security we had here," she said.

"You know," she added, "they never caught them. That means they are still out there . . . and that's hard to live with."

For Louise Brooker of Manhattan, it is just as hard to live with the fact that her husband's killer was caught, and sentenced to "only seven to thirty years in jail. I mean, a man kills in cold blood—and he could be out of prison in seven years?" she asked.

Her husband, Eugene Brooker, was in a supermarket when five armed men came in to rob the place. When Mr. Brooker, who had a license to carry a gun, drew his pistol to try to stop the robbers, one of them fired a shot that killed him.

"The police were marvelous," Mrs. Brooker recalled. "They caught three of the men the night after it happened. But it was two years before they were sentenced to prison. There was no trial, just plea bargains."

Mrs. Brooker said she was "bitter about the judicial system."

"We will never be protected as long as people know they can commit a crime and be out in a few years," she said. "There is something very wrong with a system like that."

Her husband's murder shook her faith not only in the legal system, but in people as well.

"My husband and I were liberal people—giving the benefit of the doubt to everyone, bending over backwards to be fair," she recalled. "We used to believe that some groups of people—because of circumstances—couldn't help what they did. Now I think everyone must take responsibility for what they do. There is no excuse for them."

She said her grown son and daughter were "devastated" by the murder. Although they were raised in New York and loved it, she said, "both left, and they will never be back." They, too, she said, "lost all their liberal feelings."

Mrs. Brooker said she was careful in the city before her husband's death and is even more careful now. Like Mrs. Chytillo, she now has little rituals that she follows each time she stirs from the house—streets she avoids, jewelry she won't wear, house keys she hides in a pocket.

Last month, Mrs. Brooker sold the family store, and she is now thinking of moving to another city.

SOURCE: From "For Some Victims of Crime, the Fear Never Leaves," by B. Basler, *The New York Times*, May 5, 1981, p. B6. Copyright © 1981 by The New York Times Company. Reprinted by permission.

TABLE 4.2 Crime victim's Bill of Rights

Victims of crimes have the right:

1. to protection from criminal violence
2. to be kept informed by law enforcement agencies of their investigation of a crime
3. to be kept informed by the district attorney as to the progress of a criminal case
4. to be notified of any discretionary disposition of a case
5. to be notified of any release of the defendant after conviction
6. to be notified of any change in the defendant's status
7. to be informed of financial and social services available to crime victims
8. to be provided with appropriate employer intercession services
9. to be provided with adequate witness compensation
10. to be provided with a secure waiting area during court proceedings
11. to receive adequate protection from threats of harm arising out of cooperation with law enforcement personnel
12. to have any stolen or other personal property held by law enforcement offices returned as soon as possible
13. to be represented by an attorney for certain types of cases
14. to be made whole through restitution and/or civil law recovery
15. to have perpetrators prevented from being enriched by their crimes at the victim's expense.

SOURCE: Reprinted by permission from *Victimology: An International Journal* 5 (1980): 428–37. Copyright © 1982 Victimology, Inc. All rights reserved.

important when the victim faces medical, emotional, or financial problems as a result of a crime; rape crisis centers, prosecutors' victim assistance programs, and family shelters are among the means that have been adopted. Compensation programs in most states (see Table 4.3) now supplement the assistance offered to victims of violent crime by crisis centers and provide for payment of the medical expenses of those who cannot meet them without help. When property has been stolen or destroyed, compensation programs serve to encourage judges to order restitution.

CRIMINAL JUSTICE IN AN ORGANIZATIONAL SETTING

A major factor that distinguishes modern from traditional or primitive societies is the domination of the contemporary world by large, complex, formal organizations. Modern society, characterized by a highly advanced division of labor and bureaucratization, places a premium on rationality, effectiveness, and efficiency. Organizations are designed to coordinate human activity in specific areas in ways that will enhance these qualities without producing unsatisfactory consequences. Analysis of bureaucracy's unique characteristics— hierarchical structure, division of labor, rules, and career employees—has so influenced our understanding of formal organizations that the terms **bureaucracy** and *organization* are often used synonymously.

The criminal justice system has not escaped the tendency toward the creation of formal organizations. To achieve the goals of criminal justice, many and varied organizational subunits, each with its own personnel, functions, and responsibilities, have been developed. As a result, administration of the system is presumably an orderly

bureaucracy: A form of administrative organization, characterized by depersonalized, rule-bound, and hierarchically structured relationships, that efficiently produces highly predictable, rationalized results.

TABLE 4.3 **Range of financial awards available to victims of violent crimes and qualifications to be met, by state.** The victims' rights movement has encouraged states to develop programs of compensation for those injured by violent crimes. Many victims report that they have difficulty meeting the criteria of the program in their state. Should the state compensate victims?

| State | Financial Award | To Qualify, Victim Must— | | |
		Show Financial Need	Report to Police within:	File Claim within:
Alabama	$0–10,000	No	3 days	12 months
Alaska	$0–40,000	Yes	5	24
Arizona	**	Yes	3	**
California	$100–46,000	Yes	*	12
Colorado	$25–10,000	No	3	6
Connecticut	$100–10,000	No	5	24
Delaware	$25–20,000	No	*	12
D.C.	$100–25,000	Yes	7	6
Florida	$0–10,000	Yes	3	12
Hawaii	$0–10,000	No	*	18
Idaho	$0–25,000	No	3	12
Illinois	$0–25,000	No	3	12
Indiana	$100–10,000	No	2	24
Iowa	$0–20,000	No	1	6
Kansas	$100–10,000	Yes	3	12
Kentucky	$0–25,000	Yes	2	12
Louisiana	$100–10,000	No	3	12
Maryland	$0–45,000	Yes	2	6
Massachusetts	$0–25,000	No	2	12
Michigan	$200–15,000	Yes	2	12
Minnesota	$100–50,000	No	5	12
Missouri	$200–10,000	No	2	12
Montana	$0–25,000	No	3	12
Nebraska	$0–10,000	Yes	3	24
Nevada	$0–15,000	Yes	5	12
New Jersey	$0–25,000	No	90	24
New Mexico	$0–12,500	No	30	12
New York	$0–30,000†	Yes	7	12
North Carolinaª	$100–20,000		3	24
North Dakota	$0–25,000	No	3	12
Ohio	$0–25,000	No	3	12
Oklahoma	$0–10,000	No	3	12
Oregon	$250–23,000	No	3	6
Pennsylvania	$0–35,000	No	3	12
Rhode Island	$0–25,000	No	10	24
South Carolina	$100–3,000	No	2	6
Tennessee	$0–5,000	No	2	12
Texas	$0–25,000	No	3	6
Utah	$0–25,000	**	7	12
Virgin Islands	Up to $25,000	No	1	24
Virginia	$0–15,000	No	5	24
Washington	$0–15,000†	No	3	12
West Virginia	$0–35,000	No	3	24
Wisconsin	$0–40,000	No	5	12

ªNorth Carolina's program is administratively established but not funded.
*Must report but no time limit specified
**No reference in statute
†Plus unlimited medical expenses

SOURCE: U.S. Department of Justice, *Report to the Nation on Crime and Justice,* 2nd ed. (Washington, DC: Government Printing Office, 1988), p. 37.

continuum in which a variety of professionals act upon the accused in the interests of society.

But if we are to understand the criminal justice system, we must know more than the way an organization chart says it is *supposed* to work. To assist us in this task, we can use concepts that social scientists have developed to analyze other public organizations. These concepts can help us understand how the criminal justice system functions and why it works as it does. We can then discuss possibilities of change in the administration of criminal justice.

System Perspective

Critics often say that criminal justice is a "nonsystem." They make this charge because they do not think that the administration of justice in America conforms with the formal blueprints or organization charts that outline the process or with the traditional notions of the way the system is *supposed* to work.

system: A complex whole consisting of interdependent parts whose operations are directed toward goals and are influenced by the environment within which they function.

Although the concept of **system** does imply some unity of purpose and an interrelationship among parts, it does not assume that organizations will act as rationally ordered machines. Criminal justice is a living system made up of a number of parts, or subsystems, each with its own goals and needs. The parts of an organization are interdependent; that is, changes in the operation of one unit will bring about changes in other units. An increase in the number of felony cases processed, for example, will affect the work not only of the clerks and judges of the criminal court but also of the police, prosecution, probation, and correctional subsystems. As a system, therefore, criminal justice is made up of a set of interacting parts—all the institutions and processes by which criminal justice decisions are made—and for criminal justice to achieve its goals, each must make its own distinctive contribution. None can function without at least minimal contact with at least one other part.

Before we continue to develop this conceptual framework, it is necessary to clarify certain assumptions. First, the system is an open one; new cases, changes in organizational personnel, and shifting conditions in the political system mean that the criminal justice system is forced to deal with constant variations in its environment. Second, a state of scarcity exists within the system. The shortages of resources (time, money, information, personnel) characteristic of bureaucracies prevent the system from processing every case in accordance with formally prescribed criteria. The subunits of criminal justice—police, prosecutor, courts, corrections—are forced to compete with one another for available resources. Central to these ideas is the politics of administration, the range of interactions between an agency and its environment that augment, retain, or diminish the basic resources needed to attain organizational goals.

Although understanding the dynamics of an operating system is important, we must also see how individual actors play their parts. The criminal justice system is, of course, made up of a great many persons whose jobs require them to perform specific roles. Therefore, the focus at this microlevel is on individual and group behavior. A key tool for analysis of the relationships among individual decision makers is the concept of **exchange.** Developed mainly by social psychologists, exchange theory views interpersonal behavior as resulting from the weighing by individuals of the values and costs of alternatives. A central position of exchange theory is that of reciprocity, according to which behavior responds to the rewards and punishments the individual receives.

When an agreement is made between a defense attorney and prosecutor in regard to the terms of a guilty plea, presumably an exchange takes place; that is, their decision results from some trade of valued resources. In this example, the exchange was probably a guilty plea in return for a reduction of charges. Such face-to-face relationships are found throughout the criminal justice system. The concept of exchange makes us aware that decisions are the products of interactions among individuals and that the major subsystems—police, prosecutor, court, and corrections—are tied together by the actions of individual decision makers.

The concepts of system and exchange are closely linked, and their value as tools for the analysis of criminal justice cannot be overemphasized. In this book, these concepts serve as the organizing framework within which individual subsystems and actors are described. Organizations do not exist in a vacuum, untouched by the forces around them. With this emphasis, we can hope to understand the nature of the American system of criminal justice, evaluate its components, and work toward its improvement.

System Characteristics

An organization can be described in terms of the functions it performs, the names of the actors, the value of the resources it produces, or the special ways its tasks are pursued. We have already discussed many of the agencies of criminal justice, but we have not yet looked at their methods of operation. Three special attributes—discretion, resource dependence, and sequential tasks—characterize the work of the criminal justice system. Other organizations contain one or more of these features, but few contain all three.

Discretion

At all levels of the justice process there is a high degree of **discretion,** the ability of officials to act according to their own judgment and conscience (see Table 4.4). The fact that discretion exists throughout the criminal justice system may seem odd given that our country is ruled by law and has created procedures to ensure that decisions are made in accordance with that law. However, instead of a mechanistic system in which law rather than human decision making prevails, criminal justice is a system in which the participants—police officer, prosecutor, judge, and correctional official—may consider a wide variety of circumstances and exercise many options as they dispose of a case. The need for discretionary power has been justified primarily on two counts: resources and justice. If every violation of the law were to be formally processed, the costs would be staggering. Additionally, the belief exists that in many cases justice can be more

exchange: A mutual transfer of resources; hence, a balance of benefits and deficits that flow from behavior based on decisions as to the values and costs of alternatives.

discretion: The authority to make decisions without reference to specific rules or facts, using instead one's own judgment; allows for individualization and informality in the administration of justice.

TABLE 4.4 Who exercises discretion? Discretion is exercised by various individuals throughout the criminal justice system. What influences these decisions?

These *Criminal Justice* *Officials . . .*	*. . . Must Often Decide* *Whether, or How, to:*
Police	Enforce specific laws Investigate specific crimes Search people, vicinities, buildings Arrest or detain people
Prosecutors	File charges or petitions for adjudication Seek indictments Drop cases Reduce charges
Judges or *magistrates*	Set bail or conditions for release Accept pleas Determine delinquency Dismiss charges Impose sentence Revoke probation
Correctional *officials*	Assign to type of correctional facility Award privileges Punish for infractions of discipline Determine date and conditions of parole Revoke parole

SOURCE: U.S. Department of Justice, *Report to the Nation on Crime and Justice,* 2nd ed. (Washington, DC: Government Printing Office, 1988), p. 59.

fully achieved through informal procedures. Any system that professes to promote individualized justice must allow for the use of discretion.

Resource Dependence

The criminal justice system does not produce its own resources but is dependent on others for them. It must therefore develop special links with people responsible for the allocation of resources—that is, the political decision makers. Criminal justice actors must be responsive to the legislators, mayors, and city council members who hold the power of the purse. Further, the system relies on citizens for its raw materials. Too often we think of citizens primarily in the role of violator, with the police in the role of enforcer. In fact, the discretionary decisions of citizens to report crime to the police are a principal input of the system and constitute a resource that helps to maintain it.

Sequential Tasks

Every part of the criminal justice system has distinct sequential tasks. This means that each subunit is granted jurisdiction over particular decisions and each has discretion over what to create or accept as inputs and whether to send these inputs on to the next level as outputs. Performance of the tasks must flow efficiently from police to prosecutor to judge to corrections or probation officer. Since a high degree of interdependence exists, the actions of one part directly affect the work of the others. The courts can deal only with the cases brought to them by the prosecutor, who can deal only with persons arrested by the police. Not every person arrested, however, arrives in the courtroom. On the contrary, a filtering process removes those cases that the relevant person—police officer, prosecutor, or judge—feels should not be passed on to the next level.

DECISION MAKING IN AN EXCHANGE SYSTEM

The concept of system emphasizes that organizations are made up of parts that are purposefully linked for the accomplishment of a common end. Yet systems exist in a social and political environment, which thus influences such factors as the level of resources allocated, the laws to be enforced, and the internal decisions of each of the various parts. Accordingly, the administration of criminal justice can be viewed as a system in which prosecution, the subunits of police, courts, and corrections are integrated to achieve an overriding objective, while the work of each is affected by the conditions and interests specific to its own portion of the process.

Because the criminal justice system is a continuum, with the actions of each component dependent on the work of prior units, decisions are greatly affected by the system's interrelated activities. Prosecution cannot proceed without an arrest and evidence, the judge requires the cooperation of the prosecution and defense, and the correctional caseload is influenced by the judge's sentencing practice. From this perspective one might ask the following:

1. Why do these agencies cooperate?
2. What might happen if the police refused to transfer information to the prosecutor concerning the commission of a crime?
3. What are the tensions existing between the police and the courts?
4. Do agencies maintain a form of "bureaucratic accounting" that, in a sense, keeps track of favors owed?
5. How are cues transmitted among agencies to influence decision making?

These are some of the questions posed when decisions are viewed as resulting from an exchange system.

The Basis for Exchange

The concept of exchange is based on the notion of the marketplace, in which inputs and outputs, or resources and products, are traded among persons and systems. Exchange is thus a bargaining activity that involves the transfer of certain resources among organizations and individual people and that has consequences for common goals. The person who furnishes rewarding services (favors) to another acquires a debtor; to discharge the obligation, the debtor must return some benefit. Continued exchange relationships generate a sense of trust between the system's participants, which in turn promotes a cooperative attitude that is strengthened by the organization's reward structure. For example, the help the prosecutor receives from the defense attorney who has encouraged a client to plead guilty produces benefits for both, because the case is more speedily moved.

Instead of assuming that a criminal justice agency, such as the police, needs to use only its statutory authority as it works in the bureaucratic world, we should recognize that each agency interacts with many clients on whom it depends for resources. In an exchange system, an organization owes its power and influence largely to its ability to develop clients that will support and enhance its needs. Although the justice system is characterized by the interdependence of its parts, each subunit is in competition with other public agencies outside the system. Since criminal justice agencies operate in an economy of scarcity and are faced with more claims than they can fulfill with available resources, the system must thus occupy a favorable power position vis-a-vis its clientele. Many of the exchange rela-

COMPARATIVE PERSPECTIVE
Criminal Justice in the People's Republic of China

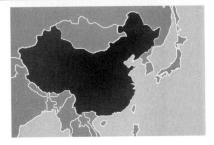

From the standpoint of the revolutionary ideology that brought about modern China under the leadership of Mao, law is viewed as a tool of the ruling class to be exercised to further the goals of the Communist Party and the workers and peasants that are the basis for government in that country. Since Mao's death a competing revisionist line has emerged that has reassessed the radical reforms of the Great Leap Forward, has restored material incentives, and has brought about a greater centralization to decision making. The new elite has emphasized the need for rapid modernization to be led by technical specialists and administrators who will work in organizations free from supervision of the party or community bodies.

Justice policy, institutional jurisdiction, and the definition of crime itself have been strained and tossed between these two lines [revolutionary and revisionist]. China has in fact developed two justice systems: a bureaucratic justice based on formal legal agencies and operated by more or less specialized professionals; and the popular justice institutions sponsored by the vast national network of community organizations and activated by millions of volunteers. . . .

Bureaucratic Justice: Order and Professionalism

The bureaucratic justice system is a natural consequence of the conserv-

ative [revisionist] notion that the Chinese revolution has been completed. Advocates argue that law is vital to consolidate past gains, regulate future changes, ensure production, and protect state authority. A set of multitiered bureaucracies is entrusted, under China's constitution, with the legal powers in a check-and-balance arrangement that in theory is designed to protect due process and maintain social order:

1. *People's courts* are a hierarchy of three-judge courts that decide cases at law and hear appeals. Law-trained professionals and lay judges serve together, with equal voting rights.
2. The *procurate* is charged with preparing evidence for prosecution at trials and with systematic review of legal procedures in other bureaus (especially the police). The procurate has been the most professional of the justice agencies, and its regular staff includes many law-trained specialists.
3. The *Ministry of Public Security* serves as local and national police and is responsible for arrests, investigation, the operation of walled prisons and the more numerous labor reform brigades, and the supervision of citizens placed under mass control (roughly analogous to probation). . . .

4. *Ministry of Control or Party Control Commissions* are internal investigation bureaus that hear complaints and prepare charges against government or party officials who have violated the law. . . .

The justice bureaucracies, especially the courts and procurate, have pressed for complete codification of criminal laws, procedures, and jurisdictional guidelines. They have asserted, in a manner not unlike Western or Soviet justice officials, that legal authority should be concentrated in the hands of trained specialists, who would themselves be regulated by law, bureaucratic routines, and professional ethics. . . . This system seeks to manage and control the process of social change and to put an end to the more revolutionary upheavals of the past.

Popular Justice: Integrative and Combative

The popular justice system has been historically linked to revolutionary-line ideals. Popular institutions do contribute to the

tionships between agencies within the system are necessitated not only by statutes mandating their participation in decision making but also by the system's needs.

The concept of an exchange system also helps clarify the influence of decisions made in one justice agency on the relationships and decisions made in the other parts of the judicial process. Figure 4.7 illustrates the exchange relationships between the prosecutor and other units in the system.

Lateral relationships are also necessary because the outputs of one subsystem become the inputs of the next (see Figure 4.8). A judge's verdict in a felony case affects the arresting officer's record, the prosecutor's conviction rate, and the credibility of the probation

protection of social order, but there is also an explicit commitment to social justice and egalitarian reform. The mass organizations at local workplaces and residential communities sponsor their own internal peacekeeping bodies, which function as auxiliaries to the regular police and as lay representative in the people's courts. . . .

While the bureaucratic ideal defines crime as a specific act proscribed and sanctioned by law, the popular justice approach emphasizes the offender's social background and motivations. The mass organizations play a crucial role in this process. Study, criticism, self-criticism, and correction within millions of intimate small groups are so continuous and ubiquitous that one hesitates to call it by such formal terms as "investigation, classification, and sanction." Only when the deviant fails to respond to informal pressures . . . or when the offense is considered extremely serious, does the state intervene with the formal agencies of control, the police, and courts.

. . .

In sum, popular justice has both an integrative and a combative function in China, the main elements of which may be summarized as:

1. The mass organizations sponsor internal peacekeeping bodies that include security defense teams and militia forces (volunteer police) and also mediation teams (to arbitrate quarrels). These bodies serve as auxiliaries to the justice professionals.

2. The local small groups involve perhaps a dozen co-workers or neighbors in weekly meetings to discuss politics and local problems and to correct conflicts, misunderstandings, and egotistic attitudes through the process of criticism and self-criticism.

3. Representatives of mass organizations participate within the bureaucratic justice agencies, most notably as people's assessors, who sit alongside professional jurists in the courts.

4. Systematic monitoring of government officials at the local level is handled by the people's supervisory committees and at other levels by the ratification committees, both of which are charged to compile and forward accusations against leadership.

5. The public has been repeatedly mobilized for mass campaigns, which have been directed at the correction of major social inequalities and fundamental political problems, resulting in massive changes in social policy and reorganization of government.

6. The suppression of class enemies, political corruption, and bureaucratic abuse has been entrusted to temporary nonprofessional judges sitting in people's tribunals. Such tribunals systematically involve mass organizations as both witnesses and as judges, but the tribunals are usually disbanded when the given mass campaign passes.

Between bureaucratic and popular justice there has been compromise, coexistence, and conflict but not steady amalgamation of the two. The bureaucrats have sought to make popular justice a reliable auxiliary, discarding the more combative functions. . . . The radicals . . . have sought to popularize the bureaucratic agencies through the infusion of critics and activists into the ranks of the police; through anti-elitist political education of judges, police, and procurators . . . and through the incorporation of the mass line principles into the national constitution of 1975 and the procedural guidelines of the justice bureaus. At present . . . the conservatives [revisionists] are very much dominant in China, and as might be expected they have pressed for extensive codification, legal professionalism, and expansion of the justice bureaus, while limiting and combating popular justice. It remains to be seen whether the more combative aspects of popular justice can be laid to rest without sacrificing public support and volunteer participation in the peacekeeping auxiliaries.

SOURCE: Adapted from "People's Republic of China," by J. P. Brady. In E. H. Johnson (ed.), Vol. 2, International Handbook of Contemporary Developments in Criminology, pp. 111–117. Copyright © 1983 by Greenwood Press. Reprinted by permission of Greenwood Publishing Group, Inc., Westport, CT.

officer's sentencing recommendation. An official's decisions are often made in anticipation of a judge's reaction. For example, knowledge that a judge customarily gives lenient sentences or fines for certain types of offenses may discourage the police from making arrests in such cases.

The interdependence of a system is often likened to "jello." Others have referred to a system's "hydraulic" effect: when one part is squeezed, there is an impact on the other parts of the system. For example, when the number of prisoners reached the riot point, the warden urged the courts to slow down the flow. Accordingly, inmates were let out on parole, and the number of persons given probation and suspended sentences increased. One could speculate that the prosecutor viewing this behavior by the judges would reduce the inputs to the courts either by not preferring charges or by increasing the pressure for guilty pleas through bargaining. Adjustments of other parts of the system could be expected to follow. For instance, the police might sense the prosecutor's reluctance to accept charges and hence be willing to present only airtight cases for indictment. One of the consequences of the problem of prison overcrowding is that correctional officials have had to let offenders out early when facilities are jammed. This has repercussions throughout the system.

Remember that interactions within organizations result from the decisions and actions of real persons; exchanges do not simply sail from one subsystem to another but take place in an institutionalized setting. Agreements are made between persons occupying boundary-spanning roles who set the conditions under which the exchange will occur. How decisions are made depends on how the actors play their roles and their perceptions of the others in the interaction.

Although the formal structures of the judicial process stress antagonistic and competitive subunits, exchange relationships strengthen cooperation within the system, thus deflecting it from its adversarial goals. For example, although the prosecutor and defense counsel play roles that are prescribed as antagonistic, continued interaction on the job, in professional associations, and in political and social groups may produce a friendship that greatly alters the way they play their roles. Combat in the courtroom, as ordained by the formal structure, may not only endanger the personal relationship

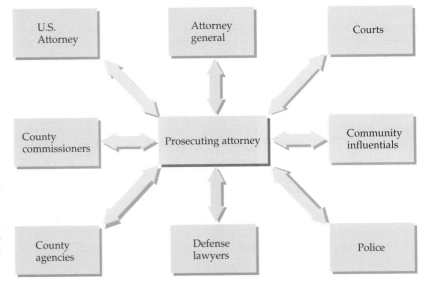

FIGURE 4.7
Exchange relationships between prosecutors and others. The prosecutor's decisions are influenced by the relationships that are maintained with other criminal justice agencies, governmental units, and community influentials.

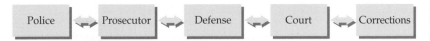

but also expose the actors' personal weaknesses to their own clienteles. Neither the judge, the prosecutor, nor the defense attorney wants to look unprepared in public. Rather than encouraging the unpredictability and professional insecurity stressed by the system, decisions on cases may be made in such a way as to bring mutual benefits to the actors in the exchange.

Exchange relationships are enhanced by the fact that each actor in the administration of justice has substantial discretionary power. Each patrol officer is able to make his or her own decisions regarding arrest in most circumstances involving minor crimes. The decision to prosecute is frequently in the hands of the individual prosecutor as a result of exchanges with individual police officers and criminal lawyers.

Thus far, this section has indicated that the justice system is composed of a number of interdependent subunits and that the work of each influences the activities of the others. Decisions concerning the operation of the system are influenced by the exchange relationships of the participants. The personal and organizational needs or goals of each member of the relationship may supersede the formally prescribed rules and procedures. Accommodations are made to maintain these relationships.

Criminal Justice as a Filtering Process

The criminal justice process may be viewed as a **filtering process** through which cases are screened: some are advanced to the next level of decision making, and others are either rejected or the conditions under which they are processed are changed. As shown by Figure 4.9, persons who have been arrested are filtered out of the system at various points in the process. Note that very few of the suspects arrested are prosecuted, tried, and convicted. At each stage decisions are made by officials as to which cases will proceed to the next level. Some arrestees go free because the police decide that a crime has not been committed or that the evidence is not sound. The prosecutor may drop charges thinking that conviction will not be possible or that justice would be better served through diversion. Great numbers of those indicted will plead guilty, the judge may dismiss the charges against others, the jury may acquit a few defendants, while most of those who go to trial will be found guilty. Various options are available to the judge at the time of sentencing and thus some offenders will go to prison, while others will serve their time in the community. The "funnel-like" nature of the criminal justice system results in many cases entering at the top, but owing to the filtering process, only a small portion are convicted and punished.

filtering process: A screening operation; hence, a process by which criminal justice officials screen out some cases while advancing others to the next level of decision making.

The System in Operation

Organizations exist within a social context in which the subunits and personnel find some activities rewarding and others tension producing. The policies followed in an exchange system will evolve to

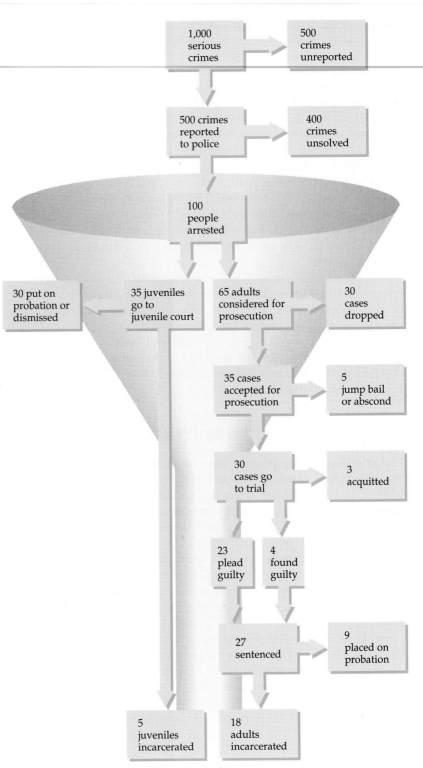

FIGURE 4.9
Criminal justice as a filtering process.
The system acts as a filtering process.
Decisions made at each point of the
criminal justice system result in some
cases being dropped, while others
pass to the next decisional point. Are
you surprised that such a small
portion of cases remains?
SOURCE: Data from this figure have been
drawn from many sources, including
U.S. Department of Justice, *Sourcebook of
Criminal Justice Statistics, 1990* (Washington,
DC: Government Printing Office, 1991);
Bureau of Justice Statistics, *Bulletin*
(January 1988, February 1989).

maximize gains and minimize stress. The administration of justice is
greatly affected by the values of decision makers, whose careers,
influence, and positions may be more important to them than consideration for the formal requirements of the law. Thus when decisions
that might be disruptive are contemplated, accommodations are
sought within the exchange system. Exchange relationships, the

norms of efficiency, good public relations, and the maintenance of harmony and esprit de corps among underlings have a great effect on the operations of the system.

The Place of the Defendant

Of central concern is the place of defendants in the administrative process. Because they pass through the system (and justice actors remain), the defendants may become secondary figures in the bureaucratic setting. Officials may view defendants and their cases as challenges or as temporarily disruptive influences. The tensions that individual cases may produce are repressed, because system personnel must be able to interact on the basis of exchange in the future. Since these relations must be maintained, pressures may be brought to dispose of cases in a manner that will help to sustain the existing linkages within the system.

The disposition of a case depends to a great extent on the negotiating skill of the accused's counsel. By exposing weaknesses in the state's case, counsel may convince the prosecutor of the futility of proceeding to trial. Alternatively, counsel may help to convince the defendant of the strength of the prosecution's case and urge bargaining for a lesser charge in exchange for a guilty plea. In some jurisdictions the filtering process works so well that, statistically, if the prosecutor says a person is guilty, the person is guilty. From the standpoint of the Crime Control Model, the courts increasingly become tribunals of last resort after the administrators of the system have made their decisions.

Most research indicates that the values of the administrative or Crime Control Model are widely held by police, prosecutors, court officials, and even defense attorneys. The tenor of comments by these actors reveals that the conditions under which decisions are made contribute to the assumption and reinforcement of those values. As one experienced prosecutor told the author, "We know that more than 80 percent of these guys are guilty. After a while you get so that you can look at the sheet [case record] and tell what is going to happen." Similar attitudes have been expressed by judges of the lower trial courts and by attorneys who depend on criminal cases for a major portion of their work. A startling example is the judge who says that he assumes that defendants who have survived the scrutiny of the police and prosecutor must be guilty.

SUMMARY

Society has charged the criminal justice system with prevention and control of crime within the framework of law and of our cultural values. Although this goal may seem clear, a view of the criminal justice system in operation reveals that a number of value decisions must be made at each point in the law enforcement, adjudication, and corrections process about the best way to fulfill the purpose of criminal justice.

In the United States, the operations of criminal justice are distributed among federal, state, and local agencies. Most criminal justice agencies, including the special agencies created to deal with juvenile crimes, operate at the local level, under the authority of counties and municipalities. The federal government has jurisdiction over only a limited number of crimes, primarily those affecting the national interest and some offenses involving the crossing of state lines. At each level of government, the law specifies the jurisdiction of the agencies and the procedures that must be followed throughout the process. The Constitution of the United States is the major tie that binds the activities together.

The criminal justice system can be viewed as an organization with goals antagonistic to those posited by the Due Process Model. Decisions concerning the disposition of cases are influenced by the selective nature of a filtering process in which administrative discretion and interpersonal exchange relationships are extremely important. At each level of decision making, judicial actors are able to determine which types of crimes will come to official notice, which kinds of offenders will be processed, and the degree of enthusiasm that will be brought to the effort to secure a conviction.

FOR DISCUSSION

1. In recent years, increased stress has been placed on the accumulation of criminal and personal data in national computer banks. What are the implications of this development for crime control? For civil liberties?
2. In our increasingly urbanized society, increased coordination among law enforcement agencies may be desirable. What problems would such a development present?
3. What means could prevent the misuse of discretion?
4. Organization of the police in metropolitan areas is often a hodgepodge of overlapping jurisdictions, with lack of cooperation among city, county, and local forces. Although some may argue that one law enforcement agency for an entire metropolitan area would be more effective, what arguments can be offered in support of the continuation of the present arrangement?
5. What are the goals of the criminal justice system? Which goals seem most important?

FOR FURTHER READING

Davis, Kenneth Culp. *Discretionary Justice*. Baton Rouge: Louisiana State University Press, 1969. A classic examination of the role of discretion in a system of law.
Lurigio, Arthur J., Wesley G. Skogan, and Robert C. Davis, eds. *Victims of Crime*. Newbury Park, CA: Sage, 1990. An excellent collection of articles concerning the impact of crime on victims and the efforts to assist them.
Poveda, Tony. *Lawlessness and Reform: The FBI in Transition*. Pacific Grove, CA: Brooks/Cole, 1990. A critical inquiry into the post-Hoover, post-Watergate FBI. Poveda asks what is distinctive about this "new" FBI?

Walker, Samuel. *Sense and Nonsense about Crime: A Policy Guide.* 2nd ed. Pacific Grove, CA: Brooks/Cole, 1989. An examination of those crime control practices that don't work (the "nonsense") and those that appear to have some potential for success (the "sense").

Wilbanks, William. *The Myth of a Racist Criminal Justice System.* Pacific Grove, CA: Brooks/Cole, 1987. Summarizes and critiques the research literature concerning racial discrimination in the criminal justice system.

NOTES

1. *New York Times,* December 23, 1984, p. 1.
2. U.S. Department of Justice, Bureau of Justice Statistics, "Profile of State and Local Law Enforcement Agencies, 1987," *Bulletin* (March 1989); U.S. Department of Justice, Bureau of Justice Statistics, *Sourcebook of Criminal Justice Statistics, 1988* (Washington, DC: Government Printing Office, 1989), p. 29.
3. Malcolm M. Anderson, *Policing the World: Interpol and the Politics of International Police Cooperation* (Oxford: Clarendon Press, 1989).
4. Ibid.
5. Ibid.
6. Joy A. Chapper and Roger A. Hanson, *Intermediate Appellate Courts: Improving Case Processing* (Williamsburg, VA: National Center for State Courts, 1990).
7. Samuel Walker, *Sense and Nonsense about Crime: A Policy Guide,* 2nd ed. (Pacific Grove, CA: Brooks/Cole, 1989), p. 22. Walker bases his analysis on the work of Lawrence M. Friedman and Robert V. Percival, *The Roots of Justice: Crime and Punishment in Alameda County, California, 1870–1910* (Chapel Hill: University of North Carolina Press, 1981) and Michael R. Gottfredson and Don M. Gottfredson, *Decision Making in Criminal Justice: Toward the Rational Exercise of Discretion* (Cambridge, MA: Ballinger, 1980).
8. President's Task Force on Victims of Crime, *Final Report* (Washington, DC: Government Printing Office, 1982).

The People versus Donald Payne

An 18-year-old named Donald Payne came handcuffed and sullen into the [courthouse] building last year—a tall, spidery, black dropout charged with the attempted armed robbery and attempted murder of a white liquor-store owner in a "changing" fringe neighborhood. The police report told it simply: ". . . At 2100 [9 p.m.] . . . August 4, 1970 . . . victim stated that two male Negroes entered his store and the taller of the two came out with a gun and announced that this is a holdup, 'give me all of your money.' With this the victim . . . walked away from the area of the cash register. When he did this, the smaller offender shouted 'shoot him.' The taller offender aimed the pistol at him and pulled the trigger about two or three times. The weapon failed to fire. The offenders then fled. . . ." It was a botched job—nobody was hurt and nothing stolen—and so Payne in one sense was only another integer in the numbing statistics of American crime.

Donald Payne's passage from stick-up to stationhouse to jail to court and finally into the shadow world of prison says more than any law text or flow chart about the realities of crime and punishment in America. The quality

Payne being fingerprinted: laboring imperfectly toward a rough approximation of justice.

of justice in Chicago is neither very much better nor very much worse than in any major American city. The agents of justice in Chicago are typically overworked, understaffed, disconnected, case-hardened, and impossibly rushed. Payne protested his innocence to them every step of the way, even after he pleaded guilty. There is, given the evidence, no compelling reason to believe him, and no one did—least of all the lawyer who represented him. So the agents of justice handed him and his case file along toward a resolution that satisfied none of them wholly. "That we really have a criminal-justice system is a fallacy," remarked Hans Mattick, co-director of the Center for Studies in Criminal Justice at the University of Chicago Law

School. "A system is artificially created out of no system. What we have is a case-disposition system." In the winter of 1970–1971, the system disposed of *People* vs. *Payne*—and the sum of Donald Payne's case and tens of thousands more just like it across the nation is the real story of justice in America.

The Defendant

They fought over Donald Payne, home against street, a war of the worlds recapitulated ten thousand times every day in the ghetto; only, when you live in a ghetto, you can never get far enough away from the street to be sure of the outcome. Payne's mother tried. Her first husband deserted her and their four kids when Donnie, the baby, was still little. But she kept them together and, thirteen years ago, was married to Cleophilus Todd, a dark, rumbly-voiced man who preaches Sundays in the store-front Greater Mount Sinai M. B. (for Missionary Baptist) Church and works weekdays to keep his family and his ministry afloat. She bore two more children and worked some of the time to supplement the family's income; and two years ago they were able to put enough together to escape the gang-infested section where Donald grew up and move into a little green-and-white frame house in a fringe working-class neighborhood called Roseland. . . . But it may have come too late for Donald. He had already begun sliding out of school: it bored him ("They'd be repeatin' the same things over and over again, goin' over the same thing, the same thing") so he started skipping, and when the school called about him, he would pick up the phone and put it back on the hook without saying anything. *Maybe I thought it was too much happenin' out there in the streets to be goin' to school.* Or church either. "They have to go to church long as they live with us," says Cleophilus Todd. For years, Donald did: he spent his Sunday mornings in the peeling, blue-curtained storefront, shouting gospel in the choir, listening to his stepfather demanding repentance of a little congregation of women and small children in the mismatched, second-hand pews and hardwood theater seats. But it got claustrophobic on Mount Sinai. "I just slowed down," Payne says. "I started sayin' I'd go next Sunday, and then I wouldn't. And then I just stopped."

The street was winning. Payne showed a knack for electricity; he made a couple of lamps

and a radio in the school shop before he stopped going and brought them home to his mother, and she would ask him why he didn't think about trade school. "He could fix everything from a light to a television set," she says. "He was all right as long as he was busy. Only time you had to worry about him was when he had nothin' to do." He did work sometimes, two jobs at once for a while and once he talked to a man working on a house about how you get into electrical work. The man told him about apprenticeships and gave him the address of his union. "But I just hated to travel. It bored me even when I was workin'—I just hated to take that trip. So I kept puttin' it off and puttin' it off." . . .

Nobody knows, really, why the street swallows up so many of them. Poverty in the midst of affluence is surely part of it, and color in the midst of whiteness; so are heroin and broken homes and the sheer get-it-now impulsiveness of life in so empty and so chancy a place as a ghetto. But no one can say which ones will go wrong—why a Donald Payne, for example, will get in trouble while three brothers and two sisters come up straight. "I told 'em all," says Todd. "I'm not going to be spending all my time and money on jail cases for you doing something you don't need to get into." Only Donald got into it. . . .

Still, he did get run in a few times for disorderly conduct, routine for kids in the ghetto street. And, in 1968, he was arrested for burglary.

It was a kid-stuff, filling-station job, two tires and a sign, and Payne was caught with the tires a few blocks away. He insisted he was only trying to help

a friend sell them, but Todd says he confessed to the family ("Sometimes it makes no difference how good a kid is or how good he is brought up") and he wound up pleading guilty in a deal for a few days in jail and two years on probation. It came to little: probation in theory is a means to rehabilitation, but probation offices in fact, in Chicago and around the country, tend to have too many cases and too little time to do much active rehabilitating. Payne's papers were lost for several months until he finally got scared and came in to find out why no one had called him. After that, he reported once every month, riding two hours on buses to see his probation officer for ten minutes. "We talked about was I workin' and how was I doin' out on the street—that was all." Once the probation officer referred him to a job counselor. Payne never went, and no one seems to have noticed.

And now, at 18, he is in big trouble. . . .

The Victim

A voice said, "I want that." Joe Castelli looked up from the till, and there across the counter stood this tall colored kid with an insolent grin and a small-caliber, blue-steel automatic not 4 feet from Castelli's face. . . .

And finally the tall one with the blue-steel .25 and the scornful half-smile—the one Castelli identified later as Donald Payne. He and another, smaller youth came in the out door that cool August evening, just as Castelli was stuffing $250 or $300 in receipts from cash register No. 2 in his pocket. "I want that," the tall one said. Castelli edged away. "Shoot him! Shoot him!" the small one yelled. The tall one started at Castelli and poked the gun across the counter at him. "Mother f---er," he said. He squeezed the trigger, maybe once, maybe two or three times.

The gun went *click*.

The two youths turned and ran. Castelli started after them, bumped against the end of the counter and went down. He got up and dashed outside, but the youths disappeared down a dark alley. An old white man emptying garbage saw them go by. The tall one pointed the pistol toward the sky and squeezed again. This time it went off.

A clerk from across the street came over and told Castelli that a woman had seen the boys earlier getting out of a black Ford. "People around here notice things like that," Castelli says. "They watch." Castelli found the car parked nearby and wrote down the license number. The driver— a third Negro youth—followed him back to the store. "What you taking my license for?" he demanded. "I was just waiting for my wife—I took her to the doctor." He stood there yelling for a while, but some of Castelli's white neighbors crowded into the store, and the black youth left. Castelli went back into the street, flagged down an unmarked police car he recognized and handed over the number, and the hunt was on.

The Cops

The evening was clear and mellow for August, a cool 67° and breezy. Patrolman Joe Higgins nosed his unmarked squad car through the night places of the Gresham police district, watching the alleys and storefronts slide past, half-listening to the low staccato of the radio, exchanging short hand grunts with his partner, Tom Cullen,

■

Cullen and Higgins work on the case.

slouched low in the seat beside him. They had been riding for three humdrum hours when, shortly after 9 p.m., they picked up the call: gunfire in the street up in the north reaches of the district. The two cops glanced at one another. Cullen got the mike out of the glove compartment and radioed: "Six-sixty going in." Higgins hit the accelerator and snaked through the sluggish night traffic toward Shop-Rite Liquors—and the middle of his own neighborhood.

. . . Higgins lives just a few blocks from Shop-Rite; he has traded there for twenty years, and when he saw Joe Castelli waving in the streets that August evening, he forgot about the shooting call and hit the brakes fast. Castelli blurted out the story and gave Higgins the license number of the black Ford. But it checked out to a fake address—a schoolyard—and Higgins and Cullen spent the next six hours

cruising the dark, fighting drowsiness and looking.

It was near first light when they spotted the car, parked in a deserted industrial area with two Negro runaways, 13 and 17 years old, curled up asleep inside. The two patrolmen rousted the boys out, searched the car—and found the blue-steel .25 under a jacket in the front seat. One of the boys, thoroughly scared, led them to a 17-year-old named James Hamilton* who admitted having driven the car but not having gone into the store. Hamilton led them to his kid cousin, Frank, who admitted having gone into the store but not having handled the gun or clicked the trigger. And Frank Hamilton led them to Donald Payne.

And so, red-eyed and boneweary, Higgins and Cullen, along with a district sergeant and two robbery detectives, went to the little green-and-white frame house in Roseland at 9 a.m. and rang the bell. Payne's sister let them in and pointed the way upstairs.

Payne was sleeping when the cops crowded into his little attic bedroom and he came awake cool and mean. "Get moving," someone said. "You're under arrest." The police started rummaging around while Payne, jawing all the while, pulled on a pair of green pants and a red jacket. "You don't have no warrant," he said. As Payne told it later, one of the cops replied, "We got a lawyer on our hands." But Higgins insists he misunderstood—"What I said was we'd get him a lawyer."

They marched him out in handcuffs past his mother, took him to the district station and shackled him to a chair while one of the officers started tapping out

*The names of Hamilton and his cousin have been changed since both are juveniles.

an arrest report: PAYNE DONALD M/N [for male Negro] 18 4-19-52. . . ." Higgins got Castelli on the phone. "It's Joe," he said, "come in—we think we've got the man." Castelli came in with DeAngelo. The cops put Payne into a little back room with a few stray blacks. Castelli picked him out—and that, for the cops, was enough. Payne was taken to the South Side branch police headquarters to be booked, then led before a magistrate who set bond at $10,000. The bounty is a paper figure: the Chicago courts require only 10 percent cash. But Payne didn't have it, and by mid-afternoon he was on his way by police van to the Cook County Jail.

Joe Higgins and Tom Cullen by then had worked twelve hours overtime; in four hours more, Tac Unit 660 was due on patrol again. They talked a little about Donald Payne. "He had a head on him," Cullen said in some wonder. "Maybe if he didn't have a chip on his shoulder. Maybe—"

The Defender

Connie Xinos disliked Donald Payne from the beginning. They met in October in the prisoners' lockup behind Judge Fitzgerald's courtroom, and all Xinos had to go on then was the police report and Payne's public-defender questionnaire ("All I know is I was arrested for attempted murder on August 5") and that insinuating half smile. *He did it*, Xinos thought; all of them except the scared children and the streetwise old pros swear they are innocent, but you get a feeling. And that smile. *He's cocky*, Xinos thought. *A bad kid.* Xinos has been at it less than four years, but four years in the bullpens is a long time. He thinks Chicago is dying. And he thinks thousands

of black street kids much like Donald Payne—his clients—are doing the killing.

Xinos is 30, the son of a Greek cafeteria owner bred in the white Chicago suburbs, a stumpy young bachelor with quizzical eyes, a shock of straight, dark hair and a Marine Reserve pin glinting gold in the lapel of his three-piece suit. He came to the building a year out of John Marshall Law School, hoping for a job as an assistant state's attorney ("It seemed to be glamorous—you don't get parking tickets and you carry a gun") but hungry enough for steady pay and trial experience to settle for what he could get.

The state's attorney had no openings, so he went upstairs to see public defender Gerald Getty. . . .

Ideals die young in a public defender's office. Chicago's is one of the oldest and best in the U.S.; it was organized in 1930, three decades before the Supreme

■

Xinos: "I was very liberal when I started."

Court asserted the right of the poor to counsel in any felony case, and its staff now numbers 68 mostly young and energetic lawyers. But they remain enormously overworked, partly because crime rates keep rising, partly because all the defendants' rights announced by the High Court in the 1960s have vastly increased and complicated their caseload. Xinos and his colleagues, squeezed in four desks to a cubicle, handle more than half of Cook County's yearly 3,700 criminal cases; their clients are 70 percent black and typically too poor either to hire private lawyers or to make bail pending trial. At any given time, says Xinos, "I got a hundred guys sitting over there in County Jail wondering if Xinos is working on my case out there." And he knows the most he will be able to do for 90 percent of them is "cop them out"—plead them guilty—"and look for the best deal you can get."

That they are all nominally innocent under the law is little more than a technicality: public and private defenders learn quickly to presume guilt in most cases and work from there. "I tell 'em I don't have to presume innocence," says one senior hand in the office. "That's a legal principle, but it doesn't have to operate in a lawyer's office." It stops operating when a rookie lawyer discovers that practically all his clients come in insisting that they didn't do it. "You can almost number the stories," says one of Xinos's colleagues, Ronald Himel. " 'I walked into the alley to urinate and I found the TV set.' 'Somebody gave me the tires.' Well, God forbid it should be true and I don't believe you. My first case out of law school, the guy told me he walked around the corner and found the TV set. So I put that on [in court]. The judge pushed his glasses down his nose, hunched up and said, 'Fifty-two years I have been walking the streets and alleys of Chicago and I have never, ever found a TV set.' Then he got me in his chambers and said, 'Are you f---ing crazy?' I said, 'That's what he told me.' The judge said, 'And you *believed* that s---? You're goofier than he is!' "

Xinos learned fast. . . . "It's our court." Xinos says. "It's like a family. Me, the prosecutors, the judges, we're all friends. I drink with the prosecutors. I give the judge a Christmas present, he gives me a Christmas present." And you learn technique. The evidence game. The little touches: "The defendant should smile a lot." The big disparities: which judge gives eighteen months for a wife-killing and which one gives twenty to forty years. How to make time and the caseload work for you. "The last thing you want to do is rush to trial. You let the case ride. Everybody gets friendly. A case is continued ten or fifteen times, and nobody cares any more. The victims don't care. Everybody just wants to get rid of the case." Then you can plead your man guilty and deal for reduced charges or probation or short time. You swing.

Xinos took an apartment in the distant suburbs, . . .

And, like any commuter, he tries to leave it all at the office. The ones you can't are the few you plead guilty when you really believe they are innocent: "When you're scared of losing. When they've got a case and you believe your guy but you lose your faith in the jury system. You get scared, and he gets scared and you plead him." But the Donald

Paynes—the great majority of his cases—are different. Xinos never liked Payne; Payne fought him, and Xinos much prefers the pros who tell you, "Hey, public defender, I killed the f---er, now get me off." Xinos thought Payne should plead guilty and go for short time. But Payne clung to Standard Alibi Number Umpty-one ("I was home at the time this was supposed to have broke out") and demanded a trial, so Xinos gave him the best shot he could. He had to lay aside his misgivings—his upset at crime in the streets and his suspicion that Payne was part of it. "Me letting ten or twenty guys out on the street isn't going to change that," he says. "This violence—it's like Niagara Falls. You can't stop it."

The Jail

He clambered down out of the van with the rest of the day's catch and was marched through a tunnel into a white-tiled basement receiving area. He was questioned, lectured, classified, stripped, showered, photographed, fingerprinted, X-rayed for TB, bloodtested for VD and handed a mimeographed sheet of RULES OF THE COOK COUNTY JAIL. (". . . You will not escape from this institution. . . . You will be safe while you are in this institution. . . .") He says he was marked down as a Blackstone Ranger over his objections—"I told them I was a little old to be gang-bangin' "—and assigned to a teen-age tier, E-4. He was issued a wristband, an ID card and a ceiling ticket, led upstairs and checked into a tiny 4-by-8 cell with an open toilet, a double bunk, two sheets, a blanket and a roommate. The door slammed shut, and Donald Payne— charged with but still presumed innocent of attempted robbery

and attempted murder—began nearly four and a half months behind bars waiting for his trial.

Jails have long been the scandal of American justice; nobody even knew how many there were until a recent federal census counted them (there are 4,037)— and found many of their 160,000 inmates locked into what one official called "less than human conditions of overcrowding and filth." And few big-city jails have had histories more doleful than Cook County's. The chunky, gray fortress was thought rather a model of penology when Anton Cermak started it in 1927. But its first warden hanged himself, and its last but two, an amiable patronage princeling named Jack Johnson, was sacked when a series of investigations found the jail ridden with drugs, whisky and homosexual rape and run by inmate bully boys.

Johnson gave way to warden (and now director of corrections) Winston Moore, 41, a round black buddha with wounded eyes, short-shaven hair, a master's and a start on a doctorate in psychology and some iron-handed notions about managing jails and jail inmates. Moore's mostly black reform administration has tamed the inmate tier bosses, cleaned up the cells and the prisoners, repainted the place for the first time, hired more guards at better pay, started some pioneering work and work-training programs, opened an oil-painting studio in the basement room where the county electric chair used to be and begged free performances by B. B. King, Ramsey Lewis, Roberta Flack, and even, minus the nude scene, the Chicago company of "Hair." But there has never been enough cash, and lately the John Howard Association, a citizens' watchdog group that gave Moore top marks for the first year, has turned on him with a series of reports charging a miscellany of cruelties within the walls. And worst of all is the desperate overcrowding. The rise in crime and the slowing processes of justice have flooded Moore's 1,300 claustrophobic cells with 2,000 prisoners, most of them doubled up at such close quarters that if one inmate wants to use the toilet, the other has to climb on the bunk to let him by.

Roughly 85 percent of the inmates are Negro, and most, like Donald Payne, are stuck inside because they are too poor to make bail—not because they have been convicted of crimes. But the presumption of guilt infects a jail as it does so much of American justice, and Moore squanders little sympathy on his charges. He came up in black New Orleans, the son of a mailman struggling for decency, and when any of his inmates blames his troubles on hard times or bad conditions, Moore explodes: "Bulls---! Don't give me that—I was there too, I know what it's like and I made it. You got in trouble because you wanted to get in trouble."

. . . He has small pity for the Donald Paynes and enormous scorn for those white liberals who seem more concerned with explaining them than with punishing them. It is there that he sees the real racism of the system—"These bleeding liberals who have so much guilt that they can justify blacks killing blacks because we're immature. They're the ones that want to keep you immature. Quit justifying why I kill my buddies on Saturday night and try to stop me from doing it."

Moore has no such tender feelings; he lays on rock concerts and painting classes but he also maintains The Hole—a tier of isolation cells into which the hard cases are thrown with no beds, no day-room privileges, no cigarettes, no candy bars, no visitors, nothing to do but lie or sit or squat on a blanket on the floor and wait for the days to go by. "You will always have to have a place like The Hole," Moore says without a hint of apology. "Much of the problem of crime is immaturity, and the greatest reflection of immaturity is rage—blind rage. There is no other way to contain it." The Hole nevertheless is a degrading place for people on both sides of the bars. The men crouch like caged animals, eyes glinting in the half light. The guards in The Hole wear white because the men throw food at them and white is easier to launder.

It took Donald Payne less than twenty-four hours to get there.

He came onto tier E-4 angry at being put with the gang kids and shortly ran into a youth from his block who had been a member of the Gangsters. "He had me classified as a Gangster, too," Payne says. "He thought I was just scared to say cause we were on a Blackstone tier. He ran up in my face and wanted to fight. We had a fight and I went to The Hole for thirty days and he got fifteen."

So they gave Payne a cage, and he sat it out. What do you do? "You sit on the toilet. You wait for the food to come around." What do you think about? "Gettin' out." How do you feel about The Hole leaving it? "It didn't matter much." Not enough, in any case, to keep him out: he went straight back in four days for sassing a guard,

emerged with a reputation as a troublemaker with a "quick attitude" and later did thirty more when Moore's men put down a noisy Blackstone hunger strike on E-4. After that, Payne was transferred to a men's tier and did a bit better. "Those Rangers," he says, "they keep talkin' about killin' up people. What they did when they was outside. What they gonna do when they get out." The older men by contrast idled away their time in the daytime playing chess and cards and dominoes. They taught Payne chess and let him sit in. "People over here been playin' five and six years," he says, grinning a little. "They're pretty good, too. But I don't wanta be that good."

All the while, his case inched through the courts. Illinois requires that the state bring an accused man to trial within 120 days or turn him loose—a deadline that eases the worst of the courthouse delays and the jailhouse jam-ups that afflict other cities. But the average wait in jail still drags out to six or seven months, occasionally because the state asks for more time (it can get one sixty-day extension for good cause), more often because delay can be the best defense strategy in an overloaded system. Evidence goes stale; witnesses disappear or lose interest; cases pile up; prosecutors are tempted to bargain. "You could get twenty years on this thing," Constantine Xinos, the assistant public defender who drew Donald Payne, told him when they met. "Don't be in a hurry to go to trial."

Waiting naturally comes easier to a man out on bail than to one behind bars, but Payne sat and waited. On August 24, nineteen days after his arrest, he went from The Hole down to the basement tunnel to the courthouse, stripped naked for a search, then dressed and was led upstairs for a hearing in Room 402—Violence Court. Room 402 is a dismal, soot-streaked place, its business an unending bleak procession of men charged with armed robbery, rape and murder, its scarred old pews crowded with cops, witnesses, wives, mothers and girl friends jumbled uncomfortably together. Payne waited in the lockup until a clerk bellowed his name, then stood before Judge John Hechinger in a ragged semicircle with his mother, the cops, the victims, an assistant state's attorney and an assistant public defender and listened to the prosecution briefly rehearse the facts of the case.

Frank Hamilton—Payne's alleged accomplice—by then had been turned over to the juvenile authorities, and Hechinger dismissed the case against James, the driver of the car, for want of evidence that he had had anything to do with the holdup. But he ordered Payne held for the grand jury. The day in court lasted a matter of minutes; Payne was shuffled back through the lockup, the nude search, the

■

Parrish: "I don't want to hurt the kid."

basement tunnel and into The Hole again. On September 18, word came over that the grand jury had indicted him for attempted armed robbery (gun) and attempted murder, and the case shortly thereafter was assigned to Circuit Judge Richard Fitzgerald for trial.

So Payne waited some more, and the rhythm and the regularity of the life inside crept into his blood. Connie Xinos, appalled by the surge in black crime, thinks it might help a little to put one of those tiny cells on display on a street corner in the middle of the ghetto as an object lesson. But, talking with Donald Payne, one begins to wonder about its power as a deterrent. Payne was irritated by the days he spent in court; nobody brings you lunch there. "I sort of got adjusted to jail life," he says. "It seems like home now."

The Trial

Everybody kept trying to talk him out of his trial. "Plead guilty, jackass, you could get ten to twenty for this," Xinos whispered when they finally got to trial. *Ain't no need for that*, said Payne. "You really want a jury?" the assistant state's attorney, Walter Parrish, teased him. "Or you want to plead?" *I want my trial*, said Payne. Everything in the building says cop out, make a deal, take the short time. "They ought to carve it in stone over the door," an old courthouse hand, then a prosecutor and now a judge, told a friend once. "NO CASE EVER GOES TO TRIAL HERE." The People vs. Donald Payne did get to trial, halfway at least. But then his case went sour, and the deal got sweeter, and in the end Donald Payne copped out, too.

Practically everybody does: Urban justice in America would

quite simply collapse if even a major fraction of the suspects who now plead guilty should suddenly start demanding jury trials. The Payne case was only one of 500 indictments on Judge Richard Fitzgerald's docket last year; it would have taken him four years to try them all. So 85 to 90 percent of them ended in plea bargaining—that backstairs haggling process by which pleas of guilty are bartered for reduced charges or shorter sentences or probation. "Plea bargaining used to be a nasty word," says Fitzgerald; only lately have the bar and the courts begun to call it out of the closet and recognize it not as just a reality but a necessity of the system. "We're saying, 'You're doing it, we know you're doing it and you have to do it; this is the way it has to be done.' "

The pressures to plead are sometimes cruel, the risks of going to trial high and well-advertised. There is, for waverers, the cautionary tale of one man who turned down one to three years on a deal—and got 40 to 80 as an object lesson when a jury convicted him. Still, Payne insisted, and Xinos painstakingly put a defense together. He opened with a pair of preliminary motions, one arguing that the pistol was inadmissible because the evidence tying it to Payne was hearsay, the other contending that the police should have offered Payne a lawyer at the line-up but didn't. The witnesses straggled in for a hearing on December 1. Joe Castelli took the stand, and Patrolman Cullen, and, for a few monosyllabic moments, Payne himself. Had anyone advised him of his rights to a lawyer? "No." Or let him make a phone call? "No." But another of the arresting officers, Robert

Krueger, said that Payne had been told his rights—and such swearing contests almost always are decided in favor of the police. Everybody admired Xinos's energy and craftsmanship. Nevertheless, Fitzgerald denied both of the defense motions and docketed the case for trial on December 14.

And so they all gathered that wintry Monday in Fitzgerald's sixth-floor courtroom, a great dim cave with marbled and oak-paneled walls, pitted linoleum floors and judge, jury, lawyers, defendant and gallery so widely separated that nobody could hear anything without microphones. Choosing a jury took two hours that day, two the next morning. Parrish, an angular, Ivy-cut Negro of 41, worked without a shopping list. "I know some lawyers say fat people are jolly and Germans are strict," he says, "but none of that's true in my experience. If you get twelve people who say they'll listen, you're all right."

But Xinos is a hunch player. He got two blacks on the jury and was particularly pleased with one of them, a light-skinned Urban League member who looked as if she might be sympathetic. And he deliberately let one hard hat sit on the panel. Xinos had a point to make about the pistol—you couldn't click it more than once without pulling back the slide to cock it—and the hard hat looked as if he knew guns.

That afternoon, slowly and methodically, Parrish began to put on his case. He opened with the victims, and Castelli laid the story on the record: "About ten after 9, the gentleman walked in. . . . He had a small-caliber pistol. . . . I edged away. . . . The other lad came up to me and he said, 'Shoot him, shoot him,

shoot him.' . . . [The first youth] pointed the gun at me and fired three times or four—at least I heard three clicks." And the gunman—did Castelli see him in court?

"Yes I do, sir."

"And would you point him out, please?"

Castelli gestured toward the single table shared by the prosecution and defense. "That," he said, "is Donald Payne."

But Xinos, in his opening argument, had promised to alibi Payne—his mother was prepared to testify for him—and now, on cross-examination, he picked skillfully at Parrish's case. Playing to his hard hat on the jury, he asked Castelli whether the stick-up man had one or two hands on the gun. "Only one, sir," said Castelli. "And was that trigger pulled in rapid succession—click-click-click?" Xinos pressed. "Yes, sir," said Castelli, and Xinos had his point: it takes two hands to keep pulling the slide and clicking the trigger. Next came Patrolman Joe Higgins, who remembered, under Xinos's pointed cross-examination, that Castelli had described the gunman as weighing 185 pounds—30 more than Payne carries on his spindly 6-foot-1 frame. Payne had nearly botched that point by wearing a billowy, cape-shaped jacket to court, but Xinos persuaded him to fold it up and sit on it so the jurors could see how bony he really was. The 30-pound misunderstanding undercut Castelli's identification of Payne—and suddenly the People and their lawyer, Walter Parrish, were in trouble.

Parrish didn't show it: he is a careful, phlegmatic man born to striving parents in the Chicago ghetto and bred to move smiling coolly through the system. He

came into it with a Howard law diploma, a few years' haphazard practice and the right sort of connections as counsel to and precinct captain for the 24th Ward regular Democratic organization. He figured on the job only as an apprenticeship for private practice, but he has stayed six years and seems rather comfortable where he is. The black kids over in the County Jail call him "The Devil," and he likes that; he fancied that the edgy hostility he saw in Donald Payne's eyes was a tribute to his hard-guy reputation. He likes his public law firm, too. It pays him $18,000—he guesses he would have to gross $50,000 in private practice to match that—and it puts all the enormous resources of the state at his service. Investigators? The state's attorney has 93 to the public defender's six. Police, the sheriff, the FBI? "All you got to do is call them." Pathology? Microanalysis? "Just pick up the phone. You've got everything at your beck and call."

What he had in *People* vs. *Payne* was the Hamilton boys, the two cousins through whom the police had tracked Payne. Parrish had hoped he wouldn't have to put them on the stand. "It was a risk," he said later. "They could have hurt us. They could have got up there and suddenly said Donald wasn't there." But he was behind and knew it. He needed Frank Hamilton to place Payne inside the store, James to connect him with the car and the pistol. So, that afternoon, he ordered up subpoenas for the Hamiltons. "We know how to scramble," said his young assistant, Joe Poduska. "That's the name of the game."

The subpoenas were being typed when Connie Xinos happened into the state's attorney's office to socialize—*it's like a family*—and saw them in the typewriter. Xinos went cold. He had talked to the mother of one of the Hamiltons; he knew their testimony could hurt. So, next morning, he headed first thing to Parrish's austere second-floor cubicle—and found the Hamiltons there. "We're going to testify," they told Xinos, "and we're going to tell the truth."

Xinos took Parrish aside. "Let's get rid of this case," he said.

"It's Christmas," Parrish said amiably. "I'm a reasonable man."

"What do you want?" Xinos asked.

"I was thinking about three to eight."

"One to five," said Xinos.

"You got it."

It's an absolute gift, Xinos thought, and he took it to Payne in the lock-up. "I can get you one to five," he said. Payne said no. Xinos thought fast. It was a dead-bang case—the kind Clarence Darrow couldn't pull out—and it was good for a big rattle, maybe ten to twenty years. Xinos went back downstairs, got the Hamiltons and sat them down with Payne in Fitzgerald's library. "They rapped," he remembers, "and one of them said, 'Donald—you mean you told them you weren't *there*?' I told him again I could get him one to five. They said, 'Maybe you ought to take it, Donald.' I said, 'You may get ten to twenty going on with the trial.' And he said, 'Well, even if I take one to five, I'm not guilty.' That's when I knew he would go."

But would Fitzgerald buy it? Xinos was worried. The judge is a handsome 57, with a pink Irish face rimmed with silver hair and creased to smile. "He looks like God would look and acts like God would act if God were a judge," says Xinos. "He doesn't take any s---." He was a suburban lawyer in Calumet City when Mayor Richard Daley's organization slated him for judge seven years ago, a reward for having backed a Daley man for governor once when it was tough to do so. He started in divorce court and hated it: "I think I'd rather have 150 lashes than go back down there. Jeez—it's a lot easier to give a guy the chair than it is to take five kids away from a mother." He is happier where he is, and he has made a considerable reputation in the building as a solid, early-rising, hard-working judge—no scholar but conscientious and good on the law. He can be stern as well: he isn't the hanging type, but he does think the pendulum has swung pretty far lately in the defendant's favor. "We've clothed 'em in swaddling clothes," he says, "and laid 'em in a manger of bliss." So Xinos fretted. "The judge is the judge," he told Payne while they waited for an audience with Fitzgerald. "He might give you three to eight. You better think about that."

But Fitzgerald agreed to talk, and the ritual began to unfold.

■

Fitzgerald: "Like God would look if God were a judge."

Xinos led Payne to the bench and announced for the record that they wanted to discuss pleading—"Is that correct, Donald?" Payne mumbled, "Correct," and, while he went back to the lockup to wait, the lawyers followed the judge into chambers. A bailiff closed the door behind them. Fitzgerald sat at his desk and pulled a 4-by-6 index card out of a box; he likes to keep his own notes. Parrish dropped into a deep, leathery sofa, his knees coming up almost to his chin. Xinos sat in a green guest chair in a row along the wall. There were no outsiders, not even a court stenographer. The conference, not the courtroom, has become the real focus of big-city criminal justice, but its business is transacted off the record for maximum flexibility.

Fitzgerald scanned Parrish's prep sheet, outlining the state case. Xinos told him glumly about the Hamiltons. "We look beat," he conceded.

"Walter," asked the judge, "what do you want?"

"I don't want to hurt the kid," Parrish said. "I talked to Connie, and we thought one to five."

They talked about Payne's record—his jobs, his family, his old gas-station burglary rap. "Two years probation," Xinos put in hopefully. "That's nothing." Fitzgerald pondered it all. He had no probation report—there isn't time or manpower enough to do them except in major cases—and no psychological workup; sentencing in most American courts comes down to a matter of instinct. Fitzgerald's instincts told him one to five was a long time for Payne to serve—and a wide enough spread to encourage him to reform and get out early. "Up to five years," he feels, "that's the area of rehabilitation. Beyond five, I think they get saturated." So he made up his mind.

"Will he take it?" the judge asked Xinos.

"I'll go back and see," Xinos replied. He ducked out to the lockup and put the offer to Payne.

"Let's do it," Payne said, "Right now."

A light snow was falling when they brought him back into court, grinning slightly, walking his diddybop walk. A bailiff led him to a table below Fitzgerald's high bench. His mother slipped into place beside him. He spread his fingers out on the tabletop and looked at them. The judge led him through the prescribed catechism establishing that he understood what he was doing and that no one had forced him to do it. Payne's "yesses" were barely audible in the cavernous room.

The choice now was his, Fitzgerald told him. He could go to the pen and cooperate and learn a trade and come out on parole in eleven months; or he could "go down there and do nothing at all and sit on your haunches . . . and you will probably be going [back] down there for twenty or thirty years." Payne brushed one hand across his eye and studied the tabletop. "I'm giving you the first break you probably ever got in your life," the judge said. ". . . The rest of it, Donald, is up to you. Do you understand that?"

"Yes," said Payne.

And then it was over. Fitzgerald called the jurors in and dismissed them. They knew nothing of the events that had buried Donald; they sat there for a moment looking stunned. Xinos slipped back to the jury room to see them before they

Payne in Joliet: "I'll be in church every day."

scattered. "But you were *ahead*," one told him.

Payne's mother walked out to a pay phone, eyes wet and flashing. "They just pressed Donnie," she insisted, "until he said he did it." Parrish packed up. "An hour, a day—even that's punishment," he said. "One to five is enough." Joe Higgins went back to Tac Unit 660. "Donald," he said, "is a very lucky man." Winston Moore heard about it in his office at the jail. "One to five?" he snorted. "S---. That's no sentence for armed robbery." Xinos went home to his apartment in the suburbs. "One to five," he said. "Fantastic. Payne *should* go to the penitentiary. He's a bad kid, he's better off there. He's dangerous. He'll be back."

And Payne was sulky sore. He shook hands with Xinos and grinned broadly when the deal went down, but when Xinos told him later what the juror had said—*you were ahead*—he felt cheated. A break? "The best

break they could have given me was letting me go." But there was nothing for him to do just then but go brooding back down to the tunnel and to jail. "Everybody do something wrong," he told himself. "Maybe my time just caught up with me."

Prison and Beyond

You can write to your lawyer, your preacher and six other people, the sergeant was saying, only remember—your letters are censored so watch what you say. No. 69656, born Donald Payne, sat half listening in the front row in his gray prison coveralls, his eyes idling over the chapel wall from the flag to the sunny poster—GOOD MORNING WORLD. Nothing controversial about prison in your letters, the sergeant was saying. "Let's keep this personal, fellas, your parents get a lot of this on TV." No sex either—"Let's keep this down to personal matters, fellas, we're not in a Sunday school class but let's keep our hands above the table." No double talk, no jive talk, no hep talk, no profanity. And fellas—don't risk your mail privileges by breaking the rules. "The more mail you get, the easier it will be for you," the sergeant was saying. "It gets depressing in here."

Payne had been marched aboard a black sheriff's bus by early light only a few days before and had been shipped with sixteen other County Jail inmates to Joliet Prison, a 112-year-old yellow-stone fortress on the Des Plaines River forty miles southwest of Chicago. The transfer, typically, was accidental. Payne was to have been held in jail until this month, when he is due in court on charges of having violated his old probation for burglary, but the papers got mixed up and he was bused out early. He didn't really mind, since by then he hated the jail so badly that even the pen seemed preferable. And so, on February 5, he checked into Joliet's diagnostic center, drew his number and his baggy coveralls, was stripped, showered and shorn and began four to six weeks of testing to see which prison he would fit into best and what if anything it could do for him. Coveralls aren't much, but Payne, sharp, flipped the collar rakishly up in back and left the front unbuttoned halfway down his chest. Cool. Good morning, world.

Except in this world, as the sergeant of the guard said, it gets depressing. Illinois's prisons, like most of America's, had fallen over the years into a sorry state of neglect until Richard B. Ogilvie made them a campaign issue at some hazard in his 1968 gubernatorial campaign and got elected. Ogilvie since has trusted the problem to a new director of corrections, Peter Bensinger, the 34-year-old heir to the Brunswick Corp. money and position, and Bensinger—an energetic beginner—has put Joliet and its neighbor, Stateville, under the management of reform-minded pros. The new team has begun upgrading the guard force, putting new emphasis on correction as against punishment and doing away with some of the pettiest dehumanizing practices; now, for example, they no longer shave a man's body hair off when he arrives, and prisoners are called to the visiting room by name, not by number. "We've taken everything else from the man," says Stateville's 33-year-old warden, John Twomey. "If we take his name, too, how can he feel he's a worthwhile human being?"

But money is short and reform painfully slow. "We've moved ahead about fifty years," says Joliet's black warden, Herbert Scott. "We're now up to about 1850." And 1850 dies hard. Donald Payne, a child of the city streets, is rousted from his bunk at 6 a.m., fed breakfast at 7, lunch at 10, dinner at 3 and locked back in his cell before sundown. The language of the place confirms his devalued humanity: men are "tickets," meals are "feeds." The battery of IQ, personality and aptitude tests he is undergoing at Joliet are exhaustive but of uncertain value, since the prisons still lack programs enough to make use of what the tests tell them. So Payne is consigned to his bars and his bitterness. In Joliet at mealtime 900 men sit at long stone tables spooning food out of tin dishes and facing an enormous American flag—"to instill patriotism," a young staff psychologist explained wryly. A visitor asked how the men respond to this lesson. "I imagine," said the psychologist, "that they think, 'F--- the flag.'"

It is here that society has its last chance with the Donald Paynes—and here that the last chance is squandered at least as often as not. The lesson of *People* vs. *Payne* and countless cases like it is that the American "system" of justice is less a system than a patchwork of process and improvisation, of Sisyphean labor and protean inner motives. Payne was arrested on chance and the tenacity of two policemen; was jailed for want of money while better-off men charged with worse crimes went free on bail; was convicted out of court and sentenced in a few minutes' bargaining among overworked men who knew hardly anything about him. It cannot be said that justice miscarried in *People* vs. *Payne*, since the evidence powerfully suggests his guilt and the result was a penalty in some relation, however uneven, to the offense. But neither was justice wholly served—not if the end of justice is more than the rough one-to-one balancing of punishments with crimes.

The punishment most commonly available is prison, and prisons in America have done far better at postponing crime than at preventing or deterring it. Joliet is a way station for Payne. He may wind up at Pontiac, where most younger offenders do their time; he would prefer the company of older men at Stateville, a vintage 1925 maximum-security prison with cells ranged in enormous glassed-in circles around a central guard tower. He says that in either event he will stick to his

Donald Payne: Twenty Years Later

Donald Payne has had a rough time since he was originally sentenced to Joilet in 1970. At that time his attorney, Connie Xinos said, "He's dangerous. He'll be back." He has been back—several times.

Payne entered Joilet Penitentiary on February 5, 1971, to serve a one- to five-year sentence as ordered by Judge Fitzgerald. He was paroled on September 28, 1973. Available records indicate that he was free for the next eleven years until he was convicted and incarcerated in California in February 1984, for possession of controlled substances. Fourteen months later he was released on parole to be served in his home state of Illinois. Payne was discharged from parole in August 1987, but was again arrested on drug charges. This time the Circuit Court of Rock Island County, Illinois, sentenced him to five years for possession of cocaine and heroin. Donald Payne is serving his time in the Vandalia Correctional Center, Illinois, and is scheduled for release on April 1, 1993.

SOURCE: Letter from Nic Howell, Chief Public Information Officer, Illinois Department of Corrections, January 15, 1991. Reprinted by permission.

cell and go for early parole. "When I get out," he told his mother once in jail, "I'll be in church every day." Yet the odds do not necessarily favor this outcome: though the Illinois prisons have made progress toward cutting down on recidivism, a fifth to a third of their alumni get in trouble again before they have been out even a year. "Well," said Payne, smiling that half-smile at a visitor during his first days as No. 69656, "I'm startin' my time now and I'm on my way home." But his time will be a long and bleak one, and, unless luck and will and the last-chance processes of justice all work for him, Donald Payne may be home right now.

SOURCE: From "How Justice Works: The People vs. Donald Payne," by P. Goldman and D. Holt, *Newsweek*, March 8, 1971, pp. 20–37. Copyright ©1971 by Newsweek, Inc. All rights reserved. Reprinted by permission.

POLICE

The police are the most visible agents of the criminal justice system in American society. In Part 2 we deal with the role of the police as the critical subunit of the system that confronts crime at the community level. Most of us have gained an image of the police from movies and television; but, as we shall see, law enforcement differs greatly from the exploits of the cops on "Miami Vice." Police work often takes place in a hostile environment with crucial questions of life and death, honor and dishonor at stake. Officers are given discretion to deal with these situations, and how that discretion is used has an important effect on the way society views policing. Chapter 5 traces the history of policing and looks at its function and organization. Chapter 6 examines the daily operations of the police, and Chapter 7 analyzes some of the current issues and trends in law enforcement.

Police

Key Terms

law enforcement
order maintenance
proactive

reactive
service
socialization

subculture
total enforcement
working personality

A democracy, like all other societies, needs order and security, but it also and equally requires civil liberty. This complexity of needs creates difficult theoretical and practical problems.

Jerome Hall

The men and women in blue are the most visible presence of government in our society. Be they members of the local or state police, sheriff's departments, or federal agencies, the more than 500,000 sworn police officers play a crucial role in American society. Citizens look to the police to perform a wide range of functions, including prevention of crime, law enforcement, maintenance of order, and services to the community. However, public expectations about the responsibilities of the police are not always clear. Unlike the courts and corrections, the police are the only unit of criminal justice whose day-to-day clientele is not exclusively accused persons, victims, and witnesses. Further, citizens necessarily form judgments about the police, and those judgments have a strong impact on the way order is maintained under law.

In a free society criticism of public agencies is to be expected. This is particularly true with respect to police since "by the very nature of their functions, [police] are an anomaly in a free society."[1] They are given a great deal of authority—to arrest, to search, to detain, and to use force (all actions disruptive of personal freedom)— yet democracy requires them to maintain order so that the free society may be possible. In fact, it has been said that the "strength of a democracy and the quality of life enjoyed by its citizens are determined in large measure by the ability of the police to discharge their duties."[2] Yet if we depend on the "thin blue line" to protect democratic society, the police and the public must clearly understand the duties and functions of policing.

History gives little help in defining police functions, because over time the agencies of law enforcement have played a great variety of often contradictory roles. These contradictions raise a number of questions:

1. Are the police to be concerned with peacekeeping or crime fighting?
2. Are the police the blind enforcers of the law or the discretionary agents of a benevolent government?
3. Are the police social workers with guns or gunmen in social work?
4. Are the police facilitators of social change or defenders of the "faith"?
5. Are the police a social agency of last resort after 5:00 P.M. or mere watchmen for business and industry?[3]

This chapter addresses the role of the police by focusing on the historical development, policies, functions, nature of decision making, and subculture of the police. The police are but one organization within the closely integrated system of criminal justice. Yet the way that the police pursue their goals greatly influences the operation of the rest of the system.

Of particular importance to our discussion of policing is the fact that order is to be maintained under law, but in contemporary society policing is performed within the context of a bureaucracy. This causes certain problems. Bureaucratic organizations emphasize the use of discretion rather than disciplined adherence to rules and regulations.

> By contrast, the rule of law emphasizes the rights of individual citizens and constraints upon the initiative of legal officials. This tension between the operational consequences of ideas of order, efficiency, and initiative, on the one hand, and legality, on the other, constitutes the principal problem of police as a democratic legal organization.[4]

A HISTORICAL PERSPECTIVE

Law and order is not a new concept; it has been a focus of discussion since the formation of the first police force in metropolitan London in 1829. Looking even further back in history to the Magna Carta, one recognizes that limitations were placed on the constables and bailiffs of thirteenth-century England. By reading between the lines of this ancient document, one can surmise that problems of police abuse, the maintenance of order, and the rule of law were similar to those encountered today. What is surprising is that the same remedies—recruiting better police, stiffening the penalties for official malfeasance, creating a civilian board of control—were suggested in that earlier time to ensure that order was kept in accordance with the rule of law.

The English Origins of the American Police

It is from the English tradition that the three major characteristics of American policing have flowed: (1) limited authority, (2) local control, and (3) organizational fragmentation. Like the British police, but unlike those in Continental Europe, the police in the United States have limited authority; their powers and responsibilities are closely circumscribed by law. England, like the United States, has no nationwide police force; each unit is under local community control. Tied to this characteristic is the fact that policing is fragmented: there are many types of agencies, each with its own special jurisdiction and responsibilities—constable, sheriff, urban police, the FBI, and so on.

Although Sir Robert Peel is credited with helping to establish the first professional police force in England, historians have shown that organizations to protect local citizens and property had existed before the thirteenth century. The **frankpledge** system required that groups of ten families, called tithings, agree to uphold the law, maintain order, and commit to a court those who had violated the law. It was mandated that every male above the age of twelve be part of the system. When a member became aware that a crime had occurred, he was obliged to raise a "hue and cry" and to join others in his tithing to track down the offender. The tithing was fined if members did not perform the obligatory duties.

The Statute of Winchester, enacted in 1285, set up a parish

frankpledge: A system in old English law whereby members of a tithing, a group of ten families, pledged to be responsible for the good conduct of all members over twelve years old.

"Night Charges on Their Way to Court" illustrates the peace-keeping, order maintenance role of the nineteenth-century police in England following the reforms of Sir Robert Peel.

constable system. It required all citizens to pursue criminals under the direction of the local constable. The position of constable was filled by selecting a man from the parish to be the law enforcement officer for one year on an unpaid basis. Watchmen were appointed to assist the constable. If a serious disturbance arose, the constable could press all members of the parish into police service.

This traditional system of community law enforcement was maintained well into the eighteenth century. The advent of the Industrial Revolution, however, brought about the growth of cities, changes in traditional patterns of life, and as a result, social disorder. As a consequence, there was an almost complete breakdown of law and order in London.

In the 1750s Henry Fielding and his brother, Sir John Fielding, led efforts to improve the police in England. Through the pages of the *Covent Garden Journal* they sought to educate the public on the problem of increased crime. They also published the *Weekly Pursuit,* a one-page flyer carrying descriptions of known offenders. Henry Fielding became a magistrate of London in 1748 and organized a small group of "thief-takers," men with previous service as constables, who became a roving band dedicated to breaking up criminal gangs, pursuing lawbreakers, and making arrests. So impressed was the government by this Bow Street Amateur Volunteer Force (known as the "Bow Street Runners") that money was provided each member, and an attempt was made to extend the concept to other areas of London. But Henry Fielding died in 1754, and Sir John was unable to maintain the high level of integrity of the original group. Effectiveness waned. Riots broke out in the summer of 1780, and for nearly a week mobs ruled much of the city. It had become obvious that a new approach to law enforcement was necessary.[5]

During the first years of the new century, various attempts were made to create a centralized police force for London. Opposition came from people who believed that police of any kind were synonymous with tyranny and the destruction of liberty.[6] It was not until

1829, under the prodding of Home Secretary Sir Robert Peel, that Parliament established the Metropolitan Constabulary for London. Structured along the lines of a military unit, the 1,000-man force was commanded by two magistrates, later called "commissioners," who were given administrative but not judicial duties. The ultimate responsibility for maintaining and, to a certain degree, supervising "bobbies" (named after Robert Peel) was vested in the home secretary. Because the home secretary was a member of the government, this first regular police force was in essence controlled by the democratically elected legislature.

The police in England during the early part of the nineteenth century had a four-part mandate:

1. to prevent crime without the use of repressive force and to avoid intervention by the military in community disturbances;
2. to manage public order nonviolently, using force to obtain compliance only as a last resort;
3. to minimize and reduce conflict between the police and the public;
4. to demonstrate efficiency by means of the absence of crime and disorder rather than by visible evidence of police actions in dealing with problems.[7]

The mandate was to keep a low profile while maintaining order. Because of fears by political leaders that a national force might emerge that would threaten civil liberties, every effort was made to keep direction of the police at a local level. In fact,

> The first "bobby" who walked the streets of London could not have foreseen the present American pattern of highly organized, rationalized, mechanized, and mobile policing, nor could he have anticipated the centrality of weaponry and the direct force applied by the modern police. It is also unlikely that he would have had much sympathy for the crime-fighting rhetoric, for at that time it was neither possible nor very wise to seek out criminals and attempt to combat them.[8]

BIOGRAPHY

Sir Robert Peel

One of the outstanding British statesmen and politicians of the nineteenth century, Sir Robert Peel had a tremendous impact on the development of policing. Appointed to the position of secretary of state for the Home Department in 1822, Peel subsequently set out to reform the criminal law through the consolidation and rewriting of all offenses. His work with the criminal law and the rise in crime led him to believe that legal reform must be accompanied by improved methods of crime prevention. In 1829, over much opposition, he was able to persuade Parliament to pass the Metropolitan Police Act, establishing the first disciplined and regular police force in the Greater London area. As a result, the patchwork of private law enforcement systems in use at the time was abolished.

Committed to governmental service, Peel sought to reduce the costs of administering justice by establishing an efficient, full-time civil service that could be relied on to serve the state, not local interests. He advocated full-time careers for the police and urged enhancement of the deterrent capacity of law enforcement. The core activity of the police, he said, should be preventive patrol by officers who were part of a civilian force, who did not carry arms, and who had been trained to prevent crime by being present in the community. He felt that effective prevention and enforcement of the laws could be substituted for harsh penalties. England's "bobbies," or "Peelers," are the legacy of Sir Robert Peel.

Development of the Police in the United States

Before the Revolution, Americans shared the English belief that community members had a basic responsibility to help maintain order. The offices of constable, sheriff, and night watchman were easily transferred to the New World. With the birth of the new nation with its federal governmental structure in 1789, police power remained with the states, again in response to the fear of centralized law enforcement activity. However, the development of the police and their mandate in the United States emerged as a response to conditions unlike those in England. Ethnic diversity, local political control, regional differences, the opening up of the West, and the more violent tradition of American society were some of the factors that brought about a different development in peacekeeping forces.

Three historical periods of American policing have been noted: the Political Era (1840–1920), the Professional Model Era (1920–1970), and the Community Model Era (1970–present).[9] This division of history has been criticized as describing policing only in the urban areas of the Northeast, without taking into account the very different development of the police in rural areas of the South and West. Even so, it is useful to us as a framework through which we can note differences in the organization of the police, the focus of police work, and the particular types of strategies employed.[10]

Political Era: 1840–1920

In the United States as in England, the growth of cities led to pressures for modernization of law enforcement. Social relations in the cities of the nineteenth century were quite different from those in the towns and countryside. In fact, from 1830 to 1870 there was unprecedented civil disorder in the major cities. Ethnic conflict as a consequence of massive immigration, hostility toward nonslave blacks and abolitionists, mob actions against banks and other institutions of property during economic declines, and violence in settling questions of morality created fears that democratic institutions would not survive.

During this period the large cities began to take steps to create constabularies. Boston and Philadelphia became the first to add a daytime police force to supplement the night watchmen. The inefficiency of separate day and night forces was soon recognized, and in 1844 the New York Legislature passed a law to create a unified force for cities under the command of a chief appointed by the mayor and council. By the middle of the century, most major American cities had followed this pattern.

This period is characterized as the Political Era, since close ties developed between the police and local political leaders.[11] In many cities this link to neighborhoods and politicians was such that the police often appeared to be adjuncts of the local party machine. This relationship served both groups, since the political machines recruited and maintained the police while the police helped ward leaders get out the vote for favored candidates. Ranks in the force were often for sale to the highest bidder, and many police officers were "on the take."

During the political era the police continued to perform the watchman and reactive patrol functions of their predecessors, focusing on crime prevention and order maintenance by foot patrol. The decentralization of authority meant that the officer on the beat dealt with crime, disorder, and other problems as they arose. In addition, the police carried out a number of service functions, such as caring for derelicts, operating soup kitchens, regulating public health, and handling medical and social emergencies.[12] Because of their closeness to the community, the police enjoyed citizen support during this era.

The police in the South developed in a different way, owing to the existence of slavery and the agrarian nature of that region. Historians have argued that the first organized police agencies with full-time officers developed in those cities in the South with large slave populations (Charleston, Savannah, and Richmond) in which the white masters lived in fear of possible uprisings.[13] "Slave patrols" were organized by white owners as a means of dealing with runaways. The patrols had full power to break into the homes of blacks suspected of keeping arms, to execute corporal punishments on those who did not obey their orders, and to arrest runaways to return them to their masters.

The westward expansion of the United States during the nineteenth century presented circumstances quite dissimilar to those in the urbanizing East and the agricultural South. Settlement preceded an ordered society, and individuals with a vested interest in "law and order" often had to take the law into their own hands through vigilante groups.

One of the first official positions to be created in rural areas was that of sheriff. Although the sheriff had responsibilities similar to those of his counterpart in seventeenth-century England, the American officer was chosen by popular election and had broad powers to enforce the law. Sheriffs depended on the men of the community for assistance, and the "posse comitatus," borrowed from fifteenth-century Europe, came into being. This institution required local men to respond to the sheriff's call for assistance. As governments were formed in the territories, marshals appointed by federal authority

■ During the political era the officer on a neighborhood beat dealt with crime and disorder as it arose. In addition, the police performed various social services.

helped enforce the law. Although the federal marshal has become a law enforcement folk hero, his duties were primarily judicial; he was responsible for maintaining order in the courtroom and for holding prisoners for trial.

Criticisms of the influence of politics on police actions in the cities of the Northeast and the spread of urbanism to other parts of the country led to efforts to promote a new type of police organization with a new orientation toward professionalism.

Professional Model Era: 1920–1970

Policing was greatly influenced by the Progressive reform movement that marked the turn of the twentieth century. The Progressives were for the most part upper-middle-class, educated Americans interested in two goals: efficient operation of government and provision of governmental services to improve the conditions of the less fortunate. They hoped at the same time to rid government of undesirable influences, such as party politics and patronage. With regard to the crime problem the Progressives called for creation of professional police forces.

The key to understanding the Progressives' concept of law enforcement professionalism is found in their slogan "The police have to get out of politics, and politics has to get out of the police." August Vollmer, chief of police of Berkeley, California, was one of the leading advocates of this position. He and other police reformers, such as Leonhard Fuld, Raymond Fosdick, Bruce Smith, and O. W. Wilson argued that the police be a professional force, a nonpartisan agency

■

The professional era emphasized the use of technological developments so as to enhance the crime-fighter goals. Rapid response was a key element of this approach.

of government committed to the highest ideals of public service. This model of professional policing comprises six essential elements:

1. the force should stay out of politics,
2. members should be well trained and disciplined, and tightly organized,
3. laws should be equally enforced,
4. the force should take advantage of technological developments,
5. merit should be the basis of personnel procedures,
6. the crime-fighting role should be prominent.

Of these six elements the redirection of the police away from a primary focus on order maintenance to crime control did more to change the nature of American policing than any of the other aspects of the professionalism model. This narrow focus on crime fighting removed the police from many of the ties that they had developed with the communities they served. Thus "between the 1890s and the end of World War I, the important public service functions that police departments had practiced disappeared or were substantially diminished, and police systems presenting viable alternatives to the subsequent system disappeared. Cops were now to be crime fighters."[14]

police were directed away from service function to crime fighting

O. W. Wilson, a student of Vollmer's, was a leading advocate of professionalism and a proponent of the use of motorized patrols, efficient radio communication, and rapid response to facilitate effective crime fighting. He felt that one-officer patrols were the best way to utilize personnel, especially since the two-way radio allowed for supervision by commanders. To combat police corruption, Wilson emphasized the importance of rotating beat assignments so that officers on patrol would not become too familiar with individuals in the community. Advocates of professionalism urged that the police be made aware of the need to act lawfully, to protect the rights of all citizens, including those suspected of criminal acts. "They sought to instill in officers a strong—some would even argue too rigid ("Just the facts, ma'am")—commitment to the supremacy of the law and the importance of equal treatment."[15]

BIOGRAPHY

August Vollmer

August Vollmer was born in New Orleans, the son of German immigrants. Despite a lack of formal education, Vollmer became a prominent figure in the history of American police reform. His career began in Berkeley, California, after his election as police marshal in 1904. He was made chief in 1909 and remained in that office until 1932.

Vollmer was an outspoken advocate of a professionalized police force staffed by dedicated crime fighters who were expertly trained and able to use science and technology in all phases of police work. In general, his desire to develop professional police forces grew out of the Progressive civic reform movement of the early twentieth century. Among the reforms that Vollmer instituted in the Berkeley Police Department were the creation of a motorcycle patrol force and the installation of a fingerprint and handwriting classification system. His advancement of police technology and administration paralleled his concept of the police officer as social worker. Accepting the belief that crime was a product of social and psychological problems, he urged that the police intervene in the lives of individuals before they entered crime.

Following his retirement as police chief in 1932, Vollmer taught and trained police professionals. His book *The Police and Modern Society* (1936), which details his vision of the professional police officer, remains a classic statement of this ideal.

By the 1930s the police emphasized their concern with serious crimes, such as murder, assault, robbery, and rape—the *UCR* Part I offenses. Fighting these crimes was important for gaining citizen support; efforts to control victimless offenses and disorderliness and to provide social services aroused citizen opposition. As emphasized by Mark Moore and George Kelling, "The clean, bureaucratic model of policing put forth by the reformers could be sustained only if the scope of police responsibility was narrowed to 'crime fighting.' "[16] Technology also helped further the emphasis on discipline, equal enforcement of the law, and centralized decision making so characteristic of professionals working in a bureaucracy.

The civil rights and anti-war movements, the urban riots, and the rise of crime in the 1960s challenged many assumptions of the professional model. In their attempts to maintain public order the police in many cities appeared to be concerned primarily with maintaining the status quo. With American cities increasingly made up of poor members of racial minorities, the professional style isolated officers from the communities they served. For many inner-city residents the police resembled more an occupying force than public servants who could be looked to for help. Although they continued to present themselves as crime fighters, the police were often seen as ineffective in this role.

Community Model Era: 1970–Present

Beginning in the 1970s there were calls for movement away from the crime-fighting focus toward greater emphasis on maintaining order and providing services to the community. Major research studies had been published since the 1960s showing the complexities of police work and the extent to which day-to-day practices deviated from the ideals of the professional model. The research also questioned the

BIOGRAPHY

Orlando Winfield Wilson

O. W. Wilson, police official and criminologist, was born in South Dakota. After his family moved to Berkeley, California, Wilson enrolled in the University of California and completed a degree in criminology in 1924. While taking courses, Wilson became a patrolman with the Berkeley Police Department and in the process became a protege of Chief August Vollmer, who was a professor at the university. After his graduation, Wilson became chief of police of Fullerton, California, on Vollmer's recommendation, and thereby launched his career as a law enforcement official and innovator.

As chief of police in Wichita, Kansas (1928–1939), Wilson attracted national attention by reorganizing the department and introducing such innovations as clearly marked police vehicles, lie detectors, and mobile crime laboratories. He gained a reputation for ridding the police of corruption and was made superintendent of the Chicago Police Department in 1960 to meet that objective. He saw corruption as a by-product of poor organization, scant planning, and tangled lines of command.

From 1939 to 1960, Wilson was professor of police administration at Berkeley. Here he developed a theory concerning the relationship of law enforcement to crime control: the police could not prevent crime, because they had little control over its social causes—poverty, neglect, and the like; the police could, however, repress and control the criminal through such aggressive tactics as preventive patrol. His most important works are *Police Records* (1942), *Police Administration* (1950), and *Police Planning* (1957).

effectiveness of the police in catching and deterring criminals. Three findings require emphasis:

1. Increasing the number of patrol officers in a neighborhood was found to have little effect on the crime rate.
2. Rapid response to calls for service does not greatly increase the arrest of criminals.
3. It is difficult if not impossible to improve rates of solving crimes.

All of these elements are major tenets of the professional crime-fighter model.

Critics have argued that the professional style isolated the police from the community and seemed not to be accountable to it. This was especially true because of the heavy emphasis on motorized patrol. The patrol car encapsulates the officer so that personal contacts with most citizens are lost. It is argued that the police should get out of their cars and spend more time directly confronting and assisting citizens with their problems. "This is mundane, prosaic work but it probably beats driving around in cars waiting for a radio call. Citizens would surely feel safer and, perhaps, might even be safer."[17]

In a provocative article, "Broken Windows: The Police and Neighborhood Safety," James Q. Wilson and George Kelling argue for a reorientation of policing to emphasize "little problems" such as the maintenance of order, provision of services to those in need, and adoption of strategies to reduce the fear of crime. They base their approach on three assumptions:

1. Neighborhood disorder creates fear. Areas with street people, youth gangs, prostitution, and drunks are high-crime areas.
2. Just as unrepaired broken windows are a signal that nobody cares and lead to more serious vandalism, untended disorderly behavior is also a signal that the community doesn't care. This leads to more serious disorder and crime.
3. If the police are to deal with disorder to reduce fear and crime, they must rely on citizens for legitimacy and assistance.[18]

■
Community policing emphasizes the need for officers to be in close contact with citizens so as to deal with problems and service needs when they arise. What would be the concerns of people such as August Vollmer and O. W. Wilson about this new trend?

Advocates of the community policing approach urge a greater emphasis on foot patrols so that officers will become known to the citizens they serve, who in turn will cooperate with and assist the police. They believe that through attention to "little problems," the police can not only reduce disorder and citizen fear but also improve public attitudes toward policing. When citizens respond positively to police order-maintenance efforts, police will have "improved bases of community and political support, which in turn can be exploited to gain further cooperation from citizens in a wide variety of activities."[19] A call for a shift in policing to a problem-oriented approach recommends that the police be prepared to handle the broad range of troublesome situations—for example, battered wives, runaway children, noisy teenagers, accidents and persons in distress—that prompt citizens to turn to them.[20] In this approach to citizen needs, the police should define the problem and look for its underlying causes.

Although the contemporary reformers have argued for a greater focus on the order maintenance and service functions of the police, they do not advocate dropping the crime-fighter role. Rather they have called for a reorientation of police priorities, placing greater attention on community needs and on better understanding the problems underlying crime, disorder, and incivility. Their proposals have been adopted by police executives in many cities and by such influential bodies as the Police Foundation and the Police Executive Research Forum. Time will tell if this new orientation will become as

COMPARATIVE PERSPECTIVE
Organization of the Police in France

Unlike the United States and England where they are organized on a local basis, the police in France are centralized as a national force divided between the Ministry of Interior and the Ministry of Defense. With a population of about 52 million, France has a unitary form of government. Political power and decision making are highly centralized in bureaucracies located in Paris. There is a single criminal code and standardized criminal justice procedures for the entire country. The country is divided into ninety-six territories known as departments and is further divided into districts and municipalities. In each department there is a Commissaire of the Republic, who represents the central government and exercises supervision over the local mayors.

Police functions are divided beween two separate forces under the direction of two ministries of the central government. With over 200,000 personnel employed in police duties, France has a ratio of law enforcement officers to the general population that is greater than that of the United States or England.

The older police force, the Gendarmerie Nationale, with over 80,000 officers, is under the military and is responsible for policing about 95 percent of the country's territory. The Gendarmerie patrols the highways, rural areas, and those communities with populations of less than 10,000. Members are organized into brigades or squads. These brigades are collectively known as the Departmental Gendarmerie. They operate from fixed points, reside in their duty area, and constitute the largest component of the force. A second agency, the Mobile Gendarmerie, may be deployed anywhere in the country. These are essentially riot police whose forces are motorized, have tanks, and even light aircraft. The Republican Guard is the third component of the Gendarmerie, is stationed in Paris, protects the president, and performs ceremonial functions.

The Police Nationale is under the Ministry of the Interior and oper-

influential and widespread as was the focus on professionalism during the first half of this century.

This call for a new orientation of the police has not gone unchallenged. Critics contend that those advocating the community focus have misread the history of the police in the United States. Samuel Walker, for example, maintains that the depersonalization of American policing by the professional crime-fighting model has been greatly exaggerated. He asserts, however, that a revitalized concept of police patrol, in light of the lessons of recent research, has merit.[21] Taking another tack, Carl Klockars doubts that the police will actually give priority to maintaining order. "Although the police are miscast in the crime-fighting role, we in the audience insist that they play the part. In the face of nearly a century of false hopes and false promises the need and desire of the public and its press to believe that police can fight crime remain strong."[22] But it has also been noted that the police shaped these expectations to begin with and, therefore, can shape them in a different direction in the future.

POLICE POLICY

Although the criminal law is written as if every infraction were expected to result in arrest and punishment, such is not the case. Limitations imposed by the law, legislatures, courts, and community

---

ates mainly in urban centers with populations over 10,000. The Police Nationale is divided into the Directorate of Urban Police, responsible for policing the cities with patrol and investigative functions, and the Directorate of Criminal Investigation, which provides regional detective services and pursues cases beyond the scope of the city police or the Gendarmerie. Another division, the Air and Frontier Police, is responsible for border protection. The Republican Security Companies are the urban version of the Mobile Gendarmerie but without the heavy armament. With sixty-one companies each with 250 officers and men, they are primarily responsible for the maintenance of order.

In addition to traditional patrol and investigative functions, the Police Nationale also contains units responsible for the collection of intelligence information and for the countering of foreign subversion. The Directorate of General Intelligence and Gambling has 2,500 officers and has as its purpose the gathering of "intelligence of a political, social, and economic nature necessary for the information of government." This includes data from public opinion surveys, mass media, periodicals, and information gathered through the infiltration of various political, labor, and social groups. The Directorate of Counter-Espionage has the mission of countering the efforts of foreign agents on French soil intent on impairing the security of the country.

Law enforcement in Paris is part of the Police Nationale, yet because it is the major city and capital, the Prefecture of Police of Paris has considerable autonomy. In other municipalities a certain amount of police responsibility devolves on the community and the office of the mayor, yet here too procedures are set by higher authority and the Code of Communal Administration.

The police system of the central government of France is powerful; the number, armament, legal powers, and links to the military are most impressive. The turbulent history of France before and after the Revolution of 1789 gave rise to the need for the government to be able to assert authority. Since the 1930s France has had to deal not only with crime but also with political instability—the Nazi invasion of 1940, weak governments following World War II, the Algerian crisis in 1958, and student rioting in 1968 all brought conditions that nearly toppled the existing regime. The need to maintain order in the streets would seem to be a major concern of the government.

SOURCE: Excerpted and adapted with permission of Macmillan Publishing Company from *The Police of France*, by P. J. Stead, pp. 1–12. Copyright © 1983 by Macmillan Publishing Company, a division of Macmillan, Inc.

greatly reduce the number of criminal acts that may become a focus of police activity. In addition, the police have wide discretion in determining how they deploy their resources, which types of behaviors are overlooked, and the particular circumstances in which officers do or do not make an arrest. Because the criminal justice system is organized as a continuum, from the police to prosecutor to court to corrections, police policies determine the extent to which agencies of adjudication and corrections function. The police are thus in a crucial position with regard to regulating the flow of cases through the system. Changes in enforcement policy—for example, increasing the size of the night patrol or tolerating certain types of vice—influence the amount of crime that comes to official attention and the system's ability to impose sanctions on offenders.

It must be emphasized that in a modern democratic society it is the police that have been designated by the community to use force against lawbreakers. The use of force by citizens acting in their private capacity is strictly circumscribed and, as we saw in Chapter 3, is restricted in the main to situations of self-defense. There are also occasions when a person may hold a lawbreaker until an officer arrives, but the police have a virtual monopoly on the right to use force to maintain order and uphold the criminal law.

As Figure 5.1 illustrates, various levels of enforcement and discretion exist within the area of police decision making. The criminal code describes acts that are prohibited, but a policy of **total enforcement**—in accordance with which the police are expected to carry out all laws without regard to civil liberties or the requirements of due process—is not a legitimate goal of American criminal justice. Such a policy might exist in a totalitarian regime, but police in a democracy are directed to work within the confines of the law, to respect the liberties of all citizens, and to proceed against suspects in accordance with the concept of due process.

Thus the police are expected to follow a policy of **full enforcement**, in accordance with which they not only are authorized but are bound to enforce fully the criminal law. It would be possible for them to do so if they had the necessary resources and if they had community support. But the policy would make life intolerable. Although every illegal act would be noted and every violator caught, the freedom of all citizens would be greatly restricted because the police would be constantly searching, patrolling, inspecting, and observing in order to root out criminals. As we know, however, com-

total enforcement: A policy whereby the police are given the resources and support to enforce all laws without regard to the civil liberties of citizens.

full enforcement: A policy whereby the police are given the resources and support to enforce all laws within the limits imposed by the injunction to respect the civil liberties of citizens.

FIGURE 5.1
Discretionary factors influencing levels of policing. One can imagine various levels of law enforcement. What are some of the advantages and disadvantages of each? What does the figure indicate about discretion? Which level would you want in your community?
SOURCE: Adapted from Joseph Goldstein, "Police Discretion Not to Invoke the Criminal Process: Low-Visibility Decisions in the Administration of Justice," 1960, *Yale Law Journal* 69: 543–594.

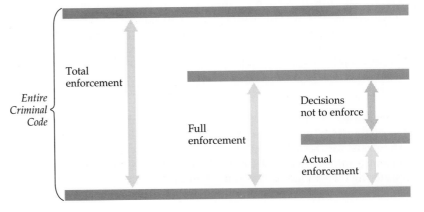

munities do not allocate their resources in such a way that law enforcement is clearly a dominating goal. The police compete for resources with such other public needs as education, recreation, and municipal services.

In reality, though legislators write laws as if full enforcement were the norm, and though every officer solemnly swears to uphold every law, the police determine the **actual enforcement,** the proportion of crimes that are reported and that result in the offender's conviction. The difference between full and actual enforcement reflects such factors as the difficulty in making arrests, the availability of resources, community disagreement on whether certain acts are to be considered unlawful, and pressure from influential persons who desire that certain laws not be rigidly enforced. Police agencies are required to fulfill their obligations but in ways that will retain community and organizational support. They resolve the dilemma by establishing procedures that minimize tension and give the greatest promise of reward for the organization and the persons involved.

actual enforcement: Enforcement of the law at a level that reflects such factors as civil liberties, discretion, resources, and community values.

Levels of Enforcement

The functions of the police are more complex than most of us assume. They are charged with maintaining order, enforcing the law, and providing a variety of social services, but the policies they follow dictate the persons and offenses that will be labeled deviant. The policies that allocate resources and set criteria for law enforcement goals are also an important variable.

In a culturally diverse society like the United States, there are bound to be differing interpretations of deviance. Should criminal justice resources be used primarily to cope with such occupational crimes as stock fraud and government corruption, with the organized crime of supplying narcotics, or with less serious but high-visibility crimes such as public drunkenness and shoplifting? Each of these and other categories involves a different social class, a different perception of deviance, and a different mode of enforcement. Each category of crime has its own political and administrative threats and rewards for enforcement organizations.

Selective Enforcement

Police executives are able to direct enforcement resources so that certain types of crimes and offenders receive special attention. As previously discussed, the police have emphasized their crime-fighting role for most of the past half-century. This means that in most communities the focus of police attention is on the categories of crimes that make up the FBI's *Uniform Crime Reports*. These are the crimes that make headlines and that politicians point to when they ask for increases in the police budget. They are also the crimes generally committed by the poor.

Much of the discussion of crime rates shows the influence of enforcement policy and the role of the police in the criminal justice system. As we have seen, the incidence of crime known to the police is a smaller portion of that committed. Presumably they are aware that their position is politically enhanced by the way certain types of offenders are processed. In terms of volume and the generation of public support, arrests of drug offenders and prostitutes have more payoff in an organizational sense than does the pursuit of white-collar criminals of upper-class social status, who may be able to challenge police decisions and whose cases may require a considerable expenditure of departmental resources.

Such a basic decision as how police resources will be deployed has an important effect on the types of persons arrested. Given the mixed social character of a metropolitan area, police administrators have to decide where they are going to send their officers and what tactics are to be employed. In part, decisions concerning the distribution of police resources are made in light of the demands of certain community groups, such as businesspeople who want special protective services. In most cities, patrol officers are expected to check the doors of downtown stores at night to make sure they are locked and to be a daytime presence in shopping areas. Policies with regard to the homeless are often developed in response to the desires of certain groups to keep "undesirables" out of the "better" areas. The use of foot patrols rather than patrol cars in such neighborhoods may also be a response to community pressures.

Community Influence on Policing

An important factor in the deployment of resources is the police administrator's perception of the style of policing that the community desires. The community's power and value structures, which are supported by the police, in turn set boundaries to the spheres of police action. James Q. Wilson found that the political culture, reflecting the socioeconomic characteristics of a city and its organization of government, exerted a major influence on whether the police acted in accordance with the watchman, legalistic, or service style of operation.[23] Table 5.1 shows the relationship between governmental structure and type of police behavior.

In the declining industrial town of Amsterdam, New York, which had a partisan elected mayor-council form of government, Wilson found the watchman style of police behavior, which emphasizes the order-maintenance activities of patrol officers. With this orientation, the administrator allowed officers to ignore minor violations, especially those involving traffic and juveniles, and to tolerate a certain amount of vice and gambling. The police were to use the law to maintain order rather than to regulate conduct and were expected to exercise discretion in judging the requirements of order, depending on the character of the group in which a violation took place.

Emphasis on professionalism and good government in Highland Park, Illinois, led to the development of a style of police work in which the police detained a high proportion of juvenile offenders, acted vigorously against illicit enterprises, and made a large number of misdemeanor arrests. In this legalistic style of enforcement, the police acted as if there were a single standard of community conduct—that which the law prescribed—rather than different standards for juveniles, minorities, drunks, and the like.

TABLE 5.1 Styles of policing. Wilson found three distinct styles of policing in the communities he studied. Each style places emphasis on different police functions, and each is associated with a particular governmental structure. What style do you believe is dominant in your hometown?

Style	Defining Characteristics	Governmental Structure	Examples
Watchman	Emphasis on maintaining order	Partisan: mayor-council	Albany, Amsterdam, and Newburgh, New York
Legalistic	Emphasis on law enforcement	Good government: council-manager	Oakland, California; Highland Park, Illinois
Service	Balance between maintaining order and law enforcement; less likely to make arrest than legalistic departments	Amenities-seeking: mayor-council or council-manager	Brighton and Nassau County, New York

SOURCE: Drawn from James Q. Wilson, *Varieties of Police Behavior* (Cambridge, MA: Harvard University Press, 1968).

In suburban communities, in which the service style predominates and police work is oriented toward providing amenities, such matters as burglaries and assaults are taken seriously, whereas arrests for minor infractions tend to be avoided when possible and replaced by informal nonarrest sanctions. In some suburbs, in which citizens feel they should be able to receive individualized treatment from their local police, plans for the development of metropolitanwide police forces have come under strong attack.

Thus even before an arrest is made, the police have formulated policies that will influence the level and type of enforcement. Since the police are the entry point to the criminal justice system, the total picture is shaped to a large extent by the decisions made by officials as to the allocation of resources and their perception of the level of law enforcement desired by the community. As discussed in Chapter 6, the current emphasis on the control of drugs has meant that the police have moved resources toward this goal and away from many of their traditional priorities.

POLICE FUNCTIONS

Police functions and responsibilities are extremely broad and complex. The police are expected not only to maintain the peace, prevent crime, and serve and protect the community but also to direct traffic, handle accidents and illnesses, stop noisy gatherings, find missing persons, administer licensing regulations, provide ambulance services, take disturbed or inebriated people into protective custody, and so on. The list is long, it varies from place to place, and much police work has little to do with the penal code. Some criminal justice planners have even suggested that the police have more in common with agencies of municipal social service than with the criminal justice system.

The American Bar Association developed a list of the objectives and functions of the police as a first step in understanding that the police are concerned with more than maintaining order, enforcing the law, and serving the public. The breadth of the police's responsibility is impressive. Among their duties are these:

1. to prevent and control conduct widely recognized as threatening to life and property (serious crime)
2. to aid individuals who are in danger of physical harm, such as the victim of a criminal attack
3. to protect constitutional guarantees, such as the right of free speech and assembly
4. to facilitate the movement of people and vehicles
5. to assist those who cannot care for themselves: the intoxicated, the addicted, the mentally ill, the physically disabled, the old, and the young
6. to resolve conflict, whether it be between individuals, groups of individuals, or individuals and their government
7. to identify problems that have the potential for becoming more serious problems for the individual citizen, for the police, or for government
8. to create and maintain a feeling of security in the community[24]

How did the police acquire such broad responsibilities? First, the police are about the only public agency that is available seven days a

A QUESTION OF ETHICS

Councilmember Peck looked over the applications of candidates to be chief of police of Shiloh, Louisiana. Five good candidates, all with experience in communities similar in size to Shiloh, and all with records indicating they had the potential to run the department. However, there was one candidate who presented a problem.

William Sherman was black. A graduate of Xavier University, he had risen to the rank of captain in the New Orleans Police Department, had been to the FBI Academy, and was highly recommended by his chief and several nationally known law enforcement experts. Sherman now wanted to be chief in a middle-sized city in his home state.

Shiloh had made great strides in race relations since the days of the freedom rides. Thirty percent of the residents were African-American, there was one black councilman, and ten of the members of the forty-man police force were black. Increasingly, Shiloh was becoming a middle-class community, with residents who commuted to Shreveport.

The city had changed, but was it ready for this change? On paper Sherman was clearly the most outstanding candidate. But what about Dave Pickens? He was born in Shiloh and had been a police officer for fifteen years. Pickens hadn't been to the FBI Academy and wasn't a college graduate, but he knew the town and he was white.

Can Councilmember Peck ethically make a decision at this stage? What issues should Peck bring up in interviews with the candidates? What factors might be relevant in determining what is best for the town? For the police? For the candidates? For Councilmember Peck?

week, twenty-four hours a day, to respond to citizens' need for help. Second, the police constitute the agency of government best able to perform the initial investigations required for the tasks just listed. Third, the capacity of the police to use force is a unifying theme of all their activity. Beyond these factors may be a political explanation for the breadth of the police function. Some commentators have suggested that since the police have been unable to control crime as their original mandate expected, they have agreed to every request to perform a new service rather than attempting to help define their crime control mandate realistically.

To aid in conceptually organizing the functions of the police, three primary categories have been developed over the years: order maintenance, law enforcement, and service. Although we usually think of the police as making arrests for the breaking of laws passed to protect persons and property, the argument can be made that their principal function is peacekeeping. Certainly, history tells us that the police were initially more involved in maintaining order than in catching criminals. Indeed, until the mid-nineteenth century, apprehension of thieves, robbers, and murderers was not considered a responsibility of the police; the victim was expected to find the guilty party.

Order Maintenance

The **order maintenance** function is a broad mandate to prevent behavior that either disturbs or threatens to disturb the public peace or that involves face-to-face conflict among two or more persons. A domestic quarrel, a noisy drunk, loud music in the night, a panhandler soliciting on the street, a tavern brawl—all are examples of disorder that may require the peacekeeping efforts of the police. Whereas most criminal laws specify acts that are illegal, laws regulating disorderly conduct deal with ambiguous situations that may be variously inter-

order maintenance: The police function of preventing behavior that disturbs or threatens to disturb the public peace or that involves face-to-face conflict among two or more persons. In such situations the police exercise discretion in deciding whether a law has been broken.

■

We expect the police to be prepared to perform a wide range of services. In this Atlanta shopping mall a gunman shot five persons. List the variety of actions the police are expected to undertake in such a situation.

■

Order maintenance is a broad mandate that includes everything from dealing with domestic violence to crowd control. Rather than invoke the law the police are expected to use discretion to "handle" a situation.

preted in accordance with the social environment and the perceptions and norms of the actors. Law enforcement comes into play when a law has been violated and only guilt must be assessed; order maintenance calls for intervention in situations in which the law may have been broken but that require interpretation of the law and determination of standards of right conduct and assignment of blame.

When we study the work of patrol officers, we can see that they are concerned primarily with behavior that either disturbs or threatens to disturb the peace. In these situations they confront the public in ambiguous circumstances and have wide discretion in matters of life and death, honor and dishonor. Walking the streets or moving about in patrol cars, officers may be variously required to help persons in trouble, to manage crowds, to supervise various services, and to assist people who are not fully accountable for what they do. When responding to a domestic disturbance, officers may find themselves in the position of mediating a squabble among family members and having to decide if one member should be removed from the home (through arrest) as a way of providing for the safety of the others. In all of these actions, patrol officers are not subject to direct external control. They have the power to arrest but also the freedom not to arrest. The order maintenance function is further complicated by the fact that the patrol officer is normally expected to "handle" a situation rather than to enforce the law, and in such cases the atmosphere is likely to be emotionally charged.

Some people argue that separating the roles of law officer and peace officer is impossible. As Wilson says, however, "to the patrolman, 'enforcing the law' is what he does when there is no dispute—when making an arrest or issuing a summons exhausts his responsibilities."[25] When patrol officers in Miami were asked what their job consisted of, they answered in police academy fashion, "protection of life and property and the preservation of peace," thus confirming what they believe to be their primary role—that of peacekeeper.[26] As we will see, studies of citizen complaints and requests for service justify this emphasis on the order maintenance function.

Law Enforcement

The **law enforcement** function of the police is concerned with situations in which the law has been violated and only the identity of the guilty needs to be determined. Police officers charged with major responsibilities in these areas are in the specialized branches of modern departments, such as the vice squad and the burglary detail. Although the patrol officer may be the first officer on the scene of a crime, in serious cases the detective usually prepares the case for prosecution by bringing together all the evidence for the prosecuting attorney. When the offender is identified but not located, the detective conducts the search; if the offender is not identified, the detective has the responsibility of analyzing clues to determine who committed the crime.

Although the police emphasize their law enforcement function, their efficiency in this area has been questioned. Especially when crimes against property are committed, the perpetrator usually has a time advantage over the police. Police efficiency is further decreased when the crime is an offense against a person and the victim is unable to identify the offender or delays notifying the police beyond the time in which apprehension might reasonably be expected.

law enforcement: The police function of controlling crime by intervening in situations in which it is clear that the law has been violated and only the identity of the guilty needs to be determined.

Service   *the dominant area of police activity*

In modern society the police are increasingly called on to perform services for the population. This **service** function—providing first aid, rescuing animals, and extending social welfare, particularly to lower-class citizens and especially at night and on weekends—has become the dominant area of police activity. Analysis of more than 26,000 calls to twenty-one police departments confirms the long-held belief that about 80 percent of citizens' requests for police intervention involve matters unrelated to crime; in fact the largest percentage of calls, 21 percent, were requests for information.[27] Because the police department is usually the only representative of local government readily accessible twenty-four hours every day, this is the agency to which people turn in times of trouble. Many departments provide information, operate ambulance services, locate missing persons, check locks on vacationers' homes, and stop would-be suicides. In cities, the poor and the ignorant—groups that few are eager to serve—rely almost solely on the police to perform service functions.

service: The police function of providing assistance to the public, usually with regard to matters unrelated to crime.

It is apparent that the police perform an important referral function. Especially in urban areas, people who call the police are often directed either to specialized units of government or to community agencies that deal with the kinds of problems they present. People who want directions, crime victims who need information, and persons who seek particular social services may all contact the police for guidance.

Although it may appear that valuable resources are being expended for police work unrelated to crime, it has been claimed that such services do have ramifications that help in crime control. It is through the service function that officers gain knowledge of the community and citizens, in turn, grow to rely on and trust the police. Checking the security of buildings is the service that most obviously helps prevent crime, but dealing with runaways, drunks, and interpersonal disturbances may help solve problems before they can lead to criminal behavior.

Implementing the Mandate

The list of police functions developed by the ABA may give the impression that each is of equal importance; in practice, however, police agencies must choose among law enforcement, maintenance of order, service, and other activities. Their choices will be made in accordance with community need, as citizens request action, and with departmental policy, as various styles of police work are emphasized.

In a comparison of police patrol work in five jurisdictions, the level of activity varied greatly with the function performed, as Table 5.2 indicates. In the urban department of the community called Midwest City, 33 percent of all activities were classified as law enforcement; in the suburban department of Pinewood, only 13 percent. Similarly, the levels of activity concerned with maintenance of order, service, traffic, and other functions varied.

The findings of this and other studies demonstrate that although the public may depend on the order maintenance and service functions of the police, citizens act as if law enforcement—the catching of lawbreakers—were the most important function. That the crime-stopping image is widely held is shown by public opinion polls and the reasons given by recruits for joining the force. Police administrators have learned that public support can be gained for budgets when the crime-fighter/law enforcement function is stressed. This emphasis is demonstrated by the internal organization of metropolitan departments, in which high status is accorded the officers who perform this function. This focus leads to the creation of specialized units within the detective division to deal with such crimes as homicide, burglary, and auto theft. The assumption seems to be that all other requirements of the citizenry will be handled by the patrol division. In some departments, this arrangement may create morale problems because of the allocation of disproportionate measures of resources and pres-

TABLE 5.2   Percentage of police patrol activities by type of department.   Patrol activities vary according to community demands and expectations.

Activity	Type of Department					
	Midwest City, Urban Department	Smithville, Suburban Department	Pinewood, Suburban Department	East Coast, State Police Station	Township Department	Total
Information gathering	8%	6%	5%	19%	12%	9%
Service	13	23	10	12	5	13
Order maintenance	24	29	16	13	26	24
Law enforcement	33	19	13	19	27	30
Traffic	18	21	52	29	30	21
Other	3	3	4	8	0	3
Total	99	101	100	100	100	100
	(N = 2835)	(N = 264)	(N = 214)	(N = 150)	(N = 168)	(N = 3631)

SOURCE: From *Police Behavior: A Sociological Perspective*, by R. J. Lundman. Copyright © 1980 by Oxford University Press, Inc. Reprinted by permission.

tige to the function that is concerned with a minority of police problems. Police are occupied with peacekeeping but preoccupied with crime fighting.

POLICE ACTION AND DECISION MAKING

Efforts by the police to carry out their functions in a democracy are mainly **reactive** (citizen invoked) rather than **proactive** (police invoked). Only in the vice, drugs, and traffic divisions of the modern police department does one find law officers acting on the basis of information gathered internally, by the organization. Because most criminal acts occur at an unpredictable time and in a private rather than a public place, the police respond to calls from persons who telephone, who signal a patrol car or officer on foot, or who appear at the station to register their need or complaint—all of which circumstances greatly influence the way the police fulfill their duties. In addition, the police are usually able to arrive at the scene only after the crime has been committed and the perpetrator has fled; the job of finding the guilty party is hampered by the time lapse and the frequent unreliability of the information the victim supplies. To a large extent, reports by victims define the boundaries of law enforcement.

The telephone, more than policies developed by community leaders or by police executives, dictates how resources will be used and the way that officers will respond to events. Studies of police mobilizations in urban areas reveal that 81 percent result from citizen telephone calls, 14 percent are initiated in the field by an officer, and 5 percent are initiated by people who request service in the field. Such a distribution not only influences the organization of a department but to a great extent also determines the response to a case. Citizens have come to expect that the police will respond quickly to *every* call, not differentiating among those that require immediate attention and those that can be handled in a more routine manner. This has the effect of what is called "incident-driven policing."[28]

reactive: Occurring in response to a stimulus, such as police activity in response to notification that a crime has been committed.

proactive: Occurring in the absence of a specific external stimulus, such as an active search for offenders on the part of the police in the absence of reports of violations of the law. Arrests for crimes without victims are usually proactive.

■
The police are primarily reactive. Generally officers are dispatched by the central communications unit to the location where an incident has occurred.

An additional problem is that in almost one-third of the cases, for example, no citizen is present when the police arrive to handle a complaint. In addition, because the patrol division of any department is organized to react to citizen requests, differences may develop between the police and citizens over what constitutes a criminal matter and the appropriate action to be taken. In short, "Police regard it as their duty to find criminals and prevent or solve crimes. The public considers it the duty of the police to respond to its calls and crises."[29]

The police do employ proactive strategies, relying on surveillance and undercover work to obtain the required information, but they do so only in connection with specific types of offenses (such as drug-related offenses), that can be detected by these means. Because of the lack of complainants, the police must rely on informers, stakeouts, wiretapping, stings, and raids. The current focus on drug offenses means that in many cities police resources have been reallocated so that a greater effort is being made to find and arrest those using or selling narcotics. Thus proactively produced crime rates are nearly always rates of arrest rather than rates of known criminal acts. The result is a direct correlation between the crime rate for these proactive operations and the allocation of police personnel.

Citizen-Police Encounters

Encounters between citizens and the police in situations that can be labeled criminal are structured by the roles each participant plays, by the setting, and by the attitudes of the victim toward legal action. The *National Crime Surveys* have shown that victims report offenses in only about half of all cases of victimization. Most often the police are not called because of the feeling that they could not or would not do anything. In other incidents, the relationship of the offender to the victim discourages reporting. The accessibility of the police to the citizen, the complainant's demeanor and characteristics, and the type of violation all structure official reaction and the probability of arrest. Although most citizens may believe that they have a civic obligation to assist the police by alerting them to criminal activity, an element of personal gain or loss exerts an important influence. Many people fail to call the police because they think it is not worth the effort and cost: filling out papers at the station, appearing as a witness, confronting a neighbor or relative. Clearly, then, citizens exercise control over the work of the police by their decisions to call or not to call them.

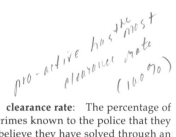

pro-active has the most clearance rate (100%)

clearance rate: The percentage of crimes known to the police that they believe they have solved through an arrest; a statistic used as a measure of a police department's productivity.

The **clearance rate**—the percentage of crimes known to the police that they believe they have solved through an arrest—varies with each category of offense. In such reactive situations as burglary, the rate of apprehension is extremely low, only about 14 percent; much greater success is experienced with violent crimes (46 percent), in which the victims tend to know their assailants.[30] Arrests made through proactive police operations against prostitution, gambling, and drug traffic have a clearance rate, theoretically, of 100 percent.

The arrest of a person often results in the clearance of other reported offenses because the police make it a practice to connect arrested persons with similar unsolved crimes when they can. Interrogation and lineups are standard procedures, as is the lesser-known operation of simply assigning unsolved crimes in the department's records to the defendant. Acknowledgment by offenders that they committed prior but unsolved crimes is often part of the bargain when guilty pleas are entered. Professional thieves know that they can gain favors from the police in exchange for "confessing" to unsolved crimes that they may not have committed.

Discretion

Discretion is a characteristic of organizations. Whether in the corporate structure of General Motors or the bureaucracy of a state welfare department, officials are given the authority to base decisions on their own judgment rather than on a formal set of rules. Thus executives and managers, but not workers on the assembly line, are given the power to make discretionary decisions. As we have noted, police officers are "street-level bureaucrats" in that discretion increases as one moves *down* the organizational hierarchy. Patrol officers, the most numerous and lowest-ranking officers and the ones who are newest to police work, have the greatest amount of discretion. In addition, they deal with clients in isolation and are charged primarily with maintaining order and enforcing highly ambiguous laws concerning disorderly conduct, public drunkenness, breach of the peace, conflicts among citizens, and other situations in which the offensiveness of the participants' conduct is often open to dispute. Wilson caught the essence of the patrol officer's role when he described it as one that "is unlike that of any other occupation . . . one in which subprofessionals, working alone, exercise wide discretion in matters of utmost importance (life and death, honor and dishonor) in an environment that is apprehensive and perhaps hostile."[31]

In the final analysis, the police officer exercises discretion through nonenforcement, arrest, or some more informal way of handling a dispute. The individual officer has the responsibility of deciding whether and how the law should be applied and is sensitive to a variety of cues. It is the officer on the scene who is able to define the situation and to decide how it is to be handled. Thus it is the officer who establishes what is defined as a violation of the law and for which no official action is to be taken.

Four factors seem particularly important in affecting the exercise of discretion by police officers:

1. *Characteristics of the crime:* Some crimes are considered trivial by the public, so, conversely, when the police become aware of a serious crime, they have less freedom to ignore it.
2. *Relationship between the alleged criminal and the victim:* The closer the personal relationship, the more variable the exercise of discretion. Family squabbles may not be as grave as they appear, and police are wary of making arrests since a spouse may, on cool reflection, refuse to press charges.
3. *Relationship between the police and the criminal or victim:* A respectful complainant will be taken more seriously than an antagonistic one. Likewise, a respectful alleged wrongdoer is less likely to be arrested.

4. *Departmental policies:* The preferences of the chief and the city administration, as reflected in the policy style, will influence the exercise of discretion.[32]

Figure 5.2 combines the types of situation with the types of police response in order to designate the offenses that belong to each category. Each type of situation offers the officials a different degree of discretion, and each has a different probability of being cleared through some kind of formal action. As mentioned earlier, law enforcement involves a situation in which the law has been violated and only the identity of the violator needs to be determined. The maintenance of order often calls for intervention in situations in which the law may have been broken but which require the law to be interpreted and standards of right conduct determined.

In encounters between citizens and police, the matter of fairness to the citizen is often intertwined with departmental policy. When should the patrol officer frisk? When should a deal be made with the addict-informer? Which disputes should be mediated on the spot and which left to adjudicatory personnel? Surprisingly, these conflicts between the demands of justice and policy are seldom decided by heads of departments but are left largely to the discretion of the patrol officers, who often act illegally without disapproval from superiors. In fact, departmental control over police actions is lacking in certain types of activities. In categories I and IV, for example, the patrol officer has great discretion, but in the former category it can be brought under departmental control and in the latter it cannot. Further, departments must resort to an internal intelligence network to suppress police corruption associated with discretion in cases of crimes without victims. In category II, patrol officers have the least amount of discretion (except when juveniles are involved), and the departmental policies and organizations are instruments of control. Category III presents an intermediate relationship between the amount of discretion and the possibility of departmental control.

In sum, police officers are street-level bureaucrats, since their encounters with citizens allow for extensive independence. Further, they are concerned primarily with order maintenance situations, in which the law is not cut-and-dried and citizens are often hostile. Because of the situational environment, they must mobilize information quickly and make decisions through the tactics of simplification and routinization, basing their perceptions of the clients on prior cases and experiences. Such a process often leads to error.

Although some people advocate the development of detailed instructions to guide the police officer, such an exercise would probably be fruitless. No matter how detailed the formal instructions, the officer will still have to fit rules to cases. In the end, police administrators must decide what measures they will take to influence the way their officers use discretion. Given the variety of functions the police are asked to perform and the influence of such factors as the nature of the crime and citizen response, administrators must develop policies that can serve to guide their officers. Controlling the actions of subordinates, according to one social scientist, "depends only partly on sanctions and inducements; it also requires instilling in them a shared outlook or ethos that provides for them a common definition of the situations they are likely to encounter and that to the outsider gives to the organization its distinctive character or 'feel.' "[33]

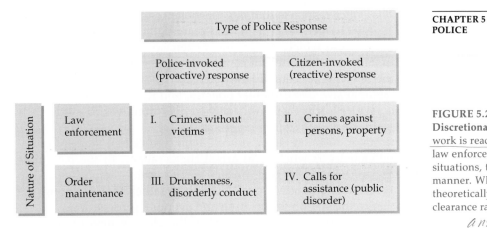

Type of Police Response		
	Police-invoked (proactive) response	Citizen-invoked (reactive) response
Law enforcement	I. Crimes without victims	II. Crimes against persons, property
Order maintenance	III. Drunkenness, disorderly conduct	IV. Calls for assistance (public disorder)

Nature of Situation

FIGURE 5.2
Discretionary situations. Most police work is reactive. For certain types of law enforcement and order maintenance situations, the police act in a proactive manner. Which type of response theoretically will result in a higher clearance rate?

ans: pro-active

police have the least amt of discretion in crimes against persons & property.

Domestic Violence: Encounters, Discretion, Action

It was not until the mid-1970s that activists succeeded in raising the level of public attention to the problem of domestic violence. By looking at police actions with respect to this problem, we can see the links between police-citizen encounters, the exercise of discretion, and actions taken (or not taken) by law enforcement officers.

Domestic violence, also called "battering" and "spouse abuse," has been defined as assaultive behavior involving adults who are married or cohabiting or who have an ongoing or prior intimate relationship. In the overwhelming number of cases, domestic violence is perpetrated by men against women. Surveys have shown that domestic violence is not rare or limited to certain socioeconomic groups and, therefore, of little concern to criminal justice policy makers. In fact, a national survey of 2,000 families led researchers to estimate that during any one year 1.7 million Americans had faced a spouse wielding a knife or gun and that well over 2 million had experienced a severe beating at the hands of their spouses.[34] Crime statistics support the belief that domestic violence may be lethal. *Uniform Crime Reports* data have shown that 30 percent of all female murder victims were killed by their husbands or boyfriends.[35] Perhaps more troubling is that domestic violence in a household is not a single isolated event. Rather, once a woman is victimized by domestic violence, she faces a high risk of being victimized again.

For too long, criminal justice agencies, and perhaps society as a whole, viewed domestic violence as a "private" affair best settled within the family. Concern was often expressed that official involvement would only make the situation more difficult for the victim, because she would have to face the possibility of reprisal.

From the viewpoint of most police departments, domestic violence was thought to be a "no-win" situation in which officers responding to calls for help were often set upon by one or both disputants. Entering a residence to handle such an emotion-laden incident was thought to be more dangerous than answering calls to investigate "real" criminal behavior. There has been a widespread belief, recently proved false, that intervention in family disputes was a leading cause of officer deaths and injury. In those situations in which an arrest is made, the police have too often found that the victim refuses to cooperate with a prosecution arising out of the incident.

The police response to domestic violence is an excellent example of a highly charged, uncertain, and potentially dangerous encounter with citizens in which officers must exercise discretion as they take action. Here is an example of maintaining order and, possibly, enforcing the law that officers are expected to handle in accordance with the criminal law, departmental policies, and the needs of the victim. Until very recently there were few formal directives to guide their actions.

A major question facing officers who confront an incident of domestic violence is whether to arrest the assailant. In the past most police departments advised officers to try to calm the parties and to make referrals to social service agencies rather than to bring the attacker to the station for booking and eventual prosecution.

The first controlled experiment of the effectiveness of arrest in preventing recidivism in cases of domestic violence was conducted in

CLOSE-UP *Battered Women, Reluctant Police*

As Joanne Tremins was moving some belongings out of her ramshackle house on South Main Street [Torrington, Connecticut] two years ago, her 350-pound husband ran over, grabbed the family cat and strangled it in front of Tremins and her children.

For more than three years, Tremins said, she had complained to Torrington police about beatings and threats from her husband. Instead of arresting him, she said, the police acted "like marriage counselors."

The cat attack finally prompted police to arrest Jeffrey Tremins on a minor charge of cruelty to animals. But four days later, outside a local cafe, he repeatedly punched his wife in the face and smashed her against a wall, fracturing her nose and causing lacerations and contusions to her face and left arm.

That Joanne Tremins is suing this New England town of 34,000 is not without historical irony. For it was here that Tracey Thurman, . . . won a $2 million judgment in 1985 against the police department in a federal civil rights case that has revolutionized law enforcement attitudes toward domestic violence.

Attorney Burton Weinstein, who won the Thurman case and represents Tremins, said he is involved in 31 suits against police by battered women. "Some involve multiple abductions and rapes," he said. "Several involve killings that were broadcast in advance."

The Thurman case marked the first time that a battered woman was allowed to sue police in federal court for failing to protect her from her husband. The ruling held that such a failure amounts to sex discrimination and violates the 14th Amendment.

The resulting spate of lawsuits has prompted police departments nationwide to reexamine their long-standing reluctance to make arrests in domestic assault cases, particularly when the wife refuses to press charges. State and local lawmakers, facing soaring municipal insurance costs, are also taking notice.

The Connecticut legislature responded in 1986 with a law requiring arrests in domestic disputes if there is probable cause to believe that an assault occurred, regardless of whether the wife wants the arrest. . . . In the 12 months after Connecticut's law took effect, the number of family-violence arrests in the state increased 93 percent, from 12,400 to 23,830.

Here in hilly Torrington . . . Police Chief Mahlon C. Sabo said [the Thurman case] had a "devastating" effect on the town and his 70-member force. "The police somehow, over the years, became the mediators," said Sabo. "There was a feeling that it's between husband and wife. In most cases, after the officer left, the wife usually got battered around for calling the police in the first place.

"We were dealing with a societal problem we weren't trained to deal with. We were trained to shoot guns, to make arrests, not to be social workers."

Although the law now requires them to make arrests, police officers here said, the courts toss out many domestic cases for the same reason that long hampered police.

"Unfortunately, many women just want the case dropped and fail to recognize they're in a dangerous situation," said Anthony J. Salius, director of the family division of Connecticut Superior Court. "If she really doesn't want to prosecute, it's very difficult to have a trial because we don't have a witness."

Court statistics bear this out. Under Connecticut's 1986 law, authorities have prosecuted only one-third of those arrested in domestic assaults, with most drawing fines or suspended sentences. Charges have been dropped against the remaining two-thirds, sometimes in exchange for their participation in counseling, alcoholic treatment or other diversionary programs.

Nearly five years after the attack by her estranged husband, Tracey Thurman remains scarred and par-

Minneapolis.[36] During the eighteen-month study period, officers systematically selected one of three different tactics—arrest, advice or mediation, and ordering the offender to leave the house for an eight-hour period—as a means of handling misdemeanor-level incidents of domestic violence. Three hundred and thirty cases occurred during the period. Interviews with the victims immediately following the incident and biweekly during a six-month follow-up period were used to discover if further violence had resulted. It was found that offenders who had not been arrested had almost twice as much repeat violence during the six-month period as those who had been arrested. This difference was not the result of the fact that the offenders were in jail rather than at home, since 86 percent were released within one week. Since only 2 percent were subjected to further actions by the criminal justice system such as prosecution and trial, the study suggests that "arrest and initial incarceration

tially paralyzed from multiple stab wounds to the chest, neck and face. Charles Thurman was sentenced to 14 years in prison.

For eight months before the stabbing, Thurman repeatedly threatened his wife and their son, 2. He worked at Skee's Diner, a few blocks from police headquarters, and repeatedly boasted to policemen he was serving that he intended to kill his wife, according to the lawsuit.

In their defense, police said they arrested Thurman twice before the stabbing. The first charges were dropped, and a suspended sentence was imposed the second time. Tracey Thurman later obtained a court order barring her husband from harassing or assaulting her.

On June 10, 1983, Tracey Thurman called police and said her husband was menacing her. An officer did not arrive for 25 minutes and, although he found Charles Thurman holding a bloody knife, he delayed several minutes before making an arrest, giving Thurman enough time to kick his wife in the head repeatedly.

Less than a year after police were found liable in the attack on Thurman, Joanne Tremins also found that a restraining order obtained against her husband was worthless. . . . Tremins recounted how she made about 60 calls to police to complain about her husband, a cook. But she acknowledges that, on most of the occasions, when the police asked if she wanted him arrested, she said no.

"How could I say that?" she asked. "He's threatening to kill me if I have him arrested. He's threatening to kill my kids if I have him arrested. He'd stand behind the cops and pound his fist into the palm of his hand."

Hours before Tremins strangled the cat on Feb. 11, 1986, according to the lawsuit, he beat and kicked his wife and her son, Stanley Andrews, 14. When an officer arrived, Joanne Tremins said, he told her that he could not make an arrest unless she filed a complaint at the police station.

"My son was all black and blue," Tremins said. "But [the officer] refused to come into my room and look at the blood all over the walls and the floor."

After Tremins was taken into custody for the cat incident, police did charge him with assaulting the son. He was released on bond, and his wife was issued a restraining order.

When her husband approached Tremins days later at a cafe in nearby Winsted, police refused to arrest him, despite the order. After the beating, Jeffrey Tremins was charged with assault and sentenced to two years in prison.

Torrington police, who have 110 restraining orders on file, said some women use them to harass their husbands or have them arrested, sometimes as evidence for a forthcoming divorce case.

Sabo said his biggest problem with the new arrest law is that police no longer can make distinctions between a shoving match and a savage beating. Even a minor, first-time altercation, he said, can result in arrest for the husband and wife.

To attorney Weinstein, however, Torrington police are still dragging their feet. "That department has the gentlest learning curve I've ever seen," he said. "Indeed, it may be flat."

SOURCE: From "Battered Women, Reluctant Police," by H. Kurtz, *The Washington Post*, February 28, 1988, p. A1. Copyright © 1988, The Washington Post. Reprinted with permission.

alone may produce a deterrent effect, regardless of how the courts treat such cases, and that arrest makes an independent contribution to the deterrence potential of the criminal justice system."[37]

The Minneapolis experiment has been replicated in a number of jurisdictions to determine if the results can be validated. A replication study in Omaha showed that arrest by itself did not appear to deter subsequent domestic conflict any more than did mediation or separating those in the dispute.[38] The researchers suggest that additional strategies need to be developed to deal with the problem. Others have suggested that arrest followed by prosecution will have a greater impact in reducing domestic violence. However, a study of prosecutorial discretion in domestic violence cases in Milwaukee showed that factors such as the victim's injuries and the defendant's arrest record influenced the decision to charge, not just the fact of spouse abuse.[39]

Meanwhile other policy changes have been enacted in many states that will force the police to confront the issue of domestic violence more directly. Legislatures in some states have expanded officers' authority to arrest in these cases. In some places the law now mandates the arrest of suspects in misdemeanor incidents of domestic violence without obtaining a warrant even if the officer did not witness the crime but has probable cause to believe that one was committed by the person arrested. Police departments have also begun to enact policy guidelines for cases of domestic violence. For example, the Seattle Police Department has listed a number of factors (gunshot wound, broken bones, intentionally inflicted burns) that should *always* be considered to involve a felony.[40] Other departments have developed procedures to assist victims and actions to be taken when protection orders are issued. Training programs on the dynamics of domestic violence have also been developed in most large departments and state academies to educate officers about this important problem.

Even though we can point to a number of dramatic changes in the ways in which the police view the problem of domestic violence, the fact remains that it is the officer in the field who must handle these situations. Laws, guidelines, and training help, but as with so much other police work, reliance must be placed on the discretionary actions of the officer.

POLICE WORK

Although we can define the formal position and legal mandate of police officers according to the duties stated in a job description, such a definition tells us little about the way individual officers act in everyday settings when they meet citizens face to face. Even if we accept the myth of the police officer as philosopher, guide, and friend, he or she plays a variety of roles according to the work situation and the persons encountered in it. The behavior of the patrol officer who arrests a boisterous young man inside a bar is very unlike that officer's behavior when an injured victim needs assistance at the scene of a traffic accident. The officer occupies the position of patrol officer in both encounters yet plays dissimilar roles and acts differently in interpersonal exchanges. We should not generalize even to this extent but recognize that the ways in which individual officers play their roles depend on such factors as personality, goals, and previous experiences. The actual behavior of police officers—their actions, perceptions, and norms—is the important dimension for discussion rather than the formal description of their duties.

To understand police work better, we need to look at the "making" of officers and the subculture of the police. First, we shall see what qualifications are required for entry into the force, examine the types of persons recruited to police work, and study their formal and on-the-job training. Second, we shall take the operational environment into account, examining the police subculture to see the impact of such factors as the officer's "working personality," isolation, and job stress.

The Making of an Officer

Gaining a fuller comprehension of the work of police officers entails our considering the factors that determine who is recruited, the values and attitudes they bring with them to the force, and the process of socialization and training that takes place. In our consideration, we must ask the extent to which the behavior of police officers is shaped by the unique demands of the job.

Qualifications

The policies that determine the types of persons recruited and retained greatly structure the behavior of the almost 800,000 sworn and unsworn persons who serve in police departments around the country. If pay scales are low, educational requirements minimal, and physical standards unrealistic, police work will attract only those from certain socioeconomic groups with certain personalities, attitudes, and objectives. At a time when police work calls for persons who are sensitive to the complex social problems of contemporary society, a majority of departments offer entrance salaries of about $20,000 and require of new members only a high school education, good physical condition, and the absence of a criminal record. Many departments examine the circumstances of the last requirement and will recruit persons who have been convicted of a misdemeanor as a youth, for example. In many cities the police receive large numbers of applications for admission to the force, but few applicants have the "right" characteristics.

Qualifying standards vary greatly and depend to a large extent on a community's level of urbanization. The fact that much of the research on the characteristics of police officers has been carried on in such major departments as those of New York City and San Francisco may have provided a false picture, because the patrol officers in rural areas and small cities may have lower education levels. Between 1969 and 1980, police officers and preservice students were encouraged to earn a college degree through the Law Enforcement Assistance Administration's (LEAA) Law Enforcement Education Program (LEEP). Although few departments require more than a high school diploma, many select recruits with a college education. In the past twenty years the educational levels of American police officers have risen significantly.

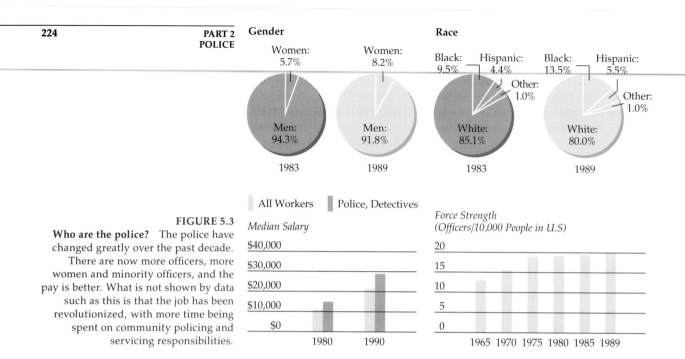

FIGURE 5.3

Who are the police? The police have changed greatly over the past decade. There are now more officers, more women and minority officers, and the pay is better. What is not shown by data such as this is that the job has been revolutionized, with more time being spent on community policing and servicing responsibilities.

The pay in relation to that of comparable occupations is one of the outstanding problems of police work, yet many recruits are attracted by the job security that is entailed, pension benefits, and, in most departments, opportunities for overtime (see Figure 5.3). Pay levels influence the personnel situation in at least three ways. Obviously, low pay scales will not attract recruits who have invested money and effort to gain additional education or skills. A second influence is more psychological. Because police officers may interpret the level of compensation as society's estimate of their worth, their self-esteem is dealt a blow. And relatively small paychecks may lead a police officer to "moonlight"—a practice that places added physical and emotional burdens on the officer and his or her family—or to yield to the temptation of corruption in order to achieve the living standard of the middle class. (See Chapter 7 for discussions of both moonlighting and corruption.)

Recruitment

Who is attracted to police work? Early studies emphasized that law enforcement tended to attract persons with authoritarian and conservative values. Later research, however, has shown that police recruits differ very little from persons who seek other civic jobs, such as fire fighters. The attraction of police work lies less in the opportunity to exert authority and use a gun than in the security and economic gains a government job offers and the opportunity to do something of worth for the community. When John Van Maanen interviewed recruits in Union City (a fictionalized name) he found that "virtually all recruits alluded to the opportunity afforded by a police career to perform in a role which was perceived as consequential or important to society."[41] The opportunity to work out of doors in a nonroutine job was another important factor. Knowledge of police work through contact with family members or friends who are officers was also found to be instrumental.

Training

Upon joining a police department, the new recruit immediately faces the reality of the organization. He or she may have a citizen's understanding of the work but little knowledge of the procedures and tactics it entails. Throughout a probationary period, the recruit learns aspects of the work and is tested. In most cities, new officers must attend a formal course of training at a departmentally run academy. Such courses range from two-week sessions in which the handling of weapons and target practice are emphasized to more academic four-month programs followed by fieldwork, such as those developed by the Los Angeles police and sheriff's departments. In the latter courses, recruits hear lectures on social relations, receive language training, and learn emergency medical treatment. Most states now require preservice training for all recruits. Large departments generally run their own programs, and a state police academy trains recruits from rural and small-town units.

The typical training program focuses on technical components of the job; it is outside the classroom, in interaction with fellow cadets and experienced officers, that the real socialization to departmental norms takes place.

Learning the Ropes

Some critics place little value on the formal instruction of the academy, for they believe that the officer is introduced to the reality of police work on the street and not in books. This attitude is often impressed on recent academy graduates the first day on the job when they are placed under the supervision of an experienced officer—often called a field training officer—whose opening remark may be "Now, I want you to forget all that stuff you learned at the academy."

It is during the first encounters with real police work that new officers learn about the culture of their chosen occupation. "Learning

Physical training is an important part of the police academy program. Increasingly departments are demanding that officers maintain good physical condition throughout their career.

the ropes" includes learning the informal ways, rather than the rule book ways, in which law enforcement operates. It includes learning about shortcuts, how to be "productive," what to avoid, and a host of other bits of wisdom, norms, and folklore that define the job in a particular department.

From the initial shock at the realization that police work is not exactly what it seemed to be, the officer settles into departmental routine. He or she readily recognizes that the crime-fighting image of television and recruiting posters bears little resemblance to reality: most police work consists of routine service and administrative tasks. The patrol officer is predominantly an order taker, a reactive member of a service organization. There are enough unpredictable elements to police work to make it interesting, however, and enough opportunities for actions that provide the self-esteem and gratification necessary to go on doing one's job well, whatever one's occupation. Thus the new police officer is "made" on the job. In the making of the officer this socialization process far outweighs in importance either the formal criteria for recruits or the background characteristics of those who seek police work.

Subculture of the Police

subculture: The aggregate of symbols, beliefs, and values shared by members of a subgroup within the larger society.

The **subculture** of the police helps to define the "cop's world" and each officer's role in it. A subculture is a subdivision of a national culture defined by such social factors as occupation, ethnicity, class, and residence, which in combination form a functioning unity that shapes the beliefs, values, and attitudes of the group's members. The police share a set of expectations about human behavior that they carry into professional contacts because they are members of the police community. Like the subculture of any occupational group that sees itself as distinctive, the subculture of the police is based on a set of value premises stemming from their view of the nature of their occupational environment and their relationship to that environment and to other people. Entry requirements, training, behavioral standards, and operational goals combine to produce a similarity of values.

socialization: The process by which the rules, symbols, and values of a group or subculture are learned by its members.

The norms and values of the police subculture are learned. From the time recruits make their first contact with the force, they become aware of the special ways they are expected to act. This process of **socialization** makes police officers attuned not only to the formally prescribed rules of the job but also, more importantly, to the informal ways in which the subculture dictates their actions. They learn that loyalty to fellow officers, professional esprit de corps, and respect for police authority are esteemed values. Although the formal training given at the police academy teaches recruits a portion of their new occupation, by actually working as police officers they become socialized by fellow officers to the "real" way the job should be performed.

Like soldiers, patrol officers work in an organizational framework in which rank carries responsibilities and privileges; yet the success of the group depends on the cooperation of its members. All patrol officers are under direct supervision and can be punished if they fail to recognize that their performance is measured by the contribution they make to the group's work. They are also influenced by the pressure exerted on them directly by their colleagues, buddies who work alongside them. Patrol officers, however, have territorial constraints dictating that they be solitary workers, dependent on their own personal skills and judgment. They move onto a social stage with an unknown cast of characters and are expected to perform in a setting and plot that can never be accurately predicted. They must be ever ready to act and to do so according to law. From arresting a fleeing assailant to protecting a fearful wife from her drunken husband to assisting in the search for a lost child, the patrol officer meets the public alone.

Although the police bureaucracy allocates duties among officers on the basis of rank and ability, the police subculture overrides these differentiations because, as organizational specialists believe, of the practice of promoting from within. There are few opportunities for lateral entry into supervisory positions; all members begin at the rank of patrol officer. Upward movement depends on the recommendations of supervisors, with the result that adherence to the rules of the occupational subculture is strengthened. The idealism of young police academy graduates may be shattered when they realize that they must operate within the structure and norms of a bureaucracy. To advance above the boredom of patrol work to the law enforcement work of the detective division may require connections (often political) and a record for acting in accordance with departmental norms. These requirements can mean that arrests that may cause fellow officers extra work are not made or that various unlawful practices within the department are not brought to the chief's attention.

advancement requires connections, often political.

The impact of the police community on the behavior of the individual officer is enhanced when situations develop that produce conflict between the group and the larger society. To endure their work, the police find they must relate to the public in ways that protect their own self-esteem. As James Ahern, former police chief of New Haven, Connecticut, has stated, most job routines in law work are boring; the idealistic recruit soon begins to question the worth of the profession.[42] If the police view the public as essentially hostile and police work as aggravating that hostility, they will segregate themselves from the public by developing strong attitudes and norms that ensure that all members of the police community conform to the interests of the group.

As these examples indicate, the subculture of the police exerts a strong impact on law enforcement operations. Further, even with the increased amount of formal training that is given to the police, law enforcement is an art, not a science. There is no body of generalized, written knowledge, theory, or rules that can chart the police officer's way. The recruit learns on the job, as an apprentice, and is thus molded to a great extent by fellow officers and the culture within which they operate.

law enforcement an art, not a science; recruit learns on the job.

Working Personality

Social scientists have demonstrated that there is a decided relationship between one's occupational environment and the way one interprets events. An occupation can be seen as a major badge of identity

working personality: The complex of emotional and behavioral characteristics developed by a member of an occupational group in response to the work situation and environmental influences.

[handwritten margin notes:] police become automatically suspicious by habit

[handwritten margin notes:] element of danger isolates police socially from citizenry

[handwritten margin notes:] always on their guard, attentive to signs of potential violence.

that a person acts to protect as an aspect of his or her self-esteem and person. Like doctors, teachers, janitors, and lawyers, the police as a group develop their own particular ways of perceiving and responding to their work environment. The police officer's **working personality** is thus developed in response to the occupational environment. Because the police role contains two important variables, danger and authority, officers develop a distinctive perspective from which they view the world. Because they operate in dangerous situations, law enforcement officers are especially attentive to signs of potential violence and lawbreaking. Hence they become suspicious persons, constantly on the lookout for indications that a crime is about to be committed or that they may become targets for lawbreakers.

As Skolnick has said, "the element of danger isolates the policeman socially from that segment of the citizenry which he regards as symbolically dangerous and also from the conventional citizenry with whom he identifies."[43] The element of authority reinforces the element of danger, because the officer is required to direct the citizenry, whose typical response denies recognition of this authority and stresses the officer's obligation to respond to danger.

The danger of their work makes police officers especially attentive to signs of potential violence and lawbreaking. Throughout the socialization process, the recruit is warned to be suspicious, to be cautious, and is told about fellow officers who were shot and killed while trying to settle a family squabble or write a ticket for speeding. In 1990, seventy-six officers were killed in the line of duty, a figure much lower than the average yearly number. The folklore of the corps emphasizes that officers must always be on their guard. They must look for the unusual, including everything from persons who do not "belong" where they are observed to businesses open at odd hours. They must watch for and interrogate persons, including:

> those known to the officer from previous arrests, field interrogations, and observations
>
> emaciated-appearing alcoholics and narcotics users, who may turn to crime to pay for their habit
>
> anyone who fits the description of a wanted suspect
>
> known troublemakers near large gatherings
>
> persons who attempt to avoid or evade the officer, who are visibly "rattled" when near the officer, and who exhibit exaggerated unconcern over contact with the officer
>
> "lovers" in an industrial area (make good lookouts)
>
> persons who loiter about places where children play or around public restrooms
>
> persons wearing a coat on a hot day
>
> cars with mismatched hubcaps, or dirty cars with clean license plates (or vice versa)
>
> uniformed "deliverymen" with no merchandise or truck.[44]

With these as examples, it is not hard to understand how police officers become suspicious of everyone and all situations.

The element of unexpected danger creates such tension in police officers that they are constantly on edge and worried about the possibility of attack. People stopped for questioning may sense this tension. A suspect may not intend to attack an officer, but the latter's gruffness may be seen as uncalled-for hostility. If the suspect shows resentment, the officer may in turn interpret it as animosity and be even more on guard. Because the work demands continual preoccupation with potential violence, the police develop a perceptual shorthand to identify certain kinds of people as possible assailants—for example, persons whose gestures, language, and attire—long hair, motorcycle jackets, "jiving"—the officers have come to recognize as connected with violence.

police learn to identify certain kinds of people as possible assailants

The police represent authority, but unlike workers whose clients have learned to recognize their professional prerogatives (such as doctors, psychiatrists, or social workers), a police officer must *establish* authority. Certainly the symbols of police authority—the uniform, badge, gun, and nightstick—help, but more important is the way police officers act within the social setting of each encounter. The officer must gain control of a situation by intervening, for example, but the right to intervene may be challenged because the patrol officer is concerned primarily with maintaining order, an area of the law in which there may be a great deal of disagreement. The maintenance of order requires that the police stop fights, arrest drunks, and settle domestic quarrels, situations in which the pertinent laws are inexact and the presence of an officer may be welcomed by neither the offender nor onlookers.

police officer must establish authority.

In law enforcement situations, the officer can usually expect the victim's support; the shopkeeper will be pleased by the officer's arrival and will assist by describing the burglar. But when officers are dispatched to investigate a report of juveniles causing trouble in a public place, a neighborhood disturbance, or a victimless crime, they usually do not find a cooperative complainant and must contend not only with the perpetrators but also with others who may gather and expand the conflict. These are the kinds of circumstances that require police to "handle the situation" rather than to enforce the law—that is, to assert authority without becoming emotionally involved. Further, they must regulate a public that, while often denying recognition of the police's authority, at the same time stresses their obligation to respond to danger. Even when verbally challenged by citizens on their personal conduct and right to enforce the law, police are expected to react in a detached or neutral manner.

The police officer, a symbol of authority with low occupational status, must at times give orders to people with high status. Professionals, business people, and others of the middle class may respond to the officer not as a person working for the community interest but as a public servant whom they do not respect. Given the blue-collar background of the cop, maintaining self-respect and refusing to take "crap" may be important ways of resolving this problem. A major emphasis of police work is on the need to assert authority on arrival at the scene, when arrival itself may generate hostility. The emphasis on authority may lead to use of excessive force or violence by officers who feel that their status has been placed in question by a person who represents a danger to them and to the community. Cries of police brutality often spring from such a circular chain of events.

professional people with high status someone look down on police.

In sum, working personality and occupational environment are so interlocked that they reinforce each other in a way that greatly

working personality √ occupational environment interlocked affects the daily work of the police. Procedural requirements and the organizational structure of policing are overshadowed by the perceived need to establish authority in the face of danger.

Isolation of the Police

National studies of occupational status have shown that the public nowadays ascribes more prestige to the police than it did in earlier decades. Public opinion polls indicate that the overwhelming majority of Americans have a high opinion of the work of the police. Even in economically depressed inner-city areas, in which the police may be viewed as the tools of an unjust society, most of the inhabitants see the police as protectors of their persons and property. But despite these findings, the police do not believe that the public regards their vocation as honorable or their work as just. They feel that they are looked upon with suspicion, probably because they must discipline those whom they serve and are given the authority to use force to ensure compliance. Because they believe that the public is hostile to them and that the nature of law work aggravates the hostility, the police tend to separate themselves from the public and develop strong in-group ties. The police culture also encourages the strong bonding that commonly occurs among people who deal with violence. This solidarity "permits fallible men to perform an arduous and difficult task, and . . . places the highest value upon the obligation to back up and support a fellow officer."[45]

Throughout the publications of police organizations runs the theme that the public is extremely critical of law enforcement agents. But the public is not the only group that is unappreciative of the police; other actors in the criminal justice system are often cited. By failing to treat the police with professional respect and by not dealing seriously with offenders whose behavior may have endangered the patrol officer, lawyers, prosecutors, and judges demean the officer's status. Part of the burden of being a police officer is that one is beset by doubt about one's professional status and worth in the public mind. This burden heightens the pressures on individual officers to isolate themselves within the police community.

Few other occupational groups are so circumscribed by the job's all-encompassing demands as are police officers. The situational context of their position limits their freedom to isolate their vocational role from other aspects of their lives. From the time they are first given badges and guns, they must always carry these reminders of the position—the tools of the trade—and be prepared to use them. The requirements that they maintain vigilance against crime even when off duty and that they work at odd hours, together with the limited opportunities for social contact with persons other than fellow officers, reinforce subculture values.

Even more important is the fact that the police uniform and membership in the force are social liabilities. Wherever they go, the police are recognized by bartenders, bookies, and waitresses who want to talk shop; others harangue them about the inadequacies of police service. The result of these occupational hazards is that officers tend to interact primarily with their families and with other officers.

When he gets off duty on the swing shift, there is little to do but go drinking and few people to do it with but other cops. He finds himself going bowling with them, going fishing, helping them paint their house or fix their cars. His family gets to know their families, and a kind of mutual protection society develops which turns out to be the only group in which the policeman is automatically entitled to respect.[46]

Job Stress

The working environment and subculture of the police expose members of the force to situations that affect their physical and mental health. This hazard has been fully recognized by law enforcement officials only during the past decade. One study of 2,300 officers in twenty departments found that 37 percent had serious marital problems; 36 percent, health problems; 23 percent, problems with alcohol; 20 percent, problems with their children; and 10 percent, drug problems.[47] Newspaper and magazine articles with such titles as "Time Bombs in Blue" discuss the effects of the pent-up emotions and physical demands of the job.

Many of the factors that produce stress in police officers have been identified by psychologists and other behavioral scientists, who have noted four general categories of stress to which police officers are subject:

1. *External stress,* produced by real threats and dangers, such as the necessity of entering a dark and unfamiliar building, responding to a "man with a gun" alarm, and pursuit of lawbreakers at high speeds.
2. *Organizational stress,* produced by elements that are inherent in the paramilitary character of police forces: constant adjustment to changing schedules, working at odd hours, requirements that detailed rules and procedures be complied with.
3. *Personal stress,* which may be generated by an officer's racial or gender status among peers, with consequent difficulty in getting along with individual fellow officers and in adjusting to group-held values not in accordance with one's own values, perceptions of bias, and social isolation.
4. *Operational stress,* the total effect of the need to confront daily the tragedies of urban life; the need to deal with thieves, derelicts, and the mentally deranged; being lied to so often that all citizens become suspect; being required to place oneself in dangerous situations to protect a public that appears to be unappreciative; and the constant awareness of the possibility of being held legally liable for one's actions.[48]

Police departments have been slow to deal with stress, but now some of the larger departments provide psychological and medical counseling for officers. As in industry, an individual is often referred to a counselor only after a problem has been identified as resulting from a work-related incident. Stress is the type of debilitating problem that may not be identified for a long time because it is usually internalized. In popular terminology, it gets "bottled up" until finally it is manifested in the person's health, habits, or behavior. Programs of prevention, group counseling, liability insurance, and family involvement have been undertaken. The legislatures of many states have instituted more liberal disability and retirement rules for police than for other public employees because their jobs are recognized to be more stressful and potentially debilitating.

SUMMARY

As the Gilbert and Sullivan operetta observes, "the policeman's lot is not a happy one." Throughout the history of policing in the United States, one can find a public that is unhappy with the level of crime and the seeming inability of the police to deal with it. Much of this unhappiness can be traced to the public's misunderstanding of the role of the police in a democratic society. Citizens evaluate the effectiveness of police work with respect to the function of law enforcement—solving crimes—though the maintenance of order and community service take the major share of the police's time and resources. Because police work is primarily reactive, law officers depend on citizens to notify them that an offense has been committed. The reluctance of many citizens to give timely notification reduces the ability of the police to prevent and control crime. In addition, the police are required to exercise discretion in situations in which decisions must be made carefully and quickly, a factor that further complicates the performance of their role.

Although some people may say that the police have a simple assignment—to maintain order through law enforcement—such is not the case. Legislators may write the laws as if full enforcement were expected, but to a large extent the police determine the extent of actual enforcement. Police administrators must make choices about the types of criminal behavior to which they will respond, the allocation of enforcement resources, and the policies governing the relationship of officers to citizens. The police are expected to perform three functions: law enforcement, maintenance of order, and service. Social and political forces will shape the extent to which each department emphasizes one or another of these functions.

As in other professions, there is a link between the work situation, the social bonds that unite police officers, and their interpretations of the world around them. Recruited because of a belief that the work will be an interesting way to serve the community, the officers often find that the assigned tasks are dull. More important, they feel that the work is not appreciated by the citizenry. On the job they are constantly aware of the danger that goes with their career and the authority they must exercise. These pressures further strengthen the bonds among officers. They may seriously interfere with the effectiveness of law enforcement in a democratic society.

FOR DISCUSSION

1. You are a police chief. What are some of the assumptions that will guide your allocation of your resources?

2. You are a police chief. How will the community's social and political characteristics influence the style of law enforcement that you create?

3. What changes could be made to enable police officers to feel that theirs is a respected profession and to integrate them more effectively into the community?

4. The police officer is taught to be on guard and watchful for suspicious activity. What influence might this stance have on encounters with the public?

5. How might officers' attitudes about drugs and possible direct experience with them influence their behavior in various encounters?

FOR FURTHER READING

Goldstein, Herman. *Problem-Oriented Policing*. New York: McGraw-Hill, 1990. Examination of the move toward problem-oriented or community policing. Argues for a shift to this focus.

Greene, Jack R., and Steven Mastrofski, eds. *Community Policing: Rhetoric or Reality?* New York: Praeger, 1988. An excellent collection of essays on community policing.

Muir, William K., Jr. *Police: Streetcorner Politicians*. Chicago: University of Chicago Press, 1979. A study of the different styles of police work as observed on the job.

Skolnick, Jerome H. *Justice without Trial: Law Enforcement in a Democratic Society*. New York: Wiley, 1966. One of the first books to look at the subculture of the police and the exercise of discretion.

Westley, William. *Violence and the Police*. Cambridge, MA: MIT Press, 1970. Based on a 1951 study of the police, this book examines the fraternal bonds of officers and addresses the question of violence by officers.

Wilson, James Q. *Varieties of Police Behavior*. Cambridge, MA: Harvard University Press, 1968. A classic study of the styles of policing in different types of communities. Shows the impact of politics on the operations of the force.

NOTES

1. Herman Goldstein, *Policing a Free Society* (Cambridge, MA: Ballinger, 1977), p. 1.
2. Ibid.
3. Bernard I. Garmire, "The Police Role in an Urban Society," in *The Police and the Community*, ed. Robert F. Steadman (Baltimore, MD: Johns Hopkins University Press, 1972), p. 2.
4. Jerome Skolnick, *Justice without Trial: Law Enforcement in a Democractic Society* (New York: Wiley, 1966), p. 6.
5. Thomas A. Critchley, *A History of Police in England and Wales* (London: T. A. Constable, 1967), p. 36.
6. Charles Reith, *The Blind Eye of History: A Study of the Origins of the Present Police Era* (London: Faber and Faber, 1952), p. 128.
7. Peter Manning, *Police Work* (Cambridge, MA: MIT Press, 1977), p. 82.
8. Ibid., pp. 82–83.
9. George L. Kelling and Mark H. Moore, "The Evolving Strategy of Policing," in *Perspectives on Policing*, U.S. Department of Justice, National Institute of Justice (Washington, DC: Government Printing Office, November 1988).
10. Hubert Williams and Patrick V. Murphy, "The Evolving Strategy of Police: A Minority View," *Perspectives on Policing*, no. 13 (Washington, DC: National Institute of Justice, 1990).

11. Kelling and Moore, *Perspectives on Policing.*

12. Eric H. Monkkonen, *Police in Urban America 1860–1920* (Cambridge: Cambridge University Press, 1981), p. 127.

13. J. F. Richardson, *Urban Police in the United States* (Port Washington, NY: National University Publications, 1974), p. 19.

14. Monkkonen, *Police in Urban America, 1860–1920,* p. 127.

15. Herman Goldstein, *Problem-Oriented Policing* (New York: McGraw-Hill, 1990), p. 7.

16. Mark H. Moore and George L. Kelling, " 'To Serve and to Protect': Learning from Policy History," *Public Interest* (Winter 1983):55.

17. Ibid., p. 280.

18. James Q. Wilson and George L. Kelling, "Broken Windows: The Police and Neighborhood Safety," *Atlantic Monthly* (March 1982) pp. 29–38.

19. George L. Kelling, "Order Maintenance, the Quality of Urban Life, and Police: A Line of Argument," in *Police Leadership in America,* ed. William A. Geller (New York: Praeger, 1985), p. 299.

20. Herman Goldstein, "Improving Policing: A Problem-Oriented Approach," *Crime and Delinquency* 25 (1979):236–257.

21. Samuel Walker, " 'Broken Windows' and Fractured History: The Use and Misuse of History in Recent Police Patrol Analysis," *Justice Quarterly* 1 (March 1984):88.

22. Carl B. Klockars, "Order Maintenance, the Quality of Urban Life and Police: A Different Line of Argument," in *Police Leadership in America,* ed. William A. Geller (New York: Praeger, 1985), p. 300.

23. Wilson, *Varieties of Police Behavior* (Cambridge, MA: Harvard University Press, 1968).

24. Goldstein, *Policing a Free Society,* p. 35.

25. Wilson, *Varieties of Police Behavior,* p. 16.

26. Jesse Rubin, "Police Identity and the Police Role," in *Police and the Community,* ed. Robert F. Steadman (Baltimore: Johns Hopkins University Press, 1972), p. 24.

27. Eric J. Scott, *Calls for Service: Citizen Demand and Initial Police Response,* U.S. Department of Justice (Washington, DC: Government Printing Office, 1981), pp. 26–37.

28. John Eck, William Spelman, Diane Hill, Darrel W. Stephens, John Stedman, and Gerald R. Murphy, *Problem Solving: Problem-Oriented Policing in Newport News* (Washington, DC: Police Executive Research Forum, 1987), pp. 1–2.

29. Albert J. Reiss, Jr. *The Police and the Public* (New Haven, CT: Yale University Press, 1971), pp. xiii, 70.

30. U.S. Department of Justice, *Crime in the United States* (Washington, DC: Government Printing Office, 1990), p. 164.

31. Wilson, *Varieties of Police Behavior,* p. 30.

32. Herbert Jacob, *Urban Justice* (Boston: Little, Brown, 1973), p. 27.

33. Wilson, *Varieties of Police Behavior,* p. 33.

34. Murray A. Straus, Richard J. Gelle, and Suzanne K. Steinmetz, *Behind Closed Doors: Violence in the American Family* (Garden City, NY: Anchor Press, 1980), pp. 25–26, 32–36.

35. U.S. Department of Justice, *Crime in the United States,* p. 39.

36. Lawrence W. Sherman and Richard A. Berk, "The Specific Deterrent Effect of Arrest for Domestic Assaults," *American Sociological Review* 49 (April 1984): 261–272.

37. Ibid.; see also Kirk R. Williams and Richard Hawkins, "The Meaning of Arrest for Wife Assault," *Criminology* 27 (1989):163.

38. Franklyn W. Dunford, David Huizinga, and Delbert S. Elliott, "The Role of Arrest in Domestic Assault: The Omaha Police Experiment," *Criminology* 28 (May 1990):204.

39. Janell Schmidt and Ellen Hockstedler Steury, "Prosecutorial Discretion in Filing Charges in Domestic Violence Cases," *Criminology* 27 (August 1989):487.

40. U.S. Department of Justice, National Institute of Justice, *Confronting Domestic Violence: A Guide for Criminal Justice Agencies* (Washington, DC: Government Printing Office, 1986), p. 34.

41. John van Maanen, "Observations on the Making of Policemen," *Human Organization* 32 (1973):407–418.

42. James F. Ahern, *Police in Trouble* (New York: Hawthorne Books, 1972), p. 27.

43. Skolnick, *Justice without Trial,* p. 44.
44. Thomas F. Adams, "Field Interrogation," *Police* (March–April 1963):28.
45. Michael K. Brown, *Working the Street* (New York: Russell Sage Foundation, 1981), p. 82.
46. Ahern, *Police in Trouble,* p. 14.
47. John Blackmore, "Are Police Allowed to Have Problems of Their Own?" *Police Magazine* 1 (1978):47–55.
48. Robert J. McGuire, "The Human Dimension in Urban Policing: Dealing with Stress in the 1980s," *Police Chief* 46 (November 1979):27; see also Francis Cullen, Terrence Leming, Bruce Link, and John Wozniak, "The Impact of Social Supports in Police Stress," *Criminology* 23 (1985):503–522.

Police Operations

Key Terms and Cases

aggressive patrol
arrest

preventive patrol
problem-oriented policing

sworn officers
Carroll v. *United States* (1925)

Terry v. *Ohio* (1968)
United States v. *Leon* (1984)

Chuck Stuart reported that his wife Carol had been murdered by a black man in the Mission Hill section of Boston. The police reacted by stopping and frisking countless African-Americans, arresting one, and causing racial tensions to rise. Stuart's subsequent suicide led to the assumption that he had been the murderer.

The story horrified racially tense Boston. A young white couple were shot driving to their suburban home through a racially mixed neighborhood after attending a birthing class at Brigham and Women's Hospital. Carol Stuart died soon after the incident. Eight-week premature Christopher Stuart was taken from his mother's dying body but died seventeen days later. Chuck Stuart suffered a gunshot wound. Later he told police that while stopped at an intersection in the racially mixed Mission Hill district, a black man in a jogging suit shot him and his wife, suspecting that they were police undercover agents.

The mayor ordered every available cop into the hunt for the man Stuart had described. Hundreds of black men were stopped and frisked. The search continued for two months until William Bennett was arrested on the basis of information from three teenagers that Bennett's nephew had boasted that his uncle had shot the Stuarts. Bennett insisted that he was innocent, but his long rap sheet did not serve him well; still, the police held off filing formal charges. Meanwhile, the Boston news media were having a field day. Portrayed as a Willie Horton, Bennett seemed to confirm for many Bostonians the link between African-Americans, drugs, and violence. It was not until January 3, when Chuck Stuart's brother went to the Boston Police, that the story began to unravel. Matthew Stuart said that the night of the shooting he had driven to a prearranged spot in Mission Hill where his brother had given him a bag and told him to "Take this to Revere" [a Boston suburb]. Matthew said he saw something on the front seat of Chuck's car but couldn't identify it. On opening the bag he discovered a gun and woman's jewelry. He threw the gun and bag into a river. It was not until two months later that he went to the police. Chuck Stuart committed suicide the next day. Police now believe that Chuck Stuart had killed his wife Carol in an attempt to collect insurance money.

The Stuart case describes the type of high-profile incident that gets attention. In much of America, law enforcement agencies are placed in difficult positions as they attempt to deal with crime, violence, racial tensions, and drugs. But as we have noted, the work of the police is multifaceted. Although the public focuses on their crime-fighter role, the police also serve the community by maintaining order and providing services to citizens in need. Chapter 5 explored the broad dimensions of the police role in a democratic society. Emphasis was placed on the discretionary aspect of police activity and the influences that are brought to bear on individual police officers as they work. Chapter 6 will focus on police operations—the actual work of agencies as the police pursue offenders and prevent crimes. Because of the demands on them, the police must be organized so that patrol efforts can be coordinated, investigations conducted, arrests made, evidence assembled, and crimes solved.

ORGANIZATION OF THE POLICE

The police have been given the resources to carry out their varied responsiblities by special organizational structures created to ensure efficient and effective operation. Tailored to meet the special needs of and demands on the police, these structures are different from those created for other organizations.

The highly decentralized nature of policing in the United States is underscored by the fact that departments vary in organization and service activities. Although a majority of police officers are employed by departments with more than 1,000 officers, a majority of departments have fewer than 30 officers each. Most departments patrol, investigate, direct traffic, and provide other services; yet others are involved in only one or two of these functions. Some communities have an officer-to-resident ratio of 3.5 to 1,000; in others (usually smaller cities), the ratio is 2.1 to 1,000. In rural communities the ratio is even smaller. One might think that population and crime levels would dictate the size of a police force, yet as seen in Figure 6.1, these variables are not always related. Such factors as the density of popu-

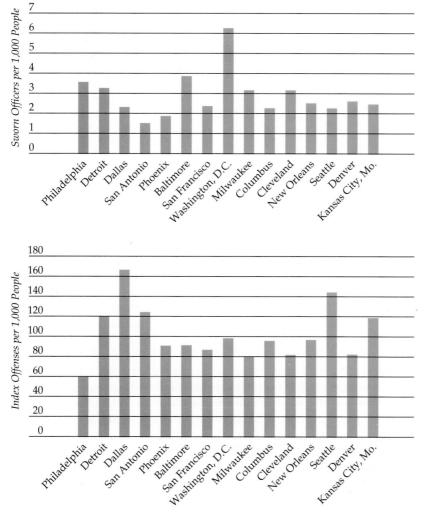

FIGURE 6.1
Sworn officers and index offenses in thirteen American cities (per 1,000 population). These major cities have varying numbers of police officers and crimes per every 1,000 residents. In some cities with less crime, the number of police is out of proportion to the population size.
SOURCE: *Issues Paper, Metropolitan Police Department Resource Allocation* (Washington, DC: Police Executive Research Forum, 1990).

lation, the number of nonresidents who spend part of their day working or visiting in a jurisdiction, local politics, and other pressures from the community influence the size of the force. In sum, there is really no model or typical police agency with reference to functions, staffing, and resources.

The police have traditionally been organized in a military manner. A structure of ranks from patrol officer to sergeant, lieutenant, captain, and up to chief helps designate the authority and responsibility of each level within the organization. Like that of the military, this operations model is designed to emphasize superior-subordinate relationships so that discipline, control, and accountability are primary values. This emphasis is thought to be important both as a means of efficiently mobilizing police resources to combat crime and as a way of ensuring that civil liberties are protected. The belief is that police objectives can be achieved most easily, effectively, and satisfactorily when the principles related to this framework are applied. The structure of a well-organized police department, shown in Figure 6.2, is designed to fulfill five functions:

1. Apportion the work load among members and units according to a logical plan.
2. Ensure that lines of authority and responsibility are as definite and direct as possible.
3. Specify a unity of command throughout so that there is no question as to which orders should be followed.
4. Place responsibility, accompanied by commensurate authority. If the authority is delegated, the user is held accountable.
5. Coordinate the efforts of members and units so that all will work harmoniously to accomplish the mission.

Allocation of Resources

In large cities, not all policing activities can be physically carried out from a central office. As a result, districts or precincts are created so that most operations affecting particular geographical areas can function within them. Accordingly, the patrol and traffic divisions tend to be dispersed throughout the city, whereas specialized units work out of headquarters. The advantage of having units already positioned in the field has the disadvantage of lessened control by headquarters. However, the modern concept of community policing emphasizes the importance of the police being located in the neighborhoods they cover. Modern communications technology provides links among units.

A major police department contains a separate functional division for each of the line units: patrol, investigation, traffic, vice, and juvenile (see Figure 6.2). Line units are the direct operations components and perform the basic law enforcement tasks of crime prevention and control. The patrol and investigation (detective) units are the core of the modern department. Patrol is traditionally the basic action arm of the police and deals with a wide range of functions, including preventing crime, apprehending offenders, arbitrating domestic quarrels, helping the ill, and assisting at the site of accidents. The investigation division is a specialized unit that is concerned primarily with apprehension and conviction of the perpetrators of the more serious crimes. The separation of patrol and investigation sometimes complicates the definition of objectives, functions, and responsibilities of each unit. Whereas the investigation unit usually concentrates on murder, rape, and major robberies, the patrol division has joint responsibility for investigating those crimes and also is responsible for investigation of lesser crimes, which of course are far more numerous.

Many departments have a traffic unit, but usually only police forces in middle-sized to large cities maintain specialized vice and juvenile units. Vice is sometimes kept as part of the investigation unit, but because operations in this field present the risk of corruption, the specialized unit reports directly to the chief in some depart-

FIGURE 6.2
Structural organization of the Police Department (Phoenix, Arizona). This is a typical police organization. Note the major divisions of patrol, special operations, investigations, and management and technical services. The Internal Affairs Bureau is closely tied administratively to the chief.
SOURCE: Courtesy of the Phoenix Police Department, *Annual Report,* 1990.

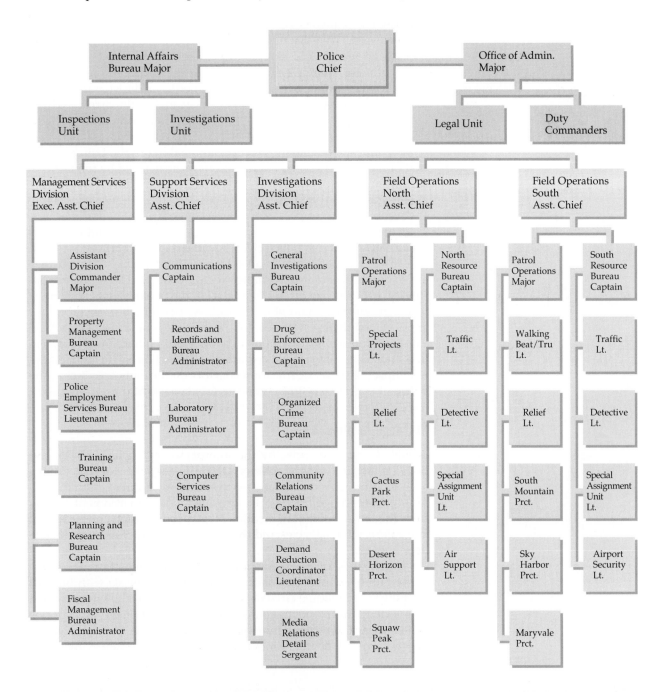

ments. As a result of the war on drugs, some cities have specialized units working only on this problem. In large departments an internal affairs section, generally reporting directly to the chief, investigates charges of corruption and other disciplinary problems associated with the staff and officers. The juvenile unit is concerned primarily with crime prevention as it relates to young people. As with the other specialized units, the carrying out of its responsibilities depends on the patrol division.

Influences on Decisions: Bureaucratic Politics

Three factors characterize the organizational context within which police decisions are made. First, the police stand as the essential gateway to the justice system, through which raw materials enter to be processed. They have the discretion not to arrest or to filter out cases they feel should not be forwarded. Those cases sent to the prosecutor for charging and then on to the courts for adjudication have their beginning with an individual officer's decision that probable cause exists to arrest. How the officer makes the arrest and collects supporting evidence to justify the action greatly influences the decisions of the prosecutor and judge.

Second, the administrative decision making of the police, unlike that of most other formal organizations, is structured by the fact that the ultimate fate of one group of clients (the accused) rests with other clients (prosecutor and judge). The police may introduce clients into the system, but the outcome of a case is largely in the hands of others. That the others are members of the legal profession and of higher social status than the police creates a potential for conflict.

Third, the police are in an odd situation because although they are expected to act in accordance with a code of ethics, possess authority, and may use discretion to decide the fate of clients, they must function within a chain of command. As part of a bureaucracy, they are expected to observe rules, follow the orders of superiors, and *also* exercise professional discretion. They are duty bound both to stay in line and to be responsible for independent choices. To understand the impact of these organizational factors on the daily activities of the police, it is necessary to examine certain aspects of these activities.

Exchange Relationships

Besides being influenced by the interpersonal relationships among decision makers, police actions are influenced by external groups such as other governmental agencies, interest groups, and citizens. This penetration of the police organizational environment results from the overlapping jurisdictions of city, county, state, and national law enforcement agencies and the political context of criminal justice decisions.

In his study of enforcement of traffic regulations in four Massachusetts towns, John Gardiner found that city officials with budgetary powers, individual citizens, and such groups as the safety council all insisted that the police conform with *these individuals'* perceptions of the way traffic regulations should be enforced. Attempts to fix tickets through the intervention of politicians or of police officials of other communities were found to be common. Massachusetts police chiefs believe that enforcement of traffic regulations can jeopardize public relations more than any other phase of their work. If ticket-writing campaigns are too active, they fear for their budget and for community support. As traffic policies must be made in a context of sporadic citizen demands and group pressures, they tend to be decided by a process of "vague picking and choosing among public values."[1]

Many of the exchange relationships between the police and their clientele are cooperative. The extensive communications network between the Federal Bureau of Investigation and local police forces is a good example. The FBI performs important and helpful services for local agencies by publicizing the names of wanted criminals, providing background information on offenders, and completing technical operations such as fingerprint analysis for departments that lack such expertise. At the same time there are organizational and political benefits to be gained by the FBI. Presumably the political support of local officials is the payment made for the services rendered.

Jurisdictional Disputes

Within the criminal justice system, the police have a peculiar connection to the prosecution and judicial subsystems. Although the police have the power to introduce clients into the larger system, they are formally required to allow other professionals to evaluate their work. Police officers' professional right to decide which clients should enter the system is thus infringed on by the bureaucratic context. Conflict among the police, prosecutor, and courts is inevitable. Prosecutors may return cases to the police for lack of evidence or because they decide not to pursue a case. The courts may criticize the police over the admissibility of evidence, techniques of interrogation, the status of a confession, and the use of force. Because the traditional index of police effectiveness has been the number of arrests rather than either the number of convictions or the nature of the sentences imposed, the police may be motivated primarily to generate information that links a person with a criminal event rather than to ensure that evidence is admissible or that other criteria of due process are met.

Prosecutors, on the other hand, may be motivated to ensure that each case brought to them by the police will easily pass the scrutiny of the judge and result in a conviction that will enhance their record. In certain cases, they may require that the police develop exceptionally strong evidence before they will consider acting. Since prosecutors know that they have more to lose than just the case if the victim refuses to cooperate, if the evidence is skimpy, and if the judge is known to dislike a certain type of case, they may persuade the police to handle the offender in some other way. The filtering system gives the police this opportunity to drop cases without the need to secure the approval of other judicial units.

In all the bargaining relationships within the criminal justice bureaucracy, the police must interact with persons who may view law enforcement with hostility. In fact, many are hired (such as defense attorneys) because of their adversarial stance toward the police. Yet these exchange relationships are not completely one-sided; the police, too, have tactics that they may use in their dealings with prosecutor and judge. Often these tactics take the form of informal and *sub rosa* practices, such as inducing suspects to plead guilty to a host of prior unsolved offenses in return for leniency, thus increasing the clearance rate.

Organizational Response

Although the police depend primarily on citizens for inputs into the criminal justice system, the nature of the police response is greatly influenced by the organizational character of the police bureaucracy. Through the functional structure of the operational divisions (patrol, vice, investigation, and so on), the quasi-military command system, and the various incentives used to induce the desired responses, the administrative environment affects the way calls for actions are processed as well as the nature of the police response.

Police organizations are increasingly being shaped by innovations in communications technology. These developments have led to growing centralization of both command and control in departments, a centralization of decision making. The core of modern police departments is the communications center, where decisions are made to activate officers. Line officers are thus in constant touch with headquarters and are required to report each of their actions. Extensive use of the two-way radio has been a primary means for police administrators to limit the discretion of the officer in the field. Whereas in former times patrol officers might have administered their own version of on-the-spot justice to a mischievously behaving juvenile, they may now be expected to file a report, take the delinquent into custody, and initiate formal proceedings.

In most cities citizens can report crimes or call for information or assistance through the standardized 911 telephone number. A dispatcher will ask for facts about the crime or need for service so that the most appropriate response can be made. Development of the 911 procedure has resulted in many departments being inundated with calls, many of which are not directly related to police responsibilities. Gilsnan has shown how 911 police operators, acting as street-level bureaucrats, interpret calls for assistance and categorize information so as to fit organizational categories. These operators handle a wide range of calls and must be able to understand the caller's request as well as to determine an appropriate response.[2]

To improve efficiency, police departments use a number of response alternatives to calls for service. The alternative chosen depends on several factors, such as whether the incident is in progress, has just occurred, or occurred some time ago, and whether anyone is or could be injured. Given these considerations, the dispatcher may send an officer immediately to the scene, may give a lower priority so that the response is delayed, or may refer the caller to another agency.

The centralization of communications and decision making has not gone unchallenged. Many researchers believe that advancements in technology tend to isolate the police from the citizens they serve. In particular, the extensive use of motorized patrols has meant that residents have only a fleeting glimpse of officers as they cruise through their neighborhoods. In many urban areas the police are perceived as an outside force having little contact with the community and little knowledge or understanding of the problems peculiar

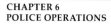

The telephone is the primary way that the police respond to events. Increasingly, departments are experiencing overload on their communication capacity as 911 programs have become the major way that urban residents call for assistance.

to a neighborhood. In addition, it is argued, officers are not in a position to build up a rapport with residents that would increase cooperation. Programs developed for community-oriented policing, discussed later in this chapter, are designed to overcome some of the negative aspects of the typical organizational response.

Productivity

Like other organizations, the modern police department is interested in maintaining quality control. But like other public agencies, the police have difficulty measuring the quantity and quality of their work. How does one measure "good" policing? Such traditional measures as the crime rate and clearance rate do not really give the true picture, and thus nebulous descriptions are used. It is not uncommon to hear a weary patrol officer say when scanning the log at the end of a busy day, "Well, we worked tonight, but we didn't get any activity for the sergeant."

Activity is one of the ways in which the police try to measure their work. It is the statistic used by sergeants to judge the productivity of their officers, by lieutenants to assure themselves that the sergeants are properly directing their officers, by captains to show their superiors that their districts are in capable hands, and by the chief to prove to the public that tax money is not being squandered. In most departments, effectiveness is based on such things as the number of parking meters tagged, illegally parked cars ticketed, suspects stopped for questioning, and arrests made and the value of stolen goods recovered.

It is obvious that police activity is more easily produced when it is police invoked (proactive) than when it is citizen invoked (reactive). Thus departmental policies concerning such offenses as traffic violations, public drunkenness, and crimes without victims greatly influence the record of police effectiveness.

DELIVERY OF POLICE SERVICES

A distinction is often made between line and staff functions. *Line functions* are those that directly involve operational activities; *staff functions* supplement or support the line. Staff functions are found in the chief's office and the auxiliary services bureau (see Figure 6.2), as well as in the staff inspection bureau. The efficient police department must have a proper balance between line and staff duties so that they can be coordinated into an effective crime control, order maintenance, and service force. The distribution of personnel in a department of the size and structure suggested by Figure 6.2 would probably be administration, 7.5 percent; operations, 84 percent; and inspection, 8.5 percent. Within the operations area, the patrol bureau accounts for 55 percent of the personnel; the investigations division, 17 percent; the special operations division, 12 percent; and the specialized units of youth and vice, the remaining 16 percent.[3] There are, however, great variations among departments, with the percentage of personnel assigned to patrol functions ranging from 40 to over 60 percent, depending on such factors as size, level of urbanism, and extent of professionalism. The allocation of personnel should *not* be used as an index of importance, because within a department the number of persons required to fulfill a function varies.

This section directs attention to the line activities of the operations bureau, including the patrol, investigation, traffic, and vice units. As each operational unit is described, consider the work of the unit and its contribution to the overall effectiveness of policing.

Patrol

Patrol is often called the backbone of police operations. The word *patrol* is thought to be derived from a French word, *patrouiller*, which originally meant "to tramp about in the mud." This translation clearly establishes what one authority has called a function that is "arduous, tiring, difficult, and performed in conditions other than ideal."[4]

sworn officers: Police employees who have taken an oath and been given powers by the state to, for example, make arrests, use force, and transverse property, in accordance with their duties.

Every modern police department in the United States has a patrol unit; even in large specialized departments, patrol officers constitute up to two-thirds of all **sworn officers.** In small communities, police operations are not specialized, and the patrol force *is* the department. The patrol officer is the police generalist and must be prepared to assume a wide variety of responsibilities.

The patrol function has three components: answering calls for assistance, maintaining a police presence, and probing suspicious circumstances. Patrol officers are well suited to these activities because they are near the scene of most situations and can render timely help or speedily move to apprehend a suspect. When not responding to calls, they engage in preventive patrol—that is, making the police presence known—on the assumption that doing so will deter crime. Walking the streets of a neighborhood or cruising in a vehicle through the beat, the patrol officer is constantly on the lookout for suspicious people and behavior.

Patrol requires officers to engage in a variety of police functions, including interviewing crime scene witnesses. Is it likely that this officer will gain the cooperation of these citizens?

The object of the patrol function is to disperse the police in ways that will eliminate or reduce opportunities for lawbreaking and increase the likelihood that a criminal will be caught while committing a crime or soon thereafter. Patrol officers also perform the important function of helping to maintain smooth relations between police and community. As the most visible members of the criminal justice system, they can have a decisive effect on the willingness of citizens to cooperate in an investigation. In addition, their effective work can help to create a sense of security among citizens.

As the essential action arm of policing, patrol forces are engaged in a variety of activities, including preventing crime, maintaining order, arresting offenders, and giving aid to citizens. Performing these activities as part of their basic responsibility to respond to calls and to make rounds on the streets may sound fairly straightforward but in practice turns out to be complex.

> With the patrol force deployed throughout the community and able to respond rapidly to calls for service, one or more of these men usually arrive first at the scene of a crime or disaster. But merely reaching the scene of an incident does not mark the end of a patrolman's mission;

it is just beginning. The measures a patrolman takes to confront a situation, the discretionary decisions he makes, the way he interacts with citizens, the skill and imagination he applies to conducting investigations, questioning suspects, interviewing complainants and witnesses, and the techniques he follows in searching crime scenes and preserving physical evidence are the hallmarks of his job. Hence, the work of a patrol officer is of far-reaching importance and the quality of service rendered by the whole department is largely dependent upon officer care and competence.[5]

One of the problems of modern police administration is that too often the patrol unit is taken for granted. Because the rank of patrol officer is close to the entry level for recruits, greater status is accorded detectives in the investigation unit. In addition, patrol work is viewed as cold, sometimes dirty, boring, and thankless. Yet patrol officers must carry the major burden of the criminal justice system. They must "confront the enraged husband, the crazed drug addict, the frightened runaway, the grieving mother, the desperate criminal, and the uninformed, apathetic, and often hostile citizen."[6] Because the patrol officer's job involves the most sensitive contact with the public, it is important that the best-qualified officers do this work. Unfortu-

CLOSE-UP   *Saturday Night in a Squad Car*

Car 120 covers an area one-half mile wide by one mile long in the heart of downtown Minneapolis. Bisecting the district along its long axis is Hennepin Avenue, a street lined with bars, nightclubs, and movie theaters. South of Hennepin Avenue lie the shopping and business areas of Minneapolis; north of Hennepin are warehouses and older office buildings. At the east end of the district lies the Mississippi River, and along it, just north of Hennepin Avenue, is the Burlington Northern Railway Station. That portion of the district is heavily populated with derelict alcoholics.

6:45 We saw some derelicts drinking wine, and the officers forced them to pour the wine out.

7:00 9 West Franklin, Apt. _____, unwanted guest The caretakers of the apartment building advised us that the ex-husband of one of their tenants was threatening harm to the tenant and abduction of the tenant's child. He had also threatened the babysitter. We determined the kind of car that the ex-husband was driving. The tenant then returned with a friend and asked us to keep out of the area so that her husband would not be afraid to find her. She then hoped to tell him that the divorce was final and that he ought not to bother her any more.

7:50 Cassius Bar, fight It had been settled by the time we arrived.

7:58 _____ Cafe, domestic A 20-year-old girl and her sister-in-law met us and advised us that the girl's stepfather, the proprietor of the cafe, had let the air out of the tires of the girl's car. He had also pulled loose some wires under the hood and then blocked their car with his. All of this had occurred in the cafe's parking lot. She also claimed that he had hit her. We

talked to the stepfather and mother of the girl, and they said that they had taken this action in order to prevent the girl from driving to Wisconsin until she had cooled down. They claimed that she had had a fight with her husband, that she wanted to get away by driving to see her grandmother in Wisconsin, and that she was too emotionally upset to drive. This was apparently evidenced by the fact that she was willing to take her baby with her in only a short-sleeved shirt. The mother also told us that the girl was a bad driver with many arrests and that the car wasn't safe. The officers advised the girl that she call a tow truck and that, if she wished, she could sign a complaint against her parents in the morning. We then left.

8:28 _____ Cafe, "settle it this time" The sister-in-law claimed that she had been verbally abused by the stepfather. The officers decided to wait until the tow truck arrived. The stepfather moved the car that was blocking. The parents of the girl began to criticize the officer in sarcastic terms, saying such things as "Isn't it a shame that the police have nothing better to do than to spend hours helping to start a car." They also threatened not to give half-price food to police officers any more. The tow truck arrived and reinflated the tires of the car. However, the tow truck driver was unable to start the car. The stepfather, although advised by one of the officers not to do so, tried to move his car in a position to block his daughter's car. The officer at that point booked him for reckless driving and failure to obey a lawful police order. The officer had the stepfather's car towed away. Another squad car came to sit on the situation until the tow truck had moved the girl's car to a service station. We took the

nately, the low status of patrol assignments encourages officers to seek more prestigious work in their departments.

Television has given citizens an image of the patrol officer as always on the go, rushing from one incident to another, and making a number of arrests during the course of a tour. Research has shown, however, that most officers, on most duty tours, do not make even one arrest. Taking formal measures against lawbreakers is clearly only a small part of patrol activity. Patrol officers are expected to be constantly "on guard," watching for suspicious persons and behaviors, providing information and assistance to the public. Because of their ability to exercise discretion, officers can handle situations without invoking formal processes. Patrol officers serve the public's need for security and assistance; their presence in a neighborhood or community, especially if they are on foot, is a major factor in reducing the fear of crime.

Patrol Activities

Historically, patrolling was done on foot, but with the development of the automobile, much patrol work is now carried out in squad cars.

---

stepfather to jail, where he immediately arranged to bail himself. The stepfather said that he was going right back. The officer replied, "We can book you more than you've got money." As soon as we left the police station, we went back to the parking lot and found that the girl's car had been started and that she had left town.

9:55 _____ Spruce, Apt. _____, unwanted guest The tenant told us that she had been ill and that she had not opened the door when her landlady knocked. The landlady then had opened the door and walked in. The officers [told] the landlady, "You can't just walk in. You are invading her privacy." The landlady replied, "The hell I can't, you damned hippie-lover. I'm going to call the mayor." "Go ahead," the officer said. He then added, "The next time this happens, we will advise the tenant to use a citizen's arrest on you."

10:35 We saw a woman crying outside a downtown bar and a man with his hands on her. We stopped but were told by both that this was merely a domestic situation.

10:50 The officers saw a drunk in an alley, awakened him, and sent him on his way.

10:55 We saw a door open in a downtown automobile dealership. When we checked, we learned that all the employees were there to carry out an inventory.

11:15 We noticed an elderly man in a car talking to a number of rather rough-looking motorcycle types. We stopped and learned from the motorcyclists that the man was very intoxicated. They offered to drive the car for him to a parking spot, and the officers allowed them to do this. The man was told by the officers to sleep off his drunk condition, and the officers took the keys from the car and threw them into the trunk so that he would be unable to drive further that evening.

11:45 15th and Hawthorne, gang fight When we arrived, the officers from two other squad cars were busy booking some young men. The officers believed that occupants of the top floor of the building adjoining this corner had been throwing things at them. When the landlord refused admittance to that building, the officers broke the door down. The apartment from which the objects had been thrown was locked, and the tenants refused admittance. Again, the officers broke down the door and booked the occupants.

12:25 Nicollet Hotel, blocked alley By the time we arrived, the car which had blocked the alley had been driven away.

12:55 11th and LaSalle, take a stolen [police radio slang] We made a report of a stolen automobile.

1:22 We saw one woman and two men standing outside an apartment building. The men appeared to be fighting. One man and the woman said that the other man was bothering them. We sent him away. The couple then went into an apartment building. As we drove away, we saw the man who had been sent returning and trying to obtain entrance to the apartment building. We returned and booked him as a public drunk.

1:45 Continental Hotel, see a robbery victim We took a report from a young man who had been robbed at knife point. We drove around the neighborhood looking, without success, for his assailant.

SOURCE: From "Policing," by J. M. Livermore, *Minnesota Law Review* 55 (1971):672–674. Reprinted by permission.

This change has created a problem of supervision and accountability. Even with modern communications and departmental policies requiring officers to check with superiors concerning their actions, it is not possible to know everything that takes place.

Methods of allocating patrol officers and arriving at decisions about various means of transportation and communications have been a subject of research during the past decade. Though the results of these studies are not definitive, they have caused police specialists to rethink some traditional aspects of patrolling.

As discussed in Chapter 5, the new focus is on community-oriented policing. Although a somewhat general term, it is most commonly associated with attempts by the police to involve the community in getting the job done. It is based on the recognition that social control is not solely a police function; the residents of a neighborhood also play a major role. Community-oriented policing may mean, for example, the permanent assignment of patrol officers to a neighborhood so that better relationships can be cultivated, the setting of priorities to focus on certain problems affecting particular communities, and the allocation of resources in ways that increase officers' responsiveness to those they serve.

Attempts to change police practices have not always been successful, because patrol methods that may appear to researchers to be the most effective often run counter to the desires of departmental personnel. We next examine some of the issues now affecting police administrators as they use their patrol forces to try to control crime while at the same time meeting community needs. The issues to be discussed are (l) allocation of patrol personnel, (2) preventive patrol, (3) response time, (4) foot patrol versus motorized patrol, (5) one-person versus two-person patrol units, (6) aggressive patrol, and (7) problem-oriented policing.

Allocation

It has traditionally been assumed that patrol officers should be assigned where and when they will be most effective in preventing crime, maintaining order, and serving the public. This assumption

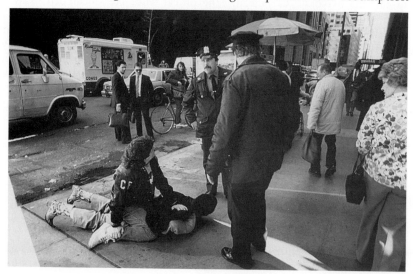

■
Are Americans becoming blasé to scenes of the police in action?

poses a basic question for the police administrator: Where should I send the troops, and in what numbers? There are no precise guidelines to answer this question, and most allocation decisions seem to be based on the assumption that patrols should be concentrated in areas where the crime is occurring or in "problem" neighborhoods. Thus, crime statistics, the degree of industrialization, pressures from business people and community groups, ethnic composition, and socioeconomic characteristics are the major factors determining the distribution of police resources.

Many citizens victimized by crime near their homes believe that crime is distributed randomly and that there are no safe places; danger lurks everywhere. Research, however, has challenged this assumption by pointing to the fact that crime "hot spots" may be identified in various cities. It is argued that direct contact predatory violations will occur when three elements converge: (1) motivated offenders, (2) suitable targets, and (3) the absence of capable guardians against the violation.[7] In a study in Minneapolis, researchers found that a relatively few "hot spots"—identified as corresponding to a place, defined as a street address or a street intersection—produced most calls to the police. By analyzing the location of calls to the police it was possible to identify those places that produced most crime.[8] Criminal offenses were thus concentrated by offense type and not scattered throughout the city. The policy implications of such research for the allocation of police resources and for the development of prevention strategies by citizens is important.

Preventive Patrol

It has long been held that **preventive patrol** is an important deterrent to crime. Since the days of Peel it has been argued that a patrol officer moving through an area prevents criminals from carrying out illegal acts. In 1972 this assumption was tested in Kansas City, Missouri, with surprising results. A fifteen-beat area was divided into three sections, with careful consideration given to ensuring similarity in crime rates, population characteristics, income levels, and calls for police service. In one area, designated "reactive," all preventive patrol was withdrawn, and the police entered only in response to citizens' calls for service. In another, labeled "proactive," preventive patrol was raised to as much as four times the normal level, and all other services were provided at the preexperimental levels. The third section was used as a control, and the department maintained the usual level of services, including preventive patrol. The Kansas City project concluded that there were no significant differences in the amount of crime reported, the amount of crime measured by citizen surveys, and the extent to which citizens feared criminal attack.[9]

The authors of the study emphasized the tentative nature of their finding that although 60 percent of officer time in all three areas was available for active patrolling, only 14.2 percent was spent in this manner. The officers were engaged instead in such administrative chores as report writing and in other matters unrelated to patrolling. This and other studies of preventive patrol have been strongly criticized by those wedded to the professional crime-fighting model of policing as attacking the heart of police work. What the research did

preventive patrol: The activity of providing regular protection to an area while maintaining a mobile presence to deter potential criminals from committing crimes.

was to call into question the inflexibility of traditional preventive patrol. The findings of this research have been one of the major factors in leading many departments to shift their focus to greater attention on maintaining order and serving the community.

Response Time

The image of the patrol officer on the beat is enshrined in American folklore. During the last half-century, however, with increased use of the squad car, the foot patrol officer has almost disappeared from many cities. With most officers in squad cars and with most citizens having ready access to a telephone, modern patrol tactics are based on the assumption that calls for assistance will come to a central dispatching section of the department, and from there officers will be directed to the site of the incident. It has been argued that because motorized officers are patrolling an area, they can respond rapidly to a call for help.

A study completed in Kansas City and since replicated in other cities across the country measured the impact of police response time on the ability of officers to intercept a crime in progress and arrest the criminal. The researchers found that the police were successful in only 29 of 1,000 cases, and it made little difference whether they arrived in two minutes or twenty. As Figure 6.3 indicates, the crucial factor was the speed with which citizens called the police.[10]

Detractors of motorized patrols say that the value of the automobile's range, flexibility, and speed is lost if citizens are the delaying factor. As Lawrence Sherman says, the rise of motorized patrols and telephone dispatching has changed the older strategy of "watching to prevent crime" to "waiting to respond to crime."[11] He believes that the officer in the patrol car is not attentive to the beat and is isolated from citizen contact. If it is also shown that the value of rapid response is lost because victims or observers do not call quickly, the entire strategy is brought into question.

If the problem of response time is one of citizen delay, it might be possible to develop education programs or technological innovations that would reduce reporting time, but it appears that such strategies would not appreciably improve crime control through arrest. As William Spelman and Dale Brown point out, there are three reasons for

FIGURE 6.3
Probability of arrest as a function of elapsed time after crime committed.
The probability of arrest declines sharply if the incident is not reported to the police within seconds. What does this mean with regard to patrol policies?
SOURCE: From *Calling the Police: Citizen Reports of Serious Crime*, by W. Spelman and D. Brown, p. 64. (Washington, DC: Police Executive Research Forum, 1981.) Reprinted by permission.

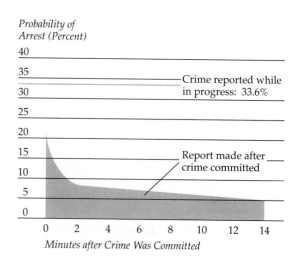

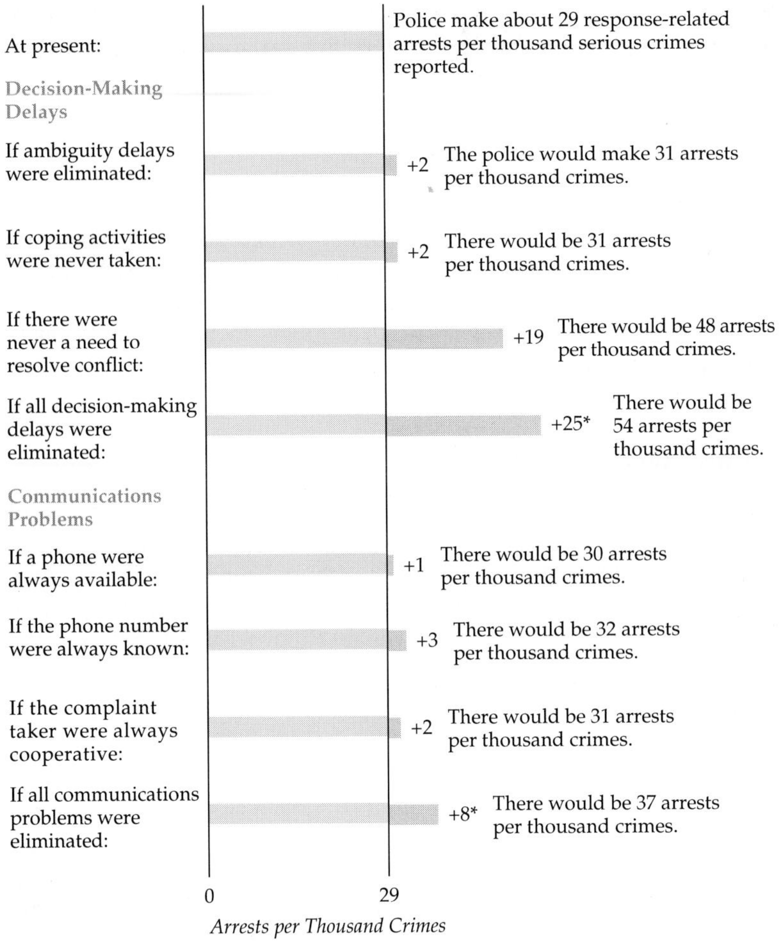

At present:	Police make about 29 response-related arrests per thousand serious crimes reported.
Decision-Making Delays	
If ambiguity delays were eliminated:	+2 The police would make 31 arrests per thousand crimes.
If coping activities were never taken:	+2 There would be 31 arrests per thousand crimes.
If there were never a need to resolve conflict:	+19 There would be 48 arrests per thousand crimes.
If all decision-making delays were eliminated:	+25* There would be 54 arrests per thousand crimes.
Communications Problems	
If a phone were always available:	+1 There would be 30 arrests per thousand crimes.
If the phone number were always known:	+3 There would be 32 arrests per thousand crimes.
If the complaint taker were always cooperative:	+2 There would be 31 arrests per thousand crimes.
If all communications problems were eliminated:	+8* There would be 37 arrests per thousand crimes.

0   29

Arrests per Thousand Crimes

FIGURE 6.4
Potential increases in response-related arrests as a result of elimination of important causes of delay. Although emphasis has been on creating opportunities for citizens to quickly call the police through the development of 911 numbers, research has shown that it is observers' delay in recognizing that a crime has been committed and the police should be called that appears to be a major factor in police response time.
* The total is more than the sum of the individual savings because of the nonlinear nature of the relationship between reporting time and arrest.
NOTE: Even if all reporting delays could be eliminated, no more than 70 crimes per thousand could result in response-related arrests.
SOURCE: William G. Spelman and Dale K. Brown, *Calling the Police: Citizen Reporting of Serious Crime* (Washington, DC: Police Executive Research Forum, 1984), p. xxix.

delay in calling the police. Some people find the situation *ambiguous;* they want to make sure that the police should be called. Others are so busily engaged in *coping activities*—taking care of the victim, directing traffic, and generally helping out—that they are unable to leave the scene. Still others experience *conflict* that they must first resolve; they may avoid making an immediate decision or may seek the advice of someone else before placing a call. In addition to these decision-making delays, there are communication problems: a phone may not be readily available, the person may not know the correct number to call, and the police complaint taker may not be cooperative.

Although citizen delay is a major problem, as Figure 6.4 shows, its elimination would only marginally increase the police's ability to make an arrest. In about three-quarters of crime calls the police are reactive, in that the offenses (burglary, larceny, and the like) are "discovered" long after they have occurred. A much smaller portion are "involvement" crimes (robbery, rape, assault) which the victims know about immediately and can call the police.[12]

Recognition that giving a high priority to rapid response to *all* calls for police assistance is unproductive has led to the development of differential response strategies. Such strategies are based on the premise that it is not always necessary to rush a patrol car out when a call is received. When calls are classified by immediacy of need, priorities can be assigned. A delayed response is often just as effective as a very prompt one and callers are satisfied as long as they know what to expect. A patrol car on the scene is not always essential, for there can be alternative ways of handling a problem, such as referral to another agency, a telephone response, or the sending of nonsworn personnel to the scene.

Studies have shown the effectiveness of differential police response. In Greensboro, North Carolina, 46.4 percent of all calls were categorized as eligible for a response other than the immediate dispatch of a patrol car; similar results were found in other test sites.[13] Differential police response permits resources to be saved, because patrol units are not diverted to nonemergency situations.

Foot Patrol versus Motorized Patrol

One of the most frequent requests of citizens is that the officer be put back on the beat. They claim that patrol officers in squad cars have become remote from the people they protect. During the 1960s such cries were especially strong, because racial upheavals were thought to have been intensified in part by the fact that white officers and the residents of black neighborhoods did not have close physical contact. Because patrol officers were not familiar faces, they were perceived as symbols of oppression.

It has been argued that the officer in the patrol car leads to ineffective policing since there is not an opportunity to really know the neighborhood.

> What the patrol car officer sees is familiar buildings with unfamiliar people around them. What the public sees is a familiar police car with an unfamiliar officer in it. The public has little chance to tell the officer what is going on in the community: who is angry at whom about what, whose children are running wild, what threats have been made, and who is suddenly living above his apparent means. Stripped of this contextual knowledge, the patrol car officer sees, but cannot truly observe.[14]

By contrast, an officer on foot is at home in the neighborhood and can more readily spot circumstances and people that warrant investigation. When patrol officers are close to the daily life of the beat, they are in a better position to detect criminal activity and to apprehend those who have violated the law.

Until the 1930s foot patrol was the dominant focus for police activity. As part of the professional crime-fighting model promoted by O. W. Wilson and others, motorized patrol came to be viewed as more effective. Officers on foot are seen as limited in their ability to respond, especially where weather and other conditions impede their actions. Squad cars increase the territory that officers can patrol, and with two-way radios officers can be quickly deployed to the sites where their assistance is needed. Wilson believed that motorized officers would still observe, talk to, and constantly interact with citizens. He thought that patrol officers would use their cars to get to a location and then walk on foot throughout their beat. He did not see them as remaining in their vehicles for most of their tour, isolated from the community. Most cities have continued to use a mixed force, assigning foot patrols to high-crime and downtown areas.

Research indicates that although foot patrol does not greatly reduce crime, it does reduce the fear of crime. What should be the response of these officers?

   The past decade has seen a revival of interest in foot patrol. This revival has come mainly in response to citizens' demands for a familiar figure walking their neighborhoods. Experiments have been carried out in a number of cities to test the cost and impact of foot patrol.[15] In general, these studies have shown that foot patrols do not greatly reduce crime but that citizens are pleased with this form of police work and fear crime less.

   The best evidence that citizens want foot patrols is probably seen in the experience of Flint, Michigan, where despite the highest unemployment rate in the nation, citizens voted in 1982 and 1985 to increase taxes in order to extend foot patrol to the entire city. In 1979 fourteen city beats had been designated for foot patrol. The three-year results showed that crime on those beats went down about 19 percent overall. And although robberies and burglaries increased in the city as a whole, even these crimes did not increase at the same rate on the experimental beats. Foot-beat residents rated their officers more effective than car-bound patrol officers, rating the motorized division higher only in its ability to respond quickly in emergencies. Sixty-four percent of the foot-beat residents were happy with the patrol program, and 70 percent said that they felt safer in their neigh-

borhoods because of it. But as Robert Trojanowicz, evaluator of the
Flint experiment, points out, " Patrolmen who operate [in the traditional way] are just motorized officers without a car. Basically, they're
doorshakers. But when the officer becomes actively involved in the
community, that's when crime problems begin to be solved."[16]

One- versus Two-Person Patrol Units

As in the controversy over beat patrol officers, the question of one- or
two-person patrol units has raged in police circles. There is variation
throughout the country in the staffing of patrol units, with two-officer
cars more prevalent in cities. Although the two-person squad car
appears to be uneconomical, officers and their union leaders argue
that safety requires the second person. On the other side, police
administrators contend that the one-person squad car is so much
more cost-effective that more cars can be deployed. Thus each car
can cover a smaller geographic sector, more sectors of the city can be
covered, and response time can be decreased. A further belief is that
an officer operating alone is more alert, because he or she cannot be
distracted by idle conversation with a fellow officer.

Research on this question has been conducted in a number of
cities.[17] What is clear is that with so many questions of organization
and personnel, factors other than effectiveness and efficiency come
into play. In specific cities policies must be developed through negotiations among individual police chiefs, the leadership of the patrol
officer's union, and the political leaders of the funding agency.

Aggressive Patrol

aggressive patrol: A patrol strategy
designed to maximize the number of
police interventions and observations
in the community.

In contrast with the community service model of team policing is the
crime attack model of **aggressive patrol.** This is a proactive strategy
that takes a wide variety of forms, from programs that encourage
citizens to identify their valuables, to "sting" operations, to repeat
offender programs. James Q. Wilson and Barbara Boland concluded
that patrol tactics that increase the risk of arrest are associated with
crime reduction. They argue that the effect of the police on crime
depends less on how many officers are deployed in a particular area
than on what they do while they are there.[18] Following an aggressive
strategy, officers maximize the number of interventions and observations in the community. This does not mean that they are encouraged to patrol in a hostile manner, for such tactics could have the
effect of merely arousing the community.

In San Diego it was found that an aggressive patrol strategy of
field interrogations and street stops was associated with a significant
decrease in certain "suppressible" crimes: robbery, burglary, theft,
auto theft, assault, sex crimes, malicious mischief, and disturbances.
It was concluded that field interrogations deterred potential offenders, especially young, opportunistic ones.[19] Officers in an "anti-
crime patrol" in New York worked the streets of high-crime areas in
civilian clothes. Although these officers represented only 5 percent
of the men and women assigned to each precinct, during one year
they made over 18 percent of the felony arrests, including more than
half of the arrests for robbery and about 40 percent of the arrests for
burglary and auto theft. The Kansas City force adopted procedures

Drug enforcement requires tactics that include the element of surprise without violating the Fourth Amendment's prohibition against unreasonable searches and seizures.

to distribute information about the most active burglars and robbers to officers before they went on patrol and created a specialized unit that staked out locations known to be likely targets of criminal activities (say, the back room of a liquor store).

Repeat offender programs have proved successful in several cities in making conviction-successful arrests of career criminals. Using proactive tactics the Washington, D.C., Repeat Offender Program targeted individuals with long records who were believed to be engaged in criminal activity. One squad of officers, the "Hunter" squad, focused on warrant targets, especially those sought for violent crimes; the "Trapper" squad initiated long-term investigations to close a large number of cases and to recover stolen property. "Fisherman" squads engaged in a variety of activities—buy/bust, follow up on tips, warrant arrests, and "cruising" targeted areas for in-process crimes. The program proved to be effective in removing repeat offenders from the streets, yet it was also costly since it moved officers away from former duties.[20]

Police antifencing operations, usually referred to as "stings," are a well-recognized and widely used law enforcement technique, particularly with regard to property offenses. Typically, a storefront operation will be set up in which the police will pose to thieves as fences and engage in the purchase of stolen property. As a result, large amounts of property are recovered and thieves are arrested and successfully prosecuted.

Questions with regard to the impact of these operations have been raised. Langworthy studied a police auto theft sting in Birmingham.[21] He argued that with respect to the department's goal of increased publicity and public support, the sting went well. However, with regard to crime prevention, an apparent increase in auto theft may have been associated with the sting operation. He noted that sting operations have costs associated with them in that the police engage in illegitimate behavior, a risk that is perhaps not worth taking.

The most cost-effective strategy for aggressive patrol seems to be to create incentives so that officers will increase the number of field interrogations and traffic stops. To achieve an aggressive patrol strategy a police executive must recruit certain kinds of officers, train them in certain ways, and devise requirements and reward systems (traffic ticket quotas, field interrogation obligations, promotional opportunities) to encourage these officers to follow the intended strategy.[22]

Problem-Oriented Policing

Regardless of whether the police focus their resources on order maintenance, law enforcement, or service, they tend to respond to specific incidents. Typically, a citizen call or an officer's field observation brings forth a police response to that event. The police are often asked to respond to a rash of similar crime-related incidents in the same location. Because the police traditionally focus on incidents, they do not seek to determine the underlying causes of these incidents. **Problem-oriented policing,** associated with community-oriented policing, tries to ascertain what is causing citizen calls for

problem-oriented policing: An approach to policing in which officers seek to identify, analyze, and respond, on a routine basis, to the underlying circumstances that create the incidents that prompt citizens to call the police.

CLOSE-UP   *The Problem-Oriented Approach*

At 1:32 A.M. a man we will call Fred Snyder dials 911 from a downtown corner phone booth. Officer Knox arrives four minutes later.

   Snyder says he was beaten and robbed twenty minutes before but didn't see the robber. Under persistent questioning Snyder admits he was with a prostitute, picked up in a bar. Later, in a hotel room, he discovered the prostitute was actually a man, who then beat Snyder and took his wallet.

   Snyder wants to let the whole matter drop. He refuses medical treatment for his injuries. Knox finishes his report and lets Snyder go home. Later that day Knox's report reaches Detective Alexander's desk. She knows from experience the case will go nowhere, but she calls Snyder at work.

   Snyder confirms the report but refuses to cooperate further. Knox and Alexander go on to other cases. Months later, reviewing crime statistics, the city council deplores the difficulty of attracting businesses or people downtown.

   Reacting to incidents reported by citizens—as this hypothetical example illustrates—is the standard method for delivering police services today. But there is growing recognition that standard "incident-driven" policing methods do not have a substantial impact on many of the problems that citizens want police to help solve. Equally important, enforcing the law is but one of many ways that police can cope with citizens' problems.

   Midnight-watch patrol officers are tired of taking calls like Snyder's. They and their sergeant, James Hogan, decide to reduce prostitution-related robberies, and Officer James Boswell volunteers to lead the effort.

   First, Boswell interviews the twenty-eight prostitutes who work the downtown area to learn how they solicit, what happens when they get caught, and why they are not deterred. They work downtown bars, they

tell him, because customers are easy to find and police patrols don't spot them soliciting. Arrests, the prostitutes tell Boswell, are just an inconvenience: Judges routinely sentence them to probation, and probation conditions are not enforced.

   Boswell works with the Alcoholic Beverage Control Board and local bar owners to move the prostitutes into the street. At police request, the Commonwealth's Attorney agrees to ask the judges to put stiffer conditions on probation: Convicted prostitutes would be given a map of the city and told to stay out of the downtown area or go to jail for three months.

   Boswell then works with the vice unit to make sure that downtown prostitutes are arrested and convicted, and that patrol officers know which prostitutes are on probation. Probation violators *are* sent to jail, and within weeks all but a few of the prostitutes have left downtown.

   Then Boswell talks to the prostitutes' customers, most of whom don't know that almost half the prostitutes working the street are actually men posing as women. He intervenes in street transactions, formally introducing the customers to their male dates. The Navy sets up talks for him with incoming sailors to tell them about the male prostitutes and the associated safety and health risks.

   In three months, the number of prostitutes working downtown drops from twenty-eight to six, and robbery rates are cut in half. After eighteen months neither robbery nor prostitution show signs of returning to their earlier levels.

SOURCE: Adapted from William Spelman and John Eck, National Institute of Justice, "Problem-Oriented Policing," in *Research in Brief* (Washington, DC: Government Printing Office, 1987).

help.[23] Knowledge of the underlying problem can then be used to enlist community agencies and citizens to resolve the situation. One result is that the police consider and respond to a wide variety of problems affecting the quality of life, not just crime.[24]

Two police departments, in Newport News, Virginia, and Baltimore County, Maryland, have gained national recognition for their implementation of problem-oriented policing. Although differing in some respects in their procedures and organization, both departments seek to involve police officers and the community in finding solutions that will reduce crime, disorder, and fear. Supervisors encourage officers who are analyzing problems to look beyond the department for information. They urge personnel to talk to residents, business people, offenders, and public officials—anyone who might know something about the problem. After analyzing this information, they might find a solution. Perhaps the incidents will cease because street lighting is made more intensive, aggressive measures are taken against streetwalkers, or closing hours of a local bar are enforced. Whatever the solution, it usually means that agencies other than those of criminal justice have had something to do with it.

Problem-oriented policing follows in the wake of other calls that the police center their attention more on maintaining order and serving the community. It is one facet of the community policing focus (discussed in Chapter 5), which stresses the importance of solving community problems and improving conditions rather than merely attacking crime.

Special Populations

In addition to the problems of crime, urban police forces must deal with a very complex population. On city streets there are an increasing number of people who are mentally ill, homeless, runaways, public inebriates, drug addicts, or infected with AIDS. Jail crowding, the deinstitutionalization of mental health facilities, decriminalization of public drunkenness statutes, economic dislocations, and reductions in public assistance programs have all contributed to an increase in the number of "problem" people on the street. Most of these people are not involved in criminal activities but their presence in the community is disturbing to residents.

Patrol officers must deal with a variety of social service agencies to assist individuals and to respond to order maintenance requests of the public. The police must walk a very fine line with regard to their authority to require individuals to go to a homeless shelter, to obtain medical assistance, or to be taken to a mental health unit.[25] Police departments have developed various organizational approaches to deal with the problem of special populations. In New York City, Los Angeles, and Philadelphia, special mobile units are equipped with restraining devices, mace, and medical equipment to handle disturbed people. Madison, Wisconsin, has approached the problem through the education of all officers to the problem and ways to deal with it. Birmingham, Alabama, uses civilian social workers to deal with the mentally ill while the police respond to persons with other problems.[26]

It is clear that the handling of special populations is a major problem now confronting police in most cities. Each community must develop policies so that the police will know when and how they are to intervene in situations where an individual may be upsetting to residents yet not have violated the criminal law.

To what extent law enforcement should engage in community policing without appearing to be mainly clearing the streets remains a question.

The Future of Patrol

A great deal of research and thinking are going on with regard to patrol, the essential element of American policing. Preventive patrol and a rapid response to calls for assistance have been the hallmarks of policing in the United States for the past half century. Because of

---

COMPARATIVE PERSPECTIVE
Patrol in Japan

Japanese policemen are addressed by the public as *Omawari-san*—Mr. Walkabout. This is an accurate reflection of what the public sees the police doing most of the time. Foot patrolling is done out of *kobans* [mini police stations in urban neighborhoods], usually for periods of an hour. Patrols are more common at night, when officers work in pairs. Patrolling by foot is more tiring than it looks. Patrolmen amble at a ruminative pace that allows thorough observation. It is like browsing or windowshopping with none of the satisfactions of actually getting somewhere. Patrolling by automobile, which is much less common than foot patrolling, can be frustrating too. Due to the narrow congested streets of Japanese cities . . . patrol cars are forced to move at a snail's pace. . . .

Patrolling is by no means a matter of high adventure. For the most part it consists of watching and occasionally answering questions. Patrolmen rarely discover genuine emergencies; the chance of coincidence between patrolmen and sudden need are simply too great. Patrolling does not reduce reaction time or particularly enhance availability. What patrolling does is to demonstrate the existence of authority, correct minor inconveniences—such as illegally parked cars—and generate trust through

the establishment of familiar personal relations with a neighborhood's inhabitants. On patrol, policemen are alert for different kinds of problems in different places. In a residential area they watch for people who appear out of place or furtive. In public parks they give attention to loitering males. Around major railroad stations they look for runaway adolescents, lured by the glamor of a big city, who could be victimized by criminal elements. They also watch for *teyhaishi*—labor contractors— who pick up and sell unskilled laborers to construction companies. In a neighborhood of bars and cabarets patrolmen stare suspiciously at stylishly dressed women standing unescorted on street corners. They determine whether wheeled carts piled with food or cheap souvenirs are blocking pedestrian thoroughfares. Throughout every city they pay particular attention to illegally parked cars and cars that have been left with their doors unlocked.

. . .

When a Japanese policeman is out on patrol he makes a special point of talking to people about themselves, their purposes, and their behavior. These conversations may be innocent or investigatory. The law provides that policemen may stop and question people only

if there is reasonable ground for suspecting they have committed or are about to commit a crime or have information about a crime. Nevertheless, standard procedure on patrol is to stop and question anyone whenever the policeman thinks it may be useful. One reason for doing so is to discover wanted persons. And the tactic has proved very effective: 40 percent of criminals wanted by the police have been discovered by patrolmen on the street. Not only do officers learn to question people adroitly on the street, they become adept at getting people to agree to come to the *koban* so that more extended, less public inquiries can be made. People are under no obligation to do so, any more than they are to stop and answer questions. The key to success with these tactics is to be compelling without being coercive. This in turn depends on two factors: the manner of the police officer and a thorough knowledge of minor laws.

this orientation, most patrol officers have been placed in squad cars that are linked to a dispatcher at the station house. But the police are still highly dependent on the community to report the occurrence of a crime, to cooperate with police investigations, and to appear in court as witnesses. Without the public's voluntary participation, the police may patrol indefinitely and have little impact on crime. The police's heavy orientation toward dispatch and preventive control may have narrowed the roles they play in the community.

The research conducted during the past twenty years has perhaps raised as many questions as it has answered. It is apparent, however, that police forces in large cities need to consider a mix of patrol tactics that fit the demographic and criminogenic characteristics of various neighborhoods. Many researchers also believe that

---

The first reduces hostility, the second provides pretexts for opening conversations justifiably. People who park illegally, ride bicycles without a light, or fail to wear helmets when riding a motorcycle are inviting officers to stop them and ask probing questions. The importance with which the police view on-street interrogation is indicated by the fact that prefectural and national contests are held each year to give recognition to officers who are best at it. One officer assumes the role of suspect and another is given eighteen minutes in which to discover essential facts about him. Judges evaluate the subtlety or technique. Senior officers continually impress upon new recruits the importance of learning to ask questions in inoffensive ways so that innocent people are not affronted and unpleasant scenes can be avoided.

. . .

Principles governing the use of discretion are not codified or set down in writing; they have the character of custom among police officers. Several factors seem to be involved in determining when illegal behavior will be tolerated. First, enforcement is modified according to place. Officers judge what the public in a particular area has become accustomed to. Second, police forces have their own traditions; over time notions about tolerable limits for different kinds of behavior become accepted within the police community. The policy of al-lowing a margin over the speed limit is an example as is toleration of sidewalk vending in prohibited areas. Third, policemen try to judge the effect of their actions upon future behavior of the individuals involved. A warning is often as effective a deterrent as an arrest, and a good deal less costly and time-consuming. Conversely, legal penalties may be an insufficient deterrent for some offenses, so rueful toleration becomes the only practical policy. Policemen appreciate an investment of time that is commensurate with results. Drunks sleeping in public places, for instance, may be more trouble to arrest than the arrests are worth in terms of changed behavior. Fourth, policemen have their own preoccupations. They may decide, for example, that it is more important to continue to patrol against sex offenders than to check upon gambling in a Mah-Jongg parlor. Fifth, policemen are sometimes motivated by sympathy for offenders. On one occasion when a minor accident occurred between a taxi and a private car, officers repressed evidence that the taxi driver had been drinking. If results of the "breath-ometer" test had been recorded, the taxi driver would have had his license suspended. The policemen decided that the punishment would be too severe, since no one had been hurt in the accident, both drivers were adequately covered by insurance, and the taxi driver had a blameless record. The taxi driver was ordered to sleep for two hours in his taxi beside the *koban* before going home. Undoubtedly, he will be more cautious about drinking and driving another time, and the police will have gained a staunch friend.

. . .

The most striking aspect of the variety of situations confronted by policemen is their compelling, unforced naturalness. The police see masses of utterly ordinary people who have been enmeshed in situations that are tediously complex and meaningful only to the persons immediately involved. The outcomes are of no interest to the community at large; the newspapers will not notice if matters are sorted out or not; superior officers have no way of recording the effort patrolmen expend in trying to be helpful; and the people themselves are incapable by and large of permanently escaping their predicaments. Policemen are responsible for tending these individuals, for showing that they appreciate—even when they are tired hurried, bored, and preoccupied—the minute ways in which each person is unique. It is perhaps the greatest service they render.

SOURCE: *Forces of Order: Police Behavior in Japan and the United States,* by D. Bayley, pp. 33–34, 37, 41, 51–52. Copyright © 1976 The Regents of the University of California. Reprinted by permission.

patrol operations have focused too narrowly on crime control, to the neglect of the order maintenance activities for which police departments were originally formed. There is also a new focus on strategies to reduce the fear of crime, which is often found to be out of proportion to the objective risk of being victimized. Critics have urged that the police become more community oriented and return to the first principle of policing: "to remain in close and frequent contact with citizens."[27]

INVESTIGATION

The fictional Sherlock Holmes has long epitomized the detective in the public's eyes. With a minimum of clues, an intuitive mind, and a careful application of logic, he and his counterparts in thousands of dramas stalk the criminal until an arrest is made in the final moments. The Holmes model of investigation has been widely copied by scriptwriters for television and the movies. As a result, citizens believe that this is how the police usually solve crimes.

In the real world, however, the investigative function is not the sole responsibility of one bureau in a police department, let alone of one detective. Patrol, traffic, vice, and sometimes juvenile units contribute to this process. In small town and rural areas, patrol officers perform investigative duties.[28] In urban areas, the patrol unit, because it is normally represented at the scene of the crime, accomplishes much of the preliminary investigative work. The patrol unit's investigation can be crucial. As Figure 6.5 indicates, successful prosecution in cases of robbery, larceny, and burglary is closely linked with the speed with which a suspect is arrested. In many incidents, however, the criminal is not immediately apprehended, and investigation must be continued to determine who committed the crime and where the person is. This section looks at the investigative function, the special police units that are set up to achieve two objectives: the identification and apprehension of offenders and the collection of evidence with which to prosecute them.

Traditionally, detectives have enjoyed a prestigious position in police departments. The pay is higher, the hours are more flexible, and the supervision is more permissive than those of patrol officers. Detectives do not wear uniforms, and their work is considered more interesting than the patrol officer's. In addition to these incentives, they are engaged solely in law enforcement rather than in order maintenance or service work; hence their activities correspond more closely to the image of the police as crime fighters.

Detective Responsibilities

Every city with a population in excess of 250,000 and 90 percent of the smaller cities have officers specially assigned to investigative duties.[29] Investigative units are normally separated from the patrol chain of command. Within the unit, detectives are frequently organized according to the type of crime they investigate—homicide, robbery, forgery—or by geographical area. Reported crimes are auto-

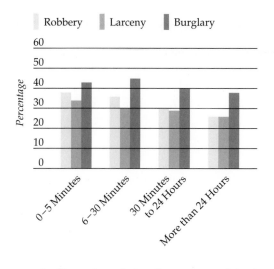

Robbery ⬛ Larceny ⬛ Burglary

FIGURE 6.5
Percentage of convictions from offense to arrest (by elapsed time). Note that for each of the offenses, the amount of time from the incident to the arrest is a major factor in successful conviction. What could be done to increase the conviction rate?
SOURCE: U.S. Department of Justice, Bureau of Justice Statistics, *Report to the Nation on Crime and Justice* (Washington, DC: Government Printing Office, 1983), p. 51.

matically referred to the appropriate investigator. One argument against separating investigation from patrol is that it results in duplication of effort and lack of continuity in the handling of cases. It often means that vital pieces of information held by one branch are not known to the other.

Detectives are concerned primarily with law enforcement activities after a crime has been reported and a preliminary investigation held. Their investigative activities depend on the circumstances of the case:

1. When a serious crime occurs and the offender is immediately identified and apprehended, the detective prepares the case for presentation to the prosecuting attorney.
2. When the offender is identified but not apprehended, the detective tries to locate the individual.
3. When the offender is not identified but there are several suspects, the detective conducts investigations aimed at either confirming or disproving his suspicions.
4. When there is no suspect, the detective starts from scratch to determine who committed the crime.[30]

In performing the investigative function, detectives depend not only on their own experience but also on the technical expertise in their department or in a cooperating police force. They require information and must therefore rely on criminal files, laboratory technicians, and forensic scientists. Many small departments turn to the state crime laboratory or the FBI for such information when serious crimes have been committed. Detectives are often pictured as working alone, but in fact they are members of a departmental team.

The Apprehension Process

Discovery that a crime has been committed is likely to set off a chain of events leading to the capture of a suspect and the gathering of the evidence required for the suspect's conviction. Unfortunately, it may also lead to a number of dead ends, ranging from a decision by the victim not to report the crime to an absence of clues pointing to a suspect or a lack of evidence linking the suspect to the crime. Where

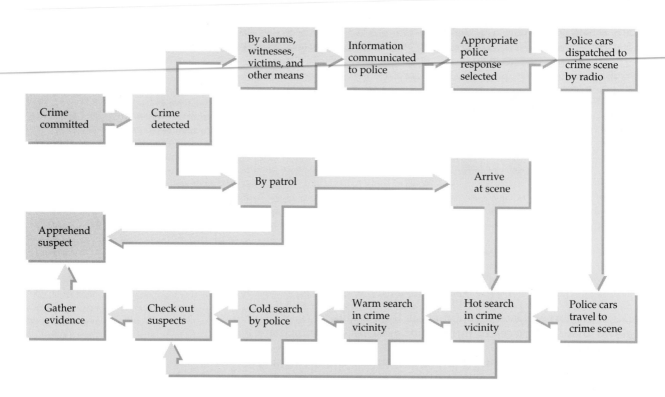

FIGURE 6.6
The felony apprehension process.
Apprehension of a felony suspect is
made up of a sequence of events taken
in response to the crime by both patrol
officers and detectives. Coordination of
police response is an important factor in
solving major crimes.

some crimes are concerned, the probability is remote that the offender will be found, especially if there is a delay between commission of the crime and arrival of the police.

As Figure 6.6 shows, the felony apprehension process can be
viewed as a sequence of actions taken in response to the commission
of a crime. The actions are designed to mount the resources of criminal justice to bring about the arrest of a suspect and to assemble
enough supporting evidence to substantiate a charge, as follows:

1. *Crime detected:* Information that a crime has been committed
usually comes in the form of a telephone call by the victim or complainant to the police. The patrol officer on the beat may also come
upon a crime, but usually the police are alerted by others. In some
cities, police are alerted to crime in business premises by automatic
security alarms that are connected to police headquarters so that
response time can be shortened and the likelihood of apprehending
the perpetrator increased.

2. *Preliminary investigation:* The first law enforcement official on
the scene is usually a patrol officer who has been dispatched by radio.
The officer is thus responsible for providing aid to the victim, for
securing the crime scene for later investigation, and for beginning to
document the facts of the crime. If a suspect is present or in the
vicinity, the officer conducts a "hot" search and possibly apprehends
a suspect. This work is crucial, because the information gathered
during this initial phase is essential. These data concern the basic
facts of the crime, including identity of the victim, description of the
suspect, and names of witnesses. After the information is collected,
it is transmitted to the investigation unit.

3. *Follow-up investigation:* After a crime has been brought to the
attention of the police and a preliminary investigation has been
made, further action is determined by a detective. In the typical big-

city department, incident reports from the previous day are analyzed the first thing in the morning. Assignments are distributed to individual investigators in accordance with their specialties. These investigators study the information, weigh each informational factor in accordance with a formula, and determine whether the factors present are sufficient to indicate that the crime can be solved.

Some departments have developed formulas for deciding the disposition of cases so that resources will be used most efficiently. For example, as Table 6.1 indicates, if the total score of the informational factors for a burglary is 10 or less, further action on the case is suspended. A study of the Kansas City (Missouri) Police Department showed that although homicide, rape, and suicide received considerable attention, fewer than 50 percent of all reported crimes received more than a minimal half-hour's investigation by detectives. In many of these cases, detectives merely reported the facts discovered by the patrol officers during the preliminary investigations.[31]

Detectives must make a number of discretionary decisions concerning any investigation. As already noted, a decision must be made about whether the preliminary investigation has produced enough information to warrant a follow-up investigation. Decisions also have to be made about the crime categories that should receive special attention and when an investigation should be discontinued.

When a full-scale investigation is thought warranted, a wider search—referred to as a "cold" search—for evidence or weapons is undertaken: witnesses may be reinterviewed, contact made with informants, and evidence assembled for analysis. The pressure of new cases, however, often requires an investigation in progress to be shelved so that resources may be directed at "warmer" incidents.

4. *Clearance and arrest:* The decision to arrest is a key part of the apprehension process. In some cases, additional evidence or links between suspects and their associates are not discovered if arrests are premature. Once in custody, suspects may be interrogated to determine whether they can provide information that will clear additional crimes. A crime is cleared when evidence supports the arrest

TABLE 6.1 **Case disposition formula: Burglary.** For each element, a weighted factor score is added. If the total is 10 or less, no further investigative action is taken.

Information Element	Weighting Factor
Estimated range of time of occurrence	
Less than 1 hour	5
1 to 12 hours	1
12 to 24 hours	0.3
More than 24 hours	0
Witness's report of offense	7
On-view report of offense	1
Usable fingerprints	7
Suspect information developed— description or name	9
Vehicle description	0.1
Other	0
Total score	—

NOTE: If the sum is less than or equal to 10, suspend the case; otherwise, follow up the case.
SOURCE: Peter B. Bloch and Donald R. Weidman, *Managing Criminal Investigations* (Washington, DC: Government Printing Office, 1975), p.33.

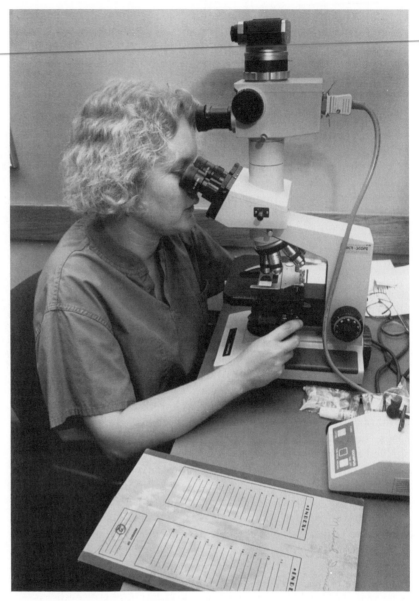

Forensic science has become a valuable tool in the fight against crime.

of a suspect or when a suspect admits having committed other unsolved offenses in department files. Clearance, then, does not mean that the suspect will eventually be found guilty. Clearance rates—which police departments use as measures of their effectiveness in solving crimes—are easily manipulated for administrative purposes and must be read with caution.

Forensic Techniques

The use of science to aid investigations in the gathering, identification, and analysis of evidence has long been a part of American police practices. The scientific analysis of fingerprints, blood, semen, hair, textiles, and weapons has assisted the police in identifying perpetrators of crimes and prosecutors to use the resulting evidence to convince jurors. Forensic laboratories exist in all states and many large cities have their own scientists to provide technical assistance.

The development of DNA "fingerprinting" techniques is the latest addition to the detective's tool kit. This technique is being used to identify people through their distinctive genotypic features. DNA, or deoxyribonucleic acid, is the basic building code for all chromosomes and is the same for all of the cells in a person's body—skin, blood, organs, and semen. The characteristics of certain segments of DNA vary from person to person and thus form a genetic "fingerprint" for each individual. It is thus possible to analyze, for example, hair samples and compare them to those of suspects. Developed in the mid-1980s, DNA typing for law enforcement use has gained much attention. The technique has been used in more than 1,000 criminal investigations since 1987, yet some researchers believe that the method is being used prematurely in that there is not yet a sound scientific foundation for the approach.[32] Courts in a number of states have accepted DNA results as evidence, yet in a New York double murder case a challenge to its introduction was successful.[33]

The full utilization of the DNA technique has been hampered by the few laboratories equipped to undertake the analysis and the general underutilization of forensic techniques. Several early studies have shown that crime laboratories play a minor role in criminal investigation yet are of potentially great value.[34] The introduction of DNA fingerprinting may have an important impact on future investigations.

DNA fingerprinting holds great promise, yet a recent case in Connecticut illustrates that what may appear to be conclusive evidence to the prosecution might not be so evaluated by a jury. In a rape trial an FBI specialist testified that DNA analysis revealed that the accused had not committed the crime. Rather than rely on this statement, the jury chose to believe the victim, since she seemed so certain in her identification of her assailant and gave a very detailed description of the car within which the rape occurred.

Evaluating Investigation

Research from a number of studies have raised important questions about the value of investigations and the role detectives play in the apprehension process. This research suggests that the police have overrated the importance of investigation as a means of solving crimes and shows that most crimes are cleared because of arrests made by the patrol force at or near the scene. As long ago as 1967 the President's Commission noted, "If a suspect is neither known to the victim nor arrested at the scene of the crime, the chances of ever arresting him are very slim."[35] Response time—the time between commission of the crime and the arrival of the police—becomes an important factor in the apprehension process. Table 6.2 shows that detectives investigate practically all serious crimes, but as Figure 6.7 indicates, large numbers of crimes against persons and a great majority of crimes against property are never cleared. Not only is response time important, but also the information given by the victim or witnesses to the responding patrol officer is also crucial.

A Rand Corporation study of 153 large police departments found that the major determinant of success in solving crimes was information identifying the perpetrator supplied by the victim or witnesses at the scene. Of those cases not immediately solved but ultimately

TABLE 6.2 **Percentage of reported crimes worked on by detectives.** Compare this table to Figure 6.7. Note that there are differences in the attention given different types of crimes by detectives and the percent cleared by arrest.

Type of Incident	Percentage
Homicide	100.0
Rape	100.0
Suicide	100.0
Forgery/counterfeiting	90.4
Kidnapping	73.3
Arson	70.4
Auto theft	65.5
Aggravated assault	64.4
Robbery	62.6
Fraud/embezzlement	59.6
Felony sex crimes	59.0
Common assault	41.8
Nonresidential burglary	36.3
Dead body	35.7
Residential burglary	30.0
Larceny	18.4
Vandalism	6.8
Lost property	0.9
All other types together	32.4

SOURCE: Peter W. Greenwood and Joan Petersilia, *The Criminal Investigation Process*, vol. l, *Summary and Policy Implications* (Washington, DC: Government Printing Office, 1975), p. 14.

cleared, most were cleared by such routine procedures as fingerprint searches, receipt of tips from informants, and mug-shot "show-ups." The report emphasizes that special actions by the investigating staff were important in only a very few cases. In summary, the study indicates that about 30 percent of the crimes were cleared by on-scene arrest and another 50 percent by the identification by victims or witnesses when the police arrived. Thus only about 20 percent could have been solved by detective work. But even among this group, the study found that most "were also solved by patrol officers, members of the public who spontaneously provide further information, or routine investigative practices."[36]

If the accumulating evidence should force a reassessment of the role of investigation, what policies might law enforcement officials adopt? The Rand research team suggests a number of reforms, including the following:

1. Reduce follow-up investigation on all cases except those involving the most serious offenses.
2. Assign generalist investigators (who would handle the obvious leads in routine cases) to the local operations commander.
3. Establish a major offenders unit to investigate serious crimes.
4. Assign serious offense investigations to closely supervised teams rather than to individual investigators.
5. Employ strike forces selectively and judiciously.
6. Initiate programs designed to impress on the citizen the crucial role he plays in solving crimes.[37]

Whether or not such changes are made, of what importance is the detective to police operations? The detective's role is important in at least two respects (apart from the ability to solve crimes). First, the prestigious rank of detective provides a goal to which the patrol officer may aspire. Second, citizens expect investigations to be carried out. As Herman Goldstein said: "One cannot dismiss lightly the public-relations value of detective work. It may fully justify the police resources that are invested. Persons treated sympathetically may offer greater assistance to the police in the future."[38]

It is clear that the realities of detective work do not match the myth, and to a large extent the belief that the investigator is the most important member of a police agency can have damaging repercussions. As a result of this myth, patrol officers may feel that their only job is to take reports, improper practices may be used to satisfy public expectations, and the citizenry may be lulled into believing that nothing more needs to be done once detectives take over. The realities of the crime problem, however, demand new responses to the traditional roles of law enforcement personnel.

Specialized Operations

Patrol and investigation are the two largest and functionally most important units within a police department. In metropolitan areas, however, specialized units are set up to deal with particular types of problems; traffic, vice, and juvenile units are the most common, but in some cities separate units are also created to deal with organized crime and narcotics. The work of the specialized units should not be permitted to overshadow the fact that patrol and investigation also have a responsibility to deal with the same problems.

Traffic

Because almost everyone in the community is a pedestrian, passenger, or driver, almost everyone is affected by the problems associated

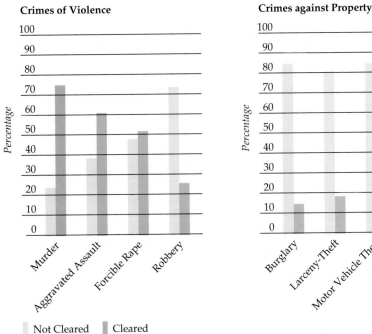

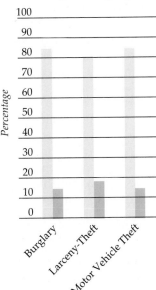

FIGURE 6.7
Crimes cleared by arrest. The probability that a reported crime will be cleared by an arrest varies greatly by the type of offense.
SOURCE: U.S. Department of Justice, *Uniform Crime Reports* (Washington, DC: Government Printing Office, 1990), p. 24.

with the use of the automobile. The police are required to regulate the flow of vehicles, to investigate accidents, and to enforce traffic laws. This work may not seem to fall within the category of crime fighting or maintenance of order, but certain dimensions of the task of traffic control further these objectives. Enforcement of traffic laws contributes to the maintenance of order; it also educates the public in safe driving habits, and it provides a visible community service. As an enforcer of traffic laws, the patrol officer has an opportunity to stop vehicles and interrogate drivers, with the result that stolen property and suspects connected with other criminal acts are often discovered. Most departments are now linked to communications systems that permit the checking of automobile and operator license numbers against lists of wanted vehicles and suspects.

Basically, the traffic control function includes accident investigation, traffic direction, and enforcement. These functions overlap with the broader goal of public safety and accident prevention. For example, accident data and observations made by the patrol officer while on duty may contribute to the pinpointing of traffic hazards that require new safety devices or even highway reconstruction.

Authorities differ with regard to the work of a specialized unit dealing solely with traffic. Most suggest that traffic control is primarily a responsibility of the patrol division and that personnel of the traffic unit should be limited to educational and preventive functions. Some argue that overemphasis on traffic control work through specialized line units can lead to morale problems owing to the privileged nature of motorcycle work and can drain resources from more important patrol duties. In some cities, the police have hired civilians to deal with nonmoving and parking violations as a way to make better use of resources. Nevertheless, in many cities police units that are assigned primarily to traffic control duties concurrently perform patrol functions.

Enforcement of traffic regulations provides one of the best examples of police discretion. This work is essentially proactive, and the level of enforcement can be considered a direct result of departmental policies and norms. Selective enforcement is the general policy, since the police have neither the desire nor the resources to enforce all traffic laws. As a consequence, many departments target particular intersections or highways for stiff enforcement, maintaining a visible presence as a deterrent to speeding motorists. Ranges in the number of tickets for moving violations issued by various departments results in part from the resources allocated to traffic control and the importance that a police chief places on this function, which are reflections of community and political values.

Traffic law enforcement is one of the areas in which police departments employ measures of productivity. Although few administrators will admit that they employ quota systems, officers seem to understand what is expected of them; that is one reason why traffic work is preferred to patrol. The traffic officer "has clearer, less ambiguous objectives, he need not 'get involved' in family fights or other hard-to-manage situations, and he need not make hard-to-defend judgments about what people deserve."[39]

Vice

Enforcement of laws against vice—prostitution, gambling, narcotics, and so forth—is dependent on proactive police work that is itself often dependent on the use of undercover agents and informers. Because of the nature of the crimes, political influence is sometimes brought to bear to dampen law enforcement efforts. At the same time, vigorous enforcement of the laws against vice requires that individual police officers be given wide latitude in the exercise of discretion. Often they are obliged "to engage in illegal and often degrading practices that must be concealed from the public."[40] The potential for corruption in this type of police work presents a number of administrative dilemmas.

A specialized vice control unit is a part of most large city departments. Regardless of the department's size, however, it is important that the police chief closely supervise this unit and that adequate controls be maintained to ensure that the department's integrity is not compromised. The special nature of vice work requires the members of the unit to be well trained in the legal procedures that must be followed if arrests are to lead to convictions. In addition, personnel are subject to transfer when their identities become known and their effectiveness is lost.

Increasingly, the police are using electronic surveillance technologies and undercover work to deal with crime.[41] Intelligence gathering that facilitates proactive police work is important for targeting individuals or organizations involved in drug-related or other crimes. The expansion of undercover work has caused concern among many who believe that this is a departure from the more traditional style of open policing. There are also concerns that the use of these tactics violate civil liberties and will result in a greater intrusion of government into private affairs, be they criminal or not.[42]

Officers engaged in vice control operations depend heavily on informants. Thus one of the major problems with these operations is that a mutually satisfactory relationship may develop between the law enforcer and the law violator. In the field of narcotics control, addicts may provide information on sellers. Frequently they are also used as decoys to help trap sellers, a practice that is of questionable legality. In exchange for cooperating with the police, addicts are sometimes rewarded by being given small amounts of drugs, freedom from prosecution for possession, or police recommendations for leniency should they be sentenced. These practices result in a paradox: the police tolerate certain levels of vice in exchange for information that will enable them to arrest other people for engaging in the same behavior they tolerate in the informant.

Drug Enforcement

Many large cities now have a separate vice bureau that deals only with drug enforcement. Within these agencies there may be task forces dedicated to dealing with organized crime or gangs that are involved in drug dealing. Other sections may use sting operations to buy drugs and arrest drug sellers on the street. Community drug education may also be a responsibility of another section.

Police drug enforcement policies may be guided by the goal of "expressive law enforcement" and allocate resources to attain a maximum number of arrests and to stop brazen street dealing. It is thought important to demonstrate to dealers and to the community that enforcement actions will be taken.[43] Some communities such as Charleston, South Carolina, have developed imaginative strategies in the drug war. A flying squad of officers unexpectedly converge on high crime and/or drug use areas and make arrests in a proactive, aggressive manner. In San Diego and Fort Lauderdale, Florida, teams of police officers and building inspectors focus on buildings and housing projects known to house drug sellers. Through safety inspections, enforcement of health and zoning codes, evictions, and the boarding up of these structures, drug dealers can be routed out of the neighborhood. As with other aspects of drug enforcement, the police are dependent on the cooperation and support of the community.

One tactic has been to disrupt the marketplace for drugs by applying law enforcement pressures on these activities. "Operation Pressure Point" was launched in New York City in 1983 through 1984. One thousand police officers were moved into the Lower East Side, an area where a "drug supermarket" operated openly on the streets, impeding the activities of law-abiding citizens, intimidating residents, and challenging law enforcement. The police made thousands of arrests, bulldozers leveled abandoned buildings, and storefronts rented to dealers were padlocked.[44] The drug supermarket was effectively shut down. Whereas in 1983 upward of one hundred dealers could be observed on the streets of the Lower East Side, by 1989 the streets had been cleared and uniformed officers were very apparent. The Operation Pressure Point approach has been used in other parts of New York, in Los Angeles, and in other cities.[45]

In cities throughout the country the police have shifted substantial portions of their resources to pursue drug offenders. The evidence shows that police efforts have been successful in disrupting drug markets, but often this has meant that other law enforcement responsibilities have been neglected. As Francis C. Hall, retired commander of the New York Police Department's narcotics division, has said: "There comes a point when you have to say, What is the optimum number of people we should have directly involved in narcotics enforcement?"[46]

Although arrests for drug sale or possession have increased dramatically in response to the latest war on drugs, some observers believe that the law enforcement approach will not be successful. Clearly there are organizational and informational limitations on police narcotic enforcement work. It can be argued that there is a contradiction between the goal of drug control and/or eradication and a due process or justice model that emphasizes procedural guarantees. Police drug work can thus be seen as merely a ritual, and enforcement activities may do "little but inflate police power, suggest to an ignorant public that something is being done, and perpetuate aspects of the police myth."[47] How should we evaluate this perspective, given the current emphasis on drug enforcement? Can the police have an impact?

POLICE ACTIONS AND THE RULE OF LAW

In a democratic society the police are expected to control crime within the framework of the law. Throughout the law enforcement processes of detection, apprehension, and arrest, police officers are required to perform their tasks in ways that conform to the law as specified in the U.S. Constitution, individual state constitutions, statutes passed by legislatures, and the interpretations of the courts. As Chapter 3 explained, the ideals of the rule of law and due process aim to ensure that justice is accorded to all citizens and that officials of the state do not use their power to thwart the law. Three police practices—search and seizure, arrest, and interrogation—are specially structured to ensure that the rule of law is upheld and that the rights of citizens are protected. Although many police officers complain that they have been handcuffed by the courts, this may be one of the prices to be paid to maintain freedom in a democratic society.

The Fourth and Fifth Amendments and to some extent the Sixth are the major articles of the Constitution that bear directly on police activities. The Fourth protects citizens from unreasonable searches and seizures, the Fifth protects them from being compelled to testify against themselves, and the Sixth upholds the right to counsel. While Earl Warren was chief justice of the United States, the Supreme Court interpreted these rights to require the states to uphold these protections.

To make certain that the police would observe the provisions of the Bill of Rights, the Supreme Court emphasized two devices: the exclusionary rule and the Sixth Amendment's right to counsel. The exclusionary rule, first developed by the Court in 1914 (*Weeks* v. *United States*), stipulates that illegally seized evidence or improperly given confessions shall be excluded from trials. The argument is made that the government must not soil its hands by profiting from police abuses of the law. It is further stated that because of the rule, the police will be deterred from acting improperly. As an additional protection, the Sixth Amendment's provision of the right to counsel has been interpreted to mean that the defendant may have a lawyer not only in the courtroom but also present during the earlier proceedings, even during interrogation in the station house. The provisions of the Bill of Rights, the decisions of the Supreme Court, and state laws may appear clear, but enough ambiguities exist to keep the police constantly aware that their actions in the field or station house may jeopardize the building of a case strong enough to be prosecuted successfully.

Search and Seizure

Evidence collected by the police in the course of an investigation must be gathered in accordance with the Fourth Amendment's strictures against *unreasonable* searches and seizures. This means that there are circumstances that are reasonable when the police may indeed invade the privacy of a home or person. One such circumstance is the issuance of a search warrant.

A search warrant is an order from a court official allowing a police officer to search a designated place. The officer must go to the court and file an affidavit, giving reasons for the search, and describe the particular place to be searched and the persons or things to be seized. Before a judge may grant the warrant authority, two conditions must be met. First, the officer must provide reliable information indicating that there is probable cause to believe that a crime has been or is being committed. Second, the particular premises and pieces of property to be seized must be identified, and the officer must swear under oath that the facts given are correct. The police cannot obtain a search warrant that vaguely describes the evidence sought or the property to be searched.

In some circumstances, however, the interests of crime control dictate that the police conduct a search without a warrant, and it is here that the courts have been most active in defining the term *unreasonable.* Searches of five kinds may be conducted without a warrant and still be in accord with the Constitution: (1) searches incident to an arrest, (2) searches during field interrogation, (3) searches of automobiles under special conditions, (4) seizures of evidence that is in "plain view," and (5) searches when consent is given.

Incident to an Arrest

When an officer has observed a crime or believes that one has been committed, an arrest may be made and a search conducted without a warrant. It is the fact of the lawful arrest that establishes the right to search and is thus reasonable under the Fourth Amendment.[48] In part, the rationale for this exception is the possibility that the suspect will destroy evidence unless swift action is taken. But in *Chimel* v. *California* (1969) the Supreme Court also said that such a search is limited to the person of the arrestee and the area within the arrestee's "immediate control," defined as that area "from within which he might [obtain] a weapon or something that could have been used as evidence against him" in order to destroy it.[49] Thus if the police are holding a person in one room of a house, they are not authorized to search and seize property in another part of the house, away from the suspect's physical presence.

Field Interrogation

Searches may be made without a warrant during field interrogations. The police often stop and interrogate persons without knowing any facts to justify an arrest. Clearly much police activity involves interrogating people who are acting suspiciously or who are disturbing the public order. These street encounters, often called "threshold inquiries," allow for brief questioning and frisking—patting down the outside of the suspect's clothing to ascertain whether there is a concealed weapon.

Terry v. *Ohio* (1968): A police officer may stop and frisk an individual if it is reasonable to suspect that a crime has been committed.

In the case of *Terry* v. *Ohio* (1968), the Supreme Court upheld the stop-and-frisk procedure.[50] In this case, a police officer noticed two men taking turns looking into a store window and then conferring. A third man joined them. Suspecting that a crime was about to be committed, the officer confronted them, removed pistols from two of the men, and charged them with carrying concealed weapons. The court ruled that this was a constitutional frisk since the officer had stopped them for the purpose of detention or interrogation and that, because he believed he was dealing with armed and dangerous individuals, the frisk could be conducted for his own safety or that of others.

On the basis of *Terry* and subsequent decisions, it is now accepted that a police officer is justified in stopping and questioning an individual if it is reasonable to assume that a crime has been committed, is being committed, or is about to be committed. The individual may be frisked for a weapon if the officer fears for his or her life, and the officer is justified in going through the individual's clothing and person if the frisk has indicated something that might be a weapon. The courts have concluded that an officer may conduct this form of field interrogation in order to investigate suspicious persons without first showing probable cause.

Automobiles

A third special circumstance in which a search can be made without a warrant is when there is probable cause to believe that an automobile contains criminal evidence. The Supreme Court has distinguished automobiles from houses and persons on the grounds that a car that has been involved in a crime can be moved and evidence lost.

A QUESTION OF ETHICS

Officer Mike Groton knocked on the apartment door. He and fellow officer Howard Reece had gone to this rundown part of town to arrest Richard Watson on the basis of evidence from an informer that Watson was a major drug seller. "Police officers, open up," said Groton. The door opened slowly, and a small tense woman peered into the hallway.

"Ma'am, we have a warrant for the arrest of Richard Watson. Is he here?"

"No. I don't know any Watson," was the answer.

"Well, let us in so that we can see for ourselves."

Groton and Reece entered the apartment. The place was a shambles and had only a few pieces of badly worn furniture. Reece quickly proceeded to a back bedroom. The window leading to a fire escape was open and the bed looked as though someone had left it in a rush. Reece started to poke around the room, opening bureau drawers and searching the closet. In the back of the closet he noticed a woman's pocketbook hanging on a hook. He opened it and found three glassine packages of a white powder.

"Hey Mike, look what I found," he called. Groton came into the bedroom. "Looks like heroin to me," said Reece. "Too bad we can't use it."

"Why can't we use it? This is his place."

"But the warrant only specified the arrest of Watson. It didn't say anything about searching his closet."

"Let's just keep those packets. When we catch him we can 'find' it in his pocket."

What are the issues here? Can the officers keep the heroin packets? Is bending the rules acceptable in some circumstances? If so, do these circumstances warrant it? What should the officers do?

First developed by the Supreme Court in 1925 (*Carroll* v. *United States*), this doctrine emphasizing the mobile nature of motor vehicles has been accepted, though the police must have reason to believe that the particular car is linked to a crime.[51]

Questions about the search of automobiles have plagued the court. If a car may be searched, does that also include the trunk? Can the police also look inside articles kept in the trunk, a suitcase for example? These questions were addressed by the Court in 1982 in *United States* v. *Ross*.[52] Here the Court said that a warrantless search of an automobile and its contents is permitted if there is probable cause to believe that it contains evidence of a crime. The right to search the containers follows from the right to search the vehicle.

In recent years two new questions have confronted the justices: whether impounded automobiles are subject to warrantless search and whether searches may be made of automobiles stopped in routine traffic inspections. A 1968 case upheld the right of the police to enter an impounded vehicle subsequent to an arrest in order to inventory its contents.[53] This position was advanced when the Court said that a validly impounded car may be searched without probable cause or warrant on the ground that it is reasonable for an inventory of the contents to be taken as a protection against theft or charges of theft while the car is in police custody.[54]

With regard to the stopping of motorists at police roadblocks for the purpose of checking licenses and to determine the health or mental state of drivers, the Court said that random stops were illegal unless the police had some reasonable suspicion that a motor vehicle law was being violated.[55] This eliminated police discretion to stop vehicles at will, but it upheld roadblocks set up to systematically check drivers in a uniform manner. In short, police may stop all cars at roadblocks designed, for example, to catch drunk drivers, but they must be able to give clear reasons for singling out cars to stop amongst moving traffic.

The warrantless search of a car's occupants is still a cloudy legal area. Currently it appears that automobiles are seen to be different than other areas considered private. Because of the importance of the automobile in American society, there will undoubtedly be additional interpretations of the Fourth Amendment with regard to unreasonable search and seizure.

"Plain View"

Another exception to the requirement of a warrant occurs when officers seize items that are in "plain view" when they have reason to believe that the items are connected with a crime. If an officer has a warrant to search a house for cocaine, for example, and during the course of the search comes upon drug paraphernalia, the paraphernalia may also be seized. But for the plain view doctrine to apply, the item must be plainly visible to a law enforcement officer who is in a lawful position when he inadvertently comes across an item the evidentiary value of which is immediately apparent. Issues of probable cause and the place where items are found may be raised to invalidate the seizure. Whether the finding of the item was inadvertent may be the basis of a challenge as well.

Two recent decisions have further defined constitutionally allowable actions by police officers under the plain view doctrine. In *New York* v. *Class* (1986) the Court said that a gun protruding from under a seat, seen by an officer when he entered the car to look for the vehicle identification number, was within the bounds of the doctrine.[56] However, in *Arizona* v. *Hicks* (1987) the Court ruled that an officer who moved a stereo system to find its identification number during a legal search for weapons had violated the Fourth Amendment ban against unreasonable search and seizure.[57] The serial number was not in

CLOSE-UP *The Case of Dolree Mapp:* Mapp *v. Ohio, 367 U.S. 643 (1961)*

In the early afternoon of May 23, 1957, three Cleveland police officers went to the home of Miss Dolree Mapp to check on an informant's tip that a suspect in a recent bombing episode was hiding there. They also had information that a large amount of materials for operating a numbers game was being kept on the premises. The officers knocked on the door and demanded entrance, but Miss Mapp, after telephoning her lawyer, refused to admit them without a search warrant.

Three hours later, the officers again sought entrance. When their knocking went unanswered, they forcibly entered the house. Miss Mapp came down the stairway, confronted the officers, and demanded to see a search warrant. One of the policemen waved a piece of paper, claimed to be the warrant, in the air. Immediately Miss Mapp snatched the paper and placed it in her bosom. One of the officers went after it anyway. In the ensuing struggle, Miss Mapp was handcuffed. At about that time her attorney, Walter Green, arrived at the house and heard Miss Mapp scream, "Take your hand out of my dress!" Green was not permitted to enter the house nor to see his client.

Meanwhile, Miss Mapp was forcibly taken upstairs to her bedroom, where her belongings were searched. A photo album and personal papers along with her child's bedroom and a trunk in the basement were included in the widespread hunt. When one officer found a brown paper bag containing books, Miss Mapp yelled, "Better not look at those. They might excite you." Disregarding the warning, he looked at the books and proclaimed them to be obscene. The trunk held additional materials that were thought to be obscene.

Miss Mapp was charged with violation of Section 2905.34 of the Ohio Revised Code, which makes illegal the possession of obscene, lewd, or lascivious materials. In the trial that followed, the state sought to show that the materials belonged to Miss Mapp, while the defense contended that they were the property of a former boarder who had just moved and left his things behind. The trial judge was unimpressed by the defense contentions and instructed the jury that under Ohio law, unlawfully obtained evidence (evidence gathered without a proper search warrant) could be introduced into the court. The jury found Miss Mapp guilty, and she was sentenced to an indefinite term in the Ohio Reformatory for Women. The effect of the sentence was that Dolree Mapp could serve between one and seven years behind bars.

On May 27, 1959, Miss Mapp appealed to the Ohio Supreme Court. She claimed, first, that the materials found in the trunk had not been in her possession; second, that the evidence had been obtained through an illegal search and seizure; and third, that the statute under which she had been charged was unconstitutional. The majority opinion found that the boarder had left the trunk with Miss Mapp for safekeeping and thus it was in her possession. The court found that while evidently no search warrant had been issued, Ohio law nevertheless allowed the admission of evidence obtained through an illegal search and seizure. Finally, concerning her claim about the obscenity statute, the court ruled that it was an unconstitutional infringement on free speech and press. However, the four-to-three ruling did not make the statute invalid, because the Ohio Constitution requires that all but one of the justices must be in the majority to overturn a law. Because of this peculiarity in the Ohio Constitution, Miss Mapp's conviction stood. Her attorney wasted no time in appealing the case to the U.S. Supreme Court.

DECISION

On June 11, 1961, a narrow majority of the Supreme Court overturned Miss Mapp's conviction on the ground that the Fourth Amendment's prohibition against unreasonable search and seizure, as applied to the states by the due process clause of the Fourteenth Amendment, had been violated. Speaking for the majority, Justice Tom Clark reviewed the history of the Court's interpretation of the amendment and then said that as

> the right to be secure against rude invasions of privacy by state officers is . . . constitutional in origin, we can no longer permit that right to remain an empty promise. . . . We can no longer permit it to be revocable at the whim of any police officer who, in the name of law enforcement itself, chooses to suspend its enjoyment.

plain view, and the police did not have probable cause to believe that the stereo had been stolen.

Consent

A citizen may waive the rights granted by the Fourth Amendment and allow the police to conduct a search or to seize items without a warrant and in the absence of special circumstances. The prosecution must be able to prove, however, that the consent was given voluntarily by the correct person. In some circumstances, as when airplane passengers' belongings are searched by airport security employees before they board a plane and by customs agents, consent is implied. But in the absence of such circumstances consent must be clearly voluntary and not given as a consequence of duress or coercion.[58] Moreover, the consenting person must understand his or her right to deny the search. Questions about who may give consent center on permission given by persons other than the defendant—for example, landlords, cohabitants, or relatives. Courts have looked at consent searches with skepticism.

Arrest

arrest: The physical taking of a person into custody on the ground that there is probable cause to believe that he or she has committed a criminal offense. Police may use only reasonable physical force in making an arrest. The purpose of arrest is to hold the accused for a court proceeding.

Arrest is the seizure of an individual by a governmental official with authority to take the person into custody. It is more than a field interrogation or threshold inquiry, since the normal consequence of arrest is that the suspect is taken to the station house, and there proceedings begin that will eventually lead to prosecution and trial. The law of arrest mixes the Fourth Amendment's protections and local rules regarding procedure. Generally this means that the arresting officer must be able to show that there is probable cause to believe (1) that a crime has been committed and (2) that the person taken into custody has committed the crime. Although this is sometimes difficult for the police to prove, the restrictions prevent them from randomly taking people into custody or using their power to limit the freedom of those whom, for one reason or another, they do not like.

Although the courts have not specifically *required* arrest only upon presentation of a warrant, they have implied that for felony arrests this is the preferred method. It is routine to make arrests without a warrant even though there may be adequate opportunity to obtain a warrant. In general, courts have upheld the common law rule stated in *Carroll* v. *United States* (1925) that "a police officer may arrest without a warrant one believed by an officer upon reasonable cause to have been guilty of a felony and he may only arrest without a warrant one guilty of a misdemeanor if committed in his presence."[59]

Interrogation

Among the rights guaranteed by the Fifth Amendment, one of the most important is the protection against self-incrimination. This means that persons shall not be compelled to be witnesses against themselves. This right is consistent with the assumption on which the adversarial process is based: that the state must prove the defendant's guilt. Although closely linked to the Fourth Amendment's prohibition of unreasonable search and seizure, the right has most force with regard to interrogations and confessions. The court will exclude from the evidence presented to the jurors any confession illegally obtained; further, because of the Sixth Amendment, the suspect has the right to counsel during the interrogation process.

The Supreme Court ruled in *Escobedo* v. *Illinois* (1964) and *Miranda* v. *Arizona* (1966) that confessions made by suspects who have not been notified of their constitutional rights cannot be admitted as evidence.[60] This development of the law is commonly called the exclusionary rule. To protect the rights of the accused, the Court emphasized the importance of allowing counsel to be present during the interrogation process. In addition, the Court said in effect that as soon as the investigation of an unsolved crime begins to focus on a particular suspect and when the suspect has been taken into custody the so-called *Miranda* warnings have to be read aloud before interrogation can commence. Suspects must be told that:

1. They have the right to remain silent.
2. If they decide to make a statement, it can and will be used against them in court.
3. They have the right to have an attorney present during interrogation, or have an opportunity to consult with an attorney.
4. If they cannot afford an attorney, the state will provide one.

Handcuffing the Police?

No sooner was the *Miranda* opinion announced than a hue and cry arose over the propriety of the new judicial rules. Criticism of the Supreme Court came from a number of sources but especially from the law enforcement community. It was argued that: (1) confessions are essential for the apprehension and conviction of law violators, (2) informing suspects of their rights would greatly reduce the ability

■
The *Miranda* warnings must be read to every suspect at the time of questioning and before being taken into custody.

of the police to secure confessions, and (3) few police would actually give the required warnings.

All of these assumptions have been challenged both by law enforcement officials and by social scientists studying the impact of the rulings. The most extensive of these studies focused on felony cases and found that fewer than 1 percent of the cases that reached the courts had been dismissed because of the exclusionary rule.[61] Similar findings were reported in a study of the rule's impact on the federal courts.[62] With some exceptions it appears that the rule is an issue only in drug cases. In 7,500 felony cases in nine counties in three states, only 46 cases (0.6 percent) were lost because of the exclusionary rule. Most of those involved offenses that might have resulted in incarceration for less than six months. Indeed it can be argued that the exclusionary rule has had only a marginal impact on the criminal court system.[63]

In most cities the police depend on either catching the accused in the act or locating witnesses who will testify. Almost all departments have limited resources for scientific investigation and so are ham-

---

CLOSE-UP   Rape on the Desert: *Miranda v. Arizona, 384 U.S. 436 (1966)*

While walking to a bus on the night of March 2, 1963, after leaving her job as a candy counter clerk at the Paramount Theater in Phoenix, Arizona, eighteen-year-old Barbara Ann Johnson was accosted by a man who shoved her into his car, tied her hands and ankles, and took her to the edge of the city, where he raped her. The man then drove Miss Johnson to a street near her home, where he let her out of his car and asked that she say a prayer for him. After piecing the girl's story together, officers of the Phoenix Police Department picked up Ernesto Miranda and asked him whether he would voluntarily answer questions about the case. In a lineup at the station Miranda was picked out by two women: one identified him as the man who had robbed her at knifepoint on November 27, 1962, and Barbara Johnson thought he was the rapist.

Ernesto Arthur Miranda was a twenty-three-year-old eighth-grade dropout with a police record going back to his arrest at the age of fourteen for stealing a car. Since that time, he had been in trouble as a peeping Tom in Los Angeles, had been given an undesirable discharge by the Army for the same offense, and had served time in a federal prison for driving a stolen car across a state line. When Phoenix police officers Cooley and Young told Miranda that he had been identified by the women, he made a statement in his own handwriting that described the incident. He also noted that he was making the confession voluntarily and with full knowledge of his legal rights. Miranda was soon charged with robbery, kidnapping, and rape.

At Miranda's trial, his court-appointed attorney, Alvin Moore, got Officers Cooley and Young to admit both that during the interrogation the defendant was not told of his right to have counsel and that no counsel

was present. Over Moore's objections the judge admitted Miranda's confession into evidence. After more than five hours of jury deliberations, Miranda was found guilty and later was given concurrent sentences of from twenty to thirty years for kidnapping and rape. In a separate trial, he was given a sentence of from twenty to twenty-five years for robbery, that term to commence after the kidnapping and rape sentences had been served. Miranda thus faced a minimum of forty and a maximum of fifty-five years in prison.

Following an unsuccessful appeal to the Arizona Supreme Court, the United States Supreme Court agreed to review Miranda's case. His counsel asked the Court to decide whether "the confession of a poorly educated, mentally abnormal, indigent defendant, not told of his right to counsel, taken when he is in police custody and without assistance of counsel, which was not requested, can be admitted into evidence over specific objection based on the absence of counsel."

DECISION

On June 13, 1966, Chief Justice Earl Warren announced the decision of the Supreme Court in *Miranda v. Arizona*. In clear terms he outlined detailed procedures that the police must use when questioning an accused person. As the chief justice said in explaining the reasons for the decision:

> The current practice of incommunicado interrogation is at odds with one of our Nation's most cherished principles—that the individual may not be compelled to incriminate himself. Unless adequate protective devices are employed to dispel the compulsion inherent in custodial surroundings, no statement obtained from the defendant can truly be the product of free choice.

pered in their efforts to amass enough evidence to arrest a suspect. In the usual situation, a suspect is not arrested until the crime is solved and conviction assured. Interrogation becomes unnecessary under these circumstances.

Although police officials, politicians, and others felt that the *Miranda* rules would stifle efforts to control a rising crime rate, no such impact occurred. Neither was *Miranda* the boon that the Supreme Court and its defenders suggested it might be. Because of noncompliance during field and station house interrogation, the difficulties of developing schemes to provide effective counsel for indigent suspects, and distrust and misunderstanding on the part of suspects, the new protections had much less effect than had been anticipated. What seems to have occurred is that the police became more conscious of their requirements under the law. *Miranda* may have improved the professional atmosphere of the police environment.

Modification of the Exclusionary Rule

In the years since the cases of Dolree Mapp, Daniel Escobedo, and Ernesto Miranda were heard, a flow of cases to the Supreme Court has raised further questions about the exclusionary rule. As the number of conservative justices increased, some people expected the Court to overturn these landmark decisions. Though it has not done so, the new conservative majority seems intent on halting the liberal thrust of previous decisions and shaping them to meet the complex demands of law enforcement. Decisions in recent cases have modified those of the Warren Court to such an extent that civil libertarians have complained that the exclusionary provisions are all but dead. They are not dead, but they have been modified by rulings in regard to particular circumstances in which searches and interrogations have been conducted.

Notable among the cases modifying the exclusionary rule as pronounced in *Miranda* was *Harris* v. *New York* (1971), in which the Court ruled that statements that are trustworthy (not coerced) may be used to attack the credibility of a defendant who takes the stand even though they have been obtained in violation of the rule.[64] The prosecution charged that Harris had lied during his trial, and the Court ruled that his statements to the police before trial could be introduced as evidence to prove the contention. In *Michigan* v. *Mosley* (1975) the Court ruled that a second interrogation session held after the suspect had initially refused to make a statement did not violate *Miranda*.[65] In *Rhode Island* v. *Innis* (1980), however, the Court broadened the application of *Miranda* by ruling that the safeguards against self-incrimination must be observed "whenever a person in custody is subjected to either express questioning or its equivalent."[66] In that case the suspect, riding with police officers in a squad car after being picked up in a murder investigation, heard one officer worry aloud to the other that because the murder had occurred near a school for handicapped children, some child might find the gun and be injured by it. At that the suspect told the officers where the gun could be found.

Three doctrines modifying the exclusionary rule have been enunciated. In the case of *New York* v. *Quarles* (1984) Justice William H. Rehnquist established a "public safety" exception to the suspect-warning doctrine.[67] Benjamin Quarles was charged with criminal possession of a weapon after a rape victim described him to the police. The officers located him in a supermarket. After frisking Quarles and discovering that he was wearing an empty shoulder holster, an officer asked where the gun was. Quarles noded in the direction of some empty cartons: "The gun is over there." The officer retrieved a loaded .38 caliber revolver from one of the cartons, formally placed Quarles under arrest, and read him his *Miranda* rights from a printed card. Rehnquist said that the case presented a situation in which concern for public safety must take precedence over adherence to the literal language of the rules. The police were justified in asking the question by "immediate necessity."

A second doctrine, called the "inevitability of discovery exception," was stated by the Court in *Nix* v. *Williams* (1984).[68] This decision followed *Brewer* v. *Williams* (1977).[69] Robert Williams had been convicted of the murder of a ten-year-old girl. During the investigation, detectives searching for the body had given Williams what became known as the "Christian burial speech." Though they had promised his lawyer not to ask questions during a drive across the state with the suspect, they asked Williams to think about the fact that the parents of the girl were entitled to have an opportunity to provide a Christian burial for their child. Williams then told them where to find the body. In 1977 the Supreme Court ruled that the detectives had violated the suspect's rights by inducing him to incriminate himself outside the presence of counsel. However, the Court left open the possibility that in a retrial the state could introduce the evidence of the body's discovery if it could be shown that it would have been found even without the defendant's testimony. Applying the "inevitability of discovery exception," the Iowa courts found Williams guilty, and in 1984 the Supreme Court upheld the conviction. The chief justice said that the doctrine was designed to put the police "in the same, not a *worse*, position than they would have been in if no police error or misconduct had occurred."

United States v. *Leon* (1984): Evidence seized using a warrant later found defective is valid if the officer was acting in good faith.

In a move likely to create a third doctrine, a "good faith exception" to the exclusionary rule, the Supreme Court has declared that evidence can be used even though it has been obtained under a search warrant that later is proved to be technically invalid. In **United States v. Leon** (1984), a six-to-three majority of the Court agreed that evidence obtained by law enforcement officers acting in reasonable reliance on a search warrant issued by a detached and neutral magistrate but ultimately found to be unsupported by probable cause could be used at trial. In dissent, Justice William Brennan, Jr., objected to the majority's effort to balance the costs and benefits of the exclusionary rule. The majority, he said, ignored the fundamental constitutional importance that was at stake in the case, and "it now appears that the Court's victory over the Fourth Amendment is complete."[70]

The Court has yet to determine the applicability of a good faith exception to evidence seized by police officers during a warrantless search. Does the exclusionary rule apply to evidence obtained by officers who reasonably but incorrectly believe they have a proper basis for a search?

Given the conservative majority on the Rehnquist Court, many observers expect that as more cases linked to the rights of defendants with regard to searches and interrogation come before the justices, the standard first enunciated by Chief Justice Warren in 1966 will be further eroded. It must be remembered, however, that although conservative justices may be concerned about crime control, they also respect legal precedent. This was illustrated in the 1990 case of *Minnick* v. *Mississippi* in which by a six-to-two vote the justices ruled that suspects have the right to have their lawyer present throughout police interrogation.[71] It is thus doubtful that the major thrust of the Warren and Burger courts will be completely overturned.

Law and Law Enforcement

As we have seen in this examination of the three major elements of the law enforcement process—detection, apprehension, and arrest—the law stipulates the actions that may be taken at each stage. Many people believe that the Supreme Court has gone too far and that criminals have gone free on technicalities as a result. Others emphasize that the Constitution protects all Americans against the unbridled exercise of power by the government and that the benefits of freedom are worth the price of letting some criminals go. It seems likely that this debate will continue and that the relationship of police actions to the rule of law will always be a subject of contention.

SUMMARY

The police, the American family, criminals, and politicians agree in at least one respect: the police have an "impossible" mandate. The police have license to carry out certain activities that others may not. They have formal rules and codes of ethics that set standards for their conduct. Yet unlike other professionals, the police in contemporary society have been unable to define their occupational mandate; rather, it has been defined for them. In addition, sociopolitical influences have added to tensions between the mandate of the police for "efficient, apolitical, and professional enforcement of the law" and their ability to define and fulfill it.[72] Police operations not only are shaped by the formal organizational structures created to allocate law enforcement resources in an efficient manner but also are influenced by social and political processes both within and outside the department. The latest war on drugs, for instance, has had an immediate effect on police operations.

The police are organized along military lines so that authority and responsibility can be located at appropriate levels. Within the modern police department, operational divisions are responsible for activities designed to achieve the goals of crime prevention and control. Although organization charts appear to show that police operations run like a well-adjusted machine, administrative leadership, recruitment, socialization of recruits to norms and values of the system, and the perspectives of the general public serve to shape the ways police activities are conducted. Police operations can likewise be influenced by pressures from community political leaders who want law enforcement resources to be allocated in ways that will further their own interests. Other portions of the criminal justice system can also shape law enforcement activities. The police are the system's crucial entry point for the disposition of offenders, and law enforcement officers are under pressure to get the evidence the prosecution needs. Yet their operations must be carried out according to law.

The traditional functions and operations of the police are being reassessed. Although the crime-fighting image is widely held among citizens, this may be a distorted notion. Research has shown that the police are engaged in a wider variety of activities. One view suggests that the modern police department has been given so many responsibilities that it is really a public service organization. New technologies, especially those of communications, have helped to alter police operations, yet research continues to describe the patrol officer as the multipurpose officer who is equipped to meet the many demands that the public places on the police. But the mandate that the police have been given is impossible. The situation cannot be changed as long as both police and public harbor misunderstandings in regard to the nature of law enforcement work, unrealistic estimates of the potential for success in efforts to control crime, and misconceptions of the role of law in a democratic society.

FOR DISCUSSION

1. The use of patrol cars instead of police officers on foot has been extensively debated. What do you see as the conflicting values underlying this argument?
2. You are a patrol officer. What things can you do to win high effectiveness ratings from your boss?
3. The military-style organization of the police is often criticized as inhibiting effective law enforcement. Do you feel this emphasis enhances or detracts from police efficiency?
4. You are a police chief. How would you allocate the personnel resources in your city?
5. Modern communications have greatly altered patrol work. What are some of the changes that a central command post has brought to police operations?

FOR FURTHER READING

Brown, Michael K. *Working the Street*. New York: Russell Sage Foundation, 1981. A study of patrol work by officers of the San Diego Police Force.
Geller, William A., ed. *Police Leadership in America*. New York: Praeger, 1985. A collection of essays written by some of the most progressive police executives.

Goldstein, Herman. *Problem-Oriented Policing.* New York: McGraw-Hill, 1990. Examination of the move toward problem-oriented or community policing with examples of its successful use.

Manning, Peter K. *Police Work.* Cambridge, MA: MIT Press, 1977. Manning offers a look at police work, arguing that the police have an "impossible mandate." They have emphasized their crime-fighting stance, a role that they do not play successfully.

Skogan, Wesley G. *Disorder and Decline: Crime and the Spiral of Decay in American Neighborhoods.* New York: Free Press, 1990. Support for community policing on the basis of studies spawned by the Wilson-Kelling thesis.

Skolnick, Jerome H., and David H. Bayley. *The New Blue Line.* New York: Free Press, 1986. A look at modern policing by two major criminal justice scholars.

NOTES

1. John Gardiner, *Traffic and the Police: Variations in Law Enforcement Policy* (Cambridge, MA: Harvard University Press, 1969), p. 116.
2. James F. Gilisnan, "They Is Clowning Tough: 911 and the Social Construction of Reality," *Criminology* 27 (May 1989):329; see also Peter Manning, *Symbolic Communication: Signifying Calls and the Police Response* (Cambridge, MA: MIT Press, 1988).
3. *Survey of Police Operational and Administrative Practices* (Washington, DC: Police Executive Research Forum and Police Foundation, 1981), pp. 22–24.
4. Samuel G. Chapman, *Police Patrol Readings,* 2d ed. (Springfield, IL: Charles C. Thomas, 1970), p. ix.
5. Samuel G. Chapman, "Police Patrol Administration," in *Municipal Police Administration,* 7th ed., ed. George D. Eastman and Esther Eastman (Washington, DC: International City Management Association, 1971), p. 77.
6. Charles D. Hale, *Fundamentals of Police Administration* (Boston, MA: Holbrook Press, 1977), pp. 105–106.
7. Lawrence E. Cohen and Marcus Felson, "Social Change and Crime Rate Trends: A Routine Activity Approach," *American Sociological Review* 44 (1979):589.
8. The results of this analysis were that 50 percent of the calls to the police were concentrated in 3 percent of all Minneapolis places and calls reporting all predatory crimes were found for robberies at 2.2 percent of places, all rapes at 1.2 percent of places, and all auto thefts at 2.7 percent of places. See Lawrence W. Sherman, Patrick R. Gartin, and Michael E. Buerger, "Hot Spots of Predatory Crime: Routine Activities and the Criminology of Place," *Criminology* 27 (February 1989):27.
9. George Kelling, Tony Pate, Duane Dieckman, and Charles E. Brown, *The Kansas City Preventive Patrol Experiments: A Summary Report* (Washington, DC: Police Foundation, 1974).
10. William G. Spelman and Dale K. Brown, *Calling the Police: Citizen Reporting of Serious Crime* (Washington, DC: Police Executive Research Forum, 1984), p. xxix.
11. Lawrence W. Sherman, "Patrol Strategies for Police," in *Crime and Public Policy,* ed. James Q. Wilson (San Francisco: ICS Press, 1983), p. 149.
12. Spelman and Brown, *Calling the Police,* p. 4.
13. Marcia Cohen and J. Thomas McEwen, "Handling Calls for Service: Alternatives to Traditional Policing," *NIJ Reports* (September 1984):4.
14. Sherman, "Patrol Strategies for Police," p. 149.
15. Lee A. Brown and Mary Ann Wycoff, "Policing Houston: Reducing Fear and Improving Service," *Crime and Delinquency* 33 (January 1987):71; *The Newark Foot Patrol Experiment* (Washington, DC: Police Foundation, 1981); Robert C. Trojanowicz, *An Evaluation of the Neighborhood Foot Patrol Program in Flint, Michigan* (East Lansing: Michigan State University, n.d.).
16. Ben Davis, "Foot Patrol," *Police Centurian* (June 1984):41.
17. In San Diego, one-officer cars were substituted for two-officer cars on a unit-for-unit basis. It was concluded that on the basis of calls handled, arrests, response time, monetary costs, and other measures, one-officer patrol was clearly as effective and more efficient than two-officer patrol. See J. Boydstun, M. Sherry, and

M. Moelter, *Patrol Staffing in San Diego: One- or Two-Officer Units* (Washington, DC: Police Foundation, 1977). On the question of officer safety, researchers in Kansas City and San Diego examined the frequency of injury for one-officer and two-officer units. Although the injury rate per officer was higher for one-officer patrols, the difference was not great, and evaluators believe that the question is still not fully answered. See U.S. Department of Justice, National Institute of Justice, *Synthesizing and Extending the Results of Police Patrol Studies* (Washington, DC: Government Printing Office, 1985), p. 94.

18. James Q. Wilson and Barbara Boland, *The Effect of the Police on Crime*, U.S. Department of Justice (Washington, DC: Government Printing Office, 1979).

19. James Q. Wilson, *Thinking about Crime*, 2nd rev. ed. (New York: Basic Books, 1983), p. 71.

20. Susan E. Martin and Lawrence W. Sherman, "Selective Apprehension: A Police Strategy for Repeat Offenders," *Criminology* 24 (February 1986):155–73; Susan E. Martin, "Policing Career Criminals: An Examination of an Innovative Crime Control Program," *Journal of Criminal Law and Criminology* 77 (Winter 1986): 1159–82.

21. Robert H. Langworthy, "Do Stings Control Crime? An Evaluation of a Police Fencing Operation," *Justice Quarterly* 6 (March 1989):27.

22. Wilson and Boland, *Effect of the Police on Crime*, p. 4.

23. Herman Goldstein, *Problem-Oriented Policing* (New York: McGraw-Hill, 1990).

24. John E. Eck and William Spelman, "Who Ya Gonna Call? The Police as Problem Busters," *Crime and Delinquency* 33 (January 1987):6.

25. Candace McCoy, "Policing the Homeless," *Criminal Law Bulletin* 22 (May/June 1986):263.

26. U.S. Department of Justice, National Institute of Justice, *Research in Action* (Washington, DC: Government Printing Office, January 1988); U.S. Department of Justice, National Institute of Justice, Peter Finn and Monique Sullivan, *Police Response to Special Populations* (Washington, DC: Government Printing Office, 1987).

27. Hubert Williams and Antony M. Pate, "Returning to First Principles: Reducing the Fear of Crime in Newark," *Crime and Delinquency* 33 (January 1987):53.

28. Vic Sims, "Criminal Investigation from a Small Town or Rural Perspective," in *Criminal Investigation: Essays and Cases*, ed. James N. Gilbert, (Columbus, OH: Merrill, 1990), p. 1.

29. Peter Greenwood and Joan Petersilia, *The Criminal Investigation Process*, vol. 1, *Summary and Policy Implications* (Santa Monica, CA: Rand Corporation, 1975).

30. Herman Goldstein, *Policing a Free Society* (Cambridge, MA: Ballinger, 1977), p. 55.

31. Greenwood and Petersilia, *Summary and Policy Implications*, p. 19.

32. Peter J. Neufeld and Neville Colman, "When Science Takes the Witness Stand," *Scientific American* 262 (May 1990):46.

33. Ibid.

34. B. Parker and J. L. Peterson, *Physical Evidence Utilization in the Administration of Criminal Justice* (Washington, DC: Government Printing Office, 1972).

35. President's Commission on Law Enforcement and Administration of Justice, *Task Force Report: The Police* (Washington, DC: Government Printing Office, 1967), p. 58.

36. Peter W. Greenwood, Jan M. Chaiken, and Joan Petersilia, *Criminal Investigation Process* (Lexington, MA: Lexington Books, 1977), p. 227.

37. Greenwood and Petersilia, *Summary and Policy Implications*, pp. x–xiii.

38. Goldstein, *Policing a Free Society*, p. 57.

39. James Q. Wilson, *Varieties of Police Behavior* (Cambridge, MA: Harvard University Press, 1967), p. 53.

40. Jonathan Rubinstein, *City Police* (New York: Farrar, Straus & Giroux, 1973), p. 375.

41. For an account of undercover police work, see James J. Ness and Ellyn K. Ness, "Reflections on Undercover Street Experiences," in *Criminal Investigations: Essays and Cases*, ed. James M. Gilbert (Columbus, OH: Merrill, 1990), p. 105.

42. Gary T. Marx, *Undercover: Police Surveillance in America* (Berkeley: University of California Press, 1988).

43. U.S. Department of Justice, National Institute of Justice, Mark H. Moore and Mark A. R. Kleiman, "The Police and Drugs," *Perspectives on Policing* (September) (Washington, DC: Government Printing Office, 1989).

44. Lynn Zimmer, "Operation Pressure Point: The Disruption of Street-Level Trade on New York's Lower East Side." Occasional papers, Center for Research in Crime and Justice, New York University School of Law, 1987.

45. Bruce D. Johnson, Terry Williams, Kojo A. Dei, and Harry Sanabria, "Drug Abuse in the Inner City: Impact on Hard-Drug Users and the Community," *Drugs and Crime*, vol. 13, *Crime and Justice*, ed. Michael Tonry and James Q. Wilson (Chicago: University of Chicago Press, 1990), p. 32.

46. David E. Pitt, "Report from the Field on an Endless War," *New York Times*, March 12, 1989, p. 14.

47. Ibid., p. 257.

48. *United States* v. *Robinson*, 414 U.S. 218 (1973).

49. *Chimel* v. *California*, 395 U.S. 752 (1969).

50. *Terry* v. *Ohio*, 392 U.S. 1 (1968).

51. *Carroll* v. *United States*, 267 U.S. 132 (1925).

52. *United States* v. *Ross*, 102 S.Ct. 2157 (1982).

53. *Harris* v. *United States*, 390 U.S. 234 (1968).

54. *South Dakota* v. *Opperman*, 428 U.S. 364 (1976).

55. *Delaware* v. *Prouse*, 440 U.S. 213 (1979).

56. *New York* v. *Class*, 54 L.W. 4178 (1986).

57. *Arizona* v. *Hicks*, 55 L.W. 4258 (1987); see also Kimberly Kingston, "Look But Don't Touch: The Plain View Doctrine," *FBI Law Enforcement Bulletin* (December 1987):17.

58. *Wren* v. *United States*, 352 F.2d 617 (1965).

59. *Carroll* v. *United States*, 267 U.S. 132 (1925).

60. *Escobedo* v. *Illinois*, 378 U.S. 478 (1964); *Miranda* v. *Arizona*, 384 U.S. 436 (1966).

61. U.S. Department of Justice, National Institute of Justice, *The Effects of the Exclusionary Rule: A Study in California* (Washington, DC: Government Printing Office, 1982).

62. U.S. Controller General of the United States, *Impact of the Exclusionary Rule on Federal Criminal Prosecutions*, Report GGD-79-45, April 19, 1979.

63. Peter Nardulli, "The Societal Cost of the Exclusionary Rule: An Empirical Assessment," *ABF Research Journal*, (Summer 1983):585–609.

64. *Harris* v. *New York*, 401 U.S. 222 (1971).

65. *Michigan* v. *Mosley*, 423 U.S. 93 (1975).

66. *Rhode Island* v. *Innis*, 446 U.S. 291 (1980).

67. *New York* v. *Quarles*, 467 U.S. 649 (1984).

68. *Nix* v. *Williams*, 52 L.W. 4732 (1984).

69. *Brewer* v. *Williams*, 430 U.S. 387 (1977).

70. *United States* v. *Leon*, 82 L.ed. 2d 677 (1984).

71. *Minnick* v. *Mississippi*, 59 L.W. 4037 (1990).

72. Ibid., p. 157.

7 CHAPTER

Policing: Issues and Trends

Key Terms and Cases

internal affairs unit
Tennessee v. *Garner* (1985)

The police in the United States are not separate from the people. They draw their authority from the will and consent of the people, and they recruit their officers from them. The police are the instrument of the people to achieve and maintain order; their efforts are founded on principles of public service and ultimate responsibility to the public.

National Advisory Commission on Criminal Justice Standards and Goals

It is a sweltering August night in Houston. Officers Katsigris and Staat have been dealing with a seemingly endless number of routine incidents—stolen car reports, a "crazie" moaning on the sidewalk, a false burglar alarm sounding, and a call to a housing project where a domestic quarrel has subsided by the time they arrive. It has been seven hours, one more to go before their shift ends. Suddenly the radio dispatcher orders them to Allen and Division Streets, a known drug sales marketplace, where gunfire is reported. Racing to the intersection at high speed and with blue lights flashing they careen around the corner, slam on the brakes, and jump out of the car with pistols drawn. They find a crowd standing around the blood-spattered body of man. It is Saturday night in Houston.

Being a police officer in an American city in the 1990s can be a debilitating experience. Hours of boring, routine work can be interrupted by short spurts of dangerous crime fighting. Although police work has always been frustrating and dangerous, today's officers must deal with a wide range of situations ranging from assisting the homeless to dealing with domestic violence to confronting shoot-outs at drug buys gone sour. Citizens demand increased protection, yet in many cities police budgets have been reduced at a time when violence is on the increase. The police are thought by many to be stuck in a bygone era, yet some of the most innovative changes in the history of police service have taken place.

In an increasingly pluralistic society there is often disagreement as to the role of the police, behavior that should be considered criminal, and the tactics of law enforcement agencies.

As the National Advisory Commission noted in the quotation that opened this chapter, the police are not separate from the people. In a democracy law enforcement draws its strength and authority from the citizenry. The police serve the people and must be responsive to them. Because of this relationship the police are now being forced to face a number of issues and trends, which Chapter 7 will discuss. Most of these issues and trends have an indirect impact on police operation, affecting the links of these agencies to the broader society and some of the enduring problems associated with police work. This does not mean that such matters as corruption, unionism, hiring practices, and accountability do not influence the effectiveness of policing; they do. Their effect, however, is indirect, because they concern police personnel and the reaction of citizens to the police.

POLITICS AND THE POLICE

Descriptions of the relationship between politics and the police have generally centered on links among the police, partisan politics, and corruption. From the beginning of this century, when the journalist Lincoln Steffens exposed corruption in American cities, to more recent times, when police scandals have rocked departments in New York City, Chicago, and Miami, politics has been entwined in the relationships that often bind criminals and the police. In addition, allocation of police resources, appointment of administrators, and determination of enforcement policies that attract public attention all have a political dimension. Thus it is a fact that police corruption occurs and that partisan politics is often the basis for it.

A number of studies have provided examples of the relationship between politics and the police that show how organized crime can forge direct links to government officials and influence the daily operations of the police.[1] In a number of cities police officials have been elected to the position of mayor as "law-and-order" candidates.

But the relationship between politics and police policy goes beyond such well-publicized incidents. In a heterogeneous and pluralistic society such as ours, there is often disagreement about the role of the police, the activities that should be labeled criminal, and the enforcement practices that should be followed. Some communities may achieve a consensus on the policies to be followed. In others, the heterogeneity of the population and existing political divisions may lead portions of the community to be antagonistic to certain police activities. For example, what appeared to whites to be a sound police strategy to deter crime in Oakland, California—namely, intensive surveillance of public places—was viewed as harassment by a substantial part of the African-American community.[2] Public controversy may develop over such matters as the treatment of juveniles, charges of police brutality, policies concerning strict or tolerant enforcement of gambling laws, and the level of protection maintained in certain neighborhoods. When such matters come to the fore in the arena of public opinion, they attract the attention of political leaders.

Although controversial issues may engender a high degree of citizen influence over decisions, studies have shown that the true nature of police work is of little interest to most citizens. Police protection may be called on to prevent things from happening; it is largely invisible, and the average citizen comes into contact with it only in the exceptional case. For most citizens, police service is difficult to evaluate. Thus while police brutality, traffic safety crackdowns, and the flagrant flouting of vice laws may bring a public outcry, most police activities are known only to people who have direct contact with the law.

An examination of eight communities disclosed that police activities were governed by the dominant values of the local political culture rather than by direct political intervention.[3] Such values were reflected in the police force's budget, pay levels, and organization, but explicit political decisions were not made about the routine handling of situations by the men and women on the force. The police were found to be sensitive to the political environment but were not governed by it in their day-to-day activities. In short, the prevailing style of policing in each community was not explicitly determined by political decisions, although a few elements were shaped by those considerations.

Police administrators are the key figures in law enforcement politics, because they link the department to other decision makers, public officials, and community elites. Through the choice of a particular type of administrator, the values of the local political culture are translated into policing policies. If conflict develops between the police chief and a politically powerful figure such as the mayor, the police department may find its operations hampered by cuts in its budget. Such political battles may even result in the firing of the chief.

During the past decade the position of police chief has become professionalized in many major U.S. cities. It used to be customary to award the job to an insider as a patronage plum; now it is becoming increasingly common to conduct a national search for the best-qualified person to fill the position. But however the chief is chosen, the department reflects the chief's policies, and the chief's approach to law enforcement must conform to the expectations of dominant local groups.

POLICE AND THE COMMUNITY

To carry out complicated tasks of law enforcement, order maintenance, and service with efficiency and discretion is a formidable assignment even under the best circumstances—that is, when the police have the public's support and cooperation. The "best circumstances" may have existed in our rural past and may exist in some suburban communities today, but they definitely do not exist in metropolitan areas, especially those populated by the poor and minorities. In city slums and ghettos—the neighborhoods that need and want effective policing—there is much distrust of the police; accordingly, citizens fail to report crimes and refuse to cooperate with investigations. Encounters between individual police officers and members of these communities are often charged with animosity and periodically turn into large-scale disorders. Yet, "the single most striking fact about the attitudes of citizens, black and white, toward the police is that in general these attitudes are positive, not negative."[4]

The relationship of the police to the urban community has been given increased attention by criminal justice officials and the media since the long hot summers of the late 1960s. Initially emphasis was placed on the special problems associated with the relations between the mostly white police officers and the mostly black inner-city residents. These issues are well demonstrated in the following incident:

> It was an incident just waiting to explode. Three flights up in a Chicago ghetto tenement, six white policemen were surrounding a furious, cursing Negro. "I didn't fire no shots," he railed. "Get your hands off me!" Neighbors, curious and uncooperative, had gathered in the hallway. A suspicious crowd was forming outside on the street. As the cops debated their next move, black patrolman George Owens and his white partner, John Bacus, rushed up the stairs from radio car 1315. Almost immediately, the elderly Negro manager of the building sought out Owens and reported having seen the suspect fire the shots. That was enough. The white cops quickly stepped aside for Owens as he approached the alleged gunman, ignoring the obscenities and racial appeals ("I'm a black man") the man shouted at him. "We've got a complaining witness," Owens announced firmly. "He says he saw the gun, saw him fire it. Book him."[5]

The presence and manner of this African-American officer were clearly very important.

Until the mid-1970s, the phrase "police-community relations" essentially meant attempts to improve police-minority relations. To this end, the recruitment to the force of minority members and the creation of programs designed to put the police in a good light before community members were stressed.

■ A key element of community policing is the assumption that the presence of foot patrol links officers to citizens and thus builds cooperative relationships.

Police-community relations have changed. There is a new recognition that in urban areas there are differences among neighborhoods with regard to the social control and policing strategies.[6] It is in the context of neighborhood characteristics and values that the police decide how they will respond to problems, exercise discretion, and manage their resources.[7]

The new community policing focus includes strategies to reduce crime, disorder, and the fear of crime. Citizens have "armed themselves, restricted their activities, rejected cities, built fortress houses and housing complexes both inside and outside the cities, and panicked about particular groups and classes of citizens."[8] The reinstatement of foot patrols and enhancement of the order maintenance function of the police have been cited as ways to reassure citizens that an arm of government cares about their needs and is determined to provide safety in their neighborhoods.

Community Crime Prevention

There is new recognition that the control of crime and disorder cannot be addressed solely by the police. Social control requires the involvement of all members of the community. In the community policing approach, there must be collaboration between government agencies and neighborhood organizations: "Voluntary local efforts must support official action if order is to be preserved within realistic budgetary limits and without sacrificing our civil liberties."[9]

Citizens' crime watch groups have proliferated in many communities. It has been estimated that more than 6 million Americans are now members of such organizations, which often have direct channels to police departments. In Detroit, Neighborhood Watch is organized on 4,000 of the city's 12,000 blocks; in New York, the Blockwatchers are 70,000 strong and are "trained at precinct houses to watch, listen and report accurately"; and in Dade County, Florida, the 175,000-member Citizens' Crime Watch has extended its operations into schools in an effort to reduce drug use.[10]

Crime Stoppers programs are designed to enlist public help in solving crimes. Originating in 1975 in Albuquerque, New Mexico, the program has quickly spread across the country so that today an estimated 600 programs assist the police.[11] Television and radio stations have been enlisted to publicize an "unsolved crime of the week," and cash rewards are given for information that results in conviction of the offender. Although these programs result in the solving of some crimes, the number solved is insignificant when compared to the total crimes committed. Problems of false arrest, defamation of character, and invasion of privacy have plagued some of the local programs.[12]

One group that gained national publicity in the 1980s was the Guardian Angels, which originated in New York City and spawned chapters in other parts of the country. The Angels are young people in distinctive apparel—red berets and T-shirts—who patrol buses, subways, and streets as self-appointed peacekeepers. Although the Angels have held lawbreakers until a police officer has arrived and have broken up fights, their main function is to act as an intimidating force against those who would otherwise be disruptive. The mere presence of the Guardian Angels has a reassuring effect on people who must travel in what they believe to be a dangerous neighborhood. In some parts of the country their presence has not been welcomed by police executives, since it is argued that only well-trained officers can maintain order and that the Angels may in fact provoke trouble in some situations. After a peak in the mid-1980s, the number of Guardian Angel organizations has declined, yet their impact has been felt and their tactics have demonstrated the need for all citizens to be involved in crime prevention.[13]

How much reliance can be placed on community organizations to reduce crime and to ensure social order? The results are mixed. Research on forty neighborhoods in six cities shows that although crime prevention strategies and the development of voluntary community organizations are successful in better-off neighborhoods, these strategies are less likely to be found in poor neighborhoods—those areas in which levels of disorder are high. In such areas, "residents typically are deeply suspicious of one another, report only a weak sense of community, perceive they have low levels of personal influence on neighborhood events, and feel that it is their neighbors, not 'outsiders,' whom they must watch with care."[14] But the control of criminal and deviant behavior cannot be the sole responsibility of the police. Law enforcement agencies require the support and assistance of the community: support when they take actions that are consistent with neighborhood values and that help to maintain order; assistance in the form of information about wrongdoing and cooperation with police investigation. The police and residents of a community must collaborate in maintaining standards of communal life, with the aim of reducing crime and—perhaps more important—the fear of crime.

The Police: A Link to Government

Police officers provide the only direct contact many people have with government, so the way the officers do their work affects the citizen's sense of the fairness of the political system. Studies of attitudes toward the police in neighborhoods characterized according to race and social class have found that African-Americans judged the police to be more corrupt, less fair, tougher, and more excitable than did whites. However, race is not the only factor that determined attitudes toward the police. Rather, race and personal experience with the police interacted to produce different results in the several areas. Attitudes toward the police may be associated with dissatisfaction about the quality of life in particular neighborhoods. When residents were asked whether "people in this neighborhood are treated as well as people living in other sections of the city," 40 percent of the ghetto blacks, 15 percent of the white working-class respondents, and 7 percent of the white middle-class respondents answered no.[15] Thus law enforcement policies and police actions clearly have a significant effect on the attitudes of some citizens toward the fairness of the political community.

As Table 7.1 and Figure 7.1 show, there is wide variation among cities in public ratings of the way the police treat people. Blacks

TABLE 7.1 **Rankings of police treatment of neighborhood residents by respondents.** Note that these are citywide responses. One might speculate about differences that may exist among residents of different neighborhoods. Boston and Baltimore residents rated the police lower than residents of most other cities.

Response	Albuquerque (N = 471)	Atlanta (N = 469)	Baltimore (N = 500)	Boston (N = 507)	Denver (N = 357)	Kansas City, Kansas (N = 193)	Kansas City, Missouri (N = 383)	Milwaukee (N = 443)	Nashville (N = 426)	San Diego (N = 517)
Very good	47%	37%	30%	29%	44%	44%	50%	52%	40%	51%
Good enough	34	38	48	44	29	42	35	32	41	34
Not so good	6	7	16	12	8	7	3	5	6	4
Not good at all	2	5	5	6	4	2	3	4	2	3
Not ascertained	11	13	1	9	15	5	9	7	11	8
Total	100%	100%	100%	100%	100%	100%	100%	100%	100%	100%

SOURCE: Floyd F. Fowler, Jr., *Citizen Attitudes toward Local Government Services and Taxes* (Cambridge, MA: Ballinger, 1974), p. 167.

consistently rated the police lower than whites, but in Kansas City, Kansas, Kansas City, Missouri, Milwaukee, and Nashville, more than 81 percent of those interviewed said that the police's treatment of people in their neighborhoods was either "very good" or "good enough."

Studies have shown that permissive law enforcement, on the one hand, and brutality, on the other, are the two basic reasons why some residents of the urban community resent the police. The police are charged with failure to give adequate protection and services in minority group neighborhoods and with abusing residents physically or verbally. The police are seen as permissive when an officer treats an offense committed against a person of the same ethnic group as the offender more lightly than a similar incident in which offender and victim are members of different groups. The police often explain such differential treatment as a result of working in a hostile environment. The white patrol officer may fear that breaking up a street fight among members of a minority group will provoke the wrath of onlookers, whereas community residents may in fact view such negligence as a further indication that the police do not care about their

FIGURE 7.1
Percentage of respondents, by race, in seven cities who say police treatment of residents is "very good" or "good enough." Race appears to be a major factor in attitudes toward the police. But is it race or social class? To what extent do these attitudes reflect greater contact with the police in poor, minority neighborhoods?
SOURCE: Floyd F. Fowler, Jr., *Citizen Attitudes toward Local Government and Taxes* (Cambridge, MA: Ballinger, 1974), p. 178.

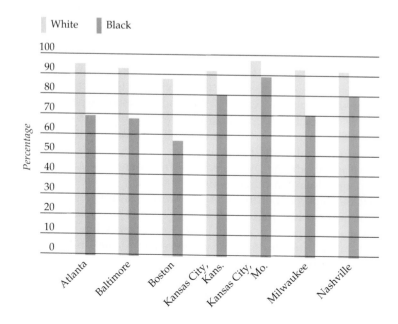

neighborhood. It is said that the police do not work effectively on such crimes as narcotics dealing, gambling, petty thievery, and in-group assault, although these are the crimes that are most prevalent in the urban neighborhoods and cause the greatest insecurity and apprehension among residents.

Interpersonal Relations

Policing is one of the few public services that is delivered via face-to-face encounters with citizens in each community and neighborhood. One might think that through the experience of their interactions, the police and citizens would develop more accurate pictures of the behavior each can expect of the other. In every situation, each must judge whether the other, in the specific social context, is hostile, friendly, or indifferent and act accordingly. Most police-community relations programs are based on this assumption, with the thought that cordial relations will develop if police officers are known to the neighborhood and have learned the special characteristics of the people among whom they work.

But learning those characteristics is not easy and is influenced by police officers' attitudes, some of which may prevent them from developing a network of acquaintances in the neighborhoods. Because of residential segregation, the minority urban community is more heterogeneous than the outsider understands; that is, African-Americans, Hispanics, or Asians of differing degrees of law-abidingness and different social class, family background, and aspirations live in close proximity. To the police, the heterogeneous, densely settled ghetto thus makes perceiving or acting on differences in social position difficult. For many officers, skin color conceals important differences in class and lawfulness among members of racial minorities. Thus because they live near or in high-crime areas, innocent citizens become not only victims of crime but also objects of police suspicion.

Practically all studies document the prejudices of the police toward the poor and members of racial minorities. These attitudes lead many police officers to see all African-Americans or Hispanics as slum dwellers and thus as potential criminals; as a result the police tend to exaggerate the extent of minority crime. If both the police and citizens view each other with intense hostility, personal encounters will be strained and the potential for explosions will be great. In such circumstances it is little wonder that the ghetto resident thinks of the police as an army of occupation and that the police think of themselves as combat soldiers.

An organizational factor also influences citizen-police encounters in lower-class neighborhoods. Just as most city school systems assign the inexperienced and incompetent to teach in the slums, in most police departments job assignment and opportunity for transfer are organized so that those with the least training and time on the job are sent to the precincts with the highest crime rates. Only officers with seniority and good effectiveness ratings win transfers to more desirable middle-income (white) neighborhoods in which crime rates are low and service calls less demanding.

POLICE ABUSE OF POWER

The rising voices of excluded groups and the urban riots of the 1960s brought incidents of police abuse of power to public attention. Although the poor have suffered these indignities for generations, only during the past quarter century has an awakened citizenry focused attention on the illegal use of violence by the police. In the racially heightened context of the contemporary city, police-resident conflicts often result when it is alleged that law enforcement has been carried out in a biased manner. Tom Wolfe's novel *The Bonfire of the Vanities* describes the racial-political context of criminality in New York City in which the actions of the police and prosecutors are seen in black–white terms. The real-life drama of Tawana Brawley, a young African-American girl whose story of being kidnapped and raped by white police officers brought a momentary storm of protest until it was proved false, illustrates the context of attitudes about the police in urban areas.

Television viewers throughout the nation were shocked in 1991 when they saw a videotape of a young African-American motorist being viciously clubbed, stomped, and kicked by three white Los Angeles police officers while eleven other officers stood by. The beating resulted in a broken skull and multiple other injuries to twenty-five-year-old Rodney King and indictments against four LAPD officers. The public storm resulting from this incident again focused attention on the issue of police brutality and its roots. Some observers point to racism, poor training, loose discipline, and the fraternal traditions of the police as the cause of such incidents. Others recognize these factors but also point to the environment within which the police must work and the resulting frustration and stress.

But stories of police incivility, physical abuse, and illegal actions are not new. In 1901 Frank Moss, a former police commissioner of New York, said:

> For three years, there has been through the courts and the streets a dreary procession of citizens with broken heads and bruised bodies against few of whom was violence needed to effect an arrest. Many of them had done nothing to deserve an arrest. In a majority of such cases, no complaint was made. If the victim complains, his charge is generally dismissed. The police are practicing above the law.[16]

Definition

Such dramatic incidents are usually popularly defined as *police brutality*, but citizens use the term to encompass a wider range of practices describing the abuse of power, including:

1. the use of profane and abusive language
2. commands to move on or get home
3. stopping and questioning people on the street or searching them and their cars
4. threats to use force if orders are not obeyed
5. prodding with a nightstick or approaching with a pistol
6. the actual use of physical force or violence

Should Handguns Be Regulated?

IN 1981, Americans were horrified to learn that President Ronald Reagan had been gunned down by a man with a handgun. Although the nation was relieved when the president recovered, there was lingering shock when it was learned that his assailant, a man with a history of mental problems, had easily purchased a handgun without any investigation into his background. The assassination attempt revived the debate about private gun ownership and helped to mobilize support for Handgun Control, Inc., an interest group that works for state and federal handgun regulations. The National Rifle Association, the highly organized and well-financed interest group that works against firearms regulations, has utilized very effective lobbying campaigns to block most efforts to regulate handguns.

Proponents of regulation point to the fact that offenders armed with handguns committed an average of 639,000 violent crimes each year between 1979 and 1987; these crimes resulted in a yearly average of 9,200 killed and 15,000 wounded. Proponents seek strong national laws that would make it more difficult to obtain handguns.

Waiting periods for purchases are advocated as a means of permitting law enforcement background checks so that criminals and mental patients can be prevented from purchasing weapons. Waiting periods may also permit angry and emo-

tional people to cool down. Not being able to purchase a gun on the spur of the moment would provide the time necessary for some to rethink any intentions to kill themselves or others.

Bans on the manufacture and importation of "Saturday Night Specials" would reduce the availability of the small, cheap, easily concealed handguns favored by many criminals. Many proponents of regulation also seek registration and licensing for gun ownership so that people who obtain weapons illegally might be readily prosecuted for owning and possessing a handgun.

As indicated in Figure B.1, opinion polls show that a significant majority of Americans favor handgun regulation. In fact, support reached an all-time high in 1991 when the Gallup Poll found that 95 percent of the public specifically expressed support for a national seven-day waiting period for handgun purchases.

The 1981 attempted assassination of President Reagan renewed the public debate over handgun control. White House Press Secretary James Brady and Police Officer Thomas Delahanty lay on the ground after being shot by John Hinkley.

For
Regulation

Supporters of regulation argue that the easy availability of handguns leads to unnecessary violence and thousands of avoidable deaths. Because criminals in the United States can readily obtain handguns, robberies and other crimes can easily lead to victims' deaths. Some homicides may even be unintended: people are killed when nervous or angry robbers with handguns make inadvertent or accidental movements with their trigger fingers.

In addition, the widespread availability of handguns increases the chances that any angry encounter may lead to death. People may use guns without thinking during arguments with spouses, neighbors, or even strangers on the highway or after an automobile accident.

The arguments in favor of regulation may be summarized as follows:

▶ Regulations will make it more difficult for people with criminal records and those with mental problems to obtain handguns. Instead of rushing out to obtain a gun while consumed with anger or depression, they would have time to rethink their intentions.
▶ Law-abiding citizens do not need handguns since very few use them to defend themselves. More commonly, guns lead to violence within families or cause tragic accidents when children find and play with weapons. Handguns are favored items

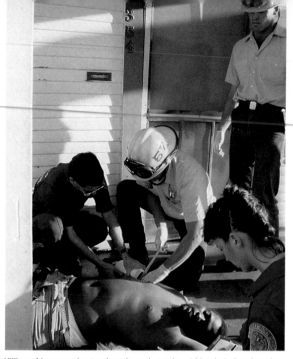

Killing of innocent bystanders through random "drive-by" shootings has increased during recent years. Advocates of gun control argue that the presence of a weapon increases the possibility that an argument will end in a shooting.

Drug turf battles have caused major increases in the homicide rate in urban areas, especially in mid-sized cities.

for theft in burglaries, and thus law-abiding citizens help provide a ready supply for criminals.
▶ Americans must pay millions of dollars each year for the costs of medical care for handgun victims. Additional financial and psychological costs are imposed on law enforcement officers, who must remain prepared to face handgun violence during all of their encounters with the public, including routine traffic stops.
▶ It is better to start reducing the harms of handguns rather than simply to surrender to a belief that nothing can be done about violence in the United States.
▶ As a legal issue, courts have consistently approved governmental regulation of firearms because the Second Amendment to the Constitution refers to the need for a militia (that is, the National Guard), not to a general right of all citizens to own guns.

Former President Reagans's endorsement of the Bill helped spur its passage. The National Rifle Association has led the opposition to all laws that might interfere with their interpretation of the right to bear arms.

Against Regulation

Opponents of handgun regulations argue that the Second Amendment forbids restrictive laws because Americans have a constitutional right to bear arms. They argue that laws will only affect law-abiding citizens because criminals will not purchase guns from licensed dealers. Criminals will steal guns or obtain them through illegal sales on the streets. Therefore, waiting periods, registration, and other regulations will not deter the people who intentionally cause harm with handguns.

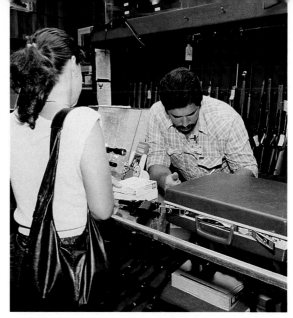

In most developed countries a gun can be obtained only after a background check and evidence that it is necessary for work or membership in a hunting or target shooting club.

Figure B.1

Public Support for Stricter Laws Covering the Sale of Firearms
Question: In general, do you feel that the laws covering the sale of firearms should be made more strict, less strict, or kept as they are now?

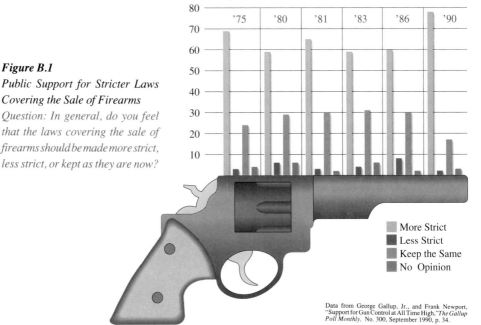

Percentage of Population

More Strict
Less Strict
Keep the Same
No Opinion

Data from George Gallup, Jr., and Frank Newport, "Support for Gun Control at All Time High," *The Gallup Poll Monthly*. No. 300, September 1990, p. 34.

The arguments against the regulation of handguns can be summarized as follows:

▶ Because there are millions of handguns already circulating in the United States, new regulations will only interfere with the ability of law-abiding citizens to obtain weapons to defend themselves. As crime rates continue to stay at high levels, Americans need to be able to obtain handguns to protect their homes and families.

▶ Criminals will easily avoid waiting periods and registration requirements by obtaining handguns from illegal sources.

▶ People who want to commit suicide or kill their spouse will find ways to accomplish their objectives whether or not they have access to handguns. The harms caused by these people do not justify placing any burdens on law-abiding gun owners.

▶ Registration of handguns is just the first step on the path toward government abolition of private firearms ownership and the seizure of all weapons. History demonstrates that people need their own weapons in order to prevent dictators from taking over their country.

▶ The government should address the crime problem by dealing harshly with people who cause harm with firearms, not by interfering with the ability of innocent people to own handguns.

Can experiences in other countries provide information to help resolve the debate? As part of its campaign, Handgun Control, Inc. circulated a poster that read: "In 1988, handguns killed 7 people in Great Britain, 19 in Sweden, 53 in Switzerland, 25 in Israel, 13 in Australia, 8 in Canada, and 8,915 in the United States. God Bless America."

Comparisons of the number of homicides per year in various American and foreign cities of equal population (Figure B.2) show that there are many fewer deaths where there are gun control laws. Canada, England, France, Germany, and Japan each have strong firearm laws that require:

- A waiting period
- An extensive background investigation by the police
- Issuance of a permit to acquire and possess the weapon
- Stiff penalties that are enforced for violation of firearms laws
- Provisions for shotguns and long guns that allow only for legitimate sporting and recreational purposes

IN 1988, HANDGUNS KILLED 7 PEOPLE IN GREAT BRITAIN 19 IN SWEDEN 53 IN SWITZERLAND 25 IN ISRAEL 13 IN AUSTRALIA 8 IN CANADA AND 8,915 IN THE UNITED STATES.

GOD BLESS AMERICA.

Help stop handgun violence.
Call 1-900-226-4455.
A letter will be sent to your name to your Member of Congress urging support of sensible gun laws. (The $2.75 cost of the call will appear on your phone bill.)
Handgun Control, Inc., 1225 Eye Street, N.W.
Washington, D.C. 20005

STOP HANDGUNS BEFORE THEY STOP YOU.

What Should U.S. Policies Be?

Given the length and vehemence of the debate, we should ask what it is about handguns that has made them such an integral part of American culture. Can waiting periods and registration requirements prevent handguns from falling into the possession of those who would misuse them? What policies might be developed to reduce levels of violence yet preserve civil liberties? Can we afford to allow unrestricted access to lethal weapons that are involved each year in an average of 9,200 murders, 12,100 rapes, 210,000 robberies, and 407,600 assaults?

Figure B.2
Do gun laws work?
International Comparisons of Homicide Rates of Cities of Similar Size

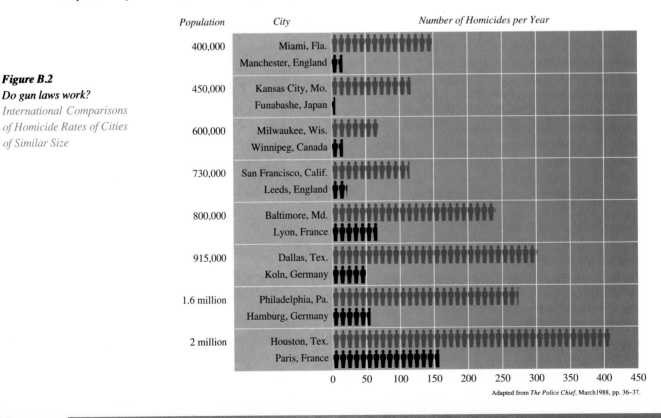

Adapted from *The Police Chief*, March 1988, pp. 36–37.

■

Television pictures shown throughout
the world recorded the savage beating
of Rodney King, a black parolee,
by Los Angeles police officers. The
officers were indicted and calls
were made for the firing of
Chief Darryl Gates.

Indeed, citizens object to any practice that debases them, restricts their freedom, annoys or harasses them, or entails the use of
unnecessary physical force. Behavior that serves only to degrade a
citizen's sense of self, including the use of belittling names, is most
upsetting. Charges of police brutality may result when citizens are
not accorded the rights and respect due them in a democratic society.

In the 1960s the issue of misconduct by law enforcement began to
be treated seriously. The 1968 report of the Kerner Commission,
which looked into the causes of the riots that shook Detroit, Los
Angeles, Newark, New York, and other cities, focused on the extent
to which police actions in dealing with citizens had triggered the
disorders.[17] The report pointed to aggressive patrol, police brutality,
and the unwarranted use of deadly force as sources of minority group
hostility.

Times have changed since the Kerner Commission submitted its
report. American cities are more racially heterogenous than they
were twenty years ago, and political leadership in many has shifted
so that members of minority groups now have positions of power.
The police have also changed, and there has been a major increase in
the number of minority officers in cities having significant African-
American and Hispanic populations. The effect of these changes on
police attitudes and behavior toward ghetto residents is yet to be
ascertained.

Dealing with officer misconduct has become a high-priority item
on the agenda of professional police administrators. It has been
shown that when the top leadership of a department disciplines officers who disregard the professional code, a standard is set and notice
given that such conduct will not be tolerated.

Because of the low visibility of police-citizen interactions and the
reluctance of victims to file charges against their assailants, we can
never know the amount of illegal force used. Although it is widely
believed that police brutality is a racial matter between white police
and black victims, Albert Reiss found that lower-class white men
were as likely to be brutalized by the police as lower-class black men
and that both were the likeliest victims.[18] In addition to the fact that
many police actions occur in situations of low visibility, such as in
the back seat of the squad car or the inner recesses of the station
house, there is the tendency for other citizens to avoid becoming
involved in cases of police brutality. Attempts to bring formal charges

against the police are often frustrated by lack of witnesses. The courts are reluctant to give credence to civilian complainants, since impeachment of a police officer may be viewed as an assault against the entire criminal justice system.

Throughout their socialization, officers are reminded that every police activity may be the basis for two legal actions: one in which they are the complainant and one in which they are the defendant. The potential for a civil suit charging false arrest, usually the citizen's only recourse, is impressed on the officer. Victims of brutality or false arrest who feel strongly enough about their case to register a formal complaint or to bring a civil suit encounter great difficulty in doing so. In one eastern city, the police department used to charge citizens who complained of police misconduct with filing false reports. In Philadelphia, the police review board found that it was standard practice to lodge a charge of resisting arrest or disorderly conduct against anyone who accused the police of brutality.

How Much Force?

Basic to the issue of police brutality is the question of the use of physical force. By law the police have the right to use force if necessary to make an arrest, to keep the peace, or to maintain public order. But just how much force is necessary and under what circumstances

---

CLOSE-UP *Response to Police Misconduct*

Two Minneapolis police officers were suspended for 30 days without pay for kicking and breaking the ribs of a man . . . , [yet] both officers, Sgt. William Chaplin and Patrolman James Thernell, were acquitted of the same criminal charge by separate Hennepin County District Court juries. Minneapolis Police Chief Tony Bouza said the jury verdicts were wrong.

"The reality is the evidence was overwhelming," Bouza said. "As I read the transcripts of the criminal trials, I came to the inescapable conclusion that they should have been found guilty."

. . .

Bouza said he was persuaded by the testimony of two other Minneapolis policemen who said Chaplin and Thernell kicked 19-year-old Steve Goodwin when he was lying face down on the ground. . . .

The chief said the primary reason the juries voted for acquittal was that Goodwin "was a terrible witness. He's a street guy. He was hostile to the police. He made silly statements on the stand," Bouza said.

In addition, he said the acquittals reflected the reluctance of juries to convict police officers.

Bouza said that the criminal process, the civil process and the internal disciplinary process "are distinct and separate. They might influence one another, but they are three separable events."

"This is an important symbolic case," because "it centers on one of the last holdouts of the old system, Bill Chaplin," Bouza said. "He is one of the leaders of this department. He has many admirable qualities and he has some qualities that make him a menace in the police world."

"He has been among the last to receive my message that brutality will not be condoned. He mistakes aggressive policing for doing anything you want on the streets." . . .

Chaplin, a 17-year veteran, previously was found guilty of "wanton and malicious" behavior in the beating of a suspect he arrested [and] was disciplined twice for incidents that occurred [earlier]. He was suspended for a few days following allegations of misuse of vice-squad funds. He was reprimanded after a fight in a northeast Minneapolis bar. Thernell, a 14-year veteran, had no disciplinary record.

Bouza said he expects the Minneapolis Police Federation to inform him that it will appeal the discipline. If the union appeals, the suspensions will be stayed until the appeals are resolved.

SOURCE: Adapted from "Bouza Suspends 2 Officers Whom Juries Acquitted," by D. J. McGrath, *Minneapolis Star and Tribune*, April 27, 1984, p. 38. Reprinted with permission from the *Minneapolis Star and Tribune*.

it may be used is an extraordinarily complicated and arguable question. In particular, the use of deadly force in the apprehension of suspects has become a deeply emotional issue that is directly connected to community relations. "There is no occurrence between the police and the community that causes more outrage [and] demoralization [or] precipitates [more] tension in a community [than] the police shooting of a civilian."[19] Estimates of the number of citizens killed annually by the police range between 300 and 600, with about 1,500 more wounded.[20] What is gratifying is that the number has declined dramatically from the high level set in the 1970s.[21] However, the drop in police killings of civilians should not obscure the fact that "the typical victim of deadly force employed in police-civilian contact has been a young black male."[22]

By no means do all cases of the use of force by police officers involve the use of *unnecessary* force. The Model Penal Code, section 307(2)(B), lists the conditions required before the use of deadly force is justified.

In a study of the deaths of 1,500 civilians killed by the police, it was discovered that the officer was punished for criminal misconduct in only three cases.[23] Statewide rates of persons killed by the police ranged from a low of 2.97 per 100,000 population in New Hampshire to a high of 37.97 in Georgia.[24] In a study of police shootings in New York City, it was found that in many of the incidents officers themselves were either injured or killed and that racial minority groups were more likely to be involved in weapons assaults than whites.[25] Lawrence Sherman reports that nationally most such incidents occur at night in central cities, that the victims are almost all males between the ages of seventeen and thirty, and that about half are black.[26] It is also clear that a high proportion of deadly force incidents occur in those large-city precincts in which forms of criminal violence are most prevalent.

What can be done about this situation? In March 1985 the Supreme Court for the first time ruled that police use of deadly force to apprehend an unarmed, nonviolent, fleeing felony suspect violated the Fourth Amendment guarantee against unreasonable seizure. The case, *Tennessee v. Garner,* arose from the killing of Edward Garner, a fifteen-year-old eighth-grader, by a member of the Memphis Police Department.[27]

Officer Elton Hymon and his fellow officer, Leslie Wright, were dispatched to answer a "prowler inside" call. Arriving at the scene,

Tennessee v. Garner (1985): Deadly force may not be used against an unarmed and fleeing suspect unless necessary to prevent the escape and the officer has probable cause to believe that the suspect poses a significant threat of death or serious injury to the officer or others.

MODEL PENAL CODE:
Use of Deadly Force

Section 307(2)(B)
The use of deadly force is not justifiable under this Section unless:

i. the arrest is for a felony
ii. the person effecting the arrest is authorized to act as a peace officer or is assisting a person whom he believes to be authorized to act as a peace officer
iii. the actor believes that the force employed creates

no substantial risk of injury to innocent persons
iv. the actor believes that:

1. the crime for which the arrest is made involved conduct including the use or threatened use of deadly force
2. there is a substantial risk that the person to be arrested will cause death or serious bodily harm if his apprehension is delayed.

they saw a woman standing on her porch and gesturing toward the adjacent house. She told them she had heard glass breaking and that someone was inside next door. While Wright radioed for help, Hymon went to the back of the house, heard a door slam, and saw someone run across the backyard toward a six-foot-high chain-link fence. With the aid of his flashlight, Hymon was able to see that Garner was unarmed. The officer called out, "Police! Halt!" but Garner began to climb the fence. Convinced that if Garner made it over the fence he would escape, Hymon fired at him, hitting him in the back of the head. Garner died on the operating table, the $10 he had stolen in his pocket. Hymon was acting under Tennessee law and Memphis Police Department policy.

Until the Supreme Court decision in *Tennessee* v. *Garner*, police in about half the states were guided by the common-law principle allowing the use of whatever force was necessary to arrest a fleeing felon. Justice Byron White ruled in his *Garner* opinion for the court that changes in the legal and technological context of police work had made the common-law rule no longer applicable. White wrote that the use of deadly force had to be interpreted according to the Fourth Amendment's requirement of reasonableness. The justices set as a new standard that the police may not use deadly force in apprehending fleeing felons "unless it is necessary to prevent the escape and the officer has probable cause to believe that the suspect poses a significant threat of death or serious physical injury to the officer or others."[28] It is this evidence of dangerousness that the officer must evaluate before taking action. Thus, for example, an officer would be justified in using deadly force if the suspect "threatens the officer with a weapon or there is probable cause to believe that he has committed a crime involving the infliction or threatened infliction of serious physical harm."[29]

In the *Garner* decision the Supreme Court in effect invalidated state laws and local police policies that had allowed officers to shoot unarmed or otherwise nondangerous suspects if they resisted arrest or attempted to flee. However, many observers believe that this landmark decision will have little impact on the day-to-day actions of the police. Many states already have laws restricting the use of deadly force to the standard set by the Supreme Court. Other states may enact legislation that will meet the new criteria but perhaps not the spirit of the new standard. For example, new standards may allow the use of deadly force against suspects fleeing "violent" or "forcible" felonies whether or not an individual actually used force or violence. However, the threat of civil litigation against officers who shoot in *Garner*like situations may limit police actions. Departmental policies and the leadership of police executives in upholding the new standards can also make the difference between a city with few civilian killings by the police and a city with many. Finally, it must be recognized that even with court rulings, departmental policies, and state laws, as long as police officers carry weapons, some incidents will occur. Training, internal review of incidents, and disciplining or discharging of trigger-happy officers may help reduce the use of unnecessary force, but the problem will undoubtedly erupt from time to time as an issue separating the community from the police.

CORRUPTION

Police corruption is an enduring problem. The nature of some laws, especially those concerning victimless crimes, places the police in positions in which favors may be extended, bribes accepted, and arrests made in the pursuit of individual goals rather than the goals of law enforcement. Police corruption is not new to America. Earlier in the century, numerous city officials actively organized liquor and gambling businesses to provide personal income and to enhance political operations. In many cities a link was maintained between politicians and police officials so that favored clients would be protected and competitors harassed. Much of the Progressive-era movement to reform the police was designed to block such associations. Although political ties have been cut in most cities, corruption is still present.

One of the difficulties in discussing police corruption is that of definition. Sometimes corruption is defined so broadly that it ranges from accepting a free cup of coffee to robbing unlocked business establishments. Herman Goldstein suggested that corruption includes only those forms of behavior designed to produce personal gain for the officer or for others.[30] This definition, however, excludes the misuse of authority that may occur in a case of police brutality when personal gain is not involved. The distinction is often not easy to make.

"Grass Eaters" and "Meat Eaters"

Corrupt police officers have been described as falling into two categories: "grass eaters" and "meat eaters." "Grass eaters" are persons who accept payoffs that the circumstances of police work bring their way. "Meat eaters" are persons who aggressively misuse their power for personal gain. "Meat eaters" are few, though their exploits make headlines; "grass eaters" are the heart of the problem. Because "grass eaters" are many, they make corruption respectable, and they en-

■

Investigations of the internal affairs unit can lead to an indictment. Here a thirty-one-year veteran undercover officer is arraigned on drug charges.

courage adherence to a code of secrecy that brands anyone who exposes corruption as a traitor.

In the past, poor salaries, politics, and recruitment practices have been cited as reasons that some police officers engage in corrupt practices. It has been said that a few "rotten apples" should not taint an entire police force, but corruption in some departments has been shown to be so rampant that the rotten-apple theory does not adequately explain the situation. An explanation based on organizational factors adds another dimension. Much police work involves the enforcement of laws in situations where there is no complainant or where there may be doubt whether a law has actually been broken. Moreover, most police work is carried out at the officer's own discretion, without direct supervision. If corruption takes place, the norms of a department and the code of the force may shield the bad cop from detection.

Enforcement of vice laws creates formidable problems for police agencies. In many cities the financial rewards to the vice operators are so high that they can easily afford the expense of protecting themselves against enforcement. More important, police operations against victimless crimes are proactive; no one complains, and no one requests enforcement of the law. In seeking out vice, police often depend on informants—persons who are willing to steer a member of the squad toward gamblers, prostitutes, or narcotics dealers in exchange for something of value, such as money, drugs, information, or tolerance. Once the exchange is made, the informant may gain the upper hand by threatening to expose the cop for offering a bribe.

A QUESTION OF ETHICS

Bianco's Restaurant is a popular, noisy place in a tough section of town. Open from 6:30 in the morning until midnight, it is usually crowded with regulars from the neighborhood who like the low prices and ample portions, teenagers congregating to plan their next adventure, and people coming in off of the street to grab a quick bite to eat.

Officer Buchanan has just finished his late night "lunch" before returning to duty on the graveyard shift. As he proceeds toward the cash register, Cheryl Bianco, the manager, takes the bill from his hand and says, "This one's on me, John. It's nice to have you with us."

Officer Buchanan protests, "Thanks, but I'd better pay for my own meal."

"Why do you say that? The other cops don't object to getting a free meal now and then."

"Well, they may feel that way, but I don't want anyone to get the idea that I'm giving you special treatment," Buchanan replies.

"Come off it. Who's going to think that? I don't expect special treatment; we just want you to know we appreciate your work."

What are the issues involved here? If Buchanan refuses to accept Ms. Bianco's generosity, what is he saying about his role as a police officer? If he accepts the offer, what is he saying? Might citizens overhearing the conversation draw other meanings? Is turning down a $4.50 meal that important?

Ellwyn Stoddard, who studied "blue-coat crime," contends that a measure of role ambivalence is inevitable among the police in a democratic society. Officers are responsible for protecting community members but are not given the powers necessary to carry out this

CLOSE-UP *Serpico*

As Serpico [the undercover name of a New York City detective] soon observed, the main function of the [7th Division] plainclothesmen was to protect the entire pad while servicing their racketeer clients. A principal safeguard was always to produce a minor arrest for the record whenever a complaint about illegal activity came down to the division for investigation. One day [his partner, Gil] Zumatto said, "Come on, I got to check out some action."

A ghetto mother had reported wide-open gambling in her neighborhood and was afraid her teenage son was being sucked into becoming a policy runner, the lowest level in the numbers racket. Policy is one of the most lucrative underpinnings of organized crime. A runner dashes around from apartment to apartment and helps take bets for a collector in a particular area; next in the intricately structured racket is the pickup man, who brings the "work"—the betting slips—from various collectors to a controller. He in turn passes it on to a "banker," the money man. The spiral continues upward with many banks interlocked into still larger ones. Playing the numbers may be basically a "poor man's game," but it is still big business, and hundreds of millions of dollars are milked annually out of ghetto areas by the underworld.

When Serpico and Zumatto arrived on the block cited in the woman's letter, it was not long before they spotted the local collector. He was a "mover," going from place to place—an alley, a tenement, a candy store—to take his action. Zumatto watched him with some amusement until he finally said, "Let's grab him." They stopped the man, frisked him, and found enough slips and money on him to make an iron-clad felony arrest. The collector was puzzled. "What's the matter?" he asked. "What's the problem? Ain't you from the division? You know, we're friends with the division. We're on."

The collector gave the name of the banker he worked for, and Zumatto said, "That's easy to check out. But we have a complaint from downtown, and we got to do something about it."

"Hey, that's cool, man. I understand, but I'm losing money just talking to you. I can't go in now. This is prime time, you know. What say I meet you at the precinct at four-thirty?"

Zumatto smiled.

"I'll bring some work," the collector said. "I'll even bring my own work, and you won't have to worry about nothing."

■ "Serpico," the undercover name of a detective, was the star witness before a New York City inquiry into police corruption. His story later became a book and a film, as seen here, with Al Pacino in the title role.

"OK. Four-thirty, remember."

"No use breaking his chops," Zumatto said to Serpico afterward. "The guy he works for is good people. He's never late."

The incident had taken place in the 42nd Precinct, and later in the day Zumatto brought Serpico to a bar called the Picadilly, across from the station house. Zumatto asked him if he wanted the collar. When Serpico said no, he didn't want this one, Zumatto looked around the bar, spied another plainclothesman, and offered it to him. He was delighted to take it, and they all adjourned to the sidewalk in front of the station house. Promptly at four-thirty, the collector, whose name Serpico learned was Brook Sims, walked up, smiling, clutching a handful of slips, although only enough for a misdemeanor arrest. The third plainclothesman marched Sims up to the desk and booked him. The case was dismissed the next day in court, but if anyone checked the record, the complaint had been investigated and an arrest had been made.

SOURCE: From *Serpico*, by Peter Maas, pp. 163–165. Copyright © 1973 by Peter Maas and Tampa Company, Inc. Reprinted by permission of The Viking Press.

mandate. As a result, conscientious police officers must often violate the law in order to perform their duties. Minor infractions by fellow officers are overlooked; but what may begin as a small departure from the rules can grow until it becomes routine: "If these reference group norms involving illegal activity become routinized with use they become an identifiable informal 'code.' "[31] Stoddard says that police officers become socialized to the code early in their careers. Those who deviate by "snitching" on their fellow officers may become objects of ridicule. If, however, corruption comes to official attention, if it exceeds the limits of the code, other members of the force will distance themselves from the accused, in this way protecting the code. Terms of this "blue coat code" are defined as follows:

- *Bribery:* The receipt of cash or a "gift" in exchange for past or future assistance in avoidance of prosecution, as by a claim that the officer is unable to make a positive identification of a criminal or by being in the wrong place at a time when a crime is to occur, or by any other action that may be excused as carelessness but not offered as proof of deliberate miscarriage of justice. Distinguished from *mooching* by the higher value of the gift and by the mutual understanding in regard to services to be performed upon the acceptance of the gift.
- *Chiseling:* Demanding price discounts, free admission to places of entertainment whether in connection with police duty or not, and the like.
- *Extortion:* A demand for placement of an advertisement in a police magazine or purchase of tickets to a police function; the practice of holding a "street court" in which minor traffic tickets can be avoided by the payment of cash "bail" to the arresting officer, with no receipt given.
- *Favoritism:* The practice of issuing license tabs, window stickers, or courtesy cards that exempt users from arrest or citation for traffic offenses (sometimes extended to wives, families, and friends of recipients).
- *Mooching:* Accepting free coffee, cigarettes, meals, liquor, groceries, or other items, justified as compensation either for being in an underpaid profession or for future acts of favoritism the donor may receive.
- *Perjury:* Lying to provide an alibi for fellow officers apprehended in unlawful activity approved by the "code."
- *Prejudice:* Treatment of minority groups in a manner less than impartial, neutral, and objective, especially members of such groups who are unlikely to have "influence" in City Hall that might cause the arresting officer trouble.
- *Premeditated theft:* Planned burglary, involving the use of tools, keys, or other devices to force entry, or any prearranged plan to acquire property unlawfully. Distinguished from *shakedown* only by the previous arrangements made in regard to the theft, not by the value of the items taken.
- *Shakedown:* The practice of appropriating expensive items for personal use during an investigation of a break-in, burglary, or unlocked door and attributing their loss to criminal activity. Distinguished from *shopping* by the value of the items taken and the

ease with which former ownership of items may be determined if the officer is caught in the act of procurement.

- *Shopping:* Picking up small items such as candy bars, gum, and cigarettes at a store where the door has been accidentally left unlocked at the close of business hours.[32]

One of the most highly publicized investigations into police corruption was launched by New York City's Knapp Commission. In its report, the commission said that it had found corruption to be widespread in the New York City Police Department. In the areas of gambling, narcotics, prostitution, and the construction industry, payments to police officers were a regular occurrence. Not only did patrol officers on the beat receive these "scores," they also shared them with superior officers. The amounts ranged from a few dollars in minor shakedowns to a narcotics payoff of $80,000. What most concerned the commission was the fact that although most police officers were not themselves corrupt, they tolerated the practices and took no steps to prevent what they knew or suspected was happening.

Over the past decade corruption scandals have rocked the Philadelphia and Miami police departments.[33] In Philadelphia the officer appointed to lead the department's corruption investigation was himself given an eighteen-year prison sentence on evidence that he not only short-circuited the investigation but was netting $50,000 a month from operators of illegal electronic poker machines. In addition, twenty-six Philadelphia officers were charged with extortion to protect illegal gambling and prostitution operations. In 1988 more than one hundred Miami officers were implicated in corrupt practices with regard to drug dealers. Ten pleaded guilty to murder conspiracy or drug-trafficking charges and now face reduced sentences of up to thirty years in prison. These ten were indicted by a federal grand jury for participation in a $13-million theft of cocaine from a boat anchored in the Miami River. Three drug smugglers drowned when they jumped into the water as the officers were approaching. The officers later sold the cocaine they had confiscated.

Impact of Corruption

Police corruption has multiple effects on law enforcement: criminals are left free to pursue their illegal activities, departmental morale and supervision drop, and the image of the police suffers. The credibility of a police agency is extremely important in light of the need for the citizenry's cooperation. When there is a generally prevalent belief that the police are not much different from the "crooks," effective crime control is impossible.

What is startling is that many people do not equate police corruption with other forms of criminal activity. That officers proceed forcefully against minor offenders yet look the other way if a payoff is forthcoming seems acceptable to some, absurd though it may be. Further, some citizens believe that police corruption is tolerable as long as the streets are safe. This attitude is unreasonable because police officers "on the take" are pursuing personal rather than community goals.

Controlling Corruption

As with other problems in a free society, the power of public opinion is crucial for the control of police corruption. The public, however, knows only about the major police scandals that are publicized in the newspapers and on television and radio. When corruption reaches this level of notoriety, government agencies other than the police—prosecutors, attorneys general, grand juries, special investigating bodies, and others—step in to solve the problem by means of indictments and organizational reforms.

To a great extent the American political and legal systems have charged the police with keeping their own house in order. It is through mechanisms internal to law enforcement organizations that the more pernicious daily acts of corruption must be exposed and corrected. Departments have policy statements that outline permissible conduct with regard to the temptations often visited upon officers. As discussed later in this chapter, every sizable department has an internal affairs unit that receives complaints about officer behavior, investigates, and makes recommendations that either clear the officer's name or result in disciplinary action.

It is well recognized in police leadership circles that the top administrators of a department must set the tone with regard to corruption. Successful police officials, such as Patrick Murphy, O. W. Wilson, Clarence Kelley, and Wyman Vernon, all took much-publicized stands that let the general public and law enforcement employees know that they would not tolerate even the slightest act of corruption and would take swift action when any such acts came to their attention.

IMPROVING COMMUNITY RELATIONS

Law enforcement requires the active cooperation of all citizens. The police depend on citizens to report crimes and to assist officers in the conduct of investigations but are too often hampered by the fear and distrust exhibited by the residents of high-crime areas. One might suppose that people who are constantly being victimized would be the most outspoken in their demands for efficient law enforcement; yet the police commonly face closed mouths and blank stares when they seek information about an event.

Improvement in community relations has become one of the foremost goals of criminal justice personnel, particularly in localities where members of minority groups live. Large sums have been expended to improve the image of the police and to educate the public about the need for cooperation in the war against crime. Recruitment of racial-minority and female officers and attempts to augment civic accountability are two means by which cities have moved toward this goal.

Minority Police Officers

Historically, the American criminal justice system has recruited few police officers among racial minorities. Though the major metropolitan areas have become increasingly populated by African-American and Hispanic citizens, law enforcement positions are still held predominantly by whites. In none of the twenty largest cities does the number of nonwhites in blue approximate the proportion of nonwhites in the community. In Washington and in Atlanta, both with populations about 70 percent black, only 41 percent and 56 percent, respectively, of the police forces are black.

The effort to recruit more minority police officers was initially spurred by the 1968 report of the National Advisory Commission on Civil Disorders, which identified police-minority relations as a major factor contributing to ghetto riots. The problem received renewed emphasis with passage by Congress of equal opportunity legislation and with court decisions promoting affirmative action. The Equal Employment Opportunity Act of 1972 prohibits state and local governments from discriminating in their hiring. To enforce this mandate and to monitor programs of affirmative action, the Equal Employment Opportunity Commission was created. Affirmative action programs are designed to reduce or eliminate patterns of underemployment of women and minorities even where there is no proof of discrimination. These efforts are based on the premise that they are needed to overcome practices that historically have limited employment of members of such groups. Typically, police departments have set goals to increase the number of female and minority officers so that the organization is more representative of the community.

At the prodding of state and federal equal opportunity commissions, most city police forces have undertaken extensive campaigns to recruit more minority officers. To a large extent, however, these efforts have failed, perhaps because departments have not been aggressive enough in their search, because young blacks have a negative view of law enforcement work, or because a poor educational background has left them unable to pass the entrance examination.

Walker conducted national surveys of the fifty largest cities in 1983 and 1988 to measure the number of minority officers in the police forces compared to the racial divisions of the population.[34] He found substantial progress over the five-year period. Twenty-eight percent of the departments reported an increase of 50 percent or more in the number of black officers, and 23 percent reported a similar increase in the number of Hispanic officers. Walker constructed an index to measure the percentage of minorities employed relative to the percentage of minorities in the local population. A department has achieved a theoretically ideal level of minority employment when the employed percentage equals the percentage of that minority group in the local population (an index of 1.00). Figure 7.2 displays the indexes for black and Hispanic representation in the twenty largest cities. As political power shifts toward minorities in some American cities, however, the composition of their police forces can be expected to reflect the change. But the election of a black or Hispanic mayor need not signal a change in the composition of the police force. Again, it is political power that is crucial, and in many cities the police are able to protect their turf from outsiders even when the outsiders are elected officials. Recruitment of minorities to the force requires a commitment by law enforcement officials.

The experience of black officers in some large police forces has encouraged them to become politicized and to form separate organi-

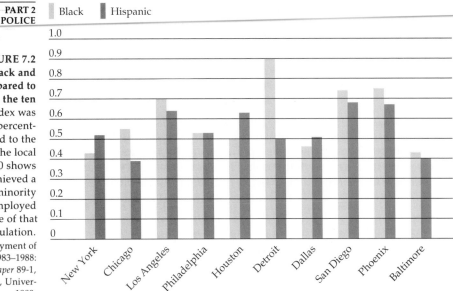

■ Black   ■ Hispanic

FIGURE 7.2

Index measuring number of black and Hispanic police officers compared to size of minority population in the ten largest U.S. cities. The index was constructed by comparing the percentage of minorities employed to the percentage of minorities in the local population. An index of 1.00 shows that a department has achieved a theoretically ideal level of minority employment in that the employed percentage equals the percentage of that minority group in the local population.

SOURCE: Samuel Walker, "Employment of Black and Hispanic Police Officers, 1983–1988: A Follow-Up Study," *Occasional paper* 89-1, Center for Applied Urban Research, University of Nebraska, Omaha, February 1989.

zations. The Afro-American Patrolman's League (AAPL) of Chicago, the Afro-American Police (AAP) of New York, and the Black Guardians of Bridgeport, Connecticut, have appealed to the courts to rule on such employment issues as seniority, minority recruitment, and discriminatory practices.

Efforts to add minority members to police forces have met with difficulty, and even when such officers are recruited, they must face the problem of becoming integrated into a department's social system. White officers have resented the hiring of minority officers to fulfill affirmative action quotas, and such reactions can have a detrimental effect on attempts to maintain a smoothly operating law enforcement organization. As public organizations continue to face limited resources in the 1990s, there may be continued reductions in the number of officers serving many financially strapped cities. Because of the important role played by seniority in layoff procedures, minority officers may be the first to go, and the gains of the past decade may thus be lost.

The importance of minority police officers cannot be overemphasized. It is not only a question of equal access to an economically desirable governmental position, it is also a question of effective policing. It is extremely difficult for members of an underrepresented group to view the police as being responsive to their needs, free of prejudice, and interested in the cause of justice if they do not see members of their group on the force. The importance of ethnic identification in American society makes it essential that the agents of justice reflect the characteristics of the community.

Civic Accountability

Relations between citizens and the police depend to a great extent on the level of confidence people have that officers will behave in accordance with the law and with departmental guidelines. Rapport is enhanced when citizens feel secure in the knowledge that the police will protect their persons and property and the civil liberties guaranteed by the Constitution. Permissive enforcement is as great a concern as police brutality in some metropolitan areas. The problem of making the police accountable to civilian control without thereby destroying their effectiveness has aroused increasing public concern.

Traditionally, Americans have relied on locally elected officials to ensure that the police carry out their tasks in accordance with the law and as the citizenry desires. Indeed, civil accountability is one reason why policing has been kept primarily a responsibility of municipal government. The appointment of the police chief by the mayor or legislature has been one way to ensure that the uniformed force is responsible to political authority. During the last half century, however, these formal ties between the police and the community have been weakened by the development of the law enforcement bureaucracy and the job security created by the civil service personnel system, which fills positions on the basis of scores obtained in competitive public examinations. More recently, the growth of urban areas has brought demands that local police units give way to centralized law enforcement agencies for the entire metropolitan region. These changes have diminished the ability of individual citizens, political leaders, and neighborhood groups to influence the way the police work.

Standards and Accreditation

One way that communities can gain greater accountability of the actions of their police is to require that operations be conducted by nationally recognized standards. The movement to accredit departments that adhere to these standards has gained momentum during the past decade. This work has been supported by the Commission on Accreditation for Law Enforcement Agencies (CALEA), a private nonprofit corporation jointly developed by four major professional associations: International Association of Chiefs of Police (IACP), National Organization of Black Law Enforcement Executives (NOBLE), National Sheriffs Association (NSA), and the Police Executive Research Forum (PERF).

The *Standards,* first published in 1983, have been periodically updated. There are now 900 standards organized according to forty-eight topics. These standards present a declarative statement that place clear-cut requirements on the agency; each is supplemented by an explanatory paragraph. For example, Standard 1.2.2. under "Limits of Authority" requires that "a written directive governs the use of discretion by sworn officers." The commentary section states:

> In many agencies, the exercise of discretion is defined by a combination of written enforcement policies, training and supervision. The written directive should define the limits of individual discretion and provide guidelines for exercising discretion within those limits.[35]

Since police departments have been almost completely silent on their use of discretion, this requirement represents an enormous shift. But the standard is not specific enough to define its coverage. Does it cover stop and frisk, handling of drunks, or the use of informants?

Police accreditation is voluntary. Organizations seeking accreditation contact CALEA, and personnel from that organization work with the department to meet the standards. This involves a self-evaluation by departmental executives, the development of management policies that meet the standards, and the training of officers with respect to those policies. CALEA personnel act in a manner comparable to the inspector general within the military, visiting the department, examining the policies, and determining if the standards are met in daily operations. Certification is given to those departments that meet the criteria. The fact that a department is accredited by a national organization can have an important local political impact. Perhaps more important, the standards can be used as a critical management tool. Officers are trained to undertand the standards and can be held accountable for their actions.

Internal Affairs

Policing the police is really an internal matter that must be given top priority by administrators. The community must feel confident that the department has developed procedures to ensure that personnel will act in ways that preserve the rights of citizens and that those procedures are effective. Unfortunately, many departments have no formal complaint machinery, and when such machinery does exist, it often seems designed to discourage civilian input. Rumor has it, for example, that a few years ago a sign over a pile of one-inch-square scraps of paper in the Internal Affairs Bureau of the San Francisco Police Department said: "Write your complaints here."[36] Internal investigators on the force may assume that a citizen's grievance is an attack on the police as a whole and reflexively move to shield individual officers. In such a situation, administrators may be deprived of valuable information and so may be unable to correct the problem. The public, in turn, may be led to believe that the questioned practices are condoned or even expected.

internal affairs unit: A segment of a police department designated to receive and investigate complaints against officers alleging violation of rules and policies.

Depending on the size of the department, a single officer or an entire section may be designated an **internal affairs unit** to investigate wrongdoing. An officer who is charged with misconduct may face criminal prosecution or departmental disciplinary action that may lead to resignation, dismissal, or suspension for a period of time. Officers assigned to the unit carry responsibilities similar to those of the inspector general's staff in the military.

The unit has the unenviable task of investigating complaints against fellow officers. The work of such units is described in the film *Internal Affairs* in which a team of investigators aggressively pursue and eventually catch a patrol officer who is involved in drug dealing and murder. As is typical for Hollywood, the film depicts the most dramatic aspects of internal affairs rather than the more common investigations of sexual harassment, alcohol or drug problems, misuse of physical force, and violations of departmental operational policies.

Officers are normally assigned to internal affairs for a specific time period, say eight years. Internal affairs investigators find the work stressful, since their status prevents them from maintaining close personal relationships with their fellow officers. A wall of silence arises between them and their fellow officers; they are shunned and are unable to partake of the social aspects of police work. This is particularly true in smaller departments in which everyone knows each other and the fraternal bonds are greatest.

The internal affairs unit must be provided with sufficient investigative resources to carry out its mission and must have direct access to the chief. Even when the top administrator supports the rooting out of misconduct, however, it is often difficult to persuade officers to testify against fellow officers. But maintenance of a "clean" force is essential if the crime prevention and law enforcement goals are to be met. When the police department demonstrates to the community that it is professionally responsible for the actions of its members, demands for review by an external body fade away.

Civil Liability

Civil suits against officers and departments for their misconduct has become another factor that has the potential for increasing civic accountability. Lawsuits arising from charges of brutality, false arrest, and negligence are increasingly being brought in both state and federal courts.

Damages to plaintiffs in the millions of dollars have been awarded by courts in a number of states, and individual police departments have settled civil suits out of court. For example, a Michigan court awarded the heirs of a man mistakenly shot by a Detroit officer $5.7 million, and the City of Boston settled with the parents of a teenager shot to death for $500,000.

The courts have ruled that generally accepted professional practices and standards must be followed in police work. It is believed that the potential for civil suits has led to policy changes within departments. For example, the successful $2 million judgment won by Tracy Thurman against the Torrington, Connecticut, police (see Close-Up: Battered Women, Reluctant Police) undoubtedly had a profound impact on departments who suddenly became aware of their liability. Plaintiff's victories in civil suits have helped spur accreditation, as police executives believe that liability can be avoided or minimized if it can be demonstrated that officers are complying with the highest professional standards. Following the lead of the courts and accreditation bodies insurance companies providing civil liability protection now offer discounts to departments that achieve accreditation.

WOMEN ON THE FORCE

Traditionally defined as "man's work," policing is increasingly attracting women into its ranks. Although Lola Baldwin, the first policewoman in the United States, was made an officer in Portland, Oregon, in 1905, the number of women officers remained small—about 1.5 percent of all officers—until 1970. At that time, as a result of passage of equal opportunity legislation and the rise of the women's movement, police departments began actively to recruit female officers. Even now, however, only 8.3 percent of sworn officers (about

■

Although the first policewoman was appointed in 1905, the number of women officers was low until the 1970s. Today women can be found in all aspects of police work, but their numbers in managerial positions are still limited.

30,000) are women, as Figure 7.3 indicates, although in some cities their proportion exceeds 10 percent. Moreover, about half of the police agencies in the United States employ no women. In the cities with large black populations (such as Atlanta, Detroit, and Washington), sexual and racial integration of the police department has gone the furthest. In contrast, "In strongly [white] ethnic-group dominated cities (Buffalo, Boston, Philadelphia, and Minneapolis) the forces of traditionalism and resistance to change . . . have retarded the hiring of policewomen."[37] Also discouraging is the fact that few women make it to supervisory positions. Further, since the rate of promotion is slow it could be "well into the twenty-first century before a significant number of women move into supervisory positions."[38]

At the federal level the FBI, DEA, and Secret Service have increased the number of women officers during the last ten years. In 1978 there were only 94 women agents in the FBI. By 1987 this figure had risen to 769. In the DEA and Secret Service, women made up 7 and 4 percent, respectively, of the special agents in those agencies. As with municipal police, an increasing number of women employed in law enforcement are from minority groups.[39]

As with racial or ethnic minorities, many departments have found it hard to recruit and retain women. What little research there is on the reasons women join the police force indicates that there is little

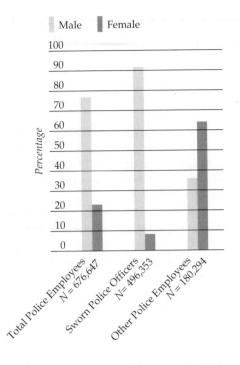

FIGURE 7.3
Percentage of male and female full-time police employees. Although their numbers have grown over the past two decades, women are still a small portion of the nation's police forces.
SOURCE: U.S. Department of Justice, *Crime in the United States* (Washington, DC: Government Printing Office, 1990), p. 157.

difference between the sexes on this question: women join because of the stability of employment, the salary, and the opportunity to serve others.[40]

Despite increases in their numbers on police forces, women still have difficulty breaking into this traditionally male stronghold. Cultural expectations of women often conflict with ideas about behavior appropriate for officers. As newcomers to the force, women have often found their upward mobility blocked and have had to contend with prejudice against their pioneering activities. Especially with regard to the assignment of women to patrol duty, such questions as the following are frequently raised:

- Can women handle situations involving force and violence?
- What changes in training and equipment must be made?
- Do women resent the loss of the "specialist" role they previously played in police work?
- Should women and men be treated equally in regard to promotion?
- Does putting men and women together on patrol as partners tend to break up families?

Women officers are required to learn a new set of behaviors, and their fellow officers and citizens must become accustomed to women's presence in their new role. In addition to mastering the technical details of arrest, weaponry, and self-defense, policewomen must learn to take control of situations assertively, to wield power, and to act authoritatively, skills seldom acquired in the socialization process most of them have undergone.

Policemen have low expectations of the law enforcement abilities of women officers but insist that they be treated just like men. Questions are raised about the physical strength of women, their willingness to take risks, and their ability to control a situation. Some are criticized for being timid in trying circumstances; if they are not timid, they are labeled bossy and unfeminine. Policemen also complain that women undermine the "emphasis on crime fighting and the masculine image that accompanies it."[41] Because of these attitudes, some departments continue to segregate female officers in specialized juvenile or women's details, whereas others keep them in the station house in clerical roles.

Most policewomen have easily met the performance expectations of their superiors. It is at the social level that they have had to overcome the greatest resistance to change. In particular, they have encountered unpredictable resistance to their exercise of authority, and they are often subjected to sexist remarks and more overt forms of sexual harassment designed to undermine their authority. Interaction with their male counterparts has brought further problems. Police work takes place in the social context of an occupational fraternity. Great emphasis is placed on the bonds that tie fellow officers together so that they will come to one another's aid, shield the force from the prying eyes of outsiders, and uphold the traditions of police work. A woman's entrance into this male domain is upsetting to many policemen. They complain that if their patrol partner is a woman, they

---

A QUESTION OF ETHICS

As the first female police officer on the fifteen-person force of Eagle, Washington, Diane Martin expected to get some kidding and pointed comments about her ability to handle the job. As a C.J. major she had read about the experiences of the women who had begun to join departments in greater numbers during the 1970s.

During her first days on the job, Diane merely smiled when she heard comments about her good looks and speculations about her reaction to the first incident involving a dead body. It was not until her second week and assignment to the graveyard shift that she became alert to the potential for troubles that might end her career.

It was a slow night. Diane and her patrol partner Steve Parent had been riding around for about four hours. The radio had been silent for the last half hour. The city of Eagle was asleep.

"Let's pull over a minute. I'd like to have a cigarette," said Steve. He pulled the squad car to the curb on the fringe of a wooded area. Diane felt sleepy, yawned, and slid back in her seat to be more comfortable. "Gee, I'm tired. Must be the lack of action tonight." Her eyes grew heavy.

With a start Diane sat bolt upright. Steve's hand was on her breast.

"Get your hand away. What do you think you're doing?" she demanded.

"Come on, I just want to be friendly," he whispered.

"Back off! What would your wife think? I'm going to report this."

"You do, sister, and your life in this department will be ended," Steve said as he started the engine.

What is your reaction to this incident? What do you think Diane should do? What will she have to consider in making her decision? With whom might she discuss her options? What could she do to help ensure that the incident does not recur, either with Steve or with another member of the force?

■

Police women have met the
performance expectations of their
superiors and today are involved in
the full range of law enforcement
activities. It is at the social level and in
their contacts with fellow officers
that they have had to overcome
resistance to change.

cannot be sure of her ability to lend assistance in times of danger—
that she simply lacks the physical stature to act effectively when the
going gets rough.[42]

Although women have encountered barriers to their acceptance
as equals of men in law enforcement work, studies conducted by the
Police Foundation and by other researchers point to a more positive
reception. A research study in Washington, D.C., found that when

CLOSE-UP *Patrol Officer Cristina Murphy*

Jim Dyer was drunk out of his mind when he called the
Rochester Police Department on a recent Saturday
night. He wanted to make a harassment complaint; a
neighbor, he claimed, was trying to kill him with a
chair. Off. Cristina Murphy, 27, a petite, dark-haired,
soft-spoken three-year veteran of the Rochester P.D.,
took the call.

"What's the problem here?" she asked when she
arrived at the scene. A crowd had gathered. Dyer's rage
was good local fun.

"You're a *woman*!" Dyer complained as Murphy
stepped from her squad car. "All they send me is
women. I called earlier and they sent me a Puerto Rican
and *she* didn't do nothing either."

"Mr. Dyer, what exactly is the problem?"

"Dickie Burroughs is the problem. He tried to kill
me." Through a drunken haze, Dyer made certain
things clear: He wanted Dickie Burroughs locked up.
He wanted him sent to Attica for life. He wanted it
done that night. Short of all that, Dyer hoped that the
police might oblige him by roughing up his foe, just a
little.

"We don't do that sort of thing," Murphy explained
in the voice she uses with drunks and children. "Mr.
Dyer, I can do one of two things for you. I can go find

Mr. Burroughs and get his side of the story; I can talk
to him. The other thing I can do is take a report from
you and advise you how to take out a warrant. You'll
have to go downtown for that."

Later, in her squad car, Murphy would say that she
isn't usually so curt to complaining citizens. "But it's
important not to take crap about being a female. Most
of the stuff I get, I just let slip by. This guy, though, he
really did not want service on his complaint, he wanted
retribution. When he saw a woman taking his call, he
figured that I wouldn't give it to him; it never struck
him that no male officer would either. You know, *everyone* has an opinion about women being police officers—
even drunks. Some people are very threatened by it.
They just can't stand getting orders from a woman.
White males, I think, are the most threatened. Black
males seem the least—they look at me and they just see
blue. Now women, they sometimes just can't stand the
idea that a woman exists who can have power over
them. They feel powerless and expect all women to feel
that way too. As I said, everyone has an opinion."

SOURCE: From "People Are Always Asking Me What I'm Trying to
Prove," by C. Dreifus, *Police Magazine* (March 1980), p. 19. Reprinted
by permission of the Edna McConnell Clark Foundation.

comparing a group of female recruits with a group of male recruits, gender "is not a bona fide occupational qualification for doing police patrol work."[43] This study, corroborated by studies in other cities, found that most citizens had generally positive things to say about the work of policewomen.

The future role of women in police work will evolve in concert with changes in the nature of policing, the cultural values of society, and the organization of law enforcement. As citizens become used to women on patrol and in other nontraditional roles, it will probably become less difficult for them to assert their authority and to gain the compliance required in law enforcement work. Finally, there are signs that more and more citizens and policemen alike are beginning to take it for granted that women will be found on patrol as sworn officers of the law.

UNIONISM

During much of this century, police employee organizations were mainly fraternal associations designed to provide opportunities for fellowship, to serve the welfare needs (death benefits, insurance) of police families, and to promote charitable activities. In some cities, however, the police were organized for the purpose of collective bargaining, and by 1919 thirty-seven locals had been chartered by the American Federation of Labor (AFL). The famous Boston police strike of 1919 was in fact triggered by the refusal of the city to recognize one of these AFL affiliates. Not until the 1950s did the police, along with other public employees, begin to join labor unions in large numbers.[44] Today nearly three-fourths of all U.S. police officers are members of unions. Yet about a third of the states do not have collective bargaining laws for public employees. This means that in those jurisdictions a police "union" is not recognized by the law, even though such an organization may have informal powers to meet with management and discuss the concerns of its membership.[45]

The dramatic rise in membership in police unions has been attributed to several factors: job dissatisfaction, especially with regard to pay and working conditions; the perception that other public employees were improving their positions through collective bargaining; the belief that the public is hostile to police needs; and an influx of young officers who hold less traditional views on relations between officer and police commissioner. Another factor is strong recruitment efforts by organized labor, which sought to make up for a decline in membership as employment opportunities shifted from the industrial to the service sectors of the economy by enrolling public employees.

The growth of police unionism has alarmed many law enforcement administrators and public officials.[46] Police chiefs fear they will be unable to manage their departments effectively because they believe that various aspects of personnel administration (transfers, promotions) will become bound up in arbitration and grievance procedures. Thus many administrators view the union as interfering with their law enforcement leadership and with the officers in the

The Boston Police Strike of 1919 paralyzed the city. The Massachusetts State Guard was activated to maintain order.

ranks. Public officials have recognized the effectiveness of unions in gaining financial advantages for their members and are thus wary of the demands that will be placed on government resources, putting them in a position no politician likes: needing to raise taxes. Some commentators have also expressed the view that the police, as the public embodiment of law enforcement, should not engage in such job actions as strikes, slowdowns, and sickouts (the "blue flu"). They wonder about the impact on the practical and symbolic aspects of criminal justice should picket lines be thrown around public buildings and the police refuse to work.

Police Unions Today

Most officers are members of a labor union, but unlike the steelworkers and other trade unionists, they have no national organization representing all police. There are, in fact, different types of organizations at the local, state, and national levels. Police unions are locally based, in the main, because the key decisions in regard to law enforcement are made at this level. There is also the feeling among some officers that the organized police of a city can achieve their ends without the need to affiliate with and pay dues to a national labor union. The local character of the employment relationship helps to explain why the relatively centralized national police organizations have failed to enroll large numbers of police officers as members.

The state is the next higher level of police unionism. Again, this structure is related to the need to bring pressure on the state government for pensions, disability benefits, and the rights of public employees. Thus state federations of the local police organizations function essentially as lobbyists in the state capital.

On the national level, the International Conference of Police Associations (ICPA) is the largest organization, with more than 100 local and state units representing more than 200,000 officers. In 1978 this organization asked its members to approve application for entrance into the AFL-CIO, but this move was rejected by the rank and file. Subsequently, a large part of the membership broke away and formed the International Union of Police Associations (IUPA), to which the AFL-CIO then granted a charter. The Fraternal Order of Police (FOP) and the International Brotherhood of Police Officers (IBPO) are other major organizations representing law enforcement interests. Police officers are also members of such national unions as the American Federation of State, County, and Municipal Employees (AFSCME), a group with members among occupational groups in all sectors of public service, and the Teamsters.

Impact of Police Unions

Clearly the police are little different from union members in other sectors of society: they are concerned primarily about wages, hours, and working conditions. Broader issues of changes in operating procedures have been touched on only when they affect these three elements. Abuses of collective bargaining procedures have occurred, according to Hervey Juris and Peter Feuille, when union leaders have appealed directly to the public or city council after failure to get police administrators to discuss contract terms in accordance with normal procedures.[47]

Of concern to some police administrators is the inclusion in union contracts of terms specifying policies and procedures that they believe interfere with their ability to run their departments. Restrictions on management's discretion in determining patrol officers' work shifts, criteria for promotion, and procedures for disciplining employees sometimes upset administrators. Officers in some localities have succeeded in having a "police officer's bill of rights" written into their contracts, specifying the procedures that will be followed when an officer must submit to an investigation that could eventuate in disciplinary action, demotion, or expulsion. Included are terms specifying the right to counsel, the right to confront accusers, the keeping of verbatim transcripts of questioning, and the conditions under which interrogation may take place.

Police unions have often been antagonistic to changes in law enforcement organization and techniques when they affect the membership. For example, attempts to shift from two-person to one-person patrol cars were opposed by unions in at least two of the twenty-two cities studied by Juris and Feuille. In addition, police unions opposed efforts to employ civilians in clerical positions, on the ground that civilians constituted a potential security risk and that all police jobs required personnel who had street experience and authority to arrest. Although the stated reasons may seem plausible, they are consistent "with the traditional trade union protectionist goal of safeguarding bargaining-unit work for incumbents."[48] In response to calls for increased recruitment of women and minorities, police unions have again tried to maintain the status quo. Affirmative action efforts, especially with regard to promotion, have been resisted by the unions because such practices threaten the prerogatives attached to seniority.

Job Actions

Slowdowns, "sickouts," and other disruptive tactics are the more common means that police unions use to exert pressure on employers. The strike has been used sparingly. It is illegal for most public employees to strike, and it was more than fifty years after the famous Boston Police Strike of 1919 before there was another such job action in a major American city. During the past decade, however, New Orleans; San Francisco; Tucson; Oklahoma City; Las Cruces, New Mexico; and Youngstown, Ohio, have all experienced strikes by law enforcement officers.[49] In some of these actions, the police returned to work within days; in others, they stayed out for as long as a month. In some cities, strikers lost their jobs; in others, they won pay raises. Aside from the legal prohibitions against such actions, individual members have ambivalent feelings about deserting their responsibilities for a strike that would leave a city to be preyed upon by criminals.

In analyzing the causes of police strikes, researchers for the International Association of Chiefs of Police concluded that a combination of factors was operating in each situation.[50] Among these factors the municipal financial crisis stands out. Beginning in the mid-1970s, American cities were faced with reduced federal allocations, local taxpayer revolts, and inflation. Since personnel costs make up as much as 85 percent of a city's operating budget, public employees usually bear the brunt of budget reductions. Many police departments had been expanded earlier in the decade because of the public clamor for increased protection. In many parts of the country an upturn in the economy during the 1980s was reflected in higher police salaries, yet in the "Rust Belt" and in the oil-producing states, allocations for public services did not keep pace. In the recession of the early 1990s similar fiscal state and local crises will undoubtedly keep salaries down.

Future of Police Unions

The increase in the use of collective bargaining by public employees during the past decade has been phenomenal. Although most police officers have preferred to join local organizations rather than to become members of an affiliate of the AFL-CIO or some other national union, the strength of police unions has increased greatly in many cities. Clearly, police officials are going to have to recognize this new influence on law enforcement administration. At the same time, in a public sector in which resources have diminished, state and local governments may not have the funds to increase salaries to keep pace with inflation. And there are still crucial questions about the role that unions should play in determining police department policies and the methods they can legitimately use to influence bargaining agreements.

PRIVATE POLICING

In the past ten years or so, uniformed security agents have been increasingly in evidence in stores, shopping malls, industrial plants, and airports. Private policing existed in Europe and the United States before the public organization of law enforcement, as witness Fielding's Bow Street Runners in England and the bounty hunters of the American West. Then, during the industrialization of the United States at the end of the nineteenth century, the Pinkerton National Detective Agency provided industrial spies and strikebreakers to thwart labor union activities, and Wells, Fargo & Company was formed to provide security for banks and other businesses. It is only in recent years that businesses have felt the need to employ private security forces to deal with shoplifting, employee pilfering, robbery, and airplane hijacking. Retail and industrial establishments spend nearly as much for private protection as all localities spend for police protection. Many private groups, too—especially residents of upper-income suburbs—have engaged private police to patrol their neighborhoods.

The rise of private agencies demonstrates one aspect of the reformulation of the concept of policing. Policing is no longer simply the catching of criminals; it must "nowadays be understood more broadly as quintessentially about *order*."[51] The growth of private policing is not merely the shifting of responsibility for policing public order "but the emergence of privately defined orders, policed by privately employed agents, that are in some cases inconsistent with, or even in conflict with, the public order proclaimed by the state."[52] Hence, we must recognize that such services are provided not only to stop lawbreakers and uphold order, as would the public police force, but also to regulate behaviors according to private policies that would not call for police action if done in a public space. For example, if you were to walk barefoot in Disney World, a behavior not permitted by the property's owner, you probably would be escorted off the premises.[53]

Private policing services are classified as either contract or proprietary. Contract security services are provided by agencies and private practitioners for a fee. Such practitioners include locksmiths, alarm specialists, and polygraph examiners; such organizations as Brink's, Burns, and Wackenhut provide guards and detectives. States and municipalities often require contract personnel to be licensed and bonded. Similar services are provided by proprietary security personnel, who are employed directly by the organization they pro-

personnel, who are employed directly by the organization they protect. Regulation by the state or municipality is not the norm for proprietary security operations, except for those individuals required to carry weapons.

Private policing has become a very large enterprise; the United States has an estimated four thousand such agencies that in the aggregate have upward of a million employees and payrolls of over $21 billion. The private policing field is thus larger in both personnel and resources than the federal, state, and local public police forces combined. As Figure 7.4 indicates, private policing is a growth industry.

Functions

The activities of private security personnel vary greatly: some employees merely act as watchmen and call the police at the first sign of trouble; others are deputized by public authority to carry out patrol and investigative duties as police officers do; and still others rely on their presence and willingness to make a "citizen's arrest" to deter lawbreakers. In most instances, private persons are authorized by law to make an arrest only when a felony has been committed in their presence. Thus private security agents or their companies face the possibility of being held civilly or even criminally liable for false arrest and the violation of an individual's civil rights. Some states have passed antishoplifting laws to give civil immunity to store personnel who reasonably but mistakenly detain people suspected of larceny. More ambiguous is the issue of a private guard's search of the person or property of a suspect. The suspect may resist and file a civil suit against the guard; if the search yields evidence of a crime, the evidence may not be admitted in court. Yet the Supreme Court

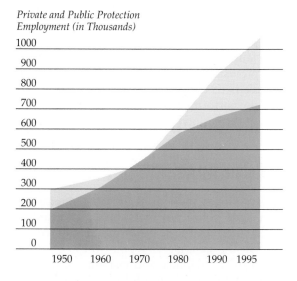

*Private and Public Protection
Employment (in Thousands)*

Private Police, Detectives, Guards, and Other Security Workers (Excluding Sales, Clerical, Manufacturing, and Other Nonoperational Personnel)

Public Law Enforcement (Federal, State, Local)

FIGURE 7.4
Employment in private and public protection, 1950-1995 (projected).
The number of people employed in the private security industry continues to grow, having surpassed the number employed by the public police. Such a large private force presents questions for the criminal justice system.
SOURCE: Adapted from U.S.Department of Justice, National Institute of Justice, *Research in Brief*, "The Growing Role of Private Security," by W. C. Cunningham and T. H. Taylor (Washington, D.C.: Government Printing Office, 1984), p. 3.

Private security firms are playing an increasingly important role in the United States. However, questions have been raised about the training, tactics, and jurisdiction of these "rent-a-cops."

has not applied the *Miranda* ruling to private police. Federal law prohibits private individuals from engaging in wiretapping, and information gathered by this means cannot be entered as evidence at trial.

A study sponsored by the National Institute of Justice indicated the willingness of proprietary and contract security managers to accept increased responsibility for minor criminal incidents that occur within their jurisdictions.[54] It was suggested that such tasks as responding to burglar alarms, investigating misdemeanors, and initiating preliminary investigations of other crimes could be undertakings that they would accept. Their counterpart law enforcement administrators indicated willingness to discuss the transfer of some of these responsibilities to private security firms. They cited a number of police tasks "potentially more cost-effectively performed by private security," such as provision of security in public buildings and courthouses and enforcement of parking regulations. Some of these tasks are already being performed by personnel provided by private firms in some parts of the country.

Private Employment of Public Police

An estimated 150,000 police officers moonlight for private security firms.[55] This means that in some police precincts the actual number of uniformed off-duty officers performing security functions exceeds those officially on duty. From the positive viewpoint these off-duty but uniformed officers swell the availability and visibility of the police. It must be remembered that even when off-duty, uniformed officers retain their full powers and status as police personnel. However, the increased use of off-duty cops patrolling department stores, directing traffic at construction sites, and walking through private housing enclaves presents a number of issues, such as potential conflicts of interest, management prerogatives, compensation, and physical stamina.

Conflict of Interest

Generally, officers are prohibited from accepting private jobs that involve conflicts of interest with their public responsibilities. For example, they may not work as process servers, bill collectors, repossessors, or preemployment investigators for industry. Bans are also placed on their work as investigators for criminal defense attorneys or as bail bondsmen. Officers are also generally prohibited from working in places that profit from gambling operations, and many departments restrict employment in bars or other places in which regulated goods or services are sold.

Management Prerogatives

What are the prerogatives of police managers with regard to officers who wish to supplement their salaries through off-duty work? Police executives have a responsibility to ensure that the public's interest is protected through the presence of a ready force. This means that the number of officers on a shift must be maintained, that officers must not appear for duty fatigued or physically weakened because of their off-duty employment, and that selection for employment by private firms must not result in conflict within the department.

Departments require that officers request permission for outside work. Permission may be denied for a number of reasons, including (1) work that lowers the dignity of the police, (2) work that is physically dangerous and where unacceptable risks may result, (3) work that is not in the "home" jurisdiction if approval is not granted by the "outside" police jurisdiction, (4) work that requires more than eight hours of off-duty service, and (5) work that interferes with scheduled routines of the police departments.

Several management models designed to coordinate off-duty employment are in use. The *department contract model* permits closer management control of off-duty work, since employers must apply to the department to have officers assigned to them. Officers selected for off-duty work are compensated by the department, which is then reimbursed by the private employer. An overhead amount for the costs of this service is charged to the employer. Departments usually screen employers to ensure that the proposed use of officers will not conflict with departmental needs or with the standards for off-duty work outlined above.

The *officer contract model* allows each officer to independently find off-duty employment and to enter into a direct relationship with the private enterprise. Officers must apply to the department for permission, which is granted if the employment criteria are met.

The *union brokerage model* means that the police union or association finds off-duty employment for its members. The union sets the conditions for the work and bargains with the department over pay, status, and conditions of the off-duty employment.

Each of these models has its backers. Reiss points out that there is an evolving case law about liability issues involving off-duty police officers. He notes that the more closely a department controls off-duty employment, the more liablity it assumes for officers' actions when they work for private firms. When the private demand for police services exceeds the supply—and many departments find this is the case—the contract model provides a way of rationally allocating manpower so as to ensure that public needs are met. Finally, there are problems with the private officer model when an individual officer takes on a broker role, thereby acting as an employment "agency" for fellow officers. This can lead to charges of favoritism and nepotism, which has disastrous consequences for dicipline and morale.

What is not known is the impact of uniformed off-duty patrol on crime prevention and the public's perception of safety. It may be that public fears are reduced owing to the visibility of officers believed to be acting in their official capacity.

Public-Private Interface

The interface between public and private law enforcement is a matter of concern to professionals charged with crime control under law. Most private policing organizations have the prevention of crime as their goal; others, however, adopt policelike methods and engage in investigation, apprehension, and prosecution. Private agents work for the people who employ them, and their goals may not always coincide with the public interest. Questions have been raised about the authority of private policing personnel to make arrests, to conduct searches, and to participate in undercover investigations. Of crucial importance is the issue of the boundary between the work of the police and that of private agencies. Lack of communication between public and private organizations has resulted in botched investigations, destruction of evidence, and overzealousness, all to the detriment of crime control. Yet most firms that provide private policing services stress that their chief concern is the prevention of crime and that their activities therefore do not conflict with the work of the public police.

These and other questions are seen to have impeded cooperation between the public and private forces. Security managers do report some sharing of information and equipment. Cooperative efforts have been reported with regard to such tasks as the transportation of hazardous materials, protection of dignitaries, crowd control, and investigation of economic crimes. Public and private police have worked together in undercover work. For example, a joint sting operation was conducted by the FBI and security personnel of IBM in regard to the sale of computer secrets in "Silicon Valley," the area around San Jose, California. Another public-private example is the National Auto Theft Bureau (NATB), a private, nonprofit organization that acts as a clearinghouse for auto theft information. In many states, law enforcement officers and insurance agents are required by law to report auto theft information to the NATB.[56]

Security managers have said that they generally report *UCR* index crimes to the police. However, incidents of employee theft, insurance fraud, industrial espionage, commercial bribery, and computer crime tend *not* to be reported to public authorities. Thus an interesting question arises: To what extent does a parallel system of private justice exist with regard to some offenders and some crimes? In such situations the chief concern of private companies is to prevent loss and protect assets. Although some such incidents are reported to the public prosecutor for action, the majority of them are resolved through internal procedures ("private justice") within the victimized company. Most businesses consider employee theft to be their greatest single crime problem. When such offenses are discovered, the offender may be "convicted" within the company and punished by forced restitution through payroll deductions or the loss of the job and the dissemination of information about the incident throughout the industry.

Private organizations often bypass the public criminal justice system in an effort to avoid the need to cope with changing prosecution policies, administrative delays in prosecution, discovery rules that would open the internal affairs of the company to public scrutiny, and bad publicity. A survey by the United States Chamber of Commerce revealed that half of 446 business executives interviewed believed that law enforcement and the criminal justice system do a poor job of fighting crimes against business.[57]

Recruitment and Training

A major concern of law enforcement officials and civil libertarians is the recruitment and training of private security personnel. Studies have shown that such personnel are generally recruited from among persons with minimal education and training; because the pay is low, the work often attracts only people who cannot find other jobs or who seek only temporary work. Thus most of the work is done by the young and the retired. A study by the Rand Corporation found that fewer than half of the private security guards surveyed had a high school education, and their average age was fifty-two. Perhaps more important, although "almost half of the respondents were armed, less than one-fifth reported having received any firearms training." Ninety-seven percent of the respondents failed to pass a "simple examination designed to test their knowledge of legal practice in typical job-related situations."[58]

As the private policing industry has grown, there have been calls for the examination and licensing of its personnel. Fewer than half of the states have such requirements. The National Council on Crime and Delinquency and the Private Security Advisory Council of the Law Enforcement Assistance Administration (LEAA) have offered model licensing statutes that specify periods of training and orientation, the wearing of uniforms that permit citizens to distinguish public from private police, and the prohibition of employing any person who has a criminal record. In some states security firms are licensed, often by the attorney general, while in others the local police have this authority. In general, however, there is little regulation of such firms.

The private policing industry arose in response to a need; it grew because the product it offered was in demand. The perceived need for the product may have resulted from the growth of crime, but it may also have developed because of the perception that the public police could not carry out a particular task. It is important that citizens distinguish between the actions of the forces of the public and private sectors. More important, private police must not hamper the work of law enforcement.

SUMMARY

Like members of any governmental agency, the police do not do their work in isolation from the social, economic, and political currents affecting society. For the police to be effective they must maintain their connection with the community and deal with the problem of brutality and corruption, demands for increased recruitment of women and minorities, pressures to unionize officers, and their competition or cooperation with private policing organizations. These are some of the problems that must be addressed by administrators and individual officers and that concern politicians and members of the general public.

The police cannot be static and unresponsive to public demands. Officers work in an environment that is both organizational and political. As the police look toward the next quarter century they must be attuned to changes in the community and adapt their tactics and approaches to new challenges. A public agency that resists change soon loses the very necessary element of public support.

FOR DISCUSSION

1. Community relations are important because the police depend on citizens to report crimes. What actions might be taken to improve community relations? What is meant by "community relations"?
2. You are a police officer. You learn that some of your fellow officers are accepting gifts from local business people. What will you do? Would your response be different if the gifts were drug related?
3. How should police administrators confront the issue of unionism?
4. As a citizen, if you feel that a police officer has been rude or has otherwise mistreated you, what actions may you take?
5. How are the issues discussed in this chapter linked to the effective functioning of the police?

FOR FURTHER READING

Juris, Hervey A., and Peter Feuille. *Police Unionism*. Lexington, MA: Lexington Books, 1973. Still the only major source of information on the development, actions, and issues of police unionism.
Maas, Peter. *Serpico*. New York: Bantam Books, 1973. The fascinating account of an undercover officer whose testimony was crucial to the Knapp Commission's investigation of police corruption.

Murano, Vincent. *Cop Hunter*. New York: Simon & Schuster, 1990. The story of an
undercover cop who worked for ten years for the Internal Affairs Division of
the New York City Police Department. Emphasizes the moral dilemmas of policing fellow officers.

Reiss, Albert J., Jr. *The Police and the Public*. New Haven, CT: Yale University Press,
1971. Now a classic study of the relationship of police officers to the public they
serve.

Shearing, Clifford, and Philip C. Stenning, eds. *Private Policing*. Newbury Park, CA:
Sage, 1987. An excellent volume that explores various aspects of the private
security industry.

NOTES

1. John Gardiner, "Wincanton: The Politics of Corruption," in President's Commission on Law Enforcement and Administration of Justice, *Task Force Report: Organized Crime* (Washington, DC: Government Printing Office, 1967), pp. 61–79;
William Chambliss, "Vice, Corruption, Bureaucracy, and Power," 4 *Wisconsin
Law Review* 1150 (1971).

2. James Q. Wilson, *Varieties of Police Behavior* (Cambridge, MA: Harvard University
Press, 1968), pp. 191–199.

3. Ibid., chap. 8.

4. James Q. Wilson, *Thinking about Crime*, 2d ed. (New York: Basic Books, 1983),
p. 91.

5. "The Black Cop: A Man in the Middle," *Newsweek* (August 16, 1971), p. 19.
Copyright © 1971 by Newsweek, Inc. All rights reserved. Reprinted by
permission.

6. Geoffrey P. Alpert and Roger G. Dunham, *Policing Multi-Ethnic Neighborhoods*
(New York: Greenwood Press, 1988), p. 20.

7. Douglas A. Smith, "The Neighborhood Context of Police Behavior," *Crime and
Justice*, vol. 8, ed. Albert J. Reiss, Jr., and Michael Tonry (Chicago: University of
Chicago Press, 1986), p. 313.

8. George L. Kelling, "On the Accomplishments of the Police," in *Control in the
Police Organization*, ed. Maurice Punch (Cambridge, MA: MIT Press, 1983),
p. 164.

9. Wesley G. Skogan, *Disorder and Decline: Crime and the Spiral of Decay in American
Neighborhoods* (New York: Free Press, 1990), p. 125.

10. *The Figgie Report Part Four: Reducing Crime in America—Successful Community Efforts* (Willowby, OH: Figgie International, 1983).

11. Dennis P. Rosenbaum, Arthur J. Lurigio, and Paul J. Lavrakas, *Crime Stoppers: A
National Evaluation*, U.S. Department of Justice, National Institute of Justice
(Washington, DC: Government Printing Office, 1986).

12. Ibid.

13. Dennis Jay Kenney, "The Guardian Angels: The Related Social Issues," *Police and
Policing: Contemporary Issues*, ed. Dennis Jay Kenney (New York: Praeger, 1989),
p. 225.

14. Skogan, *Disorder and Decline*, p. 130. See also Robert McGabey, "Economic Conditions: Neighborhood Organization, and Urban Crime," in *Crime and Justice*,
p. 230.

15. Herbert Jacob, "Black and White Perceptions of Justice in the City," paper presented at the annual meeting of the American Political Science Association,
Chicago, 1970.

16. Frank Moss, "National Danger from Police Corruption," *North American Review*
173 (October 1901): 19.

17. National Advisory Commission on Civil Disorders, *Report* (Washington, DC:
Government Printing Office, 1968).

18. Albert J. Reiss, Jr., "Police Brutality: Answers to Key Questions," *Transaction*
(July/August 1968): 10–19.

19. Amitai Schwartz, "A Role for Community Groups and Human Rights Agencies,"
in U.S. Department of Justice, *Police Use of Deadly Force* (Washington, DC: Government Printing Office, 1978), p. 54.

20. Lawrence Sherman and Robert Langworthy, "Measuring Homicide by Police Officers," *Journal of Criminal Law and Criminology* 4 (1979): 546–560; William Geller, "Deadly Force: What We Know," *Journal of Police Science and Administration* 10 (1982): 151–177.

21. Lawrence W. Sherman and Ellen G. Cohn, "Citizens Killed by Big City Police: 1970–84," unpublished manuscript, Crime Control Institute, Washington, DC, October 1986.

22. James J. Fyfe, "Reducing the Use of Deadly Force: The New York Experience," in U.S. Department of Justice, *Police Use of Deadly Force*, p. 28.

23. Arthur L. Kobler, "Police Homicide in a Democracy," *Journal of Social Issues* 31 (1975): 166.

24. Richard Kania and Wade MacKey, "Police Violence as a Function of Community Characteristics," *Criminology* 15 (1977): 27–48.

25. James J. Fyfe, "Toward a Typology of Police Shootings," paper presented at the annual meeting of the Academy of Criminal Justice Sciences, Oklahoma City, March 1980 (mimeo).

26. Lawrence W. Sherman, "What Do We Know about Homicides by Police Officers?" in U.S. Department of Justice, *Police Use of Deadly Force*, p. 9.

27. *Tennessee* v. *Garner*, 53 L.W. 4410 (1985).

28. Ibid.

29. Ibid., 4412.

30. Herman Goldstein, *Policing a Free Society* (Cambridge, MA: Ballinger, 1977), p. 190.

31. Ellwyn R. Stoddard, "The Informal 'Code' of Police Deviancy: A Group Approach to Blue-Coat Crime," *Journal of Criminal Law, Criminology, and Police Science* 59 (1968): 204.

32. Ibid., p. 205.

33. *Crime Control Digest,* November 25, 1985, June 30, 1986, August 3, 1987.

34. Samuel Walker, "Employment of Black and Hispanic Police Officers, 1983–1988: A Follow-Up Study," *Occasional Paper* 89-1, Center for Applied Urban Research, University of Nebraska, Omaha, February 1989.

35. *Standards of Law Enforcement Agencies* (Fairfax, VA: Commission on Accreditation for Law Enforcement Agencies, 1989), pp. 1–2.

36. Amitai Schwartz, "Reaching Systemic Police Abuses—The Need for Civilian Investigation of Misconduct: A Response to Wayne Kerstetter," in *Police Leadership in America*, ed. William A. Geller (New York: Praeger, 1985), p. 197.

37. Susan E. Martin, *Breaking and Entering* (Berkeley: University of California Press, 1980), p. 27.

38. Susan E. Martin, "Women in Policing: The Eighties and Beyond," in *Police and Policing*, p. 6.

39. Ibid., p. 5.

40. Marie Progrebin, "The Changing Role of Women: Female Police Officers' Occupation Problems," *Police Journal* 59 (1986): 127–133.

41. Martin, *Breaking and Entering*, p. 95.

42. See Michael Charles, "Women in Policing: The Physical Aspects," *Journal of Police Science and Administration* 10 (1982): 10–19.

43. Peter Bloch and Deborah Anderson, *Policewomen on Patrol: First Report* (Washington, DC: Police Foundation, 1974), pp. 1–7.

44. For a history of the ebb and flow of police unionism, see Anthony V. Bouza, "Police Unions: Paper Tigers or Roaring Lions?" in *Police Leadership in America*, p. 241.

45. James B. Jacobs, "Police Unions: How They Look from the Academic Side," in *Police Leadership in America*, p. 287.

46. Robert B. Kleismet, "The Chief and the Union: May the Force Be with You," *Police Leadership in America*, p. 281.

47. Hervey A. Juris and Peter Feuille, "Employee Organizations," in *Police Personnel Administration*, ed. O. Glenn Stahl and Riach A. Steufenberger (Pacific Grove, CA: Brooks/Cole, 1974), p. 214.

48. Ibid.

49. William D. Gentel and Martha L. Handman, *Police Strikes: Causes and Prevention* (Washington, DC: Government Printing Office, 1980), p. 5; Richard M. Ayres, "Case Studies of Police Strikes in Two Cities—Albuquerque and Oklahoma City," *Journal of Police Science and Administration* 5 (1977): 19–30; L. Thomas Win-

free and Frieda Gehlen, "Police Strikes: Public Support and Dissonance Education during a Strike by Police," *Journal of Police Science and Administration* 9 (1981): 451–452.

50. Ibid., p. 27.

51. Clifford D. Shearing and Philip C. Stenning, "Reframing Policing," in *Private Policing,* ed. Clifford D. Shearing and Philip C. Stenning (Newbury Park, CA: Sage, 1987), p. 13.

52. Ibid., p. 22.

53. Clifford D. Shearing and Philip C. Stenning, "Say 'Cheese!': The Disney Order That Is Not So Mickey Mouse," in *Private Policing,* p. 320.

54. William C. Cunningham and Todd H. Taylor, "The Growing Role of Private Security," in U.S. Department of Justice, National Institute of Justice, *Research in Brief* (Washington, DC: Government Printing Office, 1984).

55. Albert J. Reiss, Jr., *Private Employment of Public Police,* U.S. Department of Justice, National Institute of Justice (Washington, DC: Government Printing Office, 1988).

56. Gary T. Marx, "The Interweaving of Public and Private Police in Undercover Work," in *Private Policing,* pp. 172–189.

57. Cited in Cunningham and Taylor, "Growing Role of Private Security."

58. James S. Kakalik and Sorrell Wildhorn, *Private Police in the United States: Findings and Recommendations* (Washington, DC: Government Printing Office, 1972), p. 155.

3 P A R T

COURTS

The arrest of an individual in a democracy is only the first part of a complex process designed to separate the guilty from the innocent. Part 3 examines this process by which guilt is determined in accordance with the law's requirements. Here we shall look into the work of prosecutors, defense attorneys, bondsmen, and judges to understand the contribution each makes toward the ultimate decision. It is in the adjudicatory stage that the goals of an administrative system blunt the force of the adversarial process prescribed by law. Although we may focus on courtroom activities, most decisions relating to the disposition of a case are made in less public surroundings. After studying these chapters, we should ask ourselves whether justice is served by processes that are more akin to bargaining than to adversarial combat.

Prosecuting Attorney

Key Terms

accusatory process
count
crime construction
discovery

diversion
legal sufficiency
necessarily included offense

nolle prosequi
prosecuting attorney
state attorney general

system efficiency
trial sufficiency
United States Attorney

Nowhere is it more apparent [than in the prosecuting attorney's office] that our government is a government of men, not of laws. Nowhere do the very human elements of dishonesty, ambition, greed, lust for power, laxness or bigotry have more room for development. Also, there is no office where an able and honest public servant can be more effective.

Lewis Mayers, *The Lawyers*

On August 12, 1983, Judy Johnson telephoned the Manhattan Beach, California, police to report that her two-and-a-half-year-old son had been molested by Raymond Buckey, a teacher at the McMartin Preschool. This call precipitated the longest and most costly criminal trial in U.S. history. Five and a half years later Mr. Buckey was acquitted on fifty-two counts of sexual molestation of children, and a mistrial was declared on the remaining thirteen charges. In the interim, Mr. Buckey, his mother Peggy McMartin Buckey, his grandmother who had founded the school, his sister, and three other teachers were indicted by a grand jury on a total of 321 counts of sexual molestation of forty-eight children. While the gears of the criminal justice system ground to a conclusion, Buckey spent nearly five years and his mother two and a half years in jail awaiting trial; the Buckeys sold their preschool to pay legal fees, and taxpayers paid about $15 million for the prosecution and trial.

Raymond Buckey was arrested soon after Judy Johnson's call to the police but was quickly released for lack of evidence. Johnson then wrote a letter to the district attorney saying that her son had gone with Peggy Buckey to an armory behind her house, where "the goatman was " and where a ritual-type atmosphere prevailed. She wrote that her child was taken to a church where "Peggy drilled a child under the arms" and Ray "flew in the air." To gather evidence concerning these charges the police sent a letter to two hundred parents asking for any information from their children about possible criminal acts at the McMartin school involving oral sex, handling of genitals, and sodomy. The letter set off a panic, and hundreds of parents got in touch with the police.

Initially the children denied being molested, but in extensive taped interviews conducted by a therapist using anatomically correct dolls, the children were told that other children had divulged "yucky secrets" about the school and were urged to do likewise. About 360 children eventually described abuse, including being molested by the teachers, being photographed playing a "Naked Movie Star Game," being raped and sodomized, witnessing animal sacrifices, and being led into hidden tunnels under the school. These revelations were repeated in the press, shown on national television, and were the basis for countless radio talkshows. It was in this atmosphere that District Attorney Robert Philibosian initiated prosecution.[1]

Should a prosecution have been brought and a trial held on the basis of this evidence? To what extent was District Attorney Robert

The McMartin child molestation case
well illustrates the power of a prosecuting attorney to bring individuals to
trial on what later proves to be limited
evidence. What limitations should
there be on prosecutorial discretion?

Philibosian's decision to prosecute influenced by the police evidence,
the media-generated public panic (at times reminiscent of Salem,
Massachusetts, in 1692), or his own sagging campaign for reelection?
Should citizens in a democracy be subjected to the restrictions on
freedom and the costs associated with their case merely on the basis
of a decision by the prosecuting attorney?

The McMartin Preschool case makes us aware of the most powerful figure in the administration of justice: the **prosecuting attorney.**
It is the prosecutor who has the power to determine if charges should
be brought against a suspect, the nature of those charges, and the
extent to which they will be pursued in court. These officials (also
known in some states as district attorneys, county attorneys, or state's
attorneys) have been immortalized in novels and motion pictures and
on radio and television so that they have become almost folk heroes
who secure conviction of the guilty while upholding justice for the
innocent. In real political life there are counterparts to this crusading
image of prosecutors. Hundreds of elected officials have come into
prominence as fighting prosecutors and often based their campaigns
for higher political office on reputations gained during a widely publicized investigation or trial.

prosecuting attorney: A legal
representative of the state with sole
responsibility for bringing criminal
charges. In some states referred to as
district attorney, state's attorney, or
county attorney.

ORGANIZATION OF PROSECUTION

Since most offenders have violated state laws, their cases are
processed through the local criminal justice systems. Each state has
an elected **state attorney general,** and in most states (one exception is
Connecticut) these officials have the power to bring prosecutions
under certain circumstances. In Alaska, Delaware, and Rhode Island
the state attorney general also directs all local prosecutions. Most
criminal cases are brought to the 2,700 offices at the county level in
which the prosecuting attorney has power. In all states except Connecticut and New Jersey, prosecutors are elected, which means that
the office is heavily involved in local politics. In rural areas this office
may be composed solely of the prosecuting attorney and a part-time

state attorney general: Chief legal
officer of a state; responsible for both
civil and criminal matters.

assistant. In some urban jurisdictions, such as Los Angeles, which has 500 assistant prosecutors and additional numbers of legal assistants and investigators, the office is organized according to crime specialties. Most assistant prosecutors are young and seek to use the trial experience of the office as a means of moving on to more highly paid positions in a private law firm.

Prosecution of those accused of violating federal laws is carried out by the **United States Attorney,** who is appointed by the president and members of the U.S. Department of Justice. The 94 U.S. Attorneys and the 2,000 assistant U.S. Attorneys staff offices in each federal district court jurisdiction. Federal prosecutors are heavily involved in the prosecution of drug, white-collar, and corruption cases.

United States Attorney: Official responsible for the prosecution of crimes that are violations of the laws of the United States; appointed by the president and assigned to a U.S. District Court jurisdiction.

The office of prosecutor at the county level of government typifies the decentralization of criminal justice. Traditionally, prosecutors have been responsible only to the voters, and they enjoy an independence from the formal checks usually placed on American public officials. Although prosecutors commonly must submit to the electoral process every four years, there are few other public restraints on their actions. In most states neither the governor nor the attorney general is authorized to investigate suspected illegal activity without the permission of the local prosecutor.

The influence of prosecutors flows directly from their legal duties, but it must be understood within the context of the system's administrative and political environment. Of the many positions in the legal system, that of the prosecuting attorney is distinctive because it is concerned with all aspects of the system: from the time of arrest to final disposition of a case, prosecutors can make decisions that will determine to a great extent the cases that are to be prosecuted, the charges that are to be brought into the courtroom, the kinds of bargains that are to be made with the defendant, and the enthusiasm with which a case will be pursued. Throughout the justice process, prosecutors have links with the other actors in the system, and their decisions are usually affected not only by the types of relationships they maintain with these officials but also by the level of the public's awareness of their own actions. In most states, the prosecutors are elected officials who are able to accumulate considerable power in partisan politics, so they must be conscious of public reaction.

Rarely is the scope of the prosecutor's discretionary power either publicly recognized or defined by statute. Generally, state laws are explicit in requiring the prosecution of offenders, yet nowhere in the laws are there specific descriptions of the elements that must be present before the prosecutor can take action. Most laws describe the prosecutor's responsibility in such vague terms as "prosecuting all crimes and civil actions to which state or county may be party." On occasions when the prosecutor's decisions have been challenged, they have been shielded from judicial inquiry by an almost magical formula in the law: "within the prosecutor's discretion." In essence, the American people have placed district attorneys in a position in which they have to make choices but have not given them principles of selection.

When prosecutors feel that the community no longer considers that an act proscribed by law constitutes criminal behavior, they will probably refuse to prosecute or will expend every effort to convince the complainant that prosecution should be avoided. But like other government officials, prosecutors are sensitive to the force of public opinion. Often they must take measures to protect themselves when they believe that a course of action is likely to arouse antipathy toward agencies of law enforcement rather than toward the accused. If they hold to an exaggerated notion of duty, they can arouse a storm of protest that may gain them reputations as "persecutors" and cost them the cooperation of the community. The fact that about three-fourths of American prosecutors serve counties with populations of fewer than 100,000 accentuates the potential influence of public opinion. Local pressures may bear heavily on the single prosecution official in a community. Without the backing of public opinion, law enforcement and prosecution officers are powerless; especially with regard to victimless crimes, such as marijuana smoking, petty gambling, and prostitution, prosecutors develop policies that reflect community attitudes. A New York prosecutor has remarked, "We are pledged to the enforcement of the law, but we have to use our heads in the process."

BIOGRAPHY

Thomas E. Dewey

Twice the nomineee of the Republican party for president of the United States and three-time governor of New York, Thomas E. Dewey epitomized the "fighting prosecutor" who came to political prominence through a campaign against organized crime, racketeering, and official corruption.

Born in Michigan in 1902, Dewey began law practice in New York City in 1925. In 1931 he was appointed chief assistant U.S. Attorney for the Southern District of New York. During this period he gained his reputation as a "racket buster" for his vigorous prosecution of gangster Irving "Waxey Gordon" Wexler, who was sent to prison for ten years for income tax evasion. Dewey resumed private practice in 1933 until being appointed in 1935 to serve as investigator for a New York City grand jury that was outraged by the seeming unwillingness to prosecute gangsters demonstrated by then district attorney William C. Dodge, a Democratic party stalwart.

During the next eighteen months Dewey led a much-publicized and spirited campaign against organized crime. He targeted loan sharks, brothel keepers, numbers runners, and mob bosses. He succeeded in convicting Lucky "King of Vice" Luciano and eight others on prostitution charges. The courtroom testimony of the prostitutes kept Dewey on the front pages of the newspapers for weeks, giving him the public exposure and name recognition so sought after by politicians.

In 1937 Dewey was elected district attorney for New York County (Manhattan) on a pledge to root out corruption. A headline in the *World Telegram* read "Hoodlums Start Out as Dewey Starts In." During his term in office Dewey prosecuted such gang leaders and political bosses as James Hines, the district leader of Harlem; Richard Whitney; and the German-American Bundists Fritz Kahn and Louis (Lepke) Buchalter. It was alleged by the Hearst newspapers that in exchange for his life, Lepke offered to give evidence of corruption by a close advisor to President Roosevelt. Dewey did not accept the offer, and Lepke became the highest-ranking mobster to go to the electric chair.

With his reputation as a crime fighter, Dewey was put forward as a candidate for the Republican nomination for the presidency in 1940, only to lose to Wendell Wilkie. He was, however, elected governor of New York in 1942 and reelected for two additional terms. In 1944 he became the Republican nominee for the presidency but was overwhelmed by Roosevelt. In 1948 Dewey was the favorite throughout the campaign for the presidency. It was not until late evening of election night that it became obvious that Dewey was to lose to Harry S Truman. Returning to private practice, Dewey seemed to have lost interest in the problem of crime, refusing to testify before the Kefauver Committee investigating organized crime in 1950. He continued with his law practice until his death on March 16, 1971.

ROLES OF THE PROSECUTOR

References to the "prosecutor's dilemma" are often found in legal writings. Prosecutors face a dilemma because as "lawyers for the state" they are expected to do everything in their power to win the public's case, yet they are also members of the legal profession and are expected to engage in prosecution not to win convictions but to see that justice is done. The conditions under which they work are thought to create a "prosecutor's bias," sometimes called a "prosecution complex": they consider themselves to be instruments of law enforcement, although theoretically they are supposed to represent all the people, including the accused. This point is well made in the Canon of Ethics of the New York State Bar Association: "The primary duty of a lawyer engaged in public prosecution is not to convict, but to see that justice is done. The suppression of facts and the secreting of witnesses capable of establishing the innocence of the accused is highly reprehensible."[2] Prosecutors must define their roles by combining the professional dimensions of their work with the political context of their office.

Role definition is complicated by the fact that prosecutors must maintain constant relationships with a variety of "others"—police officers, judges, defense attorneys, political party leaders, and so forth—and these actors may have competing ideas about what the prosecutor should do. The prosecutor's decisions will vitally affect the ability of the others to perform their duties and to achieve their objectives. Because the district attorneys are at the center of the adjudicative and enforcement functions, if they decide not to prosecute, the judge and jury are helpless and the police officer's word is meaningless. If prosecutors decide to launch a campaign against drugs, pornography, or other social ills, there are likely to be repercussions in the political as well as the criminal justice arenas.

As lawyers for the state, prosecutors are expected to do everything to win their case, yet they are also expected to see that justice is done.

We can understand the work of prosecutors more clearly through use of the concept of role. A person may occupy a socially defined *position,* in this case that of prosecuting attorney, yet hold a conception of the role—the manner of action on a daily basis—that differs from those of other persons in the same position. A person's role, therefore, is a function not only of the formal aspects of the position but also of such other important factors as the individual player's personality, the environment within which he or she operates, and the individual's expectations concerning the attitudes of others with whom he or she interacts.

Four role conceptions are evident among prosecutors:

1. *Trial counsel for the police.* Prosecutors who view their primary function in this light believe they should reflect departmental views in the courtroom and take a crime-fighter stance in public.
2. *House counsel for the police.* These prosecutors believe they are there to give legal advice so that arrests will stand up in court.
3. *Representative of the court.* Such prosecutors consider their primary responsibility to be enforcement of the rules of due process to ensure that the police act in accordance with the law and uphold the rights of defendants.
4. *Elected official.* Prosecutors who view their role primarily in this way may be most responsive to community opinion. The possible political content of their decisions is a major concern of this type of prosecutor.

Each of these roles describes what the prosecutor views as his or her primary responsibility in the job. In the first two roles, prosecutors appear to believe that the police are the clients. Take a moment to consider who might be the clients of those prosecutors who view themselves as representatives of the court or as elected officials.

DISCRETION OF THE PROSECUTOR

Because of the decentralized nature of their office, their broad discretionary powers, and the low visibility of their decisions, prosecutors are able to structure their role so that they can play it in ways that are consistent with the political environment, their own personalities, and the interests of the others who are linked to the office.

Their wide power of discretion allows prosecutors to make decisions at each of the essential steps in the criminal justice process. One can readily understand that the type of case that eventually reaches the courtroom and its disposition depend to a large extent on a prosecutor's conception of his or her role within the criminal justice system as influenced by the larger political and social structure of the community. From the time the police turn a suspect's case over to the prosecutor, there are major decisions over which he or she has almost undisputed control.

That the police may arrest a person does not necessarily mean that the prosecutor will file charges against the suspect. Prosecutors can screen out cases they do not want to prosecute at their own discretion. While the proportion of such dismissals varies from place to place, estimates indicate that in most cities up to half of all arrests do not lead to the filing of formal charges. Prosecutors may decide not to press charges because of factors related to a particular case or because they have established policies dictating that charges will not be brought for certain offenses. For example, the U.S. Department of Justice provides its prosecutors with guidelines in determining whether a prosecution should be declined. The criteria include:

1. federal law enforcement priorities;
2. the nature and seriousness of the offense;
3. the deterrent effect of prosecution;
4. the person's culpability in connection with the offense;
5. the person's history with respect to criminal activity;
6. the person's willingness to cooperate in the investigation or prosecution of others;
7. the probable sentence or other consequences if the person is convicted.[3]

Having decided that a crime should be prosecuted, the prosecutor has great freedom in determining the charges to be lodged. Incidents of criminal behavior often involve the breaking of a variety of laws, so the prosecutor can bring a single charge or multiple charges.

CLOSE-UP *For the Assistant D.A., It's Nothing Like on TV*

An 8-year-old boy, his voice soft but steady, told how he had seen robbers shoot his father to death in front of the family's Brooklyn grocery store.

"He had the key and was opening the car," the child said in a small interview room in State Supreme Court in downtown Brooklyn. "Then they came, the four men. They told him if he moved they would kill him. One man had a gun."

He looked down at his feet. His mother, a woman of about 30, stared straight ahead in the chair next to him. "What was your father doing before he got shot?" asked Steven Samuel, a young assistant district attorney.

"He screamed."

There was a moment of silence. A detective who had arrested a suspect in the murder, which occurred several weeks before, pursed his lips. The widow shifted in her seat. Mr. Samuel gazed at the pen poised in his fingers, contemplating the latest of the many murder cases he has handled.

Mr. Samuel, who is 30 and five years out of law school, is typical of the 318 A.D.A.s—assistant district attorneys—in the office of the District Attorney of Brooklyn, the largest local prosecutor's office in the country behind those of Chicago and Los Angeles.

"All right," said Mr. Samuel, breaking the stillness. "Now I'm going to take you into a room, and I want you to tell what you told me to the people in that room. They like to hear little boys tell stories."

As he strode down the corridor to where the child and other witnesses would repeat their accounts before a grand jury—which later would vote a murder indictment—Mr. Samuel described his own feelings in such a case. "It used to rattle me, the tragedy of it," he said. "But now I try to keep myself as emotionally detached as possible. When you're presenting a case, it helps to be as objective as possible."

Mr. Samuel, like many of his colleagues, views his job as a chance to pursue interesting work and gain valuable experience before moving on. . . .

But perhaps the way in which Mr. Samuel most typifies his colleagues is that he and his routine often bear little resemblance to the portrayals of prosecutors on television and in the movies.

"My image of a prosecutor as a young kid was of Hamilton Burger, the District Attorney in 'Perry Mason,' " said Mr. Samuel. "He never had a guilty defendant."

Mr. Samuel, on the other hand, has won 25 convictions in the last three years, during which he has exclusively handled homicides. But he has also had three defendants who, the jury decided, were not guilty, despite his best efforts.

Then, too, in the television and movie scenarios, prosecutors generally spin their oratory in crowded, hushed courtrooms, unraveling plots complicated or clever, exciting or exotic. . . .

Suppose that Smith, who is armed, breaks into a grocery store, assaults the proprietor, and robs the cash drawer. What charges may the prosecutor file? By virtue of having committed the robbery, the accused can be charged with at least four violations: breaking and entering, assault, armed robbery, and carrying a dangerous weapon. Other charges may be added depending on the circumstances of the incident—whether the robbery was carried out during the day or night, for example.

The concept of **necessarily included offense** helps us further understand the position of the prosecutor. We can ask: Could Smith have committed crime A without committing crime B? If the answer is yes, B is not a necessarily included offense. In the example of the grocery store, Smith has committed the necessarily included offense of carrying a dangerous weapon in the course of the robbery. The prosecutor may charge Smith solely with the armed robbery or may include any number of other charges and combinations of charges in the information. By including as many charges as possible, the prosecutor increases his or her position in plea negotiations.

Selection of the charge or charges requires the prosecutor to decide also on the number of counts to be brought against the individual for the same offense. Each **count** named in an indictment or an infor-

> **necessarily included offense**: An offense committed for the purpose of committing another offense; for example, trespass committed for the purpose of committing burglary.

> **count**: Each separate offense of which a person is accused in an indictment or an information.

"Murders committed during grocery and bar holdups, during disputes among acquaintances—two guys get into a fight over a dice game—these are typical of the cases I've had," Mr. Samuel said. . . .

The day before, Mr. Samuel had won a conviction in the robbery-murder of a drug addict in East New York. But with his average workload of 15 cases awaiting trial, this simply meant that Mr. Samuel could now focus on some of his other cases. So, at 10 A.M. in the Brooklyn branch of State Supreme Court, where the borough's felony crimes are prosecuted, he was scurrying from one courtroom to another, juggling appearances in several of his cases.

In one of the wood-paneled courtrooms, Mr. Samuel and a defense lawyer, Lewis Cohen, agreed to begin the next day to try the case of a man charged with killing an off-duty corrections officer. The officer had interrupted the defendant's attempt to hold up a Crown Heights bar, Mr. Samuel said as he scurried the single block back to his office, already calculating how he would prepare his evidence and line up his witnesses on such short notice.

Mr. Samuel had hardly begun reviewing the graphic police photographs of the murder scene and other evidence in the case when the phone rang. Detective Lambert Roessner had just arrived at Supreme Court with the witnesses in the case of the grocer whose son had seen him slain.

Shunted aside was the trial beginning tomorrow; Mr. Samuel would have to work on that at home at night. Now he had to hurry back to the court and prepare the witnesses in the case of the murdered grocer for their scheduled appearance before the grand jury that afternoon.

When the trial in the killing of the corrections officer was past the jury selection stage, Mr. Samuel rose to deliver his opening statement. "The people will prove," he declared in resonant, self-assured tones, "that Leon Taft killed Rudolph Smith during the holdup of the bar at 162A Utica Avenue."

As he presented the case against Mr. Taft, the young prosecutor rarely glanced at the defendant, a man hardly older than himself, with a shaved head, sitting at the defense table only a few feet away. All the witnesses were cooperative—the defense called none of its own—and Mr. Samuel, with detailed and systematic questioning, drew forth their moment-by-moment recollections of the fatal shooting.

Within a week, the verdict was in: guilty of murder.

"Justice was served," Mr. Samuel said, pausing only briefly before turning to the next case on his still-large agenda.

SOURCE: From "For the Assistant D.A., It's Nothing Like On TV," by J. P. Fried, *The New York Times*, October 18, 1979, p. B1. Copyright © 1979 by The New York Times Company. Reprinted by permission.

mation deals with a specific criminal act, and under some conditions repeated acts result in multiple charges. A forger, for instance, may be charged with multiple counts, each carrying the potential for a similar penalty, for every act of forgery committed. It is because the prosecutor may charge multiple counts of the same criminal act that newspapers often announce that the accused may be liable for unrealistically long sentences—for example, five years for each of twenty counts. This is misleading, however, because judges may stipulate that the twenty terms of five years are to be served concurrently. In other words, the offender will serve only a total of five years, not the hundred years he would serve if the judge had stipulated consecutive terms.

The prosecutor's discretion may be limited by the procedure known as **discovery,** a legal requirement that some information in the case file be made available to the defense counsel. For example, the defense has the right to see any statements made by the accused while being interrogated by the police, as well as the results of any physical or psychological tests. Although the discovery procedure may suggest that the law unnecessarily limits the ability of the prosecution to win a case, the procedure is supported by the theory that

discovery: A prosecutor's pretrial disclosure to the defense of facts and evidence to be introduced at trial.

A QUESTION OF ETHICS

Assistant Prosecutor Debra McCoy looked at the case file. The police had arrested Leslie Wiggins, a prominent local businessman, for drunken driving. It seemed that Wiggins had been stopped after weaving on the highway at a high rate of speed. From the moment Officer Tompkins asked Wiggins to get out of the car, he knew he was very drunk. A breathalizer test revealed that he was well above the limit for sobriety. There was no question that this was an open-and-shut case. McCoy noted that Wiggins had been previously arrested, but the DWI charge had been dropped by her chief, Prosecutor Marc Gould.

"I don't know what happened last time," she thought, "but there is no question now." She recorded the charge of "driving while intoxicated" in the case file and forwarded it for review.

When the file had not yet returned for arraignment several days later, McCoy went to Gould's office.

"What happened to the Wiggins case?" she asked.

"Wiggins? Oh, that. Seems that the breathalizer wasn't reading right that night."

"Gee, I'm surprised. Tompkins didn't say anything about that when I talked with him yesterday. In fact, he was wondering when the case was coming up."

"Well, let's just not worry about this. I'm sure that Tompkins had other things to concern him. Don't think anything more about Wiggins."

McCoy left the office and wondered, "What's going on here?"

What *is* going on here? Will Gould's statement influence the case of other drivers who were tested on the breathalizer the evening that Wiggins was? Is Gould authorized to handle this matter on his own? How would dropping this case reflect on Gould or McCoy if the next time Wiggins is stopped it's at the scene of a fatal car accident?

the state has an obligation to act impartially and should not win a conviction through the use of deceit. The prosecutor has an obligation to secure justice, and knowledge of the evidence against the accused should help the accused to prepare an effective defense.

After the charge has been made, the prosecutor may reduce it in exchange for a guilty plea or enter a notation of ***nolle prosequi*** *(nol. pros.)*, indicating a freely made decision not to press the charge, either as a whole or as to one or more counts. In our system of public prosecution there is no recourse to this decision. On conclusion of a case in which a conviction is obtained, the prosecutor can exert influence over the impending sentence by submitting a recommendation concerning its nature.

nolle prosequi: An entry made by a prosecutor on the record of a case and announced in court to indicate that the charges specified will not be prosecuted. In effect, the charges are thereby dismissed.

EXCHANGE RELATIONS

The formal rules of a bureaucracy do not completely account for the behavior of the actors within it; an informal structure arises from the social environment, personal relationships, and their interaction. Thus the decisions made by the office of prosecuting attorney reflect those personal and organizational clients with whom it interacts. The influence of a particular client group depends on such things as its role in the criminal justice process, friendship, the amount of contact it has with the office, and its ability to impede the work of the prosecutor if it should choose to do so. This section examines several such exchange relationships.

Although statutes define the formal relationships among portions of the criminal justice system, research has shown that the actual ways in which the system operates are always in flux, often blurred, and usually open to negotiation. As a result, prosecutors in some jurisdictions do control the charging decision; others are mere rubber stamps for the police. Some prosecutors wield extensive influence over the operations of the court by their ability to control the calendar, to appoint counsel for indigents, and to dominate the sentencing decisions; others are beholden to the judiciary and obediently respond to directions from the bench. What must be emphasized is that the role conceptions of individual prosecutors and their clientele and the customs of particular criminal justice systems cause variations in the operation of the office. When a prosecution operation is described, it should be understood to be a picture of the exchange relations in one jurisdiction at one time.

Police

Although prosecuting attorneys have discretionary power to determine the disposition of cases, they are dependent on the police to produce the raw materials with which they work. Because of the low visibility of police decisions and their own lack of investigative resources, prosecutors are unable to control the types of cases brought to them for disposition. The police may be under pressure to establish an impressive crime clearance record and so may make many arrests without the substantiating evidence required to ensure conviction. No prosecutor wants to have poorly developed cases. They would not stand up in court and would be a wasteful expenditure of valuable resources.

In relationships with the police, prosecutors are not without means of exercising control. Their main check is the ability to return cases for further investigation and to refuse to approve arrest warrants. The police depend on the prosecutor to accept the output of their system. Rejection of too many cases can seriously affect the morale and discipline of the force.

Police requests for prosecution may be turned down for a number of reasons unrelated to the facts of the case. First, prosecutors serve as the regulators of caseloads, not only for their own office but also for the rest of the judicial bureaucracy as well. Constitutional and statutory time limits prevent them and the courts from building a backlog of untried cases. Prosecutors may also reject police requests for prosecution because they do not want to pursue cases that will not result in a conviction. Finally, prosecutors may return cases in order to check on the quality of police work. As one deputy prosecu-

COMPARATIVE PERSPECTIVE
Prosecution in the Socialist Federal Republic of Yugoslavia

Since the end of World War II the position of public prosecutor in Yugoslavia has gone from being in the style of the Soviet procurary to being a recognized part of judicial agencies, independent of both the police and the judges. The evolution reflects shifts in the Yugoslav political and legal systems as it has moved away from identity with the centralized procedures of the Soviet criminal code to a process that is now more in line with those operating in Western Europe.

Yugoslavia is a federation composed of six republics and two autonomous provinces. But unlike the United States, where a significant amount of political power resides in the national government, the Yugoslav republics have over time gained considerable autonomy. Today it is a federation in name but is de facto a confederation. The religious and ethnic complexion of Yugoslavia has contributed to this devolution of power, to calls for the secession of some republics, and to

the development of criminal justice systems that have adapted to the particular cultural values of the dominant nationality of a region.

Although contrasts are often made between the adversarial systems of common law countries and the inquisitorial (Continental) system that exists in Europe and most non-English-speaking countries, there are in fact a diversity of criminal justice processes within each of these broad models. Like most systems today, Yugoslav criminal justice contains a mixture of elements that have been drawn from both the adversarial and inquisitorial systems.

Whereas the adversarial mode takes its shape from a contest or dispute (in Anglo-American systems the adversaries activate most procedures), in Continental systems the inquisitorial mode takes the shape of an official inquiry (a single actor, the official agent, initiates all procedures). The inquisitorial mode emphasizes a search for

the truth and begins with a preparatory stage during which an investigation is carried out to determine whether there are enough grounds to believe that someone might have committed a criminal offense.

Prosecution in Yugoslavia is organized to correspond to the structure of the courts. Thus, in addition to the Office of the Federal Public Prosecutor, there is an office at each of the republic, district, and communal levels. Prosecutors are attorneys who are members of the civil service and who view their work as a career. After an eighteen-month apprenticeship following law school, prosecutors are appointed for an eight-year term. All new prosecutors are first assigned to the

■
Prosecutors are dependent on the police for the information essential for successful indictment and conviction. Their exchange relationships with officers will influence the extent to which the police cooperate.

communal courts, where they normally serve five years before being promoted to the district courts.

The Prosecution Process

In Yugoslavia, as in some other European countries, the process of establishing the facts of a case during the preparatory phase is undertaken by an investigating judge. Prosecutors receive police reports, prepare charges, and then turn the matter over to the investigating judge, who has the responsibility of determining whether the evidence exists to bring an individual to arraignment and trial.

Prosecutors play an important gate-keeping role in that they evaluate police reports before deciding whether to ask for an investigation. If a prosecutor deems it reasonable to suspect that a person has committed the offense, he is expected to file a motion with the investigating judge, thus activating the criminal process. On the basis of this motion the judge may begin the investigation, or if he believes that the evidence does not warrant further action, he must submit the motion to a three-judge panel for a final determination.

While the investigating judge, as an impartial actor, conducts a review of the evidence (and may even travel to the crime scene), the defense and prosecutor may be present to represent their positions. They both may have access to the case record. The accused has the right to remain silent and may be held up to six months while the investigation is underway if there is concern that he will leave the jurisdiction. The victim may also take part in the investigation and is entitled to be represented by counsel. If during the course of the investigation the prosecutor believes that the evidence uncovered does not justify arraignment and trial, he has the power to stop the inquiry, thus abandoning the case. The investigating judge may not stop the process on his own; if he believes that the case should not proceed, he must inform the prosecutor and ask the judicial panel for a decision. In the Republic of Croatia, about 18 percent of cases are ended at this stage.

If there is a finding of probable cause by the investigating judge, the case record is returned to the prosecutor for the filing of charges. The prosecutor, however, has the discretion to ask for a further in-vestigation on new charges, or he may drop the case. Should the case be dropped, the victim may pick up the charges and bring a prosecution.

Unlike that of his American counterpart, the scope of the Yugoslav prosecutor's discretion appears to be restricted; in every instance where he may be confronted with a choice, the law attempts to provide detailed criteria for decision making. This is part of the Continental tradition but also reflects the movement to reform prosecution in Yugoslavia from the days when it was identified almost solely with the power of the police. The Yugoslav prosecutor must operate during the crucial preparatory phase under the watchful eye of the investigative judge. It is during this prearraignment stage that the evidence is sifted, witnesses are interviewed, and weak cases are filtered out. It is perhaps not surprising, then, that events in the courtroom seem almost anticlimactic.

SOURCE: From "Prosecution in the Criminal Courts of the Socialist Republic of Croatia, Yugoslavia," by N. Cirkveni and G. F. Cole, Criminal Justice Review 15 (Spring 1990):37. Reprinted by permission.

tor told this author, "You have to keep them on their toes, otherwise they get lazy." Rather than expend the resources necessary to find additional evidence, the police may dispose of a case by sending it back to the prosecutor on a lesser charge so that it will lead to a guilty plea, or may drop the case.

In most cases a deputy prosecutor and the assigned police officer occupy the boundary-spanning roles in this exchange relationship. After repeated contacts, deputies get to know the police officers they can trust, and these perceptions may be an important consideration in the decision to prosecute. Sometimes the police perform the ritual of "shopping around" for a deputy prosecutor who, past experience has led them to believe, is likely to be sympathetic to their point of view on a case. Some prosecution offices prevent this practice by stipulating that only the prosecutor, not deputies, can make primary decisions.

Police-Prosecutor Teams

Police-prosecutor coordination has been a concern of criminal justice officials in recent decades.[4] It is argued that too often a lack of coordination between police investigators and prosecutors leads to case attrition. Part of the problem is that lawyers and police officers have different perspectives on crime and work for different criminal justice oganizations. The police often take the position that they have made a valid arrest and that there should be no reason why a case should not be indicted and tried. Prosecutors look at cases to see if there is the evidence that will result in a conviction. These contrasting orientations often result in conflicts, with some cases "slipping through the cracks." In many jurisdictions joint police-prosecution teams have been created so that representatives of both departments work on cases together.

This task force approach is often used for drug or organized crime investigation-prosecutions in which detailed information and evidence is required for a successful conviction. Cooperation between the police and prosecutor in drug cases is important, since without a network of informers, peddlers cannot be caught with evidence that can bring about convictions. One pool of informers is made up of people who have been arrested for drug violations. Through promises to reduce charges or even to *nol. pros.*, arrangements can be made to return the accused to the community to gather information for the police.

Victims

Until a very few years ago, the victim of a crime was the forgotten participant in the criminal justice process. One reason for this state of affairs lies in the nature of prosecution in the United States. In our system, a complainant depends on the prosecuting attorney to bring charges. If the prosecutor refuses, a private citizen cannot bring an indictment against a fellow citizen, as is possible in England.

Victims generally play a passive role in the criminal justice process, yet their cooperation is essential for successful prosecution.

They must assist the police and prosecuting attorney by identifying the offender, and the basic evidence to be considered often depends on their testimony. In many types of cases, the nature of a victim's prior relations with the accused, the victim's actions at the time of the offense, and the victim's personal characteristics are deemed important if the case is to come to a successful conclusion before judge and jury.

The relationship of the accused to the victim has strong bearing on a case having to do with violent crime and thus can present a major problem to the prosecutor. In one study of crimes by persons who were not strangers to their victims, difficulties with the complaining witness accounted for 61 percent of the refusals to prosecute and 54 percent of the dismissals. Barbara Boland found that the conviction rate in New Orleans for crimes of violence committed by strangers was 48 percent; by friends or acquaintances, 30 percent; and by family members, 19 percent.[5] As the closeness of the accused's relationship to the victim increased, the likelihood of conviction decreased.

A study of the prosecution and disposition of felony arrests in New York City emphasized the crucial role of the victim and the exchange relationships that may exist in the prosecution process. By analyzing a sample of felony arrests, researchers learned that a high percentage of crimes in every category, from murder to burglary, involved victims with whom the accused had had prior and often close relations. This finding was particularly true with respect to crimes of interpersonal violence: 83 percent of rape victims, 50 percent of manslaughter and attempted homicide victims, and 69 percent of assault victims knew their assailants.

Such findings are to be expected. Suspects known to their victims are more likely to be arrested than strangers, since they can more easily be identified by the complainants. The fact that the victim and the accused knew each other, however, led to the dropping of a large number of cases. Complainants were often reluctant to pursue pros-

CLOSE-UP Drug Arrests: An Example of Exchange

Lt. Roger Cirella of the drug task force of the Seattle police force entered the office of Chief Deputy Prosecutor Michael Ryan. Cirella reported that during questioning, a well-known drug dealer intimated that he could provide evidence against a pharmacist suspected of illegally selling drugs. The officer wanted to transfer the case to the friendlier hands of a certain deputy and to arrange for a reduction of charges and bail.

Cirella: Yesterday we got a break in the pharmacy case. We had arrested Sam Hanson after an undercover buy down on First Avenue. He says that a druggist at the Green Cross Pharmacy is selling out the back door. We thought that something like that was happening since we had seen these bums standing around there but we've not been able to prove it. Hanson says he will cooperate if we'll go easy on him. Now, I'd like to get this case moved to Wadsworth.

He's worked with us before and that new guy who's on it now just doesn't understand our problems.

Ryan: O.K., but what's that going to accomplish?

Cirella: We also need to be able to fix it so Hanson gets out on bail without letting the druggies out there know he has become an informer. If we can get Judge Griffin to reduce bail he can probably put up the bond. Now we also need to reduce the charges yet keep him on the string so that we can bring him right back if he doesn't play our game.

Ryan: I want to cooperate with you guys but I can't let the boss get a lot of heat for letting a pusher out on the street. How are we going to know that he's not going to screw up?

Cirella: Believe me, we'll keep tabs on him.

Ryan: O.K., but don't come here telling me we're going to get splashed with mud in the *Times*.

ecution. As the study noted, "tempers had cooled, time had passed, informal efforts at mediation or restitution might have worked, or in some instances, the defendant had intimidated the complainant."[6]

Figure 8.1 shows the outcomes of stranger and nonstranger robberies and burglaries in New York City. Note that 88 percent of the stranger robbery arrests resulted in conviction, and that 68 percent of these were on a felony charge. Sixty-five percent of those arrested were incarcerated, 32 percent for a year or more. By contrast, when the robbery victim knew the accused, only 37 percent of those arrested were convicted, 23 percent incarcerated, and none served more than a year. The same pattern exists with burglaries, although the punishments were less severe. Most of the stranger burglars were convicted, but only 8 percent on a felony charge. What is clear is that prosecutors bargained these cases down to misdemeanors probably because the evidence was not strong. As with acquaintance robberies, the burglars who knew their victims were treated much more softly by the prosecution.[7]

Research has thus substantiated that the relatively close defendant-victim relationship is by and large responsible for dismissal of felony charges, their reduction to misdemeanors, or lenient sentences even when evidence of guilt is plentiful. Prosecutors are aware of all such situations and are usually reluctant to press charges fully when there is a possibility that victims will have second thoughts as they begin to realize that the sanctions of the criminal law will be brought to bear on the offender. Many victims may not want to suffer the consequence of their role in cooperating with the prosecutor to convict a family member, friend, or neighbor.

In some cases involving strangers, the victim's personal characteristics and attitudes may influence the decision to prosecute. Prostitutes who claim rape, drug users who are assaulted by pushers, and children who may be unable to testify under pressure are viewed by prosecutors as victims whose characteristics make the securing of a

FIGURE 8.1
Outcomes of stranger and nonstranger robberies and burglaries in New York City. As can be seen, victims of burglaries and robberies are less likely to pressure for conviction when the offender is known to them. If conviction is successful the penalties tend to be less when a nonstranger is the offender. SOURCE: From *Felony Arrests: Their Prosecution & Disposition in New York City's Courts,* Vera Institute of Justice, pp. 58, 86. Copyright © 1981 by Longman Publishing Group. Reprinted by permission of Vera Institute of Justice.

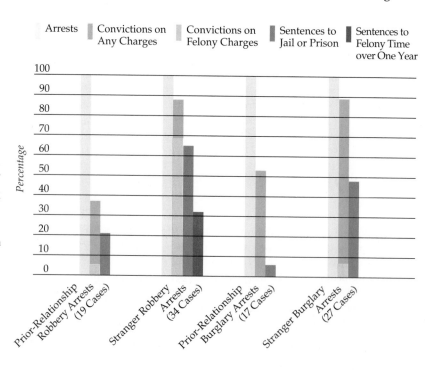

conviction difficult. Prosecutors need the evidence provided by such victims but are also wary of the jury's reaction to the victim.

Courts

The influence of the courts on the decision to prosecute is very real. The sentencing history of each judge gives prosecutors, as well as other enforcement officials, an indication of the treatment a case may receive in the courtroom. Prosecutors' expectations of the court's action may affect their decision to prosecute or not to prosecute. In the words of one prosecutor interviewed by the author: "There is great concern as to whose court a case will be assigned. After Judge Lewis threw out three cases in a row in which entrapment was involved, the police did not want to take any cases to him."

Prosecutors depend on the plea bargaining machinery to maintain the flow of cases from their office. If guilty pleas are to be successfully induced, the sentencing actions of judges must be predictable. If the defendants and their lawyers are to be influenced to accept a lesser charge or a promise of a lighter sentence in exchange for a plea of guilty, there must be some basis to believe that the judges will fulfill their part of the arrangement. Since judges are unable to announce formally their agreement with the details of the bargain, their past performance influences the actors.

Within the limits imposed by law and by the demands of the system, prosecutors may regulate the flow of cases to the court. They can regulate the length of time between accusation and trial, holding cases until they have the evidence that will convict. They may also seek repeated adjournments and continuances until the public's interest in the case dies down, witnesses become unavailable, or other difficulties make their requests for dismissal of prosecution more easily justifiable. In many cities the prosecutor is able to determine the court that will receive a case and the judge who will hear it.

In most jurisdictions, persons arrested on felony charges must be given a preliminary hearing within ten days. For prosecutors, the preliminary hearing is an opportunity to evaluate the testimony of witnesses, to assess the strength of the evidence, and to try to predict the outcome of the case should it go to trial. Subsequently, prosecutors have several options: they may recommend that the case be held for trial, seek a reduction of the charges to those of a misdemeanor, or conclude that they have no case and drop the charges.

Community

As a part of the wider political system, the administration of criminal justice responds to its environment. As shown by the McMartin case described in the opening to this chapter, public opinion and the media can play a crucial role in creating an environment either supportive or critical of the prosecutor. Like police chiefs or school superintendents, prosecuting attorneys will not be long in office if they are antagonistic to community values.

Exchange relationships between community and prosecutor can be analyzed at several levels. First, the general public is able through regulations to have its values translated into policies that criminal justice officials follow. Through the political process, especially in the election of prosecutors and in decisions concerning the budgetary resources to be placed at their disposal, the electorate affects decision making.

The public's influence is particularly acute in those "gray areas" of the law in which full enforcement is not expected. Legislatures may enact statutes that define the outer limits of criminal conduct, but this does not necessarily mean that the laws will be fully enforced. Some statutes are passed as expressions of desirable morality, and others are kept deliberately vague. Finally, some existing laws proscribe behavior that the community no longer considers criminal. Reflecting the public's attitude toward such laws, prosecutors usually disregard violations of laws regulating some forms of gambling, certain sexual practices, or obscenity.

Alternatively, the community may insist that charges be brought against people who flout its dominant values. Owners of adult bookstores and video rental shops may be harassed and the businesses closed if the prosecutor feels public pressure to wage a war on obscenity. The public is also prone to press for selective prosecution of persons who engage in some forms of "immoral" activity; for example, streetwalkers may be arrested whereas call girls and "hostesses" may remain immune.

Studies have shown that the public's level of attention to the activities of the criminal justice system is low. Still, the community remains a potential source of pressure that opinion leaders may activate against the prosecutor. The prosecutor's office always has the public in mind when it makes its decisions. It is recognized that some crimes will bring forth a vocal public reaction.

In sum, although prosecutors are free from statutory checks on their power, they must make decisions within an organizational framework and are thus subject to the influence of other actors. Because the criminal justice system requires that a number of officials participate in the disposition of each case, bargaining occurs. Prosecutors, as the link between the police and the courts, hold a strategic position in this regard, because all cases must pass through their office. Accordingly, they are able to regulate the flow of cases and also the conditions under which they will be processed. Given the caseload in metropolitan areas and the scarcity of resources to deal with it, officials are pressed to dispense justice efficiently. The prosecutors' influence over other actors is based on these stresses within the criminal justice environment. In addition, there is the dramatic aspect of their work, which can command public attention. This publicity, in turn, can be used as a weapon against the police, the courts, or other actors who do not cooperate with the efforts of their office.

DECISION-MAKING POLICIES

In view of the differences in role conceptions, exchange relationships, and sociopolitical factors that influence the decisions made by prosecutors, is it possible to generalize about how this vital sector of criminal justice operates? Research indicates that throughout the pretrial phase the prosecutor and the prosecutor's assistants are involved in a screening process to determine what action should be taken with regard to a particular case. Pretrial screening is designed to remove from the system cases that do not meet the legal test of probable cause, to divert cases that the prosecutor believes could be better handled by another agency, and to prepare appropriate charges. But the screening is influenced by the political and organizational incentives to maintain a high conviction rate, to allocate resources so that cases viewed by the community as serious are successfully prosecuted, and to keep open channels of communication and exchange with the other agencies of criminal justice.

Studies show great variation in this stage of the prosecutorial process. Differences in the way prosecutors handle felony cases in two jurisdictions are illustrated in Figure 8.2. Some offices make extensive use of screening and are less inclined to press charges. Pleas of guilty are the primary dispositional vehicle in some offices, whereas in others pleas of not guilty strain courts' trial resources to their limits. Some offices remove cases soon after they are brought to the prosecutor's attention by the police; in others, disposition occurs as late as the first day of trial. The period from receipt of the police report to the trial is thus a time of review in which the prosecutor exercises discretion to determine what charging actions should be taken.

Joan Jacoby has analyzed the management policies that prosecutors use to achieve specific goals during the pretrial process and the ways in which they staff their offices toward those ends. On the basis

FIGURE 8.2
Differences in how prosecutors handle felony cases in two jurisdictions.
The discretion of the prosecutor is seen by the way felony cases are handled in two jurisdictions. Note that different screening policies seem to be in operation and that the cases accepted for prosecution are disposed of in different ways.
SOURCE: U.S. Department of Justice, Bureau of Justice Statistics, *Report to the Nation on Crime and Justice,* 2nd ed. (Washington, DC: Government Printing Office, 1988), p. 71.

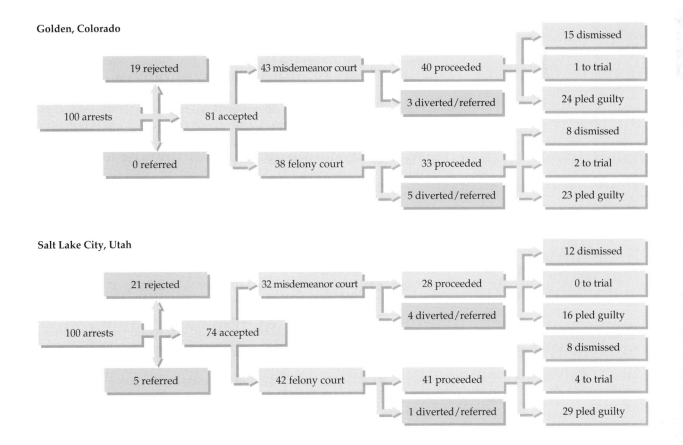

of data from more than three thousand prosecutors, she has found three policy models: Legal Sufficiency, System Efficiency, and Trial Sufficiency. She assumes that a prosecutor's choices with regard to the handling of cases are guided by a policy set forth in one of the models. The choice of policy is shaped by personal considerations of the prosecutor (such as the role conception discussed earlier), by such external factors as crime levels, and by the relationship of prosecution to the other portions of the criminal justice system.[8]

The operative policy affects the decisions made by the prosecutor and the prosecutor's assistants in screening and disposing of cases. To accomplish the basic goals stated in the model, the prosecutor adopts strategies with regard to discovery, diversion, plea bargaining, and allocation of resources. Each model thus alerts us to the point in the process at which cases are filtered out of the system. These models are valuable management tools that the prosecutor can use to ensure implementation of a particular policy choice. They also aid our understanding of criminal justice.

Legal Sufficiency

Some prosecutors believe that if a case is legally sufficient, they have a responsibility to accept it for prosecution. They ask, "Are the minimum legal elements present so that charges should be brought?" In a breaking-and-entering case, for example, if there is evidence of forcible entry and if the accused was found to have the stolen items in his or her possession, the case would be prosecuted because there is **legal sufficiency:** the required elements are there. But the force of these surface characteristics may be diminished if the police accumulated the evidence by unconstitutional tactics that would be exposed in court. Under the Legal Sufficiency Model, cases are initially screened merely for evidentiary defects before they are given a preliminary court hearing. Thus a great many cases are accepted for prosecution, and various operational strategies are employed to prevent overload of the system. Under this model, assistant prosecutors, especially those assigned to misdemeanor courts, have little time to prepare individual cases, must use plea bargaining to the utmost, and expect many dismissals and acquittals.

System Efficiency

The System Efficiency Model aims at a speedy and early disposition of cases. A prosecutor in an office that adheres to this policy asks, "What charges should be made in view of the caseload pressures on the system?" With this model, the same breaking-and-entering case would be rejected, because emphasis is placed on screening as the major technique to reduce work load. If the same unconstitutional search-and-seizure elements were present, they would be spotted and the case rejected at the outset. If the case did not appear defective, a prosecutor operating under a **system efficiency** policy might charge the defendant with a felony but agree to reduce the charge to a misdemeanor—perhaps unlawful trespass or larceny—in exchange for a guilty plea. According to Jacoby's research, this model is usually

legal sufficiency: The presence of the minimum legal elements necessary for prosecution of a case. When a prosecutor's decision to prosecute a case is customarily based on legal sufficiency, a great many cases are accepted for prosecution, but the majority of them are disposed of by plea bargaining or dismissal.

system efficiency: Operation of the prosecutor's office in such a way as to effect speedy and early disposition of cases in response to caseload pressures in the system. Weak cases are screened out at intake, and other nontrial alternatives are used as primary means of disposition.

followed when the trial court is backlogged and the prosecutor has limited resources. Thus the prosecutor must both screen out weak cases at the intake point and also use other nontrial alternatives to minimize the number of trials.

Trial Sufficiency

Under the Trial Sufficiency Model, cases are accepted and charges made only at the level that can be sustained in court. The prosecutor asks, "Will this case result in a conviction?" This does not mean that the prosecutor accepts only sure cases; rather it means that when the facts are present to sustain a conviction, every effort is made to secure that outcome—that is, there is **trial sufficiency.** In the breaking-and-entering example, given the evidence and if the constitutional problem of the police search could be overcome, the defendant would be charged with a felony, and the goal would be conviction on that charge. This model requires good police work, a prosecution staff experienced in trial work, and—because plea bargaining is minimized—court capacity. Rejected cases must be diverted from the system by alternative means.

trial sufficiency: The presence of sufficient legal elements to ensure successful prosecution of a case. When a prosecutor's decision to prosecute a case is customarily based on trial sufficiency, only cases that seem certain to result in conviction at trial are accepted for prosecution. Use of plea bargaining is minimal; good police work and court capacity are required.

Implementing Prosecution Policy

As illustrated in Figure 8.3, the policy models dictate that prosecutors select certain points in the process for disposition of the vast majority of the cases presented to them by the police. With a policy of legal sufficiency, many cases are accepted for prosecution but are then disposed of through plea negotiation and diversion after the preliminary hearing and before trial. With a policy of system efficiency, the prosecutor rejects the majority of requests for prosecution and diverts appropriate cases from the system. With a policy of trial sufficiency, most cases do not get beyond the point of intake, and the prosecutor proceeds with only those cases that will result in conviction.

Each policy requires the prosecutor to use strategies and deploy assistants in ways that are consistent with the overriding goal of the office. Accordingly, it is important for offices operating under the System Efficiency Model to have well-trained personnel at the intake point so that the critical decision to charge can be based on experience. Offices operating under the Trial Sufficiency Model require skilled courtroom advocates. And offices operating under the Legal Sufficiency Model may use less-experienced personnel at the intake point but need good plea negotiators.

DECISION TO PROSECUTE

Deciding whether to prosecute and what the charge will be is the focus of the formal aspect of prosecuting attorneys' work. These determinations can legally be made by them alone, and the consequences have a great impact not only on the defendants but also on the other agencies that participate in the administration of justice.

As the Due Process Model emphasizes, a decision to label a citizen a defendant in a criminal action should be undertaken only with full and serious understanding. Once a suspect becomes a defendant, the entire weight of the criminal justice process is brought to bear on the individual. The state may restrain the person's liberty; economic burdens are imposed by the requirement that bail be posted and a lawyer hired; and there is the nontangible penalty of damage to the person's reputation. Though the public gives lip service to the idea of "innocent until proved guilty," it may also subscribe to the notion that where there's smoke, there's fire. There are negative aspects to being arrested, but there are even greater penalties attached to being charged with a crime.

As we have seen, the decision to prosecute is not made at only one point in the criminal justice process. Although a decision to file charges is made during the initial phase, prosecutors may alter the charges at any time as they learn new facts about the case and as they interact with police, grand jury, defense attorneys, defendant, and judge. As one scholar points out, the charging decision is complex:

FIGURE 8.3

Three policy models of prosecutorial case management and allocation of staff resources. Prosecutors develop policies as to how their offices will manage cases. An assumption of these three models is that a portion of arrests will be dropped at some point in the system so that few cases reach trial.

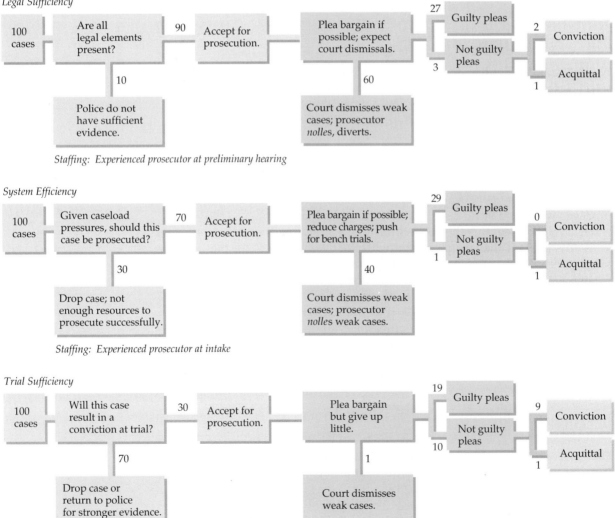

The decision to charge, unlike the decision to arrest, is not a unitary decision made at a readily identifiable time by a specific individual. It is, instead, a process consisting of a series of interrelated decisions, and the steps in the process do not always occur in the same sequence. Most often the decision is made after a suspect has already been taken into custody. In some instances, the effective decision is made when the police decide not to ask the prosecutor to charge, but to release a suspect instead. Of greater significance are the decisions made by prosecutors, acting through their assistants, whether to charge suspects already in custody, in response to requests made by the police that they do so.[9]

Accusatory Process

We can define the **accusatory process** as the series of activities that takes place from the moment a suspect is arrested and booked by the police to the moment the formal charging instrument—indictment or information—is filed with the court. During this process the activities of the police, grand jury, bail agency, and court are linked to those of the prosecuting attorney. Here the government must show only that there is a prima facie (that is, at first sight) case that a crime has been committed and that it was committed by the accused. Two issues are addressed by decision makers: (1) Is there probable cause to restrict the liberty of the individual? (2) Under the circumstances, would a reasonable person believe that the defendant committed the crime? If a grand jury or judge answers the questions affirmatively, a formal accusation instrument is presented, and the defendant is arraigned on the charges. All of these procedures are carried out within a relatively brief time, but the decisions made have an important effect on the accused: personal liberty may be taken away, and the beginnings of a defense may have to be mounted. It is during the accusatory process that we can best see the way prosecutors in various parts of the United States conduct their formal duties.

As Chapter 4 explained, the legal instrument by which charges are brought against a person is either an indictment handed down by a grand jury or a prosecutor's bill of information ruled upon by a judge at a preliminary hearing. In some states the prosecutor must present the facts of the case to a grand jury; if the jurors agree that the facts warrant formal charges, they will vote a "true bill" authorizing an indictment. In other states there is no grand jury; the prosecutor files an information directly with the court at a preliminary hearing. In addition to this difference in formal accusatory procedure, there are local variations in the responsibilities of the police and of the prosecutor at the several stages between an arrest and the filing of charges. These differences greatly influence the prosecutor's ability to exercise independent judgment in regard to the disposition of a case.

Although the formal description of these two charging processes (illustrated in Figure 8.4) seems to be clear-cut, there are operational variations that mix the roles of the city police, prosecutor, and court. The variations influence the "domain" of the prosecutor, that is, the decisions over which the prosecutor lays claim. In some places the prosecutor really controls the charging decision; in others, the police

accusatory process: The series of events from the arrest of a suspect to the filing of a formal charging instrument (indictment or information) with the court.

informally make the decision, which is then rubber stamped by the prosecutor; and in still others, the prosecutor not only controls the charging process but also is greatly involved in such judicial functions as determining the court calendar, appointing defense counsel for indigents, and sentencing.

The prosecutor's power is enhanced by the capability to screen cases early and to make accusatory decisions with the cooperation (or compliance) of the police. If, however, the police are able to hold cases until just before the filing of the information or the presentation of charges to the grand jury, the prosecutor's opportunity to assert authority is diminished.

In some cities, such as Detroit, the charging decision is made early in the process. The police decide to book a suspect and then bring the case file to the prosecutor's office for review and the institution of charges. These actions are taken within twelve hours after arrest, well before the case is filed in court. At this early point the prosecutor makes the charge that, unless it is dropped at the preliminary hearing, will become the formal charge eventually filed. This arrangement puts the prosecutor in a position to influence the bail recommendation at the defendant's initial appearance. In other juris-

FIGURE 8.4

Two models of the accusatory process. The Indictment Model and Information Model are the two models used in the United States to accuse someone of having committed a crime. Note the role of the grand jury in the Indictment Model and the presence of a preliminary hearing in the Information Model. According to the ideal of due process, each model is designed to ensure that an innocent person is spared psychological, monetary, and other costs of prosecution.

Model 1: Indictment

Model 2: Information

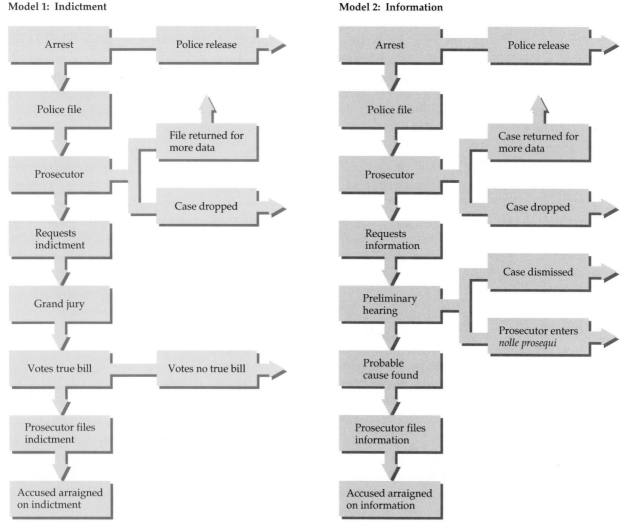

dictions, however, portions of the accusatory process are outside the prosecutor's domain.[10] In New Orleans, for example, the case does not reach the prosecutor's office until after initial charges, made by the police, are filed in court. With "police charges" already formalized, the prosecutor not only has little influence on the bail decision but also has less ability to exercise discretion. In still other jurisdictions (Greenville, South Carolina; Knox County, Tennessee; and Delaware County, Pennsylvania, for example) the prosecutor is unable to review cases until after the preliminary hearing and immediately before the filing of the information or presentation to the grand jury. With this system, the prosecutor has no say in the bail decision and is further circumscribed in making the charging decision.

Crime Construction

The charging process has been described as one in which officials "construct" crimes.[11] The term **crime construction** is used to indicate that the police and prosecutors have the authority to interpret information concerning the accused's behavior, to determine whether a crime has been committed, and to ascertain whether the legal elements necessary to prosecute are present. Naturally, not all "bad acts" are deemed to be crimes, and, among those that do violate the criminal law, many never become crimes because they go undetected, are unreported, or—even though they are detected and reported—are not prosecuted.

> **crime construction**: A process by which the police and prosecutor interpret information concerning the accused's behavior in order to determine whether a crime has been committed and to ascertain whether the legal elements necessary to prosecute are present.

In the early stages of the criminal justice process, the police have extensive discretion to determine whether formal actions will be taken against law violators. Because most crimes occur before the police arrive at the scene, officers must reconstruct the situation on the basis of physical evidence and witness reports. There is considerable ambiguity in most sets of circumstances, so that the police, relying on their training, experience, and work routines, evaluate the crime as to its potential for an arrest and prosecution. If an arrest is made and a formal complaint filed, the prosecutor is then in a position to evaluate the police reports, as well as information from other sources, in order to arrive at the exact charges.

The prosecutor's task is not simple. He or she must keep uppermost in mind that behaviors must conform to the elements of a crime—the ingredients that must be present before a person can be convicted. The law defines robbery, for example, as an act in which there is (1) forcible taking (2) of goods of another person (3) by an individual who (4) employs violence or puts victims in fear as a means to accomplish the theft. These elements also show what must be done to prove a case of robbery. The prosecutor must thus organize the evidence and witnesses so that each element can be proved to the satisfaction of judge and jury. If the prosecutor believes that this cannot be done, lesser included charges may be filed—for example, "assault with intent to rob" or "larceny from the person." The prosecutor's ability to make these decisions, however, depends not only on the evidence but also on the organizational context within which he or she operates.

Intake

In a study of twenty-one urban prosecution offices throughout the United States, Jacoby found two distinct types of intake and charging processes. In the first, the charging function is controlled by the police and the court because the prosecutor does not review cases after they have been filed in court. As a result, prosecutors in such systems can only react to the actions of others and have limited discretion. They may not decide *whether* to charge the suspect but only *at what level* to go forward with the prosecution—felony or misdemeanor. Prosecutors operating under a "transfer" system may only correct, modify, or dismiss police arrest charges; they do not have the power to decline cases for prosecution. Jacoby's survey found that in a small but significant minority of jurisdictions, prosecutors did not exercise discretion at intake, this most crucial gatekeeping function.[12]

In most jurisdictions, cases are screened in the prosecutor's office on the basis of police reports before charges are filed. Here the prosecutor exercises the greatest amount of discretion. Here crimes are "constructed" to determine whether the required legal elements are present and whether such factors as the strength of the evidence and the believability of victims or witnesses will substantiate the police report so that a conviction may be expected.

Elizabeth Stanko observed the intake and screening process in the Early Case Assessment Bureau (ECAB) of a large metropolitan prosecutor's office. Two assistant prosecutors examined forty to eighty felony arrests each day and determined the disposition of each case: drop or charge. To determine whether a case was "solid," prosecutors not only assessed the legal factors of an arrest but also evaluated extralegal factors that might influence the outcome of the case. Of importance is the prosecutor's assessment of the victim's credibility:

> Not only does the credibility of the victim become an essential organizational question—i.e., whether or not someone's story is credible is essential information when one is predicting the probable conviction of the defendant—but a victim's credibility is integrally linked to social stereotyping which predicts what *kinds* of individuals are likely to tell the truth.[13]

Case assessment is more than just a process of matching the police arrest report with the criminal code. As seen in the following Close-Up, it is an attempt by the prosecutor to determine whether the reported crime will appear credible and meet legal criteria in the eyes of judge and jury.

Charging

Determining the exact motivation of prosecutors when they select one charge over another is impossible. They can identify the factors that consciously entered into their choice, but they are seldom able to pinpoint the conversations they had or the words they read that were responsible for injecting these ideas, reinforcing them, and turning them into final decisions. Further, there are elements of the personality and attitudes of each decision maker that are difficult to unravel.

■
It is essential to crime construction and the prosecution of lawbreakers that "what happened" be accurately recorded.

To what extent, for example, are prosecutors influenced by the race, ethnicity, and gender of the accused? A study of 70,000 cases filed in the Los Angeles County District Attorney's Office found that men were more likely than women to be prosecuted and that Hispanics were prosecuted more than African-Americans, who were prosecuted more often than Anglos. The researchers believe that in marginal cases, those that could either be rejected or prosecuted, the scale is often tipped against minorities.[14]

Studies of the decision to prosecute do show a remarkable agreement on the objective elements that are considered. These considerations can be classified as evidential, pragmatic, and organizational. We cannot tell whether one of these categories is more important than

CLOSE-UP *Case Assessment*

Case 1: Robbery in the First Degree

The complainant is a professional man who works for the Better Business Bureau. He entered the Early Case Assessment Bureau with his Sunday *New York Times* tucked under his arm. His recall of the incident was clear, and he presented his story articulately. After the complainant had received instructions to appear before the grand jury the next morning and had then left the room, the Assistant District Attorney (ADA) remarked to the arresting officer (A/O):

ADA: Do you think the defendants know the complainant is a homosexual?
A/O: No.
ADA: Would have been a great alibi. They could claim that they had met and the complainant invited them up for a drink.

Being labeled a homosexual, prosecutors recognize, casts doubt on the victim's credibility; stereotypes about homosexuals, and the kinds of encounters they are alleged to have, can jeopardize the chances of winning the case. Yet in this particular instance, other factors such as the clarity of the victim's recall and his professional status compensated for this vulnerability. The charge was not altered.

Case 2: Robbery in the Second Degree

A young black complainant was accosted by two males. The defendants stopped the complainant and told him they wanted money. One put his hand on the complainant's chest and told him if he didn't produce "they would 'cap' him." The prosecutor asked the complainant what "cap" meant. The complainant replied that he didn't know. All he knew was that he didn't want to be hurt, and he assumed that whatever capping was, he didn't want to find out. He gave them his money (included was one $10 bill torn in half, which was found in the possession of the defendant). One defendant

reached inside the coat of the complainant. Then they left. The prosecutor reduced the charges from robbery in the second degree to grand larceny in the third degree. The prosecutor stated that if the grand jury asked (the complainant) what "cap" meant he couldn't answer and therefore wouldn't be able to prove the threat of force in the robbery charge.

Case 3: Robbery in the First Degree

ADA: How long have you known the defendant?
Complainant: I was a counselor in a drug program—Neighborhood Thing—and I met her there. I've seen her around since then. She was a Muslim and had a boyfriend and I didn't see her much then. But since she split I've seen her around.

ADA then asks the complainant to go out to the waiting room while he draws up the affidavit. The assessment officer says that this is the best complainant he's had in two years, but the ADA disagrees.

ADA: The people in the Supreme Court don't like prior-relationship cases. I think he was going out with her. The jury wouldn't like this. It's just a feel for the case. I don't like it.

This unknown but assumed prior relationship between the victim and the defendant somehow "normalizes" this encounter, relegating it to the range of typical everyday interactions that might occur between the victim and the defendant. The victim, in order to be seen as a "real" victim, must at least convince the prosecutor of the irregular character of the event.

SOURCE: From "The Impact of Victim Assessment on Prosecutors' Screening Decisions: The Case of the New York County District Attorney's Office," by E. A. Stanko, *Law and Society Review* 16 (1981–1982):225–238. Reprinted by permission of The Law and Society Association.

another, but we can note that at the initial stage, when a decision to file is made, the type and amount of evidence reflected in the police report appear to be dominant factors. As a former deputy prosecutor told this author, "If you have the evidence, you file, then bring the other considerations in during the bargaining phase."

Evidential Considerations

Is there a case? Does the evidence warrant the arrest of an individual and the expense of a trial? These are major questions that prosecutors ask when they think about whether to prosecute. Legally, a prosecution cannot hope to be successful without some proof that the required elements of a criminal act are present in the case, that the suspect has committed it, and that he or she formulated some intent to commit the act. Aside from the precise legal definition of the crime, prosecutors must decide whether the act is viewed as criminal within the local political context. Many offenses committed under borderline circumstances do not result in prosecution.

The nature of the crime may require the presentation of evidence that can prove such a vague charge as neglect. Prosecutors must be certain that the evidence will coincide with the court's interpretation of the term. In addition, evidence must be introduced that will connect the defendant with the criminal act: a confession, statements of witnesses, or physical evidence. All these requirements must be met within the context of the rules of evidence and guarantees of due process. For some types of offenses, such as corporate crime, the investigative and legal resources necessary for a successful prosecution are extensive and just not a part of the average district attorney's office.[15]

The nature of the complaint, the strength of the testimony of witnesses, and the attitude of the victim must also be evaluated. Thought has to be given to whose interests are being served by prosecution. Often when complaints are based on marital or neighborhood quarrels or quasi-civil offenses (for example, debt claims), the prosecutor must ensure that a violation of the criminal law has occurred and that the victim is not using the law for his or her own purposes. Evidence is weak when it is difficult to use in proving charges, when the value of a stolen article is questionable, when a case results from a brawl or other order maintenance situation, or when corroboration (supporting testimony) is lacking. As noted in Figure 8.5, problems with the evidence and witnesses were the main reasons for rejecting cases in most of the prosecution offices studied.

Pragmatic Considerations

The prosecutor is able to individualize justice in ways that can benefit both the accused and society. Especially when the offense arises from mental illness, prosecutors may feel that psychiatric treatment is more desirable than imprisonment. Diversion of the accused from the criminal justice system to a treatment facility may be a more realistic disposition of the case. Concern for the welfare of the victim may also be a reason for deciding against prosecution. In cases involving the sexual molestation of a child, prosecution may not be sought if

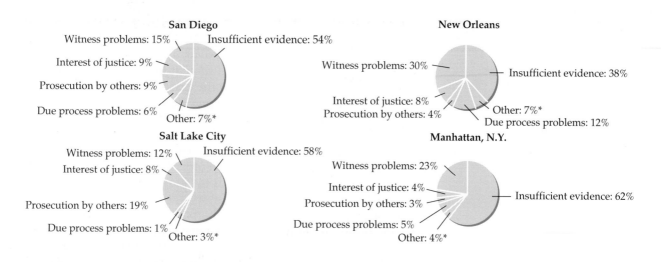

San Diego

Witness problems: 15%
Interest of justice: 9%
Prosecution by others: 9%
Due process problems: 6%
Insufficient evidence: 54%
Other: 7%*

New Orleans

Witness problems: 30%
Interest of justice: 8%
Prosecution by others: 4%
Insufficient evidence: 38%
Other: 7%*
Due process problems: 12%

Salt Lake City

Witness problems: 12%
Interest of justice: 8%
Prosecution by others: 19%
Due process problems: 1%
Insufficient evidence: 58%
Other: 3%*

Manhattan, N.Y.

Witness problems: 23%
Interest of justice: 4%
Prosecution by others: 3%
Due process problems: 5%
Insufficient evidence: 62%
Other: 4%*

conviction hinges on the victim's testimony, because the requirement of reciting the facts in court may be considered too great a psychological burden to place on the child.

The character of accused persons, their status in the community, and the impact of prosecution on their families may likewise influence the charges filed. Prosecutors may not invoke the full weight of the law when they believe that to do so would unduly punish the offender. Where the law is not flexible (mandatory sentences, for example), the prosecutor may believe that the gravity of the crime does not warrant such severe treatment. The rehabilitative potential, the seriousness of the offense, and the benefits to be gained by keeping a suspect's record clean weigh heavily in the decision to prosecute.

Organizational Considerations

The exchange relationships among units of the criminal justice system, court congestion, community pressures, and the demands placed on the system's resources all affect the decision to prosecute. The prosecuting attorney is the one criminal justice actor who has significant interactions with every other major actor. Thus the personal relationships of the participants are more influential in decision making than the written report of an incident.

The expected public reaction is a factor in most decisions. Especially if the crime is of a heinous nature, such as child rape, if publicity has aroused the electorate, and if the victim is well known, the prosecutor's discretion may be limited. In one instance, a prosecutor abandoned the practice of charging escapees from the county jail with misdemeanors and brought in felony charges instead after the newspapers publicized a rash of jailbreaks.

The expenditure of organizational resources may be another reason for withholding prosecution. If the matter is trivial or if the accused must be extradited from another state, the costs may be too high to warrant action. If the accused is on parole or has a prior deferred or suspended sentence, a prosecutor may feel that the best decision is merely to go before a judge and seek revocation of the parole.

FIGURE 8.5

Reasons for declining to prosecute felony cases in four cities. Insufficient evidence was the reason most often given for declining prosecution in the cases studied in these four cities, but note that the proportions vary. To what extent are these differences attributed to such factors as prosecution policies and system pressures?
*Includes plea to include another case and diversion.
NOTE: Percentages may not add up to 100% due to rounding.
SOURCE: Adapted from U.S. Department of Justice, Bureau of Justice Statistics, *Report to the Nation on Crime and Justice,* 2nd ed. (Washington, DC: Government Printing Office, 1988), p. 73.

Organizational influences on the decision to prosecute are many. Certainly the exchange relationships between the police and the prosecutor, congestion within the system, and community pressures are considered at this juncture. Prosecutors must decide which charge is appropriate to the facts of the case, the needs of the defendant, and the needs of society. They may decide to throw the book at the defendant, only to have it boomerang when they are unable to prove the case in court. They may charge the defendant with serious or multiple offenses to increase their latitude in plea bargaining. These options are available to prosecutors from the time the police originally file a case with them until the judge pronounces sentence, as Figure 8.6 indicates.

Prosecutors, the link between the police and the courts, hold a strategic position, because all cases must pass through their office. Accordingly, they are able to regulate not only the flow of cases but also the conditions under which the cases will be processed. Given the caseload that burdens the contemporary legal system and the scarcity of resources to deal with it, officials are hard pressed to dispense justice efficiently.

DIVERSION: ALTERNATIVES TO PROSECUTION

When prosecuting attorneys believe that the ideals of justice can be better served if they do not seek formal adjudication, they may seek alternatives that divert the offender from the criminal justice system. **Diversion** refers to formally acknowledged efforts to use alternatives to the formal processes of the justice system. Diversion by prosecutors usually takes place after a complaint has been made but before adjudication. It implies the halting or suspending of formal proceedings against a person who has violated the law in favor of a noncriminal disposition to the case.

diversion: An alternative to adjudication by which the defendant agrees to conditions set by the prosecutor (such as to undergo counseling or drug rehabilitation) in exchange for withdrawal of charges.

Although diversion from the criminal justice system is a traditional American custom—"Get out of town" or "Join the Army"—it has become formalized only during the past few decades. Cases may be dropped at the prosecutor's discretion at any time up to the moment the verdict is pronounced. As we have seen, the police often warn persons that they face arrest if they continue a particular behavior, they "handle" family crises without formal action, and they take individuals directly to treatment facilities. The extent of the diversionary activities of the police is unknown, because they are never recorded, but it is believed to be substantial. We have more knowledge about programs developed to divert accused individuals from the criminal justice system during the accusatory process, when the prosecutor is dominant.

Uses and Terms of Diversion

In most systems, such efforts are directed at diverting certain types of offenders to treatment programs for drug or alcohol abusers, to

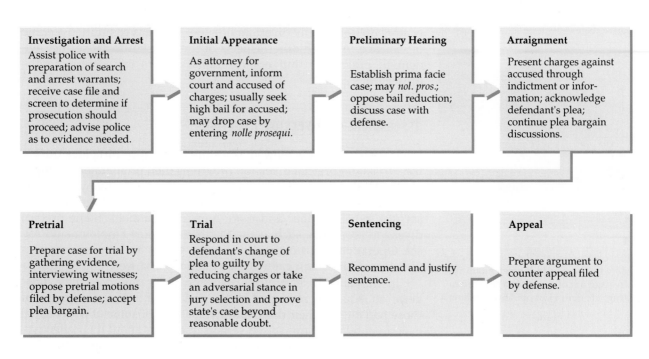

Investigation and Arrest	Initial Appearance	Preliminary Hearing	Arraignment
Assist police with preparation of search and arrest warrants; receive case file and screen to determine if prosecution should proceed; advise police as to evidence needed.	As attorney for government, inform court and accused of charges; usually seek high bail for accused; may drop case by entering *nolle prosequi*.	Establish prima facie case; may *nol. pros.*; oppose bail reduction; discuss case with defense.	Present charges against accused through indictment or information; acknowledge defendant's plea; continue plea bargain discussions.

Pretrial	Trial	Sentencing	Appeal
Prepare case for trial by gathering evidence, interviewing witnesses; oppose pretrial motions filed by defense; accept plea bargain.	Respond in court to defendant's change of plea to guilty by reducing charges or take an adversarial stance in jury selection and prove state's case beyond reasonable doubt.	Recommend and justify sentence.	Prepare argument to counter appeal filed by defense.

mental hospitals, or into voluntary public service or at persuading them to make restitution to their victims. Pretrial diversion consists of informal administrative efforts to provide alternatives to adjudication by which accused persons may receive help—medical, psychological, or social—to deal with the problems thought to be at the root of their criminal behavior. Pretrial diversion is also justified as a way to avoid the damage caused by labeling an individual as a criminal. The case of a first-time offender accused of committing a minor infraction may be informally disposed of. In some states the case is screened out of the system by the prosecutor with only minimal restrictions, or none at all; or the prosecutor may place a charge "on hold" for a specified time (say, a year), at the end of which it is dropped if the individual has not been rearrested. In other states such informal dispositions are made in court at the recommendation of the prosecutor, and so-called accelerated rehabilitation is granted. As in the case of other informal practices, the fact of the arrest, prosecution, and disposition is expunged from the record at the expiration of an arrest-free period.

Pretrial diversion may be either unconditional, in that there is no follow-up, or conditional, in that the person is monitored to ensure that the required activity has been carried out. If it has been, the defendant's case is dismissed and a criminal record avoided. Should the required activity not take place, prosecution may be reinstituted.

Several factors are considered to determine whether diversion is appropriate: the age of the offender; the willingness of the victim not to press for conviction; the likelihood that the offender has physical or psychological difficulties that are at the root of the criminal behavior and for which treatment is available; and the likelihood that the crime was related to a condition, such as unemployment or a family problem, that can be changed through rehabilitative measures. In addition, diversion is generally used only for certain types of crimes, usually those classified as misdemeanors or property felonies. Pros-

FIGURE 8.6

Typical actions of a prosecuting attorney in processing a felony case. The prosecutor has certain responsibilities at various points in the criminal process. At each point the prosecutor is an advocate for the state's case against the accused.

Prosecutors believe that justice can be more fully realized if a defendant is diverted out of the system to receive drug, alcohol, or psychiatric treatment.

ecutors do not usually divert an offender who has committed a crime of violence. As with other aspects of the decision to prosecute, evidential, pragmatic, and organizational factors can determine the prosecutor's action.

Assessment of Diversion Programs

Pretrial diversion was viewed as a simple and appealing idea during the 1970s, and pretrial diversion programs then proliferated throughout the United States. The concept was applauded by many people as offering the promise of the best of all worlds; it would result in cost savings, rehabilitation, and more humane treatment. Some pretrial diversion programs, such as the Manhattan Court Employment Project, Operation Crossroads (Washington, D.C.), and Project Intercept (San Jose, California), gained wide publicity and were emulated.

Just as quickly as pretrial diversion programs rose, their gloss began to fade. Few remained by the end of the decade, and many of those had altered their direction. Evaluations of some of the original experimental programs raised serious questions about their effectiveness. Researchers discovered that many accused persons refused to participate in pretrial diversion programs. Either because of their past experience or on the advice of counsel, they preferred to try to "beat" the formal adjudicatory process rather than accept the probationlike conditions of diversion. Almost 50 percent of the Manhattan project's eligible defendants in 1974 through 1975 chose this path. In addition, evaluators alleged that the programs were doing little to reduce prosecutorial and judicial caseloads because pretrial diversion had the effect of merely "widening the net": with some accused persons diverted, prosecutors could spend more time on cases that they would previously have dropped as minor and not worth the expenditure of resources. Other studies challenged the reported success of some pretrial programs in reducing recidivism. An overriding theme of the evaluations is that even in the absence of diversion programs, the same individuals would have been treated leniently by the prosecutor.

Why has diversion had so little success? Malcolm Feeley believes that the developers of the programs erroneously assumed that the major actors in the criminal justice system would respond positively to the goals of the programs.

> Defendants were supposed to welcome diversion as a benign alternative to an alienating courtroom. Prosecutors were expected to divert less serious cases so they could spend more time on more serious cases. Judges were expected to divert people because diversion led to rehabilitation.[16]

It appears that diversion became for many officials a further device to achieve their goals. Feeley charges that defendants learned that they could wait out the system, prosecutors used diversion as a weapon to wield against defense attorneys, and judges resented the intrusion of "outside" diversion agencies into their domain.

Most federal funding of diversion programs has ended, and few have been able to discover steady and secure alternative sources of revenue. The remaining programs seem to have changed their focus, taking on goals not directly linked to criminal justice and diversion. This is not to say that prosecutors do not use their discretion to divert offenders out of the system; they do. In fact, the long-range impact of the diversion programs may have been to legitimize alternative courses of action. In addition, pretrial diversion may have helped the police to understand that it is legitimate to find alternative means to deal with some types of deviants.

POLITICS AND PROSECUTORS

The powers that accrue to prosecutors from their legal duties may be further developed through political partisanship. Prosecutors are often able to mesh their own ambitions with the needs of a political party. The appointment of deputies to the prosecutor's office, for example, may serve the party's desire for new blood and the prosecutor's need for young lawyers. Also prosecutors may press charges in ways that enhance their own and the party's objectives. Cases may be processed so that only the few that are certain to be successful come to trial and hence help maintain the prosecutor's conviction record. Investigations may be initiated before elections to embarrass the opposition. Charges may be pressed against public officials for political gain. It is significant that certain groups and persons may receive less-than-impartial justice because of the prosecutor's determinations.

The political potential of the district attorney's office may not be realized in communities whose culture demands nonpartisanship in the system. A study of a New Orleans prosecutor's office under a reform administration and then of a prosecutor tied to a political machine found only insignificant differences in the way most cases were handled, suggesting that disposition of most cases is unaffected by direct political pressures. Indirectly, however, the part played in prosecution by political pressure may be important in that the prosecutor's office displays an intimate awareness of the problems and concerns of society that translates into a greater effectiveness in the courtroom, where testimony often needs interpretation and a grasp of different social contexts and meanings. Being attuned to the people and the community also contributes to a better use of discretion. Knowledge of the community is built into a political office, where assistant prosecutors are expected to keep their fingers on the pulse of the local attitudes and needs.

The office of prosecuting attorney has long been viewed as a stepping-stone to higher office. Because they deal with dramatic materials, prosecutors can use the communications media to create favorable public opinion. Their discretionary powers can be exercised so that voters will be impressed by their abilities. Many prosecutors have attained prominence in other political arenas, such as on the judicial bench and in the governor's mansion. Each session of Congress includes numerous senators and representatives who have been prosecutors.

Although successful prosecutor-politicians are numerous in some areas of the country, the record of upward mobility from the prosecuting attorney's office is unimpressive. However, many lawyers use a term or more in the office as a means of gaining public exposure before shifting to private law practice. Others develop contacts that can be used to secure nomination to judicial office. Further, with the recent emphasis on improving the salaries and tenure of criminal justice personnel, more lawyers may decide to embark on long-term careers in prosecution.

SUMMARY

With justification, the prosecuting attorney is called the central actor in the criminal justice system. Prosecutors not only are responsible for the decision to bring charges against defendants but also, in the vast majority of cases, participate in negotiations concerning the outcome. Thus the extent of prosecuting attorneys' influence is obvious, but the fact remains that throughout the United States little public attention is given to their role. Even when the office is elective, the amount of interest generated by the political campaign for it is usually low. In many ways the prosecutor's decisions have a potentially greater impact than those of the mayor or city council. The level of law enforcement and therefore a vital aspect of the quality of life is directly related to the actions of the prosecutor.

The office of prosecuting attorney typifies decentralization in the justice system; there are few structural checks on the powers of prosecutors, and the confidentiality of their decisions lessens the visibility of their actions. Because the decision to prosecute is the focus of their work, prosecutors are able to exercise discretion at various points in the justice process. The decision to file charges is made at the initial phase, but the charges may be altered, reduced, or dropped at a number of points for reasons pertaining to evidence, for pragmatic considerations, or in the interests of the organizational needs of the system.

FOR DISCUSSION

1. You are the prosecutor. How may factors such as an overcrowded jail, a backlog of cases, and a shortage of staff influence your decisions? Does justice consist of the decisions you make because of these factors?
2. Which policy would you follow if you were prosecutor of your county: legal sufficiency, trial sufficiency, or system efficiency? Why?
3. How can the prosecutor's decisions be made more visible? What effect would increased visibility have on the system?
4. You are the prosecutor. The director of a local business group asks you to spearhead a drive to move "undesirables" away from the sidewalks in front of the downtown stores. Should you grant the request? What should be considered?
5. You are the prosecutor. The daughter of a local minister has been caught using drugs. The minister promises that the girl will undergo therapy at a private hospital if the case is dropped. What will you do?

FOR FURTHER READING

Heilbroner, David. *Rough Justice: Days and Nights of a Young D.A.* New York: Pantheon, 1990. The experience of an assistant district attorney learning the ropes in New York's criminal courts.

Jacoby, Joan E. *The American Prosecutor: A Search for Identity.* Lexington, MA: Lexington Books, 1979. A history and survey of American prosecutors, their work and role conflicts.

McDonald, William F., ed. *The Prosecutor.* Newbury Park, CA: Sage, 1979. A collection of articles written by scholars about various aspects of prosecution.

Miller, Frank W. *Prosecution: The Decision to Charge a Suspect with a Crime.* Boston: Little, Brown, 1969. An early study of the legal ramifications of the prosecutor's discretionary powers.

Moley, Raymond. *Politics and Criminal Prosecution.* New York: Minton, Balch, 1929. A classic examination of prosecutors and their links to politics.

Naifeh, Steven, and Gregory Smith White. *The Mormon Murders.* New York: New American Library, 1989. Prosecution for murder in the context of a scandal within the Mormon Church and its political ramifications.

Rowland, Judith. *The Ultimate Violation.* New York: Doubleday, 1985. A former San Diego district attorney describes her pioneering legal strategy to prosecute rapists.

Turow, Scott. *Presumed Innocent.* New York: Farrar, Straus & Giroux, 1987. Fictional account of the indictment and trial of an urban prosecutor for the murder of a colleague. Excellent description of an urban court system.

NOTES

1. See *New York TImes,* January 24, 1990, p. 1, for a concise summary of the case and the issues surrounding it.

2. Alexander B. Smith and Harriet Pollack, *Crimes and Justice in a Mass Society* (New York: Xerox, 1972), p. 165.

3. U.S. Department of Justice, *Principles of Federal Prosecution* (Washington, DC: Government Printing Office, 1980), p. 7.

4. John Buchanan, "Police-Prosecutor Teams: Innovations in Several Jurisdictions," *NIJ Reports* (May/June 1989):2.

5. Barbara Boland, Elizabeth Brady, Herbert Tyson, and John Bassler, *The Prosecution of Felony Arrests,* U.S. Department of Justice, Bureau of Justice Statistics (Washington, DC: Government Printing Office, 1983), p. 9.

6. Vera Institute of Justice, *Felony Arrests: Their Prosecution and Disposition in New York City's Courts* (New York: Longman, 1977), p. 135.

7. Vera Institute of Justice, *Felony Arrests,* rev. ed. (New York: Longman, 1981), pp. 68, 86.

8. Joan E. Jacoby, "The Charging Policies of Prosecutors," in *The Prosecutor,* ed. William F. McDonald (Newbury Park, CA: Sage, 1979), p. 75.

9. Frank W. Miller, *Prosecution: The Decision to Charge a Suspect with a Crime.* (Boston: Little, Brown, 1969), p. 11.

10. William F. McDonald, "The Prosecutor's Domain," in *The Prosecutor,* p. 16.

11. W. Boyd Littrell, *Bureaucratic Justice* (Newbury Park, CA: Sage, 1979), p. 29.

12. Joan E. Jacoby, "The Effects of Intake Policy and Procedures on the Prosecutor's Charging Decision," paper presented at the annual meeting of the Law and Society Association, Madison, WI, June 5–7, 1980.

13. Elizabeth A. Stanko, "The Impact of Victim Assessment on Prosecutors' Screening Decisions: The Case of the New York County District Attorney's Office," in *Criminal Justice: Law and Politics,* 5th ed., ed. George F. Cole (Pacific Grove, CA: Brooks/Cole, 1988), p. 169.

14. Cassia Spohn, John Gruhl, and Susan Welch, "The Impact of the Ethnicity and Gender of Defendants on the Decision to Reject or Dismiss Felony Charges," *Criminology* 25 (February 1987):175.

15. Michael L. Benson, William J. Maakestad, Francis T. Cullen, and Gilbert Geis, "District Attorneys and Corporate Crime: Surveying the Prosecutorial Gatekeepers," *Criminology* 26 (August 1988):505.

16. Malcolm M. Feeley, *Court Reform on Trial* (New York: Basic Books, 1983), p. 103.

9 CHAPTER

Defense Attorney

Key Terms

assigned counsel
defense attorney
public defender

The case of Clarence Gideon, the "persistent defendant," resulted in the provision of defense counsel for those who could not pay for it.

Standing before Judge Robert L. McCrary, Jr., in the Circuit Court of Bay County, Florida, was Clarence Earl Gideon, drifter and former convict, now charged with breaking and entering with intent to commit a felony under Florida law. His case may sound like any of the thousands of felony and misdemeanor cases that are heard daily in America's courtrooms, yet on that summer day in 1961, Clarence Gideon made a request that eventually produced a path-breaking opinion from the U.S. Supreme Court. As the trial transcript shows, Gideon misunderstood the law, a misunderstanding that was to make history. "The United States Supreme Court," he proclaimed, "says I am entitled to be represented by Counsel."[1] It has not said so, but it shortly would remedy that oversight.

The 1963 opinion by the Supreme Court in *Gideon* v. *Wainwright* began a movement that extended the right of counsel not only to persons accused of felonies but also, with the case of *Argersinger* v. *Hamlin* (1972), to any defendant charged with commission of a crime punishable by a prison sentence. The importance of legal counsel was underscored by Justice Hugo Black when he wrote for the majority in *Gideon*:

> The right of one charged with crime to counsel may not be deemed fundamental and essential to fair trials in some countries, but it is in ours. From the very beginning, our state and national constitutions and laws have laid great emphasis on procedural and substantive safeguards designed to assure fair trials before impartial tribunals in which every defendant stands equal before the law. This noble ideal cannot be realized if the poor man charged with crime has to face his accusers without a lawyer to assist him.[2]

This chapter examines the world of criminal lawyers. It will be shown that the structure of the American bar influences the type of person who enters criminal practice. Since defense attorneys, both privately retained and publicly paid, are encouraged to handle many cases in an impersonal, bureaucratic manner, the adversarial norm of a vigorous defense is often lacking. Attorneys seek to move cases as quickly as possible by persuading clients to plea bargain in order not to upset the ongoing routine of the courthouse.

THE DEFENSE ATTORNEY: IMAGE AND REALITY

defense attorney: The lawyer who represents the accused and the convicted offender in their dealings with criminal justice officials.

Most Americans have seen a **defense attorney** in action on television. The much-rerun "Perry Mason" and more contemporary "L.A. Law" programs have shown the investigative, challenging, probing defense attorneys at their best. Through television, motion pictures, and literature, images of the great defense attorney—Clarence Darrow,

The image of the fighting, probing defense attorney was epitomized by actor Raul Julia in the film *Presumed Innocent*. The accused, prosecuting attorney Rusty Sabich (played by Harrison Ford) was tried for the murder of a female colleague.

CLOSE-UP   *The Persistent Defendant:* Gideon v. Wainwright, 372 U.S. 335 (1963)

Clarence Earl Gideon, fifty-one years old, petty thief, drifter, and gambler, had spent most of his adult life in jails serving time for burglary and larceny. On June 4, 1961, he was arrested in Panama City, Florida, for breaking into a poolroom to steal coins from a cigarette machine, plus beer, and soft drinks. After arraignment on July 31 for "unlawfully and feloniously" breaking and entering with intent to commit a misdemeanor—petty larceny—Gideon was held for trial in what appeared to be a routine case.

Standing before Judge Robert L. McCrary on August 4, Gideon surprised the court by requesting that counsel be appointed to assist with his defense.

The Court: What says the Defendant? Are you ready to go to trial?

The Defendant: I am not ready, Your Honor.

The Court: Why aren't you ready?

The Defendant: I have no Counsel.

The Court: Why do you not have Counsel? Did you know that your case was set for trial today?

The Defendant: Yes, sir, I knew that it was set for trial today.

The Court: Why, then, did you not secure Counsel and be prepared to go to trial?

The Defendant: Your Honor, . . . I request this Court to appoint Counsel to represent me in this trial.

The Court: Mr. Gideon, I am sorry, but I cannot appoint . . . Counsel to represent you in this case. Under the laws of the State of Florida, the only time the Court can appoint Counsel to represent a Defendant is when that person is charged with a capital offense. I am sorry, but I will have to deny your request to appoint Counsel to defend you in this case.

The Defendant: The United States Supreme Court says I am entitled to be represented by Counsel.

Acting as his own counsel, Gideon was unable to interrogate witnesses and present his defense in the way required by the law. The jury found him guilty, and on August 25 he was sentenced to five years in the Florida State Prison.

From his prison cell Gideon prepared a handwritten petition of appeal to the Florida Supreme Court. On October 30 it was denied without hearing. Despite the setback, Gideon persisted and filed a petition for review with the U.S. Supreme Court. On June 4, 1962, the Court granted the petition and appointed Abe Fortas, later to become a Supreme Court justice, to represent Gideon.

Fortas argued that an accused person cannot effectively defend himself and thus cannot receive due process and a fair trial. Without counsel, the accused cannot evaluate the lawfulness of his arrest, the validity of the indictment, whether preliminary motions should be filed, whether a proper search was carried out, whether the confession is admissible as evidence, and so on. Fortas noted that the indigent defendant is almost always in jail and cannot prepare his defense and that the trial judge cannot adequately perform the function of counsel. As he said, "To convict the poor without counsel while we guarantee the right to counsel to those who can afford it is also a denial of equal protection of the laws."

DECISION

On March 18, 1963, a unanimous Supreme Court said that Gideon was entitled to counsel and that the Sixth Amendment obligated the states to provide counsel to indigent defendants. Speaking for the Court, Justice Hugo Black said:

> In our adversary system of criminal justice, any person hauled into court, who is too poor to hire a lawyer, cannot be assured a fair trial unless counsel is provided for him. This seems to us to be an obvious truth.

Richard "Racehorse" Haynes, F. Lee Bailey, Melvin Belli, Gerry Spence—have become familiar.

Counsel is essential for the defense of a person accused of a crime. Criminal lawyers are advocates; that is, they are understood to support the defendant by their investigative ability before trial, by their verbal skills in the courtroom, by their knowledge of the law, and by their ability to knit these talents together in a constant creative questioning of decisions at every stage of the judicial process. As an adversary, the aggressive defense attorney insists that the government prove its case according to law. The stakes are high not only because the defendant's freedom is at stake but also because the essence of the adversary system assumes that well-qualified and active counsel keeps the system honest. Pressure from defense attorneys keep the other actors on their toes so that they do not relax into the lethargy often associated with bureaucracy.

Role of the Defense Attorney

Defense attorneys represent their clients and are generally assumed to be responsible for both the strategy and tactics of the defense. Thus the defense attorney must explain to the client the legal consequences of the facts of the case and devise tactics for the defense. The client-counselor relationship is crucial; the qualities of respect, openness, and trust between the two are indispensable. If the defendant refuses to follow the attorney's advice, the lawyer may feel obligated to withdraw from the case in order to protect his or her own reputation.

What specific functions does the defense attorney perform as an advocate or representative of the accused? Figure 9.1 describes the actions of counsel in a typical felony case. In addition to these formal activities, the defense attorney also provides psychological support to the defendant and the defendant's family. The figure deals with a

BIOGRAPHY

Clarence Seward Darrow

Born in Kinsman, Ohio, Clarence Darrow studied law for one year at the University of Michigan Law School. He was admitted to the Ohio bar in 1878 and, after practicing law in Ohio for nine years, moved to Chicago and embarked on a career that would make him one of the most famous defense attorneys in the United States.

Darrow devoted much of his career to political and labor cases. Shortly after moving to Chicago, he associated himself with those who were seeking amnesty for the Haymarket Square defendants, a group indicted in connection with a bomb thrown into the ranks of police attempting to control a labor demonstration. Because of his political beliefs, Darrow resigned his position as corporate counsel for the Chicago and Western Railway during the Pullman strike in 1894. He de-

fended socialist Eugene V. Debs against a charge of contempt of court in connection with that strike, as well as other radical political leads, such as "Big Bill" Hayward.

Darrow's two most famous cases occurred within a year of each other. In 1924 he became defense counsel in the famous trial of Richard Leopold and Nathan Loeb for the "thrill" murder of Bobby Franks. By basing his defense on a plea of temporary insanity and emphasizing the two defendants' abnormal conduct and personality development, Darrow was able to save them from the death penalty. In 1925 Darrow became defense attorney in the famous Scopes "monkey trial" in Tennessee. Here he found himself pitted against William Jennings Bryan, a longtime adversary, and though Darrow lost the case, his defense refuted the fundamentalist assertions that were at the basis of Bryan's anti-evolution argument.

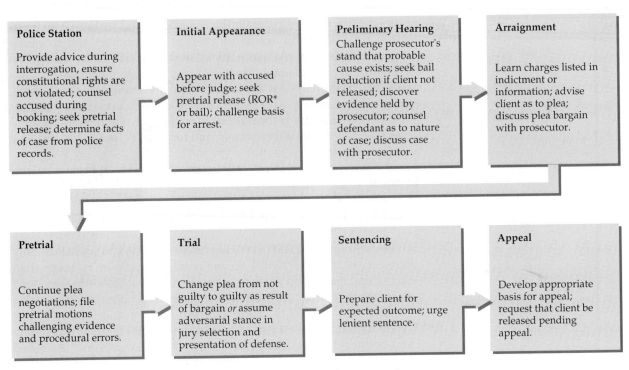

Police Station	Initial Appearance	Preliminary Hearing	Arraignment
Provide advice during interrogation, ensure constitutional rights are not violated; counsel accused during booking; seek pretrial release; determine facts of case from police records.	Appear with accused before judge; seek pretrial release (ROR* or bail); challenge basis for arrest.	Challenge prosecutor's stand that probable cause exists; seek bail reduction if client not released; discover evidence held by prosecutor; counsel defendant as to nature of case; discuss case with prosecutor.	Learn charges listed in indictment or information; advise client as to plea; discuss plea bargain with prosecutor.

Pretrial	Trial	Sentencing	Appeal
Continue plea negotiations; file pretrial motions challenging evidence and procedural errors.	Change plea from not guilty to guilty as result of bargain *or* assume adversarial stance in jury selection and presentation of defense.	Prepare client for expected outcome; urge lenient sentence.	Develop appropriate basis for appeal; request that client be released pending appeal.

case that may proceed to trial. It is important to realize, however, that counsel would normally begin discussion of a plea bargain soon after the facts were known and would continue negotiations until an acceptable agreement had been reached. Even after the trial has begun, a plea of not guilty may be changed to guilty as a result of bargaining.

FIGURE 9.1

Typical actions of a defense attorney processing a felony case. The defense attorney is an advocate for the accused and as such has an obligation to challenge within the law points made by the prosecution and to advise clients as to their rights.
*Release on recognizance.

The Realities of the Defense Attorney

The opinions of the Supreme Court and the values of the Due Process Model are based on a conception of the defense attorney as a combative element in an adversarial proceeding. How closely does this conception square with reality? The adversary system will be realized only if the exchange process and organizational setting enhance the role of the criminal lawyer. Merely to require the provision of counsel may not help if the attorney provided is ill educated and poorly paid and if the principles that structure the role of the defense attorney have been compromised by the values of the system. Rather than acting as the adversary, challenging the decisions made at each step in the process, defense counsel may, in fact, play the role of mediator for the defendant, prosecutor, and judge. A defendant with an attorney who is attuned to the administrative system may interfere less with its smooth operation than a defendant who has no counsel and whose notion of criminal justice has been formed by "Perry Mason." The latter defendant may be unwilling to cooperate because he does not know the ropes. The defense attorney may help the prosecutor and judge pull the loose ends together so that a bargain can be worked out. In whose interest the bargain is made remains an open question.

Traditionally, defense attorneys have been caught between divergent concepts of their position. According to the Perry Mason image, they owe their client a full defense at every stage of the criminal process. Too often, however, the general public feels that defense lawyers are somehow soiled by their clients and are not so much engaged in freeing the innocent as in letting the guilty escape by exploiting technical loopholes in the law. Because most defense lawyers are continually on the losing side, they must also suffer the discontent of clients who feel that they did not work hard enough. The public defender is the special focus of such complaints. In some prisons, P.D. is an abbreviation not for "public defender" but for "prison deliverer."

PRIVATE COUNSEL: AN ENDANGERED SPECIES?

Of an estimated 650,000 practicing lawyers in the United States, only between 10,000 and 20,000 accept criminal cases on a "more than occasional" basis, and of these only an additional 5,000 are employed as public defenders. In the only contemporary national study of the criminal bar, Paul Wice found that the number and quality of privately retained lawyers varied among cities, with legal, institutional, and political factors accounting for much of the variance.[3] As noted in Table 9.2, only in the rural counties studied did privately retained counsel serve more than 30 percent of felony defendants.

Recognizing the small portion of lawyers engaged in criminal practice, we might ask, Who does take criminal cases? What are the qualifications of the practitioners? Social scientists interested in this matter say that the average criminal lawyer is a solo practitioner, not a member of the law firm; comes from a middle-class, nonprofessional background; graduated from a lesser law school; and entered private criminal practice after some experience as a public lawyer. Only an estimated 4 percent are women. Wice found that 38 percent of his sample of private criminal lawyers had been prosecutors, and 24 percent had been public defenders, had worked for legal services (civil law work), or had held civil service positions.[4]

The Private Criminal Bar

When we survey the defense attorney scene it appears that three general groups of lawyers take criminal cases on a regular basis, and these might be called specialists in their field. The first group is composed of nationally known attorneys—for example, Belli, Bailey, and Spence—who have built their reputations by adhering to the Perry Mason pattern. But there are few of them, they are expensive, and they usually take only the dramatic, widely publicized cases; they do not frequent the county courthouse. A second group of lawyers practices in major metropolitan areas and is retained by professional criminals, such as drug dealers, gamblers, pornographers, and those in organized crime. In some cities—Miami, for one, with its large drug problem—lawyers who fit this category make a profitable living. But this group is fairly small because of its relatively limited clientele.

The largest group of attorneys in criminal practice consists of lawyers who accept many cases for small fees and who daily participate in the criminal justice system either as retained or assigned counsel. Surrounding most courthouses in large cities are the offices of attorneys like those called the Fifth Streeters in the District of Columbia, the Tulane Avenue bunch in New Orleans, and the Bryant Streeters in San Francisco. They routinely prowl the urban criminal courts searching for clients who can pay a modest fee or hoping to be assigned by a judge to an indigent's case.

Rather than preparing their cases for disposition through the adversary process, these attorneys negotiate guilty pleas and try to convince their clients that they have received exceptional treatment. Such lawyers are valued for their negotiating rather than their adversarial skills. They operate in a relatively closed system in which there are great pressures to process a great many cases for small fees, and they depend on the cooperation of judicial actors. These practitioners usually are less well educated, must work harder, and are financially less secure than lawyers who take the cases of business corporations.

In addition to these specialists in criminal practice are many private practitioners who are willing on occasion to take criminal cases. Often they are members of or connected with a law firm whose upper-class clients have run afoul of the law. Although this group of attorneys is fairly substantial, its members have little experience in trial work and do not have well-developed relationships with the actors in the criminal justice system. As they lack inside know-how, their clients might be better served by a courthouse regular.

Thus far we have been describing the practice of the private criminal bar in big cities. In middle-sized and small cities studies have shown that a greater portion of attorneys take defense work than one would find in large metropolitan centers, but even in "middle America" criminal law is not important either in terms of time spent or as a principal source of income.[5]

Environment of Criminal Practice

Various aspects of criminal lawyers' practice help explain the difficulties of their work. Criminal cases, as well as those concerned with matrimonial problems, tend to involve attorneys in emotional situations. Much of the service that the defense counsel renders involves preparing clients and their relatives for possible negative outcomes of their cases. Thus the client's troubles are an emotional drain. Even the lawyer's exposure to "guilty knowledge" may be a psychological burden. Lawyers have explained that they may easily become emotionally entangled because they are the only judicial actors to view the defendant in the context of social environment and family ties. Sympathy for the client is psychologically too heavy a burden for many attorneys.

Criminal lawyers must also interact continually with a lower class of clients and with police officials, social workers, and minor political appointees. They may be required to visit such depressing places as the local jail at all hours of the day and night, and after winning a case, they may find themselves unable to collect the fee. Even an appearance in court may be viewed as a disadvantage. As Thomas M.

O'Malley, an attorney in Washington, D.C., has said: "It is . . . more comforting to work in the friendly atmosphere of one's office than in an unfriendly court where otherwise discerning people sometimes miss the subtle distinctions between the criminal and the defense attorney."[6] The work setting of most criminal lawyers is thus a far cry from the mahogany paneling, plush carpets, and stimulating conversation of the "inner-circle" law firm.

The fact that criminal practice does not pay well is probably the key variable of the defense attorney's environment and one that influences other aspects of criminal practice. For the most part, criminal defendants are poor, and losing the case is likely to reduce their earning capacity even further. Thus most attorneys must make every effort to get their fees in advance or somehow to tie defendants and their families to them financially: "The lawyer goes out and tries to squeeze money from the defendant's mother or an aunt," explains Judge Charles W. Halleck, of the local trial court in Washington, D.C.

CLOSE-UP *Criminal Defenders, Law's Outcasts*

The criminal lawyer's work goes far afield from what happens in court. It is the "getting around" which is important.

And getting around Richard Daly does.

By 8:30 A.M. on any given court day, his Thunderbird is parked on Market Street in front of the courthouse and he's soon into the flow.

A prostitute who had once been helped by Daly gladeyes him in the corridor, tapping her lavender thick-soled shoes in a tattoo on the bare floor. "Stay cool, Mr. Richard," she says. Daly gives her his Jimmy Cagney smile; lots of teeth, briefly.

A clerk with a sheaf of traffic violations whispers something and Daly says thanks, which seems to please the clerk.

One after another, a variety of people move toward him like pieces of metal attracted to a magnet.

By 9 A.M., he's in the office of George Solomon, clerk of the Circuit Court of Criminal Causes. Solomon is a cousin of Sarkis Webbe, who shares Daly's office.

In Solomon's office, there is the special coterie gathered for morning coffee. The talk is easy. It's about cases. Solomon is there. And Daly. And Sidney Faber, the associate prosecuting attorney for the city of St. Louis, and Robert Wendt, an associate of Daly, and Norman London, and another lawyer, Gordian S. Benes.

Staying "tight" with Solomon's office is important to Daly because much of the processing flows through the clerk's hands. The better the relationship, the fewer the snarls and hassles.

He also is "tight" with Sidney Faber, the prosecutor. It is a mutual feeling. From Daly's point of view, he can pretty well talk out a case with Faber and get something favorable for his client. From Faber's point of view, it is profitable because by reaching an accord he doesn't have to fight Daly in court.

By 10 A.M., court opens and Daly is working the courthouse. This does not necessarily mean that he may be arguing a case. Mostly, it is filing of motions, seeing that certain things get done, seeing that he stays "tight" with the right people. James Lavin, for example. Lavin is clerk for two judges.

"Say I need a copy of all search warrants in cases I'm involved in," explains Daly. "It is proper that I get them, but getting them can be achieved efficiently and cooperatively, or can be full of hassles and delays. Of course, I want to get along with Lavin."

Which also means getting along reasonably well with the twenty or so others in the clerk's office.

At noon, the Daly coterie assembles near the chambers of Judge David Fitzgibbon. Lunch time. Cold cuts, coffee and Coke, and conversation.

The talk got around to fame and what this does to the lawyer and to his client ultimately, how it affects the performance of the criminal justice system.

"Frankly," Daly said, "becoming as well known as Morris Shenker or F. Lee Bailey or Percy Foreman could hurt my professional activity. I'd have to do something altogether different.

"Now, you might say that I have the courthouse wired. That is, I know how it works to the Nth degree. I have things functioning very smoothly. I'm not a big star, I don't draw outside attention. I'm able to accomplish a very good job as a defense lawyer."

SOURCE: From "Criminal Defenders: Law's Outcasts," by B. Gavzer, *The Washington Post*, February 18, 1973, p. E2. © 1973, The Washington Post. Reprinted with permission.

"Sometimes, he asks a jailed defendant, 'You got $15 or $25? Here, let me hold it for you.' And later that becomes part of the fee."[7]

Such financial circumstances generally force most attorneys to handle a multitude of cases for modest fees. A fifteen-minute conference with the prosecutor and a five-minute appearance in court may earn the lawyer the same fee as a three-day trial. Criminal lawyers frequently say, "I make my money on the phone or in the prosecutor's office, not in the courtroom."

One of the costs to personal esteem is the fact of being on the losing side of most cases. No one likes to lose, yet defense attorneys must quickly adjust to the fact that most of their clients are going to plead or be found guilty. Further, defense attorneys face the possibility of "losing by winning." An attorney who secures the release of a defendant accused of a heinous crime by mounting a zealous defense may be censured by the community for using "technicalities" to defeat justice. In such cases, the defense attorney faces the additional risk of embarrassing the prosecution or the judge, thus reducing the possibility of future considerations from them. The environment of criminal practice, then, involves extensive physical, psychological, and social pressures. Many attorneys get "burned out" after only a few years of such practice; few criminal law specialists are older than fifty.

COUNSEL FOR INDIGENTS

An unidentified prisoner in a Connecticut jail contributed one of the legal profession's favorite remarks when he was asked whether he had had a lawyer when he went to court. "No," he said, "I had a public defender."[8] The quality of defense counsel available to the poor is a question of national debate. The Supreme Court's requirements that counsel be appointed early in the criminal justice process and that it be provided to all indigents accused of crimes punishable by prison sentences have drastically raised the percentage of defendants who become clients of publicly supported defender programs. In

■ Criminal defense requires attorneys to deal with their clients under conditions that are not always conducive to a successful outcome.

some jurisdictions, up to 90 percent of the accused must be provided with counsel. For a brief synopsis of the major Supreme Court rulings on the accused's right to counsel, see Table 9.1.

Under ideal conditions, well-qualified counsel would be appointed early in the criminal justice process to pursue each case with zeal in the best adversary tradition. Too often, however, the right to counsel is mocked by the assignment of a lawyer in the courtroom, a brief conference with the defendant, and a quick guilty plea. These factors—the quality of counsel, conditions of defense practice, and administrative pressures to move the caseload—are major concerns of those who are committed to the principle of due process. The adversary process can be realized only if an attorney has incentives to defend indigents with the same skill and vigor brought to bear for clients who pay their own bills.

Although the *Gideon* decision required counsel to be provided, it did not set standards for indigency. Indigency is variously defined either by state law or judicial discretion around the country. Over time there has been a lessening of the requirements so that now defendants in most of the country need not be truly indigent (completely without funds) to have publicly paid counsel provided. In many areas federal poverty guidelines are used as the measure,

TABLE 9.1   The right to counsel: Major Supreme Court rulings

Case	Year	Ruling
Gideon v. *Wainwright*	1963	The Fourteenth Amendment requires that defendants in state noncapital felony cases have the right to counsel.
Escobedo v. *Illinois*	1964	The accused has the right to counsel during interrogation by the police.
Miranda v. *Arizona*	1966	The right to counsel begins when investigation of a crime focuses on a suspect. The suspect must be informed of the right to remain silent and to have counsel and informed that any statement made may be used against him or her.
United States v. *Wade*	1967	The defendant has the right to be assisted by counsel during a police lineup. (Extended to state defendants in *Gilbert* v. *California* [1967].)
Coleman v. *Alabama*	1970	Counsel must be present at a preliminary hearing.
Argersinger v. *Hamlin*	1972	Whenever a criminal charge may result in a prison sentence, the accused has the right to counsel.
Ross v. *Moffitt*	1974	States are not required to provide counsel for indigents beyond one appeal.
Moore v. *Illinois*	1977	The defendant has the right to counsel at a preliminary court hearing at which he or she appears to be identified by a witness.
United States v. *Henry*	1980	Government agents may not solicit a statement from a defendant covertly and then introduce the statement at trial.
Strickland v. *Washington*	1984	The defendant has the right to the *effective* assistance of counsel, whether privately retained or publicly provided.

Public Defender 2 3
Contract 6
Assigned Counsel 20

FIGURE 9.2
Type of indigent defense system used by the majority of the counties in each state. These aggregate descriptions often mask the fact that in a given state a combination of approaches to indigent defense may be used.
SOURCE: U.S. Department of Justice, Bureau of Justice Statistics, *Bulletin* (September 1988).

whereas in other localities the fact of being unemployed, receiving welfare, or having a low income and dependents is enough to qualify for free counsel.

Methods of Providing Indigents with Counsel

In the United States there are three basic methods of providing counsel to indigent defendants: the assigned counsel system, by which a court appoints a private attorney to represent a particular accused; the contract system, by which an individual attorney, a nonprofit organization, or a private law firm contracts with a local government to provide legal services to indigent defendants for a specified dollar amount; and public defender programs, established as public or private nonprofit organizations with full-time or part-time salaried staff. Figure 9.2 shows the system in use in the majority of counties in each of the fifty states. Differences among cities can be seen by reviewing the data in Table 9.2.

Assigned Counsel

Through the **assigned counsel** system, the court appoints a lawyer in private practice to represent an indigent defendant. This system is

assigned counsel: An attorney in private practice who is assigned by a court to represent an indigent and whose fee is paid by the government that has jurisdiction over the case.

currently used in 1,833 counties. It is widely used in small cities and in rural areas, but even some urban areas with public defender systems follow the practice of assigning counsel in some circumstances, as when a case has multiple defendants and a conflict of interest might result if one were to be represented by a public lawyer. But there are also cities such as Detroit in which the private bar has been able to insist that its members receive a major share of the cases (Table 9.2).

Assigned counsel systems are organized on two bases: the ad hoc system and the coordinated system. In ad hoc assignment systems private attorneys indicate to the judge that they are willing to take the cases of indigent defendants. When an indigent requires counsel the judge then either assigns lawyers in rotation from a prepared list or selects among attorneys who are known and present in the courtroom. In coordinated assignment systems a court administrator oversees the appointment of counsel.[9]

The competence of attorneys who are willing to be assigned cases is sometimes questionable. In many urban areas in which the assigned counsel system is used, such lawyers are largely recent law school graduates, younger, and rated by other members of the bar as less competent than retained counsel. Just as important as the quality of legal talent is the fact that a "courthouse regular" may become co-opted to serve the organizational needs of the system.

In many cities the fee schedule for defenders of indigents may be an inducement for counsel to persuade the client to plead guilty to a lesser charge. In Washington, D.C., Wice found that about fifty regulars dominated the assignment system, receiving $20 per hour for out-of-court work and $30 an hour in court.[10] In many cities, lawyers who are assigned the cases of indigents find that they can make more money by collecting a preparation fee. Such a fee usually amounts to about $50 and is payable when an indigent client pleads guilty rather than going to trial. Handling a large number of cases on this basis is

TABLE 9.2 What percentage of felony cases are handled by different types of defense attorneys in nine jurisdictions?
Jurisdictions vary according to the percentage of cases handled by each form of counsel. Note the similarities and differences among these courts. To what extent do local traditions, politics, and judicial leadership influence the type of system?

Types of Defense Attorneys	Detroit, Michigan	Seattle, Washington	Denver, Colorado	Norfolk, Virginia	Monterey, California	Globe, Arizona	Oxford, Maine	Island, Washington	San Juan, Washington
Public Defender	18.3% (84)	0.0% (0)	74.6% (276)	0.0% (0)	72.6% (297)	0.0% (0)	0.0% (0)	0.0% (0)	61.3% (19)
Assigned Counsel	64.6 (296)	1.2 (7)	5.4 (20)	71.1 (329)	19.3 (79)	0.0 (0)	52.7 (118)	0.0 (0)	0.0 (0)
Contract Attorneys	0.0 (0)	86.8 (526)	0.0 (0)	0.0 (0)	0.0 (0)	81.9 (140)	0.0 (0)	65.6 (82)	0.0 (0)
Private Counsel	17 (78)	12.0 (73)	20.0 (74)	28.9 (134)	8.1 (33)	17.5 (30)	47.3 (106)	34.4 (43)	38.7 (12)
	99.9%	100%	100%	100%	100%	99.4%	100%	100%	100%
Total Number of Cases	458	606	370	463	409	170	224	125	31
Percentage Indigent	82.9%	88.0%	80.0%	71.1%	91.9%	81.9%	52.7%	65.6%	61.3%

SOURCE: From *Indigent Defense Systems*, report to the State Justice Institute, by R. Hanson and J. Chapper. Copyright © 1991 by National Center for State Courts.

more profitable than spending an entire day in the courtroom at trial, for which the fee may be only $200. Table 9.3 shows the fees stipulated for the State of Colorado.

Contract System

In the newest method for providing defense services to poor people, currently in use in about 200 counties, the government enters into a contract with an individual attorney, a nonprofit association, or a private law firm. The majority of counties that have chosen this method are not heavily populated. Some places use public defenders for most cases but contract for services in multiple-defendant situations that might present conflicts of interest or when a case is considered to be extraordinarily complex or to require more time than the government's salaried lawyers can give to it.

The terms of contracts vary. The most common provision is for a block grant: a private law firm agrees to provide representation in all cases for a fixed amount. Fixed-price contracts are the second most frequently used type. Under such agreements lawyers agree to provide representation for a specified number of cases for a fixed amount per case. Some systems enter into a cost-plus arrangement: represen-

Contract System
1. block grant
2. fixed price

TABLE 9.3 Compensation for assigned counsel in Colorado. Colorado has a statewide fee schedule that stipulates the hourly rate that an attorney can charge for indigent defense. Note that maximum amounts for each case are stipulated.

Standard Fees

Attorney fees for trial court work:	
Out-of-court time	$25.00 per hour
Pretrial, trial, posttrial time in court	$35.00 per hour
Attorney fees for appellate court work	$25.00 per hour
Guardian *ad litem*	$25.00 per hour
Court-authorized investigative services	$25.00 per hour

Maximum Fee Payments	With Trial	Without Trial (Half Maximum)
Class 1 felonies and unclassified felonies where the maximum possible penalty is death, life, or more than 51 years	$5,000	$2,500
Class 2 felonies and unclassified felonies where the maximum possible penalty is 41 through 50 years	$2,500	$1,250
Class 3, 4, and 5 felonies and unclassified felonies where the maximum possible penalty is from 1 to 40 years	$2,000	$1,000
Class 1, 2, and 3 misdemeanors, unclassified misdemeanors, and petty offenses	$500	$250
Juvenile cases	$1,000	$500
Guardian *ad litem*	$1,000	$ —
Mental health	None	None

SOURCE: Supreme Court of Colorado, Office of the Chief Justice, "Appointment of Attorneys to Represent Indigents," Directive 85–24.

tation is provided at an estimated cost per case until the dollar amount of the contract is reached, at which point a new contract is negotiated.

Public Defender

public defender: An attorney employed on a full-time, salaried basis by the government to represent indigents.

The **public defender** is a twentieth-century response to the legal needs of the indigent. Started in Los Angeles County in 1914, the system has spread. The most recent survey shows that public defender systems exist in 1,144 counties that comprise more than 70 percent of the U.S. population.[11] The public defender system is growing rapidly and is already the dominant form in 43 of the 50 most populous counties; overall such programs serve 68 percent of the United States. Public defender systems predominate in most large cities, in populous counties, and in about twenty statewide, state-funded jurisdictions. In other states (only North Dakota and Maine do not have public defenders), they are organized and paid for by counties.

The public defender system is often viewed as superior to the assigned counsel system because the attorneys are full-time specialists in criminal law. In addition, public defenders are thought to be more efficient attorneys who do not create lengthy delays or make frivolous technical motions. Salaried public defenders represent a break with the hallowed tradition of the attorney as a private professional serving individual clients for a fee. But these claims have not been tested by researchers.

Public defense is often handled on a "zone" rather than on a person-to-person basis: public defenders are assigned to particular courtrooms and take all the cases of indigent defendants there. Thus

---

A QUESTION OF ETHICS

The call to Attorney Joy Chaplin came from Judge Henry.

"Joy, you're on the Bar Association's list for assigned counsel, and I want to assign an indigent defense case to you. It's going to be a hard case, but I hope you'll be willing to take it."

"Sure, Your Honor, what's the case?"

"Well, Joy, it's the Scott case. You've probably read about it in the papers. Alan Scott has been charged with ten counts of child molestation."

"Oh, no! Not that one. You want me to defend the guy accused of sexually abusing his two young stepdaughters? From what I've seen of him on TV, he's rotten to the core. Judge, as a woman I would have great difficulty dealing with him as a client."

"But you are also an attorney, and Scott has a right to a defense. I know it's going to be difficult, but just let me put you down as the counsel. You can pick up the case file from the D.A.'s office."

Does Attorney Chaplin have an obligation to take Alan Scott's case? Since she already has an opinion about the case, should Judge Henry look for another defense lawyer? Given the nature of the case, does it make a difference if the defense attorney is a man or a woman? Does it matter if the defense attorney has children? Can Chaplin provide a full and vigorous defense?

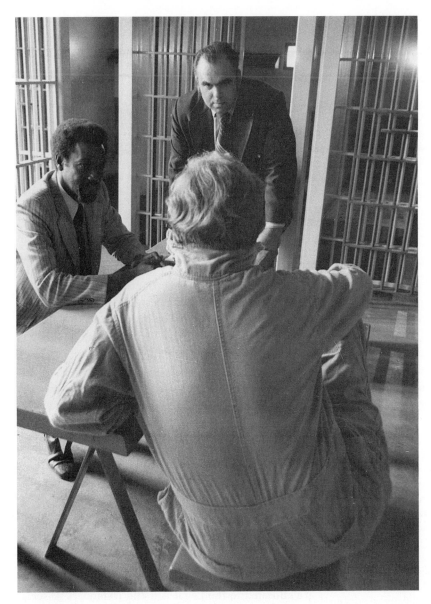

■
Counsel must often operate under
conditions that are not always
conducive to the development of
a vigorous defense.

the defendant has several attorneys, each of whom handles only a
portion of the process: one the preliminary hearing, another the arraignment, and still another the trial, if there is a trial; no one attorney is solely responsible for defending the individual accused. In a
study of Chicago felony cases, Janet Gilboy and John Schmidt found
that 47 percent of defendants received such sequential representation
by public defenders.[12] One effect of the dispersion of responsibility is
that cases are handled routinely, and many of the special elements of
an individual defense are lost. More important, because the defendant is passed from one attorney to another, no relationship of trust
is developed.

Critics point out that the defender's independence is undermined
by daily contact with the same prosecutors and judges. Private counsel has brief, businesslike encounters in the courtroom, but the public
defender has a regular work site in the courtroom and thus presents
himself or herself as one of its core personnel. He or she arrives at

the defense table in the morning with case files for the day and only temporarily leaves this post when a private attorney's case is called. As the late noted criminal lawyer Edward Bennett Williams has said:

> The public defender and the prosecutor are trying cases against each other every day. They begin to look at their work like two wrestlers who wrestle with each other in a different city every night and in time get to be good friends. The biggest concern of the wrestlers is to be sure they do not hurt each other too much. They don't want to get hurt. They just want to make a living.[13]

The style of defense in the typical public defender program is in marked contrast to the personalized relationship between client and privately retained attorney. Public defenders are street-level bureaucrats, and thus there is a tendency to routinize decision making. Typically confronted by overwhelming caseloads, they develop strategies to make decisions quickly and with a minimum expenditure of resources. Cases are standardized as much as possible, and the defense is conducted in accordance with repetitive or routinized processes so that there is little individualized treatment of the special facts of each case. With experience, defenders develop mental images of typical clients so that the characteristics of the accused will help them to "place" the case in an established category and follow a

---

CLOSE-UP *Counsel for the Indigent: Four Vignettes*

DENVER

With a population of 505,000 the city and county of Denver is the largest city in the Rocky Mountain region. The population tends to be divided between a relatively affluent majority and an impoverished class (15 percent below the poverty line) made up primarily of the 17 percent of the population that is African-American or Hispanic.

Colorado has a statewide public defender system that is responsible for all indigent cases except for those where there is a conflict (e.g., co-defendants). The federal guidelines for determining indigency are used, but the information provided by defendants is not checked for accuracy. A ten-dollar fee, waived for those in custody, is charged those who apply for a public defender. An estimated 85 percent of felony defendants qualify for a public defender.

Twenty-six attorneys staff the Denver public defender's office. They are assisted by ten investigators and clerical staff. New defenders tend to be recent law school graduates who stay six to seven years. Public defenders are paid less than their counterparts in the District Attorney's office. They are appointed at the same salary level but lose ground over time.

DETROIT

Wayne County has a population of 2,164,300. Half of the citizens live in the city of Detroit, making it the sixth largest city in the United States. Almost 40 percent of the population is nonwhite, and about 15 percent live below the poverty level. Wayne County has a crime rate of almost 10,000 index crimes per 100,000 population.

Detroit depends upon assigned counsel and a nonprofit organization similar to a public defender agency for the provision of attorneys to the indigent. The assignments are distributed betweeen two groups. Approximately 75 percent of the cases are assigned by judges to individual private attorneys; the remainder are allocated to the Legal Aid and Defenders Association (LADA), the nonprofit group. Attorneys are paid for their services on a fixed-fee based on the statutory punishment for the offense ($475 for a case where the punishment might be a maximum of twenty-four months incarceration up to $1,400 for a murder case).

In order to be eligible for appointment as assigned counsel, attorneys must complete an application form listing professional experience, education, and criminal trial experience. Each applicant must be favorably reviewed by a committee made up of five judges. Once certified an attorney can only be assigned cases where the penalty is twenty years or less imprisonment. With additional experience assignment can be granted for the full range of cases.

Six hundred and fifty attorneys are currently on the assigned counsel list. The pool is composed of about two hundred "hard core" regulars, who depend

standard procedure for disposition. Since the public defender has little time to interview clients and investigate each charge, negotiations with prosecutors and courtroom proceedings cover groups of cases. Under these circumstances the atmosphere with a public defender, who assumes that most of his or her clients are guilty of something, is different than that with an attorney, who believes clients to be innocent until the state proves them guilty.

Perspectives and Comparisons

Defendant's Perspective

Defendants interviewed by Jonathan Casper saw the criminal justice process as not much different than life on the streets as they knew it—a harsh reality divorced from the abstract values of due process.[14] They perceived a gamelike quality to the system, with the police, prosecutors, defenders, and judges manipulating the defendants and one another for their own ends. From the defendants' perspective, this was true even of their lawyers, the public defenders. As Casper commented: "Most of those who were represented by public defenders thought their major adversary in the bargaining process to be not

on assignments for a substantial portion of their caseload and income, and the remainder are "irregulars," who look to assignments to supplement their private civil and criminal practices.

The perception that the defense bar was too cozy with the judiciary and that African-Americans were not receiving vigorous defense led to creation of the Legal Aid and Defenders Association in the late 1960s. LADA is composed of twenty attorneys who by Supreme Court order must receive 25 percent of felony case assignments. At any one time each LADA attorney is carrying between thirty and thirty-five cases. In many ways LADA may be best understood as providing services as would a public defender organization with staff attorneys.

OXFORD, MAINE

With a population of only 50,200, Oxford County is located in the southwestern mountainous region of Maine. The per capita income averages $9,000, and about 13 percent of the population lives below the federal poverty level. The crime rate is low by national standards, with a *UCR* index offense rate of 1,781 per 100,000 population. Less than one-half of 1 percent of the population are minorities.

Oxford County depends wholly on assigned counsel for indigent defense. With only thirty-six members of the bar, attorneys are informally assigned cases by the one visiting superior court judge, who holds session for two to three weeks each month. By merely informing the court clerk, an attorney can receive assignments. At present only ten attorneys receive indigent cases. Most also do private criminal and civil work.

Assigned counsel are paid by a voucher system and are allowed to charge $40 per hour for both in- and out-of-court work. Indigent defense is funded completely by the state.

GILA COUNTY, ARIZONA

Gila County is a large geographic area half the size of the state of Rhode Island. Globe, the county seat, is located about ninety miles east of Phoenix in the state's copper mining country. The population is about 40,000, with 16 percent being Hispanic and Native American and 13 percent living below the poverty level. The violent crime rate is 2,500 per 100,000 population.

Gila County contracts with four local attorneys for the provision of defense services to the indigent. Compensation for each attorney averages $45,000 per year. The county provides additional support for investigators. All of the contract attorneys also maintain private criminal and civil practices.

SOURCE: From *Indigent Defense Systems,* report to the State Justice Institute, by R. Hanson and J. Chapper. Copyright © 1991 by National Center for State Courts.

the prosecutor or the judge, but rather their own attorney, for he was the man with whom they had to bargain. They saw him as the surrogate of the prosecutor—a member of 'their little syndicate'—rather than as their own representative." In the view of one defendant, "a public defender is just like the prosecutor's assistant. Anything you tell this man, he's not gonna do anything but relay it back. . . . They'll come to some sort of agreement, and that's the best you're gonna get."[15]

Attorney's Perspective

From the perspective of attorneys with public clients, criminal defendants give them little respect and trust. Roy Flemming found that attorneys who took the cases of indigents believed that their clients had doubts about their status as legal practitioners, were skeptical about their skills as advocates, and worried about whose side they were on. This makes for a complicated relationship. When asked what makes their work unsatisfying, attorneys often point to their public clients. As one member of his sample told Flemming: "Sometimes we aren't treated the best by our clients. . . . I had someone this morning whose father was yelling about how bad the public defender was right when I was appointed. That wasn't exactly thrilling."[16]

Much of an attorney's craft is based on an ability to persuade clients to follow advice. What is often referred to as "client control" requires client deference. In its absence, the defendant may ignore the advice or suggestions of the attorney. "Without the client's trust, the attorney may not be believed; in turn, attorneys are not always sure if they can trust their clients. Once attorneys secure their client's confidence, they can exercise their judgment and satisfy a desire for professional autonomy."[17] What the lawyer must engender in the defendant is a sense that the attorney can be relied upon. Only then can the attorney feel assured that the defendant will not suddenly become balky or will not unexpectedly reveal something that has been concealed.

Private versus Public Defense

Do defendants who can afford their own counsel receive better legal services than those who cannot? At one time researchers thought that public defenders entered more guilty pleas than did lawyers who had been either privately retained or assigned to cases. But recent studies have cast doubt on this assumption. With publicly funded defense counsel now representing up to 85 percent of the cases in many localities, retained counsel may be viewed as an anomaly. Retained counsel may serve only upper-income defendants who are charged with white-collar crimes or drug dealers and organized crime figures who can pay the fee.

Paul Wice made the point that recent studies indicate that little variation in ultimate case disposition can be associated with the type of defense.[18] This is supported by Peter Nardulli, who reported that the type of defense attorney made no difference in the plea packages negotiated in nine medium-sized court systems in Illinois, Michigan, and Pennsylvania.[19] In another study assigned counsel moved cases faster, but the per-case cost of public defenders offices was lower.[20] A recent study by researchers from the National Center for State Courts greatly adds to our knowledge. In their analysis of felony cases in nine courts, little difference could be found among public defenders, assigned counsel, contracted counsel, and privately retained counsel with regard to case disposition and length of sentences.[21] As Table 9.4 shows, there is little variation among the indigent defense systems in each of the four jurisdictions with regard to case dispositions.

DEFENSE COUNSEL IN THE SYSTEM

Most of the criminal lawyers in metropolitan courts work in a precarious professional environment. They work very hard for small fees in unpleasant surroundings and are not rewarded by professional or public acclaim. In a judicial system in which bargaining is a primary method of decision making, defense attorneys believe they must maintain close personal ties with the police, prosecutor, judges, and other court officials. An attorney's ability to establish and continue a pattern of informal exchange relations with these persons is essential not only for professional survival but also for the opportunity to serve the needs of clients. An experienced attorney described his work as "getting along with people—salesmanship. That's what this young lawyer in my office right now doesn't know anything about. He's a moot court champion—great at research. But he doesn't know a damn thing about people."[22]

At every step of the criminal justice process, from the first contact with the accused until final disposition of the case, defense attorneys are dependent on decisions made by other judicial actors. Even such

TABLE 9.4 **How are cases resolved by different types of defense attorneys in four jurisdictions?** Although the private versus public debate continues, these data show that there are few differences among the defense systems within each jurisdiction. Why are there differences among the cities with regard to case outcomes?

Types of Dispositions	Detroit, Michigan			Denver, Colorado		Norfolk, Virginia		Monterey, California		
	Public Defender	Assigned Counsel	Private Counsel	Public Defender	Private Counsel	Assigned Counsel	Private Counsel	Public Defender	Assigned Counsel	Private Counsel
Dismissals	11.9%	14.5%	12.8%	21.0%	24.3%	6.4%	10.4%	13.5%	8.9%	3.0%
	(10)	(43)	(10)	(58)	(18)	(21)	(14)	(40)	(7)	(1)
Trial Acquittals	9.5	5.7	10.3	1.8	0.0	3.3	5.2	1.7	1.3	0.0
	(8)	(17)	(8)	(5)	(0)	(11)	(7)	(5)	(1)	(0)
Trial Conviction	22.6	14.5	24.4	5.1	9.5	5.2	2.2	7.1	11.4	18.2
	(19)	(43)	(19)	(14)	(7)	(17)	(3)	(21)	(9)	(6)
Guilty Pleas	54.8	64.9	52.6	72.1	66.2	85.1	81.3	76.8	78.5	78.8
	(46)	(192)	(41)	(199)	(49)	(280)	(109)	(228)	(62)	(26)
Diversion	1.2	.3	0.0	0.0	0.0	0.0	.7	1.0	0.0	0.0
	(1)	(1)	(0)	(0)	(0)	(0)	(1)	(0)	(0)	(0)
	100%	99.9%	100.1%	100%	100%	100%	99.8%	101.1%	101.1%	100%

SOURCE: From *Indigent Defense Systems*, report to the State Justice Institute, by R. Hanson and J. Chapper. Copyright © 1991 by National Center for State Courts.

seemingly minor activities as visiting the defendant in jail, learning the case against the defendant from the prosecutor, and setting bail can be difficult unless defense attorneys have the cooperation of others in the system. Thus their concern with preserving their relationships within that system may have greater weight for them than their short-term interest in particular clients.

We should not assume, however, that defense attorneys are at the complete mercy of judicial actors. At any phase of the process, the defense can invoke the adversary model, with its formal rules and public battles. The effective counsel can use this potential for a trial, with its expensive, time-consuming, and disputatious features, as a bargaining tool with the police, prosecutor, and judge. A well-known tactic of defense attorneys, certain to raise the ante in the bargaining process, is to ask for a trial and to proceed as if they meant it.

COMPARATIVE PERSPECTIVE
Public Defense in Denmark

Public defenders have been a part of the legal system in Denmark as early as the sixteenth century, and by the middle of the eighteenth century laws regularizing the provision of counsel were developed. The Administration of Justice Act of 1919, as amended in 1978, sets up the modern system. Although called a "public defender" system, it is similar to an "assigned counsel" system in the United States.

Attorneys who have been designated by the judiciary are assigned on a rotation basis to provide counsel for defendants charged with crimes. Defendants, however, are also permitted to request a particular individual from among this group to represent them if they do not want the attorney assigned by the court. More than 25,000 cases per year are handled by public defenders.

Currently there are six hundred attorneys who have applied for and been selected by the judiciary to be defenders. Care is taken to ensure that very young lawyers, those with little experience, and those who are in poor professional standing are not appointed. This means that those selected are reputed to belong to the better part of the profession. They carry on their public defender role along with their private civil and criminal practices. So concerned are the Danes with the quality of the representation that defenders may not substitute members of their firm when they are called upon to be in court, fines may be levied if the defender is negligent in a case, and ultimately the bar association may impose disciplinary sanctions for unethical conduct or poor work.

Counsel is provided to all indicted persons regardless of their financial condition. If an accused is found not guilty, he or she does not have to compensate the state for defense services. Convicted persons may be required to repay the state defense in the form of restitution should their economic status warrant. Public defenders are paid on a per-case basis according to the amount of time spent in court and in preparing for the trial. The fees are calculated on a somewhat lower rate than the attorney could make if privately retained.

Recently there have been discussions about creating a centralized defender system, with salaried civil service attorneys working within a public agency. This has been opposed on the grounds that the defender should have complete freedom to take those steps considered necessary to safeguard the interests of the client, a situation, it is argued, that can best be realized outside of the bureaucratic environment of a public agency. In addition there is the feeling among some Danish lawyers that such a system would reduce the confidence that the accused should have in his or her attorneys. It is also thought that as salaried employees, public defenders would be viewed as an integral part of the judicial system that the accused finds overwhelming and hostile. It is agreed that a central public defense agency would be more cost-effective, but thus far the Danes have placed a higher value on the independence of the criminal bar and the trust that their clients have in it.

SOURCE: Adapted from "Public Counsel for the Defense: The Danish System," by H. Gammeltoft-Hansen. In W. F. McDonald (ed.), *The Defense Counsel*, pp. 195–218. Copyright © 1983 by Sage Publications, Inc. Reprinted by permission.

It is important that the defense
attorney mount a vigorous defense
yet still be able to negotiate with
the prosecutor.

Some attorneys play the adversary role skillfully. They have developed a style that emphasizes the belligerence of a professional who
is willing to fight the system for a client. Such lawyers are experienced in the courtroom and have built a practice around defending
clients who can afford the expense of a trial. These lawyers must be
willing to gamble that the trial results will benefit the accused and
counsel more than a bargain arranged with the prosecutor. For once
having broken the informal rules of the system, combative attorneys
may find that they have jeopardized future cooperation from the police and prosecutor.

Some clients may expect their counsel to play the combatant role
in the belief that they are not getting their money's worth unless
verbal fireworks are involved. Even when verbal fireworks do occur,
one cannot be certain that the adversaries are engaged in a meaningful contest. Studies in some cities have shown that attorneys with
clients who expect to get a vigorous defense may engage in the form
of courtroom drama commonly known as the "slow plea of guilty,"
in which negotiations have already determined the outcome of the
case. One attorney described a slow plea as follows:

> We had to put on one of these shows a few months ago. Well, we were
> all up there going through our orations, and the whole time the judge
> just sat there writing. Finally the D.A. reduced his charge, and the
> judge looked up long enough to say "Six months probation."[23]

In cases such as the one described, a defense attorney with a paying
client who expects a return for the fee may arrange with the prosecutor and even the judge to stage a battle that is designed to culmi-
nate in a sentence agreed on previously.

For the criminal lawyer who depends on a large volume of petty
cases from poor clients and assumes they are probably guilty of some
offense, the incentives to bargain are strong. If the attorney is to

secure cases, to serve clients' interests, and to maintain status as a practitioner, friendship and influence with judicial officials are essential. Special benefits can be obtained from these sources: informal discovery of charges and plea bargaining from the prosecutor, fact finding and favorable testimony from the police, sentencing discretion and courtroom reception by the judge, and the influence of all three on the bail decision. For these courtesies, however, a price must be paid: information elicited from the client, a less-than-vigorous defense, the cultivation of active social relationships, political support, and a general attitude of cooperativeness.

Securing Cases

As do other professions in which a potential exists for client exploitation, the American bar has rigid strictures against the solicitation of clients. Lawyers with reputations as "ambulance chasers" soon find that colleagues hold their conduct in low regard. Unlike clients of the medical profession (which has similar rules of conduct), most citizens do not have a "family lawyer" and in exceptional circumstances must seek out legal services. To a great extent, persons in need of lawyers depend on the recommendations of others; hence an attorney's reputation in the community is important. For both the lawyer trying to make a living and the accused who is in need of counsel, the difficulties of establishing contact may be severe.

Although some criminal lawyers may chase patrol wagons, many depend on a broker, a person who is able to identify and channel potential legal business to the attorney. The broker may be a bondsman, police officer, fellow attorney, prison official, or member of the clergy. Criminal lawyers seeking clients have the problem of making themselves known to a broker and creating a climate so that cases will be referred to them. Participation in social or political groups is one way to make contact with brokers. Favors to law enforcement actors, such as free legal advice on personal matters, can bring about a climate of indebtedness, but these arrangements can lead the lawyer to become more obligated to the broker than to the client. A police officer is less likely to hand the attorney's business card to a prisoner if past experience has revealed that the lawyer is not cooperative.

Relations with Clients

If criminal lawyers are not advocates using technical skills to win a case, what is the service that they perform for the accused? One of the assets they sell is their influence within the judicial system: their ability to telephone the sheriff, enter the prosecutor's office, and bargain for their clients with judicial officials. On the basis of knowledge of the accused, the charge, the evidence, and the possible sanctions, defense attorneys may view their role as getting a client's penalty set at the lowest end of the range provided by statute. All these activities are played out in such a way that clients believe they are getting their money's worth. Professional confidence, an aura of influence, and having the "inside dope" are essential.

Often the first arraignment is the greatest boon to the defense attorney. In this proceeding, the accused is told what the maximum penalty is for the charges made. When the lawyer negotiates a sentence of three to five years in prison, the client is grateful for having been spared the potential sixty-five years that the law prescribes for the multiple charges originally lodged. Thus, in one attorney's view, "the lawyer's fee is money charged for getting his client the normal penalty, which is substantially less than the maximum penalty under the law. Clients have no way of knowing what to expect from the system and one imagines attorneys do not go overboard in stressing 'I did what any attorney could do.' "[24]

Agent-Mediators

A criminal lawyer is not only an advocate for the client but also an agent-mediator—that is, an adviser who explains the judicial process and lets the accused know what to expect.[25] This facet of the attorney's role may evolve into a confidence game in which the lawyer prepares the accused for defeat and then "cools him out" when it comes, as it is likely to do. Defense attorneys help clients redefine their situation and restructure their perceptions and thus prepare them to accept the consequences of a guilty plea. In the process of preparing a client, the lawyer is often assisted by the defendant's relatives, the probation officer, the prosecutor, and the judge. All try to emphasize that they want the accused to do the right things for his or her own good. The defendant finds himself in a position similar to that of a sick person on whom various treatments are urged by people who proclaim that they are all working on the patient's behalf.

The interrelatedness of these services is evident: success in one venture depends on success in the other. If a client balks at the bargain that has been struck, the attorney's future influence with the prosecutor may be jeopardized. At the same time, the lawyer does not want to get the reputation for selling out clients; such a reputation may quickly end a career.

Public defenders have a special problem of client control. Defendants who have not selected their own counsel may not accept the bargain but insist that a trial be held. Because public defenders may fear a charge of misleading a client, they may have to invoke the "slow plea of guilty" drama. Thus the extent to which the defender *represents* the accused is open to question, for the trial may be used to impress on other defendants the fact that a cooperative attitude is important.

Criminal lawyers in their role as agent-mediator may in fact be viewed as double agents. With obligations to both client and court, they are agents seeking to effect a satisfactory outcome for both. The position is filled with conflicts of interest that must all too often be resolved in favor of the organization that provides the attorney's means of professional existence.[26]

Attorney Competence

The right to counsel is of little value if the counsel is not competent and effective. Questions about the adequacy of legal representation provided to both private and public clients have been of increasing concern to defense groups, bar associations, and the courts. There are, of course, many examples of incompetent representation. The training, the nature of the work itself, and the caseload all take their toll. In one case of note, trial counsel testified to not having conducted legal research concerning admissibility of certain physical and testimonial evidence and to making no objection to its introduction. A public defender's stamina must be enormous to handle caseloads of approximately two thousand cases a year (which works out to more than seven cases a day, five days a week, fifty-two weeks a year). One P.D., so strained, resigned from the Public Defender's office, having decided that the presence of a live body as a defender was "actually doing the defendants more harm . . . than if they had no representation at all."[27]

Other difficulties in providing effective representation can be cited as well. In jurisdictions in which assigned counsel is provided for indigents, the lawyer chosen by the court may have little experience with the criminal law, may not know the key actors in the system, and may have little interest in the case. Conflict-of-interest situations may arise when one attorney is appointed for co-defendants. Finally, caseload pressures may mean that there is little attorney-client contact before courtroom appearances, and hence key pieces of information may not be communicated to the attorney.

The U.S. Supreme Court has only recently begun to examine the issue of attorney competence and the requirements that should be met if defendants are to receive effective counsel. In two 1984 cases, *United States* v. *Cronic* and *Strickland* v. *Washington,* the Court established a new standard of what constitutes the effective assistance of counsel.[28] Cronic had been charged with a complex mail fraud scheme, which had been investigated by the government for four and a half years. Just before trial, Cronic's retained lawyer withdrew, and a young attorney with no trial experience, whose practice was primarily in the real estate field, was appointed. The trial court allowed the new attorney only twenty-five days to prepare. The Supreme Court upheld Cronic's conviction on the grounds that although the new trial counsel had made errors, there was no showing that the trial had not been a "meaningful" test of the prosecution's case or that the conviction had not been reliable.

The standard adopted in *Cronic* was applied in the capital case *Strickland* v. *Washington,* in which it was alleged that counsel had been incompetent. Washington was charged with three counts of capital murder, robbery, kidnapping, and other felonies. An experienced criminal lawyer was appointed as defense counsel. Against his attorney's advice, Washington confessed to two murders, waived a jury trial, and pleaded guilty to all charges. He then waived his right to be sentenced by an advisory capital sentencing jury and instead chose to be sentenced by the trial judge, who had a reputation for leniency. Feeling that the situation was hopeless, counsel did not adequately prepare for the sentencing hearing and sought neither character statements nor a psychiatric examination. Upon being sentenced to death, Washington appealed, asserting that counsel's failure to call witnesses, to seek a presentence investigation report, and to cross-examine medical experts constituted ineffective assistance. The Supreme Court rejected Washington's assertions, saying that his attorney was not unconstitutionally ineffective.

What emerges from the *Cronic* and *Strickland* cases is a standard of "reasonable competence" that the Supreme Court says should be applied when the issue of adequacy of representation is raised. This means that counsel's performance may be viewed as inadequate only if a reasonably competent attorney would not have acted as did the trial counsel. As noted by Justice Sandra O'Connor, the appellant must show "that there is a reasonable probability that, but for counsel's unprofessional errors, the result of the proceeding would have been different." Reviewing judges must thus determine only if the proceeding was fundamentally fair.

Gary Goodpaster wrote that four major deficiences of criminal defense attorneys have arisen in cases involving allegations that counsel was ineffective:

1. failure to attempt to develop an effective working relationship with the client
2. failure to conduct an adequate pretrial investigation
3. failure to develop an "adversarial" or "fighting" attitude toward the prosecution and its case
4. lack of knowledge or skill, and failure to seek the advice of other counsel.[29]

Central here is the adequacy of defense counsel, given the nature of the criminal justice system, the constraints of resources on the system, and the work environment of legal practitioners.

SUMMARY

The role of defense attorney is structured by the occupational environment within the criminal justice system. Recruitment of attorneys into criminal practice, financial considerations, interpersonal relations, and the demands of the system for a speedy disposition of each case in a huge caseload create needs that are met through a process of bargaining. As a result, criminal lawyers participate in a number of exchange relationships that influence case disposition. Most cases are disposed of by plea bargaining, in which the various perspectives of the defendant, prosecutor, defense lawyer, and judge play their parts. As one judge told the author: "Lawyers are helpful to the system. They are able to pull things together, work out a deal, keep the system moving." But we must ask whether that is the purpose of defense work.

FOR DISCUSSION

1. You are the defendant. How will you select an attorney? What criteria will you use? Where will you obtain the information necessary to make this decision?
2. Former chief justice Warren Burger has suggested that only lawyers with special qualifications be allowed to argue cases in court. Should the United States adopt the British distinction between solicitor and barrister?

3. You are the defense attorney. You have just learned that your client committed the crime charged. What are your responsibilities to your client? To the court?
4. We place much emphasis on the adversarial characteristics of the defense attorney. How can we create a situation in which lawyers will not be co-opted by the system?
5. If every person accused of committing a crime had access to the legal talents of a Melvin Belli or F. Lee Bailey, how would the criminal justice system be affected?

FOR FURTHER READING

Bailey, F. Lee. *The Defense Never Rests.* New York: Stein & Day, 1971. Perspectives of one of America's best-known defense attorneys.

McDonald, William R., ed. *The Defense Counsel.* Newbury Park, CA: Sage, 1983. A collection of outstanding articles by social scientists and lawyers on defense counsel in criminal cases.

McIntyre, Lisa J. *The Public Defender: The Practice of Law in the Shadows of Repute.* Chicago: University of Chicago Press, 1987. A case study of the public defender's office in Cook County (Chicago), Illinois.

Moldovsky, Joel, and DeWolf, Rose. *The Best Defense.* New York: Macmillan, 1975. As the authors note, the best defense is a good offense. Gives insights and flavor of private criminal practice.

Spence, Gerry. *With Justice for None.* New York: Penguin, 1989. A critique by a nationally known defense attorney of how law is taught, practiced, and administered.

Wice, Paul B. *Criminal Lawyers: An Endangered Species.* Newbury Park, CA: Sage, 1978. National survey of the private defense bar.

Wishman, Seymour. *Confessions of a Criminal Lawyer.* New York: Penguin, 1982. Inside view of criminal practice in major cases.

NOTES

1. Anthony Lewis, *Gideon's Trumpet* (New York: Vintage Books, 1964), p. 10.
2. *Gideon* v. *Wainwright,* 372 U.S. 335 (1963).
3. Paul B. Wice, *Criminal Lawyers: An Endangered Species* (Newbury Park, CA: Sage, 1978), p. 29.
4. Ibid., p. 75.
5. David W. Neubauer, *Criminal Justice in Middle America* (Morristown, NJ: General Learning Press, 1974), p. 70.
6. As quoted in Leonard Downie, Jr., *Justice Denied* (New York: Praeger, 1971), p. 172.
7. Ibid., p. 173.
8. Jonathan D. Casper, "Did You Have a Lawyer When You Went to Court? No, I Had a Public Defender," *Yale Review of Law and Social Change* 1 (Spring 1971):4–9.
9. Pauline Houlden and Steven Balkin, "Costs and Quality of Indigent Defense: Ad Hoc vs. Coordinated Assignment of the Private Bar within a Mixed System," *Justice System Journal* 10 (Summer 1985):159.
10. Wice, *Criminal Lawyers,* p. 208.
11. U.S. Department of Justice, Bureau of Justice Statistics, *Bulletin* (September 1988).
12. Janet A. Gilboy and John R. Schmidt, "Replacing Lawyers: A Case Study of the Sequential Representation of Criminal Defendants," *Journal of Criminal Law and Criminology* 70 (1979):2.
13. Edward Bennett Williams, *The Law,* interview by Donald MacDonald (New York: Center for the Study of Democratic Institutions, n.d.), p. 10.

14. Casper, "Did You Have a Lawyer?" p. 5.

15. Ibid., pp. 5, 6.

16. Roy B. Flemming, "Client Games: Defense Attorney Perspectives on Their Relations with Criminal Clients," *American Bar Foundation Research Journal* (Spring 1986):258.

17. Ibid.

18. Paul Wice, "Private Criminal Defense: Reassessing an Endangered Species," in *The Defense Counsel*, ed. William F. McDonald (Newbury Park, CA: Sage, 1983), p. 40.

19. Peter Nardulli, "Insider Justice: Defense Attorneys and the Handling of Felony Cases," *Journal of Criminal Law and Criminology* 79 (1986):416.

20. Larry J. Cohen, Patricia P. Semple, and Robert E. Crew, Jr., "Assigned Counsel versus Public Defender Systems in Virginia," in *Defense Counsel*, p. 143.

21. Roger Hanson and Joy Chapper, *Indigent Defense Systems,* report to the State Justice Institute (Williamsburg, VA: National Center for State Courts, 1991).

22. Jackson B. Battle, "In Search of the Adversary System: The Cooperative Practices of Private Criminal Defense Attorneys," *University of Texas Law Review* 50 (1971):66.

23. Ibid.

24. Neubauer, *Criminal Justice in Middle America*, p. 75.

25. Abraham Blumberg, "The Practice of Law as a Confidence Game," *Law and Society Review* 1 (1967):11–39.

26. Ibid., p. 38.

27. *Cooper* v. *Fitzharris*, 551 F. 2d 1162 (9th Cir. 1977).

28. *United States* v. *Cronic*, 444 U.S. 654 (1984); *Strickland* v. *Washington*, 466 U.S. 686 (1984).

29. Gary Goodpaster, "The Adversary System, Advocacy, and Effective Assistance of Counsel in Criminal Cases," *New York University Review of Law and Social Change* 14 (1986):90.

Pretrial Processes

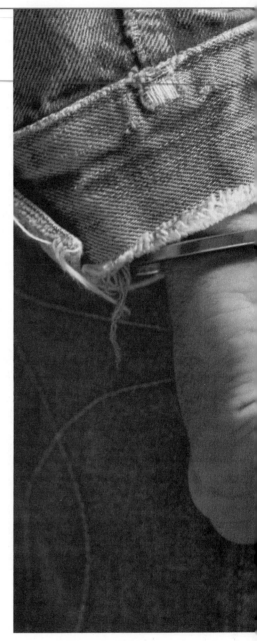

Key Terms and Cases

■ Robert Chambers, indicted in the "preppie murder case," claimed that he accidentally killed Jennifer Levin during a moment of "rough sex." He was tried, but while the jury was deliberating he changed his plea to "guilty" and was given a sentence of five to fifteen years.

From the time I first meet my client until we leave the courthouse, I have to be ready to bargain. Bail, charge, plea, and sentence—they all result from my ability to deal with the system.

Defense Attorney

For a number of years "Arrest and Trial" was a popular television drama in which audiences were permitted to see an arrest, the trial, and the sentencing. Most viewers probably assumed that arrest and trial were linked and that all persons taken into custody ended up facing a judge and jury. But most people arrested will never face trial, because a major portion of cases are dropped through the discretionary action of the police, prosecutor, or judge. Up to 90 percent of people who are arraigned on an indictment plead guilty and thus do not have a trial. The filtering process operates in such a way that only a very small portion of those who come to the attention of the police for wrongdoing are eventually given a sentence. Many who are sentenced appeal their convictions, and some have them overturned.

Different kinds of cases are handled in somewhat different fashions. The interest of the public, the nature of the case, the character of the defendant, and the tactics of the opposing attorneys all help to determine whether a case is filtered out of the system before arraignment, is given routine treatment resulting in a plea bargain, becomes one of the few highly publicized trials that occur each year, or falls somewhere in between. The vast majority of cases are handled in ways that bear little resemblance to the adversarial processes described by the Due Process Model. Chapter 10 focuses on the pretrial period, when most major decisions concerning the fate of persons arrested are made. It is during these early stages of the criminal justice system that we can best see the links among the police, prosecution, defense, and court. Of particular importance are the subjects of bail and plea bargaining, practices and procedures that are here examined in detail.

FROM ARREST TO TRIAL OR PLEA

Following the arrest, booking, and initial appearance of a defendant, the pretrial processes begin. It is at this time that the prosecution and defense prepare their cases, an indictment or information is presented to the court, and a formal **arraignment** on the charges is held. More important, this is the time for screening and filtering out of the system those cases that the prosecution believes will not pass judicial scrutiny. As we have seen, prosecutors can drop the cases of some defendants, return other cases to the police for further investigation, and recommend diversion for still others.

Figure 10.1, drawn from a study of thirty-seven urban prosecu-

arraignment: The act of calling an accused person before the court to hear the charges lodged against him or her and to enter a plea in response to those charges.

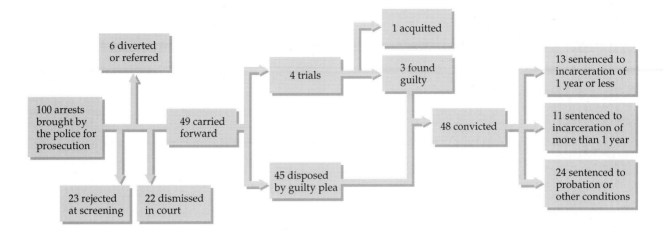

tors' offices, shows that case attrition is a major factor in the criminal justice system.[1] Also of importance is the fact that the proportion of cases dropped at the various stages of the pretrial process varies from city to city. In some jurisdictions, most cases that do not result in conviction are rejected for prosecution before court charges are filed. In other jurisdictions, rates of postfiling dismissions may be as high as 50 percent or more. As shown in Figure 10.2, prosecutorial screening is high in New Orleans, but the percentage of cases dropped after filing is low. By contrast, prosecutors in Manhattan reject a small percentage during the screening phase but drop 32 percent after filing.

The factors influencing case attrition are complex. Differences exist partly as a result of laws, administrative processes in the court-house, and traditions of the local legal culture. What is important is that somewhere in the system cases are screened, primarily with regard to the strength of the evidence, and are either removed or undergo alterations. Throughout the United States the courts are under pressure to reduce the number of cases requiring formal trial by jury. The maintenance of the system requires this type of administrative decision making by prosecutors, defense attorneys, and judges.

FIGURE 10.1

Typical outcome of one hundred urban felony cases. Crucial decisions are made by prosecutors and judges during the period before trial or plea. Once cases were bound over for disposition, guilty pleas were many; trials, few; and acquittals, minuscule in number. SOURCE: Barbara Boland with Ronald Stones, *The Prosecution of Felony Arrests*, Department of Justice, Bureau of Justice Statistics (Washington, DC: Government Printing Office, 1986), p.2.

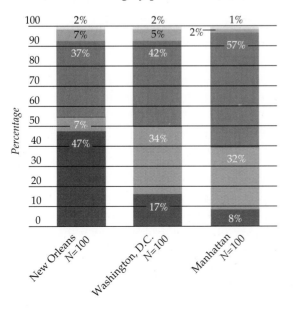

FIGURE 10.2

Disposition of felony arrests in three American cities. Note the different ways in which cases are disposed of in these cities. What factors might account for these differences? SOURCE: Derived from Barbara Boland, Elizabeth Brady, Herbert Tyson, and John Bassler, *The Prosecution of Felony Arrests* (Washington, DC: Institute for Law and Social Research, 1982).

Pretrial Motions

The defense uses the pretrial period to its own advantage. Through a pretrial **motion** to the court, counsel may attempt to suppress evidence or to learn about the prosecutor's case. A motion is an application to a court requesting that an order be issued to bring about a specified action. A court hearing is held on the motion, and the presenting attorney must be able to support the contention made about procedures used in the arrest, the sufficiency of the evidence, or the exclusion of evidence. Typical pretrial motions by the defense include:

1. motion to quash a search warrant
2. motion to exclude evidence, such as a confession
3. motion for severance (separate trials in cases with more than one defendant)
4. motion to dismiss because of delay in bringing the case to trial
5. motion to suppress evidence illegally obtained
6. motion for pretrial discovery of the evidence held by the prosecutor
7. motion for a change of venue because a fair and impartial trial cannot be held in the original jurisdiction

Aggressive use of pretrial motions has strategic as well as substantive advantages. Motions can become part of the jockeying for position between the prosecution and defense. The following reasons have been given for filing numerous motions:

1. It forces a partial disclosure of the prosecutor's evidence at an early date.
2. It puts pressure on the prosecutor to consider plea bargaining early in the proceeding.
3. It forces exposure of primary state witnesses at an inopportune time for the prosecution.
4. It raises before the trial judge early in the proceedings matters the defense may want called to his or her attention.
5. It forces the prosecutor to make decisions before final preparation of the case.
6. It allows the defendant to see the defense counsel in action, which has a salutary effect on the client-attorney relationship.[2]

Although pretrial motions are entered in only about 10 percent of felony cases and in less than 1 percent of misdemeanors, they can be used not only to secure the defendant's release but also to bargain, since the defense may want to give every indication that it is going to trial. A second, equally important function of the pretrial processes for the defense is to secure release of the defendant on bail. As the next section will explain, the defendant who is out on bail has enormous advantages over the defendant awaiting trial in jail.

BAIL: PRETRIAL RELEASE

The practice of allowing defendants to be released from jail pending trial originated in Anglo-Saxon law. In a period when the time between arrest and trial was lengthy and the cost of detention burdensome, **bail** was used as a convenience to the sheriff, allowing him to release a prisoner from his responsibility and yet be fairly certain that he or she would be in court at the appointed time. As it is today, some form of surety was required, to be forfeited if the accused did not show up as promised. This concept was transferred across the Atlantic with modifications.

The Eighth Amendment prohibits excessive bail, and most state statutes are intended to ensure that the system is administered in a nondiscriminatory manner. Nonetheless judicial personnel have a great deal of discretion in determining pretrial release. As early as 1835 the Supreme Court ruled that the purpose of bail was to ensure the presence of the accused in court to answer the indictment and to submit to trial.[3] This purpose is consistent with the belief that accused persons are innocent until proved otherwise and that they should not suffer hardship awaiting trial. Bail should not be used as punishment, for the accused has not been found guilty. The amount of bail should therefore be sufficient to ensure the defendant's presence for trial but no more than that amount. Yet concern about protection of the community while the defendant is on bail persists. Congress and some of the states have passed laws allowing the preventive detention of defendants who are believed by the judge to pose a threat to any other person or the community while awaiting trial. (Preventive detention is fully discussed later in the chapter.)

The Reality of the Bail System

The reality of the bail system is far from the ideal. The question of bail may arise at the police station, during the initial court appearance in a misdemeanor case, or at the arraignment in most felony cases. In almost all jurisdictions, the amount of bail is based primarily on the judge's perception of the seriousness of the crime and the defendant's record. In part, this emphasis stems from a lack of information about the accused. Because bail must be allowed within twenty-four to forty-eight hours after an arrest, there is no time to seek out background information on which to make a more just bail determination. The result is that judges have developed standard rates that are used in both courtroom and station house: so many dollars for such-and-such an offense. A judge may in certain instances set high bail in response to the police's wish to keep a defendant in custody. Defense attorneys have reported that bail of any amount has the effect of scaring the defendant but that a high bail implies that the judge believes the crime was vicious or that the defendant may not otherwise appear in court.

Critics of the bail system argue that the emphasis on monetary bail operates to penalize the poor and to punish in advance of trial those whom society does not like. They say that the emphasis on monetary bail raises problems about the equality of the administration of justice. Imagine that you have been arrested and you have no money. Should you be denied a chance for freedom before trial simply because you are poor? What if you have little money and are forced to make a decision between bail and hiring a defense attorney? Big-time drug dealers can readily make bail and continue their criminal activities while awaiting trial; a poor person arrested for a minor

bail: An amount of money specified by a judge to be posted as a condition of pretrial release for the purpose of ensuring the appearance of the accused in court as required.

violation may spend the pretrial period in jail. Should the dangerous rich be allowed out on bail and the undangerous poor kept in?

To post bail, a prisoner is required to give the court some form of monetary surety, usually cash, property, or a bond from a bonding company. For persons arrested for lesser offenses who have ties to the community, release on their own recognizance is often permitted. The effect of the system on the poor often means that they must remain in jail awaiting trial. Meanwhile, the more affluent and the professional criminals have no difficulty in making bail. In Mary Toborg's study of eight urban jurisdictions, about 85 percent of all defendants were released on bail prior to trial.[4]

The inequity of the system is further shown by the fact that those who cannot make bail must remain in jail, where they are treated the same as convicted prisoners. Given the length of delay between arraignment and trial in most courts, the effect of pretrial detention on defendants and their families can be disastrous. Not only is their freedom eroded, but they almost always lose their jobs, and their personal relationships are jeopardized. Judges commonly give suspended sentences to people convicted of less serious crimes if they have already spent time in jail awaiting trial.

Bondsmen: Beneficiaries of Bail

A central figure in the bail system is the professional bondsman, whose services are available twenty-four hours a day to those who need to produce sufficient cash to be released. Across from most courthouses his bright neon sign spells out "Bonds," a reminder of the freedom that can be had for a price.

Using their own assets or those of an insurance company, bondsmen will provide the surety required for a fee of between 5 and 10 percent. They are licensed by the state, choose their own clients, and

may set their own collateral requirements. In addition, they may track down and return bail jumpers without extradition and by force if necessary.

Providing cash bonds for criminal defendants may be financially rewarding, but like other services, it is driven by local market forces. The demand for bail bonds is influenced by such factors as arrest rates and the willingness of judges to release defendants on their own recognizance. The supply of these services is determined by the number of bondsmen in the local surety market, the amount of credit available for bonding, the willingness of the agents to take risks, and the force with which the courts foreclose on defaulted bonds.

Like other actors who have an interest in the judicial system, bondsmen exert a strong influence on the court through their ability to cooperate with police officers who recommend their services rather than those of another bondsman. In return they may refuse to provide bail for defendants whom the police do not wish to see released. Reformers view bondsmen as a cardinal flaw in the bail system, because although they are private individuals with no formal ties to the judicial process, they still have the power to overrule, in effect, a judge's decision. Bondsmen may withhold their services arbitrarily. Bondsmen, as the late Judge J. Skelly Wright succinctly said,

> hold the keys to the jail in their pockets. They determine for whom they will act as surety—who in their judgment is a good risk. The bad risks, in the bondsmen's judgment, and the ones who are unable to pay the bondsmen's fees, remain in jail. The court and the commissioner are relegated to the relatively unimportant chore of fixing the amount of bail.[5]

Although the bonding profession has an unsavory reputation, these businesspeople of criminal justice facilitate court operations. Their most important function is to maintain social control over the defendant during the pretrial period. Bondsmen stress to their clients the importance of appearing in court on the correct date, and they emphasize the penalties that may result if they fail to do so. Often pressure on friends and relatives, as well as telephone calls and mailed reminders, are used to ensure appearance. Like defense attorneys, bondsmen help prepare their clients for the probable fate in store for them, often encourage a plea of guilty, and usually forecast the sentence quite accurately. Bondsmen also share responsibility with judges for the defendant's release, thus providing a buffer should the defendant upset the public by committing further crimes before trial. In this era of crowded jails, bail bondsmen relieve some of the pressure.[6]

Bail Setting

Although the judiciary is responsible for setting bail, its powers are often delegated to other officials. When the offense is a misdemeanor, bail is generally set by a police officer according to a judicially prescribed schedule. In most jurisdictions, bail for those charged with felonies is set by a judge exercising discretion that takes into account the severity of the offense, the characteristics of the defendant, and community protection. With jails in many communities crowded, the

TABLE 10.1 The bail process in eleven major cities.   Note that different actors in different places make bail decisions. One can see that in most places the initial level for misdemeanors is set by a police officer, who is to follow a schedule provided by the court.

	Who Sets the Bail		Where It Is Done		How It Is Done	
City	Misdemeanor	Felony	Misdemeanor	Felony	Misdemeanor	Felony
Washington	Desk sergeant	Judge	Station house	Court of Gen'l Sessions	Schedule	Discretion
San Francisco	Clerk of criminal court	Judge	Hall of Justice	Hall of Justice	Schedule	Discretion
Los Angeles	Police captain	Judge	Station house	Regional	Schedule	Discretion
Oakland	Police captain	Judge	Station house	Courthouse		
Detroit	Desk sergeant Arresting magistrate	Arresting magistrate	Police station	Hall of Justice	Schedule	Discretion
Chicago	Desk sergeant	Judge of bond court	Police station	Bond court or electronically	Schedule	Discretion
St. Louis	Desk sergeant	County circuit court judge	Police station	Police station or courthouse	Schedule	Flexible schedule
Baltimore	Desk sergeant	Judge	Police station	Police court	Schedule	Schedule
Indianapolis	Turnkey	Turnkey	City jail	City jail	Schedule	Schedule
Atlanta	Police	Police	Police headquarters	Police headquarters	Discretion schedule	Discretion schedule
Philadelphia	Desk sergeant	Magistrate and district attorney	Station house	Police headquarters	Schedule	Discretion

SOURCE: Paul B. Wice, *Freedom for Sale* (Lexington, MA: D.C. Heath, 1974), p. 26.

availability of pretrial detention space has become an additional factor. Table 10.1 shows who sets bail in eleven large cities, where the process is carried out, and how the amount is determined.

When the judge or magistrate determines the amount of bail, he or she is influenced by the formal criteria but also the expectations of the prosecutor, defense counsel, police, and sometimes the bondsman. Exchanges among these actors affect the judge's decision. Inevitably, the prosecutor supports high bail, and the defense attorney asks that it be low, pointing out that the defendant must "take care of his family," "has a good job," or "is well liked in the neighborhood." The police may be particularly active in some settings in urging high bail, especially if they have expended extensive resources to apprehend the suspect or have had contact with the victims. It is not unknown for detectives to visit judge's chambers before an arraignment to tell the judge about aspects of the case that the police do not want brought out in open court.

Frederic Suffet studied bail settings in New York County Criminal Court. Recording the interactions of the prosecutor, defense attorney, and judge, Suffet noted the way norms emerged and guided the decision. The acknowledged standards or "rules of the game"—seriousness of the charge, prior record, defendant's ties to the community—provided the accepted boundaries for the interactions. With these standards accepted by the participants, negotiations could proceed with a minimum of conflict.[7]

The study showed that the prosecutor had more prestige in the courtroom than did the defense attorney. The latter was less likely to make the initial bail suggestion and had less chance of getting the judge to accede to it if he did make it. The prosecutor's request for higher bail was granted in more than four out of five cases, no matter who had made the original suggestion. By contrast, the defense attorney, when arguing against the first suggestion of the prosecutor, got the bail lowered only a little over half the time (57.8 percent). In a direct conflict with the judge, the defense attorney affected the bail decision a little more than a fourth of the time (28 percent). Suffet's further analysis shows that the judge and prosecutor hold similar conceptions as to the level of bail required and are reciprocally supportive.

Although the "manifest," or formal, purpose of the bail hearing is to stipulate an amount that will ensure the defendant's appearance in court, the latent purpose, or by-product, of this interaction is to spread responsibility for the defendant's release. By including the prosecutor and defense counsel in the process, the judge can create a buffer between the court and the outraged public if an accused criminal released from custody pending a court appearance should commit a crime.

In addition to interpersonal influences, the local legal and political culture have been found to be important factors in the setting of bail. In a study of Detroit and Baltimore, Roy Flemming learned that

A QUESTION OF ETHICS

Jim Rourke stood in front of Desk Sergeant Jack Sweeney at the Redwoods City Police Station. Rourke was handcuffed and waiting to be booked. He had been caught by Officers Davis and Thatcher outside of a building in a prestigious neighborhood soon after the police had received a frantic 911 call from a resident who reported that someone had entered her apartment. Rourke was seen loitering in the alley with a flashlight in his back pocket. He was known to the police because of his prior arrests for entering at night. As Thatcher held Rourke, Davis went around behind the desk and spoke to Sergeant Sweeney in a soft voice.

"I know we don't have much on this guy, but he's a bad egg and I bet he was the one who was in that apartment. The least we can do is set the bail high enough so that he'll know we are on to him."

"Davis, you know I can't do that. You've got nothing on him," said Sweeney.

"But how's it going to look in the press if we just let him go? You know the type of people who live in Littleton Manor. There will be hell to pay if it gets out that this guy just walks."

"Well, he did have the flashlight . . . I suppose that's enough to indicate that he's a suspect. Let's make the bail $1,000. I know he can't make that."

What is the purpose of bail? Was the amount set appropriate in this instance? Should Rourke be held merely because of the suspicion that he might have burglarized the apartment? Would the case have been handled in the same way if the call had come from a poorer section of town?

the two cities approximated the extremes of pretrial treatment of felony defendants among larger American cities. In Detroit's Recorder's Court, nearly 48 percent of felony defendants arraigned were freed on their own recognizance, the median bail for the remainder was $2,000, and 32 percent were detained for the entire predisposition period. In Baltimore's District Court, only 12 percent of the accused were freed on their own recognizance, the median bail was $4,650, and 41 percent awaited disposition in jail.[8]

Among the influences contributing to these differences was the political climate in Detroit, described as "prodefendant" following reforms instituted after the riots in 1967, when thousands of black citizens were detained by means of exorbitant bail; a formal limit on the Wayne County Jail population; and bail-setting judges who held secure positions. In Baltimore, in contrast, bail was set by "low-status court officials or commissioners with insecure tenure who were more highly vulnerable" to criticism of bail reforms on the part of the police and other public officials. Thus there was a high level of uncertainty among the people responsible for setting bail, and there were no population limits on detention facilities.

From a constitutional viewpoint, it has been argued that bail should be set in accordance with six presumptions, namely that:

1. the accused is entitled to release on his or her own recognizance
2. nonfinancial alternatives to bail will be used when possible
3. the accused will receive a full and fair hearing
4. reasons will be stated for the decision
5. clear and convincing evidence will be offered to support a decision
6. there will be a prompt and automatic review of all bail determinations.

Many people claim that requiring bail to be set in accordance with these criteria greatly hampers the ability of the justice system to deal with offenders and to protect society. Others counter that personal freedom is so precious that failure to afford a person every opportunity to remain at large is a greater injustice.

Reform of the System

There has been a concerted effort for three decades to reform the bail system. Activated by early studies of pretrial detention in Philadelphia and New York, the movement has spread across the country. Criticisms of the pretrial release process have focused on judicial discretion in setting bail amounts, poor people's being deprived of their freedom while better-off citizens can afford bail, the perceived unsavory role of bondsmen, and jail conditions for those detained while awaiting trial.

As measured by the increased portion of defendants who are not detained, the bail reform movement can be judged a success. One study of twenty cities showed that the release rate increased from 48 percent in 1962 to 67 percent in 1971 for felony defendants.[9] By 1981 a study of eight jurisdictions found that 85.3 percent of defendants had been released prior to trial,[10] and in the Philadelphia Municipal Court about 90 percent had been released prior to adjudication or final disposition of their cases.[11] These changes have been brought about by several alternative methods developed to facilitate pretrial release. Some of these methods are highlighted in Table 10.2.

Citation

The police have long been accustomed to issuing a **citation,** or summons, to appear in court—a "ticket"—to a person accused of committing a traffic offense or some other minor violation. By issuing the citation, the officer avoids the need to take the accused to the station house for booking and to court for arraignment and determination of bail. Such citations are being used with increasing frequency for more serious offenses, in part because the police want to reduce the amount of time they must spend booking minor offenders and waiting in arraignment court for their cases to come up for decision. In most jurisdictions fewer than 5 percent of those given citations fail to appear. In some cities bail bondsmen have opposed this threat to their livelihood.

citation: A written order issued by a law enforcement officer directing an alleged offender to appear in court at a specified time to answer a criminal charge; referred to as a summons in some jurisdictions.

Release on Recognizance (ROR)

Pioneered in the 1960s by the Vera Institute of Justice in New York City, the **release on recognizance (ROR)** approach is based on the assumption that judges will grant releases if they are given verified information about defendants' reliability and roots in the community. Court personnel talk to defendants soon after their arrest about job, family, prior criminal record, and associations and then determine whether release should be recommended. In the first three years of

release on recognizance (ROR): Pretrial release granted on the defendant's promise to appear in court because the judge believes that the defendant's ties in the community are sufficient to guarantee the required appearance.

TABLE 10.2 Pretrial release methods

Financial Bond

Fully secured bail. The defendant posts the full amount of bail with the court.

Privately secured bail. A bondsman signs a promissory note to the court for the bail amount and charges the defendant a fee for the service (usually 10 percent of the bail amount). If the defendant fails to appear, the bondsman must pay the court the full amount. Frequently, the bondsman requires the defendant to post collateral in addition to the fee.

Percentage bail. The courts allow the defendant to deposit a percentage (usually 10 percent) of the full bail with the court. The full amount of the bail is required if the defendant fails to appear. The percentage bail is returned after disposition of the case although the court often retains 1 percent for administrative costs.

Unsecured bail. The defendant pays no money to the court but is liable for the full amount of bail should he fail to appear.

Alternative Release Options

Release on recognizance (ROR). The court releases the defendant on his promise that he will appear in court as required.

Conditional release. The court releases the defendant subject to his following of specific conditions set by the court such as attendance at drug treatment therapy or staying away from the complaining witness.

Third-party custody. The defendant is released into the custody of an individual or agency that promises to assure his appearance in court. No monetary transactions are involved in this type of release.

SOURCE: U.S. Department of Justice, Bureau of Justice Statistics, *Report to the Nation on Crime and Justice*, 2nd ed. (Washington, DC: Government Printing Office, 1988), p. 76.

the New York project, more than 10,000 defendants were interviewed, and approximately 3,500 were released. Only 1.5 percent failed to appear in court at the appointed time, an appearance rate almost three times better than the rate for those being released on bail.[12] Comparable programs in other cities have had similar results, yet studies have shown that the percentage of those released on their own recognizance does not greatly increase with the creation of a formal pretrial release program.[13]

Today ROR programs exist in almost every major jurisdiction.[14] Often a pretrial release agency is a part of the court organization. In some places it is closely tied to the probation department and in some jurisdictions persons working to secure the release of individuals on their own recognizance are supported by private foundations.

Ten Percent Cash Bail

Although ROR is an attractive alternative to money bail, judges are unwilling to release some defendants on their own recognizance. For this group, some states (Illinois, Kentucky, Nebraska, Oregon, Pennsylvania) have inaugurated bail programs in which the defendants deposit with the court cash equal to 10 percent of their bail. When they appear in court as required, 90 percent of this collateral is returned to them. Begun in Illinois in 1964, this plan is designed primarily to release as many defendants as possible without enriching the bondsmen.

Bail Guidelines

To deal with inequities caused by the unfettered exercise of judicial discretion, reformers have written guidelines for setting bail. The guidelines, designed to bring about consistency, specify the criteria that judges should use in setting bail and list appropriate amounts. Judges are expected to follow the agreed-upon criteria but may deviate when they believe special circumstances are present. Guidelines aim at the rational setting of bail amounts in concert with concerns about the use of pretrial detention, the problem of fleeing, and the potential for additional crimes by the defendant awaiting trial. When guidelines were experimentally tested in the Philadelphia Municipal Court (see Figure 10.3), a greater consistency among the judges was found.[15]

Preventive Detention

Reforms have been suggested not only by those concerned with inequities in the bail system but also by those concerned with crime.[16] Critics point to a relationship between release on bail and commission of crimes, arguing that the accused may commit other illegal acts while awaiting trial. As one more reflection of the debate over due process versus crime control, **preventive detention** has been proposed so that judges can hold suspects without bail if they are accused of committing a dangerous or violent crime and locking them up is deemed necessary for community safety. Civil libertarians, however, call preventive detention a threat to basic constitutional values.

preventive detention: The holding of a defendant for trial, based on a judge's finding that if released on bail, he or she would endanger the safety of any other person and the community.

Least Serious Charges . . . . .　. . . . . Most Serious Charges

Positive "P" = "p"
Negative "n" = "n"

	1	2	3	4	5	6	7	8	9	10	11	12	Risk Severity	Risk Severity Dimension—Risk Groups
Lowest risk of failure to appear and rearrest	ROR 01*	ROR 06	ROR 11	ROR 16	ROR 21	ROR 26	ROR 31	ROR-$1,500 36	ROR-$1,500 41	$800-$3,000 46	$1,000-$3,000 51	$2,000-$7,500 56	I (+19 to +13)	CONSTANT / crim. categ.
	ROR 02	ROR 07	ROR 12	ROR 17	ROR 22	ROR 27	ROR 32	ROR-$1,500 37	ROR-$1,500 42	$500-$3,000 47	$1,000-$3,000 52	$2,000-$7,500 57	II (+12 to +10)	arrests / cr. + arrs.
	ROR 03	ROR 08	ROR 13	ROR 18	ROR 23	ROR 28	ROR-$500 33	ROR-$1,500 38	$500-$1,500 43	$1,000-$3,000 48	$1,000-$3,000 53	$2,000-$7,500 58	III (+9 exactly)	pend'g chgs. / FTAs
	ROR 04	ROR 09	ROR 14	ROR-$1,000 19	ROR-$1,000 24	$500-$1,000 29	$500-$1,500 34	$500-$2,000 39	$800-$2,500 44	$1,000-$5,000 49	$1,000-$5,000 54	$2,000-$7,500 59	IV (+8 to +4)	age of def't / age + FTAs
Greatest risk of failure to appear and rearrest	ROR 05	ROR-$500 10	ROR-$1,000 15	$500-$1,000 20	$500-$1,000 25	$500-$1,500 30	$500-$2,000 35	$500-$2,000 40	$800-$3,000 45	$1,500-$5,000 50	$1,500-$5,000 55	$3,000-$10,000 60	V (+3 to -13)	comm'ty ties
RISK GROUPS points	1	2	3	4	5	6	7	8	9	10	11	12		Col. Total / Subtract "n" (if smaller) / TOTAL POSITIVE

Charge Severity Dimension—Charge Levels

Selected Guidelines Range:

_____

→

Actual Decision:

☐ ROR　☐ _____
(amount)

If outside guidelines, check reason below:

IF YOU GO BELOW THE GUIDELINES AMOUNT—show reason for departing from guidelines by using a lower figure (ROR or lower financial bail than in the guidelines decision) and by checking the applicable box(es) below.

IF YOU GO ABOVE THE GUIDELINES AMOUNT—show reason for departing from guidelines by using a higher bail amount (money bail instead of ROR, or greater money amount) by checking the applicable box(es) below.

A* ☐ (LIKELY) Prosecution will be withdrawn　VERSUS　Will be convicted (LIKELY) ☐ G

B ☐ (GOOD)　Court room demeanor of defendent　(POOR) ☐ H

C ☐　Physical or mental health concerns　☐ I _____

D ☐ (VERY UNLIKELY)　Interference with witnesses　(LIKELY) ☐ J _____

E ☐ Sponsor at prelim. arr.　VERSUS　Cause guardian to be notified of arrest ☐ K _____

N/A　POSSIBILITY of mandatory sentence　☐ L _____

N/A　CURRENT/OUSTANDING warrants/detainers/wanted cards　☐ M _____

F ☐　OTHER (indicate DIRECTION OF DEPARTURE)　☐ N ⇨ SHOW REASON ABOVE

Guidelines decision by: _____

FIGURE 10.3
Bail guidelines worksheet for judges. Judges in Philadelphia use this worksheet to first determine in which risk group the accused should be placed. Next the severity of the charges are noted. The box in which the two variables cross contains the guideline for either ROR or bail. *Numbers and letters for coding purposes. SOURCE: John Goldkamp and Michael Gottfriedson, *Judicial Decision Guidelines for Bail: The Philadelphia Experiment* (Washington, DC: National Institute of Justice, 1983).

Preventive detention was authorized by Congress in the Bail Reform Act of 1984. Under the Act, federal judges may consider whether the defendant poses a danger to the community in deciding whether (and under what conditions) to release him or her before trial. The legislation allows outright detention on the basis of presumed danger to particular persons or the community at large. This decision is made at a hearing to consider the prosecution's contention that (1) there is a serious risk that the person will flee; (2) the person will obstruct justice or threaten, injure, or intimidate a prospective witness or juror; or (3) the offense is one of violence or one punishable by life imprisonment or death. As shown in Table 10.3, three-fourths of the states now have one or more provisions in the laws designed to ensure community safety in pretrial release.

Preventive detention would seem to be at odds with the Constitution's prohibition of excessive bail and the due process clause, since the accused is held in custody until a verdict at trial is rendered.

TABLE 10.3 **States with one or more provisions to ensure community safety in pretrial release.**   Concern that some persons on bail are committing additional crimes while they await trial has caused some states to enact laws limiting pretrial release under some circumstances.

Type of Provision	States that Have Enacted the Provision
Exclusion of certain crimes from automatic bail eligibility	Colorado, District of Columbia, Florida, Georgia, Michigan, Nebraska, Wisconsin
Definition of the purpose of bail to ensure appearance and safety	Alaska, Arizona, California, Delaware, District of Columbia, Florida, Hawaii, Minnesota, South Carolina, South Dakota, Vermont, Virginia, Wisconsin
Inclusion of crime control factors in the release decision	Alabama, California, Florida, Georgia, Minnesota, South Dakota, Wisconsin
Inclusion of release conditions related to crime control	Alaska, Arkansas, Colorado, Delaware, District of Columbia, Florida, Hawaii, Illinois, Iowa, Minnesota, New Mexico, North Carolina, South Carolina, South Dakota, Vermont, Virginia, Washington, Wisconsin
Limitations on the right to bail for those previously convicted	Colorado, District of Columbia, Florida, Georgia, Hawaii, Indiana, Michigan, New Mexico, Texas, Utah, Wisconsin
Revocation of pretrial release when there is evidence that the accused committed a new crime	Arizona, Arkansas, Colorado, District of Columbia, Georgia, Hawaii, Illinois, Maryland, Massachusetts, Michigan, Nevada, New Mexico, New York, Rhode Island, Texas, Utah, Vermont, Wisconsin
Limitations on the right to bail for crimes alleged to have been committed while on release	Arizona, Arkansas, Colorado, District of Columbia, Florida, Georgia, Illinois, Indiana, Maryland, Massachusetts, Michigan, Minnesota, Nevada, New Mexico, New York, Rhode Island, Tennessee, Texas, Utah, Vermont, Wisconsin
Provisions for pretrial detention to ensure safety	Arizona, Arkansas, California, Colorado, District of Columbia, Florida, Georgia, Hawaii, Illinois, Indiana, Maryland, Massachusetts, Michigan, Nebraska, Nevada, New Mexico, New York, Rhode Island, South Dakota, Texas, Utah, Vermont, Virginia, Washington, Wisconsin

SOURCE: U.S. Department of Justice, Bureau of Justice Statistics, *Report to the Nation on Crime and Justice* 2nd ed. (Washington, DC: Government Printing Office, 1988), p. 77.

However, in two cases the Supreme Court has upheld the constitutionality of preventive detention. In *Schall* v. *Martin* (1984) the Court said that the detention of a juvenile was useful to protect both the welfare of the minor and the community as a whole.[17] The preventive detention provisions of the Bail Reform Act of 1984 were upheld in *United States* v. *Salerno* (1987).[18] The justices said that preventive detention was a legitimate use of governmental power, since it was designed not to punish the accused but to deal with the problem of people committing crimes while on bail. Prevention of further damage to the community from these crimes was within the powers of Congress. By upholding the federal law the Court also legitimized comparable state laws dealing with preventive detention.

Proponents of preventive detention point to the fact that studies

Schall v. *Martin* **(1984)**: Pretrial detention of a juvenile is constitutional to protect the welfare of the minor and the community.

United States v. *Salerno* **(1987)**: Preventive detention provisions of the Bail Reform Act of 1984 are upheld; legitimate use of governmental power is designed to prevent people from committing crimes while on bail.

CLOSE-UP   *Preventive Detention: Two Sides of an Issue*

For Ricardo Armstrong, there is the despair of trying to reunite his family after spending four months in a Cincinnati jail for bank robbery before being acquitted of the crime.

For friends and family of Linda Goldstone, there is the anguish of knowing that she would still be alive if there had been a way to keep Hernando Williams in jail while he was facing rape and assault charges in Chicago. . .

The cases illustrate the debate over preventive detention, which allows defendants to be held in jail awaiting trial if a judge deems them a danger to the community. . .

Ricardo Armstrong was one of the first defendants held under the federal law's [Bail Reform Act of 1984] provision. The twenty-eight-year-old janitor, who had a prior burglary conviction, was denied bail after being charged with robbing two Ohio banks.

From the start, Mr. Armstrong had insisted that bank robbery charges against him were part of some nightmarish mix-up.

A Cincinnati jury agreed. After viewing bank photographs of the robber, the jury acquitted Mr. Armstrong in what was apparently a case of mistaken identity.

Justice, it seemed, had been served—but not before Mr. Armstrong had spent four months in jail. [Mr. Armstrong's] life crumbled as he sat in a jail cell, while his wife left their home and moved with their children a thousand miles away.

"Who's going to get me back those four months?" he now asks bitterly. "Who's going to get me back my kids?" The Bail Reform Act makes no provision for compensating defendants who are jailed and later acquitted.

Legal scholars believe that prosecutors and judges who favored preventive detention were nonetheless cautious about imposing it before the Supreme Court ruling [*United States* v. *Salerno*] because they believed the law might be overturned. The ruling has emboldened judges who might otherwise have feared being reversed on appeal.

"Until now, the courts have been a little cautious about detaining people," said Judy C. Clarke, the federal public defender in San Diego. "No more. Now the federal courts will read the law much more broadly. And the states will take the cue, too."

Proponents, including Justice Department officials, say preventive detention is needed to stop dangerous criminals from committing still more crimes while free on bond. They say it ensures that drug dealers, who often view bail as merely a business expense, cannot flee before trial.

They concede that some injustices inevitably occur. But they note that other cases, involving dangerous defendants set free on bond, ring just as tragically for victims of crimes that could have been prevented. . . . Prosecutors point to the release of Hernando Williams as the classic example of the need for preventive detention. Even as Mr. Williams, free on $25,000 bond, drove to court to face charges, [of raping and beating a woman he abducted at a shopping mall], another woman lay trapped inside his car trunk. This victim, Linda Goldstone, a twenty-nine-year-old birthing instructor, was abducted by Mr. Williams as she walked to Northwestern Hospital and was forced at gunpoint to crawl into his trunk.

Over a four-day period, Mrs. Goldstone was removed from the trunk periodically to be raped and beaten until she was shot to death. Mr. Williams has been sentenced to death.

"Linda Goldstone might well be alive today if we'd had this law then," said Richard M. Daley, the Cook County State's Attorney.

SOURCE: Adapted from "Preventive Detention: Two Sides of an Issue," by D. Johnston, *The New York Times,* July, 13, 1987, p. A13. Copyright © 1987 by The New York Times Company. Reprinted by permission.

have shown that somewhere between 7 and 20 percent of persons under pretrial release commit crimes, and for some crimes the figure is as high as 34 to 70 percent. Martin Sorin argues that "pretrial criminals may account for as much as one-fifth of our nation's total crime problem."[19] Such findings have led planners to argue that there is a small but identifiable group of defendants who are immune to the imposition of stringent release conditions and the prospect of revocation of their bail: they are not deterred. Research has shown that the nature and seriousness of the charge, a history of prior arrests, and the presence of drug addiction all have a strong bearing on the probability that a defendant will commit a pretrial criminal act.[20] Other scholars, however, have contended that the criteria normally used to set bail are poor indicators of the probability a defendant will not appear in court as scheduled or will commit another crime while awaiting trial.[21]

What is the likely impact of preventive detention? One study by Stephen Kennedy and Kenneth Carlson suggests that although preventive detention has had an impact on federal pretrial release practices, the percentage of defendants released before trial remains relatively stable.[22] They believe that this apparent contradiction results from the fact that prior to the Bail Reform Act, judges set high bail for those accused whom they did not want to release. The new provisions no longer mean that they must use this ruse. The study showed that preventive detention was used most often when the case involved violence, drugs, and immigration offenses.

PRETRIAL DETENTION

Individuals who are unable to secure bail or to be released on their own recognizance are remanded to jail to await their court appearance. American jails have been called the ultimate ghetto; in fact, most of the more than 350,000 people in jails are poor. About half are in pretrial detention, and the remainder are serving sentences (normally of less than one year) or awaiting transfer to state prison or to

The period immediately after arrest is extremely stressful. It is at this time that jail suicides are most prevalent, yet most jails are ill-equipped to handle the multiple problems presented by detainees.

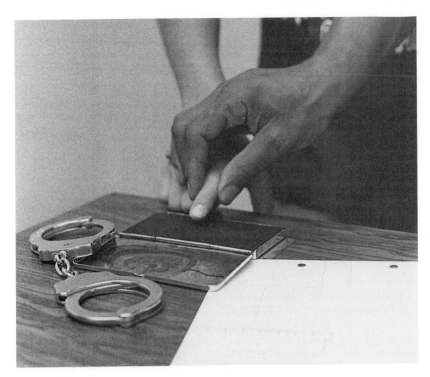

■
One of the first steps upon entering
the criminal justice system.

another jurisdiction. The function and characteristics of the jail
are fully discussed in Chapter 14; here we will be dealing only with
that portion of the incarcerated population that is being held
awaiting trial.

For most suspects the period immediately after arrest is the most
frightening. Imagine yourself in such circumstances. After being fingerprinted, photographed, and questioned, you are taken to the detention section of the jail. In some newer facilities you may be asked
further questions about your background, physical condition, and
mental health so that treatment may be provided if necessary. More
than likely, there is no formal intake procedure, and you are simply
put in a holding "tank." If you are a man, there are probably three or
more strangers in the cell with you, men whose stories you do not
know and whose behavior you cannot predict. If you are a woman,
you are probably by yourself. In either case, the guard leaves, and
you are on your own. You now have time to think and to worry about
your situation.

For most people this is a threatening scenario; they might approach panic in such circumstances. That is why the initial hours
following arrest are often referred to as a period of crisis for the
defendant. The vulnerability, the sense of hopelessness and fright,
and the ominous threat of loss of freedom are never more stressful
than in those first few hours of confinement. It is understandable that
most jail suicides occur within the first six to ten hours of detention
and that most psychotic episodes occur during or just after intake.

The crisis nature of arrest and detention can be exacerbated by
other factors. Often the newly arrested person is intoxicated by alcohol or another drug; indeed, intoxication may have contributed to the
very crime for which the person is being held. Sometimes the criminal behavior that has put the accused in jail stems from an emotional
instability that may become more severe in detention. For young of-

fenders, the oppressive threat and reality of personal violence can set off debilitating depression. Without question, one of the most crucial times for the administrator and the offender comes immediately after arrest.

COMPARATIVE PERSPECTIVE
Magistrates' Court in England

When readers of Agatha Christie and Sir Arthur Conan Doyle imagine an English criminal court, they probably picture a judge in robe and wig, barristers similarly attired, and a jury about to determine the fate of the person in the dock. The skill of argument, the ceremony of the proceedings, and the Victorian architecture combine to produce high drama usually absent from American courtrooms. But what they have imagined is the Crown Court, and it differs significantly from the 500 Magistrates' Courts where most of the work of criminal justice is accomplished.

American visitors are usually impressed with the Magistrates' Court because its lay justices convey an air of dignified informality in their work. Unlike the pomp and ceremony of trials in the Crown Court, the ambience of the Magistrates' Court is that of a "people's court." The room is usually without decoration; it contains only tables where the magistrates and solicitors sit, and a few chairs for defendants, relatives, and onlookers. Sitting in panels of twos and threes, and with the assistance of a legally qualified clerk, the lay magistrates call the cases, receive evidence, listen to circumstances of mitigation, and make dispositions without the conveyor-belt atmosphere so typical of urban courts in the United States.

The 2,400 magistrates in England and Wales (Scotland has a separate criminal justice system) are unpaid volunteers who are expected to donate one day every two weeks to their judicial duties. Selection as a lay magistrate is an honor given

to those who have exhibited a concern for civic activities. They are appointed on behalf of the Crown by the Lord Chancellor upon the recommendation of local advisory committees after secret deliberations.

Critics argue that the appointment process results in a judiciary composed mainly of persons from the upper and professional classes, with the consequence that justice is biased against the poor. That result has been questioned; in fact, it is said that magistrates from working-class backgrounds tend to be harder on offenders. There have been recent efforts to ensure that the magistery has a broader social base, yet the fact remains that it is those from the more privileged groups in the community who are able to give the time and who present themselves as being interested in performing this civic duty. As a result, the foreign visitor is immediately struck by the gulf in vocabulary and accent that usually exists between those on the bench and the person in the dock.

The English divide offenses into three classes: indictable, and therefore triable by judge and jury at the Crown Court; summary, and therefore triable before the Magistrates' Court; or so-called "either way," in which the defendant decides at which level he or she wishes to be tried. Magistrates' Courts are the setting for summary trials and for committal proceedings for trials to be held in the Crown Court. Thus almost anyone charged with a crime appears before the lay justices. One result is that even with indictable offenses, 87 percent of the dispositions result from sentences given by the Magistrates' Courts.

The penalties that the magistrates are authorized to impose for each offense reach a maximum of six months imprisonment and/or a £1,000 fine. But magistrates may also use other correctional alternatives such as community service, suspended sentences, and probation. Of particular interest is the fact that the fine is the most frequent sanction, with 55 percent of all offenders receiving that sanction.

The English Magistrates' Courts dispense an informal brand of justice in a manner that is quite different from lower courts in the United States, in which prosecutors and defense attorneys argue over the introduction of evidence and due process rules. In England, police officers give their testimony, and defendants present their cases with the assistance of counsel. There are usually questions from the bench, followed by a huddled conversation among the magistrates and then announcement of guilt or innocence. Sentences are then imposed, more in the manner of a stern lecture than the swift recitation of the terms of the punishment; this is followed by the sound of the gavel and the call, "Next case."

Impact of Pretrial Detention

The fact that a defendant is being held in jail seriously affects the ultimate disposition of his or her case. Consider the effect on a judge and jury of two hypothetical defendants: one steps neatly dressed from among the onlookers to the counsel's table; the other, in jail garb, is escorted by guards from a nearby cell to the counsel's table. What would you think if you were on the bench or in the jury box? Although it would be difficult to prove that these contrasting scenes affect the justice dispensed, various theories of human behavior suggest that the accused who has been detained is more likely to be labeled guilty. The ways we present ourselves to others have important effects on their actions toward us.

Are people who are detained awaiting trial more often convicted and receive harsher treatment than those out on bail? The evidence is unclear. A study by Eric Single revealed that defendants held for trial in lieu of bail are more often convicted and, when convicted, go to prison more often and receive longer sentences than those who post bail.[23] However, John Goldkamp found no such relationship in his study of the bail-custody question in Philadelphia. What he did find was that those held in custody were more likely to get prison terms than those not detained.[24] One problem with research on this question is that it is difficult to isolate the detention factor from such other variables as the severity of the offense and the evidence supporting a guilty verdict.

One of the facts about U.S. jails that is significant is that the conditions under which inmates (half of whom have not been convicted of the crimes for which they are being detained) are detained are deplorable. For a goodly number, their pretrial detention is long: in many states the average delay between arrest and trial is six months or more. The hardship of detention before trial is serious, for it creates pressures on defendants to waive their rights and to plead guilty.

PLEA BARGAINING

The Supreme Court has ruled that plea bargaining is constitutional. Other courts, and prosecutors, say it is absolutely necessary. Defense lawyers say it is often a boon to their clients. Former chief justice Warren Burger has said, "It is an elementary fact, historically and statistically, that the system of courts—the number of judges, prosecutors, and of courtrooms—has been based on the premise that approximately 90 percent of all defendants will plead guilty, leaving only 10 percent, more or less, to be tried."[25] By contrast, the National Advisory Commission on Criminal Justice Standards and Goals called for the abolition of plea bargaining.

The process of plea bargaining—also called negotiating a settlement or **"copping out"**—was for many years one of the best-kept secrets of criminal justice practitioners; only in recent years has the public become aware of it as the method by which the great bulk of criminal offenders are sanctioned. It was little discussed earlier because there were doubts about its constitutionality and because it did

copping out (slang): Entering a plea of guilty, normally after bargaining. The copping out "ceremony" consists of a series of questions that the judge asks the defendant as to the voluntary nature of the plea.

■ Plea bargaining has now become so much a part of the system that judges frequently take part in negotiations.

not seem appropriate to a system committed to the adversary procedure.

But decisions by the Supreme Court have clearly said that plea bargaining is legitimate. In *Blackledge* v. *Allison* (1976), for example, the justices said: "Whatever might be the situation in an ideal world, the fact is that the guilty plea and the often concomitant plea bargain are important components of this country's criminal justice system. Properly administered, they can benefit all concerned."[26] The Court has noted that plea bargaining flows from "the mutuality of advantage" to defendants and prosecutors, each with his or her own reasons for wanting to avoid trial.

In the broadest sense, plea bargaining is the process that produces a defendant's agreement to plead guilty to a criminal charge with the reasonable expectation of receiving some consideration from the state for doing so. Some defendants plead guilty without entering into negotiations but expect to receive some benefit nevertheless, a practice called *implicit* plea bargaining. It is distinguished from *explicit* plea bargaining, an arrangement between the prosecutor and defendant—sometimes with the participation of the judge—whereby a plea of guilty is exchanged for the prosecutor's agreement to press a charge less serious than that warranted by the facts and perhaps to recommend leniency in sentencing to the judge.

The defendant's usual objective is to be charged with a crime carrying a lower potential maximum sentence, thus limiting the judge's discretion in sentencing. A plea may also be entered on one charge on agreement that the prosecutor will drop other charges in a multicount indictment. Another reason for seeking a lesser charge may be the defendant's wish to avoid charges with legislatively mandated sentences or stipulations against probation or to escape a charge that carries an undesirable label, such as rapist or child molester. The prosecutor seeks to obtain a guilty plea to avoid combat in the courtroom. Although the imposition of the sentence remains a function of the court, the prosecutor draws up the indictment and usually has an important influence on the judge's sentencing deci-

TABLE 10.4 Plea bargaining in five jurisdictions: Robbery and burglary.   The percentage of guilty pleas is about the same in all five jurisdictions regardless of such factors as the number of judges, number of felony trials, and number of indictments or informations.

	Jurisdiction				
	New Orleans	Seattle (King County)	Norfolk	Tucson	(Delaware County)
Population	562,000	1,157,000	285,500	500,000	600,000
Estimated Annual Indictments or Informations Filed	5,063	4,500	2,800	2,309	3,000
Number of Felony Judges	10	8	3	7	4
Number of Prosecutors	63	69	15	39	30
Percentage of Robbery and Burglary Defendants Pleading Guilty	81%	86%	78%	87%	80%
Number of Felony Trials per Year	1,069	4,567	648	270	491
Type of Defense Counsel and Estimated Percentage of Defendants Covered	Public 65% Assigned 10% Retained 25%	Public 64% Assigned 16% Retained 20%	Assigned 75% Retained 25%	Public 70% Assigned 3% Retained 27%	Public 65% Retained 35%
Prosecutorial Restrictions on Plea Bargaining	Limited charge bargaining	For high-impact cases	Minimal	For career criminals	Minimal

SOURCE: William F. McDonald, *Plea Bargaining: Critical Issues and Common Practices* (Washington, DC: National Institute of Justice, 1985), p. 7.

sion. Clearly, plea bargaining is the most crucial stage in the criminal justice process and is the primary example of "bargain justice."

According to the traditional conception of adversarial justice, criminal cases are not "settled," as in civil law; the outcome is determined by the symbolic contest of the state versus the accused. Table 10.4 shows the percentages of guilty pleas in robbery and burglary cases in five jurisdictions. Note that the percentage of guilty pleas varies little among the cities even given the number of trials, judges, and prosecutors. Figure 10.4 shows the types of plea concessions

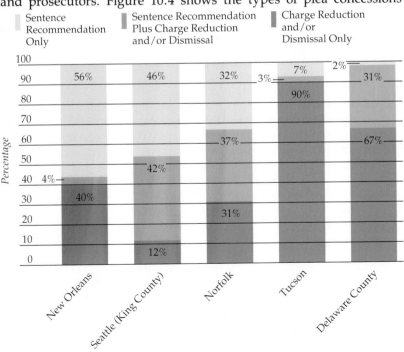

Sentence Recommendation Only

Sentence Recommendation Plus Charge Reduction and/or Dismissal

Charge Reduction and/or Dismissal Only

FIGURE 10.4

Types of plea concessions in robbery and burglary cases in five jurisdictions.   Although about the same percentage of cases ends in a guilty plea, the type of concession differs. SOURCE: William F. McDonald, *Plea Bargaining: Critical Issues and Common Practices* (Washington, DC: National Institute of Justice, 1985), p. 7.

made in these cases in the same jurisdictions. This study is consistent with other studies. It is generally accepted that up to 90 percent of felony defendants in the United States plead guilty.

Exchange Relationships in Plea Bargaining

Plea bargaining is essentially a series of exchange relationships in which the prosecutor, the defense attorney, the defendant, and sometimes the judge participate. All enter the contest with particular objectives; all attempt to structure the situation to their own advantage and come armed with a number of tactics designed to improve their position; and all will see the exchange as a success from their own perspective. The exchange may be considered successful by the prosecutor who is able to convict the defendant without trial; by the defense attorney who is able to collect a fee with a minimum of effort; and by the judge who is able to dispose of one more case from a crowded calendar.

Tactics

Plea bargaining between defense counsel and prosecutor bears a striking resemblance to a formal ritual in which friendliness and joking mask the forceful advancement of antagonistic views. The pattern is a familiar one: initial humor, the stating of each viewpoint, resolution of conflict, and a final period of cementing the relationship. Throughout the session, each side tries to impress the other with its confidence in its own case while indicating weaknesses in

---

A QUESTION OF ETHICS

Attorney Larry Bowman came bustling into the office of Assistant Prosecutor Wayne Shannon with an armload of case files. Shannon had been expecting the visit and knew what Bowman was likely to do.

"Wayne, I'd like to talk with you about these ten cases that I have for tomorrow. Most of them are just garbage, so I think we can get rid of them quickly. For example, here is the Buckley and Dickens case. They're codefendants and I've got them both. They're each charged with armed robbery, but Dickens says he did not have the gun. You've got to admit that the whole case is pretty flimsy, since the victim is confused as to what happened. How about a guilty plea on a reduced charge of robbery 2 for Dickens? He's a young kid and deserves a break. He told me that Buckley actually planned this whole thing and held the gun to the woman's head. Buckley's not been very cooperative with me. I just don't like his attitude."

"Well Larry, I don't know. These guys have been in trouble before. If I go for the plea for Dickens, where does that place Buckley?"

How should Prosecutor Shannon react to Bowman's statement? What are the ethical questions that would arise from this case should the offer of a guilty plea and charge reduction for Dickens be accepted? What should happen to Buckley? How might the resolution of this case affect future negotiations between Shannon and Bowman?

the opponent's presentation. During the discussion, there appears to be a norm of openness and candor designed to maintain the relationship. Little effort seems to be made to conceal information that may later be useful to the adversary in the courtroom. There seems to be a standing rule that confidences shared during negotiations will not be used in court.

Some attorneys, of course, do not conform to this norm. One prosecutor said: "There are some attorneys with whom we never bargain, because we can't. We don't like to penalize a defendant because he has an ass for an attorney, but when an attorney cannot be trusted, we have no alternative." Defense attorneys often feel that prosecutors are insulated from the human factors of a case and are thus unwilling to individualize justice. Since defense lawyers get to know the defendants, their problems, and their families, they may become emotionally attached to cases. As one defense lawyer told this author: "We have to impress the chief deputy prosecutor with the fact that he is dealing with humans, not with just a case. If the guy is guilty he should be imprisoned, but he should get only what's coming to him, no more."

A tactic that prosecutors commonly bring to plea bargaining sessions is the multiple-offense indictment. One defense attorney commented: "Prosecutors throw everything into an indictment they can think of, down to and including spitting on the sidewalk. They then permit the defendant to plead guilty to one or two offenses, and he is supposed to think it's a victory."[27] Multiple-offense charges are especially important to prosecuting attorneys when they are faced with difficult cases—cases in which, for instance, the complainant is reluctant, the value of the stolen item is in question, and the reliability of the evidence is in doubt. Narcotics officers often file charges of selling a drug against defendants when they know they can convict only for possession. Since the accused persons know that the penalty for selling is much greater, they are tempted to plead guilty to the lesser charge.

Defense attorneys may approach these negotiations by threatening to ask for a jury trial if concessions are not made. Their hand is further strengthened if they have filed pretrial motions that require a formal response by the prosecutor. Another tactic is to seek rescheduling of pretrial activities in the hope that because of the delay, witnesses will become unavailable, public interest will die, and memories of the incident will be weakened by the time of the trial. Rather than resort to such legal maneuverings, some attorneys prefer to bargain on the basis of friendship. An Oakland attorney commented:

> I never use the Constitution. I bargain a case on the theory that it's a "cheap burglary" or a "cheap purse-snatching" or a "cheap whatever." Sure, I could suddenly start to negotiate by saying, "Ha, ha! You goofed. You should have given the defendant a warning." And I'd do just fine in that case, but my other clients would pay for this isolated success. The next time the district attorney had his foot on my throat, he'd push too."[28]

Often the bargain is struck in ways that might go unnoticed by the casual observer. To maintain some psychological distance between the adversaries, vague references are often made to disposition of the case. Such statements as "I think I can sell this to the boss" or "I'll see what can be done" signal the completion of a bargaining session and are interpreted by the actors as an agreement on the terms of the exchange. On other cases, negotiations are more specific, with a direct promise made that certain charges will be altered in exchange for a guilty plea.

Because negotiations are conducted primarily between the prosecutor and the defense attorney, the interests of the public and even of the defendant may become secondary considerations. Without the possibility of a trial in which evidence gathered in a legal manner must be presented, plea bargaining can shield unconstitutional practices by justice system actors from public view.

Neither the prosecutor nor the defense attorney is a free agent. Each must count on the cooperation of both defendants and judges. Attorneys often cite the difficulty they have convincing defendants that they should uphold their end of the bargain. Judges must cooperate in the agreement by sentencing the accused according to the prosecutor's recommendation. Although their role requires that they uphold the public interest, judges may be reluctant to interfere with a plea agreement in order to maintain future exchange relationships. Thus both the prosecutor and the defense attorney usually confer with the judge regarding the sentence to be imposed before agreeing on a plea. At the same time, however, the judicial role requires that judges hold in reserve their power to reject the agreement. Because uncertainty is one of the hazards of the organizational system, prosecutors and defense attorneys will use each judicial decision as an indication of the judge's future behavior.

Pleas without Bargaining

Recent studies have alerted scholars to the fact that in many courthouses the marketplace tactics of plea bargaining do not exist in certain types of cases, yet guilty pleas remain as high as the national average.[29] The term *bargaining* may be misleading in that it implies haggling. Many scholars now argue that guilty pleas emerge after a consensus is reached to "settle the facts" by professionals—the prosecuting and defense attorneys and sometimes the judge.[30] From this perspective the parties first examine the facts of a case. What were the circumstances of the event? Is it *really* an assault, or is it more of a pushing and shoving match? Did the victim first antagonize the accused? By settling the facts the defense and prosecution fit the behavior into "normal crime" categories—the way that charges are locally defined. With the facts of the crime settled and agreement on the appropriate charges, there can next be agreement as to the sentence according to the locally defined "going rates" (the usual sentences given for such an offense). The shared expectations as to the definition of the crime event into charge categories, coupled with a sentence that is consistent with the going rate, can be referred to as implicit bargaining.

Douglas Maynard found that many cases are concluded when one party offers a disposition and the other simply agrees to it. Because courthouse actors are familiar with the definition and categorization of criminal acts, and know the going rate, bargaining is limited. In only a small number of cases did Maynard discover extensive bargaining carried out visibly and unambiguously. As he notes, the sharing of expectations

> means simply that participants are able to read situations in like manner and infer what resolution will be mutually acceptable. Such a process in plea bargaining is surely aided by the participants' knowledge of the courtroom subculture. The establishment by legal practitioners of "going rates" for run-of-the-mill, "normal" crimes . . . in local jurisdictions and the administration of these rates as a matter of course . . . is a well-documented practice.[31]

We should expect to find implicit plea bargaining in courtrooms in which the going rates are known to the participants. If there is much turnover among the actors, uncertainty would be likely to reduce the number of guilty pleas offered without negotiation. We should also expect bargaining to be more explicit over serious offenses, when the possible sentence would be incarceration. But underlying both the implicit and explicit models of plea bargaining is the assumption that there is a penalty for going to trial. The nature of that penalty may be an added factor that looms over all plea considerations.

We should also be alert to the fact that the local courtroom culture has a decided impact on the bargaining process; similar issues are not decided in the same manner from courthouse to courthouse. Particular ways of disposing of cases develop in each setting. In some courts a "slow plea" process will be the dominant method: defendants initially plead not guilty but change their pleas as the trials progress. In other courts, various portions of the caseload may be filtered out by the prosecutor through the dropping of cases or the diversion of offenders. The variety of routines, norms, and expectations may be much greater than was originally thought, and observers of any one courthouse may discover patterns that are not exactly like the textbook description.

Legal Issues in Plea Bargaining

The constitutionality of the guilty plea has evolved over the last several decades. Questions concerning the voluntariness of the plea and the sancity of the agreement have forced the U.S. Supreme Court to confront these issues. In deciding these questions the justices have upheld the general constitutionality of the practice and sought to ensure that due process rights have been upheld within the context of administrative decision making.

The voluntariness of the defendant to plead guilty is a central concern. In *Boykin* v. *Alabama* (1969) the Court ruled that defendants must make an affirmative statement that the plea was made voluntarily before a judge may accept the plea.[32] Courts have created standardized forms listing a series of questions for the defendant to affirm before the plea is accepted. Trial judges are also required to learn whether the defendant understands the implications of an agreement to plead guilty and to ensure that pressures were not brought by either the prosecutor or defense attorney to coerce the plea.

Boykin v. *Alabama* (1969): Defendants must make an affirmative statement that they are voluntarily making a plea of guilty.

Can a trial court accept a guilty plea if the defendant maintains his innocence? In *Alford* v. *North Carolina* (1970) the Court approved, in principle, a plea of guilty by a defendant who nevertheless said he was innocent, for the purpose of obtaining a lesser sentence.

Henry C. Alford was accused of killing a man in Forsyth County, North Carolina. He was charged with first-degree murder, a capital offense. Although maintaining his innocence, Alford plea bargained to second-degree murder, a charge for which the death penalty was not authorized. After receiving a thirty-year sentence, he complained to the Supreme Court that the plea had been coerced by the death penalty threat. He argued that throughout the proceedings he had never admitted his guilt. The Court disagreed with Alford's contention that he was an innocent person who had been sent to prison without trial. It ruled that it was Alford's privilege to plead guilty to avoid a possible death penalty even though he continued to maintain his innocence. One result of this ruling is that courts in many parts of the country now routinely accept pleas based on the "Alford Doctrine," by which defendants plead guilty but say they are not guilty.[33]

A second issue concerns fullfillment of the plea agreement. If the prosecutor has given a promise of leniency, it must be kept. In *Santobello* v. *New York* (1971), the Supreme Court ruled that "when a [guilty] plea rests in any significant degree on a promise or agreement of the prosecutor, so that it can be said to be part of the inducement or consideration, such promise must be fulfilled."[34] That defendants must also keep their side of the bargain was decided by the Court in *Ricketts* v. *Adamson* (1987). Here, Ricketts agreed to plead guilty and testify against a codefendant in exchange for a reduction of the charges from first- to second-degree murder. He carried out the bargain but refused to testify a second time when the codefendant had his conviction reversed on appeal. The prosecutor then withdrew the offer to reduce the charge. The Supreme Court upheld the recharging and said that Ricketts had to suffer the consequences of his voluntary choice not to testify at the codefendant's second trial.[35]

May prosecutors threaten to penalize defendants who insist on their right to a jury trial? Paul Hayes was indicted in Kentucky for forging an $88.50 check. The prosecutor offered to recommend a sentence of five years' imprisonment if a guilty plea was entered but said that if Hayes pleaded not guilty, he would be indicted under the state's habitual criminal act. If Hayes was then found guilty, a mandatory life sentence would result, because he had two prior convictions. Hayes rejected the guilty plea, went to trial, and was sentenced to life imprisonment. On appeal, the U.S. Supreme Court ruled in *Bordenhircher* v. *Hayes* (1978) that in the "give and take" of plea bargaining, the prosecutor's conduct did not violate constitutional protections.[36] Milwaukee Judge Ralph Fine has charged that prosecutors around the country are now using this decision as a tool to extract guilty pleas from hesitant defendants.[37]

Plea bargaining, then, is no longer a secret of the courthouse. The Supreme Court has accepted the constitutionality of the practice and has emphasized the importance of protecting due process rights within this administrative context. As noted, when a plea is given, the judge is required to ask a series of questions to ensure that the method by which the bargain was struck adheres to these principles.

Alford v. *North Carolina* (1970): A plea of guilty may be accepted for the purpose of a lesser sentence by a defendant who maintains his or her innocence.

Santobello v. *New York* (1971): When a guilty plea rests on a promise of a prosecutor, it must be fulfilled.

Ricketts v. *Adamson* (1987): Defendants must uphold plea agreement or suffer the consequences.

Bordenhircher v. *Hayes* (1978): A defendant's rights were not violated by a prosecutor who warned that not to accept a guilty plea would result in a harsher sentence.

At one time, this charade of the "copping out ceremony" was one of the regular features of the courtroom day. But judges are increasingly discussing plea bargaining openly in their courts and admitting on record that they are aware of plea negotiations. In many cases, judges have entered into plea discussions with respect to sentences in cases before them.

Justification for Plea Bargaining

As early as the 1920s the legal profession was united in opposition to plea bargaining. Roscoe Pound, Raymond Moley, and others associated with the crime surveys of the period stressed the opportunities for political influence as a factor in the administration of criminal justice. Today, owing to the pressures generated by crime in an urban society and the reality of bargaining, a shift has occurred so that professional groups are primarily interested in procedures that will allow for the review of guilty pleas and for other safeguards. Plea bargaining is now justified on the grounds that it individualizes justice and that it is administratively necessary.

Individualized Justice

One of the most common justifications for plea bargaining is that it is necessary to individualize justice. Traditionally, judges have performed this function by fashioning sentences to the severity of the offense and the characteristics of the offender. Some people have argued, however, that developments in the system have limited the discretion of the judge while increasing the opportunity for the prosecutor to allocate justice. This view suggests that if the criminal law is to be even minimally fair, the prosecutor's office must be able to determine case outcomes administratively.

One factor that promotes the guilty plea is related to the legislatures that have dictated extreme sentence lengths. Legislatures respond to public pressures by fixing severe punishments. Criminal justice personnel soften the punishments through the plea bargaining process in the interests of justice, to serve the needs of the bureaucracy, and to gain the acquiescence of the accused. In this way, courthouse practitioners develop shared norms as to the sentencing value attached to a particular offense. Courthouse regulars believe that defendants who insist on a trial and are then found guilty and those who refuse to cooperate should receive harsher sentences than those who "go along." It is often claimed that the acceptance of the guilty plea by the prosecutor and judge may help to soften the occasional overharshness of the law.

Administrative Necessity

A second justification for plea bargaining is administrative necessity. As we have seen, the problem of criminal justice is that of mass production. The demands on the judicial process—including calendar congestion, the size of the prison population, and strains on judicial personnel—are overwhelming. A Manhattan prosecutor has said, "Our office keeps eight courtrooms extremely busy trying 5 percent of the cases. If even 10 percent of the cases ended in a trial, the system would break down. We can't afford to think very much about anything else."[38] Yet there are courts in large urban areas where guilty pleas are used considerably less frequently than the average.[39]

Studies have also cast doubt on the assumption that plea bargaining is a contemporary practice that developed as a response to increased caseloads. In fact, one study of case dispositions found that plea bargaining was practiced extensively in both high- and low-volume courts as early as 1880 and that trials have resulted from fewer than 10 percent of indictments since that time.[40] Others have shown that plea bargaining has been a major feature of American criminal justice since the Civil War.

CLOSE-UP *Plea Bargaining in Detroit Recorder's Court*

The lawyer pushed through the swinging gate in the dark wood railing that separates court officials from the public and walked up and down past packed rows of spectators.

It was 10 o'clock on an August morning in Recorder's Court, which is the criminal court for the city of Detroit. In many ways, the scene could have been any criminal courtroom in the United States.

"Jackson," the lawyer called out. "Sam Jackson."

He was trying to find a client he had seen only once before, months ago, when he had been appointed to defend the man for a $100 fee paid by the state of Michigan. On the first day, he stood briefly beside his client as Jackson was arraigned and a date was set for his trial. Until this morning, when a courtroom clerk handed him a copy of the official court "paper" for the case, the lawyer had done nothing more.

"Jackson," he called again.

A slightly built black man in a polo shirt and work pants rose hesitantly a few rows back in the audience. Sam Jackson, a sometime laborer and truck driver, had, his record showed, been connected on and off with gambling and dope. He had been arrested nearly a year earlier for possession of a concealed pistol, which was found when a police detective stopped and searched his car, and he had been free on bail since then, waiting for his trial. That day, he was one of many defendants, mostly black, crowded together with relatives and friends in the worn wooden pews of Courtroom 8.

To these benches and to the barred cells hidden behind the courtroom are brought each day scores of men and women charged with such felonies as murder, rape, robbery, burglary, serious assault, the sale or possession of narcotics, or the illegal possession of a weapon. Many, like Jackson, wait a year or longer to be tried. But, for most of them, trial before a judge and jury never comes.

"Jackson?" the lawyer asked, pushing down his glasses to peer at his client. "Okay, okay. Sit back down. I'll be with you in a minute."

Turning, he walked through the gate again toward a cluster of policemen, all in street clothes, standing and gossiping idly near the empty jury box. In the confusion and cacophony that characterize the criminal courtroom scene, the policemen, numbering about thirty, were balanced by a swirling, changing mass of as many men opposite them. These are the criminal lawyers, most of whom work in Courtroom 8 every day. Their only clients, whose fees are usually paid by the state, are those assigned to them by the court. Some keep dingy offices in squat, grimy buildings across narrow Clinton Street from the courthouse; others have no offices at all and operate out of the courtroom itself. Known collectively as the "Clinton Street bar," they carry no briefcases and seldom consult law books; their case preparation consists of marking trial dates in dog-eared date books and scanning court papers hurriedly on the day a case comes up.

By this time, as the lawyer passed by, the judge was seated atop a two-tiered wooden platform, surrounded by clerks, bailiffs, and other functionaries shuffling through and stamping papers just below him. Save for the few persons standing immediately before him to conduct business, nobody seems really aware of the judge's presence. Lawyers, policemen, clerks, and others criss-crossed noisily in front of his bench, streamed back and forth through the swinging gate, and generally kept up a roar of conversation that crashed around the pronouncements of the judge, occasionally drowning out his words altogether.

"Detective Sanders," Jackson's lawyer said, "You got the Jackson case?" The policeman, recognizing the attorney, nodded. "Good," said the lawyer. Then, ignoring the judge nearby, the lawyer shouted the question that, in Recorder's Court, takes the place of trials, juries, legal rules, and the rest: "Hey, Sanders, what can you do for me today?"

Coming together in the middle of the courtroom, the lawyer and policeman began to haggle amiably over what reduction the government might make in its

Malcolm Feeley argues that the prevalence of plea bargaining has increased in direct proportion to the adversariness of the system. From a historical perspective, he says, the modern criminal justice system has expanded requirements of due process, has allocated increased resources to both the prosecution and the defense, has developed a substantive criminal law, and has increased the availability of defense counsel. If one looks at conditions in the nineteenth century, a period often referred to nostalgically as the "golden era of trials," one finds

a process that is difficult for the contemporary observer to recognize; those accused of criminal offenses—misdemeanor or felony alike—

charge against Jackson if he agreed to plead guilty rather than go to trial. If convicted of the felony charge by a jury, Jackson would be given a prison sentence of several years. The law required it. The policeman suggested that the charge might be reduced to "failure to present a gun for licensing," a misdemeanor carrying a penalty of only ninety days in jail, *if* Jackson pleaded guilty immediately. Together, the lawyer and Detective Sanders then joined a line of other attorneys and policemen that stretched to a back room occupied by the prosecutor—an official who is himself seldom seen in the courtroom.

Case by case, the prosecutor and each lawyer, usually joined by the policeman involved, hammer out a bargain for a guilty plea, similar to the one that Jackson's lawyer was seeking. If the accused agrees to admit guilt rather than insisting on a trial by jury, the government reduces the charge against him, often ensuring a lighter sentence. Thus, a man charged with armed robbery, which carries a mandatory twenty-year prison sentence, might plead guilty to unarmed robbery or attempted robbery and receive a much shorter sentence. Another, charged with burglary, might "admit" to attempting "unlawful entry." The changes are not made simply to fit the facts of the crimes involved; usually, in fact, the robber *had* used a gun or the burglar *had* succeeded in entering a house and stealing valuables. Instead, the change is made to induce the defendant to trade the possibility of a long prison term (against the chance for freedom if acquitted by a jury) for the promise of a shorter sentence.

In Sam Jackson's case, the prosecutor readily agreed to the bargain offered by the lawyer and policeman. The lawyer took Jackson into the bustling hallway outside the courtroom.

"I got you ninety days," he told Jackson enthusiastically. He did not refer at all to the crime itself or to his client's actual guilt or innocence. "It's a good deal. You have a record. You go to trial and get convicted on the felony and you're in trouble."

Jackson nodded in agreement.

"Remember," the lawyer cautioned as they returned to the courtroom, "don't hem and haw in front of the judge, or he might insist on a trial."

Jackson's turn came quickly. He stood mute, while the judge sorted through papers and read out the defendant's name and address and the charge originally placed against him. A court stenographer recorded everything.

"The prosecutor has signed a statement that he will accept your plea of guilty to a lesser charge," the judge announced. Then, like a clergyman reading a litany, with Jackson responding at appropriate pauses, he intoned, "You are pleading guilty because you are guilty?"

"Yes, sir."

"No one has threatened you or promised you anything?"

"No."

"No one has induced you to plead guilty?"

"No."

"You understand your constitutional right to a trial, and you are freely waiving that right?"

"Yes."

Turning sideways to stare out a window, the judge wearily recited, as he had again and again already that morning, "Let the record show that counsel was present, that the defendant was advised of his rights and that he understood them, and that the defendant waived his right to trial by jury or this court, and that he freely withdrew his plea of not guilty and entered a plea of guilty."

The court stenographer took down every word. The judge swiveled around again and sentenced Jackson to ninety days in jail.

SOURCE: From *Justice Denied*, by L. Downie, Jr., pp. 18–22. Copyright © 1971 by Praeger Publishers. Reprinted by permission of the author.

were typically rushed through crowded and noisy courts either sub-ject to a perfunctory trial lasting an hour or two or pressured to plead guilty by overbearing prosecutors whose practices were condoned by judges. All this took place without benefit of counsel.[41]

In the contemporary system, Feeley believes, the relationship be-tween the state and the accused is more evenly balanced. It is this new relationship—"a relationship that did not hold in a great many criminal cases when trials were more prevalent but the accused more dependent"—that has increased the adversariness of the system and thus the opportunity for negotiation.[42]

Criticisms of Plea Bargaining

Although plea bargaining is pervasive in the American criminal jus-tice system, its practice has been deplored by a number of scholars and by such prestigious groups as the American Bar Association and the National Advisory Commission of Criminal Justice Standards and Goals. The criticisms are mainly of two kinds. The first emphasizes due process considerations and argues that plea bargaining does not provide procedural fairness to individual defendants because they forfeit the exercise of some of their constitutional rights, especially the right to trial by jury. The second criticism emphasizes sentencing policy and points out that society's interest in awarding appropriate sentences for criminal acts is diminished by plea bargaining. It is believed that in urban areas in which caseloads are burdensome, harried prosecutors and judges make concessions on the grounds of administrative expediency, with the result that sentences are lighter than those required by the penal code. Such a sentence may have little relationship either to the seriousness of the crime or to the rehabilitation and deterrence of the offender. Thus plea bargaining is criticized by both civil libertarians and law-and-order advocates, groups that usually are not on the same side of the fence.

Plea bargaining also comes under fire because it is hidden from judicial scrutiny. Since the agreement is most often made at an early stage of the proceedings, the judge has little information about the crime or the defendant and cannot evaluate the prosecutor's appraisal of each. Nor can the judge make a knowledgeable review of the terms of the bargain—that is, a check on the amount of pressure applied to the defendant to plead guilty. The result of "bargain justice" is that the judge, the public, and sometimes even the defendant cannot know for certain who got what from whom in exchange for what.

Another criticism leveled at plea bargaining is that it is inconsis-tent with the espoused values of the adversarial system. Some critics feel that overuse of plea bargaining breeds disrespect and even con-tempt for the law. It is said that criminals look at the judicial process as a game or a sham, little different from other "deals" that one makes in life.

Critics also contend that it is unjust to penalize persons who assert their right to a trial and are convicted by giving them stiffer sentences than they would have received if they had pleaded guilty. The evidence in this regard is unclear, although courthouse mythol-ogy upholds the view that a penalty is exacted from defendants who take up the court's time. In their analysis of robbery and burglary data from three California counties, David Brereton and Jonathan Casper found that a greater proportion of defendants who went to trial received prison sentences than of those who pleaded guilty.[43] Likewise, Mark Cuniff's study of twenty-eight large jurisdictions revealed that defendants pleading guilty were less likely to be sent to prison than those found guilty after a jury trial. Of interest is the fact that cases decided by the judge alone in a bench trial resulted in about the same proportion of offenders going to prison as cases in which the defendant pleaded guilty.[44] It is important to view these results cautiously, since it is difficult to determine the strength of the evidence against a defendant and the reason why a plea was not the method of dispostion. We know that when defendants view the stakes as high, they will more likely choose to take a chance on a jury trial.

Finally, there is concern that innocent people will plead guilty to acts they did not commit. Although it is difficult to substantiate such suspicions, evidence exists that some defendants have indeed entered guilty pleas when they have committed no criminal offense. For example, the Colorado courts overturned a sentence on the ground that the defendant had been coerced by the judge's statement that he would "put him away forever if he did not accept the bargain."[45] In California, Benjamin M. Davis, a San Francisco attorney, represented a man charged with kidnapping and forcible rape. Though Davis was confident that the defendant was not guilty, the defendant elected to plead guilty to the lesser charge of simple battery. When Davis informed him that conviction on the original charges seemed improbable, he simply replied, "I can't take the chance."[46]

Reforming Plea Bargaining

As we've seen, some people believe that plea bargaining should be abolished. Others believe that as long as negotiations are in the open and that counsel for the defense is present, then plea bargaining should be retained.

In a number of jurisdictions (Honolulu, New Orleans, El Paso), efforts have been made to ban plea bargaining. The most noteworthy instance was in Alaska, where the state attorney general instructed district attorneys to stop the practice as of August 15, 1975. Criminal justice practitioners feared that the courts would be immediately flooded and that there would be a massive slowdown in moving the docket. Neither fear was realized. What happened was that direct bargaining was eliminated but the "implicit" form remained. In addition, there was some increase in the punishment given minor cases, but there was little impact on the sentences received for serious cases.[47]

In 1982 California voters passed Proposition 8, a "victims' Bill of Rights." Included in this new law was a stipulation that plea bargaining was not to occur in cases before the Superior Courts that involved serious crimes. However, the ban did not extend to cases decided in the Municipal Court. Candace McCoy has shown how the effect of Proposition 8 was to shift plea bargaining to the lower courts, with

preplea conference: A discussion, in which all the parties openly participate, of ways to bring about an agreement on a sentence in return for a plea of guilty.

only the most serious and disputatious felonies being bound over to the Superior Court.[48]

To meet many of the criticisms of plea bargaining, several jurisdictions have instituted the **preplea conference** in which all the parties—judge, victim, defendant, police, and prosecutor—take part. Persons supporting this approach argue that the guilty plea is an important part of the criminal justice system and that many of the charges against plea bargaining will be blunted if there is full and open participation of all concerned. For the purpose of the conference, the defendant's guilt is assumed, and the discussion is of issues that may contribute to a settlement. The presence of the judge ensures that the facts and the defendant can be fully evaluated before sentence is passed.

Evaluating Plea Bargaining

Pleading guilty, either in the expectation of a lighter sentence or as part of a bargain, is one of the most typical phenomena of the American criminal justice system. The guilty plea occurs in up to 90 percent of felony cases before state and federal courts. Although often explained in terms of the heavy caseloads being processed through the system, plea bargaining can be shown to be in the interests of all the participants: the prosecutor secures a guilty plea and does not have to go to trial; the defense attorney is able to use time more efficiently; the judge moves the caseload; and the defendant receives a sentence that is less than the law could impose.

Do those who plead guilty rather than going to trial receive lesser sentences? The data presented in Figure 10.5 appear to support this conclusion. With the exception of burglary, the mean prison sentence is less for offenders who choose to plead guilty rather than to be convicted at either a bench or jury trial. To the unwary, these results appear to conclusively support the idea that it is in the best interest

FIGURE 10.5
Conviction by guilty plea, bench trial, or trial by jury: A comparison of prison sentences.   Although it would appear that for most crimes it is in the offender's interest to plead guilty, there is not enough information in this table to support such a conclusion. What else would you need to know?
SOURCE: U.S. Department of Justice, Bureau of Justice Statistics, *Bulletin* (February 1990).

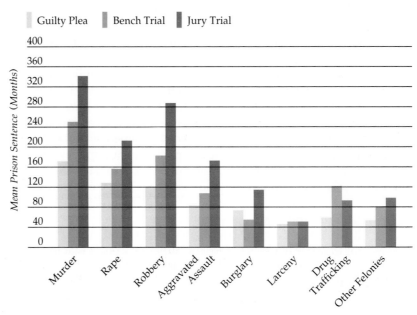

of the defendant to plead guilty. However, there is really not enough information in the figure to support the conclusion. We do not know anything about such factors as the criminal records of the offenders, the nature of the original charges, or the particular circumstances of the crime.

Attempts to abolish or limit plea bargaining have not altered the results: consideration in sentencing in exchange for a guilty plea. The system appears to require some means of serving the interests of the participants. With the recent decisions of the Supreme Court and the increased public awareness of plea bargaining, the practice will continue and will be increasingly aboveboard.

SUMMARY

During the last two decades, the period from arrest to acceptance of a guilty plea has been recognized as the most crucial in our system of justice. Until then, most Supreme Court decisions focused on the trial in efforts to ensure an impartial jury and courtroom procedures in accordance with the Constitution. The pretrial processes, especially bail setting and plea bargaining, offer some of the best insights into the making of administrative decisions that affect the future of criminal defendants within the context of law.

FOR DISCUSSION

1. The Constitution prohibits the levying of excessive bail. Should money be the sole determinant of whether someone is forced to await trial in jail? What other criteria might be used?
2. You are the judge. When you set bail, how may the nature of the crime, the characteristics of the defendant, and community pressure influence your decision? If the crime involved drugs, what additional factors would weigh in your decision?
3. Is discovery fair? Should the defense be allowed to see information held by the state?
4. Is plea bargaining really necessary? Whom does it help?
5. You, the defendant, have been arrested and charged with a crime. Your attorney has begun to bargain with the prosecutor for a reduction of the charges. Do you feel that you will be able to resist the temptation to "cop out" if you did not commit the offense charged? What will be weighing in your mind as you decide?

FOR FURTHER READING

Eskridge, Chris W. *Pretrial Release Programming.* New York: Clark Boardman, 1983. A survey of the history and trends of pretrial release programs.
Fine, Ralph A. *Escape of the Guilty.* New York: Dodd, Mead, 1986. A trial court judge's critical view of plea bargaining.
Flemming, Roy B. *Punishment before Trial.* New York: Longman, 1982. Study of bail

and pretrial release in Detroit and Baltimore that shows the punishments imposed on defendants before trial.

Heumann, Milton. *Plea Bargaining.* Chicago: University of Chicago Press, 1978. The ways that prosecutors, judges, and defense attorneys adapt to plea bargaining.

Mather, Lynn M. *Plea Bargaining or Trial?* Lexington, MA: Lexington Books, 1979. An early study of plea bargaining in Los Angeles.

Maynard, Douglas W. *Inside Plea Bargaining.* New York: Plenum, 1984. Examination of the discourse that plea bargaining takes as settlements are made by prosecutors and defense attorneys.

Taubman, Bryna. *Preppy Murder Trial.* New York: St. Martins, 1988. A description of the events leading up to the plea bargain of Robert Chambers in the death of Jennifer Levin.

Wice, Paul. *Freedom for Sale.* Lexington, MA: Lexington Books, 1974. One of the few major surveys of bail and its operation.

NOTES

1. Barbara Boland, Elizabeth Brady, Herbert Tyson, and John Bassler, *The Prosecution of Felony Arrests* (Washington, DC: Institute for Law and Social Research, 1982).
2. Paul Wice, *Criminal Lawyers: An Endangered Species* (Newbury Park, CA: Sage, 1978), p. 148.
3. *Ex Parte Milburn,* 34 U.S. 704 (1835).
4. Mary Toborg, *Pretrial Release: A National Evaluation of Practices and Outcomes* (Washington, DC: National Institute of Justice, 1982).
5. *Pannell* v. *United States,* 320 F. 2d 698 (D.C. Cir.) (1963).
6. Mary Toborg, "Bail Bondsmen and Criminal Courts," *Justice System Journal* 8 (Summer 1983):144.
7. Frederic Suffet, "Bail Setting: A Study of Courtroom Interaction," *Crime and Delinquency* 12 (October 1988):318.
8. Roy B. Flemming, *Punishment before Trial* (New York: Longman, 1982), pp. 136–38.
9. Wayne H. Thomas, Jr. *Bail Reform in America* (Berkeley: University of California Press, 1976), pp. 37–38, 65–66.
10. Toborg, *Pretrial Release,* p. 6.
11. John Goldkamp and Michael E. Gottfredson, *Policy Guidelines for Bail: An Experiment in Court Reform* (Philadelphia: Temple University Press, 1985), p. 69.
12. Ronald Goldfarb, *Ransom: A Critique of the American Bail System* (New York: Harper & Row, 1965), p. 137.
13. Malcolm Feeley, *Court Reform on Trial* (New York: Basic Books, 1983), pp. 68–70.
14. Chris W. Eskridge, *Pretrial Release Programming* (New York: Clark Boardman, 1986), p. 27.
15. Goldkamp and Gottfredson, *Policy Guidelines for Bail,* p. 198.
16. John Goldkamp, "Danger and Detention: A Second Generation of Bail Reform," *Journal of Criminal Law and Criminology* 76 (1985):1–75.
17. *Schall* v. *Martin,* 467 U.S. 253 (1984).
18. *United States* v. *Salerno,* 481 U.S. 739 (1987).
19. Martin D. Sorin, "How to Make Bail Safer," *Public Interest* 76 (Summer 1984):102–110; Steven R. Schlesinger, "Criminal Procedure in the Courtroom," in *Crime and Public Policy,* ed. James Q. Wilson (San Francisco: Institute for Contemporary Studies, 1983), p. 188.
20. *Pretrial Release and Misconduct in the District of Columbia* (Washington, DC: Institute for Law and Social Research, 1980).
21. Goldkamp, "Danger and Detention."
22. Stephen Kennedy and Kenneth Carlson, *Pretrial Release and Detention: The Bail Reform Act of 1984,* Bureau of Justice Statistics (Washington, DC: Government Printing Office, 1988).
23. Eric W. Single, "The Consequence of Pretrial Detention," paper presented at the 1973 annual meeting of the American Sociological Association, New Orleans.
24. John Goldkamp, *Two Classes of Accused* (Cambridge, MA: Ballinger, 1979).

25. Warren Burger, "Address at the American Bar Association Conference," *New York Times,* August 11, 1970, p. 1.
26. *Blackledge* v. *Allison,* 431 U.S. 63 (1976), 71.
27. Albert Alschuler, "The Prosecutor's Role in Plea Bargaining," *University of Chicago Law Review* 35 (1968):54.
28. Ibid., p. 79.
29. James Eisenstein, Roy B. Flemming, and Peter F. Nardulli, *The Contours of Justice: Communities and Their Courts* (Boston: Little, Brown, 1988), p. 118.
30. Pamela Utz, *Settling the Facts* (Lexington, MA: Lexington Books, 1978).
31. Douglas Maynard, "The Structure of Discourse in Misdemeanor Plea Bargaining," *Law and Society Review* 18 (1984):81.
32. *Boykin* v. *Alabama,* 395 U.S. 238 (1969).
33. *Alford* v. *North Carolina,* 400 U.S. 25 (1970).
34. *Santobello* v. *New York,* 404 U.S. 257 (1971).
35. *Ricketts* v. *Adamson,* 481 U.S. 1 (1987).
36. *Bordenhircher* v. *Hayes,* 343 U.S. 357 (1978).
37. Ralph Adam Fine, *Escape of the Guilty* (New York: Dodd, Mead, 1986), p. 84.
38. Ibid., p. 55.
39. James Eisenstein and Herbert Jacob, *Felony Justice* (Boston: Little, Brown, 1977), p. 291. For example, Eisenstein and Jacob found that of Baltimore defendants who came to trial, only 34.7 percent pled guilty, whereas in Chicago and Detroit this rate was 62 and 63 percent, respectively.
40. Milton Heumann, *Plea Bargaining* (Chicago: University of Chicago Press, 1978).
41. Malcolm M. Feeley, "Plea Bargaining and the Structure of the Criminal Process," *Criminal Justice: Law and Politics,* 5th ed., ed. George F. Cole (Pacific Grove, CA: Brooks/Cole, 1988), p. 467.
42. Ibid.
43. David Brereton and Jonathan Casper, "Does It Pay to Plead Guilty? Differential Sentencing and the Function of Criminal Courts," *Law and Society Review* 16 (1981–82):56–61.
44. Mark Cuniff, *Sentencing Outcomes in Twenty-Eight Felony Courts,* (Washington, DC: National Institute of Justice, 1987).
45. *People* v. *Clark,* 515 2d 1242 (Colorado, 1973).
46. Alschuler, "Prosecutor's Role in Plea Bargaining," p. 61.
47. Michael L. Rubenstein and Teresa J. White, "Alaska's Ban on Plea Bargaining," *Law and Society Review* 13 (1979):367.
48. Candace McCoy, "Determinate Sentencing, Plea Bargaining Bans and Hydraulic Discretion," *Justice System Journal* 9 (Winter 1984):256.

Court

Key Terms

grouping
jurisdiction
local legal culture

merit selection
nonpartisan election
partisan election

trial court of general jurisdiction
trial court of limited jurisdiction
workgroup

Yet trial-court fact-finding is the toughest part of the judicial function. It is there that court-house government is least satisfactory. It is there that most of the very considerable amount of judicial injustice occurs. It is there that reform is most needed.

Jerome Frank

The traditional image of the courthouse is of a building standing prominently on the central square of a town or city. It usually has a marble exterior, and it often is in the style of a Greek temple. The courthouse's location and structure symbolize the prominence of the rule of law in the American social and governmental system. But not all judicial decisions are made in this idealized version of the courthouse. The buildings vary from community to community. In some large cities it is difficult to distinguish the courthouse from the office buildings that surround it. In rural areas "court" is often held in a small office or even in the converted living room of the justice of the peace.

A visitor might be at a loss to find a particular court, for courts are given a somewhat bewildering collection of names—municipal court, superior court, county court, district court, justice court, and so on. Further, these names rarely tell us much about what the courts do. Upon entering one of these buildings, we would probably be still further confused by signs that read "Clerk of Court," "Criminal Division, Part I," "Arraignment Court," "Juvenile Court." Venturing ahead, we might come upon a crowded and noisy room in which groups of people appear before a judge and then move on in rapid succession; or we might watch a trial in progress that has all the dignity of our image of the administration of justice; or we might see a circular table around which four or five adults and a fourteen-year-old girl are seated.

It is obvious that *court* refers to a variety of physical structures, names, functions, processes, and settings. Because of the fragmented and local nature of American governmental units, our courts have developed in a somewhat irregular fashion. Each has been influenced by political and cultural aspects of its community's history. Although all of our courts are alike in that they follow the basic patterns of the Anglo-American legal tradition, each is distinctive in the way it is structured to perform particular functions and to deal with certain problems.

Differences aside, courts in the United States have many problems in common. Court congestion is one of them. Governmental and civic groups deplore the fact that defendants in criminal cases often wait in jail for months before they come to trial. Yet the conditions in the criminal courts also point up the reality of the filtering process, the administrative determination of guilt, and the exchange relationships that characterize the system. Additional judges and courtrooms cannot serve to emphasize due process as long as the system is able to function in a way that is consistent with the needs of the actors within it.

This chapter examines the structure of the American court system and looks at the conditions that influence decision making within it. It focuses on the key player—the judge—but it also shows that decisions on guilt or innocence, probation or prison are essentially made collectively by a small courtroom workgroup. As you read this chapter, put yourself in the position of each of the courtroom players. Is justice being served?

STRUCTURE AND MANAGEMENT OF AMERICAN COURTS

Before we can analyze the problems of American criminal courts, we must understand the structure and management of these essential instruments of justice. As Chapter 4 emphasized, the United States has a dual court system, federal and state. The U.S. Supreme Court oversees both systems and the Constitution protects the rights of defendants in criminal cases, yet most crime is processed in state systems. Within the state systems, it is the trial courts of county and city governments that deal with most of the criminal business.

American courts are strikingly decentralized. Throughout our history it has been felt that courts should be close to the people and responsive to them. Only in a few relatively small states is the court system completely unified on a statewide basis, centrally administered, and funded by state government. In much of the rest of the country, the criminal courts operate under the state penal code but are staffed, managed, and financed by county or city government. Thus local political influences and community values are brought to bear on the courts; local officials determine their resources, residents comprise the staff, and justice operations are adjusted to fit commu-

■

Courthouses come in all shapes and sizes, their names vary and the relationships of the people who work in them differ, yet all processes are under law.

nity needs. This situation leads to overstaffing of the courts in some communities while others have tremendous case backlogs, to leniency toward offenders in some courts and severity in others, and to the processing of cases in ways that accord with local practices.

The Movement for Reform

In 1906 Roscoe Pound, one of the nation's greatest judicial thinkers, delivered a speech to the American Bar Association (ABA) with the memorable title "The Causes of Popular Dissatisfaction with the Administration of Justice."[1] Later referred to as "the spark that kindled the white flame of progress," the speech was a broadly based analysis that struck mainly at the organizational inadequacies of the judicial system.[2] Pound claimed that there were too many courts and, in consequence, duplication and inefficiency; further, there was a great waste of judicial power because of rigid jurisdictional boundaries, poor use of resources, and the frequent granting of new trials.

Calls for the upgrading of the organization and administration of the state courts have continued. What is the malady that affects the courts, and what are the proposed remedies? Although a range of symptoms is usually cited, such as insufficient resources and the poor quality of politically appointed judges, the reform literature generally points to the fragmented and decentralized structure of state courts as impeding the effective administration of justice. The remedy most often prescribed: creation of a unified court system with four objectives:

1. elimination of overlapping and conflicting jurisdictional boundaries (of both subject matter and geography)
2. a hierarchical and centralized court structure, with administrative responsibility vested in a chief justice and court of last resort
3. financing of the courts by state government
4. a separate personnel system, centrally run by a state court administrator.

BIOGRAPHY

Roscoe Pound

As jurist and educator, Roscoe Pound had a profound influence on American jurisprudence and court reform. Born in Lincoln, Nebraska, he studied botany at the University of Nebraska, then attended Harvard Law School, and in 1890 was admitted to the Nebraska bar. From 1916 to 1936 he served as dean of Harvard Law School, and he retired from that institution as a professor in 1947.

Pound is principally known as the most prominent American exponent of a theory of law known as *sociological jurisprudence*, which asserts that the law must recognize contemporary social conditions, and there-fore rules must be adapted to a changing world. This theory contrasted sharply with nineteenth-century formalism, which emphasized the mechanical application of legal rules and principles to all situations, without regard to societal conditions. Pound's most important works include *The Spirit of the Common Law* (1921), *The Formative Era of American Law* (1938), and *Jurisprudence* (1959).

As a court reformer, Pound is remembered for his 1906 speech "The Causes of Popular Dissatisfaction with the Administration of Justice." This speech called attention to the organizational inadequacies of the judicial system and helped to spark reform efforts by the ABA and the American Judicature Society.

These themes—(1) structure, (2) centralization of administrative authority, (3) funding, and (4) a separate personnel system—have been at the forefront in the movement to reform the state courts so that they are more efficient and more effectively dispense justice. These efforts have been influential in bringing about changes in certain states and cities but not in others. But to achieve the objectives of court reform, one must go beyond simple structural and process reforms. Where judicial reform has succeeded, its architects have recognized the system's political nature and been able to move the system in the necessary direction.

The Structure of State Courts

The basic structure and organization of American state courts were borrowed, with some modification, from the English heritage. During the prerevolutionary period, each of the American colonies adapted the English court system to the local customs, religious practices, needs, and nature of its commerce. With formation of the United States, efforts were made to ensure that the courts would be responsive to the local community. Legislatures created court systems that were decentralized, linked to the local political system, and dependent for resources on the nonjudicial branches of government.

The growth of commerce and population during the nineteenth century brought new types of disputes requiring judicial attention. Litigation increased, and there were more specialized cases. The states and localities responded to this challenge mainly by creating new courts, each having a particular legal or geographical **jurisdiction.** Small claims courts, juvenile courts, and family relations courts were added in many states. In the larger cities, more courts of general jurisdiction were added, in part to meet the demands of the increased population and in part to create jobs that could be filled through patronage appointments beneficial to the political machines. In most states these changes produced a confusing structure of multiple courts with varying jurisdictions, overlapping responsibilities, and intercounty differences.

The court structure of all fifty states is now organized into three tiers: the **appellate court** (court of last resort and having intermediate appellate jurisdiction), the **trial court of general jurisdiction,** and the **trial court of limited jurisdiction.** Although this basic structure is found throughout the United States, the number of courts, their names, and their specific functions vary widely. Table 11.1 contrasts the court structure of Alaska, a reformed state, with that of Georgia, in which the court structure has not been reformed. Both are organized according to the three-tier model, but Georgia has more courts and greater jurisdictional complexity, with multiple courts of limited jurisdiction.

At the heart of reform efforts is the wish to consolidate and simplify court structures. A simple court structure is appealing because it creates an impression of clarity of purpose and efficiency. It must be recognized, however, that the presence of various courts within one structure provides desirable alternatives. Overlapping jurisdictions may be of benefit to some litigants. Likewise, the existence of

jurisdiction: The territory or boundaries within which control may be exercised; hence, the legal and geographical range of a court's authority.

appellate court: A court that does not try criminal cases but hears appeals of decisions of lower courts.

trial court of general jurisdiction: A criminal court that has jurisdiction over all offenses, including felonies, and that may in some states also hear appeals.

trial court of limited jurisdiction: A criminal court of which the trial jurisdiction either includes no felonies or is limited to some category of felonies. Such courts have jurisdiction over misdemeanor cases, probable cause hearings in felony cases, and, sometimes, felony trials that may result in penalties below a specified limit.

TABLE 11.1   Court structures of Alaska (reformed) and Georgia (unreformed).
Reformers have pushed for states to reduce the number of courts, to standardize
the nomenclature, and to clearly demarcate their jurisdictions.

Alaska	Georgia
Appellate Courts	
Supreme Court	Supreme Court
Court of Appeals	Court of Appeals
Trial Courts of General Jurisdiction	
Superior Court	Superior Court
Trial Courts of Limited Jurisdiction	
District Court	County Recorder's Court (also known as City Court)
	Probate Court (also known as Courts of Ordinary [probate])
	State Court
	Juvenile Court
	Magistrates' Court
	Municipal and Civil Court

SOURCE: National Center for State Courts, *State Court Caseload Statistics: Annual Report*
(Williamsburg, VA: National Center for State Courts, 1989), pp. 185, 194.

courts in many locations means that decisions of appellate courts may
conflict with those handed down by trial judges. Without the authority to enforce uniformity, members of the appellate courts have to put
up with a fair amount of independence of the trial court judges,
which means conflicting judicial policies within the state. Further,
judicial decentralization and autonomy make it possible for local
courts to become integral parts of the local political systems, thus
providing community interest groups with access to judicial decision
makers.

Centralization of Administrative Authority

Who runs the courts? Who is in charge? These questions address not
only the issue of authority within the court structure but also the
autonomy of the judiciary. In decentralized court systems there is no
overall authority to ensure continuity in procedures, to supervise, or
to protect the judiciary from encroachment by the legislative and
executive branches of government. The day-to-day administration of
a state judiciary necessitates that some person or body handle such
matters as assignment of judges, assignment of cases, record keeping,
personnel, and financing. Contemporary proponents of a unified
court system argue that either the supreme court of the state or its
chief justice should be given the power to assign judges, set rules,
and institute systemwide procedures.

Today each of the fifty states has a state court administrator, appointed either by the chief judge or by a committee of the state's
highest court. In many states an analogous position exists in the trial
courts. During the the 1960s, a number of academic programs were
created to train court administrators; the Institute for Court Management of the National Center for State Courts offers one of the leading
programs. Its graduates now are found in court management positions throughout the country.

Although the movement toward centralized management continues, experience has shown that the granting of these powers to a

supreme court does not necessarily ensure the expected results. In most states the local judges, clerks, and administrators are still able to resist dominance by the centralizing authority. Systems may look unified on an organization chart but be operationally fragmented nevertheless.

State Funding

Of all the elements that make up the ideal unified state court system, the method of funding is probably the most influential to bring into being the centralized administration model. Control of the purse strings is a crucial ingredient of power in any organization. Funding involves both the amount of resources that come from the state (as opposed to the local treasury) and the procedure by which the needs of the judiciary are made known to the funding body. It is on this portion of the unified court model that reformers have been most consistent during the past two decades; they have proposed that the state fully fund the courts and that the court administrator, under the direction of the chief justice, prepare for the legislature a budget for the entire system.

In the most recent study of judicial funding, Marcia Lim found that although the state share of funding varied from 13 percent to 100 percent, the court systems of only twenty-one states receive substantial or full support of their budget from the state.[3] Of costs for the judiciary, 62 percent is from local government, almost twice the amount spent by state governments. A more striking fact is that the larger a state's population, the lower its percentage of court funding by state government. Thus five of the ten largest states (California, Texas, Ohio, Michigan, and Pennsylvania) are among the fourteen with the lowest percentage of state funding. States smallest in area and population show the highest levels of funding by the central government: Connecticut, Hawaii, Delaware, Rhode Island, Vermont, and New Mexico all provide more than 80 percent.

During the past few years there has been a slow but significant move toward increased funding by a number of states. As court costs rise in an increasingly litigious society, local political leaders seem willing to let the state government appropriate money for the judiciary.

Separate Court Personnel System

It is logical that the judiciary should have its own personnel system. Without a separate civil service system for judicial employees, a state-wide unified court system cannot come into being, and the courts are beholden to local political powers. The 1974 ABA Standards Relating to Court Organization recommended a system of position classification, levels of compensation, and procedures for personnel evaluation.

Identifying the employees of the court is not so simple an undertaking as it may seem. There are many persons, such as sheriffs, probation officers, and social workers, whose work is closely tied to the judicial process but who report to other officials and agencies. With the growth of the unified court concept, especially with regard to state funding, separate personnel rules for the judicial branch have been developed in a number of states. In other states, however, court employees are still subject to the rules that cover all public workers.

Trend toward Unified Court Systems

In recent years, deficiencies in the administration of justice have received much attention from state and federal governments. The rise in crime and the caseload problems of the courts have led to increased funding as a means of improving the administration of justice. Judicial expenditures in the states have more than doubled during the past decade. Several populous states have moved toward a unified court system, and employment in state and local courts has increased. Although these facts may portend eventual realization of the reformers' dream, questions are now being raised about the impact of the unified court system. It is now argued that the conventional wisdom of centralized management of state court systems is out of date both in fact and theory and that the traditional model does not deal adequately with the reality of administration because it assumes that formal structures determine behavior. Many fear that the emphasis on centralization and unity through structural change neglects the need for better management. A tidy organization chart in no way reflects either a more efficient or more equitable administration of justice.

TO BE A JUDGE

Of the many actors in the criminal justice process, judges are perceived to hold the greatest amount of leverage and influence over the system. Decisions of the police, defense attorneys, and prosecutor are greatly affected by their rulings and sentencing practices. Although we tend to think of judges primarily in connection with trials, their work is much more varied. They are a continuous presence throughout the activities leading to the disposition of each case. Many portions of a judge's work—signing warrants, fixing bail, arraigning defendants, accepting guilty pleas, scheduling cases—fall outside the formal trial process.

More than any other person in the system, the judge is expected to *embody* justice, thereby ensuring that the right to due process is respected and that the defendant is fairly treated. The black robes and gavel symbolize the impartiality we expect from our courts. The judge is supposed to act within and outside the courthouse according to a well-defined role designed to prevent involvement in anything that could bring the judiciary into disrepute. (For a discussion of Italy's concerns in this regard, see the Comparative Perspective.) Yet such are the pressures of today's justice system that the ideals of the judge's position have often been subordinated to the need to dispose of cases speedily.

Although we think of the judiciary primarily with reference to activities in the courtroom, much of a judge's work falls outside of formal trial procedures.

The traditional image of the courtroom stresses the individuality, aloofness, and loneliness of the judge, sitting in robed splendor above the battle to control the actors before the bench. The law emphasizes the crucial role of the judge: within hours after arrest, accused persons shall be brought before a judge and informed of their rights. From that moment until final disposition of the case, accused persons face a judge whenever decisions affecting their future are made: bail, arraignment, preliminary hearing, pleading, trial, and sentencing. Because courtroom activities are primarily concerned with fact finding, judges function as lawgivers. They interpret legal precedents and apply them to the specific circumstances of the case. They are believed to be isolated from the social context of the courtroom participants and to base their decisions on their own interpretation of the law after thoughtful consideration of the issues.

Like patrol officers, lower court judges have many of the attributes of street-level bureaucrats. They exercise discretion in the disposition of summary offenses without the constant supervision of a higher court, and they have wide latitude in fixing sentences. Although judges are popularly portrayed as being forced to decide complex legal issues, in reality their courtroom tasks are routine. Because of the unending flow of cases, they operate with assembly-line precision, and, like workers on an assembly line, many judges soon tire of the repetition. One can often observe bored judges paying little attention to the arguments of the lawyers before them.

Who Becomes a Judge?

Judges of the criminal courts have socioeconomic characteristics very different from those of judges in the upper appellate courts, and they operate in a different organizational environment. One national survey of trial judges revealed that they were overwhelmingly white and male, had an average age of 53.4 years, and came from families connected to the local legal-political community. A majority (53.8 percent) had been in private legal practice, and 24 percent became trial judges after serving in lower courts—municipal, juvenile, or probate.[4] Before their accession to the bench most judges have been in private or public law practice (many as prosecuting attorneys). The average salaries for trial court judges of general jurisdiction range from about $50,000 in some southern states to near $100,000 in New York and California; the national average being about $70,000.[5] For some attor-

---

A QUESTION OF ETHICS

Judge Harold Abrams of the Euclid District Court was angry. He had been sitting on the bench all Monday morning arraigning, setting bail, and taking pleas from a steady stream of people who had been arrested over the weekend. Most of the people appearing before him were charged with such offenses as possession of a controlled substance, solicitation for the purpose of prostitution, drunk and disorderly conduct—samples of the range of behaviors that had attracted police attention on Saturday night. He had seen many of the accused before, and a steady banter emanated from the bench as the judge took each case.

"So it's you again, Lucille. When are you girls going to learn that you can't walk up and down First Avenue? In that eight-inch skirt, you're a menace to traffic. We can't have every Tom, Dick, and Harry—and I mean mostly Dick—screwing his eyes on you and not on the road. Get what I mean?"

"But this time I was just going to the store to buy a loaf of bread."

"Sure. You mean you were walking to make some bread? In fact you don't do much walking, do you Lucille; you're mainly on your back! How do you plead?"

"Guilty, but I didn't do no soliciting."

Fifty dollars and costs. Now, I suppose you'll be back on the Avenue to earn the fine. See you again Lucille."

Throughout this exchange the courtroom regulars grinned. You could really see quite a show in Judge Abrams's courtroom.

Is this the way justice should be allocated? Are Judge Abrams's banter and manner appropriate? What are the defendants learning about the administration of justice? Should the judge be removed from the bench?

neys a position as a judge may carry with it an income comparable to what they could get in private practice, and certainly the position is more secure. For others, to return to private practice might result in a 50 to 100 percent increase in personal income. The position of judge, however, has a significance for most that overshadows considerations of wealth. Public service, politics, and prestige in the community may be more important than dollars to these individuals.

In many cities political factors dictate that judges be drawn from specific racial, religious, and ethnic groups. In Philadelphia, Paul Wice found that practically every judge he interviewed was either Jewish, Irish, or Italian.[6] Racial minorities, primarily black and Hispanic, are underrepresented on the bench. One study found only 1 percent of the nation's judges were black and that half of that 1 percent were in six large cities.[7] When one compares the racial and ethnic composition of the defendant population in urban courts with the overwhelmingly white judiciary, one might raise questions about the symbolic aspects of the allocation of justice.

In most cities, criminal court judges occupy the lowest place in the judicial hierarchy. Lawyers and citizens alike fail to accord them the prestige that is part of the mystique usually surrounding members of the bench. Even their peers who hear civil cases may look down on them. As in other professional relationships, the status of criminal trial judges may be linked to the status of the defendants. The judges are so close to the type of client they serve and work under such unpleasant conditions that, although they may retain some of the charisma of the judiciary, their reputation becomes tarnished and somewhat mundane. For many, the possibility of moving up to civil or appellate courts sustains them while they deal with the heavy caseloads and unpleasant working conditions of the criminal court.

Functions of the Judge

With so much public discussion about case backlogs in the criminal courts, many citizens who have visited the local courtroom have been surprised to find the bench empty, the judge and staff absent. Where are the judges? What do they do? A study of the criminal courts in New York City revealed that, on the average, judges were on the bench only three hours and three minutes a day. Although this period is shorter than that prevailing in most parts of the country, it does highlight questions about the work and function of the criminal court judge. If the judge is on the bench less than half a workday, how does he or she spend the rest of it? What *do* judges do?

We tend to think that the judge's functions are primarily concerned with presiding at trials, but the work of most judges extends to all parts of the judicial process. Defendants see a judge whenever decisions about their future are being made: when bail is set, when pretrial motions are made, when pleas of guilty are accepted, when a trial is conducted, when sentence is pronounced, and when appeals are entered. But in addition to responsibilities directly related to the processing of defendants, judges have functions that are performed outside the courtroom and that are related to the administration of

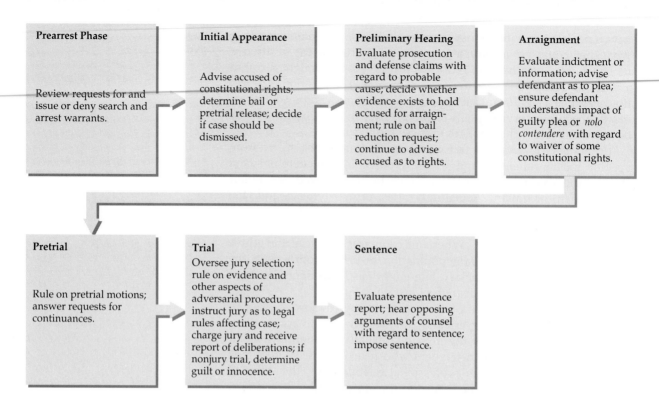

Prearrest Phase	Initial Appearance	Preliminary Hearing	Arraignment
Review requests for and issue or deny search and arrest warrants.	Advise accused of constitutional rights; determine bail or pretrial release; decide if case should be dismissed.	Evaluate prosecution and defense claims with regard to probable cause; decide whether evidence exists to hold accused for arraignment; rule on bail reduction request; continue to advise accused as to rights.	Evaluate indictment or information; advise defendant as to plea; ensure defendant understands impact of guilty plea or *nolo contendere* with regard to waiver of some constitutional rights.

Pretrial	Trial	Sentence
Rule on pretrial motions; answer requests for continuances.	Oversee jury selection; rule on evidence and other aspects of adversarial procedure; instruct jury as to legal rules affecting case; charge jury and receive report of deliberations; if nonjury trial, determine guilt or innocence.	Evaluate presentence report; hear opposing arguments of counsel with regard to sentence; impose sentence.

FIGURE 11.1
Typical actions of a trial court judge in processing a felony case. Throughout the entire process judges ensure that legal standards are upheld; they maintain courtroom decorum, protect rights of the accused, uphold speedy trial rules, and ensure proper maintenance of case records.

the judicial system. Judges are adjudicators, negotiators, and administrators (see Figure 11.1).

Adjudicator

In a criminal justice system based on the ideals of due process and the adversary system, judges must play a role of neutrality between the prosecution and the defense. They must apply the law to ensure that the rights of the accused are upheld as decisions are made concerning detention, plea, trial, and sentence. In discharging these responsibilities, judges are given a certain amount of discretion—for example, in setting the level of bail—but they must also conduct the proceedings according to law. Judges are the final arbiters of the law in the cases before them unless, on appeal, they are overruled by a higher court. If a nonjury trial is held, the judge not only rules on the issues of law but also decides issues of fact and ultimately determines the defendant's guilt or innocence. Judges may exercise discretion in the sentencing of convicted persons. In doing so, it is of great importance that they be fair and also give the appearance of fairness. They must avoid any conduct that may give the appearance or impression of being less than totally unbiased.

Negotiator

Much of the criminal justice process is carried out through negotiation in the privacy of areas shielded from public view. Judges spend much of their time in their chambers talking with prosecutors and defense attorneys and often encourage the litigants to compromise or to agree to conduct proceedings in a specific manner. Although judicial ethics generally prohibit judges from directly discussing a pending case with the victims, witnesses, defendants, and arresting officers, members of the bench often are called on to mediate disputes that have not yet escalated to a formal trial. In lower misdemeanor courts, the remarks of the judge from the bench often take the form of advice to the disputants rather than formal points of law. It is in the plea bargaining process that many judges act as negotiators. Although there is a new openness toward this practice, the court rules in seven states and in the federal jurisdiction prohibit judicial participation in these discussions. In other states, case law and dicta place additional restraints on the role that judges may play in plea bargaining.

Administrator

A seldom-recognized function of most judges is the administration of the courthouse. In urban areas a professional court administrator may direct the personnel who are assigned to record keeping, case scheduling, and the many logistical operations that keep a system functioning. Even in cities, however, judges are responsible for the administration of their own courtroom and staff. In rural areas, the administrative responsibilities of judges may be more burdensome, because professional court administrators are not usually employed.

In discharging these duties, judges must be concerned not only with the administration of the judicial process itself but also with the operation of the courthouse and with its personnel. Budgeting, labor relations, and the maintenance of the physical plant may all come under their supervision. As administrator, the judge is required to maintain contact with such nonjudicial political actors as county commissioners, legislators, and members of the state executive bureaucracy.

How to Become a Judge

The quality of justice depends to a great extent on the quality of those who dispense it. As the American jurist Benjamin Cardozo once said, "In the long run, there is no guarantee of justice except the personality of the judge."[8] Because government has been given the power to deprive a citizen of his or her liberty, good judges are essential. Because society wants protection from wrongdoers, good judges are essential. Although the connection between these needs and the character and experience of those appointed to our highest courts has long been recognized, less interest has been focused on trial judges of the criminal courts. Yet it is in the lower courts that citizens most often have contact with the judiciary, and the public's impression of the criminal justice system is shaped to a great extent by the trial judge's behavior in the courtroom. When a judge is rude or inconsiderate or allows the courtroom to become a noisy, crowded dispensary of rapid-fire justice, public confidence in the fairness and effectiveness of the criminal justice process is diminished.

All judges are addressed as "Your Honor," and we deferentially stand whenever they enter or leave the courtroom, yet too often they are chosen for reasons that have very little to do with either their legal qualifications or their judicial temperament. The variety of processes by which judges are selected may reflect confusion about their work and about the justice system as a force in society. There is a strong reform movement to place men and women of quality on the bench. Reformers urge that judges be experts and believe that selection on a nonpolitical basis will produce higher-quality, more efficient, more independent, and consequently more impartial and just members of the judiciary.

In opposition are those who argue that in a democracy the voters should elect the people charged with carrying out public policies, including judges. The attorney who earned a degree at a less prestigious law school and whose general practice has focused on the representation of people rather than of corporations, they contend, would have a better sense of the justice to be meted out in the lower

CLOSE-UP   The Criminal Court Judge: Time Management and the Flow of a Typical Day

A typical day for the judge of criminal assignment began around 9:00 A.M., when the judge arrived in chambers, read mail, and skimmed the day's case files. The call of criminal cases generally started soon after but might be delayed if the judge were in conference with lawyers, or if lawyers were in conference with each other. More times than not, the judge and the court were forced to wait while lawyers concluded bargains, talked with clients, or hurried from another courtroom. In many courts the call itself tended to be a rather chaotic process, with attorneys coming in and out of court, whispered plea negotiations continuing throughout the room, and a variety of people approaching the clerk's desk (usually immediately adjacent to the bench). In most instances, the criminal call not only served an attendance-taking function but afforded a review of the status of each case. The call could also assume some legal importance as defense lawyers jockeyed for advantageous (i.e., later) trial dates, while the judge used the threat of immediate trial as a form of bargaining leverage. Often, short hearings, arraignments, the taking of guilty pleas, sentencings, and probation violations were disposed of in the criminal call.

After the completion of the call (or the first round), the judge might attend to some minor administrative matters, socialize with attorneys or court personnel, take a coffee break, or participate in case-related discussions with attorneys. Then the judge might begin formal court proceedings—a motions hearing, a bench trial, or (most likely) a jury trial. These proceedings would continue for the rest of the morning, with adjournment around noon for a lunch break. While some judges gulped sandwiches at their desks and worked through lunch, most criminal judges lunched with court or law enforcement personnel, lawyer acquaintances, former political associates, or other judges. Occasionally judges attended bar luncheons, spoke at civic meetings, or participated in more specialized meetings such as judicial seminars, advisory board meetings of a halfway house, and the like. Frequently lunch conversations included mention of past and current cases, and from time to time some judicial business of a minor nature was transacted (usually pertaining to scheduling). However, politics, financial affairs, and travel plans were also common topics of conversation.

Returning to chambers somewhere between one hour and ninety minutes later, the judge might meet with some lawyers, catch up on correspondence, sign orders, or glance through the "advance sheets" (early publication of recent appellate cases) before the afternoon court session. After the court was reconvened, unfinished matters of the morning might again be taken up, whether continuation of the call or of a bench or jury trial. Jury proceedings were planned to begin and end for juror convenience; but while there might be a half-hour comfort break during the afternoon, many judges preferred to finish as much of the scheduled proceedings as possible before leaving for the day. Departure ranged anywhere from 3:00 to 6:00 P.M. or later, though the majority probably left sometime around 4:30 or so. The judge might attend to some minor matters after adjourning court or go to a meeting of the judiciary before leaving the building, but such activities were generally infrequent and not very lengthy. Most of the criminal judges whom we observed did not take case files or journals home, though some may have read the latter at home.

SOURCE: Reprinted with permission of The Free Press, a Division of Macmillan, Inc., from *American Trial Judges*, by J. P. Ryan, A. Ashman, B. D. Sales, and S. Shane-Dubow, pp. 17–19. Copyright © 1980 by The American Judicature Society.

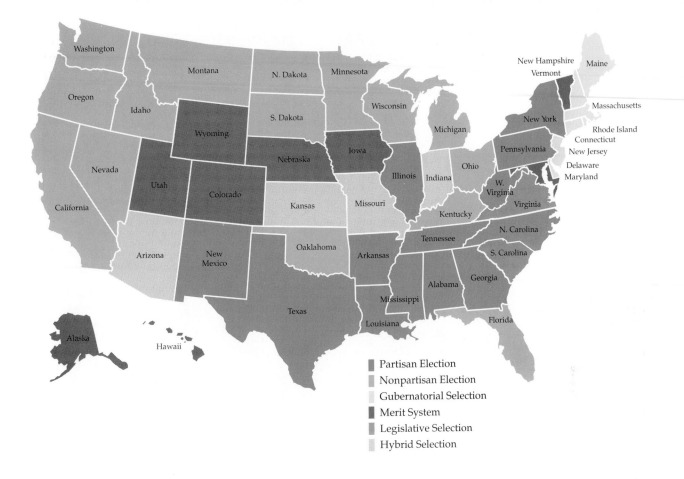

criminal courts than the Harvard graduate who can discuss the philosophy behind the elements of a fair trial but may be ill equipped to handle the steady stream of human problems confronting the judges of the nation.

Methods of Selection

The states and the federal government use essentially six methods to select trial court judges. Figure 11.2 shows the methods used in each of the states: (1) gubernatorial selection, (2) legislative selection, (3) merit selection, (4) **nonpartisan election,** (5) **partisan election,** and (6) hybrid selection. Methods vary depending on the circumstances. Throughout all the arguments advanced in support of one method or another runs a persistent concern about the desired qualities in a judge and the assumption that the type of selection process will lead to a particular judicial style. On the one hand is the view that judges should be concerned only with the law; on the other, the view that they must feel the pulse of the people in order to render justice. Each approach heightens opportunities for certain people and interests and diminishes them for others.

Selection by the electorate, as occurs in more than half the states, seems to go against the traditional notion that judges are specially trained to "find the law" and to exercise power in a manner worthy of Solomon. In Europe, prospective judges are trained in law schools for careers in the judicial profession. By contrast, choice by the com-

FIGURE 11.2
Methods used by states for selection of trial judges. States use different methods for the selection of judges; however, many are initially appointed to fill a vacancy, thus having an advantage if they subsequently must run for election.
[a]Partisan or merit, depending on locale.
[b]Nonpartisan or merit, depending on locale.
SOURCE: Council of State Governments, *The Book of the States* (Lexington, KY: Council for State Governments, 1986), p. 19.

nonpartisan election: An election in which candidates who are not endorsed by political parties are presented to the voters for selection.

partisan election: An election in which candidates endorsed by political parties are presented to the voters for selection.

Judges are elected in about half the states. Critics of this practice argue that it compromises the idea that the judiciary is above politics. Supporters argue that judges should be responsive to the people. What do you think?

munity of the individuals to sit on the bench has long been part of this nation's tradition. One result is that upon assuming office, judges in the United States must learn on the job.

Campaigns for judgeships are generally low-key, low-visibility contests marked by little controversy: usually only a small portion of the voters participate, judicial positions are not prominent on the ballot, candidates are constrained by ethical considerations from discussing issues, and public attention is centered on executive and legislative races. The situation was summarized well by Judge Samuel Rosenman of New York:

> I learned at first hand what it meant for a judicial candidate to have to seek votes in political clubhouses, to ask for support of political district leaders, to receive financial contributions for his campaign from lawyers and others, and to make nonpolitical speeches about his own qualifications to audiences who could not care less—audiences who had little interest in any of the judicial candidates, of whom they had never heard, and whom they would never remember.[9]

Although popular election of judges may be an important part of our political heritage, these elections rarely capture the voters' notice.

The selection of judges is complicated by the regular occurrence of vacancies owing to deaths and retirements. In a majority of states, the governor has the power to fill these judicial vacancies, and the person appointed normally wins a full term in the next election. In California, for example, although nonpartisan election is the formal selection system, 88 percent of the trial court judges were initially selected by the governor to fill a vacancy. One study has shown that in states where nonpartisan elections are held, only 43 percent of the judges initially assumed the bench following election, a finding that indicates the importance of political connections in obtaining the position.[10]

In many cities judgeships provide much of the fuel for the party machine. Because of the honors and material rewards that may be gained from a place on the bench, parties are able to secure the energy and money of attorneys who seek a judgeship as the capstone of their career. In addition, a certain amount of courthouse patronage may be involved because clerks, bailiffs, and secretaries—all jobs that may be filled by active party workers—are appointed by the judge.

Merit selection, combining appointment and election, was first instituted in Missouri in 1940 and has now spread to nine other states and the District of Columbia. When a vacancy occurs, a nominating commission of citizens and attorneys for the empty bench sends the governor the names of three candidates from among whom the replacement is selected. After one year, a referendum is held to determine the judge's retention. The voter is asked, "Shall Judge X remain in office?" With a majority vote, the judge serves out the term and can then come before the citizens on another ballot. Designed to remove partisan politics from the judiciary, merit selection is also supposed to have the advantage of giving the electorate an opportunity to unseat judges. However, most judges selected under this procedure are in fact returned to the bench. Studies have shown that only a handful have been removed by the voters in merit selection states.[11]

Despite the impressive support of bar groups, merit selection has not gone unchallenged. It is said that although political party politics may have been removed, it has merely been replaced by politics within the legal profession. Many lawyers regard it as a system favoring "blue-bloods" (high-status attorneys with ties to corporations) to the detriment of the "little guy."[12]

merit selection: A reform plan by which judges are nominated by a committee and appointed by the governor for a given period. When the term expires, the voters are asked to signify their approval or disapproval of the judge for a succeeding term. If the judge is disapproved, the committee nominates a successor for the governor's appointment.

Results of Selection Methods

What are the dynamics and consequences of using one selection method over another? Does each have class implications, as some believe, so that judges of only a certain social background reach the bench? Do some methods favor the choice of politically oriented judges as opposed to legally oriented judges? If each method has built-in biases, do these biases find their way into judges' decisions? Does one method elevate judges who sentence lawbreakers more leniently than judges chosen by a different method?

These questions have been hotly debated in the judicial reform and legal literature. It seems apparent that the selection method does influence the type of judge chosen. Some appointed judges would probably never have reached the bench if they had to win it through a partisan political campaign. Others who ran and won their election, probably wouldn't have been selected by a governor. In states where the legislature makes the decision, the evidence shows that former legislators are preferred. But do these differences result in better or worse judges? Findings from a number of studies seem to conclude that no one of the systems is superior to the others.[13]

Martin Levin's comparison of the criminal courts of Pittsburgh and Minneapolis is the major investigation of the relationship between selection methods and judicial decisions.[14] He singled out those two cities because of major differences in their political systems and methods of judicial selection and consequent differences in judges. In Pittsburgh, judges were chosen through the highly politicized environment of a city controlled by the Democratic machine: "Public and party offices are filled by party professionals whose career patterns are hierarchical and regularized. They patiently 'wait in line' because of the party's needs to maintain ethnic and religious 'balance' even on a judicial ticket."[15] Partisan politics is so much a part of the culture of that city that the public accepts the idea that the courts should be staffed by party workers; the bar association plays a very limited role in judicial selection. There was little enthusiasm for efforts to reform the selection process.

Minneapolis has a system that is formally nonpartisan. The parties have almost no place in the selection of judges, but the bar association is influential. Before a judicial election, the Minneapolis Bar Association polls its members and publicizes the results. The winner in this straw vote among lawyers almost always wins in the general election. When vacancies occur, Minnesota governors have traditionally appointed judges according to the preference of the attorneys. Out of the Minneapolis system came judicial candidates who were usually members of large, business-oriented law firms and who had not been active in partisan politics.

The differing selection methods and political settings of these two cities produced judges with opposing judicial philosophies and, as a result, contrasting sentencing decisions in the criminal courts. In general, judges in Pittsburgh were more lenient than those in Minneapolis. Not only did white and black defendants receive more sentences of probation and shorter terms of incarceration in Pittsburgh, but the pattern was maintained when the defendants' prior records, pleas, and ages were held constant. The relationship between selection method and judicial philosophy held in regard to all nine offenses analyzed. A portion of Levin's findings, illustrated in Figure 11.3, demonstrates this relationship. Among white defendants with prior records, the percentage of those convicted who received probation rather than incarceration was higher in Pittsburgh than in Minneapolis.

The background of judges and the method of their selection seem to exert strong influence on their decisions. An elimination process may operate, so that only certain types of persons who have had certain kinds of experiences are available for selection in each judicial system. Levin believes that any relationship between judges' background and their decisions is indirect. What is crucial is the variable of the city's political culture and its influence on judicial selection methods.

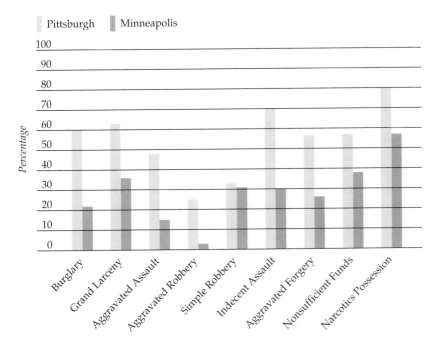

FIGURE 11.3
Percentage of white defendants with prior records receiving probation in Pittsburgh and Minneapolis (by charge). The leniency of Pittsburgh judges is shown by the percentage of defendants receiving probation as compared to those sentenced in Minneapolis. What does this say about the judicial recruitment and selection process?
SOURCE: Adapted from "Urban Politics and Policy Outcomes: The Criminal Courts," by Martin Levin. In G. F. Cole (ed.) *Criminal Justice: Law and Politics,* 5th ed., pp. 335–336 (Pacific Grove, CA: Brooks/Cole, 1988).

THE COURTROOM: HOW IT FUNCTIONS

With some variations, justice is allocated in fairly similar ways throughout this large and diverse country. There are some differences from state to state in the structure and organization of courts, various methods are used to select judges, and the rules of criminal procedure may be somewhat dissimilar, yet there are nationally shared values about how persons accused of crimes should be treated. These values are espoused in the laws and constitutions of the states and the United States. A person who grew up in New Jersey but was arrested in Idaho is going to find that guilt or innocence will be determined in approximately the same way as it would have been back home.

We do recognize that even with the overall similarity of the formal processes of adjudication, differences are discernible to anyone who has visited American courts. A study of criminal courts in nine communities in three states revealed that it is not the laws and procedures that are different but rather the way defendants are treated—the results of the judicial process.[16] Some courts sentence offenders to longer terms than do others. Delays and tight release policies keep some accused in jail awaiting trial, whereas in other jurisdictions similar defendants are out on bail or have had their cases expeditiously resolved. Guilty pleas may make up 90 percent of dispositions in some communities but only 60 percent in others. How can we explain these differences among courts in various cities and even among different courtrooms in the same city?

Social scientists have long recognized that culture—the shared beliefs and attitudes of a community—has a great influence on the way members behave. Culture implies a consensus as to the definition of proper behavior. Researchers have identified a **local legal culture**—norms shared by members of a particular court community (judges, attorneys, clerks, bailiffs, etc.) as to case handling and participants' behavior in the judicial process.[17] The local legal culture influences court operations since the norms:

1. Help participants distinguish between "our" court and other jurisdictions. Often a judge or prosecutor will expound upon how "we" do the job so much better than in the neighboring county or central city.

2. Stipulate how members should treat one another. For example, mounting a strong adversarial defense may be viewed as not in keeping with the norms of court, whereas this may be the expected behavior in another locality. In Montgomery County, Pennsylvania, a local attorney told researchers that "suits challenging the operation of the criminal system 'upset' the bar, and that 'upsetting the bar would be rocking the boat.' "[18]

COMPARATIVE PERSPECTIVE
Erosion of Judicial Legitimacy in Italy

Independence and impartiality are cornerstones of the judicial role in western cultures. Judges are expected to act in a professional manner, overcoming personal or political preferences in accordance with the requirement that decisions be made according to the law. Judges must act in ways that buttress their legitimacy so that citizens will accept judicial policies and decisions.

Judicial independence is usually secured through a system of separation of powers, but in the Italian case that works in only one direction. The judiciary is protected from the powers of other branches of government but judges are allowed to hold posts in those agencies. Thus, judges may also be employed full-time in the executive branch and in Parliament by taking temporary leave from their judicial tasks without losing either their place or seniority within the judiciary. About 200 of the 7,000 magistrates are involved full-time in the activities of the legislative and ex-

ecutive branches of government while ten times that number participate on a part-time basis. One result is a widely held perception that the agencies of government influence judicial decisions by playing on the ambitions and aspirations of the magistrates. Partisan politics are thought to have permeated the judicial ranks by the activities of its members; in fact, the National Magistrates Association is divided into three political factions pushing conservative, moderate, and leftist agendas. The press regularly makes innuendos about political influences on judicial decisions by citing overzealous investigations of individuals later vindicated and investigations that are halted prematurely. Involvement of several judges in the famous P2 Masonic Lodge that allegedly was plotting a right-wing coup added to public skepticism of judicial impartiality.

Judicial objectivity was, until late 1989, complicated by the inquisitorial nature of the justice system, which placed both the judge

and the prosecutor on the same side of a criminal case. Sometimes these functions were merged into a single individual. Judges and prosecutors were jointly regarded as magistrates, shared the same training, were recruited in the same manner, were promoted by the same rules, and were able to shift from one position to another.

At the lowest level of the judiciary, the *pretura*, where prison sentences of up to four years may be given, the same person served simultaneously as prosecutor and "impartial" third party. This role conflict was aggravated by the power of the prosecutor to direct the police, to manage the investigation, and even to initiate charges

3. Describe how cases *should* be processed. The best example of this is what is often referred to as the **going rate**—the local view of the appropriate sentence given the offense and defendant's prior record and other characteristics. The local legal culture also includes attitudes about such issues as the appropriateness of judicial participation in plea negotiations, when continuances should be given, and who is eligible for a public defender.

Differences among local legal cultures have been used to explain why court decisions are dissimilar even though the formal rules of criminal procedure are basically the same. Informal rules and practices arise within particular settings, and "the way things are done" differs from place to place. As one might expect, the local legal culture of Albuquerque differs from that of Tolland County or Baltimore. The customs and traditions of each jurisdiction vary because local practices are influenced by such factors as size, politics, and population characteristics. Among these, urban–rural differences are a major factor.

going rate: Local view of the appropriate sentence given the offense and the defendant's prior record and other characteristics.

and arrests. The blurring of the prosecutor-judge was also found at higher court levels by participation of the judge in the pretrial phases of more than nine-tenths of all prosecutions that never come to trial.

Role confusion and work demands among Italian judges have also been heightened by the political terrorism and increased Mafia activity during the past two decades. These problems were perceived as threats to the state, which passed various internal security laws granting the police, prosecutors, and judges strong tools to deal with terrorism or the Mafia. Pretrial preventive detention of suspects for up to one year for each stage of the criminal process (a total of eight years for some crimes) was allowed. Use of *pentiti*, those who "repent" their crimes by implicating others (often after such inducements as cash, plastic surgery, and new identities), was authorized. Laws reinstated the Fascist practice of allowing suspects to be interrogated without the presence of counsel and allowing electronic eavesdropping without prior approval of a judge.

The laws designed to counter political terrorism and Mafia activity pushed the Italian judges to use prosecution weapons that were inconsistent with notions of independence and objectivity. The role of judge became merged with that of the police and prosecution so that they were no longer impartial umpires. Some were so committed to the prosecution of terrorists and mafioso that they became known as "assault judges," those who no longer separate politics and social issues from the law but try to make a name for themselves in the press by "attacking" the problem.

Use of these new laws raised a storm of protest among civil libertarians, who criticized the unbridled discretion of judges, prosecutors, and the police. In November 1987, 80 percent of those casting ballots voted to remove the shield against civil liability of magistrates, a judicial protection found in most Western democracies. The Italian government then took additional actions to bolster the legitimacy of the judiciary. In 1988 it passed legislation for determining the civil liability of judges. These

procedures allow courts to assess damages caused by the magistrate's alleged mistake. The state, not the jurist, pays the damages, but the offending magistrate may be penalized through a reduction of annual salary.

More sweeping legislation was passed to replace the procedures of the civil code with those in line with American practices, labeled in the press "*Processo* Perry Mason." More in keeping with the adversarial system, the new code separates prosecution from the arrest function, separates judicial from prosecutor functions, requires that investigations be completed in thirty days, shifts the burden of proof to the prosecution, and creates a new position of judge of first audience who will determine, through an adversarial proceeding, if a prosecution should go forward. All of these procedures are designed to restore the independence, impartiality, and legitimacy of the Italian judiciary.

SOURCE: Adapted from "The Judical Role in Italy: Independence, Impartiality and Legitimacy," by M. L. Volcansek, *Judicature* 73 (April/May, 1990): 322–327. Reprinted by permission of the author.

Urban–Rural Differences

It is well recognized that there are differences in the way people treat each other in a city as compared to a rural area. In their nine-court study, James Eisenstein, Roy Flemming, and Peter Nardulli found that community size was a major ingredient in determining local legal culture and thus the way justice was allocated.[19] The operation of criminal courts in small towns is different, and more personal, than in cities. In rural communities people know and interact with each other on personal terms. Thus a small town judge probably knows not only the accused and the victim but also their family circumstances. In addition, the amount of crime is low, and a small number of officials are involved in the disposition process. By contrast, cities are impersonal. Decisions there are made in a bureaucratic context— offenders are known only by their case record, multiple courtrooms are used, the courthouse has a large staff, and caseload pressures are great.

In a study of criminal courts in a rural Pennsylvania county, Klingler found that there was little crime, a part-time judge, prosecutor, and public defender, and a desire to avoid trials. "Everyone was thoroughly familiar with the principals in each case—the arresting officer, the defendant and his or her family, the victim, witnesses, and the attorneys."[20] This familiarity made the actions of the judge, opposing attorneys, and the defendant highly visible to the community. In small communities there is a strong desire to avoid conflict, given the extent of the personal relationships. One result is that the guilty plea is the predominant means of case disposition. A second factor is that going rates play a lesser role, since with fewer cases precedents cannot be established. Third, with a low caseload, there is greater individualization because there are too few matters to be handled in a routine manner. These factors combine in small jurisdictions and increase the give-and-take among participants and thus raise the percentage of guilty pleas.

One of the problems with much of our knowledge of criminal justice is that it is based primarily on urban felony courts in which the court community is large, where there are a great number of cases, and where bureaucratic routines have been developed to guide decisions. It is in crowded urban courts that scholars have noted the importance of the workgroup.

The Courtroom Workgroup

The traditional picture of the courtroom emphasizes adversarial attitudes, but a more realistic picture might emphasize the interactions among the major actors within the normative context of the local legal culture. Adjudication is also influenced by the fact that courtroom participants are organized as a **workgroup.** From this perspective, the reciprocal relationships of the judge, prosecutor, and defense attorney, along with those of the support cast (clerk, reporter, and bailiff), are necessary to complete the group's basic task: the disposition of cases. The workgroup concept seems especially important for the analysis of urban courts, in which there are many separate court-

workgroup: A collectivity of individuals who interact in the workplace on a continuing basis, share goals, develop norms in regard to the way activities should be carried out, and eventually establish a network of roles that serves to differentiate this group from others.

■

Even though ours is an adversarial system, courtroom participants form a workgroup that requires constant interaction, cooperation, and negotiation.

rooms in the same system, the number of judicial actors is great, and the caseload is heavy.

Merely placing the major actors in the courtroom does not instantly make them into a workgroup. A judge, prosecutor, defense attorney, defendant, and others together might be called a **grouping,** a conglomerate of persons. It is only when the following conditions are met that a workgroup exists:

grouping: A collectivity of individuals who interact in the workplace but because of shifting membership do not develop into a workgroup.

1. There must be *interaction* of the members.
2. The members share (that is, have the same attitudes about) one or more *motives* or *goals* that determine the direction in which the group will move.
3. The members develop a set of norms that determine the boundaries within which interpersonal relations may be established and activity carried out.
4. If interaction continues, a set of roles becomes stabilized and the group differentiates itself from other groups.
5. A network of interpersonal relationships develops on the basis of the members' likes and dislikes for one another.[21]

The degree to which these conditions are met distinguishes a workgroup from a grouping. We might think of this as a continuum, with the players simply grouped together in some circumstances but working together as a workgroup in other circumstances.

Given this conceptual framework, research might place different sets of courtroom actors at different points on the continuum (see Figure 11.4). For example, a rotation of judges among the courtrooms may limit the opportunity to develop workgroup norms and roles. Although the same prosecutors and defense attorneys may be present every day, bringing in a new judge, perhaps on a weekly basis, will require them to learn and accommodate to the various special ways that the judges on the circuit expect the proceedings to be run. In such circumstances there is some basis for shared norms and role stability because some of the actors are regularly present, but there is

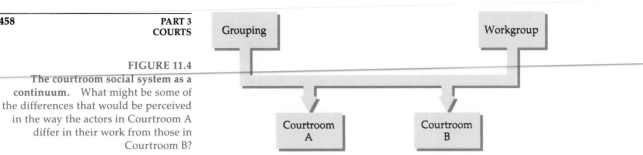

FIGURE 11.4

The courtroom social system as a continuum. What might be some of the differences that would be perceived in the way the actors in Courtroom A differ in their work from those in Courtroom B?

enough interruption in this social network to keep strong relationships from developing. Cases proceed more formally, with less reliance on agreed-upon routines, than with a workgroup that has a well-developed pattern of interactions.

Alternatively, if the same actors are in the courtroom on a continuing basis, we may expect that, through interaction, the cooperative relationships among the judge, prosecutor, and defense attorney, along with those of the staff, will shape the manner in which decisions are made. Thus the defendant, a person from outside the workgroup, will confront "an organized network of relationships, in which each person who acts on his case is reacting to or anticipating the actions of others."[22] Through cooperation it is possible for each member to achieve individual goals as well as for the group to achieve its collective goals.

Although norms and goals are shared, each member of the courtroom workgroup occupies a specialized position and is expected to fit into the socially accepted definition of that status. Because the occupant of each position has specific rights and duties, there is no exchange of roles. When a lawyer moves from the public defender's office to the prosecutor's and ultimately to the bench, each status mandates a different role in the courtroom workgroup. Because each actor is expected to act in a certain way, there can be a high degree of stability in the interpersonal relations among members: each member can become proficient at the work routines associated with his or her role, and the group can develop stable expectations about the actions of the members. Thus the business of the courtroom proceeds in a regularized, informal manner, with many understandings among the members that are never being recorded but nonetheless easing much of the work.

In addition to sharing norms with the other members of the courtroom group, each actor represents a different sponsoring organization.[23] One organization, loosely called the court, sends judges; the prosecuting attorney's office sends assistant prosecutors; the public defender's office sends counsel for indigents. Sponsoring organizations determine and provide the resources for the courtroom workgroup and—perhaps more important—attempt to regulate the behavior of their representatives in the courtroom. Policies of a particular sponsoring organization may stipulate rules to be followed, may encourage or discourage plea bargaining, or may insist that police evidence conform strictly to formal requirements. Thus the judge, prosecutor, or public defender must meet the needs and goals of the workgroup while at the same time satisfying superiors in their own sponsoring organization. The degree to which the chief judge, prosecuting attorney, or chief public defender oversees the work of the representative greatly influences the degree to which each courtroom member can adjust practices to meet the workgroup's goals.

Playing supporting roles in the courtroom drama, members of the judge's staff, such as clerks and reporters, have access to vast amounts of confidential information. This resource, as well as their access to the judge, may be used to enhance their own power within the group. Bailiffs to keep order in the courtroom and to escort prisoners are supplied by the sheriff. Probation officers who provide presentence reports are often present in the courtroom and work closely with the judge. Although not directly tied to the close interactions of the judge, prosecutor, and defense attorney, they provide information and carry out duties in support of the major actors. Finally, the courtroom actors must keep in mind those others with whom they have ties. Prosecutors must not endanger their relationships with the police; defense attorneys know that the accused persons and their families expect a defense; judges must be alert to reactions to their decisions on the part of the news media as well as of members of higher appellate courts. These pressures may have two effects. First, they may require that the actors give "performances" to satisfy their clients and that the dramatizations in turn have the support of other members of the courtroom cast. Second, these pressures may bolster the shared norms of the group—that is, the secrets of stage technique that must be shielded from the audience's view— with the effect that cohesion is increased.

The elements of the courtroom workgroup and the influences that have a bearing on decision making are depicted in Figure 11.5. Note that the workgroup operates in an environment in which the local legal culture, recruitment and selection processes, cases, and the socioeconomic, political, and legal structures of the broader community are conceived as having an impact on decision making.

Physical Setting

The work site of the courtroom group strengthens the interaction patterns of its members and separates them from their clientele groups. The physical surroundings separate the individual courtroom from other social spaces so that communications with those outside the group are limited. Opportunities for social interaction occur during recesses, but the irregularity of these breaks means that refreshment and conversation are shared with other members of the group, not with members of other courtroom teams working in adjoining space.

The low visibility of courtroom activities to both the public and government officials is an additional characteristic of the judicial system. Judges enjoy a great deal of independence from supervision because few people are watching. The members of the courtroom team could be an important instrument for quality control, but they are bound into the process and depend on the judge for favors. The higher courts may supervise the administration of justice, but only a small percentage of criminal cases are appealed. Members of the general public may observe, but few citizens attend criminal court.

The bench is usually elevated to symbolize the judge's authority. Because it faces the lawyers' table, persons in the audience, and sometimes even the defendant, are unable to observe all the verbal and

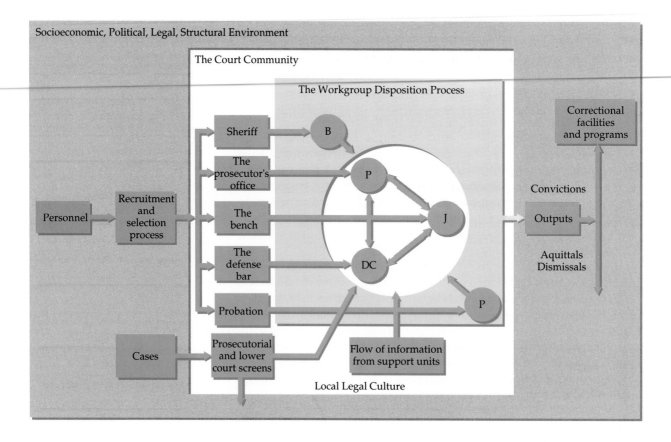

FIGURE 11.5

Model of criminal court decision making. This model ties together the elements of the courtroom workgroup, sponsoring organizations, and local legal culture. Note the influences brought to bear on decision making. Are there other factors that should be considered? SOURCE: Adapted from *Tenor of Justice: Criminal Courts and the Guilty Plea Process*, by P. Nardulli, J. Eisenstein, and R. Flemming. Copyright © 1988 by the University of Illinois Press. Reprinted by permission.

nonverbal exchanges. In some courts the attorneys for both sides sit toward either end of a long table; the furniture does not define them as adversaries. Throughout the proceedings, lawyers from both sides periodically engage in muffled conversations with the judge out of the hearing range of the defendant and spectators. When judges call the attorneys into their chambers for private discussion, the defendants remain in the courtroom. In most settings, the defendants sit isolated either in the "dock" or in a chair behind their counsel to symbolize their status as silent observers with no power to negotiate their own fate.

Since public defenders often represent as many as 90 percent of the court's clients, they occupy a "permanent" place in the courtroom and only temporarily relinquish their desks to the few lawyers who have been privately retained. Whereas the courtroom encounters of private attorneys are brief, businesslike, and temporary, public defenders view the courtroom as their regular workplace and thus give the impression that they are core members of the courtroom group. From the defendants' perspective, the adversarial system must appear to be a myth as these agent-mediators decide their fate.

Role of the Judge

In the view of some defendants, the judge is a peripheral figure who does not play an important part in determining the outcome of their case. In their eyes the lawyer and prosecutor play much more significant roles. From the perspective of these defendants, the judge's behavior shows the ultimate failure of the system and the complete submission of due process ideals to bureaucratic goals.

Yet judges are leaders of the courtroom team and are supposed to ensure that procedures are correctly followed. They are also administrators who are responsible for coordinating the process. Even so, there is latitude for each judge to play the role somewhat differently. Judges who run a loose administrative ship see themselves as somewhat above the battle. They give other members of the team considerable freedom to discharge their responsibilities and will usually ratify decisions made by the group. One might expect that although the task goals of the organization, in terms of the number of cases processed, would be low, the social relations within the courtroom group would be high.

More aggressive judges see themselves as necessary leaders of the courtroom team. These judges run tighter ships; they anticipate problems; provide cues for other actors, threaten, cajole, and move the group toward an efficient accomplishment of goals. Such judges command respect and fully participate in the ongoing courtroom drama.

Because of their position within the judicial process, judges possess the potential leadership resources to play their role according to these polar types or somewhere in between. The way they define their role will greatly influence the structure of interpersonal relations within the courtroom. As a consequence, the way the group performs its task, as measured by the output of its case decisions, is influenced by the role of the judge.

Encounters: The Labeling Process

The criminal court provides a social context for encounters between the defendant and the agents of the law who fasten the label "criminal" onto the guilty. The courtroom appearance of the accused, the plea of guilty, and the process of sentencing can be viewed as containing many of the elements of a degradation ceremony.

We should emphasize, however, that the new label on the defendant is the culmination of a process that began at the time of arrest (some would argue even before). From civilian to accused to defendant to convict, the entire journey through the criminal justice system can be viewed as a "moral career," a sequence of changes in the person's conception of self and the framework within which he or she interacts with others and they, in turn, react to the person. Erving Goffman explains:

> Each moral career, and behind this, each self, occurs within the confines of an institutional system, whether a social establishment such as a mental hospital or a complex of personal and professional relationships. The self, then, can be seen as something that resides in the arrangements prevailing in a social system for its members. The self in this sense is not a property of the person to whom it is attributed, but dwells rather in the pattern of social control that is exerted in connection with the person by himself and those around him. This special kind of institutional arrangement does not so much support the self as constitute it.[24]

The courtroom is a meeting place for professionals (lawyers, probation officers, and social workers) who proclaim that they work in the service of accused persons, supposedly to treat their needs and those of society. These are the agent-mediators who help the defendants redefine themselves and prepare them for the next phase of the moral career.

Dress may communicate the role each performer plays. Group members wear appropriate uniforms: the judge in robes, the attorneys, both male and female, in conservative suits. One may even observe differences between the clothing of the prosecutor and the defense attorney. Prosecutors dress in more somber colors (to identify their role with that of the judge?); some defense attorneys tend toward more flamboyant outfits (to conform to their clients' expectations?). Even the defendants may be dressed in uniforms—jail garb—if they are being detained for lack of bail. Because most defendants are poor, their clothing helps to define their role and differentiates them from the group of court actors.

The role played by defendants in courtroom encounters will greatly influence the perceptions of the agent-mediators and guide their decisions. Defendants are expected to present themselves according to the "ideal form" as conceived by the other persons along the moral career journey. If the defense attorney, social worker, family members, and other agent-mediators have been successful during the pretrial phase in getting defendants to redefine themselves, they should understand how they must act out their part. Ideally, they will act guilty, repentant, silent, and submissive. The guilty plea "ceremony" allows others in the courtroom to meet administrative needs within a legal context. For example, when the accused acknowledges guilt in public and testifies that he or she is entering the plea willingly and voluntarily, acceptance of the plea can be followed by a brief lecture from the judge about the seriousness of the wrongful act or the unhappiness the defendant has caused his or her family. Thus the defendant's contrite demeanor allows the judge to justify the lesser sentence negotiated by the prosecutor and defense lawyer. The judge can "give a break" to the defendant for having cooperated.

The defendant who pleads not guilty or who otherwise gives an inappropriate performance may incur severe sanctions. Maureen Mileski observed that the judge's harsh manner in encounters was not related to the seriousness of the charge. More important, a minor disruption in the courtroom or a show of disrespect for its personnel led to reprimands from the judge or sentences that were more severe than usual. But she noted few cases in which the defendant's behavior was not according to form; only 5 percent elicited a harsh response from the judge. The vast majority conformed to the expectations of a routine bureaucratic encounter.[25]

Felony Justice: The Impact of Courtroom Workgroups

The research of James Eisenstein and Herbert Jacob on the felony disposition process in the courtrooms of Baltimore, Chicago, and Detroit gives us important insights into the influence of the workgroup on decisions in felony cases and provides comparative evidence showing differences in the criminal justice systems of three cities.[26]

They found that the same type of felony case was handled very differently in each, yet the dispositions were remarkably similar for those defendants who reached the trial court. It was not the law, rules of procedure, or crime rate that produced the variation but rather the structure of the courtroom workgroups, the influence of the sponsoring organizations, and the sociopolitical environment of each city.

Before examining the trial courtroom dispositions discussed by Eisenstein and Jacob, we must first look at the screening process that occurred in the felony defendants' preliminary hearings. And we note a basic fact of American criminal justice: the courts convict fewer than half of those arrested by the police on felony charges and brought forward for prosecution (see Chapter 10). Many felony defendants never reach a trial court because their cases are dismissed, charges against them are reduced, or they are diverted at a preliminary hearing.

The preliminary hearings in the three cities had very different outcomes. In Chicago almost two-thirds of the cases presented were dismissed, whereas in Baltimore and Detroit about three-fifths and four-fifths, respectively, were moved on to the trial courtroom after probable cause was found. Although these differences are striking, they do not tell the entire story. Bail and pretrial motion decisions are also made at preliminary hearings, and bail outcomes disagree substantially. About half of Baltimore defendants remained in jail, compared with two-fifths in Chicago and Detroit. Baltimore released 21 percent on recognizance but levied high money bail for the remainder; practically no one was let out on recognizance in Chicago, but money bail was kept low; in Detroit, almost half were released on recognizance, and when money bail was required it was fairly low. Pretrial motions concerning the state's evidence were also treated variously. Since most Baltimore defendants went directly to a trial courtroom without a preliminary hearing, there was little opportunity to present pretrial motions to suppress evidence. The preliminary examination was conducted in an adversarial fashion in Detroit, less so in Chicago.

What influence did the courtroom workgroups have on these preliminary hearings? Eisenstein and Jacob found that the stable courtroom workgroups in Chicago developed informal procedures for screening cases. Because of the groups' close links to the trial courtrooms, they felt pressure to screen out many cases; hence the very high dismissal rate. In Detroit, also a city with stable workgroups, the prosecutors had already screened cases before they reached the courtroom; thus most of the defendants who appeared at preliminary hearings were sent to trial. Baltimore was characterized as having unstable workgroups, in part because members were frequently rotated and the sponsoring organizations exercised little supervisory control. As a result, fewer guilty pleas occurred and most defendants were forwarded to the grand jury and ultimately to the trial courts.[27]

Findings in regard to the trial court stage were similar to those in regard to the preliminary hearing: the conviction rates of the cities were similar (Table 11.2), but the methods used to produce the dispositions differed substantially. It must be remembered, however, that Baltimore processed largely unscreened cases, whereas 40 per-

TABLE 11.2 Trial court dispositions of felony defendants in three cities. With other variables being similar, the cities varied as to the method of case disposition. What might account for the lesser use of the guilty plea in Baltimore?

	Baltimore	Chicago	Detroit
Defendants sent to trial whom court convicted	68.0%	75.5%	72.2%
Median number of days between grand jury indictment or information and trial courtroom disposition	178	151.5	56
Median number of days between arrest and trial courtroom disposition	226	267.5	71.2
Disposition methods			
Guilty pleas	34.7%	61.7%	63.9%
Bench trials	33.9%	19.9%	6.8%
Jury trials	9.4%	6.7%	7.3%
Dismissals	22.0%	11.7%	22.0%
	100.0%	100.0%	100.0%
	(N = 549)	(N = 519)	(N = 1,208)

SOURCE: From *Felony Justice: An Organizational Analysis of Criminal Courts,* by J. Eisenstein and H. Jacob, p. 233. Copyright © 1977 by James Eisenstein and Herbert Jacob. Reprinted by permission of the authors.

cent of felony arrests in Detroit and 85 percent in Chicago had been pruned at the preliminary hearing. The data also make it apparent that each of the cities arrived at the results in a different way. Detroit operated at a pace three times faster than that of Chicago and Baltimore. Chicago and Detroit relied primarily on guilty pleas, whereas Baltimore processed more cases through trials than through plea bargaining. But in all three cities the workgroups shunned the jury trial: fewer than 10 percent of the cases were disposed of in this manner.

Differential dispositions among the cities were reflections of, among other things, the organizational structure of the courtroom workgroups. The way the workgroups dealt with cases was also influenced by defendants' characteristics, the strength of the evidence, and the nature of the offense, factors that were inputs into the ongoing social system of the courtroom.

The disposition of felony cases results from the interaction of the courtroom members. The tasks that they perform require full participation, but they in turn are influenced by the policies of their sponsoring organizations. The degree to which the interdependence of these factors affects the processes of felony justice varies between jurisdictions, over time in each jurisdiction, and from courtroom to courtroom. The stability of workgroup interactions can be upset by such changes as a new docket system, a shift by the public defender's office from a zone to a person-to-person strategy, or a decision by the prosecutor to institute policies where only cases expected to result in a conviction are brought to trial. When such shifts occur, new factors are brought to bear on the courtroom, and its members must adapt, with the result that an altered felony disposition configuration will evolve.

One of the oldest concepts of the common law is that justice delayed is justice denied. Ever since the English nobles forced King John to sign the Magna Carta and promise not to "deny or delay right or justice," there has been concern over the slowness with which courts sometimes process cases. In the United States a speedy trial is guaranteed by the Sixth Amendment to the Constitution, and the Supreme Court has characterized adherence to swift justice as an important safeguard to prevent undue incarceration prior to trial, to minimize anxiety accompanying public accusation, and to limit the possibilities that long delay will impair the abilities of accused persons to defend themselves.

Nowadays the pace of the criminal courts is usually assumed to be slowed by the huge caseloads thrust upon mismanaged and inefficient operations. Because of the courts' deficiencies, defendants must wait unreasonably long for trial (often in jail), and prosecution is hampered by victims' loss of interest and witnesses' fading memories of crucial facts as time passes.

Delay is usually described as an aberration and dysfunction of the system. Much of the research on delay has emphasized structural and resource problems associated with the organization of the courts. It has been suggested that the problems would go away if the numbers of judges and courtrooms were increased, if professional administrators were hired, and if sound management were instituted.

Studies by the National Center for State Courts question assumptions about the causes of delay and about the remedies traditionally advanced.[28] When researchers examined the size, caseload, and management procedures of urban trial courts, they found major exceptions to the assumption that criminal cases are disposed of expeditiously only where there is a small volume of cases that are neither serious nor complex. As shown in Table 11.3, the researchers

TABLE 11.3   Court structure and case delay.   As the data show, there is little relationship among the number of judges, the case filings per judge, and processing time. If these are not the variables that explain delay, what might be at work here?

	FTE* Judges	Filings per FTE Judge	Median Processing Time (Days)
Salinas, CA	3.50	383	22
Detroit, MI	34.00	480	38
New Orleans, LA	10.50	595	42
Dayton, OH	4.00	555	42
San Diego, CA	19.00	487	50
Phoenix, AZ	13.54	917	85
Portland, OR	7.00	905	94
Denver, CO	6.75	431	109
Providence, RI	5.40	559	111
Miami, FL	24.00	995	112
Boston, MA	8.00	206	233

*Full time equivalent.

SOURCE: From *Examining Court Delay*, by J. Goerdt, p. 72. Copyright © 1989 by National Center for State Courts. Reprinted by permission.

uncovered very little relationship between processing time and the number of felony filings per judge. The data show that the courts with the largest caseloads are not those with the slowest disposition times, nor are the comparatively underworked courts speedier.

The court in Pittsburgh handles more cases and is slower than the small-volume courts in Oakland and San Diego, but the Wichita and Jersey City courts are substantially slower than might be expected for their size, and the large Detroit court processes criminal cases at a faster pace than others like it. The courts of Boston are not particularly distinguished by the numbers of their filings, judges, or populations, yet they are the slowest of those examined.

Why, then, do some courts process cases much more quickly than others? The answer appears to be that it is not the formal, structural

CLOSE-UP | *Making Things Happen: The Genius of Judge Harold Rothwax*

Seated behind an elevated desk in the high-ceilinged courtroom, Judge Harold Rothwax does not look at all pleased. His broad face, an appealing face with something of the lumpy quality of an old prizefighter's, is set and pale, and his head is pulled down between his shoulders. The two lawyers before him—a young assistant district attorney clutching a confusion of documents and a defense counsel whose brown toupee gleams in contrast to his own dull sideburns—place their hands on the massive desk and seem to brace themselves against his next words. A few spectators stare from the highbacked wooden benches, and in the well of the court, the clerks and uniformed officers are still.

At a table perhaps 20 feet from the judge and behind the lawyers, the defendant stands waiting. He is a handsome white man in his early thirties, and his face above the light turtleneck projects a kind of distaste, as if his straight nose were picking up bad odors at this tawdry proceeding. But he has been in such surroundings many times before. As his record attests, he is a specialist in burglarizing the rooms of first-class hotels, and he often carries a gun to impress anyone unfortunate enough to discover him. He is, in short, a dangerous thief whose devotion to his work led most recently to his capture on one job while he was out on bail after another. He uses different names for different occasions, and he is in bad trouble this morning.

"Tell the defendant," says Judge Rothwax to the defense attorney, in a voice that cannot be heard beyond his desk, "that this is the last day for three and a half to seven. After this, it goes up. If he's going to take the offer, he has to decide now. If he doesn't take it, he's going to trial. We've had enough of this delay. Either he takes the plea, or we set a trial date *today*."

The lawyer looks at the judge for a moment without speaking and then turns and walks back to his client.

It is clear that Rothwax is not going to tolerate further stalling. The defendant either must plead guilty to the reduced burglary charge offered by the district attorney—for which Rothwax had earlier indicated he would hand down a sentence of no more than three and a half to seven years in prison—or must prepare to go to trial. Then if a jury convicts him on the original charge (and the prosecution's case seems very good), the trial judge will surely give him a much heavier sentence. And if the defendant wants to delay now and enter plea later, to avoid trial, the bargain offered today will be unavailable. This is the hard moment of truth in the plea bargaining process for the handsome burglar, and his face, empty now of any disdain, is taut and angry. He speaks in a rapid whisper to his attorney, stares at Rothwax, shrugs and whispers to his lawyer again.

The lawyer comes back to the bench. "This guy is crazy," he says to Rothwax. "We'll go to trial."

"All right, gentlemen," the judge says briskly. "Let's settle on a date certain for trial."

"Judge, I'd like to be relieved of this case," says the defense lawyer. "This guy won't listen."

Rothwax shakes his head. "No," he replies. "You're the fourth lawyer he's had. That's enough. Let's pick a trial date." It is clear that there is no more room for discussion on this matter. A day two weeks later is selected. The defendant is taken out of the courtroom and back into detention. His case, of course, may still never go to trial, but it has been brought one step closer, largely because of pressure brought by Judge Rothwax. The calendar proceeds.

elements of courts that are important in this regard but rather the local legal culture and the social organization of the criminal justice system. The participants become adapted to a certain pace of litigation, and these expectations are translated into others in regard to the way cases should proceed. What is viewed as the normal speed for the disposition of criminal cases in one system may be viewed as undue haste in another. As this book has emphasized throughout, decisions are made in the context of an organization in which discretion is widely exercised. This means that local norms, role relationships, and the incentives of the major actors determine the manner in which cases are processed. Unless the defendant is being held without bail while awaiting trial, there is little incentive for speed.

Impact of Drug Cases on Urban Trial Courts

One consequence of the war on drugs is the influx of drug sale and possession cases on urban trial courts throughout the United States. The increase in drug arrests, the aggressive prosecution of drug cases, and the severe sentences mandated by legislatures have all worked to overload many trial courts already weighted down by heavy caseloads (see Figure 11.6).

A study of twenty-six urban courts found that drug sale, drug possession, and intent to sell cases constituted an average of 26 percent of felony cases in 1987.[29] Wide variation among the courts was found, with cities such as Dayton, Ohio, registering only a 12 percent drug caseload, whereas 46 percent of the cases in the Bronx, New York, were in this category. The study found that over four years there had been an average increase of 56 percent in the drug caseload. Since more recent data is not available, one must interpolate these trends and look to other sources. As discussed in Chapter 6, drug testing by the police has shown that in many cities 60 to 90 percent of arrestees display positive signs of drug use. By 1991 some urban courts such

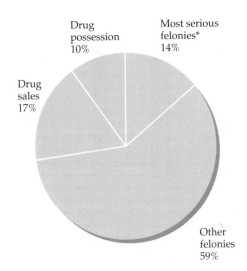

FIGURE 11.6
Average caseload mix of twenty-three large urban trial courts.   An increasing portion of cases before urban trial courts involves drugs. One result may be that less attention is being given to other serious felonies.
*Most serious cases: murder, rape, robbery.
SOURCE: From *Examining Court Delay,* by J. Goerdt, p. 59. Copyright © 1989 by National Center for State Courts. Reprinted by permission.

as Jersey City, New Jersey, were reporting that more than 70 percent of their caseload concerned drugs. It must also be remembered that these data concern only drug sale, possession and intent to sell cases; they do not reflect the number of robberies, thefts, and burglaries often associated with drug users.

Drug cases not only add to the number and composition of cases before the trial courts, but they also, because of the severity of sentences and the complexity of the evidential rules, take much longer to resolve than most felonies (see Figure 11.7). Drug cases tend to be dismissed much later in the court process than do other types of felonies. Research suggests that this is because "package deals" involving multiple drug cases and multiple defendants are put together.[30] As part of these bargains additional pending drug charges may be dropped late in the justice process. Other problems that contribute to delay in drug cases include the time necessary to get lab test results and the resolution of pretrial motions related to search and seizure.

Continuances: Accommodations in the System

continuance: An adjournment of a scheduled case until a future date.

The **continuance** is a prime example of the type of accommodation that causes delay. From a legal standpoint, the judge has the discretion to grant continuances so that the defense will have an opportunity to prepare its case. The need for time to obtain counsel, to prepare pretrial motions, to obtain evidence, or to find a witness can be used as a reason for postponement. The prosecution can also request continuances. Although they are less likely to have a request granted than the defense, especially if the defendant is being held for trial, prosecutors do receive a significant number of continuances in most courts. Although the law is specific, the granting and denial of

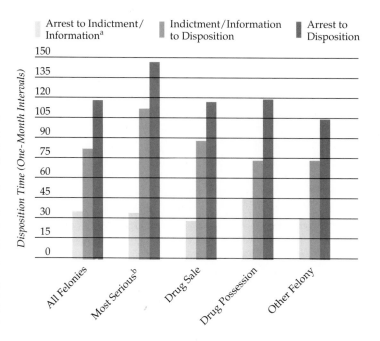

FIGURE 11.7
Median felony case processing time for large urban trial courts. Owing to the complexity of the evidence and the potential severity of the sentence, drug cases take longer to resolve than do most felonies.
NOTE: Medians are from among the median CPTs for 18 to 26 courts, depending on case type and whether total or upper court time.
[a]Arrest to disposition minus indictment/information to disposition.
[b]Murder, rape, and robbery.
SOURCE: From "The Impact of Drug Cases on Case Processing in Urban Trial Courts," by J. A. Goerdt and J. A. Martin, *State Court Journal* (Fall 1989): 8.

motions for continuances go on almost unaffected by the legal framework. The important rules that the system follows are rules of administrative practice rather than of law, and thus continuances are accommodations to the goals of judicial actors rather than to technical factors of a case.

Using data gathered from five urban court systems, Martin Levin estimated that the percentage of cases in which continuances are granted ranges from ten in Minneapolis District Court to more than seventy in Chicago Criminal Division Court.[31] Research also shows that continuances have the effect of decreasing the number of guilty dispositions as the number of court appearances increases. Defendants with retained counsel are often able to put off a trial as a way of wearing out witnesses, remaining out on bail as long as possible, or waiting for community interest to die. This tactic has the additional effect of discriminating in favor of defendants who can afford counsel. The poor, represented by the public defender, do not receive the same treatment, in part because they must await disposition of their cases in pretrial detention.

Rules for Speedy Trials

Congress and several states have tackled the problem of delay by enacting rules for speedy trials. These rules typically require that cases be moved from arrest to trial within certain strict time limits, and they provide for the dismissal of charges if the case is not brought to trial within the time specified. Many federal and state courts have long had such requirements, and in 1974 Congress passed the Federal Speedy Trial Act. The maximum limits established by the act are thirty days from arrest to indictment and seventy days from indictment to trial. Cases that do not meet these requirements may be dismissed either with or without the option of reinstatement of the charges, but it is expected that charges will not be reinstated without good reason. Although defendants may waive their right to a speedy trial under the rules, the prosecution can get an extension of the limits only if the "ends of justice" will thus be served or if there is a "judicial emergency."[32]

In assessing the results of the Speedy Trial Act, Malcolm Feeley found that it has not been taken seriously by most federal judges.[33] The legislation has had some indirect effects, however: the planning process has spurred administrative modernization of the courts, and procedures have been tightened in the interest of improved allocation of resources. The backlog of civil cases has grown as the courts have worked to bring criminal cases to trial before the charges have to be dismissed. In many courts it appears that only the formal requirements of the act have been met and that the problem of delay remains, because the "ends of justice" exception is used extensively.

Although speedy trial statutes give the impression of having caused a revolution in some state courts, the policies at that level also contain enormous loopholes. Surveys have discerned "no correlation between the stringency of provisions in state speedy trial rules and actual disposition times."[34]

Assessing Delay

Delay benefits not only defendants seeking lenient treatment but also defense attorneys, prosecutors, and judges. The major goals of defense attorneys are to collect their fees and to minimize their court time per case. They are further motivated to avoid a conviction or severe punishment for their clients. Thus delay not only is in the defendants' interest but also helps the attorneys maximize their fees, please their clients, and enhance their reputations for skill. Although a move to delay a case is usually initiated by the defense attorney, it cannot succeed without the cooperation of the prosecutor and judge. Levin found that prosecutors generally did not oppose motions for continuances. Prosecutors presumably understand the need to reach accommodations that will result in a bargained plea. Judges also realize that postponement usually helps prevent a full-length trial that would tie up the courtroom for an extended period. But the prosecutor and judge recognize that by assisting the defense attorney, they ensure the attorney's cooperation in turn.

Although formal changes have been proposed to reduce delay in the criminal courts, such changes will not be successful unless it is recognized that courtroom actors have individual and multiple goals. The personal needs of the defense attorney, prosecutor, and judge have been shown to be stronger than the broader goal of processing offenders quickly. Thus system goals cannot be expected to dominate the criminal court until incentives are provided that are more rewarding to the actors than the fulfillment of their current needs.

SUMMARY

Assembly-line justice is the means that enables court administrators to move the enormous caseloads with which they must contend. Judicial decisions are dispensed in wholesale lots because actors in the system work on the basis of three assumptions: (1) any person who is brought before the court is probably guilty; (2) the vast majority of defendants will plead guilty; and (3) those charged with minor offenses will be processed in volume. Guilt or innocence, probation or prison are usually decided by a small group of courtroom actors.

The judge is the most important figure in the criminal court. Decisions of the police, defense attorneys, and prosecutors are greatly affected by judges' rulings and sentencing practices. In most cities the criminal court judge occupies the lowest rung in the judicial hierarchy.

In more than half the states, judges are popularly elected, which usually means that candidates must be active in politics and are often nominated for a judgeship as a reward for party work. In other states judges are either appointed by the governor or legislature or selected by merit. Arguments have been advanced in support of each method, but the important question concerns the decisions made by the judges once they are seated. Levin's comparison of the criminal courts of

Pittsburgh and Minneapolis provides an opportunity to examine the types of persons selected to be judges under each system and the types of decisions that they make.

The concepts of role and group help to clarify the operations of courtroom actors. Although norms and goals are shared, each member of the courtroom group—judge, prosecutor, defense attorney, defendant, bailiff, and clerk—occupies a specialized position and is expected to fit into the socially accepted definition of that status. The cohesion of the workgroup is enhanced by the physical setting and by the delineation of roles. The delays in the courts result from the conflicts between the goals of the system and the personal needs of the members of the courtroom team. The influx of drug cases during the past decade has exacerbated demands on the courts. The criminal court provides a social context for personal encounters between the defendant and the agents of the law who fasten the label "criminal" onto the guilty.

FOR DISCUSSION

1. Case overload is one of the major problems facing the criminal courts. Is multiplication of judges and facilities likely to solve this problem?
2. Discuss the effects that partisan election of judges may have on the administration of justice. Which system of judicial selection do you prefer?
3. The judge plays several roles. What are they? Do any of them conflict?
4. If you are being prosecuted on a drug charge, what tactics might your attorney use to get you a light sentence? How would these tactics influence court operations?

FOR FURTHER READING

Blumberg, Abraham S. *Criminal Justice.* Chicago: Quadrangle Books, 1967. A classic examination of the criminal courts as organizations.

Eisenstein, James, Roy Flemming, and Peter Nardulli, *The Contours of Justice: Communities and Their Courts.* Boston: Little, Brown, 1988. A study of nine felony courts in three states. Emphasizes the impact of the local legal culture on court operations.

Eisenstein, James, and Herbert Jacob. *Felony Justice.* Boston: Little, Brown, 1977. Examines felony courts in three cities. Develops the concept of the courtroom workgroup and its impact on decision making.

Feeley, Malcolm M. *Court Reform on Trial.* New York: Basic Books, 1983. Study of court reform efforts such as diversion, speedy trial, bail reform, and sentencing reform. Notes the difficulties of bringing about change.

Satter, Robert. *Doing Justice: A Trial Judge at Work.* New York: Simon & Schuster, 1990. A judge's view of the cases he faces daily and the factors influencing his decisions.

NOTES

1. Roscoe Pound, "The Causes of Popular Dissatisfaction with the Administration of Justice," *Journal of the American Judicature Society* 20 (1937):178–187.
2. John H. Wigmore, "Roscoe Pound's St. Paul Address of 1906," *Journal of the American Judicature Society* 20 (1937):136.
3. Marcia Lim, "A Status Report on State Court Financing," *State Court Journal* 11 (Summer 1987):7.
4. John Paul Ryan, Allan Ashman, Bruce D. Sales, and Sandra Shane-DuBow, *American Trial Judges* (New York: Free Press, 1980), p. 182.
5. U.S. Department of Justice, *Sourcebook of Criminal Justice Statistics* (Washington, DC: Government Printing Office, 1989), p. 109.
6. Paul B. Wice, *Chaos in the Courthouse* (New York: Praeger, 1985), p. 96.
7. Ibid., p. 96.
8. Benjamin N. Cardozo, *The Nature of the Judicial Process* (New Haven, CT: Yale University Press, 1921), p. 149.
9. Samuel I. Rosenman, "A Better Way to Select Judges," *Journal of the American Judicature Society* 48 (1964):86.
10. Ryan et al., *American Trial Judges*, p. 124.
11. Lawrence Baum, "The Electoral Fates of Incumbent Judges in the Ohio Court of Common Pleas," *Judicature* 66 (1983):420; William K. Hall and Larry T. Aspin, "What Twenty Years of Judical Retention Elections Have Told Us," *Judicature* 70 (April-May 1987):340.
12. Richard A. Watson and Rondal G. Downing, *The Politics of the Bench and the Bar: Judicial Selection under the Missouri Nonpartisan Court Plan* (New York: Wiley, 1969).
13. James Alfini, "Mississippi Judicial Selection: Election, Appointment, and Bar Appointment" in *Courts and Judges,* ed. James A. Cramer (Newbury Park, CA: Sage, 1981), p. 253.
14. Martin A. Levin, "Urban Politics and Policy Outcomes: The Criminal Courts," in *Criminal Justice: Law and Politics,* 5th ed., ed. George F. Cole (Pacific Grove, CA: Brooks/Cole, 1988), p. 330.
15. Ibid., p. 332.
16. James Eisenstein, Roy B. Flemming, and Peter F. Nardulli, *The Contours of Justice: Communities and Their Courts* (Boston: Little, Brown, 1988), p. 12.
17. Thomas W. Church, Jr., "Examining Local Legal Culture," *American Bar Foundation Research Journal* (Summer 1985):449.
18. Eisenstein, Flemming, and Nardulli, p. 30.
19. Ibid., p. 261.
20. As cited in Eisenstein, Flemming, and Nardulli, *Contours of Justice,* p. 263.
21. A. Paul Hare, *Handbook of Small Group Research* (New York: Free Press of Glencoe, 1962), pp. 9–10.
22. Edward J. Clynch and David W. Neubauer, "Trial Courts as Organizations," *Law and Policy Quarterly* 3 (1981):59–94.
23. James Eisenstein and Herbert Jacob, *Felony Justice* (Boston: Little, Brown, 1977), p. 43.
24. Erving Goffman, *Asylums* (Garden City, NY: Doubleday, 1961), p. 169.
25. Maureen Mileski, "Courtroom Encounters," *Law and Society Review* 5 (1971):524.
26. Eisenstein and Jacob, *Felony Justice,* pp. 19–39.
27. Ibid.
28. Thomas Church, Jr., Alan Carlson, Jo-Lynn Lee, and Teresa Tan, *Justice Delayed* (Williamsburg, VA: National Center for State Courts, 1978); Barry Mahoney et al., *Implementing Delay Reduction and Delay Prevention Programs in Urban Trial Courts* (Williamsburg, VA: National Center for State Courts, 1985).
29. John Goerdt, *Examining Court Delay* (Williamsburg, VA: National Center for State Courts, 1989), p. 54.
30. John A. Goerdt and John A. Martin, "The Impact of Drug Cases on Case Processing in Urban Trial Courts," *State Court Journal* (Fall 1989):4–12.

31. Martin A. Levin, "Delay in Five Criminal Courts," *Journal of Legal Studies* 4 (1975):83.
32. Title 18 U.S.C. 3166.
33. Malcolm M. Feeley, *Court Reform on Trial* (New York: Basic Books, 1983), p. 173.
34. Church et al., *Justice Delayed,* pp. 48–49, 78.

Trial and Posttrial Processes

Key Terms and Cases

appeal
bench trial
challenged for cause
circumstantial evidence

direct evidence
habeas corpus
jury
peremptory challenge

presentence report
real evidence
reasonable doubt

testimony
voir dire
Williams v. Florida (1970)

"For instance, now [the Queen says to Alice] . . . there's the King's Messenger. He's in prison now, being punished; and the trial doesn't even begin till next Wednesday; and of course the crime comes last of all." Alice replies, "Suppose he never commits the crime?" "That would be all the better, wouldn't it?" the Queen responds.

Lewis Carroll

From the time that Washington, D.C., mayor Marion Barry was indicted by a federal grand jury on three perjury and eleven drug charges until his conviction on only one misdemeanor charge for possession of cocaine, the national media provided almost continuous attention to the activities surrounding the affair. At his trial the prosecution entered into evidence the "sting video" that showed Barry taking long pulls from a crack pipe as FBI agents burst into his room at the Vista International Hotel. Other testimony portrayed him as a drug addict eager to snort cocaine or smoke crack and as a womanizer. Perhaps most damaging to the mayor was the testimony of former model turned FBI informant, Rasheeda Moore, who goaded Barry into taking the drug while the video camera rolled on.

The prosecution of Barry, one of the nation's highest elected black officials, raised questions of a politically motivated prosecution, racism, corruption, and personal tragedy. The frequent showing on television of the FBI videotape gave national attention to Barry's arrest and the events leading to his trial. That the mayor of the nation's capital, a city with a major drug problem, should behave in the manner depicted was thought by many to be inexcusable. Others, however, argued that the civil liberties of Barry had been violated by the FBI's use of entrapment. The sequence of events surrounding Barry's prosecution had all of the elements of a gripping drama. As one observer said, "This case has everything. It has sex, drugs, politics, and race."

As with every drama there was an ending. After eight days of jury deliberation Marion Barry stood by his attorney's side and heard the verdict—he had "beaten rap." The jury of ten blacks and two whites found him guilty of only one misdemeanor, cocaine possession. He was acquitted of a second possession count, and the jury was hung on the other counts. Judge Thomas Penfield Jackson ruled a mistrial on the undecided counts. Barry's supporters claimed victory, and the mayor, who earlier had announced that he would not run again for that office, filed papers to run for the Washington, D.C., city council.

Like other famous trials of the past, such as those of Bruno Hauptmann, kidnapper of the Lindbergh baby; Leopold and Loeb; Patty Hearst; and Sacco and Vanzetti, the trial of Barry contained all the ingredients of soap opera, and the public was eager for every tantalizing tidbit. The case is the type that occupies the very top of Walker's criminal justice wedding cake: those celebrated cases that go to trial, command great public attention, and result in endless

High-interest cases such as that of District of Columbia Mayor Marion Barry give the public the impression that the trial is the key to understanding the criminal process.

appeals. Meanwhile judges were handing out hundreds of sentences to less famous defendants whose crimes were perhaps no less heinous but who did not receive the trial by judge and jury guaranteed by the Bill of Rights. As we have seen, the vast majority of defendants plead guilty or are judged in a bench trial without jury. The number of full-fledged trials with a judge and jury is tiny compared with the total number of cases processed by the judicial system.

TRIAL: THE EXCEPTIONAL CASE

According to the assumptions underlying the adversarial system, a trial by **jury** is a search for the truth. In reality, however, many other values, some of them in conflict, combine in a jury trial. The search must be conducted within the framework of the constitutionally guaranteed protections accorded the defendant. Thus the quest for truth must step aside when it conflicts with the individual's rights against self-incrimination, unlawful searches and seizures, and other abuses of governmental authority. A trial by a jury composed of members of the community is one of the greatest safeguards against arbitrary and unlawful actions by criminal justice officials.

A trial is also a contest, a symbolic combat between the prosecution and the defense in which one party normally emerges the winner. The spirit of rivalry permeates the proceedings, with the result that the determination to win may override the search for the truth.

Because trials are conducted in public, they are also a kind of stylized drama, though the totality of this living theater often assumes proportions greater than those intended.

> It is also politics, in both the noblest and the basest senses of the word. A criminal trial is an almost primordial confrontation between the individual and society. At stake are values no less important than individual liberty on the one hand, and the need for social order on the other. It is also pragmatic, grass-roots clubhouse politics in its rawest form. Trial by jury is publicity, the news media, and the making and unmaking of reputations. Many a political career has begun or ended in a criminal courtroom.[1]

jury: A panel consisting of a statutorily defined number of citizens selected according to law and sworn to determine matters of fact in a criminal action and to render a verdict of guilty or not guilty.

Who goes to trial? What are the characteristics of defendants who demand and receive the constitutionally stipulated trial by jury? Because the data on which to base answers to these questions have not yet been accumulated, we must respond broadly that trials result when other forms of disposition (dismissal, diversion, plea negotiation) fail or are not sought. Often a dispute over the facts of a case is so irreconcilable that either the prosecutor or defense attorney seeks a trial. The fact-finding function of the jury trial serves to resolve such a dispute. The defendant's prior record may also play a part in the state's decision to go to trial. If the evidence against a repeat offender is weak, the prosecutor may prefer to have a jury find the accused innocent rather than to strike a bargain that would yield only a minimal sanction. The state may lose the trial but still convey to the defendant the message that "we are after you."

The seriousness of the charge is probably the most important factor influencing the decision to go to trial. A trial is rarely demanded by defendants charged with property crimes. Murder, armed robbery, or drug sales, all of which bring long prison terms, are more likely to require judge and jury. When the penalty is harsh, many defendants seem willing to take the risk inherent in a trial.

Since the adversarial process is designed to get to the truth, the rules of criminal law, procedure, and evidence govern the conduct of the trial. Trials are based on the idea that the prosecution and defense will compete before a judge and jury so that the truth will emerge. Above the battle, the judge sees to it that the rules are followed and that the jury impartially evaluates the evidence and reflects the community's interest. The jury is the sole evaluator of the facts in a case.

Among the legal systems of the world, it is only in common law countries such as Great Britain, Canada, Australia, and the United States that a group of laypersons determines guilt or innocence. In civil law countries, this function is usually performed by a judge or judges, often assisted by two or three lay assessors. Eighty percent of all jury trials worldwide take place in the United States.[2]

In the United States, a jury in a criminal trial is traditionally constituted of twelve citizens, but some states now allow as few as six persons. This reform was recommended as a way to modernize court procedures and reduce expenses. It was upheld by the Supreme Court in *Williams v. Florida* (1970) and has been extended nationally, although twelve-person juries still are required in capital cases.[3] In *Burch v. Louisiana* (1979) the Supreme Court ruled that in juries of six a unanimous vote for conviction is required, but with larger juries a majority verdict is enough for conviction[4] (see Figure 12.1). The change to six-person juries has its critics, who charge that the smaller group is less representative of the conflicting views in the community and too quick to bring in a verdict.

Williams v. Florida (1970): Juries of fewer than twelve members are constitutional.

The right to trial by jury is one of the most ingrained features of the American ideology—it is mentioned in the Declaration of Independence, three amendments to the Constitution, and countless opinions of the Supreme Court. Yet only about 8 percent of criminal cases are decided in this manner and fewer than half of all trials are conducted before a jury. Even so, jury trials have a decided impact on decisions made throughout the criminal justice system. We have already indicated that the anticipated reactions of juries play a major

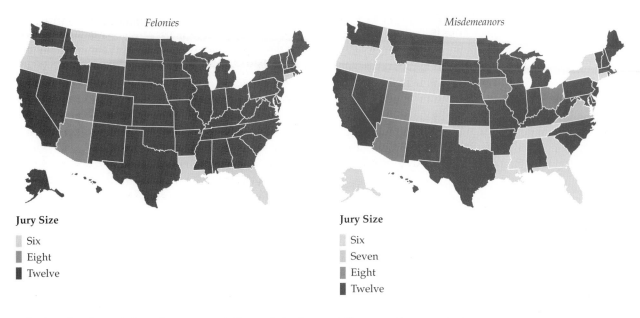

Felonies

Misdemeanors

Jury Size

- Six
- Eight
- Twelve

Jury Size

- Six
- Seven
- Eight
- Twelve

role in plea bargaining, but even at the point of arrest the question that enters the decisional thinking of police officers is 'Would a jury convict?' The decision to prosecute and even the sentencing behavior of judges are influenced by the potential call for a jury.

Juries perform six vital functions in the criminal justice system:

1. prevent government oppression by safeguarding citizens against arbitrary law enforcement
2. determine the guilt or innocence of the accused on the basis of the evidence presented
3. represent diverse community interests so that no one set of values or biases dominates decision making
4. serve as a buffer between the accused and the accuser
5. educate citizens selected for jury duty about the criminal justice system
6. symbolize the rule of law and the community foundation that supports the criminal justice system

Apart from legal stipulations, the choice of trial by jury is left to the accused, and the option becomes a major strategy of the defense. If the accused waives the right to trial by jury (in some states the prosecutor must agree), the case is decided by the judge, who serves as finder of fact and determines issues of law. Such a trial is called a **bench trial.** Nationally about 40 percent of felonies are decided by judges alone. As might be expected the more serious the charge, the greater the likelihood of a case going to trial (see Table 12.1). But note the variation among the cities listed. What reasons might be given for these differences?

The decision to avoid a jury trial by having the case resolved solely by the bench varies considerably according to the offense and to regional customs. A principal consideration is the question Will a jury believe the defendant's story? In addition, attorneys must estimate whether a harsher penalty will be incurred if a guilty verdict is returned by a jury rather than handed down by a judge. A defense lawyer in "Prairie City" said, "No question there is a harsher penalty

FIGURE 12.1

All states require twelve-member juries in capital cases; six states permit less than twelve-member juries in felony cases. Does a fewer number of people on a jury have advantages or disadvantages? Would you rather have your case decided by a twelve- or a six-person jury?

SOURCE: U.S. Department of Justice, Bureau of Justice Statistics, *Report to the Nation on Crime and Justice,* 2nd ed. (Washington, DC: Government Printing Office, 1988), p. 86.

bench trial: Trial conducted by a judge who acts as both a finder of fact and a determiner of issues of law. No jury participates.

TABLE 12.1   Percent of indicted cases going to trial (by offense).   There are differences in both offense and the jurisdiction in the percentage of cases going to trial. It would seem that the stiffer the possible penalty, the greater possibility of a trial. What other factors might be an influence?

Jurisdiction	Homicide	Sexual Assault	Robbery	Larceny	Drug Offenses
Indianapolis	38%	18%	21%	12%	9%
Los Angeles	29	20	12	5	7
Louisville	57	27	18	10	11
New Orleans	22	18	16	7	7
St. Louis	36	23	15	6	6
San Diego	37	2	12	5	3
Washington	43	32	22	12	10
Total	262	140	116	57	53

SOURCE: Adapted from U.S. Department of Justice, Bureau of Justice Statistics, *Report to the Nation on Crime and Justice,* 2nd ed. (Washington, DC: Government Printing Office, 1988), p. 84.

if there is no plea. An unwritten rule of practice here is that if you go to trial and lose, there will be a harsher penalty. Maybe in one case in 500 there will be an exception and the defendant will get the same after the trial as . . . with a plea. Otherwise the penalty is always more."[5]

Trial Process

Although variations are found among the states, the trial process generally follows eight steps: (1) selection of the jury, (2) opening statements by prosecution and defense, (3) presentation of the state's evidence and witnesses, (4) presentation of the defense's evidence and witnesses, (5) presentation of rebuttal witnesses, (6) closing arguments by each side, (7) instruction of the jury by the judge, and (8) decision by the jury. Though the number of trials may be proportionately small, it is essential to understand each step in the process and consider the broader societal impact of this institution.

Twelve Angry Men depicted the tensions that often emerge in a jury room. The 1957 film showed how one juror's belief in the innocence of the defendant could sway the other members.

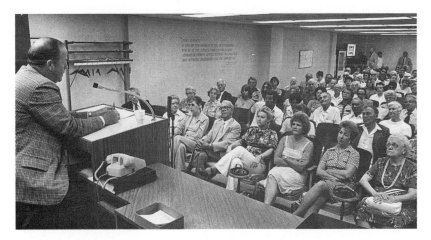

Citizens are called to jury service and enter a pool from which individuals are randomly selected for each case.

Jury Selection

Although history shows that juries were used in Ancient Greece, the use of disinterested citizens to try the facts of a case is relatively new in Anglo-American law. Early English juries were composed of those most knowledgeable and on occasion even those involved in a dispute. Later evolved the idea that juries should be made up of a cross section of the community. But until the mid-twentieth century there were many states in which women and members of minority groups were legally denied membership on juries.

Of a jury's various functions, that of representing diverse community interests seems to lie at the heart of the selection process. A cross section of the community is necessary to ensure that there will be a counterbalancing of biases so as to minimize those who might convict on inadequate evidence. Unfortunately, the reality of jury selection processes often means that a cross section of the community is not included and that class and racial bias influences decision making within the jury room.

Creation of the pool   Theoretically, every citizen of the community should have an equal chance of being chosen for jury duty in accordance with the process shown in Figure 12.2, but various stipulated qualifications have the effect of keeping certain citizens out of the jury pool. In most states, jurors are drawn from the list of registered voters, but research has shown that nonwhites, the poor, and the young register to vote at substantially lower rates than the remainder of the population. In addition, the Bureau of the Census has reported that only about 70 percent of those eligible actually register to vote and that in some areas the rate is as low as 40 percent. Over the past decade, the proportion of registered voters has continued to decrease.

Researchers agree that jury unrepresentativeness can best be attacked by the use of a comprehensive list from which citizens are randomly selected for duty.[6] Supplementary pools of citizens—for instance, licensed drivers, utility customers, taxpayers—would bring new names to the roster. Ideally, a cross section of the community could be found if the jury were randomly and scientifically selected from an up-to-date list of all adult citizens.

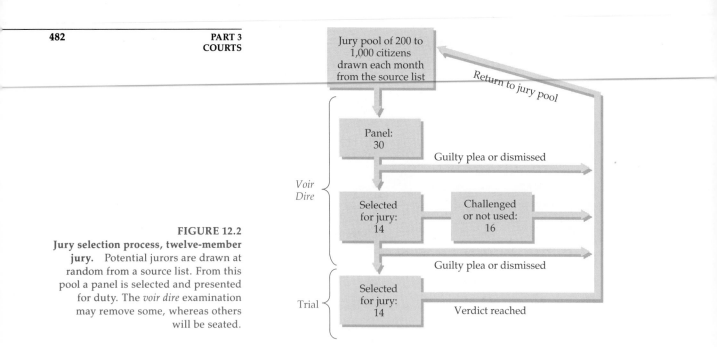

FIGURE 12.2
Jury selection process, twelve-member jury. Potential jurors are drawn at random from a source list. From this pool a panel is selected and presented for duty. The *voir dire* examination may remove some, whereas others will be seated.

Persons in some occupations—doctors, lawyers, teachers, police officers—are not called because their professional services are needed; others are not called because of their connection with the criminal justice system. Some legislatures, particularly in states where jurors are required to serve thirty days, have added other categories because of pressures for exemption. In many localities,

---

A QUESTION OF ETHICS

The return address on the official-looking envelope read "Jury Commissioner, District Court, Plainville, Massachusetts." Having a good idea of the contents, David Rotman tore open the envelope and pulled out a computer-generated form that read:

"*David A. Rotman*, You are hereby summoned to be available for duty as a trial juror and are directed to report to the District Court of the Commonwealth of Massachusetts located at 61 South Street, Plainville, at 9:00 A.M. on July 10. Failure to appear as instructed by law may subject you to a penalty as provided by law. Your Juror Number is: 89367. The term of your jury duty will be one day or one trial."

"Hell! I can't do that, I want to go to Cape Cod that week. There must be some way out of this." Rotman looked at the bottom of the form and read, "You may apply to be excused from this duty if you are: an attorney; caring for a child under three; student or teacher during the school year, . . ." and about five other categories, none of which applied to him.

"This is no big deal. Everyone does it. I'll just tell them I'm going to summer school. They won't check."

Is getting out of jury duty no big deal? What are the implications of David's action? If David is required to serve on a jury, how might justice be affected by the fact that he had planned to spend that week on vacation? What exemptions to service should exist?

citizens may be excused if jury duty would cause economic or physical hardship. One result is that only about 15 percent of adult Americans have ever been called for jury duty. Because of this narrowing of the sources of potential jurors, there is a tendency for retired persons, housewives with grown children, the unemployed—those who would not be inconvenienced by the duty—to be overrepresented on juries.

Voir dire As a protection against bias, prosecution and defense are allowed to challenge the seating of some jurors. This process of *voir dire* ("to speak the truth") examination is designed for the constitutional purpose of ensuring a fair trial. Attorneys for each side and the judge may question each potential juror about background, knowledge of the case, or acquaintance with the persons involved. If it appears that the juror will be unable to be fair, he or she may be **challenged for cause.** The challenge must be ruled on by the judge, and if it is sustained, the juror will be excused from participation in that specific case. There is usually no limit to the number of challenges for cause that both lawyers can make, and in some complex or controversial cases the *voir dire* is extremely time consuming.

The **peremptory challenge** has a more important influence on the composition of the jury. It is used to exclude a person from service, and no reason need be given. An attorney may exercise this prerogative because of a hunch or because someone appears to be unsympathetic. Normally the defense is allowed eight to ten peremptory challenges and the prosecution six to eight.

Instances of "jury stacking" raise questions about *voir dire.* In several highly publicized trials the assistance of social scientists has been sought; often with much success. In fact, one consulting firm has boasted that where their advice has been used, their clients have succeeded in 95 percent of their cases.[7]

Lawyers reason that if they can determine the social and attitudinal characteristics of persons most likely to sympathize with their side, such knowledge can be used to select a sympathetic jury. For example, in the trial of Ford Motor Company executives in being criminally prosecuted for defective gasoline tanks in Pinto automobiles, jury scholar Hans Zeisel was hired by the defense. He advised that Ford's interests would best be served by selecting older men, who would be most likely to remember that Ford had put American industry on the world map.[8]

Whether these methods may become standard practice is still not known. In the past, *voir dire* was attacked as too time consuming. If investigation of potential jurors' backgrounds and exclusion of those whose attitudes are deemed to be not in the interest of one side become widespread, the opportunity for challenge may be limited by future changes in the law. One suggested reform holds that only the judge should examine the jurors for bias; another, that the number of challenges allowed should be sharply reduced.

Any change would not come easily, however, for in addition to removing potential jurors who might be biased, *voir dire* also serves the important purpose of introducing the prosecutor and defense attorney to the panel. As the nationally recognized lawyers F. Lee Bailey and Henry B. Rothblat have said:

voir dire: An examination of prospective jurors by means of which the prosecution and defense screen out persons who might be biased or incapable of rendering a fair verdict.

challenge for cause: Removal of a prospective juror by showing bias or some other legal disability. The number of such challenges permitted is unlimited.

peremptory challenge: Removal of a prospective juror without assignment of any cause. The number of such challenges permitted is limited.

As you interrogate the jurors you meet them personally for the first time. You are given a chance to start selling the defense. Your questions should educate each prospective juror to the legal principles of your defense.[9]

Opening Statements

After the jury has been selected, the trial begins. The clerk reads the complaint (indictment or information), and the prosecutor and the defense attorney may, if they desire, make opening statements to the jury to summarize the position that each side intends to take. The statements are not evidential, and judges normally keep tight control so that no prejudicial or inflammatory remarks are made. Lawyers use this period of trial to establish themselves with the jurors and emphasize points they intend to make later.

Presentation of the Prosecution's Evidence

One of the basic protections of the American criminal justice system is the assumption that the defendant is innocent until proved guilty. The prosecution has the burden of proving beyond a reasonable doubt, within the demands of the court procedures and rules of evidence, that the individual named in the indictment committed the crime. This does not mean that absolute certainty is required, only that the evidence is such that there is no reasonable doubt.

By presenting evidence to the jury, the state must establish a case showing that the defendant is guilty. Evidence is classified as real evidence, testimony, direct evidence, and circumstantial evidence. **Real evidence** might include such objects as a weapon, records, fingerprints, or stolen property. Most evidence in a criminal trial, however, consists of the **testimony** of witnesses. Witnesses at a trial must be legally competent; thus the judge may be required to determine whether the witness whose testimony is challenged has the intelligence to tell the truth and the ability to recall what was seen. **Direct evidence** refers to eyewitness accounts—for example, "I saw John Smith fire the gun." **Circumstantial evidence** requires that the jury infer a fact from what the witness observed. Thus: "I saw John Smith walk behind his house with a gun. A few minutes later I heard a gun go off, and then Mr. Smith walked toward me holding a gun." The witness's observation that Smith had a gun and that he heard a gun go off does not provide the direct evidence that Smith fired his gun; yet the jury may link the described facts and infer that Smith fired his gun. After a witness has given testimony, he or she may be cross-examined by counsel for the other side.

The rules of evidence govern the facts that may be admitted into the case record. Real evidence that has been illegally seized, for example, may be excluded under the Fourth Amendment's protection against unreasonable searches and seizure. Likewise, statements by the defendant given outside the Supreme Court's requirements developed by the *Miranda* decision may also be excluded. Testimony that is hearsay or opinion cannot become a formal part of the trial record. It is the judge who decides, with reference to these rules, what evidence may be heard. In making such decisions, the judge must weigh the importance of the evidence and balance it against the

real evidence: Physical evidence, such as a weapon, records, fingerprints, stolen property.

testimony: Oral evidence provided by a legally competent witness.

direct evidence: Eyewitness accounts.

circumstantial evidence: Evidence provided by a witness from which a jury must infer a fact.

need for a fair trial. Because the purpose of an adversary proceeding is to get the truth, the attorney for each side contests the presentation of evidence with reference to the rules, to the trustworthiness of statements, and to the relevance of the information presented to the points at issue.

Once the prosecution has presented all of the state's evidence against the defendant, the court is informed that the people's case rests. It is common for the defense then to ask the court to direct the jury to bring forth a verdict of not guilty. Such a motion is based on the defense contention that the state has not presented enough evidence to prove its case; it has not established all the elements of the crime charged. The judge rules on this motion, sustaining or overruling it. If the motion is sustained (it rarely is), the trial is ended; if it is overruled, the defense has its chance to present its evidence.

Presentation of the Defense's Evidence

There is no requirement that the defense answer the case presented by the prosecution. Since it is the state's responsibility to prove the case beyond a reasonable doubt, it is theoretically possible—and in fact sometimes happens—that the defense rests its case immediately. Usually the accused's attorney employs one strategy or a combination of three strategies: (1) contrary evidence is introduced to rebut or cast doubt on the state's case, (2) an alibi is offered, or (3) an affirmative defense is presented. If the last strategy is employed, the attorney presents a legal excuse that permits the jury to find the defendant not responsible for the crime. The affirmative defenses include self-defense, insanity, duress, and necessity.

One of the most important questions that the defense must consider is whether the accused will take the stand. The Fifth Amendment protection against self-incrimination means that the defendant does not have to testify. The Supreme Court has ruled that the prosecutor may not comment on, nor can the jury draw inferences from, the defendant's decision not to appear in his or her own defense.[10] The decision is not taken lightly, because if the defendant does testify, the prosecution may cross-examine. Cross-examination is broader than direct examination, and the prosecutor may question the defendant not only about the crime but also about his or her past and often is able to introduce testimony about prior convictions. In addition, many criminal lawyers believe that juries expect to hear both sides of what happened; to deny them this opportunity may prejudice

The jury listens as defending counsel questions a witness during a murder trial in Orange County Superior Court, California. Jurors must play a passive role throughout the trial. It is only when they deliberate over guilt or innocence that they play an active role.

them against the client. Given the suspiciousness of human nature, jurors wonder what the defendant who chooses not to testify is hiding.

Presentation of Rebuttal Witnesses

On completion of the defense's case, the prosecution may present witnesses whose testimony is designed to discredit that of preceding witnesses. Evidence previously introduced by the prosecution may not be rehashed, but new evidence may be presented. If the prosecution brings rebuttal witnesses, the defense has the opportunity to examine them and also to present new witnesses in surrebuttal.

Closing Arguments by Each Side

When each side has completed its presentation of the evidence, prosecution and defense make closing arguments to the jury. The attorneys lay out the facts of the case in a manner that is most favorable to their side. The prosecutor may use the summation to tie together the evidential and legal elements and to try to show that isolated bits of evidence form a cohesive whole that proves the accused to be guilty. The defense, on the other hand, may set forth the applicable law and try to show that the prosecution has not proved its case, that the testimony raised questions instead of providing answers, and that the need to prove beyond a reasonable doubt is very demanding. Each side reminds the jury of its duty not to be swayed by emotion and to evaluate the evidence impartially.

Veteran attorneys feel that the closing argument is a major chance to appeal directly to the members of the jury. Some lawyers use the emotional and spellbinding techniques of experienced actors in making their summations in an attempt to sway the jury. But for many it is also an opportunity to show the defendant, the agent-mediators, or their supervisors that they have really put their full effort into the task.

Judge's Instructions to the Jury

The jury decides the facts of the case, but the judge determines the law. Before the jurors retire to consider the defendant's fate, the judge instructs them about the manner in which the law bears on their

The prosecutor must prove the case against the defendant beyond all reasonable doubt.

decision. The judge may discuss such basic legal principles as proof beyond a reasonable doubt, the legal requirements necessary to show that all the elements have been proved by the prosecution, or the rights of the defendant. More specific aspects of the law bearing on the decision, such as complicated court rulings on the nature of the insanity defense or the manner in which certain types of evidence have been gathered, may be included in the judge's instructions.

The concept of **reasonable doubt** is at the heart of the jury system. The prosecution is not required to prove the guilt of the defendant beyond *all* doubt. Instead, if a juror is

> satisfied to a moral certainty that this defendant . . . is guilty of any one of the crimes charged here, you may safely say that you have been convinced beyond a reasonable doubt. If your mind is wavering, or if you are uncertain . . . you have not been convinced beyond a reasonable doubt and must render a verdict of not guilty.[11]

A vote for acquittal should not be based on sympathy or the reluctance of a jury to perform a disagreeable task.

The experience of listening to the judge may become an ordeal for the jurors, who must assimilate perhaps two or three hours of instruction on the law and the evidence. It is assumed that somehow they will be able to absorb these details so that when they are in the jury room they will be able to draw on their instant expertise. Finally, the judge explains the charges and the possible verdicts. Trials usually involve multiple charges, and the judge must instruct the jurors in such a way that their decisions will be consistent with the law and the evidence.

Decision by the Jury

After they have been instructed, the jurors retire to a room where they have complete privacy. A foreperson to run the meeting is elected from among them, and deliberations begin. Until now, the jurors have been passive observers of the trial, unable to question witnesses; now they can discuss the facts that have been presented. Throughout their deliberations the jurors may be sequestered; if they are allowed to spend nights at home, they are ordered not to discuss the case with anyone. The jury may request that the judge reread to them portions of the instructions, ask for additional instructions, or seek portions of the transcript.

In almost every state and in the federal courts, the verdict must be unanimous. Only Louisiana, Montana, Oregon, Oklahoma, and Texas permit majority decisions in a criminal case whose jury is composed of twelve people. If the jury becomes deadlocked and cannot reach a verdict, the trial ends with a hung jury. When a verdict is reached, the judge, prosecution, and defense reassemble in the courtroom to hear it. The prosecution or the defense may request that the jury be polled: each member tells his or her vote in open court. This procedure presumably ensures that there has been no pressure by other members. If the verdict is guilty, the judge may continue bail or may incarcerate the convicted person to await a presentence report. If the verdict is not guilty, the defendant is freed. Because the Fifth Amendment guarantees that a person shall not be "twice put in jeopardy of life or limb," prosecutors may not appeal a jury's finding or reinstitute the same charges.

reasonable doubt: The standard used by a juror to decide if the prosecution has provided enough evidence for conviction. Jurors should vote for acquittal if they can give a reason to support this position.

Evaluating the Jury System

The 1957 film *Twelve Angry Men* gives an inside view of jury deliberations and the emotions that often rule decision making. Henry Fonda, initially the lone holdout against conviction, gradually turns other members to his side as doubts are raised about the evidence that the prosecution has presented. After hours of deliberation in a hot cramped room, a vote for acquittal is finally achieved.

The question of which factors in a trial lead to the jurors' verdict is always intriguing. Social scientists have been hampered in studying the process of decision making because of the secrecy of actual juries. Simulated juries have been often been used with interesting results. Early research at the University of Chicago Law School found that, consistent with theories of group behavior, participation and influence in the process are related to social status. Men were found to be more active than women, whites more active than minority members, and the better educated more active than those less educated. Much of the discussion in the jury room was not directly concerned with the testimony but rather with trial procedures, opinions about the witnesses, and personal reminiscences.[12] In 30 percent of the cases, a vote taken soon after sequestration was the only one necessary to reach a verdict; in the rest of the cases, the majority on the first ballot eventually won out 90 percent of the time.[13] Because of group pressures, only rarely did a lone juror produce a hung jury. More recent findings have upheld the importance of group pressure on decision making.[14]

In evaluating the jury system, researchers have tried to discover whether juries and judges view cases differently. Harry Kalven and Hans Zeisel attempted to answer this question by examining more than 3,500 criminal trials in which juries played a part. They found that the judge and jury agreed on the outcome in 75.4 percent of the trials but that a jury was more lenient than a judge: the total conviction rate by juries was 64.5 percent; that by judges, 83.3 percent.[15] The very high rate of conviction supports the idea that the filtering process removes doubtful cases before trial. A study by Robert Roper and Victor Flango has challenged the earlier Kalven-Zeisel findings.[16] In examining data from all fifty states, Roper and Flango found that juries convicted felons at a higher rate than did judges and that judges were more conviction-prone in regard to nonfelons.

Kalven and Zeisel's analysis of the factors that caused disagreement between judge and jury revealed that 54 percent of disagreements were attributable to "issues of evidence," about 29 percent to "sentiments on the law," about 11 percent to "sentiments on the defendant," and about 6 percent to other factors. Thus juries clearly do more than merely deal with questions of fact. Much of the disagreement between the judge and jury was favorable to the defendant, an indication that citizens recognize certain values that fall outside the official rules. In weighing the evidence, the jury was strongly impressed by a defendant who had no criminal record and took the stand, especially when the charge was serious. Juries tend to take a more liberal view of such issues as self-defense and are likely to minimize the seriousness of an offense if they are impressed by some attribute of the victim. Presumably because judges have more experience with the process, they are more likely to confer the guilty label on defendants who survive the examination of the police and prosecutor.

CHAPTER 12   **489**
TRIAL AND POSTTRIAL PROCESSES

Jury Duty

The *Juror's Manual* of the U.S. District Court says that jury service is "perhaps the most vital duty next to fighting in the defense of one's country." Every year nearly 2 million Americans respond to the call to perform this civic duty even though doing so usually entails personal and financial hardships. Unfortunately, most jurors experience great frustration with the system as they wait for endless hours in barren courthouse rooms to be called for actual service. Often they are placed on a jury only to have their function preempted by a sudden change of plea to guilty during a portion of the trial. The result is wasted juror time and wasted money. Compensation is usually minimal, and not all employers pay for time lost from the job. What could be an important part of a civic education is often sacrificed to boredom. An unnecessarily negative impression of the entire criminal justice system may be the result.

To deal with some of the more distasteful aspects of jury duty, some courts have introduced the "one-day–one-trial" system. Traditionally, citizens are asked to be jurors for a thirty-day term, and although only a few may be needed for a particular day, the entire pool may be present in the courthouse for the full thirty-day period. In the new system, jurors serve either one day or for the duration of one trial. Prospective jurors who are challenged at *voir dire* or not called to a courtroom are dismissed at the end of their first day and have thus fulfilled their jury duty for the year. Those who are accepted on a jury are required to serve for the duration of that trial, normally about three days. The consensus of jurors, judges, and court administrators is that the one-day–one-trial system is a great improvement.

THE SENTENCING PROCESS

Regardless of how and where the decision has been made—misdemeanor court or felony court, plea bargain or adversarial contest, bench or jury trial—judges have the responsibility for imposing sentence. In the process of fixing the punishment, judges are guided by the penal code, their own evaluation of the offender, and organizational pressures that bear on the criminal justice system. Chapter 13 is devoted to an examination of the goals of the criminal sanction and the forms that punishment may take such as prison, fines, death, probation. Here we need to look at the environment of the courts and the various factors that influence the sentencing behavior of judges. For as the distinguished jurist Irving A. Kaufman has said:

> If the hundreds of American judges who sit on criminal cases were polled as to what was the most trying facet of their jobs, the vast majority would almost certainly answer "sentencing." In no other judicial function is the judge more alone; no other act of his carries greater potentialities for good or evil than the determination of how society will treat its transgressors.[17]

The building looks like it was once a factory, its brick walls showing in places where the facade had peeled away. Its one identifying feature is a plaque that reads Moscow City Court. This is a court of general jurisdiction; it hears appeals from the lower People's Court and is the court of first instance for such serious crimes as murder, treason, counterfeiting, and terrorism.

Inside, in one of the twenty courtrooms, the public benches are jammed, and the steamy air smells of sweat and old wool.... The three-judge panel mounts the raised platform. Sitting in the center is an older woman, her hair in a tight bun, dressed in a severely cut blue suit. On either side are her cojurors, two younger women. All three had been elected by the Moscow City Soviet, not directly by the people, for a five-year term. In the dock is a thickset young man, slouched in his chair, guarded by a soldier.

The charge is intentional murder with aggravating circumstances—a capital offense. A tall, gray-haired woman speaking from the front desk addresses the court: "Comrade Judges! A man's life is at stake, we must be very careful. We face only one real issue in this case: the mental condition of the accused. . . . Two psychiatrists, who examined him directly after the incident, have concluded that he was disturbed, and not responsible for his actions. The court has not called them; I urge it to do so now. Hearing this case without them would only violate the defendant's rights and prevent us from doing justice."

"Your opinion, Comrade Procurator?"

From the table opposite another woman rises. "I remind the court that the accused was carefully examined at the best criminal-psychiatric institutions in Moscow. I see no reason to question the competence of those doctors. I request that the petition be denied."

After a whispered conversation among the three on the dias, the chief judge announces: "The Court has decided to deny the petition. The record shows that the accused was observed for fifty days in the Serbski Institute. Further psychiatric expertise would be superfluous. We will proceed to a reading of the indictment."

It charges that the accused, Chernov, killed his wife on a Sunday evening six months before, soon after the friends they had been entertaining left their apartment. Why? The prosecution cites "hooliganistic" motives, points to a record of minor misbehavior including excessive drinking, truancy, lack of interest, and poor work habits.

"Chernov, stand. Is the charge clear to you?"

"Clear."

"Do you admit your guilt?"

"I-Yes . . . I admit . . . my guilt."

"Tell the court what happened, everything you know about it."

There is a silence in the room as Chernov gazes at the wall. Finally he whispers, "Comrade Judges, I cannot look you in the face. I know that I deserve to be shot. . . ."

"Chernov, you may say all of that at your last word. We are interested now only in what happened."

Chernov recites a long sad tale about a woman, Klavda, he had met last winter while working at Coal Depot Number 4. She worked in the office; he drove a truck. She was recently divorced. They went out together, she moved into his room, and they were married in April. Her children moved in with them. They were happy.

That fatal Sunday began normally. Things were fine at home. Chernov and Klavda drank together as they often did on days off and then invited their friends over. "Then—I don't remember what happened. . . . Nothing remains in my memory about Klavda that night. . . . Oh, I know now what I did to her, but when the police came I couldn't tell them—I didn't know myself. I didn't know anything. . . . It was as if there was a heavy veil over my eyes and mind."

"Is that all? Have you finished?"

"Yes."

"What do you mean, you can't remember? Tell us exactly what you *do* remember. Do you remember drinking vodka?"

"Of course I remember that."

"How much?"

"I don't know exactly. Perhaps a bottle. I didn't keep count."

"You don't remember but it was too much vodka in any case, wasn't it? There were four empty bottles on the table. You were drunk weren't you?"

"I suppose I was high. We started in the afternoon—"

"Chernov, it would be better for you to tell the court everything you can. What really happened when you were alone with your wife? Did you quarrel?"

"I can't say. Honest."

"Do you remember hitting her?"

"I can't remember."

"You can't remember. You choose a convenient moment to forget, don't you? Can you remember anything at all about what passed between you?"

"No. Yes, I think I hit her. I think I remember fragments. It's all vague, like in a haze, like it was someone else and I was watching. I think I slapped her three times. Like in a silent movie. I didn't feel anything when my hand hit her."

. . .

"When the door to your room was opened, the floor was sopping wet. You were scrubbing the blood from the floor. Now, does a man in a haze carry out such logical actions, or did you really know quite well what you were doing?"

"I can't say. I didn't think Klavda was dead. I thought she was sleeping."

This dialogue continues, with the judge asking Chernov about his actions, his attitude, and his past. When the judge has finished there is little for the advocates to pursue. The prosecutor asks about his character and his job record. The defense emphasizes Chernov's support of Klavda's children, his excellent military record, and his unhappy childhood, summarizing with the statement, "The defendant clearly has less than a normal emotional make-up."

After a break for lunch witnesses are called—relatives, the invited friends, the police officers. They appear not for the prosecutor or for the defense but to assist the court in finding the truth. As with the accused, questions are directed by the judge. All agree as to the facts of the case. Again and again the sordid tale is repeated, with each witnesses adding his or her own nuance to the basic story.

Tearfully sitting in the audience is Klavda's mother. Under Soviet law she is the "victim" and thus has the right to participate in the trial, asking questions, challenging the court, and giving her own testimony. In the Soviet Union it is believed that justice should be done not only to the defendant but also to others directly affected by the crime. Klavda's mother seems bewildered. After each witness testifies the judge asks her if she has questions. Each time she mutters "No." The other silent individual is the *obshchestvenni* (community) accuser, a fellow worker. She too answers "No" when asked if she wished to question the witnesses.

Two expert witnesses sit at the prosecutor's table. The first gives a medical report on the cause of death. The second provides a psychiatric report from the Serbski Institute. Chernov was found to be an alcoholic with an unstable personality, but he is not mentally ill. Two questions are then asked by the defense counsel. Was there anything unusual about the defendant's sexual behavior? There had been a satisfactory sexual relationship with Klavda, he sometimes beat her, but she did not protest. But these are not grounds, the experts emphasize, on which to call him mentally ill. What was his exact mental condition at the moment of the crime? This was not possible to determine. He was drunk but he was mentally healthy in the legal sense.

The defense counsel again rises. "Comrade Judges!" . . . "The procedural code permits the naming of additional experts in cases where expert testimony has been insufficiently clear or comprehensive. This is surely such a case. . . . I urgently request, therefore that these doctors be called, or that Chernov be examined again by new doctors to find out why he killed. Again, I want to emphasize that a life is at stake in this case. We can afford no doubts."

After a fifteen-minute recess to consider this request, the judges return and announce that it has been denied. The trial examination phase has now ended. With agreement as to the facts, it is time for closing arguments and a decision as to Chernov's fate.

The first presentation is by the community accuser, who says that "the collective held a general meeting on August 5, discussed Chernov's case thoroughly, and on the basis of these considerations instructed me to ask the court to apply to him the highest measure of punishment for the crime. 'Comrade Judges, we earnestly recommend that he be shot.' "

The prosecutor reminds the judges about the seriousness of the crime. "Our law is the most humane in the world. But we must fight determinedly against murder. And, indeed, this too is humane: it means freeing our society of those who impede the building of a just society, the building of Communism. . . . Our law provides for the death penalty for those who hinder honest Soviet toilers, beloved toilers like Klavda. . . . I agree, therefore, with the *obshchestvenni* accuser and ask the court to prescribe the highest measure of punishment, shooting. We have no room for such people in Soviet society."

The gray-haired counsel for the defense next rises. In an impressive, clearly reasoned talk she challenges the prosecutor's interpretation of the motive and method of killing, hoping to reduce the charge from capital murder. "Chernov and Klavda lived happily together. . . . Yet he killed her, just a few minutes after kissing her. Why? The prosecution never explained why. All its talk of 'hooliganistic' motives explains nothing. We still do not know *why*, and that is why the defense feels that further psychiatric examination is essential. . . . The prosecutor's request for the highest measure of punishment is too cruel. In our law the death sentence is . . . justified only in exceptional cases. . . . Chernov is a young man, he can be cured, reeducated, and returned to society as a useful member. This is the task that awaits us. I would like to believe that *this* is what socialist society means."

Chernov now addresses the court. He swallows, waits, and hangs his head. Few spectators can look at him.

"Comrade Judges, I am terribly sorry. I have done an awful thing. My life with Klavda was good. I miss her more than anyone. I don't know why I did it. I didn't mean to do it."

"Is that all?"

"I deserve to be shot. But I beg the court to spare my life. And nothing more."

Everyone stands as the judges retire. They return two hours later and the sentence is read; the accused stands, flanked by two soldiers. The judge drones on reviewing the case, rejecting mitigating circumstances, and since the crime was committed with cruelty, it remains a capital offense. The court orders that Chernov be shot. He is handcuffed and led from the room.

SOURCE: Drawn from *Justice in Moscow* by G. Feifer, pp. 257–285. Copyright © 1964 by George Feifer. Reprinted by permission of the author.

Assembly-Line Justice: Misdemeanor Courts

The lower courts are of limited jurisdiction because the law restricts the severity of the punishments they can allocate, usually to less than a year in prison. In a sense they are "people's courts." The judges hear the full range of infractions, but most cases involve defendants who have committed minor violations of the law. It is here that about 90 percent of criminal cases are heard either for arraignment and preliminary hearing or through to completion in the form of dismissal or sentence (see Table 12.2).

Because most lower courts are overloaded, the time allotted an individual case is minimal. Acceptance of a guilty plea takes no more than fifteen minutes, and a summary trial following a plea of not guilty typically lasts less than thirty minutes. Judicial decisions are mass produced because actors in the system work on the basis of three assumptions. First, there is a high probability that any person brought before a court is guilty; doubtful cases will be filtered out of the system by the police and prosecution. Second, the vast majority of defendants will plead guilty. Third, those charged with minor offenses will be processed in volume. The citation will be read by the clerk, a guilty plea given, and sentence pronounced by the judge.

Although the lower criminal courts have been criticized because of their assembly-line characteristics, social scientists are now beginning to reassess this view. Susan Silbey has argued, for example, that the informality, availability, and diversity of the lower courts are their most valuable qualities. As she pointed out, the lower courts have a unique capacity to resolve cases effectively because they are placed at the entry point of the system, are dispersed throughout the nation, and are embedded within local communities.[18] These courts are more oriented toward individualized justice that is responsive to the community. The judges appear to be more interested in responding to "problems" than to formally defined "crimes." Thus they seek to use their discretion to impose sentences that will fit the needs

TABLE 12.2 Choice of sanction in four misdemeanor courts. Only a minority of cases adjudicated in four lower courts ends in jail sentences; instead, the preponderance of offenders are sanctioned through fines and probation.

	Austin (Texas) (N = 1,216)	Columbus (Ohio) (N = 1,281)	Mankato (Minnesota) (N = 803)	Tacoma (Washington) (N = 565)
Probation	15.0%	NA	5.6%	3.0%
Jail	6.7	5.1	10.7	4.2
Fine	6.7	57.2	62.7	54.4
Fine and probation	49.0	NA	4.4	4.8
Fine and jail	22.2	29.6	2.0	3.2
Other Combinations	0.4	—	4.8	2.1
None of above	—	8.1[a]	9.8[b]	28.3[c]
	100.0%	100.0%	100.0%	100.0%

[a]Includes fines and jail terms suspended in their entirety; possibly also probation sentences, for which data are unavailable.
[b]Includes fines and jail terms suspended in their entirety, as well as community work and counseling/treatment programs.
[c]Includes court costs imposed in lieu of fines, as well as community work.
SOURCE: Anthony J. Ragona and John Paul Ryan, "Misdemeanor Courts and the Choice of Sanctions: A Comparative View," *Justice System Journal* 8 (Summer 1983): 203.

of the offender and the community rather than sticking strictly to the harshness of the sentences provided by law.

In addition to the formal sanctions prescribed by law, other punishments are imposed on persons who get caught in the criminal justice system, even on those who ultimately are not convicted. If one is arrested and released without having been charged, if the case is dismissed at a preliminary hearing or if it is "nolled" at trial, various tangible and intangible costs are still to be borne. Social scientists have become increasingly aware of these costs; indeed, one book describing sentencing in a misdemeanor court is titled *The Process Is the Punishment.*[19] In a study of felony courts in Baltimore, Chicago, and Detroit, James Eisenstein and Herbert Jacob found that consid-

---

CLOSE-UP   *Quiet, Efficient Justice in a Small City Court*

City Court in this quiet upstate community [Saratoga Springs] sometimes looks very much like Criminal Court in New York City. The public defender meets his clients for the first time in the courtroom. Much of the judicial action takes place briskly before the bench. And the prosecutor is amenable to "down charging" for first offenders. . . .

The process is efficient, the atmosphere is dignified, and case disposition is fairly predictable, with dismissals and adjournments granted on merit. And as Judge Lawrence J. LaBelle puts it, "Our 'don't shows' amount to only one percent."

The differences of scale, of course, are enormous. The one hundred cases that represent a month's work [here] are equal to a single day's calendar for many judges in Criminal Court in Manhattan. Misdemeanors are handled only twice a week, on Mondays and Thursdays.

The contrast between the court here and in New York City is well known to defendants. "They'll say that in the city they wouldn't bother with this," said the public defender, John P. Pastore. . . .

Judge LaBelle, a practicing lawyer, works part time in the $21,000-a-year post of City Court judge, as his father did from 1934 to 1950.

"When I began in 1970," he said, "there was less than an hour and a half's work a day. Today, it's sixty percent of my time. We're bordering on a full-time judgeship."

The judge described courtroom conditions as "horrendous," but they seemed orderly and efficient on a recent day, when the court handled more than two dozen cases.

The day began, as it often does in most courts, with informal discussions in chambers. Judge LaBelle's court assistant . . . went over some of the cases as Frank B. Williams, an assistant district attorney, and the public defender discussed the scheduled trial of a woman charged with welfare fraud. It seemed that the charges might be dropped.

The judge looked up. "Are you telling me it was a bad arrest?" he asked. . . . Although the defendant "had not given notice that her husband had moved back in," [Mr. Williams] said, she had accurately reported the number of family members living with her, making it difficult to prove intentional fraud.

There were roughly thirty people in the courtroom, a few sitting inside the railing after being escorted from the local jail. The rest, in the rows of wooden benches, were other defendants, family members or friends, lawyers and potential jurors.

In the first cases, the defendants were defended by Mr. Pastore. Then Judge LaBelle said, "Now we'll take cases where attorneys are ready." They included traffic violations, petty larceny, disorderly conduct and aggravated harassment—with many offenses, including intoxication.

Judge LaBelle was relatively tough on drunken drivers. One man who pleaded guilty to speeding and failing to keep to the right, but with no drinking charges, was fined $45. The next case, a man who was charged with driving while intoxicated, received a $250 fine, a civil surcharge of $10, and was required to attend a course for drunken drivers.

One by one, the defendants appeared before the bench, the majority pleading guilty to reduced charges, many paying fines ranging from $25 to $50, and none going to jail that day. Cases were put over, defendants were encouraged to settle civil disputes, and, finally, the case of the *People* v. *Debbie Millington*, the woman who had been charged with wrongfully acquiring welfare funds, was "dismissed in the interests of justice," as Judge LaBelle put it.

The potential jurors filed out, the judge returned to his chambers, and Mrs. Millington left, passing a sign behind the bench that reads, "Not All Are Guilty."

SOURCE: Adapted from "In an Upstate City Court, a Feeling of Quiet, Efficient Justice," by J. Feron, *The New York Times*, June 30, 1983, p. B4. Copyright © 1983 by The New York Times Company. Reprinted by permission.

TABLE 12.3   Sanctions imposed on unconvicted defendants in three cities

	Baltimore	Chicago	Detroit
Percentage not released on bail	38.1%	19.2%	33.8%
Percentage of those released on bail who spent a week or more in jail	48.2%	22.9%	n.a.
Percentage with bond set at $5,000 or more	31.6%	19.4%	25.1%
Median number of days from arrest to disposition	42.0	102.0	65.5

SOURCE: Adapted from "Sentences and Other Sanctions in the Criminal Courts of Baltimore, Chicago, and Detroit," by H. Jacob and J. Eisenstein, *Political Science Quarterly*, 90 (Winter 1975–1976): 617–635.

erable penalties had been imposed on unconvicted defendants.[20]

For most people, simply being arrested is a frightening and costly experience. It is impossible to measure the psychic and social price of being stigmatized, separated from family, and deprived of freedom. Even on release, one's associates may have lingering suspicions about one's alleged participation in a criminal act. Many employment applications ask whether the applicant has ever been arrested. Other costs are more easily measured: the amount of time the case took, the sum of money posted to obtain bail, the defense attorney's fee, and lost wages. Some of the costs for unconvicted defendants are shown in Table 12.3.

Although the law decrees that only those the court finds guilty are to be punished under the penal code, many citizens find the process of criminal justice expensive. It might be argued that such costs are part of the price we pay for having an adversarial system under law and that inconvenience or financial drain for a few is unavoidable. Malcolm Feeley believes that the pretrial costs not only have an impact on the unconvicted but also encourage rapid and perfunctory practices in the courtroom and guilty pleas. As he notes, the costs to the individual defendant of the pretrial process may serve to answer a number of puzzling questions: Why do so many waive their right to free appointed counsel? Why do so many people not show up for court at all? Why do people choose the available adversarial options so infrequently?[21] In addition, many defendants do not "take advantage" of diversion, simply increasing their contact with the criminal justice system. All told, defendants seem to have as their principal goal getting out from the control of the police and courts as rapidly as possible—perhaps a rational strategy in view of the exactions of the process. In short, a series of costly informal punishments is inflicted on those arrested, whether they are quickly released, plead guilty, or are found guilty or innocent. Some of these penalties are unavoidable in an adversarial system, but others serve the needs of the principal actors in the system to move cases and to achieve organizational goals.

Felony Court

Felony cases are processed and offenders are sentenced in courts of general jurisdiction. Because of the seriousness of the punishment, the atmosphere is more formal and generally lacks the hurly-burly of

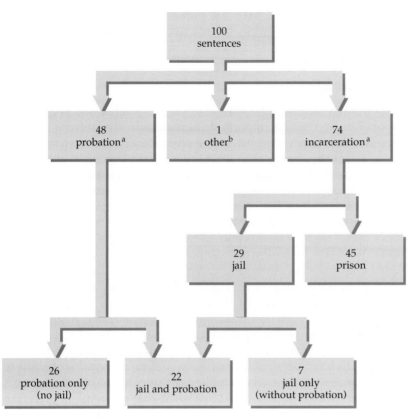

FIGURE 12.3
Types of sentences imposed for one hundred typical cases disposed of in felony court.   Note that although we often equate a felony conviction with a prison sentence, this sentence is imposed in less than half of the cases, when those sent to jail and then given probation are discounted.
[a]Sentences to jail with probation are counted twice, once with incarceration and again with probation. For this reason, the sum of incarceration, probation, and other exceeds 100.
[b]Other includes such sentences as restitution to the victim or a fine.
SOURCE: Mark A. Connif, *Sentencing Outcomes in Twenty-Nine Felony Courts,* U.S. Department of Justice, Bureau of Justice Statistics, (Washington, DC: Government Printing Office, 1987), p. 5.

misdemeanor court. But even here, where judges may send an individual to prison for a long term or even impose the death penalty, administrative pressures bear on judicial decision making.

A study of sentencing practices in twenty-eight felony courts provides data on the type of sanction imposed on one hundred typical offenders. Figure 12.3 graphically portrays the sentencing options used by judges in these felony cases. Table 12.4 relates the conviction offense to the type of sentence imposed. It must be emphasized that these are outcomes in typical felony convictions. In deciding the pun-

TABLE 12.4   Percentage of sentence by type of sentence and conviction offense. The sentence varies greatly depending on the conviction offense. Note that some offenders receive jail and probation.

Conviction Offense	Type of Sentence Imposed					
	Prison	Jail Only	Jail and Probation	Probation Only	Other	Total
Homicide	84%	1%	7%	8%	—	100%
Rape	65	1	17	16	—	100
Robbery	67	7	13	13	—	100
Aggravated assault	42	7	26	24	1	100
Burglary	49	7	20	25	—	100
Larceny	32	10	19	38	1	100
Drug trafficking	27	6	34	32	1	100
Total	45%	7%	22%	26%	1%	100%

—Less than 0.5%

SOURCE: Mark A. Connif, *Sentencing Offenders in Twenty-Nine Felony Courts,* U.S. Department of Justice, Bureau of Justice Statistics (Washington, DC: Government Printing Office, 1987), p. 5.

ishment the judge will have the presentence report, prepared by a probation officer as a guide, but the decision will also be influenced by organizational considerations and community norms.

Presentence Report

presentence report: A report prepared by a probation office after an investigation into the background of a convicted offender, which is designed to help the judge determine an appropriate sentence.

Even though sentencing is the judge's responsibility, the **presentence report** has become an important ingredient in the judicial mix. Although the primary purpose of the presentence report is to help the judge select the appropriate sentence for the offender, it also assists in the classification of probationers, prisoners, and parolees with respect to treatment planning and risk assessment. Usually a probation officer investigates the convicted person's background, criminal record, job status, and mental condition in order to suggest a sentence that is in the interests both of the person and of society. In some areas, however, probation officers present only factual material to the judge and make no sentencing recommendation. The probation officer may weigh hearsay as well as firsthand information.

Given the crucial role of the presentence report and the manner in which the information it contains is collected, one might expect that the offender would have a right to examine it and to challenge the contents. In 1949 the Supreme Court ruled in *Williams* v. *New York* that a convicted person did not have a Sixth Amendment right to cross-examine persons who supplied the information in the report.[22] Since then, however, the Court has ruled that a defendant is denied due process if a sentence is based on information that the defendant is not given the opportunity to deny or explain.[23]

The presentence report is one means by which judges ease the strain of decision making: they can shift responsibility to the probation department. Because a substantial number of sentencing alternatives are open to them, they often rely on the report for guidance. After studying sentencing decisions in California, Robert Carter and Leslie Wilkins found a high correlation (96 percent) between a recommendation for probation in the presentence report and the court's disposition of individual cases.[24] When the probation officer recommended incarceration, there was a slight weakening of this relationship, an indication that the officers were more punitive than the judges.

In most jurisdictions the probation department is part of the judiciary and under the institutional supervision of the judges; hence it is not as independent as one might expect. A close relationship between the probation officers and the members of the court is often justified on the ground that judges will place greater trust in the information provided by staff members under their immediate supervision. Rather than presenting an independent and impartial report, probation officers may be more interested in second-guessing the judge. Yet one should also be concerned that because of the pressure of their duties, judges may rely totally on the presentence recommendations and merely ratify the suggestions of the probation officers without applying their own judicial perspective to the decisions.

The impression of the offender that the presentence report conveys is a very important factor. The probation officer's use of language is crucial. Summary statements may be written in a totally noncommital style or may convey the notion that the defendant is worth saving or is unruly. Judges say that they read the report to get an understanding of the defendant's attitude. A comment such as "the defendant appears unrepentant" can send a person to prison. One

CLOSE-UP *Presentence Report: State of New Mexico*

STATE OF NEW MEXICO

Corrections Department
Field Service Division
Santa Fe, New Mexico 87501

To: The Honorable Manuel Baca   Date: January 4, 1990
From: Presentence Unit, Officer Claire Verduin
Re: Richard Knight

Evaluation

Appearing before Your Honor for sentencing is twenty-year-old Richard Knight, who on November 10, 1989, pursuant to a Plea and Disposition Agreement, entered a plea of guilty to Aggravated Assault upon a Peace Officer (Deadly Weapon) (Firearm Enhancement), as charged in Information Number 89-5736900. The terms of the agreement stipulate that the maximum period of incarceration be limited to one year, that restitution be made on all counts and charges whether dismissed or not, and that all remaining charges in the Indictment and DA Files 39780 be dismissed.

The defendant is an only child, born and raised in Albuquerque. He attended West Mesa High School until the eleventh grade, at which time he dropped out. Richard declared that he felt school was "too difficult" and that he decided that it would be more beneficial for him to obtain steady employment rather than complete his education. The defendant further stated that he felt it was "too late for vocational training" because of the impending one-year prison sentence he faces, due to the Firearm Enhancement penalty for his offense.

The longest period of time the defendant has held a job has been for six months with Frank's Concrete Company. He has been employed with the Madrid Construction Company since August 1989 (verified). Richard lives with his parents, who provide most of his financial support. Conflicts between his mother and himself, the defendant claimed, precipitated his recent lawless actions by causing him to "not care about anything." He stressed the fact that he is now once again "getting along" with his mother.

Although the defendant contends that he doesn't abuse drugs, he later contradicted himself by declaring that he "gets drunk every weekend." He noted that he was inebriated when he committed the present offense.

In regard to the present offense, the defendant recalled that other individuals at the party attempted to stab his friend; he and his companion left and returned with a gun in order to settle the score. Richard claimed remorse for his offense and stated that his past family problems led him to spend most of his time on the streets, where he became more prone to violent conduct. The defendant admitted being a member of the 18th Street Gang.

Recommendation

It is respectfully recommended that the defendant be sentenced to three years incarceration, on Information Number 89-5736900, and that the sentence be suspended. It is further recommended that the defendant be incarcerated for one year as to the mandatory Firearm Enhancement and then placed on three years probation under the following special conditions:

1. That restitution be made to Juan Lopez in the amount of $622.40.
2. That the defendant either maintain full-time employment or obtain his GED, and
3. That the defendant discontinue fraternizing with the 18th Street Gang members and terminate his own membership in the gang.

seventeen-year-old Connecticut offender was sent to a reformatory in large measure because he was reported to be unrepentant and unconcerned with what he had done. His father protested that the probation officer who drafted the report had talked to the boy twice for no longer than two minutes each time and could not have formed a reasonable impression of the boy's attitude. This protest had no effect on the judge.[25]

Sentencing Behavior of Judges

That judges exhibit different sentencing tendencies is taken as a fact of life by criminal lawyers and the court community. As early as 1933 one report noted that "some recidivists know the sentencing tendencies of judges so well that the accused will frequently attempt to choose which is to sentence them, and . . . are frequently able to do this."[26]

The sentence differences among judges can be ascribed to a number of factors: the conflicting goals of criminal justice, the fact that judges are products of different backgrounds and have different social values, the administrative pressures on the judge, and the influence of community values on the system. Each of these factors to some extent structures the judge's exercise of discretion in sentencing offenders. In addition, a judge's perception of these factors is dependent on his or her own attitudes toward the law, toward a particular crime, or toward a type of offender.

Evaluating Convictions and Sentences

Our initial impression may be that minorities and poor people receive the longest prison terms and are placed on probation the fewest times. Although some investigations sustain these assumptions, the evidence is not totally conclusive. The prison populations of most states are more heavily made up of African-Americans and Hispanics than the general population. Is this situation a result of the prejudicial attitudes of judges, police officers, and prosecutors? Are poor people more liable to commit violations that elicit a strong response from society? Are enforcement resources distributed so that certain groups are subject to closer scrutiny than other groups? Unfortunately, the research evidence on these and similar questions is inconclusive. Although some studies have shown that members of racial minorities and the poor are treated more harshly by the system, other research has been unable to demonstrate a direct link between harshness of sentence and race or social class. The jury seems to still be "out" on these questions.

One study of sentencing in Texas found that African-Americans received longer prison terms than whites for most offenses but shorter terms than whites for others. Blacks received longer sentences when they were convicted of burglary (largely an interracial offense) but shorter sentences when they were convicted of murder (a predominantly intraracial offense). Intraracial rape, too, elicits short sentences when blacks are the offenders. Thus racial attitudes concerning property and morals show the important role played by local and regional values. As the author concluded: "Those who enforce the law conform to the norms of the local society concerning racial prejudice, thus denying equality before the law."[27]

Analysis of a sample of 2,366 sentencing files for blacks and whites drawn from 50,000 felony convictions in "Metro City" also indicated discrimination on the basis of race. When Cassia Spohn, John Gruhl, and Susan Welch took into account prior record, charge, legal representation, and severity of sentence, they found that black men received harsher sentences than white men but that this disparity could be accounted for primarily by the fact that blacks were charged with more serious offenses and had more serious prior criminal records. They also found that defendants who had private attorneys or had been released pending trial received less severe sentences. Because of the racial link to social class, these factors were an indirect form of racial discrimination. But even after both legal and extralegal factors were taken into account, the researchers found that the incarceration rate for black men was 20 percent higher than that for white men. Whites were more likely to receive long periods of probation; blacks were more likely to receive short prison terms.[28]

A most serious dilemma for the criminal justice system concerns those who are falsely convicted and sentenced. Although much public concern is expressed over those who "beat the system" and go free, comparatively little attention is paid to those who are innocent, yet convicted. Each year several such cases of persons convicted but innocent come to national attention. For example, the case of Randall Dale Adams, whose story was portrayed in the film *The Thin Blue Line,* had his murder conviction overturned in 1989 after spending twelve years on death row. Likewise, James Richardson was freed after twenty-one years in Florida prisons for the poisoning deaths of seven children. How prevalent are miscarriages of justice such as these? C. Ronald Huff and Arye Rattner estimate that about 1 percent of felony convictions are in error.[29] They cite eyewitness error, unethical conduct by police and prosecutors, community pressure, false accusations, inadequacy of counsel, and plea bargaining pressures as contributing to wrongful convictions. Not only does it hurt society that an innocent person has been wrongfully convicted, but also it must be emphasized that the real criminal is presumably still at large.

APPEALS

Imposition of a sentence does not mean that it must be served immediately; the defendant has the right to appeal the verdict to a higher court. An **appeal** is based on a contention that one or more errors of law were made during the criminal justice process. A defendant might base an appeal, for example, on the contention that evidence was improperly admitted, that the judge did not charge the jury correctly, or that a guilty plea was not made voluntarily. Note that appeals are based on questions of procedure, not on the defendant's guilt or innocence. It is for the government to prove, in the ways required by the law, that the individual is guilty. If mistakes

appeal: A request to a higher court that it review actions taken in a completed trial.

were made by the prosecution or judge, a conviction may be reversed. The conviction is then set aside, and the defendant may be retried. Many states provide for an automatic appeal in capital cases.

Basis for Appeals

Unlike most other Western countries, the United States does not allow the terms of the sentence to be appealed in most circumstances. An appeal may be filed when it is contended that the judge selected penalties that did not accord with the law or that there were violations of either due process or equal protection. But if the law gives the judge the discretion to impose a sentence of, for example, ten years in a particular case and the defendant thinks that his or her actions warranted only eight, it would be quite unusual for the sentence to be overturned on appeal unless some procedural defect could be shown. It would be necessary to show that the decision was illegal, unreasonable, or unconstitutional.

A case originating in a state court is usually appealed through that state's judicial system. If a state case involves a constitutional question, however, it may be appealed to the U.S. Supreme Court. Almost four-fifths of all appeals are decided by state courts.

There has been an increase in the number of appeals in both the state and federal courts during the past decade. What is the nature of these cases? A recent five-state study by Joy Chapper and Roger Hanson showed that: (l) although a majority of appeals occur after trial convictions, about a quarter result from nontrial proceedings such as guilty pleas and probation revocations; (2) homicides and other serious crimes against persons make up over 50 percent of appeals; (3) most appeals come from cases in which the sentence is five years or less; and (4) the issues raised at appeal tend to concern the introduction of evidence, the sufficiency of evidence, and jury instructions.[30]

It is commonly believed that since appeals are free, there is little incentive not to ask a higher court to review a conviction. The public seems to believe that many offenders are being "let off" through the appellate process. With this perspective it might be expected that most appeals are successful. In fact, Chapper and Hanson found that in almost 80 percent of the cases they examined the decision of the trial court was affirmed. Table 12.5 shows the percentage distribution

TABLE 12.5 Percentage distribution of alternative outcomes in five state appellate courts. Although the public seems to believe that persons exercising their right of appeal will "get off," this study shows that although 20 percent have their convictions reversed, only a few defendants are acquitted by the appellate court.

Appeal Outcome	Percentage of Appeals	Percentage Nonaffirmance
Affirmed	79.4	—
Reversed	20.6	100.0
Acquittal	1.9	9.4
New trial	6.6	31.9
Resentencing	7.3	35.3
Other	4.8	23.4

SOURCE: From *Understanding Reversible Error in Criminal Appeals,* by J. Chapper and R. Hanson, p. 16. Copyright © 1989 by National Center for State Courts. Reprinted by permission.

of the outcomes from the appellate process. The right of appeal performs an important function not only of righting wrongs but its presence is a constant influence on the daily operations of the criminal justice system.

Habeas Corpus

Known as "the great writ," **habeas corpus** is a command by a court to a person holding a prisoner in custody requiring that the prisoner be brought before a judge. This procedure permits a judge to decide whether the person is being legally held. Article III of the U.S. Constitution has been interpreted to extend the application of *habeas corpus* to federal prisoners, and over time the use of the writ led to a kind of appellate review of the conviction. The right was extended by Congress in 1867 to state prisoners, allowing review of their convictions in federal court after state remedies had been exhausted.

Although very few *habeas corpus* petitions are successful in federal court (about 3 percent), the number filed has increased by almost 700 percent since the 1870s. This increase has caused concern among federal judges, who find their criminal caseloads greatly expanded. Various tactics, such as allowing magistrates to review petitions and eliminate those that are frivolous, have been used to deal with this problem.

habeas corpus: A writ or judicial order requesting that a person holding another person produce the prisoner and give reasons to justify continued confinement.

Evaluating the Appellate Process

Frustrated by the problems of crime, some conservatives have argued that opportunities for appeal should be limited. It is said that too many offenders delay imposition of their sentences and that others completely evade the sanctions by filing appeals endlessly. This practice not only increases the work load of the courts but puts the concept of the finality of the justice process at risk. It is thought that punishment should be swift and certain. But critics fail to note that since 90 percent of accused persons plead guilty, the number of cases that might be appealed is greatly diminished.

A successful appeal for the defendant, one that results in reversal of the conviction, normally means that the case is remanded to the lower court for a new trial. At this point the state must consider whether the procedural errors in the original trial can be overcome and whether it is worth additional expenditure to bring the defendant into court again.

SUMMARY

The public's assumptions about the criminal justice system are greatly influenced by newspapers and television. Most people are exposed to only the most noteworthy cases—the criminal trials that become public dramas. Chapter 12 has explained the process of the trial from jury selection to decision. The sentencing process, introduced here, will be explored further in Chapter 13. Throughout, this book has argued that the sanction imposed by the court—"the time to be served"—is a factor that heavily influences the actions of many portions of the system. The judge's crucial decision concerning whether the offender will receive probation or prison is evaluated by the prosecutor, the defense attorney, and the defendant. The final portion of this chapter introduced the appellate process. Offenders may appeal their convictions on legal grounds, but in most jurisdictions in the United States it is not possible to appeal the sentence. This, then, is the final chapter in the section on adjudication. Part 4 focuses on postconviction strategies.

FOR DISCUSSION

1. Since there are so few jury trials, what types of cases would you expect to find adjudicated in this manner? Why?
2. If most cases are decided through a guilty plea or a bench trial, what is the purpose of appellate courts? Who is likely to use them?
3. How might your counsel's knowledge of the judge's sentencing behavior influence decisions in your case?
4. Should probation officers be required to make a presentence investigation and report in plea bargained cases?

FOR FURTHER READING

Harris, Jean. *Stranger in Two Worlds.* New York: Macmillan, 1986. The autobiography of Jean Harris, whose trial and murder conviction occupied public attention. This book tells of her experience through the trial and while incarcerated.

Hastie, Reid, Steven Penrod, and Nancy Pennington. *Inside the Jury.* Cambridge, MA: Harvard University Press, 1983. A study of the jury process and the elements of decision making.

Kalven, Harry, Jr., and Hans Zeisel. *The American Jury.* Boston: Little, Brown, 1966. The classic study of American juries by two well-known social scientists and legal scholars.

Phillips, Steven. *No Heroes, No Villains.* New York: Random House, 1977. An exciting story of the frustrations of a murder trial.

Wishman, Seymour. *Anatomy of a Jury.* New York: Times Books, 1986. An account of inside the jury room.

NOTES

1. Steven Phillips, *No Heroes, No Villains* (New York: Random House, 1977), p. 109.
2. Valerie P. Hans and Neil Vidmar, *Judging the Jury* (New York: Plenum, 1986), p. 109.
3. *Williams* v. *Florida,* 399 U.S. 78 (1970).
4. *Burch* v. *Louisiana,* 441 U.S. 130 (1979).
5. David Neubauer, *Criminal Justice in Middle America* (Morristown, NJ: General Learning Press, 1974), p. 229.
6. David Kairys, Joseph B. Kadane, and John P. Lehoczky, "Jury Representativeness: A Mandate for Multiple Source Lists," *California Law Review* 65 (1977):776.

7. Hans and Vidmar, *Judging the Jury*, p. 90.

8. Paula D. Perna, *Juries on Trial* (New York: Dembner Books, 1984), p. 137.

9. F. Lee Bailey and Henry B. Rothblat, *Successful Techniques for Criminal Trials* (New York: Lawyers Cooperative, 1971), p. 83.

10. *Griffin v. California*, 380 U.S. 609 (1965).

11. Phillips, *No Heroes, No Villains*, p. 214.

12. Fred Strodtbeck, Rita James, and Gordon Hawkins, "Social Status in Jury Deliberations," *American Sociological Review* 22 (1957):713–719.

13. David W. Broeder, "The University of Chicago Jury Project," *Nebraska Law Review* 38 (1959):774.

14. Hastie Reid, Steven Penrod, and Nancy Pennington, *Inside the Jury* (Cambridge, MA: Harvard University Press, 1983), p. 199.

15. Harry Kalven, Jr., and Hans Zeisel, *The American Jury* (Boston: Little, Brown, 1966), p. 62.

16. Robert Roper and Victor Flango, "Trials before Judges and Juries," *Justice System Journal* 8 (Spring 1983):186.

17. As quoted in Ronald L. Goldfarb and Linda R. Singer, *After Conviction* (New York: Simon & Schuster, 1973), p. 138.

18. Susan S. Silbey, "Making Sense of the Lower Courts," *Justice System Journal* 6 (Spring 1981):20.

19. Malcolm Feeley, *The Process Is the Punishment* (New York: Russell Sage Foundation, 1979).

20. James Eisenstein and Herbert Jacob, *Felony Justice* (Boston: Little, Brown, 1977).

21. Feeley, *Process Is the Punishment*, p. 200.

22. *Williams v. New York*, 337 U.S. 241 (1949).

23. *Gardner v. Florida*, 430 U.S. 349 (1977).

24. Robert M. Carter and Leslie T. Wilkins, "Some Factors in Sentencing Policy," *Journal of Criminal Law, Criminology, and Police Science* 58 (1967):503.

25. Rosemary B. Zion, *Sentencing Practices in the Supreme Courts of Connecticut*, study prepared for the Judicial Department, State of Connecticut, 1972, p. 51.

26. Frederick J. Gaudet, G. S. Harris, and C. W. St. John, "Individual Differences in Sentencing Tendencies of Judges," *Journal of Criminal Law and Criminology* 23 (1933):814.

27. Henry A. Bullock, "Significance of the Racial Factor in the Length of Prison Sentences," *Journal of Criminal Law, Criminology, and Police Science* 52 (1961):411.

28. Cassia Spohn, John Gruhl, and Susan Welch, "The Effect of Race on Sentencing: A Reexamination of an Unsettled Question," *Law and Society Review* 16 (1981–82):85.

29. C. Ronald Huff and Arye Rattner, "Convicted but Innocent: False Positives and the Criminal Justice Process," in *Controversial Issues in Crime and Justice*, ed. Joseph E. Scott and Travis Hirschi (Newbury Park, CA: Sage, 1988), p. 130.

30. Joy A. Chapper and Roger A. Hanson, *Understanding Reversible Error in Criminal Appeals* (Williamsburg, VA: National Center for State Courts, 1989), p. 4.

4

P   A   R   T

CORRECTIONS

Part 4 looks at the various ways in which the American system of criminal justice deals with offenders. The processes of sentencing and corrections are intended to penalize the individual found guilty and also to impress upon others that those who transgress the law will be punished. Historically, there has been no agreement about the best measures to use against lawbreakers. Unfortunately, over the course of time the corrections system has risen to peaks of excited reform, only to drop to valleys of despairing failure. Chapters 13 through 16 will discuss how offenders are treated and how various influences have structured our correctional system. As these chapters unfold, recall the processes that have occurred before the imposition of sentence, especially as they determine the goals of the correctional portion of the criminal justice system.

13

Sentencing

Key Terms and Cases

community service
determinate sentence
fine
forfeiture
general deterrence
house arrest

incapacitation
indeterminate sentence
intensive probation supervision
intermediate sanctions
mandatory sentence
probation

rehabilitation
restitution
retribution
selective incapacitation
sentence disparity
sentencing guidelines

shock probation
special deterrence
Furman v. *Georgia* (1972)
Gregg v. *Georgia* (1976)
McCleskey v. *Kemp* (1987)

You sit on the bench . . . and you get this terrible sense that you can't help anyone who could be helped. Sometimes you look at a young man or woman and you feel that if someone could really get hold of them maybe something good could come of their lives.

Judge Joel L. Tyler, Manhattan Night Court,
City of New York

"All rise!" The courtroom audience stands as Judge Frank A. Bianco, robed in black, strides from his office and mounts the dais. Although the noise level subsides during the entrance of the judge, it immediately returns to a constant hum as offenders, their families, attorneys, and friends await the beginning of proceedings. Today there is a current of tension, unlike the easy give-and-take apparent on other days. Everyone knows that during the next hour Judge Bianco will be imposing sentences on the felony offenders whose presentence reports he has studied during the previous week.

As each case is called, the offender steps forward. After statements by the prosecution and defense regarding an appropriate punishment, Judge Bianco asks the offender if he or she has anything to add. Most hang their heads and mumble, "No, Your Honor." The judge then stipulates the conditions of the sentence. Some offenders receive probation, others are given terms of incarceration, still others are required to perform some kind of community service or to enter a drug treatment program, a few are fined. As each sentence is read, the offender is led to a van for transfer to jail or prison, approached by a probation officer and told when and where to report, or directed to the clerk's office to pay a fine. Newly sentenced, each offender has now entered the world of corrections.

The criminal justice system aims to solve the three basic problems in the law: What conduct should be designated as criminal? What determinations must be made before a person can be found to have committed a criminal offense? What should be done with persons who are found to have committed criminal offenses? Earlier chapters have emphasized the first two problems, but, as we have seen, the assumptions a society makes about any of the three problems greatly affect its interpretation of the others. The answers given by the legal system to the first question constitute the basic norms of the society: do not murder, rob, sell drugs, commit treason. The process of determining guilt or innocence is stipulated by the law and is greatly influenced by the administrative and interpersonal considerations of criminal justice actors. The remainder of this book will focus primarily on the third problem: the sanctions or punishments specified by the law.

Sentencing, or the specification of the sanction, can be viewed as both the beginning and the end of the criminal justice system. When guilt has been established, a decision must be made concerning what to do with the convicted person. Public interest seems to wane at this point; usually the convicted criminal is out of sight and thus out of mind as far as society is concerned. But for the offender, the passing of sentence is the beginning of corrections, with its restriction of freedom and its promise of rehabilitation.

For the regular participants and observers of the criminal justice system, the terms of the sanction will to some degree determine their future behavior. As we have seen, a great part of the efforts of the defendant, prosecutor, and defense attorney during the presentencing phase is based on assumptions concerning the sanction that may follow conviction. Although police officers are generally removed from the courtroom at the time of sentencing, they, too, will be influenced by the judge's decision. Law enforcement officials may wonder whether arresting certain types of violators is worthwhile if their effort is not reflected in the sentences imposed. For the general population, punishment is expected to perform a deterrent function that reinforces societal values by serving as a warning of the consequences of wrongdoing.

PURPOSE OF THE CRIMINAL SANCTION

Throughout the history of Western civilization, punishment for violations of the criminal law has been shaped by philosophical and moral orientations. Although the ultimate purpose of the criminal sanction is assumed to be the maintenance of social order, different justifications have emerged in different eras to legitimize the punishment imposed by the state. The ancient custom of severing a limb of a thief who stole was once justified as an act of retribution; in later periods, similar penalties were exacted—capital punishment, for example—on the grounds of incapacitation or deterrence. Over time, Western countries have moved away from the imposition of physical pain as a form of retribution and toward greater reliance on restrictions of freedom and the use of social and psychological efforts to change behavior.

In the United States today the term *punishment* often has an ideological connotation that links it to retribution and not to the other justifications for the criminal sanction. It is difficult for some people to reconcile the goal of rehabilitation with punishment. Are individuals being punished if they are in a correctional facility that emphasizes therapy? Is probation a punishment?

Herbert Packer argues that punishment can be described as any way of dealing with people that is marked by these elements:

1. the presence of an offense
2. the infliction of pain on account of the commission of the offense
3. a dominant purpose that is neither to compensate someone injured by the offense nor to better the offender's condition but to prevent further offenses or to inflict what is thought to be deserved pain on the offender.[1]

Note that Packer emphasizes two major goals of criminal punishment: the deserved infliction of suffering on evildoers and the prevention of crime.

In the twentieth century four goals of the criminal sanction are acknowledged in the United States: retribution (deserved punishment), deterrence, incapacitation, and rehabilitation. Although no

one goal is the sole reason for a particular sentence, from the 1940s
until the 1970s most legislatures stipulated that rehabilitation was to
be given priority. That judges often acknowledged the importance of
other goals, and legislatures failed to appropriate money to implement the rehabilitative goal did not strike many people as odd.

RETRIBUTION

retribution: Punishment inflicted
on a person who has infringed on the
rights of others and so deserves to be
penalized. The severity of the sanction
should fit the seriousness of the crime.

"An eye for an eye, a tooth for a tooth" has been a purpose of the
criminal sanction since biblical times. Although the ancient saying
may sound barbaric, it can be thought of as a definition of **retribution:**
those who do a wrong should be punished alike, in proportion to the
gravity of the offense or to the extent to which others have been made
to suffer. Retribution is punishment that is deserved.

Some people claim that the desire for retribution is a basic human
emotion. If the state does not provide criminal sanctions so that the
community may express its revulsion at offensive acts, citizens will
take the law into their own hands. Retribution is thus an expression
of the community's disapproval of crime. This view argues that if
retribution is not exacted, the disapproval may also disappear. A
community that is too ready to forgive a wrongdoer may end up
approving the crime.

One of the developments in criminal justice in recent years has
been the resurgence of interest in retribution as a justification for the
criminal sanction. Using the concept of "just deserts," some theorists
have advanced the idea that one who infringes on the rights of others
does wrong and deserves blame for that conduct.[2] Andrew von
Hirsch, a leading contemporary writer on punishment, has said that
in such instances "the sanctioning authority is entitled to choose a
response that expresses moral disapproval: namely, punishment."[3]
The argument is made by von Hirsch and others that punishment
should be applied only for the wrong inflicted and not primarily to
achieve utilitarian benefits (deterrence, incapacitation, rehabilitation). Offenders should be penalized for their wrongful acts because
fairness and justice dictate that they deserve punishment.

DETERRENCE

general deterrence: Punishment
of criminals intended to serve
as an example to the general
public and thus to discourage the
commission of offenses.

The eighteenth- and nineteenth-century reformers called utilitarians,
followers of Jeremy Bentham, were struck by what seemed to be the
pointlessness of retribution. Holding that human behavior was governed by the individual calculation of the excess of pleasure over pain
to be derived from an act, the Benthamites argued that punishment
by itself is unjustifiable unless it can be shown that more "good"
results if it is inflicted than if it is withheld. The presumed good was
the prevention of the greater evil, crime. The basic objective of punishment, they said, was to deter potential criminals by the example
of the sanctions laid on the guilty.

Modern ideas of deterrence have incorporated two subsidiary
concepts: **general deterrence,** which is probably most directly linked

to Bentham's ideas, and **special deterrence.** General deterrence is the idea that the general population will be dissuaded from criminal behavior by observing that punishment will necessarily follow commission of a crime and that the pain will be greater than the benefits that may stem from the illegal act. The punishment must be severe enough so that all will be impressed by the consequences. For general deterrence to be effective, the public must be informed of the equation and continually reminded of it by the punishments of the convicted. Public hanging was once considered to be important for its effect as a general deterrent.

Special deterrence (often called specific or individual deterrence) is concerned with changes in the behavior of the convicted. It is individualized in that the amount and kind of punishment are calculated to deter the criminal from repeating the offense. What does the criminal need? becomes the most important question here.

There are some obvious difficulties with the concept of deterrence. In many cases, for example, the goals of general and special deterrence are incompatible. The level of punishment necessary to impress the populace may be inconsistent with the needs of an individual offender. The public disgrace and disbarment of an attorney, for example, may be effective in preventing him from committing criminal acts, but the sanction may seem inconsequential to many persons who cannot believe he has been sufficiently punished.

A more important problem with the goal of deterrence is obtaining proof of its effectiveness. General deterrence suffers because social science is unable to measure its effects; only those who are *not* deterred come to the attention of criminal justice researchers. Thus a study of the deterrent effects of punishment would have to examine the impact of different forms of the criminal sanction on various potential lawbreakers. An additional factor to be considered is how the criminal justice system influences the effect of deterrence through

BIOGRAPHY

Jeremy Bentham

Born in London, Jeremy Bentham was the foremost writer on jurisprudence and criminology of his time. He earned a master's degree in law at Oxford and was admitted to the bar in 1767 but spent little time in the practice of law. Instead, he soon became well known for pursuit of his three major interests: politics, jurisprudence, and criminology.

Wishing to depart from the social control jurisprudence of his day, Bentham substituted a new theory termed *utilitarianism.* He believed that human beings are essentially hedonistic calculators of the relative values of pleasure and pain and that all laws should therefore be guided by a principle of rational utility. Law is a balance between what society demands and what humanity needs. When applied to punishment, the principle of utility demands that a relationship be established between the value of committing a crime and the punishment to be expected for it. A person who chose a course of crime rationally would be deterred by the likelihood of a quick, certain, and commensurate penalty.

Bentham applied utilitarian principles to prison management and discipline as well. His *Principles of the Penal Code* contains the basis for many reforms in the treatment of prisoners, including reform of their morals, preservation of their health, and the provision of education so that society would be relieved of their burden. His planned "panopticon" prison was of circular design to reduce the number of guards required (they were to be able to keep all prisoners in view from the center of the circle) and was to be operated by a manager who would employ the convicts in contract labor. The prison in Stateville, Illinois, built between 1916 and 1924, was modeled on Bentham's design.

the speed, certainty, and severity of the allocated punishment. While deterrence is believed to play a prominent role as a purpose of the criminal sanction, the exact nature of that role and the extent to which sentencing policies may be altered to meet the purpose rest on an unfirm scientific foundation.

Incapacitation

"Lock them up and throw away the key!" Such sentiments are heard often from citizens outraged by some illegal act. The assumption of **incapacitation** is that a crime may be prevented if criminals are physically restrained. In primitive societies, banishment from the community was the usual measure taken to prevent a recurrence of forbidden behavior. In early America, agreement by the offender to move away or to join the army was often presented as an alternative to some other form of punishment. Prison is the typical mode of incapacitation, since offenders can be kept under control so that they cannot violate the rules of society. Capital punishment is the ultimate method of incapacitation.

Any policy that incarcerates or in some way physically restricts the offender has some incapacitative effect, even when retribution, deterrence, or rehabilitation is the espoused goal. But the incapacitative sanction is different from these other goals in that it is future oriented (unlike retribution); is based on personal characteristics of the offender, not on characteristics of the crime (unlike general deterrence); and is not intended to reform the criminal. Incapacitation is thus imposed because a person of a certain type of personality has committed a particular type of crime and is believed to be likely to repeat the offense. It is important to note that we are really dealing with a policy of selective incapacitation, not general incapacitation, which would require the incarceration of all offenders.

One of the problems of this concept is that of undue severity. If the object is prevention, imprisonment may be justified for both a trivial and a serious offense. More important is the question of the length of incarceration. Presumably, offenders are not released until the state is reasonably sure that they will no longer commit crimes. Not only is such a prediction difficult to make, but the answer may be that such offenders can never be released.[4]

The extreme of the incapacitative position may seem foolish, but many states do have habitual offender laws that seem to be based on this assumption. Under such statutes, people who have committed two or more serious offenses at different times can be sentenced to extended imprisonment, even for life, on the grounds that they have not learned from their past mistakes and so society must be protected from them.

In recent years greater attention has been paid to the concept of **selective incapacitation.** Research has suggested that a relatively small number of offenders are responsible for a large number of violent and property crimes. Burglars, for example, tend to commit many offenses before they are caught, so it is argued that they should receive long terms in prison. Under the assumption that offenders com-

incapacitation: Deprivation of capacity to commit crimes against society, usually by detention in prison.

selective incapacitation: The strategy of making optimum use of expensive and limited prison space by targeting for incarceration those individuals whose incapacity will do the most to reduce crime.

mit only one type of crime, it has been estimated that an individual commits between 2 and 3.5 robbery offenses per year, 6 or 7 burglaries, or 3 to 3.5 auto thefts. Sentencing policies, it is asserted, should be so directed that such career criminals will be locked up for long periods of time.[5] The costs of such a policy, however, are worth considering: correctional facilities would have to be expanded; it would be more difficult to obtain convictions if the accused were aware that a long prison term would result; and policing activities would have to be upgraded to catch and convict these serious offenders.

Rehabilitation

Rehabilitation is undoubtedly the most appealing modern justification for use of the criminal sanction. That the offender should be treated and resocialized while under the care of the state is not an entirely new idea and is even found in some of Bentham's writings. What is new is the belief that techniques are available to identify and treat the causes of the offender's behavior. If the criminal behavior is assumed to result from some social, psychological, or biological imperfection, the treatment of the disorder becomes the primary goal of corrections. Because rehabilitation is oriented solely toward the offender, no relationship can be maintained between the severity of the punishment and the gravity of the crime.

According to the concept of rehabilitation, offenders are not being punished; they are being treated and will return to society when they are well. The assumption that offenders are in need of treatment, not punishment, requires that they remain in custody only until they are "cured." Consequently, the judge should set not a fixed sentence but rather one with maximum and minimum terms so that correctional officials, through the parole board, may release inmates when they have been rehabilitated. The indeterminate sentence is also justified by the belief that if prisoners know when they are going to be released, they will not make an effort to engage in the treatment programs prescribed for their cure.

Until the 1970s the rehabilitative ideal was so widely shared that it was almost assumed that matters of treatment and reform of the offender were the only questions worthy of serious attention in the whole field of criminal justice and corrections. Since then, however, the model has come under closer scrutiny and in some quarters has been discredited. Indeed, some social scientists have wondered whether the causes of crime can be diagnosed and treated.

rehabilitation: The goal of restoring a convicted offender to a constructive place in society through some form of vocational, educational, or therapeutic treatment.

Sentencing Today

Although the goals and justifications of criminal sanctions can be discussed as if they were distinct, there is great overlapping among most of the objectives. A sentence of life imprisonment can be philosophically justified in terms of its primary goal of incapacitation, but the secondary functions of retribution and deterrence are also present. Deterrence is such a broad concept that it mixes well with all the other purposes, with the possible exception of rehabilitation, which logically would only be connected with specific deterrence. Bentham's notion that the pain of criminal punishment must be present as an example to others cannot be met if the prescribed

---

CLOSE-UP *A Trial Judge at Work: Judge Robert Satter*

I am never more conscious of striving to balance the scales of justice than when I am sentencing the convicted. On one scale is society, violated by a crime, on the other is the defendant, fallible, but nonetheless human.

As a trial judge I am faced with the insistent task of sentencing a particular defendant who never fails to assert his own individuality. I hear each cry out, in the words of Thomas Wolfe, "Does not this wonderful and unique I, that never was before and never will be again; this I of tender favor, beloved of the gods, come before the Eye of Judgment and always plead exception?"

In my early years on the bench, I presided mainly over misdemeanors, which are crimes punishable by a sentence of less than one year in jail. Because they are not so serious, I could be more creative, or even experimental, in sentencing.

When sparing a defendant from going to jail, I often imposed conditions related to the crime or the underlying cause of the crime. Young boys charged with destroying public property might be required to spend several Saturdays weeding the flower beds in the town green. A man charged with exposing himself in public might be required to obtain psychiatric treatment. If a husband was accused of beating his wife for the first time, I would get the court family relations officer to counsel the couple. When a crime stemmed from alcoholism, I would order that the offender attend Alcoholics Anonymous.

Later in my career when I came to hear felony cases, I found to my surprise that sentencing for minor crimes is more difficult than sentencing for serious ones. The decision for misdemeanors is whether to incarcerate; that is the hard one. The decision for felonies is the number of years in the state prison; that is much easier. But sometimes even felony cases present the dilemma of whether to imprison or not to imprison.

George Edwards was tried before me for sexual assault, first degree. The victim, Barbara Babson, was a personable woman in her late 20s and a junior executive in an insurance company. She described on the stand what had happened to her:

> I was returning to my Hartford apartment with two armloads of groceries. As I entered the elevator, a man followed me. He seemed vaguely familiar but I couldn't quite place him. When I reached my floor and started to open my door, I noticed him behind me. He offered to hold my bags. God, I knew right then I was making a

mistake. He pushed me into the apartment and slammed the door. He said, "Don't you know me? I work at Travelers with you." Then I remembered him in the cafeteria and I remembered him once staring at me. Now I could feel his eyes roving over my body, and I heard him say, "I want to screw you." He said it so calmly at first, I didn't believe him. I tried to talk him out of it. When he grabbed my neck, I began to cry and then to scream. His grip tightened, and that really scared me. He forced me into the bedroom, made me take off my clothes. "Then," she sobbed, "he pushed my legs apart and entered me."

"What happened next?" the state's attorney asked.

"He told me he was going to wait in the next room, and if I tried to leave he would kill me. I found some cardboards, wrote HELP! on them, and put them in my window. But nobody came. Eventually I got up the courage to open the door, and he had left. I immediately called the police."

Edwards's lawyer cross-examined her vigorously, dragging her through the intimate details of her sex life. Then he tried to get her to admit that she had willingly participated in sex with the defendant. Through it all, she maintained her poise. She left the stand with her version of the crime intact.

Edwards took the stand in his own defense. A tall man with bushy hair, he was wearing baggy trousers and a rumpled shirt. In a low voice he testified that the woman had always smiled at him at work. He had learned her name and address and gone to her apartment house that day. When he offered to help her with her bundles, she invited him into her apartment. She was very nice and very willing to have sex. He denied using force.

I did not believe him. I could not conceive that Miss Babson would have called the police, pressed the charges, and relived the horrors of the experience on the stand if the crime had not been committed as she testified. The jury did not believe him either. They readily returned a verdict of guilty.

First-degree sexual assault is a class B felony punishable by a maximum of 20 years in the state prison. If I had sentenced Edwards then, I would have sent him to prison for many years. But sentencing could take place only after a presentence report had been prepared by a probation officer.

The report was dropped off in my chambers a few days before the sentencing date. Unlike the trial, which had portrayed Edwards in the context of the crime, the presentence report portrayed the crime in the context of Edwards's life.

treatment for the rehabilitation of offenders requires a therapeutic environment.

CHAPTER 13
SENTENCING

515

For the trial judge, the burden of determining a sentence that accommodates these values as applied to the particular case is ex-

It revealed that Edwards was 31 years old, born of a black father and white mother. He had graduated from high school and had an associate's degree from a community college. He had served in Vietnam, where he had been decorated with the Purple Heart for wounds in action and the Bronze Star for bravery under fire. After the army, Edwards had worked successfully as a coordinator of youth programs in the inner city of Hartford. Simultaneously he had taken computer courses. At the time of the crime, he was a computer programmer at Travelers Insurance Company. Edwards was separated from his wife and child, and fellow employees had recently noticed a personality change in him; he seemed withdrawn, depressed, and sometimes confused. His only criminal offense was a disorderly conduct charge three months before the crime, which had not been prosecuted.

I gazed out the window of my chambers and reflected. What should be my sentence?

Before the rescheduled date, I had weighed the factors, made up my mind, and lived with my decision for several days. In serious criminal cases I do not like to make snap judgment from the bench. I may sometimes allow myself to be persuaded by the lawyers' arguments to reduce a preconceived sentence, but never to raise it.

I nod to the state's attorney to begin. He asks to have Miss Babson speak first. She comes forward to the counsel table. "That man," she says, pointing to Edwards, "did a horrible thing. He should be severely punished not only for what he did to me, but for what he could do to other women. I am furious at him. As far as I am concerned, Judge, I hope you lock him up and throw away the key."

She abruptly stops and sits down. The state's attorney deliberately pauses to let her words sink in before he stands up. Speaking with less emotion but equal determination, he says,

This was a vicious crime. There are not many more serious than rape. The defendant cynically tried to put the blame on the victim. But it didn't wash. She has been damaged in the most fundamental way. And the defendant doesn't show the slightest remorse. I urge the maximum punishment of 20 years in prison.

Edwards's lawyer starts off by mentioning his client's splendid Vietnam war record and his lack of a criminal record. The he goes on, "George and his wife have begun living together again with their child, and they are trying to pick up the pieces of their lives. More important," the lawyer continues, "George started seeing a psychiatrist six weeks ago."

The lawyer concludes, "If you will give George a suspended sentence, Your Honor, and make a condition of probation that he stay in treatment, he won't be before this court again. George Edwards is a good risk."

I look at Edwards. "Do you have anything you want to say, Mr. Edwards?"

The question takes him by surprise. Gathering his thoughts, he says with emotion, "I'm sorry for what I did, Judge. I'm sorry for Barbara, and I understand how she feels. I'm sorry for my wife. I'm . . ." His voice trails off.

I gaze out the courtroom window struggling for the words to express my sentence. I am always conscious that the same sentence can be given in a way that arouses grudging acceptance or deep hostility.

Mr. Edwards, you have committed a serious crime. I am not going to punish you to set an example for others, because you should not be held responsible for the incidence of crime in our society. I am going to punish you because, as a mature person, you must pay a price for your offense. The state's attorney asks for 20 years because of the gravity of the crime. Your attorney asks for a suspended sentence because you are attempting to deal with whatever within you caused you to commit the crime. Both make valid arguments. I am partially adopting both recommendations. I herewith sentence you to state prison for six years.

Edwards wilts. His wife gasps. I continue.

However, I am suspending execution after four years. I am placing you on probation for the two-year balance of your term on the condition that you continue in psychiatric treatment until discharged by your doctor. The state is entitled to punish you for the crime that you have committed and the harm you have done. You are entitled to leniency for what I discern to be the sincere effort you are making to help yourself.

Edwards turns to his wife, who rushes up to embrace him. Miss Babson nods to me, not angrily, I think. She walks out of the courtroom and back into her life. As I rise at the bench, a sheriff is leading Edwards down the stairwell to the lockup.

SOURCE: From *Doing Justice: A Trial Judge at Work*, by R. Satter, pp. 170–181. Copyright © 1990 by Robert Satter. Reprinted by permission of Simon & Schuster, Inc.

tremely difficult. In one case, a forger may be sentenced to prison as an example to others despite the fact that she is no threat to community safety and is probably not in need of correctional treatment. In another case, the judge may impose a light sentence on a youthful offender who, although he has committed a serious crime, may be a good risk for rehabilitation if he can move quickly back into society.

That judges have wide powers of discretion with regard to sentencing is reflected in how they combine sentences to tailor the punishment to fit the offender. The judge may stipulate, for example, that the prison terms for two charges are to run either concurrently or consecutively or that all or part of the period of imprisonment is to be suspended. In other situations, the offender may be given a combination of a suspended prison term, probation, and a fine. Execution of the sentence may be suspended as long as the offender stays out of trouble, makes restitution, or seeks medical treatment. The judge may also delay imposing any sentence but retain power to set penalties at a later date if conditions warrant. The variety of choices emphasizes the fluidity of sentencing, especially if bargaining is a part of the process. This condition, too, has come under fire.

The penal code of each state and the federal government defines the behaviors that are considered illegal and specifies the punishments. Unfortunately, the legal standards for sentencing—applying the punishment—have been less well developed than the definitions of the offenses or the procedures used to determine guilt. Because of the complexity of the goals of the criminal sanction and because of our insistence that the punishment should be appropriate to the crime, judges are given discretion to determine the appropriate sentence. As a result, observers have raised questions about the rationality and fairness of sentencing practices.

FORMS OF THE CRIMINAL SANCTION

intermediate sanctions: A variety of punishments that are more restrictive than traditional probation but less stringent and less costly than incarceration.

Incarceration, **intermediate sanctions,** probation, and death are the basic forms that the criminal sanction takes in the United States. Although less than one-third of adults under correctional supervision are in prison or jail, it would seem that incarceration has held a dominant position throughout most of American history. In the popular mind it is the expected fate for most felons and serious misdemeanants; this image has been maintained through books, songs, and films. As a consequence, much of the public views the use of alternatives to incarceration, such as probation, as sanctions that allow offenders to "get off."

Many scholars believe that sentencing structures in the United States are both too severe and too lenient: many offenders who do not warrant incarceration are sent to prison, and many who should be given more restrictive punishments receive little probation supervision. It is because there seems to be little use of sanctions more severe than probation but less severe than incarceration that Norval Morris and Michael Tonry have advocated the more widespread use of intermediate sanctions.[6] These punishments provide a variety of

restrictions on freedom, such as fines, house arrest, intensive supervision probation, restitution, and community service. They can be
used singly or in combination so as to exact a punishment equal to
the severity of the offense and the characteristics of the offender.
With prisons now overcrowded and probation caseloads overwhelming in many urban areas, intermediate punishments are attracting
renewed attention.

Finally, among the forms of the criminal sanction is capital punishment. Questions about the morality and usefulness of capital
punishment have been argued throughout recent history. We will
look at this in some detail and ask why there has been a revival of
death sentences and so few executions during the past decade.

Incarceration

Imprisonment is the most visible penalty imposed by U.S. courts.
Though fewer than 30 percent of persons under correctional supervision are in prisons and jails, incarceration remains the almost exclusive means for punishing those who commit serious crimes, and it is
also widely used against misdemeanants. Because of its severity, imprisonment is thought to have the greatest effect in deterring potential offenders, but it is expensive for the state to carry out and may
prevent the offender's later reintegration into society.

A QUESTION OF ETHICS

Seated in her chambers, Judge Ruth Carroll read the presentence
investigation report of the two young men she would sentence when
court resumed. She had not heard these cases. As often happened in
this overworked courthouse, the cases had been given to her only for
sentencing. Judge Krisch had handled the arraignment, plea, and
trial.

The codefendants had held up a convenience store in the early
morning hours, terrorized the young manager, and taken $47.50
from the till.

As she read the reports Judge Carroll noticed that they looked
pretty similar. Each offender had dropped out of high school, had
held a series of low-wage jobs, and had one prior conviction for
which probation was imposed. Each had been convicted of Burglary
1, robbery at night with a gun.

Then she noticed the difference. David Bukowski had pled guilty
to the charge in exchange for a promise of leniency. Richard Leach
had been convicted on the same charge after a one-week trial. Judge
Carroll pondered the decisions that she would soon have to make.
Should Leach receive a stiffer sentence because he had taken the
court's time and resources? Did she have an obligation to impose
the light sentence recommended for Bukowski by the prosecutor and
defender?

There was a knock on the door. The bailiff stuck his head in.
"Everything's ready, Your Honor." "OK Ben, let's go."

How would you decide? What factors would weigh in your decision?
How would you explain your decision?

While incarcerated the offender is not on the streets committing crimes. The amount of time actually served in prison varies not only with the sentence but with such other factors as good time and the level of crowding.

Penal codes vary as to the structure of the sentences permitted. Each structure makes certain assumptions about the goals of the criminal sanction, and each allocates discretionary authority. It is also from the structure of the sentences authorized by the legislature that the problems of disparity, unchecked discretion, and excessive terms derive.

Indeterminate Sentences

indeterminate sentence: A period set by a judge in which there is a spread between the minimum date for a decision on parole eligibility and a maximum date for completion of the sentence. In holding that the time necessary for treatment cannot be set, the indeterminate sentence is closely associated with the rehabilitation model.

In accord with the goal of rehabilitation, which dominated corrections for much of the past half century, state legislatures also have adopted the **indeterminate** (often termed *indefinite*) **sentence.** On the basis of the notion that correctional personnel must be given the discretion to make a release decision on the grounds of successful treatment, penal codes with indeterminate sentences stipulate a minimum and maximum amount of time to be served in prison: one to five years, three to ten years, ten to twenty years, one year to life, and so on. At the time of sentencing, the offender knows only the range and that he or she will probably be eligible for parole at some point after the minimum term (minus "good time") has been served.

State penal codes vary in the degree of sentencing discretion they permit judges. Court discretion can be described as narrow if the range of sentencing options available to the judge is restricted by law to a third of the statutory maximum sentence for each offense. Thus for a person convicted of a crime carrying a twelve-year statutory maximum, judges with narrow discretion must select a sentence from within, at most, a four-year range (six to ten years, say, or eight to twelve). Even so, the sentences imposed may bear little relation to the amount of time actually served, because parole boards in most of these states have broad discretion in making release decisions.

Determinate Sentences

Growing dissatisfaction with the rehabilitative goal led to efforts in support of determinate sentences based on the assumption of deserved punishment. With a **determinate sentence,** a convicted offender is given a specific length of time to be served (two years, five years, ten years). At the end of this term, again minus credited "good time," the prisoner is automatically freed (there is no parole board). Hence release is not tied to participation in a treatment program or the judgment of the parole board about the future recidivism of the offender.

determinate sentence: A sentence that fixes the term of imprisonment at a specified period of time.

As states have moved toward determinate structures, some have adopted penal codes that stipulate a specific term for each crime category; others still allow the judge to choose a range of time to be served. Some states emphasize a determinate presumptive sentence; the legislature or often a commission specifies a term from a range into which it assumes most cases will fall. Only in special circumstances should judges veer from the presumptive sentence. Whichever variant is used, however, the offender theoretically knows at sentencing the amount of time to be served. One result of determinate sentencing is that legislatures have tended to reduce the discretion of the judiciary as a means of limiting sentencing disparities and ensuring that terms will correspond to those deemed appropriate by the elected body.

Sentencing Guidelines

In recent years **sentencing guidelines,** designed to constrain the discretion of judges, have been established in the federal courts, in several states, and in selected jurisdictions in other states. The approach is viewed as a constructive middle ground between legislatively mandated determinate sentences and indeterminate sentences. Although statutes provide a variety of sentencing options for particular crimes, guidelines attempt to direct the judge to more specific actions that *should* be taken. Sentence ranges provided for most offenses are based on the seriousness of the crime and the criminal history of the offender.

sentencing guidelines: An instrument developed to indicate to judges the usual sanctions given in the past in particular types of cases.

After voluntary experimentation in several courts during the 1970s, Minnesota adopted guideline sentencing in 1980, followed by Washington and Pennsylvania. In 1984, Congress created the U.S. Sentencing Commission and directed that it produce guidelines that would avoid unwarranted sentencing disparities while retaining enough flexibility to permit individualized sentencing when called for by mitigating or aggravating factors. The commission guidelines went into effect on November 1, 1987.

For sentencing guidelines, as for parole guidelines (discussed in Chapter 16), a grid is constructed on the basis of two scores, one related to the seriousness of the offense, the other to characteristics of the offender that indicate the likelihood of recidivism (see Table 13.1). The offender score is arrived at by summing the points allocated to such factors as the number of juvenile, adult misdemeanor, and adult felony convictions; the number of times incarcerated; whether the accused was on probation or parole or had escaped from confinement at the time of the last offense; and employment status or educational achievement. Judges are expected to provide a written explanation when they depart from the guidelines.

Sentencing guidelines are expected to be reviewed and modified periodically so that decisions in the most recent past will be included. Some critics argue that because the guidelines reflect only what has happened, they in no way really reform sentencing. Others question the choice of characteristics included in the offender scale and wonder whether some are used to mask racial criteria. However, as noted by Terance Miethe and Charles Moore, the Minnesota guidelines have resulted in sentences that are "more uniform, more predictable, and more socioeconomically neutral than before the guidelines."[7] Unlike some reforms designed to limit the discretion of judges, guidelines attempt to structure that discretion so as to reflect the collective experience of sentencing in a particular city. Some prefer the use of guidelines to legislative enactment of a penal code based on mandatory or definite sentences.

Mandatory Sentences

Recent years have brought allegations that many offenders are being set free by lenient judges and that the objective of crime control

TABLE 13.1 **Minnesota sentencing guidelines grid (presumptive sentence length in months).** The italicized numbers within the grid denote the range within which a judge may sentence without the sentence being deemed a departure. The criminal history score is computed by adding one point for each prior felony conviction, one-half point for each prior gross misdemeanor conviction, and one-quarter point for each prior misdemeanor conviction.

Severity Levels of Conviction Offense	Criminal History Score						
	0	1	2	3	4	5	6 or More
Unauthorized use of motor vehicle Possession of marijuana	12	12	12	15	18	21	24 _23–25_
Theft-related crimes ($150–$2500) Sale of marijuana	12	12	14	17	20	23	27 _25–29_
Theft crimes ($150–$2500)	12	13	16	19	22 _21–23_	27 _25–29_	32 _30–34_
Burglary—felony intent Receiving stolen goods ($150–$2500)	12	15	18	21	25 _24–26_	32 _30–34_	41 _37–45_
Simple robbery	18	23	27	30 _29–31_	38 _36–40_	46 _43–49_	54 _50–58_
Assault, second degree	21	26	30	34 _33–35_	44 _42–46_	54 _50–58_	65 _60–70_
Aggravated robbery	24 _23–25_	32 _30–34_	41 _38–44_	49 _45–53_	65 _60–70_	81 _75–87_	97 _90–104_
Assault, first degree Criminal sexual conduct, first degree	43 _41–45_	54 _50–58_	65 _60–70_	76 _71–81_	95 _89–101_	113 _106–120_	132 _124–140_
Murder, third degree	97 _91–100_	119 _116–122_	127 _124–130_	149 _143–155_	176 _168–184_	205 _195–215_	230 _218–242_
Murder, second degree	116 _111–121_	140 _133–147_	162 _153–171_	203 _192–214_	243 _231–255_	284 _270–298_	324 _309–339_

NOTE: First-degree murder is excluded from the guidelines by law and is punished by life imprisonment.
SOURCE: Minnesota Sentencing Guidelines Commission, *Report to the Legislature* (1983).

requires greater certainty that criminals will be incapacitated. More than thirty legislatures have responded by stipulating that persons convicted of violent or drug crimes, if they are habitual offenders or used a firearm, must be confined a minimum of some specified amount of time. No consideration may be given to the circumstances of the offense or to the background of the individual; the judge has no discretion and is not allowed to suspend the sentence.

The Massachusetts gun law, which decrees that anyone convicted of possessing an unregistered firearm *must* spend one year in jail, is one such piece of legislation requiring a **mandatory sentence.** Like the 1973 Rockefeller drug law of New York, the Massachusetts law has had no deterrent or incapacitative effects.[8] In the New York case, the draconian sentences prescribed by the law merely raised the stakes for the defendant so high that the prosecution had to bargain to move cases. Research in several states shows that the mandatory sentence is imposed in only a small portion of the cases in which it could be used. What appears to happen is that courtroom workgroups view the mandatory penalties as too harsh, given the circumstances of many cases. The mandatory provisions are avoided by exacting a guilty plea to a lesser charge or by interpreting the record so that the requirements do not apply. Studies of the Michigan Felony Firearms Statute found that although the law was intended to reduce judicial discretion in sentencing, the result was to transfer wide discretion to the prosecuting attorney.[9] Sentence disparity remains, because some offenders are punished according to the mandatory requirements and others are not.

Challenging the argument that mandatory sentences do not achieve their purpose is research conducted on Florida's mandatory minimum sentences.[10] These are designed to ensure that certain categories of offenders are not released early through good time and other provisions before a certain portion of their sentence has been served. Eleven categories of offenders, for example, those convicted of capital offenses, certain drug and firearms offenses, and those designated habitual offenders come under the mandatory minimum provisions. The impact of these laws has been cited as a major cause for increased incarceration lengths with a resulting growth in the prison population.

Good Time

Although not a type of sentence, good time and its impact on sentencing should be mentioned here; it is more fully discussed in Chapter 16. In all but four states, days are subtracted from prisoners' minimum or maximum terms for good behavior or for participation in various types of vocational, educational, and treatment programs. Correctional officials consider these sentence reduction policies necessary for the maintenance of institutional order and as a mechanism to reduce overcrowding. Good time is also taken into consideration by prosecutors and defense attorneys during plea bargaining.

The amount of good time that can be earned varies among the states, from five to ten days a month. The amounts are written into the penal codes of some states and stipulated in department of corrections policy directives in others. In some states, once ninety days of good time are earned, they are vested; that is, they cannot be taken

mandatory sentence: A type of sentence by which statutes require that a certain penalty shall be imposed and executed on certain convicted offenders.

away because of misbehavior. Prisoners in those systems who violate the rules risk losing only days not vested.

The Sentence versus Actual Time Served

Judges in the United States often prescribe long periods of incarceration for serious crimes. But there is a great difference between the length of the sentence announced in the courtroom and the amount of time actually served by offenders. Credit for time spent in jail awaiting the sentence, the application of good time, and in most states release to the community on parole greatly reduce the period of incarceration (see Figure 13.1). The figures give credibility to the belief that the average felony offender spends about two years in prison.

Because of the variation in sentencing and releasing laws, it is difficult to compare the amount of time served with the length of sentence imposed throughout the United States. It is possible, however, to make comparisons in regard to different offenses in the same state. The Bureau of Justice Statistics has brought to light an interesting phenomenon: the more serious the offense, the smaller the proportion of the sentence served. An auto thief, say, may be sentenced to twenty-four months in prison but actually serve twenty months, or 83.3 percent of the sentence; a murderer may well be sentenced to thirty years but be released after fifteen years, or 50 percent of the sentence.[11] As you will see in Chapter 16, these examples are not atypical.

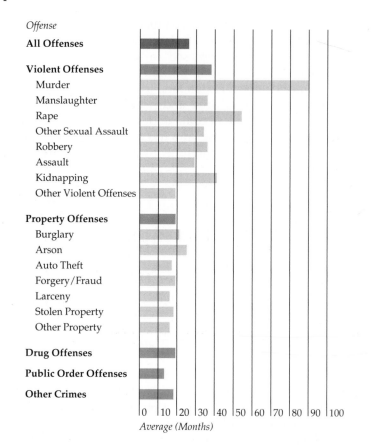

FIGURE 13.1

Average time served by state inmates (by offense type). The data give credibility to the observation that the average felony offender spends about two years in prison. What would be the public's reaction to this fact?

NOTE: Time served includes jail credits.
SOURCE: Adapted from U.S. Department of Justice, Bureau of Justice Statistics, *Report to the Nation on Crime and Justice,* 2nd ed. (Washington, DC: Government Printing Office, 1988) p. 100.

Should the Death Penalty Be Abolished?

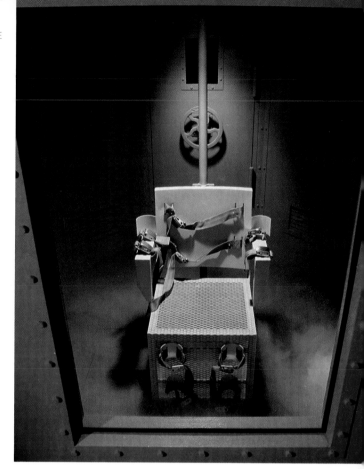

A television station in San Francisco recently sued the state for permission to provide live coverage of California executions. The suit and the publicity it generated helped to revive a debate that has continued for more than two hundred years in this country: Should the state make use of the death penalty, and if so, should executions be public?

The debates over these issues are inexorably linked, since part of the supposed deterrence value of executions has traditionally been the effect on those who witnessed them. Clearly, the country has changed since the days of public hangings in the Old West, but is the need for the death penalty any different today?

Executions in the United States ceased in 1967 when the Supreme Court and legislatures questioned whether the death penalty was an appropriate punishment for criminal offenders. In 1976, the Court declared that the death penalty is permissible as long as judges and juries consider all relevant factors before condemning a murderer to death. In 1977, the ten-year moratorium ended when convicted killer Gary Gilmore asked the state of Utah to carry out his execution by firing squad.

As illustrated in Figure C.1, reinstatement of capital punishment coincided with a steady increase in public support for the death penalty. Whereas in 1966 only 40 percent supported the death penalty, by 1990 80 percent of Americans expressed support for capital punishment. A majority of the American public apparently still believe that the death penalty is needed to punish violent criminals severely and thereby deter other people from committing murders.

Gary Gilmore was the first individual to be put to death following *Gregg* v. *Georgia.* Gilmore asked that his lawyers stop appealing his sentence and that he be executed. Many people believe that the state of Utah, in effect, provided the means for Gilmore to commit suicide.

Although thirty-seven states have reinstated the death penalty, opponents of capital punishment continue to fight for its abolition. Opponents argue that poor people and members of racial minority groups receive a disproportionate number of death sentences. In addition, they argue that it is barbaric to execute people who do not fully understand the consequences of their actions, such as murderers who are teenagers, insane, or mentally retarded. Although the Supreme Court has prevented the execution of those under sixteen years of age and those judged to be insane, it has rejected other arguments that seek to limit capital punishment because of racial discrimination, inconsistent sentences, or a defendant's mental retardation.

Even the proponents of capital punishment remain dissatisfied with its application. They point to the fact that although there are more than 2,400 convicted murderers on Death Row, fewer than 150 executions have been carried out since 1977. The appeals process is a major factor in this pace, since executions are delayed for years as cases are appealed through the courts. To change this, judges and legislators are attempting to develop ways to limit the number and length of appeals filed by prisoners.

Despite the strong support for the death penalty among politicians and the public, policies vary and vigorous debate continues. Several populous states, including New York, Michigan, and Massachusetts, still reject capital punishment in favor of life sentences for murderers. What are some of the arguments for and against this ultimate criminal sanction?

IN looking at capital punishment worldwide (see Figure C.2), we see that the United States policy is not shared by many other developed countries. Nearly all of the industrialized countries in the world, with the exception of formerly communist countries and South Africa, have abolished the death penalty. Since the end of communism in Eastern Europe most of the former Warsaw Pact countries have abolished the death penalty. The United States, the Soviet Union, and South Africa remain the only major developed countries using the death penalty.

Supporters of capital punishment say that when a country has a high level of violence it will generally enact the death penalty. Yet economic and political development may be the more important variables, since capital punishments tend to be used most often in the Third World.

In some countries the death penalty is implemented without legal safeguards and the most basic elements of respect for humanity.

International bodies such as the United Nations, the Council of Europe, and the Organization of American States have submitted to member states, for their ratification, treaties or protocols pledging abolition. These actions are based on the premise that the death penalty is a violation of human rights.

What Should U.S. Policies Be?

What would be the reaction of the American people if executions were broadcast live into every home? Some theorists argue that having the public exposed to executions in this way would increase the deterrence value of capital punishment. Abolitionists undoubtedly hope that the sight would so repel most citizens that public opinion would turn against capital punishment and put an end to it.

With more and more persons on Death Row but fewer than twenty-five individuals executed each year, the policy issue seems at a significant crossroads. Will the United States increase the pace of executions, allow the number of capital offenders in prison to grow, or provide some alternatives such as life imprisonment without parole for convicted murderers?

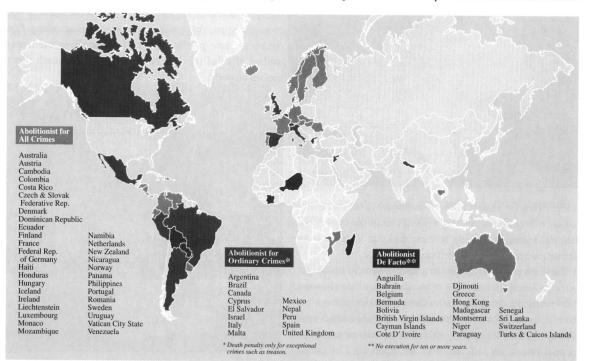

Abolitionist for All Crimes

Australia
Austria
Cambodia
Colombia
Costa Rica
Czech & Slovak
  Federal Rep.
Denmark
Dominican Republic
Ecuador
Finland
France
Federal Rep.
  of Germany
Haiti
Honduras
Hungary
Iceland
Ireland
Liechtenstein
Luxembourg
Monaco
Mozambique

Namibia
Netherlands
New Zealand
Nicaragua
Norway
Panama
Philippines
Portugal
Romania
Sweden
Uruguay
Vatican City State
Venezuela

Abolitionist for Ordinary Crimes*

Argentina
Brazil
Canada
Cyprus   Mexico
El Salvador   Nepal
Israel   Peru
Italy   Spain
Malta   United Kingdom

* Death penalty only for exceptional
  crimes such as treason.

Abolitionist De Facto**

Anguilla
Bahrain
Belgium
Bermuda
Bolivia
British Virgin Islands
Cayman Islands
Cote D' Ivoire

Djinouti
Greece
Hong Kong
Madagascar   Senegal
Montserrat   Sri Lanka
Niger   Switzerland
Paraguay   Turks & Caicos Islands

** No execution for ten or more years.

Figure C.2 *Major Countries that Have Abolished the Death Penalty*

Data from Amnesty International, October 1991

Prison crowding and low levels of probation supervision have renewed interest in the development and use of intermediate sanctions, those punishments less severe than incarceration and more restrictive than probation. Joan Petersilia and Susan Turner have estimated that if murderers and rapists, plus those who had been previously incarcerated and those with a prior sentence for violence, are excluded from consideration for intermediate punishments, 29 percent of those who are now prison bound would be sanctioned in the community.[12] Punishments such as fines, house arrest, intensive probation supervision, restitution and community service, boot camp, and forfeiture are among the sentencing forms that fit this category. In this chapter we will describe each of these forms. Later, in Chapter 16 on community corrections, we will examine the way these punishments are being carried out. There we will analyze the role that they can be expected to play in corrections of the 1990s.

In advocating increased use of intermediate punishments, Morris and Tonry stipulated that these sanctions not be used in isolation from each other but that they be combined to reflect the severity of the offense, the characteristics of the offender, and the needs of the community.[13] For intermediate sanctions to be effective there is need for the development of "exchange rates" consistent with the principle of interchangeability so that one form can be substituted for or added to another form. For example :

$$
\begin{aligned}
\text{two weeks of jail} \; &= \; \text{30 days intermittent confinement} \\
&= \; \text{two months' home detention} \\
&= \; \text{100 hours community service} \\
&= \; \text{one month's salary}
\end{aligned}
$$

A second requirement for effective use of intermediate punishments is that they be enforced and backed up by mechanisms that take seriously any breach of the conditions of the sentence. Too often criminal justice agencies have put few resources into the enforcement of nonincarcerative sentences. If the law does not fullfill its promises, offenders may feel that they have "beaten" the system, with the result that the punishment is meaningless. Citizens viewing the ineffectiveness of the system also develop the attitude that nothing works and that there is a need for stiffer sentences.

Fines

Although the **fine** was leveled in the nineteenth century primarily in connection with crimes of a financial character, it is routinely imposed today for offenses ranging from traffic violations to felonies. Recent studies have shown that the fine is used very widely as a criminal sanction and that probably well over $1 billion is collected annually by courts across the country.[14] Judges in the lower courts were found to be more positively disposed to fines than were judges of higher courts, yet fines are extensively imposed by courts that handle only felonies. Perhaps most important, however, is the fact that fines are rarely used as the *sole* punishment for crimes more serious than motor vehicle violations. Typically, fines are used in

fine: A sum of money to be paid to the state by a convicted person as punishment for an offense.

conjunction with other sanctions, such as probation and incarceration. Hence, it is not unusual for a judge to impose, say, two years' probation and a $500 fine.

Many judges cite the difficulty of collecting and enforcing fines as the reason that they do not make greater use of this punishment.[15] For most other sanctions, the judge can generally rely on another agency of government, usually in the executive branch, to carry out the sentence; monetary penalties are typically the only criminal sanction carried out directly by the court. Perhaps the judiciary sees little incentive to expend its own resources in administering the collection of fines. Judges report that fine enforcement receives a low priority.

In addition, judges indicate that since offenders tend to be poor, the judges are concerned that fines would be paid from the proceeds of additional illegal acts. Further, reliance on fines as an alternative

---

COMPARATIVE PERSPECTIVE
Day Fines in Germany: Could the Concept Work Here?

The idea that the amount of a fine should be related not only to the offense but also to the income of the offender is hardly new. As long ago as the twelfth century it was recognized that criminal punishments weigh more heavily on some offenders than on others. Thus by imposing different levels of fines on offenders who have committed the same offense but have different levels of financial assets, it is believed that greater fairness can be achieved.

Modern implementation of relative fines began with creation of the day-fine system in Finland in 1921, followed by its development in Sweden (1931) and Denmark (1939). The Federal Republic of Germany instituted day fines in 1975. Since then, there has been a major change in the punishments of offenders so that now more than 80 percent of those convicted receive a fine-alone sentence.

The German day-fine system is essentially calculated as the cost of a day of freedom. One day-fine unit is equal to a day's income without deductions for family maintenance. It is the amount of income an offender would have forfeited if incarcerated for a day. Judges determine the amount of this monetary sanction through a two-stage process. First, judges must relate the crime to offense guidelines. These guidelines have established the minimum and maximum number of day-fine units for each offense. For example, according to the guidelines theft may be punished by a day-fine within the range of ten to fifty units. Judges are to choose the number of units by considering the culpability of the offender by examining the offender's motivation and the circumstances surrounding the crime. During the second stage the value of these units is determined by calculating the offender's average net daily income (considering salary, pensions, welfare benefits, interests, etc.), so long as the offender and the offender's dependents have a minimal standard of living. Finally, the law calls for publication of the number of units and their value for each day-fine set by the court so that the sentencing judgment is publicly known.

To illustrate the impact of the day-fine system, let us say that a judge is faced with two defendants who have separately each been convicted of theft. One defendant is a truck driver who earns an average of DM 100 per day and the other is a business manager whose earnings average DM 300 per day. The judge uses the guidelines and decides that the circumstances of the theft and the criminal record of each offender is the same. It is decided that forty day-fine units should be assessed to each. By multiplying these units by the average daily income for each, the truck driver's fine is DM 4,000 and the manager's is DM 12,000.

Since the day-fine system was introduced in Germany, there has been an increase in the use of fines and a decrease in the amount of short-term incarceration. The size of fines has also increased, reflecting the fact that affluent offenders now are being punished at levels corresponding to their worth. Likewise, fines for poor offenders have remained relatively low. All of this has been accomplished without an increase in the default rate.

Might a day-fine system work in the United States? How might the day fine for a truck driver and a cocaine dealer compare?

■
Installment plans for the payment
of fines are being used increasingly
by courts.

to incarceration might mean that the affluent would be able to "buy"
their way out of jail and that the poor would have to serve time.

In Europe fines are used extensively, and they are enforced. They
are normally the sole sanction for a wide range of crimes. The
amounts are geared to the severity of the offense and the resources
of the offender. To deal with the concern that fines exact a heavier toll
on the poor than on the wealthy, Sweden and West Germany have
developed the "day fine." Under this system fines are levied so as to
take into account the differing economic circumstances of offenders
who have committed the same crime.

Greater use of the fine is gaining increased attention from judges
and criminal justice planners as they struggle with overcrowded jails
and prisons and overwhelming probation caseloads and as their dissatisfaction with present sentencing alternatives mounts.

House Arrest

With the increase in prison crowding and technological innovations
that provide for electronic monitoring, **house arrest** has gained new
attention from criminal justice planners. House arrest is a sentence
imposed by a court requiring convicted offenders to spend all or part
of the time in their own residence. Conditions are placed on permissible actions; some offenders are allowed to go to a place of employment during the day but must return to their residence by a specific
hour. House arrest is viewed as a sanction that is tougher than probation but less harsh and less expensive than incarceration. It also
has the advantage of flexibility, since it can be used as a sole sanction
or in combination with other penalties and can be imposed at almost
any point in the criminal justice process: during the pretrial period,
after a short term in jail or prison, or as a condition of probation
or parole.

house arrest: A sentence requiring
the offender to remain inside his or
her home during specified periods.

House arrest coupled with electronic monitoring is becoming more common as an intermediate sanction.

The development of electronic monitoring equipment makes house arrest in its contemporary version a viable sentencing alternative. The devices now being used are all designed to allow officials to know if the conditions of the sentence are being followed. One form of electronic monitoring requires the offender to wear a transmitter that emits a radio signal that is picked up by a receiver attached to the home telephone. During periods when the offender is supposed to be in residence, a computer randomly dials the phone to determine if the signal is being received. If the computer does not receive the signal, it alerts officials to the possibility that the offender has violated the conditions of house arrest. Another type of device is a wrist band worn by the offender. When the computer dials the residence, the offender must insert the identification bracelet into a receiver attached to the phone, which, in turn, sends a signal confirming that there is no violation.

This form of punishment has received much favorable publicity, yet there are legal, technical, and correctional questions that need to be resolved before house arrest with electronic monitoring takes its place as a standard form of the criminal sanction. Some have questioned the constitutionality of the sanction, in that it may violate the Fourth Amendment's protection against unreasonable searches and seizures. Here the issue is privacy and the invasion of one's domicile by government. Technical problems with the monitoring devices have dogged many experiments. Failure rates among those under house arrest may prove to be high. Being one's own warden is a difficult task, and visits by friends and enticements of the community may become too great for many offenders. Tolerance levels for house arrest have not yet been researched, but some observers believe that four months of full-time monitoring is about the limit before a violation will occur.

Restitution and Community Service

restitution: Compensation for injury one has inflicted, in the form of payment of money to the victim.

In its simplest form, **restitution** is repayment to a victim who has suffered some form of financial loss as a result of the offender's crime. In the Middle Ages it was a common way to settle a criminal case: the offender was ordered to do the victim's work or to give the victim money. The growth of the modern state meant that less attention was given to "private" arrangements between offender and victim and greater attention to the wrong done to the community by the offender.

Victim restitution has always been a part of the U.S. criminal justice system, but a largely unpublicized one, effected by informal agreements between enforcement officials and offenders, at the station house and during plea bargaining, and by sentence recommendations. It is only during the past decade that it has been institutionalized in many areas. It is usually carried out as one of the conditions of probation.

community service: Compensation for injury to society by the performance of service to the community.

Community service is unpaid service to the public to overcome or compensate society for some of the harm caused by the crime; it may take the form of work in a social service agency, cleaning parks, assisting the poor, and so on. The sentence specifies the number of hours to be worked and is usually supervised by a probation officer.

Community service can be tailored to the economic and ability levels of the offenders. There is also symbolic value in the offender's effort to make reparation to the community offended by the crime. In some jurisdictions community service has been criticized by labor unions and workers who charge that offenders are taking jobs from crime-free citizens.

Although restitution and community service have many supporters, some believe that if it is used as the sole sanction, it may allow some offenders to purchase relatively mild punishments. This is particularly true, they argue, when it is the sanction applied to upper-class and white-collar criminals. Others point out that although it can be a useful criminal justice sanction for a property crime, it is of little value if violence figured in the offense.

Forfeiture

With passage of the Racketeer Influence and Corrupt Organizations Act (RICO) and the Continuing Criminal Enterprise Act (CCE) in 1970, Congress resurrected forfeiture, a criminal sanction that had lain dormant since the American Revolution. Through amendments in 1984 and 1986, Congress improved procedures for implementing the forfeiture provisions of the law.[16] **Forfeiture** is seizure by the government of property derived from or used in criminal activity. Forfeiture proceedings can take both a civil and a criminal form. Using the civil law, property utilized in criminal activity (contraband, equipment to manufacture illegal drugs, automobiles) can be seized without a finding of guilt. Criminal forfeiture is a punishment imposed as a result of conviction at the time of sentencing. It requires that the offender relinquish various assets related to the crime.

forfeiture: Seizure by the government of property and other assets derived from or used in criminal activity.

Forfeiture as an intermediate punishment has been added to other pieces of federal legislation since 1970, and similar laws are now found in a number of states, particularly with respect to controlled substances and organized crime. An estimated one billion dollar's worth of assets has been confiscated from drug dealers by state and federal officials during the past five years.[17]

Boot Camp/Shock Incarceration

One of the most publicized intermediate sanctions, boot camps now operate in more than fourteen states. Although programs vary, they are all based on the belief that young offenders can be "shocked" out of their criminal ways if they undergo a physically rigorous, disciplined, and demanding regimen for a short period, usually three or four months, before being returned to the community for supervision. The boot camp concept is drawn from the military, but most boot camps also include educational and job training programs as well as other rehabilitative services.

Although boot camps have proved to be popular with the general public, critics charge that their effectiveness has yet to be proved.[18] Larry Meachum, formerly Oklahoma's Commissioner of Corrections and an early advocate of boot camps, has changed his mind. He says that it is hard to control the power of the staff so that they do not go too far and abuse offenders.[19]

Intensive Probation Supervision

intensive probation supervision: Probation granted under conditions of strict reporting to a probation officer with a limited caseload.

During the past decade **intensive probation supervision** has been added to the sentencing menu of intermediate punishments and is usually employed because of prison crowding. Often referred to as "old style" probation, the major characteristic of this sanction is strict and frequent reporting to an officer who carries a limited caseload; electronic monitoring is often used with it. Through this approach, the number of rearrests may be cut, and offenders who might otherwise go to prison can be released to the community. Intensive probation supervision is discussed fully in Chapter 16.

Probation

probation: A sentence allowing the offender to serve the sentence imposed by the court in the community under supervision.

Probation is designed as a means of simultaneously maintaining control and assisting offenders while permitting them to live in the community under supervision. Because probation is a judicial act, given by grace of the state and not extended as a right, conditions are imposed that specify how the offender will serve the term. If the conditions are not met, the supervising officer may bring the offender back to court and recommend that the probation be revoked and that the sentence be served in prison.

Probation gives hope for the rehabilitation of the offender who has not committed a serious crime or whose past record is clean. It is also viewed as a way of maintaining surveillance over offenders so that they do not fall back into criminal ways. Probation is granted to more than 60 percent of the offenders sentenced in the United States, and the proportion is increasing. Although probationers serve their sentences in the community and not in prison, the sanction is often tied to incarceration. Judges may set a prison term but suspend it upon successful completion of a period of probation. In some jurisdictions the court is authorized to modify an offender's prison sentence after a portion is served by changing it to probation. Ohio, for example, has tried **"shock probation"** (called "split probation" in California), in which an offender sentenced to incarceration is released after a period of incarceration (the shock) and resentenced to probation. An offender on probation may be required to spend intermittent periods, such as weekends or nights, in jail. Whatever the specific terms of the probationary sentence, its emphasis is on guidance and supervision in the community.

shock probation: A sentence during which an offender is released after a short incarceration and resentenced to probation.

The success of probation in preventing recidivism is hard to document. Most studies of revocation either for commission of a new offense or for violation of the conditions of probation indicate that from one-fifth to one-third of probationers fail. A Rand Corporation study has cast doubt on more optimistic reports of probation effectiveness.[20] A sample of offenders from two urban California counties who had been placed on probation for FBI index crimes was followed up after forty months. It was found that 34 percent had been reincarcerated for technical violations of their probation or for new offenses; 65 percent had been arrested for another felony or misdemeanor; and 51 percent had been convicted of another crime. It should be noted, however, that the California study looked at offenders who had committed serious crimes; most probationers are first-time offenders who have been convicted of misdemeanors or lesser felonies.

Death

Between 1930 and 1967, when the Supreme Court ordered a stay of executions pending a hearing on the issue, more than 3,800 men and women were executed in the United States. In 1935, a particularly active year for use of this sanction, 199 persons were executed. During recent decades, however, public attention has focused on capital punishment and the question of its consistency with the Eighth Amendment's prohibition against cruel and unusual punishment.

In the 1972 case of *Furman* v. *Georgia,* the Supreme Court ruled for the first time that the death penalty, as administered, constituted cruel and unusual punishment, thereby voiding the laws of thirty-nine states and the District of Columbia.[21] Every member of the Court wrote an opinion, for even among the majority, agreement could not be reached on the legal reasons to support the ban on the death penalty. Three of the five members of the majority emphasized that judges and juries had used their discretion with regard to imposition of capital punishment in such an arbitrary, capricious, and discriminatory manner that it constituted cruel and unusual punishment. Justices Marshall and Brennan argued that capital punishment per se was cruel and unusual, in violation of the Eighth Amendment.

Furman v. *Georgia* (1972):   Death penalty, as administered, constituted cruel and unusual treatment.

Although headlines declared that the Court had banned the death penalty, many legal scholars felt that state legislators could write capital punishment laws that would remove the arbitrariness from the procedure and thus pass the test of constitutionality. By 1976 thirty-five states had enacted new legislation designed to eliminate the faults cited in *Furman* v. *Georgia.* These laws took two forms. Some states removed all discretion from the process by mandating capital punishment on conviction for certain offenses; other states provided specific guidelines for judges and juries to use in deciding whether death is the appropriate sentence in a particular case. The new laws were tested before the Supreme Court in June 1976 in the case of *Gregg* v. *Georgia;* (described more fully in the Close-up on page 532).[22] The Court struck down the mandatory death penalty provisions of the new laws but upheld those that required the sentencing judge or jury to take into account specific aggravating and mitigating factors in deciding which convicted murderers should be sentenced to death. Many state legislatures, citing public opinion polls showing that a great majority favored the death penalty for murder, quickly revised their laws to accord with those of Georgia. The federal government and thirty-six states now have laws providing for the death penalty. The methods of execution authorized in these states are shown in Figure 13.2, the number of persons on death row and executed is shown in Figure 13.3.

Gregg v. *Georgia* (1976):   Upheld death penalty law in which judge and jury considered mitigating and aggravating circumstances in deciding which convicted murderers should be given death sentence.

For opponents of the death penalty, the U.S. Supreme Court may have dealt a fatal blow to their hopes in April 1987. In the case of *McCleskey* v. *Kemp,* the Court rejected a constitutional challenge to administration of the death penalty in Georgia.[23] Warren McCleskey, a black man, had been convicted of two counts of armed robbery and one count of murder following the robbery of an Atlanta furniture store and the killing of a white police officer during the incident. McCleskey appealed his sentence arguing that the death penalty in Georgia was being unconstitutionally administered in a racially discriminatory manner.

McCleskey v. *Kemp* (1987):   Rejected a challenge of Georgia's death penalty on grounds of racial discrimination.

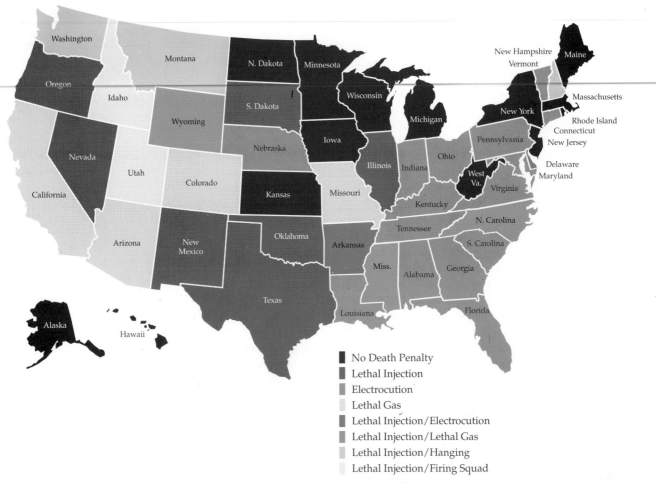

Legend:
- No Death Penalty
- Lethal Injection
- Electrocution
- Lethal Gas
- Lethal Injection/Electrocution
- Lethal Injection/Lethal Gas
- Lethal Injection/Hanging
- Lethal Injection/Firing Squad

FIGURE 13.2

Methods of execution authorized by state. An increasing number of states authorize the use of lethal injections. What reasons might be given for the attractiveness of this execution method? SOURCE: U.S. Department of Justice, Bureau of Justice Statistics, *Report to the Nation on Crime and Justice*, 2nd ed. (Washington, DC: Government Printing Office, 1988), p. 99.

After McCleskey lost two appeals in lower federal courts, his case was presented before the U.S. Supreme Court. McCleskey's attorneys cited research conducted by Professor David Baldus and his associates that showed a disparity in the imposition of the death sentence in Georgia based on the race of the murder victim and, to a lesser extent, the race of the defendant. Baldus examined over two thousand Georgia murder cases and found that defendants charged with killing white persons had received the death penalty eleven times more often than had those charged with killing black victims. Even after compensating for 230 factors, such as viciousness of the crime or quality of the evidence, he showed that the death sentence was four times more likely to be imposed when the victim was white. Although 60 percent of Georgia homicide victims are black, all seven people put to death in that state since 1976 had been convicted of killing white people; six of the seven murderers were black.

By a 5-to-4 vote, the justices rejected McCleskey's assertion. Justice Lewis Powell, for the majority, said that the appeal challenged the discretionary aspects of the criminal justice system, especially with regard to prosecutors, judges, and juries. He wrote that discretion would certainly lead to disparities but that to show the Georgia law was being administered in an unconstitutional manner, McCleskey would have to prove that the decision makers in his case had acted with a discriminatory purpose by producing evidence specific to the case and not the generalized statistical study conducted by Baldus.

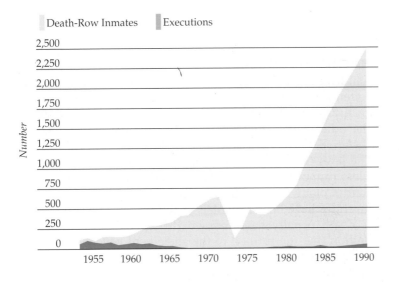

■ Death-Row Inmates ■ Executions

FIGURE 13.3
Persons under sentence of death and persons executed, 1953–1990. Since 1976 approximately 250 new offenders have been added to death row each year, yet the number of executions has never been greater than twenty-five. What explains this situation?
SOURCE: NAACP Legal Defense and Educational Fund, *Death Row, USA*, January 21, 1991.

CLOSE-UP *"I Didn't Like Nobody"*

On the night of June 3, 1973, a Chevrolet Caprice, driven by a woman, was forced off Interstate 57 in southern Cook County, Ill., by a car carrying four men. One of them pointed a 12-gauge pump shotgun at her, ordered her to strip and then to climb through a barbed-wire fence at the side of the road. As she begged for her life, her assailant thrust the shotgun barrel into her vagina and fired. After watching her agonies for several minutes, he finished her off with a blast to the throat. Less than an hour later, the marauding motorists stopped another car and told the man and woman inside it to get out and lie down on the shoulder of the road. The couple pleaded for mercy, saying that they were engaged to be married in six months. The man with the shotgun said, "Kiss your last kiss," then shot both of them in the back, killing them. The total take from three murders and two robberies: $54, two watches, an engagement ring, and a wedding band.

The man ultimately convicted of the "I-57 murders" now sits confined in the Menard Condemned Unit, the official name for death row in the Illinois prison system. Yet Henry Brisbon, Jr., 28, does not face execution for those three killings nearly ten years ago. Illinois' death penalty was invalidated in 1972 and was not restored until 1977, the year that Brisbon was finally brought to trial. At that time, the judge sentenced him to a term of 1,000 to 3,000 years in prison. It took Brisbon less than one year to kill again, this time stabbing a fellow inmate at Stateville Correctional Center with the sharpened handle of a soup ladle. At the trial for this murder, Will County State's Attorney Edward Petka described Brisbon as "a very, very terrible human being, a walking testimonial for the death penalty." The jury agreed.

Brisbon's eleven months on death row have been quiet, compared with his Stateville years, when he took part in 15 attacks on inmates and guards, instigated at least one prison riot, trashed a courtroom during a trial and hit a warden with a broom handle. "I'm no bad dude," he says, "just an antisocial individual." The third of 13 children, Brisbon thinks that his upbringing by a strict black Muslim father made him indifferent: "I was taught to be a racist and not like whites. As I grew up, I decided I didn't like nobody."

Brisbon has 90 well-supervised minutes each day outside his small (7 ft. 7 in. by 5 ft. 10 in.) cell. He works out with weights, keeping his 155 lbs. (on a 5-ft. 9-in. frame) in shape. He complains about his confinement: "Can't take two steps in this cage. It's inhuman. And that dull-ass color blue on the walls in no way brightens my life." He has devised a novel idea about judicial reform: "All this talk about victims' rights and restitution gets me. What about my family? I'm a victim of a crooked criminal system. Isn't my family entitled to something?" The shadow of the death penalty does not faze him: "I don't see that happening to me. What would killing me solve? Isn't that just another murder? If I got to die, it's going to be of natural causes." The state of Illinois thinks otherwise. Says Michael Ficaro, who prosecuted the I-57 case: "On the day he dies in the chair at Stateville, I plan to be there to see that it's done. Nobody I've heard of deserves the death penalty more than Henry Brisbon."

SOURCE: From "I Didn't Like Nobody," *Time*, January 24, 1983, p. 30. Copyright 1983 Time Warner, Inc. Reprinted by permission.

AUTHOR'S NOTE: As of April 1991, Henry Brisborn was still listed as being on death row at Stateville. See NAACP Legal Defense and Education Fund, *Death Row, U.S.A.*, April 24, 1991.

What Is the Future of the Death Penalty?

Three issues related to the death penalty have occupied the attention of jurists and activists during recent years. Opponents of capital punishment have argued that it is cruel and unusual punishment to execute offenders who committed their crimes as minors and that the Eighth Amendment also prohibits the execution of retarded people. On the other side, Chief Justice Rehnquist has proposed that the lengthy appeals process be streamlined.

The laws of thirteen states do not specify an age below which offenders cannot be given capital punishment. Since 1642 when the Plymouth Colony, Massachusetts, hanged a teenage boy for bestiality, 281 juveniles have been executed in the United States.[24] Opponents of the death penalty have focused their position on the long-held recognition that the turmoil of the adolescent psyche is in a kind of diminished capacity, thus exempting juveniles from execution.

CLOSE-UP *Death by the Highway:* **Gregg v. Georgia** *(1976)*

As they stood trying to hitch a ride from Florida to Asheville, North Carolina, on November 21, 1973, Troy Gregg and his sixteen-year-old companion, Sam Allen, watched car after car whiz past. Finally, as they were beginning to lose hope, one came to a stop, the door was opened, and they entered and were off. Fred Simmons and Bob Moore, both of whom were drunk, continued toward the Georgia border with their passengers. Soon, however, the car broke down. Simmons purchased another, a 1960 Pontiac, using a large roll of cash. Another hitchhiker, Dennis Weaver, was picked up and then dropped off in Atlanta about 11 P.M. as the car proceeded northward.

In Gwinnett County, Georgia, just after Simmons and Moore got out of the car to urinate, Gregg told Allen, "Get out, we're going to rob them." Gregg leaned against the car to take aim at the two men, and as they were climbing up an embankment to return to the car, he fired three shots. Allen later told the police that Gregg circled around behind the fallen bodies, put the gun to the head of one and pulled the trigger, and then quickly went to the other and repeated the act. He rifled the pockets of the dead men, took their cash, and told Allen to get into the car. Then they drove away.

The next morning the bodies were discovered beside the highway. On November 23, after reading about the discovery in an Atlanta newspaper, Weaver—the other hitchhiker—called the police and described the car. The next afternoon Gregg and Allen, still in Simmons's car, were arrested in Asheville. A .25-caliber pistol, later shown to be the murder weapon, was found in Gregg's pocket. After receiving the *Miranda* warnings, Gregg signed a statement in which he admitted shooting and then robbing Simmons and Moore. He justified the slayings on the grounds of self-defense.

Georgia uses a two-stage procedure in which one jury decides questions of guilt or innocence and a second jury determines the penalty. At the conclusion of the trial, the judge instructed the jury that charges could be either felony murder or nonfelony murder, and either armed robbery or the lesser included offense of robbery by intimidation. The jury found Gregg guilty of two counts of armed robbery and two counts of murder. At the penalty stage, the judge instructed the jury that it could not authorize the death penalty unless it first found that one of three aggravating circumstances was present: (1) that the murder was committed while the offender was engaged in committing two other capital felonies; (2) that Gregg committed the murders for the purpose of acquiring the money and automobile; (3) that the offense was outrageously and wantonly vile, horrible, and inhuman and showed the depravity of the mind of the defendant. The jury found the first and second circumstances to be present and returned verdicts of death on each count.

The sentence was affirmed by the Supreme Court of Georgia in 1974. Gregg appealed to the U.S. Supreme Court, arguing that imposition of the death penalty was cruel and unusual punishment in violation of the Eighth Amendment.

DECISION

On July 2, 1976, the Supreme Court upheld the Georgia law under which Gregg had been sentenced. In a widely split opinion, seven of the justices said that capital punishment is not inherently cruel and unusual and thus upheld the laws in those states in which the judge and jury had discretion to consider the crime, the particular defendant, and mitigating or aggravating circumstances before ordering death.

The Supreme Court has been divided on the issue of the death penalty for juveniles. In *Thompson* v. *Oklahoma* (1988), the court narrowly decided that William Wayne Thompson, who was fifteen years old when he committed murder, should not be executed.[25] A plurality of four justices held that executing juveniles did not comport with the "evolving standards of decency that mark the progress of a maturing society." The dissenters said that Thompson had been correctly sentenced under Oklahoma law. Within a year the Court again considered the issue and this time upheld the death sentence. In two cases, *Stanford* v. *Kentucky* (1989) and *Wilkins* v. *Missouri* (1989), the justices upheld the convictions of offenders who were sixteen and seventeen years old at the time of their crime.[26] On May 18, 1990, Dalton Prejean, a juvenile at the time of the offense, was executed by Louisiana.

An estimated 250 offenders on the nation's death rows are classified as retarded. It is argued that retarded people have difficulty defending themselves in court since they have problems remembering details, locating witnesses, and testifying credibly in their own behalf. It is also asserted that executing the retarded serves no deterrent purpose, is only minimally retributivist, and is disproportionate to the crime.[27] In 1989 the Supreme Court upheld the Texas death penalty statute and said that the Eighth Amendment does not prohibit execution of the mentally retarded. The case involved Johnny Paul Penry, a convicted killer with an IQ of about 70 and the mental capacity of a seven-year-old.[28]

One aspect of the modern dilemma over capital punishment is the long appeals process. The average length of time between imposition of the sentence by a trial court to the date that the sentence is carried out is between seven and eight years. During this time sentences are reviewed by the state courts and through the writ of *habeas corpus* by the federal courts. Chief Justice Rehnquist has been particularly active in pushing to limit the appeals process in death penalty cases. He set up a committee headed by retired Justice Lewis Powell that recommended that only one *habeas corpus* appeal to the federal courts be allowed. This position was upheld by the Supreme Court in a 6-to-3 ruling in April 1991 when it said that only in exceptional circumstances should a prisoner be allowed to use the writ more than once when appealing a death sentence in the federal courts.[29] Appellate review is a time-consuming and expensive process, but it also has an impact. From 1977 (the year after *Gregg*) to 1988, 3,057 persons were sentenced to death and 104 people were executed; however, 1,249 were removed from death row as a result of appeal, commutation by a governor, or death while awaiting execution.[30] Would these death sentences have been overturned with the expedited appeals process advocated by the Chief Justice?

The philosophical and legal arguments over capital punishment continue. Of the four goals of criminal sanction, deterrence has had the greatest appeal. Although research has tended to support both sides of the issue, recent studies by Ehrlich have engendered great controversy.[31] Using economic modeling and sophisticated statistical techniques, Ehrlich argued that use of the death penalty deterred murderers and saved innocent lives. This research has been critiqued by many scholars, including researchers at the National Academy of

■ Opponents of capital punishment point to the possibility of error. Here Randall Dale Adams, whose murder conviction in the 1976 slaying of a Dallas police officer was questioned in the film *Thin Blue Line*, had his conviction overturned after 13 years.

Science, and found to have measurement errors that biased the results. Most scholars today question the deterrent effect of the death penalty.

If deterrence cannot be shown to result from use of the death penalty, what then is the justification? Ernest van den Haag, a leading supporter of the penalty, has argued that retribution justifies the sanction.[32] He and others argue that there are some people whose crimes are so heinous that they deserve to be executed. Yet others point to the discriminatory aspects of the penalty, noting that of the approximately 20,000 murders per year in the United States, only 250 offenders receive a sentence of death and upward of 25 are executed yearly.

The number of persons under sentence of death has increased dramatically in the past decade. About 2,400 incarcerated persons were awaiting execution in thirty-four of the death penalty states in 1990 (see Figures 13.2 and 13.3). Two-thirds of those on death row were in the South, with the greatest number in that area concentrated in Florida, Georgia, and Texas (see Figure 13.4).

More than 250 new death sentences are now being given out each year, but since the penalty was reinstated in 1976, there have never

FIGURE 13.4
Death row census, race, region, December 1990. As can be seen, the number of inmates on death rows are mainly concentrated in certain states. Blacks make up about 13 percent of the U.S. population, yet they make up 39.42 percent of the death row population. Is it interracial homicide that results in a death sentence? SOURCE: NAACP Legal Defense and Education Fund, *Death Row, U.S.A.*, January 21, 1991.

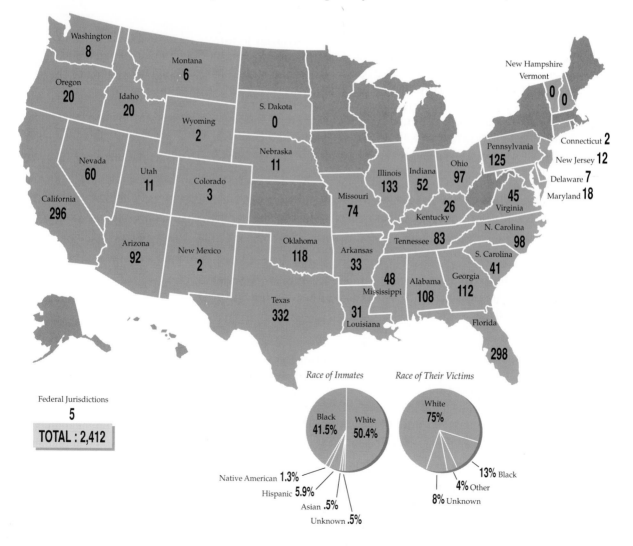

been more than 25 offenders executed in any one year. Is this situation the result of a complicated appeals process or of lack of will on the part of both political leaders and a society that is perhaps uncertain about the taking of human life? Why is public opinion in support of capital punishment growing? Maybe the death penalty has more significance as a political symbol than as a deterrent to crime. Is it possible that in the future the United States will stop executing criminal offenders, thereby joining the other industrial democracies that (with the exception of South Africa) do not have the death penalty?

SENTENCING REFORM
Calls for Reform

It could be said that the United States had a national system of sentencing from 1935 to 1975. Anchored on the goal of rehabilitation, every state, the District of Columbia, and the federal system had indeterminate sentences and discretionary release on parole. In the short period of 1975 to 1988 major changes in the structures, practices, and laws of sentencing were considered or adopted in practically every jurisdiction. As noted by Michael Tonry, there is no longer an American system of sentencing.[33]

The reform movement of the past two decades raised questions about the assumptions of rehabilitation and the forms of sentencing—indeterminate terms and release on parole—linked to it. Beginning in 1969 a series of books criticized the goals and forms of the criminal sanction. Among them were Kenneth Culp Davis's *Discretionary Justice* (1969), Norval Morris's *The Future of Imprisonment* (1974), and Andrew von Hirsch's *Doing Justice* (1976).[34] These works and other publications by scholars and practitioners drew attention to a number of problems that had resulted from what at that time was almost nationwide consensus supporting rehabilitation. They pointed to (1) the failure of treatment programs and (2) disparities in the sentences received by similar offenders that were a product of the broad discretion exercised by judges and parole boards. Independent of this scholarly critique were the calls of political leaders for legislatures to change the sentencing process by "toughening" criminal penalties, making greater use of incarceration, and ending or limiting the parole release decision.

Failure of Treatment Programs

Robert Martinson's research was probably one of the most influential factors in the campaign to reform sentencing practices.[35] Using rigorous standards, Martinson surveyed all studies of rehabilitation programs in correctional systems written in English and published between 1945 and 1967; 231 met his criteria. The studies used various measures of offender improvement—recidivism, adjustment to prison life, vocational success, educational achievement, personality and attitude change—to compare the results for offenders who had received treatment with results for those who had not. Included in his analysis were such standard rehabilitative programs as educational and vocational training, individual counseling, group counseling, etc. Martinson's findings: "With few and isolated exceptions, the rehabilitative efforts that have been reported so far have had no appreciable effect on recidivism." Widely interpreted as "nothing works," publication of Martinson's finding in 1974 fueled the reform movement.

Sentence Disparities and Discretion

sentence disparity: Divergence in the lengths and types of sentences imposed for the same crime or for crimes of comparable seriousness when no reasonable justification can be discerned.

A lack of uniformity in sentences is justifiable, given rehabilitative goals and the aim that punishment should fit the criminal. **Sentence disparity** becomes a problem when no reasonable basis for it can be adduced. Release decisions of parole boards are highly discretionary and can thus have the same problem.

Sentencing disparities (see Figure 13.5) not only present a constitutional issue that challenges the ideal of equal justice under law but also create problems that interfere with criminal justice goals. Predictably consistent differences among judges within an urban court system can act to interfere with the scheduling and processing of cases when defense attorneys request continuances in the hope that they can bring a client's case to a more lenient judge. Also, prisoners compare sentences. Those who feel they have been the victims of prejudice become embittered. In many cases, serious disciplinary problems have erupted because of perceived injustices. At the heart of the rehabilitation goal is the need for judges and correctional officials to individualize the amount of probation or incarceration time. Early advocates of treatment argued that there could be no set time for an offender to be rehabilitated, just as there could be no set time for a sick person to be hospitalized. What was necessary was that decision makers have the discretion to determine the type of sanction to be imposed, the treatment to be prescribed, and the time when the offender could be released from correctional supervision.

Reform critics in the 1970s argued that indeterminate sentences were being imposed and parole board release decisions were being made on the basis of racial, ethnic, and class biases. Although the research findings on criminal justice discrimination were equivocal, it *appeared* to many that discretion was being misused. The fact that an increasing portion of offenders were African-American and Hispanic heightened the impression that members of minority groups were being discriminated against by criminal justice officials. The need to rein in the discretion of judges and parole boards became one of the major stimuli for reform.

Tougher Sentences

During a period of heightened awareness of the crime problem, legislators and other public officials called for increased use of incarceration and longer sentences, particularly for repeat offenders. This effort was consistent with the shift to a more conservative period in the United States epitomized by the election of Ronald Reagan in 1980. Research supporting the concept of selective incarceration, the belief that parole boards were too lenient, and awareness

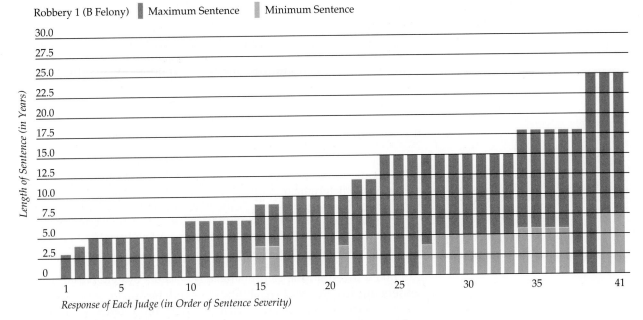

Robbery 1 (B Felony) ▮ Maximum Sentence ▮ Minimum Sentence

Response of Each Judge (in Order of Sentence Severity)

that the actual time served in prison was much less than either the law allowed or the judge had imposed all contributed to calls for tougher sentences.

Results of Reform

Much of the reform activity of the past two decades was based on the assumption that deserved punishment should be the goal of the criminal sanction. Advocates of this approach say that justice should be humane and simple and that it can be achieved if discretion is harnessed by the specification of definite sentences. Unlike rehabilitation, which emphasizes that the sanction should fit the needs of the individual offender, "just deserts" focuses on the seriousness of the crime that the offender has committed and the number of his or her prior convictions. "Seriousness" depends on the harm done by the act and the degree of the offender's responsibility for it.

Although reformers of the 1970s all articulated the same basic set of criticisms, the proposals submitted to state legislatures met a mixed fate. Many of the proponents argued that the new laws should not result in an increase in the length of incarceration. A goodly number of the legislators, in contrast, responded to the public demand for crime control by structuring penal codes to ensure that most offenders would stay in prison for longer periods. Correctional officials, although content to have the discretion of independent parole boards restricted, were concerned that they would not have the resources to manage the expected increase in prison populations. Judges, who might have responded favorably to attempts to reduce sentence disparities, became alarmed when it appeared that the new schemes would shift power away from the judiciary to prosecutors, whose plea bargaining leverage would thereby increase. In short, the well-thought-out schemes of the reformers to constrain discretion and shift criminal justice to the goal of deserved punishment came face to face with the political reality of legislatures and governmental

FIGURE 13.5

Minimum and maximum sentences hypothetically imposed by forty-one New York judges in a case of first-degree robbery. Each bar of the chart represents the sentence that each judge would have given in the case of an elderly man robbed at knife point. The defendant, a heroin addict, was unemployed, lived with his pregnant wife, and had a minor criminal record. The sentences range from zero to three years to the statutory maximum of eight and one-third to twenty-five years; the defendant received an actual sentence of incarceration for a minimum of no time to a maximum of five years.

SOURCE: From "Sentence Disparity in New York: The Response of Forty-One Judges," *The New York Times,* March 30, 1979, p. B3. Copyright © 1979 by The New York Times Company. Reprinted by permission.

537

bureaucracies. Compromise, that key element of politics and policy change, came to guide reform attempts.

In reviewing sentencing reform developments, Michael Tonry has noted that they have been unprecedented in their diversity.[36] In a national survey he found that many jurisdictions retained the indeterminate arrangement, having much the same approach as they did in 1936. But in the jurisdictions that made major changes, although there was agreement that the traditional system was undesirable, there was no agreement on what to establish in its place.

> Some jurisdictions have abolished parole release, parole supervision, or both. Some have adopted parole guidelines. Some have enacted statutory determinate sentencing laws. Some have adopted presumptive sentencing guidelines. Some have adopted "voluntary" sentencing guidelines at the state or local levels, for some or all offenses. Most have enacted mandatory sentencing laws. A few have tried to invigorate appellate sentence review.[37]

Taken together, the reforms have replaced a system based on the sentencing structures of rehabilitation—indeterminate sentences and discretionary parole release—with a variety of systems, each developed in part as a consequence of a particular set of political and organizational forces that came together in an individual state at a particular time. After a decade of innovation we must ask a number of questions: What has been the impact of changes in the penal codes? Is there more consistency in sentencing? Have the new laws resulted in longer prison terms and, hence, prison crowding? Have the costs to the criminal justice system increased or decreased? What have the changes meant with respect to crime control?

Researchers have provided only tentative answers to these questions. If we posit that the goals of the sentencing reforms were "consistency and predictability in outcomes, accountability on the part of decision makers, [and] reduction of disparities and anomalies," some of the innovations can be judged as successes and some as failures.[38] Tonry lists parole guidelines, comprehensive plea bargaining bans, and presumptive sentencing guidelines as having achieved these stated goals. Contrariwise, voluntary sentencing guidelines, mandatory sentencing laws, and partial plea bargaining bans have largely failed. Determinate sentencing laws, he says, defy easy generalization.[39]

With regard to the other questions posed—about lengths of prison terms, crowding, costs, and crime control—the answers are either not available or unclear. A major problem that criminal justice researchers must face in carrying out impact studies is the difficulty of isolating the change being tested from other factors at work in the system. It is clear that prison terms have grown longer, but is that owing to determinate sentencing or public pressure for judges to dole out stiffer penalties? If it is shown that the number and duration of trials have increased since reform, can it be proved that the new penal code is the cause, or are changes in prosecution policies the dominant factor? With the exception of drug-related offenses, crime rates have leveled off since the early 1980s, yet violence remains at all-time highs in most urban areas. Have the sentencing reforms had any effect other than to crowd prisons and probation caseloads?

SUMMARY

Sentencing—the specification of the sanction—can be viewed as both the beginning and the end of the criminal justice system. With guilt established, a decision must be made concerning what to do with the person who has been convicted. Much of the effort of the defendant, prosecutor, and defense attorney during the presentencing phase is based on assumptions about the sanction that may follow conviction. Various justifications for the criminal sanctions have been given in succeeding eras to legitimize the punishment imposed by the state. Although the goals of retribution, deterrence, incapacitation, and rehabilitation can be viewed as distinct, there is a great deal of overlapping among them. Rehabilitation appears to be the one goal that, if carried out according to its model, does not overlap with the other objectives.

When a judge sentences an offender in open court, the effect is felt not only by the individual facing the bench but by the official actors in the criminal justice system and by the general public as well. So much of the emphasis of the values and culture of the criminal justice system is on the sentence that its impact is felt throughout the system. Each person will view the sentence through his or her own perceptual screen and evaluate its contents as one element to be considered when personal decisions are made. As long as judges are given discretion in sentencing; as long as the corrections process is expected to serve the multiple goals of rehabilitation, deterrence, and retribution; and as long as it is agreed that the punishment should fit the criminal, disparities will exist. The excesses are what concern those bothered by the "sentencing wonderland."

FOR DISCUSSION

1. You are the judge. What personal characteristics do you feel justify you in giving different sanctions to offenders who have committed the same crime?
2. In some states the jury not only decides guilt but also fixes the sentence. What problems do you see with this approach?
3. Many white-collar offenders are given short terms that they serve in minimum security institutions that have extensive recreational facilities and campuslike surroundings. Poor persons who are found guilty of committing property crimes serve long terms in the "big house." Is this justice?
4. You are the judge. The law in your state sets terms of five to fifteen years for the offense of armed robbery. The parole board usually releases individuals when half their sentence has been served. How might these facts influence your sentencing decisions?
5. You have been commissioned by your state legislature to devise a criminal sanction that will deter crime yet treat offenders humanely. What will you suggest?

FOR FURTHER READING

American Friends Service Committee. *Struggle for Justice.* New York: Hill & Wang, 1971. Critique of indeterminate sentences and discretionary parole release. The book that raised the battle cry for sentencing reform.

Gaylin, Willard. *The Killing of Bonnie Garland.* New York: Simon & Schuster, 1982. True story of the murder of a Yale student by her boyfriend and the reaction of the criminal justice system to the crime. Raises important questions about the goals of the criminal sanction and the role of the victim in the process.

Goodstein, Lynne, and John Hepburn. *Determinate Sentencing and Imprisonment: A Failure of Reform.* Cincinnati: W. H. Anderson, 1985. Analysis of the movement for determinate sentencing and its impact.

Haas, Kenneth C. and James A. Inciardi, eds. *Challenging Capital Punishment: Legal and Social Science Approaches.* Newbury Park, CA: Sage, 1988. An excellent collection of articles concerning various aspects of the death penalty debate.

Hirsch, Andrew von. *Doing Justice.* New York: Hill & Wang, 1976. The modern restatement of retributist theory with its implications for sentencing.

Johnson, Robert. *Death Work.* Pacific Grove, CA: Brooks/Cole, 1989. A look at those on death row—prisoners and correctional officers—and the impact of capital punishment on their lives.

McDonald, Douglas Corry. *Punishment without Walls: Community Service Sentences in New York City.* New Brunswick, NJ: Rutgers University Press, 1986. Explores use of community service as an intermediate sentence.

Morris, Norval, and Michael Tonry. *Between Prison and Probation: Intermediate Punishments in a Rational Sentencing System.* New York: Oxford University Press, 1990. Urges development of a range of intermediate punishments that can be used to sanction offenders more severely than probation but less severely than incarceration.

Wheeler, Stanton, Kenneth Mann, and Austin Sarat. *Sitting in Judgment: The Sentencing of White-Collar Criminals.* New Haven, CT: Yale University Press, 1988. Describes how federal district court judges think about the sentencing of criminals, particularly white-collar criminals.

Zimring, Franklin E., and Gordon Hawkins. *Capital Punishment and the American Agenda.* Cambridge, England: Cambridge University Press, 1986. Examines the fall in use and support for the death penalty until the 1970s. Raises important questions about the future of capital punishment.

NOTES

1. Herbert L. Packer, *The Limits of the Criminal Sanction* (Palo Alto, CA: Stanford University Press, 1968), pp. 33–34.
2. Twentieth Century Fund, Task Force on Criminal Sentencing, *Fair and Certain Punishment* (New York: McGraw-Hill, 1976).
3. Andrew von Hirsch, *Doing Justice* (New York: Hill & Wang, 1976), p. 49.
4. Packer, *Limits of the Criminal Sanction,* p. 51.
5. Peter Greenwood, "Controlling the Crime Rate through Imprisonment," in *Crime and Public Policy,* ed. James Q. Wilson (San Francisco: ICS Press, 1983), p. 258.
6. Norval Morris and Michael Tonry, *Between Prison and Probation: Intermediate Punishments in a Rational Sentencing System* (New York: Oxford University Press, 1990).
7. Terance D. Miethe and Charles A. Moore, "Sentencing Guidelines: Their Effect in Minnesota," *Research in Brief* (Washington, DC: National Institute of Justice, 1989).
8. U.S. Department of Justice, "Mandatory Sentencing: The Experience of Two States," *Policy Briefs* (Washington, DC: Government Printing Office, 1982).
9. Milton Heumann and Colin Loftin, "Mandatory Sentencing and the Abolition of Plea Bargaining: The Michigan Felony Firearm Statute," *Law and Society Review* 13 (Winter 1979):393–430.

10. Florida, Department of Corrections, "Mandatory Minimum Sentences in Florida: Past Trends and Future Implications," February 11, 1991.

11. U.S. Department of Justice Statistics, *Bulletin* (January 1988).

12. Joan Petersilia and Susan Turner, "The Potential of Intermediate Sanctions," *State Government* (March/April 1989):65.

13. Morris and Tonry, *Between Prison and Probation*, p. 37.

14. Sally T. Hillman, Joyce L. Sichel, and Barry Mahoney, *Fines in Sentencing* (New York: Vera Institute of Justice, 1983).

15. George F. Cole, Barry Mahoney, Roger Hanson, and Marlene Thornton, *Attitudes and Practices of Trial Court Judges toward the Use of Fines* (Denver: Institute of Court Management, 1987).

16. Karla R. Spaulding, " 'Hit Them Where It Hurts': RICO Criminal Forfeitures and White-Collar Crime," *Journal of Criminal Law and Criminology* 80 (1989):197.

17. *New York Times*, July 16, 1990.

18. Dale K. Sechrest, "Boot Camps Do Not Measure Up," *Federal Probation* 53 (September 1989):15–20; see also Dale G. Parent, *Shock Incarceration: An Overview of Existing Programs* (Washington, DC: Government Printing Office, 1989).

19. *Newsweek* (May 22, 1989), p. 42.

20. Joan Petersilia, Susan Turner, James Kahan, and Joyce Peterson, *Granting Felons Probation: Public Risks and Alternatives* (Santa Monica, CA: Rand Corporation, 1985).

21. *Furman v. Georgia*, 408 U.S. 238 (1972).

22. *Gregg v. Georgia*, 428 U.S. 153 (1976).

23. *McCleskey v. Kemp*, 478 U.S. 1019 (1987).

24. Ron Rosenbaum, "Too Young to Die?" *New York Times Magazine*, March 12, 1989, p. 60.

25. *Thompson v. Oklahoma*, 108 S. Ct. 2687 (1988).

26. *Stanford v. Kentucky* 109 S. Ct. 2969 (1989) and *Wilkins v. Missouri* 109 S. Ct. 2969 (1989).

27. Philip L. Fetzer, "Execution of the Mentally Retarded: A Punishment without Justification," *South Carolina Law Review* 40 (1989):419.

28. *Penry v. Lynaugh*, 45 Cr. L. Rptr. 3188 (1989).

29. *McCleskey v. Zant*, No. 89–7024 (1991).

30. U.S. Department of Justice, Bureau of Justice Statistics, *Bulletin* (July 1989).

31. William J. Bowers, "The Effect of Executions Is Brutalization, Not Deterrence," *Challenging Capital Punishment*, ed. Kenneth C. Haas and James A. Inciardi (Newbury Park, CA: Sage, 1988), p. 49.

32. Ernest van den Haag, *Punishing Criminals* (New York: Basic Books, 1975).

33. Michael Tonry, "Structuring Sentencing," *Crime and Justice*, vol. 10, ed. Michael Tonry and Norval Morris (Chicago: University of Chicago Press, 1988), p. 267.

34. Kenneth Culp Davis, *Discretionary Justice* (Baton Rouge: Louisiana State University Press, 1969); Norval Morris, *The Future of Imprisonment* (Chicago: University of Chicago Press, 1974); Andrew von Hirsch, *Doing Justice* (New York: Hill & Wang, 1976).

35. Robert Martinson, "What Works? Questions and Answers about Prison Reform," *Public Interest* 35 (Spring 1974):22.

36. Tonry, "Structuring Sentencing," p. 268.

37. Ibid.

38. Michael Tonry, *Sentencing Reform Impacts*, U.S. Department of Justice, National Institute of Justice (Washington, DC: Government Printing Office, 1987). p. 97.

39. Ibid., p. 98; see also Sandra Shane-DuBow, Alice P. Brown, and Erik Olsen, *Sentencing Reform in the United States: History, Content, and Effect*, U.S. Department of Justice, National Institute of Justice (Washington, DC: Government Printing Office, 1985).

Corrections

Key Terms

community corrections
congregate system

penitentiary   separate confinement
penology

When a sheriff or a marshal takes a man from a courthouse in a prison van and transports him to confinement for two or three or ten years, this is our act. We have tolled the bell for him. And whether we like it or not, we have made him our collective responsibility. We are free to do something about him; he is not.

Chief Justice Warren Burger

For most citizens, prison comes to mind when they think of corrections. This perception is perhaps understandable, given the history of corrections in this country, the folklore, films, and songs about prison life, and the fact that incarceration is the most visible aspect of the process. Almost everyone has unexpectedly come across the looming walls, barbed-wire fences, and searchlights of the modern prison on a drive through the countryside. The prison is also brought to our attention by the media whenever there is inmate unrest or an escape. And it is the prison that legislators and politicians seem to keep uppermost when they consider changes in the penal code or the annual appropriation for corrections.

For students of criminal justice, it should be no surprise that *corrections* refers to the great number of programs, services, facilities, and organizations responsible for the management of people who have been accused or convicted of criminal offenses. In addition to prisons and jails, corrections also includes probation, halfway houses, education and work release programs, parole supervision, counseling, and community service. One can find correctional programs operating in Salvation Army hostels, in forest campsites, along roadsides, in medical clinics, and in urban storefronts. Almost 4 million adults and juveniles are given correctional supervision by more than 400,000 administrators, psychologists, officers, counselors, social workers, and others. It is a system authorized by all levels of government, administered by both public and private organizations, and with a total cost of over $15 billion yearly.[1]

DEVELOPMENT OF CORRECTIONS

As we look at U.S. corrections today, we must ask: How did we get here? Why are offenders now placed on probation or incarcerated rather than whipped or burned? Why is most of corrections organized on a state and local rather than a national basis? Why do the great hopes of one period seem to turn into the dismay of another? How do political and social attitudes influence the allocation and type of punishment?

The correctional system did not just spring up full blown: over time its goals and practices have undergone marked shifts that in part reflect social and political currents. In looking at corrections over the past two hundred years, we can discern swings in the pendulum as one approach and then another were undertaken to deal with the

During the seventeenth and eighteenth centuries American justice relied heavily on punishments that were physically brutal, such as death, flogging, and branding, legacies from Europe.

problem of the criminal offender. As we examine these shifts, it is important to reflect on our present situation and to speculate about the future of criminal punishment.

An Age of Reform

The latter part of the eighteenth century stands out as a remarkable period, one in which scholars and social reformers in Europe and America engaged in an almost complete rethinking of the nature of society and the place of the individual in it. The Enlightenment, as the philosophical movement was called, challenged traditional assumptions by emphasizing the individual, the limitations on government, and rationalism. It was the major intellectual force behind the American Revolution and had a direct impact on views of the way the criminal law should be administered and on the goals and practices of corrections. Questions were raised about such matters as the procedures used to determine guilt, the limits on government's power to punish, the nature of criminal behavior, and appropriate means to correct offenders. At a time of overcrowded and unmanaged jails, brutal corporal punishment, and rising levels of crime, the great period of correctional reform was launched.

During the colonial and early postrevolutionary years, Americans used physical punishment, a legacy from Europe, as the main criminal sanction. Fines, stocks, flogging, branding, and maiming were the primary means used to control deviancy and to maintain public safety. For more serious crimes, the gallows was used with frequency. In the state of New York about 20 percent of all crimes were capital offenses, and criminals were regularly sentenced to death for picking pockets, burglary, robbery, and horse stealing.[2] Recidivists especially usually ended on the gallows during the early years of the republic. Jails existed throughout the country, but they served only the limited purpose of holding people awaiting trial or punishment or those unable to pay their debts. Jails were not a part of the correctional scheme.

The early American preference for physical punishment was reinforced by the Puritans' belief in human depravity and the ever-present temptations of the devil. The Calvinist notion of predestination—that is, that people had no control over their fate in the next life—did not encourage efforts to rehabilitate offenders in this one.

The French scholar Michel Foucault has chronicled the spread of humanistic ideas during the latter portion of the eighteenth century. In Europe, the period following the French Revolution led to the disappearance of torture as a public spectacle and the adoption of "modern" penal codes that emphasized adapting punishment to fit the individual offender. Most important, those decades "saw the disappearance of the tortured, dismembered, amputated body, symbolically branded on face or shoulder, exposed alive or dead to public view." As punishment moved away from the infliction of pain, the offender's body was no longer the major target of penal policy. Now the body served as the instrument for correctional intervention to change the individual and set him or her on the right path. Foucault notes, "The expiation that once rained down upon the body must be replaced by a punishment that acts in the depths of the heart."[3]

penitentiary: An institution intended to isolate prisoners from society and from one another so that they can reflect on their past misdeeds, repent, and thus undergo reformation.

Of the many persons who actively promoted the reform of corrections, John Howard (1726–1790), sheriff of Bedfordshire, England, stands out. His book, *The State of Prisons in England and Wales* (1777), led to the development of the **penitentiary.**[4] Howard's book is an

John Howard's *The State of the Prisons in England and Wales* fed the reform effort of the late eighteenth century. His depictions of the conditions struck a responsive chord among reformers on both sides of the Atlantic.

unsentimental, factual account of his observations of the prisons that he visited. He found the conditions to be horrible, and he was particularly concerned about the lack of discipline. The book aroused the interest of certain members of Parliament, who sought passage of the Penitentiary Act of 1779. The act called for the creation of a house of hard labor in which people convicted of crimes would be imprisoned for up to two years. The institution would be based on four principles set down by Howard: (1) a secure and sanitary structure, (2) systematic inspection, (3) the abolition of fees, and (4) a reformatory regime. During the night prisoners were to be confined to solitary cells, and during the day they were to labor silently in common rooms. The regimen was to be strict and ordered. Perhaps influenced by his Quaker friends, Howard believed that the new institution should be not merely a place of industry but also one for contrition and penance. The purpose of the penitentiary was to punish and to reform.

Howard saw the legislation passed but not implemented. The war in the American colonies diverted English public attention, and the resources to carry out the changes were not appropriated. It was not until 1842, with the opening of Pentonville in North London, that Howard's plan came to fruition. Meanwhile, however, his conception of the penitentiary had traveled across the Atlantic and was planted in the more fertile soil of Pennsylvania and New York, where it blossomed.

Reform in the United States

During the first fifty years after the birth of the American republic, a revolution occurred in the conception of criminal punishment. Part of the impetus for change came from the postrevolutionary patriotic fervor that blamed recidivism and criminal behavior on English laws. Still more, however, the new correctional philosophy coincided with

The idea of the penitentiary was first tested in Philadelphia's Walnut Street Jail, where a section was set aside to house offenders in isolation from each other and the outside world.

ideals found in the Declaration of Independence, with its optimistic view of human nature and its implied belief in each person's perfectibility. Accordingly, social progress was seen to be possible through reforms carried out according to the dictates of "pure reason." Emphasis shifted from the assumption that deviance was part of human nature to a belief that crime was a result of forces operating in the environment. If the humane and optimistic ideals of the new nation were to mean anything, it must include reformation of the criminal.

In the first decades of the nineteenth century the creation of penitentiaries in Pennsylvania and New York attracted the attention of legislators in other states and also investigators from Europe. In 1831 France sent Alexis de Tocqueville and Gustave Auguste de Beaumont, England sent William Crawford, and Prussia dispatched Nicholas Julius. Travelers from abroad with no special interest in penology made it a point to include a penitentiary on their itinerary, much as they planned visits to a southern plantation, a textile mill, or a town on the frontier. The U.S. penitentiary had indeed become world famous by the middle of the century.

The Pennsylvania System

Reform of the penal structure became the goal of a number of humanist groups in the United States. The first of these groups was the Philadelphia Society for Alleviating the Miseries of Public Prisons, formed in 1787. Under the leadership of Dr. Benjamin Rush, this group, which included a large number of Quakers, urged replacement of capital and corporal (bodily) punishment by incarceration. The Quakers believed that criminals could best be reformed if they were placed in solitary confinement so that, alone in their cells, they could consider their deviant acts, repent, and reform themselves. The word *penitentiary* is rooted in the Quaker idea that criminals need an opportunity for penitence (sorrow and shame for their wrongs) and repentance (willingness to change their ways).

BIOGRAPHY

Benjamin Rush

Benjamin Rush (1745–1813), physician, patriot, signer of the Declaration of Independence, and social reformer, was born in Pennsylvania and began practicing medicine in Philadelphia in 1769. Although widely recognized for his work in medicine, particularly his insistence on the importance of personal hygiene, Rush was also a humanitarian. He helped organize the Pennsylvania Society for the Abolition of Slavery and served as surgeon general under Washington during the Revolutionary War.

Following his military career, Rush became active in various reform movements, especially those dealing with treatment of the mentally ill and with prisoners. His interest in methods then being used to punish criminals led him to protest laws assigning such punishments as shaved heads, whippings, and other public displays. In *An Enquiry into the Effects of Public Punishment upon Criminals* (1787) he maintained that such excesses served only to harden criminals. Opposed to capital punishment, he wrote *On Punishing Murder by Death* (1792), condemning the practice as an offspring of monarchical divine right, a principle contrary to a republican form of government. He is probably best known for advocating the penitentiary as a replacement for capital and corporal punishment.

In a series of legislative acts in 1790, Pennsylvania provided for the solitary confinement of "hardened and atrocious offenders" in the existing three-story, stone Walnut Street Jail in Philadelphia. This plain building, forty feet by twenty-five feet, housed eight cells on each floor, and there was an attached yard. Each cell was small and dark (only six feet by eight feet, and nine feet high). Inmates were alone in their cells, and from a small, grated window high on the outside wall they "could perceive neither heaven nor earth." No communications of any kind were allowed. It was from this limited beginning that the Pennsylvania system of **separate confinement** evolved. In accordance with this approach, each inmate was held in isolation from other inmates. It was believed that only under such conditions could true rehabilitation occur.

Pressed by the Philadelphia Society, the legislature was persuaded to build additional institutions: Western Penitentiary on the outskirts of Pittsburgh and Eastern Penitentiary near Philadelphia. The opening of Eastern in 1829 marked the culmination of forty-two years of reform activity by the Philadelphia Society. On October 25, 1829, the first prisoner arrived. Charles Williams, eighteen years old and sentenced to a two-year term for larceny, was assigned to a cell twelve by eight by ten feet that had an individual exercise yard some eighteen feet long. Designed according to the system, the prison isolated inmates not only from the community but also from one another. In each cell was a fold-up steel bedstead, a simple toilet, a wooden stool, a workbench, and eating utensils. Light came from an eight-inch window in the ceiling. Solitary labor, Bible reading, and reflection were the keys to the moral rehabilitation that was supposed to occur within the prison walls. Although the cell was larger than most in use today, it was the only world the prisoner would see for the duration of the sentence. The only other human voice the prisoner heard would be that of a clergyman who would visit on Sundays. Nothing was to distract the penitent prisoner from the path toward reform.

As described by Robert Vaux, one of the original Philadelphia reformers, the Pennsylvania system was based on the following principles: (1) prisoners should be treated not vengefully but in ways to convince them that through hard and selective forms of suffering they could change their lives; (2) to prevent the prison from being a corruptive influence, solitary confinement of all inmates should be practiced; (3) in seclusion offenders have an opportunity to reflect on their transgressions so that they may repent; (4) solitary confinement is a punishing discipline because humans are by nature social animals; (5) solitary confinement is economical, because prisoners do not need long periods of time to acquire the penitential experience, fewer keepers are needed, and the costs of clothing are reduced.[5]

Unfortunately for Vaux and the Quakers, their ideals were short-lived. The Walnut Street Jail became overcrowded as more and more offenders were held for longer periods of time. It turned into a warehouse of humanity dominated by Philadelphia politicians, who took over its operation. The Western Penitentiary (near Pittsburgh) was soon declared outmoded because isolation was not complete and the cells were too small for solitary labor. Like the other institutions, it became overcrowded and was recommended for demolition in 1833.

separate confinement: A penitentiary system, developed in Pennsylvania, in which each inmate was held in isolation from other inmates. All activities, including craft work, were carried on in the cells.

■

The Auburn system featured congregate labor during the day but isolation at night. It was favored by most states over the harsher Pennsylvania system.

The Auburn System

In 1819 the Auburn system of New York evolved as a rival to Pennsylvania's. The use of incarceration was not questioned, only the regimen to which the prisoners were to be exposed. Under the Auburn system, prisoners were kept in individual cells at night but congregated in workshops during the day. In this **congregate system,** however, inmates were forbidden to talk to one another or even to exchange glances while on the job or at meals. One of the advantages of the Auburn system was that it cost less because one guard could supervise an entire group of prisoners. In addition, Auburn reflected some of the growing emphases of the Industrial Revolution. The men were to have the benefits of labor as well as meditation. They were to live under tight control, on a simple diet, and according to an undeviating routine, but they would work to pay for a portion of their keep.

congregate system: A penitentiary system, developed in Auburn, New York, in which each inmate was held in isolation during the night but worked with fellow prisoners during the day under a rule of silence.

American reformers saw the Auburn approach as a great advance in penology, and it was copied throughout the land. At an 1826 meeting of prison reformers in Boston, the Auburn system was described in glowing terms:

> At Auburn, we have a more beautiful example still, of what may be done by proper discipline, in a Prison well constructed. . . . The unremitted industry, the entire subordination, and subdued feeling among the convicts, has probably no parallel among any equal number of convicts. In their solitary cells, they spend the night with no other book than the Bible, and at sunrise they proceed in military order, under the eye of the turnkey in solid columns, with the lock march to the workshops.[6]

During this period of reform, advocates of both the Pennsylvania and Auburn plans debated on public platforms and in the nation's periodicals. Although the two approaches seem similar in retrospect, an extraordinary amount of intellectual and emotional energy was spent on the arguments. Often the two systems have been contrasted by noting that the Quaker method aimed to produce honest persons, whereas the New York system sought to mold obedient citizens. Advocates of both systems agreed that the prisoner must be isolated from society and placed on a disciplined routine. They believed that deviancy was a result of corruption pervading the community and that such institutions as the family and the church were not providing a counterbalance. Only when offenders were removed from these temptations and subjected to a steady and regular regimen could they become useful citizens. The convicts were not inherently depraved but, rather, the victims of a society that had not protected them from vice. As the word *penitentiary* connotes, while offenders were being punished, they would become penitent, see the error of their ways, and want to place themselves on the right path.

The Cincinnati Declaration

By the middle of the nineteenth century, reformers had become disillusioned with the results of the penitentiary movement. Deterrence and rehabilitation had been achieved in neither the Auburn nor the Pennsylvania system nor in their copies. The failure of the penitentiaries, however, was seen as a problem of poor administration rather than as an indictment of the concept of incarcerative penalties. Within forty years of their advocates' optimistic proclamations, penitentiaries had become overcrowded, understaffed, and minimally financed. Discipline had become lax, administrators were viewed as corrupt, and the institutions had become places of brutality. At Sing Sing penitentiary in Ossining, New York, in 1870, for example, investigators discovered "that dealers were publicly supplying prisoners with almost anything they would pay for" and that convicts were "playing all sorts of games, reading, scheming, trafficking."[7]

In 1870 the newly formed National Prison Association, meeting in Cincinnati, issued a Declaration of Principles, which sounded the trumpet for a new round of penal reform. Although proponents of the Pennsylvania system continued to condemn congregate prisons and looked with suspicion on the advocates of a new order, they were outnumbered by such progressive penologists as Franklin Sanborn, Enoch Wines, and Zebulon Brockway. The association advocated a new design for **penology.** The goal should be the treatment of criminals through their moral regeneration: the reformation of criminals, "not the infliction of vindictive suffering." To achieve this goal, corrections should provide for progressive classification of prisoners, the indeterminate sentence, and the development of the inmate's self-respect. Penitentiary practices as developed during the first half of the nineteenth century—the fixed sentence, lockstep, rules of silence, and isolation—were now seen as debasing, humiliating, and destructive of initiative.

penology: A branch of criminology dealing with the management of prisons and treatment of offenders.

The Declaration of Principles asserted that prisons should be operated in accordance with a philosophy of inmate change that would reward reformation with release. Peremptory sentences should be replaced by sentences of indeterminate length, and proof of reformation should replace the "mere lapse of time" in bringing about the prisoner's freedom. This reformation program should be encouraged through a progressive classification of prisoners based on character and improvement. But in this connection it should be remembered that, like the Quakers, these progressive reformers looked to institutional life as the way to effect rehabilitation. Inmates should be made into well-adjusted citizens, but the process should be done behind walls. The declaration could thus in good faith insist: "Reformation is a work of time; and a benevolent regard to the good of the criminal himself, as well as to the protection of society, requires that his sentence be long enough for reformatory processes to take effect."[8]

Elmira Reformatory

The new progressive approach, which had an early advocate in Zebulon Brockway, a career prison administrator, took shape at Elmira, New York, in 1876. According to Brockway, the key to reform and rehabilitation lay in education:

> The effect of education is reformatory, for it tends to dissipate poverty by imparting intelligence sufficient to conduct ordinary affairs, and puts into the mind, necessarily, habits of punctuality, method and perseverance. . . . If culture, then, has a refining influence, it is only necessary to carry it far enough, in combination always with due religious agencies, to cultivate the criminal out of his criminality, and to constitute him a reformed man.[9]

Brockway's approach at Elmira Reformatory was supported by legislation passed by New York providing for indeterminate sentences, permitting the reformatory to release inmates on parole when their reform had been assured. At Elmira, attempts were made to create a schoollike atmosphere, with courses in both academic and moral subjects. Inmates who performed well in the courses and who lived according to the reformatory discipline were placed in separate categories so that they could progress to a point where they were eligible for parole. Poor grades and misconduct extended the inmates'

BIOGRAPHY

Zebulon Brockway

Zebulon Brockway of Connecticut began his distinguished career in penology at the age of twenty-one as a clerk at the Wethersfield Prison. In 1852 he became superintendent of the Albany Municipal and County Almshouse, where he founded the first county hospital for the insane. In 1854, at the age of twenty-seven, he became superintendent of the Monroe County Penitentiary in Rochester, New York, where he began to experiment with ideas on making prisons more humane and rehabilitative. Believing that his energies should be devoted to youthful offenders, who offered the greatest possibility for reformation, Brockway moved to Detroit in 1861 to head the Michigan House of Correction, an institution for young men between the ages of sixteen and twenty-one.

Brockway welcomed the opportunity to put his theories into practice as superintendent of Elmira State Reformatory, New York, in 1876. In the following twenty-five years he made it a model for other institutions through the development of educational instruction and training for trades. He persuaded the New York Legislature to enact indeterminate sentences and ran Elmira on a graded system that rewarded inmates for their progress. He believed that incarceration had one purpose—to protect society against crime—and that reform of the criminal should be the ultimate goal.

Brockway retired from Elmira in 1900 and served in a variety of public and charitable offices for the next twenty years. He was a charter member of the National Prison Association (predecessor of the American Correctional Association) and was its president in 1898. His autobiography, *Fifty Years of Prison Service*, was published in 1912.

tenure. Society could reform criminals, Enoch Wines said, only "by placing the prisoner's fate, as far as possible, in his own hands, by enabling him, through industry and good conduct, to raise himself, step by step, to a position of less restraint; while idleness and bad conduct, on the other hand, keep him in a state of coercion and restraint."[10]

By 1900 the reformatory movement had spread throughout the nation, but by World War I it was already in decline. In most institutions the architecture, attitudes of the guards, and emphasis on discipline differed little from orientations of the past. Too often the educational and rehabilitative efforts took a back seat to the traditional punitive emphasis. Even Brockway admitted difficulty in distinguishing between inmates whose attitudes had changed and those who superficially conformed to prison rules. Being a good prisoner, the traditional emphasis, became the way to win parole in most of these institutions.

Reforms of the Progressives

The first two decades of the twentieth century were also a period of reform as social and political thought confronted such modern developments as industrialization, urbanization, and the advancement of science. This was the era of the Progressives, who attacked the excesses of urban society, in particular those of big business, and advocated state action to deal with the social problems of slums, vice, and crime. They believed that civic-minded people could apply the findings of science to social problems in ways that would be of benefit to all. Application of the concepts of the social and behavioral sciences, rather than religious or moral precepts, was believed to be the means by which criminals could be rehabilitated.

The new activists relied on the developments of modern criminology associated with a scientific approach to crime and human behavior known as the positivist school, which focused on the behavior of the offender.

Armed with this positivist view of criminal behavior and faith in the efficacy of state action to reform offenders, the Progressives fought for changes in correctional methods. Their efforts centered on two strategies: one designed to improve conditions in the environments they believed to be breeding grounds of crime, the other emphasizing ways to rehabilitate the individual deviant. The presentence report, with its extensive personal history, would enable judges and correctional officials to analyze the individual's problem and to take action toward rehabilitation. By the 1920s, probation, indeterminate sentence and parole, and treatment programs were being espoused by reform penologists as the instruments of this more scientific approach to criminality.

Although the Progressives were instrumental in advancing the new penology, it was not until the 1930s that attempts were made to implement fully what became known as the rehabilitation model of corrections. Then penologists, operating under the banner of the newly prestigious social and behaviorial sciences, helped shift the emphasis of the postconviction sanction to treatment of criminals, whose social, intellectual, or biological deficiencies were seen as the causes of their illegal activities. With the essential structural elements of parole, probation, and the indeterminate sentence already in place in most states, incorporation of the rehabilitation model required only the addition of classification systems to diagnose offenders and treatment programs that would rehabilitate them. Advocates of this approach held that the goal of rehabilitation could be achieved by using modern scientific theories of criminality. Because they likened the new correctional methods to those used by physicians in hospitals, this approach was often referred to as the medical model. Under this approach, correctional institutions were to be staffed with persons who could diagnose the causes of an individual's criminal behavior, prescribe a treatment program, and determine when a cure had been effected so that the offender could be released to the community.

Following World War II rehabilitation won new adherents. Group therapy, behavior modification, counseling, and numerous other approaches all became part of the "new penology." Yet even during the 1950s, when the medical model was at its zenith, only a small proportion of state correctional budgets was allocated for rehabilitation. What frustrated many persons committed to treatment was that although states adopted the rhetoric of the rehabilitation model, the institutions were still being run with custody as an overriding goal. The failure of these new techniques to stem crime, the changes in the characteristics of the prison population, and the misuse of the discretion required by the model prompted another cycle of correctional reform, so that by 1970 rehabilitation as a goal had become discredited.

Community Model

As we have seen, correctional goals and methods have been greatly influenced by the social and political values of particular periods. During the 1960s and early 1970s U.S. society experienced the civil rights movement, the war on poverty, and resistance to the war in Vietnam. It was a time in which the traditional ways of government were challenged. In 1967 the President's Commission on Law Enforcement and Administration of Justice reported that

> crime and delinquency are symptoms of failures and disorganization of the community. . . . The task of corrections, therefore, includes building or rebuilding social ties, obtaining employment and education, securing in the larger sense a place for the offender in the routine functioning of society.[11]

community corrections: A model of corrections based on the assumption that the reintegration of the offender into the community should be the goal of the criminal justice system.

Community corrections was based on the assumption that the reintegration of the offender into the community should be the goal of the criminal justice system.

Proponents of the community model pointed to the need for the rehabilitation of offenders but said that it should occur in the community, not in prisons. Prisons were viewed as artificial institutions that interfered with the offender's ability to develop a crime-free lifestyle. It was argued that corrections should turn away from an emphasis on psychological treatment to programs that would increase the opportunities for offenders to be successful citizens. Imprisonment was to be avoided, if possible, in favor of probation, so that offenders could engage in vocational and educational programs that would increase their chances of adjusting to community life. For the small proportion of offenders who had to be incarcerated, the amount of time in prison should be only a short interval until release on parole. To further the goal of reintegration, correctional workers were to serve as advocates for offenders as they dealt with governmental agencies providing employment counseling, medical treatment, and financial assistance. This swing was, however, shortlived. By the middle of the 1970s the reform movement seemed so dispirited that many penologists threw up their hands in despair.

Corrections in the 1990s

As the political climate changed in the seventies and eighties, legislators, judges, and corrections officials responded with a new emphasis on incarceration as a way to solve the crime problem. Attacks were mounted against such structures of rehabilitation as indeterminate sentences, treatment programs, and discretionary release on parole. It was argued that treatment should be available only on a voluntary basis and that longer sentences should be imposed, especially on career criminals and those who had committed violent crimes.

The doubling of the probation and prison populations during the 1980s put such great pressure on correctional approaches that most states found they were only able to provide minimal services. Probation departments shifted to an emphasis on risk assessment as a means of supervising those offenders with the greatest propensity to recidivate. Officials supervising jammed correctional institutions had to deemphasize treatment programs because of space and fiscal limitations. Prison crowding necessitated a greater emphasis on custody goals and the provision of a secure environment.

To a great extent corrections in the 1990s will be driven by the war on drugs. As greater police resources are allocated to the arrest of drug dealers and as the courts respond with stiffer penalties for those offenders, corrections will reap a bumper harvest of probation and prison populations.

In a recent sudy of twelve states, the National Council on Crime and Delinquency (NCCD) estimated that the prison population will expand by 68 percent in five years, twice that projected in 1988.[12] Figure 14.1 shows the increase in drug offense prison admissions in selected states. With incarceration being the sentence of choice for most drug violations, the NCCD expects that most of the prison increase can be accounted for by this focus. In addition they expect that there will be a great increase in the number of offenders returned to prison for drug-related parole violations. During the 1980s those sentenced for drug offenses comprised about 10 percent of the inmate population in most states. They now represent about 35 percent in most prisons, and the percentage is rising. The NCCD also projects that the war on drugs will increase the proportion of African-

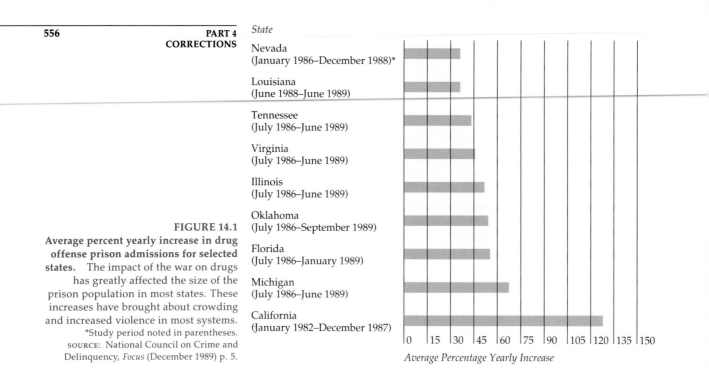

FIGURE 14.1

Average percent yearly increase in drug offense prison admissions for selected states. The impact of the war on drugs has greatly affected the size of the prison population in most states. These increases have brought about crowding and increased violence in most systems. *Study period noted in parentheses. SOURCE: National Council on Crime and Delinquency, *Focus* (December 1989) p. 5.

American and Hispanic-American offenders and offenders with AIDS. Because of new sentencing laws and the fact that drug users and traffickers persist in their criminal behavior longer than other offenders, there will be an increase in the number of inmates over fifty years of age.

Extensive prison construction and the expansion of probation resources are now taking a greater and greater portion of state budgets. In some states more money is going to corrections than to higher education. At some point the public may begin to question these expenditures, especially if there does not appear to be any reduction in criminality. At that point one may expect a different swing of the correctional pendulum.

ORGANIZATION OF CORRECTIONS IN THE UNITED STATES

Although we tend to think of corrections with reference to institutions of incarceration, only about a quarter of the persons under correctional supervision live in institutions. Persons under probationary supervision constitute more than twice the population maintained in prisons and jails (see Figure 14.2).

As we shall see, corrections includes a great variety of programs and facilities. In this chapter and the next, the focus is on institutions and programs of incarceration. Community corrections including programs of probation, work and educational release, and parole supervision, are discussed in Chapter 16.

The administration of corrections is fragmented in that various levels of government are involved. The federal government, the fifty states, the District of Columbia, the 3,047 counties, and most cities each have at least one facility and many programs. The scope of the

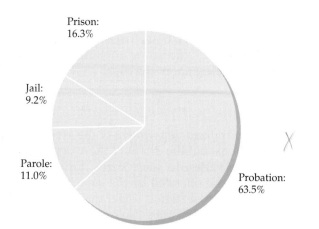

Prison:
16.3%

Jail:
9.2%

Parole:
11.0%

Probation:
63.5%

FIGURE 14.2
Percentage of persons under
correctional supervision in all
categories of supervision.   Although
most people think of corrections as
prisons and jails, in fact almost three-
quarters of offenders are being
supervised in the community.
SOURCE: U.S. Department of Justice, Bureau
of Justice Statistics, *Bulletin* (November 1989).

criminal laws of the national government is less broad than that of
the laws of the states; as a result, only about 100,000 adults are under
federal correctional supervision. State and local governments pay
about 95 percent of the cost of all correctional activities in the nation.[13] Jails are operated mainly by local governments (usually sheriff's departments), but in six states they are integrated with the state
prison system. Most correctional activities are part of the executive
branch of government, but most probation offices are attached to the
judiciary and are paid for by county government.

Each level of government has some responsibility for corrections,
and often one level exercises little supervision over another. The federal government has no formal control over corrections in the states.
In most areas, maintaining prisons and parole is the responsibility of
the state, while counties have some misdemeanant jails but no authority over the short-term jails operated by towns and cities. In
addition, there is a division between juvenile and adult corrections.
The fragmentation of corrections reminds us that within the physical
boundaries of a state there are many correctional systems, each with
its own special orientation.

The Federal Correctional System

The U.S. Bureau of Prisons was created by Congress in 1930. Before
that time, the administrators of the seven federal prisons then in
operation functioned with relative freedom from control. Since 1930
the Bureau of Prisons has grown until it operates an integrated system of prisons containing over 50,000 inmates. Facilities and inmates
are classified in a security-level system ranging from Level 1 (the least
secure, camp-type settings) through Level 6 (the U.S. Penitentiary,
Marion, Illinois). Between these extremes are Levels 2 through 5
federal correctional institutions—other U.S. penitentiaries, administrative institutions, medical facilities, and several other specialized
institutions for women or juveniles. Because of the nature of federal
criminal law, prisoners in most of these facilities are quite different
from those in state institutions. In general, the population contains
more inmates who have been convicted of white-collar crimes, although drug offenders are increasing. There are fewer who have committed crimes of violence than are found in most state institutions.

Probation and parole supervision for U.S. offenders are provided by the Division of Probation, a branch of the Administrative Office of the United States Courts. Officers are appointed by the federal judiciary and serve at the pleasure of the court.

State Corrections

Every state has a centralized department of the executive branch that administers corrections, but the extent of these departments' responsibility for programs varies. In some states, for example, probation and parole programs are operated by the department of corrections, whereas in other states probation is under the judiciary, and parole is handled separately. Wide variation also exists in the way correctional responsibilities are divided between the state and local governments. The differences can be seen in the proportion of correctional employees who work for the state. In Connecticut, Rhode Island, and Vermont, for example, the proportion is 100 percent, whereas in California it is only 47 percent.

State correctional institutions for adult felons include a great range of facilities and programs, including prisons, reformatories, industrial institutions, prison farms, conservation campuses, forestry campuses, and halfway houses. Despite this variety, most state prisons are generally old and large. Over half of the nation's inmates are in institutions with average daily populations of more than 1,000, and about 35 percent are in prisons built more than fifty years ago. Some states have created facilities that are small and are designed to meet individual correctional needs, but most inmates are in very large "megaprisons" that are antiquated and have many of the maintenance and operational deficiencies associated with other old, intensively used buildings.

Correctional institutions are classified according to the level of security they afford, and the type of population shifts according to the special needs of the offenders. The security level is easily recognized by the physical characteristics of the buildings: the massive stone walls of maximum security prisons are topped by barbed wire and strategically placed guard towers; minimum security institutions are often indistinguishable from college campuses or apartment complexes.

The maximum security prison (44 percent of state inmates): Built like a fortress, surrounded by stone walls with guard towers, the maximum security prison is designed to prevent escape. Inmates live in cells that have plumbing and sanitary facilities. The barred doors may be operated electronically so that an officer can confine all prisoners to their cells with the flick of a switch. The purpose of the maximum security facility is custody and discipline; there is a military-style approach to order. Prisoners wear uniforms, march to meals and work, and follow a strict routine. Some of the most famous prisons, such as Stateville, Attica, Yuma, and Sing Sing, are maximum security facilities.

The medium security prison (44 percent of state inmates): Although in appearance it resembles the maximum security prison, this prison is organized on a somewhat different basis, with the result that its atmosphere is less rigid and tense. Prisoners have more privileges, and contact with the outside world through visitors, mail, and access to radio and television is freer. One can expect to find a greater emphasis on rehabilitative programs in the medium security prison because, although in most states the inmates of this type of facility have probably committed serious crimes, they are not perceived to be hardened criminals.

The minimum security prison (12 percent of state inmates): Housing the least violent offenders, principally white-collar criminals, the minimum security prison does not have the guard towers and walls usually associated with correctional institutions. Often the buildings are surrounded by Cyclone fencing. Prisoners usually live dormitory style or even in small private rooms rather than barred cells. There is a relatively high level of personal freedom: inmates may have television sets, choose their own clothes, and move about casually within the buildings. Particular reliance is placed on treatment programs, and there are opportunities for education and for work release. Although outsiders may sometimes feel that little punishment is associated with the minimum security facility, it is still a prison; restrictions are placed on inmates, and they remain segregated from society.

Jails: Local Correctional Facilities

The U.S. jail has been called the "poorhouse of the twentieth century."[14] It is a strange correctional hybrid: part detention center for people awaiting trial, part penal institution for sentenced misdemeanants, and part holding facility for social misfits of one kind or another taken off the street. Although there has been much emphasis on the importance of correctional facilities and programs located in the community to serve those who do not require long-term incarceration, local jails and short-term institutions in the United States are generally held to be poorly managed custodial institutions.

There are approximately 3,500 locally administered jails in the United States with the authority to detain individuals for more than forty-eight hours. The hundred largest hold 40 percent of the nation's jailed inmates. Most jails are much smaller—63 percent hold fewer than fifty persons—and they are becoming less numerous because of new construction and the creation of regional multicounty facilities.

The most recent census of the jail population found 395,553 inmates (148 inmates per 100,000 residents), a 61 percent increase in five years. The characteristics of these inmates are shown in Figure 14.3. But the number of persons held at any one time in jail does not tell the complete story. Many people are held for less than twenty-four hours, others may reside in jail as sentenced inmates for up to one year, a few may await their trial for more than a year. In fact, the turnover rate is so great that almost 19 million Americans experience jail in one year. More citizens see the insides of jails than see the insides of prisons, mental hospitals, and halfway houses combined.[15]

Jails are usually locally administered by elected officials (sheriffs or county administrators). Only in Alaska, Connecticut, Delaware, Hawaii, Rhode Island, and Vermont are they run by the state government. Traditionally jails have been run by law enforcement agencies, though about half of the inmates are sentenced offenders under correctional authority. It seems reasonable that the agency that arrests and transports defendants to court should also administer the facility

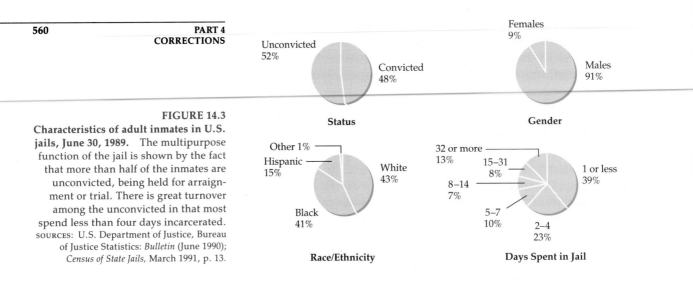

FIGURE 14.3
Characteristics of adult inmates in U.S. jails, June 30, 1989.   The multipurpose function of the jail is shown by the fact that more than half of the inmates are unconvicted, being held for arraignment or trial. There is great turnover among the unconvicted in that most spend less than four days incarcerated.
SOURCES: U.S. Department of Justice, Bureau of Justice Statistics: *Bulletin* (June 1990); *Census of State Jails,* March 1991, p. 13.

that holds them, but generally neither sheriffs nor their deputies have much interest in corrections. They think of themselves as police officers and of the jail as merely an extension of law enforcement activities. Remember, though, that about half of the inmates are sentenced offenders under correctional authority.

Function

The primary function of jails is to hold persons awaiting trial and persons who have been sentenced as misdemeanants to terms of no more than one year. But this figure is deceptive since on a national basis about 50 percent of jail inmates are pretrial detainees. In some states, convicted felons may serve terms of more than one year in jail rather than in prison. But for a high proportion (87 percent) of the sentenced population, stays in jail are less than one month.

Increasingly, jails are housing sentenced felony offenders for whom space is lacking at the state prison. Others held in jail are persons awaiting transportation to prison, persons convicted of parole or probation violations. This backup in the flow has caused difficulties for judges and jail administrators, who must often put misdemeanants on probation for lack of jail space.

Jails and police lockups shoulder responsibility for housing not only criminal defendants and offenders but also those persons viewed as problems by society. Here we can see how the criminal justice system is linked to other agencies of government. The deinstitutionalization of mental patients in particular has shifted a new population to criminal justice. Many such people are unable to cope with urban living and come to the attention of the police through reports of deviant behavior (urinating in public, appearing disoriented, shouting obscenities, and so on) that although not illegal, is upsetting to the citizenry. The police must handle such situations, and temporary confinement in the lockup or jail may be necessary if no appropriate social service facilities are immediately available. In Denver, for example, the situation has been described as a revolving door that shifts these "street people" from the police station to the wing of the jail designated for psychiatric cases, often to court, and then back to the street.

The national concern about drunk driving has also placed an additional burden on jails. In response to such groups as MADD (Mothers Against Drunk Driving), legislators have passed mandatory jail sentences for persons convicted of driving while intoxicated. These campaigns cause the police to devote additional resources to catching drunk drivers, the courts become overloaded, with the result that the jail is often inundated with offenders. Such campaigns can bring the local jail to the point of organizational breakdown.

Because of the great turnover and because local control provides an incentive to keep costs down, correctional services are usually lacking. Recreational facilities and treatment programs are not found in most jails. Medical services are generally minimal. Such conditions add to the idleness, tensions, and pangs of incarceration. High levels of violence and suicides are a hallmark of many jails. In any one year almost half of the number of persons who die while in jail have committed suicide.

The mixture of offenders of widely diverse ages and criminal histories is another often-cited problem in U.S. jails. Because most inmates are viewed as temporary residents, little attempt is made to classify them for either security or treatment purposes. Horror stories of the mistreatment of young offenders by older, stronger, and more violent inmates occasionally come to public attention. The physical condition of most jails aggravates this situation, because most are old, overcrowded, and often lacking in basic facilities. Many sentenced felons are pleased to move on to state prison in which the conditions are likely to be better.

As criminal justice policy has become more punitive, jails, like prisons, have become crowded. Surveys have documented annual increases averaging 10 percent during the past five years. Even with new construction, release on recognizance programs, diversion, intensive probation supervision, and house arrest with electronic monitoring, the jail population continues to rise. With the cost of building new facilities as high as $100,000 per cell and the cost of incarcerating an inmate about $12,000 per year, the $4.5 billion cost of operating jails places a great financial burden on local governments.

Jails hold a variety of individuals, both pretrial and sentenced misdemeanants. In most states jails are administered by county sheriffs. Many are overcrowded and poorly maintained.

Institutions for Women

Because so few women are sent to prison, the number and adequacy of facilities for them are limited. Although the ratio of arrests is approximately six men to one woman, the ratio of admissions to state and federal correctional institutions is twenty-one men to one woman. Of inmates in state and federal prisons, 5 percent are women. The proportion is low, but the number of women in prison is

---

CLOSE-UP *Specific Strategies for Reducing Jail Populations*

Reducing Bookings

Diversion for alcoholics: To keep the jail from being an expensive drunk tank, communities must do more than merely decriminalize public drunkenness, which most states have already done. The community must provide detoxification centers . . . designed to meet the needs of police and health officials as well as alcoholics. A study of two cities in Kentucky showed that Lexington had a jail population two and a half times larger than Louisville's because Louisville used a diversion program for alcoholics, whereas Lexington did not.

Taking Care of the Mentally Ill

Community mental health centers can provide support to keep people from getting into trouble in the first place and can be a refuge for those picked up on nuisance charges or for minor crimes. Many of these are people who have been released from mental hospitals but not given outpatient treatment. In Galveston, Texas, specially trained deputies identify mental health arrestees and divert them to special facilities.

Keeping Juveniles Out of Jail

Juveniles end up in jail not because authorities think they belong there but because there is nowhere else to put them. Even for communities without separate juvenile institutions, there are many options. . . . Police can find beds for runaway or troubled youths in hospitals, nursing homes, or mental health facilities. Foster families can be trained to take in juveniles on short notice. Using a network of these and other resources, Pennsylvania has kept all juveniles out of adult facilities since 1980.

Citation Release

For those charged with misdemeanors, there is often no need to book into jail at all; a police officer can issue a summons or citation. The pioneer project in this area, the Manhattan Summons Project . . . saved $6.7 million in police time in its first four years and had a low failure-to-appear rate of 5 percent.

Getting Inmates Out of Jail Quickly

Release on recognizance: Known as ROR, this system . . . uses a point scale that counts ties to the community, including job, family, and length of residence, to determine which defendants are most likely to show up for trial; they can be released on their own recognizance without posting cash bond. Across the country, 135 formal programs do such screening; in smaller jurisdictions, probation officers often handle it. . . .

Percentage bail: Under this option, a defendant can post 10 percent of the amount of bail with the court rather than with a bail bondsman. If he shows up for trial, he gets most or all of his money back, unlike the fee he pays a bail bondsman. If he does not show up, he owes the other 90 percent, plus he is charged with a separate offense for bail-jumping. Philadelphia estimated that it saved $1 million a year and reduced its jail population 29 percent using this system.

Conditional release: For those who cannot be released on their own recognizance but do not present a major threat to the community, judges can impose special conditions, such as requiring that the defendant attend a drug treatment program or call the probation office every day.

Speeding up the courts: By introducing measures to reduce court delays, Providence, Rhode Island, was able to reduce the median time a case was in court from 277 days to 61 days. These measures included bringing in extra judges to clear up a backlog, enforcing strict time limits, and introducing new management practices. . . .

Warrants and detainers: Many jurisdictions automatically keep people in jail even on petty charges if they have a warrant lodged against them. Investigating these warrants and discriminating between types of warrants can speed releases from jail.

Programs for sentenced inmates: Alternative programs such as restitution, community service, intensive probation, work-release, and halfway houses can be run on a county level. These programs keep convicted petty offenders from taking up jail space for months on minor charges.

SOURCE: Adapted from *Time to Build?*, pp. 40–41. Copyright © 1984 by Edna McConnell Clark Foundation. Reprinted by permission.

increasing annually at a rate of about 12 percent; the growth of the male correctional population is about 7 percent annually.[16]

Until the beginning of the nineteenth century, women offenders in Europe and North America were treated no differently than men offenders and were not separated from men when they were incarcerated. Only with John Howard's exposé of prison conditions in England in 1777 and development of the penitentiary in Philadelphia did attention begin to focus on the plight of the woman offender. Elizabeth Gurney Fry, a middle-class English Quaker, was the first person to press for changes. When she and fellow Quakers visited London's Newgate Prison in 1813, they were shocked by the conditions in which the female prisoners and their children were living. She agitated for separate facilities for women, staffed by women and with a domestic atmosphere. In 1818 a parliamentary committee heard the evidence that she had gathered, and reforms were ordered.

News of Fry's efforts spread to the United States, and the Women's Prison Association was formed in New York in 1844. Its goal was to improve the treatment of female prisoners and to separate them from men. It was not until 1873 that the first U.S. prison intended exclusively for women was built in Indiana. Within fifty years thirteen other states had followed this lead. There are now forty state institutions for women and two federal institutions. In some states with no separate facilities for women, women offenders are assigned to a section of the state prison for men; other women offenders are housed in neighboring states by intergovernmental contract.

Conditions in correctional facilities for women are more pleasant than those of similar institutions for men. Usually the buildings are attractive, without gun towers and barbed wire. Because of the small population, however, most states have only one facility, and that is located in a rural setting far removed from urban centers. Thus women prisoners may be more isolated than men from their families

BIOGRAPHY

Elizabeth Fry

Born in Norwich, England, Elizabeth Fry was second only to John Howard as a nineteenth-century advocate of prison reform in Europe. She came from an old Quaker family that had long been active in efforts to improve society. Her devotion to her religion was strengthened in 1798 under the fiery influence of the American Quaker William Severy.

Elizabeth Fry devoted much of her life to caring for the poor and neglected, and her most notable work was in prison reform. In April 1817 she helped to organize the Association for the Improvement of Female Prisoners in Newgate, then the major prison in London. The group was made up of the wives of Quaker businessmen who believed that prison to be a "den of wild beasts." Their aim was to establish prison discipline, separation of the sexes, classification of criminals, female supervision for the women inmates, adequate provision for religious and secular instruction, and the useful employment of prisoners. The positive results at Newgate were dramatic.

Largely through the personal effort of Fry, methods similar to those at Newgate were rapidly extended to other prisoners in England and abroad. Publication of the notes that she took while visiting the prisons of Scotland and northern England in 1818 brought her recognition on an international scale. Her *Observations on Visiting, Superintendence, and Government of Female Prisons* (1827) was influential in the movement to reform American prisons for women. She made personal inspection tours of prisons throughout Europe: Ireland in 1827; France and Switzerland in 1838; Belgium, Holland, and Prussia in 1840; and Denmark in 1841. By the time of her death in 1845, her reform approaches had been widely accepted.

and communities. Pressure from the women's movement and the apparent rise in the incidence of crime among women may bring about a greater equality in corrections for men and women. For more information on life in correctional institutions for women, see Chapter 15.

Private Prisons

One response to prison crowding has come from private entrepreneurs who argue that they can build and run prisons at least as effectively, safely, and humanely as any level of government can. Their efficiency, they believe, can lower costs for taxpayers while allowing a profit for themselves. The contracting of correctional services on a piecemeal basis is not new and varies from jurisdiction to jurisdiction; such services as food and medical care, educational and vocational training, maintenance, security, and industrial programs are provided by private businesses. But the idea of running entire institutions for adult felons under private contract is new.

The first privately operated correctional institution was the Intensive Treatment Unit, a twenty-bed, high-security, dormitory-style training school for delinquents opened in 1975 by the RCA Corporation in Weaversville, Pennsylvania. In January 1985 Kentucky's Marion Adjustment Center became the first privately owned and operated (by U.S. Corrections Corporation) facility for the incarceration of adult felons sentenced to a level of at least minimum security. By mid-1989 Logan counted about a dozen companies running about two dozen adult confinement institutions totaling some 7,000 beds in about a dozen states. He notes that it is difficult to be precise in this count since it is not always clear how to classify institutions and because contractual prisons and jails can spring so rapidly into and out of existence.[17] Currently adult confinement institutions under private operation include jails, state and county prisons, prerelease facilities, lockups for parole violators being returned to custody, and detention centers for the U.S. Immigration and Naturalization Service (INS).

The major advantages cited by advocates of privately operated prisons are that such prisons provide more cheaply and flexibly the same level of care provided by the states. Logan's study of private prisons points to the difficulties of measuring the costs and quality of these institutions. One of the problems is that many of the "true costs" (fringe benefits, contracting supervision, federal grants) are not taken into consideration. The quoted rates of existing private facilities range greatly. A report for the National Institute for Corrections, for example, cites a cost of $30 a day at Okeechobee and $110 a day at the Weaversville facility. The INS facilities for illegal aliens operate on average daily rates of $23 to $28.[18] In regard to the issue of care, we have only the evaluation of juvenile justice expert James Finkenauer that the Weaversville facility is "better staffed, organized, and equipped than any program of its size that I know."[19] In regard to flexibility, it is argued that because correctional space requirements rise and fall, private entrepreneurs can provide additional space when it is needed, and their contracts can go unrenewed when space is in oversupply.

■

Corrections Corporation of America is one of several private businesses that contract with government to build and operate prisons. As with this facility in Santa Fe, New Mexico, CCA says that its prisons are better and provide more services at a lower cost than can the states or counties.

A number of political, fiscal, and administrative issues must be considered and resolved before corrections can become too heavily committed to the private ownership and operation of prisons. The political issues, including ethical questions of the propriety of delegating social control functions to persons other than the state, may be the most difficult to overcome. Some people believe that the administration of justice is one of the basic functions of government and that it should not be delegated. There is also concern that correctional policy would be skewed because contractors would use their political influence to continue programs not in the public interest; would press for the maintenance of high occupancy levels, thus widening the net of social control; and would be interested only in skimming off the "cream of the crop," leaving the most troublesome inmates to the public correctional system. Though it is not yet possible to demonstrate the fiscal value of private corrections, labor unions have opposed these incursions into the public sector, pointing out that the salaries, benefits, and pensions of workers in such other spheres as private security are lower than those of their public counterparts. Finally, there are questions about quality of services, accountability of service providers to corrections officials, and problems related to contract supervision. Opponents cite the many instances in which privately contracted services in group homes, day-care centers, hospitals, and schools have been terminated upon reports of corruption, brutality, and provision of only minimal services.

The idea of privately run correctional facilities has stimulated much interest among the general public and within the criminal justice community. There may be further privatization of criminal justice services, or privatization may become only a limited venture that was spawned at a time of prison crowding, fiscal constraints on governments, and revival of the free enterprise ideology. The controversy about privatization has, however, forced corrections to rethink some strongly held beliefs. In this regard the possibility of competition from the private sector may be a positive factor.

PRISON POPULATIONS: TRENDS AND CHARACTERISTICS

For most of the last fifty years the numbers of persons incarcerated in the United States remained fairly stable and the characteristics of those individuals was little changed. During the era of the "big house," the incarceration rate was maintained at about 120 per 100,000 population, and the prisoners were overwhelmingly white, poor, and convicted for nonviolent crimes.

For a brief period in the early 1970s when the trend in correctional circles was to stress deinstitutionalization and community corrections, the incarceration rate actually decreased. By the mid-1970s the size of the prison population started its meteoric climb, and the charactistics of inmates changed, with increased numbers of African-Americans and Hispanics and persons sentenced for violent offenses. By 1990 the American prison was a much changed institution from just two decades before.

Incarceration Trends

Every year on December 31 a census of the U.S. prison population is carried out for the Bureau of Justice Statistics. Every year during the past decade the results of this enumeration have shown new record highs for the number of men and women incarcerated in state and federal prisons. As shown in Figure 14.4, this rise has been dramatic, and no end appears in sight.

In many states the influx of new adult inmates has crowded al-

COMPARATIVE PERSPECTIVE
Corrections in Sweden

The Swedish corrections system is run by an independent agency called *Kriminalvardsstyrelsen*—literally the Criminal Care Administration. Inmates often make fun of this designation. "We are not prisoners, or inmates, or convicts," said one man mockingly. "We are consumers of criminal care." Swedish officials translate the title as the National Correctional Administration. This is the agency responsible for pretrial detention, probation supervision, prisons, and parole supervision.

On a given day, the Correctional Administration is responsible for about 3,000 inmates serving sentences and about 600 awaiting trial. In most countries, a half dozen institutions would be considered more than enough to hold the small number of inmates. But in Sweden

they believe in small institutions; hence the inmates are housed in 103 different facilities. There are 20 national prisons, 57 local, and 26 remand institutions for pretrial detainees. The maximum capacity ranges from 10 to 435, most between 20 to 40, and thus appear to be more akin to halfway houses in the United States. The prisons have a total capacity for 1,700 inmates housed in "open" institutions— without walls or fences—and 2,400 in closed facilities.

Sixty-five percent of Swedish prisoners serve sentences of three months or less; 13 percent, three to six months; 9.5 percent, six to twelve months; 8 percent, twelve to twenty-four months; and only 4 percent, more than two years. But these figures are meaningless when compared with time served in the

United States. The Swedish data include drunk drivers, draft resisters, and other minor offenders who would not be incarcerated in the United States or who would serve time in the county jail. In Sweden there is no distinction between felons and misdemeanants: all enter the same correctional system.

The time served by serious Swedish offenders, however, is indeed shorter than in the United States. Burglars, embezzlers, and others found guilty of "gross theft" serve between six months and three years in prison. The minimum sen-

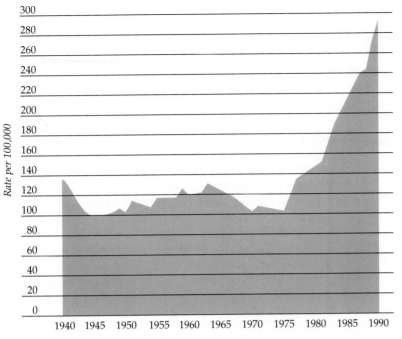

FIGURE 14.4
Incarceration per 100,000 population, 1940–1990. For most of the past fifty years the incarceration rate has been steady. It has only been since 1975 that there has been a continuing increase. Today the incarceration rate is about double what it was in 1980.
SOURCE: U.S. Department of Justice, Bureau of Justice Statistics, *Bulletin* (May 1991, p. 1).

ready bulging institutions; some offenders have had to be held in county jails and temporary quarters while others made do in corridors and basements. Faced with such conditons, courts in a number of states demanded that changes be made because they viewed the overcrowding as a violation of the equal protection and cruel and unusual punishment portions of the Bill of Rights. In most states

tence for most violent crimes is one or two years; the maximum, up to ten. Most murderers get ten years. Some receive life imprisonment but are almost always pardoned after ten to twelve years.

Legislation passed in 1974 puts great emphasis on the reintegration of prisoners into the community. It states that the "natural" form of correctional care is noninstitutional and that every effort should be made to keep offenders out of prison and to maximize contacts with the outside world for those who are incarcerated. To accomplish this goal judges were instructed to make greater use of probation; inmates in local institutions were to be given the right to leave the facility during the day to work, study, and participate in recreation; furlough programs were to be developed; and long-term prisoners not viewed as security risks

were to be given short-term periods of release to study or secure treatment or for other reasons that would facilitate the prisoner's adjustment to society.

These policies have served to place greater emphasis on community corrections, particularly probation and parole. The Correctional Administrator supervises 13,000 offenders on probation and 4,000 on parole. There are 689 probation/parole officers who carry an average caseload of 26. They are assisted by 10,000 "private supervisors"—volunteers who supervise two or three probationers or parolees in their spare time for a nominal salary.

Since the 1930s Sweden has gained the reputation of taking social welfare policies further than any developed nation. The Swedish political ideology emphasizes the similarities among citizens rather than the differences and encour-

ages a sense of collective responsibility that seeks to protect the rights and needs of its weakest members. Governmental policies have been developed to assist these citizens, even those who have broken the law. As Claes Amilon, Deputy Director of the Correctional Association, wrote in a United Nations report: "A society without slums cannot let its prisoners live under slum conditions; a society which has accepted collective responsibility for the physical and economic welfare of its citizens cannot abuse the rights even of those who transgress its laws."

SOURCE: Adapted from "Profile/Sweden," by M. S. Serrill, *Corrections Magazine* 3 (June 1977):11. Reprinted by permission of the author; adapted from "Sweden," by A. Nelson. In G. F. Cole, S. J. Frankowski, and M. G. Gertz (eds.), *Major Criminal Justice Systems*, 2nd Ed., p. 134. Copyright © 1987 by Sage Publications, Inc. Reprinted by permission.

prison construction has become a growth industry, with massive public expenditures for new facilities that immediately become filled when they open.

Why this increase? Several hypotheses have been advanced to explain the surge. These issues are fully explored in Policy Issue number four. Here we will summarize four reasons often given to account for the growth of the American prison population.

Regional Attitudes

Some people point to the high incarceration rates in the states of the "Old Confederacy" to explain the population increase. As Figure 14.5 shows, some of the highest ratios of prisoners to the civilian population are found in these states. In 1990 that region incarcerated at the rate of 315 persons for each 100,000 inhabitants, a ratio higher than the national average of 293. Those favoring these regional perspective point to the high levels of violence in the South, the long sentences provided by the penal codes, and to a long history of racial conflict. It is suggested that black men are prime candidates for incarceration in these states. But as Figure 14.5 reveals, there are exceptions to the regional hypothesis: Alaska, Arizona, Delaware, District of Columbia, Michigan, and Nevada all have incarceration rates above the national average.

Public Attitudes

A second hypothesis is that a hardening of public attitudes toward criminals during the past decade has been reflected in longer sentences, in a smaller proportion of those convicted being granted probation, and in fewer being released at the time of the first parole hearing. As discussed in Chapter 13, some states have passed penal codes that greatly limit the discretion of judges in sentencing offenders who have committed certain types of crimes. In addition, the shift to determinate sentences has removed the safety valve of discretionary parole release, which has been important to corrections administrators when prison populations have risen in the past. Evidence from determinate sentencing states suggests that offenders are now spending more time incarcerated.

Better Police and Prosecution

A third hypothesis is that the billions of dollars spent on the crime problem, especially with regard to the war on drugs, may be paying off. Although crime rates overall have been fairly steady during the last decade, arrest and prosecution rates for drug-related offenses and the violence drugs spawn have gone up. Accordingly, the impact of the success of the police and prosecution is being felt by the corrections subsystem.

Construction

Finally, the increased rate of incarceration may be related to the creation of additional space in the nation's prisons. Again, public atti-

Washington 162
Montana 174
N. Dakota 67
Minnesota 72
Wisconsin 149
Michigan 366
New Hampshire 117
Vermont 117
Maine 118
New York 304
Massachusetts 132
Rhode Island 157
Oregon 221
Idaho 201
S. Dakota 187
Iowa 139
Pennsylvania 183
Connecticut 238
New Jersey 271
Wyoming 237
Nebraska 140
Illinois 234
Indiana 223
Ohio 289
West Va. 85
Delaware 321
Maryland 347
Nevada 444
Utah 143
Colorado 209
Kansas 227
Missouri 287
Kentucky 241
Virginia 274 ★
District of Columbia 1,125
California 311
Tennessee 207
N. Carolina 264
Arizona 375
New Mexico 184
Oklahoma 383
Arkansas 277
S. Carolina 451
Mississippi 311
Alabama 370
Georgia 327
Texas 290
Louisiana 427
Florida 336
Alaska 348
Hawaii 150
Federal System 21

tudes in favor of more punitive sentencing policies may have influenced legislators to build more prisons. Organization theorists have contended that available public resources will be utilized; in other words, "beds will be filled." After new cells are constructed, judges may feel little hesitation in sentencing offenders to prison; when space was short, the same judges reserved incarceration for only the most violent convicts. The escalating incarceration rates in some states may primarily reflect the impact of prison expansion programs in these states.

The contemporary rise in the incarceration rate has brought increased pressures to build more prisons. With courts sentencing more and more offenders to imprisonment, some people argue that space must be made available. For reasons of both health and security, the crowded conditions in existing facilities cannot be tolerated or permitted to worsen. But others say that, once built, prisons will stay filled because of the organizational needs of the correctional bureaucracy. Cells will not remain empty. Society, it is argued, penalizes less serious offenses at times when serious crime is not viewed as a problem and lets off minor offenders when serious crime has become endemic. Thus, if murder is relatively uncommon, criminal justice resources will be diverted to shoplifters, drug abusers, or prostitutes. Similarly, when violent offenses are more prevalent, there may be proposals to decriminalize the victimless crimes, such as drug use, prostitution, and gambling.

Perhaps building costs are one of the greatest deterrents to prison expansion. Legislatures typically discuss new construction in terms of $25,000 to $125,000 per cell, but recent analyses by economists have shown that these levels are very low. One study computed the true cost of constructing and operating a hypothetical 500-bed medium security prison, using real designs and construction estimates. In

FIGURE 14.5
Sentenced prisoners in state institutions per 100,000 civilian population at year end 1990. What can be said about these differences with respect to incarceration among the states? There are regional differences, but differences also exist between contiguous states that would seem to have similar socioeconomic and crime characteristics.
SOURCE: U.S. Department of Justice, Bureau of Justice Statistics, *Bulletin* (May 1991, p. 2).

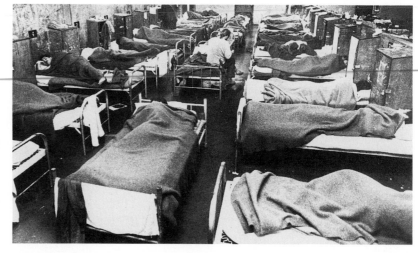

■ The crowding of correctional facilities is a national crisis. The great increase in prison population during the past decade has meant that most institutions hold offenders in numbers greater than rated capacity. How do the states solve this problem?

CLOSE-UP | Overcrowding in South Carolina: "Don't Be Afraid of Public Opinion"

The South Carolina Prison Overcrowding Project, a panel of key state and local officials and private citizens, was created in 1981 to find solutions to the state's severe prison overcrowding problem. Dispelling ignorance about that problem, both in the legislature and among the citizens of the state, was one of the panel's primary tasks.

"When we started out, I was probably the most conservative member of the Senate," State Senator John Drummond said. "I was in favor of putting more of these s.o.b.s in jail, not turning them loose." That has certainly been the prevailing attitude about imprisonment in South Carolina for the last decade. The number of state inmates there tripled between 1972 and 1982; at the end of 1982, the prison population was 9,161. The state's incarceration rate of 270 per 100,000 is one of the highest in the nation.

But a closer look at the inmates serving time in the state's prisons surprised Drummond (as chairman) and other members of the prison overcrowding panel. South Carolina sends everyone sentenced to ninety days or more, including misdemeanants, to state prison. This was originally a reform measure designed to remove lesser offenders from the harsh and primitive conditions of county road camps. Although corrections officials are unable to say precisely how many misdemeanants are in state facilities, a survey made for the overcrowding panel showed that more than 400 inmates were admitted to the corrections system during fiscal 1982 for the offenses of writing bad checks and failing to make child support payments. About 40 percent of the state's prisoners have been convicted of nonviolent property offenses.

"When I got the facts," Drummond said, "I was solidly sold on going the other way"—that is, finding punishments other than imprisonment. "I could see

that we had been totally wrong in the direction we had been going. I didn't see any point in ruining someone's life by sending him to prison for a first-time minor offense."

The panel eventually produced two short-term remedies for overcrowding that would require legislative action. One was an emergency powers act that would legally establish a capacity for the state prison system of 7,630 inmates and permit the release of inmates when that capacity was reached or exceeded. The other was the creation of a sentencing guidelines commission. It will report to the legislature . . . on a proposed sentencing system that will set up uniform sentencing standards that take the prison system's capacity into account.

All of the panelists fulfilled pledges to lobby for the measures; they traveled throughout the state, speaking before civic clubs and newspaper editorial boards. "We wanted to take the fire away from the opposition before these measures went to the floor," Drummond said. "We wanted to let the people know that we were not talking about turning rapists loose, or turning murderers loose."

Drummond's foresight paid off. . . . The measures passed in the House in the final hours of the last day of the session.

Drummond has some advice for legislators in other states who want to change the direction of their corrections systems. "First," he said, "arm yourself with the facts. And don't be afraid of public opinion. The public will be with you if you give them the facts. I don't know of a more conservative state than South Carolina, and we were able to get the public behind us."

SOURCE: Adapted from *Time to Build?*, pp. 12–13. Copyright © 1984 by Edna McConnell Clark Foundation. Reprinted by permission.

addition to the base cost of $61,015 per bed, or approximately $30 million for the facility, hidden (but expected) costs such as architects' fees, furnishings, site preparation expenses, and so on, pushed the estimate to $82,246 per bed ($41 million for the facility). At a conservative estimate of $14,000 per inmate per year, the operating cost would be $7 million a year. Thus the thirty-year bill to the taxpayers for construction and operation would be $350 million versus $30 million as originally described.[20]

Given current public attitudes on crime and punishment, continued high crime rates, and the expansion of prison space, it is likely that incarceration rates will remain high. Perhaps only when the costs of this form of punishment have a direct impact on the pocketbooks of taxpayers will there be a shift in policies. It may also be that at some point the correctional pendulum will again swing, with a greater emphasis being placed on intermediate punishments that do not require incarceration.

Who Is in Prison?

The size of the inmate population directly affects the ability of correctional officials to do their work, because crowding reduces the placing of offenders in rehabilitative programs, increases the potential for violence, and greatly strains staff morale. In addition, the makeup of the inmate community in terms of age, race, and criminal record has a determining impact on the operation of correctional institutions.

What are the social characteristics of the inmates in our nation's prisons? Following a survey of state prisons, the Bureau of Justice Statistics said that this population is predominantly made up of

> poor young adult males with less than a high school education. Prison is not a new experience for them; they have been incarcerated before, many first as juveniles. The offense that brought them to prison was a violent crime or burglary. On the average they already served 1½ years on a maximum sentence of 8½ years. Along with a criminal history, they have a history of drug abuse and are also likely to have a history of alcohol abuse.[21]

What is clear from recent studies is that inmates who are recidivists and those convicted of a violent crime make up an overwhelming portion of prison populations. More than 60 percent of inmates in nineteen states have been either incarcerated or on probation at least twice; 45 percent of them, three or more times; and nearly 20 percent, six or more times. Two-thirds of the inmates were serving a sentence for a violent crime or had previously been convicted of a violent crime.[22] These are major shifts from the prison populations of earlier decades, when only about 40 percent of all inmates had committed such offenses.

Correctional officials have recently become aware of the increasing number of prison inmates who are older than fifty-five. Nationally that number is now more than 20,000, with about 400 over eighty-five years old. About half of these inmates are serving long sentences; the other half committed crimes late in life. Whereas older prisoners are still a small portion of the total inmate population, their numbers are doubling every four years. Elderly prisoners have security and medical needs that are different from the average inmate. In a number of states special sections of the institutions have been designated for this older population so that they will not have to mix with the younger, tougher inmates. Costly medical needs are also a problem that corrections must carry. For this aging group, chronic illnesses such as heart disease, stroke, and cancer may develop. The average yearly maintenance and medical costs for inmates over fifty-five is about $69,000, triple that of the norm. Will some prisons be renamed Centers for the Correctional Treatment of Old Folks?[23]

It's also known that nearly three-quarters of the adults under

---

A QUESTION OF ETHICS

The policy directive was precise:

> All inmates will be tested for HIV. All inmates found to be positive will be placed in Wing A, regardless of their physical condition, conviction offense, or time remaining in their sentence.

Testing for the deadly virus began at Elmwood State Prison soon after Warden True's directive was posted. All of the 753 inmates were tested over a three-week period, and every new prisoner entering the institution first went to the medical unit to have blood drawn for laboratory examination.

Six weeks after the directive was posted, the test results were known. For most of the inmates there was relief in the knowledge that they had not contracted the virus. For a few, however, the notice that they were to report to the prison doctor was a prelude to knowledge that a medical death sentence had been issued. Hearing the news that they had tested positive was traumatic. Most responded with an expletive, others burst into tears, still others sat in stunned silence.

Word of the new policy at the prison was leaked to the press. There was an immediate response from the state chapter of the American Civil Liberties Union and the Howard Association for Prisoners' Rights. The groups called for a meeting with Warden True. In a press conference they protested the "state's invasion of privacy" and the "discriminatory act of segregating gay and drug users, most of the latter being African American and Hispanic." They emphasized that it would be years before most of the infected would come down with a "full" case of AIDS; compassion, not stigmatization, should be the response of corrections to the disease.

Warden True told reporters that he had a responsibility for the health of all inmates and that the policy had been developed to prevent transmission of the disease. He said that although the HIV inmates would be segregated, they would have access to all of the facilities available to the general population, but at separate times. He denied that he intended to stigmatize the twenty prisoners who had thus far tested positive.

What do you suppose Warden True considered in developing this policy? Is his policy likely to cause harm or good? Is it ethical to segregate the prison population? Is it ethical to add conditions to parole for prisoners who test HIV positive?

correctional supervision are between the ages of twenty-five and forty-four. In addition to other longstanding issues that corrections must address (violence, boredom, drug use, homosexual behavior in prison), there is now the problem of AIDS (Acquired Immune Deficiency Syndrome) and related health issues. It is precisely this age group, so heavily represented in prison, for which AIDS is expected to be the leading cause of death among males in the United States.

AIDS and Corrections

Statistical probabilities based on the demographic characteristics of the correctional population tell only part of the story of the impact of AIDS. The potential impact on corrections is further heightened by the fact that the probation, parole, jail, and prison populations contain a high concentration of individuals at particular risk for this disease—those with histories of intravenous drug use and, to a lesser extent, homosexual behavior. Not surprisingly, studies have shown that offenders with AIDS tend to be concentrated in those areas of the country where drug use is highest (District of Columbia, New York, New Jersey). Among heterosexual males with AIDS, the ratio of African-Americans to whites is 12.0 to 1; for Hispanics 9.3 to 1.[24] A survey of state and the federal prison systems conducted in October 1990 found that 1,312 inmates had AIDS. Sixty-three percent of the cases were found in three prison systems. An additional 560 cases were found in the twenty-seven city and county jails surveyed.[25]

Although the offender with AIDS, either a person with the illness itself or a person who has been infected with the HTLV-III virus, confronts probation and parole officials with a number of problems, jail and prison administrators are most affected by questions and policy issues related to this problem. Institutional administrators must develop policies covering such matters as methods to prevent transmission of the disease, the housing of those infected, and medical care for inmates who have the full range of symptoms. In determining what actions should be taken, administrators have found that a host of legal, political, medical, budgetary and attitudinal factors impinge on their ability to make what they believe are the best decisions.

In the context of overcrowded facilities, the contemporary inmate population presents correctional workers with a challenge. Even if resources are not available to provide rehabilitative programs for most inmates, the goal of maintaining a safe and healthy environment may tax the ability of the staff. The difficulties of this task are multiplied still further by the problem of AIDS. In addition, corrections is being asked to deal with a different type of inmate, one who is more prone to violence, and with a prison society in which racial tensions are great. At the other end of the scale is the problem of elderly inmates, a new segment of the prison population. Further, there are the problems inherent in trying to deal with individuals in crowded, out-of-date facilities. How well this correctional challenge is met will have an important impact on crime in American society.

SUMMARY

At various times in the history of the United States, various methods of imposing criminal sanctions have been considered appropriate. With the development of the penitentiary at the beginning of the nineteenth century, incarceration was the primary means of dealing with serious offenders. Although keeping offenders in custody has been a dominant goal, rehabilitation and reintegration into the community have been alternative objectives since the end of World War II to the early 1970s. With the shift to an emphasis on deserved punishment and crime control, corrections had to develop new policies and programs. Today corrections is faced with higher rates of incarceration and probation. In most states the number of facilities and correctional workers has increased. One wonders when there will be a leveling off in the number of offenders under correctional supervision and what alternatives to traditional programs will emerge.

Corrections in the United States is organized along several lines: the Federal Bureau of Prisons, state prison systems, and local (mainly county run) jails are the three major instruments of incarceration. The characteristics of the inmate populations differ in accord with these structures. There are also separate prison facilities for women, and some institutions are run on a cocorrectional basis. The number and type of inmates in an institution greatly influence the character of that facility and the problems faced by administrators. The chapters that follow will first examine the internal structure of prison society and then consider the community corrections alternative.

FOR DISCUSSION

1. If prisons don't work, why do we use them?
2. You are the administrator of a local jail. What are some of the management problems that you face?
3. Correctional officials must compete with other public agencies for resources. What are some of the special problems that they face in this quest?
4. A legislative committee has hired you as a consultant to advise on the prison crowding problem. Would you support the building of new facilities? Why? Why not?

FOR FURTHER READING

Clear, Todd R., and George F. Cole. *American Corrections,* 2nd ed. Pacific Grove, CA.: Brooks/Cole, 1990. An overview of American corrections designed for classroom use.

Foucault, Michel. *Discipline and Punish,* trans. by Alan Sheridan. New York: Pantheon, 1977. Describes the transition from a focus of correctional punishment on the body of the offender to use of the penitentiary to reform the individual.

Irwin, John. *The Jail.* Berkeley: University of California Press, 1985. A description of the multiple functions and problems of the American jail.

Logan, Charles. *Private Prisons: Cons and Pros.* New York: Oxford University Press, 1990. A definitive view of the issues surrounding the private prison question.

Rothman, David J. *Conscience and Convenience.* Boston: Little, Brown, 1980. Argues that conscience activated the Progressives to reform corrections yet the new structures for rehabilitation operated for the convenience of administrators.

Rothman, David J. *The Discovery of the Asylum: Social Order and Disorder in the New Republic.* Boston: Little, Brown, 1971. Rothman notes that prior to the nineteenth century, deviants were cared for in the community. The coming of urbanization and industrialization brought into being government institutions to handle this function.

NOTES

1. U.S. Department of Justice, Bureau of Justice Statistics, *Sourcebook of Criminal Justice Statistics* (Washington, DC: Government Printing Office, 1989), pp. 2, 12, 150.
2. David J. Rothman, *The Discovery of the Asylum: Social Order and Disorder in the New Republic* (Boston: Little, Brown, 1971), p. 49.
3. Michel Foucault, *Discipline and Punish*, trans. Alan Sheridan (New York: Pantheon, 1977), pp. 8, 16.
4. John Howard, *The State of Prisons in England and Wales* (London: J. M. Dent, 1929).
5. Thorsten Sellin, "The Origin of the Pennsylvania System of Prison Discipline," *Prison Journal* 50 (Spring–Summer 1970):15–17.
6. Ronald L. Goldfarb and Linda R. Singer, *After Conviction* (New York: Simon & Schuster, 1973), p. 30.
7. David J. Rothman, *Conscience and Convenience* (Boston: Little, Brown, 1980), p. 18.
8. Ibid., p. 32.
9. As quoted in Goldfarb and Singer, *After Conviction*, p. 40.
10. As quoted in ibid., p. 41.
11. President's Commission on Law Enforcement and the Administration of Justice, *The Challenge of Crime in a Free Society* (Washington, DC: Government Printing Office, 1967), p. 7.
12. National Council on Crime and Delinquency, *Focus* (December 1989).
13. U.S. Department of Justice, Bureau of Justice Statistics, *Report to the Nation on Crime and Justice*, 2nd ed. (Washington, DC: Government Printing Office, 1988), p. 117.
14. Ronald Goldfarb, *Jails: The Ultimate Ghetto* (Garden City, NY: Doubleday, 1975), p. 29.
15. U.S. Department of Justice, Bureau of Justice Statistics, *Bulletin* (June 1990).
16. U.S. Department of Justice, Bureau of Justice Statistics, *Bulletin* (May 1991, p. 1).
17. Charles Logan, *Private Prisons: Cons and Pros* (New York: Oxford University Press, 1990), p. 16.
18. Camille G. Camp and George M. Camp, *Private Sector Involvement in Prison Services and Operations*, Report to the National Institute of Corrections (Washington, DC: Government Printing Office, February 1984).
19. Cited in Kevin Krajick, "Punishment for Profit," *Across the Board* 21 (1984):25.
20. *Time to Build?* (New York: Edna McConnell Clark Foundation, 1984), pp. 18–19.
21. U.S. Department of Justice, Bureau of Justice Statistics, *Bulletin* (December 1982), p. 1.
22. Ibid., May 1991, p. 4.
23. *Newsweek*, (November 20, 1989):70.
24. Mark Blumberg, "Issues and Controversies with Respect to the Management of AIDS in Corrections," in *AIDS: The Impact on the Criminal Justice System*, ed. Mark Blumberg (Columbus, OH: Merrill, 1990), p. 195.
25. Theodore M. Hammett and Andrea L. Daughtery, *AIDS in Correctional Facilities: Issues and Options—1990 Update*, report submitted to the National Institute of Justice (Cambridge, MA: ABT Associates, 1991).

15

Incarceration

Key Terms and Cases

classification
community model
custodial model
good time
inmate code

rehabilitation model (institutions)
total institution
totality of conditions
Bell v. *Wolfish* (1979)
Bounds v. *Smith* (1977)

Cooper v. *Pate* (1964)
Cruz v. *Beto* (1972)
Fulwood v. *Clemmer* (1962)
Hudson v. *Palmer* (1984)
Johnson v. *Avery* (1969)

Rhodes v. *Chapman* (1983)
Ruffin v. *Commonwealth* (1871)
Ruiz v. *Estelle* (1980)
Wolff v. *McDonnell* (1974)

Born in this jailhouse
Raised doing time
Yes born in this jailhouse
Near the end of the line

Malcolm Braly, On the Yard

The blue van passes through a small town and then veers off the highway onto a secondary road where only occasional houses punctuate the fields and woods. We are heading toward a looming fortress. As we approach it we see gray stone walls, barbed-wire fences, gun towers, steel bars. The van passes through opened gates and comes to a stop. Blue-uniformed guards move briskly to the rear doors, and in a moment four men, linked by wrist bracelets on a chain, stand on the asphalt and look about nervously.

Although this description may read like the beginning of a 1940s "big house" movie starring James Cagney, Pat O'Brien, or George Raft, it could be filmed today at Brushy Mountain, Tennessee; Ossining, New York; or Soledad, California. Incarceration in American prisons for adult felons has changed since the 1940s: the characteristics of the inmates are different, rehabilitative personnel are employed in addition to guards, and the population is crowded. But the physical dimensions of the fortress institution remain the same, and the society of captives within may be only slightly changed.

Incarceration—what does it mean to the inmates, the guards, and the public? What goes on in our prisons? Is prison society a mirror image of American culture? How does incarceration fit with the goals of the criminal sanction? Are correctional institutions really training schools for criminals? These are a few of the questions that this chapter explores.

In many ways the interior of the American maximum security prison is like a foreign land. As observers we need guidance in trying to gain an awareness of the social dimensions of prison life: its traditions, the roles played there, and the prevailing patterns of interpersonal relations. Although the walls and guns may give the impression that everything goes by strict rules and with machinelike precision, a human dimension exists that we may miss if we study only the formal organization and routines. This human element and the lives of the incarcerated—both inmates and keepers—are the subjects of this chapter.

THE MODERN PRISON: LEGACY OF THE PAST

For someone schooled in criminal justice history, entering most American prisons of today is like entering a time machine. Elements from each of the major reform movements can be seen within the walls. In accord with the early notion that the prison should be located away from the community, most correctional facilities are in

The achievement of correctional goals is affected by architecture, yet prisons are built to last. This means that over time institutions thought suitable for one era are not appropriate for their contemporary function.

rural areas—Somers, Connecticut; Stateville, Illinois; Attica, New York—far from the urban residences of the inmates' families. The fortress style, built to secure the population, remains typical of today's prison architecture. Prison industries, founded on the principles of the Auburn system, occupy many inmates. Treatment programs, including vocational education, group therapy, and counseling, are available. Whether called a correctional facility or a treatment center, a prison remains a prison whatever it is called.

Hollywood's picture of the big house is still the image in the minds of most citizens, even though it is no longer realistic, if indeed it ever was. American correctional institutions have always been more variegated than one might suspect from viewing films or reading some of the landmark prison studies. Although big houses predominated in much of the country during the first half of this century, some prisons, especially in the South, did not conform to this model. There, racial segregation was maintained, prisoners were involved in farm labor, and the massive walled structures were not so dominant a form. In many other states the correctional systems had not emerged from the cruelty and corruption, silence systems, hard labor, and corporal punishment that had characterized American prisons during the late nineteenth century.

The typical big house of the 1930s and 1940s was a walled prison made up of large, tiered cell blocks, a yard, shops, and industries. The prisoners, averaging about 2,500, came from both urban and rural areas, were poor, and, outside the South, were predominantly white. The prison society was essentially isolated; access to visitors, mail, and other kinds of communication was restricted. Prisoners' days were strictly structured, with rules enforced by the guards. There was a basic division between inmates and staff; rank was observed and discipline maintained. In the big house there was little in the way of treatment programs; custody was the primary goal.

Since World War II many changes have come to American prisons. It is now difficult to find an institution that conforms exactly to the big house depicted in films and analyzed by such social scientists as Donald Clemmer and Gresham Sykes.[1] During the 1950s and early 1960s most penologists accepted the rehabilitation model of corrections. Many states built new facilities and converted others into "correctional institutions." Although the new name was often the principal evidence of an alternative philosophy, in some states the medical model was widely accepted, and treatment programs became a major part of institutional life. Indeterminate sentences, classification, treatment, and parole, the chief emphases of this approach, brought changes to the prison. In particular, treatment personnel—counselors, educators, and psychologists—were added to the staff. Often conflict erupted over the competing claims of the treatment and custody goals. The shift toward rehabilitation occurred at a time when outside forces were beginning to penetrate the prison walls.

The ending of corrections' isolation from the wider community has had the most far-reaching influence on correctional institutions during the past twenty-five years. As the population of the United States changed, so did that of the inmate population. The proportion of African-American and Hispanic inmates increased, and inmates from urban areas became more numerous, as did inmates convicted of drug-related and violent offenses. The average age was younger. The civil rights movement of the early 1960s had a profound effect on minority prisoners. There was an infusion of political activism, with demands that prisoners be more fully integrated into the society and that there be greater sensitivity to their needs. The courts began to take notice of the legal rights of prisoners. Former street gangs regrouped inside prisons, disrupting the existing inmate society, raising the level of violence in many institutions. Finally, with the rise of public employees' unions, correctional officers were no longer willing to accept the paramilitary work rules of the warden.

As prisons have responded to community influences, they have shifted away from the treatment model of corrections. The rehabilitative programs touted in the 1960s have been either deemphasized or abandoned. The determinate sentence has replaced the indeterminate sentence in many states; as a consequence, the parole board no longer has much discretion to return prisoners to the community. On top of these policy shifts there has come a great increase in the number of persons being held in prisons, so that most are overcrowded and under increased tension. Humane incarceration seems to have become the contemporary goal of correctional administrators.

Goals of Incarceration

Various parts of the correctional subsystem tend to emphasize one or a combination of the broad goals of the criminal sanction: punishment, deterrence, incapacitation, and rehabilitation. It is natural to regard security as the dominant purpose of a prison, given the nature of the inmates and the need to protect the staff and the community. High walls, barbed-wire fences, searches, checkpoints, and regular counts of inmates serve the security function because few inmates escape. More important, they set the tone and strongly color the daily operations. Thus prisons are expected to be impersonal, quasi-military places where strict discipline, a minimal level of amenities, and restrictions on freedom are thought to serve the goals of the criminal sanction.

Correctional models have been developed to describe the purposes and approaches that should be used in handling prisoners in an institutional setting. Although models may provide a set of rationally linked criteria and aims, the extent to which a given model is fully implemented is a question for empirical investigation. As with the stated purpose of the criminal sanction, the plan for a particular model may have little relation to the ongoing process of corrections and the experience of the inmates. New terms to describe the key elements of each model may be adopted to signify changes in day-to-day practices, yet the new terminology may have no relationship to actual conditions. For example, many state legislatures have decreed that prisons be referred to as "correctional facilities" and that guards be designated "correctional officers" to signify a shift in goals from a custodial to a rehabilitative model (Table 15.1). Too often, however, the same legislatures have not provided resources to implement the essential shifts in facilities and personnel required by the new model.

Three models of incarceration have been prominent since the early 1940s: the custodial, rehabilitation, and community models. Each can be viewed as an ideal type that summarizes the assumptions and characteristics associated with one style of institutional organization. The **custodial model** is based on the assumption that prisoners have been incarcerated for the protection of society and for the purpose of incapacitation, deterrence, or retribution. It emphasizes maintenance of security and order through the subordination of the prisoner to the authority of the warden. Discipline is strict, and most aspects of behavior are regulated. This model was prevalent within corrections prior to World War II, and it dominates most maximum security institutions today.

custodial model: A model of corrections that emphasizes security, discipline, and order.

With the onset of the treatment orientation in corrections during the 1950s, the **rehabilitation model** of institutional organization was developed. In prisons organized according to this model, security and housekeeping activities are viewed primarily as a framework for rehabilitative efforts. Professional treatment specialists enjoy a higher status than that accorded other employees, in line with the idea that all aspects of the organization should be directed toward rehabilitation. During the past two decades, with the rethinking of the goal of rehabilitation, the number of institutions geared toward this end has declined. Treatment programs still exist in most institutions, but very few prisons can be said to conform to this model.

rehabilitation model (institutions): A model of corrections that emphasizes the provision of treatment programs designed to reform the offender.

TABLE 15.1 Nomenclature associated with correctional models

Custodial Model	Rehabilitative Model	Community Model
Prison	Correctional facility	Community correctional facility
Guard	Correctional officer	Counselor
Prisoner	Inmate	Resident
Solitary confinement	Adjustment center	n/a

The **community model,** sometimes known as the reintegration model, is linked to the structures and goals of community corrections (see Chapter 14). Although inmates are confined in a prison during the early part of their sentences, they may gradually be given greater freedom and responsibility and often move to a halfway house or community correctional center before being released under supervision. The community model is based on the assumption that it is important for the offender to maintain or develop ties with the free community. It is believed that without strong bonds to family, church, and workplace, people are more likely to commit criminal acts; hence their reintegration with these groups is necessary if they are going to resume a normal life. The structures of this model—community corrections, probation, and parole—will be extensively discussed in Chapter 16.

This chapter describes the operation of the vast majority of prisons in the United States that fall between the extremes of the highly authoritarian custodial institution and those designed to maintain a purely rehabilitative atmosphere. An assumption is that in the long run the two goals of custody and rehabilitation cannot be equally served in the same institution. Both may be pursued, but one will predominate and the other will be relegated to secondary status. The goal that predominates is almost invariably custody. Wardens and other prison administrators must deploy staff and resources to service inmates to the extent budgetary contraints permit. "The bottom line is storage; it must retain and restrain inmates."[2] But because all but a few inmates can be expected to return to society at some point, even the most thoroughly custodial institution cannot neglect the reintegrative needs of prisoners.

Prison Organization

The prison differs from almost every other institution or organization in modern society. Not only are its physical features different from those of most institutions, but it is a place where a group of persons devotes itself to managing a group of captives. Prisoners are required to live according to the dictates of their keepers, and their movements are sharply restricted.

Corrections is a unique governmental agency. Unlike other government agencies, corrections:

- cannot select its clients.
- has little or no control over release of its clients.
- services clients who are there against their will.
- relies on clients to do most of the work in the day-to-day operation of the institution and to do so by coercion and without fair compensation for their work.
- usually has no clear, comprehensive law defining what it should do with its clients.
- can have its capacity grossly overloaded.
- depends on the maintenance of satisfactory relationships between its clients and its staff.

The Total Institution

Much research on prisons has assumed that they share with some other organizations, such as the mental hospital and the monastery, the characteristics of a **total institution.**[3] This concept, developed by Erving Goffman, emphasizes that the prison completely encapsulates the lives of those who work and live there. Whatever prisoners do or do not do begins and ends in the prison; every minute behind bars must be lived according to the institution's rules as enforced by the staff. Adding to the totality of the prison is a basic split between the large group of persons (inmates) who have very limited contact with the outside world and the small group (staff) who supervise on an eight-hour shift within the walls and are socially integrated with the outside world where they live. Each sees the other in terms of stereotypes. Staff members view inmates as secretive and untrustworthy, whereas inmates view staff as condescending and mean. Staff members feel superior and righteous; inmates, inferior and weak.

This view of the prison has been challenged by social scientists who have noted the extent to which the modern correctional institution has been permeated by outside influences. They argue that today's inmates have greater access to news of the outside world than they once did, that racial and ethnic cliques have divided the prison population, and that community advocacy groups using the power of the law have diluted the total power of institutional administrators. Given these changes, we must use the total institution concept cautiously; yet the contemporary prison is still far enough removed from the free world for Goffman's term to remain useful for purposes of analysis.

total institution: An institution (such as a prison) that completely encapsulates the lives of those who work and live within it. Rules govern behavior, and the group is split into two parts, one of which controls all aspects of the lives of the other.

The film *Brubaker* was based on the work of reform warden Tom Murton (played by Robert Redford) at the notorious Cummins Farm Unit of the Arkansas State Penitentiary.

Management

The administrative structure of prisons is organized down to the lowest level. Unlike the factory or the military, in which there are separate groups of supervisors and workers or officers and enlisted personnel, the lowest-status prison employee (the guard) is both a supervisor *and* a worker. The correctional officer is seen as a worker by the warden but as a supervisor by the inmates. Guards are thus subject to role conflict that makes them susceptible to corruption by the inmates. The warden judges their efficiency on the basis of their ability to manage the prisoners, which often depends in large part on their ability to secure at least some cooperation by the inmates.

Although the organizational structure of most prisons exhibits a similar bureaucratic form, management styles vary. Political scientist John DiIulio studied the management of selected prisons in Texas, California, and Michigan.[4] He found differences that were related to the leadership philosophy, political environment, and administrative style of individual wardens. DiIulio has argued that the quality of prison life as measured by levels of order, amenity, and service is mainly a function of the management. He believes that prisons can be governed, violence can be minimized, and services can be offered to the inmates if leadership is provided by correctional executives and wardens.

DiIulio believes that prison systems will perform well if administrators successfully manage those political and other pressures that make for administrative uncertainty and instability. In particular, management will be successful if prison directors

1. are in office long enough to learn the job, make plans, and implement them.
2. are highly hands-on and proactive, paying close attention to details and not waiting for problems to arise. They must know what is going on inside yet also recognize the need for outside support. In short, they are strangers neither to the cell blocks nor to the aisles of the state legislature.
3. project an appealing image to a wide range of people both inside and outside of the organization. They are leaders.
4. are dedicated and loyal to the department, seeing themselves as engaged in a noble and challenging profession.[5]

From this perspective making prisons work is a function of administrative leadership and the application of management principles.

Multiple Goals

Most prisons are expected to carry out a number of goals related to keeping (custody), using (working), and serving (treating) inmates. Because individual staff members are not equipped to perform all functions, there are separate organizational lines of command for the groups of employees that fulfill these different tasks. One group is charged with maintaining custody over the prisoners, another group

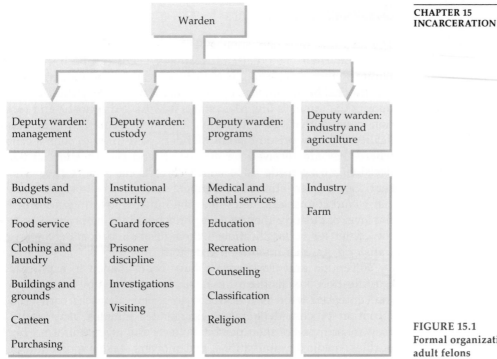

Warden

Deputy warden: management

Deputy warden: custody

Deputy warden: programs

Deputy warden: industry and agriculture

Budgets and accounts

Food service

Clothing and laundry

Buildings and grounds

Canteen

Purchasing

Institutional security

Guard forces

Prisoner discipline

Investigations

Visiting

Medical and dental services

Education

Recreation

Counseling

Classification

Religion

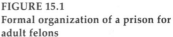

Industry

Farm

FIGURE 15.1
Formal organization of a prison for adult felons

supervises them in their work activities, and a third group attempts to rehabilitate them.

The custodial employees are normally organized along military lines, from warden to captain to guard, with accompanying pay differentials and job titles that follow the chain of command. The professional personnel associated with the using and serving functions, such as clinicians and teachers, are not part of the regular custodial organizational structure, and they have little in common with the others. All employees are responsible to the warden, but the treatment personnel and the civilian supervisors of the workshops have their own salary scales and titles. They are not part of the custodial chain of command, and their responsibilities do not include providing specialized advice to the custodial employees. The formal organization of staff responsibilities in a typical adult prison is shown in Figure 15.1.

As a result of multiple goals and separate employee lines of command, the administration of correctional institutions is often filled with conflict and ambiguity. Under these circumstances, how do prisons function? What are the means by which prisoners and staff attempt to meet their own distinct goals? In view of the conflicting purposes and the complex set of role relationships within the prison society, it is amazing that prisons are not a chaotic mess of social relations. Although the U.S. prison may not conform to the ideal goals of corrections and although the formal organization of staff and inmates may bear little resemblance to the ongoing reality of the informal relations, order *is* kept and a routine *is* followed.

Classification of Prisoners

The idea that prisoners should be diagnosed and then classified according to their custodial and treatment needs can be traced to the Elmira Reformatory and Zebulon Brockway. In the modern prison, this process has been developed so that it plays a major role in determining the inmate's life. Most states now have diagnostic and reception centers that are physically separated from the main prison facility. All new prison-bound offenders pass through such a center, where they are received for evaluation and **classification** so that a decision can be made as to which correctional facility they will be sent. Specialized clinical personnel, such as psychologists, physicians, and counselors, determine the inmates' treatment needs and the level of custody they require. Prisoners may be brought back to the center for reclassification if their needs and goals change or if transfer to another institution is desired.

classification: The act of assigning a new inmate to a type of custody and treatment appropriate to his or her needs.

Reception and classification have been likened to a process of mortification. Just as the army recruit is socialized by basic training, the sentenced felon is introduced to a new status as convict. The reception process deliberately exaggerates inmates' new status as they are stripped of their personal effects and given uniforms, books of rules, medical examinations, and showers. Take a moment to read through the rules set forth in the list that follows. Although substantial, they represent just a small part of the rulebook that the state of Michigan issues to new inmates. During the six weeks in which a new prisoner normally undergoes classification, every element of the process—from the rules to the communal showers—underscores the fact that the newcomer is now an inmate and not a citizen of the free community.

Rules of general conduct, Michigan Department of Corrections[6]
1. All residents are expected to obey directions and instructions of members of the staff. If a resident feels he/she has been dealt with unfairly, or that he/she has received improper instructions, he/she should first comply with the order and then follow the established grievance procedure outlined later in this booklet.
2. Any behavior considered a felony or a misdemeanor in this state also is a violation of institutional rules. Such acts may result in disciplinary action and/or loss of earned good time in addition to possible criminal prosecution.
3. Any escape, attempt to escape, walk-away or failure to return from a furlough may result in loss of good time and/or a new sentence through prosecution under the escape statute. At one time or another, most persons in medium or minimum custody have felt restless and uneasy. When this happens, we urge you to see your counselor or the official in charge for guidance and advice. Occasionally, the department has asked that those who have walked away impulsively not be prosecuted when they have turned themselves in immediately after the act, realizing their mistake.
4. Any residents may, if they feel they have no further recourse in the institution, appeal to the Director of Corrections, Deputy Director, the Attorney General, state and federal courts, Michi-

Should Less Use Be Made of Incarceration?

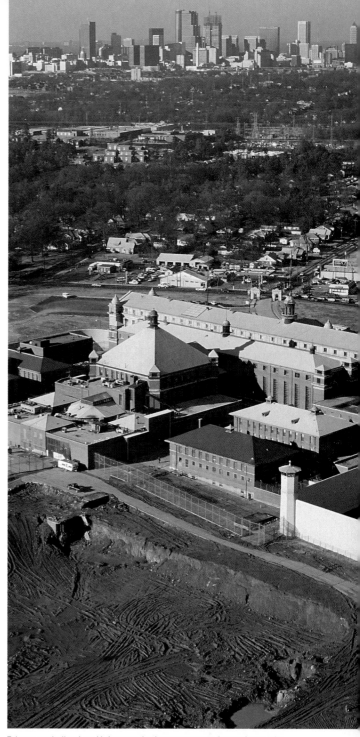

Every American who reads the newspapers or watches television knows of the serious problem of prison crowding. Over the last decade, the incarceration rate has more than doubled and the trend seems to be ever upward. One response has been to build more institutions, resulting in a prison construction boom across the nation. Critics have called for a moratorium on further expansion, saying that more prison cells will only lead to higher levels of incarceration. Supporters of current policies argue that the prison population is high because the level of violent crime is also high. However, reformers have urged that alternatives to incarceration be developed, so that less serious offenders can serve their sentences in the community and not in prison.

What reasons might be offered to explain the rate of incarceration in the United States? Are less serious offenders being sent to prison rather than being put on probation? Is there cause for concern in the fact that the rates of incarceration for some minorities far surpass their relative percentages in the population at large? Recent public polls have consistently shown that about 85 percent of those interviewed believe that the courts do

Prisons are built to last. Unfortunately, those constructed to conform to the correctional goals of one era cannot be readily adapted to changing goals. This addition to the Atlanta Federal Penitentiary will look quite different from the older buildings.

Prison construction is one of the few growth industries in the current economy. Here a new facility is being built to be added to the New York State prison system.

not deal with criminals harshly enough. This response is particularly significant since the overall crime rate for index offenses is lower than it was in 1973. Is incarceration being overused in the United States? Are people being institutionalized who are not a threat to the community? Are there other, more effective ways to achieve the goals of justice?

For Incarceration

Supporters of the use of incarceration for offenders who have committed serious felonies say that the large numbers of persons now in prison reflect the fact that crime is a major national problem and must be dealt with severely. They believe that to use incarceration *less* would be a serious mistake. In fact, some argue that on cost-benefit grounds it is less costly to society to incarcerate felons than it is to let them live in the community where they will continue their criminal ways. One analyst has calculated that incarcerating 1,000 felons costs society $25 million per year, yet to not put these same individuals behind bars costs society about $430 million per year.

Other supporters of current correctional policies argue that the recent spurt in prison populations is mainly a return to levels that existed prior to 1960. There is some evidence that during the period 1980 to 1989, changes in criminal justice policies increased a serious offender's probability of being incarcerated from levels that existed throughout the 1960s and 1970s. As shown in Figure D.1, in 1960 there were 62 prison commitments for every 1,000 serious offenses (that is, murder, nonnegligent manslaughter, forcible rape, robbery, aggravated assault, and burglary) reported to law enforcement agencies. During the next decade this ratio steadily declined, as did the ratio of prison commitments to adult arrests (from 299 per 1,000 arrests in 1960 to 170 per 1,000 in 1970). It was not until the late 1980s that incarceration rates began to return to the 1960 level.

In further defense of contemporary sentencing policies supporters say that the growth of the prison population during the past decade has helped to lower the crime rate. Those taking a philosophical position argue that it is just to treat criminals severely and that incarcerated felons deserve to be punished because their crimes are serious.

Overcrowded prisons present administrators with a great number of problems, including those related to health, security, and violence. Are conditions such as these in violation of constitutional rights?

The arguments against less use of incarceration may be summarized as follows:

▶ Incarceration is being used to punish individuals who have committed serious offenses. Justice demands that they be punished in this manner.

▶ Analysis of prison populations indicates that most inmates have committed serious crimes, often with violence, and they are repeat offenders. There are few inmates who should have received a community sentence as the laws are now written.

▶ Incarceration is not racially biased. The high number of minorities in American prisons and jails reflects the fact that minorities commit crimes out of proportion to their numbers in the general population.

▶ Incarceration policies have been successful in lowering the crime rate as reflected in the *National Crime Survey*.

▶ The public's support of current incarceration policies is reflected by the actions of Congress and the state legislatures.

The maintenance of personal relationships with loved ones is at best difficult for the incarcerated. What would be the impact on your spouse and children if you were in prison?

Against Incarceration

Critics of current policies argue that incarceration is being overused. They say that the harsher sentencing policies of the past decade have not reduced crime. They recognize that there are some offenders who deserve to be given prison terms, but they argue that many first-time offenders and those who have committed only property crimes are also being incarcerated. These critics believe that American society is increasingly vindictive toward minorities and the poor, the groups most likely to be sentenced to prison.

The current building programs will only increase the prison population, since empty cells will be filled. Critics say that the almost $16 billion per year that is used to incarcerate could be better spent on programs that address the causes of crime. In addition, corrections should be geared toward the rehabilitation of offenders, and greater use should be made of sanctions in the community.

Prisoners spend most of their time in idleness, since there are few opportunities to be employed. These prisoners are the exception in that they are working at the front line of a forest fire and are housed in a work camp.

The arguments in favor of less use of incarceration may be summarized as follows:

▶ Changes in penal policies have resulted in a misuse of incarceration, with the result that offenders whose crimes do not warrant the severe deprivation of prison are nonetheless being sent to prison.

▶ Race and class bias in American society are reflected in the disproportionate numbers of members of minorities and poor people who are incarcerated.

▶ Expansion of prison capacities will only lead to greater numbers of incarcerated individuals.

▶ Money spent on incarceration could be better used to attack the problems in society that breed crime such as unemployment, poor education, and family instability.

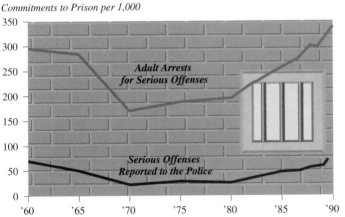

Commitments to Prison per 1,000

Adult Arrests for Serious Offenses

Serious Offenses Reported to the Police

Data from U.S. Department of Justice, Bureau of Justice Statistics, *Bulletin*, May 1991, p. 7.

Figure D.1
Commitments to State Prison Relative to Offenses and Arrests, 1960 to 1989

Boot camps are a new intermediate sanction being tried in a number of states. The concept is based on the assumption that with hard labor, physical training, and the development of leadership skills, young first-time offenders may be turned away from crime.

Release from prison is a joyous occasion, yet the stigma of incarceration will remain.

We've seen that incarceration is used extensively in the United States. In fact, one researcher has reported that the United States has the highest incarceration rate in the developed world, even surpassing the Soviet Union and South Africa (see Figure D.2). Although this analysis has been criticized on methodological grounds, the point is well taken. How do other Western, developed countries punish offenders?

Some analysts have pointed to the higher crime rate in the United States as accounting for higher incarceration rates. Research comparing the likelihood of imprisonment for robbery, burglary, or theft in the United States, Canada, England, and Germany (prior to unification) showed little difference. For example, the percentages of arrested adults who are incarcerated after a conviction for robbery are: United States, 49 percent; Canada, 52 percent; England, 48 percent; and Germany, 58 percent.

It can be argued that international comparisons are not really appropriate since there are cultural, legal, and criminality differences among the various nations. Is the situation in the United States so different from countries such as Canada, England, and Germany that we cannot learn from their policies?

What Should U.S. Policies Be?

Incarceration is expensive in terms of prison construction and operation as well as the human costs to offenders and their families. In addition, one cannot measure the psychological, economic, and social costs that years of incarceration extract from prisoners, their families, and friends. Some analysts believe that incarceration is necessary for serious offenders and that the governmental and human costs do not outweigh the costs of crime to crime victims and the community. They dispute the idea that there are prisoners whose offense and criminal record do not require their incarceration.

A number of questions with respect to incarceration warrant serious attention in the years ahead. Does incarceration have an impact on the crime rate? Should greater use be made of nonincarcerative punishments? Will the American public support less severe punishments?

Required community service has been advocated as one way of keeping lesser offenders out of prison.

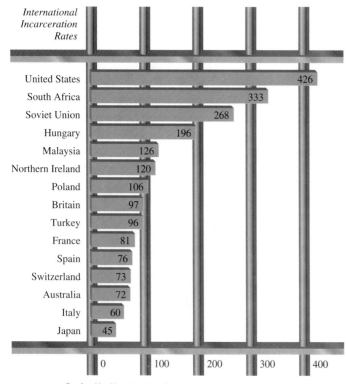

International Incarceration Rates

Country	Rate
United States	426
South Africa	333
Soviet Union	268
Hungary	196
Malaysia	126
Northern Ireland	120
Poland	106
Britain	97
Turkey	96
France	81
Spain	76
Switzerland	73
Australia	72
Italy	60
Japan	45

0   100   200   300   400

Data from Marc Mauer, "Americans Behind Bars: A Comparison of International Rates of Incarceration" (Washington, DC: The Sentencing Project, 1991).

Figure D.2
International Incarceration Rates
(inmates per 100,000 population)
Among industrialized nations, the United States would seem to lead the world with respect to incarceration. Are criminals really more likely to be incarcerated in the United States than in South Africa and the U.S.S.R.? What factors should be considered in this analysis?

gan Civil Rights Commission or the Governor in the form of sealed and uncensored mail.

5. Reasonable courtesy, orderly conduct and good personal hygiene are expected of all residents. Standards for haircuts, beards and general appearance are listed later in this rule book.

6. Residents cannot hold any group meetings in the yard. Meetings for all legitimate purposes require staff approval; facilities, if available, will be scheduled for this purpose and necessary supervision provided.

7. While residents are permitted to play cards and other games, gambling is not allowed. In card playing areas there shall be no more than four persons at a table. Visible tokens or other items of value will be sufficient evidence of gambling. Games are prohibited during working hours on institutional assignments.

8. All typewriters, calculators, radios, TV's, electric razors and other appliances, including musical instruments, must be registered with the institutional officials by make, model and serial number.

9. Items under Para. 8 cannot be traded, sold or given away without written approval of the Deputy Warden or Superintendent.

10. Residents cannot operate concessions, sell services, rent goods or act as loan sharks or pawnbrokers.

11. All items of contraband are subject to confiscation.

12. When residents desire to go from one place to another for a specific and legitimate reason, they should obtain a pass from the official to whom they are responsible, such as the housing unit supervisor, work foreman, teacher, etc.

13. No resident is allowed to go into another resident's cell or room unless specifically authorized.

A classification committee usually consists of the deputy warden and the heads of departments for security, treatment, education, industry, and the like. At the hearing caseworkers or counselors present information gathered from the presentence reports, police records, and the reception process. The inmate appears before the committee, personal needs and assignments are discussed, and decisions are made.

Unfortunately, classification decisions are often made on the basis of administrative needs rather than inmate needs. Certain programs are limited, and the demand for them is great. Thus inmates may find that the few places in the electrician's course are filled and that there is a long waiting list. Another problem is that the institution's housekeeping work must be carried out by the inmates. Inmates from the city may be assigned to farm work because that is where they are needed. What is most upsetting to some prisoners is that release on parole often depends on a good record of participation in treatment or educational programs. They have difficulty explaining to the parole board that they really did want to learn plumbing but that there was no opportunity to do so.

The Society of Captives

The public widely believes that prisons are operated in an authoritarian manner. In such a society of captives, guards *give* orders and inmates *follow* orders. Rules specify what the captives may and may not do, and these rules are strictly enforced. Because the guards have a monopoly on the legal means of enforcing rules and can be backed up by the state police and the National Guard if necessary, many people believe that no question should arise as to how the prison is run. Members of the staff have the right to grant rewards and to inflict punishment, and, in theory, any inmate who does not follow the rules should end up in solitary confinement.

We could imagine a prison society made up of hostile and un-cooperative captives ruled in an authoritarian manner. Prisoners can legally be isolated from one another, physically abused until they cooperate, and put under continuous surveillance. Although such a regime is theoretically possible, a prison would probably not be run long in this fashion because the public expects correctional institutions to be run humanely. Besides, there are defects in the view that the guards have total power over the captives. As Gresham Sykes has noted: "The ability of the officials to physically coerce their captives into the paths of compliance is something of an illusion as far as the day-to-day activities of the prison are concerned and may be of doubtful value in moments of crisis."[7] Forcing people to follow commands is basically an inefficient method of making them carry out complex tasks. Efficiency is further diminished by the realities of the usual 1-to-40 guard-to-inmate ratio and the potential danger of the situation. Thus correctional officers' ability to threaten the use of physical force is limited in practice.

Rewards and Punishments

Faced with the necessity of running the prison, correctional officers often rely on a system of rewards and punishments to induce cooperation. Extensive rules of conduct are imposed on prisoners, and rewards in the form of privileges may be offered for obedience: **good time** allowances, choice job assignments, and favorable parole reports. Informers may be rewarded, and administrators may purposely ignore conflicts among inmates on the assumption that such dissension prevents the prisoners from organizing to work together as a united force against the authorities.

good time: A reduction of a convict's prison sentence awarded for good behavior at the discretion of the prison administrator.

The system of rewards and punishments also has limitations, however. One of the problems is that the punishments for rule breaking do not represent a great difference from the prisoners' usual status. Because they are already deprived of many freedoms and valued goods—heterosexual relations, money, choice of clothing, and so on—the punishment of not being allowed to attend a recreational period does not carry much weight. Further, the system is often defective because the authorized privileges are given to the inmate at the start of the sentence and are taken away only if rules are broken. Thus few additional authorized rewards can be granted for progress or exceptional behavior, although a desired work assignment or transfer to the honor cell block will induce some prisoners to maintain good behavior.

In recent years the ability of correctional officials to discipline prisoners who resist authority has been somewhat weakened by the prisoners' rights movement and the demands of the courts for due process. The extent to which these forces have actually limited official sanctions is not known, but wardens are undoubtedly aware of the fact that their actions may be subject to legal action or censure by groups outside the prison.

Exchange Relations

One way that correctional officers obtain inmates' cooperation is through the types of exchange relationships described in earlier chapters. The guard is the key official in the exchanges within the custodial bureaucracy:

> It is he who must supervise and control the inmate population in concrete and detailed terms. It is he who must see to the translation of the custodial regime from blueprint to reality and engage in the specific battles for conformity. Counting prisoners, periodically reporting to the center of communications, signing passes, checking groups of inmates as they come and go, searching for contraband or signs of attempts to escape—these make up the minutiae of his eight-hour shift.[8]

Thus the guards are in close and intimate association with the prisoners throughout the day: in the cell block, workshop, or recreation area. Although the formal rules stipulate that a social distance must be maintained between guards and inmates and that they speak and act toward each other accordingly, their closeness makes them aware that each is in many ways dependent on the other. The guards need the cooperation of the prisoners so that they will look good to their superiors, and the inmates depend on the guards to relax the rules or occasionally look the other way. Even though guards are backed by the power of the state and have the formal authority to punish any prisoner who does not follow their orders, they often discover that their best path of action is to make "deals" or "trades" with the captives in their power. As a result, guards exchange or "buy" compliance or obedience in some areas by tolerating violation of the rules elsewhere.

Correctional officers must be careful not to pay too high a price for the cooperation of their charges. *Sub rosa* (secret) relationships that turn into manipulation of the guards by the prisoners may result in the smuggling of contraband or other illegal acts. The guards are under public pressure to be humane and not to use coercion—in short, to be "good guys"—yet there are risks to the use of the carrot rather than the stick.

By working through the leaders of the inmate social system—the convict society—correctional administrators secure their cooperation in helping to maintain order. In fact, the institution generally gives the inmate hierarchy covert support and recognition by assigning better jobs and quarters to its high-status members—if they are "good inmates." In this and other ways the institution buys peace with the system by avoiding battle with it.[9]

"Good" inmates do not withdraw from the convict society but rather maintain a position that permits control over other inmates. Convict society leaders tend to have extensive prison experience. They have been "tested" through relationships with other inmates so that they are neither pushed around by inmates nor distrusted by them as stool pigeons. Because staff can also rely on them, these leaders serve as the essential communications link between the two. With the ability to acquire inside information and access to decision makers, inmate leaders command respect from other prisoners. They benefit from the corruption of the formal authority of the staff by receiving illicit privileges and favors from the guards. In turn, they can distribute these benefits to other prisoners, thus bolstering their own influence within the society.

In sum, there is a striking difference between the formal chain of command as displayed on an organization chart of the prison and the reality of the existing social relationships. The prison conforms to an authoritarian model of control only in a formal sense; an informal network of social and exchange relationships maintains order and secures correctional goals. Riots may occur as a result of forces that disrupt the social equilibrium of the prison. Changes in the institution's leadership, attempts to shift from custodial to treatment goals, and political pressures to tighten discipline have all been cited as forces that destroy the stability of the ongoing system. Struggles for leadership within the convict society and the racial antagonisms of the contemporary prison have likewise caused unrest.

One of the amazing aspects of prisons is that they "work," in the sense that order is maintained, chaos is avoided, and activities are carried out. Staff and prisoners are bound together so that potential conflicts and misunderstandings are generally avoided, the routine is followed, and the institution functions.

THE CONVICT WORLD

What is it like to be incarcerated? Because a prison population is made up of felons, many of whom are prone to violence, one might expect much rebellion if it were not for the discipline imposed by the authorities. As we have seen, however, there are definite limits to the ability of correctional administrators to impose their will on inmates. Scholars have looked at the convict world to try to understand the prison subculture and the means by which prisoners adapt to their social and physical environment.

A widely recognized fact is that the inmate population is *not* made up of persons who serve their terms in internal isolation. Rather, prisoners form a society with traditions, norms, and a leadership structure. Some members may choose to associate with only a few close friends; others form cliques along racial or "professional" lines. Still others may be the politicians of the convict society: they attempt to represent convict interests and distribute valued goods in return for support. Just as there is a social culture in the free world, there is a prisoner subculture on the "inside."

As in any society, the convict world has certain norms and values. Often described as the **inmate code,** the values and norms emerge within the prison social system and help to define the inmate's image of the model prisoner. The code also helps to emphasize the solidarity of all inmates against the staff. One feature is that cons are not to interfere with other cons' interests; they must, for example, never rat

inmate code: The system of values and norms of the prison social system that defines for inmates the characteristics associated with the model prisoner.

■

Increasingly, prison populations are divided along racial and ethnic lines, with the result that friendship groups are important. As a result a prisonwide inmate code is no longer as strong as in the past.

on a con, be nosy, have a loose lip, or put another con on the spot. They must be tough and not trust the guards or the things for which they stand. According to the code, guards are hacks or screws; the officials are wrong and the prisoners are right.

Although some sociologists believe that the code is something that emerges from within the institution as a way to lessen the pain of imprisonment, others believe that it is part of the criminal culture that prisoners bring with them. The inmate who follows the code can be expected to enjoy a certain amount of admiration from other inmates. He may be thought of as a "right guy" or a "real man." Those who break the code are labeled "rat" or "punk" and will probably spend their prison life at the bottom of the convict social structure, alienated from the rest of the population and preyed upon.[10]

Because contemporary prison society has become more heterogeneous, a single overriding inmate code may not exist in some institutions. The variety of cultural and subcultural orientations (ethnic, class, and criminal), the variety of preprison experiences, and the intense, open hostility between segments of the prison population may preclude this. Race has become a key variable dividing convict society. Perhaps reflecting tensions in the broader community, many prisons now have been plagued by racially motivated violence, the formation of organizations based on racial symbolism, and the voluntary segregation of inmates by race whenever possible (recreation areas, dining halls).

For its members the friendship group affords mutual protection from theft and physical assault, serves as the basis of wheeling-and-dealing activities, and provides a source of cultural identity. In the absence of a single code accepted by the entire population, however, administrators find their task more difficult. They must be aware of the variations that exist among the groups, recognize the norms and rules that members hold, and deal with the leaders of many cliques rather than with a few inmates who have risen to top positions in the inmate society.

Adaptive Roles

On entering prison, a newcomer ("fish") is confronted by the question How am I going to do my time? Some may decide to withdraw into their own world and isolate themselves from their fellow prisoners. Others may decide to become full participants in the convict social system, which "through its solidarity, regulation of activities, distribution of goods and prestige . . . helps the individual withstand the 'pains of imprisonment.' "[11] In other words, some inmates may decide to identify mainly with the outside world, and others may orient themselves primarily toward the convict world. This choice of identity is influenced by prisoners' values. Are they interested primarily in achieving prestige according to the norms of the prison culture, or do they try to maintain or realize the values of the free world? Their preference will influence the strategies that they will follow during the prison sentence.

Four categories have been used to describe the lifestyles of inmates as they adapt to prison. "Doing time" and "gleaning" are the choices of those who try to maintain their links with the free world and its perspectives. "Jailing" is the style used by those who cut themselves off from the outside and try to construct a life within the prison. The fourth category, "disorganized criminal," includes those who are unable to develop role orientations to prison life. Often of low intelligence or afflicted with a psychological or physical disability, they have difficulty functioning within the prison society; they are the human putty of the prison social world who are exploited by others. John Irwin believes the great majority of imprisoned felons can be classified according to these orientations.[12]

"Doing time"

The "doing time" lifestyle is adopted by those who see the period in prison as a temporary break in their outside careers. They tend to be professional thieves—that is, criminals who look at their "work" as a legitimate businessperson would. A prison sentence to these inmates is one of the risks or "overhead" costs of the way they make their living. Such inmates try to serve their terms with the least amount of suffering and the greatest amount of comfort they can manage. They avoid trouble by adhering to the inmate code, find activities to fill their days, form friendships with only small groups of other convicts, and generally do what they think is necessary to get out as soon as possible.

"Gleaning"

With the prevalence of rehabilitative programs, some prisoners decide to spend their time "gleaning," taking advantage of opportunities to change their lives by trying to improve themselves, improve their minds, or "find themselves." They use every resource at hand: library, correspondence courses, vocational training programs, school. Some prisoners make a radical conversion to this prison lifestyle. Irwin's study of San Quentin shows that such persons tend to be those who are not committed to a life of crime.[13]

"Jailing"

Some convicts never acquire a commitment to the outside social world. While in prison, they adopt a "jailing" lifestyle and make a world out of the prison. They are likely to be "state-raised youth," persons who have known foster homes, juvenile detention facilities, reformatories, and adult prisons for most of their lives. Because they know the institutional routine, have the skills required to "make it," and view the prison as a familiar place, they often aspire to leadership within the convict society. These are the inmates who seek positions that carry power and influence in the larger prison society. For example, an assignment as a runner for a staff member gives a convict greater freedom of movement within the institution and thus access to information. As clerk in the kitchen storeroom, an inmate is able to steal food to exchange with other prisoners for cigarettes, the prison currency. By constantly dealing in goods that are valued— food, clothes, information, drugs—he can live more comfortably in prison. This lifestyle has its rewards: first, the consumption itself, and second, "the reward of increased prestige in the prison social system because of the display of opulence."[14]

Although only four of the potential adaptive models chosen by inmates are described, we can see that prisoners are not members of an undifferentiated mass; individual members choose to play specific roles in the convict society. These models reflect the physical and social environment of the prison and contribute to the development of the system that maintains the institution's ongoing activities.

Making It

In prison, as in the outside world, individuals desire goods and services that are not freely provided. Although the state feeds, clothes, and houses all prisoners, amenities are sparse; institutional life is a type of enforced destitution. In prison one is deprived of everything but bare necessities and subjected to monotony in diet and routine, loss of individual identity due to uniformity of treatment, scarcity of recreational opportunities, and lack of responsibility. It is true that since the mid-1960s the items that a prisoner may purchase or receive through legitimate channels have increased. In some institutions, inmates may own television sets, civilian clothing, and hot plates. Yet the prison community has been deliberately designated an island of poverty in the midst of a society of relative abundance.

The state has decreed that a life of extreme simplicity is part of the punishment of incarceration. And correctional administrators feel that rules must be enforced so that all prisoners are treated alike and none can gain higher position or status or comfort because of wealth or access to goods. Thus prisoners are limited as to what they may have in their cells, visitors are restricted as to the gifts that they may bring into the institution, and money may not be in the inmate's possession.

Recognizing that prisoners do have some needs that are not met, officials have created a formal economic system in the form of a commissary or "store" in which inmates may, on a scheduled basis, purchase a limited number of items—toilet articles, tobacco, snacks, and other food items—in exchange for credits drawn on their "bank accounts." The size of a bank account depends on the amount of money deposited on the inmate's entrance, gifts sent by relatives, and amounts earned in the low-paying prison industries. In some prisons, the amount that may be spent weekly is limited.

But the peanut butter, soap, and cigarettes of the typical prison store in no way satisfy the consumer needs and desires of prisoners. In consequence an informal, *sub rosa* economy exists as a major element in the society of captives. Many items taken for granted on the outside are inordinately valued on the inside. For example, talcum power and deodorant take on added importance because of the limited bathing facilities. Goods and services not consumed at all outside prison can attain exaggerated importance inside prison. As examples Vergil Williams and Mary Fish cite offenders who, unable to enjoy their accustomed drink of bourbon, will find that somewhat the same effect can be achieved by sniffing glue; or those who, to distinguish themselves from others, pay laundry workers to iron a shirt in a particular way, a modest version of conspicuous consumption.[15]

The informal economy reinforces the norms and roles of the social system, influences the nature of interpersonal relationships, and is thus one of the principal features of the culture. The extent of the economy and its ability to produce desired goods and services—food, drugs, alcohol, sex, preferred living conditions—vary according to the extent of official surveillance, the demands of the consumers, and the opportunities for entrepreneurship. Much inmate activity revolves around the "hustle."

The standard medium of exchange in the prison economy is cigarettes. Because possession of coins or currency is prohibited and a barter system is somewhat restrictive, "cigarette money" is a useful substitute. Cigarettes are not contraband, are easily transferable, have a stable and well-known standard of value, and come in denominations of singles, packs, and cartons. Further, they are in demand by smokers. Even those who do not smoke keep cigarettes for trading purposes.

Certain positions in the prison society provide opportunities for entrepreneurs. Access to food, clothing, materials, and information allows inmates assigned to work in such places as the kitchen, warehouse, and administrative office to ply their trade. As Susan Sheehan found in Green Haven, a New York prison, almost every job offered possibilities for "swagging" (stealing from the state):

> Kitchen workers can take far more food than they can eat, and sell it or swap it. One [inmate] who receives five cartons of cigarettes a month from a crime partner he didn't rat on, doesn't smoke but loves to eat. His recent purchases from a kitchen worker have included a dozen eggs (two packs of cigarettes), a pound of rice (one pack), a pound of coffee (one pack), and several steaks (three packs apiece). He also has a contract with his friend in the kitchen for a daily loaf of soft bread (one carton a month). Kitchen workers have access to the various ingredients used at Green Haven to make booze—yeast, raw dough, sugar, fruit, potatoes, cereal—and either sell the raw ingredients or make and sell the finished product.[16]

"Sales" in the economy are one to one and are also interrelated with other *sub rosa* transactions. Thus the exchange of a dozen eggs for two packs of cigarettes may result in the reselling of the eggs in the form of egg sandwiches made on a hot plate for five cigarettes each, whereas the kitchen worker who swagged the eggs may use the income to get a laundry worker to starch his shirts or a hospital orderly to provide drugs or to pay a "punk" for sexual favors. The economic transactions wind on and on.

Disruptions of the economy may occur when officials conduct periodic "lockdowns" and inspections. Confiscation of contraband may result in temporary shortages and price readjustments, but gradually hustling will return. The law of supply and demand will be back in force.

CLOSE-UP *A Day in the Life*

George Malinow, a self-described "professional criminal," was asked by Susan Sheehan to keep a diary of four ordinary days of incarceration in Green Haven, one of New York State's maximum security prisons. As the following excerpt makes obvious, he knows the ropes of prison life. As he says, "I hustle, I swag, same as on the street."

Tuesday, August 10, 1976

6:30 A.M. Bell rings very loud and long. A certain C.O. [correction officer, or guard] does this (rings bell long) whenever he comes on duty, and I and many other inmates here would like to hit him with a shoe, as he seems to do this on purpose!

God—I hate to get up, I feel so tired!! Serves me right for staying up doing glass painting till 1:55 this morning. But—get up I must and do so. Wash up, shave and get dressed in my work clothes which is green regulation issued pants and shirt and work shoes. Put on water to be boiled for my coffee. Have coffee and 2 do-nuts. Smoke a cigarette and listen to the news, via earphones.

7:15 A.M. Doors open up. I immediately rush off to the mess hall entrance area on the West Side entrance, being I'm one of the first inmates up—no one is near that area at this time of the morning. Terry, a friend of mine (inmate) who works in the kitchen, is there awaiting me. He hands me a large cardboard box which contains 20 dozen fresh eggs, about 20 pounds of raw bacon, and about 20 pounds macaroni, 20 to 30 oranges, 2 large cans orange juice and one large can of olive oil for cooking. I immediately *rush* back to my cell, to avoid the other inmates about due to start going to the mess hall for their breakfast.

Hide food in my cell and my friend Andy's cell. Andy is just up and washing. We joke together about our sudden good windfall.

7:40 A.M. Andy and I proceed to go to work, the parole-clothing department located at the basement of the Administration Building. Terry stops us to ask us to please get him some shorts, 2 white shirts and black socks. We tell him that we'll give it to him next morn-ing. We reach the check point gate of the Administration Building, get pat frisked, and sign the logbook to verify at what time we arrived to work. Also left our institutional passes at this check point, as must be done.

We arrive at the basement parole-clothing area where we work. C.O.s Stevens and Barton are there already.

The coffee pot is ready as C.O. Stevens always plugs in this pot early. So Andy, I and Stevens all have coffee and cake. C.O. Barton is busy checking papers for the inmate he is due to take to the hospital so he doesn't join us. We have the radio playing and listening to the local news broadcast. Meanwhile, there are 4 men going home on parole this morning and they just arrived and are getting dressed. Andy and I both help and make certain that these inmates have all their clothes and personal property packages. They have cups of coffee and relax in casual and happy conversation—about the steaks, drinks and women they'll soon enjoy out there, etc.

Does seeing men talk like this and seeing them go home each day bother us? Andy and I . . . feel very glad to see as many as possible leave any prison as prison represents "hell" in all respects!!

7:50 A.M. All the men due to go home now, leave with C.O. Stevens, to go upstairs to an office where they'll all receive their $40 gate money and whatever's in their inmate account and their release papers. Then C.O. Stevens will escort them out and drive them in the prison van bus to Hopewell Jct. station where they will board a bus for N.Y. City. I sorted out all their state issued clothing they turned in to our dept. and also gathered all the earphones they brought to our dept. upon departure. Bagged all state clothes to be sent to State Shop, their final destination.

8:05 A.M. We have an extra relief C.O. to stay with us, as C.O.s Stevens & Barton are out on assignments. Said relief C.O.s name is Officer Dover (works in officers' mess from 10 A.M. onward), who is one of the best

(continued)

One must acknowledge that the economy of the prison society meets the members' needs for goods and services. It permits some inmates to live better than others and to exert power over them. Economic transactions may lead to violence when goods are stolen, debts are not paid, or agreements are violated. The guards may also become enmeshed in the prison economy as they, too, see opportunities to provide goods for payment. The prison economy, like that of the outside world, allocates goods and services, rewards and sanctions, and is closely linked to the cultural and social systems of the society it serves.

CLOSE-UP (continued)

natured officers in all respects that I have ever come across. Good sense of humor, always smiling & happy go lucky. Very well mannered, fair and easy to relate with. Should be made a warden.

Andy and I . . . relax and talk about general topics on the outside.

8:30 A.M. Another 3 inmates that work with us now arrive to work also. They are Danny, Benno, and Ned.

This morning—we have to take a full inventory of all the stock garments we have and record each item in our general inventory stock so we will know what to order, we are short of. After Danny, Ned, and Benno all have their coffee and buns, all 5 of us get ready to do the inventory.

8:50 A.M. Andy and I start counting the jackets, slacks, socks, handkerchiefs, belts, shoes and shirts. Danny and Ned start to count the ties, topcoats and the other apparel that the men wear to go out on furloughs, death visits and to courts.

10:35 A.M. We all are caught upon our inventory and go to have coffee again and relax. During inventory taking, Benno sat at the desk to answer all phone calls of general inquiry and also made up lists for calling men the next day—that have to be fitted out with civilian clothes for their due release dates soon.

11:05 A.M. Benno starts to prepare the foods that he will cook for our lunch as we are not going to go to the mess hall as there is only franks for lunch. Benno is making steaks, fried onions, French fried potatoes, sauce gravy and sweet green peas for our lunch meal. Benno is an exceptional cook! When he cooks, we all leave the kitchen to be out of his way and also, not to distract him then. One or more of us are available to help him—if he calls us, but most times he does it all by himself.

Of course, he cooks—so all others of us do the cleaning up and wash the pots & dishes.

11:40 A.M. We are just about ready to start eating. We all are in conversation about how good Benno cooked the steaks, the high price of food outside, etc. The radio is playing a late song hit and we all are enjoying the food and are in a good mood.

12:25 P.M. We are done eating—so Andy, Danny and I all take out the dishes, silver ware, pots to the sink area away from the kitchen and wash & dry all. Meantime, Ned swept out kitchen while Benno went to his desk to relax.

12:45 P.M. No inmates to dress this afternoon so Danny and I re-check all the men due to go home the next morning—on our out going releases sheet. We line up all the clothing outfits and their packages containing personal property at the benches where they will get dressed in the morning.

1:15 P.M. We all now sit around the desks and are in conversation about many topics. The parole board's unjust decisions, rehabilitation, politics and prison mismanagement, etc.

2:05 P.M. Phone rings and we have to go to the store house to pick up 6 large cases containing jackets and slacks. Andy, Danny and I all take a strong push wagon and check out from the check out gate at the administration area, get pat frisked and proceed to go to the store house. Along the way, we stop off at E block, on the East Side, to find out if 2 of the men locking there will be at our Jaycee's meeting tonight? They said they will. We leave for the store house.

We arrive at the store house, load our wagon with all the large cases and pick up a copy of the order-form. We arrive at the front administration check point and again are pat frisked. We get all boxes to the rack area. We open all boxes, take out garments and count them. The total checks out correctly. C.O. Stevens signs the receipt form copy and I take it back to the store house civilian clerk. When I return, Andy, Danny, Benno, and Ned are about half way done placing the slacks on the shelfs in their respective sizes, and the jackets on the line racks, in their respective sizes.

I join them in doing this and I sort the jackets. We stop this work at 2:45 P.M. I check and pull out coffee pot plug, stove plug, radio plug and toaster plug. Meanwhile—Andy dumps out all the trash into plastic trash bags due to go out to the dump area, via truck, in the morning. Benno dumps out all water from wash

PRISON PROGRAMS

One of the major ways in which modern correctional institutions differ from those of the distant past is in the number and variety of programs. Although prison industries were a part of such early penitentiaries as Auburn, under the stimulus of the rehabilitative goal many educational, vocational, and treatment services have been added to the correctional institution. In some states such programs have not been well developed, and prisoners spend their time working at tasks that do not prepare them for jobs on the outside.

pails in kitchen. Danny washes out coffee pot and prepares it for next morning's use.

2:55 P.M. All of us leave our job area in basement, get pat frisked again at check out gate, pick up our passes and proceed to our cells in C block, all except Ned as he locks in J block.

3:05 P.M. I arrive at my cell, change clothes, wash up and go to the wash room to wash out and hang up the clothes I left there to soak yesterday.

3:25 P.M. Returned to cell, put water on for my thermos bottle to make my coffee. Layed down, smoked a cigar and relaxed listening to some soft music via earphones.

4:10 P.M. Got up, made cup of coffee, had a ham and Swiss cheese sandwich. Cleaned up table, brushed teeth and started to get materials ready to do my glass painting. Worked on glass painting until lock in.

5:05 P.M. Bell rings—lock in time. Doors close and 2 C.O.s walk by & check the doors & count as they walk past my cell. I continue on working on the glass pictures.

5:25 P.M. C.O. stops at my cell and hands me 8 letters (personal), 2 more business letters and 1 magazine on real estate. C.O. continues on handing out mail to other cells.

Read 3 of these letters which come from the Philippines. One from my sweetheart, one from her sister & the 3rd from her mother. Finish reading all mail and lay down to catch the prison phone bulletin announcements on prison news.

5:55 P.M. Get up, wash up, brush teeth and get all my papers and materials ready for my Jaycees meeting due tonight at the school class building at J block, from 6 to 8:30 P.M.

6:00 P.M. Doors open up. I proceed to block door exit where many other men are waiting to go to different night classes and program classes. The block C.O. checks each one of us out on his master sheet.

I arrive at my Jaycee class room and start writing out on the black board the agenda for tonight's meeting. An outside male Jaycee coordinator arrives and our Jaycee meeting starts. We discuss various project pos-

sibilities. One project involves bringing boys from high schools within a few miles of Haven to the prison to see what it is like so that they will never want to commit crimes and will never wind up in prison. We also form committees for each project. Meeting ends at 8:25 P.M. and all of us leave to return to our blocks.

8:35 P.M. Returned to cell. Wash and make cup of coffee & smoke 2 cigarettes. Start to work again on my glass pictures and continue until 10 P.M. I stop to eat a salami & cheese with lettuce and tomatoe sandwich. Smoke 2 cigarettes and relax on my bed.

I start to think of my sweetheart in the Philippines. What's she doing, etc.? That's rather silly cause since it is a 12 hour difference in time from N.Y. City, it goes without saying it has to be about 10 a.m. there so of course, she can't be sleeping.

10:20 P.M. I start working on my glass pictures again. I accidently spill over the bottle of drawing paint all over my glass and I am angry as hell at myself for my carelessness! Finally get that particular portion on my glass cleaned and I have to re-draw that part of the picture again.

10:55 P.M. The bell rings and that means it's time to lock in for the night. Doors close and the 2 C.O.s again check the doors & take the count. I continue on working on the glass pictures. I feel very tired tonight so I stop working on these pictures at 11:40 P.M. I clean up all paint brushes, table and put away to a safe area, the glass paintings to dry during the night. Have a fast cup of coffee, then wash up, brush teeth and get undressed.

11:55 P.M. Put on only small night lamp, put on phones to catch midnight news. Light up cigarette and listen to the news on phones. Music (Western songs) comes on by some local Poughkeepsie disc jockey and I listen to it until 12:30 A.M.

12:35 A.M. I put out light, pull out phone plug and go to sleep.

SOURCE: Adapted from *A Prison and a Prisoner* by S. Sheehan, pp. 96–102. Published by Houghton Mifflin Company. Copyright © 1978 by Susan Sheehan. Reprinted by permission.

Administrators must use institutional programs to manage the problem of time. They know that the more programs they are able to offer, the less likely it is that inmates' ideleness and boredom will turn to hostility. The less cell time, the fewer tensions. Activity is the administrator's tool for controlling and stabilizing prison operations.

Educational Programs

Most correctional facilities offer academic programs so that courses passed by inmates are credited in accordance with state requirements. Since a great majority of adult felons lack a high school diploma, it seems natural that many could make good use of their prison time in the classroom. In many institutions, inmates without at least an eighth-grade education are assigned to school as their main occupation. In some facilities, college-level courses are offered in the evening through an association with a local community college. Studies have shown that inmates who were assigned to the prison school are good candidates to achieve a conviction-free record after release. Evidence has also suggested, however, that this outcome may be due largely to the type of inmate selected for schooling rather than the schooling itself.

Vocational Education

The idea that inmates can be taught a trade that will be of service to them in the free world has great appeal. Programs in modern facilities are designed to teach a variety of skills: plumbing, automobile mechanics, printing, computer programming. Unfortunately, most such programs are unable to keep abreast of technological advances and needs of the free market. Too many programs are designed to train inmates for trades that already have an adequate labor supply or in which new methods have made the skills taught obsolete. Some vocational programs are even designed to prepare inmates for careers on the outside that are closed to former felons. The restaurant indus-

Most prisons provide vocational education programs, such as here at the Connecticut Correctional Facility for Women. Unfortunately, in most systems the number of inmates that can be handled in the more popular programs is limited.

try, for example, is a place where former felons might find employment, yet in many states they are prohibited from working where alcohol is sold.

Prison Industries

Early prison reformers felt that inmates should develop good work habits and that prisoners should be productive so that their labor would help pay the costs of their incarceration. Others cited the usefulness of work in keeping inmates out of mischief and declared that work was consistent with the goal of incapacitation. Some scholars now point to the early industries established at Auburn as a reflection of the industrialization of the United States and the need for prison to instill good work habits and discipline in potential members of the labor force.

Traditionally, prisoners have been required to work at tasks that are necessary to maintain and run their own and other state facilities. Accordingly, food service, laundry, and building maintenance jobs are assigned. In some states, prison farms produce food for the institution. Industry shops make furniture, repair office equipment, and fabricate items. Prisoners receive a nominal fee (perhaps 50 cents an hour) for such work.

The prison industries system has had a checkered career. During the nineteenth century, factories were set up inside many prisons, and inmates manufactured items that were sold on the open market. With the rise of the labor movement, however, state legislatures and Congress passed laws restricting the sale of prison-made goods so that they would not compete with those made by free workers. Whenever unemployment became extensive, political pressures mounted to prevent prisons from engaging in enterprises that might otherwise be conducted by private business and free labor. In 1940 Congress passed the Sumners-Ashurst Act prohibiting the interstate transportation of convict-made goods for private use. With the outbreak of World War II, however, President Franklin Roosevelt issued an executive order permitting the federal government to procure goods for the military effort from state and federal prisons. Under labor pressure, the wartime order was revoked in 1947 by President Harry Truman, and prisoners returned to idleness.[17] By 1973 the National Advisory Commission found that throughout the correctional system "only a few offenders in institutions have productive work."[18] In 1979 Congress lifted restrictions on the interstate sale of prison-made products and urged correctional administrators to explore with the private sector the possibilities for improving prison industry programs.[19]

The 1980s saw renewed interest in the channeling of prison labor into industrial programs that would relieve idleness, allow inmates to earn wages that they could save until release, and reduce the costs of incarceration to the state. Through initiatives promoted by the federal government, efforts have been made to encourage private sector companies to set up "factories within fences" so as to effectively use prison labor. A 1987 study found that thirty-eight private sector prison industry programs employed over 1,000 inmates in twenty-six prisons and two jails in fourteen states.[20]

Although the idea of employing inmates sounds attractive, the economic value may be offset by inefficient aspects of prison industries. Turnover among prisoners is great since many spend less than two years incarcerated and are often transferred among several institutions during that period. Supervisors have found that because of low education levels and the absence of steady work habits, it is difficult to utilize prisoners to perform many of the tasks related to modern production. The absence of steady work habits also means that some prisoners are inefficient. The cost of maintaining security so that materials are not pilfered must also be figured into the business formula. Mechanisms for more productive use of inmate labor to provide goods and services that are competitive in the free market are in experimental stages. These activities deserve watching to see if prison industries can become one way to deal with idleness and to inculcate habits and skills that will be beneficial when inmates are released.

Treatment Services

Rehabilitative programs aim at reforming the offender's behavior through treating defects thought to have brought about the criminality. There is little dispute about the desirability of providing for the rehabilitative needs of offenders, but there is much dispute about the degree of emphasis that should be given to these programs and the types that should be offered.

Reports in the mid-1970s cast doubt on the ability of treatment programs to stem recidivism and raised questions about the ethics of requiring inmates to participate in such programs in exchange for the promise of parole. Their findings led to a rethinking of rehabilitation as an element of sentencing decisions. Treatment programs still have their supporters who argue that certain programs work for certain offenders, but such happy outcomes require more accurate diagnosis and fine-tuned sentencing by judges than are now possible.

In most correctional systems a range of psychological, behavioral, and social services is available to inmates. The extent of their use seems to vary greatly according to the goals of the institution and the attitudes of the administrators. Nationally less than $100 a year per inmate is spent for treatment services, and these programs reach only 5 percent of the inmate population.[21] Treatment services remain a part of correctional institutions, but the overemphasis of the past has diminished. Incarceration's current goal of humane custody implies no effort to change inmates.

CORRECTIONAL OFFICERS

A survey of American teenagers by the pollster Louis Harris revealed that only 1 percent had considered a career in corrections. This finding is not surprising, because a prison guard or correctional officer has no opportunity to acquire the prestige accorded the Secret Service agent, who may come to share in the glamour of the person he guards. The correctional officer's occupational prestige is tarnished

The correctional officer is often caught between differing role expectations. The officer is expected to maintain a certain distance from inmates yet be close enough to counsel and serve them.

by the company he or (increasingly) she must keep: the adult felon. The prisoner, of course, is not pleased at being guarded, and the community—the beneficiary of the correctional officer's activities—seems not to care except when a riot or escape occurs. Officers who are primarily concerned with inmate security make up more than half of all correctional employees. Their hours are long, their pay is low, entry requirements are minimal, and turnover is very high.

Role

Correctional officers are another example of street-level bureaucrats within the criminal justice system. As discussed in Chapter 3, street-level bureaucrats are public service workers who must deal with their clients in an organizational environment of scarce resources and who must exercise discretion. The correctional officer must cope with the human problems of inmates on a personal level—that is, treat prisoners as individuals and help them with their institutional and personal problems. But the officer also functions as a member of a complex bureaucratic organization and thus is expected to deal with clients impersonally and to follow formally prescribed procedures. Fulfilling these contradictory role expectations is difficult in itself, and the difficulty is exacerbated by the physical closeness of the officer and inmate over long periods of time.

Although prison work is widely perceived to be largely routine, guarding is not an undifferentiated occupation and includes a range of activities, as described by James Jacobs and Norma Crotty:

> Guards supervise the cell houses, dining areas, and shops; transport prisoners to hospitals and courts; take turns serving on the disciplinary board; sit perched with rifles in the towers on top of the walls; and protect the gates leading into and out of the interior. Unscheduled activities range from informal counseling to breaking up fights to escorting prisoners on family visits in the community.[22]

Of all the correctional staff, the officers in the cell blocks have the closest contact with the prisoners, and one might assume that they would have the greatest potential for inducing behavioral change in their charges. As the President's Commission noted:

> They can, by their attitude and understanding, reinforce or destroy the effectiveness of almost any correctional program. They can act as effective intermediaries or become insurmountable barriers between the inmates' world and the institution's administrative and treatment personnel.[23]

This points up one of the problems that has faced most correctional systems during recent decades: the unclear role that the guard is expected to play in an institution that combines both custodial and treatment goals. Officers are held responsible for preventing escapes, for maintaining order, and for the smooth functioning of the institution. At the same time, they are expected to cooperate with treatment personnel by counseling inmates and assuming an understanding attitude. In addition to such incompatible roles, officers must conform to the rehabilitative ideal, which stresses that each person be dealt with as a unique being, a task that seems impossible in a large people-processing institution. Guards are expected to use discretion yet somehow to behave both custodially and therapeutically. As Donald Cressey noted, "If they enforce the rules, they risk being diagnosed as 'rigid,'" whereas "if their failure to enforce rules creates a threat to institutional security, orderliness or maintenance, they are not 'doing their job.'"[24]

A QUESTION OF ETHICS

After three years of daily contact, Correctional Officer Bill MacLeod and Jack Douglas, who was serving a three-to-five-year sentence, knew each other very well. They both were devoted to the Red Sox and the Celtics. Throughout the year they would chat about the fortunes of their teams and the outlook ahead. MacLeod got to know and like Douglas. They were about the same age and had come from similar backgrounds. Why they were now on opposite sides of the cell bars was something that MacLeod could not figure out.

One day Douglas called to MacLeod and, instead of pointing out that "The Bird" had scored thirty points for the Celtics, said that he needed money since he had lost a bet gambling on their team. Douglas said that his wife would send him the money but that it couldn't come through the prison mail to him in cash. A check or money order would have to go into his commissary account.

"The guy wants cash. If he doesn't get it I'm dead." Douglas took a breath and then rushed on with his request. "Could you bring it in for me? She'll mail the money to you at home. You could just drop the envelope on my bed."

"You know the rules. No gambling and no money," said MacLeod.

"But I'm scared shitless. It will be no big deal for you and it will make all the difference for me. Come on, we've gotten along well all these years. I think of you as being different from those other officers."

What should MacLeod do? Is this likely to be a one-time occurrence with Douglas? What if MacLeod's sergeant finds out? What if other inmates learn about it?

Guards complain that the rules are constantly changing and therefore that neither they nor the inmates know where they stand. Many guards look back with nostalgia to the days when their purpose was clear, their authority was unchallenged, and they were respected by the inmates.

The position of correctional officer is more complicated than may be realized. The guard is both a manager and a worker—a low-status worker in relationships with supervisors but a manager of the inmates. Placed in an environment where most interactions while on duty are with the prisoners, the guard is nevertheless expected to maintain a formal distance from them. As the member at the lowest level of the correctional staff, the guard is constantly under scrutiny by superiors in the same way that the inmate is under surveillance. Because of the fear of trafficking in contraband, guards are often shaken down, just as inmates are. As guards write disciplinary reports on inmates, captains write up rule infractions of the guards. James Jacobs and Harold Retsky commented that even "the disciplinary board for guards is quite similar to the tribunal that hears inmate cases."[25]

Correctional officers follow a code of behavior that encourages solidarity among them, as the following list illustrates.

The officer code[26]

1. Always go to the aid of an officer in distress.
2. Don't "lug" drugs.
   Bringing drugs or alcohol into the prison places fellow officers in danger.
3. Don't rat.
   Never rat on an officer to an inmate.
   Never testify against a fellow officer.
4. Never make a fellow officer look bad in front of inmates.
5. Always support an officer in a dispute with an inmate.
6. Always support officer sanctions against inmates.
7. Don't be a white hat.
   Don't be too lenient or sympathetic to inmates.

CLOSE-UP *Gaining Respect*

The hardnose, thick-headed, bull correctional officer of the movies in the Jimmy Cagney era doesn't exist. And if he comes in here, he doesn't last very long. Your first goal ought to be to gain the respect of an inmate.

You can't gain respect from an inmate from being an easy mark. They don't respect easy marks. You don't gain respect through bully tactics, then everyday he comes into the joint it's going to just wear him down a little bit more. Things just don't work that way anymore.

You gain respect by attempting to treat everyone the same . . . equally . . . no matter what they're in for.

As a matter of fact, myself, I try not to find out what a man's in here for. It might change me a little bit. . . . I might not feel that it showed, but it shows. Now, someone will ask me to do something, send a request out to the visiting desk or something like that. . . . His request might sit in my pocket where someone else's request would be expedited right off the bat because of maybe what he did on the street . . . so I try not to even know what he's here for.

SOURCE: From "Prison Guards: The Inside Story," by E. May, *Corrections Magazine* (December 1976), p.36. Copyright © 1976 by Edna McConnell Clark Foundation. Reprinted by permission.

8. Maintain officer solidarity versus all outside groups.
   Don't talk about the institution to outsiders.
9. Show positive concern for fellow officers.
   Never leave another officer a problem.
   Help your fellow officer with problems outside the institution.

Prison Personnel Issues

Recruitment

As we know, employment as a correctional officer is not one of the glamorous, sought-after occupations. The work is thought to be boring, the pay is low, and career mobility is almost nonexistent. Studies have shown that one of the primary incentives for becoming a guard is the security that civil service status provides. In addition, prisons offer better employment options than most other jobs available in the rural areas where most correctional facilities are located. Because correctional officers are recruited locally, most of them are rural and white, whereas the majority of prisoners come from urban areas and are either black or Hispanic.

With the great increase in the prison population there has been a great expansion of the number of correctional officers. Salaries have been increased so that now the yearly average entry level pay runs between $15,000 and $20,000.[27] Special efforts have been made to recruit women and minorities. Women are no longer restricted to working with female offenders, and the number of correctional officers from minority groups has increased dramatically, though not in proportion to the inmate population in most states. Yet for most correctional workers a position as a custody officer is a dead-end job. Though guards who perform well may be promoted to higher ranks within the custodial staff, very few ever move into administrative positions. In effect, career officers commit themselves to life sentences in prison. The conventional wisdom among many officers is: "We're all doing time; some of us are just doing it in eight-hour shifts."

Collective Bargaining

The unionization of prison guards is a fairly recent phenomenon. It was not until the 1970s, when many states passed laws permitting collective bargaining by public employees, that the unions made inroads in prisons. By 1981 correctional employees in twenty-nine of fifty-two jurisdictions (state, federal, and District of Columbia) were unionized.[28] Like other labor organizations, unions representing prison employees seek better wages and working conditions for their members. Because the members are public employees, most are prevented by law from engaging in strikes, but work stoppages have occurred in a number of prisons nonetheless. As a result of unionization, relationships between employees and the administration are now more formalized, with the rights and obligations of each side stipulated by contract.

WOMEN IN PRISON

Women constitute only a small portion of the entire prison population. For every twenty-five men convicted as felons, only one woman is convicted. Perhaps because the number of women among both prisoners and corrections researchers has been so small, the literature on women's institutions is sparse. In general, it compares life in women's prisons with that in men's. Women's prisons are smaller; security is less tight; the relationships between inmates and staff are less structured; physical aggression seems less common; the *sub rosa* economy is not so well developed; and female prisoners appear to be less committed to the convict code. Women serve shorter sentences, and there is perhaps more fluidity in the prison society as new members join and others leave.

Surveys have shown that incarcerated women are young (average age twenty-nine), poorly educated (less than half have finished high school), employed at unskilled jobs, and often nonwhite. Nearly half were caring for dependents when they were admitted, yet most had no male companion. Few had alcohol problems, but about half were drug abusers. Compared to men, a higher proportion of incarcerated women are in prison for property offenses (39 percent versus 33 percent) and drug-related offenses (11 percent versus 7 percent).[29]

One impact of the war on drugs has been the great increase in the number of women incarcerated for drug offenses. With greater police resources being allocated for "sweeping" drug-infested neighborhoods, greater numbers of drug users and sellers are being caught and sentenced to prison terms. New York City has seen a fourfold increase in the number of women in their jails since 1981, and nationally there has been a threefold increase of incarcerated women during this same period.[30] Women incarcerated for drug offenses tend to be young, and most have children (85 percent of jailed inmates in New York City).

■
Although they make up only a small percentage of all incarcerated individuals, women have special problems that must be addressed.

The problem of inmates with dependents is a major difference between the correctional task of dealing with female rather than male prisoners. Because their time has largely been taken up with child rearing during their early adult years, most do not have the skills necessary to enter the job market on their release from prison. Whatever their crime, women prisoners as a group tend to be dependent, and it is argued that the prison environment increases this weakness.

Separate Institutions for Women

It was not until the end of the nineteenth century that separate prisons for women were created in the United States. Although women had been housed in penitentiaries since the 1820s, they were usually segregated from men in out-of-the-way areas where they had no ac-

To what extent is the convict society in women's prisons different from that of men's?

cess to exercise yards, visiting rooms, or even fresh air and light. In 1873 the Indiana Women's prison, the first physically separate women's institution, was opened. There are now 47 state institutions for women in the United States, compared with 613 for men and 34 that house both men and women.[31]

Although institutional facilities for women are generally smaller, better staffed, and less fortresslike than those for men, these advantages may disappear when the problems of remoteness and heterogeneity are considered. Because only three states operate more than one prison for women and some operate none, inmates are generally far removed from their families, friends, and attorneys. In addition, because the number of inmates is small, there is less pressure to design programs to meet an individual offender's security and treatment needs. Rehabilitation programs are few, and dangerous inmates are not segregated from those who have committed minor offenses.

Social Relationships

Researchers have been most interested in the types of social relationships that women prisoners maintain. As in all types of penal institutions, homosexual relationships are found, though among women they appear to be more voluntary than coerced. More important, female inmates tend to form pseudofamilies in which they adopt various roles—father, mother, daughter, sister—and interact as a unit. Esther Heffernan views these "play" families as a "direct, conscious substitution for the family relationships broken by imprisonment, or . . . the development of roles that perhaps were not fulfilled in the actual home environment."[32] Such interpersonal links help to relieve the tensions of prison life, to assist the socialization of the new inmate, and to allow individuals to act according to clearly defined roles and rules.

Rose Giallombardo believes that in most respects the subcultures of prisons for males and females are similar, with one major exception: the informal social structure of the female prison helps inmates "resist the destructive effects of imprisonment by creating a substitute universe—a world in which the inmates may preserve an identity which is relevant to life outside the prison." The orientation of female inmates is somewhat collectivist, with warmth and mutual aid being extended to an extended network of "family" members. This emphasis, Giallombardo contends, is in sharp contrast to male inmates' strategy of combating the pains of imprisonment through the development of a convict code and by the showing of solidarity with other inmates.[33]

Adaptive Roles

Esther Heffernan discovered that three terms in prison argot—*square, cool,* and *in the life*—correspond to the noncriminal, professional, and habitual offenders in women's correctional institutions; these adaptations correspond to identities brought in from the outside. *Square* is used, as in the larger community, to describe a person who holds conventional norms and values. A "square" is a noncriminal who perhaps killed her husband in a moment of rage. She attempts to maintain a conventional life while incarcerated, strives to gain the respect of officers and fellow inmates, and seeks to be a "good Christian woman." Female prisoners are "cool" if they make a "controlled, pleasurable, manipulative response to a situation." They are the professionals who "keep busy, play around, stay out of trouble, and get out." They attempt to manipulate others and intend to get through this term of incarceration on "easy time" through unity with others in their group, gaining as many amenities as they can without risking a longer stay. To be "in the life" is to be antisocial in prison

---

A QUESTION OF ETHICS

Elizabeth Hanson was the new superintendent of the Woman's Reformatory in Sunrise, California. As the youngest person to be appointed superintendent, she saw an opportunity to make a name for herself professionally. Perhaps she would one day become Commissioner of Corrections for California or some other state.

Ms. Hanson had inherited a poorly run institution that had a reputation for violence, inadequate training programs, and an uncaring staff. Problems, yes, but also a chance to show what she could do. Within weeks she had instituted a new code of inmate conduct, had begun a staff evaluation, and had requested a financial audit. The grumbling among staff and inmates was immediate. She knew that familiar ways were hard to break, but the intensity of the criticisms directed at her by key staff members was surprising.

When the audit of the food and supplies accounts revealed major irregularities and shortages, Hanson launched her own investigation. She detailed Deputy Superintendent Lewis to examine the accounts and interview the inmate workers and staff in the warehouse; this investigation pointed to Deputy Superintendent for Services Frank Grandy.

Grandy was a nineteen-year correctional veteran. He had risen from correctional officer in an institution for males to his present administrative position mainly on the basis of his easy ways and knowledge of the system. Lewis's report indicated that over the years Grandy had entered into arrangements with selected suppliers who overcharged the state and then gave him cash kickbacks. Hanson was furious and immediately called her superior, Commissioner Ray Morgan.

"Ray, we've got a problem. It looks like Frank Grandy has been getting kickbacks from vendors. I want him out of state service."

"Now hold on Betty, you're making serious charges. I can't imagine Frank doing something like that. Besides, he's close to Senator Leffingwell and our budget's up for review. Let's think this through. You're making charges about a very respected member of this department. Remember, you're new here and frankly have some things to learn about our ways of doing things. I want you to be a team player and not a loose cannon. Now why don't you just put this aside and get that institution shaped up."

Are Morgan's arguments valid? Should Hanson go over her superior's head to pursue her investigation? Should she drop the issue or pursue it on her own? What options does she have if she wants to enhance her career?

just as one had been on the outside. Such persons—about 50 percent of the prison population— are the habitual offenders who have been involved in prostitution, drugs, numbers, and shoplifting. They have been in prison previously; interact with others with similar experiences, and find community within the prison. It is important to them to stand firm against authority.[34]

Male versus Female Subcultures

In comparing research on the subcultures in prisons for men and for women, one discovers a great deal of correspondence but also a number of major differences. Comparisons are complicated somewhat by the nature of the research, for most studies have been of single-sex institutions. In addition, it seems that theories and concepts have been studied first in male prisons and then replicated in female institutions. Thus the concepts of argot roles, the inmate code, indigenous versus imported values, the prison economy, and so on are central to this entire body of literature; all have been found to have explanatory value in both types of institution. Heffernan's "square," "cool," and "in the life" are the female counterparts of John Irwin's "square john," "thief," and "convict" in a male prison. In both types of institution, to "make it" is to adapt to prison life in some way that makes the experience as painless as possible, as is illustrated in the following box. Prisoners who cannot come to terms with incarceration can expect to do "hard time" and suffer from the experience.

A principal difference between these two gender-specific societies lies in interpersonal relations. Male prisoners seem to have a greater sense that they act as individuals and that their behavior is evaluated by the yardstick of the prison culture. As James Fox noted in a comparative study of four prisons for men and one for women, male prisoners have their gangs or cliques but not the network of "family" relationships that has been found in prisons for women. Men are expected to do their *own* time. The norms stress autonomy,

CLOSE-UP *Surviving in Prison*

I was scared when I went to Bedford Hills. But I knew a few things by then. Like if you act quiet and hostile, people will consider you dangerous and won't bother you. So when I got out of isolation and women came up and talked to me, I said, "I left my feelings outside the gate, and I'll pick 'em up on my way out." I meant I wasn't going to take no junk from anyone. I made a promise if anybody hit me, I was gonna send 'em to the hospital.

When you go in, if you have certain characteristics, you're classified in a certain way. First of all, if you are aggressive, if you're not a dependent kind of woman, you're placed in a position where people think you have homosexual tendencies. If you're in that society long, you play the game if it makes it easier to survive. And it makes it easier if people think you're a stud broad. I played the game to make it easier so they would leave me alone. I didn't have money to use makeup and I couldn't see going through any changes. You're in there and the women are looking for new faces. Since I was quiet and not too feminine-looking, I was placed in a certain box in other people's mind. I let them think that's what box I was in—'cause it was a good way to survive. My good friends knew better. But I had three good friends and they were considered "my women"—so they in turn were safe, too. You have to find ways to survive. You cultivate ways to survive. It's an alien world and it has nothing to do with functioning in society better. What I learned there was to survive there.

SOURCE: Kathryn Watterson Burkhart, *Women in Prison* (New York: Doubleday, 1976), pp. 89–90.

self-sufficiency, and the ability to cope with one's problems. Fox found little sharing.[35]

Women at the Bedford Hills Correctional Facility in New York were less likely to look toward achievement of status or recognition within the prisoner community or "to impose severe restrictions on the sexual (or emotional) conduct of other members."[36] In prisons for women, close ties seem to exist among small groups of inmates. These extended families, which may include homosexual dyadic relationships, provide emotional support and emphasize the sharing of resources.

Some researchers have ascribed the distinctive female prison subculture to the nurturing, maternal qualities of women. Others have criticized this analysis as a stereotype of female behavior, imputing to women sex-specific personality characteristics.

Programs and the Female Role

Two major criticisms of women's prisons are that they do not have the variety of vocational and educational programs available in male institutions and that existing programs for women tend to conform to sexual stereotypes of "feminine" occupational roles: cosmetology, food service, housekeeping, sewing. It is suggested that such activities reflect the roles of women before World War II but have little correspondence to the occupations open to women today. Most educational programs for women stop at the secondary level; the large numbers of male inmates are said to make it more feasible to offer courses at the college level. Yet vocational and educational opportunities during incarceration are crucial: upon release most women have to support themselves, and many are financially responsible for children as well.

Recent studies have shown that there has been an increase in the number and variety of educational and vocational programs in women's prisons. Earlier research had emphasized that programs in women's prisons were generally limited, as compared to those in male institutions, and that they were primarily geared to traditionally "feminine" jobs.[37] National surveys by Ralph Weishet and T. E. Ryan conducted in the mid-1980s revealed that educational programs are found in almost all women's institutions and that vocational programs exist in about 90 percent of the institutions.[38] Perhaps more important is the fact that the range of courses now offered in many prisons for women has increased so that now business education, computer training, auto repair, and carpentry have been added to the more traditional offerings.

The lack of medical, nutritional, and recreational services in women's prisons has also been noted. In particular, the numbers game affects the provision of medical services, with most female institutions sharing physicians and hospital facilities with male prisons. Because the health delivery system at Bedford Hills Correctional Facility was deficient—no full-time physician or continuous medical care and inadequate screening for medical problems—a ruling in a lawsuit filed on behalf of the inmates found the institution in violation of the Eighth Amendment's prohibition of cruel and unusual punishment. The court declared that the state had been deliberately indifferent to known medical needs.

Mothers and Their Children

Of greatest concern to incarcerated women is the fate of their children. The best available data indicate that about 65 percent of women inmates are mothers and that on average they have two dependent children. It is thus estimated that on a typical day 21,000 children in the United States—two-thirds of whom are under ten years of age—have mothers who are in jail or prison.[39] Few of these mothers have husbands or male partners who are able or willing to maintain a home for the children. When Phyllis Jo Baunach studied the effects of separation on 133 inmates and their children, she found that the children were most often taken care of by their maternal grandmothers.[40] The knowledge that her children were with their

■ What is the impact on the child of a woman inmate? How would you react to visiting your mother in prison?

grandmother gave the inmate peace of mind. When an inmate had no relative who would care for the children, they were often put up for adoption or placed in state-funded foster care.

Enforced separation of children from their mothers is bad for the children and bad for the mothers. It is a stress-producing experience that is not fully shared by male prisoners. In most states a baby born in prison must be placed with a family member or social agency within three weeks, to the detriment of the early mother–child bonding thought to be important for the development of a baby. But anxiety about the care of their children is not confined to mothers of infants; it affects all mothers, especially if the children are being cared for by strangers.

Mothers have difficulty maintaining contact with their children because of the distance of prisons from the children's homes, restrictions on visiting hours, only intermittent telephone conversations, and the conditions for interacting with their offspring when they do come to the institution. In some correctional institutions, child visitors must abide by the rules governing visits by adults: physical contact is not allowed, and visiting time is strictly limited.

Increasingly, programs are being developed to deal with the problems of mothers and their children. In some states, children may meet with their mothers at almost any time, for extended periods, and in playrooms or nurseries where contact is possible. Transportation for visits is arranged in some states, and in some it is even possible for children to stay overnight. In both South Dakota and Nebraska, for example, children may stay with their mothers for up to five days a month. Virginia Neto and LaNelle Marie Bainer found in a study of forty prisons that four had family visiting programs that allowed the inmate, her legal husband, and her children to be together, often in a mobile home or apartment, for periods ranging up to seventy-two hours.[41]

Although most states do not allow women to keep their newborns in prison with them for more than a few weeks, some innovative programs make longer periods possible. The emphasis on community corrections as it developed in the 1970s gave rise to programs that permitted mothers and their children to live together in halfway houses. These programs have not expanded as much as it was first thought they might, in part because the presence of children upsets the routine of the facility.

In view of the gains made by women in the United States during the past decade, one might have expected the differences between men's and women's prisons to diminish. But the proportion of arrested women who are sent to prison is rising, and their offenses are becoming more like those of men. One wonders whether a new generation of researchers will find future female inmates engaged in the nurturing enterprise of the pseudofamily and female prisons being run in a different manner.

PRISON VIOLENCE

A recipe for violence: confine in cramped quarters a thousand men, some of whom have a history of engaging in violent interpersonal

■ Conditions in some prisons may lead to violence, as with the burning of the U.S. Penitentiary in Atlanta.

acts, restrict their movement and behavior, allow no contact with women, guard them with guns, and keep them in this condition for an indefinite period of time. Although collective violence such as the prison riots at Attica (1971), Santa Fe, New Mexico (1980), and Atlanta (1987) is well known to the public, little has been said about interpersonal violence in U.S. prisons. Each year more than 100 inmates are "killed by another," and countless others are assaulted. Still other prisoners live in a state of constant uneasiness, always on the lookout for persons who might subject them to homosexual demands, steal their few possessions, and in general increase the pangs of imprisonment.

It is true that some of the violence is perpetrated by the guards and not always in the performance of their duties. But most violence in prison occurs among inmates. The correctional systems of some states seem more prone to violence than others, yet the problem is one that all must face. Assaultive behavior in our correctional institutions raises serious questions for administrators, criminal justice specialists, and the general public. What are the nature and causes of prison violence, and what can be done about it? What is the responsibility of the state to the prisoners whom it holds in these institutions?

Causes of Prison Violence

Too often explanations of prison violence merely recite the deprivations and injustices of life in penal institutions. Mention is usually made of the rules enforced by brutal guards, the loss of freedom, and the boredom. Although such statements may identify the speaker as humane, they usually do not explain the violence itself. Must physcial assault or death be a fact of incarceration? Incidents of prison violence in Western Europe are relatively rare, possibly because those countries also have lower rates of violent crime. Hence the relative lack of

■ Prisons are organized with special emphasis on maintaining security by keeping count of the numbers incarcerated and restricting movement within the walls.

violence may be explained by the character of the general population and the culture that inmates bring with them to the prison.

Alternatively, the absence of assaultive behavior may stem from a more effective prison management that provides few opportunities for attacks. DiIulio argued that no group of immates is "unmanageable" and "no combination of political, social, budgetary, architectual, or other factors makes good management impossible."[42] He pointed to such varied institutions as the California Men's Colony, New York City's Tombs and Rikers Island, the Federal Bureau of Prisons, and the Texas Department of Corrections under the leadership of George Beto as evidence that good management practices can result in prisons and jails in which inmates can "do time" without fearing for their personal safety. In a study of major prison riots from 1971 through 1986, Bert Useem and Peter Kimball found that factors related to prison organization and management were the single most important determinants of the violence.[43]

The importance of prison management should not be downplayed as it has by social scientists in the past, yet every warden and correctional officer must exercise leadership with a full recognition of the types of people with whom they are dealing, the role of prison gangs, and the structure of institutions.

Inmate Characteristics

Violent behavior in prisons is undoubtedly related in part to the types of people who are incarcerated and their characteristics. Three of these characteristics stand out: age, attitudes, and race.

Age

Studies have shown that young people, both inside and outside prison, are more prone to violence than their elders. The group most likely to commit violent crimes is made up of males between the ages of fifteen and twenty-four. Not surprisingly, 96 percent of adult prisoners are males, and their average age at the time of admission is twenty-seven. Prisoners committed for crimes of violence are generally a year or two younger than the average. Not only do the young have greater physical strength, they also lack those commitments to career and family that are thought to restrict antisocial behavior. In addition, many young men have difficulty defining their position in society; thus many of their interactions with others are interpreted as challenges to their status. *Machismo,* the concept of male honor and the sacredness of one's reputation as a man, has a bearing on violence among the young. To be macho is, for one thing, to have a reputation for physically retaliating against those who make slurs on one's honor. The potential for violence among prisoners with these attributes is obvious.

Attitudes

One of the sociological theories advanced to explain crime is that among certain economic, racial, and ethnic groups there is a subculture of violence. Attitudes developed in this subculture influence behavior. It is argued that persons brought up in certain environments are accustomed to violent behavior in their families and among their peers. Arguments are settled and decisions made by the fist rather than by verbal persuasion. These attitudes are brought into the prison as part of an inmate's heritage.

Race

Race has become the major factor that divides the contemporary prison population, reflecting tensions in the larger society. Racist attitudes seem to be acceptable in most institutions and have become part of the convict code. The fact of forced association, having to live with persons with whom one would not be likely to associate on the outside, exaggerates and amplifies racial conflict. The presence of gangs organized along racial lines contributes to violence, and prisoners may be coerced to join the gang of their racial or ethnic group.

Prison Gangs

In recent years the influence of outside groups on prison violence has been documented. In many prison systems racial or ethnic gangs have been linked to acts of violence. In essence the gang wars of the streets are often continued in prison. Gangs are organized primarily with the intention of controlling an institutions's narcotics, gambling, loan sharking, prostituion, extortion, and debt collection rackets. In addition, gangs provide protection for their members from other gangs and instill a sense of macho camaraderie.

A national survey found that prison gangs existed in the institutions of thirty-two states and in the federal system (see Figure 15.2). The survey identified 114 individual gangs, overall a membership of more than 12,000.[44] Although the gangs are small, they are tightly organized and have even been able to arrange the killing of opposition gang leaders housed in other institutions. Administrators say that prison gangs, like organized crime groups, tend to pursue their "business" interests, yet they are also a major source of inmate–inmate violence as they discipline members, enforce orders, and re-

FIGURE 15.2
Prison gangs reported to exist in most jurisdictions
SOURCE: U.S. Department of Justice, Office of Legal Policy, *Prison Gangs: Their Extent, Nature and Impact on Prisons* (Washington, DC: Government Printing Office, 1985).

Prisons with Gangs
Prisons without Gangs

taliate against other gangs. The racial composition of prison gangs in Texas is shown in Table 15.2.

Institutional Structure

It is not enough to point to the personal characteristics of inmates as the cause of prison violence. Lee Bowker has listed five contributing factors: (1) inadequate supervision by staff members, (2) architectural design that promotes rather than inhibits victimization, (3) the easy availability of deadly weapons, (4) the housing of violence-prone prisoners near relatively defenseless persons, and (5) a general high level of tension produced by close quarters.[45] The social and physical environment of the institution also plays a part. Such variables as the physical size and condition of the prison and the relations between inmates and staff all have a bearing on violence.

The gray walls of the fortress prison certainly do not create a likely atmosphere for normal interpersonal relationships. In addition, the prison that houses up to 3,000 inmates presents problems of both crowding and management. The massive scale of some institutions provides opportunities for aggressive inmates to hide weapons, carry out private justice, and engage in other illicit activities free from supervision. As the prison population rises and the personal space of each inmate is decreased, we may expect an increase in antisocial behavior.

As we have seen, the staff is greatly dependent on the inmate society for the functioning of the prison. The degree to which inmate leaders are allowed to take matters into their own hands may have an impact on the amount of violence among inmates. When prison administrators run a tight ship, security is maintained within the

TABLE 15.2   Prison gangs in Texas

Name of Gang	Racial Composition	Size of Membership	Year Formed
Texas Syndicate	Predominantly Hispanic	296	1975
Texas Mafia	Predominantly white	110	1982
Aryan Brotherhood	All white	287	1983
Mexican Mafia	All Hispanic	351	1984
Nuestro Carneles	All Hispanic	47	1984
Mandingo Warrriors	All black	66	1985
Self-Defense Family	Predominantly black	107	1985
Hermanos de Pistolero	All Hispanic	21	1985
Others		115	1985

SOURCE: From "The Organizational Structure of Prison Gangs: A Texas Case Study," by R. S. Fong, *Federal Probation* (March, 1990):36. Reprinted by permission.

institution so that rapes do not occur in dark corners, "shivs" (knives) are not made in the metal shop, and conflict among inmate groups does not take place. "A prison should be the ultimate exemplar of 'defensible space.' It should be an irreducible and primary principle of prison administration that every inmate is entitled to maximum feasible security from physical attack."[46]

The warden is ultimately responsible for the management of a correctional institution.

In sum, prisons must be made safe places. Because the state puts offenders there, it has a responsibility to prevent violence and maintain order. These purposes may conflict with the goals of correction and restriction of freedom. If violence is to be excluded from prisons, limitations may have to be placed on movement within the institution, contacts with the outside, and the right to choose one's associates. These measures may seem to run counter to the goal of producing men and women who will be accountable when they return to society.

PRISONERS' RIGHTS

Ruffin v. *Commonwealth* (1871): As a result of his crime, the prisoner is the slave of the state.

Until the 1960s, the courts, with few exceptions, took the position that the internal administration of prisons was an executive, not a judicial, function. They maintained a hands-off policy with regard to corrections. Judges accepted the view that they were not penologists and that their intervention would be disruptive of prison discipline. The view was a continuation of a position taken more than a century earlier by a Virginia court that said in *Ruffin* v. *Commonwealth* (1871) that the prisoner "has, as a consequence of his crime, not only forfeited his liberty, but all his personal rights except those which the law in its humanity accords to him. He is for the time being the slave of the state."[47] Even in 1951, in a case involving the "bird man of Alcatraz," a federal circuit judge declared, "We think it well settled that it is not the function of the courts to superintend the treatment and discipline of persons in penitentiaries, but only to deliver from imprisonment those who are illegally confined."[48]

With the civil rights movement of the 1960s and the expansion of due process by the Supreme Court, prisoner groups and their sup-

Knowing one's way around the law library has become such a marketable skill that some jailhouse lawyers charge other prisoners for legal advice.

porters pushed to secure inmate rights. Some have expressed the belief that prisoners were—like blacks, women, and the handicapped—a deprived minority whose rights were not being protected by the government. To achieve such protection, the American Civil Liberties Union and various legal services agencies, including the federally funded Office of Economic Opportunity, began to counsel prisoners. Clinic programs for law students and committees of the American Bar Association soon discovered that their services were needed. Alliances were formed between prisoners and groups outside the institutions that could promote the redress of inmates' grievances in the courts.

The most far-reaching departure from the hands-off policy occurred in 1964 when the Supreme Court ruled in *Cooper* v. *Pate* that prisoners are entitled to the protections of the Civil Rights Act of 1871.[49] This legislation designated as 42 United States Code 1983 asserts that any person who violates the rights of another shall "be liable to the party injured in an action at law, suit in equity, or other proper proceedings for redress."[50]

Cooper v. *Pate* (1964): Prisoners are entitled to the protection of the Civil Rights Act of 1871 and may challenge conditions of their confinement in federal courts.

Because of the decision in *Cooper* v. *Pate*, the federal courts now recognize that prisoners are *persons* whose rights are protected by the Constitution, and prisoners in both state and federal institutions may challenge the conditions of their confinement in the federal courts. Thus prisoners may sue the state or public officials for such abuses as brutality by guards, inadequate nutritional and medical care, theft of personal property, and the denial of basic rights. These changes had the effect of decreasing the custodian's power and the prisoners' isolation from the larger society. In addition as James Jacobs has pointed out, "the litigation . . . heightened prisoners' consciousness and politicized them."[51]

Subsequently, the amount of prisoner-inspired litigation in the courts skyrocketed. In 1969, for example, the Supreme Court ruled in *Johnson* v. *Avery* that prison officials could not prohibit one inmate from acting as a jailhouse lawyer for another inmate unless the state provided the inmate with free counsel to pursue a claim that rights had been denied.[52] This was followed by *Bounds* v. *Smith* (1977) in which the Court required that inmates have access to law libraries or the help of persons trained in the law.[53] By the mid-1970s inmates and wardens had learned that in the view of the courts, a prisoner is not wholly stripped of constitutional protection when imprisoned.

Johnson v. *Avery* (1969): The use of jailhouse lawyers may not be prohibited unless free counsel is provided by the state.

Bounds v. *Smith* (1977): Inmates have the right to access to adequate law libraries or the assistance of those trained in the law.

The first successful cases concerning prisoner rights involved the most excessive of prison abuses: brutality and inhuman physical conditions. In 1967, for example, the Supreme Court invalidated the confession of a Florida inmate who had been thrown naked into a "barren cage," filthy with human excrement, and kept there for thirty-five days.[54] Gradually, however, prison litigation has focused more directly on the daily activities of the institution, especially on the administrative rules that regulate inmates' conduct. The result has been a series of court decisions in three general areas of the law. Probably the greatest gains have been made in the upholding of such First Amendment rights as the free exercise of religion. Fourth Amendment protections against unreasonable searches and seizures have been upheld in some circumstances. Courts have found the conditions of confinement in some prisons to be in violation of the

Eighth Amendment's protection against cruel and unusual punishments, and they have required that some of the elements of due process be included in the disciplinary procedures of institutions. Finally, prisoners have been successful in challenging individual situations in which the conditions of confinement as defined by the Civil Rights Act have been violated.

First Amendment

Because the Supreme Court has long maintained that the First Amendment holds a special position with respect to the Constitution, it is not surprising that litigation concerning prisoner rights has been most successful in this area. The First Amendment guarantees freedom of speech, press, assembly, petition, and religion. Many of the restrictions of prison life—access to reading materials, censorship of mail, and some religious practices—have been challenged by prisoners in the courts.

Since 1970 the federal and state courts have extended the rights of freedom of speech and expression to prisoners and have required correctional administrators to show why restrictions on these rights must be imposed. For example, in 1974 the Court said that censorship of mail could be allowed only when there is a substantial governmental interest in maintaining security.[55] The result has been markedly increased communication between inmates and the outside world. It is only when officials have been able to prove that limitations on speech are necessary and when they have proved that an inmate poses a threat to himself or herself, other inmates, or the staff that courts have supported these institutional rules. For instance, the justices upheld federal rules prohibiting inmate interviews with journalists since it was believed that this might enhance the reputation of the prisoner.[56] Yet a lower circuit court has held that prisoners do have a right to correspond with newspapers unless they discuss escape plans or their letters contain contraband material.[57]

The First Amendment also prevents Congress from making laws respecting the establishment of religion or prohibiting its free exercise. The history of the Supreme Court's interpretation of this clause has been long and complex, and its application to the prison setting is no exception. Although freedom of belief has not been challenged, challenges concerning the free exercise of religion have caused the judiciary some problems, especially when the practice may interfere with prison routine.

The arrival in the 1960s of the Black Muslim religion in prisons holding large numbers of urban blacks set the stage for litigation demanding that this group be granted the same privileges as other faiths (special diets, access to clergy and religious publications, opportunities for group worship). Many prison administrators believed that the Muslims were primarily a radical political group posing as a religion, and they did not grant them the benefits accorded to persons who practiced conventional religions.

Fulwood v. Clemmer (1962): The Muslim faith must be recognized as a religion and officials may not restrict members from holding services.

In an early case (*Fulwood v. Clemmer,* 1962), the U.S. District Court of the District of Columbia ruled that correctional officials must recognize the Muslim faith as a religion and not restrict members from holding services. It did not accept the view of the commissioner of corrections that the Muslims were a "clear and present danger."[58] In *Cruz v. Beto* (1972), the justices of the Supreme Court declared that it was discriminatory and a violation of the Constitution for a Buddhist prisoner to be denied opportunities to practice his faith comparable to those accorded fellow prisoners who belonged to conventional religions.[59]

Cruz v. Beto (1972): Prisoners who adhere to other than conventional beliefs may not be denied the opportunity to practice their religion.

In many respects, Muslims and other prisoners have succeeded in gaining some of the rights considered necessary for the practice of their religion. For example, Native Americans have the right to wear their hair long if it is a sincere part of religious belief.[60] However, there is no accepted judicial doctrine in this area, and courts have varied in their willingness to order institutional policies changed to meet the requests of minority religions.[61]

Fourth Amendment

It must be emphasized that the Fourth Amendment prohibits "unreasonable" searches and seizures; thus regulations reasonable in light of the institutions' needs for security and order may be justified. The courts have not been active in extending Fourth Amendment protections to prisoners. In 1984 the decision in *Hudson v. Palmer* upheld the right of officials to search cells and confiscate any materials found.[62]

Hudson v. Palmer (1984): Officials may search cells without a warrant and seize materials found there.

The Fourth Amendment opinions by the Supreme Court illustrate the difficulty of balancing the right to privacy with institutional needs. Body searches have been harder for administrators to justify than cell searches, for example, but they have been upheld when they are part of a clear policy demonstrably related to an identifiable legitimate institutional need and when they are not intended to humiliate or degrade.[63] Courts have ruled that staff members may not supervise inmates of the opposite sex during bathing or use of the toilet or carry out strip searches of the opposite sex. Any inconvenience that administrators may experience in ensuring that the supervisor is of the same sex as the inmate does not justify such intrusion.[64] Yet the right of female guards to "pat down" male prisoners, exclusive of the genital area, has been upheld. These cases illustrate the lack of clear-cut constitutional principles in such matters.

Eighth Amendment

The Eighth Amendment's prohibition of cruel and unusual punishments has been tied to prisoners' rights in relation to their need for decent treatment and minimal standards of health. Most claims involving the failure of prison administrators to provide minimal conditions necessary for health, to furnish reasonable levels of medical care, and to protect inmates from assault by other prisoners have taken the form of suits against specific officials. Three principal tests have been applied by courts to determine whether conditions violate the protection of the Eighth Amendment: (1) whether the punishment shocks the general conscience of a civilized society, (2) whether the punishment is unnecessarily cruel, and (3) whether the punishment goes beyond legitimate penal aims.

Federal courts have ruled that although some aspects of prison life may be acceptable, the combination of various factors, the **"totality of conditions,"** may be such that life in the institution may constitute cruel and unusual punishment. When suits have been brought by pretrial detainees, the totality of conditions in jails has been ruled to constitute unjustifiable punishment without due process of law. The result has been that specific institutions in some states and the entire prison system in other states have been declared violative of the constitution.

Wardens have been held liable for maintaining an environment that is suitable to prisoners' health and security, but recoveries of damages by inmates have been rare. Most often the judge has ruled that specific actions must be taken by correctional administrators to remedy conditions so that they meet constitutional standards.[65] In particular, courts have required that prison populations be reduced to prevent crowding, that treatment programs be instituted, that internal administration be conducted to ensure prisoner safety, and that health or nutritional standards be raised.

There have been several dramatic cases in which prison conditions were shown to be so bad that judges have demanded change. On January 13, 1976, Federal Judge Frank M. Johnson, Jr., issued a precedent-setting order listing minimal standards for the prisons of Alabama and threatened to close all the institutions in that state if the standards were not met. He appointed a special committee empowered to oversee implementation of the standards. Judge Johnson's opinion was that imprisonment in Alabama constituted cruel and unusual punishment because prison conditions were barbaric and inhumane.[66]

In an earlier suit a federal court cited the notorious Cummins Farm Unit of the Arkansas State Penitentiary as being in violation of the Eighth Amendment. This case was the basis for the film *Brubaker,* in which Robert Redford played the role of the reform warden Tom Murton. The federal court found that brutal punishments were administered for minor offenses. The court also cited the use of inmates as prison guards and said that prisoners had a constitutional right of protection by the state while they were incarcerated. As the judges noted, a system that relies on trusties for security and that houses inmates in barracks, leaving them open to "frequent assaults, murder, rape and homosexual conduct," is unconstitutional.[67]

A more wide-ranging order was issued in December 1980 in the case of *Ruiz. v. Estelle*[68] The case, as discussed in the following Close-Up, has been far reaching and controversial; some observers have argued that its impact was to increase prison violence. Judicial supervision of the Texas prison system as a result of this case lasted for a decade and ended on March 31, 1990.

Of particular concern to correctional officials have been rulings that overcrowding is in violation of the Eighth Amendment and must be ended. Among the conditions that the courts have found to violate the Constitution is the crowding of inmates into cells that afford each

totality of conditions: Although specific conditions in prisons might not violate the Constitution, the totality of the conditions may violate the cruel and unusual punishment provisions of the Eighth Amendment.

Ruiz v. *Estelle* (1980): Conditions of confinement in the Texas prison system were unconstitutional.

person less than sixty square feet of floor space. However, the Supreme Court upheld double bunking in Ohio (*Rhodes* v. *Chapman*, 1981) as not constituting a condition of cruel and unusual punishment.[69] In other cases courts have ruled overcrowded conditions to be unconstitutional. Judges have issued orders requiring that space be increased or the prison population decreased.

Many conditions that violate the rights of prisoners may be corrected by administrative action, training programs, or a minimal expenditure of funds, but overcrowding requires an expansion of facilities or a dropping of the intake rate. Prison officials have no control over the capacities of their institutions or over the number of offenders that are sent to them by the courts. New facilities are expensive, and they require appropriations by legislatures and, often, approval of bond issues by voters. In some states, reduction of prison overpopulation has only added to jail populations later. In other states, building programs have not been able to keep pace with the number of new prisoners.

Due Process in Prison Discipline

Administrative discretion in determining disciplinary procedures can usually be exercised within the prison walls without challenge. The prisoner is physically confined, lacks communication with the outside, and is legally in the hands of the state. Further, either formal codes stating the rules of prison conduct do not exist, or the rules are written vaguely. Disrespect toward a correctional officer, for example, may be called an infraction of the rules but not be defined. Normally, disciplinary action is taken on the word of the correctional officer, and the inmate has little opportunity to challenge the charges.

Yet in a series of decisions the Supreme Court has insisted that procedural fairness be included in the most sensitive of institutional decisions: the process by which inmates are sent to solitary confinement and the method by which "good time" credit may be lost because of misconduct. Certain procedural rights must be granted to inmates: to receive notice of the complaint, to have a fair hearing, to confront witnesses, to be assisted in preparing for the hearing, and to be given a written statement of the decision. In 1974 *(Wolff* v. *McDonnell),* the Supreme Court issued an opinion guaranteeing prisoners these fundamental rights of due process.[70] Yet the Court also said that there is no right to counsel at a disciplinary hearing.[71] Rather than consistency, the courts have emphasized the need to balance the rights of the prisoner against the interest of the state.

Wolff v. *McDonnell* (1974): Basic elements of procedural due process must be present when decisions are made concerning the discipline of an inmate.

As a result of the Supreme Court decisions, rules have been established in most prisons to provide some elements of due process in disciplinary proceedings. In many institutions, a disciplinary committee receives the charges, conducts hearings, and decides guilt and punishment. Such committees are usually made up of administrative personnel, but sometimes inmates or citizens from the outside are included. Even with these protections, the fact remains that prisoners are powerless and may fear further punishment if they too strongly challenge the disciplinary decisions of the warden.

Conditions of Confinement

Although decisions of the U.S. Supreme Court make headlines, they are only the very tip of the iceberg. Almost 20,000 suits are filed annually in the lower federal courts by state prisoners contesting aspects of the conditions by which they are being confined. These are filed under the Civil Rights Act of 1871 (42 U.S.C. 1983). In these suits prisoners make claims that the conditions of their confinement violate their rights—for example, that they are not receiving proper medical care, that the state has lost items of their personal property, that they are not being protected from violent inmates, or that crowding limits their freedom.

Few of these suits are successful. Most petitions to the court are written without the assistance of counsel and are often filed in error because of misinterpretations of the law. Screening processes have been developed in most courts so that clerks evaluate the complaints for errors and return it to the prisoner without it having been seen by the judge. There have nonetheless been many cases in which individual inmates secured redress of their grievances. Some have received monetary compensation for neglect; others have been given the medical attention they desired; still others have elicited judicial orders that end certain correctional practices.

Courts may respond to prisoners' requests in specific cases, but judges cannot possibly oversee the daily activities within institutional walls. As a result of the increase in conditions-of-confinement cases, correctional authorities have taken steps to ensure that fair procedures are followed and that unconstitutional practices are foregone. Publication of institutional rules, obligations, and procedures is one of the first and most important steps required to meet this goal. In most states grievance procedures have been developed so that prisoner complaints may be addressed before they result in a suit. Correctional officials often claim that they spend too much of their time answering prisoner complaints in court, yet most would also agree that the judiciary has been most helpful in pressuring legislatures and the executive branch to appropriate the resources necessary to remedy admittedly bad situations.

A Change in Judicial Direction?

Throughout the 1960s and most of the 1970s, the prisoners' rights movement was buoyed by decisions of the U.S. Supreme Court and those of lower federal courts supporting its claims. Beginning in 1979 with *Bell* v. *Wolfish,* the Court seems to have indicated that it wishes to slow the expansion of rights, if not to return to the hands-off policy.[72] The *Bell* case involved the Metropolitan Correctional Center (MCC) in New York City, a newly constructed federal detention unit designed with the most advanced and innovative features. The inmates, however, complained that soon after it opened it was overcrowded, regulations prevented them from receiving hardcover books from anyone but a publisher, they were not allowed to receive packages containing items available in the jail's commissary, and they were not allowed to be present during shakedown inspections of

Bell v. *Wolfish* (1979): Strip searches, including body cavity searches after contact visits, may be carried out when the need for the search outweighs the invasion of personal rights.

their quarters. The Supreme Court found no constitutional violations in the conditions at MCC and said further that the restrictions were a rational response by correctional officials to security concerns. In addition the Court's majority seemed to go out of its way to emphasize that "prison administrators . . . should be accorded wide-ranging deference in the adoption and execution of policies." This is consistent with the 1981 statement in *Rhodes* v. *Chapman* challenging conditions in Ohio's maximum security prison that unless the conditions were "deplorable" or "sordid," the courts should defer to correctional authorities.[73]

That the Supreme Court under the chief justiceship of William Rehnquist is less sympathetic to such civil rights claims is discerned in several cases that limit the ability of prisoners to sue correctional officials. In particular, the court ruled in 1986 that prisoners could sue for damages in federal court only if officials had inflicted injury intentionally or deliberately.[74] The chief justice wrote for the majority that "the due process clause is simply not implicated by a negligent act of an official causing unintended loss or injury to life, liberty or property." He said that the due process clause was put into the Constitution only to prevent an "abuse of power" by public officials and that "lack of due care" or carelessness is not included.

Some observers have detected a return by the Rehnquist Court to the hands-off doctrine. They note that recent decisions with respect to the use of force, inmate privacy, and procedural requirements for disciplinary matters support this belief. In 1991 the Court ruled that a prisoner's conditions of confinement are not unconstitutional unless it can be shown that prison administrators had acted with "deliberate indifference" to basic human needs.[75] Even with regard to First Amendment rights (inmate to inmate correspondence and attendance at Muslim religious services), the Court upheld prison policies.[76] Increasingly, the Court has deferred to the expertise of prison officials with regard to the maintenance of order in their institutions. All of this is not to say that prisons are likely to revert to the conditions found in earlier eras, but it is probable that there will be little forward motion to extend rights and that in some areas there will be a retreat.

Impact of the Prisoners' Rights Movement

It is difficult to measure accurately the impact of the prisoners' rights movement.[77] There are problems in identifying the impact of specific cases and in defining success or failure in many instances. Individual cases may make only a dent in such correctional bureaucracies, but over time basic shifts may occur.

The prisoners' rights movement can probably be credited with some general changes in American corrections since the late 1970s. The most obvious are concrete improvements in institutional living conditions and administrative practices. Law libraries and legal assistance are now generally available; communication with the outside is easier; religious practices are protected; inmate complaint procedures have been developed; and due process requirements are emphasized. Prisoners in solitary confinement undoubtedly suffer less

Rhodes v. *Chapman* (1983): Double bunking and crowding do not necessarily constitute cruel and unusual punishment. Conditions must involve "wanton and unnecessary infliction of pain" and be "grossly disproportionate to the severity of the crime warranting imprisonment."

neglect. Although overcrowding is still a major problem in many institutions, one suspects that the deplorable conditions described in the film *Brubaker* no longer exist in any U.S. prison. This is not to say that prison life has become a bed of roses, but conditions have been improved, and the more brutalizing elements have been diminished.

The prisoners' rights movement has also had an impact on correctional officials. Surely the threat of suit and public exposure has placed many in the correctional bureaucracy on guard. It can be argued that this wariness has merely led to the increased bureaucratization of corrections, with staff now required to prepare extensive and time-consuming documentation of their actions as a means of protecting themselves from suits. On the other hand, judicial intervention has forced corrections to rethink many of the existing procedures and organizational structures. As part of the wider changes in the "new corrections," new administrators, increased funding, reformulated policies, and improved management procedures were, at least in part, influenced by the prisoners' rights movement.

CLOSE-UP | The Impact of Ruiz v. Estelle

In December 1980 William W. Justice, federal judge for the Eastern District of Texas, issued a sweeping decree against the Texas Department of Correction in the case of *Ruiz* v. *Estelle*. He ordered prison officials to face a host of unconstitutional conditions, including overcrowding, unnecessary use of force by personnel, inadequate numbers of guards, poor health-care practices, and a "building-tender" system that allowed some inmates to control others.

The Eastham Unit of the Texas penal system is a large, maximum security institution housing recidivists over the age of twenty-five who have been in prison three or more times. It is tightly managed and has been the depository for troublemakers from other Texas prisons. To help deal with these hard-core criminals, the staff relied on a select group of inmates known as building tenders (BTs). By co-opting the BTs with special privileges, officials were able to use them and their assistants, the "turnkeys," to handle the rank-and-file inmates.

Officially, the building-tender system was an information network. The BTs could help officials penetrate and divide the inmate society. In turn, the BTs and turnkeys had snitches working for them. Information about troublesome inmates, guards, and conditions were passed along by the BTs to officials. With this information, the staff was able to exercise enormous power over the inmates' daily activities. The BTs and turnkeys were rewarded, enjoying power and status far exceeding those of ordinary inmates and even those of lower-ranking guards. Unofficially, the BTs kept order in the cell blocks through intimidation and the physical disciplining of those who broke the rules.

In May 1982 Texas signed a consent decree, agreeing to dismantle the building-tender system by January 1983. BTs were reassigned to ordinary prison jobs; stripped of their power, status, and duties; and moved to separate cell blocks for their protection. At the same time Eastham received 141 new officers, almost doubling the guard force, to help pick up the slack. These reforms were substantial and set off a series of shifts that fundamentally altered the guard and inmate societies.

With the removal of the BTs and turnkeys, with restrictions on the unofficial use of force by guards, and with institution of a prisoner discipline system emphasizing due process, fairness, and rights, the traditional social structure of Eastham came under severe strain. Criminologists Marquart and Crouch found that the reforms had brought about three major changes within the prison community, in interpersonal relations between the guards and inmates, reorganization within the inmate society, and the guard subculture and work role.

Guards and Inmates

Formerly, ordinary inmates had been subject to an all-encompassing, totalitarian system in which they were "dictated to, exploited, and kept in submission." With the new relationship between the keepers and the kept, inmates challenge the authority of correctional officers and are more confrontational and hostile. In response to the verbal and other assaults on their authority, the guards have cited inmates for infractions of the rules. The changes in the relationship between guards and inmates result from a number of factors:

The extension of constitutional rights to prisoners has by no means been speedy, and the courts have spoken only to limited areas of the law. The impact of these decisions on the actual behavior of correctional officials has not yet been measured, but evidence suggests that court decisions have had a broad effect. Because prisoners and their supporters have asserted their rights, wardens and their subordinates may be holding back from traditional disciplinary actions that might result in judicial intervention. In sum, after 200 years of judicial neglect of the conditions under which prisoners are held, courts have begun to look more closely at the situation.

SUMMARY

Since the mid-1970s, there have been calls for reduced use of imprisonment as a form of the criminal sanction. Some critics have argued

---

there are more guards, restrictions on the guards mean that physical reprisals are not feared, the guards no longer have the BTs to act as intermediaries, and the social distance between guards and prisoners has diminished. The last factor is important because one result of the civil rights movement is that prisoners are no longer viewed as "nonpersons." Inmates have rights and may invoke due process rules to challenge decisions of guards and other officials. Although guards control the prison, they must negotiate, compromise, or overlook many difficulties with inmates.

Reorganization within the Inmate Society

The purging of the BT–turnkey system created a power vacuum characterized by uncertainty. One outcome was a rise in the amount of inmate–inmate violence. Without the BTs to help settle disputes among inmates, these conflicts more often led to violence in which weapons were used. Self-defense became a social necessity. As personal violence escalated, so did the development of inmate gangs. Gang members know that they will have the assistance of others if they are threatened, assaulted, or robbed. Nongang prisoners must rely on themselves and avoid contact with inmates known for their toughness.

Guard Subculture and Work Role

The court-imposed reforms upset the foundations of the guard subculture and work role, making the work no longer well ordered, predictable, or rewarding. Upon removal of the BTs, guards were assigned to cell block duty for the first time. This placed them in close

contact with inmates. The fact that most of the guards were new to prison work meant that they were hesitant to enforce order. Many officers believe that because they cannot physically punish inmates and their supervisors do not back them up, it is better not to enforce the rules at all. They think that their authority has been undermined and that the new disciplinary process is frustrating. Many would rather look the other way.

Conclusion

The court-ordered reforms brought Eastham's operations more in line with constitutional requirements of fairness and due process but disrupted an ongoing social system. Before the *Ruiz* decision the prison had been run on the basis of paternalism, coercion, dominance, and fear. Guards exercised much discretion over inmates, and they used the building tenders to help maintain order and as a source of information. During the transition to a new bureaucratic and legal order, levels of violence and personal insecurity increased. Authority was eroded, combative relations between inmates and officers materialized, and inmate gangs developed to provide security and autonomy for members.

An overriding question remains: Can a prison be administered in ways that conform to the requirements of fairness and due process yet maintain security for the inmates and staff?

SOURCE: Drawn from "Judicial Reform and Prison Control: The Impact of *Ruiz* v. *Estelle* on a Texas Penitentiary," by J. W. Marquart and B. M. Crouch, *Law and Society Review* 19 (1985): 557–586. Reprinted by permission.

that prisons are not humane, that they are schools of crime, that they do not rehabilitate, and that they are used to oppress minorities. Yet the size of the prison population in the United States continues to reach record levels.

Although the prison facility depicted in old movies remains, many of the characteristics of the convict population, the programs, the guards, and the rules have changed. The social relations of the convict world have therefore changed, too. The most striking feature of many contemporary prisons is the racial composition of the population and the tensions arising from it. In many institutions, convict solidarity against the "screws" has been broken. Instead, observers report, the convict society has divided along racial lines, with resultant societal instability and the potential for intergroup clashes.

A wide variety of correctional institutions exists, and none is exactly the same as another. Each has its own traditions, organization, and environment, though in many respects the characteristics described apply generally to most institutions. Although less emphasized than in the past, treatment, educational, and vocational programs remain. Efforts to improve prison industries by making them productive has gained prominence in some states. The correctional officers are the real linchpin to the system. They are constantly in close contact with prisoners and are the first to become aware of prisoners' problems and needs. The effectiveness of the institution weighs heavily on officers' shoulders.

The prisoners' rights movement has brought about many changes in the administration and conditions of American prisons. Through litigation in the federal courts, prisoners have challenged the conditions of their confinement. In many cases judges have responded by ordering that unconstitutional procedures and conditions be changed.

That incarceration will continue to be widely used is clear. To reduce the size of the correctional bureaucracy and tear down the physical plants devoted to incarceration would be all but impossible. As the National Advisory Commission has said: "The prison . . . has persisted, partly because a civilized nation could neither turn back to the barbarism of an earlier time nor find a satisfactory alternative."[78]

FOR DISCUSSION

1. You have just accepted a position as a correctional officer. What should be your attitude toward the prisoners?
2. What are some of the problems likely to arise between custodial and treatment staffs?
3. Should prisoners have the right to organize a union? What might the impact of a prisoners' union be on the inmate society?
4. What can be done to reduce prison violence?
5. You have just arrived in a maximum security prison to serve a sentence. What goals and fears are you likely to have? How would you cope with them?

Baunach, Phyllis Jo. *Mothers in Prison.* New Brunswick, NJ: Transaction Books, 1985. A survey of incarcerated mothers and their relationships with their children.

DiIulio, John J., Jr. *Governing Prisons.* New York: Free Press, 1987. A critique of the sociological perspective on inmate society. DiIlulio argues the need to view the problems of prisons as one of governance.

Goodstein, Lynne, and Doris Layton MacKenzie, eds. *The American Prison: Issues in Research and Policy.,* New York: Plenum, 1989. An excellent collection of essays on various prison issues.

Johnson, Robert. *Hard Time: Understanding and Reforming the Prison.* Pacific Grove, CA: Brooks/Cole, 1987. A significant contribution to understanding prison society.

Kauffman, Kelsey. *Prison Officers and Their World.* Cambridge, MA: Harvard University Press, 1988. Looks at the work of correctional officers, their roles and place within the prison environment.

Lockwood, Daniel. *Prison Sexual Violence.* New York: Elsevier, 1980. Analysis of the problem of sexual violence within prisons.

Martin, Steve J., and Sheldon Ekland-Olson. *Texas Prisons: The Walls Came Tumbling Down.* Austin: Texas Monthly Press, 1987. Impact of the federal courts on the Texas prison system.

Useem, Bert, and Peter Kimball. *States of Siege: U.S. Prison Riots, 1971–1986.* New York: Oxford University Press, 1989. Analysis of collective riots in American prisons during the last two decades.

Zimmer, Lynn. *Women Guarding Men.* Chicago: University of Chicago Press, 1986. Exploration of the innovative policy of employing women as correctional officers in prisons for men.

NOTES

1. Donald Clemmer, *The Prison Community* (New York: Holt, Rinehart & Winston, 1940); Gresham M. Sykes, *The Society of Captives* (Princeton, NJ: Princeton University Press, 1958).
2. Robert Johnson and Hans Toch, "Introduction," in *The Pains of Imprisonment,* eds. Robert Johnson and Hans Toch (Newbury Park, CA: Sage, 1982); p. 15.
3. Erving Goffman, *Asylums* (Garden City, NY: Anchor Books, 1961).
4. John DiIulio, Jr., *Governing Prisons* (New York: Free Press, 1987).
5. Ibid., p. 242. See also DiIulio, *No Escape: The Future of American Corrections* (New York: Basic Books, 1990); *Barbed Wire Bureaucracy: Leadership and Administration in the Federal Bureau of Prisons* (New York: Oxford University Press, 1991).
6. Michigan Department of Corrections, *Resident Guide Book* (Lansing, MI: Department of Corrections, n.d.).
7. Sykes, *Society of Captives,* p. 49.
8. Ibid., p. 53.
9. Richard Korn and Lloyd W. McCorkle, "Resocialization within Walls," *Annals* 293, (1954):191.
10. Sykes, *Society of Captives,* pp. 84–90.
11. John Irwin, *The Felon* (Englewood Cliffs, NJ: Prentice Hall, 1970), p. 47.
12. Ibid., pp. 67–79.
13. Ibid., p. 78.
14. Ibid., p. 75.
15. Vergil L. Williams and Mary Fish, *Convicts, Codes, and Contraband* (Cambridge, MA: Ballinger, 1974), p. 50.
16. Susan Sheehan, *A Prison and a Prisoner* (Boston: Houghton Mifflin, 1978), p. 90. Reprinted by permission.

17. Gordon Hawkins, "Prison Labor and Prison Industries," in *Crime and Justice*, eds. Michael Tonry and Norval Morris, vol. 5 (Chicago: University of Chicago Press, 1983), p. 90.

18. U.S. National Advisory Committee on Criminal Justice Standards and Goals, *Task Force Report: Corrections* (Washington, DC: Government Printing Office, 1973), p. 188.

19. Justice System Improvement Act of 1979, P.L. 96–157, 93 Stat. 1167, 1215.

20. U.S. Department of Justice, *Report to the Nation on Crime and Justice*, 2nd ed. (Washington, DC: Government Printing Office, 1988), p. 110.

21. Paul Gendreau and Robert R. Ross, "Effective Correctional Treatment: Bibliotherapy for Cynics," in *Effective Correctional Treatment*, eds. Robert R. Ross and Paul Gendreau (Toronto: Butterworths, 1980), p. 25.

22. James Jacobs and Norma Crotty, "The Guard's World," in *New Perspectives on Prisons and Imprisonment*, ed. James B. Jacobs (Ithaca, NY: Cornell University Press, 1983), p. 135.

23. U.S. President's Commission on Law Enforcement and Administration of Justice, *Task Force Report: Corrections* (Washington, DC: Government Printing Office, 1967), p. 96.

24. Donald R. Cressey, "Limitations on Organization of Treatment in the Modern Prison," in *Theoretical Studies in Social Organization of the Prison*, eds. Richard A. Cloward, Donald R. Cressey, George H. Grosser, Richard McCleery, Lloyd E. Ohlin, Gresham M. Sykes, and Sheldon L. Messinger (New York: Social Science Research Council, 1960), p. 103.

25. James B. Jacobs and Harold G. Retsky, "Prison Guard," in *The Sociology of Corrections*, eds. Robert E. Leger and John R. Stratton (New York: Wiley, 1977), p. 54.

26. Drawn from Kelsey Kauffman, *Prison Officers and Their World*, by K. Kauffman, pp. 86–114. Copyright © 1988 by Harvard University Press. Reprinted by permission.

27. U.S. Department of Justice, Bureau of Justice Statistics, *Report to the Nation on Crime and Justice*, 2nd ed. (Washington, DC: Government Printing Office, 1988), p. 126.

28. David Duffee, "Careers in Criminal Justice: Corrections," in *Encyclopedia of Crime and Justice*, ed. Sanford H. Kadish (New York: Free Press, 1983), p. 1232.

29. Joycelyn M. Pollock-Byrne, *Women, Prison, and Crime* (Pacific Grove, CA: Brooks/Cole, 1990), p. 57.

30. *New York Times*, April 17, 1989, p. 1.

31. U.S. Department of Justice, Bureau of Justice Statistics, *Sourcebook of Criminal Justice Statistics* (Washington, DC: Government Printing Office, 1989), p. 627.

32. Esther Heffernan, *Making It in Prison* (New York: Wiley, 1972), p. 88.

33. Rose Giallombardo, *Society of Women: A Study of a Women's Prison* (New York: Wiley, 1966), pp. 102–103.

34. Heffernan, *Making It in Prison*, pp. 41–42.

35. James G. Fox, *Organizational and Racial Conflict in Maximum-Security Prisons* (Lexington, MA: Lexington Books, 1982).

36. Ibid., p. 100.

37. Ruth M. Glick and Virginia V. Neto, *National Study of Women's Correctional Programs*, U.S. Department of Justice, National Institute of Law Enforcement and Criminal Justice (Washington, DC: Government Printing Office, 1977).

38. T. E. Ryan, *Adult Female Offenders and Institutional Programs: A State of the Art Analysis* (Washington, DC: National Institute of Corrections, 1984), p. 24; Ralph Weishet, "Trends in Programs for Female Offenders: The Use of Private Agencies as Service Providers," *International Journal of Offender Therapy and Comparative Criminology* 29 (1985):35–42.

39. Brenda G. McGowan and Karen L. Blumenthal, *Why Punish the Children?* (Hackensack, NJ: National Council on Crime and Delinquency, 1978), p. 3.

40. Phyllis J. Baunach, "You Can't Be a Mother and Be in Prison . . . Can You? Impacts of the Mother-Child Separation," in *The Criminal Justice System and Women*, ed. Barbara Rafel Price and Natalie J. Sokoloff (New York: Clark Boardman, 1982), pp. 155–169.

41. Virginia V. Neto and LaNelle Marie Bainer, "Mother and Wife Locked Up: A Day in the Family," *Prison Journal* 63 (Autumn-Winter 1983):124.

42. John J. DiIulio, Jr., *No Escape: The Future of American Corrections* (New York: Basic Books, 1990), p. 12.

43. Bert Useem and Peter Kimball, *States of Siege: U.S. Prison Riots 1971–1986* (New York: Oxford University Press, 1989).

44. U.S. Department of Justice, Office of Legal Policy, *Prison Gangs: Their Extent, Nature and Impact on Prisons* (Washington, DC: Government Printing Office, 1985).

45. Lee Bowker, "Victimizers and Victims in American Correctional Institutions," in *Pains of Imprisonment*, eds. Robert Johnson and Hans Toch (Newbury Park, CA: Sage, 1982), p. 62.

46. James B. Jacobs, "Prison Violence and Formal Organization," in *Prison Violence*, eds. Albert K. Cohen, George F. Cole, and Robert G. Bailey (Lexington, MA: Lexington Books, 1975), p. 79.

47. *Ruffin* v. *Commonwealth*, 62 Va. 790 (1871).

48. *Stroud* v. *Swope*, 187 F. 2d 850 (9th Circ. 1951).

49. *Cooper* v. *Pate*, 378 U.S. 546 (1964).

50. 42 U.S.C. 1983.

51. James B. Jacobs, "The Prisoners' Rights Movement and Its Impact, 1960–1980," in *Crime and Justice*, vol. 2, eds. Norval Morris and Michael Tonry (Chicago: University of Chicago Press, 1980), p. 433.

52. *Johnson* v. *Avery*, 393 U.S. 483 (1969).

53. *Bounds* v. *Smith*, 430 U.S. 817 (1977).

54. *Brooks* v. *Florida*, 389 U.S. 413 (1967).

55. *Procunier* v. *Martines*, 416 U.S. 396 (1974).

56. *Saxbe* v. *Washington Post*, 417 U.S. 396 (1974).

57. *Nolan* v. *Fitzpatrick*, 451 F. 2d 545 (1st Cir. 1985).

58. *Fulwood* v. *Clemmer*, 206 F. Supp. 370 (1962).

59. *Cruz* v. *Beto*, 92 S. Ct. 1079 (1972).

60. *Callahan* v. *Hollyfield*, 516 F. Supp. 1004 (E.D.Va. 1981).

61. *Abdullah* v. *Kinnison*, 769 F. 2d 345 (6th Circ. 1985).

62. *Hudson* v. *Palmer*, 52 L. W. 5052 (1984).

63. *Bell* v. *Wolfish*, 441 U.S. 420 (1979).

64. *Lee* v. *Downs*, 641 F. 2d 1117 (4th Cir. 1981).

65. *Estelle* v. *Gamble*, 429 U.S. 97 (1976).

66. *Pugh* v. *Locke*, 406 F. Supp. 318 (1976).

67. *Holt* v. *Sarver*, 300 F. Supp. 825 (E.D. Ark. 1970).

68. *Ruiz* v. *Estelle*, No. 74-329 (E.D. Tex. 1980).

69. *Rhodes* v. *Chapman*, 45 U.S. 337 (1981).

70. *Wolff* v. *McDonnell*, 94 S. Ct. 2963 (1974).

71. *Baxter* v. *Palmigiano*, 425 U.S. 308 (1976).

72. *Bell* v. *Wolfish*, 99 S. Ct. 1861 (1979).

73. *Rhodes* v. *Chapman*, 45 U.S. 337 (1983).

74. *Daniels* v. *Williams*, 54 L. W. 4090 (1986).

75. *Wilson* v. *Seiter*, No. 89-7376. (June 17, 1991).

76. *Turner* v. *Saley*, 107 S. Ct. 2254 (1987); *O'Lone* v. *Shabazz*, 107 S. Ct. 2400 (1987).

77. Malcolm M. Feeley and Roger A. Hanson, "The Impact of Judicial Intervention on Prisons and Jails: A Framework of Analysis and a Review of the Literature," in John J. DiIulio, Jr., ed., *Courts, Corrections and the Constitution* (New York: Oxford University Press, 1990), pp. 12–46.

78. U.S. National Advisory Committee on Criminal Justice Standards and Goals, *Task Force Report: Corrections* (Washington, DC: Government Printing Office, 1973), p. 343.

16

C H A P T E R

Community Corrections: Probation, Intermediate Sanctions, Parole

Key Terms and Cases

community correctional center
community corrections
discretionary release
furlough

mandatory release
parole
presumptive parole date

probation
recidivism
work and educational release

Gagnon v. *Scarpelli* (1973)
Mempa v. *Rhay* (1967)
Morrissey v. *Brewer* (1972)

*The general underlying premise for the new directions in correc-
tions is that crime and delinquency are symptoms of failures
and disorganizations of the community as well as of individual
offenders.*

*President's Commission on Law Enforcement
and Administration of Justice (1967)*

It is often said that the way a society deals with its criminals reflects the forces operating in that society. As we have seen, the invention of the penitentiary reflected the values of nineteenth-century religion and culture. Prisons were intended to instill discipline and good work habits and to give inmates an opportunity to reflect on their misdeeds. During the early part of the twentieth century, with the rise of the social and behavioral sciences, correctional institutions became places for treatment of offenders. Reflecting the belief that science could solve the criminal's problems, most prison systems incorporated rehabilitative programs. During the social and political turmoil of the late 1960s, a shift took place in assumptions about how offenders should be handled. This new shift became known as "community corrections"; it emphasized the reintegration of the offender into the community.

American corrections has not underscored incarceration to the exclusion of other forms of the criminal sanction. Even during the nineteenth-century reform period it was recognized that supervision in the community was a more appropriate means to bring about the desired change in some offenders. The development of probation by John Augustus in Boston in the 1840s and the transplantation of parole from England in the 1880s best exemplify this approach. Until the 1950s, however, many states still relied more on incarceration than on probation and parole, and it was not until the 1960s that a variety of community alternatives was developed. In the 1980s, with prison crowding becoming a major national problem, there was new interest in creating methods—intensive probation supervision, home arrest, and electronic monitoring—by which offenders, who might normally be sent to prison, could be supervised in the community. Today almost two-thirds of all persons under correctional supervision are living in the community.

This means that corrections must deal with the fact that release under supervision in the community is one way in which judges, parole boards, and correctional officials can reduce the number incarcerated. A different type of offender, one who has committed more serious crimes, is on the street under correctional supervision. Given the characteristics of these offenders, community corrections has taken a tougher stance, with surveillance outweighing the rehabilitative and reintegrative thrust of the past.

COMMUNITY CORRECTIONS: ASSUMPTIONS

Community corrections aims at building reintegrating ties between the offender and the community: the restoration of family links, help in obtaining employment and education, and development of a sense of place and pride in daily life. The community model of corrections assumes that the offender must change, but it also recognizes that factors within the community that might encourage criminal behavior (unemployment, for example) must change, too. Whereas the rehabilitation model focuses on social and psychological imperfections in the criminal, the community, or reintegration, model emphasizes that social conditions in the community have an influence on the criminal as well.

Four factors are usually cited in support of community corrections. First, there are some offenders whose background characteristics or crimes are not serious enough to warrant incarceration. Second, community supervision is cheaper than incarceration. Third, if rehabilitation is measured by **recidivism** rates, prison is no more effective than community supervision. In fact, some studies show that just being in prison raises the offender's potential for recidivism. Fourth, incarceration is more destructive to both the offender and society. In addition to the pangs of imprisonment and the harmful effects of prison life, there is the suffering of family members, particularly the children of women offenders.

Central to the community corrections approach is a belief in the "least restrictive alternative," the notion that the criminal sanction should be applied only to the minimum extent necessary to meet the

community corrections: Programs designed to rehabilitate offenders through probation, diversion, halfway houses, and parole.

recidivism: A return to criminal behavior.

The halfway house provides a supportive atmosphere for parolees, probationers, and those diverted from the system. In this San Francisco halfway house a prospective new resident is interviewed by the director and present residents.

community's need for protection, the gravity of the offense, and society's need for deserved punishment. It is argued that personal freedom is so valuable that it is unjust to incarcerate individuals needlessly when community-based alternatives can achieve correctional goals. Supporters of community corrections urge that efforts be made to expand halfway houses, work release and furlough programs, probation and parole services to assist and reintegrate the offender into the community. All of these features of community corrections reflect the belief that actions should be taken to increase offenders' opportunities to succeed in law-abiding activities and to reduce their contact with the criminal world.

To ease the transition of released offenders from prison to the community and to assist probationers and parolees, community corrections asserts that a variety of educational, medical, and social services should be available. Provision of these services should involve not only correctional authorities but also public and private agencies. The provision of services in the community rather than in the prison is believed to be in the interest of both offenders and society. The offender is able to develop community ties at a cost to the taxpayer that is much less than the cost of prison. Consistent with the belief that corrections should prepare offenders for return to society, the approach emphasizes services that will help the reintegrative process and provide a gradual adjustment to freedom.

Community corrections appeals to people who believe that most prison terms in the United States are too long and that institutionalization has important negative consequences for the offender's reintegration. In this view, incarceration of some types of offenders not only imposes punishment out of proportion to the crime but also unnecessarily exposes first-timers to the prison "crime factory," so that the possibility of successful reintegration is reduced. If the objective is to avoid the negative impact of separation from the community, severing of family ties, and the culture of the prison, for many offenders the alternative of corrections in the community may be more beneficial. With the tougher sentencing policies instituted in the 1980s, a greater percentage of felony offenders are being supervised in the community because prison space is in such short supply. In fact, some argue that the ideals of community corrections have been preempted by concerns over public safety.[1] As Joan Petersilia has said: "The goal is not offender rehabilitation, but offender control, with public safety the central concern."[2]

This chapter describes and evaluates the major alternatives that constitute community corrections:

- probation, the most widely used community sanction
- intermediate sanctions, such as house arrest and intensive probation supervision
- programs for easing the transition from prison to the community
- parole, the primary means that released felons are supervised

Each approach attempts to deal with the problems of a particular type of offender in a somewhat distinctive manner, and each has organizational characteristics of its own. As each mode is discussed, consider its likely contribution to the goals of corrections. Is community corrections effective? What changes might be made?

PROBATION: CORRECTION WITHOUT INCARCERATION

Probation denotes the conditional release of the offender into the community under supervision. It is a sentence, usually not involving confinement, that imposes conditions and retains the authority of the sentencing court to modify the conditions of sentence or to resentence the offender if he or she violates those conditions. Often the judge imposes a prison term but then suspends execution of it and instead places the offender on probation. Increasingly, however, judges in some states are using the tactics of shock incarceration or split sentences, in which a period in prison is followed by probation.

Judges normally stipulate a set of conditions as to how the probationer is to live in the community. Depending on the offense and background characteristics, these conditions may require that the probationer obtain drug, alcohol, or mental health treatment. If the offense was a result of domestic violence or sexual abuse an order may be given stipulating that the probationer not have contact with the victim. Restitution, community service, or a fine may be ordered as part of the punishment. These rules are in addition to the standard conditions that the client cooperate with the probation officer and not commit another offense. The probationer who meets the conditions set by the court may remain in the community. Violations of these terms or arrest for another offense may cause the probation to be revoked and the prison sentence carried out.

The number of probationers is at a record level and is still rising. Much has been written about overcrowded prisons, yet the adult probation population has also been increasing—over 7 percent a year, up 40 percent since 1984. At the same time the political climate has supported harsher correctional policies, with the result that probation goals are now oriented more toward punishment of the offender and protection of the community than toward rehabilitation. Probation budgets in many states have been cut and caseloads increased as greater resources are diverted to prison expenditures. However, the reality of corrections in the 1990s will undoubtedly mean that with prisons filled, judges will be forced to place more offenders convicted of serious crimes, especially drug crimes, on probation. This means that probation will be dealing with an increasing number of "high-risk" clients.

> **probation**: A sentence allowing the offender to serve the sentence imposed by the court in the community under supervision.

Origins of Probation

Although historical antecedents for probation can be found in the procedures of reprieves and pardons of early English courts, John Augustus, a prosperous Bostonian, has become known as the world's first probation officer. By persuading a judge in the Boston Police Court to place a convicted offender in his custody for a brief period, Augustus was able to assist his probationer so that the man appeared to be rehabilitated when he returned for sentencing.

Probation continued to be a voluntary activity in Boston until 1878, when it was formalized; the mayor was given the power to hire officers, who would report directly to the criminal courts. Massachusetts developed the first statewide probation system in 1880, and by 1920 twenty-one other states had followed suit. The federal courts were authorized to hire probation officers in 1925, and by the beginning of World War II, forty-four states had implemented the concept.

Today over 60 percent of offenders in the United States are placed on probation. Estimates are that at any one time there are almost two million probationers. Such groups as the National Council on Crime and Delinquency have urged that probation be the disposition of choice for most first offenders, although several questions have been raised about probation's effectiveness. Some observers say that to place an offender on probation nowadays is to do almost nothing. Given the huge caseloads of probation officers, offenders are given very little guidance, supervision, or assistance. A Philadelphia criminal court judge, Lois Forer, has remarked: "Probation is not a penalty. The offender continues with his life style. . . . If he is a wealthy doctor, he continues with his practice; if he is an unemployed youth, he continues to be unemployed. Probation is a meaningless rite; it is a sop to the conscience of the court."[3]

Organization

Probation may be viewed as a form of corrections, but in many states it is administered by the judiciary, and it is very much a local affair. In about 25 percent of the states probation is a responsibility of county and local government; in them the state provides only financial support, training courses, and setting standards. This locally based approach accounts for about two-thirds of all persons under probation supervision.[4] Although in many jurisdictions the state is formally responsible for all probation services, the locally elected county judges are really in charge. Some persons argue that judges

BIOGRAPHY

John Augustus

John Augustus (1785–1859) was a Boston bootmaker who became a self-appointed probation officer, thereby developing the concept of probation as an alternative to incarceration. His initial probation effort occurred in the Boston Police Court in 1841 when he posted bail for a man charged with being a common drunkard. Because his philanthropic activities made Augustus a frequent observer in the courts, the judge was willing to defer sentencing for three weeks, and the man was released into Augustus's custody. At the end of this brief probationary period, the man convinced the judge of his reform and therefore received a nominal fine. The concept of probation had been born.

Continuing his interest in criminal justice reform, Augustus was often present in Boston courts, acting as counsel and furnishing bail. He found homes for juvenile offenders and frequently obtained lodging and employment for adults accused or convicted of violating Boston's vice or temperance laws. Between 1842 and 1858 he bailed out 1,946 people, making himself liable to the extent of $243,235 and preventing these individuals from being held in jail to await trial. He reported great success with his charges and asserted that, with help, most of them eventually led upright lives. Since Augustus belonged to no charitable or philanthropic society, his primary sources of financial support were his own business and voluntary contributions. He never received a salary from any organization. Augustus persisted in his efforts, and as a result, criminal justice gained a practice that has since become commonplace.

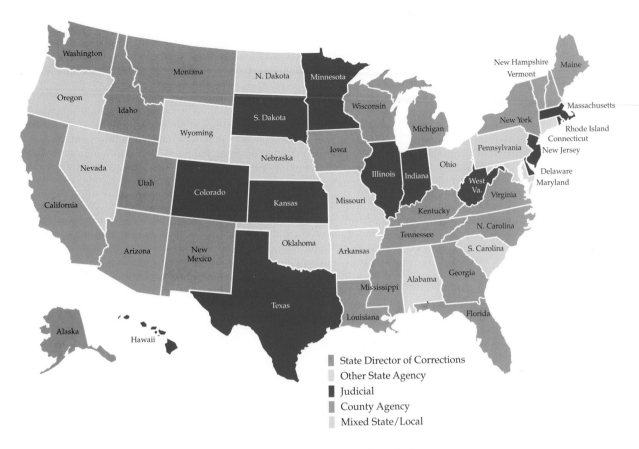

State Director of Corrections
Other State Agency
Judicial
County Agency
Mixed State/Local

know little about corrections and that probation increases the administrative duties of the overworked courts. Others contend that probationers would be unduly stigmatized if they were under the supervision of the corrections since most citizens equate that department with prisons. Figure 16.1 shows the organizational structure of probation in the United States.

Perhaps the strongest argument in favor of judicial control is that probation works best when there is a close relationship between the judge and the supervising officer. Proponents say that judges need to work with probation officers they can trust, whose presentence reports they can accurately evaluate, and whom they can rely on to report on the success or failure of individual cases. These views have been extensively argued in the literature. At the same time, judges also may well be interested in their ability to appoint probation officers who are responsive to the local political system.

Yet it is in the executive branch of government that corrections and other human service agencies are found. Probation officers have a greater chance of using such services for their clients' benefit if they have direct access to the services. In a number of states this consideration has led to the combining of probation and parole services in the same agency. Proponents of this move argue that it increases effectiveness and efficiency. Others point out, however, that probationers are quite different from parolees, for they have not developed the same degree of criminal lifestyles and do not have the same problems of reintegration into the community.

FIGURE 16.1
Probation organizational structures.
Probation is primarily a local responsibility. Even when probation operates under the jurisdiction of a state agency, it is the county judge who really influences probation decisions.
SOURCE: *Research in Action* (Washington, DC: National Institute of Justice, 1988), p. 2

Offenders meet with their probation officers on a regular basis. Officers often face conflict in achieving the twin goals of supervision and service.

Probation Services

Probation officers are expected to be both police personnel and social workers. In addition to assisting the judiciary with presentence investigations and reports, they are to supervise clients in order to keep them out of trouble and to help them secure treatment and other services. Not surprisingly, individual officers may emphasize one role over the other, and the potential for conflict is great. But studies have shown that most probation officers have backgrounds in social service and are partial to the treatment role.

Probation originated as a humanitarian way of giving first-time and minor offenders a second chance. To this end, probation officers were to use a casework model and intervene in the client's life, guiding him or her toward the "right" path. The offender was not only to refrain from criminal acts but also to behave in a morally acceptable fashion. Early officers were thus actively involved in all levels of the offender's lifestyle: family, religion, employment, and free time. They were to provide a role model or moral leadership for those who had been in trouble.

With the rise of psychology in the 1920s, the probation officer continued as a caseworker, but the emphasis was now on therapeutic counseling in the office rather than on assistance in the field. This shift in emphasis brought a number of important changes. First, the officer was no longer primarily a community supervisor charged with enforcing a particular morality. Second, the officer became more of a clinical social worker whose goal was to help the offender solve psychological and social problems. Third, the offender was expected to become actively involved in the treatment program. As in other aspects of the Rehabilitation Model, the probation officer had to be given extensive discretion to diagnose the problem and treat it.

During the 1960s, perhaps reflecting the emphasis of the war on poverty, a third shift occurred in the orientation of probation work. Rather than counseling offenders in their offices, probation officers provided them with concrete social services, such as assistance with employment, housing, finances, and education. Probation officers backed away from direct involvement in the lives of offenders, on the assumption that when offenders exercised more control over their own goals and activities, their chances of adjustment to the community were improved. Finally, instead of being a counselor or therapist, the probation officer was to be an advocate, dealing with the private and public institutions on the offender's behalf.

In the late 1970s the orientation of probation again changed. The goals of rehabilitation and reintegration gave way to an orientation widely referred to as risk control. This approach, dominant today, tries to minimize the probability that an offender will commit a new offense. Risk control combines values of the just desserts model of the criminal sanction, which holds that punishment should be commensurate with the offense and that correctional intervention should neither raise nor lower the level of punishment, with the commonly accepted idea that the community deserves protection. Hence, the amount and type of supervision of the probationer are a function of estimates of risk that he or she will return to criminal behavior.

One of the continuing issues related to probation services is the size of the caseload that is both efficient in the use of resources and effective in the guidance of offenders. The oversized caseload is usually identified as one of the major obstacles to successful operation of probation. The 50-unit caseload established in the 1930s by the National Probation Association was reduced to 35 by the President's Commission in 1967; yet the national average is currently about 115, and in extreme cases it reaches more than 300. Recent evidence indicates that the size of the caseload is less significant than the nature of the supervision experience, the classification of offenders, the professionalism of the officer, and the services available from the agencies of correction.

During the past decade probation officials have developed methods of classifying clients according to their service needs, the element of risk that they pose to the community, and the chance of recidivism. It is through this process that probationers may be granted less supervision as they continue to live without violation of the conditions of their sentence. Risk classification schemes are consistent with the deserved punishment model of the criminal sanction in that the most serious cases receive the greatest restrictions and supervision.[5]

Because the probation officer is also responsible for filing presentence reports, assistance and supervision obviously have to be on a catch-as-catch-can basis. In some urban areas, probationers are merely required to telephone or mail reports of their current residence and employment. Under such conditions, it must be asked which justification for the criminal sanction—deserved punishment, rehabilitation, deterrence, or incapacitation—is being realized. If none is being realized, the offender is getting off free.

The war on drugs has had a significant impact on probation in urban areas. Probation is now "the dominant place to put drug traffickers and people convicted of drug possession."[6] Many of these offenders have committed violent acts and live in inner-city areas where drug selling, turf battles, and attempts to control drug markets are a fact of life. Estimates vary but some reports indicate that upwards of 75 percent of probationers are addicted to drugs or alcohol. Direct supervision is dangerous under these conditions.

Probation is at a crossroads. Some people advocate a continuation of the service provider orientation; others object that the individual probation officer cannot possibly know all that is required to be effective in the specialized fields of human services. Thus it is urged that the probation unit contract with community agencies for these services and that the probation officer return to supervision. Finally, there is dissatisfaction with probation itself. In many quarters it is argued that, especially in urban areas, it does nothing. Because of huge caseloads and indifferent officers, probation is regarded as a "free ride" by offenders, who can easily avoid supervision and check in only perfunctorily with the officers. Such a situation does little for crime control.

Revocation of Probation

Probationers who violate the provisions of their sentences may be taken to court for further disposition. Since probation is usually granted in conjunction with a suspended jail or prison sentence, if the terms of probation are not fulfilled, incarceration may follow. Probation officers and judges have widely varying notions of what constitutes grounds for revoking probation. Once the officer has decided to call a violation to the attention of the court, the probationer may be arrested or summoned for a revocation hearing. Revocation for technical violation of supervision rules was fairly common in the 1950s and 1960s, but the contemporary emphasis is on avoiding incarceration except for flagrant and continual violation of the conditions of probation. Most revocations today occur because of a new arrest or conviction.

Mempa v. *Rhay* **(1967)**: Probationers have the right to counsel at a hearing considering revocation of a suspended sentence.

Gagnon v. *Scarpelli* **(1973)**: Requirement that before probation may be revoked, a two-stage hearing must be held and the offender provided with specific elements of due process.

Not until 1967 did the Supreme Court of the United States give an opinion concerning the due process rights of probationers at a revocation hearing. In *Mempa* v. *Rhay* it determined that a state probationer had the right to counsel at a revocation proceeding, but nowhere in the opinion did the Court refer to any requirement for a hearing.[7] This issue was addressed by the Court in *Gagnon* v. *Scarpelli* (1973).[8] Here the justices ruled that revocation of probation and parole demands a preliminary and a final hearing. When a probationer is taken into custody for violating the conditions of probation, a preliminary hearing must be held to determine whether probable cause exists to believe that the incident occurred. It there is a finding of probable cause, a final hearing, where the revocation decision is made, becomes mandatory. At these hearings the probationer has the right to cross-examine witnesses and to be given notice of the alleged violations and a written report of the proceedings. The Court ruled, though, that there is no automatic right to counsel: this decision is to be made on a case-by-case basis. It is then that the judge decides on incarceration and its length. If the violation has been minor, the judge may simply continue probation, but with greater restrictions.

Assessing Probation

Although probation is under less attack than parole, its effectiveness is increasingly being questioned. Probation produces less recidivism than incarceration, but researchers now wonder if this effect is a direct result of supervision or an indirect result of the maturation process. Most offenders placed on probation do not become career

COMPARATIVE PERSPECTIVE
Community Corrections in Japan

Probation, parole, and after-care services in Japan are characterized by the extensive participation of community volunteers. In the period after World War II when Japan reorganized its correctional services, it was argued that probation and parole should be developed along the lines of common law countries. The new organization was to be a combination of professional staff and *hogoshi*, volunteer probation workers. A shortage of funds precluded an expanded professional service, and there was a historical record of volunteer services that had contributed to the rehabilitation of offenders. Japan also has a tradition of voluntary social welfare systems that is firmly rooted in the community. The Offender's Rehabilitation Law called on all people to "render help, in accordance with their position and ability, in order to achieve the goals (of rehabilitation of offenders, etc.)." With passage of the Volunteer Probation Officer Law in 1950, nominations were made of people to serve in this capacity. They were charged with helping offenders to rehabilitate themselves in society and to foster a constructive public attitude that would help to promote crime prevention. Currently, 47,000 volunteers are supervised by about 800 professional probation officers.

Volunteer probation officers are appointed for two-year terms and are assigned according to their place of residence to one of 764 "rehabilitation areas." They are supervised by a professional probation officer and work on an individual basis, with the two to ten cases assigned to them. The volunteers in each area form an association of officers that is nationally linked so as to provide for solidarity with others to coordinate training and to gain resources.

Volunteer officers come from a variety of backgrounds; the largest group (23 percent) comes from such primary industries as agriculture, fishing, and forestry. The second largest category (18 percent) is made up of those individuals officially classified as unemployed but composed mainly of housewives and the retired. Religious professionals make up the next largest category. Lawyers, doctors, and other professionals account for only 5 percent of probation officers, a factor somewhat in contrast to the community activities of this group in Western countries. Although there is a diversity of backgrounds, most volunteers come from the middle class.

The Volunteer as Counselor and Friend

The volunteer probation officer regularly meets his client at his own home and also visits the client and the client's family. He continues to observe the offender in these contacts and tries to advise, assist, and support him. Assistance is also given to the offender's family, with due respect to the dignity and freedom of the individual. Sometimes the volunteer has to visit the client's place of employment. The greatest concern of the volunteer is also how to maintain contact with his charge while at the same time keeping knowledge of the offender's criminal background from his neighbors and employer. Generally, the frequency of contact with the client is about twice a month, but in special cases it occurs almost every day. The volunteer feels that he should be readily available to the client and his family, even over the weekend or late at night in case of emergency, particularly in remote areas where professional services are very scanty.

The volunteer probation service in Japan is believed to have unique merits lacked by the professional officer. The nonofficial nature of the relationship between volunteer and offender is thought to be a positive factor. It is believed that through this relationship the offender can regain his self-respect and identify with the law-abiding culture. Another factor is the "local" nature of the volunteer. As a member of the community in which the client lives, the volunteer knows the particular setting and local customs. Officers try to shield their clients' identities so as to avoid clients being viewed as criminals by neighbors.

The Japanese approach to probation and parole is quite different from ours. Perhaps it would only be successful in a country where there is not great cultural diversity and where community pressures are a major aspect of social control.

SOURCE: From "Use of Volunteers in the Noninstitutional Treatment of Offenders in Japan," by Y. Shiono, *International Review of Crime Policy* 27 (1969): 25–31. Reprinted by permission; from "Japan," by K. Nakayama. In G. F. Cole, S. Frankowski, and M. G. Gertz (eds.), *Major Criminal Justice Systems*, p. 168. Copyright © 1987 by Sage Publications, Inc. Reprinted by permission.

criminals; their criminal activity is short-lived, and they become stable citizens as they get jobs and marry. Even most of those who are arrested a second time do not repeat their mistake again. It is disturbing to some observers that intensive supervision may have little influence on the likelihood of "success." What rallies support for probation is its relatively low cost. Estimates vary, but it takes roughly $700 a year to keep an offender on probation and about $18,000 a year to keep one behind bars.

In recent years, as prison space has become scarce and overcrowding institutions a problem, many felony offenders have been placed on probation. Today over one-third of the nation's probationers have been convicted on felony charges. This situation presents a new challenge for probation, because it means that officers can no longer assume that their clients pose little threat to society and that they are capable of living a productive life in the community.

If probation is to be a viable alternative to incarceration, the resources must be made available so that it can do its job of supervision and assistance. The new demands upon probation have given rise to calls for increased electronic monitoring and for risk management systems that will differentiate the levels of supervision required for different offenders.

INTERMEDIATE SANCTIONS IN THE COMMUNITY

Dissatisfaction with the traditional means of probation supervision and the crowding of American prisons has resulted in a call for intermediate sanctions that will allow serious offenders to be punished in the community. As discussed in Chapter 13 the emphasis of this approach is to create sanctions that are more restrictive than probation, that are punishments equal to the offense and the characteristics of the offender, and that can be carried out in ways that protect the community. Supervision of offenders by probation officers is a central focus of intensive probation supervision, house arrest, and shock incarceration/boot camps—the three major intermediate sanctions that have a community supervision component.

Intensive Probation Supervision (IPS)

In response to research findings indicating that a small core of high-risk offenders commits a disproportionate amount of crime and adds to the overcrowded conditions of prisons, various localities have developed programs for the intensive supervision of certain offenders.[9] Intensive supervision is viewed as a way of using probation as an intermediate punishment. It is thought that daily contact between the probationer and officer may cut rearrests and may permit offenders who might otherwise go to prison to be released into the community. Other restrictions are often imposed on offenders receiving intensive probation supervision, as noted in Table 16.1. Programs of intensive supervision have been characterized as "old-style" probation, because one officer has only twenty clients and frequent face-to-face contacts are required. Because the intention is to place in the com-

TABLE 16.1   Key features of selected IPS programs in thirty-one states.

IPS is more than daily contacts with a probation officer; other restrictions are often imposed. Would you choose IPS or a short prison term?

Program Feature	Number	Percentage
Curfew/house arrest	25	80.6
Electronic monitoring	6	19.3
Mandatory (high needs) referrals/special conditions	22	70.9
Team supervision	18	58.1
Drug monitoring	27	87.1
Alcohol monitoring	27	87.1
Community service	21	67.7
Probation fees	13	41.9
Split sentence/shock incarceration	22	70.9
Community sponsors	4	12.9
Restitution	21	67.7
Objective risk assessment	30	96.7
Objective needs assessment	29	93.5

SOURCE: From "The Effectiveness of the New Intensive Supervision Program," by J. M. Byrne, A. I. Lurigio and C. Baird, *Research in Corrections* 2 (September, 1989):16. Reprinted by permission.

munity high-risk offenders who would normally be incarcerated, it is expected that resources will be saved. But questions have been raised about how much difference constant surveillance can make to probationers who also need help to secure employment and to deal with emotional and family situations as well as their own drug or alcohol problems.

A Georgia program requires probationers to meet with a probation officer or a surveillance officer five times a week and to provide 132 hours of community service work; except in unusual cases, it imposes a 10 PM curfew. The standards are enforced by teams of one probation officer and one surveillance officer, each of whom supervises twenty-five probationers. Evaluation of the Georgia program suggests that it has played a significant role in reducing the flow of offenders to prison and that the cost of intensive supervision, although higher than that of regular probation, is much less than the cost of a stay in prison. Recidivism rates are lower for those under intensive supervision than for either regular probationers or those released from prison on parole.[10]

Intensive supervision has proved to be popular among probation administrators, judges, and prosecutors. Programs have been instituted in a large number of states, with most requiring a specific number of monthly contacts with probation officers, performance of community service, curfews, drug and alcohol abuse testing, and referral to appropriate job training, education, or treatment programs. Evaluations of these intensive supervision programs have been undertaken in a number of states. Observers have warned that intensive supervision should not be viewed as a panacea, since evidence from earlier attempts at the approach showed that as caseloads were reduced, recidivism increased. A larger number of probationers were sent to prison because officers were in a position to more easily detect violations.

One interesting aspect of the intensive probation supervision experience is that given the option of serving prison terms or participating in IPS, many offenders have chosen prison. In New Jersey 15 percent of offenders withdrew their applications for IPS once they knew the conditions and requirements. Likewise, when offenders in Marion County, Oregon, were asked if they would participate in IPS, one-third chose prison.[11] It would seem that these offenders would rather spend a short time in prison, where conditions differ little from their accustomed life, to a longer period under conditions that are quite different from the customs and habits of their community. IPS does not represent freedom to these offenders since it is so much more intrusive and the risk of revocation is perceived as high.

It is clear that intensive probation supervision is not the solution for many of corrections' goals. There are problems associated with the "high-risk" target group, with the methods of supervision, and the operational context within which it operates. Yet IPS has rejuvenated probation; some of the most effective offender supervision is being carried out by these programs.[12]

House Arrest

With the increased interest in intermediate punishments, probation departments have assumed responsibility for many of the house arrest programs that have emerged in recent years. As explained in Chapter 13, house arrest is a form of intensive supervision that requires the offender to remain at home except under court-ordered conditions. It may be coupled with electronic monitoring or supervision by probation officer visits or telephone calls. In many states house arrest programs are distinct from intensive probation supervision, but the trend seems to be to add this feature to IPS.[13]

Two basic types of electronic devices are now in use. A continuously signaling device has a transmitter that is attached to the probationer. A receiver-dialer is attached to the probationer's home telephone. It reports to a central computer at the monitoring agency when the signal stops, indicating that the offender is not in the house, alerting correctional officials of the unauthorized absence. A second device uses a computer programmed to telephone the probationer randomly or at specific times. The offender has a certain number of minutes to answer the phone and to verify that he or she is indeed the person under supervision.[14]

Electronic monitoring has not been as widely adopted as might be expected. Probation departments have found that the devices are both expensive and not foolproof. Thirty-three states now have some type of permanent or experimental program using electronic monitoring, but offenders sentenced in those states still represent only about 3,000 persons.[15] Of interest is the type of offender under electronic monitoring. As shown in Figure 16.2, major traffic and property offenses are the major categories but a few probationers who have committed serious crimes are also being monitored. Presumably these are the offenders who might otherwise been incarcerated.

Some have expressed concerns that house arrest has merely widened the net of social control. That persons who in the past would not have been sent to prison but placed on "regular" probation will now be given house arrest with its greater restrictions. Others, however, have pointed out that with increased numbers of high risk offenders on probation, home arrest is a necessary shift in correctional policy.

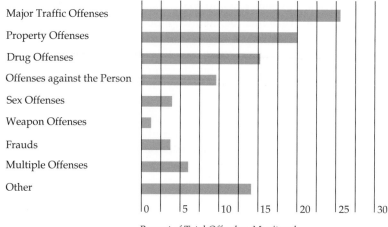

Percent of Total Offenders Monitored

FIGURE 16.2
Electronically monitored offenders (categorized by offense). Although most offenders currently being monitored have committed offenses for which prison is not the normal disposition, there are a few who have committed crimes that might have resulted in their incarceration.
SOURCE: Annesley K. Schmidt, "Electronic Monitoring of Offenders Increases," *Research in Action* (Washington, DC: National Institute of Justice, 1989), p. 2.

Shock Incarceration/Boot Camp

The idea that some, especially youthful offenders, will benefit if they are shocked into facing up to their criminal ways has become a part of correctional policy in a number of states. Eleven states now have shock incarceration programs, and another eleven are developing them.[16]

Offenders are typically sentenced to a short period (90 to 180) days in a military-style boot camp where they receive physical training and perform hard labor under a regimen of strict discipline. Boot camp inmates are housed separately from the regular prisoners and spend six hours a day at work and two to three hours in military drills and physical training. Like the Marine Corps, most programs emphasize a spit-and-polish environment to build self-esteem.

Only now are evaluations of these programs being conducted. Some advocates argue that the boot camp programs do build self-esteem among offenders, which will help keep them out of future trouble. A study of shock incarceration in Louisiana found that those completing the course left the boot camp with more positive attitudes

Boot camps for young offenders have received much publicity since they were first introduced in the 1980s. Advocates believe that boot camps build self-esteem and discipline. Skeptics wonder if this is another correctional panacea.

in regard to their experience and toward society in general, compared with those who were incarcerated in prison.[17] Critics believe that the emphasis on physical training does not get to the bottom of the real problems affecting young offenders. Others point out that like the military, shock incarceration builds esprit de corp and solidarity, characteristics that have the potential for improving the leadership qualities of the young offender and that when taken back to the streets may actually enhance a criminal career.[18]

On successful completion of the program, offenders are released to the community and remain under supervision. At this point probation officers take over, and the conditions of the sentence are imposed. It is too early to tell what impact shock incarceration will have on recidivisism.

COMMUNITY PROGRAMS FOLLOWING RELEASE

Community corrections entails continuous evaluation and testing of the offender to ensure that the least-restrictive-alternative goal is being met and that the individual is steadily moved toward reintegration into the community. In pursuit of the latter goal, programs of partial confinement are used to test the readiness of the offender for full release. Throughout the period of correctional supervision, staff members must therefore ask such questions as: Is it necessary for this offender to be held in a maximum security facility, or is he ready for a less structured environment? With only a year remaining before she appears before the parole board, should this offender be moved to a halfway house? Is work release an option, given the offender's skills? Notice that community-based corrections assumes that multiple alternatives to incarceration are available and that the goal is to choose the least restrictive situation consistent with eventual reintegration.

Among the many programs developed to assist offenders in their return to the community, three are especially important: work and educational release, furloughs, and residential programs. Although they are similar in many ways, each offers a specific approach to helping the formerly incarcerated individuals reenter the community. This may be a period of anxiety, for offenders must adjust to changes that have taken place in society while they were in prison. This is believed to be the decisive period with regard to whether the offender returns to crime.

Transfer of the offender from prison to the community has taken on a new dimension in the states that have adopted the just deserts model of the criminal sanction, with fixed sentences and the abolition of release on parole. No longer is the decision to release a matter for the parole board to consider; rather, correctional authorities have gained new discretionary powers with regard to the reintegration process. In some states, offenders leave prison on the expiration of their sentence minus good time and are then required to live under supervision in the community. In other states, a more gradual process has developed, with release first to a halfway house or community center and then to supervision status. There are some jurisdictions with "home supervision" under which the former inmate lives with his or her family and has contact with a corrections officer on a regular basis. What must be emphasized is that in the jurisdiction with reformed sentencing patterns, community corrections has acquired fresh significance.

Work and Educational Release

Programs of **work and educational release** were first established in Vermont in 1906, but the Huber Act, passed by the Wisconsin Legislature in 1913, is usually cited as the model on which such programs are based. By 1972 most states and the federal government had release programs that allowed inmates to go into the community to work or to attend school during the day and return at night to an institution. Although most of the programs are justifiable in terms of rehabilitation, many correctional administrators and legislators like these programs because of their low cost. In some states, a portion of the inmate's employment earnings may even be deducted for room and board. One of the problems of administering the programs is that the person on release is often viewed by other inmates as being privileged, and such perceptions can lead to social troubles within the prison. Another problem is that in some states organized labor complains that jobs are being taken from free citizens. Further, the releasee's contact with the community makes it possible for contraband to be brought into the institution. To deal with such bootlegging and to assist in the reintegration process, some states and counties have built special work and educational release units in urban areas.

work and educational release: The release of inmates from correctional institutions during the day so that they may work or attend school.

Furloughs

Isolation from loved ones is one of the pains of imprisonment. Although conjugal visits have been a part of correctional programs in many countries, they have rarely been used in the United States. Many penologists view the **furlough** as a meaningful alternative. Consistent with the focus of community corrections, brief home furloughs have come into increasing use in the United States. In some states an effort is made to ensure that all eligible inmates are able to use the furlough privilege on Thanksgiving and Christmas. In other

furlough: The temporary release of an inmate from a correctional institution for a brief period, usually one to three days, for a visit home. Such programs are designed to maintain family ties and prepare inmates for release on parole.

■
Release to the community under supervision presents a host of problems including housing, employment, and reforging ties with loved ones.

states, however, the program has been much more restrictive, and often only those about to be released are given furloughs.

Furloughs are thought to offer an excellent means of testing an inmate's ability to cope with the larger society. Through home visits, family ties can be renewed and the tensions of confinement lessened. Most administrators also feel that furloughs are good for morale. To the detriment of the program, the general public is sometimes aroused when an offender on furlough commits another crime or fails to return. The "Willie Horton" syndrome, in which a furloughed offender commits a heinous crime while in the community, makes correctional authorities nervous.

Residential Programs

community correctional center: An institution, usually located in an urban area, housing inmates soon to be released. Such centers are designed to help inmates maintain community ties and thus to promote their reintegration with society.

The **community correctional center** is an institution designed to reduce the inmate's isolation from community services, resources, and support. It may take a number of forms and serve a variety of offender clients. Throughout the country, halfway houses, prerelease centers, and correctional service centers can be found. Most require offenders to live there, although they may work in the community or visit with their families. Others are designed primarily to provide services and programs for parolees. Often these facilities are established in former private homes or small hotels, which permit a less institutional atmosphere. Individual rooms, group dining rooms, and other homelike features are maintained whenever possible.

Halfway Houses

The term *halfway house* has been applied to a variety of community correctional facilities and programs. Halfway houses range from secure institutions in the community with programs designed to assist inmates preparing for release on parole to shelters where parolees, probationers, or persons diverted from the system are able to live with minimal supervision and direction. Some halfway houses are organized to deliver special treatment services, such as programs designed to deal with alcohol, drug, or mental problems. A national survey found that there were about 800 halfway houses in the United States, most operated under contract by private organizations, with an average capacity of twenty-five residents. Eight to sixteen weeks was found to be the average length of stay.[19] There are three models of release or transfer to halfway houses, as shown in Figure 16.3.

Problems of Residential Programs

Not unexpectedly, few neighborhoods want halfway houses or treatment centers for convicts; community resistance has been an important roadblock and has forced the closing of many facilities. Community corrections, along with programs to deinstitutionalize mental patients and the retarded, has become a major political issue. One of the results of the "not in my backyard" theme often used by protest groups is that the only available facilities are in deteriorating

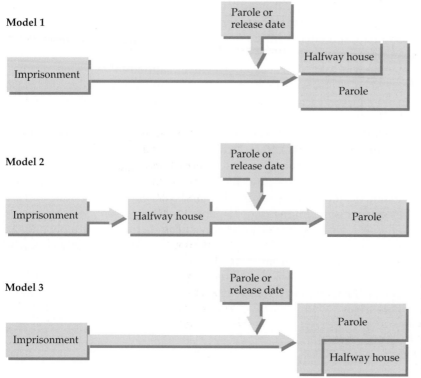

FIGURE 16.3
Three models of release or transfer from prison to a halfway house. The offender may be released on parole either directly to a halfway house (model 1) or into a community in which a halfway house is available, should the parolee need its services (model 3). In model 2 (an increasingly popular alternative), the halfway house is a waystation where the offender stays for a time before being released on parole. SOURCE: From "Halfway Houses and Parole: A National Assessment," by E. Latessa and H. Allen, *Journal of Criminal Justice* 10 (1982):156. Copyright © 1982 by Pergamon Press. Reprinted by permission.

neighborhoods inhabited by the poor, who lack the political power to resist placement of a center in their midst. One wonders whether such locations assist or hinder a former offender.

The future of residential programs is unclear. Originally advocated for both rehabilitative and financial reasons, they do not now seem to be realizing the expected economies. Medical care, education, vocational rehabilitation, and therapy are expensive. Comparisons with incarceration are difficult, but it can probably be said that the costs of quality community programs differ little from those of prisons. The expenditures might be justified if it could be shown that recidivism rates of offenders who have been involved in community treatment were lower, but the available data are not encouraging. One evaluation of a federally administered prerelease guidance center found a recidivism rate of 37 percent among its clients and a 32 percent rate among a control group. The excitement and optimism of the community correctional movement may have been unwarranted. Because of cutbacks in federal funding and resistance by local governments, these programs may be diminished at the very time when they might be helping relieve the overcrowding in prisons.

PAROLE: REENTRY INTO SOCIETY

Historically, the term **parole** referred to both a release mechanism and a method of community supervision. Parole has meant the conditional release of a prisoner from incarceration but not from the legal

parole: The conditional release of an inmate from incarceration under supervision after a portion of the prison sentence has been served.

custody of the state. It is still used in this general sense, but since adoption of the just desserts model of the criminal sanction and determinate sentencing (discussed in Chapter 13), the dual usage is no longer appropriate. We must now distinguish between a release mechanism and supervision. However, although releasing mechanisms have changed in many states during the past decade, most former prisoners are still required to serve a period of time under parole supervision.

Only felons are released on parole; adult misdemeanants are usually released directly from local institutions on expiration of their sentences. Every year more than 300,000 convicted felons are released from prison and allowed to live in the community. Until the recent advent of determinate sentencing and guidelines to be followed in release decisions, upward of 75 percent of the persons serving prison sentences were returned to society through the discretionary decision of the parole board. As shown by Figure 16.4 now only about 40 percent of releases from state prisons came about as a result of a parole board decision. An increasing number of felons returned to society through mandatory release, as specified by the terms of their sentences.

Origins of Parole

Rather than being the product of a single reformer or reform movement, parole in the United States evolved during the nineteenth century as a result of such English, Australian, and Irish practices as conditional pardon, apprenticeship by indenture, transportation of criminals from one country to another, and the issuance of "tickets-of-leave" or license. All these methods have as their common denominator the movement of criminals out of prison, and in most cases, such problems as overcrowding, unemployment, and the cost of incarceration appear to have motivated the practice rather than any rationale linked to a goal of the criminal sanction.

As early as 1587 England had passed the Act of Banishment, which provided for the movement of criminals and "rogues" to the

FIGURE 16.4
Percentage of state prisoners released by various methods, 1977–1989. With determinate sentences and mandatory release gaining momentum, fewer prisoners are released by parole boards.
SOURCE: U.S. Department of Justice, Bureau of Justice Statistics, *Bulletin* (November 1990), p. 4.

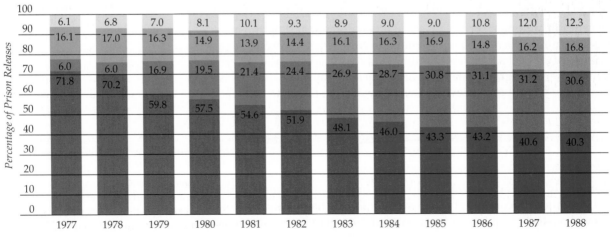

colonies as laborers for the king in exchange for a pardon. The pardons were initially unconditional but evolved to become conditional on the completion of a period of service. In later periods, especially during the eighteenth century, English convicts were released and indentured to private persons to work in the colonies until the end of a set term, at which time they were freed.

With the independence of the United States, the English were deprived of a major dumping ground for their criminals, and their prisons soon became overcrowded. The opening up of Australia met the need for an outlet when in 1790 the power to pardon felons was granted to the governor there and a system was developed for the transporation of criminals. Although unconditional pardons were at first given to offenders with good work records and good behavior, problems arose—as before—and the pardons became conditional— that is, having the requirement that prisoners support themselves and remain within a specific district. This method of parole became known as a "ticket-of-leave." It was like the modern concept of parole, except that the released prisoner was not under supervision by a government agent.

In the development of parole, two names stand out: Captain Alexander Maconochie and Sir Walter Crofton. In 1840, when Maconochie was in charge of the penal colony on Norfolk Island in the South Pacific, he criticized definite prison terms and devised a system of reward for good conduct, labor, and study. He developed a classification procedure by which prisoners could pass through five stages of increasing responsibility and freedom: (1) strict imprisonment, (2) labor on government chain gangs, (3) freedom within a limited area, (4) a ticket-of-leave or parole resulting in a conditional pardon, and (5) full restoration of liberty. Like modern correctional practices, this procedure assumed that prisoners should be prepared gradually for release.

BIOGRAPHY

Alexander Maconochie

A naval officer, geographer, and penal reformer, Alexander Maconochie was born in Edinburgh, Scotland, in 1787. He entered the Royal Navy in 1803 and served in the Napoleonic Wars. A founder of the Royal Geographic Society (1813), Maconochie became private secretary to the lieutenant governor of the colony of Van Diemen's Land (now Tasmania) in 1836. This appointment was to lead to a more important post in the colony's administration, but after completing a report condemning the condition of discipline in the island's penal colony, he was removed from his position.

Maconochie held two views in regard to penology: (1) punishment should be aimed at reform, not at vengeance; and (2) a sentence should be indeterminate, with release depending on the prisoner's industriousness and effort, not on time served. In 1840 he was given an opportunity to apply these principles as superintendent of the Norfolk Island penal settlement in the South Pacific. Under his direction, task accomplishment, not time served, was the criterion for release. Marks of commendation were given to prisoners who performed their tasks well, and they were released from the penal colony as they demonstrated willingness to accept society's rules.

Returning to England in 1844 to campaign for penal reform, Maconochie was appointed governor of the new Birmingham Borough Prison in 1849. But he was unable to institute his reforms there because he was dismissed from his position in 1851 by visiting justices, who had power over the prison, on the ground that his methods were too lenient. He died in 1860.

Although Maconochie's idea of requiring prisoners to earn their early release did not gain immediate acceptance in England, it was used in Ireland, where Crofton had built on Maconochie's idea that an offender's progress in prison and a ticket-of-leave were linked. Prisoners who graduated through Crofton's three successive levels of treatment were released on parole with a series of conditions. Most important, parolees were required to submit monthly reports to the police. In Dublin a special civilian inspector helped releasees find jobs, visited them periodically, and supervised their activities. This concept of assistance and supervision can be viewed as Crofton's contribution to the modern system of parole.

In the United States, parole developed during the prison reform movement of the nineteenth century. Relying on the ideas of Maconochie and Crofton, such American reformers as Zebulon Brockway of Elmira, New York, began to experiment with the concept of parole. Following New York's adoption of indeterminate sentences in 1876, Brockway started to release prisoners on parole. Under the new sentencing law, prisoners could be released when their conduct during incarceration showed that they were ready to return to society. The parole system in New York as originally implemented did not require supervision by the police, as in Ireland; rather, responsibility for assisting the parolees was assumed by private reform groups. With increased use of parole, states replaced the volunteer supervisors with correctional employees who were charged with helping and observing the parolees.

The idea that convicts should be released before they had paid full price for their crimes was opposed by many individuals and groups in the United States. Yet by 1900, twenty states had parole systems; by 1932, forty-four states and the federal government had adopted this method. Today all jurisdictions have some mechanism for the release of offenders into the community.

Although parole in the United States is now more than 100 years old, it is still controversial. Once the public opposed the concept because it seemed to allow for lenient treatment of offenders; today it is being attacked for contributing to the unjust exercise of discretion by parole boards and correctional authorities. It has also charged that paroled felons serve much less time than the interests of crime control and justice dictate. These contemporary criticisms have led about half the states and the federal government to restructure their sentencing laws and release mechanisms.

Release Mechanisms

mandatory release: The required release of an inmate from incarceration upon the expiration of a certain time period, as stipulated by a determinate sentencing law or parole guidelines.

The use of determinate sentences and parole guidelines to fix the end of a prisoner's incarceration is referred to as **mandatory release,** because the correctional authority has little leeway in considering whether the offender is ready to return to society. The new sentencing laws are based on the assumption that it is the judge who gives the offender a specific amount of time to serve. Under the older method, a minimum and maximum period were specified by the judge, allowing the parole board to decide the release date within those limits. With mandatory release the prisoner is automatically

■

Discretionary release is made by
the parole board, often viewed by
offenders as a "roomful of strangers"
who do not really know them yet are
making decisions that affect their lives.

discharged to community supervision at the end of the term, less
credited good time (see Figure 16.4).

In states retaining indeterminate sentences, **discretionary release**
by the parole board is the manner by which most felons leave prison.
This approach is tied to the rehabilitation model and the idea that the
parole board should assess the prisoner's fitness for reentry and
determine the appropriate release. In the context of discretionary
release, it is underscored that the offender's past, the nature of the
offense committed, the inmate's behavior and participation in rehabilitative programs, and the prognosis for a crime-free future should
guide the decision.

Although the formal structures by which felons are released from
prison may seem cut-and-dried, these mechanisms have an impact
on other parts of the system; they influence sentencing, plea bargaining, and the size of prison populations. In sum, the actual amount of
time that a prisoner serves before release is crucial.

discretionary release: The release of
an inmate from incarceration at the
discretion of the parole board within
the boundaries set by the sentence
and the penal law.

Impact on Sentencing

U.S. judges are often said to impose the longest prison sentences in
the Western world, yet little attention has been paid to the amount of
time that offenders actually serve. One of the important results of
discretionary release is that an administrative body, the parole board,
can shorten a judge's sentence. States that have moved to determinate
sentencing or to the use of parole guidelines have attempted to eliminate or severely circumscribe such discretion, but various reductions
built into the sentence mean that the full time is rarely served.

To understand the impact on criminal justice of discretionary
release, one needs to compare the amount of time actually served in
prison with the sentence specified by the judge. In some jurisdictions
up to 80 percent of felons sentenced to the penitentiary are released
to the community after their first appearance before the parole board.
Eligibility for discretionary release is ordinarily determined by the
minimum term of the sentence minus good time and jail time. As we

have seen, good time allows the minimum sentence to be reduced for good behavior during incarceration or for exceptional performance of assigned tasks or personal achievement. Jail time—credit given for time spent in jail while the offender awaited trial and sentencing—also shortens the period that must be served before the inmate's first appearance before the parole board.

Although there is considerable variation among the states, it is estimated that, on a national basis, felony inmates serve on the average less than two years before release. The amount of time served in prison varies with the nature of the offense. In fact, most people would probably be shocked to learn that the actual time served is so much less than the sentences announced in court and published in the newspapers.

Figure 16.5 helps us understand how the indeterminate sentence, good time, and discretionary release on parole shortened the amount of time that inmates were incarcerated in federal prisons. Note that although offenders who received longer terms did remain in prison for longer periods, the proportion of the sentence actually served dropped rapidly as the length of the sentence increased. For example, the robbery offenders who were sentenced to terms of 12 to 60 months actually served 76 percent of their terms; those sentenced to terms of 181 to 240 months actually served only 38 percent. Because

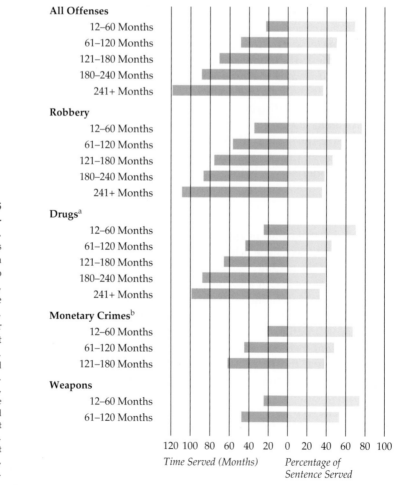

FIGURE 16.5
Average time served by adults convicted of selected federal offenses.
This figure includes all adult offenders who had their initial hearing between July 1, 1979, and June 30, 1980, and who were released prior to January 1, 1987, or had a release date scheduled by the Parole Commission for a later date. Offenders sentenced to one year or less, and therefore not eligible for parole, are excluded. [a]Includes marijuana, drug, and controlled substance offenses. [b]Includes counterfeiting, forgery, fraud, mail theft, embezzlement, interstate transportation of stolen securities, and receiving stolen property with intent to sell. Excludes burglary and theft. SOURCE: Adapted from U.S. Department of Justice, Bureau of Justice Statistics, *Special Report* (June 1987), p. 4.

the defendant is primarily concerned about when he or she will be freed and because the prosecutor is concerned about a sentence that the public will view as appropriate to the crime but that will still encourage a plea bargain, the impact of parole on the time actually served is in the interests of both sides.

Supporters of discretion for the paroling authority argue that the courts do not adequately dispense justice and that the possibility of parole has invaluable benefits for the system. Discretionary release mitigates the harshness of the penal code, it equalizes disparities inevitable in sentencing behavior, and it is necessary to assist prison administrators in maintaining order. Supporters also contend that the postponement of sentence determination to the parole stage offers the opportunity for a more detached evaluation than is possible in the atmosphere of a trial and that early release is economically sensible because the cost of incarceration is considerable.

A major criticism of the effect of parole is that it has shifted responsibility for many of the primary decisions of criminal justice from a judge, who holds legal procedures uppermost, to an administrative board, in which discretion rules. In most states that allow discretion, states' parole decisions are made in secret hearings, with only the board members, the inmate, and correctional officers present. Often there are no published criteria to guide decisions, and the prisoners are given no reason for either the denial or granting of their release. One might ask whether such uncontrolled discretionary power is something that should be entrusted to individuals.

Organization of Releasing Authorities

By the statutes they enact, legislatures either grant authority to parole boards to release prisoners or stipulate the conditions for mandatory release from a determinate sentence. Parole boards tend to be organized either as a part of a department of corrections or as an independent agency of government. It has been argued that the parole board must be autonomous so that members can be insulated from the ongoing activities of the institutional staff. Some people feel that an independent decisional process shields the board members from influence by such staff considerations as reducing the size of the prison population and punishing inmates who do not conform to institutional rules. Recently there has been a movement to locate the parole board within the department of corrections or in a multifunctional human services department. This trend has appeared in response to the criticism that autonomous boards are insensitive to institutional programs and treatment goals. It is believed that when parole decisions are made by persons who are closely connected with corrections, the treatment of a particular offender can be more closely linked with the suitability of release.

Whichever organizational structure is used, the parole board cannot exist in a vacuum, immune to political and organizational influences. An autonomous parole board may develop conflicts with correctional authorities so that the information needed for decision making is "unavailable" or biased. A board that is closely tied to corrections runs the risk of being viewed by prisoners and the general public as merely the rubber stamp of the department. Both types of boards have to operate under the pressure of public opinion. Members of one parole board said that they had to be very cautious in releasing prisoners because if parolees became involved in further violations of the law, the news media always pointed to the board as having let them out.

Membership on the parole board is often based on the assumption that persons with training in the behavioral sciences are able to discern which candidates have been rehabilitated and are ready to return to society. But in many states political considerations dictate that membership include persons with specific racial or geographical qualifications. In the recent past, for example, the Mississippi board consisted of a contractor, a businessman, a farmer, and a clerk; the Florida board included a newspaperman, an attorney, and a man with experience in both business and probation; the state of Washington board had persons with training and experience in sociology, government, law, the ministry, and juvenile rehabilitation.

The Decision to Release

An inmate's eligibility for parole depends on the requirements set by law and the sentence imposed by the court. In the states with determinate sentences or parole guidelines, release from prison to com-

---

A QUESTION OF ETHICS

The five members of the parole board questioned Jim Allen, an offender with a long history of sex offenses involving teenage boys. Now approaching forty-five and having met the eligibility requirement for a hearing, Allen respectfully answered the board members.

Toward the end of the hearing, Richard Edwards, a dentist who had recently been appointed to the board, spoke up:

"Your institutional record is good, you have a parole plan, a job has been promised, and your sister says she will help you. All of that looks good, but I just can't vote for your parole. You haven't attended the behavior modification program for sex offenders. I think you're going to repeat your crime. I have a thirteen-year-old son, and I don't want him or other boys to run the risk of meeting your kind."

Allen looked shocked. The other members had seemed ready to grant his release.

"But I'm ready for parole. I won't do that stuff again. I didn't go to that program because electroshock to my private area is not going to help me. I've been here five years of the seven year max and have stayed out of trouble. The judge didn't say I was to be further punished in prison by therapy."

After Jim Allen left the room, the board discussed his case. "You know, Rich, he has a point. He has been a model prisoner and has served a good portion of his sentence," said Brian Lynch, a long-term board member. "Besides, we don't know if Dr. Hankin's program works."

"I know, but can we really let someone like that out on the streets?"

Are the results of the behavior modification program for sex offenders relevant to the parole board's decision? Is the purpose of the sentence to punish Allen for what he did or for what he might do in the future? Would you vote for release on parole? Would your vote be the same if his case had received media attention?

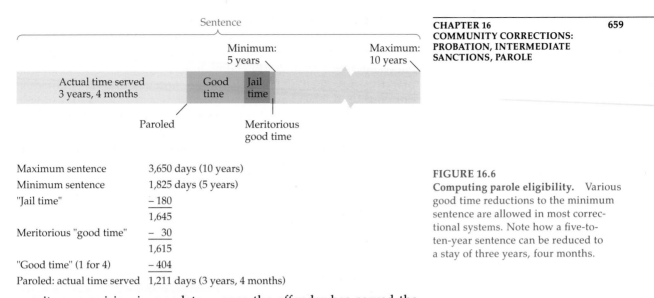

Maximum sentence	3,650 days (10 years)
Minimum sentence	1,825 days (5 years)
"Jail time"	− 180
	1,645
Meritorious "good time"	− 30
	1,615
"Good time" (1 for 4)	− 404
Paroled: actual time served	1,211 days (3 years, 4 months)

FIGURE 16.6
Computing parole eligibility. Various good time reductions to the minimum sentence are allowed in most correctional systems. Note how a five-to-ten-year sentence can be reduced to a stay of three years, four months.

munity supervision is mandatory once the offender has served the required amount of time. In these states, mandatory release becomes a matter of bookkeeping to ensure that the correct amount of good time and other credits have been allocated and that the court's sentence has been accurately interpreted so that on expiration of the period, the offender moves automatically into the community. In nearly half of the states, however, the decision to release is discretionary, and the parole board has the authority to establish a date on the basis of the sufficiency of rehabilitation and the individual characteristics of each inmate. Most inmates serving an indeterminate sentence become eligible for parole automatically at the expiration of one-third of the maximum term or three years, whichever comes first.

As an example of the computation of parole eligibility, we'll look at the case of Richard Scott (see Figure 16.6). At the time of sentencing Scott had been held in jail for six months, awaiting trial and disposition of his case. He was given a sentence of a minimum of five years and a maximum of ten years for robbery with violence. Scott did well in the maximum security prison to which he was sent. He did not get into trouble and was thus able to amass good time credit at the rate of one day for every four that he spent on good behavior. In addition, he was given thirty days' meritorious credit when he completed his high school equivalency test after attending the prison school for two years. After serving three years and four months of his sentence, he appeared before the Board of Parole and was granted release into the community.

In 1933 the American Prison Association asserted that the prisoner's fitness for reentry to the community should determine the release time.

> Has the institution accomplished all that it can for him; is the offender's state of mind and attitude toward his own difficulties and problems such that further residence will be harmful or beneficial; does a suitable environment await him on the outside; can the beneficial effect already accomplished be retained if he is held longer to allow a more suitable environment to be developed?[20]

Although parole boards may subscribe to these principles, the nature of the criteria presents difficulties that cannot be resolved by "hard" data. Some boards have used prediction tables specifying the qualities of an inmate that have been shown over time to correlate with parole success. Not only has the reliability of these data been questioned, but civil liberty claims have been raised on the ground that the described characteristics do not account for individual differences.

What criteria guide board members as they determine whether inmates can be released? Although a formal statement of standards may list such elements as inmates' attitude toward their family, their insights into the causes of their past conduct, and the adequacy of their parole plan, the decision is a discretionary act that is probably based on a combination of information and moral judgment. It is frequently said that parole boards release only good risks, but as one parole board member has said: "There are no good-risk men in prison. Parole is really a decision of when to release bad-risk per-

CLOSE-UP *Parole Hearing*

Michael Gardner is 22 and looks 16. Frail, narrow-shouldered, quavery-voiced, pale, he seems out of place here. He ought to be at the high school dance, standing uncomfortably against a wall. He grew up in a small textile mill town in the poorest part of the state. Kicked out of school at 16, he retaliated by ransacking the building. At 17 it was larceny; at 18, breaking into a car. A reformatory sentence. An escape. Thirteen more months in the reformatory. Then a string of robberies, finally a sentence of two to eight years. He looks frightened, anxious. He brings out the grandfather in Gates [the parole board chairman].

"This is your first time in prison," Gates begins in a soft voice. "Now you've had some time to think. What's the story? What causes you to do this, do you think?"

Gardner looks at the floor. "I think it was my own stupidity. I didn't stop to think."

"Well, a young fella your age, it's a waste of time if you don't come up with some ideas about where all this is coming from and where you're going. . . ."

Gardner answers slowly, the words measured: "I know where it's coming from and I know where I'm going. I've done something to better myself in here. I've become an apprentice carpenter. And I've taken the time to think. . . ."

Gardner is ringing bells with the board. He's done something to *better himself.* He may be *rehabilitated.* And maybe he is. He wasn't a carpenter when he came in. He was a thief, and not much of one. "If they've got the tiniest bit of smarts they know what this board wants to hear," an ex-inmate has told me. "If you show some inclination to self-help, don't just do your time the old-con way. They want to see you run a little."

Gates seems particularly impressed. He believes in work, and here's a man with a trade. "We live to work, we don't work to live," Gates likes to say. "We've been growing away from that in this country."

Gates is gentle with him, avuncular. "Well, you know you got a long sentence this time, but it's nothing to what you'll get next time."

"Yessir." Gardner almost swallows his reply.

Sacks [a board member] has taken his coat off. He has a sudden thought: "Do you think prison is a good thing for rehabilitation or not? Do you think we ought to close the prisons?" It's time for a commercial.

Gardner sees the opening. "No," he says, "I wouldn't say close the prisons. I may have a different outlook than some of the people in here, but I mean to me it's helped me to see myself. I made my apprenticeship."

Rawlins [the third member] is looking thoughtful, puffing on his pipe. Sacks is toying with his glasses. Gates looks like a statue—erect in his chair, not a wrinkle. His eyes have the cool, subdued glow of a distant star.

"When was the last time you saw your father?" Sacks asks. They have seen the probation officer's presentence report; Gardner's father has been stepping on him for years.

"About four weeks ago."

"How do you get along with him?"

"I get along with him good now." The answer comes too quickly.

"I mean, we have our arguments like every family does, but. . . ."

His last parole officer had reported: "His father and him beat the hell out of each other whenever they saw each other. I couldn't even talk to the old man if I wanted to get anywhere with Mike."

Rawlins senses something: "Did you say you wanted to live with your family?"

sons."[21] Other considerations, such as internal prison control and morale, public sentiment, and the political implications of their decisions, weigh heavily on board members.

How to Win Parole

"If you want to get paroled, you've got to be in a program." This statement reflects one of the most controversial aspects of the rehabilitation model: the link between treatment and discretionary release. Although penal authorities emphasize the voluntary nature of most treatment services, although clinicians will argue that therapy cannot be successful in a coercive atmosphere, the fact remains that inmates believe they must "play the game" so that they can build a record that will look good before the parole board. Most parole boards stipulate that an inmate's institutional adjustment, including

"Yes. I figure I owe them something. I mean they done a lot for me."

A week earlier, the father had told me: "The kid's asked me to speak to the parole board for him, but the way I look at it he's on his own now. Why should I lose a day's pay and go down there? He can live here if he wants to, but he's got to behave." The mother was no softer: "The doctor told us when he was 10 that he wasn't getting enough affection at home. He got the same as the rest. He got clothes, food, all a kid could want."

Gardner looks close to tears now. He gets up and leaves the room. The board did not ask his feelings about parole, but the day before, Gardner had described it as a "bunch of crap. You got to go out and live like a human being, not with someone watching you all the time. Out there you can't listen to anyone, you gotta look out for yourself." "I'm going to vote to parole," Gates says. "He's just a youngster, younger than his age. I think this might be the time, prison might have awakened him. This is a kid. He's different from the others with long records and set in their ways."

"I vote for parole," says Sacks. "One thing that impressed me was his answer on what prison does. It made sense."

Rawlins still wonders. "My concern is that he may have problems at home. I see a fragile guy. . . . He may be hurting more deeply than he showed here." ("One of the weaknesses of our operation," Sacks will say later, "is that usually nobody checks out the family, what he's going out to. We should know what it's like.")

All three agreed to parole. Of the seventeen men who come before the board on this day, six will be granted parole, nine denied and the decisions in two cases will be postponed; usually, between 50 and 60 percent win parole. Gardner is expressionless when he gets the word. "I'll probably still get in trouble if I stay in that little town," he had said. "Everybody knows me there. I gotta get some money and then take off." The old parole officer had said he felt Gardner had a chance "if he can latch onto something for his ego, a good job, a girl, so he can say, 'Look, Dad'. . . ." Now, the board members are saying they want to get Gardner in a work-release program, but they are not sure they can. It means a month's delay in his release. Gardner doesn't understand, and Gates doesn't feel he can explain it. "We think you can stand at least another month because you're learning something," he says instead. "Okay? Now take care of yourself."

Gardner looks uncertain as he walks out.

"Gee," Sacks says quietly, "he looked so downhearted."

"He's a kid," Gates says.

Just over three months after Michael Gardner was released on parole, he was arrested and charged with a number of counts of breaking and entering with criminal intent and larceny. He pled guilty and was sentenced to a total effective sentence of three to eight years. Thirty-one months after this term began, he was released on parole. A month later, he was again arrested and charged with breaking and entering, larceny, and criminal trespassing. He pled guilty to one count of third-degree burglary and received a one-year suspended sentence and probation. Later that year, he was arrested and charged with third-degree burglary and fourth-degree larceny. He was sentenced to serve a one-year sentence for the burglary charge and the larceny charge was nolled. As a result of these new sentences, the board voted to revoke Gardner's parole.

SOURCE: From "Parole Board," by Donald Jackson, LIFE Magazine © 1970 Time Warner, Inc. Reprinted by permission.

participation and progress in self-improvement programs, is one of the criteria to be considered in a release decision. A Connecticut inmate noted, "The last time I went before the board they wanted to know why I hadn't taken advantage of the programs. Now I go to A.A. and group therapy. I hope they will be satisfied." Playing the "parole board game" may be the dominant motivation of many inmates.

Unfortunately, many offenders come up for parole only to find either that they have not done enough to satisfy the board or that they have been in the wrong program. This problem may result from changes in the personnel of the board or the limited number of places in the educational and rehabilitative programs in American prisons. Offenders report that they often must wait long periods before they can gain admission to a program that fits their needs or that will impress the board. Observation of the classification proceedings described in Chapter 14 confirms the impression that offenders are assigned to work, education, and rehabilitative programs in keeping with the organizational needs of the institution.

Structuring Decision Making

In response to the criticism that parole boards' release decisions are somewhat arbitrary, at least sixteen states have adopted guidelines to assist their members. As with other guideline schemes, there is a "severity scale" that ranks crimes according to their seriousness and a "salient factor" score that is based on the offender's characteristics (drug arrests, prior record, age at first conviction, etc.) as they are thought to relate to successful completion of parole. By placing the offender's salient factor score next to his or her particular offense on the severity scale, the board, the inmate, and correctional officials are able to know the **presumptive parole date** soon after the offender enters prison. This is the date by which the inmate can expect to be released if there are no problems during incarceration.

presumptive parole date: The presumed release date stipulated by parole guidelines should the offender serve time without disciplinary or other incidents.

Guidelines have been opposed by civil libertarians and others who feel that to deny freedom on the basis of characteristics such as race over which a person may have no control is at odds with the concepts of equal protection and due process. Others have argued that the guidelines result in fixed and mechanical decisions that do not consider the impact of rehabilitative programs or institutional behavior.

Supervision

Parolees are released from prison on condition that they do not further violate the law and that they live according to rules designed both to help them readjust to society and to control their movements. These rules may require them to abstain from alcoholic beverages, to keep away from bad associates, to maintain good work habits, and not to leave the community without permission. The restrictions are justified on the ground that people who have been incarcerated must gradually readjust to the community with its many temptations and not easily fall back into their preconviction habits and associations. This orientation creates a number of problems not only for the parolee but also for the administration of this type of community treatment program. Some people feel that the attempt to impose on parolees standards of conduct that are not imposed on law-abiding persons is absurd.

When they first come out of prison, the parolees' personal and material problems are staggering. In most states they are given only clothes, a token amount of money, the list of rules governing their conditional release, and the name and address of the parole supervisor to whom they must report within twenty-four hours. Although a promised job is often a condition for release, actually becoming employed may be another matter. Most ex-convicts are unskilled or semi-skilled, and the conditions of parole may restrict their movement to areas where a job may be available. If the parolee is black and under thirty, he joins the largest group of unemployed in the country, with the added handicap of having ex-convict status. In most states, laws prevent former prisoners from being employed in certain types of establishments—where alcohol is sold, for example—thus placing many jobs automatically off limits. In many trades, union affiliation is a requirement for employment, and there are restrictions on the admission of new members. The situation of the newly released parolee has been described as follows:

> He arrives without a job in an urban area, after years in prison, with perhaps $20 or $30 in his pocket. Surviving is a trick, even if he's a frugal person, not inclined to blow his few dollars on drinks and women. The parole agents—with some remarkable exceptions—don't give a damn. He's deposited in the very middle of the city, where all he can find is a fleabag hotel in the Tenderloin. He has an aching determination to make it on the outside, but there are hustlers all over him; gambling con games, dollar poker.[22]

On the Outside

The reentry problems of parolees are seen in the fact that many parolees are rearrested soon after release. As shown in Figure 16.7 about 25 percent are arrested during the first six months, almost 40 percent within the first year, and 62 percent within three years.[23]

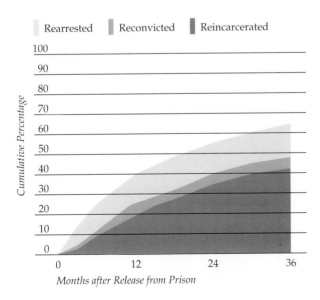

FIGURE 16.7
Cumulative percent of state prisoners rearrested, reconvicted, and reincarcerated thirty-six months after release. The first year after release is the period of greatest probability for recidivism. What separates those who are successful on parole from those who return to prison?
SOURCE: U.S. Department of Justice, Bureau of Justice Statistics, *Special Report* (April 1989), p. 4.

About 40 percent will be reincarcerated. With little preparation, the ex-offender moves from the highly structured, authoritarian life of the institution into a world that is filled with temptations, that presents complicated problems requiring immediate solution, and that expects him to assume responsibilities to which he has long been unaccustomed. The parolee must go through a role change that requires him suddenly to become not only an ex-convict but also a workman, father, husband, son. The expectations, norms, and social relations in the free world are quite different from those learned under the threat of institutional sanction. The parolee's adjustment problems are not only material but social and psychological as well.

It is perhaps not too surprising that the recidivism rate, the percentage of former offenders who return to criminal behavior after release, is so high given the fact that the average felon who has served time in today's prisons has been convicted of serious crimes (83 percent for violent or property offenses), has a criminal record of multiple arrests (8.4 prior arrests) and prior incarcerations (67 percent).[24] Few can be characterized as situational offenders who have run afoul of the law only once; instead most prisoners have committed serious crimes and have a long history of difficulties with the criminal justice system. From the viewpoint of many observers, a large number of today's inmates are career criminals who will resort to their old habits upon release.

Parole Officer: Cop or Social Worker?

After release, a parolee's principal contact with the criminal justice system is through the parole officer. It is the officer who is responsible for seeing that the conditions imposed by the parole board are followed. The conditions imposed are substantial, as can be seen by those of Connecticut's Board of Parole, which are not atypical:

1. Upon release from the institution, you must follow the instructions of the institutional Parole Officer (or other designated authority of the Division of Parole) with regard to reporting to your supervising parole officer, and/or fulfilling any other obligations.
2. You must report to your Parole Officer when instructed to do so and must permit your Parole Officer or any Parole Officer to visit you at your home and place of employment at any time.
3. You must work steadily, and you must secure the permission of your Parole Officer before changing your residence or your employment, and you must report any change of residence or employment to your Parole Officer within twenty-four hours of such change.
4. You must submit written reports as instructed by your Parole Officer.
5. You must not leave the State of Connecticut without first obtaining permission from your Parole Officer.
6. You must not apply for a Motor Vehicle Operator's License, or own, purchase, or operate any motor vehicle without first obtaining permission from your Parole Officer.
7. You must not marry without first obtaining written permission from your Parole Officer.
8. You must not own, possess, use, sell, or have under your control at any time, any deadly weapons or firearms.

9. You must not possess, use, or traffic in any narcotic, hallucinatory, or other harmful drugs in violation of the law.
10. You must support your dependents, if any, and assume toward them all moral and legal obligations.
11. A. You shall not consume alcoholic beverages to excess.
    B. You shall totally abstain from the use of alcoholic beverages or liquors. (Strike out either A or B, leaving whichever clause is applicable.)
12. You must comply with all laws and conduct yourself as a good citizen. You must show by your attitude, cooperation, choice of associates, and places of amusement and recreation that you are a proper person to remain on parole.

Huge caseloads make effective supervision practically impossible in some states. A national survey has shown that parole caseloads range from fifty to seventy; this is smaller than probation caseloads, but the services required by former inmates are greater. Thus only periodic check-ins may be required.

Parole officers are asked to play two different roles: cop and social worker. As police officers, they are given the power to restrict many aspects of the parolee's life, to enforce the conditions of release, and to initiate revocation proceedings if violations occur; they are street-level bureaucrats. In many states they have the authority to search the parolee's house without warning, to arrest him or her without the possibility of bail for suspected violations, and to suspend parole pending a hearing before the board. Like other officials in the criminal justice system, the parole officer has extensive discretion in low-visibility situations. The authoritative component of the parole officer's role relationship with the ex-offender produces a sense of insecurity in the latter that can only hamper the development of mutual trust.

Parole officers are also expected to assist the parolee's readjustment to the community. They must act as social workers by helping the parolee to find a job and restore family ties. Parole officers must be prepared to serve as agent-mediators between parolees and the organizations with which they deal and to channel them to social agencies, such as psychiatric clinics, where they can obtain help. As caseworkers, parole officers must be able to develop a relationship that allows parolees to feel free to confide their frustrations and concerns, something they are not likely to do if they are constantly aware of the parole officer's ability to send them back to prison. It has been suggested that parole officers' conflicting responsibilities of cop and social worker should be separated. Parole officers could maintain the supervisory aspects of the position while other persons perform the casework functions. Alternatively, parole officers could be charged solely with social work duties while local police check for violations.

The parole officer works in a bureaucratic environment. In addition, the difficulties faced by many parolees are so complex that the officer's job is almost impossible. Like most other human service organizations, parole supervision departments are short on resources and expertise. This means that they classify parolees, giving priority to those most in need. To serve those with the greatest need, most parole officers spend more time with the newly released than with those who have been in the community for some time. As the officer gains greater confidence in the parolee, the level of supervision can be adjusted to "active" or "reduced" surveillance. Depending on how the releasee has functioned in the community, only check-in periods may be required. This system is illustrated in Table 16.2.

Revocation of Parole

Always hanging over the ex-inmate's head is the potential revocation of parole for either committing a crime or failing to live according to the rules of the parole contract. Since the paroled person still has the status of inmate, many people believe that parole should be easily revoked without adherence to due process or the rules of evidence. In some states, liberal parole policies have been justified to the public on the ground that revocation is swift and can be imposed before a crime is committed. For example, some state statutes provide that if the parole officer has a reasonable cause to believe that the parolee has lapsed, or is probably about to lapse, into criminal ways or company, or has violated the conditions of parole, a report of these suspicions should be made to the parole board so that the parolee can be apprehended, or the officers may personally retake the parolee. The parole officer's power to recommend revocation because the parolee is "slipping" must hang over the parolee like the sword of Damocles, suspended by a thread. The parolee who leaves the state or has been charged with a new offense is usually detained by an arrest warrant until a revocation hearing or a criminal trial is held.

Morrissey v. Brewer **(1972)**: Due process requires that before parole may be revoked a prompt, informal inquiry before an impartial hearing officer is required. The parolee may present relevant information and question adverse informants.

If the parole officer alleges that a technical (noncriminal) violation of the parole contract has occurred, a revocation proceeding will be held. The U.S. Supreme Court, in the case of *Morrissey v. Brewer* (1972), distinguished the requirements of such a proceeding from the normal requirements of the criminal trial but held that many of the due process rights must be accorded the parolee.[25] The Court has required a two-step hearing process whereby the parole board determines whether the contract has been violated. Parolees have the right to be notified of the charges against them, to know the evidence

TABLE 16.2 Frequency of officer–parolee contacts, by level of supervision.
Different levels of supervision dictate the frequency and types of contacts between the officer and the parolee.

Type of Contact	Intensive Supervision	Active Supervision	Reduced Supervision
Reporting to parole office	Weekly or semimonthly	Monthly or up to but not exceeding every two months	Quarterly, or less frequently up to and including annually
Employment check	Monthly	Every two months	Same as reporting
Employment visit	Every three months	Every three months	At least as frequently as reporting
Home visit	Every three months	Monthly	
Other and collateral visits	More frequently than active or reduced		

SOURCE: David T. Stanley, *Prisoners among Us* (Washington, DC: Brookings Institution, 1976), p. 170.

against them, to be heard, to present witnesses, and to confront the witnesses against them.

The number of parole revocations is difficult to determine since the data do not distinguish between parolees returned to prison for

CLOSE-UP *On His Own*

Lloyd Nieman is white and thirty-six years of age. He has served two separate terms for forgery and had been on parole for a short time when interviewed. A professional musician, Lloyd was reared by his mother, who worked in a factory. His friends have usually been cons. He attended school through the eighth grade only, which he has regretted most of his life.

The first few days I was out were about the roughest days of this entire period. I've only been out a short time—five weeks—but the first three days was a hassle . . . no money, no transportation, no job, and no place to live. Now these things have a way of working themselves out in time, but you have to contact the right people, and sometimes it's hard to find the right people. I was lucky enough to make a contact with a fellow at the Service Center and he gave me enough money to tide me over out of a fund that they had. [. . .]

I was lucky that I had two friends here, too, that could help me. Nick gave me a place to stay, because I was out of money within four days. They give you $60, and out of that you got to buy your own clothes, and I couldn't just move in without paying something, so I gave him $25, you know, for room and board. He didn't want it, but I think there's a lot of guys getting out that don't particularly want charity. They like to pay their own way. Even a convict's got pride.

I'd met Nick four or five times, and he kind of gave me a little coming home party. There was several people there that we'd call "squares." But he explained the whole thing to them and they just kind of accepted me as a person. They didn't shy away from me because I was an ex-con. Everybody was very nice, very friendly. They didn't go out of their way to please but they were just comfortable, nice. I think that's a big thing, being able to be comfortable.

I put in several job applications when I first got out, and I went through the ex-con bit on the applications. In fact, I thought about going back to music, so I joined a musicians' union. I was hired and fired by a club in 20 minutes because I was an ex-con.

Job training is a farce, as far as the institutions are concerned. I was a musician, but they want you to have a manual trade, so they recommended silk screening, which is fine. I have no objection to silk screening, you know. . . . I might as well learn something while I'm there. . . . "You got to have this for the [Parole] Board," they say. Well . . . all of a sudden, they have an opening at camp. So they send me to camp and tell me, "This training isn't really necessary. You don't need it to go to the Board." They need bodies up at camp, so it's not a question of what's good for you, but of what's good for the institution.

Now I'm at State College on the EOP [Equal Opportunities Program]. Whoever thought I'd go to college at 36? I'm having a hard time studying [because] I've been away from it for so long a time that nothing seems to sink in. Well, I'm going after my B.A., and we'll work on an M.A. from there. But I want to make it through education. I really do.

Financially, I'm not too bad off. I've got enough money now for about another six weeks, and I hope to get a job to supplement that income. I have a few friends and, right now, things are pretty good.

When I was in the joint, I kind of thought I might have to go back to hanging paper [forgery]. I thought, "I'm not going to get what I want. I'll probably go out and get a job. I don't want to go back to playing in the bars if I can get away from it because I think that's part of my problem." I have always put on a front. I have an eighth-grade education and the institution should be proud of the fact that I am in college.

But if this [college] had not come to pass, I probably would have gone back to work in the bars and associate with the middle-class crowd or the high-paid bracket crowd, and invariably, I would go to cashing checks to keep up this front, you know.

I didn't expect it to turn out as well as it has. It's getting better all the time. My major disappointment is trying to do too many things too fast and realizing that I can't. The time that you're locked up is gone, you know, and you want to do all the things you've missed. When you get out, you're three or four years behind, or whatever it happens to be, and you try to make these things up. It's a disappointment when you find out that you can't do it, that it's going to take you a while to catch up. You got to go slow.

I have mixed emotions. I'm happy to be out, but I have a thing about being my own man. I realize it is necessary, but I do resent a parole officer telling me what I can do and what I cannot do. I believe that every man is different, every case is different, and there can be no set policy.

Lloyd didn't make it. Shortly after his interview, he jumped parole and left the state. A year later, he still had not been located.

SOURCE: Adapted from *Paroled but Not Free*, by R. J. Erickson, W. J. Crow, L. A. Zurcher, and A. V. Connett, pp. 17–20. Copyright © 1973 by Behavioral Publications. Reprinted by permission of Human Services Press, Inc.

technical violations and those sent back for new criminal offenses. Given today's crowded prisons, most revocations occur only after arrest on a serious charge or when the parolee cannot be located by the parole officer. Given the normal caseload, most parole officers are unable to maintain close scrutiny over parolees and so are not aware of technical violations. Under the new requirements for prompt and fair hearings, parole boards are discouraging the issuance of violation warrants following infractions of parole rules without evidence of serious new crimes.

The effectiveness of corrections is usually measured by rates of recidivism, the percentage of former offenders who return to criminal behavior after release. As discussed above, studies have shown that about 60 percent of parolees are rearrested within thiry-six months of their release from prison. About 40 percent will be reincarcerated. It is perhaps not too surprising that the recidivism rate is so high given the fact that in today's correctional environment most prisoners are individuals who have committed serious crimes and have a long history of difficulties with the criminal justice sytem.

The Future of Parole

Parole has been under attack for the past decade. Sentencing laws were changed in about half of the states to remove the discretionary release authority of parole boards. Guidelines have been adopted in a number of jurisdictions to structure the decision to release. Supervision of most adult felons released from prison has been maintained. Parole officers still have extensive supervisory responsibilities, although their efforts to provide client services have been curtailed.

As prison populations rise, demands that felons be allowed to serve part of their time in the community will undoubtedly mount. In states with discretionary release, parole provides one of the few mechanisms available to correctional officials to relieve institutional pressures. In many states in which mandatory release is the way out of prison, offenders nearing expiration of their terms are being moved to community facilities so that they can begin the reintegration process.

PARDON

References to pardon are found in ancient Hebrew law, and in medieval Europe the church and the monarch had the power of clemency. Later, pardon became known as the "royal prerogative of mercy" in England.

Pardons are acts of the executive. In the United States, the president or governors of the states may grant such clemency in individual cases. In each state the executive receives recommendations from the state's board of pardons (often combined with the board of parole) in regard to individuals who are thought to be deserving of the act. In contemporary times, pardons serve three main purposes: (1) to remedy a miscarriage of justice, (2) to remove the stigma of a conviction, and (3) to mitigate a penalty. Although full pardons for miscarriages of justice are rare, newspaper readers are from time to time alerted to the story of some individual who has been released from prison after it has been discovered that he or she was incarcerated by mistake. The more typical activity of pardons boards is to expunge the criminal records of first-time offenders—often young people—so that they may enter the professions, obtain certain types of employment, and in general not have to bear the stigma of a single indiscretion. In states that have abolished release on parole and have adopted fixed sentences, the pardons board may become a more important agency for the mitigation of penalties.

CIVIL DISABILITIES

We may believe that once a person has been released from prison, paid a fine, or been discharged from parole or probation, the punishment has ended; the "debt" to society has been paid. For many offenders, however, a criminal conviction is a lifetime burden. In most states it is not enough to have served time, to have reestablished family ties, to have gotten a job, and otherwise to have become a law-abiding member of the community; certain civil rights are forever forfeited, some fields of employment may never be entered, and some insurance or pension benefits may be foreclosed.

The extent of civil disabilities varies greatly among the states, but generally persons who have been convicted of a felony are treated as a group. In some states, persons who have been convicted of certain crimes are subjected to specific restrictions; forgery, for example, prevents employment in the banking or stock-trading fields. In other states, blanket restrictions are placed on all felons regardless of the circumstances of the crime. These restrictions are removed only upon completion of the sentence, after a period subsequent to completion of the sentence, or upon action of the board of pardons. The forfeiture of rights can be traced to Greek and Roman times, and American courts have generally upheld the constitutionality of such restrictions.

The right to vote and to hold public office are two civil rights that are generally limited upon conviction. Three-fourths of the states return the right to vote after varying lengths of time, whereas the remainder keep felons off of the voting lists unless they are pardoned or restored to full citizenship. Nineteen states permanently restrict the right to hold public office to felony offenders unless pardoned or given back their full citizenship, and twenty-one states return the right following discharge from probation, parole, or prison. Other civil rights such as eligibility to serve on juries and access to public employment are denied felons in many states.[26]

Although most former felons may not believe that restrictions on their civil rights will make it difficult for them to lead normal lives, limitations on entry into certain fields of employment are a problem. Many observers assert that the restrictions force offenders into menial jobs at low pay that may lead them back to crime. Until the turn of the century, only members of the professions—lawyers, doctors, teachers—were licensed by the state; the withholding of such licenses from felons was quite common. With the rise of the labor movement and the professionalization of many occupations, states began to require licenses to enter hundreds of fields. Originally justified in terms of safety and quality standards, licensing appears now to have been designed primarily to restrict the number of persons in a field so that the fees for services could be kept high.

Occupations that currently restrict the entry of former offenders include nurse, beautician, barber, real estate salesperson, chauffeur, employee of a place where alcoholic beverages are served, cashier, stenographer, and insurance agent. Richard Singer has noted: "In all, nearly six thousand occupations are licensed in one or more states; the convicted offender may find the presumption against him either difficult or impossible to overcome."[27] The fact that many prison vocational programs promoted for rehabilitative purposes lead to restricted occupations seems to have been ignored.

Although some states provide no procedures for the restoration of rights, others provide discretionary mechanisms—often through the pardoning process—for the expunging of a criminal conviction after the passage of time. But questions remain as to whether a person may legally deny a conviction on an employment application even after the conviction has been expunged.

Critics of civil disability laws point out that upon fulfilling the penalty imposed for a crime, the former offender should be assisted to full reintegration into society. They argue that it is counterproductive for government to promote rehabilitation with the goal of reintegration while at the same time preventing offenders from fully achieving that goal. Others, however, say that the possibility of recidivism and the community's need for protection justify these restrictions. In the middle ground there is the belief that not all persons convicted of felonies should be treated equally and that society can be protected adequately by the placement of restrictions on only certain individuals.

SUMMARY

Methods for dealing with criminal offenders have come a long way since the reform activities of Philadelphia's Quakers, but uncertainty remains about the methods that should be used. Community supervision through probation and parole have long been major elements of U.S. corrections. During the 1960s and 1970s the concept of community corrections, a model that emphasized the reintegration of the offender, drew the attention of penologists. In the more conservative environment of the 1980s, much of the fervor of community corrections waned. Community supervision, prerelease orientation, and halfway houses have remained, but the focus today is less on the provision of services to offenders and more on surveillance. The development of intermediate sanctions with a community supervision component have added to the demand placed on probation and other correctional agencies.

Upon release from incarceration, offenders face problems in finding housing and employment. Just as important is their need to reforge links to family and friends. It is during this period that former offenders need assistance. Research has shown that supervision often is of limited effectiveness unless it is structured to deal individually with offenders and their particular problems.

Of all the various subsystems of criminal justice, corrections appears to be going through the most sustained soul searching. As incarceration rates climb, one can expect that public pressures will build to deal more effectively with the criminal population. Supervision in the community through probation is one alternative to incarceration, and postrelease supervision of parolees is another. Both have the potential to help stem the tide of persons who commit crimes.

FOR DISCUSSION

1. You are on the parole board. Before you is a young man with little education and a history of trouble with the law since he was a child. He has been incarcerated for stealing to support a drug habit and is now eligible for parole. What should you consider as you make your decision?

2. What restrictions does your state place on former convicts with regard to occupation?

3. You are a prisoner. You have been sentenced to three to ten years in your prison's maximum security facility. How should you act so that you can win parole at the earliest date? How will you act in relation to your fellow prisoners?

4. The department of corrections wants to build a halfway house in your neighborhood. What will be your reaction?

5. Is community corrections a viable alternative to incarceration? What are its advantages and disadvantages?

FOR FURTHER READING

Clear, Todd R., and Vincent O'Leary. *Controlling the Offender in the Community*. Lexington, MA: Lexington Books, 1983. Examination of risk assessment, classification, and supervision in the context of community corrections.

McCarthy, Belinda, and Bernard McCarthy. *Community-Based Corrections*. Pacific Grove, CA: Brooks/Cole, 1983. A thorough overview of community corrections and its role in the criminal justice system.

McCleary, Richard. *Dangerous Men*. Newbury Park, CA: Sage, 1976. A classic study of the operation of a parole office and the routines used for risk classification.

Stanley, David. *Prisoners among Us.* Washington, DC: Brookings Institution, 1975. Still the only major published account of parole release decision making. Emphasis on the role of discretion.

Von Hirsch, Andrew, and Kathleen J. Hanrahan. *The Question of Parole.* Cambridge, MA: Ballinger, 1979. Examines parole from the "just deserts" perspective and urges its reform.

NOTES

1. Peter J. Benekos, "Beyond Reintegration: Community Corrections in a Retributive Era," *Federal Probation* (March 1990), p. 52.
2. Joan Petersilia, "Probation Reform," in *Controversial Issues in Crime and Justice,* eds. Joseph E. Scott and Travis Hirschi (Newbury Park, CA: Sage, 1988), p. 167.
3. As quoted in Keven Krajick, "Probation: The Original Community Program," *Corrections Magazine* 6 (December 1980), p. 7.
4. As quoted in Randall Guynes, "Difficult Clients, Large Caseloads Plague Probation Parole Agencies," *Research in Action* (Washington, DC: National Institute of Justice, 1988).
5. Todd Clear and Vincent O'Leary, *Controlling the Offender in the Community* (Lexington, MA: Lexington Books, 1983), pp. 77–100.
6. *New York Times,* June 19, 1990, p. A16.
7. *Mempa* v. *Rhay,* 389 U.S. 128 (1967).
8. *Gagnon* v. *Scarpelli,* 411 U.S. 778 (1973).
9. See *Crime and Delinquency* 36 (January 1990); entire issue is devoted to Intensive Probation Supervision.
10. Billie S. Erwin and Lawrence A. Bennett, "New Dimensions in Probation: Georgia's Experience with Intensive Probation Supervision," *Research in Brief,* National Institute of Justice (Washington, DC: Government Printing Office, 1987); Joan Petersilia, *Expanding Options for Criminal Sentences* (Santa Monica, CA: Rand Corporation, 1987), pp. 10–32.
11. Joan Petersilia, "When Probation Becomes More Dreaded Than Prison," *Federal Probation* (March 1990), p. 24.
12. Todd Clear and Patricia L. Hardyman, "The New Intensive Supervision Movement," *Crime and Delinquency* 36 (January 1990):42.
13. Billie S. Irwin, "Old and New Tools for the Modern Probation Officer," *Crime and Delinquency* 36 (January 1990):61.
14. Annesley K. Schmidt, "Electronic Monitoring of Offenders Increases," *Research in Action* (Washington, DC: National Institute of Justice, 1989).
15. Ibid.
16. Doris Layton MacKenzie and Deanna Bellew Ballow, "Shock Incarceration Programs in State Correctional Jurisdictions—An Update," *Research in Action* (Washington, DC: National Institute of Justice, 1989). See also National Institute of Justice, *Shock Incarceration: An Overview of Existing Programs* (Washington, DC: Government Printing Office, 1989).
17. Doris Layton MacKenzie and James W. Shaw, "Inmate Adjustment and Change during Shock Incarceration: The Impact of Correctional Boot Camp Programs," *Justice Quarterly* 7 (March 1990):125–150.
18. *New York Times,* March 4, 1988, pp. B1, B4.
19. Edward Latessa and Harry Allen, "Halfway Houses and Parole: A National Assessment," *Journal of Criminal Justice* 10 (1982):156.
20. As quoted in Edwin H. Sutherland and Donald R. Cressey, *Criminology* (Philadelphia: Lippincott, 1970), p. 587.
21. As quoted in Donald J. Newman, "Legal Models for Parole: Future Developments," in *Contemporary Corrections,* ed. Benjamin Frank (Reston, VA: Reston, 1973), p. 246.
22. As quoted in Jessica Mitford, *Kind and Usual Punishment* (New York: Knopf, 1973), p. 217.

23. U.S. Department of Justice, Bureau of Justice Statistics, *Special Report,* (April 1989).

24. Ibid.

25. *Morrissey* v. *Brewer,* 408 U.S. 471 (1972).

26. Velmer S. Burton, Jr., Francis T. Cullen, and Lawrence F. Travis III, "The Collateral Consequences of a Felony Conviction: A National Study of State Statutes," *Federal Probation* 51 (September 1987):52–60.

27. Richard Singer, "Conviction: Civil Disabilities," in *Encyclopedia of Crime and Justice,* ed. Sanford H. Kadish (New York: Free Press, 1983), p. 246.

JUVENILE JUSTICE SYSTEM

Crimes committed by juveniles have become a serious national problem. The *Uniform Crime Reports* show that just over a third of the people arrested for an index crime are under eighteen years of age. Children who are charged with crimes, who have been neglected by their parents, or whose behavior is deemed to require official action come in contact with the juvenile justice system, an independent process that is interrelated with the adult system. As Chapter 17 will demonstrate, many of the procedures used in the handling of juvenile problems are similar to those used with adults, but the overriding philosophy of juvenile justice is somewhat different, and the extent to which the state may intrude into the lives of children is much greater.

Juvenile Justice

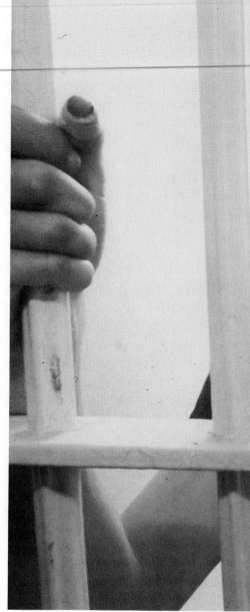

Key Terms and Cases

delinquents
dependent child
detention
neglected child

parens patriae	Breed v. Jones (1975)	McKeiver v. Pennsylvania (1971)
PINS	Fare v. Michael C. (1979)	New Jersey v. T.L.O. (1985)
status offense	In re Gault (1967)	Schall v. Martin (1984)
	In re Winship (1970)	

There is evidence . . . that there may be grounds for concern that the child receives the worst of both worlds: that he gets neither the protections accorded to adults nor the solicitous care and regenerative treatment postulated for children.

Justice Abe Fortas

At 10:00 A.M. on Monday, June 8, 1964, fifteen-year-old Gerald Gault and his friend Ronald Lewis were taken into custody by the sheriff of Gila County, Arizona, on the complaint of a neighbor who had received a telephone call in which the caller had made lewd and indecent remarks. On her arrival from work late that afternoon, Gerald's mother became alarmed that her son was not at home. Neighbors told her that the sheriff's car had been at the house earlier in the day. Because Gerald was on probation as a result of an incident in January 1964, when he had been apprehended in the company of another youth who had stolen a woman's purse, Mrs. Gault anxiously called the sheriff's office and learned that her son was being held at the Children's Detention Home for appearance in Juvenile Court the following day.

At hearings conducted before Judge McGhee on June 9 and 15, Gerald said that he had only dialed the number and that Lewis had done the talking. In attendance at the hearings were only Gerald, his parents, Judge McGhee, and probation officers Flagg and Henderson. The proceedings were informal, no one was sworn, no transcript was made, and no record was prepared. Mrs. Gault asked why the complaining neighbor was not present "so she could see which boy had done the talking." The judge said her presence was not necessary. The only other item that played a role in the hearing was a "referral report" filed with the court by the probation officers; none of the three Gaults was told what it said.

After the end of the hearing, Judge McGhee announced that he was committing Gerald as a juvenile delinquent to the state industrial school "for the period of his majority [that is, until the age of twenty-one] unless sooner discharged by due process of law." Had he been an adult, the maximum punishment for such a telephone call would have been a fine of $5 to $50 or imprisonment for not more than two months. As a minor, Gerald Gault was committed to the state school for six years.

With the aid of Amelia Lewis, an attorney and member of the Arizona Civil Liberties Union, the Gaults appealed the decision on the ground that the safeguards of due process had not been accorded. They stated that the juvenile court had not given them adequate notice of the nature of the charges and the hearing; had not advised them of their constitutional rights, including the right to counsel, the right to confront witnesses, and the privilege against self-incrimination; had not made a record of the proceedings; and had used hearsay testimony from unsworn witnesses.

Appealing to the U.S. Supreme Court, Mr. and Mrs. Gault argued that their son had not been accorded the procedural guarantees required by the due process clause of the Fourteenth Amendment. Before focusing on these rights, the brief examined the historical background of juvenile court systems. It argued that **parens patriae**—the legal concept that the state may intervene to protect the welfare of children—had been substituted for procedural due process and had resulted in detrimental effects on many children in juvenile proceedings. Although conceding that the juvenile court movement had led to advances in the treatment accorded juveniles, the brief went on to say that "juvenile court proceedings, which were instituted to protect the young, led in many jurisdictions to findings of delinquency in proceedings that conspicuously failed to protect the child." It further reasoned that neither *parens patriae* nor the theory that a juvenile proceeding was a civil matter dealing with treatment rather than punishment could justify "the refusal to accord Gerald Gault and other juveniles the protection of the Bill of Rights."

parens patriae: The state as parent; the state as guardian and protector of all citizens (such as juveniles) who are unable to protect themselves.

On May 15, 1967, almost three years after Gerald Gault had first been sent to the Children's Detention Home, the United States Supreme Court reversed the Arizona decision. In its decision **In re Gault** the justices held that a child in a delinquency hearing must be afforded certain procedural rights, including notice of charges, right to counsel, right to confrontation and cross-examination of witnesses, and protection against self-incrimination. Writing for the majority, Justice Abe Fortas emphasized that due process rights and procedures adhere to juvenile justice. "Under our Constitution the condition of being a boy does not justify a kangaroo court."[1] The opinion went on to specify that juveniles had (1) the right to notice, (2) the right to counsel, (3) the right to confront witnesses, (4) the privilege against self-incrimination, (5) the right to transcripts, and (6) the right to appellate review.

In re Gault (1967): Juveniles have the right to counsel, to confront and examine accusers, and to have adequate notice of charges when there is the possibility of confinement as a punishment.

Of the two dissenters, Justice Potter Stewart expressed a more traditional conception of juvenile justice:

> Juvenile proceedings are not criminal trials. They are not civil trials. They are simply not adversary proceedings. Whether treating a delinquent child, a neglected child, a defective child, or a dependent child, a juvenile proceeding's whole purpose and mission is the very opposite of the mission and purpose of a prosecution in a criminal court. The object of the one is correction of a condition. The object of the other is conviction and punishment for a criminal act.[2]

The Supreme Court decision points to a constant tension within the juvenile justice system between those who think that children should be given all the due process guarantees accorded adults and those who think that children must be handled in a less adversarial, more treatment-oriented manner so that legal procedures will not interfere with efforts to secure the justice that is in the children's best interest.

You may wonder why a chapter on juvenile justice appears in this book, since it is often assumed that the system organized to deal with delinquency and the problems of young people is administrative rather than adversarial, with diagnosis and rehabilitation as its main goals. It is true that the formal processes of juvenile justice differ from those used with adults, but these differences lie primarily in emphasis. The juvenile justice system is a separate but interrelated part of the broader criminal justice system. Whether involved in policing, courts, or corrections, one cannot be divorced from the problems of youth. With juveniles composing a significant portion of those who violate the criminal law, serious attention must be paid to this system.

YOUTH CRIME IN THE UNITED STATES

To a great extent, crime in the United States is a phenomenon of youth. Fewer than 12 percent of Americans are aged fifteen to twenty-one, yet they account for 29.7 percent of all arrests for violent index crimes and 45.9 percent of all arrests for property index crimes (see Figure 17.1). It is estimated that about one in twenty in the cohort is taken into police custody each year. In all, more than 1.7 million juveniles under eighteen years are arrested each year; nearly a million are processed by juvenile courts yearly. That we are speaking of crimes committed primarily by young males should be emphasized, since only 23 percent of arrestees under eighteen years of age were females. The youthfulness of persons prone to crime is underscored by two other facts: about one-third of those arrested each year are under twenty-one, and about half are under twenty-five. Some researchers have estimated that one boy in three will be arrested by the police at some point before his eighteenth birthday.

The contemporary concern about drugs has again focused attention on juveniles. Data supplied by the National Council of Juvenile and Family Court Judges show that drug abuse is a problem in between 60 and 90 percent of the cases referred to them.[3] Surveys of high school students show that drug use is on the decline yet there are clearly young people who are either drug users or heavily involved in the sale of drugs. A study of four hundred detained juveniles in Florida showed that 41 percent tested positive for drug use. Of those who tested positive for cocaine, 51 percent were rearrested

FIGURE 17.1
Percentage of arrests for index crimes of persons under twenty-one years.
Those age fifteen to twenty-one make up fewer than 12 percent of the population and are arrested out of proportion to their numbers. Although property offenses are most often committed by young people, the number of violent crimes committed by this group is rising.
SOURCE: U.S. Department of Justice, *Crime in the United States* (Washington, DC: Government Printing Office, 1990), p. 127.

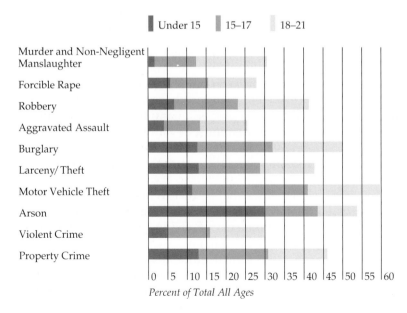

or referred to juvenile authorities for a property misdemeanor within eighteen months of the testing.[4] The homicide rate among young urban males engaged in turf battles over drug sales is viewed with alarm.

The presence of youth gangs in most large American cities has also brought new attention to the problem of juvenile crime. There have been periods in the past when gang violence has rocked cities, but during the past ten years there has been renewed evidence of this problem. Many of the same gangs now apparent in the adult correctional system have their younger counterparts on the streets. Today's gangs have become a major element in the drug trade—and the resulting crimes of violence.

HISTORY OF JUVENILE JUSTICE

The *Gault* decision was the first major challenge to a system and philosophy of juvenile justice that had its inception in the United States during the period of social reform in the latter part of the nineteenth century. The origin of the idea that children should be treated differently from adults, however, is found in the common law and in the chancery courts of England. The common law had long prescribed that children under seven years of age were incapable of felonious intent and were therefore not criminally responsible. Children aged seven to fourteen could be held accountable only if it could be shown that they understood the consequences of their actions. Under the doctrine of *parens patriae,* which held the king to be the father of the realm, the chancery courts exercised protective jurisdiction over all children, particularly those involved in questions of dependency, neglect, and property. These courts, however, had civil jurisdiction, and juvenile offenders were dealt with by the criminal courts. But the concept of *parens patriae* was important for the development of juvenile justice, for it legitimized the intervention of the state on behalf of the child.

The English procedures were maintained in the American colonies and continued into the nineteenth century. In 1838, for example, the Supreme Court of Pennsylvania upheld the doctrine of *parens patriae* in a suit brought by a father objecting to the commitment of his daughter (by his wife without his knowledge) to the Philadelphia House of Refuge on the ground that she was "incorrigible." The court said that the courts as guardians of the community could supersede the desires of the natural parents when they were unequal to the task of rearing a child. If the parents fail to fulfill their responsibility of training their children to be productive, law-abiding adults, the state should assume it by training the children "to industry [and] by imbuing their minds with the principles of morality and religion."[5]

The doctrine of *parens patriae* was to fall on hard times in the latter half of the twentieth century, but it had wide appeal throughout the Civil War era. During the nineteenth century, as the United States came to grips with dynamic social changes, there were shifts in the ways in which juveniles were treated. The major influences on this development were the movement of the population from rural to urban areas and the flood of newly arriving immigrants. The stages through which the concepts of treatment of delinquent and dependent children have passed from the seventeenth century to the present are outlined in Table 17.1.

The Child Savers

Reform of the criminal law pertaining to juveniles was among the social movements that arose in the United States to cope with the problems associated with rapid industrialization and urbanization in the nineteenth century. The reformers were stimulated by growing concern about the influence of environmental factors on behavior; the rise of the social sciences, which claimed they could treat the problems underlying deviance; and an awareness of the brutality of the conditions under which children were incarcerated.

These middle-class reformers sought to use the power of the state to "save" children from a life of crime. They were concerned primarily with the urban immigrant poor, and they sought to have parents declared "unfit" if their children roamed the streets and apparently were "out of control." It was not that the children were engaged in

TABLE 17.1   Juvenile justice developments

Period	Major Developments	Causes and Influences	Juvenile Justice System
Puritan **1646–1824**	Massachusetts Stubborn Child Law (1646)	A. Christian view of child as evil B. Economically margin agrarian society	Law provides: A. Symbolic standard of maturity B. Support for family as economic unit
Refuge **1824–1899**	Institutionalization of deviants; New York House of Refuge established (1824) for delinquent and dependent children	A. Enlightenment B. Immigration and industrialization	Child seen as helpless, in need of state intervention.
Juvenile Court **1899–1960**	Establishment of separate legal system for juveniles: Illinois Juvenile Court Act (1899)	A. Reformism and rehabilitative ideology B. Increased immigration, urbanization, large scale industrialization	Juvenile court institutionalized legal irresponsibility of child.
Juvenile Rights **1960–1980**	Increased "legalization" of juvenile law; *Gault* decision (1966); Juvenile Justice and Delinquency Prevention Act (1974) calls for deinstitutionalization of status offenders	A. Criticism of juvenile justice system on humane grounds B. Civil rights movement by disadvantaged groups	Movement to define and protect rights as well as to provide services to children.
Crime Control **1980–Present**	Concern for victims, punishment for serious offenders, transfer to adult court of serious offenders, protection of children from physical and sexual abuse	A. More conservative public attitudes and policies B. Focus on serious crimes by repeat offenders	System more formal, restrictive, punitive; increased percentage of police referrals to court; incarcerated youths stay longer periods

SOURCE: Adapted from U.S. Department of Justice, *A Preliminary National Assessment of the Status Offender and the Juvenile Justice System* (Washington, DC: Government Printing Office, 1980), p. 29; Barry Krisberg, Ira M. Schwartz, Paul Litsky, and James Austin, "The Watershed of Juvenile Justice Reform," *Crime and Delinquency* 32 (January 1986):5–38.

criminal acts (though many were) but—the belief went—that children who were not disciplined and trained by their parents to abide by the rules of society would eventually find themselves in prison. The state's power was to be used to prevent delinquency. The solution was to create institutions for these children where they could learn good work and study habits, live in a disciplined and healthy environment, and develop "character." The first such institution was the House of Refuge of New York, which opened in 1825. It was followed by similar facilities in Boston, Philadelphia, and Baltimore. Children were placed in these homes by court order and often stayed there until they reached the age of majority.

By the middle of the nineteenth century, the more "progressive" states had begun to develop new institutions—reform schools—to provide the discipline needed by wayward youth in a "homelike" atmosphere where education would be emphasized. The first, the Lyman School for Boys, was opened in Westboro, Massachusetts, in 1848. A similar school for girls was opened in Lancaster, Massachusetts, in 1855. Ohio created the State Reform Farm in 1857, and the states of Maine, Rhode Island, New York, and Michigan soon followed suit.

■

Jane Addams, the Chicago social worker, was one of the major leaders of the child savers movement. Founder of the settlement house Hull House, she worked for development of programs for juvenile justice.

At the same time that some groups were advocating creation of reform schools, other groups, such as the Children's Aid Society of New York, were emphasizing the need to place neglected and delinquent children in private homes. During this period the city was viewed as a place of crime and bad influences, in contrast to the clean, healthy, crime-free country. Like the advocates of reform of adult corrections, the children's aid societies of the 1850s emphasized placement in rural areas. The additional hands thus acquired provided an economic incentive for farmers to "take in" these juveniles.

Establishment of the Juvenile Court

With services to neglected youth widely established in most states by the end of the nineteenth century, the problem of juvenile criminality became the focus of attention during another period of reform. As Chapter 14 pointed out, members of the Progressive movement sought to use the power of the state to provide individualized care and treatment of deviants of all kinds—adult criminals, the mentally ill, juvenile delinquents. They pushed for adoption of probation, treatment, indeterminate sentences, and parole for adult offenders and were successful in establishing similar programs for juveniles. They also campaigned successfully for creation of a juvenile court.

Juvenile delinquency created a dilemma for the state. It could either deal with young accused persons under the adult criminal law, calling upon its full powers to prosecute, try, sentence, and imprison them, or it could refrain from such strictness and merely return them to their parents and the community; both options were viewed as poor policy for juveniles and for society. It was argued that a separate juvenile court system should be created so that the problems of the individual youth could be treated in an atmosphere in which flexible procedures would, as one reformer said, "banish entirely all thought of crime and punishment."[6]

With passage of the Juvenile Court Act by Illinois in 1899 the first comprehensive system of juvenile justice was established. The act brought together under one jurisdiction cases of dependency, neglect, and delinquency ("incorrigibles and children threatened by immoral associations as well as criminal lawbreakers"). Such activists as Jane Addams and Julia Lathrop, of the settlement house movement; Henry Thurston, a social work educator; and the National Congress of Mothers were successful in promoting the juvenile court concept, so that by 1904 ten states had implemented procedures similar to those of Illinois, and by 1920 all but three states provided for a juvenile court.

Undergirding the philosophy of the juvenile court was the idea that the state should deal with a child who broke the law much as a wise parent would deal with a wayward child. The doctrine of *parens patriae* helped legitimize the system. Procedures were to be informal and private, records were to be confidential, children were to be detained apart from adults, and probation and social worker staffs were to be appointed. Even the vocabulary and physical surroundings of the juvenile system were changed to emphasize diagnosis and treatment rather than findings of guilt. The term *criminal behavior* was replaced by *delinquent behavior* as it pertained to the illegal acts of children. This shift in terminology serves to underscore the view of these children as wayward; they could be returned to society as law-abiding citizens.

Because procedures were not to be adversarial, lawyers were unnecessary. Psychologists and social workers, who could determine the juvenile's underlying behavior problem, were the main professionals attached to the system. Judge Julian Mack, one of the pioneers of the movement, summarized the questions to be placed before a juvenile court: "The problem for determination by the judge is not, Has this boy or girl committed a specific wrong, but What is he, how has he become what he is, and what had best be done in his interest and in the interest of the State to save him from a downward career."[7]

Although the child savers may have been imbued with good intentions, contemporary scholars have pointed out that the reforms (1) served to expedite traditional policies rather than create alternatives, (2) assumed the natural dependence of juveniles, (3) maintained a paternalistic approach to youths, and (4) promoted correctional programs designed to inculcate middle-class values and lower-class skills.[8]

Juvenile Rights

Until the 1960s, the ideology and practices of juvenile justice were dominated by the philosophy expressed by Judge Mack and others, such as Ben B. Lindsey, Denver's juvenile court judge from 1901 to 1929, and Gustav L. Schramm, who served for a long time on the bench of Pittsburgh's juvenile court. During recent years, however, reformers have sought to emphasize a concern for the rights of juveniles and the importance of the family as the means of controlling children's behavior.

BIOGRAPHY

Julian W. Mack

A federal judge for thirty years, Julian Mack (1866–1943) ranks as one of the foremost innovators in juvenile justice. Born in San Francisco, he received his law degree at Harvard and went into practice in Chicago in 1890. He was elected to a judgeship for the Circuit Court of Cook County, Illinois, in 1903, and between 1904 and 1907 he presided over Chicago's juvenile court, the first in the world. This court had been established by the Illinois legislature in 1899. Under Mack, the court dealt with neglected and abused children, runaways, school dropouts, and juveniles who had committed crimes. Juveniles were to be seen not as criminals but as wards of the state, thereby achieving a new legal status. The court was to become a social agency mixing services, discipline, probation, and the use of reformatories. Mack believed that the proper work of the system depended to a large extent on the judge and how well he was supported by probation officers, caseworkers, and psychologists. The judge and the staff had to be intellectually and temperamentally suited for work with juveniles; they had to be professionals and not political hacks. To this end, Mack supported the founding of the National Probation Officers Association. He sought as much as possible to avoid using reformatories and tried to bring the expertise of social service professionals to work for the courts.

In 1907 Mack was promoted to the Illinois Appeals Court, and in 1911 he was appointed by President William Howard Taft to a seat on the U.S. Court of Appeals for the 7th Circuit, from which he retired in 1941.

In re Winship (1970): The standard of proof of beyond a reasonable doubt applies to juvenile delinquency proceedings.

McKeiver v. Pennsylvania (1971): There is no constitutional right for a jury trial for juveniles.

Breed v. Jones (1975): Juveniles cannot be found delinquent in juvenile court and then be waived to adult court without violating double jeopardy.

Schall v. Martin (1984): Juveniles can be held in preventive detention if there is concern that additional crimes may be committed while awaiting court action.

The Supreme Court opinion in *Gault* (1967) and the earlier ruling in *Kent* v. *United States* (1966) extended due process rights to children.[9] These cases were followed by **In re Winship** (1970), in which the Court held that proof must be established "beyond a reasonable doubt" before a juvenile may be classified as a delinquent for committing an act that would be a crime if it were committed by an adult.[10] Perhaps signifying the extent to which the Court was willing to extend the concept of due process, it held in **McKeiver v. Pennsylvania** (1971) that "trial by jury in the juvenile court's adjudicative stage is not a constitutional requirement."[11] But in **Breed v. Jones** (1975) the Court extended the protection against double jeopardy to juveniles by requiring that before a case is adjudicated in juvenile court, a hearing must be held to determine if it should be transferred to the adult court.[12] However, in 1984 in **Schall v. Martin**,[13] the Court significantly departed from the trend toward increased juvenile rights. Noting that any attempt to structure such rights "must be qualified by the recognition that juveniles, unlike adults, are always in some form of custody," the Court confirmed the general notion of *parens patriae* as a primary basis for the juvenile court, equal in importance to the Court's desire to protect the community from crime. Thus, juveniles may be detained before trial if they are found to be a "risk" to the community, even though this rationale is not applicable to adult pretrial detention.

COMPARATIVE PERSPECTIVE
The Hidden Juvenile Justice System in Norway

There is no punishment for crimes in Norway for a child who is under fifteen. No special courts have been established with jurisdiction to try criminal cases against juvenile offenders. Older teenagers may be tried in ordinary courts of law and sentenced to prison. Sentences for most crimes, however, consist of only a suspended sentence or probation or several months in an open prison.

In practice, the public prosecutor, who represents the police, will transfer the juvenile cases directly to a division of the "social office," the *barnevern*—literally, child protection. Alternatively, the judge, after the trial, will refer the youth to the *barnevern*. Police evidence is turned over to the social workers, not for prosecution, but for "treatment."

The usual first step in "treatment" is that the *barnevern* takes

emergency custody of the child and places the child in a juvenile institution, *ungdomshjem* (youth home). If the parents or guardians do not give consent, there will be a meeting of the . . . child welfare committee [at which an] attorney may represent the parents. . . . At the meeting [the social welfare committee] will hear the lawyer's and parents' arguments against the placement. The concern is not with evidence about the crimes but rather with appropriate treatment for the child.

. . .

The *barnevern* is most often associated in the public mind with handling of cases of child abuse and neglect. In such case, the board will turn over custody of the child to the *barnevern* social workers, who will place the child in a foster home or youth home. Once the custody is removed from the parents, the

burden of proof is on the parents to retain custody. Social workers in alcoholism treatment are well aware of numerous such cases of recovering alcoholics who, even after recovery, have been unable to retain custody of their children.

. . .

In contrast to the American juvenile court, the Norwegian model is wholly social worker dominated. . . . The child welfare office presents the evidence and recommendations [to the judge] and directs the course of the case. The five laypersons who constitute the [social welfare committee] are advised by the child welfare office well before the hearing of the "facts" of the

The *Schall* decision reflects the ambivalence permeating the juvenile justice system. On one side are the liberal reformers, who call for increased procedural and substantive legal protections for juveniles accused of crime: on the other side, conservatives devoted to crime control policies are alarmed by the rise in juvenile crime. Like the Supreme Court, various state courts considered issues involving the right to treatment, equal protection, and cruel and unusual punishments and had to acknowledge the vagueness of certain laws affecting juveniles.

The system has also responded to charges that correctional institutions for children were being operated in ways that reinforced delinquent behavior and that too many children were being incarcerated. During the 1970s there was a movement to attack these problems. In 1972 Massachusetts became the first state to close most of its reformatories and to place the children in group homes and community treatment centers instead. Other states less dramatically reduced the number of children they held in institutions.

Thus much of the reform effort of the past two decades has been directed away from the broad jurisdiction of the juvenile court, with its lack of due process protections and its overarching treatment orientation. At the same time, juvenile crime has become recognized as a serious problem. By the mid-1980s greater attention was being focused on repeat offenders, with policymakers calling for heavier pun-

case. *Before* the hearing, the youth will have been placed in a youth home or mental institution "on an emergency basis"; the parents' rights to custody will have already been terminated. The process of the hearing itself is thus a mere formality after the fact. . . .

Proof of guilt brought before the committee will generally consist of a copy of the police report of the offenses admitted by the accused and a school report written by the principal after he or she has been informed of the lawbreaking. Reports by the *barnevern*—appointed psychologist and social worker— are also included. The *barnevern*, in its statement, has summarized these reports from the point of view of its arguments (usually for placement). Otherwise, the reports are ignored.

The hearing itself is a far cry from standard courtroom procedure. The youth and his or her parents may address the board briefly. The attorney sums up the case for a return to the home. Expert witnesses may be called and questioned by the board concerning, for instance, their treatment recommendations.

Following the departure of the parties concerned, the *barnevern* office presents what amounts to "the case for the prosecution." There is no opportunity to rebut the testimony and no opportunity for cross-examination.

. . .

Children receive far harsher treatments than do adults for similar offenses. For instance, for a young adult first offender the typical penalty for thievery is a suspended sentence. A child, however, may languish in an institution for years for the same offense.

. . .

A *barnevern's* first work ought to be to create the best possible childhood. However, the *barnevern* also has a control function in relation to both the parents and child, and the controller often feels a stronger duty to the community than to the parents and child. The fact of insti-

tutionalization of children with behavior problems clearly reflects this social control function.

. . .

The system of justice for children accused of crimes or behavioral problems is therefore often very harsh in Norway. This is in sharp contrast to the criminal justice system in general, which is strikingly lenient.

. . .

What we see in Norway today is a process of juvenile justice that has not changed substantially since the 1950s. Due to flaws within the system, including the lack of external controls, the best intentions of social workers "have gone awry." Where care and protection were intended, power and secrecy have prevailed. Juvenile justice in Norway today is the justice of America yesterday.

SOURCE: Adapted from "The Hidden Juvenile Justice System in Norway: A Journey Back in Time," by K. Van Wormer, *Federal Probation* (March 1990): 57–61. Reprinted by permission.

ishment for juveniles who commit crimes. Several states have passed laws broadening the waivers of juvenile court jurisdiction over youths accused of violent crime, and public support for a get-tough stance toward older juveniles seems to be growing. The juvenile court, long a bastion of discretion and rehabilitative zeal, has become a system of rules and procedures similar in many respects to adult courts. With deserved punishment assuming more prominence as a correctional goal, sentences for juveniles who have been adjudged repeat offenders have become more severe.

OPERATION OF JUVENILE JUSTICE

Juvenile justice operates through a variety of procedures in different states, and even within states, but a national pattern can fairly easily be discerned. In general, the system functions through many of the existing organizations of the adult criminal justice system but often with specialized structures for activities having to do with juveniles. Thus, although some large cities have specialized juvenile sections in their police departments, it is usually the patrol officer who has contact with delinquents when a disturbance or crime has been reported. In many states, special probation officers work with juveniles, but

FIGURE 17.2

Youngest age at which juveniles may be transferred to adult criminal court by waiver of juvenile jurisdiction. States vary greatly with regard to waiver provisions. There does not seem to be a clear regional or other factor that can explain the different provisions. This is perhaps another example of the role of politics in the system. NOTE: Many judicial waiver statutes also specify offenses that are waivable. This map shows the youngest age for which judicial waiver may be sought without regard to offense, by state. SOURCE: U.S. Department of Justice, Bureau of Justice Statistics, *Report to the Nation on Crime and Justice,* 2nd ed. (Washington, DC: Government Printing Office, 1988), p. 79.

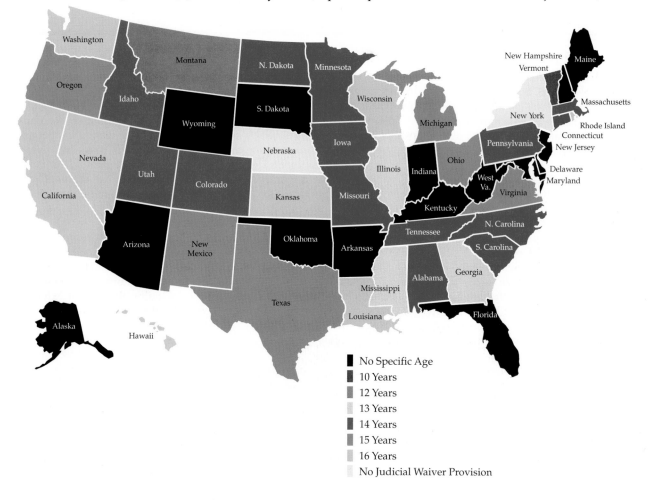

A disposition in keeping with the needs of the offender holds a high priority in the juvenile justice system.

they function as part of the larger probation service. Indeed, there are even some correctional systems that, although they maintain separate facilities for children, are organized under a commissioner who is responsible for both adult and juvenile institutions. The one portion of the system that is distinctive is the jurisdiction and procedures of the juvenile court, where only actions concerning children are heard, where the judge usually has a special concern for such cases, and where many of the processes of the adversarial system are absent. The broad outlines of the juvenile justice system are shown inside the back cover of this book.

Age normally determines whether a person is processed through the juvenile or adult justice system. The upper age limit for a juvenile varies from sixteen to eighteen: in thirty-eight states and the District of Columbia it is the eighteenth birthday; in eight states, the seventeenth; and in the remainder, the sixteenth. In most states, judges have the discretion to transfer juveniles to adult courts (see Figure 17.2). Although juveniles may be tried by the adult system when they "are not amenable to treatment in juvenile court" or "not a fit subject" for juvenile court jurisdiction, the severity of the offense and a prior record are the underlying reasons for the transfer. Thus in some states children charged with serious crimes, such as rape, murder, or armed robbery, may be processed in the adult criminal courts. In a growing number of states, youths charged with a particularly serious offense or who may have a history of repeated offenses may have charges filed against them directly in the criminal court, with no process of transfer from the jurisdiction of the juvenile court.

Which cases enter the juvenile justice system? Generally, there are four types: delinquency, status offenses, neglect, and dependency. Delinquent children have committed acts that if committed by an adult would be criminal—for example, auto theft, robbery, and assault. Acts that are illegal only if they are committed by juveniles—such as playing truant, running away, or refusing to obey the orders of adults—are known as **status offenses** and may lead to a correctional term in most states. Rather than having committed a violation of the penal code, status offenders have been designated as ungovernable or incorrigible: as runaways, truants, or persons in need of supervision **(PINS)**.

status offense: Any act committed by a juvenile that would not be a crime if it were committed by an adult but that is considered unacceptable for a child, such as truancy or running away from home.

PINS: This acronym (for "person in need of supervision") is used to designate juveniles who either are status offenders or who are thought to be on the verge of getting into trouble. Related acronyms often used are CINS (for "child in need of supervision") and JINS (for "juvenile in need of supervision")—juveniles who either are status offenders or who are thought to be on the verge of getting into trouble.

delinquents: Children who have committed criminal or status offenses.

Some states do not distinguish between delinquent offenders and status offenders and label both as juvenile **delinquents.** Those judged to be ungovernable and those judged to be robbers may be sent to the same correctional institution. Beginning in the early 1960s, many state legislatures attempted to distinguish status offenders and to exempt them from a criminal record. Efforts were made to divert such children out of the system, to reduce the possibility of incarceration, and to rewrite the laws with regard to status offenses. The breadth of the law defining status offenses is a matter of concern, because the language is often vague and all-encompassing: "growing up in idleness and crime," "engaging in immoral conduct," "in danger of leading an immoral life," "person in need of supervision." A child may be judged incorrigible and therefore delinquent for "refusing to obey the just and reasonable commands of his parents." The jurisdictional net is so broad in many states that almost any child can be described as requiring the protection of the juvenile justice system.

Juvenile justice also deals with problems of neglect and dependency—situations in which children are viewed as being hurt through no fault of their own, because their parents have failed to provide a proper environment for them. Such situations have been the jurisdictional concern of most juvenile justice systems since the turn of the century, when the idea gained currency that the state should act as a parent to a child whose own parents are unable or unwilling to provide proper care. Illinois, for example, defines a

neglected child: A child who is not receiving proper care because of some action or inaction of his or her parent(s).

dependent child: A child whose parent(s) is unable to give proper care.

neglected child as one who is neglected as to proper or necessary support, education as required by law, medical or other remedial care recognized under state law, or other care necessary for his well-being; or who is abandoned by his parents, guardians or custodians; or whose environment is injurious to his welfare; or whose behavior is injurious to his own welfare or that of others. A **dependent child** is

The juvenile justice system deals with those who are neglected or dependent as well as those who are delinquent.

either without a parent or guardian or is not receiving proper care because of the physical or mental disability of that person. The jurisdiction here is broad and includes a variety of situations in which the child can be viewed as a victim of adult behavior.

The laws of the State of Connecticut outlining the powers of the juvenile court provide a good example of the range of authority of the system, as follows:

> Juvenile matters include all proceedings concerning uncared-for, neglected or dependent children and youth and delinquent children within this state, termination of parental rights of children committed to a state agency, matters concerning families with service needs and contested termination of parental rights transferred from the probate court, but do not include matters of guardianship and adoption or matters affecting property rights of any child or youth over which the probate court has jurisdiction.[14]

Nationally about 75 percent of the cases referred to the juvenile courts are delinquency cases, of which a fifth are concerned with status offenses (see Table 17.2); about 20 percent are dependency and

TABLE 17.2   Delinquency and status offenses referred to juvenile court.   The work of the juvenile court concerns cases of delinquency, status offenses, and such noncriminal matters as neglect, adoption, and dependency. Note the distribution of the delinquency and status offense matters in this table. Do you think that these divisions will change in the future?

Percentage of Total Referred

11%	*Crimes Against Persons*	
	Criminal homicide	1%
	Forcible rape	2
	Robbery	17
	Aggravated assault	20
	Simple assault	59
		100%
46%	*Crimes Against Property*	
	Burglary	25%
	Larceny	47
	Motor vehicle theft	5
	Arson	1
	Vandalism and trespassing	19
	Stolen property offenses	3
		100%
5%	*Drug Offenses*	100%
21%	*Offenses Against Public Order*	
	Weapons offenses	6%
	Sex offenses	6
	Drunkenness and disorderly conduct	23
	Contempt, probation, and parole violations	21
	Other	44
		100%
17%	*Status Offenses*	
	Running away	28%
	Truancy and curfew violations	21
	Ungovernability	28
	Liquor violations	23
		100%

SOURCE: U.S. Department of Justice, Bureau of Justice Statistics, *Report to the Nation on Crime and Justice*, 2nd ed. (Washington, DC: Government Printing Office, 1988), p. 78.

neglect cases; and about 5 percent involve special proceedings, such as adoption. The system, then, deals with both criminal and non-criminal cases, and a concern has been expressed that juveniles who have done nothing wrong are categorized either officially or in the public mind as delinquents. In some states little effort is made in pre-judicial detention facilities or in social service agencies to keep the classes of juveniles separate.

More discretion is exercised in the juvenile than in the adult justice system. Turn-of-the-century reformers believed that juvenile justice officials should have wide discretion in their efforts to serve the best interests of the child. Currently there are pressures to nar-row the scope of this discretion, yet to a great extent decision makers may still individualize justice. At the same time, because of the insti-tutional needs of the bureaucracy and the presence of the others with whom they interact, juvenile officials must be attuned to considera-tions of efficiency, public relations, and the maintenance of harmony and esprit de corps among their underlings.

Juvenile justice is a particular type of bureaucracy that is based on an ideology of social work and is staffed primarily by persons who think of themselves as members of the helping professions. The judge may find that justice must be dispensed in an organizational context in which the public's demand for punishment conflicts with pres-sures from probation officers and social workers who blame environ-mental conditions for deviant behavior and urge treatment for the offender. The juvenile court judge does not have the explicit sanctions described in the criminal law to guide decisions and justify actions.

Like the adult criminal justice system, juvenile justice functions within an organizational and political context in which exchange relationships among officials of various agencies influence decisions. The juvenile court must deal not only with children and their parents but also with patrol officers, probation officers, welfare officials, so-cial workers, psychologists, and the heads of treatment institutions. These others all have their own goals, their own perceptions of delin-quency, and their own concepts of treatment.

The Police Interface

Most complaints against juveniles are brought by the police, although they may be initiated by an injured party, by school officials, or even by the parents. The police must make three major decisions with regard to the processing of juveniles: (1) whether to take the child into custody, (2) whether to request that the child be detained follow-ing apprehension, and (3) whether to refer the child to court.[15]

As might be expected, the police exercise enormous discretion with regard to these decisions. The police perform extensive screen-ing and informal adjustment in the street and the station house. In communities and neighborhoods where law enforcement officials have developed close relationships with the residents or where law enforcement policy dictates, the police may simply give warnings to the juveniles and notify their parents. Figure 17.3 shows that more than half (63.1 percent) of those taken into police custody have their cases referred to the juvenile court; about a third (29.1 percent) are

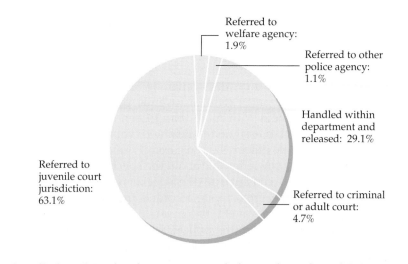

Referred to
welfare agency:
1.9%

Referred to other
police agency:
1.1%

Handled within
department and
released: 29.1%

Referred to criminal
or adult court:
4.7%

Referred to
juvenile court
jurisdiction:
63.1%

FIGURE 17.3

Disposition of juveniles taken into police custody. The police have discretion with regard to the disposition of juvenile arrest cases. What factors may explain the different ways that cases are handled?
SOURCE: U.S. Department of Justice, Bureau of Justice Statistics, *Sourcebook of Criminal Justice Statistics* (Washington, DC: Government Printing Office, 1990), p. 456.

handled within the department and then released; and 7.7 percent are referred to other agencies or to an adult court.

In a study of four communities in the Pittsburgh metropolitan area, a wide variation was found in arrest rates and a corresponding variation in the portion of those arrested who were selected for appearance in juvenile court.[16] Only about half of those who come to the attention of the police for law violations are taken to the station house, and only a small proportion of those officially registered on police records (35.4 percent) are referred to the court for action. Thus whether a child is declared a delinquent is to some extent determined by the police officer in selective reporting of juvenile offenders to the court. Such factors as one's attitude toward the juvenile, the juvenile's family, the offense, and the court; the predominant attitude of the community; and one's conception of one's own role as a police officer influence this selection process.

In a study of police in a metropolitan industrial city of 450,000, the choice of disposition of juvenile cases was found to depend very much on the prior record of the child; second in importance was the offender's demeanor.[17] Juveniles who had committed minor offenses but were respectful and contrite were defined by the officers as worthy candidates for rehabilitation and were given an informal reprimand. Those who were argumentative or surly were defined as "punks" who needed to be taught a lesson through arrest. The researchers found that only 4 percent of the cooperative youths were arrested, in comparison with 67 percent of those who were uncooperative.

To summarize, a number of factors play a role in the way that the police dispose of a case of juvenile delinquency. These factors include:

- the seriousness of the offense
- the willingness of the parents to cooperate and discipline their child
- the child's behavioral history as reflected in school and police records
- the extent to which the child and his or her parents insist on a formal court hearing
- the local political and social norms with regard to dispositions in such cases

Because the law specifies that persons classified as juveniles (usually those under eighteen) and adult offenders be treated differently, and because of the belief that prevention should be a dominant goal of efforts to deal with youth crime, most large police departments have specialized juvenile units. It is generally recommended that depending on the nature and extent of juvenile problems in a given community, a department with more than fifteen employees should have at least one member assigned to deal with youth.

The special juvenile officer is often carefully selected and trained to relate to youths, is knowledgeable about the special laws concerned in these cases, and is sensitive to the special needs of young offenders. Because of the importance accorded the goal of diverting juveniles from the justice system, the juvenile officer is also viewed as an important link between the police and other community institutions, such as the schools, recreation facilities, and organizations serving young people. Because of the emphasis on the prevention of delinquency, many authorities urge that juvenile officers not be involved in the investigation of serious juvenile crimes. Other authorities believe that police resources should not be used to enhance recreational activities as a delinquency prevention strategy.

Although young people commit many serious crimes, the juvenile function of police work is concerned largely with the maintenance of order. In many instances, the law is ambiguous, and blame cannot easily be assigned. In terms of physical or monetary damage, many offenses committed by juveniles are minor infractions: breaking windows, hanging around the business district, disturbing the peace, adolescent sexual behavior, shoplifting. In such instances the function of the investigating officer is not so much to solve crimes as to handle the often legally uncertain complaints involving juveniles. The officer must seek both to satisfy the complainant and to keep the youth from future trouble. Given this emphasis on settling trouble cases within the community rather than an emphasis on strict enforcement of the law, the police power to arrest provides a weapon that can be used to deter juveniles from criminal activity and to encourage them to conform to the dictates of the law.

It is important not to minimize the amount of serious crime that juveniles perpetrate. At the opening of Part 5 it was noted that, according to the *UCR*, over a third of those arrested for index crimes were under eighteen. These are the offenses that are of major concern to the public, and in urban areas especially the police must devote more of their resources to these offenses than to the less serious and status offenses of juveniles. Data from interviews conducted by the *National Crime Survey* in 60,000 U.S. households indicate:

- Rates of personal crimes were higher for juveniles than for adults. Juveniles were also more likely to commit crimes in groups of three or more.
- The seriousness and types of injuries inflicted in crimes committed by juveniles and youthful offenders (eighteen- to twenty-year-olds) were similar to those of injuries inflicted by adults.
- No relationship was found between general economic conditions (unemployment rate, consumer price index, and gross national product) and crime. However, juvenile crime rates were higher in urban neighborhoods with high unemployment.

- In poor neighborhoods, juveniles and youths, but not adults, were more likely to use weapons than were their counterparts in wealthier neighborhoods.
- Males committed offenses about four to fifteen times more frequently than females did, depending on the type of crime.[18]

Do the *Miranda* and *Mapp* Decisions Apply to Juveniles?

Throughout the 1960s and 1970s the Supreme Court of the United States extended due process rights to adult defendants in state courts. Although the Court also extended certain rights to persons brought before the juvenile court, such as the right to counsel (*In re Gault*) and the right to certain procedural elements (*In re Winship*), the court was not as active in applying the *Miranda* self-incrimination doctrine and the *Mapp* unreasonable search and seizure ruling to juveniles. This does not mean, however, that states have not extended these protections; most have for some circumstances. Juveniles today have almost as much protection as do adults in the criminal courts.

The Uniform Juvenile Justice Act was drafted in 1968 by the National Conference of Commissioners on Uniform State Laws, a nongovernmental body interested in achieving uniformity of procedures among the states throughout the nation. The Conference recommended that the states adopt the Uniform Juvenile Justice Act including *Miranda*-type safeguards designed to implement the *Gault* and other Supreme Court decisions. It appears that jurisdictions throughout the nation now provide the *Miranda* protections, but issues remain as to the ability of juveniles to waive these rights. In 1979 the Court ruled in *Fare v. Michael C.* that a child may waive rights to an attorney and to self-incrimination but that juvenile court judges must evaluate the totality of circumstances under which the minor made these decisions.[19]

Fare v. *Michael C.* (1979): Trial court judges must evaluate the voluntariness of confessions by juveniles by examining the totality of circumstances.

On the issue of unreasonable searches and seizures as required by the Fourth Amendment, the Court has not been as forthcoming. State courts interpreted *Gault* to extend these provisions, but in 1985 the Supreme Court ruled in *New Jersey v. T.L.O.* that school officials can search students and their lockers if they have reasonable suspicion that the search will produce evidence of a school or criminal law violation.[20] The justices recognized that children do have Fourth Amendment rights yet also noted that under the concept of *in loco parentis*, school officials may act in place of the parent under certain conditions when the child is under their jurisdiction.

New Jersey v. *T.L.O.* (1985): School officials may search a student based on a reasonable suspicion that the search will produce evidence that a school or civil law has been violated.

Intake

When the police believe that formal actions should be taken by the juvenile justice system, a complaint is filed with a special division of the juvenile probation department for preliminary screening and evaluation. During this intake stage, an officer reviews the case to determine whether the alleged facts are sufficient to cause the juvenile court to take jurisdiction or whether some other action would be in the child's interest. If it appears that the case warrants formal judicial processing, a formal petition may be filed with the court. If the police referral does not contain sufficient legal evidence or if the juvenile has committed only a minor violation, has no prior record, and is living with a caring parent, the case may be dismissed. Alternatively, a child may be diverted out of the system to an appropriate mental health, educational, or social agency. In some instances, juveniles are put on informal probation by the intake officer so that the department can provide counseling or other services. The intake officer thus has considerable discretion and power. Nationally, between 40 and 50 percent of all referrals from the police are disposed of at this stage, without formal processing by a judge.

The numbers and types of cases sent to the juvenile court are influenced by the decisions of political and enforcement agencies. The size of the court staff and the resources at its disposal depend on the maintenance of cooperative relations with community leaders. The actions of the juvenile court judge must be consistent with local values. Acts of delinquency that outrage the community will inspire pressures on the court to deal severely with transgressors. Politicians feel that they can gain support by advocating a "get tough" policy rather than by pushing for the rehabilitation of offenders. When the sons of influential persons are charged with delinquency, the informality and treatment orientation of the system allow a variety of lenient dispositions, including probation, outpatient care at a psychiatric clinic, and incarceration in a therapeutic community. Not all cases end up in the reform school or industrial school.

In most juvenile justice systems the probation officer plays a crucial role during the intake phase. Because intake is essentially a screening process to determine whether a case should be referred to the court or to a social agency, it often takes place without judicial supervision. Informal discussions among the probation officer, the parents, and the child are important means of learning about the child's social situation, of diagnosing behavioral problems, and of recommending treatment possibilities. It has been estimated that nationally about half the delinquency cases each year are settled informally and unofficially during this pre-judicial stage.[21]

Diversion

Although there have always been informal ways of diverting alleged delinquents away from the courts and toward community agencies, the number and types of diversion programs have greatly expanded during the past two decades. In keeping with the philosophy of the juvenile court, many people believe that diversion should be promoted as much as possible. Because of the court's extraordinary powers, many persons believe that it should intervene only as a last resort. When behavioral problems can be identified early, the child should be given access to the necessary remedial resources without being taken before a judge and labeled delinquent. Diversion has also been advocated as one way of reducing the court's work load. Perhaps more important is that children respond more readily to the treatment provided by community-based services than to the correctional services available through the court. Diversion, it is argued, permits the juvenile court to allocate its resources more wisely by concentrating on cases of repeat and serious offenders.

But diversion is not without its critics. Although diversion programs have greatly expanded during the past decade, the number of young people committed to institutions has not decreased appreciably. It appears to many observers that the increase in diversion programs has widened the juvenile justice net and that children who in the past would not have been formally handled are so handled now.

Detention

After the decision is made that some formal action should be taken, should the juvenile be put in **detention** until disposition of the case? This decision is usually made by an intake officer of the juvenile court. One of the early reforms of the juvenile justice system was to ensure that children were not held in jails in company with adults who were also awaiting trial or sentencing. To mix juveniles—some of whom are status offenders or under the protection of the court because they are neglected—in the same public facility with adults accused of crimes has long been thought unjust, but in many areas separate detention facilities for juveniles do not exist.

detention: A period of temporary custody of a juvenile before disposition of his or her case.

Children are held in detention for a number of reasons. For some youths, it is the possibility that they will commit other crimes while awaiting trial. For others, it is the possibility of harm from gang members or parents if they are released. For still others, it is the possibility that they may not appear in court as required. Finally, youths are detained when there is no responsible adult who is willing to care for them. These are the formal reasons, but detention may also be used as punishment, to teach a lesson.

Although much attention is focused on the juvenile court and the sanctions imposed by judges as a result of the formal processes of adjudication, many more children are punished through confinement in detention centers and jails before any court action has taken place. An estimated half million juveniles are detained each year, sometimes for several months; but only about 15 percent are eventually confined to a group home, training school, or halfway house. These figures seem to indicate that detention and intake decisions have a greater impact than the decisions of the court. They may also underscore the belief that a brief period of detention is a good device to "shake up the kid and set him straight." The fact remains: juveniles held in detention have not been convicted.

Adjudication

Each year more than a million cases of delinquency are disposed of by the juvenile courts. During the adjudicatory, often referred to as the "fact finding" process, the judge hears evidence concerning the alleged behavior.

The questions of attaching the label "delinquent" to a juvenile and determining a sanction are the primary matters before the court. In accordance with the Progressives' belief that adjudication should be informal and nonadversarial, the normal rules of criminal procedure were modified; the rules of evidence were not strictly followed, hearsay testimony could be admitted, there was no prosecutor (a police or probation officer presented the case), and the sessions were closed to the public. From a formal standpoint, the purpose of the hearing was not to determine a child's guilt or innocence of a specific charge but rather to establish the child's status as either delinquent or not delinquent and to help the child to become law abiding.

The role of the juvenile court has been described by a former judge of the Denver Juvenile Court as a complex mixture.

It is law, and it is social work; it is control, and it is help; it is the good parent and, also, the stern parent; it is both formal and informal. It is concerned not only with the delinquent, but also with the battered child, the runaway and many others. . . . The juvenile court has been all things to all people.[22]

CLOSE-UP | Crime at an Early Age: The Violent Streets of Luis Guzman

Luis Guzman is one of tens of thousands of violent youths who prowl the streets of the nation's cities, instilling fear and limiting in countless ways the manner in which urban Americans live.

By [the time he was sixteen], Luis Guzman had become a familiar figure to the police. He was arrested in September on charges of stealing a teacher's purse at a public school. His history made him a natural suspect for the police in the slaying later that month of a lawyer in a robbery in a riverside park, and he spent two weeks in jail before three other youths were arrested in the crime.

Before the murder charge was dropped, the authorities learned that eight months earlier Luis had violated probation for an armed-robbery conviction by running away from a halfway house for juvenile delinquents in East Harlem. So, for now, he remains in custody at Rikers Island.

Like many other young criminals, Luis has spent much of his life in institutions. Thousands of dollars of public money have been spent on trying to turn him into a responsible member of society. He has had hundreds of hours of group therapy and counseling. He has repeatedly run away from the institutions, most of which had no locked doors or fences.

Luis Guzman is slender and short. He wears his dark hair in a crew cut and looks out at the world through black eyes, his jaw set. His speech is slow and direct. . . .

What is wrong with robbing, Luis said, is that "you could run into the wrong person. He could turn around and shoot you. That's what I was afraid of. But I still done it anyway. I took big risks for the money. I like to support myself. I do it to support myself, that's why."

About the victims Luis said, "We'd just say, 'We got over. We took the money without getting busted.' I don't be thinking about them. I just think of getting the money and hanging out."

Sometimes Luis mugged with his bare hands, sometimes with an .007 knife with a six-inch blade that he bought for $8.

"Sometimes you run up in the back and yoke 'em," with an arm around the neck, Luis said, "and the other boys take the money out of his pockets." With a knife, "You just put it in front of them and say, 'Give me your money.' We tell them to walk one way, then we walk the other way. When we get to the corner we run."

Luis's victims were always men. "Women scream. One, I just went up to her, I didn't have my knife out and she started screaming. So I just ran. The men just stop and get scared."

Anyone who tried to rob Luis would have to kill him. If someone resisted him, "I'd probably put them to sleep. My friend would yoke 'em." If he had a knife, he said, "I'll probably stick 'em."

. . .

Luis's criminal records do not include the jewelry-store robbery he described. Either the information was lost or the case was dropped, or Luis invented it. All are equally plausible in the realm of juvenile delinquency, where prosecution and record-keeping are uneven and where tales of self-aggrandizement are not rare.

Luis passed a few more months in Spofford. Then in late January, he went to the Great Valley Youth Camp in the densely wooded foothills of the Allegheny Mountains, near the junction of the New York, Pennsylvania and Canadian borders—about as far from New York City as you can get and still be in New York State. The camp has no locked doors, barred windows or fences.

[That fall] Luis made a trip to the city on a public bus, and, three days later, returned to Great Valley on schedule. He seemed to be coming along nicely.

While in the city, Luis made an appearance in State Supreme Court in Manhattan before Justice Harold J.

The changes in criminal proceedings mandated by the due process decisions of the Supreme Court following *Gault* have brought about shifts in the philosophy and actions of the juvenile court. Copies of formal petitions with specific charges must be given to the parents and child, counsel may be present and free counsel appointed if the juvenile is indigent, witnesses may be cross-examined, and a transcript of the proceedings must be kept. In thirteen states, juveniles have a right to a jury trial.

As with other Supreme Court decisions, the reality of local practice may differ sharply from the stipulations in the opinion. Juveniles and their parents often waive their rights in response to suggestions made by the judge or probation officer. The lower social status of the offender's parents, the intimidating atmosphere of the court, and

---

Rothwax. There he pleaded guilty to pulling his .007 knife on a man on a subway platform [the year before] and stealing a man's oversized radio: armed robbery.

Justice Rothwax placed Luis on probation for five years. The judge said in an interview that he had done so in a plea-bargaining arrangement after being assured that Luis would spend the time in a locked facility of the Division for Youth.

Luis did not go to a secure facility. He returned to Great Valley.

Four months later, after he had been at Great Valley for 13 months, Luis was transferred to the state's Judge Harold A. Stevens Youth Development Center No. 2 in East Harlem, an unlocked six-story sandstone-and-brick building at 112th Street and Lexington Avenue. There were 16 boys there. Luis stayed three days before taking flight.

He headed for his father's tenement apartment on the Lower East Side. On March 4, Felix Guzman returned his son to the center. . . . [Luis left the same day.] This time he went to his mother's apartment on Avenue D.

Law enforcement officials say that a warrant was issued for Luis's arrest, that youth workers searched for him on the Lower East Side, to no avail.

Over the next seven months, Luis made a joke of the attempts to rehabilitate him. He roamed the streets with the "Little Wild Boys" gang, later renamed "The Baddest Boys Around." He snatched gold chains on the Upper East Side, and he went out mugging with "my boys." He drifted in and out of his parents' and friends' apartments.

In April, Luis was arrested and charged with stealing a Father's Day plaque from a card shop on East 14th Street. The charge was conditionally dismissed and Luis went free. No one noticed the outstanding warrant against Luis for running away from the youth center and violating the terms of his probation.

In the summer, a policeman caught Luis trespassing on a construction site, where he had gone to steal sheets of plywood. The policeman took Luis to his mother's apartment and let him go with a warning. That officer was also apparently unaware of the arrest warrant.

Shortly after the start of school in September, the police said, Luis stole a teacher's purse from a classroom at Junior High School 22, where his sister Evelyn is a student. An undercover policeman from the Seventh Precinct saw him sprinting down the street with the purse and took him into custody.

He was taken to Rikers Island for the first time. But in four days he was free again after promising to appear in Criminal Court. Once again, the arrest warrant had been overlooked.

Luis said he had intended to return to court on October 7, but, he added, "then I got busted for this murder, something I didn't do. If I did it," he said, "I would admit it. I wouldn't be scared to admit it. Every time I do a robbery I admit it."

At Rikers Island, after talking for more than two hours, sitting still, seldom even moving a hand, Luis began to twist and turn in his straight-backed chair. He was tired of answering questions, he said. He was tired of the way his life had been going, too. He wanted to get out of New York, go to Puerto Rico.

"There's too much trouble around here," he said. "My boys be instigating. . . . But now when I get out of here, if I work this case, I ain't going to hang out with them. My mother's going to try to get me a ticket to Puerto Rico. I ain't never coming back."

SOURCE: Adapted from "Crime at an Early Age: The Violent Streets of Luis Guzman," by J. B. Treaster, *The New York Times*, November 9, 1981, p. B1. Copyright © 1981 by The New York Times Company. Reprinted by permission.

judicial hints that the outcome will be more favorable if a lawyer is not present are reasons the procedures outlined in *Gault* are not demanded. The litany of "treatment," "doing what's right for the child," and "working out a just solution" may sound enticing, especially to people who are unfamiliar with the intricacies of formal legal procedures. In practice, then, juveniles still lack many of the protections accorded adult offenders. Some of the differences between the juvenile and adult criminal justice systems are shown in Table 17.3.

Adjudicatory Process

In some jurisdictions the adjudication process is more adversarial than it was before the *Gault* and *Winship* decisions. Like adult cases, however, juvenile cases tend to be adjudicated in a style that conforms to the crime control (administrative) model: most are settled in preliminary hearings by a plea agreement, and few go on to formal trial. At the preliminary hearing the youth is notified of the charges and his or her rights, and counsel may be present. Since in most cases the juvenile has already admitted guilt to the arresting or intake officer, the focus of the hearing is on the disposition. In contested

TABLE 17.3   Adult and juvenile criminal justice compared.   Compare the basic elements of the adult and juvenile systems. To what extent does a juvenile have the same rights as an adult? Are the different decision-making processes necessary because a juvenile is involved?

	Adult System	Juvenile System
Philosophical assumptions	Decisions made as result of adversarial system in context of due process rights	Decisions made as result of inquiry into needs of juvenile within context of some due process elements
Jurisdiction	Violations of criminal law	Violations of criminal law, status offenses, neglect, dependency
Primary sanctioning goals	Punishment, deterrence	Treatment
Official discretion	Widespread	Widespread
Entrance	Official action of arrest, summons, or citation	Official action, plus referral by school, parents, other sources
Role of prosecuting and defense attorneys	Required and formalized	Sometimes required; less structured; poor role definition
Adjudication	Procedural rules of evidence in public jury trial required	Less formal structure to rules of evidence and conduct of trial; no right to public jury in most states
Treatment programs	Run primarily by public agencies	Broad use of private as well as public agencies
Application of Bill of Rights amendments		
4th: Unreasonable searches and seizures	Applicable	Applicable
5th: Double jeopardy	Applicable	Applicable (re waiver to adult court)
Self-incrimination	Applicable (*Miranda* warnings)	Applicable
6th: Right to counsel	Applicable	Applicable
Public trial	Applicable	Applicable in half of states
Trial by jury	Applicable	Applicable in half of states
8th: Right to bail	Applicable	Applicable in half of states
14th: Right to treatment	Not applicable	Applicable

cases, a prosecutor presents the state's case and the judge oversees the proceedings, ruling on the admission of evidence and the testimony of witnesses. Because juries are used only sparingly, even in states where they are authorized, guilt or innocence is generally determined by the judge, who then passes sentence.

With the increased concern about due process and the legal rights of juveniles, prosecuting attorneys are taking a more prominent part in the system. In keeping with the traditional child-saver philosophy, prosecuting attorneys rarely appeared in juvenile court until after the *Gault* decision. Now, with the presence of a defense attorney, it is felt to be important that the state's interest be represented by legal counsel. In many jurisdictions prosecutors are assigned to deal specifically with juvenile cases by advising the intake officer, administering diversion programs, negotiating pleas, and acting as an advocate during judicial proceedings.

Disposition

If the court makes a finding of delinquency, a dispositional hearing is required. This hearing may be held immediately following the entry of a plea or at a later date. Typically, the judge receives a social history or predispositional report before passing sentence. Few juveniles are found by the court to be not delinquent at trial, since the intake and pretrial processes normally filter out cases in which a law violation cannot be proved. In addition to dismissal of a petition, five other choices are available: (1) dismissal or suspended judgment, (2) probation, (3) community treatment, (4) institutional care, and (5) waiver to an adult court.

The traditional belief of juvenile court advocates was that rehabilitation through treatment was the only goal of the sanction imposed on young people. Throughout most of this century judges have sentenced juveniles to indeterminate sentences so that correctional administrators would have the discretion to determine when release was appropriate. As with the adult criminal justice system, indeterminate sentences and unbridled discretion have been under attack during the past decade. A number of states have tightened the sentencing discretion of judges, especially with regard to serious offenses. The state of Washington, for example, has adopted a determinate sentencing law for juveniles. The emphasis in other states is that a youth may be transferred to the adult court for adjudication and sentencing. Jurisdictions such as the District of Columbia, Colorado, Florida, and Virginia have passed laws requiring mandatory sentences for certain offenses committed by juveniles.

What seems to have occurred during the past decade is that the same "get tough" emphasis that has been brought to bear on the adult system is also being reflected in juvenile justice.

Corrections

Many aspects of juvenile corrections are similar or identical to those of adult corrections; for example, both systems mix rehabilitative and retributive sanctions. Juvenile corrections differs in many respects from the adult system, however. Some of the differences flow from the *parens patriae* concept and the youthful, seemingly innocent persons with whom the system deals. At times the differences are expressed in formal operational policies, such as contracting for residential treatment; at other times the differences are apparent only in the style and culture of an operation, as in juvenile probation.

One predominant aim of juvenile corrections is to avoid unnecessary incarceration. When children are removed from their homes, they are inevitably damaged emotionally, even when the home is harsh, for they are forced to abandon the only environment they know. Further, placing children in institutions has labeling effects; the children begin to perceive themselves as "bad," because they have received punitive treatment, and children who see themselves as bad are likely to behave that way. Finally, treatment is believed to be more effective when the child is living in a normal, supportive home environment. For these reasons, noninstitutional forms of corrections are seen as highly desirable in juvenile justice, and they have proliferated in recent years.

Alternative Dispositions

Although probation and commitment to an institution are the major dispositional alternatives, judges have wide discretion to warn, to fine, to arrange for restitution, to refer a juvenile for treatment at either a public or a private community agency, or to withhold judgment. In making this decision, the judge relies on a social background report, developed by the probation department. Often it includes reports from others in the community, such as school officials or a psychiatrist. When psychological issues are involved, a disposition may be delayed pending further diagnosis.

Judges sometimes suspend judgment, or continue cases without a finding, when they wish to put a youth under supervision but are reluctant to apply the label "delinquent." Judgment may be suspended for a definite or indefinite period of time. The court thus holds a definitive judgment in abeyance for possible use should a youth misbehave while under the informal supervision of a probation officer or parents.

Probation

By far the most common method of handling juvenile offenders is to place them on probation. Juvenile probation operates in much the same way as adult probation, and it is sometimes carried out by the same agency. In two respects, however, juvenile probation can be very different from adult probation. Traditionally, juvenile probation has been more satisfactorily funded; hence caseloads of officers are much lower in number. Second, juvenile probation itself is often infused with the sense that the offender can change, that the job is enjoyable, and that the clients are worthwhile. Such attitudes make for greater creativity than is possible with adult probation.

The probation officer can choose among an array of options in working out supervision approaches for juveniles. One of the most common choices is to pair the juvenile with a "big brother" or "big

Big Brother/Big Sister programs are viewed as one way to provide role models for young people and thus prevent delinquency.

sister" who spends time with the offender, providing a positive adult role model. Another much-used approach, possible because the officer normally has more discretionary control over the caseload than the adult probation officer, is "contingency contracting," in which something the juvenile hopes for (less frequent reporting, perhaps, or termination of supervision) is linked to the juvenile's achievement of some goal (such as passing grades). It is also common for the probation officer to engage in supervision activities that involve the juvenile's family or school. Probation is the most widely used sanction in juvenile corrections, and it is also the most creative.

Community Treatment

Treatment in community-based facilities has greatly expanded during the past decade. In particular, the number of private, nonprofit agen-

Much emphasis in juvenile justice is
on treating the needs of individual
delinquents in a community setting.

cies that contract with the states to perform services for troubled
youths has grown. Demands for deinstitutionalization emphasized
that juveniles could receive better and less costly treatment in the
community from private and social service agencies.

Foster homes are families in which juvenile offenders live, usually for a short period of time. Foster parents often have children of
their own, and they treat the foster child more or less as a member of
the family. The foster home concept was developed as a means for
implementing a policy of limited intervention into juvenile lives. It
reflects the sentiment of the Standard Juvenile Court Act (a model
law developed by The National Council on Crime and Delinquency)
that when a child "is removed from the control of his parents, the
court shall secure for him care as nearly as possible equivalent to [the
home]."[23]

Group homes are small, often privately run facilities for groups
of juvenile offenders. They are usually older houses that have been
remodeled to fit the needs of twelve to twenty juveniles. Each group
home has several staff personnel who work as counselors or house-
parents on eight-hour or twenty-four-hour shifts. Typically, group
home placements are for longer terms than foster home placements,
and they may be more suited to seriously delinquent youths because
they can allow juveniles to attend local schools, can provide individual and group counseling, and can otherwise maintain a more structured day than most of the residents received in their own homes.
Most group homes are nonsecure, in the sense that the residents are
expected to abide by rules, including curfews, but staff members take
little responsibility for seeing to it that the rules are obeyed; juveniles
who flout the rules are returned to court for placement elsewhere.

Institutional Care

Incarceration of juveniles has traditionally meant commitment to a
state institution often called a training school, reform school, or industrial school. An assumption of the Progressive movement was
that juveniles could be helped only if they were removed from "the
crowded slum-life of the noisy, disorderly settlement where 70 percent of the population is of foreign parentage." The children were to
be "taken away from evil association and temptations, away from the
moral and physical filth and contagion, out of the gas light and sewer
gas; away out into the woods and fields, free from temptation and

contagion; out into the sunlight and the starlight and the pure, sweet air of the meadows."[24] Once in a rural setting, the children were to learn a vocation and be trained to middle-class standards. This usually meant that juveniles were taught outdated farming skills and trades no longer practiced in the urban areas to which they were destined to return. The remoteness of these institutions meant the further loss of meaningful personal and family relationships. Even today, state correctional facilities for children tend to be in rural areas.

Large custodial training schools located in outlying areas remain the typical institutions to which juveniles are committed, although during the past decade there has been an increase in the number of privately maintained facilities that accept residents sent to them by the courts. The last census revealed that more than 83,402 juveniles were housed in 2,900 public and private centers; 62 percent of the residents were in public facilities.[25]

There is a major difference between the public and private facilities, with training schools holding only 13 percent of all juveniles in private facilities. The census found that the average age in all facilities was about fifteen years and that boys outnumbered girls three to one. In addition to the juveniles in the institutions named, unknown numbers of children are under the care of the juvenile court but have been placed in noncorrectional private facilities such as schools for the emotionally disturbed, military academies, and even preparatory schools. Although courts usually maintain jurisdiction over delinquents until they attain the age of majority, data from the training

---

A QUESTION OF ETHICS

Residents of the Lovelock Home had been committed by the juvenile court because they were either delinquent or neglected. All twenty-five boys, aged seven to fifteen, were streetwise, tough, and interested only in getting out. The institution had a staff of social services professionals who tried to deal with the residents' educational and psychological needs. Since state funding was short, these services looked better in the annual report than to an observer who might visit Lovelock. Most of the time the residents watched TV, played basketball in the backyard, and just hung out in one anothers' rooms.

Joe Klegg, the night supervisor, was tired from the eight-hour shift that he had just completed on his "second job" as a daytime convenience store manager. The boys were watching television when he arrived at seven. Everything seemed calm. It should have been, since Joe had placed a tough fifteen-year-old, Randy Marshall, in charge. Joe had told Randy to keep the younger boys in line. Randy used his muscle and physical presence to intimidate the other residents. He knew that if the home was quiet and there was no trouble, he would be rewarded with special privileges such as a "pass" to go see his girlfriend. Joe wanted no hassles and a quiet house so that he could doze off when the boys went to sleep.

Does the situation at Lovelock Home raise ethical questions, or does it merely raise questions of poor management practices? What are the potential consequences for the residents? For Joe Klegg? What is the state's responsibility?

schools indicate that nationally the average length of stay is approximately ten months.

What types of juveniles are placed in custodial institutions? Results from a national survey showed that 40 percent were incarcerated for violent offenses, 60 percent used drugs regularly, and 50 percent said that a family member had been in prison at some time in the past. Most of the residents (94 percent) were male, only 30 percent had grown up in a household with both parents, and the percentage of African-American (41.1 percent) and Hispanic (18.9 percent) are considerably greater than the portion of those groups in the general population (12 percent and 6 percent, respectively).[26]

Placement in the more desirable private treatment centers may be sought for preferred juveniles. Often the availability of treatment alternatives depends upon negotiations between the court and the private agencies. Some private institutions desire referrals as a way of maintaining and expanding their clientele, but they want the "right" type of patients. The private agencies select "motivated" and high-status clients and pass on to public agencies the harder-to-work-with, more resistant clients. In return for opening their doors to court referrals, the treatment centers expect to be able to transfer their troublesome cases to state institutions.[27]

JUVENILE TREATMENT STRATEGIES

Because of the emphasis on rehabilitation that has dominated juvenile justice for much of the past fifty years, a wide variety of treatment programs has been used. Counseling, education, vocational training, and an assortment of psychotherapy methods have been incorporated into the juvenile correctional programs of most states. Unfortunately, there is much dissatisfaction with the results. For many offenders, incarceration in a juvenile training institution appears to be mainly preparation for entry into adult corrections. John Irwin's concept of the state-raised youth (Chapter 15) is a useful way of looking at children who come in contact with institutional life at an early age, lack family relationships and structure, become used to living in a correctional environment, and are unable to move out of this cycle.

Optimism about treatment and rehabilitation has turned to dismay and soul searching. During the 1950s and 1960s some experimental programs based on the community treatment idea were thought to hold much promise. Highfields was a New Jersey program in which a small number of boys lived with staff members and in which control was fostered through the development of a group culture. The recidivism rate of Highfields graduates was lower than that of comparable juveniles who left the Annandale State Reformatory (37 percent versus 53 percent). This rate, the lower cost of Highfields, and the shorter period of confinement seemed to indicate that Highfields's program provided a better form of corrections than total incarceration. Likewise, the Community Treatment Program in California was widely acclaimed in the 1960s. Rather than being sent to an institution, the members of an experimental group were diagnosed, classified, and placed on parole in the community under the close supervision of a parole officer specially trained to meet juveniles' needs. These children were compared with a control group released on regular parole after confinement, and a higher success rate was claimed for the experimental group.[28]

But these and other rehabilitative programs have come under critical examination. Reanalysis of the research findings often shows that experimental groups were preselected and would probably have been more successful in leading a crime-free life even without treatment. Some critics argue that the manner in which recidivism has been defined and calculated often leads to a misreading of results. Others concede that experimental therapies do produce positive results but claim that when the particular treatment method is incorporated in the regular correctional program, it loses much of its special quality, with the result that resources are diminished, staffs become overburdened, and the bureaucratic milieu deadens the participants' enthusiasm. The warehousing of juveniles until they reach the age of majority may become the underlying goal of many institutions.

PROBLEMS AND PERSPECTIVES

Much of the criticism of juvenile justice has emphasized the disparity between the treatment ideal and the institutionalized practices of an ongoing bureaucratic system. Commentators have pointed to the ways in which the language of the social reformers has been used to disguise day-to-day operations in which elements of due process are lacking and custodial incarceration is all too frequent. Other criticisms have stressed the apparent inability of the juvenile justice system to control juvenile crime.

We remember that the juvenile court, in both theory and practice, is a remarkably complex institution called on to perform a wide variety of functions from administrating what are essentially welfare functions to providing a forum for criminal prosecution (as, for example, in cases of adults alleged to have contributed to the delinquency of minors). The juvenile court is a court as well as a governmental agency charged with administrative responsibilities and, in some localities, clinical services.[29] Given the range of roles played by the juvenile justice system, it is inevitable that goals and values will collide. In many states the same judges, probation officers, and social workers are asked to deal with neglected children as well as with young criminals. Although departments of social services may deal primarily with neglect cases, the distinction is often not maintained.

In addition to recognizing the organizational problems of the juvenile system, we must acknowledge that our understanding of the causes of delinquency and its prevention or treatment is extremely limited. Over the years, various social and behavioral theories have been advanced to explain delinquency. Where one generation looked to slum conditions as the cause of juvenile crime, another now points to the affluence of the suburbs. Freudians may stress masculine insecurity in a matriarchal family structure, and some sociologists note the peer group pressures of the gang. The array of theories has occasioned an array of proposed—and often contradictory—treatments. With this type of confusion, those interested in the problems of youth may well throw up their hands in despair. What is clear is that additional research is needed to give insights into the causes of delinquency and the treatment of juvenile offenders.

Using a different perspective, other social scientists have deemphasized the importance of juvenile crime. Observers point out that the majority of juvenile delinquents "both convicted and unconvicted do not subsequently pursue criminal careers; only a minority become recidivists."[30] With this evidence, some authorities maintain that it is inappropriate to say that there are certain "causes" of youth crime. They argue instead that young people go through stages of development and that such earmarks of youth crime as vandalism and auto theft do not necessarily indicate a criminal in the making.[31]

But there remains much concern about the serious repeat offender who continues a life of crime as an adult. For example, the unavailability of juvenile court records to judges in the adult courts means that persons who have already served several periods of time on probation and in juvenile institutions are thought to be first offenders when they reach the age of majority. It is believed very important that juvenile records be made available and that efforts be made to treat young criminals more severely in order to deter them from future illegal activity.

What trends may foretell the future of juvenile justice? In many ways the same trends that are found in the adult criminal justice system can be seen in the juvenile counterpart. However, there is often a delay between reform of the adult system and that of the juvenile system. Hence, restriction of the discretion of judges and parole boards, a major thrust of the 1970s, has now surfaced for juvenile justice. The toughening of sentencing standards and increases in the amounts of time served in adult prisons are now becoming a part of the juvenile system. Youthful offender laws have elevated many delinquents to the adult system for adjudication and correction.

Although the future of juvenile justice may reflect the more conservative attitudes of the 1980s and 1990s, it must be recognized that the reforms of the 1970s have had an important impact. These changes have been referred to as the "Big Ds" of juvenile justice: diversion, decrimininalization, deinstitutionalization, and due process.[32] Diversion consisted of the attempt to reduce to a minimum the juvenile's penetration into the justice system. The decriminalization movement sought to limit the range of behaviors for which juveniles could be held liable by the justice system. Deinstitutionalization, which reached its peak in Massachusetts under Jerome Miller, was an attempt to force communities to deal with their own delinquency problems. And the due process revolution was made possible by the U.S. Supreme Court's extension of rights to juveniles at various stages in the court process.

Barry Krisberg, president of the National Council on Crime and Delinquency, has added disarray as a fourth D. He believes that the conservative revolution that hit the adult criminal justice system, with its emphasis on deterrence, deserts, and a get tough policy, has had its impact on juvenile justice.[33] He points to growing levels of overcrowding in juvenile institutions, increased litigation challenging the abuse of children in training schools and detention centers, and increased rates of minority youth incarceration. All of these problems have emerged during a period of declining youth populations and fewer arrests of juveniles. With the demographic trend now reversing and the increased concern about drugs, Krisberg sees a surge of adolescents going through their criminally high-risk years in a system and community not able to cope with them.

The Big Ds—whether four or five—have left a lasting mark on juvenile justice. Lawyers are routinely present at court hearings and other stages of the process, adding a note of formalism that was simply not present twenty years ago. Status offenders seldom end up in secure, punitive environments such as training schools. The juvenile justice system looks more like the adult justice system than it did, but it still is less formal. Its stated intention is also less harsh: to keep juveniles in the community whenever possible.

Some observers declare that the themes of the 1970s and 1980s have been played out and that we are entering a new era based on a more realistic assessment of the possibilities of corrections for juveniles. Such an assessment takes into account the burdensome heritage created by juvenile correctional practices of the past: a large proportion of the adults in our prisons learned about crime and criminal justice as juveniles in training schools, foster homes, group homes, and the like. These "state-raised youth" are, experts speculate, a particular control problem. There is also greater willingness today to confront the problem of violent offenders and to take drastic steps to control the damage these youths do. Yet even these aims are disputed; critics deny that the numbers of violent and state-raised youth are large enough to warrant our making them the centerpiece of juvenile corrections policy. The next decade will see all these many forces at work.

SUMMARY

The juvenile justice system has not lived up to its ideals. Its goals have often been subverted by a jurisdictional overreach in an attempt to use the law to solve a host of moral and social problems. Within the bureaucratic context of the system, the needs of the organization have often subverted the needs of the child. After years of neglect, the juvenile justice system went through a period of rapid change in the 1970s. The case of Gerald Gault and the due process revolution brought into the open many practices long obscured from public view. As a result, the emphasis on discretion that characterized the juvenile justice of earlier periods has dwindled. At the same time there is renewed concern about youth crime. Legislatures have adopted more of a crime control focus to deal with juvenile delinquency in the 1990s.

The incidence of juvenile delinquency has increased during the past twenty years until youth crime is now a national concern. Many people contend that the courts treat violent juvenile offenders too leniently. Juveniles are primarily property offenders, but they also are responsible for a fairly large share of predatory crimes.

Decisions by police officers and intake workers of the juvenile justice system dispose of a large portion of cases without their being referred to the court for formal processing. Diversion is a major aspect of this process. Institutional and noninstitutional programs for those judged to be offenders are available in great variety. The predominant aim of juvenile corrections is to avoid unnecessary incarceration.

Some observers declare that the reforms of the past have not addressed the problem of juvenile justice and that we are entering a new era based on a more realistic assessment of the possibilities of dealing with youthful offenders. There seems to be a greater willingness today to confront the problem of violent offenders and to take drastic steps to control these youths.

FOR DISCUSSION

1. What are some of the legal and social implications of extending due process rights to minors?
2. Under what circumstances should a juvenile be incarcerated?
3. Should the law consider the acts of young people and those of adults differently? Why?
4. You are the judge. Jane, an eight-year-old, has been placed under the care of the juvenile court because her father has disappeared and her alcoholic mother is unable to care for her. How would you provide for Jane's upbringing?

FOR FURTHER READING

Cicourel, Aaron V. *The Social Organization of Juvenile Justice.* New York: Wiley, 1968. A description and analysis of the organization of the juvenile justice system.

Emerson, Robert. *Judging Delinquents.* Chicago: Aldine, 1971. Describes the exercise of discretion and the role played by the characeristics of the juvenile in the decision.

Mahoney, Anne Rankin. *Juvenile Justice in Context.* Boston: Northeastern University Press, 1987. A view of juvenile justice in the context of the social and political environment.

Matza, David. *Delinquency and Drift.* New York: Viking, 1974. A classic examination of the role of the juvenile court. Describes the impact of "kadi" justice on the system.

Platt, Anthony. *The Child Savers: The Invention of Delinquency.* Chicago: University of Chicago Press, 1970. A history of the Progressive "child saver" movement.

Rubin, H. Ted. *Behind the Black Robes.* Newbury Park, CA: Sage, 1985. A juvenile court judge discusses his role and the decision making process.

NOTES

1. *In re Gault*, 387 U.S. 9 (1967).
2. Ibid.

3. Metropolitan Court Judges Committee Report, "Drugs—The American Family in Crisis" (Reno: National Council on Juvenile and Family Court Judges, University of Nevada, 1988).

4. U.S. Department of Justice, National Institute of Justice, *Research in Brief* (May 1990).

5. *Ex parte Crouse,* 4 Wharton (Pa.) 9 (1838).

6. David J. Rothman, *Conscience and Convenience* (Boston: Little, Brown, 1980), p. 213.

7. Julian Mack, "The Juvenile Court," *Harvard Law Review* 2 (1909):119.

8. Anthony Platt, *The Child Savers: The Invention of Delinquency* (Chicago: University of Chicago Press, 1969), p. 116.

9. *Kent v. United States,* 383 U.S. 541 (1966).

10. *In re Winship,* 397 U.S. 358 (1970).

11. *McKeiver v. Pennsylvania,* 403 U.S. 528 (1971).

12. *Breed v. Jones,* 421 U.S. 519 (1975).

13. *Schall v. Martin,* 467 U.S. 253 (1984).

14. State of Connecticut, General Laws, Sec. 46b–121.

15. H. Ted Rubin, *Juvenile Justice: Policy, Practice, and Law,* 2nd ed. (New York: Newbury Award Records, 1985), p. 87.

16. Nathan Goldman, "The Differential Selection of Juvenile Offenders for Court Appearance," in *The Ambivalent Force: Perspectives on the Police,* eds. Arthur Niederhoffere and Abraham S. Blumberg (Waltham, MA: Ginn, 1970), p. 156.

17. Irving Piliavin and Scott Briar, "Police Encounters with Juveniles," in *Back on the Street,* eds. Robert M. Carter and Malcolm W. Klein (Englewood Cliffs, NJ: Prentice-Hall, 1976), pp. 197–206.

18. U.S. Department of Justice, *Justice Assistance News* (September 1981).

19. *Fare v. Michael C.,* 442 U.S. 707 (1979).

20. *New Jersey v. T.L.O.,* 105 S. Ct. 733 (1985).

21. Mark Creekmore, "Case Processing: Intake, Adjudication, and Disposition," in *Brought to Justice? Juveniles, the Court, and the Law,* eds. Rosemary C. Saari and Yeheskel Hasenfeld (Ann Arbor: National Assessment of Juvenile Corrections, University of Michigan, 1976), p. 126.

22. H. Ted Rubin, *The Courts: Fulcrum of the Justice System* (Santa Monica, CA: Goodyear, 1976), p. 66.

23. *Standard Juvenile Court Act,* 6th ed. (New York: National Council on Crime and Delinquency, 1959), p. 4.

24. Ronald Goldfarb and Linda R. Singer, *After Conviction* (New York: Simon & Schuster, 1973), p. 514.

25. U.S. Department of Justice, Bureau of Justice Statistics, *Bulletin* (October 1986), p. 2. See also U.S. Department of Justice, *Children in Custody—Public Juvenile Facilities, Juvenile Justice Bulletin* (Washington, DC: Government Printing Office, 1988), p. 3.

26. U.S. Department of Justice, *Special Report* (September 1988).

27. Richard A. Cloward and Irwin Epstein, "Private Social Welfare's Disengagement from the Poor: The Case of the Family Adjustment Agencies," in *Social Welfare Institutions: A Sociological Reader,* ed. Mayer N. Zald (New York: Wiley, 1965), p. 626.

28. Lamar T. Empey, *American Delinquency,* (Homewood, IL: Dorsey, 1978), p. 460.

29. Francis A. Allen, *The Borderland of Criminal Justice* (Chicago: University of Chicago Press, 1964), p. 44.

30. Norval Morris and Gordon Hawkins, *The Honest Politician's Guide to Crime Control* (Chicago: University of Chicago Press, 1970), p. 155.

31. Marvin E. Wolfgang, Robert Figlio, and Thorstein Sellin, *Delinquency in a Birth Cohort* (Chicago: University of Chicago Press, 1973).

32. James O. Finckenauer, *Juvenile Delinquency and Corrections: The Gap between Theory and Practice* (Orlando, FL: Academic Press, 1984), p. 190.

33. Barry Krisberg, *The Juvenile Court: Reclaiming the Vision* (San Francisco: National Council on Crime and Delinquency, 1988).

Crime and Justice in the Year 2010

In her State of the Union Address on January 23, 2010, the president called for an enormous increase in federal funding for criminal justice agencies and for new legislation to deal with the dramatic rise in crime. She noted that although criminologists declared in the 1980s that street crime would decrease as the population aged, this had not happened. Citing data from the UCR and NCS, she explained that property crimes rose during the economically stagnant 1990s and that violent crime, especially among members of the underclass, skyrocketed as the social fabric of inner-city areas deteriorated and drug dealers became powerful forces. Compounding the crime problem, the president said, were advances in computer technology that made fraud and other types of occupational crime much more difficult to detect.

The president urged Congress to heed public demands for law and order. She proposed that legislation be enacted to control the possession of handguns, to free the police from the "shackles" of the exclusionary rule, to allow release on bail only to persons without criminal records, and to institute a national identification system that would permit criminal justice agencies to keep track of individuals.

Editorials in leading newspapers and commentators on television supported the president's call for action and urged bipartisan support in Congress to deal quickly with the proposals. A few voices were raised about risk to civil liberties, but they were drowned out by the thunder of public approval of get-tough policies.

Is it likely that the beginning of the twenty-first century will find the United States in a situation such as that just described? Certainly we can point to other periods in history when the United States was racked by what was perceived as a crime wave. An aroused public at various times has demanded and gotten government action to restrict civil liberties and due process in the interest of crime control. But is there any evidence that we are headed for still another "war on crime" during the early years of the new century? Or is it possible that crime and concern about it will taper off during the next decade so that resources can be reallocated to other pressing social problems, such as environmental pollution, the homeless, and poverty among children?

What will be the crime and justice environment in the United States in the year 2010? This is an important question that requires serious thought not only by researchers, planners, and government officials but also by you. If you become a criminal justice manager, the question will have direct bearing on your professional role. In any case, issues having to do with crime and justice will impinge on your life as a citizen, taxpayer, and potential victim. The new century will soon be here. Will we be ready to deal with the crime problem in very different circumstances when that milestone is passed?

SCANNING THE FUTURE

Most people generally leave the depiction of coming events and conditions in the social environment to fortune tellers and science fiction writers. During the past several decades, however, "futures research" has emerged as a field whose concepts and methods are designed to help planners and policy makers better understand conditions that might prevail in the longer term. There is an older kind of economic and demographic forecasting by which what is known about present and past conditions is extrapolated to construct a probable future. Futurists use these methods, but they also are willing to *speculate* about events and conditions that might occur in periods to come. It is not possible to predict social conditions with meaningful levels of certainty, but researchers can alert planners and policy makers to alternative possibilities so that strategies can be developed to deal with them.

Environmental scanning and scenario writing are two major aspects of contemporary futures research. Environmental scanning is a systematic effort to put a social problem under a microscope, with an eye toward the future. The major objective is to identify, track, and assess the prospects of emerging changes in the environment, changes that could improve or adversely affect society in important ways. Through scanning, crime and justice researchers can examine the factors that seem likely to "drive" the environment. "Drivers" would be economic conditions, demographic shifts, governmental policies, international developments, social attitudes, technological advances, resource availability, and so on. The criminal justice literature contains evidence that these and other drivers have a bearing on future conditions.

Futurists also depend on the opinions of experts to assess the probability of developments and to describe their potential impacts. For example, social scientists furnish evidence that indicates the significant extent to which street crime is mainly committed by young males in the sixteen- to twenty-four age group. Demographers have pointed to the decline of this cohort as a portion of U.S. society. But surely we would not want to make predictions regarding crime and justice in the year 2010 based solely on what we conclude from these two pieces of information. Through scanning, other elements can be evaluated to see if there are countervailing trends that might negate or diminish the possibility of crime reduction solely on the basis of the demographic element. Environmental scanning gives notice to decision makers of advancing potential difficulties and opportunities.

After scanning the environment for elements deemed likely to play some part in determining the future, researchers attempt to collate them by writing scenarios—that is, descriptions of a possible set of future conditions. A scenario may provide a "snapshot," capturing conditions at a particular instant. Thus, from the list of drivers, those thought to be most important can be evaluated as to their impact on one another and on the environment.

Scenarios are not forecasts. They are plausible descriptions of what might come about, portrayals of events and trends as they could evolve. One can point to such authors as Jules Verne *(20,000 Leagues under the Sea, A Voyage to the Moon)*, Aldous Huxley *(Brave New World)*, and George Orwell *(1984)* as writers of scenarios, although they did not write in the systematic manner just described. Modern futurists prepare scenarios as a means of developing and testing the value of policies and descriptions. Environmental scanning and scenario writing together provide an especially useful way of systematically surveying the prospects for change in the environment and exploring the value of potential policies, given such prospects.

In this epilogue let us approach the crime and justice future of the United States by listing the drivers that may have an impact on society in the year 2010. In compiling the list, we should include the factors for which reliable evidence exists but also think about possible developments, such as technological innovations (a drug to prevent heroin addiction, for instance), political shifts (war), or environmental catastrophes (say, a major nuclear accident) that would have a decided impact on criminal justice. Our goal is to conjecture within reason, yet we must allow our minds to range freely so that we take into account even what initially may seem farfetched. We probably will not arrive at definitive conclusions, but through this exercise we shall become aware of factors that may have an effect on the future crime and justice environment.

FACTORS INFLUENCING THE FUTURE CRIME AND JUSTICE ENVIRONMENT

Three categories of drivers will serve to identify possible trends and events impacting the U.S. criminal justice system by the year 2010. Social and economic conditions are one category; size and age of the population, immigration patterns, nature of employment, and lifestyle characteristics fit into this grouping. Shifts in the amount and types of crimes constitute a second driver category; we shall consider the potential for new types of criminality and for technological advances that may be related to illegal behavior. For the third category we shall explore possible developments with regard to the criminal justice system itself. For example, what changes are indicated in the ways the police, the courts, and corrections operate? What important innovations are on the horizon?

As we consider drivers, we list them so that we may reflect on the probability of their occurring, and if a particular driver should occur by the year 2010, we want to reflect on its potential impact on the crime and justice environment. In addition to the limited number of drivers noted on the pages that follow, what others do you believe should enter into our thinking? Throughout the exercise consider the interlinking of the drivers and the weights you would give them were you to write a scenario.

Social and Economic Conditions

Major theories of criminality focus on such environmental factors as population characteristics, family structure, urbanism, and economic conditions as influencing criminality and the administration of justice. Should any of the following drivers occur, what would be their probable impact on the crime and justice environment in the year 2010?

1. Demographic Factors
   a. The total population of the United States reaches 300 million.
   b. Differing birth and migration rates result in a greater proportion of minorities in the United States.
   c. The population has aged, and persons over forty make up more than 45 percent of the total population.
   d. The size of the "crime-prone" age group declines as a portion of the total population. An "echo boom" is not realized; couples have fewer children. The number of new workers entering the labor force drops.
   e. Urbanization continues. Gentrification of sections of inner cities causes further displacement of the poor. Homelessness continues to be a major problem.
   f. There is much changing of places within the country: the elderly migrate to warmer climates, rural people move off the land, and workers seek employment wherever opportunities beckon. Some African-Americans move from the North to the South.
2. Economic Factors
   a. Economic growth proceeds slowly, in part because of erosion of the international competitive edge historically held by the United States.
   b. Restructuring of the postindustrial economy increases income disparities between those in high-tech and professional positions and those in the service sector.
   c. An increasing portion of the population lacks the skills necessary to enter the job market.
   d. Restructuring the economy means that geographic areas of distress appear where traditional industries were located.
   e. Checks and credit cards assume a larger portion of consumer monetary transactions.
   f. Agriculture becomes more technologically advanced and organized in a corporate manner. The family farm is viewed as a historical artifact.

3. Social Factors
   a. Levels of education of the population increase, yet illiteracy remains a problem. Education is continued throughout life for a larger number of people.
   b. Trends in marriage and divorce rates do not drastically change.
   c. Households headed by single women increase. Because of the lower income of these families, more children are growing up in poverty.
   d. Day care for preschool children becomes the accepted way to allow parents to pursue their careers.
   e. Membership in organized religions continues to decline.
   f. The urban underclass is viewed as a major problem without solution.

Crime

The public has traditionally been most concerned about the types of crimes found in the *Uniform Crime Reports*. What drivers may alter the frequency of various types of crimes? What technological innovations may shift the focus of crime control efforts? Is it likely that reductions of certain types of crimes will shift attention to other types? We can consider these questions and their relation to the crime environment of the year 2010 by listing drivers that may affect each of the major crime categories:

1. Index Offenses
   a. Aging of the baby-boom cohort results in a decrease in violent crime.
   b. Participation of women in criminal activity increases as their societal role is redefined.
   c. The elderly, as a larger portion of the population, become targets of opportunity, especially for financial scams.
   d. Wider use of credit cards and electronic monetary transfers reduces robberies from persons. Microchip implants render stolen credit cards useless.
   e. Handguns continue to be owned by a significant portion of the population.
2. Occupational Crime
   a. A new class of crimes and criminals emerges due to computerization and other technological advances.
   b. Illegal manipulation of computer financial records and securities increases.
   c. Disposal of toxic and nuclear wastes remains a major problem. Corporate producers of these materials engage in illegal dumping.
   d. As competition becomes more intense in some industries, the stealing of technological secrets becomes more extensive.
   e. As the financial services industry develops worldwide links, stock manipulation takes on an international dimension.
3. Organized Crime
   a. Asian and Latin American groups play more prominent roles in organized crime. This results in the use of tactics, structures,

and interests that are different from those of organized crime groups of the past.

b. Drug trafficking activities continue to be a major source of income for organized crime groups. More sophisticated money laundering schemes are developed.

c. Disposal of nuclear and toxic wastes becomes a major organized crime activity.

4. Drugs

a. The war on drugs of the 1990s has been cut back as cocaine use has decreased and enforcement been proved costly.

b. Calls for the legalization of drugs continue, but these proposals have not been realized. Toleration of personal use of small amounts of some drugs has become a de facto situation.

c. The homicide rate in urban areas declines as organized crime provides greater stability in the marketplace.

Criminal Justice System

The third group of drivers includes factors that will influence the operations of the criminal justice system in the year 2010. We assume that the basic configuration of the system remains as it is today but that there will be changes in processes, techniques, and levels of resources that affect the way justice is administered. We consider two sets of drivers: laws and policy, and operations. Again, the factors listed are only a few of those that can be expected to work upon the system in the twenty-first century:

1. Laws and Policy

a. Determinate sentencing and parole guidelines are rethought as their link to prison overcrowding is validated.

b. Preventive detention in the interest of community safety is widely accepted.

c. The soaring costs of incarceration impel a renewed effort to find suitable intermediate punishments.

d. Greater priority is given to the concerns of victims. Increasing numbers of states allow victims to make sentencing recommendations. Private prosecution by individuals is proposed.

e. Privacy of the individual from government intrusion remains a basic yet unresolved issue.

f. Some states enact registration and control laws to reduce the availability of handguns.

g. Very few convicts are executed, yet thousands of offenders are on death row.

h. Levels of criminal justice funding reflect public concerns and the strength of the economy.

2. Operations

a. Computer technology and advanced information systems become major operational components of the police, the courts, and corrections.

b. Police allocate greater resources to maintaining order and providing service, in response to public demand.

c. Miniaturization of computers gives patrol officers instant access to crime information files.

d. Private policing continues to grow.
e. Electronic surveillance is extensively used by probation and parole agencies.
f. Contracting with private organizations for the operation of certain types of correctional institutions expands.

REFLECTIONS ON THE FUTURE

We can expect that crime will continue to be a major social problem in the year 2010. As is evident from the list of drivers, however, the level of criminal activity, the types of illegal behaviors, and the response of the criminal justice system will be different. How the drivers will interconnect and interact we do not know. What we do know is that in the modern era, very little has stayed the same for very long. The appearance of new technologies, shifts in political concerns, and transformations in the economy and in social variables seem to be fast-paced and never-ending. There remain, however, certain basic factors that apparently are static.

What will the new century be like with respect to crime and justice? If we consider all that has happened during the past quarter century, we should expect a very different future. But what will be the levels of criminality, the place of crime control on the public agenda, and the capacity of the criminal justice system? One can imagine a scenario in which, although there are high levels of crime, crime control declines as a top public issue relative to other matters, and consequently resources are not made available to justice agencies so that they can effectively deal with the problem. Alternatively, lower crime levels may coexist with a high public commitment to crime control and a swelling of resource allocations to the police, the courts, and corrections. Should such an unlikely circumstance come about, one would expect a widening of the criminal justice net, with the system enforcing all laws more strictly.

It is fitting that at the close of this text we consider the future. It is hoped that by speculating about the United States in the year 2010, you will recognize that concerns about crime and justice do not end. Regardless of your personal plans and concerns, the American system of criminal justice warrants your continuing attention.

Constitution of the United States: Criminal Justice Amendments

The first ten amendments to the Constitution, known as the Bill of Rights, became effective on December 15, 1791.

IV. The right of the people to be secure in their persons, houses, papers, and effects, against unreasonable searches and seizures, shall not be violated, and no warrants shall issue but upon probable cause, supported by oath or affirmation, and particularly describing the place to be searched, and the persons or things to be seized.

V. No person shall be held to answer for a capital or otherwise infamous crime, unless on a presentment or indictment of a grand jury, except in cases arising in the land or naval forces or in the militia when in actual service in time of war or public danger; nor shall any person be subject for the same offence to be twice put in jeopardy of life or limb; nor shall be compelled in any criminal case to be a witness against himself, nor be deprived of life, liberty, or property, without due process of law; nor shall private property be taken for public use without just compensation.

VI. In all criminal prosecutions the accused shall enjoy the right to a speedy and public trial, by an impartial jury of the State and district wherein the crime shall have been committed, which district shall have been previously ascertained by law, and to be informed of the nature and cause of the accusation; to be confronted with the witnesses against him; to have compulsory process for obtaining witnesses in his favor, and to have the assistance of counsel for his defense.

VIII. Excessive bail shall not be required, nor excessive fines imposed, nor cruel and unusual punishments inflicted.

The Fourteenth Amendment became effective on July 28, 1868.

XIV. Section 1. All persons born or naturalized in the United States, and subject to the jurisdiction thereof, are citizens of the United States and of the State wherein they reside. No State shall make or enforce any law which shall abridge the privileges or immunities of citizens of the United States; nor shall any State deprive any person of life, liberty, or property, without due process of law; nor deny to any person within its jurisdiction the equal protection of the laws.

accusatory process: The series of events from the arrest of a suspect to the filing of a formal charging instrument (indictment or information) with the court.

actual enforcement: Enforcement of the law at a level that reflects such factors as civil liberties, discretion, resources, and community values.

aggressive patrol: A patrol strategy designed to maximize the number of police interventions and observations in the community.

Alford v. North Carolina (1970): A plea of guilty may be accepted for the purpose of a lesser sentence by a defendant who maintains his or her innocence.

anomie: Social conditions in which rules or norms to regulate behavior have weakened or disappeared.

appeal: A request to a higher court that it review actions taken in a completed trial.

appellate court: A court that does not try criminal cases but hears appeals of decisions of lower courts.

Argersinger v. Hamlin (1972): Defendants have a right to counsel when imprisonment might result.

arraignment: The act of calling an accused person before the court to hear the charges lodged against him or her and to enter a plea in response to those charges.

arrest: The physical taking of a person into custody on the ground that there is probable cause to believe that he or she has committed a criminal offense. Police may use only reasonable physical force in making an arrest. The purpose of arrest is to hold the accused for a court proceeding.

assembly-line justice: The operation of any segment of the criminal justice system with such speed and impersonality that defendants are treated as objects to be processed rather than as individuals.

assigned counsel: An attorney in private practice who is assigned by a court to represent an indigent and whose fee is paid by the government that has jurisdiction over the case.

bail: An amount of money specified by a judge to be posted as a condition of pretrial release for the purpose of ensuring the appearance of the accused in court as required.

Bell v. Wolfish (1979): Strip searches, including body cavity searches after contact visits, may be carried out when the need for the search outweighs the invasion of personal rights.

bench trial: Trial conducted by a judge who acts as both a finder of fact and a determiner of issues of law.

Bordenkircher v. Hayes (1978): A defendant's rights were not violated by a prosecutor who warned that not to accept a guilty plea would result in a harsher sentence.

Bounds v. Smith (1977): Inmates have the right to access to adequate law libraries or the assistance of those trained in the law.

Boykin v. Alabama (1969): Defendants must make an affirmative statement that they are voluntarily making a plea of guilty.

Breed v. Jones (1975): Juveniles cannot be found delinquent in juvenile court and then be waived to adult court without violating double jeopardy.

bureaucracy: A form of administrative organization, characterized by depersonalized, rule-bound, and hierarchically structured relationships, that efficently produces highly predictable, rationalized results.

Carroll v. United States (1925): Because it is mobile, an automobile may be searched if the police have probable cause to believe it contains criminal evidence.

challenge for cause: Removal of a prospective juror by showing bias or some other legal disability. The number of such challenges permitted is unlimited.

circumstantial evidence: Evidence produced by a witness from which a jury must infer a fact.

citation: A written order issued by a law enforcement officer directing an alleged offender to appear in court at a specified time to answer a criminal charge; referred to as a summons in some jurisdictions.

civilian review board: A citizen board independent of the police, established to receive and investigate complaints against police officers.

classification: The act of assigning a new inmate to a type of custody and treatment appropriate to his or her needs.

clearance rate: The percentage of crimes known to the police that they believe they have solved through an arrest; a statistic used as a measure of a police department's productivity.

common law: The Anglo-American system of uncodified law, in which judges follow precedents set by earlier decisions when they decide new but similar cases. The substantive and procedural criminal law was originally developed in this manner but was later codified by legislatures.

community correctional center: An institution, usually located in an urban area, housing inmates soon to be released. Such centers are designed to help inmates maintain community ties and thus to promote their reintegration with society.

community corrections model: A model of corrections based on the assumption that the reintegration of the offender into the community should be the goal of the criminal justice system.

community service: Compensation for injury to society by the performance of service to the community.

conflict model: A legal model that asserts that the political power of interest groups and elites influences the content of criminal law.

congregate system: A penitentiary system, developed in Auburn, New York, in which each inmate was held in isolation during the night but worked with fellow prisoners during the day under a rule of silence.

consensus model: A legal model that asserts that criminal law, as an expression of the social consciousness of the whole society, reflects values that transcend the immediate interests of particular groups and individuals.

continuance: An adjournment of a scheduled case until a future date.

control theories: Theories postulating that criminal behavior occurs when the bonds that tie an individual to others in society are broken or weakened.

Cooper v. Pate (1964): Prisoners are entitled to the protection of the Civil Rights Act of 1871 and may challenge conditions of their confinement in federal courts.

copping out: (slang) Entering a plea of guilty, normally after bargaining. The "copping out ceremony" consists of a series of questions that the judge asks the defendant as to the voluntary nature of the plea.

count: Each separate offense of which a person is accused in an indictment or an information.

crime: A specific act of commission or omission in violation of the law, for which a punishment is prescribed.

crime construction: A process by which the police and prosecutor interpret information concerning the accused's behavior in order to determine whether a crime has been committed and to ascertain whether the legal elements necessary to prosecute are present.

crime control model: A model of the criminal justice system that assumes that freedom is so important that every effort must be made to repress crime; it emphasizes efficiency and the capacity to apprehend, try, convict, and dispose of a high proportion of offenders, and it also stresses speed and finality.

crime rate: The number of reported crimes per 100,000 people as published in the *Uniform Crime Reports*.

crimes without victims: Offenses involving a willing and private exchange of illegal goods or services for which there is a strong demand. Participants do not feel that they are being harmed. Prosecution is justified on the ground that society as a whole is being injured by the act.

criminal justice wedding cake: A model of the criminal justice process in which criminal cases form a four-tiered hierarchy with a few celebrated cases at the top, and each succeeding layer increasing in size as its importance in the eyes of officials and the public diminishes.

criminogenic factors: Factors thought to bring about criminal behavior in an individual.

critical criminology: A school of criminology that holds that criminal law and the criminal justice system have been created to control the poor and have-not members of society.

Cruz v. Beto (1972): Prisoners who adhere to other than conventional beliefs may not be denied the opportunity to practice their religion.

custodial model: A model of corrections that emphasizes security, discipline, and order.

dark figure of crime: A metaphor that emphasizes the dangerous dimension of crime that is never reported to the police.

defense attorney: The lawyer who represents the accused and the convicted offender in their dealings with criminal justice officials.

delinquents: Children who have committed criminal or status offenses.

dependent child: A child whose parent(s) is unable to give proper care.

detention: A period of temporary custody of a juvenile before disposition of his or her case.

determinate sentence: A sentence that fixes the term of imprisonment at a specified period of time.

deterrence: Discouragement of criminal behavior on the part of known offenders (special deterrence) and of the public (general deterrence) by the threat of punishment.

differential association theory: A theory that people become criminals because they encounter a large number of influences that regard criminal behavior as normal and acceptable, with these influences outnumbering the influences hostile to criminal behavior.

direct evidence: Eyewitness accounts.

discovery: A prosecutor's pretrial disclosure to the defense of facts and evidence to be introduced at trial.

discretion: The authority to make decisions without reference to specific rules or facts, using instead one's own judgment; allows for individualization and informality in the administration of justice.

discretionary release: The release of an inmate from incarceration at the discretion of the parole board within the boundaries set by the sentence and the penal law.

diversion: An alternative to adjudication by which the defendant agrees to conditions set by the prosecutor (such as to undergo counseling or drug rehabilitation) in exchange for withdrawal of charges.

double jeopardy: The subjecting of a person to prosecution more than once for the same offense; prohibited by the Fifth Amendment.

dual court system: A system consisting of a separate judicial structure for each state in addition to a national structure. Each case is tried in a court of the same jurisdiction as that of the law or laws broken.

due process model: A model of the criminal justice system that assumes that freedom is so important that every effort must be made to ensure that criminal justice decisions are based on reliable information; it emphasizes the adversarial process, the rights of defendants, and formal decision-making procedures.

Duncan v. Louisiana (1968): States must provide a jury trial for defendants charged with serious offenses.

Durham rule: A test of the defense of insanity that requires it to be shown that the accused is not criminally responsible because the act resulted from mental disease or mental defect.

entrapment: The defense that the individual was induced by the police to commit the criminal act.

Escobedo v. Illinois (1964): Counsel must be provided suspects when taken into police custody.

exchange: A mutual transfer of resources; hence, a balance of benefits and deficits that flow from behavior based on decisions as to the values and costs of alternatives.

exclusionary rule: The principle that illegally obtained evidence must be excluded from a trial.

Fare v. Michael C. (1979): Trial court judges must evaluate the voluntariness of confessions by juveniles by examining the totality of circumstances.

felonies: Serious crimes carrying a penalty of death or incarceration for more than a year. Persons convicted of felonies lose the right to vote, to hold public elective office, and to practice certain professions and occupations.

filtering process: A screening operation; hence, a process by which criminal justice officials screen out some cases while advancing others to the next level of decision making.

fine: A sum of money to be paid to the state by a convicted person as punishment for an offense.

forfeiture: Seizure by the government of property and other assets derived from or used in criminal activity.

frankpledge: A system in Old English law whereby members of a tithing, a group of ten families, pledged to be responsible for the good conduct of all members over twelve years of age.

full enforcement: A policy whereby the police are given the resources and support to enforce all laws within the limits imposed by the injunction to respect the civil liberties of citizens.

Fulwood v. Clemmer (1962): The Muslim faith must be recognized as a religion, and officials may not restrict members from holding services.

furlough: The temporary release of an inmate from a correctional institution for a brief period, usually one to three days, for a visit home. Such programs are designed to maintain family ties and prepare inmates for release on parole.

Furman v. Georgia (1972): Death penalty, as administered, constituted cruel and unusual treatment.

Gagnon v. Scarpelli (1973): Requirement that before probation may be revoked, a two-stage hearing must be held and the offender provided with specific elements of due process.

general deterrence: Punishment of criminals intended to serve as an example to the general public and thus to discourage the commission of offenses.

Gideon v. Wainwright (1963): Defendants have a right to counsel in felony cases.

going rate: Local view of the appropriate sentence given the offense and the defendant's prior record and other characteristics.

good time: A reduction of a convict's prison sentence awarded for good behavior at the discretion of the prison administrator.

Gregg v. Georgia (1976): Upheld death penalty law in which judge and jury considered mitigating and aggravating circumstances in deciding which convicted murderers should be given death sentence.

grouping: A collectivity of individuals who interact in the workplace but because of shifting membership do not develop into a workgroup.

habeas corpus: A writ or judicial order requesting that a person holding another person produce the prisoner and give reasons to justify continued confinement.

house arrest: A sentence requiring the offender to remain inside his or her home during specified periods.

Hudson v. Palmer (1984): Officials may search cells without a warrant and seize materials found there.

incapacitation: Deprivation of capacity to commit crimes against society, usually by detention in prison.

inchoate offenses: Conduct made criminal even though it has not yet produced the harm that the law seeks to prevent.

incorporation: The extension of the due process clause of the Fourteenth Amendment to make binding on state governments the rights guaranteed in the first ten amendments to the U.S. Constitution (the Bill of Rights).

indeterminate sentence: A period set by a judge in which there is a spread between the minimum date for a decision on parole eligibility and the maximum date for completion of the sentence. In holding that the time necessary for treatment cannot be set, the indeterminate sentence is closely associated with the rehabilitation model.

inmate code: The system of values and norms of the prison social system that defines for inmates the characteristics associated with the model prisoner.

In re Gault (1967): Juveniles have the right to counsel, to confront and examine accusers, and to have adequate notice of charges when there is the possibility of confinement as a punishment.

In re Winship (1970): The standard of proof beyond a reasonable doubt applies to juvenile delinquency proceedings.

intensive probation supervision: Probation granted under conditions of strict reporting to a probation officer with a limited caseload.

interest groups: Private organizations formed to influence government policies so that they will coincide with the desires of its members. Such organized pressure groups operate at all levels of government.

intermediate sanctions: A variety of punishments that are more restrictive than traditional probation but less stringent and less costly than incarceration.

internal affairs unit: A segment of a police department designated to receive and investigate complaints against officers alleging violation of rules and policies.

irresistible impulse test: A test of the defense of insanity that requires it to be shown that although the accused knew right from wrong, he or she was unable to control an irresistible impulse to commit the crime.

Johnson v. Avery (1969): The use of jailhouse lawyers may not be prohibited unless free counsel is provided by the state.

jurisdiction: The territory or boundaries within which control may be exercised; hence, the legal and geographical range of a court's authority.

jury: A panel consisting of a statutorily defined number of citizens selected according to law and sworn to determine matters of fact in a criminal action and to render a verdict of guilty or not guilty.

labeling theories: Theories emphasizing that the causes of criminal behavior are not to be found in the individual but in the social process through which certain acts are labeled deviant or criminal.

law enforcement: The police function of controlling crime by intervening in situations in which it is clear that the law has been violated and only the identity of the guilty needs to be determined.

learning theories: Theories postulating that criminal behavior, like legal and normative behavior, is learned.

legal sufficiency: The presence of the minimum legal elements necessary for prosecution of a case. When a prosecutor's decision to prosecute a case is customarily based on legal sufficiency, a great many cases are accepted for prosecution, but the majority of them are disposed of by plea bargaining or dismissal.

local legal culture: Norms shared by members of a court community as to case handling and participants' behavior in the judicial process.

McCleskey v. *Kemp* (1987): Rejected a challenge of Georgia's death penalty on ground of racial discrimination.

McKeiver v. *Pennsylvania* (1971): There is no constitutional right for a jury trial for juveniles.

M'Naghten Rule: A test of the defense of insanity which requires it to be shown that at the time of committing the act the accused was unable to distinguish right from wrong because of a disease of the mind.

mala in se: Offenses that are wrong by their very nature, irrespective of statutory prohibition.

mala prohibita: Offenses prohibited by statute but not inherently wrong.

mandatory release: The required release of an inmate from incarceration upon the expiration of a certain time period, as stipulated by a determinate sentencing law or parole guidelines.

mandatory sentence: A type of sentence by which statutes require that a certain penalty shall be imposed and executed on certain convicted offenders.

Mapp v. *Ohio* (1961): Fourth Amendment protects citizens from unreasonable searches and seizures by the state.

Mempa v. *Rhay* (1967): Probationers have the right to counsel at a hearing considering revocation of a suspended sentence.

mens rea: "Guilty mind," or blameworthy state of mind, necessary for the imputation of responsibility for a criminal offense; criminal, as distinguished from innocent, intent.

merit selection: A reform plan by which judges are nominated by a committee and appointed by the governor for a given period. When the term expires, the voters are asked to signify their approval or disapproval of the judge for a

succeeding term. If the judge is disapproved, the committee nominates a successor for the governor's appointment.

Miranda v. *Arizona* (1966): Confessions made by suspects who have not been notified of the due process rights cannot be admitted as evidence.

misdemeanors: Offenses less serious than felonies and usually punishable by incarceration for no more than a year, a fine, or probation.

Morrissey v. *Brewer* (1972): Due process requires that before parole may be revoked a prompt, informal inquiry before an impartial hearing officer is required. The parolee may present relevant information and question adverse informants.

motion: An application to a court requesting that an order be issued to bring about a specified action.

National Crime Surveys: Interviews of samples of the U.S. population conducted by the Bureau of Justice Statistics to determine the number and types of criminal victimizations and thus the extent of unreported crime.

necessarily included offense: An offense committed for the purpose of committing another offense; for example, trespass committed for the purpose of committing burglary.

neglected child: A child who is not receiving proper care because of some action or inaction of his or her parent(s).

New Jersey v. *T.L.O.* (1985): School officials may search a student based on a reasonable suspicion that the search will produce evidence that a school or civil law has been violated.

nolle prosequi: An entry made by a prosecutor on the record of a case and announced in court to indicate that the charges specified will not be prosecuted. In effect, the charges are thereby dismissed.

nolo contendere: A defendant's formal answer in court in which it is stated that the charges are not contested and which, while not an admission of guilt, subjects the defendant to the same sentencing consequences as a plea of guilty. Often used to preclude civil action against the accused by the victim.

nonpartisan election: An election in which candidates who are not endorsed by political parties are presented to the voters for selection.

occupational crime: Conduct in violation of the law that is committed through opportunities created in the course of a legal occupation.

order maintenance: The police function of preventing behavior that disturbs or threatens to disturb the public peace or that involves face-to-face conflict between two or more persons. In such situations the police exercise discretion in deciding whether a law has been broken.

organized crime: A social framework for the perpetration of criminal acts, usually in such fields as gambling, narcotics, and prostitution, in which illegal services that are in great demand are provided.

overcriminalization: The use of criminal sanctions to deter behavior that is acceptable to substantial portions of society.

parens patriae: The state as parent; the state as guardian and protector of all citizens (such as juveniles) who are unable to protect themselves.

parole: The conditional release of an inmate from incarceration under supervision after a portion of the prison sentence has been served.

partisan election: An election in which candidates endorsed by political parties are presented to the voters for selection.

penitentiary: An institution intended to isolate prisoners from society and from one another so that they can reflect on their past misdeeds, repent, and thus undergo reformation.

penology: A branch of criminology dealing with the management of prisons and treatment of offenders.

peremptory challenge: Removal of a prospective juror without assignment of any cause. The number of such challenges permitted is limited.

PINS: This acronym (for "person in need of supervision") is used to designate juveniles who either are status offenders or who are thought to be on the verge of getting into trouble. Related acronyms often used are CINS (for "child in need of supervision") and JINS (for "juvenile in need of supervision")—juveniles who either are status offenders or who are thought to be on the verge of getting into trouble.

plea bargaining: A defendant's pleading of guilty to a criminal charge with the reasonable expectation of receiving some consideration from the state for doing so, usually a reduction of the charge. The defendant's ultimate goal is a penalty lighter than the one formally warranted by the offense originally charged.

political considerations: Matters taken into account in the formulation of public policies and the making of choices among competing values—who gets what portion of the good (justice) produced by the system, when, and how.

political crime: Act that constitutes threat against the state (such as treason, sedition, espionage).

positivist criminology: A school of criminology that views behavior as stemming from social, biological, and psychological factors. It argues that punishment should be tailored to the individual needs of the offender.

Powell v. *Alabama* (1932): Counsel must be provided defendants in a capital case.

preplea conference: A discussion, in which all parties openly participate, of ways to bring about an agreement on a sentence in return for a plea of guilty.

presentence report: A report prepared by a probation officer after an investigation into the background of a convicted offender, which is designed to help the judge determine an appropriate sentence.

presumptive parole date: The presumed release date stipulated by parole guidelines should the offender serve time without disciplinary or other incidents.

preventive detention: The holding of a defendant for trial, based on a judge's finding that if released on bail, he or she would endanger the safety of any other person and the community.

preventive patrol: The activity of providing regular protection to an area while maintaining a mobile police presence to deter potential criminals from committing crimes.

proactive: Occurring in the absence of a specific external stimulus, such as an active search for offenders on the part of the police in the absence of reports of violations of the law. Arrests for crimes without victims are usually proactive.

probation: A sentence allowing the offender to serve the sentence imposed by the court in the community under supervision.

problem-oriented policing: An approach to policing in which officers seek to identify, analyze, and respond, on a routine basis, to the underlying circumstances that create the incidents that prompt citizens to call the police.

procedural due process: The constitutional requirement that all persons be treated fairly and justly by government officials. This means that an accused person can be arrested, prosecuted, tried, and punished only in accordance with procedures prescribed by law.

prosecuting attorney: A legal representative of the state with sole responsibility for bringing criminal charges. In some states referred to as district attorney, state's attorney, or county attorney.

public defender: An attorney employed on a full-time, salaried basis by the government to represent indigents.

reactive: Occurring in response to a stimulus, such as police activity in response to notification that a crime has been committed.

real evidence: Physical evidence, such as a weapon, records, fingerprints, stolen property.

reasonable doubt: The standard used by a juror to decide if the prosecution has provided enough evidence for conviction. Jurors should vote for acquittal if they can give a reason to support this position.

recidivism: A return to criminal behavior.

rehabilitation: The goal of restoring a convicted offender to a constructive place in society through some form of vocational, educational, or therapeutic treatment.

rehabilitation model (institutions): A model of corrections that emphasizes the provision of treatment programs designed to reform the offender.

release on recognizance (ROR): Pretrial release granted on the defendant's promise to appear in court because the judge believes that the defendant's ties in the community are sufficient to guarantee the required appearance.

restitution: Compensation for injury one has inflicted, in the form of payment of money to the victim.

retribution: Punishment inflicted on a person who has infringed on the rights of others and so deserves to be penal-

ized. The severity of the sanction should fit the seriousness of the crime.

Rhodes v. *Chapman* (1983): Double bunking and crowding do not necessarily constitute cruel and unusual punishment. Conditions must involve "wanton and unnecessary infliction of pain" and be "grossly disproportionate to the severity of the crime warranting imprisonment."

Ricketts v. *Adamson* (1987): Defendants must uphold plea agreement or suffer the consequences.

Ruffin v. *Commonwealth* (1871): As a result of his crime, the prisoner is the slave of the state.

Ruiz v. *Estelle* (1980): Conditions of confinement in the Texas prison system were unconstitutional.

Santobello v. *New York* (1971): When a guilty plea rests on a promise of a prosecutor, it must be fulfilled.

Schall v. *Martin* (1984): Pretrial detention of a juvenile is constitutional to protect the welfare of the minor and the community.

selective incapacitation: The strategy of making optimum use of expensive and limited prison space by targeting for incarceration those individuals whose incapacity will do the most to reduce crime.

self-incrimination: The act of exposing oneself to prosecution by being forced to answer questions that may tend to incriminate one; it is protected against by the Fifth Amendment. In any criminal proceeding the prosecution must prove the charges by means of evidence other than the testimony of the accused.

sentence disparity: Divergence in the lengths and types of sentences imposed for the same crime or for crimes of comparable seriousness when no reasonable justification can be discerned.

sentencing guidelines: An instrument developed to indicate to judges the usual sanctions given in the past in particular types of cases.

separate confinement: A penitentiary system, developed in Pennsylvania, in which each inmate was held in isolation from other inmates. All activities, including craft work, were carried on in the cells.

service: The police function of providing assistance to the public, usually with regard to matters unrelated to crime.

social conflict theories: Theories that assume criminal law and the criminal justice system are primarily means of controlling the poor and have-nots.

social process theories: Theories that see criminality as normal behavior. Everyone has the potential to become a criminal, depending on the influences that impel one toward or away from crime and the ways in which one is regarded by groups and other persons.

social structure theories: Theories that blame crime on the creation of a lower-class culture based on poverty and deprivation, and the response of the poor to this situation.

socialization: The process by which the rules, symbols, and values of a group or subculture are learned by its members.

sociological explanations: Explanations of crime that emphasize the social conditions that bear on the individual as causes of criminal behavior.

special deterrence: Punishment inflicted on criminals with the intent to discourage them from committing crimes in the future.

stare decisis: "To stand by the decision." The principle that judges should be bound by precedents (decisions made in previous similar cases) when they decide the cases before them.

State Attorney General: Chief legal officer of a state who is responsible for both civil and criminal matters.

status offense: Any act committed by a juvenile that would not be a crime if it were committed by an adult but that is considered unacceptable for a child, such as truancy or running away from home.

statutes: Laws passed by legislatures. Statutory definitions of criminal offenses are embodied in penal codes.

strict liability: An obligation or duty whose breach constitutes an offense that requires no showing of *mens rea* to be adjudged criminal; a principle usually applied to regulatory offenses involving health and safety.

subculture: The aggregate of symbols, beliefs, and values shared by members of a subgroup within the larger society.

substantive criminal law: Law defining the behaviors that are subject to punishment, and the sanctions for such offenses.

sworn officers: Police employees who have taken an oath and been given powers by the state to, for example, make arrests, use force, and transverse property, in accordance with their duties.

system: A complex whole consisting of interdependent parts whose operations are directed toward goals and are influenced by the environment within which they function.

system efficiency: Operation of the prosecutor's office in such a way as to effect speedy and early dispositions of cases in response to caseload pressures in the system. Weak cases are screened out at intake, and other nontrial alternatives are used as primary means of disposition.

Tennessee v. Garner (1985): Deadly force may not be used against an unarmed and fleeing suspect unless necessary to prevent the escape and the officer has probable cause to believe that the suspect poses a significant threat of death or serious injury to the officer or others.

Terry v. Ohio (1968): A police officer may stop and frisk an individual if it is reasonable to suspect that a crime has been committed.

total enforcement: A policy whereby the police are given the resources and support to enforce all laws without regard to the civil liberties of citizens.

total institution: An institution (such as a prison) that completely encapsulates the lives of those who work and live within it. Rules govern behavior, and the group is split into two parts, one of which controls all aspects of the lives of the other.

totality of conditions: Although specific conditions in prisons might not violate the Constitution, the totality of conditions may violate the cruel and unusual punishment provisions of the Eighth Amendment.

trial court of general jurisdiction: A criminal court that has jurisdiction over all offenses, including felonies, and that may in some states also hear appeals.

trial court of limited jurisdiction: A criminal court of which the trial jurisdiction either includes no felonies or is limited to some category of felonies. Such courts have jurisdiction over misdemeanor cases, probable cause hearings in felony cases, and, sometimes, felony trials that may result in penalties below a specified limit.

trial sufficiency: The presence of sufficient legal elements to ensure successful prosecution of a case. When a prosecutor's decision to prosecute a case is customarily based on trial sufficiency, only cases that seem certain to result in conviction at trial are accepted for prosecution. Use of plea bargaining is minimal; good police work and court capacity are required.

underclass: Disadvantaged members of the urban community, mainly blacks and Hispanics, who are at the bottom of the economic and social hierarchy. Membership is characterized by poverty, unemployment, criminal behavior, drug use, and welfare dependency.

Uniform Crime Reports: An annually published statistical summary of crimes reported to the police based on voluntary reports to the FBI by local, state, and federal law enforcement agencies.

United States Attorney: Official responsible for the prosecution of crimes that are violations of the laws of the United States; appointed by the president and assigned to a U.S. District Court jurisdiction.

United States v. Leon (1984): Evidence seized using a warrant later found defective is valid if the officer was acting in good faith.

United States v. Salerno (1987): Prevention detention provisions of the Bail Reform Act of 1984 is upheld; legitimate use of governmental power is designed to prevent people from committing crimes while on bail.

victimization rate: The number of victimizations per 1,000 people or households as reported by the *National Crime Surveys*.

victimology: A subfield of criminology that examines the role played by the victim in precipitating a criminal incident.

visible crimes: Offenses against persons and property committed primarily by members of the lower class. Often referred to as "street crimes" or "ordinary crimes," these are the offenses most upsetting to the public.

voir dire: An examination of prospective jurors by means of which the prosecution and defense screen out persons who might be biased or incapable of rendering a fair verdict.

Williams v. Florida (1970): Juries of fewer than twelve members are constitutional.

Wolff v. *McDonnell* (1974): Basic elements of procedural due process must be present when decisions are made concerning the discipline of an inmate.

work and educational release: The release of inmates from correctional institutions during the day so that they may work or attend school.

workgroup: A collectivity of individuals who interact in the workplace on a continuing basis, share goals, develop norms in regard to the way activities should be carried out, and eventually establish a network of roles that serves to differentiate this group from others.

working personality: The complex of emotional and behavioral characteristics developed by a member of an occupational group in response to the work situation and environmental influences.

Group. **404**, George Godoy. **414**, © Rhoda Sidney/Leo de Wys, Inc. **415**, © Gale Zucker 1990. **418**, © Jim Pickerell 1985/Stock, Boston, Inc.

CHAPTER 11

434–435, Stephen Whalen/Picturesque. **437**, (left) © Mary Kate Denny/PhotoEdit; (right) © Paul Conklin/PhotoEdit. **438**, Courtesy of Harvard College Library. Reproduced by permission. **443**, Laima Druskis Photography. **450**, © Granitsas/The Image Works. **457**, © David Lissy/Leo de Wys, Inc.

CHAPTER 12

474–475, John J. Lopinot/Black Star. **477**, James Colburn/PhotoReporters. **480**, Movie Still Archives. **481**, John J. Lopinot/Black Star. **485**, © Jon Kral/The Miami Herald. **486**, Spencer Grant/Stock, Boston, Inc.

PART 4

504–505, Tom Cheek/Stock, Boston, Inc.

CHAPTER 13

506–507, AP/Wide World Photos. **511**, The Library of Congress. **518**, © Cornell Capa/Magnum Photos, Inc. **525**, Szabo Photography. **526**, Bi-Corp. **533**, AP/Wide World Photos.

POLICY ISSUE NUMBER THREE

p. 1, Sygma. **p. 2**, (top) Randy G. Taylor/Leo de Wys, Inc.; (bottom) Bettmann. **p. 3**, (top) © Orlando Sentinel/The Gamma-Liaison Network; (middle) © Phil Huber; (bottom) S. Elbaz/Sygma. **p. 4**, (clockwise from top) Reuters/Bettmann; © Tom Wright/The Gamma-Liaison Network; Mike Brown/Gamma-Liaison; Wide World Photos.

CHAPTER 14

542–543, © Kent Reno 1987. **545**, The Library of Congress. **546**, Historical Picture Service, Inc. **547**, Pictorial History Research. **548**, The Library of Congress. **550**, Richard Lawson, Illinois State Archives, Southern Illinois University. **552**, American

Correctional Association. **561**, Peter Menzel/Stock, Boston, Inc. **563**, The Library of Congress. **565**, © Ed Kashi/Gamma-Liaison. **570**, AP/Wide World Photos.

CHAPTER 15

576–577, Neil Leifer/Time Magazine. **579**, (left) David J. Wallace/Aerial Photography; (right) Culver Pictures, Inc. **583**, Hollywood Book and Poster. **591**, Ruth Morgan. **598**, Gale Zucker. **601**, © Charles Harbutt/Actuality Inc. **605**, © Gale Zucker. **606**, Jeroboam Inc. **611**, © Gale Zucker. **613**, AP/Wide World Photos. **614**, Tom O'Brien Correction Magazine © 1988/Frost Publishing Group. **617**, Bohdan Hrynewych/Stock, Boston, Inc. **618**, AP/Wide World Photos.

POLICY ISSUE NUMBER FOUR

p. 1, (top) Stephen Ferry/Gamma-Liaison; (bottom) Bob Daemmrich/Stock, Boston, Inc. **p. 2**, (top) © Joe Traver/The Gamma-Liaison Network; (bottom) © Mike Schwarz/Gamma/Liaison. **p. 3**, (top) © Mark Richards; (bottom) Ed Kashi/Gamma-Liaison. **p. 4**, (top) Adam Zetter/Leo de Wys, Inc.; (bottom) Bob Daemmrich/Stock, Boston, Inc.

CHAPTER 16

632–633, Bob Daemmrich/Stock, Boston, Inc. **635**, Bruce Kliene/Jeroboam. **638**, Courtesy of Connecticut Criminal Justice Training Academy. **640**, Cathy Cheney/Stock, Boston, Inc. **647**, UPI/Bettmann. **649**, David Woo. **653**, David Redfern Photography. **655**, Joseph M. Luns, Pennsylvania Board of Probation and Parole.

PART 5

674–675, © Kevin Beebe 1988/The Stock Broker.

CHAPTER 17

676–677, Rhoda Sidney/Leo de Wys, Inc. **683**, Library of Congress. **685**, Painting by Boardman Robinson. Courtesy of Harvard Law Art Collection. **689**, Billy E. Barnes. **690**, Jeffrey High/Image Productions. **703**, Maurice Cohn Band/The Miami Herald. **704**, Frost Publishing Group.

Index

Juvenile Justice System

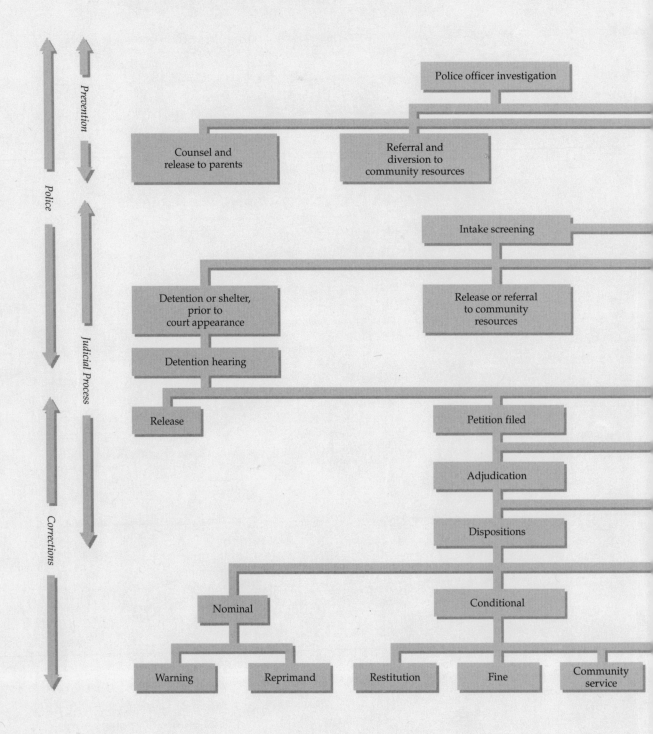

Prevention

Police

Judicial Process

Corrections

Police officer investigation

Counsel and release to parents

Referral and diversion to community resources

Intake screening

Detention or shelter, prior to court appearance

Release or referral to community resources

Detention hearing

Release

Petition filed

Adjudication

Dispositions

Nominal

Conditional

Warning

Reprimand

Restitution

Fine

Community service